Medieval Allegory as Epistemology

OXFORD STUDIES IN MEDIEVAL LITERATURE AND CULTURE

General Editors

Ardis Butterfield and Christopher Cannon

The monograph series Oxford Studies in Medieval Literature and Culture showcases the plurilingual and multicultural quality of medieval literature and actively seeks to promote research that not only focuses on the array of subjects medievalists now pursue—in literature, theology, and philosophy, in social, political, jurisprudential, and intellectual history, the history of art, and the history of science—but also combines these subjects productively. It offers innovative studies on topics that may include, but are not limited to, manuscript and book history; languages and literatures of the global Middle Ages; race and the post-colonial; the digital humanities, media and performance; music; medicine; the history of affect and the emotions; the literature and practices of devotion; the theory and history of gender and sexuality, ecocriticism and the environment; theories of aesthetics; and medievalism.

Medieval Allegory as Epistemology

Dream-Vision Poetry on Language, Cognition, and Experience

MARCO NIEVERGELT

Great Clarendon Street, Oxford, OX2 6DP,
United Kingdom

Oxford University Press is a department of the University of Oxford.
It furthers the University's objective of excellence in research, scholarship,
and education by publishing worldwide. Oxford is a registered trade mark of
Oxford University Press in the UK and in certain other countries

© Marco Nievergelt 2023

The moral rights of the author have been asserted

All rights reserved. No part of this publication may be reproduced, stored in
a retrieval system, or transmitted, in any form or by any means, without the
prior permission in writing of Oxford University Press, or as expressly permitted
by law, by licence or under terms agreed with the appropriate reprographics
rights organization. Enquiries concerning reproduction outside the scope of the
above should be sent to the Rights Department, Oxford University Press, at the
address above

You must not circulate this work in any other form
and you must impose this same condition on any acquirer

Published in the United States of America by Oxford University Press
198 Madison Avenue, New York, NY 10016, United States of America

British Library Cataloguing in Publication Data
Data available

Library of Congress Control Number: 2022947788

ISBN 978–0–19–284921–2

DOI: 10.1093/oso/9780192849212.001.0001

Printed and bound in the UK by
Clays Ltd, Elcograf S.p.A.

Links to third party websites are provided by Oxford in good faith and
for information only. Oxford disclaims any responsibility for the materials
contained in any third party website referenced in this work.

Acknowledgements

This book has been a long time in the making, and its slow gestation in many ways reflects the meandering trajectories followed by the dreamer/protagonists of the three poems that constitute the main focus of this study. Just like the quest-narratives I discuss, my own search was punctuated by frustrations, pitfalls, false starts, breakdowns, delusions, and premature conclusions that needed to be unmade and rethought. But the time I spent with these poems—or rather *inside* them—also brought incredible rewards, both intellectual and personal. Even though this book was written in an academic register that values depersonalized scientific objectivism, and despite the often meticulous work of historical contextualization required to allow these texts to speak with something like their own 'true voices', I was struck again and again by the ability of these three poems to trigger much deeper responses within me. The struggles of the semi-fictional dreamer/protagonist often counterpointed, informed, and possibly lent meaning to my own personal struggles and vicissitudes—*contreres choses, les unes des autres gloses*. I was relieved and delighted, then, to find that despite the scholarly nature of my own interest, and even after years spent working on this project, I was able to vibrate and resonate with these old books with something I believe approaches human empathy. I found myself thinking that this is, after all, the great power of poetry—an idea that kept me going throughout the long dry stretches, and the many moments of crisis, despair, or paralysis. This, I further kept telling myself, must be what Langland intended by 'kynde knowyinge'—an experience of the 'cors' as much as an experience of the disembodied intellect, and one that often passes through visceral 'suffering'. The greatest benefit I have derived from all this, then, is that perhaps I too have been able to transform my own inadequate understanding of what it means 'to know' something.

It has been a long journey, and I have been fortunate to be able to rely on the support and assistance of many friends, colleagues, and institutions. The project was begun in Lausanne, where I held an 'Ambizione' research fellowship awarded by the Swiss National Science Foundation, and where the English Department and the Centre for Medieval Studies provided support and inspiration. Particular thanks are due to Denis Renevey, Juliette Vuille, and later Christiania Whitehead— fine scholars but even finer people. The project was kick-started during a visiting fellowship at Corpus Christi College, Oxford, in 2013, where the President, fellows, and larger college community provided me with an ideal, stimulating, and supportive environment for my forays into medieval scholastic philosophy and theology. Particular thanks are due to Helen Moore, Anna Marmodoro, Fr. Rob Gay (OP), Richard 'Padrino', Rowley, and of course to 'the brotherhood of the *Rose*'—i.e. Jonathan Morton, Philip Knox, and other participants in our reading group—but also to Laura Ashe, Helen Swift, Mishtooni Bose, Vincent Gillespie, and Kantik Ghosh. I was equally fortunate in receiving a EURIAS junior fellowship at the Paris Institute for Advanced Studies in 2015–16, where I was able to benefit from stimulating interdisciplinary conversations, and to rely on impeccable research support and on generous assistance for the organization of scientific activities, including an international conference. Particular thanks are due to Gretty Mirdal, Simon Luck, and Geneviève Marmin at the Institute, and to the wider community of medievalist intellectual historians in Paris, who provided such a wonderfully welcoming environment—in particular Irène Rosier-Catach, Christophe Grellard, Aurélien Robert, Véronique Decaix, and Antonio Montefusco among many others. This wonderful experience was followed by a difficult period of exile to a dark and unhappy place in a field in the vicinity of Coventry, made bearable by some happy encounters with my students and with Jonathan Skinner, Eileen John, Jayne Sweet, and some of the medievalists and early modernists gravitating around the Centre for the Study of the Renaissance there. I suppose everyone encounters their own personal Slough of Despond sooner or later, and I am glad I was able to put mine behind me.

As I write this, I find myself—again—at a crossroads, with an exhausted Will and yet an unremitting Conscience wanting to hit the road again in search of Truth. But I also write this in the knowledge that some things *have* come full circle, and that something much more durable has been achieved. This book was begun in 2013, the year of the birth of little Louis, and it was completed in 2021, when baby Héloïse was added to the family. I dedicate the book to both of them, in the hope that they will always cherish books as much as I do in their own quest to balance 'experience' and 'auctoritee', whatever their chosen path in life.

Leamington Spa
20 October 2021

Contents

Abbreviations	ix
Introduction	1
1. Medieval Allegory: Poetry as Philosophy	3
2. Medieval Epistemology	16
3. Agency, Experience, and Subjectivity in the Later Middle Ages	40
4. This Book	46

PART I. JEAN DE MEUN

1. In the Beginning was the *Rose*	55
1. 'Une vraye mappemonde de toutes choses celestes et terriennes'	56
2. Jean de Meun and the Schools	70
3. Allegory, Signification, and Equivocation	77
4. The Poetics of Faux Semblant	97
5. The Body of Experience: *Choses* and *Gloses*, *Reliques* and *Roses*	107

PART II. DEGUILEVILLE

Introduction to Part II	117
2. Language	121
1. *Predicatio*: Allegory and the Place of Authority	121
2. Learning to Argue	129
3. Learning to Read	140
4. Signs and Sacraments	159
5. 'Parler proprement des choses [...], sanz metre gloses' (*RR* 7049–50): Exposé sur le *Roman de la Rose*	168
3. Cognition: Theory and Practice	175
1. Augustine's Soul, Avicenna's Flying Man, and Deguileville's Hermeneutics of the Subject	177
2. Theory: Divine Illumination and Active Cognition	193
3. The Body of Sin and the Carnal Poetics of the *Rose*	202
4. Practice: Eyes, Ears, and the Spectre of Aristotle	220
5. The Long Shadow of the *Rose*: Didacticism, Embodiment, and Experiential Hermeneutics	236

viii   CONTENTS

4. Experience   246
   1. Conversion I: The ABC of Grace and Will   247
   2. Language Redeemed, Language Remade   263
   3. *Hortus Conclusus*: Lyric, Stasis, and Fruition   275
   4. 'Car les signes puent faillir' (*PVH2* 14,377): The *fleur de lis*,
      the Revised *Pèlerinage de Vie Humaine*, and the Search for a
      Perfect Semiotics   295
   5. The Breakdown of Language and the Experiential Subject   309

PART III. LANGLAND

Introduction to Part III   323
Langland and French Allegory   325
5. The Desire for Knowledge and the Experience of
   Conversion: (*Piers Plowman* B VIII–XIII.215)   331
   1. Learning, Crisis, and Conversion   331
   2. Vision and Penitence: 'to se moche and suffre more'   344
   3. The Legitimacy of Poetry: Bidding of Bedes or Meddling
      with Makynges   357
   4. Eucharistic and Sapiential Knowledge in Deguileville and Langland 366
   5. 'Til I haue preued moore' (B XIII.183)   375

6. The Experience of Failure and the Architecture of Vision:
   (*Piers Plowman* B XIII.215–XV)   380
   1. Starting Over   382
   2. Haukyn, Guillermus, and Will   397
   3. Willing and Longing; *Makyng* and Suffering   411
   4. Vision and Re-Vision: Deguileville's and Langland's Reiterative Poetic 425

7. The Ends of Experience: Incarnation and Apocalypse:
   (*Piers Plowman* B XVI–XX)   437
   1. Incarnation and Embodiment: Pilgrimage '*à rebours*'   441
   2. The Coming of Antichrist and the Ends of Allegory   459
   3. The Ends of Allegory   470
   4. False Conclusions   496

Bibliography   501
General Index   548
Index of passages, motifs, and debates relating to main poetic corpus 556

Abbreviations

AHDLMA	*Archives d'histoire doctrinale et littéraire du Moyen Âge*
B	William Langland, '*Piers Plowman*', B-text. As edited in William Langland, '*Piers Plowman*': *A Parallel Text Edition of the A, B, C, and Z Versions*, ed. A. V. C. Schmidt, 2nd edn, 2 vols. Kalamazoo: Medieval Institute Publications, 2011.
CCCM	*Corpus Christianorum Continuatio Mediaevalis*
CCSL	*Corpus Christianorum Series Latina*
CHMP	*The Cambridge History of Medieval Philosophy*, ed. By Robert Pasnau and Christina Van Dyke, 2 vols. Cambridge: Cambridge University Press, 2010.
CHLMP	*The Cambridge History of Later Medieval Philosophy: From the Rediscovery of Aristotle to the Disintegration of Scholasticism, 1100–1600*, ed. by Norman Kretzmann, Anthony Kenny, and Jan Pinborg. Cambridge: Cambridge University Press, 1982.
CIMAGL	*Cahiers de l'Institut du Moyen-Âge grec et latin*
Cole and Galloway	Andrew Cole and Andrew Galloway, eds, *The Cambridge Companion to 'Piers Plowman'*. Cambridge: Cambridge University Press, 2014.
DFL	Guillaume de Digulleville, *Le Dit de la Fleur de Lis*, ed. Fréderic Duval. Paris: École des Chartes, 2014.
DMF	*Dictionnaire du Moyen Français*, version 2020 (DMF 2020). ATILF—CNRS and Université de Lorraine. http://www.atilf.fr/dmf
Duval and Pomel	Fréderic Duval and Fabienne Pomel, eds, *Guillaume de Digulleville: les pèlerinages allégoriques*. Rennes: Presses Universitaires de Rennes, 2008.
FEW	Walther von Wartburg, *Französisches Etymologisches Wörterbuch: Eine Darstellung des Galloromanischen Sprachsatzes*. 25 vols. Basel, Berlin, Bonn, Leipzig, 1922–2002.
Godefroy	Frédéric Godefroy, *Dictionnaire de l'ancienne langue française: et de tous ses dialectes du IXe au XVe siècle*. Paris. 10 vols. F. Vieweg, 1881–1902.
JEGP	*Journal of English and Germanic Philology*
Kablitz and Peters	Andreas Kablitz and Ursula Peters, eds, *Mittelalterliche Literatur als Retextualisierung. Das 'Pèlerinage'-Corpus des Guillaume de Deguileville im europäischen Mittelalter*. Heidelberg: Winter, 2014.

X ABBREVIATIONS

Kamath and Nievergelt — Stephanie A. V. G. Kamath and Marco Nievergelt, eds, *The Pèlerinage Allegories of Guillaume de Deguileville: Tradition, Authority and Influence*. Cambridge: D. S. Brewer, 2013.

Morton and Nievergelt — Jonathan Morton and Marco Nievergelt, eds, *The Roman de la Rose and Thirteenth-Century Thought*. Cambridge: Cambridge University Press, 2020.

PA — Guillaume de Deguileville, *Le Pèlerinage de l'Âme*, ed. J. J. Stürzinger. London: Roxburghe Club, 1895.

PIMS — Pontifical Institute of Mediaeval Studies

PJC — Guillaume de Deguileville, *Le Pèlerinage de Jhesucrist*, ed. J. J. Stürzinger. London: Roxburghe Club, 1897.

PL — *Patrologiae cursus completus, series Latina*, ed. J.-P. Migne, 221 Vols. Paris: 1844–65.

PVH1 — Guillaume de Deguileville, *Le Pèlerinage de vie humaine*, ed. J. J. Stürzinger. London: Roxburghe Club, 1893 [1st version, *c.* 1331].

PVH2 — Guillaume de Deguileville, *Le Livre du pèlerin de vie humaine (1355)*, ed. by Philippe Maupeu and Graham Robert Edwards. Paris: Le Livre de Poche, 2015 [2nd version, *c.* 1355–6].

RES — *Review of English Studies*

RR — Guillaume de Lorris and Jean de Meun, *Le Roman de la Rose*, ed. Jean Lecoy. 3 vols. Paris: Champion, 1965–70. English translations of the poem from *The Romance of the Rose*, trans. Frances Horgan. Oxford: Oxford World's Classics, 1994.

ST — Thomas Aquinas, *Summa Theologiae, Opera Omnia iussu impensaque Leonis XIII edita*, 4–12. Rome: Ex Typographia Polyglotta, 1888–1906.

Tobler-Lommatzsch — *Altfranzösisches Wörterbuch*, ed. Adolf Tobler, Erhard Lommatzsch, Achim Stein, Peter Blumenthal. Wiesbaden: Franz Steiner, 2002.

YLS — *Yearbook of Langland Studies*

Introduction

O Aristotle! If you had had the advantage of being 'the freshest modern' instead of the gravest ancient, would you not have mingled your praise of metaphorical speech, as a sign of high intelligence, with a lamentation that intelligence so rarely shows itself in speech without metaphor—that we can so seldom declare what a thing is, except by saying it is something else?

George Eliot, *The Mill on the Floss*, Book II, Chapter 1

This book is concerned primarily with one central question: what is the relation between language—specifically poetry—and knowledge, individual agency, and personal salvation? In the chapters that follow, I analyse the tentative and evolving answers provided by three major medieval poets who employ the literary form of the first-person dream vision to explore this question. The three poets are Jean de Meun, author of the 'continuation' of the *Roman de la Rose* (*c.* 1269–78);[1] Guillaume de Deguileville, author of a trilogy of allegorical *Pèlerinages* (1331–58), the *Dit de la Fleur de Lys* (1338), and a corpus of undated Latin poems;[2] and William Langland, author of the multiple versions of *Piers Plowman* (*c.* 1360–90).[3]

The *Roman de la Rose*, the *Pèlerinages*, and *Piers Plowman* are among the lengthiest, most complex, and intellectually most challenging vernacular works produced during this period. However, they were also among the most popular

---

[1] I will be using Guillaume de Lorris and Jean de Meun, *Le Roman de la Rose*, ed. Félix Lecoy. 3 vols (Paris: Champion, 1965–70).

[2] The first of these, the *Pèlerinage de Vie Humaine*, exists in two substantially different versions, which I will refer to respectively as *PVH1* (1331), and *PVH2* (1355) throughout. Editions used are as follows: *PVH1*: Guillaume de Deguileville, *Le pèlerinage de vie humaine*, ed. J. J. Stürzinger (London: Roxburghe Club, 1893); and *PVH2*: Guillaume de Deguileville, *Le Livre du pèlerin de vie humaine (1355)*, ed. by Philippe Maupeu and Graham Robert Edwards (Paris: Le Livre de Poche, 2015). For the two further *Pèlerinages*, see Guillaume de Deguileville, *Le Pèlerinage de l'Âme*, ed. J. J. Stürzinger (London: Roxburghe Club, 1895), henceforth cited as *PA*; ibid., *Le Pèlerinage de Jhesucrist*, ed. J. J. Stürzinger (London: Roxburghe Club, 1897), henceforth cited as *PJC*. I will also be referring to Guillaume de Digulleville, *Le Dit de la Fleur de Lis*, ed. Fréderic Duval (Paris: École des Chartes, 2014), henceforth *DFL*. For details on Deguileville's Latin poetry, unavailable in a critical edition, see especially Graham Robert Edwards, 'Making Sense of Deguileville's Autobiographical Project: The Evidence of Paris, BnF MS Latin 14845', in Kamath and Nievergelt, pp. 129–50; and Frédéric Duval, 'Deux prières latines de Guillaume de Digulleville: Prière à Saint Michel et prière à l'ange gardien', in Duval and Pomel, pp. 185–211.

[3] I will be using the Schmidt parallel-text edition unless otherwise noted: William Langland, '*Piers Plowman': A Parallel-Text Edition of the A, B, C, and Z Versions*, ed. A. V. C. Schmidt, 2nd edn. 2 vols (Kalamazoo: Medieval Institute Publications, 2011).

Medieval Allegory as Epistemology. Marco Nievergelt, Oxford University Press.
© Marco Nievergelt (2023). DOI: 10.1093/oso/9780192849212.003.0001

2 MEDIEVAL ALLEGORY AS EPISTEMOLOGY

and influential works of vernacular literary fiction in the late Middle Ages, and early readers responded by engaging with these texts in sustained and intense fashion.[4] Given their popularity, all three poems have attracted considerable modern scholarly attention, with the possible exception of the *Pèlerinages*. Existing work has often noted the formal and thematic similarities between these texts, but no sustained study of their relationship to each other has been produced. More importantly, existing work has tended to comment on the relations between these poems in strictly comparative terms, without examining their deeper intellectual affinities and intertextual relations in any depth and detail. This study, by contrast,

---

[4] With more than 300 MSS, the *Rose* is the second most widely copied and circulated medieval poetic work in the vernacular after Dante's *Divina Commedia*. For a catalogue of Manuscripts, see the list provided in Catherine Bel and Herman Braet, eds, *De la Rose: texte, image, fortune* (Leuven: Peeters, 2006), pp. 541–4, and the regularly updated online census at https://dlmm.library.jhu.edu/en/extant-manuscripts. On the dissemination and reception of the *Rose* in Europe, see particularly Pierre-Yves Badel, *Le Roman de la Rose au XIVe siècle: Etude de la Réception de l'Oeuvre* (Geneva: Droz, 1980); Kevin Brownlee and Sylvia Huot, eds, *Rethinking the Romance of the Rose: Text, Image, Reception* (Philadelphia: University of Pennsylvania Press, 1992); Sylvia Huot, *The Romance of the Rose and its Medieval Readers: Interpretation, Reception, Manuscript Transmission* (Cambridge: Cambridge University Press, 1993); Catherine Bel and Herman Braet, eds, *De la Rose: texte, image, fortune* (Louvain: Peeters, 2006). On the 'querelle de la Rose' see Christine de Pizan, et al., *Le Débat sur le 'Roman de la Rose'*, ed. Eric Hicks (Paris: Champion, 1977); Christine de Pizan, *The Debate of the Romance of the Rose*, ed. and trans. David Hult (Chicago: University of Chicago Press, 2010); Christine McWebb, ed., *Debating the Roman de la Rose: A Critical Anthology* (New York: Routledge, 2007); Andrea Valentini, *Le remaniement du Roman de la Rose par Gui de Mori. Étude et édition des interpolations d'après le manuscrit* (Leuven: Peeters, 2007). On the reception of the *Rose* in England, see Philip Knox, *The 'Romance of the Rose' and the Making of Fourteenth-Century English Literature* (Oxford: Oxford University Press, 2022), and Stephanie A. V. G. Kamath, '*Le Roman de la Rose* and Middle English Poetry', *Literature Compass* 6.6 (2009), 1109–26. On its printed fortunes, see e.g. Philippe Frieden, 'Le *Roman de la Rose*: de l'édition aux manuscrits', *Perspectives Médiévales* 34 (2012), n.p.

Deguileville's *Pèlerinages* are preserved both as individual poems and, more rarely, grouped into manuscripts containing two or all three items. To date, 84 MSS contain *PVH* (of which only 9 feature *PVH2*), 48 contain *PA*, and 29 *PJC*. For a work in progress census, see the table published by Géraldine Veysseyre, with Julia Drobinsky and Émilie Fréger, in Duval and Pomel, pp. 425–53, also available online on open access: https://books.openedition.org/pur/35136?lang=en. Géraldine Veysseyre is currently finalizing an annotated catalogue, to be published with Viella: http://www.opvs.fr/?q=fr/ content/préparation-du-catalogue-des-manuscrits-du-pèlerinage-de-vie-humaine-versions-françaises-et. On the circulation and influence of Deguileville's work, as well as on the various prose *remaniements*, multiple translations into English, German, Dutch, Castilian, and Latin, and sixteenth-century printed editions (10 separate ones), see variously the collections by Kamath and Nievergelt, Kablitz and Peters, as well as the monographs by Philippe Maupeu, *Pèlerins de vie humaine: Autobiographie et allégorie narrative, de Guillaume de Deguileville à Octovien de Saint-Gelais* (Paris: Champion, 2009); Stephanie A. Viereck Gibbs Kamath, *Authorship and First-Person Allegory in Late Medieval France and England* (Cambridge: D. S. Brewer, 2012); Marco Nievergelt, *Allegorical Quests from Deguileville to Spenser* (Cambridge: D. S. Brewer, 2012).

For synthetic accounts of the popularity and reception history of *Piers Plowman*—surviving in 50 manuscripts, which makes it 'the single most popular verse text disseminated in the fourteenth century' (Ralph Hanna, 'The Visions and Revisions of *Piers Plowman*', in Cole and Galloway, p. 33)—see Simon Horobin, 'Manuscripts and Readers of Piers Plowman', and Lawrence Warner, 'Plowman Traditions in Late Medieval and Early Modern Writing', both in Cole and Galloway, pp. 179–97 and 198–213. For a more in-depth study of the intricate and disputed reception history of the poem among its earliest readers, see Lawrence Warner, *The Lost History of Piers Plowman: The Earliest Transmission of Langland's Work* (Philadelphia: University of Pennsylvania Press, 2011).

is grounded in two broad contentions. Firstly, it argues that the three poems constitute a tightly knit intertextual community, where later works engage with earlier ones through dialogue, critique, and sustained rewriting and rethinking. Secondly, and more importantly, this study argues that the reasons for these extremely close intertextual relations are to be found in the shared interest in human knowledge that runs through these poems. All three poets grapple with a number of shared, closely related epistemological problems that emerged in Western Europe during the thirteenth century, in the wake of the reception of the complete body of Aristotle's works on logic and the natural sciences, with important consequences for the development of vernacular poetry in the period.

The epistemological questions confronted by these three poems can be broken down into a three broad areas of interest. To adopt a modern terminology, we might tentatively describe these as follows: (1) hermeneutics and philosophy of language; (2) philosophy of mind and cognition; (3) debates on the operation of the human will and divine grace. All three poems explore a subset of more specific and closely interconnected questions, with particular attention to the cognitive potential of poetry itself: what is 'knowledge', and how does it obtain in ordinary humans? Does knowledge occur in the body, or in the soul, or across that divide? What is the relationship between knowledge, learning, and individual salvation? What *kind* of knowledge is necessary to salvation? Does this knowledge require a particular kind of learned understanding and systematic intellectual training mediated by written 'auctoritee' and textual interpretation, scriptural or otherwise? Or does this knowledge obtain through individual 'experience'? Or does this knowledge emerge from the dialectic between 'experience' and 'auctoritee'? Does knowledge amount to an act, or is it best understood in terms of a passive experience? What are the respective roles of human volition and divine grace in enabling such knowledge to crystallize? What is the role of Christ's Incarnation, the sacraments of the Church, and the scriptural text in this process of (self-)discovery or self-recovery? And, finally: what is the role of specifically *poetic* writing in enabling access to such salvific knowledge?

1. Medieval Allegory: Poetry as Philosophy

As will be clear by now, this study is not primarily intended as a contribution to literary history, but as an account of how a specific poetic tradition emerged in the later Middle Ages as a response to a number of complex philosophical problems and contemporary debates regarding the nature of human knowledge. Accordingly, in what follows I will not be focusing on literary questions in themselves, but will be examining how literary and fictional forms are used to conduct philosophical speculation. Furthermore, I will be examining the philosophical affinities of late medieval dream vision poetry through the lens of *medieval*, as opposed to *modern*

4   MEDIEVAL ALLEGORY AS EPISTEMOLOGY

notions of philosophical thinking and intellectual speculation. This means that rather than engaging in sustained fashion with modern theories of allegory, for instance, I will be concentrating on medieval poetic practice in its own, medieval intellectual context. In disciplinary terms, then, the present book also wants to make the case for putting more intellectual history into literary history—and vice versa. I therefore hope that the book will be of interest to both literary scholars and intellectual historians.

The *Rose*, the *Pèlerinages*, and *Piers Plowman* engage with contemporary intellectual traditions in ways that are perhaps more sustained, polemical, intense, creative, and sophisticated than those found in any other medieval literary tradition in the Anglo-French orbit, and in ways that are broadly comparable to texts in the Italian tradition of this same period, which have received more careful scholarly attention in this respect.[5] Far from being invested in a narrowly encyclopaedic or didactic project, then, and 'far from peddling moralizing and edifying banalities',[6] all three poems insistently question the textual, interpretive, and cognitive processes involved in the transmission and production of knowledge, and indeed end up questioning the very definition of what knowledge might be. More specifically, the three poems are marked by their determination to initiate conversations with several areas of advanced intellectual enquiry that tackled epistemological problems during the later Middle Ages—from scholastic philosophy and theology to the natural sciences, faculty psychology, and the language arts of the *trivium* (grammar, logic, and rhetoric). Far from being passively 'influenced' by contemporary developments in the late medieval schools and Universities, however, the poems studied here also develop a series of distinctive, active strategies for philosophical speculation in poetic form, and often do so by challenging or interrogating the cultural and intellectual dominance of the scholastic tradition itself. The poems studied here often do this by drawing inspiration from older and more firmly established intellectual traditions such as monastic and patristic thought, or earlier traditions of 'philosophical poetry'—from the late classical *prosimetra* of Boethius and Martianus Cappella, to the medieval Ovidian tradition, twelfth-century philosophical allegory, and later traditions of lyric and romance in both Latin and the vernacular.

This means that rather than simply situating the work of my three authors synchronically in terms of the direct and binary relation to contemporary scholastic thought, I want to place these texts within a richer, more pluralistic, layered,

---

[5] See especially Joël Biard and Fosca Mariani Zini, eds, *Ut philosophia poesis: Questions philosophiques dans l'œuvre de Dante, Pétrarque et Boccace* (Paris: Vrin, 2008); Carla Casagrande and Gianfranco Fioravanti, eds, *La filosofia in Italia nell'età di Dante* (Bologna: Il Mulino, 2016); Filippo Andrei, *Boccaccio the Philosopher: An Epistemology of the Decameron* (Cham: Palgrave Macmillan, 2017); and the classic study by Ruedi Imbach, *Dante, la philosophie et les laïcs, Initiations à la philosophie médiévale, 1* (Paris/Fribourg: Cerf/Éditions Universitaires, 1996).

[6] As noted by Adrian Armstrong and Sarah Kay, *Knowing Poetry: Verse in Medieval France from the Rose to the Rhétoriqueurs* (Ithaca: Cornell University Press, 2011), p. 5.

INTRODUCTION 5

and capacious, but also more conflicted intellectual context.[7] While each of my three authors wrote within a unique, highly distinctive historical and cultural context, it seems important to emphasize that each of them inhabited a space that was, in different ways, liminal, ill-defined, and porous, straddling the boundary between the schools and very different, non-scholastic forms of theological and philosophical thought and/or expression. Their poetic thought accordingly cannot be understood in terms of a binary interface between poetry and contemporary scholastic debates alone, and will need to be situated in relation to a much wider range of available sources, ideas, and discourses, gradually produced, accumulated, and rearranged over a much longer historical *durée*. Furthermore, instead of looking to the literary works in order to validate an overarching and pre-existing intellectual-historical narrative—about, say, the ostensible rise of scepticism, fideism, or 'nominalism' in the fourteenth century—I have adopted an inductive approach. I have preferred to work outwards from the poems themselves towards the specific philosophical concerns and multi-faceted intellectual context(s) that each of these poems mobilizes in order to conduct its own, distinctive exploration of epistemological problems. This means taking into account a much longer, incremental, and increasingly complex and articulated intellectual history, one that recognizes the discursive fluidity and heterogeneity of the cultural environment in which authors such as Jean de Meun, Deguileville, and Langland actually moved.

As well as resisting any easy and direct ideological alignment with contemporary intellectual positions as articulated by the scholastics,[8] these three dream vision allegories also assert their claims to speculative agency and intellectual independence by adopting an emphatically *poetic* form. This implies a qualified resistance to scholastic forms of thought and analysis more broadly, and in this study as a whole I seek to emphasize the intellectual-historical significance of

---

[7] My comments here converge closely with those of e.g. David Aers, *Salvation and Sin: Augustine, Langland, and Fourteenth-Century Theology* (Notre Dame, IN: University of Notre Dame Press, 2009), pp. 55–8, and Nikolaus Largier, 'Das Glück des Menschen: Diskussionen über *beatitudo* und Vernunft in volkssprachlichen Texten des 14. Jahrhunderts', in Jan A. Aertsen, Kent Emery, and Andreas Speer, eds, *Nach der Verurteilung von 1277/After the Condemnation of 1277: Philosophie und Theologie an der Universität von Paris im letzten Viertel des 13. Jahrhunderts. Studien und Texte/Philosophy and Theology at the University of Paris in the Last Quarter of the Thirteenth Century. Studies and Texts* (Berlin and New York: Walter de Gruyter, 2001), pp. 827–55 (832–4).

[8] The dynamics of scholastic debate itself, it must be said, were far more fluid and heterogeneous than is often assumed, and recent scholarship by intellectual historians has consistently dismantled the older, reductive model that sought to understand late medieval scholasticism predominantly in terms of a clash between rival 'schools' or even 'currents' of thought. See e.g. William J. Courtenay, *Schools and Scholars in Fourteenth-century England* (Princeton: Princeton University Press, 1987), pp. 171–92 on the misconceptions underpinning the model pitching 'nominalism' against 'realism'; and Stephen P. Marrone, *The Light of thy Countenance: Science and Knowledge of God in the thirteenth Century*, 2 vols (Leiden: Brill, 2001), I:1–25 on the distortions created by the narrative opposing 'Augustinians' and 'Aristotelians'.

6 MEDIEVAL ALLEGORY AS EPISTEMOLOGY

these three texts *as poems*.[9] Following recent theoretical accounts of the interface between poetry and philosophy, I am particularly interested in the ability of poetry to function as a distinctive, and comparatively independent vehicle for intellectual speculation, enabling a form of inherently poetic thinking and knowing that cannot necessarily be translated back into the more academic register of systematic philosophical reasoning. As Angela Leighton has recently argued, 'poetic knowing' is an essentially processual and predicative activity, as opposed to the largely objectivist and objectifying project of systematic philosophical analysis.[10] A very similar point has been made by Adrian Armstrong and Sarah Kay about late medieval francophone poetry very specifically: beginning with the appearance of Jean de Meun's *Roman de la Rose* during the 1270s, late medieval francophone literary culture underwent a paradigm shift, resulting in the emergence of a new kind of 'knowing poetry', where the writing and reading of *poetrie* is widely understood as a distinctive type of cognitive activity.[11] Furthermore, during the late medieval period the different cognitive prerogatives of poetry and philosophy are reflected at the level of the socio-cultural formations associated with these two forms of intellectual speculation. Leaving aside the vexed issue of the emergence of 'philosophy' as an independent discipline distinct from theology,[12] it is undeniable that scholasticism as a whole is a highly institutionalized form of intellectual activity, inextricably tied up with the rise of medieval universities in the period 1200–1400. Late medieval poetry, by contrast—and vernacular poetry in particular—is characterized by its eminently unregulated and exploratory character, free from any clear disciplinary, institutional, or discursive affiliations and constraints. Even though poets demonstrably engaged with scholastic learning in a variety of ways throughout this period, they did so under the assumption that they were granted considerable 'poetic licence', entitling them to work creatively with academic methods and ideas, consciously appropriating, modifying, and interrogating the intellectual habits and structures that underpin the culture of the schools.[13] Within the main body of this study, the question of each poet's

---

[9] For a call to pay more careful attention to the formal specificities and theoretical sophistication of specifically 'literary' vernacular poetry—on its own terms and not those employed in contemporary scholastic discourse—see especially Nicolette Zeeman, 'Imaginative Theory', in Paul Strohm, ed., *Middle English*. Oxford Twenty-First Century Approaches to Literature (Oxford: Oxford University Press, 2007), pp. 222–40: 'the literary text—especially in the vernacular—was in a disciplinary sense "different", a site from which to enter into dialogue with, or even counter, the teachings of the schools' (p. 225).

[10] See especially Angela Leighton, 'Poetry's Knowing: So What Do We Know?', in John Gibson, ed., *The Philosophy of Poetry* (Oxford: Oxford University Press: 2015), pp. 162–82.

[11] Armstrong and Kay, *Knowing Poetry*, esp. pp. 16–22. See also Rebecca Dixon and Finn E. Sinclair, eds, *Poetry, Knowledge, and Community in Late Medieval France* (Cambridge: D. S. Brewer, 2008), emerging from the same research project.

[12] On which see Jan Aertsen and Andreas Speer, eds, *Was ist Philosophie im Mittelalter?* (Berlin and New York: de Gruyter, 1998).

[13] See e.g. Nicolette Zeeman, 'The Schools Give a License to Poets', in Rita Copeland, ed., *Criticism and Dissent in the Middle Ages* (Cambridge: Cambridge University Press, 1996), pp. 151–80; and ibid.,

INTRODUCTION 7

evolving attitude towards institutionalized academic culture will therefore constitute a recurrent topic. Ultimately I suggest that each of these three poets points to
the perceived limitations of scholastic forms, as each of them attempts to define
with greater precision the nature of 'poetic knowing' as they understood it. In
doing so, all three of them display a conflicted, critical but intellectually productive engagement with scholastic thought, focusing in particular on the endemic rift
between *parola poetica* and *parola pensante* in Western culture.[14]

Instead of attempting to align poetic texts with a particular intellectual project,
individual figure, school, agenda, or controversy, this study is therefore primarily
interested in tracing the trajectories of poetic thinking as they emerge, crystallize,
evolve, dissolve, and reform within and through the poetry itself. I will therefore
be paying particular attention to the distinctive formal and expressive features
of allegorical poetry: its narrative and figurative character; its reliance on discursive ambiguity and irresolution; its ubiquitous use of multiple and variously
unreliable personifications to mediate any claims to larger truth and authority.
Presented within the notoriously unstable narrative framework of a first-person
allegorical dream vision,[15] all three poems clearly foreground their own tentative
and fluctuating epistemic status, constantly threatened by the cognitive shifts, ruptures, hesitations, and abrupt changes of direction experienced by the first-person
subject/dreamer/narrator. Ultimately, however, it is not so much *despite* such pitfalls and *aporias*, but specifically *because of them* that these poems manage to
question—if maybe not quite 'challenge'—the intellectual dominance of scholastic
thought during this period. In doing so they manage to assert their own claims
to producing very different, alternative, or complementary form of knowing and
(self-)understanding:[16] whereas scholastic thought is essentially conceived as a

---

'Philosophy in Parts: Jean de Meun, Chaucer, and Lydgate', in Dallas G. Denery II, Kantik Ghosh,
and Nicolette Zeeman, eds, *Uncertain Knowledge: Scepticism, Relativism and Doubt in the Middle Ages*
(Turnhout: Brepols, 2014), pp. 213–38.

[14] See Giorgio Agamben, *Stanze*: *La parola e il fantasma nella cultura occidentale* (Torino: Einaudi,
1977), p. xiii.

[15] The late medieval tradition of dream vision poetry has been analysed in considerable detail,
but only rarely have scholars examined the role of late medieval scholastic/Aristotelian debates in
shaping the formal organization of the *Roman de la Rose*, which is the foundational poem in this tradition. Particularly the role of commentaries on Aristotle's *parva naturalia* produced in the mid- to
late thirteenth-century Paris in shaping Jean's poem deserves much closer scrutiny, as is suggested by
numerous close resonances, for which see especially Christophe Grellard, 'Mechanisms of Belief: Jean
de Meun's Implicit Epistemology', in Morton and Nievergelt, pp. 27–44 (esp. 33–5, and material in
notes); and Fabienne Pomel, 'Visual Experiences and Allegorical Fiction: The Lexis and Paradigm
of *Fantaisie* in Jean de Meun's *Rose*', in Morton and Nievergelt, pp. 45–64 (49–59). For some of
the most important discussions of dream vision poetry and dream theory in the period, see especially Anthony C. Spearing, *Medieval Dream-Poetry* (Cambridge: Cambridge University Press, 1976);
Stephen Russell, *The English Dream Vision: Anatomy of a Form* (Columbus: Ohio State University
Press, 1988); Stephen Kruger, *Dreaming in the Middle Ages* (Cambridge: Cambridge University Press,
1992); Katherine L. Lynch, *The High Medieval Dream Vision: Poetry, Philosophy, and Literary Form*
(Stanford: Stanford University Press, 1998); Mireille Demaules, *La corne et l'ivoire: étude sur le récit
de rêve dans la littérature romanesque des XIIe et XIIIe siècles* (Paris: Champion, 2010).

[16] See also Armstrong and Kay, *Knowing Poetry*, pp. 7, 20, and *passim*.

8 MEDIEVAL ALLEGORY AS EPISTEMOLOGY

systematic project of linguistic disambiguation of propositions, aimed at producing scientific certainty and epistemic closure, poetic thinking is far more interested in exploring unstable, incomplete, or uncertain cognitive states that appear to play such a large part in the ordinary lives of ordinary humans.

As I will discuss in more detail in the next section of this introduction, even scholastic thinkers themselves acknowledged that the very large majority of ordinary cognitive acts carried out by ordinary humans under normal circumstances occurred in the realm of contingency, and thus could not in fact produce certain, reliable scientific knowledge in the strict sense. In particular, the scholastics agreed that knowledge of physical objects through the senses could never attain the status of scientific certainty, as Robert Grosseteste observed in his influential commentary on Aristotle's *Posterior Analytics* (*c.* 1220): 'it is evident that no scientific knowledge can be obtained with regard to physical contingent objects that are grasped through sensation' [manifestum est quod scientia non est circa res transmutabiles que cadunt sub signatione sensibili].[17] While the status of sense perception was explored in depth within the medieval universities as part of the emerging 'discipline' of faculty psychology, this study argues that poetic thinking provided an alternative, complementary vehicle for analysing the nature of knowledge *as experienced by an individual*.[18] More specifically, this study suggests that the tradition of allegorical first-person dream-vision poetry growing out of the seminal *Roman de la Rose* defined a particularly suitable, almost natural space to explore the nature and operation of specifically *contingent* knowledge. Precisely because it lacked the systematic and objectivist character of scholastic *scientia*, first-person poetic fiction displayed a striking affinity with its objects, and was thus ideally suited to facilitate the analysis of the nature of uncertain, contingent, and subjective 'knowing'.[19]

The lack of certainty that for medieval thinkers characterized sensory experience also applied, *a fortiori*, to any mental experience performed or mediated by the imagination. If the senses could only be trusted within the framework of contingent, probable belief, the ontological nature of mental images and concepts was far more problematic still, and accordingly became the subject of intense debates among medieval intellectuals between the late thirteenth and mid-fourteenth century, which I review in some greater detail below. The *Roman de la Rose* shows

---

[17] Robert Grosseteste, *Commentarius in Posteriorum Analyticorum libros*, ed. by Pietro Rossi (Firenze: Olschki, 1981), I.19, p. 281. Translation mine.

[18] On natural affinities between the poetic and the contingent, see also Zeeman, 'Philosophy in Parts', pp. 217–19.

[19] For an account of how the *Roman de la Rose* signals the particular suitability of poetic thinking to explore contingency as defined by the scholastics, see especially Grellard, 'Mechanisms of Belief'. For a more extended analysis of the *Rose* in terms of its 'poetics of contingency', more broadly defined and including modern and contemporary thinkers in the conversation, see Daniel Heller-Roazen, *Fortune's Faces: The 'Roman de la Rose' and the Poetics of Contingency* (Baltimore and London: Johns Hopkins University Press, 2003). On the 'anti-systematic' character of this tradition, see also Zeeman, 'Philosophy in Parts', p. 217 and *passim*.

INTRODUCTION 9

clear evidence of engaging with such debates in very close, knowledgeable, sophisticated, but also critical and creative fashion.[20] While the broadly Aristotelian faculty psychology developed by scholastic thinkers played an important role in focusing the attention of non-scholastic intellectuals on the function of the imagination, both Jean de Meun and later poets were also able to draw on a wide range of rather different, non-scholastic discourses on knowledge. These included broadly Augustinian accounts of cognition, which often assigned a central place to direct divine intervention in the human cognitive processes—a model that was postulated on what came to be identified as a 'theory of divine illumination', discussed in further detail in the next section of this introduction. Augustine had also established a tripartite hierarchy of vision, featuring, in ascending order, physical/material vision; spiritual vision; and purely intellectual vision.[21] Later in his life Augustine also went on to develop an elaborate theory of language based on the notion of the inner word (*verbum mentis/in corde*), which in turn had major cognitive implications and was widely used and elaborated by medieval thinkers and commentators before the rise of scholasticism.[22] To these strands of thought ought to be added late antique theories of the imagination, as elaborated by philosophers and rhetoricians alike.[23] These continued to influence late medieval thought alongside the newly rediscovered works of Aristotle and their commentaries by Arabic philosophers that were privileged by scholastic writers, and were in some places absorbed within later scholastic culture, but also flowed into such hybrid textual traditions such as the increasingly popular *artes poetriae* that were produced throughout the late twelfth and thirteenth centuries.[24]

---

[20] See also Pomel, 'Visual Experiences and Allegorical Fiction'.

[21] On Augustine's threefold vision, see especially Margaret Miles, 'Vision: The Eye of the Body and the Eye of the Mind in Saint Augustine's *De Trinitate and Confessions*', *The Journal of Religion* 63.2 (1983), 125–42; and Eugene Vance, 'Seeing God: Augustine, Sensation, and the Mind's Eye', in Stephen G. Nichols, Alison Calhoun, and Andreas Kablitz, eds, *Rethinking the Medieval Senses: Heritage / Fascinations / Frames* (Baltimore: Johns Hopkins University Press, 2008), pp. 13–29.

[22] On the concept and its history, see Claude Panaccio, *Le Discours Intérieur: de Platon à Guillaume d'Ockham* (Paris: Seuil, 1999), esp. 94–119 on Augustine specifically; and Alberto Romele, *L'esperienza del 'verbum in corde': Ovvero l'ineffettività dell'ermeneutica* (Milan: Mimesis, 2013). For an account of the interplay between visual and verbal figures in Augustine's understanding of cognition, see Mary Sirridge, '*Quam videndo intus dicimus*: Seeing and Saying in De Trinitate XV', in Sten Ebbesen and Russell L. Friedman, eds, *Medieval Analyses in Language and Cognition* (Copenhagen: Royal Danish Academy of Sciences and Letters, 1999), pp. 317–30.

[23] Mireille Armisen-Marchetti, 'La notion d'imagination chez les Anciens. I: Les philosophes', *Pallas* 26 (1979), 11–51; ibid., 'La notion d'imagination chez les Anciens. II: La rhétorique', *Pallas* 27 (1980), 3–37.

[24] On the impact of late antique and scholastic theories of the imagination as well as literary theory on late medieval poetry, see especially Vincent Gillespie, 'From the Twelfth Century to *c.* 1450', and Alastair Minnis, 'Medieval Imagination and Memory', both in Alastair Minnis and Ian Johnson, eds, *The Cambridge History of Literary Criticism. Volume 2: The Middle Ages* (Cambridge: Cambridge University Press, 2005), pp. 145–235 and 239–74 respectively; and Gregor Vogt-Spira, 'Senses, Imagination, and Literature: Some Epistemological Considerations', in Nichols, Calhoun, and Kablitz, *Rethinking the Medieval Senses*, pp. 51–72.

10 MEDIEVAL ALLEGORY AS EPISTEMOLOGY

While none of these imaginative theories was primarily or even explicitly concerned with accounting for the role of the imagination in specifically *poetic* processes, all of them touched on questions that were directly relevant to the relation between words, mental images, and external objects. Poets were naturally drawn to such questions, and responded in creative and critical ways that are reflected in their own poetic practice. The nature and degree of engagement depended on material circumstances (availability of texts and commentaries) as well as on the immediate context and purpose, personal interest and inclination. I will accordingly refrain from proposing a general theoretical 'model' to describe or analyse such engagement. Instead, I have again privileged an inductive approach, preferring to assess each author's engagement with a variety of overlapping discourses and debates according to the cues and prompts provided by the poetry itself. This has involved considerable amounts of close reading informed by discussion of both broader intellectual trends and at times far more localized and circumscribed developments that appear to have shaped specific details in the work of individual poets. It seems important to stress from the beginning, therefore, that intellectually curious late medieval poets were able to tap into a capacious and diverse pool of very different discourses on language and cognition. Instead of adopting a binary model where authors of poetic fiction are univocally 'influenced' by contemporary scholastic debates, then, I suggest that it might be more productive to see such poetic work as being more loosely 'informed' by a wider range of existing debates and ideas, scholastic and not. Poets employed such diverse elements liberally and eclectically to forge their own, distinctive and often idiosyncratic path through a series of complex philosophical questions regarding human ways of knowing.

In addition to emphasizing the general sensitivity of poets to discussions of imagination and cognition by medieval intellectuals, I want to argue that specifically *allegorical* poetry provided a discursive form that was particularly well suited to the exploration of epistemological concerns. At its most basic, *allegoria* was defined as a rhetorical trope characterized by a clear disjunction between the verbal surface and its deeper meaning. This disjunction, however, was not absolute, and the two terms were linked by an oblique, ill-defined, but fundamentally figurative or 'metaphorical' relation: as Donatus had influentially noted, 'Allegory is a trope by which something else is signified than what is said' [Allegoria est tropus, quo aliud significatur quam dicitur].[25] While modern notions of allegorical poetry as a 'genre' or 'mode' are largely anachronistic,[26] it is nonetheless accurate to note that allegorical poetry, loosely defined, is grounded in the

---

[25] Donatus, *Ars Maior*, 3.6, in Louis Holtz, *Donat et la tradition de l'enseignement grammatical: etude et edition critique* (Paris: CNRS, 1981), p. 671.

[26] I examine this question in more detail elsewhere: Marco Nievergelt, 'Allegory', in Robert Rouse and Sian Echard, eds, *Blackwell Encyclopaedia of British Medieval Literature*, 4 vols (Oxford: Blackwell, 2017), I:50–9. On the difficulties of the term, see also Vladimir Brljak, 'Introduction: Allegory Past

INTRODUCTION 11

same principle of oblique signification that underpins the medieval notion of *allegoria* as a rhetorical trope.[27] It is precisely because of its inherent dependence on this principle of oblique figuration that allegorical signification becomes a particularly suitable, indeed ideal tool to explore problems of human cognition and representation. The figurative relation at the heart of the allegorical mode, then, to some extent reproduces the 're-presentational' disjunction between objects and their mental concepts or images as described in the Aristotelian tradition of faculty psychology. In examining both the natures of, and reciprocal relations between, physical objects, mental constructs, and human language, allegorical poetry ultimately explores the relations between the three principal terms involved in human cognitive processes as identified by Aristotle in a hugely influential passage of the *De Interpretatione/Periermeneias* (16a3–9): things, mental concepts, and words (see below, Section 2 of this introduction for fuller discussion).

Because of its insistently *figurative* character and its particularly pronounced reliance on visual/mental imagination, allegorical poetry is therefore able to define an experimental mental 'space' where narrative fiction can be harnessed to stage a series of thought experiments that examine a whole series of representational and cognitive processes of great complexity. More specifically, allegorical poetry consciously harnesses the imaginative potential that is the defining characteristic of 'the poetic' as understood in the Arabo-Latin scholastic tradition, recently re-examined by Vincent Gillespie but already reviewed by Gilbert Dahan.[28] As Gillespie highlights, thinkers like Al-Fārābī, Averroës, and Western scholastics who follow their lead concurred in identifying the imagination as the distinctive and defining characteristic of 'the poetic', separating it from the more strictly rhetorical, persuasive power which was widely seen as being an extrinsic, second-order response to vivid poetic images. This does not, I hasten to add, imply that vernacular writers somehow developed their own poetic experiments on the basis of scholastic theories of 'the poetic', or even that they were familiar with such theories. As Gillespie himself observes, what is remarkable about such

---

and Present', in ibid., ed., *Allegory Studies? Contemporary Perspectives* (London: Routledge, 2022), pp. 1–40.

[27] The point is made concisely in relation to the *Rose* by Fabienne Pomel in her discussion of the cognitive underpinnings of Jean de Meun's allegory, 'Visual Experiences and Allegorical Fiction', pp. 60–1. Among the rich scholarly literature on the subject of allegory, I have relied in particular on Angus Fletcher, *Allegory: The Theory of a Symbolic Mode* (Ithaca, NY: Cornell University Press, 1964); Stephen A. Barney, *Allegories of History, Allegories of Love* (Hamden CT: Archon Books, 1979); Maureen Quilligan, *The Language of Allegory: Defining the Genre* (Ithaca, NY: Cornell University Press, 1979); Carolynn Van Dyke, *The Fiction of Truth: Structures of Meaning in Narrative and Dramatic Allegory* (Ithaca, NY: Cornell University Press, 1985); Jon Whitman, *Allegory: The Dynamics of an Ancient and Medieval Technique* (Oxford: Clarendon Press, 1987); Rita Copeland and Peter T. Struck, eds, *The Cambridge Companion to Allegory* (Cambridge: Cambridge University Press, 2010); and Brljak, *Allegory Studies?*

[28] Vincent Gillespie, '*Ethice Subponitur*? The Imaginative Syllogism and the Idea of the Poetic', in Philip Knox, Jonathan Morton, and Daniel Reeve, eds, *Medieval Thought Experiments: Poetry, Hypothesis, and Experience in the European Middle Ages* (Turnhout: Brepols, 2018), pp. 297–32; and Gilbert Dahan, 'Notes et textes sur la Poétique au Moyen Âge', *AHDLMA* 47 (1980), 171–239 (esp. 188–90).

12   MEDIEVAL ALLEGORY AS EPISTEMOLOGY

scholastic accounts is that they converge so closely with much older discussions of the affective power of literature (*enargeia*) produced by classical rhetoricians such as Cicero and Quintilian.[29] These discussions were available throughout the medieval period as part of the Horatian tradition, and recur with increasing frequency within late thirteenth-century *artes poetriae*.[30] Beyond this, discussions of the *modus poeticus* by scholastic theologians likewise emphasized the cognitive potential of metaphors, figures, and tropes: the latter were considered not merely as stylistic and rhetorical tropes, but as supports for a hermeneutics hinging on the ontological 'leap' enabled by the imagination.[31] This accumulation of concurrent discussions of the imaginative and affective power of 'the poetic' during the later thirteenth century underscores, then, a much more widespread awareness of poetry as a distinctive, powerfully imaginative cognitive activity. Instead of merely 'responding' to scholastic accounts of the imaginative power of poetry, poets thus appear to have harnessed the intrinsic imaginative and speculative potential of poetic fiction for exploratory, heuristic, and actively speculative purposes. This allowed them to reflect on the cognitive possibilities of poetic fiction through the very act of producing poetic images. As will be seen in Chapter 1, the *Roman de la Rose* played a particularly important, seminal role in triggering this epistemic turn in late-medieval vernacular poetry in the Anglo-French as well as the Italian sphere, lending such vernacular poetry a distinctly philosophical, but also poetological and metapoetic character.

As Gillespie illustrates, the vividness and imaginative plasticity of such counterfactual poetic thought experiments lends them an embodied, quasi-performative quality, making them accessible not only to the rational intellect but also to pre- or sub-rational affective responses in the mind. This enables a kind of *embodied* thinking that is 'palpably' different from the purely rational thinking based on syllogistic demonstration that dominates scholastic *scientia* in the strict sense. The scholastics themselves accordingly described such thinking as being dependent on the use of the 'imaginative syllogism'. Predictably—and in line with Aristotle's own definition of *scientia*, to which I turn below—the cognitive value of the syllogism

---

[29] Gillespie, '*Ethice Subponitur?*', pp. 317–20.

[30] On *enargeia*, its terminology, and its impact, see variously Mary Carruthers, *The Craft of Thought: Meditation, Rhetoric, and the Making of Images, 400–1200* (Cambridge: Cambridge University Press, 1998), pp. 130–41; Vogt-Spira, 'Senses, Imagination, and Literature', pp. 52–4, 63–4 and *passim*. The notion of *enargeia* was still widely invoked during the early modern period, and, significantly, was applied to explain the imaginative status of dreams, on which see Pierrine Galand-Hallyn, 'Le songe et la rhétorique de l'*enargeia*', in Françoise Charpentier, ed., *Le songe à la Renaissance: colloque international de Cannes, 29–31 mai 1987* (Saint-Etienne: Institut d'Études de la Renaissance et de l'Âge classique, Université de Saint-Etienne, 1990), pp. 125–36.

[31] Gilbert Dahan, 'Saint Thomas d'Aquin et la métaphore: Rhétorique et herméneutique', *Medioevo* 18 (1992), 85–117. More broadly, the relations between the parallel discussions of language and signification found in both the Arts and Theology Faculties during the twelfth and thirteenth centuries still remain largely unclear. See especially the important study by Christopher Ocker, *Biblical Poetics before Humanism and Reformation* (Cambridge: Cambridge University Press, 2002), notably pp. 5–7, 31–71.

secundum imaginationem was considered inferior to that of both the demonstrative and the dialectical syllogism. Crucially, however, the scholastics also widely accepted that the imaginative syllogism held far greater appeal for the human mind compared to the proper, truly scientific demonstrative syllogism.[32] As Dominicus Gundissalinus stated in his *De divisione philosophiae* (after 1150), closely following Al-Fārābī, 'the imagination is always more powerfully at work in humankind than knowledge or thought' [imaginacio enim quandoque plus operatur in homine quam scientia vel cogitatio].[33]

In the light of all this, it seems important to stress that so-called 'allegorical poetry' attained its greatest cultural prominence at a time when Western European intellectual culture furnishes particularly abundant evidence for a widespread consensus concerning poetry's strong imaginative appeal—from scholastic theories of the poetic influenced by Arabic commentators on Aristotle, to the increasingly popular rhetorical theory of *enargeia* derived from late classical rhetoric, and found in late medieval treatises on the art of poetry,[34] and the spectacular growth of broadly 'allegorical' literature itself that comes to dominate European literary culture in the fourteenth century.[35] Indeed this tendency to 'allegorise' was so predominant in late medieval francophone poetry as a whole that Sarah Kay and Adrian Armstrong have suggested that the one medieval term that comes closest to being a synonym for our modern idea of 'allegory' is, quite simply, the middle French *poetrie*.[36]

What is even more striking, it seems to me, is that the medieval notion of a distinctly plastic and embodied figurative imagination should converge so closely with *modern* accounts of metaphor and figurative thinking that have been

---

[32] See especially Deborah L. Black, 'The "Imaginative Syllogism" in Arabic Philosophy: A Medieval Contribution to the Philosophical Study of Metaphor', *Mediaeval Studies* 51 (1989), 242–67.

[33] Dominicus Gundissalinus, *De divisione philosophiae*, ed. Alexander Fidora and Dorothee Werner (Freiburg: Herder, 2007), p. 156, quoted and discussed in Gillespie, '*Ethice Subponitur?*', p. 303, and Dahan, 'Notes et textes sur la Poétique', p. 190.

[34] Philippe Maupeu has argued for an impact of the late classical theory of *enargeia* on Deguileville's poetry in particular, providing what seems to me compelling arguments if not indisputable 'evidence' for influence. See Philippe Maupeu, 'Statut de l'image rhétorique et de l'image peinte dans le *Pèlerinage de Vie Humaine* de Guillaume de Deguileville', *Le Moyen Age* 114.3 (2008), 509–30.

[35] On the topic, see variously Armand Strubel, *La Rose, Renard et le Graal. La littérature allégorique en France au XIIIe s.* (Paris: Champion, 1989); ibid., '*Grant senefiance a*': *Allégorie et littérature au Moyen Âge* (Paris: Honoré Champion, 2002); Fabienne Pomel, *Les Voies de l'au-delà et l'essor de l'allégorie au Moyen Âge* (Paris: Champion, 2001); Sarah Kay, *The Place of Thought: The Complexity of One in Late Medieval French Didactic Poetry* (Philadelphia: University of Pennsylvania Press, 2007); Armstrong and Kay, *Knowing Poetry*. See also the older studies by Pierre-Yves Badel, 'Le poème allégorique', in Daniel Poirion, ed., *Grundriss der Romanischen Literaturen des Mittelalters, vol. VIII.1: La littérature française aux XIVe et XVe siècles*, 11 vols, gen. eds Hans U. Gumbrecht and Ulrich Mölk (Heidelberg: Carl Winter, 1988), pp. 139–60; and Hans Robert Jauss. 'Entstehung und Strukturwandel der allegorischen Dichtung', in Hans Robert Jauss and Erich Koehler, eds., *Grundriss der romanischen Literaturen des Mittelalters, vol. VI: La Littérature didactique, allégorique et satirique*, 11 vols, gen. ed. Hans U. Gumbrecht and Ulrich Mölk. Heidelberg: Winter, 1968, pp. 146–244.

[36] Armstrong and Kay, *Knowing Poetry*, p. 9.

14 MEDIEVAL ALLEGORY AS EPISTEMOLOGY

developed by present-day cognitive science and psycholinguists.[37] On the one hand, cognitive scientists have insisted on the 'need to recognize how imagery is accompanied by sensorimotor sensations, or whole "body-loops", which give imagistic experience its rich phenomenal quality'.[38] On the basis of a review of empirical studies of this question, Raymond W. Gibbs has called for a fundamental modification of the dominant accounts of cognition, all of which are ultimately derived from a tacit, implicit acceptance of Cartesian mind-body dualism. For Gibbs, we need to

> create an embodied model of mind that is not internal to people's heads, but is distributed as a 'cognitive web' across brains, bodies, and world. This distributed, embodied view of cognition offers a vision of human thought that is far less internally computational and far more bodily extended into the real world of action than is traditionally understood in cognitive science.[39]

On the other hand, recent generations of psycholinguists have examined the role in metaphorical representation in enabling various forms of embodied simulation, arguing that

> significant aspects of metaphor use involve people simulating what it must be like to engage in specific bodily actions referred to in metaphorical expressions. These mental reenactments demonstrate how the imagination is tied to bodily action and more specifically suggest the ongoing role that imaginative processes play in verbal metaphor understanding.[40]

While in this study I will not be *applying* the insights of modern-day psycholinguistics to the study of medieval literature, it seems important to note that there are powerful affinities and resonances at work here. Despite the dominance of broadly dualist models of the mind/soul vs. body from Augustine to Descartes,[41] then, Western culture also appears to be characterized by a residual, latent but

---

[37] Much of this recent work has developed ideas originally proposed by George Lakoff and Mark Johnson, especially in *Metaphors we Live By* (Chicago: University of Chicago Press, 1980); and ibid. *Philosophy in the Flesh* (New York: Basic Books, 1999). For more recent work that resonates closely with some of the readings presented here, see especially Raymond W. Gibbs, *Embodiment and Cognitive Science* (Cambridge: Cambridge University Press, 2005); and ibid., ed., *The Cambridge Handbook of Metaphor and Thought* (Cambridge: Cambridge University Press, 2008). The relevance of such contemporary work to the study of medieval poetry, and more specifically to the study of its figurative qualities in relation to an 'incarnational poetics' has been suggested by Maria Cristina Cervone, *Poetics of the Incarnation: Middle English Writing and the Leap of Love* (Philadelphia: University of Pennsylvania Press, 2013), p. 21. See further below, Chapter 3.5.

[38] Gibbs, *Embodiment and Cognitive Science*, p. 138.

[39] Gibbs, *Embodiment and Cognitive Science*, p. 157.

[40] Raymond W. Gibbs and Teenie Matlock, 'Metaphor, Imagination, and Simulation: Psycholinguistic Evidence', in Gibbs, *The Cambridge Handbook of Metaphor and Thought*, pp. 161–76 (173).

[41] On the similarities and differences between Augustinian and Cartesian dualism, see Peter King, 'Why Isn't the Mind-Body Problem Medieval?', in Henrik Lagerlund, ed., *Forming the Mind: Essays*

persistent interest in the possibilities of embodied knowing associated with the faculty of the imagination—an interest shared by the *antiqui*, the *moderni*, and the *post-moderni*.

This persistent interest in the affective and imaginative potential of poetic fiction raises the more difficult question of the cognitive, speculative, and 'philosophical' value of poetry. What kind of knowledge do such mental images convey, and what kind of cognitive operations are enabled by poetic figures in general, and by allegorical poetry in particular? In what ways can poetry really serve the ends of philosophy or at least intellectual speculation? I already mentioned that late medieval intellectuals generally considered imaginative processes to have a far lower cognitive value than demonstrative Aristotelian *scientia*.[42] Thus, as Jonathan Morton has observed, allegory's reliance on linguistic and mental figuration entails a *deliberate*, self-conscious transgression of the strictures imposed by Aristotle on the language of strictly philosophical reasoning and demonstration, which ought to be rigorously univocal and unambiguous. As Aristotle observes in book IV of the *Metaphysics* (IV.4 1006b7-8), 'not to have a single meaning is to signify nothing at all' [non unum significare nichil significare est],[43] and this notion constitutes the foundation upon which rests Aristotle's principle of non-contradiction (cf. *Metaph* IV.3 1005b19-20): 'And it will not be possible for the same thing to be and not to be, except in virtue of an ambiguity' [Et non erit esse et non esse idem nisi secundum equiuocationem] (*Metaph* IV.3 1006b19-20).[44] In the *Sophistical Refutations*, too, Aristotle identifies unnoticed cases of equivocation (or homonymy) as the first and gravest of the six linguistic fallacies that will entail erroneous conclusions (165b24 ff.). This insistence on the necessity of univocity—i.e. the univocal and unambiguous signification of terms—for philosophical reasoning remains constant throughout the medieval period, and is reiterated in numerous early commentaries that shape the later evolution of logic, such as Boethius's second commentary on the *De Interpretatione* (*Periermeneias*), where he asserts that verbal equivocation renders determinations of any kind simply impossible.[45] The entire philosophical project of late medieval scholastic logic, and particularly the study of the semantics of terms, in turn arises out of the need

---

on the Internal Senses and the Mind/Body Problem from Avicenna to the Medical Enlightenment (Dordrecht: Springer, 2007), pp. 187–205.

[42] Gillespie, '*Ethice subponitur?*', pp. 300–4.

[43] Aristotle, *Metaphysica, lib. I–XIV, Recensio et Translatio Guillelmi de Moerbeka*, ed. Gudrun Villemin-Diem (Leiden: Brill, 1995). See Jonathan Morton, 'Sophisms and Sophistry in the *Roman de la Rose*', in Morton and Nievergelt, p. 91. See also Morton's discussion of the *Rose* in terms of its relation to scholastic methods, in his *The Roman de la Rose in its Philosophical Context: Art, Nature, and Ethics* (Oxford: Oxford University Press, 2018), pp. 13–35.

[44] See further Wouter Goris, 'The Foundation of the Principle of Non-Contradiction. Some Remarks on the Medieval Transformation of Metaphysics', *Documenti e studi sulla tradizione filosofica medievale* 22 (2011), 527–55.

[45] Lambertus Marie de Rijk, *Logica Modernorum. A Contribution to the History of Early Terminist Logic.* 2 vols (Assen: Van Grocum, 1962–7), I:25–7, on *De Interpretatione* 129.14–132.21.

to reduce argumentative and demonstrative language to univocal signification.[46] Being produced within an intellectual context that places an extremely high value on the elimination of ambiguity, allegorical poetry therefore ought to be understood as a form of thought and expression that, I argue, *deliberately* transgresses such rules of univocity. This further reinforces the intimate link between allegorical expression and contingency: as a form of thought that foregrounds and intensifies the representational and meta-representational character of the poetic imagination, allegorical dream-poetry defines a space whose formal qualities are self-consciously contingent. Allegorical poetic fiction thus enables an exploration of contingency that can rely on a natural, intrinsic affinity of its language with its object, both pertaining to the realm of contingency.

My analysis in the chapters that follow is therefore grounded in the desire to illuminate what is most distinctive about allegorical poetry when compared to scholastic methods of analysis: instead of being organized around the principle of disembodied syllogistic demonstration and depersonalized objective causal proof that characterizes Aristotelian *scientia*, the epistemology of allegorical poetry is fundamentally contingent, relativistic, and subjectivistic. Allegorical dream-poetry is concerned with the nature of emphatically probabilistic, experiential, uncertain knowledge, as apprehended by an embodied individual subject whose cognitive abilities are both radically impaired yet infinitely perfectible. This study therefore aims to foreground the intellectual dynamism and exploratory character of late medieval allegorical dream vision poetry, recognizing its ambition to function as a tool of active intellectual speculation that provides an important supplement or alternative to the strictures of scholastic reasoning based on logical proof and demonstration. Such an approach, I hope, can provide a useful model for a more articulated, inclusive, pluralistic, and interconnected intellectual history that recognizes the distinctive contribution of vernacular poetic fiction.

2. Medieval Epistemology

Before going on to examine how exactly each individual poem develops its own reflections on the workings of human language, cognition, and experience, it will be necessary to provide a condensed overview of some of the most important epistemological issues debated by scholastic philosophers in the period in question, *c.* 1250–1400.

Intellectual historians invariably point out that the late medieval curriculum did not, in fact, define a separate area of inquiry that would correspond to the

---

[46] See Lambertus Marie de Rijk, 'Semantics and Ontology: An Assessment of Medieval Terminism', *Vivarium* 51 (2013), 11–59 (30–1).

modern discipline of 'epistemology'.[47] This does not mean, however, that medieval intellectuals did not theorize and debate the nature of knowledge or analyse processes of human cognition—quite the opposite. Discussion of epistemological problems was widespread from the middle of the thirteenth century onwards, occurring within a wide range of different disciplines, from the language arts to the natural sciences, faculty psychology, and theology. For the period in question, the most fundamental framework for the categorization of knowledge was provided by Aristotle's *Analytica posteriora*, hugely influential in the Latin West after James of Venice produced the first translation during the second quarter of the twelfth century.[48] It has been argued that James's translation of the *Analytica posteriora* was the single most important event of the larger cultural process that saw the full range of Aristotle's writings on logic and on the natural sciences being 'rediscovered' in the Latin West, leading to a fundamental overhaul of the entire system of knowledge in late medieval culture. The influence of the *Analytica posteriora* is accordingly foundational, and provides the inescapable framework for any discussion of human knowledge during the late medieval period, in any of the scientific disciplines studied within the medieval Universities.

Crucially, the Latin translation of the *Analytica posteriora* established the opposition between certain knowledge (*scientia*) and probable belief (*opinio*), and stipulated the conditions under which *scientia* in the strict sense could be obtained. To qualify as *scientia* or *epistēmē*, conclusions had to be the result of syllogistic demonstration based on self-evident, necessary first principles. Among the many difficulties caused by Aristotle's definition of apodictic *scientia*, the most notable is that it appears to demand impossibly strict standards for the attainment of 'certainty':[49] in fact, only a small set of first principles in metaphysics and mathematics deserve to be categorized as 'necessary' truths. In his recent work, Robert Pasnau has accordingly argued that the definition of *scientia* provided by the *Analytica*

---

[47] See for instance Joseph Owens, 'Faith, Ideas, Illumination, and Experience', in *CHLMP*, pp. 440–59(459); and Robert Pasnau, *After Certainty: A History of our Epistemic Ideals and Illusions* (Oxford: Oxford University Press, 2017), pp. 1–2 and *passim*.

[48] For useful brief overviews, see for instance Christophe Grellard, 'Epistemology', in Henrik Lagerlund, ed., *Encyclopedia of Medieval Philosophy: Philosophy between 500 and 1500*, 2 vols (Dordrecht: Springer, 2011), I: 294–300; Robert Pasnau, 'Science and Certainty', in *CHMP*, I:357–68. For an overview of issues in the medieval reception of the *Posterior Analytics*, see Joël Biard, ed., *Raison et démonstration. Les commentaires médiévaux sur les Seconds Analytiques* (Turnhout: Brepols, 2015). For a fuller and historically far-reaching discussion of Western epistemology in the wake of the *Posterior Analytics*, see Pasnau, *After Certainty*. For the Latin versions, see Aristotle, *Analytica posteriora. Translationes Iacobi, Anonymi sive Ioannis Gerardi et Recensio Guillelmi de Moerbeke*, ed. Lorenzo Minio-Paluello and Bernard G. Dod (Bruges/Paris: Desclée de Brouwer, 1962).

[49] This concern with 'certainty' is, rather characteristically, not strictly Aristotelian, but is the result of the lexical choices during the translation of his works into Latin, where *akribeia* (precision, accuracy, exactitude) is rendered as *certitudo*. See further Jakob Leth Fink, 'Aristotle and the Medievals on Certainty', in Sten Ebbesen, David Bloch, et al., eds, *History of Philosophy in Reverse: Reading Aristotle through the Lenses of Scholars from the Twelfth to the Sixteenth Centuries* (Copenhagen: The Royal Danish Academy of Sciences and Letters, 2014), pp. 148–65; and Pasnau, *After Certainty*, pp. 31–2.

posteriora, and widely adopted by medieval scholasticism, was not so much operative in practice, but rather defined a liminal, ideal state of certainty that was all but unattainable in our daily experience.[50] All of the ordinary conclusions, insights, deductions, and experiences of the physical world are accordingly situated in the domain of contingency, and thus can only ever attain the level of *opinio*.[51]

This state of affairs did not, however, automatically entail a radically sceptical attitude towards knowledge. For the most part, scholastic writers broadly accepted that our knowledge of contingent objects, as opposed to necessary ones, was for the most part reliable. Thus Robert Grosseteste observes in his influential commentary on the *Analytica posteriora* that the term *scientia* is also commonly used in a looser sense to refer to knowledge of contingent objects, in the mind and through the senses:

> It does not escape us, however, that having *scientia* is spoken of broadly, strictly, more strictly, and most strictly. *Scientia* commonly so-called is merely comprehension of truth. Unstable contingent things are objects of *scientia* in this way. *Scientia* strictly so-called is comprehension of the truth of things that are always or most of the time in one way. Natural things—namely, natural contingencies—are objects of *scientia* in this way. Of these things there is demonstration broadly so-called. *Scientia* more strictly speaking so-called is comprehension of the truth of things that are always in one way. Both the principles and the conclusions in mathematics are objects of *scientia* in this way ... *Scientia* most strictly so-called is comprehension of what exists immutably by means of the comprehension of that from which it has immutable being. This is by means of the comprehension of a cause that is immutable in its being and in its causing.[52]

The fact remains that most cognitive states that we would commonly identify as conveying reliable 'knowledge' fall well short of the exacting standards of *scientia* in the strictest sense. While radical scepticism was for the most part avoided, this was achieved at the cost of leaving the specific mechanics of mental operations and cognitive acts unexplained. It was therefore largely within individual

---

[50] See Pasnau, *After Certainty*, pp. 3–6. See also Pasnau's earlier discussion building up to this conclusion, 'Science and Certainty'.

[51] For a discussion of the place of the *Roman de la Rose* very specifically within this scholastic scheme, see Christophe Grellard, 'Mechanisms of Belief'.

[52] 'Sed non lateat nos quod scire dicitur communiter et proprie et magis et maxime proprie. Est enim scientia communiter veritatis comprehensio, et sic sciuntur contingentia erratica; et dicitur scientia proprie comprehensio veritatis eorum que semper vel frequentius uno modo se habent, et sic sciuntur naturalia, scilicet contingentia nata, quorum est demonstratio communiter dicta. Dicitur etiam scientia magis proprie comprehensio veritatis eorum que semper uno modo se habent, et sic sciuntur in mathematicis tam principia quam conclusiones. ... [E]st quod maxime proprie dicitur scire comprehensio eius quod immutabiliter est per comprehensionem eius a quo illud habet esse immutabile, et hoc est per comprehensionem cause immutabilis in essendo et in causando' Grosseteste, *Commentarius in Posteriorum Analyticorum libros*, I.2, p. 99.

INTRODUCTION   19

branches or disciplines of scientific learning that such epistemological problems and challenges were explored in detail. The emphasis was placed less explicitly on the question of *whether* true knowledge was at all possible and under what conditions it could be obtained—the primary concern of epistemology in the strict sense as currently understood—and more specifically on attempting to provide accurate descriptions of *how* knowledge of different kinds was produced, occurred, crystallized, or simply 'happened' in an individual human subject.

In the remainder of this section, I will provide a brief, highly condensed and non-exhaustive overview of some of the most important debates within the area of epistemology in specific branches and disciplines of scientific thought. These debates, I argue, provide the broader context for the interest in epistemological questions that characterizes late medieval poetry as a whole, and more specifically the work of Jean de Meun, Guillaume de Deguileville, and William Langland. I have organized my survey of late medieval debates in epistemology under three headings: language, cognition, and experience. Just like the term 'epistemology' itself, these terms are anachronistic, and establish categories that do not neatly overlap with the disciplinary structures of medieval intellectual culture. However, the three terms have the advantage of facilitating examination of a set of recurrent philosophical problems that were often debated in very different areas or 'pockets' of medieval intellectual culture, allowing me to group together apparently disparate developments under an overarching thematic concern. It may be added, moreover, that in practice medieval intellectuals themselves routinely crossed the extremely fluid boundaries among 'disciplines', variously moving between the different faculties of the medieval universities—arts, theology, law, and medicine—or leaving the university world altogether to take up administrative roles within various political and ecclesiastical institutions, thus facilitating a kind of interdisciplinary thinking *avant la lettre*. As I will explore in some greater detail later in this study, each of the three poets I will be concerned with was particularly well placed to access a wide range of very different, and at time divergent and competing discourses on these three themes. While they worked within very different, unique socio-cultural environments, they all occupied a somehow hybrid position in terms of their institutional and intellectual affiliations, and this allowed each of them to engage critically with a wide range of very different discourses and ideas.[53]

---

[53] Alain Corbellari has argued convincingly that the emergence of a certain kind of intellectually challenging and ethically engaged but often socially critical vernacular literary culture in France becomes possible precisely thanks to the work of such *clercs* with close ties to the schools and universities. See Alain Corbellari, *La voix des clercs: Littérature et savoir universitaire autour des dits du XIIIe siècle* (Geneva: Droz, 2005). For a study of the development of francophone vernacular literary culture in the context of the rise of early Aristotelian logic in the twelfth century, see especially Sarah Kay, *Courtly Contradictions: The Emergence of the Literary Object in the Twelfth Century* (Stanford: Stanford University Press, 2001); and Virginie Greene, *Logical Fictions in Medieval Literature and Philosophy* (Cambridge: Cambridge University Press, 2014).

20 MEDIEVAL ALLEGORY AS EPISTEMOLOGY

Language

While epistemologically orientated discussions of language emerged to particular prominence during the scholastic period, it is worth stressing that the interest in language was firmly established in the culture of the Latin Christian Middle Ages long before the advent of scholasticism from 1200 onwards. This meant that authors of the late medieval period—scholastic and monastic, Latin and vernacular, conservative or innovative—were able to tap into a much longer history of medieval ideas and discussions of language or signification. As will be seen, my three authors all engaged with such non-scholastic theories of language and signification as well as more recent developments in semantics and supposition theory. While in the chapters that follow I will provide additional background on some of these earlier ideas about language and cognition where relevant, in this section I will concentrate primarily on late medieval scholastic developments.[54]

Scholastic discussions of language and signification are, like scholasticism as a whole, largely grounded in the rediscovery of Aristotle's full corpus of works on logic and natural philosophy from the twelfth century onwards. The rise of the Universities during the thirteenth century enabled more focused study of various aspects of linguistic signification from the perspective of an Aristotelian examination of natural causation: thinkers now examined the relationship of linguistic reference (*suppositio*) linking words to physical and mental objects; the mental and cognitive processes involved in language use; and the causal processes involved in various kind of speech acts, including ordinary utterances, interjections, sacramental formulas, and magic spells, among many other types of utterances. While

---

[54] For some broad overviews see, on grammar and rhetoric, Rita Copeland and Ineke Sluiter, eds, *Medieval Grammar and Rhetoric: Language Arts and Literary Theory, AD 300–1475* (Oxford: Oxford University Press, 2009). On Theology, see Marcia L. Colish, *The Mirror of Language: A Study of the Medieval Theory of Knowledge*, rev. edn (Lincoln and London: University of Nebraska Press, 1983); and Luisa Valente, *Logique et théologie: Les Écoles Parisiennes entre 1150 et 1220* (Paris: Vrin, 2008). On biblical hermeneutics, see Ocker, *Biblical Poetics before Humanism and Reformation*; and Gillian R. Evans, *The Language and Logic of the Bible: the Earlier Middle Ages*. Vol. 1, and *The Road to Reformation*. Vol. 2 (Cambridge: Cambridge University Press, 1984 and 1985). In addition to the logical, referential, and cognitive concerns of the scholastic language arts I discuss in what follows—which, I assume, will be largely unfamiliar to most literary historians—I will also be referring to the more strictly textual and hermeneutic concerns of scholastic 'literary criticism', which have been far more extensively studied, only where they are directly relevant to my arguments. This tradition has been thoroughly examined and its impact on vernacular literature abundantly discussed. See notably the important work by Alastair Minnis, especially *Medieval Theory of Authorship: Scholastic Literary Attitudes in the later Middle Ages*, 2nd edn (Philadelphia: University of Pennsylvania Press, 2010); Ian R. Johnson and Alastair J. Minnis, eds, *The Cambridge History of Literary Criticism: The Middle Ages* (Cambridge: Cambridge University Press, 2008); Alastair Minnis, *Translations of Authority in Medieval English Literature: Valuing the Vernacular* (Cambridge: Cambridge University Press, 2009). See also Rita Copeland, *Rhetoric, Hermeneutics, and Translation in the Middle Ages: Academic Traditions and Vernacular Texts* (Cambridge: Cambridge University Press, 1995). On the *Rose* more specifically and its relation to such traditions, see Alastair Minnis, *Magister Amoris: The 'Roman de la Rose' and Vernacular Hermeneutics* (Oxford: Oxford University Press, 2001).

these inquiries were conducted in a register largely determined by Aristotle's ideas about natural causation, it was ultimately the Augustinian notion of words as 'signs' that was the starting point for *all* major developments in the study of language throughout the thirteenth and early fourteenth centuries, both in the *trivium* and in theology. It is within the context of this widespread rise of interest in semiotics, semantics, and Aristotelian principles of causation that the interest in the specifically cognitive function of language ought to be situated.[55]

One recurrent difficulty that was hotly debated by logicians but which also affected a number of other disciplines concerned the question of the 'object' of knowledge: what is, ultimately, the 'thing' that is known through a cognitive act? Do humans know particular, natural, and contingent objects in the physical world (Peter John Olivi), an intentional and purely conceptual *verbum* (Thomas Aquinas), the propositions themselves as constituted by linguistic or mental objects (William of Ockham and Robert Holcot), or the notorious *complexe significabile*, i.e. an abstract but extra-mental entity signified by linguistic constructs (Adam of Wodeham and Gregory of Rimini)?[56] Debates on the nature of the object of knowledge thus often took the form of an examination of mental operations involved in the thinking process, leading to the development of elaborate theories of mental representation and mental language. The primary concern of such discussions was essentially the analysis of the relationships between language, empirical reality, and mental/conceptual objects. This interest culminated in the early fourteenth century with the generation of Burley, Ockham, and Buridan, whose works effected the 'semiotical turn' of scholasticism from the

---

[55] The most reliable and accessible introduction to thirteenth- and early fourteenth-century debates in 'philosophy of language', both within the Arts and Theology faculties, can be found in Costantino Marmo, *La Semiotica del XIII secolo: Tra Arti Liberali e Teologia* (Milano: Bompiani, 2010), esp. pp. 1–92 (a translation into French, *La Sémiotique du XIIIe siècle*, by Hélène Leblanc, is in preparation). See also Irène Rosier, *La Parole Comme Acte: Sur la Grammaire et la Sémantique au XIIIe Siècle* (Paris: Vrin, 1994), esp. pp. 95–112 on Augustine's theory of signs and its thirteenth-century elaborations; and Costantino Marmo, *Semiotica E Linguaggio Nella Scolastica: Parigi, Bologna, Erfurt, 1270–1330. La Semiotica Dei Modisti* (Rome: Istituto Storico Italiano Per il Medio Evo, 1994), pp. 19–108. On the vexed question of the relations and exchanges between debates in the Arts and Theology faculties, see especially Ocker, *Biblical Hermeneutics before the Reformation.*

[56] On these, see notably Panaccio, 'Mental Representation', in *CHMP*, I:346–56 (350–1), and Pasnau, 'Science and Certainty', *CHMP*, I:357–68 (361–2). For a fuller study of the figures mentioned here see, among other studies, Juhana Toivanen, *Perception and the Internal Senses: Peter of John Olivi on the Cognitive Functions of the Sensitive Soul* (Leiden: Brill, 2013); José Filipe Silva and Juhana Toivanen, 'The Active Nature of the Soul in Sense Perception: Robert Kilwardby and Peter Olivi', *Vivarium* 48.3 (2010), 245–78; Claude Panaccio, 'Semantics and Mental Language', in Paul Vincent Spade, ed., *The Cambridge Companion to Ockham* (Cambridge: Cambridge University Press, 1999), 53–75; Claude Panaccio, *Ockham on Concepts* (Aldershot: Ashgate, 2004); E. A. Moody, 'A Quodlibetal Question of Robert Holcot, O.P., on the Problem of the Objects of Knowledge and Belief', *Speculum* 39 (1964), 53–74; Jeffrey E. Brower and Susan Brower-Toland, 'Aquinas on Mental Representation: Concepts and Intentionality', *Philosophical Review* 117.2 (2008), 193–243; Katherine H. Tachau, *Vision and Certitude in the Age of Ockham: Optics, Epistemology, and the Foundations of Semantics, 1250–1345* (Leiden: Brill, 1988), pp. 39–55, 123–30, 244–55, 303–10; Pascale Bermon, *L'assentiment et son objet chez Grégoire de Rimini* (Paris: Vrin, 2007).

22 MEDIEVAL ALLEGORY AS EPISTEMOLOGY

fourteenth century onwards.[57] While such a turn was undeniably innovative, the turn had roots in earlier developments. The most important traditions to shape this development were the works of twelfth- and thirteenth-century terminist logicians (language); thirteenth-century analysis of the soul's faculties, cognition, and perception (cognition); and the theologians' discussion of the theory of divine illumination (experience). I shall discuss each of these in turn.

Terminist logicians were primarily concerned with explaining the referential function of language, and developed an elaborate system to analyse the semantics of linguistic terms and their signifying operation in spoken and written use.[58] Linguistic terms were treated as signs endowed with psycho-physical qualities enabling them to signify—a process of causation that was explained with reference to Aristotle's seminal, and hugely problematic, semiotic triangle described in the opening lines of the *De Interpretatione* (*Periermenias,* 16a3–9):

> Now spoken sounds are symbols of affections in the soul, and written marks symbols of spoken sounds. And just as written marks are not the same for all men, neither are spoken sounds. But what these are in the first place signs of—affections of the soul—are the same for all; and what these affections are likenesses of— actual things—are also the same. These matters have been discussed in the work on the soul and do not belong to the present subject [cf. *De anima*, III.5–8].[59]

It is hard to overestimate the impact of this passage on medieval approaches to language, semiotics, and semantics, and it has been observed that the entirety of 'the medieval debate on signification can be regarded as a commentary on

---

[57] See especially the contributions in Guyla Klima, ed., *Intentionality, Cognition, and Mental Representation in Medieval Philosophy* (New York: Fordham University Press, 2015); Panaccio, *Ockham on Concepts*; and Elizabeth Karger, 'Mental Sentences According to Burley and to the Early Ockham', *Vivarium* 34.2 (1996), 193–230. Martin M. Tweedale, 'Mental Representations in Later Medieval Scholasticism', in J-C. Smith, ed., *Historical Foundations of Cognitive Science* (Dordrecht: Kluwer, 1990), pp. 35–51; and ibid., 'Representation in Scholastic Epistemology', in Henrik Lagerlund, ed., *Representation and Objects of Thought in Medieval Philosophy* (London: Routledge, 2007), pp. 73–90. On the impact and reception of Ockham in England, see especially Courtenay, *Schools and Scholars*, pp. 193–306; ibid. *Ockham and Ockhamism: Studies in the Dissemination and Impact of his Thought* (Leiden: Brill, 2008), esp. pp. 91–228.

[58] For useful introductory overviews, see Lambertus Marie de Rijk, 'The Origins of the Theory of the Properties of Terms', and Paul Vincent Spade, 'The Semantics of Terms', both in *CHLMP*, pp. 159–73 and 188–96; and E. Jennifer Ashworth, 'Terminist Logic', in *CHMP*, I:146–58. For more thoroughgoing discussion, see Marmo, *La Semiotica del XIII Secolo*; Rosier, *La parole comme acte*. For a collection of relevant primary texts and discussions, see de Rijk, *Logica Modernorum*.

[59] In the Moerbeke translation, 'Sunt quidem igitur que in voce earum que in anima passionum symbola et que scribuntur eorum que in voce. Et sicut neque littere omnibus eedem, sic neque voces eedem; quorum tamen hec signa primum, eedem omnibus passiones anime, et quarum hee similitudines, res iam eedem. De hiis quidem igitur dictum est in hiis que de anima'. See Aristotle, *De interpretatione vel Periermenias. Translatio Boethii*, ed. L. Minio-Paluello; *Translatio Guillelmi de Moerbeka*, ed. G. Verbeke, rev. L. Minio-Paluello. Bruges and Paris: Desclée De Brouwer, 1965, p. 41. All Aristotle translations, except where otherwise noted, are from Aristotle, *The Complete Works of Aristotle: The Revised Oxford Translation*, ed. Jonathan Barnes. 2 vols (Princeton: Princeton University Press, 1984).

these few lines'.[60] Starting from this scheme, terminist logicians theorized the relations of signification obtaining between verbal signs or sounds, written signs, and mental concepts, and their relation to contingent, physical objects in the real world. As well as developing the central notions of reference or supposition that described various types of signification, terminist logicians also elaborated associated notions of connotation (i.e. the evocation of associated meanings, as for instance the term 'black' will connote the notion of 'white', or the idea of 'blindness' will connote the idea of 'sight'), ampliation and restriction (processes through which the signification of a word is expanded or narrowed down, for instance through the addition of adjectives or relative clauses, or with reference to context), debated the truth value of specific utterances and different types of supposition, analysed cases of improper, figurative, or equivocal utterances, and examined in depth the question of the conventional imposition of meaning (*significata*), and the authority and stability of such impositions (developing, notably, Aristotle's observations in *Categorieae* 7a5–7).

Twelfth- and thirteenth-century terminist logic and semantics became an important tool for tackling a wide range of philosophical and theological problems, ranging from analysis of Trinitarian theology and the sacraments, to the resolution of apparent contradictions in Scripture for biblical exegetes, and the disambiguation of apparent fallacies or instances of paradox and equivocation in later sophismatic literature.[61] William of Ockham's innovation in the early fourteenth century essentially consisted in applying the full range of insights about signification, supposition, connotation, and representation developed by the earlier terminists to a fully fledged, systematic analysis of discursive thought as such.[62] This ultimately allowed him and his successors to develop an elaborate analysis of 'mental language', describing conceptual processes in terms of their signifying operations. Since mental concepts were the correlatives of linguistic terms, concepts themselves functioned as signs within a wider semiotic system endowed with its own syntax and semantics. Crucially, however, many of Ockham's innovations amounted to elaborations of ideas already present in the work of earlier

---

[60] Giorgio Pini, 'Species, Concept and Thing: Theories of Signification in the Second Half of the Thirteenth Century', *Medieval Philosophy and Theology* 8.1 (1999), 21–52 (22). See also Norman Kretzmann, 'Aristotle on Spoken Sounds Significant by Convention', in J. Corcoran, ed., *Ancient Logic and its Modern Interpretations* (Dordrecht: Reidel, 1974), pp. 3–21.

[61] See especially the range of themes covered by contributors in Ebbesen and Friedman, eds, *Medieval Analyses in Language and Cognition*. On sacramental theology, see Irène Rosier, *La parole efficace: Signe, rituel, sacré* (Paris: Éditions du Seuil, 2004). On Trinitarian theology, see e.g. Simo Knuuttila, 'Supposition and Predication in Medieval Trinitarian Logic', *Vivarium* 51 (2013), 260–74; and Courtenay, *Schools and Scholars*, pp. 276–82. On *sophismata*, see Paul Vincent Spade, 'Sophismata', in *CHMP*, I:185–95.

[62] Stephen Read, 'Concepts and Meaning in Medieval Philosophy', in Klima, *Intentionality, Cognition, and Mental Representation*, pp. 9–28; Panaccio, 'Semantics and Mental Language'. On the terminist basis and semantic orientation of many of the new theological debates in Ockham's generation more broadly, see Courtenay, *Schools and Scholars*, pp. 221–40; 258–62.

24 MEDIEVAL ALLEGORY AS EPISTEMOLOGY

generations of writers on semantics, reference, and linguistic equivocation.[63] As will be seen in Chapter 1—and contrary to a well-established assumption—it is not necessarily Ockham's nominalist semantics, but the thought of earlier terminist logicians on supposition, and particularly that of Roger Bacon, that appears to have had the deepest and most long-lasting impact on the development of allegorical poetry in the late medieval period.

Cognition

Another, closely related problem in the debate about the objects of knowledge concerned the ability to grasp not only particular entities and objects ('existents' in medieval scholastic parlance), but their ultimate 'essences' (also known as 'substances', 'common natures', or 'quiddities').[64] While most scholastics, following book II of the *Analytica posteriora*, concluded that 'perception instils the universal' (100b5), opinions on how such essences were grasped and how they were related to mental concepts, verbal signs, and external objects or existents varied dramatically. As Pasnau observes, 'the only common ground among authors with respect to the details of this process is their inability to supply persuasive details'.[65] While undeniably grounded in Aristotle's own authority, the appeal to essences created additional complications because of its loosely Platonizing undertones. This was a symptom of the pervasive presence of 'residual Platonism' in Aristotle's thought more widely, and debates on this question accordingly dovetailed with the larger, ongoing controversy over the status of universals, which resulted in the endemic conflict between realist and nominalist positions.[66] Commentators therefore agonized in the attempt to reconcile the decidedly Platonic implications of Aristotle's appeal to essences with the strongly empiricist orientation of Aristotle's overall account of knowledge through sense perception—encapsulated in the famous Aristotelian dictum that 'Nihil est in intellectu quod non prius fuerit in sensu' ('nothing is in the intellect that was not previously in the senses').[67]

---

[63] See further the articles in Egbert P. Bos, *Medieval Supposition Theory Revisited* (Leiden: Brill, 2013), a special issue of *Vivarium* 51 (2013). See especially de Rijk, 'Semantics and Ontology', 11–59.

[64] For a discussion of essence and existence in terms of their implications for cognitive theory, see Deborah L. Black, 'Mental Existence in Thomas Aquinas and Avicenna', *Mediaeval Studies* 61 (1999), 45–79. On the strictly metaphysical implications of the distinction between 'essence' and 'existence' see John F. Wippel, 'Essence and Existence', *CHLMP*, pp. 383–410; and ibid., 'Essence and Existence', *CHMP* II:609–22.

[65] Pasnau, 'Science and Certainty', p. 363.

[66] See further e.g. Alain de Libera, *La quérelle des universaux de Platon à la fin du Moyen Âge* (Paris: Seuil, 1996), from whom I borrow the expression 'platonisme résiduel', p. 29. For a concise overview, see Marilyn McCord Adams, 'Universals in the Early Fourteenth Century', *CHLMP*, pp. 411–39.

[67] Paul F. Cranefield, 'On the Origin of the Phrase, *Nihil est in intellectu quod non prius fuerit in sensu*', *Journal of the History of Medicine*, 25 (1970), 77–80. See also Aristotle's fuller discussion in *Posterior Analytics*, II.19.

INTRODUCTION 25

Given this predominance of a broadly empiricist bias in Aristotle's definition of knowledge, medieval discussions of the mind's grasp of universals was often conducted with reference to Aristotle's account of cognitive processes in his writings on natural science and the human soul, the most important of which was the *De anima*. As Aristotle himself observes in *De interpretatione* 16a3–9, quoted and discussed above, it is in this text that the cognitive mechanics underpinning linguistic reference and signification are more fully discussed. Aristotle's *De anima*, however, posed formidable challenges to Latin commentators. On the one hand, Aristotle's description of the human being as a hylomorphic compound of body and soul challenged the established notion of the body and soul as separate or at least theoretically separable substances inherited from Augustine.[68] Whereas Augustine had argued that the soul existed as a purely intellectual substance that was ontologically separate and superior to the body (e.g. *De trinitate*, VII–X),[69] Aristotle argued that 'the soul is an actuality of the first kind of a natural body having life potentially within it' [Vnde anima est primus actus corporis phisici potencia uitam habentis] (*De anima*, II.1.412a27–8).[70] This determined an understanding of human nature as being constituted as an inseparable compound of matter and form, soul and body:

That is why we can dismiss as unnecessary the question whether the soul and body are one: it is as though we were to ask whether the wax and its shape were one, or generally the matter of a thing and that of which it is a matter (*De anima*, II.1.412b5–8).[71]

---

[68] For late medieval developments, I have relied on the following discussions, in ascending order of complexity and detail: John Haldane, 'Soul and Body', in *CHMP*, I:293–304; Peter King, 'Body and Soul', in John Marenbon, ed., *The Oxford Handbook of Medieval Philosophy* (Oxford: Oxford University Press, 2012), pp. 505–24; ibid., 'Why Isn't the Mind-Body Problem Medieval?', in Henrik Lagerlund, ed., *Forming the Mind: Essays on the Internal Senses and the Mind/Body Problem from Avicenna to the Medical Enlightenment* (Dordrecht: Springer, 2007), pp. 187–205; Robert Pasnau, 'The Mind-Soul Problem', in Paul J. J. M. Bakker and Johannes M. M. H. Thijssen, eds, *Mind, Cognition and Representation: The Tradition of Commentaries on Aristotle's 'De anima'* (Aldershot: Ashgate, 2008), pp. 3–20; ibid., 'Mind and Hylomorphism', in Marenbon, *Oxford Handbook of Medieval Philosophy*, pp. 486–504; M. W. F. Stone, 'The Soul's Relation to the Body: Thomas Aquinas, Siger of Brabant and the Parisian Debate on Monopsychism', in Tim Crane and Sarah Patterson, eds, *History of the Mind-Body Problem* (London: Routledge, 2000), pp. 34–69; Magdalena Bieniak, *The Soul–Body Problem at Paris, ca. 1200–1250: Hugh of St Cher and his Contemporaries* (Leuven: Leuven University Press, 2010); Richard Dales, *The Problem of the Rational Soul in the Thirteenth Century* (Leiden: Brill, 1995); Sander W. De Boer, *The Science of the Soul: The Commentary Tradition on Aristotle's De anima, c. 1260–c. 1360* (Leuven: Leuven University Press, 2013).

[69] Augustine of Hippo, *De Trinitate Libri XV*, ed. W. J. Mountain and F. Glorie, 2 vols, CCSL 50 and 50 A (Turnhout: Brepols, 1968). English translations are from Saint Augustine, *The Trinity*, trans. Edmund Hill (New York: New City Press, 1991). For a full account, see Gerard O'Daly, *Augustine's Philosophy of Mind* (Berkeley and Los Angeles: University of California Press, 1987); and Ludger Hölscher, *The Reality of the Mind: St Augustine's Philosophical Arguments for the Human Soul as a Spiritual Substance* (London: Routledge, 1986).

[70] *De anima. Translatio 'nova': Iacobi Venetici translationis recensio; Guillelmus de Morbeka revisor translationis Aristotelis secundum Aquinatis librum* (Turnhout: Brepols, 2011).

[71] In the Moerbeke version, 'Vnde anima est primus actus corporis phisici potencia uitam habentis' [. . .] 'Si autem aliquod commune in omni anima oportet dicere, erit utique actus primus corporis

26 MEDIEVAL ALLEGORY AS EPISTEMOLOGY

Aristotle's hylomorphic understanding of the soul as the body's substantial form, then, was all but incompatible with the Augustinian view that had dominated Western accounts of the soul and its faculties until the twelfth centuries, and which had advocated a form of substance dualism in line with a Platonic ontology.[72] Thirteenth-century commentators accordingly racked their brains in the attempt to reconcile the two accounts, creating a variety of hybrid models and providing sometimes dramatically divergent interpretations of Aristotle's writings. The problem was not helped by the fact that the surviving text of the *De anima* itself was already Aristotle's 'most frustratingly incoherent and incomplete [. . .] work', and ultimately presented a series of 'notoriously murky' considerations on the nature of the soul that were very far from constituting a tightly unified and systematically organized account.[73] Indeed, Aristotle's comments appear openly self-contradictory: while he generally denied the possibility of the soul's existence separately from the body, on at least one occasion he also allowed that the contrary view *might* apply (*De anima* II.2 413b25–6).

These difficulties were further exacerbated by the specific circumstances in which Aristotle's *De anima* was transmitted to the Latin West. It was mediated and very substantially inflected by the strongly Neoplatonizing interpretations of Arabic commentators, first among them Avicenna (Ibn Sînâ), author of his own treatise on the soul. Avicenna's *De anima* was hugely influential in the West, precisely because it foregrounded the residual Platonism found in Aristotle's own writings on the soul.[74] Avicenna thus presented an account of the soul's ontology and cognitive faculty that was far more easily compatible with Augustine's substance dualism, and his text easily outstripped Aristotle's own *De anima* in terms of influence and popularity. While it may be misleading to speak of an 'augustinisme avicennisant' along the lines suggested by Etienne Gilson in the earlier twentieth century, it is undeniable that Aristotle's writings on the soul were often read

---

phisici organici. Vnde non oportet querere si unum est anima et corpus, sicut neque ceram et figuram neque omnino uniuscuiusque materiam et id cuius est materia. Vnum enim et esse cum multipliciter dicatur, quod proprie est, actus est.'

[72] This view was ubiquitous, and discussions widely available in popular texts such as pseudo-Augustinian *De spiritu et anima*, Isaac of Stella's *Epistola de anima*, William of St Thierry's *De naturae corporis et animae*, or Hugh of St Victor's *De unione corporis et spiritus*. Translations of the first three of these works are included and discussed in Bernard McGinn, *Three Treatises on Man: A Cistercian Anthropology* (Kalamazoo: Cistercian Publications, 1977).

[73] Quotations are taken respectively from Dales, *The Problem of the Rational Soul*, p. 9; and Robert Pasnau, *Theories of Cognition in the Later Middle Ages* (Cambridge: Cambridge University Press, 1997), p. 12.

[74] See especially Dag Nikolaus Hasse, *Avicenna's 'De anima' in the Latin West: The Formation of a Peripatetic Philosophy of the Soul, 1160–1300* (London: Warburg Institute, 2000). For a concise overview, see ibid., 'The Soul's Faculties', in *CHMP*, I:305–19. For a fuller account of Avicenna's Aristotelianism, see the revised edition of Dimitri Gutas, *Avicenna and the Aristotelian Tradition*, 2nd edn (Leiden: Brill, 2014), especially pp. 4–8, 67–76, 80–6, 155–9, 288–96, 335–58 on Avicenna's theory of soul and knowledge. On how Avicenna's theory of knowledge was shaped by Neoplatonism, see Peter Heath, *Allegory and Philosophy in Avicenna (Ibn Sînâ): With a Translation of the Book of the Prophet Muhammad's Ascent to Heaven* (Philadelphia: University of Pennsylvania Press, 1992), pp. 80–106.

through the lens of Avicenna's Neoplatonism, emboldening Latin commentators in their attempts to interpret Aristotle along Augustinian lines.[75]

Such debates over the nature of the soul, its functions, and its relation to the body raised troubling questions about some of the most fundamental dogmas of the Christian Church. Since the immortality of the soul was an axiomatic truth of Christianity, it was often claimed that such immortality also presupposed the human soul's ability to exist as a separate incorporeal substance independently from the body. This was a view that was difficult to accommodate with Aristotelian hylomorphism, i.e. the theory that matter and form, or body and soul, were mutually actualizing principles. The problem was to some extent obviated by the appeal to the existence of multiple souls or internal subdivisions within the soul: vegetative, animal/sensitive, and rational/intellectual. The idea went back to Plato, and was already current in the Latin West well before the arrival of Aristotle's *De anima*. In the context of the rise of interest in faculty psychology during the thirteenth century, Aristotle's typically evasive comments on the matter (*De anima*, II.2–3) prompted scholastic commentators to elaborate more sophisticated models to describe the structure and 'topography' of the soul.[76] Only the intellectual/rational soul, which was concerned with the apprehension of essences and universals, was deemed to be immortal—a view that managed to circumvent the problem of the materialist reduction of rational/intellectual powers to corporeal operations. The latter were the prerogative of the sensitive or animal soul, which was mortal, and concerned itself with the apprehension of contingent, outward realities through the mediation of corporeal sense perception.[77]

While the solutions invoked by various scholastic thinkers managed to circumvent the problem of the potential material reduction of the intellectual soul, this was achieved only at the price of displacing the problem. If the sensitive soul concerned itself with perception and cognition of ordinary particulars, and the intellectual soul only concerned itself with the apprehension of universal essences, what were their respective roles in the process of cognition, and how did

---

[75] See Étienne Gilson, 'Les Sources gréco-arabes de l'augustinisme avicennisant', *AHDLMA* 4 (1929–30), 5–149. For a discussion of more recent revisions of Gilson's hypothesis, emphasizing the greater fluidity of intellectual traditions, and widespread tendency to attempt a syncretistic alignment of Augustine and Aristotle, see especially Marrone, *The Light of thy Countenance*, I:1–25.

[76] On earlier medieval treatments of the three souls (s. IX–XII), see David N. Bell, 'The Tripartite Soul and the Image of God in the Latin Tradition', *Recherches De Théologie Ancienne Et Médiévale* 47 (1980), 16–52. For two focused studies of the views of two individual thinkers from the later, scholastic period, see Toivanen, *Perception and the Internal Senses*; and José Filipe Silva, *Robert Kilwardby on the Human Soul: Plurality of Forms and Censorship in the Thirteenth Century* (Leiden: Brill, 2012). Both studies contain useful general descriptions of the problems around the theory of soul and knowledge in the period, respectively pp. 1–18 in Toivanen, and pp. 27–42 in Silva.

[77] See especially the studies in Simo Knuuttila and Pekka Kärkkäinen, eds, *Theories of Perception in Medieval and Early Modern Philosophy* (New York: Springer, 2008). For concise overviews, see A. Mark Smith, 'Perception', *CHMP*, I:334–45; and Dominik Perler, 'Perception in Medieval Philosophy', in Mohan Matthen, ed., *The Oxford Handbook of Philosophy of Perception* (Oxford: Oxford University Press, 2015), pp. 51–65.

28 MEDIEVAL ALLEGORY AS EPISTEMOLOGY

they interact or communicate? How did the transition from perception to intellectual cognition occur, and which element, object, or faculty was the efficient cause of cognition and understanding? If the rational soul really was potentially separable—a notion that even Aristotle was able to contemplate on occasion (*De anima*, II.2 413b25–6)—and if it was the primary agent in the cognitive process, was it still possible for the rational soul to be individuated and embodied, being 'the first actuality of a natural body having life potentially within it', as Aristotle put it (*De anima*, II.1 412a27–8)?

Such questions of faculty psychology were widely debated by intellectuals who straddled the boundaries of natural science, cognitive theory, faculty psychology, philosophy, and theology in the period. While different thinkers produced a wide range of theories, the vast majority of scholastics adopted variations of the 'abstraction' theory of cognition. According to this theory, the sensitive soul's internal senses played a mediating role between sensation and intellect by 'abstracting' information from sense data, thus making it accessible to the higher-order rational powers of the intellective soul. The process was imagined as a progressive de-materialization of sense data, during which the information received by the sense organs in the form of the material *species in medio* emitted by the objects of perception was first transformed into a mental image or sensible *species*, and thence further distilled into immaterial, purely intellectual *species*.[78] Discussions of this process of abstraction resulted in a multiplication of increasingly sophisticated and convoluted accounts of human cognition, from the early thirteenth to the middle of the fourteenth century. While different thinkers explained the mechanics of this process in highly original and increasingly complex ways, nearly every scholastic writer accepted the existence of multiple forms of *species* (material, sensible and intellectual), and recognized the centrality of the internal senses in this process. Mediating between raw sense data and intellect, it was the operation of the internal senses that abstracted sense data and thus allowed the intellect to perform its own, strictly intellective cognitive operation.[79]

---

[78] See Leen Spruit, *Species Intelligibilis: From Perception to Knowledge*, 2 vols (Leiden: Brill, 1994 and 1995), especially I:29–174. See however Tachau, 'The Notion of Intentional Existence', in Ebbesen, *Medieval Analyses in Language and Cognition*, pp. 331–54 (p. 337 n. 20) for reservations about the accuracy of Spruit's wide-ranging study, and the tendency to reduce the relevance of Bacon. For more meticulous studies of *species* in the late thirteenth and early fourteenth century, see also Tachau, *Vision and Certitude*, esp. pp. 1–84; and Rega Wood, 'Imagination and Experience: In the Sensory Soul and Beyond: Richard Rufus, Roger Bacon and their Contemporaries', in Lagerlund, ed., *Forming the Mind*, pp. 27–57. On the particular relevance of optics for the development of species-theory—an issue to which I shall return in Chapter 3—see David C. Lindberg, ed., *Roger Bacon's Philosophy of Nature: A critical ed., with English transl., introd., and notes of De multiplicatione specierum and De speculis comburentibus* (Oxford: Clarendon Press, 1983); ibid., ed., *Roger Bacon and the origins of 'Perspectiva' in the Middle Ages: A critical edition and English translation of Bacon's 'Perspectiva' with introduction and notes* (Oxford: Clarendon Press, 1996).

[79] The notion of the internal senses had its bases in Aristotle, *De anima*, III.1–3, but was considerably expanded by Arabic commentators. For a short introduction, see Simo Knuuttila and Pekka

INTRODUCTION   29

While the number (between three and five), functions, and designations of the various internal senses varied widely,[80] particular emphasis was invariably placed on the imaginative faculty. The process of abstraction was widely represented as the production of a mental 'image', as a way of mediating the material *species* transmitted by the sense organs and in turn enabling an immaterial, intellectual *species* to crystallize at the level of the intellectual soul. This notion again partly finds its origin in Aristotle's ideas in *De anima*, III.7 432a6–9, where he insists that 'the soul never thinks without an image' [nequaquam sine phantasmate anima intelligit]. This insistence on the mediating power of the imagination and of mental *phantasma*, however, ultimately amounted to little more than yet another evasion technique, and ended up displacing the epistemological problem one step further: if the image allowed the human mind to mediate between the material and the purely intellectual, what, then, was the ontological status and cognitive role of the *phantasma* or *imago*, of the sensible *species*, and of the intellectual *species*?[81] How are we to understand Aristotle when he says that 'images are like sensuous contents except in that they contain no matter' [fantasmata autem sicut sensibilia sunt preter quod sunt sine materia] (*De anima*, III.8 432a9–10). If 'the soul never thinks without an image', and if 'nothing is in the intellect that was not previously in the senses', how can some form of materialist reduction of the intellect to corporeally based functions be avoided at all?[82]

Kärkkäinen, 'Medieval Theories of Internal Senses', in Simo Knuuttila and Juha Sihvola, eds, *Sourcebook for the History of the Philosophy of Mind* (Dordrecht: Springer, 2014), pp. 131–45. See further the essays in Lagerlund, ed., *Forming the Mind*. For a more detailed discussion of Avicenna's model and its influence in particular, see Carla Di Martino, *Ratio particularis: La doctrine des sens internes d'Avicenne à Thomas d'Aquin: Contribution à l'étude de la tradition Arabo-Latine de la psychologie d'Aristote* (Paris: Vrin, 2008). See also more recently Seyed N. Mousavian and Jakob Leth Fink, eds, *The Internal Senses in the Aristotelian Tradition* (Cham: Springer, 2020).

[80] For a concise account of Avicenna's model, comprising five internal senses, see Hasse, 'The Soul's Faculties', *CHMP*, I:309. For a detailed but concise account of the main variations in the scheme, see also the classic study by Harry Austryn Wolfson, 'The Internal Senses in Latin, Arabic, and Hebrew Philosophic Texts', *Harvard Theological Review* 28.2 (1935), 69–133. Encyclopaedic texts from the late thirteenth century often adopted a simplified model consisting of three senses: the common sense (which comprised the imagination); the logical/rational faculty (not to be confused with the rational soul); and memory. See e.g. Bartholomaeus Anglicus, *De proprietatibus rerum*, in the Trevisa translation (1398): *On the Properties of Things: John Trevisa's Translation of Bartholomaeus Anglicus' De Proprietatibus Rerum': a Critical Text*, ed. Michael C. Seymour. 2 vols (Oxford: Clarendon Press, 1975), p. 98.

[81] On the development of the controversy in the late thirteenth century, see Spruit, *Species Intelligibilis*, I: 175–255. Further see also Tachau, *Vision and Certitude*; Pasnau, *Theories of Cognition*; and Dominik Perler, 'Things in the Mind: Fourteenth-Century Controversies over "Intelligible Species"', *Vivarium* 34 (1996), 231–53. On the status of concepts as mental images, see also references above, nn. 56 and 57.

[82] This view indeed became widespread during the fourteenth century, in the form of a philosophical materialism, especially with Ockham and Buridan. Proponents of this position effectively postulated an embodied, hylomorphic nature of the intellectual soul—but only insofar as this conclusion was based on strictly rational, philosophical principles. Its proponents invariably reiterated their commitment to the orthodox Christian dogma of the rational soul's immateriality, but on the basis of faith alone as opposed to reason. See further Pasnau, 'Mind and Hylomorphism', pp. 493–95; Jack Zupko, 'John Buridan on the Immateriality of the Intellect', and Olaf Pluta, 'How Matter Becomes Mind', both in in

30   MEDIEVAL ALLEGORY AS EPISTEMOLOGY

Debates over the chain of causalities in the cognitive process accordingly threatened to compromise the agency and independence of the intellectual soul and its cognitive operations. Various attempts were made to try and solve the conundrum, notably by appealing by the respective operations of the 'possible' (also 'material' or 'potential') intellect on the one hand, and the 'agent' (or 'active') intellect on the other. Again these were notions that Aristotle had brought into play, respectively in III.4 and III.5 of his treatise on the soul—the latter being 'the most cryptic and contentious chapter in Aristotle's *De anima*'.[83] Quite apart from Aristotle's failure to answer question of whether the agent and possible intellects actually were individuated functional parts of individual souls or separate transcendent powers (*De anima*, III.4 429a10–12)—a problem that led to the controversy over the 'unicity' or 'plurality' of the intellect during Aquinas's lifetime[84]—Aristotle infuriatingly suggested that 'mind . . . in order to know . . . must be pure from all admixture' [Necesse est itaque, quoniam omnia intelligit, inmixtum esse] (*De anima*, III.4 429a18–19). He further insisted that 'for this reason, [mind] cannot reasonably be regarded as blended with the body' [Vnde neque misceri est rationabile ipsum corpori] (*De anima*, III.4 429a24–5)—a point that once more stood in open contradiction with the hylomorphist model that predominates in the *De anima*. Scholastics accordingly saw in Aristotle's comments on the agent and possible intellect, mediated by Avicenna's considerable development of these notions,[85] the opportunity to preserve the independent causal agency of the incorporeal intellect, and variously argued that while cognition may be *initiated* by sense-perception, it was *caused* in the final instance by the action of the agent intellect upon the potential intellect. As Aristotle suggests—but fails to develop or explain—it is this higher form of agency that ultimately causes thought:

> And in fact thought, as we have described it, is what it is by virtue of becoming all things, while there is another which is what it is by virtue of making all things: this is a sort of positive state of light; for in a sense light makes potential colours into actual colours.
>
> Thought in this sense of it is always separable, impassible, unmixed, since it is in its essential nature activity (for always the active is superior to the passive factor, the originating force to the matter) (*De anima*, III.4 430a14–19).[86]

Lagerlund, *Forming the Mind*, pp. 129–47 and 149–67 respectively; and discussion below, Chapters 3.1 and 3.5.

[83] On the Agent and Possible Intellect, see Deborah Black, 'The Nature of Intellect', in *CHMP*, I: 320–33 (quotation from p. 321).

[84] Alain de Libera, *L'unité de l'intellect: Commentaire du 'De unitate intellectus contra Averroistas' de Thomas d'Aquin* (Paris: J. Vrin, 2004). For a concise discussion of the issue, see Stone, 'The Soul's Relation to the Body'.

[85] Hasse, *Avicenna's De Anima in the Latin West*, pp. 174–223.

[86] 'et est huiusmodi quidem intellectus in quo omnia fiunt, ille uero quo omnia est facere, sicut habitus quidam, ut lumen: quodam enim modo et lumen facit potencia existentes colores actu colores.

INTRODUCTION 31

For Albert the Great, who followed the lead of Al-Kindī and Al-Fārābī, the action of the agent on the material intellect would ultimately 'elevate' the cognitive faculties to attain a state of perfected or accomplished intellect (*intellectus adeptus*), transcending the realm of materially based, contingent knowledge, and preserving the immateriality of the intellect while allowing it to become individuated through its action upon the data abstracted from perception.[87] Aquinas, by contrast, emphasizes continuous and unconscious activity of the agent intellect upon the possible intellect in the production of universals (or essences), and saw this operation as a process reflecting upon the intelligible species abstracted from the senses. Intellectual *species*, accordingly, was not so much the *object* but merely the *means* of cognition—a position that allowed Aquinas to preserve the agency of the higher intellect.[88] For Bonaventure, the agent and possible intellect were not so much instances but powers in the soul, which allowed them both to perform passive and active operations simultaneously. Richard Rufus, John Pecham, and many others ultimately envisaged the existence of two different kinds of agent intellect, one personal and individuated, the other transcendent and divine. Roger Marston followed suit in accepting the existence of two agent intellects but adopted an even more radical position, seeing the transcendent agent intellect quite simply as identical with God, and making it responsible for illuminating human cognitive acts from above.[89]

As the dizzying multiplication of increasingly elaborate models and theories attests, the central difficulty remained: no matter how many intermediary stages and additional mediating instances one was willing to postulate, the final step in this process of abstraction or de-materialization of the *species* necessarily eluded formal description and analysis, because it was *by its very definition* a process of strictly immaterial nature. With its insistence on the centrality of the mediating function of the imaginative faculty in the sensitive soul, the *species*-based account of cognition ultimately made itself endemically vulnerable to charges of either representationalism or materialist reduction, posing a number of epistemological and ontological problems that were all but insurmountable in practice. While this did not precipitate a crisis of scepticism during the fourteenth century—as the now

---

Et hic intellectus separabilis et inpassibilis et inmixtus, substancia actu ens. Semper enim honorabilius est agens paciente et principium materia.'

[87] Hasse, 'The Soul's Faculties', pp. 318–19. On Aquinas's position, see Black, 'The Nature of Intellect', 331–2.

[88] For an accessible overview, see Anthony Kenny, 'Body, Soul, and Intellect in Aquinas', in M. James and C. Crabbe, *From Soul to Self* (London: Routledge, 1999), pp. 33–48. See further the overview of arguments presented in the work of Robert Pasnau—who disputes the established view—in 'Id quo cognoscimus', in Knuuttila and Kärkkäinen, *Theories of Perception in Medieval and Early Modern Philosophy*, 131–49; ibid., *Theories of Cognition*, esp. pp. 126–30 and 134–8 on the agent intellect, and 195–219 on *species*. See also Pasnau's commentary on the relevant portions from Aquinas, *Thomas Aquinas on Human Nature: A Philosophical Study of Summa Theologiae, 1a 75–89* (Cambridge: Cambridge University Press, 2002).

[89] On Bonaventure, Pecham, and Marston, see the overview in Noone, 'Divine Illumination', *CHMP*, I: 369–83.

32 MEDIEVAL ALLEGORY AS EPISTEMOLOGY

outdated account popularized by Gordon Leff led earlier generations of scholars to believe—the difficulties posed by the *species*-based model nevertheless focused minds more intensely on the difficulty of accounting for the precise mechanisms of human cognition in the period.[90] This triggered a much more widespread interest in epistemology, relativism, and cognitive error during the early fourteenth century, among scholastics but also among writers and thinkers beyond the schools, including vernacular poets.[91] A number of scholastic thinkers ultimately started questioning the viability of a *species*-based account of perception—notably by denying the role of the *species* as the efficient cause of cognition, as Olivi did, or indeed by denying the existence of sensible *species* altogether, as in the case of William of Ockham.[92] These difficulties also appear to have preoccupied the writers of allegorical dream visions discussed in the following chapters, prompting them to use their literary craft to interrogate the status and function of mental images and the imaginative faculty in general, as well as the nature and value of their own poetic imaginings.

Experience

In what precedes, I have identified some of the main epistemological problems created by the dominant, broadly Aristotelian understanding of cognition, perception, and mental and linguistic representation during the late medieval period. Most of these problems arose specifically because of the perceived incompatibility of Aristotle's cognitive model with traditional Christian doctrine, and its more strongly Platonizing and dualist models of the soul's relation to the body as derived from Augustine, which asserted the greater degree of independence and agency of the rational/intellectual soul. Augustine's views, however, remained influential throughout the scholastic period. Rather than resulting in a large-scale confrontation between Aristotelians and Augustinians—as early twentieth-century scholarship had suggested—recent work has argued that scholastic thinkers responded by attempting to accommodate elements from both models.[93] Beyond his broadly dualist model of the soul-body relation, discussed above, two further elements

---

[90] See especially Gordon Leff, *The Dissolution of the Medieval Outlook* (New York: New York University Press, 1976), which already presents a more mature and mitigated version of his earlier arguments over the rise of scepticism. For recent reassessments of scepticism in the period, see especially the work of Dominik Perler, e.g. 'Skepticism', *CHMP*, I:384–96; and ibid. *Zweifel und Gewißheit: Skeptische Debatten im Mittelalter* (Frankfurt am Main: Klosterman, 2006); and Christophe Grellard, 'Comment peut-on se fier à l'expérience? Esquisse d'une typologie des réponses médiévales au scepticisme', *Quaestio* 4 (2004), 113–35. See further Henrik Lagerlund, ed., *Rethinking the History of Skepticism: the Missing Medieval Background* (Leiden: Brill, 2010).

[91] See Denery, Ghosh, and Zeeman, *Uncertain Knowledge*.

[92] See especially the relevant chapters in Pasnau, *Theories of Cognition*, and in Tachau, *Vision and Certitude*.

[93] On the need to revise the paradigmatic account of the conflict between Augustinians and Aristotelians, and the 'triumph' of the latter, see for instance Silva, *Kilwardby on Soul*, p. 275: 'Why not

in Augustine's thought lay at the heart of the Church Father's enduring appeal for later Christian writers interested in the cognitive and psychological processes that underpin individual salvation. The first was his commitment to a doctrine of divine illumination, according to which God directly intervenes in the cognitive process of individual humans. The second was his analysis of the operation of the individual will—an entity that had no pendant whatsoever in Aristotle's model of the soul. I shall discuss the significance of these two elements in turn, sketching the development of late medieval debates in both areas. I will then offer some considerations on my reasons for presenting this discussion under the heading of 'experience', which will allow me to anticipate the argument I will trace in the main body of this study.

It is only during the thirteenth century that intellectuals began to refer to a specific 'doctrine' of divine illumination.[94] This was a consequence of the recently increased circulation of Aristotle's model of the soul, which differed from Augustine's in a number of important ways that I have already described. It was therefore only in the context of the threat posed by Aristotle's alternative account of the soul that intellectuals began to elaborate a fully fledged 'doctrine' of divine illumination from the scattered and largely unsystematic observations that Augustine had provided on the topic throughout his works. While the mechanisms of divine illumination were theorized in a variety of ways by scholastics sympathetic to Augustine, especially Franciscans, the great advantage of a theory of divine illumination was constituted by its radically different anthropological implications. Unlike Aristotle's empiricism, which for the most part attempted to explain the cognitive process by appealing almost exclusively to natural causes, Augustine's theory of divine illumination ultimately located agency not in natural, but *supernatural* causes. According to Augustine's observations, human sense faculties ultimately depended on the action of a divine, transcendent principle upon the individual human subject. Such a model placed clear limits on the cognitive remit of corporeal phenomena derived from sensation, and correspondingly enhanced the agency of man's strictly intellectual faculties, which were variously seen as being sustained, guided, or infused by divine agency.

The argument over the relative place of divine illumination within human cognitive processes was the subject of heated debates. During the late thirteenth

---

tell the story from the point of view of the thinkers aligned with the thought of Augustine, who were challenged when the new Aristotelian corpus came to circulate in the Latin West? . . . This means, however, that we cannot reduce the struggle to a dispute between two fields, the Aristotelians and the anti-Aristotelians—or the conservatives and the reactionaries'. See further Gilson, 'Les sources gréco-arabes de l'augustinisme avicennisant'. For a discussion of more recent revisions of Gilson's hypothesis, away from a binary model, see Marrone, *The Light of thy Countenance*, I:1–25.

[94] For a lucid study of Augustine's doctrine of divine illumination and its legacy, see Lydia Schumacher, *Divine Illumination: The History and Future of Augustine's Theory of Knowledge* (Oxford: Wiley-Blackwell, 2011). For a more detailed study of the decline of theories of divine illumination at the end of the thirteenth century, see Marrone, *The Light of Thy Countenance*.

century the debate became particularly intense, and in an important study Stephen Marrone has argued that it would be preferable to speak not so much of a single 'doctrine' of divine illumination, but rather of 'a cluster of theories, not all of which were applied to precisely the same philosophical purpose and thus not all of which were equally vulnerable to the threat from apodictic [i.e. Aristotelian] science'.[95] Views on the precise mechanics and cognitive effects of divine illumination accordingly varied substantially. Thinkers often seized on the more nebulous aspects of Aristotle's theory in order to accommodate the action of divine illumination, initially with reference to the agent intellect that Arabic commentators had already brought into the foreground in their own discussions. For Avicenna, notably, intellection was ultimately caused not by the process of abstraction, but by the action of the agent intellect upon the lower, sense-bound cognitive faculty considering the image previously abstracted from sense perception.[96] Latin commentators responded by variously adjusting Avicenna's comments, involving divine illumination both in ordinary cognitive processes of everyday objects as well as in more exceptional instances of intellection, notably the knowledge of God or divine realities. As Marrone insists, it is precisely this second element that lies behind the passionate interest of many thinkers in the doctrine of divine illumination:

> Because it argued for direct, or nearly direct, cognitive access to the divinity under normal conditions of intellection, it stood as eloquent testimony to an extraordinary intimacy between God and mind, even in the world of sin. Confirmation of such intimacy was particularly important for the Augustinians, more valuable than any specific philosophical creed taken for itself, since upon mind's intimacy with God depended a host of traditional religious inclinations and devotional practices. [...] The complex of ideas and associations involved could be summed up in what was almost a philosophical mantra for Augustinians, the description of the soul as created in God's image, traditionally taken to indicate that mind was directed to God as to its object and intellective light.[97]

In the present study, I am not directly concerned with the precise history of the fortunes and transformations of various theories of divine illumination within scholasticism itself, which Marrone outlines in the main body of his study. I am, however, deeply interested in the wider and more diffuse long-term effects of these debates. As Marrone and other scholars have rightly noted, the theory of divine illumination essentially disappears from scholastic debates at the very beginning of the fourteenth century, for a series of complex reasons that Marrone's study examines in detail. But the appeal of divine illumination palpably persisted for

---

[95] Marrone, *The Light of Thy Countenance*, I:21.
[96] Hasse, *Avicenna's De Anima in the Latin West*, pp. 174–89.
[97] Marrone, *The Light of Thy Countenance*, I:22.

readers and thinkers who moved outside of the narrow orbit of the universities. As I will argue in Chapter 3, Guillaume de Deguileville, for one, espouses a strongly illuminationist epistemology in his attempt to reject several elements that characterize the 'standard', Aristotelian account of the soul and cognition. This has important implications that reach well beyond the problem of our understanding of Deguileville's poetry: it suggests that much remains to be done in order to assess the ulterior influence and transformation of scholastic theories and ideas by authors and thinkers who move outside the strictly academic environment, particularly those writing in the vernacular. If we are willing to write an intellectual history that looks beyond the schools, and one that includes the evidence of texts and ideas that do not fit into a linear narrative of the 'evolution' of strictly scholastic arguments, it is clear that an 'anthropology' of divine illumination—if not a fully fledged 'theory' of divine illumination—continues to shape the religious and intellectual culture of the late Middle Ages well beyond the early fourteenth century.

Within the broader epistemological perspective adopted by this study, and within a more inclusive history of late medieval philosophical and theological thought that includes vernacular and literary texts, then, the controversy over divine illumination is best understood in terms of its place within the larger legacy of Augustine's distinctive philosophy of mind. As I have already anticipated, Augustine's model is also characterized by its inclusion of the Will—an entity that has strictly no equivalent in Aristotle's system, and which accordingly exercised the minds of late medieval scholastic philosophers and theologians. Augustine's most fundamental model of the human mind, as presented in the *De trinitate* X, comprised three entities: Understanding, Memory, and the Will (*intellectus, memoria, voluntas*).[98] In the context of the available Greco-Roman theories of cognition, Augustine's appeal to the Will was unprecedented and revolutionary, but the theory rapidly gained acceptance within Christian thought and culture, and thus became uncontroversial and all but ubiquitous before the twelfth century in the Latin West.[99] Augustine argued for the interdependence of Will, Memory, and Understanding, observing that they operated through one another and were contained within each other, with each of these three powers able to stand in for the soul as a whole. Augustine thus appears to have thought of them as faculties or aspects of the single (rational) soul, opening the door to further speculation about the operation of the rational/intellectual soul as a whole (see esp. *De trinitate* X.11.17–18).

---

[98] For discussions of the will-intellect-memory triad that have a close bearing on the present issues, see e.g. O'Daly, *Augustine's Philosophy of Mind*, pp. 133–8; Schumacher, *Divine Illumination*, pp. 43–6; and Colish, *The Mirror of Language*, pp. 51–4.

[99] Neal Ward Gilbert, 'The Concept of Will in Early Latin Philosophy', *Journal of the History of Philosophy* 1.1 (1963), 17–35.

36 MEDIEVAL ALLEGORY AS EPISTEMOLOGY

But the model became more problematic once it was scrutinized more closely through an Aristotelian lens: what, for instance, was the ontological status of the Intellect, Will, and Memory? Are they powers, or faculties, appetites, or separate 'parts', subdivisions of the soul? While the Intellect and Memory had rough equivalents in the Aristotelian system and therefore did not pose any particular difficulties, the Will did not, and became the focus of sustained analysis and heated debate. The debates were particularly intense at the theology faculties of late medieval Europe, since the salvation of the human soul depended on free human choice (*liberum arbitrium*), and the latter constituted the arena for the competing operations of the Will and the Intellect. In parallel with the strictly cognitive considerations of thirteenth-century faculty psychology, scholastic theologians now produced elaborate theories of moral psychology, assessing the respective roles of the human Will and Understanding in determining individual moral choice—a debate that eventually culminated in the controversy between 'intellectualists' and 'voluntarists'.[100] A range of solutions was put forward. Peter Lombard established the interdependence of the Will and Intellect that underpinned human agency, and this notion was widely adopted by later thinkers. But the Lombard had also stressed that while the Will depended on the prior operation of Reason in order to act, its actions were not however 'determined' by the Intellect, establishing the principle of primacy of the Will over the Intellect. The idea was consolidated in the work of later voluntarists, often Franciscans like Bonaventure or Olivi, who stressed the ability of the Will to act against the judgment of Reason. Thomas Aquinas, by contrast, predictably argued that while the Will was the subject of free choice, its ultimate cause was Reason/the Intellect. This made the Will a passive potency acted upon by the intellect, although Aquinas also stressed the inextricable interdependence of the two powers in practice. More radical positions were advocated by Siger of Brabant in his early career and later by Godfrey of Fontaines: Siger presented a necessitarian argument for the operation of the Will—although he tried to defuse the determinism of such a position by introducing the notion of 'conditional necessity'—whereas Godfrey stressed the lack of autonomy of the Will on metaphysical grounds, arguing that no passive power is able to achieve its own transition to agency on its own strength, and is necessarily impelled from outside/above.

While the controversy itself subsided at the end of the century, it had profound long-term effects upon the overall trajectory of fourteenth-century theological debate. In a striking break from the more adventurous metaphysical speculations of the late thirteenth and early fourteenth century, later fourteenth-century

---

[100] For a concise overview, see Thobias Hoffmann, 'Intellectualism and Voluntarism', in *CHMP*, I:414–27. Further see Bonnie Kent, *Virtues of the Will: The Transformation of Ethics in the Late Thirteenth Century* (Washington, DC: Catholic University of America Press, 1995); Tobias Hoffmann, Jörn Müller, Matthias Perkams, eds, *Das Problem der Willensschwäche in der mittelalterlichen Philosophie / The Problem of Weakness of Will in Medieval Philosophy* (Leuven: Peeters, 2006).

INTRODUCTION 37

scholasticism was, broadly speaking, characterized by a return to markedly more pragmatic moral and soteriological concerns. Interest no longer focused on problems such as the analysis of the precise psycho-moral mechanics of self-determination in terms of Aristotelian causality, but shifted to address matters such as human freedom and predestination, determinism, the respective roles of human action ('works'), individual faith, and divine grace, God's power or *potentia* (*absoluta* and *ordinata*), and the role of the Incarnation and personal devotion in the attainment of individual salvation.[101] In most of these debates, the question of the nature and operation of the Will and its interaction with other powers both within and outside the individual human soul took up a central place, even though the power of the Will itself was no longer explored in terms of moral psychology or cognitive processes during the fourteenth century.[102] One of the notable consequences of voluntarist debates was the introduction of the notion that the Will, ostensibly located in the immaterial intellectual soul, was in effect susceptible of experiencing passions and emotions: this was, ultimately, the reason why the Will could chose to disregard the guiding light of reason in Franciscan/voluntarist theories of the Will. This created serious problems in terms of the ontology of *voluntas*: if it was susceptible to affections and emotions, how could it be maintained that it was not a physiological power inhering in the sensory soul but an intellective power inhering in the supposedly immaterial rational soul? Again, 'Diverse folk diversely they seyde' in the attempt to preserve the Will from subjection to contingent and material causes, mostly arguing for an indirect and mediated impact of emotion upon the Will and thus, indirectly, upon the Intellect.[103]

The discussion of the weakness of the Will also entailed a more meticulous scrutiny of the dynamics of grace another favourite topic that looms large among the preoccupations of fourteenth-century theologians. In order to lend greater technical precision to Augustine's often unsystematic observations, thirteenth-century scholastics initially resorted to the Aristotelian language of causality to develop an elaborate account of the mechanics of grace. Grace was increasingly conceptualized as a *habitus*, instilled in the soul in the manner of other virtues, and operating as a form or formal cause enabling personal salvation. Since grace therefore tended to be viewed as a *habitus* or disposition inhering in the soul— much in the same manner of the three theological virtues, and for whose inherence the *habitus* of grace was often seen as a precondition, notably by Aquinas—the focus of discussions increasingly came to rest on the larger question of agency and

---

[101] See among others Oberman, 'Fourteenth-Century Religious Thought'; Courtenay, *Schools and Scholars*, pp. 250–8, 327–82; E. A. Moody, 'Empiricism and Metaphysics in Medieval Philosophy', *Philosophical Review* 67 (1958), 145–63.

[102] For a fertile and nuanced overview of the full complexity of various views, discourses, and controversies on the will, scholastic and not, available to a late fourteenth-century poet like Langland, see John M. Bowers, *The Crisis of Will in 'Piers Plowman'* (Washington, DC: Catholic University of America Press, 1995), pp. 1–78.

[103] Richard Cross, 'Weakness and Grace', *CHMP*, I:441–53.

38 MEDIEVAL ALLEGORY AS EPISTEMOLOGY

causation: what, ultimately, lay at the roots of the *habitus* of grace, and to what extent was it inherent or acquired, or even sufficient? And how could the notion of grace as *habitus* be reconciled with the freedom of the Will and the wide differences in virtuous dispositions between individuals on the one hand, and with the notion of a universal Atonement brought about by the Incarnation on the other? Aquinas responded by differentiating between Habitual Grace—the predisposition to receive salvation—and Actual Grace, i.e. the causal action of the divine operation upon the individual that could transform the potentiality into act. Such a distinction was in turn critiqued by other thinkers such as Scotus and Ockham, and despite increasingly subtle differentiations between different levels of efficient causality within the operation of sacramental grace itself—such as the distinction of efficient cause into principal and instrumental (Aquinas, *ST* 3a d. 62, 1)[104]—the question of the ultimate cause and source of individual salvation remained as vexed as ever.[105]

The debate on the nature and operation of divine grace in many ways culminated in the famous anti-Pelagian tirades of Thomas Bradwardine and Gregory of Rimini during the second quarter of the fourteenth century. Here too Augustine's thought played a major role, as is suggested by the various designations adopted to describe the radically anti-Pelagian arguments that were developed during the fourteenth century—from 'Radical Augustinianism' to 'Neo-Augustinianism'.[106] This current of theological thinking was primarily developed in England, and emerged as a reaction against the perceived 'Pelagian heresies' put forward by the likes of William of Ockham—views condemned as heretical after examination at Avignon between 1324–6, but adopted by influential theologians such as Robert Holcot. At the heart of these new Pelagian heresies was the contention that humans could indeed achieve their own salvation by living a morally righteous life thanks to the efforts of their own individual Will, even without requiring the intervention of divine grace—a view that was ascribed to Ockham, but which he never actually articulated in those terms.[107] While Ockham and his followers accepted, in line with Scotus, that God had determined a certain set of conditions and requirements to attain salvation, they also argued that the acts in question had no intrinsic moral and salvific qualities: they had merely been established as part of a *pactum* or covenant between God and man, incurred under the circumstances of *potentia*

[104] Rosier, *La parole efficace*, pp. 135–9; Aers, *Salvation and Sin*, pp. 48–9.

[105] Cross, 'Weakness and Grace'. For a retrospective overview from a late fourteenth-century perspective, see Christopher Levy, 'Grace and Freedom in the Soteriology of John Wyclif', *Traditio* 60 (2005), 279–337 (279–306).

[106] See e.g. Christopher Ocker, 'Augustinianism in Fourteenth-Century Theology', *Augustinian Studies* 18 (1987), 81–106; William J. Courtenay, 'Augustinianism at Oxford in the Fourteenth Century', *Augustiniana* 30.1/2 (1980), 58–70, and *Schools and Scholars*, pp. 307–24. On the precise doctrinal outlines of such fourteenth-century Augustinianism, especially in terms of the differences between radical 'Augustinian' anti-Pelagianism and Augustine's own, arguably more moderate and articulated position on grace vs. works, see especially Aers, *Salvation and Sin*.

[107] On this, and on Ockham's often overlooked reaffirmation of the necessity of grace under the dispensation *de potentia dei ordinata*, see Levy, 'Grace and Freedom', 301–4.

dei ordinata. From the perspective of *potentia dei absoluta*, however, an omnipotent God was at least theoretically free to waive, suspend, or entirely disregard the covenant, overruling his own agreement by choosing to recognize *any* human act as worthy of salvation—even one that contravened the ten commandments. The notion of God's freedom to accept human moral efforts despite their inherent insufficiency was encapsulated in the famous Pelagian 'mantra' that achieved wide currency during this period: *facientibus quod in se est Deus non denegat gratiam* ('God does not deny grace to those who perform to the best of their abilities').[108] In response, Bradwardine and Gregory categorically rejected the possibility that humans might attain salvation through their own natural powers (*ex puris naturalibus*), and accordingly assigned a central, indeed supreme role to the operation of grace. Gregory developed earlier formulations of Habitual and Actual Grace as articulated by Aquinas, and argued that while before the Fall Habitual Grace or *gratia creata* was sufficient to ensure Adam's salvation, after the Fall man also depended on God's additional gift of Special Grace, or *auxilium dei speciale*. Even in this case, however, theologians of such radical 'Augustinian' persuasion insisted that salvation was not achieved on individual merit, but only through the direct agency and special dispensation of God. Given the resolutely impaired condition of the human will after the fall, salvation could never be 'earned' but was freely given as the result of God's gratuitous choice to reward human striving, albeit dramatically insufficient, through the free gift of salvation. While the possibility of earning salvation through full merit (*meritum de condigno*) was thus utterly unimaginable, the special gift of divine grace acted as recognition of *meritum de congruo*. More importantly, perhaps, both Bradwardine and Gregory insisted that the path to attaining such a state of justified *meritum de congruo* did not lead through works, but only through faith: 'man is justified solely by faith, and not by preceding works' [sola fide sine operibus paecedentibus fit homo iustus].[109]

Literary scholars have long argued that such debates on the nature of grace and individual will had a discernible impact on fourteenth-century literature, particularly on *Piers Plowman*.[110] By providing a much broader overview of thirteenth- and fourteenth-century philosophical and theological debates in the area of epistemology and cognition, however, and especially by highlighting the

---

[108] Heiko A. Oberman, '*Facientibus quod in se est Deus non denegat gratiam*: Robert Holcot, OP and the Beginnings of Luther's Theology', *Harvard Theological Review* 55.4 (1962), 317–42.

[109] Thomas Bradwardine, *De Causa Dei Contra Pelagium, et de Virtute Causarum, ad suos Mertonenses, libri tres* (London: 1618) 1.43, fol. 394B. On the debates surveyed in this paragraph, see variously Ocker, 'Augustinianism in Fourteenth-Century Theology'; Oberman, 'Fourteenth-Century Religious Thought'; Courtenay, *Schools and Scholars*, pp. 210–16, 250–306; ibid., *Ockham and Ockhamism*, pp. 107–54, 349–58; Levy, 'Grace and Freedom'; Hester Gelber, *It Could Have Been Otherwise: Contingency and Necessity in Dominican Theology at Oxford, 1300–1350* (Leiden: Brill, 2004), esp. pp. 191–222; 309–50; and John T. Slotemaker and Jeffrey C. Witt, *Robert Holcot* (Oxford: Oxford University Press 2015).

[110] Among the most influential discussions it is worth retaining the following three: Joyce Coleman, '*Piers Plowman*' and the Moderni (Rome: Edizioni di Storia e Letteratura, 1981); Bowers, *The Crisis of Will*; and Aers *Salvation and Sin*.

40 MEDIEVAL ALLEGORY AS EPISTEMOLOGY

relation of this specific controversy over human *voluntas* to those other debates, I want to place such an interest in the mechanics of grace and the individual will back within the broader and more articulated intellectual environment in which it developed. One larger contention of this study, therefore, is that in order to understand the precise nature of the interface between vernacular poetic texts and theological controversies in the fourteenth century—both in terms of the specific issue of grace and will, as well as larger philosophical and theological concerns with cognition and self-understanding—it is necessary to move beyond the narrow focus on a single specific issue. I believe that this can be achieved precisely by focusing on the larger topic of epistemology broadly defined, and specifically its subdivisions into various clusters of concerns under the headings of language, cognition, and experience.

3. Agency, Experience, and Subjectivity in the Later Middle Ages

A few words will be required to explain my choice of the rather vague heading of 'experience' under which to organize the preceding considerations on the questions of divine illumination, the relation between Intellect and the Will, and the operation of grace. In grouping these discussions under the heading of 'experience', I specifically intend to draw attention to the wider problems of individual moral and cognitive agency that underpin all of these questions. More specifically, I have chosen the term 'experience' because of three related reasons that have an important bearing on my arguments pursued in what follows.

Firstly, the notion of experience is particularly useful in terms of its philosophical implications for the argument I shall be making. 'Experience' is in fact a widely used but notoriously nebulous concept. Even within the modern branch of philosophy that is commonly known as 'phenomenology', and which is concerned with the study of experiential phenomena, the notion of 'experience' itself remains philosophically opaque and disputed.[111] What do we, or medieval thinkers, mean when we speak of having 'experienced' something? Does an experience occur in the soul, in the body, or across that divide? Is experience an active state, endogenously generated by the self, or is experience the result of external action upon a passive subject? What is the degree of ontological reality and cognitive reliability of individual, personal experience—especially in a culture that displays a high degree of deference to often dogmatic 'auctoritees' of all kinds (religious, political, intellectual)? All of these questions also shade into the larger project of epistemology, since the definition of 'experience' that will be adopted in what follows is grounded

---

[111] The dispute runs through the history of twentieth-century phenomenology, in the work of Husserl, Heidegger, Merleau-Ponty, and Derrida. See Dermot Moran, *Introduction to Phenomenology* (London and New York: Routledge, 2000). For a historically more wide-ranging philosophical discussion of the problem of experience, see the articles in Pasquale Porro and Costantino Esposito, eds, *Experience / Expérience / Die Erfahrung / L'esperienza*, a special issue of the journal *Quaestio* 4 (2004).

INTRODUCTION   41

in the etymological understanding of phenomenology as 'the study of appearances as opposed to reality'.[112] The notion of 'experience', therefore, is particularly useful for my argument because it raises questions about the definition of the human subject in terms of the boundaries between action and passion, thought and sensation, truth and appearance, interiority and exteriority, self and non-self, individual agency and external powers both contingent and providential.

Secondly, the thirteenth and fourteenth centuries saw a rapid rise of interest in the problem of experience and related notions of *experimentum* and *scientia experimentalis* among the scholastics themselves, and it has even been suggested that in the area of theological speculation such a concern with *experientia* is 'the central theme of the [fourteenth] century'.[113] The acceleration of the general interest in experience and scientific experimentation was particularly marked in insular intellectual culture, shaped by the contributions of influential figures such as Robert Grosseteste, Roger Bacon, and William of Ockham.[114] Historians during the first half of the twentieth century insistently argued that this early interest in experimental methods prefigured and enabled the emergence of a fully empirical modern science, but the suggestion has proven misleading.[115] Indeed, the late medieval interest in experience appears predominantly geared

[112] David Woodruff Smith, 'Phenomenology' (3), *The Stanford Encyclopedia of Philosophy* (Summer 2018 Edition), Edward N. Zalta (ed.), URL = https://plato.stanford.edu/archives/sum2018/entries/phenomenology.

[113] Oberman, 'Fourteenth-Century Religious Thought', p. 89. Among recent discussions of experience, experimentation, and empiricism, see e.g. the contributions contained in Alexander Fidora and Matthias Lutz-Bachmann, eds, *Erfahrung und Beweis. Die Wissenschaften von der Natur im 13. und 14. Jahrhundert / Experience and Demonstration. The Sciences of Nature in the 13th and 14th Centuries* (Berlin: De Gruyter, 2009); and Jürgen Sarnowsky, '*Expertus—experientia—experimentum*: Neue Wege der wissenschaftlichen Erkenntnis im Spätmittelalter', *Das Mittelalter: Perspektiven mediävistischer Forschung*, 17.2 (2012), 47–59; Mark J. Barker, 'Experience and Experimentation: The Meaning of *Experimentum* in Aquinas', *The Thomist: A Speculative Quarterly Review* 76.1 (2012), 37–71.

[114] See e.g. Andreas Speer, '*Scientia demonstrativa et universaliter ars faciens scire*: Zur methodischen Grundlegung einer Wissenschaft von der Natur durch Robert Grosseteste', in Fidora and Lutz-Bachmann, eds, *Erfahrung und Beweis*, pp. 25–40; Jeremiah Hackett, '*Scientia experimentalis*: From Robert Grosseteste to Roger Bacon', in James McEvoy, ed., *Robert Grosseteste: New perspectives on his thought and scholarship* (Turnhout: Brepols, 1995), pp. 89–119; ibid., 'Roger Bacon on *Scientia Experimentalis*', in Jeremiah Hackett, ed., *Roger Bacon and the Sciences: Commemorative Essays 1996* (Leiden: Brill, 1997), pp. 277–315; ibid., 'Experience and Demonstration in Roger Bacon: A Critical Review of Some Modern Interpretations', in Fidora and Lutz-Bachmann, *Erfahrung und Beweis*, pp. 41–58; ibid., 'Roger Bacon's Concept of Experience: A New Beginning in Medieval Philosophy?', *The Modern Schoolman* 86.1/2 (2008), 123–46; Gerhard Leibold, 'Ockham und Buridan—Vorgestalten neuzeitlicher Wissenschaft?', in Fidora and Lutz-Bachmann, eds, *Erfahrung und Beweis*, pp. 225–31; Courtenay, *Schools and Scholars*, pp. 206–10; and the selection of texts and commentary in John Lee Longeway, *Demonstration and Scientific Knowledge in William of Ockham. A Translation of 'Summa Logicae' III-II: De 'Syllogismo Demonstrativo', and Selections from the Prologue to the 'Ordinatio'* (Notre Dame, IN: University of Notre Dame Press, 2007); and Peter King, 'Two Conceptions of Experience', *Medieval Philosophy and Theology* 11.2 (2003), 203–26.

[115] See notably the work of Pierre Duhem, and, more specifically on experimental methods, Herbert Butterfield, *The Origins of Modern Science, 1300–1800* (London: Bell & Sons, 1949); and Alistair C. Crombie, *Robert Grosseteste and the Origins of Experimental Science, 1100–1700* (Oxford: Clarendon Press, 1953).

For a useful critique of Duhem's contribution, see especially John E. Murdoch, 'Pierre Duhem and the History of Late Medieval Science and Philosophy in the Latin West', in Ruedi Imbach and Alfonso

42 MEDIEVAL ALLEGORY AS EPISTEMOLOGY

towards mental, cognitive, and emotional experience—both as objects of study in their own right and as tools for further philosophical inquiry. As Peter King has argued, 'the method of medieval science was thought-experiment rather than actual experiment or testing',[116] and recent work has begun examining the centrality of thought-experiments in medieval intellectual culture more closely.[117] A more useful framework for situating the rise of interest in experience, I believe, is therefore provided by the intensified scrutiny of individual subjectivity that marks the thirteenth and fourteenth centuries.

This growing interest in subjectivity—not to be confused with misleading and reductive grand narratives about the ostensible 'discovery of the (modern) individual self' in the period[118]—is manifested in variable ways across very different areas of late medieval intellectual culture, popular as well as *élite*. On the *élite* side, this includes a wide range of developments already discussed: the growing interest in cognitive and mental operations in faculty psychology; the discussions of the mechanics and interactions of the individual will, intellect, and grace; the development of 'nominalist' as well as 'empiricist' theories of cognition based on the intuitive apprehension of singular realities in the material world; careful and systematic scrutiny of individual spiritual development, conversion, and justification in terms of the quantitative methods of physics and mathematics.[119] But this growing interest in individual subjectivity is also manifested in large-scale cultural shifts taking place in vernacular culture outside the schools. This includes, for instance, the growing focus on interiority entailed by the reforms of sacramental and penitential practice instituted by the fourth Lateran Council in 1215,[120] or the emergence of literary subjectivity and late medieval (pseudo-)autobiography or 'autography', which I will discuss in greater detail in Chapter 1.[121]

Maierù, eds, *Gli studi di filosofia medievale fra otto e novecento* (Rome: Edizioni di Storia e Letteratura, 1991), pp. 253–301.

[116] See Peter King, 'Medieval Thought–Experiments: The Metamethodology of Medieval Science', in Tamara Horowitz and Gerald J. Masey, eds, *Thought Experiments in Science and Philosophy* (Savage, MD: Rowman and Littlefield, 1991), pp. 43–64(43).

[117] See Knox, Morton, and Reeve, eds, *Medieval Thought Experiments*; and Katerina Ierodiakonou and Sophie Roux, eds, *Thought Experiments in Methodological and Historical Contexts* (Leiden: Brill, 2011).

[118] Two particularly crass and unhelpful examples of this reductive narrative can be found in Norman Cantor, *The Last Knight: The Twilight of the Middle Ages and the Birth of the Modern Era* (New York: Free Press, 2004); and Stephen Greenblatt, *The Swerve: How the World Became Modern* (New York and London: W. W. Norton, 2011). For useful critiques, see Jean-Claude Schmitt, 'La découverte de l'individu: une fiction historiographique?', in ibid., *Le corps, les rites, les rêves, le temps: essais d'anthropologie médiévale* (Paris: Gallimard, 2001), pp. 241–62; Barbara H. Rosenwein, 'Y avait-il un "moi" au haut Moyen Age?', *Revue historique* 633 (2005), 31–52. For a more extended analysis and critique of this tendency in terms of its impact on vernacular literature, specifically first-person allegorical narratives in the tradition of the *Rose*, see my previous monograph, *Allegorical Quests from Deguileville to Spenser* (Cambridge: D.S. Brewer, 2012), pp. 6–15.

[119] On this latter topic, see Courtenay, *Schools and Scholars*, pp. 282–94.

[120] For a discussion of its effect on pastoral literature and practice and on vernacular culture more widely, see e.g. Masha Raskolnikov, 'Confessional Literature, Vernacular Psychology, and the History of the Self in Middle English', *Literature Compass* 2.1 (2005), n.p.

[121] See items listed below Chapter 1, n.42 and Michel Zink, *La subjectivité littéraire: autour du siècle de Saint Louis* (Paris: Presses Universitaires de France, 1985).

INTRODUCTION   43

Alongside such late medieval developments, however, it is important to stress the continuing influence of a much older, and culturally more deeply ingrained understanding of 'experience' as formulated by early medieval traditions of mysticism and monasticism, with its roots in the work of the church fathers, particularly Gregory and Augustine.[122] This tradition proposed an alternative understanding of notions of corporeal experience based on deeply ingrained, specifically Christian ideas of embodiment shaped by the theology of the Incarnation and by image theology. Radically different from the Aristotelian, hylomorphic model of embodiment, the tradition was durably shaped by the work of mystical and contemplative authors such as Origen, Pseudo-Dionysius, Scotus Eriugena, and St. Bernard, influencing the mystical tradition as a whole together with the work of later scholastics, particularly Franciscans like Bonaventure. The tradition developed an elaborate but largely unsystematic set of beliefs and ideas concerning the soul's potential for 'spiritual sensation', which accordingly shaped the Christian understanding of 'experience' in fundamental ways.[123] These traditions exercised a complex, often indirect influence upon the development of late medieval affective theology and mysticism—both Latin and vernacular, lay and institutional.[124] Furthermore, such ideas had become deeply ingrained in the fabric of Christian culture at all levels, and permeated Christian thought, doctrine, devotion, and liturgical practice well beyond the spheres of advanced learning and even beyond the confines of literacy.[125] These elements too shaped the complex understanding of experience in the work of my three authors, particularly Deguileville and Langland, as will be seen.

---

[122] See Pierre Miquel, *Le vocabulaire Latin de L'expérience spirituelle dans la tradition monastique et canoniale de 1050 à 1250* (Paris: Beauchesne, 1989), esp. pp. 98–9, 109–10, 120–2 on the 'passive' nature of experience in the monastic tradition. See also Piroska Nagy, 'Individualité et larmes monastiques: Une expérience de soi ou de Dieu?', in Gert Melville and Markus Schürer, eds, *Das Eigene und das Ganze. Zum Individuellen im mittelalterlichen Religiosentum* (Münster: Lit Verlag, 2003), pp. 107–30. See further the analysis below, in Chapter 3.

[123] See variously Paul L. Gavrilyuk and Sarah Coakley, eds, *The Spiritual Senses: Perceiving God in Western Christianity* (Cambridge: Cambridge University Press, 2011); Gordon Rudy, *The Mystical Language of Sensation in the Later Middle Ages* (London: Routledge, 2002). On Bonaventure, see Kevin L. Hughes, 'By its Fruits: The Spiritual Senses in Bonaventure's "Tree of Life"', *Medieval Mystical Theology* 28.1 (2019), 36–47.

[124] See variously John C. Hirsh, 'The Experience of God: A New Classification of Certain Late Medieval Affective Texts', *The Chaucer Review* 11. 1 (1976), 11–21; Barbara Newman, 'What Did it Mean to Say "I saw"? The Clash between Theory and Practice in Medieval Visionary Culture', *Speculum* 80.1 (2005), 1–43; Vincent Gillespie, 'Vernacular Theology', in Strohm, *Medieval English*, pp. 401–19.

[125] Evidence for this transfer is by necessity anecdotal and difficult to document. On the specific question of the role of the liturgy in propagating a shared understanding of sacramental 'experience', see for instance Nicholas Love's notorious contention that a Wycliffite 'tasteþ not þe swetnes of þis precious sacrament nor feleþ þe gracious wirching þerof in himself', in Nicholas Love, *The Mirror of the Blessed Life of Jesus Christ*, ed. Michael Sargeant (Exeter: Exeter University Press, 2004), p. 152. See also the discussion of this contention in David Aers, *Sanctifying Signs: Making Christian Tradition in Late Medieval England* (Notre Dame, IN: Notre Dame University Press, 2004), pp. 23–4. On how this notion of liturgical 'experience' shapes late medieval textual/literary aesthetic and the performativity of devotional reading acts, see further Jessica Brantley, *Reading in the Wilderness: Private Devotion and Public Performance in Late Medieval England* (Chicago: Chicago University Press, 2007).

44   MEDIEVAL ALLEGORY AS EPISTEMOLOGY

Thirdly, and finally, the question of 'experience' appears to have been one that held particular appeal for the poets discussed in the main body of this study—along with others such as Chaucer, who is palpably obsessed with the recurrent opposition between 'experience' and 'auctoritee'.[126] I suggest that this concern with experience arises from the underlying interest in the questions of individual moral, ethical, and cognitive agency that are equally at the heart of late medieval debates among scholastic theologians over grace, works, the will, and individual salvation. More specifically, I argue that Augustine becomes a crucially important source of inspiration for the ruminations on such topics found in the works of Jean de Meun, Deguileville, and Langland, and that their engagement with Augustine often serves as a filter for their response to more recent, scholastic debates on epistemology. In particular, Augustine's major writings on language, cognition, and experience—including the *De trinitate*, the *Confessiones*, and the *De doctrina christiana*—ultimately provided late-medieval poets with a model for exploring questions of agency and epistemology in a language and in an imaginative register that was utterly different from that of the late medieval Aristotelian scholasticism. In this respect, it seems appropriate to conclude this section by commenting on Augustine's use of conspicuously unsystematic, even inconsistent language and terminology in his major writings on the soul, cognition, and the experience of conversion. As Ludger Hölscher has observed in his book on Augustine's theory of the incorporeal soul:

> There might be two main reasons why Augustine was not a very systematic thinker and writer: his training as a rhetorician which rendered his style close to poetic language, and his ingenious capacity of constantly discovering new and surprising phenomena which he tried to describe in all their aspects by a variety of terms: non-systematicity was 'the heavy price for being so prodigal and flexible a writer'.[127]

Citing Peter Brown's classic study of Augustine, Hölscher invites readers to exercise leniency towards Augustine's 'non-systematic' approach, all but overlooking the language itself: 'we should look at the meaning of the things themselves *(rerum ipsarum intellectus)* when discussing an issue, without being concerned too much with how it can or cannot be expressed linguistically'.[128] What I would take away from Hölscher's observation, however, is the obverse point: the 'prodigality' of Augustine's prose reminds us that the latter's use of language is *not* merely intended

---

[126] See e.g. the classic discussion by Robert B. Burlin, *Chaucerian Fiction* (Princeton: Princeton University Press, 1977), pp. 3–22. While Chaucer's attitude to 'auctoritee' has been amply documented and analysed in work produced over the last four decades, no equivalent account of Chaucer's poetics of 'experience' is available.

[127] Hölscher, *The Reality of the Mind*, p. 5, citing Peter Brown, *Augustine of Hippo* (Berkeley and Los Angeles: University of California Press, 1967), p. 123.

[128] Hölscher, *The Reality of the Mind*, p. 5.

INTRODUCTION   45

to convey his theory of soul, but equally captures Augustine's own *experience* of the process of grasping and formulating such truths about the nature of his own mind. Augustine's use of language may be infuriatingly unsystematic—but it also conveys to the reader a precious and powerful sense of the author's protracted struggle, as a tenaciously *embodied* being, to capture the fluidity of his own, constantly evolving spiritual experience, as part of a never-ending process of conversion.

Augustine's language, then, is not the rigorous and systematic language of scholastic logic and syllogistic demonstration. It is a distinctive kind of language that signifies not merely denotatively, but also connotatively through its distinctive *form*—with its figurations, allusions, displacements, slippages, tropes, repetitions, hesitations, equivocations, and *aporias*. What is signified by such language, then, is not merely a *theory* of a disembodied intellectual soul, but—in a wonderful paradox—the *practical*, embodied experience of the struggle to apprehend the possible outlines and capabilities of such a disembodied, 'theoretical' soul. It is this unique, exploratory ability to capture the tentative, searching, groping, but also evolving quality of human self-understanding that ensures Augustine's enduring appeal for late medieval readers.[129] Far more than the dispassionate and supposedly unambiguous language of scholastic reasoning, demonstration, and Aristotelian causality, Augustine's oblique, 'poetic' language carries the hallmark of the existential condition from within which it is spoken and written. This is not the language of the perfected, purely intellectual and disembodied soul already arrived in its heavenly *patria* and with its *imago dei* fully restored, but rather the language of an as yet alienated and deregulated *viator*, a pilgrim on the way (*in via*) towards a heavenly homeland through a 'region of dissemblance' (*regio dissimilitudinis*).[130]

Even the scholastics themselves—at least in principle—accepted Augustine's description of human life as such a journey, and adopted it as a conceptual and terminological framework for their own analysis of the cognitive abilities of the exiled human *viator*, measuring his/her limited cognitive abilities *in via* against the fully restored powers of understanding of the blessed *in patria*.[131] But only a language like Augustine's could capture the nature of the human *experience* of this slow forward movement. For late medieval readers who are themselves attempting

---

[129] For a similar appreciation of the poetic in Augustine's thought, see also Eugene Vance, *Marvelous Signals: Poetics and Sign Theory in the Middle Ages* (Lincoln and London: University of Nebraska Press, 2002), pp. 43–50.

[130] On such notions of pilgrimage and alienation in Augustine's thought, see e.g. Paul G. Kuntz, 'Augustine: From *Homo Erro* to *Homo Viator*', in Leonard J. Bowman, ed., *Itinerarium: The Idea of Journey* (Salzburg: Institut für Anglistik und Amerikanistik, Universität Salzburg, 1983), pp. 34–53; Étienne Gilson, '*Regio dissimilitudinis* de Platon à saint Bernard de Clairvaux', *Mediaeval Studies* 9 (1947), 108–30; Gerhart B. Ladner, '*Homo Viator*: Mediaeval Ideas on Alienation and Order', *Speculum* 42.2 (1967), 233–59. See also discussion below, Chapter 2.3.

[131] For the wide currency of these terms of reference and the significance of the implied figuration of life as 'pilgrimage' as developed by Augustine, see e.g. Severin Valentinov Kitanov, *Beatific Enjoyment in Medieval Scholastic Debates: The Complex Legacy of Augustine and Peter Lombard* (Plymouth: Lexington, 2014), esp. pp. 1–18. See also Courtenay, *Schools and Scholars*, pp. 282–98.

46 MEDIEVAL ALLEGORY AS EPISTEMOLOGY

to make sense of their own, elusive and constantly shifting cognitive and spiritual experience on their way to a heavenly homeland that could only be conjured up in a tentative 'vision' but never properly 'seen', the unsystematic words and ideas of Augustine were a source of endless philosophical fascination and poetic inspiration. These readers included, notably, Jean de Meun, Guillaume de Deguileville, and William Langland.

4. This Book

As I have anticipated, the *Roman de la Rose* plays a seminal role not only in the development of late medieval allegorical literature in the Anglo-French tradition, but also in helping to trigger the wider epistemic turn within late medieval vernacular poetry more broadly. The *Rose* will accordingly play a pivotal role in this study, and I will begin Chapter 1 by providing a sustained discussion of the cognitive and epistemological challenges raised by the poem, particularly in terms of the relations between language and knowledge. I will however return to the *Rose* on multiple occasions throughout this book. The *Rose* in effect sows the seeds for many of the specific philosophical and epistemological problems that Deguileville and Langland will pick up in turn. By returning to the *Rose* periodically throughout this book, instead of dealing with it in a set of separate chapters, I also aim to highlight its inescapable, tenacious, haunting, and often troubling presence at the heart of the speculative and compositional processes that produce the poetry of both Deguileville and Langland. This, I hope, provides an appropriate *mimesis* for a difficulty that both poets encountered in their conversations with the *Rose*: as a poem that poses formidable interpretive and epistemic challenges, the *Rose* can never simply be 'dealt with' in any conclusive or satisfactory fashion.

As I will argue throughout the study, the unprecedented appeal of the *Rose* is ultimately a function of its unique ability to conjure up epistemological problems without proposing any viable solutions. As a poem that promises elucidation on a wide, encyclopaedic range of subjects, the *Rose* constantly publicizes its own ability to serve as a gateway for some sort of totalizing knowledge: 'a poem driven by the intense desire to account for the totality of experience' [un poème animé par la volonté intense de rendre compte de la totalité de l'expérience].[132] This knowledge, however, is repeatedly and deliberately withheld, turning the *Rose* into a uniquely frustrating work that simultaneously articulates an irresistible desire for cognitive and epistemic closure, yet systematically undermines this very possibility. This lends it an almost inexhaustible potential to provoke thought, to prompt further speculation, and to serve as a critical interlocutor and sounding board for later poets. The *Rose*, then, is not only a text that later poets often 'go back to', but is

---

[132] Badel, *Le Roman de la Rose au XIVe siècle*, p. 53.

also a text that 'talks back to them': it is a garrulous, indomitable, evasive, and at times devious interlocutor, maybe best imagined as a formidable opponent in an extended poetic *disputatio*, supplying incisive objections to any potential answers or *determinationes* its readers might be attempting to formulate. As David Hult notes, the *Rose* 'manages to anticipate in uncanny fashion, through its manipulative and indecisive debate structure, any response we are likely to make, either by including that response within the text, or by deferring responsibility (which is to say, pronounced authorial intention), through verbal or vocal chicanery'.[133] The *Rose* therefore also manages to become a poem that, as Sarah Kay puts it, 'reads like a parody of texts that in fact come after it',[134] invariably managing to critique, rebut, and deconstruct any doctrinaire *sententia* or imperfect *determinatio*, real and hypothetical, past and future—including, of course, its own ostensible *diffinitive sentance* (definitive sentence; *RR* 19,474). While the *Rose* clearly is the product of a very specific cultural moment and milieu, and of a highly idiosyncratic individual poetic mind, it manages to crystallize a kind of intellectual relativism that ends up haunting multiple generations of poets and intellectuals throughout Western Europe over the next three centuries. It is within this framework, I argue, that we ought to place both Deguileville's and Langland's attempts to forge their own poetics of knowledge.

Formally and conceptually speaking, it is a different poem that lies at the heart of this book. That is Guillaume de Deguileville's *Pèlerinage de Vie Humaine* (*PVH*), existing in two substantially different versions (*PVH1*, 1331 and *PVH2*, 1355), and successively integrated within what is commonly referred to as Deguileville's 'Pilgrimage trilogy', including the *Pèlerinage de l'Âme* (*PA*, 1356) and the *Pèlerinage Jhesucrist* (*PJC*, 1358). The *Pèlerinages* have long had a bad press, and in this study I propose to modify critical consensus on the poem itself and its influence in a number of important ways. The possibility that Deguileville's poetry may have influenced Langland has been repeatedly invoked, but specialists have rarely ventured beyond pointing out general similarities and occasional parallels in the use of allegorical imagery and personifications. The question is in need of serious reassessment, but this also presupposes a sustained reconsideration of Deguileville's own poetry in its own right. More specifically, this study attempts to move beyond reductive assessments of Deguileville's allegories, which see them as pursuing a narrowly didactic and homiletic agenda. In contrast, I will argue that the *Pèlerinage de Vie Humaine* in particular is a poem primarily concerned with the nature of subjectivity, understanding, and interpretation in a soteriological perspective. Instead of merely placing emphasis on 'doing' what is morally right, as has long been assumed, Deguileville's poem is far more interested in exploring

---

[133] David F. Hult, 'Language and Dismemberment: Abelard, Origen and the Romance of the Rose', in Brownlee and Huot, *Rethinking the Romance of the Rose*, pp. 101–30 (106).
[134] Kay, *The Place of Thought*, p. 18.

48 MEDIEVAL ALLEGORY AS EPISTEMOLOGY

the mechanisms of 'knowing' that subtend human choices and experiences within an overarching salvific concern. Like Langland's allegory, then, Deguileville's pilgrimage poems are only incidentally concerned with dispensing reliable normative precept: the principal focus falls on the task of 'figuring out', through allegorical imagination, a path towards the knowledge of salvific truth. This will be the primary focus of Part II (Chapters 2 to 4). I will variously address Deguileville's treatment of language, dialectic, and interpretation (Chapter 2); his model of the soul and its cognitive powers (Chapter 3); and his treatment of the pilgrim's encounter with Grace and the ensuing experience of conversion (Chapter 4). I will conclude by arguing that this latter experience not only leads to a major reorientation within the plot of his *Pèlerinage de Vie Humaine*, but that it finally leads to a radical reorientation of Deguileville's entire poetics. More specifically, in Chapter 4 I will argue that Deguileville becomes deeply disillusioned with the cognitive and salvific aspirations of his allegorical poetry. This initially prompts him to produce a modified, defensive rewriting of his original poem (*PVH2*, *c.* 1355–6), augmented by a closely related second poem recounting the judgement of the pilgrim's soul after death (*PA*, *c.* 1356). In a second phase, however, Deguileville can be seen to abandon the allegorical mode altogether, developing a radically different poetics shaped by two main traditions: on the one hand he foregrounds devotional and Christological concerns, which loom large in the third poem in his so-called pilgrimage 'trilogy' (*PJC, c.* 1358); on the other, he becomes immersed in the tradition of contemplative mysticism, producing a series of Latin poems that fit clearly within the tradition of monastic poetry. This chapter will therefore propose a radically new model for understanding the evolving nature of Deguileville's poetics and the trajectory of his literary career.

While this book was not conceived as a study of textual and intellectual influence, I will nevertheless argue that Deguileville must be seen as a major influence on Langland's poem, as well as shaping the development of Langland's poetics and his poetic project over time—an argument I develop in Part II (Chapters 5 to 7). This influence cannot be understood without taking into account the internal dynamics and complexities of Deguileville's own *Pèlerinage de Vie Humaine* (*PVH*)—a poem that is already conceived as an 'exposé sur le roman de la rose'.[135] It appears that Langland, like many other readers in the period, was clearly aware of this dialogic configuration between the *Rose* and *PVH*. Langland does, however, appreciate the complexities of this relationship far more sharply than any other medieval reader I am aware of. Indeed, I suggest that he was a much better reader of Deguileville's poetry than most modern critics over the last century. By this I mean that he was not only aware of *PVH*'s origin as a moralizing response or spiritual

---

[135] See Sylvia Huot, '"Exposé sur le *Roman de la Rose*": Rewriting the *Rose* in the *Pelerinage de vie humaine*', in *The Romance of the Rose and its Medieval Readers*, pp. 207–38, and further discussion below in Chapter 2.

exposé on the *Rose*, but that he also registered the difficulties of engaging in such a project, rich in potential pitfalls, paradoxes, and *aporias*. Langland's meticulous attention and keen interest in human cognitive processes allowed him to appreciate the strikingly ambivalent, conflicted, and at times self-contradictory position of Deguileville as manifested in his *PVH*, and to understand its origin in the latter's attempt to solve some of the epistemic and logical challenges posed by the *Rose*. I will therefore argue that Langland produces and revises his own poem by actively engaging with this pre-existing and highly conflicted dialogue between the *Rose* and *PVH*, using these two French allegories as 'glosses' on each other. To mix my metaphors, it could be said that Langland uses these two poems as mirrors for each other, or lenses through which the other poem could be viewed, re-viewed, and re-configured: each poem thus refracts, but also deforms and refigures images and ideas from its counterpart in order to develop its own specific epistemology. Langland therefore steps into an already fraught and conflicted disputation, mediating and alternating between a series of conflicting voices and positions already established within these earlier poems in order to craft his own idiosyncratic and highly conflicted poetic vision. I will be arguing that the very existence of *Piers Plowman* in the form(s) familiar to us is therefore predicated on the availability of this earlier, francophone tradition of allegorical writing and rewriting, vision and revision.

Somewhat paradoxically, then, it is precisely because this book is *not* primarily intended as a literary historical study that the arguments presented in the following chapters enable us to revise a number of unexamined assumptions about 'English' literary history. Despite its uniquely idiosyncratic form, Langland's *Piers Plowman* can, and indeed ought to be understood as emerging out of an intense, layered, and recursive dialogue with the two earlier dream poems written in French. This argument therefore runs counter to two closely related and well-established assumptions that continue to shape *Piers Plowman* scholarship: first, that *Piers Plowman* is a formidably complex, endlessly frustrating, idiosyncratic, and fundamentally unique piece of writing that eludes categorization and frustrates comparisons of any kind; second, that Langland's poem is a quintessentially 'English' or 'insular' work.[136] While it has often been observed that *Piers Plowman* displays considerable formal similarities with both the *Rose* and with Deguileville's *Pèlerinages*, the relationship between them has not been adequately examined in existing work. In what follows I argue that the three poems are not merely part of a common textual tradition, but constitute a tightly knit intertextual community, where later works engage in sustained and sometimes obsessive conversations with the earlier ones.

---

[136] On the latter issue, see also my 'William Langland: European Poet?', in Sif Ríkharðsdóttir and Raluca Radulescu, eds, *A Companion to Medieval English Literature in a Trans-European Context, 1100–1500*. London: Routledge, forthcoming 2022.

50 MEDIEVAL ALLEGORY AS EPISTEMOLOGY

The present study also makes a contribution to several long-standing debates in Langland studies more specifically. Firstly, it calls for a modification of the framework within which we approach the vexed questions of 'Langland's learning', shedding light on the origins and development of his idiosyncratic, critical, and ambivalent attitude towards scholasticism.[137] In particular, I want to suggest that instead of postulating a binary model that sees Langland's poetry as being engaged in a dialogue and/or conflict with scholasticism, we should acknowledge that both the *Pèlerinages* and the *Rose* played a crucial role in shaping Langland's encounter with, attitude towards, and use of scholasticism. Not only were these two earlier poems important channels through which Langland came into contact with scholastic texts, debates, and ideas, but they also provided him with a powerful model for how poetry could resist, critique, and interrogate the prerogatives of scholastic discourse while pursuing intellectual objectives of its own. Secondly, the following chapters also have important implications in terms of our approach to the question of Langland's 'Semi-Pelagianism' and his ideas about grace. Rather than suggesting where Langland might be 'placed' on a spectrum of ideological positions running from 'Pelagian' to 'Augustinian', however, the readings presented in what follows tend to point up the impossibility of doing so. Instead, a careful analysis of his response to Deguileville suggests that Langland thought of this question not in terms of ideological affiliation, but rather in terms of a fluctuating, endlessly protracted and reiterated dialectic between human will and divine grace, action and passion, determination and frustration, 'doing' and 'experience'.[138] Langland appears far less interested in 'settling' the question through his commitment to a particular 'doctrine' than in highlighting the fundamentally mysterious, and profoundly illogical and paradoxical nature of the quest for salvation as experienced by the individual will/Will. Both the distinctive texture and

---

[137] See especially A. V. C. Schmidt, 'Langland and Scholastic Philosophy', *Medium Ævum* 38 (1969), 134–56; Coleman, *Piers Plowman and the Moderni*; Andrew Galloway, 'Piers Plowman and the Schools', *YLS* 6 (1992), 89–107; John A. Alford, 'Langland's Learning', *YLS* 9 (1995), 1–8; Christopher Cannon, 'Langland's *Ars Grammatica*', *YLS* 22 (2008), 3–25; Andrew Galloway and Andrew Cole, 'Christian Philosophy in *Piers Plowman*', in Cole and Galloway, pp. 136–59; Christopher Cannon, *From Literacy to Literature: England, 1300–1400* (Oxford: Oxford University Press, 2016), esp. pp. 125–58. Discussions of Langland's learning can now also avail themselves of the increasingly detailed picture of Langland's putative 'biography' as a member of the Rokele family, on which see especially Robert Adams, *Langland and the Rokele Family: The Gentry Background to Piers Plowman* (Dublin: Four Courts Press, 2013); and, more recently, Michael Johnston, 'The Clerical Career of William Rokele', *YLS* 33 (2019), 111–25.

[138] My overarching conclusions therefore converge most closely with those proposed by Nicolette Zeeman, who sees the poem as being animated by a 'narrative mechanism of failure and recuperation', in *Piers Plowman and the Medieval Discourse of Desire* (Cambridge: Cambridge University Press, 2006), p. 17; and David Aers, who emphasizes the centrality of an Augustinian understanding of 'double agency' in the poem: according to this 'distinctive grammar of grace . . . [t]he initiative of divine agency, often hidden or obscurely mediated, is prevenient and pervasive but addresses human desire and elicits human agency'. 'The model is not of an irresistible power overwhelming a passive creature, or of a grace whose action is extrinsic, but of a transforming gift whose work is intrinsic to the will.' See Aers, *Sanctifying Signs*, pp. 16, 20.

the continuously shifting trajectory of Langland's thinking on this topic crystallize out of his recursive dialogue with the *Rose* and with the *Pèlerinages*.

To conclude, then, in this study I ultimately argue that the two French allegories constitute the single most important influence on Langland's poetic thought and compositional method—at the level of form, theme, narrative development, and even at the level of its evolving structure over time, through its multiple manifestations in the A, B, and C texts. While this argument is not meant to minimize or overshadow the influence of many other textual and intellectual traditions, this, I realize, is a very substantial claim for me to make. It is, however, a claim I believe to be based on structured evidence and a nuanced and meticulous argument as opposed to mere local borrowings and anecdotal correspondences. Accordingly, both the presentation of the evidence and the argument to support this claim are complex, and will have to be elaborated over the entire length of this study, tracing the overlapping trajectories of the evolving conversations, debates, and reconfigurations across all three poems in their multiple versions. What follows is therefore a rather unusual study, in the sense that it presents a single, overarching but highly articulated argument that develops across all chapters—not, as is more frequently the case, a sequence of chapters proposing a series of studies organized around a central set of themes. Because of this incremental character, individual chapters contain abundant cross-references to other sections in this book, and I have decided to number the subsections within chapters in order to facilitate cross-referencing. As well as arguing for the centrality of an epistemological 'urge' at the heart of all three poems, the present book is therefore intended as a contribution to what I would call the archaeology of the speculative and compositional processes that produce Langland's *Piers Plowman*. I believe that a close intertextual study of these three texts, with particular attention to their interest in questions of linguistic signification, knowledge, and human volition and divine grace, ultimately sheds light on the workings of Langland's mind, and does so in ways that sharpen our understanding of the idiosyncratic and at times erratic shifts and ruptures that 'structure' his thinking process and poetic career.

PART I

JEAN DE MEUN

1

In the Beginning was the *Rose*

Here the third mode of equivocation occurs. For the name of something universal is transferred to a person, and this can readily happen because names are at our pleasure [. . .] and we see that some name is common and it is transferred to a particular of another species. For example, 'rose' is the name of a flower and is the name of a woman, and the basis for the transference is the beauty of both, in which they agree.[1]

Roger Bacon, On Signs, § 48

Concerning this third question, it remains to be seen whether in the case of a non-existent rose, it can be maintained that a rose is known or understood. [. . .] Man can understand what does not exist, because what does not exist can be intelligible and understood through the imagination.

Against this we pitch the opinion of those that argue that if Socrates were to obtain knowledge of an existing rose, and the rose should cease to exist while Socrates' knowledge remains conserved, and he understands nothing else, the proposition that Socrates understands something or that the rose is understood by Socrates would not be true. And by analogy it is also not true to say that before the creation of the world God understands the world or that some creature is understood by God.[2]

Robert Holcot, Questions on Peter Lombard's Sentences,
II, q.2, art.3

---

[1] '[A]ccidit hic tertium modus aequivocationis. Transsumitur enim nomen ipsius universalis ad personam, et bene potest hoc fieri, quia nomina sunt ad placitum ... et nos videmus quod aliquod nomen est commune et transsumitur ad particularius alterius speciei, ut "Rosa" est nomen floris et est nomen mulieris, et ratio transsumptionis est pulchritudo utrobique in qua conveniunt' (Roger Bacon, *De signis*, § 48). For an edition and translation, see respectively K. M. Fredborg, L. Nielsen, J. Pinborg, 'An Unedited Part of Roger Bacon's *Opus Majus*: *De Signis*', *Traditio* 34 (1978), 75–136 (99); and Roger Bacon, *On Signs*, trans. and intr. Thomas S. Maloney (Toronto: PIMS, 2013), p. 64.

[2] 'Circa tertium articulum restat videre an nulla rosa existente, haec sit concedenda: rosa concipitur vel rosa intelligitur. [. . .] Potest etiam homo intelligere illud quod nihil est, secundum istos, concedunt enim illud quod nihil est, est intelligibile et cognoscibile, immo cui repugnat esse potest intelligi et a nobis imaginando cognosci. [. . .] Econtra est opinio aliorum talis quod posita intellectione rosae

---

Medieval Allegory as Epistemology. Marco Nievergelt, Oxford University Press.
© Marco Nievergelt (2023). DOI: 10.1093/oso/9780192849212.003.0002

When I said.
'A rose is a rose is a rose is a rose'. [...]
I made poetry and what did I do I caressed completely caressed
and addressed a noun.[3]

Gertrude Stein, 'Poetry and Grammar'

1. 'Une vraye mappemonde de toutes choses celestes et terriennes'

The *Roman de la Rose* is not only a hugely popular literary work, but also a poem that sparks a major surge of interest in 'poetic knowledge' in late medieval France.[4] The impact of the *Rose*, however, reaches far beyond France, and plays a central role in triggering a much broader epistemic turn within late medieval European literary culture. A good illustration of this widely shared awareness of the *Rose* as a paradigm for intellectual speculation in poetic form is provided by Laurent de Premierfait's observations in his 1409 translation of Giovanni Boccaccio's *De Casibus virorum illustrium* into French. Laurent here provides a brief account of Dante's life, and identifies the latter's encounter with the *Rose* as a particularly important moment: the 'noble book of the *Rose*', Premierfait claims, provided Dante with 'a true *mappa mundi* of all heavenly and earthly things'[5] and inspired the Florentine poet to write his own *magnum opus*, the *Divina Commedia*, in imitation of Jean de Meun.[6] Whatever the historical accuracy of Premierfait's statement— almost certainly spurious—the anecdote confirms a widely shared awareness of

in mente Sortis et conservata post adnihilationem et corruptionem rosae, ita quod Sortes nihil aliud intelligat, dicunt quod haec propositio est neganda: aliquid intelligitur a Sorte, et haec similiter: rosa intelligitur a Sorte. Et eadem ratione, . . . quod ante creationem mundi, haec fuisset falsa si fuisset: Deus intelligit mundum, et haec simliter: aliquae creatura intelligitur a Deo'. In Oxford, Oriel College MS 15, f. 149va, and the early printed edition, *Quatuor Libros Sententiarum Questiones* (Lyon: 1518), f. h6ra, quoted in Hester Gelber, *It Could Have Been Otherwise: Contingency and Necessity in Dominican Theology at Oxford, 1300–1350* (Leiden: Brill, 2004), pp. 345–6. Translation adapted from Gelber.

[3] Gertrude Stein, *Lectures in America* (Boston: Beacon Press, 1985), p. 231.

[4] See especially Armstrong and Kay, *Knowing Poetry*, pp. 73–80, and discussion above, 'Introduction', pp. 5–9, 46–7.

[5] Laurent de Premierfait, *Laurent de Premierfait's Des cas des nobles hommes et femmes*, ed. Patricia May Gathercole (Chapel Hill, NC: The University of North Carolina Press, 2017), quoted in McWebb, *Debating the Roman de la Rose*, pp. 422–3.

[6] On Dante's debt to the *Rose*, on his possible role as the author of the Tuscan translations/adaptations known as *Il Fiore* and *Il Detto d'Amore*, and on the *Rose*'s broader role in Italian literary culture, see further e.g. Gianfranco Contini, 'Un nodo della cultura medievale: la serie *Roman de la Rose, Fiore, Divina commedia*', in his *Un Idea di Dante: Saggi Danteschi* (Torino: Einaudi, 1973), pp. 345–83; Kevin Brownlee, 'The Conflicted Genealogy of Cultural Authority: Italian Responses to French Cultural Dominance in *Il Tesoretto, Il Fiore*, and *La Commedia*', in Kevin Brownlee and Valeria Finucci, eds, *Generation and Degeneration: Tropes of Reproduction in Literature and History, from Antiquity to the Early Modern Period* (Durham and London: Duke UP, 2001), pp. 262–86; and the recent work of Antonio Montefusco, e.g. 'Contini e il "nodo": l'avventura del *Fiore* (tra *Roman de la Rose* e *Commedia*), *Ermeneutica Letteraria* 10 (2014), 55–66; ibid., 'Sull'autore e il contesto del *Fiore*:

the *Rose* as a summative *précis* of physical and metaphysical knowledge, circulating among an international community of élite poets and intellectuals. Premierfait's observation is not an isolated occurrence. Almost a century later, in 1500, Jean Molinet observes in his moralized rewriting of the *Rose* that the poem had by then been thoroughly 'absorbed into the memories of men' ['incorporé en la mem-oire des hommes'].[7] It is hardly a coincidence that another major 'philosophical poet' and monumental figure of European literary history, Geoffrey Chaucer, was deeply invested in the *Rose*. As Alcuin Blamires observes, together with Boethius's *Consolation*, the *Rose* is 'another of the central medieval writings that Chaucer comprehensively imbibed by translating it into English'.[8] While Chaucer's famil-iarity with the *Rose* is well known and widely acknowledged, as Alastair Minnis has suggested many Chaucerians continue to underestimate both the 'details' and the 'profundity' of Chaucer's engagement with Jean's poem.[9] As Mark Miller observes, not only did the *Rose* 'play a central role in mediating philosophy and poetry for Chaucer', but it also served as a paradigm for a new kind of philosophical poetry in the vernacular: 'Chaucer found the questions explored in the *Roman de la Rose* [. . .] immensely productive even—and perhaps especially—when the *Rose* functioned for him more as an intellectual interlocutor than as a direct literary source'.[10]

It is therefore reductive to see the *Roman de la Rose* merely as a strictly 'lit-erary' work that simply happens to have been very fashionable with aristocratic readers during the late medieval period. Prominent poets, intellectuals, and more shadowy readers did not just express a bewildering array of divergent views on the poem and its interpretation, but many of them were only too happy to tam-per with the text itself—variously emending, annotating, augmenting, abridging, rewriting, reformulating, censuring, vilifying, condemning, and especially *debat-ing* the poem in ways that are unprecedented in European literary history.[11] To adapt Miller's remark, it can be said that Jean de Meun's poem thus became a privileged and active 'intellectual interlocutor' for later readers, and its reception history is accordingly generative and dialogic.[12] Much of the controversy about the *Rose* revolved around the poem's obscenity and its apparent incompatibil-ity with Christian moral strictures, particularly during the famous and frequently

---

Una Nuova Proposta di Datazione', in Natascia Tonelli, ed., *Sulle tracce del Fiore* (Firenze: Le Lettere, 2017), pp. 136–58.

[7] Jean Molinet, *Le Roman de la rose moralisé* (Lyon: Guillaume Balsarin, 1503) sig. 5v.

[8] Alcuin Blamires, 'Philosophical Sleaze? The "Strok of thought" in the Miller's Tale and Chaucerian Fabliau', *Modern Language Review* 102/3 (2007), 621–40 (629–30).

[9] Minnis, *Magister Amoris*, pp. 119–20.

[10] Mark Miller, *Philosophical Chaucer: Love, Sex and Agency in the Canterbury Tales* (Cambridge: Cambridge University Press, 2004), pp. 33, 12.

[11] Badel, *Le Roman de la Rose au XIVe siècle*; Huot, *The Romance of the Rose and its Medieval Readers*. See further above, 'Introduction', n. 4.

[12] See especially de Pizan, *et al.*, *Le Débat sur le 'Roman de la Rose'*, ed. Hicks; ibid., *The Debate of the Romance of the Rose*, ed. Hult; McWebb, ed., *Debating the Roman de la Rose*.

58   MEDIEVAL ALLEGORY AS EPISTEMOLOGY

discussed *Quérelle de la Rose* (c. 1401–3). While the controversy itself addresses a number of important moral, ethical, and aesthetic questions that have been thoroughly examined by existing scholarship, it is important to recognize that the controversy as a whole ultimately crystallizes as a result of the poem's underlying referential ambiguity. Beneath the debate over the moral and ethical legitimacy of the poem, then, lies a much wider and more fundamental problem of linguistic reference and equivocation that is characteristic of allegorical expression.[13] Just how insistently and self-consciously Jean de Meun foregrounded referential ambiguity becomes evident if the *Rose* is compared with some of its immediate sources. Those are primarily the Latin allegorical poems and commentaries produced during the twelfth century by Platonizing poet-philosophers such as Alan of Lille and Bernardus Silvestris, many loosely associated with the Chartrian 'movement'.[14] Jean de Meun's use of such sources has been discussed in numerous important studies, and I shall return to this complex question at various points throughout subsequent chapters.[15] For the time being, however, I merely want to identify some most fundamental and general features that differentiate Jean de Meun's use of allegorical poetry from that of his predecessors.

In its twelfth-century incarnation, allegorical interpretation was at least in part conceived as a method of philosophical enquiry and even spiritual development. Such an approach assumes the ability of readers to produce an interpretation that is broadly concordant with a deeper, truer, and objectively real level of meaning. The hermeneutic process is thus often imagined as a gradual 'uncovering'

---

[13] For an illuminating (and brilliant) discussion of the 'hermeneutics of censorship' in the *Rose*, which takes into account both sexual ethics, social constructions of obscenity, and theories of signification and representation, see David Hult, 'Words and Deeds: Jean de Meun's *Romance of the Rose* and the Hermeneutics of Censorship', *New Literary History* 28.2 (1997), 345–66.

[14] See especially Winthrop Wetherbee, *Platonism and Poetry in the Twelfth Century: The Literary Influence of the School of Chartres* (Princeton: Princeton University Press, 1972); Lynch, *The High Medieval Dream Vision*; Whitman, *Allegory*, pp. 161–260. On the notion of *integumentum*, see especially Édouard Jeanneau, 'L'usage de la notion d'*integumentum* à travers les gloses de Guillaume de Conches', *AHDLMA* 24 (1957), 35–100.

[15] See notably Winthrop Wetherbee, 'The Literal and the Allegorical: Jean de Meun and the *de Planctu Naturae*', *Mediaeval Studies* 33 (1971), 264–91; ibid., *Platonism and Poetry*, pp. 187–265; Maureen Quilligan, 'Allegory, Allegoresis, and the De-allegorization of Language: the *Roman de la Rose*, the *De planctu naturae*, and the *Parlement of Foules*', in Morton W. Bloomfield, ed., *Allegory, Myth, and Symbol* (Cambridge, Mass.: Harvard University Press, 1981), pp. 163–83; Sarah Kay, 'Sexual Knowledge: The Once and Future Texts of the *Romance of the Rose*' in Judith Still and Michael Worton, eds, *Textuality and Sexuality: Reading Theories and Practices* (Manchester: Manchester University Press, 1993), pp. 69–86; ibid., 'Women's Body of Knowledge: Epistemology and Misogyny in the *Romance of the Rose*' in Sarah Kay and Miri Rubin, eds, *Framing Medieval Bodies* (Manchester: Manchester University Press, 1994), pp. 211–35; ibid., *The Romance of the Rose* (London: Grant & Cutler, 1995), pp. 73–113; ibid., 'The Birth of Venus in the *Roman de la rose*', *Exemplaria* 9 (1997), 7–37; Jill Mann, 'Jean de Meun and the Castration of Saturn', in John Marenbon, ed., *Poetry and Philosophy in the Middle Ages: A Festschrift for Peter Dronke* (Leiden: Brill, 2000), pp. 309–26; Minnis, *Magister Amoris*, pp. 82–118, 126–59, and *passim*; Noah Guynn, *Allegory and Sexual Ethics in the High Middle Ages* (New York: Palgrave Macmillan, 2007), pp. 93–170; David Rollo, *Kiss My Relics: Hermaphroditic Fictions of the Middle Ages* (Chicago: University of Chicago Press, 2011), pp. 77–213; Morton, *The 'Roman de la Rose' in its Philosophical Context*, pp. 36–61; Morton and Nievergelt, pp. 5–9.

of the truth concealed beneath the veil of poetic fiction. This view implies a fundamentally positive, productive, and developmental understanding of the hermeneutic process that is broadly consonant with notions of Christian spiritual development—an idea I will explore more fully in Chapter 2. Nonetheless, twelfth-century authors themselves often questioned, destabilized, or subverted this central principle through various forms of irony and ambiguity. Writing in a very different kind of cultural and intellectual environment over a century later, Jean de Meun deliberately amplified and exacerbated such latent slippages and ironies at work in earlier philosophical allegory, and did so by directing the reader's attention very specifically to the referential ambiguities of allegorical expression.

As is often noted, Jean de Meun's poem explicitly references this twelfth-century principle of spiritualized allegorical interpretation during Raison's extended conversation with the first-person dreamer/narrator. Any fabulous poetic narrative, Raison argues, ought to be understood figuratively, with a view to uncovering the philosophical truth concealed beneath the veil of the poetic fiction:

qui bien entendroit la letre,	he who understood the letter well,
le sen verroit en l'escriture,	would see the meaning in the writing
qui esclarcist la fable occure.	that would shed light on the dark fable.
La verité dedenz reposte	The truth hidden within would be
seroit clere, s'el iert esposte;	clear, if it were exposed/explained. You
bien l'entendras, se bien repetes	will understand it well if you rehearse
les integumanz aus poetes.	the integuments of the poets. There you
La verras une grant partie	will see a great portion of the secrets of
des secrez de philosophie.	philosophy.[16]
(RR 7132–40)	

Quite apart from the fact that the theory is presented by the often erratic character of Raison—and not by the poem's authorial voice—this principle does not ultimately provide an accurate and satisfactory description of how the *Rose* itself generates meaning(s). As is often noted, this is at least in part a function of the dreamlike nature of the events recounted, and Guillaume de Lorris's narrator tells readers at the start of the poem that the dream needs to be interpreted for its prophetic meanings to become apparent (*RR* 15–30). The significance of whatever appears obscure at present will become evident in due course (*RR* 19–20), once a full exposition of its meaning is provided:

Qui dou songe la fin ora,	I can assure you that whoever hears the
je vos di bien que il porra	end of the dream will be able to learn a
des jeus d'Amors assez aprendre,	great deal about the games of Love,

---

[16] Translations from the *Rose* are based on *The Romance of the Rose*, trans. Frances Horgan (Oxford: Oxford World's Classics, 1994), often, as here, emended and accordingly noted.

60 MEDIEVAL ALLEGORY AS EPISTEMOLOGY

puis que il veille tant atendre	provided that he is willing to wait until I
que je die et que j'encomance	have begun to expound the significance
dou songe la senefiance.	of the dream. The truth, which is
La verité, qui est coverte,	hidden, will be completely plain when
vos sera lores toute overte	you have heard me explain the dream,
quant espondre m'oroiz le songe,	
(RR 2065–73)	

But despite many similar, insistent, and reiterated promises of elucidation throughout the poem (RR 980–4; 1598–1600; 7132–42; 16,821–4; 21,183–4), no exposition is ever provided—a disjunction exacerbated by the arrival of a second author/narrator dreamer, Jean de Meun, who claims to have continued and concluded Guillaume de Lorris's unfinished dream poem after an interval of some forty years (cf. RR 10,465–650). As we finally reach the end of this long and digressive poem, we are still awaiting clarification, and remain in the dark about the significance of the dream as much as the intended meaning of the poem. This strategy of promise, deferral, and repeated frustration clearly plays with the reader's desire for clarification and exposition, and thus presupposes a hermeneutic approach that is broadly consonant with that pursued by twelfth-century philosophical poets like Alain de Lille, whose *De Planctu Naturae* is indeed one of Jean de Meun's most important direct sources. But this broadly Neoplatonist understanding of allegorical interpretation is conjured up only in order to be deliberately and systematically undermined, and the desire for exposition frustrated. In the words of Jill Mann, here the '"integuments of the poets" are invoked only to be dismissed, banished along with Reason'.[17] Maureen Quilligan has similarly argued that what occur here are ultimately a 'deallegorization of language' and a 'perfect inversion of the normal allegorical process of metaphor'.[18]

As I have argued elsewhere in more detail, together with Jonathan Morton, Jean's ironic use of such twelfth-century ideas militates against the assumption that there might be some direct, binary, recoverable, and objectively viable relation between the fabulous surface of his own poetic text and its supposed philosophical depths:

[i]n this 'Romanz de la Rose, / ou l'art d'Amors est tote enclose' (Romance of the Rose, in which the whole art of love is enclosed; RR 37–8, translation emended), any philosophical truth remains stubbornly 'enclosed', contained yet

---

[17] Mann, 'Jean de Meun and the Castration of Saturn', pp. 322–3.

[18] Maureen Quilligan, 'Words and Sex: the Language of Allegory in the *De planctu Naturae*, the *Roman de la rose*, and Book III of the *Faerie Queene*', *Allegorica*, 2 (1977), 195–215 (199–200); ibid., 'Allegory, Allegoresis, and the De-allegorization of Language'.

imprisoned, locked up—just as the Rose, the object of the lover's quest, remains confined within Jalousie's tower. But whereas the Rose is ultimately won by the lover/dreamer/narrator, the philosophical secrets of the text remain inaccessible to the reader, impenetrably wrapped up in the body of the text, and ultimately inextricable from its poetic, fictional, and linguistic texture. Indeed, the standard hermeneutic binaries opposing surface to meaning, husk to kernel, and the literal to the allegorical no longer obtain and we are left with an unstable, inextricable compound of poetic fictions and philosophical truths. For all of its ostensible commitment to a Platonic hermeneutic dualism, then, at the level of its own poetic practice the *Rose* remains a deliberately impenetrable, inscrutable, stubbornly hylomorphic text that resists any attempt to be fully 'known'.

Rather than writing poetry that demonstrably contains an encrypted, but ultimately discernible and retrievable truth, Jean's poem appears deliberately designed to interrogate the kind of confidence in interpretive teleology that structures the universe of allegorical signification developed by his twelfth-century predecessors.

Jean de Meun's determination to frustrate any desire for interpretive closure engenders a more widespread crisis of discursive authority in the poem, casting doubt on the veracity of the statements of its many fictional characters. Personified abstractions such as Nature, Reason, and the God of Love *may* embody and give voice to the universal entities or realities they represent, but they do so only insofar as the reader accepts to believe in the artifice of *prosopopoeia*. Through the very act of speaking, such personifications inevitably draw attention to their artificial and re-presentational nature, constantly forcing the reader to acknowledge that the truth-value of *any* statement within the *Rose* is invariably mediated and fabricated, and as such ultimately unreliable. This is most evident when Jean de Meun's narrator himself reminds us of his ostensible neutrality as a purely objective compiler of pre-existing voices and authorities, during the one of the rare moments where he *appears* to speak *in propria persona*:

D'autre part, dames honorables,
s'il vos samble que je di fables,
por manteür ne m'an tenez,
mes aus aucteurs vos an prenez
qui an leur livres ont escrites
les paroles que g'en ai dites,
et ceus avec que g'en dirai;
    [...]

Moreover, honourable ladies, if it seems to you that I am making things up, do not call me a liar, but blame those authors who have written in their books what I have said, along with the things I have yet to say.
[translation emended]
    [...]

62 MEDIEVAL ALLEGORY AS EPISTEMOLOGY

je n'i faz riens fors reciter,	I merely rehearse their
se par mon geu, qui po vos coute,	pronouncements, except for making
quelque parole n'i ajoute,	a few additions on my own account
si con font antr'eus li poete,	which cost you little. Poets do this
quant chascuns la matire trete	among themselves, each one dealing
don il plest a antremetre;	with the subject that he wants to
car si con tesmoigne la letre,	work on, for, as the text tells us, their
profiz et delectation,	intention is solely to edify and to
c'est toute leur entencion.	please.
(*RR* 15,185–90; 15,204–12)	[translation emended]

This denial of authorial bias is palpably disingenuous, and indeed appears deliberately designed to arouse precisely the kinds of suspicion it pretends to allay.[19] By reminding us of the presence of a narrator who is more than willing to interject (*antremetre*) extraneous materials and opinions amongst the pre-existing materials (*matire*) he purports merely to transmit (*reciter*), Jean effectively draws attention to the mediated, compromised, fabricated, and potentially mendacious nature of his own text. This uncertainty is exacerbated by the use of *prosopopoeia* within the framework of a narrated dream, whose epistemic status is fundamentally unclear: far from being 'real' and realistic *personae*, the speaking characters and multiple embedded narrators within this poem are all speaking puppets at the mercy of an author who, however, declines to assume responsibility for their utterances—an author who furthermore claims to have encountered them in a dream that turns out *not to be his own*, as emerges at the midpoint of the poem, when the God of Love names its *two* authors, Guillaume de Lorris and Jean de Meun. What is ostensibly intended to reassure the poem's readers, then, only compounds our suspicions about the fundamentally equivocal and duplicitous status of the poem in its entirety.[20]

This untrustworthiness applies *a fortiori* to the statements and utterances ascribed to real historical *auctoritates* cited by name within the text, but whose pronouncements are mediated in various ways: Aristotle, Horace, Boethius, Alan of Lille, and a host of others.[21] As Sylvia Huot puts it, in Jean's *Rose* 'plenty of

---

[19] This pervasive concern with discursive agency and authorial intention appears to have been one of the features of the *Rose* that most intrigued Chaucer, who can be seen grappling with the question throughout his poetic career. For a discussion of such issues in relation to the Pardoner and the Wife of Bath, both of whom are direct descendants of characters of Jean's *Rose*, see especially Alastair Minnis, *Fallible Authors: Chaucer's Pardoner and Wife of Bath* (Philadelphia: University of Pennsylvania Press, 2013).

[20] Susan Stakel, *False Roses: Structures of Duality and Deceit in Jean de Meun's 'Roman de la rose'* (Saratoga: Anma Libri, 1991).

[21] On the citational logic of the *Rose*, see also Nancy Freeman Regalado, '"Des contraires choses": la fonction poétique de la citation et des *exempla* dans le *Roman de la rose* de Jean de Meun', *Littérature* 41 (1981), 62–81; David F. Hult, 'Closed Quotations: The Speaking Voice in the *Roman de la rose*', *Yale*

IN THE BEGINNING WAS THE ROSE 63

Latin authors are indeed glossed [. . .] to within an inch of their lives',[22] and Mary Franklin-Brown observes that 'Jean's speakers are dodgier than those of earlier allegories, their expositions more confused. One after the other, they regale the Lover with often warped interpretations of authorities from Ptolemy to Ovid to Albert the Great'.[23] It is precisely this endemic tendency of the poem to pervert, misread, or falsify authoritative statements that Jean Gerson found so objectionable as part of the *Quérelle de la Rose*. In Jean's poem, Gerson argues,

> sont translatés, assemblés et tirés come a violance et sans propos autres livres plusseurs, tant d'Ovide come des autres, qui ne sont point moins deshonnestes et perilleux.[24]

> are translated, assembled, and as it were violently disfigured—without reason— many other books, by Ovid and others, which are hardly less infamous and dangerous. [translation mine]

It is particularly the treatment inflicted upon impeccably orthodox Christian authors that horrifies Gerson. He singles out Jean's manipulative *translacion* of Alan of Lille's *De Planctu Naturae*. Jean is not only plundering the works of others, but is deliberately distorting their originally intended meanings:

> ceste fiction poétique fut corumpuement estraitte du grant Alain, en son livre qu'il fait *De la Pleinte Nature*; car aussy tres grant partie de tout ce que fait nostre Fol Amoureulx n'est presques fors translacion des dis d'autruy.
> [. . .]
> je reviens a Alain et dy que par personnaige quelconque il ne parla onques en tele maniere.[25]

> this poetic fiction has been perversely extrapolated from Alan's book *The Plaint of Nature*, since a great part of what our Foolish Lover undertakes is almost entirely a translation of the writings of other people.
> [. . .]
> and I return once more to Alan, and maintain that he never spoke in such fashion through the mouthpiece of any of his characters.

Gerson's attack here is undoubtedly motivated primarily by moral concerns, and it is these concerns with the perceived immorality of the *Rose* that loom large

---

French Studies 67 (1984), 248–69; and ibid., 'Language and Dismemberment: Abelard, Origen and the *Romance of the Rose*' in Brownlee and Huot, *Rethinking the 'Romance of the Rose'*, pp. 101–30.

[22] Sylvia Huot, *Dreams of Lovers and Lies of Poets: Poetry, Knowledge, and Desire in the Roman de la Rose* (London: Legenda, 2010), p. 24.

[23] Mary Franklin-Brown, *Reading the World: Encyclopaedic Writing in the Scholastic Age* (Chicago and London: University of Chicago Press, 2012), p. 184.

[24] Jean Gerson, *Traité*, in Hicks, *Le debat sur le roman de la rose*, pp. 76–7.

[25] Jean Gerson, *Traité*, in Hicks, *Le debat sur le roman de la rose*, p. 80.

64 MEDIEVAL ALLEGORY AS EPISTEMOLOGY

in the *Querelle* as a whole, involving Christine de Pizan, the Col brothers, and Jean de Mentreuil as well as Gerson. In the present context, however, I'm less interested in Gerson's outrage about the strictly moral and ethical implications of Jean's unorthodox *translacion* of Alan of Lille's poetic fiction. Instead, and following David Hult's reading,[26] I want to focus on the semiotic slippages at work within Jean's poem, since it is that referential instability that enables Jean's poem to develop its uniquely evasive, rampant yet implicit obscenity in the first place.[27] As Hult observes, 'Jean manages to create a sequence of images that by imaginative contagion all end up suggesting obscene possibilities'.[28] Gerson's attack, then, seems to me to highlight Jean de Meun's exceptional skill in exploiting the intrinsic slipperiness of allegorical expression to interrogate and subvert any notion of 'orderly' hermeneutics and textual *auctoritas*, postulated on the tacit respect for a supposedly transparent *intentio auctoris*.

What are we to make of such determined effort to resist and subvert any textual and discursive authority by means of underhand *translatio*? For Marc-René Jung, 'Jean de Meun effectively warns us against any kind of argumentation that relies, *a priori*, on any citation of an antecedent *auctoritas*'.[29] This point is taken up by Hult, who sees the poem's handling of textual authorities as performing a kind of transfer of meaning that is not so much translation in the strict sense as 'adaptation gone berserk'.[30] As Hult argues elsewhere, this is a strategy that fits within a much 'broader ideological preoccupation within the *Rose* as a whole', namely Jean's persistent interest in 'stressing language's independent expressivity outside the bounds of specific authority and intentionality'.[31] Jonathan Morton sees the poem's philosophical value as being 'perversely anti-authoritative',[32] while Pierre-Yves Badel memorably sums up the ideological agenda of Jean's poem as being that of an 'œuvre contre les structures',[33] that is, a poem that militates against pre-existing structures of all kinds—textual, institutional, political, cultural, intellectual, poetic, hermeneutic, and imaginative.

It is worth noting, then, that despite the disagreements over the larger ideological objectives and affinities of the *Rose*, there is a broad consensus about the poem's *method*: whatever the larger meaning or purpose of Jean's hermeneutic

---

[26] Hult, 'Language and Dismemberment'.

[27] Hult, 'Language and Dismemberment'. On obscenity and its mechanisms of signification, see also Alastair J. Minnis, 'From *Coilles* to *Bel Chose*: Discourses of Obscenity in Jean de Meun and Chaucer', in Nicola F. McDonald, ed., *Medieval Obscenities* (Woodbridge: Boydell & Brewer/York Medieval Press, 2006), pp. 156–78; and ibid., *Magister Amoris*, esp. pp. 164–208.

[28] David F. Hult, 'Poetry and the Translation of Knowledge in Jean de Meun', in Dixon and Sinclair, *Poetry, Knowledge and Community in Late Medieval France*, pp. 19–41 (35).

[29] Marc-René Jung, 'Jean de Meun et l'allégorie', *Cahiers de l'Association internationale des études françaises* 28 (1976), 21–36 (35).

[30] Hult, 'Poetry and the Translation of Knowledge', p. 26.

[31] Hult, 'Language and Dismemberment', p. 124.

[32] Morton, *The 'Roman de la Rose' in its Philosophical Context*, p. 108.

[33] Badel, *Le RR au XIVe siècle*, pp. 53–4.

IN THE BEGINNING WAS THE ROSE   65

shenanigans, it is undeniable that the poem actively and expertly labours to frustrate any definitive and satisfying interpretation. As Sylvia Huot shows in a concise overview of critical opinion on the poem, the *Rose* is widely seen as being 'a masterfully complex text that refuses to cohere into a single viewpoint. Noah Guynn, for example, describes it as "hybrid, encyclopaedic, polyphonic"; Alastair Minnis terms it "incorrigibly plural"; and for Sarah Kay it is "not just dialectical but infinitely slippery".[34] More importantly in the present context, it is precisely this ability to mobilize a multiplicity of voices, discourses, and perspectives without adjudicating between them that helps to explain the enduring popularity of the *Rose* with later readers, who continued meddling with it to produce such a remarkably lively and dialogic reception history: 'It is this capacity to stage conflicting readings of itself—rival voices vying with each other in the citational density of the text—that has enabled the *Rose* to remain a controversial, much-debated poem for well over seven hundred years'.[35]

The *Rose*'s deliberate evasiveness about its own, irreducibly plural meanings determines how we understand the *Rose*'s ability to mediate knowledge, and thus indelibly shapes its wider, and largely implicit poetic epistemology. It will be useful to provide some general considerations on the poem's attitude to knowledge before moving on to a broader discussion of the poem's 'philosophical' aspirations within its specific intellectual context. Three points seem particularly important. Firstly, if we step back from the poem's concern with strictly textual and linguistic 'authority'—which has understandably figured so prominently in the analyses of literary scholars—Jean de Meun's interest in language comes into focus as part of a much larger web of concerns with the nature of knowledge more broadly. I would therefore suggest that the *Rose* is *fundamentally* concerned with human knowledge, since this is the only topic that has a direct bearing on every single aspect, detail, and apparent digression in this otherwise massive, crushing, baggy, meandering, and 'monstrous' poem.[36] As Sarah Kay has previously suggested, while '[e]pistemology may be an anachronistic term to speak of medieval thought, since questions of knowledge are dispersed among a wide variety of different kinds of intellectual investigation . . . these areas of academic study are, however . . . united in the literary form of the *Rose*'.[37] The *Roman de la Rose*, then, is fundamentally and principally concerned with the nature of human knowledge,

---

[34] Huot, *Dreams of Lovers*, p. 4, citing Guynn, *Allegory and Sexual Ethics*, p. 137; Minnis, *Magister Amoris*, p. 194, n. 83; Kay, *Place of Thought*, p. 197.

[35] Huot, *Dreams of Lovers*, pp. 6–7.

[36] I echo the remarks of Joseph Bédier: 'Ce monstre qui est le *Roman de la Rose*', in *Les Fabliaux* (Paris: Champion, 1893), p. 370, cited and discussed in Alain Corbellari, *Joseph Bédier: Écrivain et Philologue* (Genève: Droz, 1997), p. 95. See also Edmond Faral, '*Le Roman de la rose* et la pensée française au XIIIe siècle', *Revue des deux mondes* 96 (1926), 430–57 (440–1)

[37] Kay, 'Women's Body of Knowledge', p. 211. On the recurrence of epistemological considerations across a wide range of different disciplines in the late medieval period, see 'Introduction' above, pp. 16–19.

66 MEDIEVAL ALLEGORY AS EPISTEMOLOGY

constantly examining and interrogating its ontological status, its origins, its different modalities, its mechanics, its uses, abuses, and its purpose. This, I suggest, was abundantly clear to many of its later readers, particularly those who were philosophically inclined, such as Deguileville and Langland, but also Dante, Chaucer, and Guillaume de Machaut among many others.[38]

The second and third points I wish to make about the centrality of knowledge in Jean's *Rose* concern the specific nature of the knowledge conveyed by the poem. To put it succinctly, the *Rose*'s concerted, if largely implicit attack on textual *auctoritee*, ultimately draws attention to an alternative, very different form of knowledge based on *experience*. But far from simply promoting experiential knowledge at the expense of knowledge mediated by textual *auctoritee*, the poem ultimately interrogates the nature of experiential knowledge in turn, highlighting its often slippery and unstable truth-value, and its intricate and indissoluble link to *auctoritee* itself. More particularly, the *Rose* explores the mechanics, dangers, and limitations of experiential knowledge specifically in terms of its relation to erotic desire broadly defined—and this too appears a constant in the work of later poetico-philosophical 'interlocutors' of the *Rose*. For Sarah Kay, '[t]he twin themes of the *Rose*, desire and knowledge, are dialectically intertwined so that desire for knowledge generates knowledge of desire and vice-versa'.[39] This points to the poem's underlying concern with the interference between the rational and the appetitive, matter and intellect, body and soul—pairs that are regularly invoked by the poem itself, but whose binarism is repeatedly blurred, questioned, and broken down.[40] Sylvia Huot has similarly stressed that Jean de Meun is interested in the nature of specifically *embodied* knowledge: the *Rose* holds out 'the promise of a different sort of knowledge altogether—a knowledge accessed not through language, but through the body'.[41] My second point, therefore, is that the *Rose* is interested in examining the nature of specifically embodied and experiential knowledge, which is variously imperfect, compromised, and provisional.

My third and final point concerns the formal and narrative means engaged by the poem in order to conduct such an examination. As literary histories

---

[38] On Machaut's creative engagement with problems of truth, knowledge, and epistemology, and on his debt to the *Rose*, see especially Jacqueline Cerquiglini-Toulet, '*Un engin si soutil': Guillaume de Machaut et l'écriture au XIV e siècle* (Genève: Droz, 1985); and Huot, *The Romance of the Rose and its Medieval Readers*, pp. 239–72. On the broader impact of the *Rose* on the Francophone tradition of 'philosophical' *poetrie*, see Armstrong and Kay, *Knowing Poetry*, esp. pp. 73–80.

[39] Kay, *Place of Thought*, p. 179.

[40] For the *Rose*'s systematic dismantling of binaries such as centre-margin, text-commentary, body-soul, 'tiexte'-'glose', 'diz'-'fez' see especially Kay, *Rose*, pp. 94–113; and ibid., 'Sexual Knowledge', pp. 83–4; Sylvia Huot, 'Bodily Peril: Sexuality and the Subversion of Order in Jean de Meun's *Roman de la Rose*', *Modern Language Review* 95 (2000), 41–61 (46 and passim); Hult, 'Words and Deeds', 357 and *passim*.

[41] Huot, *Dreams of Lovers*, p. 5. See further Huot, 'Bodily Peril'; and Kay, 'Sexual Knowledge', pp. 81–5; ibid., 'Women's Body of Knowledge', pp. 222–32.

IN THE BEGINNING WAS THE *ROSE*   67

consistently point out, the principal innovation of the *Rose* is the carefully controlled combined use of the dream frame and of a complex, stratified first-person
narrator/dreamer/protagonist *persona*.[42] In the present context I am less interested
in the strictly literary innovation that this constitutes, except insofar as it is through
such narrative devices that a split subject can actually be articulated or 'thought'
in the first place. As Michel Zink pointed out long ago, it is essentially this combination of the dream-frame and first-person narrative that enables the exploration
of a distinctive, internally self-divided subjectivity.[43]

The first person subject in the *Rose* and in the tradition that develops from
it, then, is invariably fragmented, multiple, and unstable, making it impossible
to understand the 'I' as a simple authorial, let alone autobiographical figure. As
Cynthia Brown observes, 'in many medieval works, especially from the *Roman
de la Rose* on, the presentation of the author occurs in a complex layering of sub-
jectivities, which proceed from a kind of external authoritative figure [. . .] to a
more internal fictional one'. Whereas the author 'previously [. . .] had been relegated to distinctly defined positions outside the text, to prologues and epilogues,
[. . .] [i]n the *Rose* [. . .] the persona of the first person voice is multiplied in an
intricate meshing of narrative levels as the narrator occupies positions before, during, and after the recounted events'.[44] The 'I' is therefore neither wholly exemplary
nor strictly authorial, let alone 'autobiographical' in any simple sense. Instead it
is invariably fluctuating, generic in its openness to being explored, inhabited, and
gradually filled by the reader in ways that are never merely descriptive or prescriptive. Because the 'I' is fundamentally unspecific, the dream-narrative thus creates
the space to accommodate the first-person subject in its role as 'reader', as an inter-
preter and expositor of its own dream. By degrees this capacious 'I' thus comes to
subsume the subjectivity of the external reader, drawn in to inhabit the poem and
investing the narrated 'I' by sharing in its hermeneutic, cognitive, and emotional

---

[42] For traditional literary historical accounts of such innovations, see especially Badel, 'Le poème
allégorique'; Jauss, 'Entstehung und Strukturwandel der allegorischen Dichtung'; and Strubel, *La Rose,
Renard et le Graal*; ibid., *'Grant senefiance a'*. For a more recent, challenging and illuminating scrutiny
of the complexities of the first-person poetic voice in late medieval poetry, and for a call to abandon
traditional and reductive literary-historical constructs such as 'authors' and 'narrators', see especially
the important work of A. C. Spearing, *Textual Subjectivity: The Encoding of Subjectivity in Medieval
Narratives and Lyrics* (Oxford: Oxford University Press, 2005); and ibid., *Medieval Autographies: The
"I" of the Text* (Notre Dame: University of Notre Dame Press, 2012). See also Laurence De Looze,
*Pseudo-Autobiography in the Fourteenth Century: Juan Ruiz, Guillaume De Machaut, Jean Froissart,
and Geoffrey Chaucer* (Gainesville: University of Florida Press, 1997). More specifically on the tradition of first-person narrative allegory in the tradition of the *Rose* in the Anglo-French tradition
c. 1330–1600, see variously Maupeu, *Pèlerins de vie humaine*, esp. pp. 32–5, 98–107; Pomel, *Les voies
de l'au-delà*, pp. 397–456; Kamath, *Authorship and First-Person Allegory*; Nievergelt, *Allegorical Quests*.

[43] On this aspect of the *Rose*, see especially Zink, *La Subjectivité littéraire*, pp. 127–35, 140–5, 160–70.

[44] Cynthia J. Brown, 'Text, Image, and Authorial Self-Consciousness in Late-Medieval Paris', in Sandra Hindman, ed., *Printing the Written Word: The Social History of Books, circa 1450–1520* (Ithaca:
Cornell University Press, 1991), pp. 103–42 (111).

68   MEDIEVAL ALLEGORY AS EPISTEMOLOGY

labour, and finally coming to experience the narrated subject as its own.[45] The unstable referential status of the 'I', then, functions as a sort of trapdoor, allowing the reader to penetrate within the multiple fictional enclosures of the poem/*verger* and experience—Narcissus-like and refracted in the mirror of allegory—its own subjectivity as that of another: *soi-même comme un autre*.[46]

An essential element that determines and maintains the internal division of this 'I' is its existence *in time*, suspended between the various temporalities of the dream, the narration, the past waking life, the prophesied future, as well as the temporal duration of the experience of reading and/or writing.[47] As we are told at the beginning of the *Rose* (*RR* 15–30), all of these multiple temporalities overlap in the dream narrative, in ways that make it impossible to disentangle them definitively from each other. Because the 'I' of such an allegorical narrative is never simply affirmed or 'given', it remains temporally distended and unfinished, in perpetual movement, caught up in a process of narrative becoming and transformation. The 'I' of dream vision poems thus represents a realm of possibilities, inviting the reader to engage hermeneutically in ways that that reach far beyond strictly textual exegesis and beyond the boundaries of the poem itself. Since the 'I' of the external subject is invited to become the 'co-author' of the first-person fiction through its interpretive engagement,[48] this means that the reader's own 'I' is simultaneously authoring the fictional narrative and being authored by it. In this sense, late medieval first-person narrative allegory provides a neat, almost perfect exemplification of Ricœur's theory of fiction in *Soi-même comme un autre*: fictional narrative as a whole relies on the reader's ability to 'identify' with a fictional instance in order to achieve the 'narrativization' of the reader's own subjectivity through an act of projective *mimesis*.[49] In asking its readers to accomplish such labour, dream-vision poetry makes the hermeneutic work of allegory coterminous with a distinctive form of self-awareness, an awareness of a self in movement, in time, engaged in a process of constant becoming that is bound to fall short of any stable and definite 'being'. As I will develop in the remainder of this chapter, this is a divided self that is neither specifically 'modern' nor essentially 'medieval', but one that finds some of its most important historical roots in the thought of Augustine.

---

[45] On such strategies of 'seduction', see David F. Hult, *Self-Fulfilling Prophecies: Readership and Authority in the First 'Roman de la rose'* (Cambridge: Cambridge University Press, 1986), pp. 8–9 and *passim*. See also Maupeu, *Pèlerins de vie humaine*, pp. 101–4; and A. C. Spearing, *Medieval Autographies*, pp. 16–18.

[46] See especially Paul Ricœur's discussion of the internal split of the subject in *Soi-même comme un autre* (Paris: Seuil, 1990), pp. 137–98.

[47] Emmanuèle Baumgartner, 'The Play of Temporalities or, the Reported Dream of Guillaume de Lorris', in Brownlee and Huot, *Rethinking the 'Romance of the Rose'*, pp. 21–38.

[48] Ricœur, *Soi-même comme un autre*, pp. 115–16, 189, 191 and *passim*.

[49] For 'narrativization', see Ricœur, *Soi-même comme un autre*, pp. 188–9 n. 2, 195–6, and *passim*; for Ricœur's third type of mimesis, defined as a readerly re-enactment of the narrated story, see *Temps et Récit 1: L'intrigue et le récit historique* (Paris: Seuil, 1983), pp. 136–62.

IN THE BEGINNING WAS THE ROSE   69

To conclude my third point and summarize the previous two, then, I suggest that Jean de Meun's highly skilful and deliberate use of the first-person dreamer/narrator allows him to articulate and explore a distinctive, internally self-divided subjectivity that is fundamentally narrative and distended in time. This also enables, or indeed requires him to engage in a series of thought experiments that raise a number of important epistemological questions concerning the cognitive powers of such an embodied individual, who is the 'subject' of potentially endless change. This, I believe, is a hugely important factor that is often neglected in traditional literary-historical accounts of the *Rose*, which tend to reduce the significance of the dream frame and first-person dreamer/narrator figure to that of literary devices. As I have suggested in what precedes, I believe that the truly innovative implications of Jean's slippery first-person narrator/dreamer/protagonist *persona* are to be sought on a rather different level. Indeed, it is ultimately the 'invention' of this uniquely complex, layered first-person narrated subject that enables allegorical dream-poetry to scrutinize the nature of thought, emotion, and consciousness as experienced by an individual subject.[50] It is this same reliance on a first-person narrator/protagonist figure that allows poets to reflect on a kind of cognitive experience that scholastic philosophers and theologians could only account for with great difficulty. As was seen in the introduction, scholasticism primarily aimed at producing certain, scientific knowledge (*scientia*) by using the unequivocal and disembodied language of logical demonstration. Scholasticism also produced elaborate but strictly theoretical accounts of contingent knowledge in the area of faculty psychology, and did so by using the objectivist language of empirical description, observation, and Aristotelian causality. Poets, by contrast, were able to explore the nature of contingent, experiential knowing from the inside, relying on the subjectivist language of first-person allegorical fiction.[51] Only the equivocal, ambiguous language of allegorical fiction was able to account for the process whereby knowledge crystallizes and metamorphoses within an individual, embodied subject engaged in a temporal process of constant becoming, and who seeks to understand the nature and significance of that experience *as it happens*. This, I believe, has important consequences for our understanding of the place of vernacular fiction in the history of phenomenology and philosophical

[50] For the avoidance of doubt, I want to stress again that I am *not* proposing a version of the familiar narrative about the putative 'invention' of modern selfhood. See further below.

[51] One exception here is constituted by scholastic accounts of proprioception, on which see Mikko Yrjönsuuri, 'Perceiving One's Own Body', in Knuuttila and Kärkkäinen, eds, *Theories of Perception*, pp. 101–16. Significantly, such accounts emphasize the distinctly sensory, 'embodied', and often tactile nature of self-awareness, and almost invariably rely on fictionalized counterfactuals that function 'allegorically' in ways that that are closely reminiscent of dream vision narratives. See also further discussion in Chapter 3, and Marco Nievergelt, 'Can Thought Experiments Backfire? Avicenna's Flying Man, Self-Knowledge, and the Experience of Allegory in Deguileville's *Pèlerinage de Vie Humaine*', in Knox, Morton, and Reeve, *Medieval Thought Experiments*, pp. 41–69.

70 MEDIEVAL ALLEGORY AS EPISTEMOLOGY

hermeneutics writ large. This seems particularly important at a time when considerable energy is being invested in the writing of a new archaeology of the subject that finally recognizes the crucial importance of medieval forms of thought and expression in the evolution of western ideas of the self.[52]

2. Jean de Meun and the Schools

The *Rose* marks a crucial watershed moment in the history of late medieval vernacular consciousness, and its impact is accordingly seminal and unprecedented. But for all of its self-consciously innovative and generative force, the *Rose* also crystallizes a wide range of intellectual, cognitive, and representational problems that are already being discussed within the wider cultural environment that Jean de Meun inhabits during the 1260s and 1270s. More importantly, Jean engages in uniquely creative and critical fashion with contemporary scholastic debate, specifically in areas that we would now define as 'philosophy of language' and 'philosophy of mind'. In this section, I therefore want to examine how exactly Jean engages with contemporary scholastic culture, and specifically contemporary discussions of reference and signification. I will be arguing that rather than merely 'echoing' the debates of the scholastics, the *Rose* actively engages with such debates, and thus provides an influential model for how to 'do philosophy' through poetry. Far from simply dismissing, subverting, or ridiculing the scholastic project, Jean's *Rose* engages with it in genuinely 'critical', intellectually enabling, and philosophically positive ways. More specifically, I argue that Jean finally uses poetry to test some of the most fundamental epistemic assumptions and limitations that define the scholastic project, and does so in the attempt to elaborate alternative and/or complementary ways of thinking that find their natural expression in allegorical dream poetry.

Ever since the publication of Ernest Langlois's *Origines et sources du 'Roman de la Rose'* in 1890, Jean de Meun's familiarity with scholastic authors has never been in doubt. It has proven far more difficult, however, to determine the extent and depth of Jean's learning, and especially its relevance for our interpretation of the poem. In the 1940s Gérard Paré could still claim that Jean was merely 'a vulgarizer and translator who continues to make the rudiments of university learning accessible to lay readers', but whose 'loosely scientific digressions [. . .] amount to

---

[52] I refer to Alain de Libera's monumental project on *L'Archéologie du sujet: I. Naissance du sujet* (Paris: Vrin, 2007); *II. La Quête de l'identité* (Paris: Vrin, 2008); *III. L'Acte de penser: 1. La Double révolution* (Paris: Vrin, 2014). On the centrality and complexity of notions of the 'individual' in fourteenth-century philosophy—avoiding any reductionist appeals to the rise of 'nominalism'—see also Jorge J. E. Gracia, 'The Centrality of the Individual in the Philosophy of the Fourteenth Century', *History of Philosophy Quarterly* 8.3 (1991), 235–51.

IN THE BEGINNING WAS THE *ROSE*   71

little more than child's play [...] and are deprived of any genuinely scientific aspiration.'[53] It is becoming increasingly clear that this is an unsatisfactory assessment. On the one hand, Jean's understanding of philosophical problems debated in Paris during the 1260s and 70s appears to have been far more precise and informed than Paré allowed for; on the other hand Jean's handling of such materials is often provocative, critical, and creative rather than merely derivative or incompetent. Gisela Hilder already provided an important and often overlooked study in 1972, assessing the linguistic evidence for Jean's familiarity with scholastic culture, which notably helped to shed light on Jean's close familiarity with schoolroom practice.[54]

Recent work has woken up to the remarkably wide range of advanced scientific discourses that are refracted within the poem. Scholarship has only just begun to provide serious discussions of Jean's familiarity with Aristotelian natural philosophy,[55] Aristotelian Ethics,[56] Boethian and Aristotelian ideas of contingency, fortune, and free will,[57] medieval optics, cognition, and epistemology,[58] the language arts of the *trivium* and medieval semantics,[59] *sophismata* literature,[60] medieval theories of the law, natural law, and political philosophy.[61]

---

[53] 'un vulgarisateur et un traducteur [qui] continue de mettre à la portée des laïcs les rudiments de sa science universitaire'. '[Ses] vagues dissertations scientifiques [...] apparaissent comme de l'enfantillage [...] et n'[ont] aucune prétention scientifique' Gérard Paré, *Les idées et les lettres au XIIIᵉ siècle: 'Le Roman de la Rose'* (Montreal: Bibliothèque de Philosophie, 1947), pp. 265, 311. See also ibid. *Le 'Roman de la Rose' et la scholastique courtoise* (Paris: Vrin/Ottawa: Institut d'études médiévales, 1941).

[54] Gisela Hilder, *Der scholastische Wortschatz bei Jean de Meun: die artes liberales* (Tübingen: Niemeyer, 1972), esp. pp. 185–96.

[55] Kellie Robertson, *Nature Speaks: Medieval Literature and Aristotelian Philosophy* (Philadelphia: University of Pennsylvania Press, 2017), pp. 127–76; Morton, *The 'Roman de la Rose' in its Philosophical Context*.

[56] Jessica Rosenfeld, *Ethics and Enjoyment in Late Medieval Poetry: Love After Aristotle* (Cambridge: Cambridge University Press, 2011), pp. 45–73; Morton, *The 'Roman de la Rose' in its Philosophical Context*.

[57] Heller-Roazen, *Fortune's Faces*; Philip Knox, 'Desire for the Good: Jean de Meun, Boethius, and the "homme devisé en deuz"', in Knox, Morton, and Reeve, eds, *Medieval Thought Experiments*, pp. 223–50; John Marenbon, 'Jean de Meun, Boethius, and Thirteenth-Century Philosophy', in Morton and Nievergelt, pp. 173–93.

[58] Suzanne Conklin Akbari, *Seeing Through the Veil: Optical Theory and Medieval Allegory* (Toronto: University of Toronto Press, 2004), pp. 78–113; Stephen G. Nichols, 'The Pupil of Your Eye: Vision, Language, and Poetry in Thirteenth-Century Paris', in Nichols, Calhoun, and Kablitz, *Rethinking the Medieval Senses*, pp. 286–308; Christophe Grellard, 'Mechanisms of Belief: Jean de Meun's Implicit Epistemology', pp. 27–44 in Morton and Nievergelt; Pomel, 'Visual Experiences and Allegorical Fiction'.

[59] Minnis, *Magister Amoris*, pp. 82–163; Stephen G. Nichols, 'Rethinking Texts through Contexts: The Case of le *Roman de la Rose*' in Jan-Dirk Müller and Elizabeth Müller-Luckner, eds, *Text und Kontext: Fallstudien und Theoretische Begründungen einer kulturwissenschaftlich angeleiteten Mediävistik* (München: Oldenbourg, 2007), pp. 245–70; Marco Nievergelt, 'Imposition, Equivocation, and Intention: Language and Signification in Jean de Meun's *Roman de la Rose* and Thirteenth-Century Grammar and Logic', in Morton and Nievergelt, pp. 65–89.

[60] Morton, 'Sophisms and Sophistry in the *Roman de la Rose*'.

[61] Luciano Rossi, 'Du nouveau sur Jean de Meun', *Romania* 121 (2003), 430–60; ibid. 'Encore sur Jean de Meun: Johannes de Magduno, Charles d'Anjou et le *Roman de la Rose*', *Cahiers de civilisation médiévale* 51 (2008), 361–77; Juhana Toivanen, 'The Personal and the Political: Love and Society in the *Roman de la Rose*', in Morton and Nievergelt, pp. 111–30; Philip Knox, 'Human Nature and Natural

72 MEDIEVAL ALLEGORY AS EPISTEMOLOGY

Clearly, then, Jean appears to have come into contact with a number of theories and debates that were at the cutting edge of intellectual developments in the Arts Faculty at Paris during the 1260s and 70s, where he has traditionally been situated. This has been confirmed by more circumstantial studies of the topical allusions to internal University polemic, notably in the work of Ian Wei, who observes that

> [w]hile Jean de Meun's continuation of the *Romance of the Rose* is frequently and rightly analysed in relation to literary genres and other literary texts, it is also clearly a product of the university milieu. More specifically, it seems to offer the perspective of a secular clerk educated in the faculty of arts.
>
> [...]
>
> [A]lmost every line of Jean's continuation seem to invoke debates that gripped the university or to make reference to some aspect of its basic culture.[62]

More specifically, Wei demonstrates Jean de Meun's sensitivity to a number of debates in the Theology faculty at Paris as well as the endemic tensions between theologians and *artistae* that would culminate in the condemnation of radical Aristotelian propositions in 1270 and 1277—events that have long been assumed to have had an impact on the poem.[63] Further elements of Jean's intellectual biography have come into focus thanks to Luciano Rossi's tireless work on archival materials relating to 'Iohannes de Magduno/Mauduno', a cleric from the diocese of Orleans who spent time studying law in Bologna in the 1260s before returning to Paris in 1269. While definitive proof of a link between this figure's identity and 'our' Jean de Meun is difficult to come by, the bulk of the evidence speaks overwhelmingly in its favour.[64]

Law in Jean de Meun's *Roman de la Rose*', in Morton and Nievergelt, pp. 131–48; Morton, *The 'Roman de la Rose' in its Philosophical Context*, pp. 88–109 and *passim*.

[62] Ian Wei, *Intellectual Culture in Medieval Paris: Theologians and the University, c. 1100–1330* (Cambridge: Cambridge University Press, 2012), pp. 359, 363.

[63] Wei, *Intellectual Culture in Medieval Paris*, pp. 356–74. For discussions of the poem's relation to the condemnations of 1270 and 1277, see also Morton, *The 'Roman de la Rose' in its Philosophical Context*, pp. 18–23, and references therein; David F. Hult, '1277, 7 March: Jean de Meun's *Roman de la Rose*' in Denis Hollier, ed., *A New History of French Literature* (Cambridge MA: Harvard University Press: 1994), pp. 97–103; and Kay, 'Women's Body of Knowledge', pp. 229–31. On the condemnations themselves, see David Piché and Claude Lafleur, eds, *La condamnation parisienne de 1277: Nouvelle édition du texte latin, traduction, introduction et commentaire* (Paris: Vrin, 1999); and the contributions in Aertsen, Emery, and Speer, *Nach der Verurteilung von 1277/After the Condemnation of 1277*. On Jean's relation to debates in Theology, see further Earl Jeffrey Richards, '"Les contraires choses": Irony in Jean de Meun's Part of the *Roman de la Rose* and the Problem of Truth and Intelligibility in Thomas Aquinas', in Dulce M. Gonzalez-Doreste and Maria del Pilar Mendoza Ramos, eds, *Nouvelles de la Rose: Actualités et persepectives du 'Roman de la Rose'* (La Laguna: Servicio de Publicaciones, Universidad de La Laguna, 2011), pp. 383–98; and Robertson, *Nature Speaks*, pp. 127–76.

[64] Among the many items, all listed in the bibliography, see especially Rossi, 'Du nouveau sur Jean de Meun', containing transcriptions of many of the most relevant documents; ibid. 'Encore sur Jean de Meun'; and, more recently, ibid., 'Jean de Meun e Chrétien de Troyes', *Studi Romanzi* 13 (2017), 9–41; and '"Frere Seier", i "frati Alberti" e le "pulzellette". Sulla diffusione del *Roman de la Rose* in Italia: da Jean de Meun, a Cino da Pistoia, a Dante', in *Letteratura Italiana Antica* 21 (2020), 21–58. For further

IN THE BEGINNING WAS THE ROSE   73

Jean's Bolognese experience not only helps to put into perspective Jean's interest in ethics, theories of the natural law, or the exegetical practices of the 'post-glossator' legal tradition—among several other topics relevant to medieval jurisprudence that are refracted in the *Rose*—but also provides a good illustration of the remarkable intellectual fluidity and pluralism of the social and cultural environment in which Jean appears to have moved. The mention of Iohannes de Magduno in a document from 1260, where he is identified as 'magister', suggests that he had already obtained his title of Master of Arts before his departure to Bologna, and he appears to have spent time studying in both Paris and in Orléans near his native Meung-sur-Loire. According to further documentation, Jean returned to Paris in 1269 before being appointed Archdeacon in his native Orléannais the following year. The hypothetical biography that can be reconstructed on the basis of Rossi's findings fits remarkably well with the internal evidence provided by the poem itself. Jean's deep familiarity with ancient poets, for instance, can in many ways be explained in terms of his likely early association with the schools at Orléans, where the study of the classics continued despite the rising tide of Parisian logic from the early thirteenth century onwards.[65] Regardless of the exact details of Jean de Meun's intellectual trajectory, it is important to stress that the elements provided by Rossi's outline are in many ways characteristic of the career of a late thirteenth-century intellectual, in the sense that they present us with an itinerant scholar who cannot be firmly identified with any specific branch of learning or indeed any specific faculty or institution. Masters and students often moved between different schools, universities, or faculties (Arts; Theology; Law; Medicine), often situated in different parts of Europe. More often than not, their association with a particular institution was limited in time, and many of them went on to pursue careers in the ecclesiastical and secular administration. Iohannes de Magduno too appears to have entertained close associations with secular rulers, as Rossi and others have shown, notably with the House of Anjou, and his presence is recorded on an embassy sent by Charles of Anjou to Alfonso X of Castille in 1269. Crucially, then, Jean de Meun, cannot be thought of in terms of an exclusive relation to a single intellectual environment—that of

---

discussion of biographical evidence, see also Jean Mesqui, 'La Famille De Meung et ses alliances: Un lignage Orléanais du XIe au XVe siècle', in *Bulletin archéologique et historique de l'Orléanais* 117 (2014), 5–66; for an argument against the identification, see Charles Vulliez, 'Autour de Jean de Meun, esquisse de bilan des données prosopographiques', in Jean-Patrice Boudet, Philippe Haugeard, et al., eds, *Jean de Meun et la culture médiévale: Littérature, art, sciences et droit aux derniers siècles du Moyen Âge* (Rennes: Presses Universitaires de Rennes, 2017), pp. 23–46; Patricia Stirnemann, 'Jean de Meun: Où et pour qui a-t-il travaillé?', in *Jean de Meun et la culture médiévale*, pp. 107–19; and Rossi's response, 'Jean de Meun et la culture de Panurge', *Revue de linguistique romane* 82 (2018), 289–310.

[65] This confrontation between logicians and grammarians is also the topic—rather fittingly—of an allegorical, mock-epic poem by Henri D'Andeli, *La Bataille des Sept Arts* (c. 1230), pitching the army of *grammatica* (Orléans) against the forces of *logica* (Paris). See Henri d'Andeli, *Les dits d'Henri d'Andeli*, ed. Alain Corbellari (Paris: Champion, 2003).

74 MEDIEVAL ALLEGORY AS EPISTEMOLOGY

Bologna, Orléans, Paris, the Angevin Court, or indeed any other location and/or institution.[66]

But how, then, can we best characterize Jean's attitude towards the kind of advanced intellectual speculation of the scholastics, which is undeniably echoed throughout his poem? Readings of the *Rose* as a strongly 'partisan' text have proven untenable, not least because of Jean's determined strategy for discursive evasion, which may well have been conditioned by the climate of heightened suspicion at the Paris Arts Faculty in the 1270s.[67] Already in 1980 Badel cautioned readers against the hasty attempt to align the elusive Jean with any particular intellectual position—'Averroistic' or otherwise.[68] Badel instead suggested that the poem is 'driven by the intense desire to account for the totality of experience' [animé par la volonté intense de rendre compte de la totalité de l'expérience], but that in doing so 'the poet exhausts himself in pursuing an impossible objective' [le poète s'épuise à une tâche impossible]. Critics since Badel, however, have increasingly argued that the discontinuities and ruptures that derail this totalizing pursuit may be due to more than mere 'exhaustion'. The multiple fragmentations and dislocations within the poem may well be the result of deliberate design, and suggest a rather more complex, critical but philosophically enabling relation to scholastic learning. Mary Franklin-Brown, for instance, observes that the poem deliberately 'pushed some of the dominant textual practices of scholasticism over the edge of absurdity'.[69] For Ian Wei, 'the *Romance of the Rose* represented a profound challenge to conceptions of knowledge and authority that were articulated by university scholars'. Such 'entertaining distortions' ultimately threaten to push the very presuppositions underlying scholastic methods over the brink: 'Most threatening of all, the possibility of certain meaning was denied'.[70]

Jean's attitude towards scholastic methods and ideas is therefore clearly 'subversive'—but what exactly is being subverted, and why? On one level, the *Rose* evidently pursues a satirical agenda, and it is inevitable that it should therefore satirize the divergence between theory and practice, ideals and institutions. It is entirely possible that here Jean may be alluding to the imperfect standards of scholastic disputation as he encountered them in practice, often characterized by

---

[66] For a more extended overview of Jean's fluid intellectual environment and its possible impact on the poem, see Morton and Nievergelt, pp. 15–21.

[67] See especially Morton, *The 'Roman de la Rose' in its Philosophical Context*, pp. 18–23; Richards, '"Les contraires choses"'; and Hult, '1277, 7 March'.

[68] See Badel, *Le RR au XIVe siècle*, pp. 32–8. For the earlier view about Jean's 'Averroism', see Franz Müller, *Der 'Rosenroman' und der lateinische Averroismus des 13. Jahrhunders* (Frankfurt: Klostermann, 1947). On the many problems with term 'Averroism' and the assumptions that underlie it, see John Marenbon, 'Latin Averroism' in Anna Akasoy, James E. Montgomery, and Peter E. Pormann, eds, *Islamic Crosspollinations: Interactions in the Medieval Middle East* (Cambridge: The E. J. W. Gibb Memorial Trust, 2007), pp. 135–47.

[69] Franklin-Brown, *Reading the World*, p. 184.

[70] Wei, *Intellectual Culture in Medieval Paris*, pp. 363, 374.

rhetorical bluster and a lack of logical consistency and genuine intellectual rigour. As Olga Weijers has shown, thirteenth-century scholasticism inherited two rival traditions of disputation: the first, which she designates the 'dialectical disputation', is primarily conceived as a polemical and rhetorical performance, and aims to overwhelm one's opponent rather than produce any kind of reliable or scientific knowledge; this form was widely practised within the arts faculties to develop the argumentative skills of the various disputants, and culminated with the various *sophismata* and *obligationes* that become fashionable during this period. On the other hand, we have what Weijers calls the 'scholastic disputation', which on the contrary relies on syllogistic reasoning and aims at solving genuine philosophical questions by applying rigorous definitions and restricting the signification of terms.[71] Given that nearly all speakers in the *Rose* give speeches whose structure is mostly rambling and digressive, and whose arguments are often developed in ad-hoc and inconsistent fashion, it is certainly possible to read Jean's poem as satirizing the pettiness of contemporary diatribes in the classroom.

There are however, I believe, more deep-seated and genuinely philosophical reasons behind Jean's determination to push scholastic discourse to its limits. Several recent studies have suggested independently and concurrently that Jean's poem is not so much dismissive of scholastic culture in a broadly parodic, satirical, and anti-intellectual sense, but rather that it interrogates the very principles and presuppositions that underlie the scholastic project as a whole. The *Rose* does this by conducting a series of counterfactual thought experiments in order to test the validity of a whole range of scholastic methods, formulations, axiomatic assumptions, and specific theories and ideas. Variations of this argument have recently been presented in relation to a whole range of issues and debates: theories and definitions of Natural Law;[72] supposition theory in logic and semantics;[73] Boethian ideas of necessity;[74] scholastic definitions of natural sexuality;[75] the freedom of the will in the context of the clash between voluntarist and intellectualist positions;[76] Aristotelian theories of economic sufficiency;[77] *species*-based theory of visual perception and cognition.[78] Rather than mocking scholasticism, then, Jean's poem appears to stress-test its assumptions and formulations by consistently

---

[71] Olga Weijers, 'De la joute dialectique à la dispute scolastique', *Comptes rendus des séances de l'Académie des Inscriptions et Belles-Lettres*, 143.2 (1999), 509–18.

[72] Knox, 'Human Nature and Natural Law', pp. 140, 143, 148.

[73] Nievergelt, 'Imposition, Equivocation, and Intention', p. 82. See also the discussion offered in Chapter 1.3.

[74] Marnebon, 'Jean de Meun, Boethius, and Thirteenth-Century Philosophy', p. 187.

[75] Knox, 'Desire for the Good', p. 225. On sexuality and scholastic debates on the natural, see further Morton, *The 'Roman de la Rose' in its Philosophical Context*, pp. 62–87; Wei, *Intellectual Culture in Medieval Paris*, pp. 356–74; Rosenfeld, *Ethics and Enjoyment*, pp. 45–73.

[76] Robertson, *Nature Speaks*, p. 157.

[77] Morton, *The 'Roman de la Rose' in its Philosophical Context*, pp. 138, 141.

[78] Akbari, *Seeing Through the Veil*, p. 111; Pomel, 'Visual Experiences and Allegorical Fiction', pp. 45, 46, 61. For further discussion of the *species*-theory, see also Chapter 3.5.

76 MEDIEVAL ALLEGORY AS EPISTEMOLOGY

working through them, extrapolating their utmost consequences and implications, relentlessly pursuing them to their absolute limits—often *ad absurdum*.[79]

This strategy is particularly evident in the poem's many pseudo-*disputationes* that make up the bulk of the lover's dream, and which appear designed to test the precision and effectiveness of the scholastic dialectical method in terms of its practical application. The lack of focus and discipline in such extended polemical diatribes often arises from fundamental inconsistencies in terminology, or from disagreements between the disputants about the definition of a limited set of key conceptual terms:[80] justice (*joutice*),[81] knowledge (*connoissance*),[82] truth (*verité*),[83] nature (*nature*),[84] freedom (*franchise*),[85] pleasure (*delit*),[86] imagination (*fantaisie*),[87] the nature of the good (*bon/bonte*)[88]—and, above all, the primary subject of the poem, love (*amor*).[89] As Jean le Bel (or Jean d'Arkel) will similarly observe a century later, *amours* is undeniably a 'nons équivokes'[90] that functions exactly like the term 'chiens' (*canis*)—the stock textbook example for equivocal nouns.[91] Rather than invoking these terms to designate stable concepts, then, the poem seems to delight in exposing their fundamental polysemy and slipperiness. Most importantly, many of the concepts denoted by the terms I just listed were also the subject of intense discussions among contemporary scholastic thinkers. The poem thus appears to reference very specifically a wide

[79] I borrow the expression from Knox, 'Human Nature and Natural Law', p. 144.

[80] To cite only one recent example in extended form, see Knox, 'Human Nature and Natural Law': 'Raison's argument is largely that *amor* in her sense is superior to *joutice*. But after an account of the end of the Golden Age (when the figure of Joutice reigned) and the castration of Saturn (*RR* 5505–24), her use of these terms shifts confusingly . . . [at 5537–40] she seems to have shifted her viewpoint, making *amor* the force that prevailed in a lapsed phase of human society, during which dominium (in the sense of both lordship and property ownership) held no sway' (pp. 139–40).

[81] E.g. Knox, 'Human Nature and Natural Law'; Toivanen, 'The Personal and the Political'; Morton, *The 'Roman de la Rose' in its Philosophical Context*, pp. 88–109.

[82] See further discussion in Chapter 1.5.

[83] Minnis, *Magister Amoris*, p. 88.

[84] E.g. Morton, *The 'Roman de la Rose' in its Philosophical Context*, pp. 36–61.

[85] E.g. Knox, 'Human Nature and Natural Law', pp. 140–3; Robertson, *Nature Speaks*, pp. 149–57.

[86] E.g. Rosenfeld, *Ethics and Enjoyment*, pp. 45–73.

[87] E.g. Pomel, 'Visual Experiences and Allegorical Fiction'.

[88] Jon Whitman, 'Dislocations: The Crisis of Allegory in the *Romance of the Rose*' in Sanford Budick and Wolfgang Iser, eds, *Languages of the Unsayable: The Play of Negativity in Literature and Literary Theory* (New York: Columbia University Press, 1989), pp. 259–80 (263–4, 272–4).

[89] On the how the equivocal meaning of 'love' is explored in the *Rose*, see further e.g. Morton, *The 'Roman de la Rose' in its Philosophical Context*, pp. 13–35.

[90] See Jehan le Bel, *Li Ars d'Amour, de Vertu, et de Boneurté*, ed. Jules Petit, 2 vols (Brussels: Victor Devaux, 1867–9), I:15, discussed in John M. Fyler, *Language and the Declining World in Chaucer, Dante, and Jean de Meun* (Cambridge: Cambridge University Press, 2007), p. 221, n. 327.

[91] The example of *canis* (dog) is a stock textbook example of equivocation, widely referred to in semantic treatises of the period. It can designate either a) the common mammal 'dog' (*canis latrabilis*); b) a marine animal, 'dog-fish' or 'shark'; c) the 'dog star' Sirius. It is discussed, for instance, by Roger Bacon in the *De Signis*, § 61 and § 93. See further e.g. Jennifer E. Ashworth, 'Signification and Modes of Signifying in Thirteenth-Century Logic: A Preface to Aquinas on Analogy', *Medieval Philosophy and Theology* 1 (1991), 39–67 (61–3).

range of contemporary philosophical debates, pointing to the endemic difficulty in defining key conceptual terms in logically viable and unambiguous fashion.

I have already suggested that the *Rose* very deliberately contravenes the strictures placed on the language of philosophical reasoning as defined by Aristotle, who had stipulated that terms ought to be defined in rigorously univocal and unambiguous fashion: 'for not to have a single meaning is to signify nothing at all' [non unum significare nichil significare est].[92] But rather than merely contravening such strictures in his poetry, Jean appears to point up the far more fundamental, radical opacity of the terms in themselves. It is not only Jean's many unreliable and undisciplined disputants such as Raison, Genius, and Nature who variously misunderstand, obfuscate, trivialize, misuse, manipulate, and distort the main terms of their debates—whether deliberately or not; Jean rather suggests that the terms themselves elude accurate definition and unequivocal understanding. Jean thus appears to be crafting his poem very deliberately as a sequence of largely abortive, unsystematic, and scientifically inconsequential *disputationes* around philosophically central terms that are insufficiently defined and fundamentally equivocal, and whose meanings cannot be usefully disambiguated, either *in* the poem or, by implication, *outside* it. Such referential slipperiness ultimately threatens to undermine the very possibility of knowledge of any kind as defined by Aristotle, and therefore harbours the potential to implode the scholastic project as a whole. This, it seems to me, is not so much an anti-intellectual project, but rather an indicator of Jean's commitment to an intellectual project of a very different kind, and one that cannot be accommodated within scholastic forms and discourses as Jean encountered them.

3. Allegory, Signification, and Equivocation

Despite Jean de Meun's fundamentally critical attitude towards scholasticism as a whole, I want to argue that his understanding of language as a radically equivocal sign-system, *does*, somewhat paradoxically, emerge out of his engagement with late thirteenth-century semantics, and more specifically with the highly controversial theories of reference and supposition formulated by Roger Bacon, which in turn had their roots in the thought of Augustine.[93] To be sure, Jean's understanding of linguistic signification appears to have relied on a broad spectrum of sources and discourses. It has been suggested, for instance, that Jean's conspicuous interest in linguistic instability results from his belief in the fundamentally fallen, postlapsarian status of human language, leading him to develop what John

---

[92] Aristotle, *Metaphysics* IV.4, 1006b7–8, and *Sophistical Refutations*, 165b24 ff. See introduction, pp. xx–yy.
[93] I discuss the issue in greater detail in a separate article, 'Imposition, Equivocation, and Intention', in Morton and Nievergelt, pp. 65–89.

78   MEDIEVAL ALLEGORY AS EPISTEMOLOGY

Fyler calls a 'lapsarian poetic'.[94] I believe Fyler is fundamentally correct in situating Jean's work in relation to this exegetical tradition stemming from Augustine and other Church Fathers,[95] and which also continued to shape scholastic developments during the thirteenth century.[96] Rather than providing an alternative to Fyler's account then, I propose to complement it by pointing to a set of more localized contemporary debates that took place around the University of Paris during the 1260s. Those debates seem to have helped to focalize Jean's attention on problems of linguistic equivocation in particular, and may well have provided the immediate impetus for Jean to elaborate a wider, distinctive theory of language and signification that is implicit in the narrative structure of the *Rose* as a whole.

Before discussing in some detail the close affinities between Jean de Meun's attitude to linguistic signification and the theories of Roger Bacon, it is worth stressing that the two figures appear to occupy a similarly liminal zone on the margins of Parisian scholastic culture in the period between about 1260 and 1280. We have no concrete details regarding the precise nature of Jean's relationship to the University of Paris, formal or informal, before or after his stay in Bologna (1265–9)—if we accept Rossi's suggestion about the identity of 'Iohannes de Magduno/Mauduno'. As evidenced by the *Rose* itself, however, it seems abundantly clear that Jean occupies an 'eccentric' position in relation to standard scholastic culture, and his attitude is best described as critical and ironic along the lines traced in what precedes. Jean would have found in Bacon an irresistibly unconventional thinker, writing on the margins of the University world and developing a highly idiosyncratic personal philosophical project, particularly in the *Opus maius*, written in secret for pope Clement IV in Paris between 1266 and Clement's death in 1268.[97] In the *Opus maius*, Bacon in fact aimed to do nothing less than overhaul the entire system of theological and philosophical thought of the medieval university, criticizing a whole range of contemporary scholastic practices as mechanical and intellectually sterile.[98] Jean would thus have found in Bacon a like-minded, profoundly irreverent, endlessly vituperative but also formidably

---

[94] See Fyler, *Language and the Declining World*, pp. 60–100 (here 52).

[95] I am less convinced, however, by Fyler's more specific claim that the famous exchange between Amant and Raison on the acceptability of the term *coilles* is intended to evoke notions of prelapsarian language, *Language and the Declining World*, pp. 74–95. See below for my reading of this passage within the rather different context of scholastic theories of reference, imposition, and supposition.

[96] See especially Irène Rosier, 'Babel: Le péché linguistique originel?', in Gianluca Briguglia et Irène Rosier, eds, *Adam, la nature humaine, avant et après: épistémologie de la chute* (Paris: Presses Universitaires de la Sorbonne, 2016), pp. 63–86.

[97] For Bacon's biography, see Jeremiah Hackett, 'Roger Bacon: His Life, Career, and Works', in Jeremiah Hackett, ed., *Roger Bacon and the Sciences*, pp. 9–25; and George Molland, 'Bacon, Roger (c.1214–1292?)', *Oxford Dictionary of National Biography*, Oxford University Press, 2004 [http://www.oxforddnb.com/view/article/1008, accessed 10 September 2019]. For an edition of the *Opus maius*, see *The Opus Maius of Roger Bacon*, ed. John Henry Bridges, 3 vols (Oxford, 1897–1900). See also subsequent notes for discussion of its structure and complex textual history.

[98] Bacon was particularly critical of the scholastic method, specifically the new vogue for Sentence commentary in theology, which he considered an aberration. See *Opus maius*, part 1; and *Opus minus*, in Brewer, ed., *Opera quaedam hactenus inedita* 1 (London, 1859), pp. 328–30.

IN THE BEGINNING WAS THE *ROSE* 79

challenging and engaging thinker, who sought to shake up the entire academic establishment of his day and redefine the very foundations of learning by writing a uniquely idiosyncratic *summa* of the most diverse sciences. Jean's *Roman de la Rose*—covering pretty much every subject under the sun from the refractive properties of mirrors to improper signification, astral determinism, the coming of Antichrist, and the nature of human justice—may be seen as doing something similar, in its own, inimitable and uniquely challenging fashion. Jean's critical attitude towards scholastic culture, too, may well be motivated by a broadly reformist or idealistic agenda that is not entirely unlike Bacon's. It is certainly striking that Jean should be particularly interested in a whole range of distinctly 'Baconian' questions addressed within the *Opus maius* in particular:[99] astrology, astral determinism, and divination; processes of natural generation and the relation of the individual to the species; the question of the ontological priority of particulars or common natures (universals); alchemy; theories of linguistic equivocation; astronomical phenomena and meteorology; the importance of translations to ensure a renewal of knowledge; the imminent coming of Antichrist; and, first and foremost, perspectivist optics, *species*-theory, and their epistemological and theological implications. This latter interest is evidenced, among other things, by Jean's verbatim translation of an extract from Bacon's *Perspectiva* (Part V of the *Opus maius*) as part of Nature's lecture on mirrors, to which I will return in Chapter 3.5.[100] The resonances and affinities between the *Rose* and the *Opus maius* certainly deserve further study.

Whether Jean would have subscribed to the ambitious holistic vision that Bacon pursued in the *Opus maius* is more dubious, especially given the relentlessly centrifugal, anti-systematic, and interrogative energies at work in the *Rose*—a poem that has variously been described as 'an encyclopaedia in disorder', an 'anti-encyclopaedia', or a mirror reflecting 'the epistemological fragility of the encyclopedic project'.[101] More specifically, it is difficult to imagine Jean having much truck with Bacon's ambitions for integrating the study of language and signification within an overarching theological project. Bacon in fact clearly saw his own works on grammar and semantics as a preparatory stage in what is a

---

[99] For an overview of Bacon's eclectic and wide-ranging interests, with particular reference to the *Opus maius*, see especially Hackett, *Roger Bacon and the Sciences*. See further Jeremiah Hackett, 'Roger Bacon', *The Stanford Encyclopedia of Philosophy* (Spring 2015 Edition), ed. Edward N. Zalta, https://plato.stanford.edu/archives/spr2015/entries/roger-bacon.

[100] For the identification, see Akbari, *Seeing through the Veil*, pp. 92–3. cf. Roger Bacon, *Opus maius*, Book V, part 3, dist. 3, ch. 3, text edited in *Roger Bacon and the Origin of Perspectiva in the Middle Ages*, ed. Lindberg, pp. 332–5. Bacon's discussion of *species*-theory was closely linked to his language theory—on which see Tachau, *Vision and Certitude*, pp. 1–26—a connection that seems highly relevant to its possible impact on Jean's *Rose*. See also the previous suggestions by Akbari, *Seeing through the Veil*, pp. 101–4; and Nichols, 'The Pupil of Your Eye'.

[101] See respectively Gaston Paris, *Esquisse historique de la littérature française au Moyen Âge* (Paris: A. Colin, 1907), p. 198; Sarah Kay, *The Romance of the Rose*, p. 71; Franklin-Brown, *Reading the World*, p. 214.

80 MEDIEVAL ALLEGORY AS EPISTEMOLOGY

fundamentally theological and sapiential endeavour, as is evident from the inclusion of an extended section on *De utilitate grammaticae* in part three of the *Opus maius*, essentially drafted in 1267.[102] The only surviving part of this section of the *Opus maius* was rediscovered in 1978, and is published under the title *De signis*.[103] It is doubtful whether Jean would have known the *De signis* in its surviving form. It may also be objected that it is somewhat perverse to be arguing for Jean's familiarity with a treatise whose writing was apparently shrouded in secrecy, and which survives in a single manuscript rediscovered only in 1978. However, it is abundantly clear from the allusions in the writings of many other contemporary Parisian authors that Bacon's unusual theory of signification was highly controversial, widely debated, and almost universally critiqued, often in highly polemical and aggressive language that echoed Bacon's own style.[104] Bacon himself in the *De signis* already refers to a 'not inconsiderable contention among famous men' [non modica [...] contentio inter viros famosos] (*De signis*, § 163), and Duns Scotus still speaks of this as a 'great dispute' [magna altercatio] more than a generation later. We also know that Bacon circulated fragments of his work in progress on the *Opus*

---

[102] See *The Opus Maius of Roger Bacon*, ed. Bridges, 3:80–125. Particularly the third section of part three of the *Opus maius* appears to have combined discussion of grammatical and exegetical problems. This part of the *Opus maius* survives only in fragmentary form, but its structure and contents can be inferred from the summary given by Bacon himself in Chapters XXV–XXVII of the *Opus tertium*, ed. J. S. Brewer, in *Fr. Rogeri Bacon Opera quaedam hactenus inedita*, vol. 1 (London: Longman, Green, Longman and Roberts, 1859), chs. XXV–XXVII, pp. 88–102.

[103] See Fredborg, Nielsen, and Pinborg, 'An Unedited Part of Roger Bacon's *Opus Majus: De Signis*'. For a recently published translation, see Bacon, *On Signs*, trans. Maloney. In its original form, part 3 of the *Opus maius* appears to have included three sections: section 1 is included in Bridges' edition, along with section 2, although parts of the second section may be missing. Only the *De signis* from part 3, section 3 has been rediscovered. In the remaining portions of the third section of part 3 of the *Opus maius*, following the more strictly semiotic considerations of the *De signis*, Bacon had discussed 'quomodo vox in Scriptura Sacra significat sensum spiritualem cum literali', and 'quomodo sensus literalis significat spiritualem' (*Opus tertium*, p. 101). Such remarks provide a striking example of how some of Jean de Meun's more eclectic contemporaries integrated the language arts and theology when it came to discussions of reference, signification, and the function of poetic figures and tropes—on which see more broadly Ocker, *Biblical Poetics Before Humanism and Reformation*, pp. 31–71; and Rosier, *La parole efficace*, pp. 166–72. For a more detailed overview of part 3 of the *Opus maius*, see Rosier-Catach, 'Roger Bacon and Grammar', in Hackett, *Roger Bacon and the Sciences*, pp. 67–102 (74–81). A new critical edition of the *De signis* was published as the present volume goes to press, and will certainly facilitate work on this important aspect of Bacon's thought: Roger Bacon, *Des Signes*, translation and commentary by Irène Rosier-Catach, Laurent Cesalli, Frédéric Goubier and Alain de Libera (Paris: Vrin, 2022).

[104] See the remarks by Alain de Libera, 'Roger Bacon et la Logique', in Hackett, *Roger Bacon and the Sciences*, pp. 103–32 (111–14, 121–32). For further examples of clearly anti-Baconian positions in contemporary texts, see ibid., 'Roger Bacon et la référence vide: Sur quelques antécédents médiévaux du paradoxe de Meinong', in Jean Jolivet, Zenon Kaluza, Alain de Libera, eds, '*Lectionum varietates*', Hommage à Paul Vignaux (1904–1987) (Paris: Vrin, 1991), pp. 85–120; ibid., 'Roger Bacon et le problème de l'*appellatio univoca*', in Henricus A. G. Braakhuis, Corneille H. Kneepkens, and Lambertus M. de Rijk, eds, *English Logic and Semantics, from the End of the Twelfth Century to the Time of Ockham and Burleigh. Acts of the 4th European Symposium on Mediaeval Logic and Semantics*, Leiden-Nijmegen, 23–27 April 1979 (Turnhout: Brepols, 1981) pp. 193–234 (200–3); ibid., *La Référence vide: Théories de la proposition* (Paris: Presses Universitaires de France, 2002),especially 35–61. See also the relevant sections of Paris, BnF MS Lat 16,135, ed. in Alain de Libera, *César et le Phénix. Distinctiones et sophismata parisiens du XIIIe siècle* (Pisa: Scuola Normale superiore/Florence: Opus libri, 1991), xxvii–xxx and 133–243 (esp. 219–43); and Alain de Libera et Leone Gazziero, 'Le sophisma "Omnis homo de necessitate est animal" du parisinus latinus 16135, f. 99rb–103vb', *AHDLMA* 75/1 (2008), 323–68.

maius to a number of friends and associates.[105] Furthermore, Bacon's ideas about signification had been elaborated well before he begun work on the *Opus maius* in 1266, and may have been available in other forms: Bacon's general theory of reference underwent only very minor changes between its earliest articulation in the *Summulae dialectices* (1252), the fuller exposition offered in the *De signis* (1267), and his final, synthetic overview in the *Compendium studii theologiae* (1292).[106] While his theories were certainly not 'common knowledge' outside Parisian University circles, it seems difficult to imagine that a keen and irreverent intellectual like Jean de Meun would not have come into contact with Bacon's views in one form or another. For the sake of convenience, then, in what follows I will mostly be quoting from the *De signis*.

In the remainder of this section, I want to argue that the influence of Baconian semantics on the *Rose* is discernible on two related levels. Firstly, Jean appears to be alluding to current debates over reference and supposition directly in the famous exchange between Raison and Amant on the nature of linguistic signification. Secondly, and far more importantly, Bacon's theory of the imposition of names informs Jean's poem at a much deeper level, shaping the overall plot of the *Rose* as a whole as well as the signifying mechanisms at work in it, helping Jean to develop a new kind of radically equivocal poetics. I will begin by examining the more localized resonances in the debate between Raison and Amant, before offering some considerations on what I see as a much deeper level of convergence between Jean's poetics and Bacon's semiotics and semantics.

The debate between Raison and Amant on the nature of linguistic signification develops in seemingly unexpected and incidental fashion, on the back of Raison's passing use of the world *coilles* ('balls' or testicles) during her account of Saturn's castration (*RR* 5505–8; 6898–912), an episode relayed by earlier authors including Cicero and Isidore.[107] This quarrel over the acceptability of the term *coilles* lends the exchange the air of a comical, anecdotal, and fundamentally pointless digression. This, however, is a recurrent strategy in the poem, often used to signal some of its most provocative interventions, and to invite readers to extrapolate and ponder some of the deeper, philosophically serious implications of such 'digressions'.[108]

---

[105] See Francis A. Gasquet, 'An Unpublished Fragment of a Work by Roger Bacon', *English Historical Review* 12 (1897), 494–517 (500).

[106] See Alain de Libera, ed., 'Les *summulae dialectices* de Roger Bacon: Parts 1–2: *De termino, De enuntiatione*', and 'Part 3: *De argumentatione*', *AHDLMA* 53 (1986), 139–289; 54 (1987), 171–278; for an English translation, see Roger Bacon, *The Art and Science of Logic*, trans. Thomas S. Maloney (Toronto: PIMS, 2009); and Roger Bacon, *Compendium of the Study of Theology*, ed. and trans Thomas S. Maloney (Leiden: Brill, 1988).

[107] Cicero, *De natura deorum*, ed. Teubner (Turnhout: Brepols, 2010), II.64. Isidore of Seville, *Etymologiae sive origines*, ed. W. M. Lindsay. 2 vols (Oxford: Clarendon Press, 1911), VIII.xi.77.

[108] The strategy serves as a perfect illustration of what Sarah Kay calls the continuous reversals obtaining between 'what is central, and what is marginal in this poem' (*The Romance of the Rose*, p. 65), and what Nicolette Zeeman in turn describes as 'local "parts" that no longer seem to fit into an epistemological "whole"' ('Philosophy in Parts', p. 219).

82   MEDIEVAL ALLEGORY AS EPISTEMOLOGY

Raison begins by asserting her prerogative to speaking 'properly' and calling things by their 'proper' names. This, Raison claims,

Dex
   [...]
m'aprist ceste maniere.
Par son gré sui je coutumiere
de parler proprement des choses,
quant il me plest, sanz metre gloses.
   [...]
ainceis m'opposes
que, tout ait Dex fetes les choses,
au meins ne fist il pas le non,
ci te respoing:
   [...]
il vost que nons leur trovasse
a mon plesir et les nomasse
proprement et communement
por craistre nostre entendement;
et la parole me dona
ou mout tres precieus don a.
   (*RR* 7043–50; 7053–6; 7061–6)

It was God who taught me this habit, and it is by his will that I am accustomed to call things by their names when I want to, without glossing them.
   [...]

And you object that although God made things, he did not make their names—yet this is my reply:
   [...]

he wanted me to find proper and common names, at my pleasure, in order to increase our understanding, and he gave me speech, a most precious gift. [translation emended]

Raison then signals her refusal to adopt a newly assigned, different word to name the male genitals, insisting that the name assigned during the original imposition of terms is entirely 'proper', beautiful, and adequate:

Et quant tu d'autre part obices
que lez et vilain sunt li mot,
je te di devant Dieu qui m'ot,
se je, quant mis les nons aus choses
   [...]
coilles reliques apelasse
et reliques coilles clamasse,
tu, qui m'en morz et depiques,
me redïsses de reliques
que ce fust lez moz et vilains.
Coilles est biauz noms et si l'ains,
si sunt par foi coillon et vit,
onc nus plus biaus guieres ne vit.
   (*RR* 7076–9; 7081–8)

And if you object on the other hand that the words are ugly and base, I tell you before God who hears me that if, when I put names on things

I had called balls 'relics' and relics 'balls', then you who thus attack and reproach me would tell me instead that 'relics' was an ugly, base word.
'Balls' is a good name and I like it, and so, in faith, are both 'bollocks' and 'cock'; none more beautiful have ever been seen. [translation emended]

Despite its undeniably comical tone, the exchange is saturated with the terminology of contemporary language arts, and points to a whole series of important

IN THE BEGINNING WAS THE *ROSE*   83

debates in this area. Alastair Minnis has already provided a brilliant analysis of the multiple echoes, both philosophical and obscene, triggered by the extended play on the notion of 'proper speaking' in this passage.[109] It seems evident that the most important immediate 'source' for this exchange is actually constituted by a passage from Augustine's discussion of the 'power of words' (*vis verbi/virtus verborum*) in figurative expressions, taken from the *De dialectica*.[110] There Augustine differentiates between the signifying power of obscene words and that of ordinary and acceptable ones by invoking the example of male genitals:

> Why is the chastity of the ears not offended when one hears 'he had squandered his patrimony by hand, by belly, and by penis'? It would be offended if the private part of the body would be called by a low or vulgar name, though the thing with a different name is the same. If the shamefulness of the thing signified were not covered over by the propriety of the signifying word, then the base character of both would affect both sense and the mind (*De dialectica* VII.13).[111]

I am not the first reader of the *Rose* to suggest that this passage, echoing Cicero, may be the ultimate source for the argument between Raison and the Amant.[112] But it seems to me that earlier critics have not appreciated the very specific resonance of this source text within the poem's immediate intellectual environment, i.e. the Arts Faculty at Paris during the 1260s and 70s. In fact, what is remarkable about the citation is not so much its detail or its content, but rather its very existence: the *De dialectica* was in fact an almost totally neglected and ignored source in the work of contemporary logicians and grammarians—with the crucial exception of Roger Bacon, and, a generation later, Henry of Ghent.[113] Not only did Bacon cite the *De dialectica* repeatedly, but as I will discuss in greater detail below, he built his entire, highly controversial theory of signification on the foundations of Augustine's *De dialectica*—a text otherwise utterly ignored by every single scholastic author of

---

[109] Minnis, *Magister Amoris*, pp. 119–63.

[110] On the later developments of these ideas, see Costantino Marmo, '*De virtute sermonis/verborum*: L'autonomie du texte dans le traitement des expressions figurées ou multiples', in Nicole Bériou, Jean-Patrice Boudet, and Irène Rosier-Catach, eds, *Le pouvoir des mots au Moyen Âge* (Turnhout: Brepols, 2014), pp. 49–69; William Courtenay, 'Force of Words and Figures of Speech: The Crisis over *virtus sermonis* in the Fourteenth Century', in *Ockham and Ockhamism*, pp. 209–28.

[111] 'Unde enim, quod non offenditur aurium castitas, cum audit manu ventre pene bona patria laceraverat? Offenderetur autem, si obscena pars corporis sordido ac vulgari nomine appellaretur, cum res eadem sit cuius utrumque vocabulum est, nisi quod in illo turpitudo rei quae significata est decore verbi significantis operitur, in hoc autem sensum animumque utriusque deformitas feriret'. Augustine of Hippo, *De dialectica*, ed. Jan Pinborg and trans. by B. Darrell Jackson (Dordrecht and Boston: Reidel, 1975), pp. 102–3.

[112] See John V. Fleming, *Reason and the Lover* (Princeton: Princeton University Press, 1984), pp. 110–11, who misunderstands Augustine's point. For a more balanced reading, see Hult, 'Language and Dismemberment', pp. 113–14.

[113] See *De dialectica*, ed. Pinborg and trans. Jackson, pp. 18–22. On Henry of Ghent, see Irène Rosier-Catach, 'Henri de Gand, le *De dialectica* d'Augustin, et l'imposition des noms divins', *Documenti e studi sulla tradizione filosofica medievale* 6 (1995), 145–253.

84   MEDIEVAL ALLEGORY AS EPISTEMOLOGY

this generation.[114] The very use of the *De dialectica* as a source for the *Rose* would therefore be a remarkable 'coincidence' in itself; however, given that Jean de Meun follows Bacon in using Augustine's work very specifically in order to discuss the question of linguistic imposition, it seems to me that it becomes almost unavoidable to postulate some form of direct connection between the thought of these two Parisian authors on questions of linguistic reference and signification.

Crucially, then, Raison's response to Amant's criticism hinges on a series of observations pertaining to the nature, status, and authority of the original imposition of terms—questions that ultimately are at the heart of the 'non modica contentio' opposing Bacon to the near-totality of his contemporaries. Raison first asserts her own, divinely conferred authority to name things according to her own private will: '[Dieu] vost que nons leur trovasse / a mon plesir et les nomasse' (*RR* 7061–2). This claim echoes the widely accepted idea that the signifying operation of human language is based on the relations of signification imposed through convention, according to the will of the original impositor. Raison's notion of the assignation of names *a mon plesir* in fact provides a remarkably precise translation of the Latin notion of *impositio ad placitum meum*—a far better translation than the modern English expression generally employed, 'imposition by convention'.[115] Raison in fact not only insists on the conventional, and thus potentially arbitrary, nature of this act of imposition by the individual will, but emphasizes its 'reasonable' circumstances, lending it normative authority: since she herself is human 'Reason' personified, an act of imposition performed according her own individual will necessarily conforms to human reason, and accordingly acquires normative, and to some degree 'natural' authority.

Raison's arguments are unmistakeably borrowed from the discussions of *impositio* in the work of contemporary grammarians and logicians, who universally agreed on three points: words signified by convention; signification was conferred through the original imposition of names; original imposition needed to conform to the dictates of reason.[116] Boethius of Dacia, for instance, explains how in order to exercise his authority as name-giver, the original *impositor* needed to have knowledge of the ontological nature of the thing signified (*res significata*), and was thus required to combine the qualities of the grammarian and the metaphysician (*grammaticus* and *philosophus realis*).[117] The authority of the *ratio significandi* (signifying logic) that was assigned during the act of *impositio ad placitum* was not therefore entirely arbitrary, but was endowed with something approximating

---

[114] Rosier, *La parole comme acte*, pp. 133–4.

[115] See the remarks by Thomas S. Maloney, 'The Semiotics of Roger Bacon', *Medieval Studies* 45 (1983), 120–54 (149).

[116] Marmo, *Semiotica e linguaggio nella scolastica*, pp. 56–63.

[117] Boethius of Dacia, *Modi significandi sive quaestiones super Priscianum maiorem*, ed. J. Pinborg and H. Roos (Copenhagen: GAD, 1969), I, 48–51. See also Michel de Marbais, *Summa de modi significandi*, ed. Louis G. Kelly (Stuttgart/Bad Cannstatt: Frommann/Holzboog, 1995), pp. 6 and 12. See further Marmo, *Semiotica e linguaggio nella scolastica*, pp. 56–63, 485–90.

IN THE BEGINNING WAS THE *ROSE* 85

natural authority: 'imposition has the status of nature with respect to significative words' [natura in dictionibus est earum impositio].[118] To some extent, then, the authority of the original *impositio* carried out by a qualified and 'reasonable' *impositor* determined the stability and authority of the term once assigned. In this respect, Raison's claim is perfectly aligned with the mainstream view on linguistic imposition held by nearly all contemporary scholastics—except for Roger Bacon, as will be seen below. More specifically, Raison's insistence on her prerogative to impose names on things, and her insistence on the normative authority of imposition and the 'proper' use of linguistic signs, aligns Raison with the mainstream position of contemporary grammatical and logical textbooks.

The natural authority and stability of the *ratio significandi* imposed at origin occupied a particularly important place in the system developed by the *modistae* or speculative grammarians, and which gained momentum between the 1260s and 1300 at the Paris Arts Faculty.[119] At the heart of the modistic project lay the desire to produce a truly scientific, and therefore universal grammar that would be able to explain the mechanisms of linguistic signification regardless of the specific language in question and regardless of the immediate linguistic and extralinguistic context in which an utterance occurs. Modistic grammarians therefore moved attention away from the semantics of individual words in context that characterized the approach of earlier terminist logicians, and concentrated on the signifying mechanisms at work within language itself, and particularly the function of different grammatical categories such as nouns, verbs, cases, tenses, etc. Various modes of signifying (*modi significandi*), essential and accidental, were associated with each word (*dictio*), and such modes of signifying were in turn associated with corresponding modes of understanding and modes of being (*modi intelligendi* and *modi essendi*).[120] In order to guarantee the stability of these correspondences between *modi significandi*, *modi intelligendi*, and *modi essendi*, however, signifying relations in language had to remain stable, and modists accordingly insisted on the normative authority and stability of *significata* as originally imposed. Modists

---

[118] See e.g. John of Dacia, *Summa grammatica*, in *Johannis Daci Opera*, ed. Alfred Otto, 2 vols (Copenhagen: GAD, 1955), I:184, cited and discussed in Marmo, *Semiotica e linguaggio nella scolastica*, p. 58, n. 94; and Anon., *Quaestiones super 'Sophisticos elenchos'*, ed. Sten Ebbesen (Copenhagen: GAD, 1977), p. 76 (cf. Marmo, *Semiotica e linguaggio nella scolastica*, p. 129).

[119] Modists often invoked the authority of Petrus Helias's commentary on Priscian in this matter (*Summa super Priscianum*, ed. Leo Reilly, 2 vols, Toronto: PIMS, 1993), II:1045: 'Natura ergo dictionis dicitur esse significatio'; II:914: 'Vox est materia nominis. Impositio vero facta est ad significandam quasi formam nominis que additur ipsi voci'. I reproduce the references given in Sten Ebbesen, 'The Odyssey of Semantics from the Stoa to Buridan', in *Greek-Latin Philosophical Interaction: Collected Essays of Sten Ebbesen*, 2 vols (Aldershot: Ashgate, 2008), I. 21–33 (28).

[120] The fullest study is Marmo, *Semiotica e linguaggio nella scolastica*. For a concise but reliable overview, see Irène Rosier, 'Modisme, pré-modisme et proto-modisme: vers une définition modulaire', in Ebbesen and Friedman, *Medieval Analyses in Language and Cognition*, pp. 45–81.

86 MEDIEVAL ALLEGORY AS EPISTEMOLOGY

therefore insisted that this original signification was inalienable, rehearsing the common dictum that: 'words cannot deviate [lit. "fall away"] from that which they signify' [voces non cadunt a suis significatis].[121] First-generation modists, active in the early 1270s when Jean de Meun was writing or completing his *Rose*, were particularly insistent on this point.[122]

The idea of the stability of the *ratio significandi* was well established before the emergence and modism, and is attested in slightly earlier texts—although chronology is difficult to establish. This is the case, for instance, with the discussion of *impositio* found in Pseudo-Kilwardby's commentary on the *Priscianus maior*. This treatise too affirms that the act of imposition is carried out by a wise man or philosopher 'who has authority over other wise men, and is a first philosopher' [qui habet auctoritatem super omnes alios sapientes, qui est philosophus primus].[123] Crucially, however—and in contrast to the modistic insistence on the inalienable authority and stability of imposition—Pseudo-Kilwardby adds that signification may be modified:

> Once a vocal sound has received a signification through institution, if it is pronounced in the same fashion, it will signify the same thing by reason of this first institution, *unless it be given a new signification*, as sometimes happens with equivocal utterances. (my emphasis)[124]

First imposition is accepted as being authoritative and binding in the manner of a law (*lex*)[125]—*unless* another meaning is re-imposed for a word at an ulterior moment. Original imposition can therefore be modified by ulterior acts of imposition, transforming the signification of previously instituted words.

This is an important distinction that would be elaborated by a different current of grammatical and logical theory, which, in contrast to the modistic model, emphasized the possibility for modifying the originally imposed *significatio* of words through later, supplementary acts of imposition. In contrast to the *modistae* who focused exclusively on grammatical and semantic relations within the

---

[121] E.g. John of Dacia, *Summa grammatica*, I:183–5.

[122] Later modistic authors began to nuance the rigidity of the original imposition, as they addressed the evident problems and limitations of a theory that essentially disregarded any pragmatic questions of reference in the real world, outside of language itself. See Costantino Marmo, 'A Pragmatic Approach to Language in Modism' in Sten Ebbesen, ed., *Sprachtheorien in Spätantike und Mittelalter* (Tübingen: Günther Narr, 1995), pp. 169–83.

[123] Pseudo-Robert Kilwardby, *Commentum super Priscianum Maiorem*, ed. K. M. Fredborg, N. J. Green-Pedersen, and L. Nielsen, J. Pinborg, in 'The Commentary on Priscianus Maior Ascribed to Robert Kilwardby', *CIMAGL* 15 (1975), 1–143 (76).

[124] 'Postquam enim vox est instituta ad significandum consimiliter prolata idem significat ratione primae institutionis, **nisi de novo detur alia significatio** sicut contingit in equivocis', ibid., 63.

[125] Ibid., 73.

sentence, grammarians associated with this current of thought examined the immediate linguistic and communicative circumstances that were likely to have an incidence on the signifying operation of a particular utterance within a specific linguistic and pragmatic context. In particular, they argued that the communicative *intention* of specific speakers was able to modify the signification of words according to context, which has led Irène Rosier to refer to this group as 'intentionalist grammarians'.[126] Practically speaking, intentionalist grammarians argued that the meaning of specific words was modified by the immediate circumstances of their use. A recurrent, well-trodden example to illustrate this point was the expression *prata rident* ('the meadows smile'): here the original signification (smiling) was modified according to the immediate semantic and communicative context (speaking about a meadow) in order to signify that the meadow was 'in bloom'.[127] Poetic tropes more widely played a central role in the development of intentionalist theories of signification, since they provided ample illustration for the modification of 'proper', originally imposed meanings through semantic *translatio* or *transumptio*. Indeed, Rosier has demonstrated that the entire model of signification developed by intentionalist grammarians ultimately relies on the study of poetic tropes.[128] Instead of insisting on the normative role of imposition, then, intentionalists maintained that the original signifying relationship could be modified through an oblique or metaphorical use. Along with the primary, literal, or 'proper' understanding of an utterance (*intellectus primus/proprius*) based on the originally imposed signifying logic (*ratio significandi*), speakers were thus able to convey a 'transposed', 'secondary', or 'improper' meaning (*intellectus secundus/translatus/improprius*). This transposition was understood as a modification of the original imposition, and was generally determined by the immediate locutionary and illocutionary context, by the immediate intention of the speaker (*intentio proferentis*), or by specific usage (*usus loquendi*) that deviated from the original *ratio significandi/impositionis*. Effective understanding consisted largely in the ability to grasp the secondary, improper meaning of utterances, which ultimately allowed the listener to arrive at the understanding intended by the speaker (*intellectus intentus*).[129]

---

[126] See especially Rosier, *La Parole comme acte*; Irène Rosier-Catach, 'Speech Act and Intentional Meaning in the Medieval Philosophy of Language', *Bulletin de philosophie médiévale* 52 (2010), 55–80.

[127] Irène Rosier-Catach, 'Prata rident', in Alain de Libera, Abdelali Elamrani-Jamal, and Alain Galaonnier, eds, *Langages et philosophie: Hommage à Jean Jolivet* (Paris: Vrin, 1997), pp. 155–76.

[128] Rosier, *La Parole comme acte*, pp. 41–55.

[129] For a representative example of this characteristically intentionalist position, see Bacon, *Summa grammatica*, pp. 17–27. See further Corneille H. Kneepkens, 'Roger Bacon on the Double *Intellectus*: A Note on the Development of the Theory of *Congruitas* and *Perfectio*', in Osmond P. Lewry, ed., *The Rise of British Logic* (Toronto: PIMS, 1985), pp. 115–43 (119–28); Irène Rosier-Catach and Alain de Libera, 'Intention de signifier et engendrement du discours chez Roger Bacon', *Historie, Épistémologie, Langage*, 8.2 (1986), 63–79 (69–74); de Libera, 'Roger Bacon et la Logique', especially pp. 107–9, 123–32.

88   MEDIEVAL ALLEGORY AS EPISTEMOLOGY

Nobody took this intentionalist approach to signification further than Roger Bacon.[130] He provided a markedly pragmatic analysis of language use in practice—a sort of pragmatics *avant la lettre*—and it has been claimed that 'Bacon devotes more time than any other medieval author [. . .] to elucidating what happens in ordinary discourse'.[131]

Like other grammarians, Bacon accepts the idea that words acquire significance through convention, as determined at the time of the original imposition of meanings (*secundum rationem impositionis*), and that imposition is the fruit of a deliberate free choice (*ad placitum*—cf. *De signis*, henceforth *DS*, § 10 and *Compendium studii theologiae*, henceforth *CST*, § 41 and 59).[132] He also accepts that this first imposition is carried out by a wise man or philosopher (*sapiens, DS*, § 156). Following Pseudo-Kilwardby's commentary on the *Priscianus maior*—and in complete opposition to the *modistae*—however, Bacon sees the authority of this original imposition as being unstable and susceptible of modification.[133] Behind such an approach lies Bacon's distinctive theory of signification more generally: Bacon—uniquely and controversially—claimed that a word signifies an extramental thing (*res extra animam*) directly,[134] not its essence or concept, as Aristotle had argued in the *De interpretatione* and as all of Bacon's contemporaries believed.[135] For Bacon, accordingly, first imposition could only be carried out only on the basis of present, *existing* objects, and not on the basis of mere concepts or objects that had ceased to exist or did not (yet) exist (*DS*, § 134–42, 163).

Bacon's unusual theory requires that after initial imposition has taken place, a change in the status of the object will naturally prompt language users to modify the *significatum* of the word originally imposed to signify that particular *res*. So, for instance, after the death of Socrates, the word 'Socrates' will continue to be used to designate Socrates, but no longer signifies in the same manner: 'Socrates' designates not the living person, but rather his corpse (*DS*, § 148); similarly, a sign displaying barrel hoops outside a tavern no longer signifies the presence of

---

[130] There is a substantial body of secondary literature on Bacon's semantics. Along with works already cited, see also Thomas S. Maloney, 'Roger Bacon on Equivocation', *Vivarium*, 22. 2 (1984), 85–112; ibid,. 'Roger Bacon on the *Significatum* of Words', in Lucie Brind' Amour and Eugene Vance, eds, *Archéologie du signe* (Toronto: PIMS, 1983), pp. 187–211; Karin Margareta Fredborg, 'Roger Bacon on *Impositio vocis ad significandum*', in Braakhuis, Kneepkens, and de Rijk, *English Logic and Semantics*, pp. 167–91; de Libera, 'Roger Bacon et le problème de l'appellatio *univoca*'.

[131] Maloney, 'Introduction', in Bacon, *On Signs*, p. 16.

[132] Translations from *Compendium of the Study of Theology*, ed. and trans. Maloney.

[133] See especially Rosier, *La parole comme acte*, and ibid., 'Grammaire, Logique, Sémantique, deux positions opposées au XIIIème siècle: Roger Bacon et les modistes', *Histoire Epistémologie Langage* 6.1 (1984), 21–34.

[134] See especially Maloney, 'Roger Bacon on the *Significatum* of Words'.

[135] Thomas Aquinas, *Expositio libri peryermenias*, ed. René-Antoine Gauthier, Opera Omnia iussu impensaque Leonis XIII edita, 1*. 1 (Rome: Commissio Leonina/Paris: Cerf, 1989), 1. 2 (p. 11): 'voces significant intellectus conceptiones immediate, et eis mediantibus res' (Words directly signify concepts in the mind, and through the latter, things). See also above, 'Introduction', pp. 22–3.

wine once all of the wine has been drunk (*DS*, § 1, § 147).[136] If change in the *res* occurs, the first imposition decays or falls away (*cadit*, cf. *DS*, § 147, § 148), with the result that the word designating the *res* in question no longer maintains its original meaning. Bacon's use of the term *cadit* here confirms that this is unmistakably a direct attack on a key principle upheld by the *modistae*, who insisted that 'voces non cadunt a suis significatis', as discussed above.[137] Bacon vehemently rejects this idea, denouncing the opinions of the 'ignorant plebs' [*vulgus insensatus, DS*, § 143] who believe that signification remains unaltered despite the change or even destruction of the thing signified (*res significata, DS*, § 143–53). This characteristically Baconian argument is in turn explicitly condemned and denounced by contemporaries, such as Siger of Brabant, who insists that despite the annihilation of a *res*, or the material referent (*suppositum*) of a term, its essential being nevertheless persists insofar as it is understood by the mind.[138]

Bacon develops the implications of his theory much further. Since first imposition is by nature unstable and subject to modification, the value and authority of imposition needs to be reactivated or renewed through each ulterior utterance of the same word (*DS*, §143–53). But since the meaning of words employed by an individual speaker for a communicative act in context is necessarily contingent upon that very context, the *significatum* of a specific word can be radically altered by usage (*usus*) within that context. Each utterance of a word/term 'renews' an original *significatio*—but this can mean two different things according to Bacon: it either reactivates and reiterates the original imposition (*DS*, §147) or modifies it, even potentially replacing it with a new one. In such a case the utterance also coincides with a new act of imposition, tacitly carried out by an individual speaker at the very moment the word is used with a modified or new meaning (see especially *DS*, §149). More often than not, the second imposition will be somehow guided and co-determined—through natural inference, connotation, or concomitance (*DS*, § 102–3, 165–9)—by the first one, which places some limits on the kinds of re-imposition that is likely to occur. This is the case, for instance, with the name 'Rosa' when it is transferred to a woman because of the beauty she shares with the flower (*DS*, § 48, and epigraph above). Although most cases of re-imposition will thus follow a discernible logic based on a principle of analogy (the *ratio qua potest fieri*), for Bacon it remains theoretically possible to re-impose an entirely new *significatum* for the sign, and he insists on this point repeatedly:

---

[136] On the recurrence of the classic example of the *circulum vini*, see Rosier-Catach, *La parole efficace*, pp. 64–5, 72–3, 496 n. 35.

[137] E.g. John of Dacia, *Summa grammatica*, pp. 183–5.

[138] Siger of Brabant, *Quaestio utrum haec sit vera: Homo est animal, nullo homine existente*, ed. Bernardo Bazàn (Leuven: Publications universitaires de Louvain/Paris: Beatrice Nauwelaerts, 1974), p. 56: 'corruptio rerum non pervertit earundem conceptionem' (the destruction of a thing does not modify its conception in the mind). See further Bernardo Carlos Bazàn, 'La signification des termes communs et la théorie de la supposition chez Maître Siger de Brabant', *Revue Philosophique de Louvain*, 77.35 (1979), 345–72.

90 MEDIEVAL ALLEGORY AS EPISTEMOLOGY

[A] vocal sound can be transferred to an infinite number of things in accord with our good pleasure.[139]

[A]ny word can be taken equivocally, as we wish, for an unlimited number of significates, because we can impose and transfer at out pleasure.[140]

Bacon's model of signification thus emphasizes the fundamental fluctuation of signifying relations, largely determined by the will of the speaker in a specific communicative situation. This places him in stark opposition to the modists, who insisted on the inalienable authority and stability of the *ratio significandi* assigned through original imposition, in line with mainstream scholastic thinking in the period.

It is precisely this divergence of opinion that is the key issue at the heart of the 'magna altercatio'—and it is this divergence that is refracted in the disputation between Raison and Amant in the *Rose*. I have already insisted on Raison's determination to assert her own right to 'speak properly' by invoking her own, eminently 'reasonable' act of original imposition of signification *ad placitum*. But Raison's determined defence of 'proper speaking' in line with the *ratio significandi* she herself originally established, 'proprement et communement', appears rather pathetic in the face of practical language use. Indeed, rather than 'speaking properly', language users in practice constantly transgress the supposedly normative authority of imposition—a fact that Raison herself reluctantly acknowledges, by rehearsing the numerous improper terms used by 'the women of France' to designate male genitals, instead of 'speaking properly' about *coilles*:

Se fames nes noment en France,	If women do not name them in France,
ce n'est fors desacoutumance,	it is only because they are not
car li propres nons leur pleüst,	accustomed to do so, for they would
qui acoutumé leur eüst;	have liked the proper name had it been
et se proprement les nomassent,	made familiar to them, and in giving
ja certes de riens n'i pechassent.	them their proper name they would
(*RR* 7101–6)	certainly have committed no sin.

Chascune qui les va nomant	The women who name them call them
les apele ne sai conmant,	all sorts of things: purses, harness,
borses, harnais, riens, piches, pines,	things, torches, pricks, as though they
ausint con se fussent espines;	were thorns!
[. . .]	[. . .]

---

[139] 'vox potest transsumi ad infinita iuxta bene placitum nostrum', *DS*, § 87.

[140] 'dictio quaelibet potest aeccipi aequivoce, ut volumus, pro infinitis significatis quia possumus imponere et transsumere ad placitum nostrum', *DS*, § 82.

Or les nomment conme el seulent,	Now they may call them whatever is
quant proprement nomer nes	usual if they do not want to give
veulent.	them their proper names!
(RR 7111–18)	

Women in France fail or refuse to adopt the proper term originally imposed to signify the male genitals, and instead employ language 'improperly' for purposes of euphemism and circumlocution. Reason protests but remains utterly powerless to force language users to conform to her original, 'reasonable', and divinely sanctioned act of imposition. Unable to regulate language use, she can only bewail, rather pathetically, the irresistible force of *acoutumance* (custom, usage):

Acoutumance est trop poissanz,	Custom is very powerful, and if I am
et se bien le sui connoissanz,	any judge, many things that offend
mainte chose desplest novele,	when they are new become beautiful
qui par acoustumance est bele.	through custom.
(RR 7107–10)	(Translation emended)

In this respect at least, Raison in the *Rose* thus appears to advocate a distinctly modistic understanding of the *ratio significandi* of words, asserting the unalterable authority of first impositions carried out by a grammarian who is also a *philosophus realis* or metaphysician. Such claims to regulate language and signification, however, are happily ignored by the 'women of France' and ordinary language users more broadly, who are all subject to the power of *acoutumance*—what the contemporary language arts refer to as *usus loquendi*.[141]

What, then, is Jean de Meun's larger purpose in exposing Raison's failure to ensure that ordinary speakers conform to her own, normative and 'Reason-able' practice of 'proper speaking'? To some extent Raison's pathetic failure to regulate language use tends to expose the fundamental principles that underpin modism as untenable once they are measured against actual, practical language use—let alone the gleefully subversive linguistic play that pervades the *Rose* itself. As already mentioned, the modistic project as a whole must be understood as a large-scale attempt to develop a strictly scientific, universalizing analysis of linguistic signification conforming to the demands of Aristotelian *scientia*. This presupposed that the object of study had to be real, unchanging, and universal substances endowed with an ontology. This meant that modistic grammar was inevitably conditioned to disregard the practical, real-life circumstances of communicative practice and language use, since the latter were strictly contingent and could not be objects

---

[141] On the notion of *usus loquendi* as employed in contemporary debates, see variously Marmo, 'A Pragmatic Approach to Language in Modism'; Rosier, 'Modisme, pré-modisme et proto-modisme', pp. 66–70; Marmo, '*De Virtute Sermonis/Verborum*'.

92 MEDIEVAL ALLEGORY AS EPISTEMOLOGY

of an Aristotelian *scientia* of language.[142] Indeed, it is precisely modism's inability to consider how contingent, extralinguistic circumstances shape language use and communicative practice that eventually led to its rapid demise at the end of the thirteenth century.[143] By reminding us that ordinary language such as that employed by the 'women of France' is invariably 'improper',[144] Jean draws attention precisely to such limitations. While Raison's point of view is clearly aligned with modistic insistence on the authority of first imposition, the outcome of the exchange suggests that the attempt to produce a strictly Aristotelian *scientia* of language understood as a normative, ordered, and regulated process is ultimately a hopeless endeavour.

Such an interpretation fits well with the broadly anti-systematic orientation of the *Rose*, and more specifically with its tendency to interrogate the practical viability and logical consistency of scholastic *scientia* more broadly.[145] In this sense, Jean de Meun's project seems more closely aligned with Bacon's rather more disruptive theories of signification, which emphasize the slipperiness of language as determined by individual intention and contingent circumstances. Jean's poem cannot be said, however, to simply subscribe or conform to a Baconian and anti-modistic position. Instead, I want to suggest that the *Rose* is best understood as an experimental testing ground for some of Bacon's ideas, subjecting those ideas to a more subtle critique in turn. More specifically, I want to argue that the *Rose* ultimately extrapolates some of the more extreme consequences and implications of Bacon's controversial theories, specifically Bacon's theory of metaphor and other tropes.

I have already mentioned that the kind of 'intentionalist' approach to grammar by Bacon and others originates from the analysis of poetic figures and tropes in the work of mid-century authors such as Robert Kilwardby.[146] Vocabulary borrowed from such mid-century discussions of figures and tropes accordingly abounds in the writings of Bacon, whose preferred terms to designate a modification of an original imposition of meaning are *translatio* or *trasumptio* (see *DS*, § 82 and 87, cited above, and e.g. § 149 and 155, and *passim*), which were commonly used to designate metaphorical speech in contemporary writings on rhetoric and grammar. Like earlier intentionalist grammarians, Bacon used such discussions of figures and tropes to formulate a far more ambitious theory of communication based the existence of two related, complementary levels of understanding— proper and improper, primary and secondary. Most intentionalist grammarians

---

[142] See Marmo, *Semiotica e linguaggio*, especially pp. 137–59.

[143] See Marmo, *Semiotica e linguaggio*, pp. 473–96, especially pp. 478–9, 485–8, 495–6.

[144] On the 'femininity' of this kind of evasive rhetorical play in the *Rose* more widely, see also the brilliant essay by Lee Patterson, '"For the Wyves love of Bathe": Feminine Rhetoric and Poetic Resolution in the *Roman de la Rose* and the Canterbury Tales', *Speculum* 58.3 (1983), 656–95.

[145] I concur with Zeeman, 'Philosophy in Parts', who uses the term 'skeptical' in a similarly qualified and contextualized sense, e.g. pp. 219–20.

[146] Rosier, *La parole comme acte*, pp. 16–22.

also associated these two levels of understanding with two different types of speakers and interpreters.[147] On the one hand we have the ordinary speakers (*rudes*), whose understanding of an utterance is often limited to the primary level of understanding (*intellectus primus*), understood strictly according to the original meaning of a word (*ad sensum*); on the other hand we have the *sapientes*, *poetae*, or *auctores* who have access to a secondary level of understanding (*intellectus secundus*), where comprehension results from the listener's intellectual ability to extrapolate an ulterior, intended but implicit meaning (*ad intellectum*).[148] Bacon, however, departed from this traditional view: while he accepted the existence of two complementary levels of signification, he also assigned—uniquely—a much larger place to 'improper signification' in human language. For Bacon, the existence of a secondary, improper level of meaning was not limited to the statements of ancient *sapientes* and *auctores*, but characterized human language *as such*— including the speech of the *rudes*, i.e. perfectly ordinary speakers who would nonetheless constantly use language in oblique, metaphorical, or 'improper' fashion. This contention had dramatic implications for the understanding of the fundamental nature of human language and communication, as it tended to suggest that human speech was *fundamentally* equivocal, as I explain in what follows. It is also this question, I believe, that lies behind Jean de Meun's interest in Baconian semantics, and that constitutes the main philosophical reference point for the dispute between Amant and Raison in Jean's *Rose*.

After her defence of 'proper speaking', Raison abruptly shifts gears and starts attacking Amant because of his limited, literalistic understanding of *coilles*. Raison now claims to have spoken in the language of the poets, in order to convey a second, deeper understanding (*ad intellectum*) that differs from Amant's merely literal understanding (*ad sensum*)—a claim that sits rather oddly, incidentally, with her earlier defence of 'proper speaking':

Si dit l'en bien en noz escoles	In our schools many things are
maintes choses par paraboles,	expressed through parables that are fair
qui mout sunt beles a entendre;	to hear, and not everything one hears
si ne doit l'en mie tout prendre	should be taken literally. In my speech
a la letre quan qu l'en ot.	there is a different meaning—at least
En ma parole autre sen ot,	when I spoke of 'balls', which I only
au mains quand des coillons parloie,	mentioned in passing: there is a
don si briefment parler voloie,	different meaning from the one you
que celui que tu i veuz metre;	want to assign to the word, and

---

[147] See Rosier, *La parole comme acte*, pp. 50–1, discussing Gosvin de Marbais' *Tractatus de constructione*, Robert Kilwardby's *Sophismata grammaticalia*, Nicholas of Paris' *Quaestiones super primum Priscianum*, Magister Johannes' *Sicut dicit Remigius*, Pseudo-Kilwardby's *Commentum super Priscianum maiorem*, and the anonymous *Glosa admirantes*.

[148] A typical formulation is found in Pseudo-Kilwardby, *Commentum super Priscianum maiorem*, p. 99.

et qui bien entendroit la letre,	anyone who understood the letter well,
le sen verroit en l'escriture,	would see the sense in the text, bringing
qui esclaircist la fable occure.	light to the obscure fable. The truth
La verité dedenz reposte	concealed within would be clear if it
seroit clere, s'el iert esposte;	were exposed/explained. You will
bien l'entendras, se bien repetes	understand it well if you rehearse the
les integumanz aus poetes.	integuments of the poets. You will find
La verras une grant partie	there a great number of the secrets of
des secrez de philosophie.	philosophy.
(*RR* 7123–40)	

The intentionalist notion of a twofold understanding is here grafted upon the principles of allegorical interpretation that underpin twelfth-century philosophical allegory. Reason accordingly differentiates between two separate categories of speakers: those who take literally (*a la letre*) whatever they hear, and those who are able to decrypt the 'integumanz aus poetes', which contain a wealth of 'secrez de philosophie'.

In invoking this differentiation, Raison now appeals to distinctly intentionalist models of communication, but does so in a context that again casts doubt on the practical viability of her views. As her preceding rant against the refusal of 'women of France' to abide by the normative standards of original imposition suggests, 'improper' and loosely figurative speech is far from being the exclusive preserve of philosophically inclined *poeatae, sapientes,* or *auctores.* Instead, it occurs in perfectly ordinary everyday language too, for instance when instead of using the proper term *coilles*, the women of France resort to terms such as 'borses, harnais, riens, piches, pines' (*RR* 7113). Strikingly, this appears to echo Bacon's contention that whereas first imposition is carried out by a wise person, a *sapiens* (*DS*, § 156), second imposition is carried out by ordinary language users without any particular qualifications: 'now anyone can do this because names are at our pleasure' [et tunc potest quilibet hoc facere, quia nomina sunt ad placitum, *DS*, § 157]. For Bacon alone, second imposition based on *transsumptio* or *translatio* is not an exceptional process, taking place only in very specific cases such as poetic or philosophical utterances: instead, it is perfectly normal, banal even, and occurs all the time, often silently and without the speaker's full awareness (*DS*, § 154–61). Indeed, the act of second imposition is not a separate act that precedes the use of a word to express a new *significatum*, but coincides with any speech act that employs a specific term in ways that deviate from its original, 'proper' meaning:

All day long we impose names and pay no attention to when or how.[149]

---

[149] 'Nos tota die imponimus nomina et non avertimus quando nec quomodo' (*DS*, § 51).

IN THE BEGINNING WAS THE ROSE   95

Again, we see an infinite number [of names] being transferred in this way. [. . .] We act this way throughout the day and renew the significates of words without vocally and explicitly imposing a new meaning for them, as we would do in the case of the naming of newborn infants. [translation emended][150]

Second imposition, and indeed multiple imposition, thus becomes something ubiquitous and automatic, and occurs almost invariably as soon as we open our mouths. Not only poetry—relying on figures and tropes for expressive reasons that can be justified (*ratio excusans*)—but language as a whole becomes radically equivocal.

While all other thirteenth-century grammarians would have considered such improper uses as relatively innocuous cases of usage (*usus*) that were compatible with the principle of *univocatio* (i.e. usages that did not alter the fundamental, primary signification of the term itself as conferred through original imposition), Bacon did not. For Bacon any improper use of a particular term based on *translatio* or *transsumptio* could no longer be accommodated as a mere variation (ampli- ation or restriction) of an originally imposed, existing meaning, but amounted to the semantic re-imposition of the terms themselves, performed by the speaker according to his own pleasure and according to his communicative intention in the context of the utterance (*DS*, § 89–99). Such 'improper' uses of an existing term required—or indeed *caused*—an ulterior, additional signification to be imposed upon an existing term, producing a case of fully fledged *equivocatio* or polysemy:[151]

in this way there is a double imposition and a double signification and equivocation, and all these things can happen because vocal sounds are to be imposed at our pleasure.[152]

Bacon's contention that ordinary speech is fundamentally equivocal because it makes abundant use of figures and tropes may seem like a trivial detail. But in its late thirteenth-century context it constituted a fundamental challenge to tradi- tional and institutionally established paradigms, and stood in direct opposition to axiomatic assumptions that underpinned scholastic logic as a whole.

---

[150] 'Item, nos videmus infinita sic transumi. [. . .] Et sic tota die facimus et renovamus significata dictionum sine forma imponendi vocaliter expressa, ut datur nomen infantibus' (*DS*, § 155).

[151] See especially Rosier, *La parole comme acte*, pp. 133–4. In the technical terminology of grammar- ians and logicians, *aequivocatio* describes the case where a same word has different meanings based on multiple instances of imposition. The classical example is *canis* (dog), for which see above, n. 91. In this case, we have three different acts of imposition. *Univocatio*, on the other hand, designates the case where a single word is used with multiple meanings, but relies on a single act of imposition. This usually includes cases of modified signification determined by context, and transfer of meaning as in figurative uses. For all authors such modifications do not entail a new act of imposition, but for Bacon they do.

[152] 'sic duplex impositio et duplex significatio et aequivocatio, et haec omnia fieri possunt, quia voces sunt ad nostrum placitum imponendæ' (*DS*, § 162).

96   MEDIEVAL ALLEGORY AS EPISTEMOLOGY

Bacon's theory was distinctive and highly controversial at the time, and is indeed highly problematic as has been pointed out by a wide range of commentators, both modern and medieval. Since for Bacon all linguistic activity relies on re-imposition of terms, and since multiple impositions continuously transform univocal terms into equivocal ones, Bacon's model leads to an understanding of language as a radically polysemous, inherently equivocal sign system. In particular, as Maloney observes, Bacon 'fails to develop the conditions for interpretation peculiar to signs at pleasure', and while, he 'grants that cases of tacit imposition are also cases of use, [. . .] he fails to spell out the conditions for use'.[153] Costantino Marmo observes, more fundamentally, that Bacon is victim to a form of 'extensionalist fallacy', since he 'is compelled to make appeal to an infinite (and mainly unconscious) process of new imposition of words, and this puts in danger the possibility of communicating at all'.[154] Bacon himself, however, assumes that individual speakers will be able to handle the theoretically infinite possibilities for equivocation: he simply assumes that the listener (*audiens*) will usually be able to reconstruct the intention of the speaker (*proferens*) without too much difficulty, and feels no need to theorize or defend such an assumption, in the *De signis* or elsewhere.[155] Bacon merely observes that such re-impositions of meaning occur, and can be deciphered, because

> it pleases an intellect in the presence of such predicates and subjects to transfer names and to ampliate or restrict because of the conformity of such predicates and subjects with the significates to which the intellect transfers when ampliating or restricting.[156]

While Jean demonstrates a distinctly 'Baconian' interest in the equivocal possibilities of language, he clearly does not share Bacon's optimism about the human ability to reconstruct the *intentio proferentis* that is necessary for communication to take place effectively. Indeed, if anything, much of the *Rose* reads like an experiment in multi-voiced *mis*-communication, as I have already suggested. This applies not only to the conversations between the dreamer/narrator and the many fictional characters within the poem, but also to the poem's use of pre-existent linguistic utterances, specifically fragments and snippets from venerable Latin *auctores*. Rather than being quoted in line with something like an original

---

[153] Maloney, 'The Semiotics of Roger Bacon', p. 149.

[154] Costantino Marmo, 'Bacon, Aristotle and (all) the Others on Natural Inferential Signs', in Jeremiah Hackett, ed., *Roger Bacon and the Sciences: Commemorative Essays* (Leiden: Brill, 1997), pp. 136–54 (153).

[155] I paraphrase Sten Ebbesen, 'Theories of Language in the Hellenistic Age and in the Twelfth and Thirteenth Centuries', in *Greek-Latin Philosophical Interaction: Collected Essays*, I. 79–96 (95). See also de Libera, 'Roger Bacon et la logique', pp. 109, 131–2.

[156] 'placet tamen intellectui in praesentia talium predicatorum et subiectorum transsumere nomina et ampliare vel restringere propter conformitatem talium predicatorum et subiectorum cum significatis ad quae intellectus transsumit ampliando vel restringendo' (*DS*, § 97).

intentio proferentis or *intentio auctoris*, such fragments are often appropriated to serve the many divergent ulterior motives of the poem's many speakers, and are thereby stretched, bent, 'translated', transformed beyond recognition—and thus, ultimately, re-imposed at the pleasure of ulterior speakers according to their own, private intentions in accordance with the modified context of utterance.[157] *A fortiori*, the same remark applies to the poem as a whole, constituted by a multitude of equivocal utterances by unreliable speakers—ostensibly encountered within a dream, but in reality fabricated wholesale by an elusive author who declines to assume authorial responsibility for any of these pronouncements.

4. The Poetics of Faux Semblant

The radically equivocal nature of the poem's language destabilizes any hope of gaining a satisfactory interpretation of localized pronouncements, characters, and episodes, and *a fortiori* undermines any possibility of agreeing on something like an overarching interpretation for the poem. Indeed, even the *literal* meaning of the dream narrative remains unclear: although the reader is told in the poem's first lines that the dream itself would come to be realized in waking reality, the nature of this correspondence is never elucidated, and the reader is left without any chance of deriving any kind of interpretation from this dream—'literal', 'figurative', or 'allegorical'. This radical uncertainty compromises our ability to understand even the most fundamental terms that shape the poem's narrative, first among them the nature of the quest for this elusive 'Rose' itself. The poem provides an account of Amant's quest for a metaphorical object, framed by a dream, but the nature of that object remains fundamentally unclear. We surmise that the 'Rose' represents the beloved, but we are never actually *told* so. We are also told that this poem is dedicated to one who 'must be called Rose' [doit estre Rose clamee, *RR* 44], but again the formulation appears deliberately equivocal, drawing attention to the radical rupture between naming and being: there is a strong implication here that while we may *call* her 'Rose', we may never be able to identify who or what the referent (*suppositum*) of the word 'Rose' ultimately *is*.[158] In the concluding scene of the poem, the metaphorical flower equivocates in yet another, more radically 'improper' manner, since 'Rose' now turns out to be merely another name for the female genitals. Indeed, the poem ends with an accumulation of obscene allegories of sexual defloration: cast as a devout pilgrim, Amant kneels down reverently in front of the 'relics' he wishes to touch and kiss (*RR* 21,555; 21,573); he moves aside the curtain that conceals the 'sanctuary', and finally inserts his phallic pilgrim staff into a narrow opening between two solid marble pillars, while his pilgrim satchel,

---

[157] See also Jung, 'Jean de Meun et l'allégorie', pp. 34–6.
[158] See also Fyler, *Language and the Declining World*, p. 99; Kay, *Romance of the Rose*, p. 18.

98   MEDIEVAL ALLEGORY AS EPISTEMOLOGY

containing two constantly labouring hammers, is left hanging outside the narrow opening. The obscene climax is described in abundant detail until Amant finally scatters some of his seed amidst the petals of the rose (*RR* 21,185–750).

The basic premise upon which the entire poem is postulated, a quest for the 'Rose', is thus already beset with a range of insoluble referential difficulties. This seems to me to suggest something about the deeper intellectual affinities of Jean's poetico-philosophical project, and his use of narrative allegorical fiction to articulate a number of serious epistemological challenges. By producing a poetic narrative whose very plot is fundamentally equivocal, Jean does not merely 'apply' Bacon's ideas about equivocation, but pursues such reflections much further in order to work out their larger, and more extreme, troubling implications. This, I suggest, is Jean's way of affirming the ability of poetry to expand the range of intellectual speculation beyond the usual, scholastic forms that philosophical thinking would have taken in the late thirteenth century, venturing where scholastics were unable, did not want, or did not quite dare to go. This included, notably, the exploration of linguistic slipperiness in terms of both its obscene potentialities and its ethical implications. Thus, while it may be true that 'it is a pity that none of these [grammarians and logicians] considered puns and double entendre, let alone the possibility to mislead through using equivocal language'—as Jennifer Ashworth has observed, as part of her analysis of thirteenth-century scholastic discussions of equivocation and analogy[159]—this is precisely a step that is taken by Jean de Meun's *Rose*, picking up the reflection where the scholastics left it off. Both *double entendre* and deliberate deception are absolutely central concerns of the *Rose*, since the entire poem is structured as a sequence of sexual puns that raise a range of both ethical and epistemological questions about representation, and about the manipulative uses of equivocal language that is not only 'double' but also 'duplicitous'.[160]

Jean's analysis of duplicitous speech crystallizes in particular around the figure of Faux Semblant, who inhabits the (hollow?) centre in the exact numerical middle of the poem. It is surely not coincidental that Faux Semblant should present himself as the embodiment of fallacious discourse impenetrable by any sort of dialectical disambiguation. Faux Semblant is a perfect walking sophism, a speaker who eludes the thirteen traditional categories used to classify fallacious reasoning according to Aristotle's *Sophistici elenchi* (*Sophistical Refutations*):[161]

---

[159] Ashworth, 'Signification and Modes of Signifying in Thirteenth-Century Logic', 62.

[160] See especially Stakel, *False Roses*.

[161] The reference to the 'xiii branches' of 'Elanches' points to Aristotle, *Sophistical Refutations* I.4, 165b, 23–6, and 166b, 20–2. The distinction between these thirteen subcategories of fallacious reasoning—six of which were strictly dependent on language, and seven on extra-linguistic factors— were traditional in thirteenth-century work on fallacy and ambiguity. See e.g. Roger Bacon, *Summulae dialectices*, ed. Robert Steele, Opera hactenus inedita Rugeri Baconi 15 (Oxford, 1940), 330. See also comments in Hilder, *Der Scholastische Wortschatz*, 44, 79–80. For further discussion of the passage, see Morton, 'Sophisms and Sophistry in the *Roman de la Rose*'.

IN THE BEGINNING WAS THE ROSE   99

Il font un argument au monde
ou conclusion a honteuse:
cist a robe religieuse,
donque est il religieus.

Cist argumenz est tout fieus,
il ne vaut pas un coustel troine:
la robe ne fait pas le moine.
Ne porquant nus n'i set respondre,

tant face haut sa teste tondre,
voire rere au rasoer d'Elanches,
qui barat tremche en .XIII. branches;

nus ne set si bien distinter
qu'il en ose un seul mot tinter.
   (*RR* 11,021–34)

They offer to the world a syllogism that has a shameful conclusion: a man wears a religious habit, therefore he is religious. This argument is entirely specious, not worth a privet-knife: the habit does not make the monk. And yet no one can answer it, no matter how high he tonsures his head or shaves it with the razor of *Elenchis*, which cuts fraud into thirteen branches; no one is so good at making distinctions that he dare utter a single word about it.

The immediate purpose of the passage is simply to highlight Faux Semblant's hypocrisy, but allegorically speaking this is also a way of suggesting that Faux Semblant crystallizes a kind of fallacious use of language that eludes the reach of traditional Aristotelian tools of analysis employed for identifying and classifying fallacies as discussed in the *Sophistici elenchi*. Faux Semblant signals, and embodies, the existence of problems of equivocation that are by definition beyond the grasp of the usual, institutionally established scholastic tools and methods for resolving ambiguity, and thus fall entirely outside of the traditional area of activity accessible to institutionalized philosophy in the period. Faux Semblant's flattering appeal to the reader's own 'subtlety' is self-defeating, encapsulating the paradox embodied by Faux Semblant himself:

Mes ja ne verrez d'apparance
conclurre bone consequance
en nul argument que l'en face,
se deffaut existance efface;
toujorz i troverez soffime
qui la consequance envenime,
se vos avez soutillité
d'entendre la duplicité.
   (*RR* 12,109–16)

But in any argument, if deficiency cancels existence, you will not find that mere appearance can produce a good consequence; if you have the subtlety to see through the deception, you will always find that the consequence is undermined by a sophism.

Regardless of the reader's 'soutillité' and his ability to hear the 'duplicité', a further level of 'soffime' remains always lurking at the heart of utterance, constantly beyond the grasp of a hermeneutics condemned to remain within the realm of

100   MEDIEVAL ALLEGORY AS EPISTEMOLOGY

mere 'apparance'. If such words contain any truth, it is a truth that remains resolutely inaccessible. Any truthful *conclusiones* are buried within an infinite regress
of 'Chinese boxes', by analogy with the 'senefiance' (*RR* 16) of the *Rose* itself, a
poem where 'l'art d'Amors est tote *enclose*' (*RR* 38; my emphasis).[162] If there is any
truth here, Jean suggests that it remains endlessly deferred, concealed under multiple layers of 'apparence'—not merely enclosed but imprisoned, like the Rose itself
locked up in a tower.

Several critics have pointed out that Faux Semblant's 'duplicitous' manipulation
of appearances recalls the duality at the heart of allegorical representation more
broadly.[163] More specifically, Faux Semblant embodies the disjunction between
surface and substance, appearance and reality, 'saying' and 'signifying' that underpins the principle of allegorical expression. Faux Semblant's speech is accordingly
riddled with allusions to integumental and hermeneutic binaries—kernel and
husk (*grain* and *paille*, *RR* 11,787); bark and marrow (*escorce* and *moële*, *RR*
11,828–30); words and objective fact (*diz* and *fet*, *RR* 11,192); or between words
and works (*paroles* and *euvres*, *RR* 11,043–6). But in the mouth of a wolf in
sheepskin (*RR* 11,096–8; 11,687–8), the appeal to such apparently stable binary
categories only draws attention to their instability, making them utterly useless as
analytical tools. The very fact that Faux Semblant indulges in ample self-revelation
is a logical paradox that debilitates the potential truth-value of his own words,
turning him into an embodiment of the 'liar paradox' of which Jean de Meun is
so fond.[164] But Faux Semblant also functions as an alter-ego for Jean de Meun, the
evasive and duplicitous author/narrator figure who fabricates the poetic fiction in
which Faux Semblant appears. Structures of doubleness and duplicity are fundamental to Jean's authorial presentation, beginning with the reduplicated status of
the authorial persona itself, presented as an improbable conflation of Guillaume
de Lorris and Jean de Meun. Significantly, the presentation of the two authors
at the midpoint of the poem (*RR* 10,465–888) is introduced by the appearance
of Faux Semblant at one end, and capped off by his extended speech at the other.
This underlines the fallacious and improbable 'absent presence' of the two authors
within the dream that is ostensibly being recorded by the narrator/author himself,

[162] I build in particular on Akbari, *Seeing through the Veil*, pp. 45–76. 'Chinese boxes', or 'poupées
russes' are also invoked by Barney, *Allegories of History*, p. 188, and Paul Verhuyck, 'Guillaume de Lorris
ou la multiplication des cadres', *Neophilologus* 58.3 (1974), 283–93, both discussed by Akbari, p. 46.

[163] Stakel, *False Roses*, pp. 46–82; Kevin Brownlee, 'The problem of Faux Semblant: Language,
History, and Truth in the *Roman de la Rose*', in Marina Scordilis Brownlee, Kevin Brownlee, and
Stephen G. Nichols, eds, *The New Medievalism* (Baltimore: Johns Hopkins University Press, 1991),
pp. 253–71; Fabienne Pomel, 'L'art du faux-semblant chez Jean de Meun ou "la langue doublée en
diverses plications"', *Bien dire et bien aprandre* 23 (2005), 295–313.

[164] Morton, 'Sophisms and Sophistry in the *Roman de la Rose*', pp. 100–1; Greene, *Logical Fictions*, pp. 118–25; Heller-Roazen, *Fortune's Faces*, pp. 132–5; De Looze, *Pseudo-Autobiography in the
Fourteenth Century*, pp. 35–8.

raising troubling questions about issues of agency and temporality, not to mention the problem of a unified, stable, or reliable *intentio auctoris*.[165]

Significantly, Faux Semblant imperceptibly slips into the role of *expositor* as well as author at this moment in the poem, coming to occupy the role of exegete previously played by Jean de Meun's elusive narrator:

Or vos ai dit du sen l'escorce, qui fet l'entencion repondre; or en veill la moële *espondre*. (*RR* 11,828–30)	I have given you the shell of the meaning which hides the real intention; now I will *explain* the kernel [lit. 'marrow'] to you.

It is worth noting that Faux Semblant here employs exactly the term (*espondre*) that is repeatedly used by the *Rose*'s own, highly unreliable and duplicitous narrator/exegete, in order to reassure his readers about the supposedly imminent 'exposition' of the dream-poem's allegorical meaning:[166]

La verité, qui est coverte, vos sera lores toute overte quant *espondre* m'oroiz le songe (*RR* 2071–3)	The truth, which is hidden, will be completely plain when you have heard me *explain* the dream.

Et se vos i trovez riens trouble,
g'esclarcirai ce qui vos trouble
quant le songe m'orrez *espondre*
    (*RR* 15,115–17; cf. also *RR* 980–4;
    1598–1600; 16,821–4; 21,183–4)
	If you find anything nebulous, I will
	explain what troubles you when you
	hear me *expounding* the significance of
	the dream.
	[translation emended]

The God of Love, too, employs the term at the very moment where he prophecies the birth of Jean De Meun:

car quant Guillaumes cessera, Jehans le continuera (*RR* 10,557–8)	For where Guillaume stops, Jean will continue

Puis vodra si la chose *espondre* que riens ne s'i porra repondre. (*RR* 10,573–4)	Then he will *explain* the story in such a way that nothing shall remain hidden.

It is again this same term that is used by Raison in order to promise that she too, by encouraging Amant to read the 'integumanz aus poetes' allegorically, will help him to 'expound' their significance:

---

[165] See references given above in n. 15.

[166] See also Renate Blumenfeld-Kosinski, 'Overt and Covert: Amorous and Interpretive Strategies in the *Roman de la Rose*', *Romania* 111 (1990), 432–53.

102 MEDIEVAL ALLEGORY AS EPISTEMOLOGY

qui bien entendroit la letre,	he who understood the letter well,
le sen verroit en l'escriture,	would see the meaning in the writing
qui esclarcist la fable occure.	that would shed light on the dark fable.
La verité dedenz reposte	The truth hidden within would be
seroit clere, s'el iert *esposte*;	clear, if it were *exposed/explained*.
(*RR* 7132–6)	[translation emended]

All of these repeated promises of 'exposition' ultimately work to suggest a direct homology between Faux Semblant, Raison, and the poem's author/narrator. This exacerbates any existing difficulties of interpretation, and ultimately suggests that both Raison's allegorical/integumental poetics as well as Jean's poetic craft are cut from the same cloth as Faux Semblant's mantle (*habit*) of sophistical and rhetorical deception. Far from assuaging any doubts about the poem's truth value, then, all of this underlines that Jean de Meun deliberately embraces a paradoxical poetics of Faux Semblant, whose signifying processes can never be disambiguated according to the principles of Aristotelian logic that dominate contemporary scholastic methods of analysis.

This commitment to a theory of signification that sees human language as fundamentally equivocal has serious implications in terms of the cognitive possibilities available to ordinary postlapsarian humans. More specifically, the very possibility of proper Aristotelian *scientia*, which presupposes the univocal signification of its terms, appears seriously compromised. Jean addresses this problem directly towards the very end of his poem, in yet another pivotal 'digression':

Ainsinc va des contreres choses,	The nature of opposites is that one
les unes sunt des autres gloses;	glosses the other: if you want to define
et qui l'une an veust *defenir*,	one, you must be mindful of the other,
de l'autre li doit souvenir,	or else you will never achieve a
ou ja, par nule antancion,	definition, however good your
n'i metra *diffinicion*;	intentions. Unless you know both, you
car qui des .II. n'a *connoissance*,	will never understand the difference
ja n'i connoistra *differance*,	between them, without which no
san quoi ne peut venir en place	proper definition can be made.
diffinicion que l'an face.	[translation emended]
(*RR* 21,543–52)	

This frequently cited passage is often taken to contain something like a condensed 'poetics' of the *Rose*.[167] It is striking that this miniaturized poetic programme should use language that has unmistakeably Aristotelian affinities: *differance*, *diffinicion*, *connoissance*. Despite the poem's apparent desire to signal its alignment

---

[167] Jung, 'Jean de Meun et l'allégorie', pp. 28–31; Regalado, '"Des contraires choses"'; Whitman, 'Dislocations: The Crisis of Allegory in the *Romance of the Rose*', pp. 275–6; Morton, 'Sophism and Sophistry in the *RR*', pp. 93–5.

with notions of Aristotelian *scientia*, however, the passage in effect tends to question the viability of Aristotelian ideas of relational and positional 'definition': how exactly is one expected to define A in opposition to B, if B in turn needs to be defined in terms of yet another relationship of difference and opposition? Since the model of definition proposed here is radically relational, and does not appear to allow for the possibility of a reduction to undemonstrable first principles, it necessarily entails a potentially infinite regress through a chain of binary relations that make any chance of genuine 'definition' appear impossible.

On closer scrutiny, the process of 'definition' that is being described here has nothing 'Aristotelian' or truly demonstrative about it at all—despite the rather heavy-handed use of scholastic terminology. Indeed, Jean's narrator is using the terms of Aristotelian logic and syllogistic demonstration to talk about strictly *experiential*, 'empirical' knowledge, encouraging readers to 'try out' the greatest possible range of sexual and alimentary experiences (*RR* 21,414–27). It is only by expanding the range of one's sense experience, both pleasurable and painful, that one can gain true *connaissance* of opposites:

Ausinc sachiez, et n'an doutez,	I assure you also, and there is no doubt
que qui mal essaié n'avra	about it, that no one can know anything
ja du bien guieres ne savra;	of good if he has not experienced evil,
ne qui ne set d'aneur que monte	and no one who does not know the
ja ne savra connoistre honte;	meaning of honour will be able to
n'onc nus ne sot quel chose est ese	understand shame. No one ever knew
s'il n'ot avant apris mesese,	what comfort was without first learning
ne n'est pas digne d'ese avoir	about discomfort: if a man is unwilling
qui ne veust mesese savoir;	to encounter discomfort and unable to
et qui bien ne la set soffrir,	endure it, he is unworthy to enjoy
nus ne le devroit ese offrir.	comfort and no one should offer it to
Ainsinc va des contreres choses,	him. The nature of opposites is that one
les unes sont des autres gloses;	glosses the other;
(*RR* 21,532–44)	

Here the vocabulary of Aristotelian *scientia* is itself being used in equivocal, ironic, 'improper', and ultimately sophistical fashion,[168] and this threatens to implode the significance of the very principle of Aristotelian demonstration along with the oppositional definitional processes it relies upon.[169] This raises serious questions about the practical viability of Aristotelian *scientia* of demonstration more widely,

---

[168] See also Morton, 'Sophism and Sophistry in the *RR*', pp. 93–5.

[169] This is a principle that infuses the *Rose* in its entirety. According to Morton, *The 'Roman de la Rose' in its Philosophical Context*, p. 34, the poem does 'more than just demand that its readers consider and choose between contradictory positions. It works to undermine the very articulation of positions in the first place: in the knotty ambiguity of its discourse, the poem's own style works against any commitment to propositionally transparent accounts of the phenomena it describes'.

104 MEDIEVAL ALLEGORY AS EPISTEMOLOGY

rooted in the principle of non-contradiction, and presupposing a stable, unambiguous definitions of terms (cf. *Metaph* IV.3–4).

If we return to view the poem as a whole through the lens of such pervasive linguistic ambiguity, the many dialogues, speeches, citations, and verbal altercations between the various characters appear in a very different light. The entire poem reads like a series of pseudo-scholastic *disputationes* that can never in fact produce a demonstration of anything at all because of the fundamental disagreements on the significance of their fundamental terms. This emerges with particular clarity whenever some of the poem's fictional characters actually attempt to offer some kind of authoritative pronouncement or magisterial *determinatio*, as is the case with Genius's notoriously outrageous 'diffinitive santance' (*RR* 19,474).[170] As Gerson noted:

> il enhorte et commande sans differance user de toute charnalité, et meudit toux ceulx et celles qui n'en useront. [...] et promet paradys a tous qui ainssy le feront.[171]

> He encourages and enjoins everyone to indulge in carnality, without any differentiation, and curses all who refuse to do so [...] while promising life in paradise to all who will.

Jean thus invites his readers to question the limits of Aristotelian *scientia*, and to envisage a radically different kind of knowledge. Instead of pursuing knowledge through the disambiguation and restriction of the semantic meaning of terms—a principle echoed in the narrator's repeated promises to provide an 'exposition' of the poem's meaning—the *Rose* ultimately points to a knowledge that lies beyond language altogether. *Connoissance* through contraries as defined by the *Rose*, then, is not so much the result of a semantic restriction of linguistic terms through *differance*, eventually leading to proper *diffinicion*, but rather an ever-expanding web of practical, sensory, corporeal experience. If there is an underlying poetic epistemology to be extrapolated from the *contreres choses* passage, then, it appears to be a radically experiential one. Despite its own verbosity and *prolixité* (*RR* 18,222), the *Rose* ultimately culminates with a defence of resolutely experiential knowledge, while remaining fundamentally evasive and non-committal about the precise cognitive and epistemic status of this kind of experiential knowledge. It may not be an accident that Roger Bacon—a fierce critic of traditional scholastic principles and teaching methods, and insisting on the radically equivocal status of all human language—was similarly committed to promoting 'experiential' knowledge: while it has often been misunderstood as a pre-figuration of modern

---

[170] See e.g. Kay, *Place of Thought*, pp. 180–5; Zeeman, 'Philosophy in Parts', pp. 221–5.
[171] Gerson, 'Traité contre le *Roman de la Rose*', in *Le Débat sur le Roman de la Rose*, ed. Hicks, p. 80.

IN THE BEGINNING WAS THE *ROSE*   105

empiricism, such *scientia experimentalis* is actually best described as a distinctly medieval 'phenomenology of experience'.[172]

While this strong experiential bias in Jean's poetry points to a profound suspicion about the operations of language and signification, such ideas are neither strictly sceptical nor radically innovative or anti-intellectual. Instead, Jean simply provides a rigorous, albeit admittedly extreme elaboration of a number of ideas that were already available to him in his cultural and intellectual environment. Alongside Baconian semantics, Jean de Meun would have been able to engage with closely related ideas about the nature of linguistic signs in the writings of Augustine—ideas that did, indeed, provide the primary impetus for the development of thirteenth-century semiotics as a whole.[173] Augustine's sign theory in fact emphasized the relational nature of signs—an important idea echoed in the very first sentence of Bacon's *De signis*: 'A sign is the visible manifestation of a relation' (or 'stands in the category of Relation') [Signum est in praedicamento relationis].[174] More importantly, he would also have been able to trace to Augustine the idea that words, understood as relational signs, were unable in themselves to produce knowledge of any kind:

we don't learn anything by these signs called words. As I have stated, we learn the meaning of a word—that is, the signification hidden in the sound—once the thing signified is itself known, rather than our perceiving it by means of such signification.[175] (*De magistro* X.34)

To give them as much credit as possible, words have force only to the extent that they remind us to look for things; they don't display them for us to know. [. . .] From words, then, we learn only words—rather, the sound and noise of the words. [. . .] when words are spoken, we either know what they signify or we don't; if we do, then it's reminding rather than learning; if we don't, it isn't even reminding, though perhaps we recollect that we should enquire.[176] (*De magistro* XI.36)

---

[172] Jeremiah Hackett, 'Introduction', in ibid., ed., *Roger Bacon and the Sciences*, p. 6, and Hackett's article in that same collection, 'Roger Bacon on *Scientia Experimentalis*', pp. 277–315; and ibid., 'Experience and Demonstration in Roger Bacon: A Critical Review of Some Modern Interpretations', in Fidora and Lutz-Bachmann, eds, *Erfahrung und Beweis*, pp. 41–58.

[173] See especially Marmo, *La semiotica del XIII secolo*, pp. 14–16; ibid., *Semiotica e linguaggio nella scolastica*, pp. 20–36; Rosier, *La parole comme acte*, pp. 96–111.

[174] See further Laurent Cesalli and Irène Rosier-Catach, '"Signum est in praedicamento relationis": Roger Bacon's Semantics Revisited in the Light of his Relational Theory of the Sign', *Oxford Studies in Medieval Philosophy* 6 (2018), 62–100.

[175] 'per ea signa, quae uerba appellantur, nos nihil discere; potius enim ut dixi uim uerbi, id est significationem, quae latet in sono, re ipsa, quae significatur, cognita discimus, quam illam tali significatione percipimus', in Augustine of Hippo, *De magistro*, in *Contra academicos; De beata vita; De ordine; De magistro; De libero arbitrio*, ed. W. M. Green and K. D. Daur, CCSL 29 (Turnhout: Brepols, 1970). Translation from Augustine of Hippo, *Against Academicians; The Teacher*, ed. and trans. by Peter King (Indianapolis: Hackett, 1995).

[176] 'Hactenus uerba ualuerunt, quibus ut plurimum tribuam, admonent tantum, ut quaeramus res, non exhibent, ut norimus. [. . .] Verbis igitur nisi uerba non discimus, immo sonitum strepitumque

106   MEDIEVAL ALLEGORY AS EPISTEMOLOGY

Since the entirety of the thirteenth-century discussions of natural and artificial signs is rooted in Augustine's sign theory, this was an idea that continued to be evoked in later, strictly scholastic texts—such as the *Summa fratris alexandri* (*c.* 1241–59) or the work of Gregory of Rimini, particularly in the context of discussions of angelic speech (*locutio angelica*)[177]—and the idea ultimately resonates deeply with Jean de Meun's principle of the experiential knowledge of opposites.

Although presented in very different terms, the principle of 'contreres choses, les unes des authres gloses' similarly tends to question the value of any linguistic grounding for human knowledge in favour of more immediate, non-linguistic kinds of experiential knowledge. In doing so, Jean appears to be simultaneously radical and yet true to tradition: while on the one hand his insistence on the limitations of language's ability to convey knowledge breaks with the primary objective of Aristotelian logic that dominates late thirteenth-century scholasticism, it also returns to the Augustinian foundations of the Western Latin language arts, upon which much of thirteenth-century 'Aristotelian' semiotics and semantics was built. In doing so Jean appears to be less interested in participating in any bipartisan controversies or in subscribing to any specific ideology—'radical' or 'reactionary'—than in testing the internal rigour and consistency of the scholastic method as a whole. As well as pointing to the potential internal *aporias* of the scholastic project, Jean's insistence on the referential, didactic, and cognitive possibilities of language also raises troubling question about the epistemic status of the poem itself: if language is thoroughly equivocal, how can the *Rose*—or indeed any other linguistic construct—ever produce convincing proof or argument for this very idea? Conversely, if the *Rose* truly advocates the primacy of experiential knowledge, how is it possible to take this very notion seriously, since it is being conveyed by a poem, i.e. a medium that is entirely and exclusively *linguistic*? It seems we are back once more in the paradoxical realm of Faux Semblant, and indeed the poem ultimately suggests that among the many binary opposites whose definitions are eroded we should include also any notions of (empirical) 'experience' and (textual) 'auctoritee'. In the face of the poem's refusal to resolve and clarify its own epistemic status, then, the only possibility appears to be the deliberate suspension of disbelief in accordance with Faux Semblant's invitation to the God of Love: 'Take the risk, for if you require sureties you will not be any more secure as a result' [Metez vos en en aventure, / car se pleges en requerez, / ja plus asseür n'en serez, *RR* 11,960–2]. Just as with Faux Semblant's own duplicity, the poem stubbornly refuses to be understood in terms of binary oppositions, and

---

uerborum; [. . .] cum uerba proferentur, aut scire nos quid significent aut nescire; si scimus commemorari potius quam discere, si autem nescimus nec commemorari quidem, sed fortasse ad quaerendum admoneri'.

[177] Marmo, *La Semiotica del XIII Secolo*, pp. 14–15; ibid. 'Gregorio da Rimini: Segni, linguaggio e conoscenza: Il pensiero umano tra cani dialettici e angeli introversi', in Francesco Bottin, ed., *Gregorio da Rimini Filosofo* (Rimini: Raffaelli Editore, 2003), pp. 127–54 (151–2).

advocates instead a self-consciously unsettled, contingent epistemology based on the simultaneous availability of what appear to be mutually contradictory positions. In doing so, the *Rose* also points up its own, consistently equivocal status, as a poem that is both true and false, affirming both everything and nothing.

5. The Body of Experience: *Choses* and *Gloses, Reliques* and *Roses*

Given the radically equivocal nature of human language as understood by Jean de Meun, echoing both Bacon and Augustine, it seems difficult to claim that the *Roman de la Rose*, as a poem, actually conveys or produces anything like 'knowledge' in the ordinary sense. Instead, the *Rose* situates knowledge largely outside and beyond language—and therefore outside of itself—and thus remains fundamentally evasive about its own epistemic status. I have already cited Sylvia Huot's contention that the *Rose* is interested in examining the nature of specifically *embodied* knowledge, as experienced by an individuated subject: the *Rose* holds out 'the promise of a different sort of knowledge altogether—a knowledge accessed not through language, but through the body'.[178] Jill Mann has similarly argued that in the *Rose* ultimately 'the body becomes the goal of reading'.[179] But rather than simply affirming the superiority of such experiential knowledge over disembodied, depersonalized Aristotelian *scientia*, Jean merely 'holds out this promise', and ultimately interrogates the nature of corporeal knowing in turn. As Sylvia Huot has suggested elsewhere, the ending of the poem also forces its readers to contemplate the disturbing possibility that the 'body no longer signifies anything beyond itself'.[180] What is the nature and value of corporeal experience, and does the body really become an instrument of knowledge? Is there even such a thing as purely corporeal, unmediated experience? And if so, what is the relation between experience and mental reality, and between experiential knowledge and linguistic expression, and specifically poetic craft? These are once more questions that Jean's poem asks but does not allow us to answer in any definitive fashion. Rather than labouring to determine the cognitive and epistemic value of experience, then, Jean appears more interested in producing a poem that reads like a phenomenology of cognitive experience, with all its uncertainties kept in play. The closing sections of the poem are therefore consecrated to interrogating the nature of experiential knowledge, in endlessly challenging and frustrating ways that will preoccupy readers of the *Rose* for successive generations. I will briefly trace the main lines of that interrogation in the remaining pages of this chapter, emphasizing in particular the elusive role of corporeality in the conception of experience.

---

[178] Huot, *Dreams of Lovers*, p. 5. See further Sylvia Huot, 'Bodily Peril'; and Kay, 'Sexual Knowledge', pp. 81–5; ibid., 'Women's Body of Knowledge', pp. 222–32.
[179] Mann, 'Jean de Meun and the Castration of Saturn', p. 326.
[180] Huot, 'Bodily Peril', p. 52.

108   MEDIEVAL ALLEGORY AS EPISTEMOLOGY

If the human body really becomes the primary site of knowledge in the *Rose*, then the sexual climax that concludes the poem also denotes some sort of culmination of the 'I's quest for knowledge. The consummation brings narrative closure, and indeed appears to instantiate the poem's *diffinitive santance* as proclaimed by Genius, reasserting the imperatives of natural sexuality and procreation. Given the radically equivocal nature of the poem as a whole, however, and given the ability of allegory to signify what is perpetually 'other' to itself (*alieniloquium*), it is legitimate to ask whether the poem's conclusion really centres on the body, or whether this sexualized body signifies something fundamentally other than itself. On a primary level of interpretation, the body does indeed appear to be the ultimate referent of allegory that concludes the poem: the pilgrim arrives at his destination, and finally inserts his pilgrim staff into a narrow opening to 'touch' the much adored relics, and ultimately inseminates the young Rose—an elaborate, oblique, but unmistakeable allegory of sexual penetration. As many commentators have pointed out, however, the figuration of the sexual act here is so overdetermined that this episode appears not so much 'allegorical'—i.e. oblique, allusive, indeterminate—but aggressively literal.[181] In a poem that is otherwise so consistently evasive about its own meanings, this single-minded focus on a distinct, unambiguously sexual *significatum* is highly suspect. While maintaining an insistently sexualized valence, the allegory here once more draws attention to its own figurative operations, foregrounding its restlessly metamorphic character by figuring the sexualized human body through metaphor: as statue, pillar, tower, arrow-slit, pilgrim staff, sanctuary, curtain, rosebush, relics—a sequence of objects/body parts that cannot be mapped onto an organic and organized human body with any degree of certainty, let alone construed as denoting a natural heterosexual act.[182] Particularly in the wake of Jean's appeal to an epistemology of *contreres choses*, the oblique-yet-overdetermined description of a sexual act that concludes the poem may well signify something radically 'other', and even something 'contrary' to its apparent primary meaning.

The defloration scene also highlights the rupture between *natural* forms produced by actual sexual reproduction and *representational*, poetic, and imaginative forms produced by human artifice and the human mind—or, in simpler terms, between art and nature.[183] The *Rose* appears to end by reiterating the question it purports to answer, and that produces the poem in its entirety, with its manifold digressions and developments: what is the relation of poetic language to the experience of sexuality and desire? This question is also signalled more explicitly

---

[181] See especially Quilligan, 'Words and Sex'; and ibid. 'Allegory, Allegoresis, and the Deallegorization of Language', pp. 169–70, 185.

[182] Simon Gaunt, '*Bel Acueil* and the Improper Allegory of the *Romance of the Rose*', *New Medieval Literatures* 2 (1998), pp. 65–93; Rollo, *Kiss my Relics*, pp. 201–9.

[183] For a recent discussion, reviewing the abundant earlier literature on this once-popular topic, see Morton, *The 'Roman de la Rose' in its Philosophical Context*, pp. 36–61.

in the narrator's final 'digression', an extended retelling of Ovid's account of the fable of Pygmalion from book X of Ovid's *Metamorphoses* (*RR* 20,787–21,184). While Jean's handing of the Pygmalion fable is susceptible of multiple interpretations, it clearly provides a proleptic *glose* for the obscene defloration that concludes the poem, focusing attention on the relation between art and sex, figuration and embodied experience. I have argued elsewhere that Jean's retelling does much to trouble the ostensible transparency of the poem's seemingly reductive carnal conclusion: rather than providing a more 'naturalistic' and truly 'generative' alternative to the courtly Narcissism of Guillaume de Lorris, as has often been argued, the fable works as yet another warning against the lures and seductions of art— from Narcissus's infatuation with his own image, to Pygmalion's work as a sculptor, to Jean's craft as a writer.[184] In doing so, however, it also raises the more difficult question of the value and 'fertility' of artistic production: what, exactly, is being created through processes of artistic (re-)production?

Whatever our chosen answer, it seems undeniable that the poem's 'multiple endings' prompt the reader to reflect on the relation between artistic and natural forms with a new kind of intensity and urgency.[185] This meta-poetic dimension also reminds us that Amant's prolonged and meandering quest for the Rose is in fact doubled by a parallel hermeneutic quest on the reader's part, longing to discover the significance of the Rose as a metaphor and as the object of an interpretive quest. As I have already noted, the centrality of this hermeneutic quest is periodically reiterated by the narrator, who promises repeatedly to 'expound' (*espondre*) the significance of the entire dream. The defloration of the Rose thus marks a moment of symbolic penetration into the heart of this mystery, a defloration that is also an exfoliation of the leaves/petals/pages of the poem/flower/text. But as Amant finally attains the Rose, and as the reader finally reaches the climax of this long poem, the nature of this 'exposition' is, once more, revealed as deeply equivocal and ultimately fallacious:

A la parfin, tant vos an di,	I can tell you that at last, when I had
un po de greine i **espandi**	shaken the bud, I **scattered** a little seed
quant j'oi le bouton elloichié'	there.
(*RR* 21,689–91)	

The earlier promise to 'expound' the significance of the dream (*espondre . . . le songe, RR* 2073, cf. also 7126, 10,573, 11,830, 15,117) is simultaneously frustrated and fulfilled: rather than providing an *expositio* of the poem's meaning (*espondre* with an O, from Lat. *exponere*), we are given a simple scattering of seed, an

---

[184] Marco Nievergelt, 'Textuality as Sexuality: The Generative Poetics of the *Roman de la Rose*', in Elisabeth Dutton and Martin Rhode, eds, *Medieval Theories of the Creative Act* (Fribourg: Presses Universitaires de Fribourg, 2017), pp. 103–30.

[185] Kevin Brownlee, 'Pygmalion, Mimesis, and the Multiple Endings of the *Roman de la Rose*', *Yale French Studies* 95 (1991), 193–211.

'expansion' of meaning (*espandre* with an A, from Lat. *expandere*: to scatter, to disperse, or simply to expand).[186] Jean turns his description of the insemination of the Rose into a meta-polysemous joke: the joke not only hinges on the equivocal homophony of *esponde* and *espandre*, but is also *about* interpretive equivocation, suggesting that any attempt to 'expound' or 'expose' the significance of the dream merely ends up 'expanding' its meaning beyond any manageable proportion, resulting in the accretion of supplementary 'gloses' that invariably occlude the real, ultimate nature of the 'Rose' or 'chose' that remains enclosed at the heart of this infuriating poem. Instead of receiving a long-awaited, definitive explanation of the significance of the dream, we witness only a further scattering of metaphorical 'seed'—an uncontrolled multiplication of semantic meanings. In doing so, Jean ultimately forces his readers to confront the inevitable proliferation of semantic meanings brought about by any act of interpretation.

The scattering of seed that concludes the *Rose* marks, quite literally, one of the most 'seminal' moments of late medieval European poetry. More specifically, it inaugurates the point of origin for the incredibly fertile reception history of the *Rose* itself—a history that is to a very large extent inextricable from the evolution of European literary culture over the next two and a half centuries. The paradoxical, euphemistic-pornographic scattering of seed itself becomes a major target of later condemnations: Gerson, for instance, stigmatizes Jean's *Rose* for its ability to 'sow evil doctrine in the hearts of people' [semer mauvaise doctrine es cuers des gens].[187] Yet Gerson's attack merely feeds the process it seeks to denounce and suppress: it acts as yet another confirmation of the *Rose*'s semantic vitality, revealing its ability to proliferate beyond itself in the form of an endless textual offspring: glosses, commentary, interpretation, debate, rewriting, revisions, and polemical attacks. Each intervention in the poem's reception history attempts to impose some form of 'conclusion', yet finally enhances the poem's uncanny ability to pre-empt interpretive closure, allowing the seeds scattered during the defloration to germinate in new ground, gradually producing a bewildering textual maze or forest.

It seems rather fitting that the conclusion of Jean's poem, with its emphasis on the scattering of seed (*greine*), should resonate so uncannily with Jacques Derrida's much later reflections on the analogy between the processes of organic 'dissemination' and the dispersal of 'semantic' meaning through language. To borrow my words from Peter Travis—another medievalist who finds such proto-Derridean speculations at work in medieval poetry—'playing upon the fortuitous resemblance between "semen" and "seme", Derrida is gesturing towards the dispersal of semantic meaning in every text—a dispersal that is both a wasteful dissipation

---

[186] See respectively http://www.atilf.fr/dmf/definition/esponde and http://www.atilf.fr/dmf/definition/épandre.

[187] Jean Gerson, *Traité*, in Hicks, *Le debat sur le roman de la rose*, p. 69.

of semiological meanings and at the same time an excessive surplus of unlimited meanings.'[188] It seems to me that such a poetic 'programme' first crystallizes precisely at the end of the *Rose*, where under the pretext of providing a definitive 'exposition' of the poem's ultimate *senefiance*, Jean de Meun in reality enacts its expansion and dispersal into an irreducible plurality of possible meanings.

This move also has important implications in terms of Jean de Meun's ideas of literary authorship and their impact on later generations of writers across Europe: rather than inaugurating a new, proto-humanistic and fundamentally 'modern' notion of individual authorship, as has often been argued, Jean ultimately declines to claim any authorial intention and control.[189] Against the background of a medieval theory of authorship dominated by the notion of an *intentio auctoris*, Jean thus produces a poem that tenaciously affirms something approaching an *intentio operis* as theorized by Umberto Eco. According to Eco's theory, the significance of a literary work is thus not primarily determined by the author's design, but rather reconstructed and constantly renegotiated by its readers as a result of their own culturally situated position.[190] As Costantino Marmo has suggested, Eco's model also provides a strikingly close analogue to the kind of semantics theorized by Roger Bacon, based on the principle of a continuous re-imposition of meanings, and leading to an understanding of language as a system in perpetual movement, engaged in a process of unlimited semiosis:[191]

> [E]ven if an author wants to convey a certain meaning through a certain expression, his text once produced lives independently of the original intentions of its producer and can give rise to all the possible readings allowed by its manifestation.[192]

By ending his poem with the scattering of such a surplus of meanings, Jean effectively declines to exercise any firm authorial control over his own poem, transferring agency to the *Rose* itself, and leaving the burden of inferring some form of *intentio operis* to the poem's many readers.

---

[188] Peter Travis, *Disseminal Chaucer: Rereading the Nun's Priest's Tale* (Notre Dame: Notre Dame University Press, 2010), p. 17, referring to Jacques Derrida, *La Dissémination* (Paris: Seuil, 1972).

[189] See discussion above, and items cited in n. 15.

[190] Umberto Eco, *I limiti dell'interpretazione* (Milan: Bompiani, 1990).

[191] While there is nothing strictly 'nominalist' about this kind of semantics, many of its principles prepared the ground for Ockham's elaboration of a fully nominalist philosophical system two generations later. On Bacon as a 'proto-nominalist', see especially Jeremiah Hackett, 'Roger Bacon', *The Stanford Encyclopedia of Philosophy* (Spring 2015 Edition), Edward N. Zalta (ed.), https://plato.stanford.edu/archives/spr2015/entries/roger-bacon, § 4. 5, [retrieved on 3 June 2021] and the observations in de Libera, 'Roger Bacon et le Logique', especially p. 122. Further see also Tachau, *Vision and Certitude*. On the parallels of Bacon's and Ockham's approach to semantics, see also e.g. Marmo, '*De Virtute Sermonis/Verborum*: L'autonomie du texte dans le traitement des expressions figurées ou multiples', p. 69.

[192] Marmo, 'A Pragmatic Approach to Language in Modism', pp. 178–9.

112   MEDIEVAL ALLEGORY AS EPISTEMOLOGY

What, then, are we to make of the defloration scene, which at least *appears* to denote some sort of culmination? Although it is the vanishing point of the narrative, the defloration does not bring any hermeneutic resolution, but rather performs yet another, final deferral of interpretive closure. Rather than standing apart from the narrative that precedes it, the defloration itself is in desperate need of the kind of 'exposition' that Jean ostentatiously promises but refuses to supply. The ending thus functions not so much as a corporeal, experiential release from the allegorical indirections and linguistic equivocations of the poem that precedes, but as a reminder of the difficulty of disentangling *experience* and *auctoritee—contreres choses* that are also mutually constitutive opposites: rather than simply affirming the role of the body as the site of experiential knowing, the ending displaces such pleasure onto language, underlining the strictly textual, figural, rhetorical, and thus vicarious nature of the pleasure we experience. The poem's conclusion of course supplies not one, but three complementary representations of penetrative sex:[193] Venus' dart thrown at the *ymage*; the pilgrim inserting his staff into the shrine; and the Lover's defloration of the Rose. But none of this amounts to even a *description* of a sexual act: instead, the extended and metamorphic conclusion functions as a rhetorical simulation of penetrative sex, a *simulacrum* produced by literary artifice. The origin of the pleasure is not the encounter with a woman or even a female body, but, as in Pygmalion's case, the ability to wrap up that *imagined*, phantasmatic experience in tantalizing, always new, always changing layers of verbal artifice, to dress it up in always new metaphors and rhetorical colours. There is simply no female 'Other' in this poem— there is 'no body', merely an unsubstantial poetic trope.[194] For all the poem's talk about sex, bodies, and genitals, then, the *Rose* is no more than that: *talk* about sex, bodies, and genitals. On the one hand, this is symptomatic of the intellectual context that produces the poem, an all-male clerical milieu where the presence of women can only be conjectured, talked about, dreamt of, but never experienced as a bodily reality.[195] On the other hand, however, Jean's *Rose* also foregrounds a far more abstract and philosophical problem, the difficulty of grasping the mysterious nature of desire and the embodied human experience of *eros*. Jean finally anticipates Lacan's observation that whenever we put the experience of sexuality into words, the thing itself recedes into infinite distance: despite its obsession with every imaginable facet of human sexuality, and despite its claim to being a 'miroir

---

[193] Brownlee, 'Pygmalion, Mimesis, and the Multiple Endings of the *Rose*'.
[194] I here echo the analyses of Sarah Kay, 'Sexual Knowledge'; ibid., 'The Birth of Venus'; and Huot, 'Bodily Peril', and ibid., *Dreams of Lovers and Lies of Poets*, especially pp. 10–54, 99–104. Both Kay and Huot similarly stress the fundamentally mysterious, unspeakable nature of sexual desire, and its challenge to common intellectual categories in medieval Western culture.
[195] See especially Minnis, *Magister Amoris*, pp. 164–208, especially 192–4.

IN THE BEGINNING WAS THE ROSE   113

aus amoureus' (10,621), the *Roman de la Rose* is a poem in which, finally, 'il n'y a pas de rapport sexuel'.[196]

By eroding the significance of such fundamental binary opposites—body and soul, experience and authority, embodiment and figuration—this conclusive leap into a corporeal void troubles the didactic, philosophical aspirations of the *Rose* in even more radical fashion. This philosophical and introspective urge of the *Rose* had begun, in many respects, with Raison's exhortation to the Lover/reader to embrace a productive logic of profitable pleasure in his reading of the 'integuments of the poets'—an approach that readers, in turn, are invited to adopt in their interpretation of the *Rose*, as discussed above:

La verras une grant partie	There you will see a great number of
des secrez de philosophie	the secrets of philosophy, in which you
ou mout te vodras deliter,	will wish to take much delight, and so
et si porras mout profiter:	you will be able to profit greatly; while
en delitant profiteras	profiting you will be delighted, while
en profitant deliteras	delighting in it, you will profit; for in
car en leur geus et en leur fables	the games and fables of the poets lie
gisent deliz mout profitables	most profitable delights under which
souz cui leur pensees covrirent,	they covered their thoughts when they
quant le voir des fables vestirent.	clothed the truth in fables.
(*RR* 7139–48)	[translation emended]

Clearly this Horatian precept is difficult to reconcile with the eroticized rhetorical pleasure procured by the *Rose*'s playful ending. If anything, memories of this Horatian principle suggest that the ending procures a kind of pleasure that is largely self-serving, self-consuming, and eminently *un*-profitable. Far from actualizing Genius's preposterous *diffinitive santance* about the primacy of natural reproduction, then, the ending marks the triumph of a different, deeply unnatural kind of rhetorical pleasure that is fundamentally sterile, and thus ultimately amounts to a perversion of the natural order of sexuality and reproduction. The association of between sexual perversion and overindulgence in rhetorical tropes is of course well established at least since the twelfth century, particularly in Alain de Lille's *De Planctu Naturae*, a major influence on Jean's *Rose*. In Alan's poem all sorts of grammatico-rhetorical aberrations are used as tropes to denote unnatural, homosexual behaviour,[197] and Jean's Genius similarly castigates all those

---

[196] I echo the title of a talk by Alexandre Leupin, 'Il n'y a pas de rapport sexuel dans le *Roman de la Rose*', given at the University of California, Berkley, in April 1996.

[197] See Ian Ziolkowski, *Alan of Lille's Grammar of Sex: The Meaning of Grammar to a Twelfth-Century Intellectual* (Cambridge, MA: Medieval Academy of America, 1985); and more recently, including discussion of the *Rose*, Rollo, *Kiss my Relics*.

114 MEDIEVAL ALLEGORY AS EPISTEMOLOGY

who refuse to engage in procreative sex by using metaphors of writing and reading, speaking of those who 'pervert the writing when they get to the reading' [pervertissent l'escriture / quand ils viennent à la lecture', *RR* 19,631–2]. But of course such analogies always cut both ways, and Jean de Meun can always be relied upon to turn any analogical correspondence on its head: if homosexuality is figured by an overindulgence in artful tropes, then oblique, metaphorical, poetic expression is in turn inherently deviant, deeply unnatural, and implicitly sodomitical.[198]

This is nowhere more evident than in the heavy-handed metamorphic overkill that concludes the poem, and which amounts to an extended imaginative *simulacrum* of a sexual climax. Whereas the pleasure produced by this culmination is undeniable, Jean seems to delight in questioning the origin, nature, and purpose of such *deliz*. As Sylvia Huot has suggested, the ending of the *Rose* leaves open the possibility that 'the poem will be the euphemistically worded, if thinly disguised, story of a nocturnal, or more properly matitudinal emission', triggered by a dream that is a projection of the Lover's own, exacerbated fanciful desire. The *Roman de la Rose* 'is being offered, in effect, as a pornographic text, a cornucopia of sexual fantasies and erotic *doux parler* that culminates in a sexual *jouissance* not only for the poetic persona, but also for the willing reader'.[199] Such sexual *jouissance* is nothing if not sterile and 'unnatural', and in a culture where the definition of sodomy subsumes all forms of non-reproductive sexuality, it is also fundamentally sodomitical.[200] The reader inevitably becomes complicit in the guilty, sterile pleasures afforded by such densely metaphorical poetry. In her analysis of the imagery of reading practices in late-medieval poetic culture, Jacqueline Cerquiglini has pointed out that the female genitalia are increasingly figured as a book, as a library, as a set of inscribed pages to be 'leafed through', particularly in the works of such dedicated rhodophiles like Machaut, Deschamps, and Molinet.[201] In Jean de Meun's *Rose*— which plays a crucial role in popularizing this analogy—the leaves of the page also become the leaves of the Rose, its petals to be parted, one by one, by the male readerly desire in the attempt to get to the bottom of the '*Romanz de la Rose*, / ou l'art d'Amors est tote enclose' (*RR* 37–8).

But of course when the Lover penetrates the Rose, and when we get to the end of the poem, there is nothing there—'no thing', no object, no *senefiance* apart from

---

[198] Jonathan Morton, 'Queer Metaphors and Queerer Reproduction in Alan de Lille's *De Planctu Naturae* and Jean de Meun's *Roman de la Rose*', in Manuele Gragnolati et al., eds, *Desire in Dante and the Middle Ages* (Abingdon and New York: Legenda, 2012), pp. 208–26. For the gender trouble at work in the *Rose*, see especially Gaunt, '*Bel Acueil* and the Improper Allegory', and Rollo, *Kiss my Relics*.

[199] Huot, *Dreams of Lovers and Lies of Poets*, p. 101.

[200] On the slipperiness and inclusiveness of the concept of 'sodomy' in the period, see the influential work of Mark D. Jordan, *The Invention of Sodomy in Christian Theology* (Chicago: Chicago University Press, 1997), esp. pp. 41–4. See also Allen J. Frantzen, 'The Disclosure of Sodomy in Cleanness', *PMLA* (1996), 451–64.

[201] Jacqueline Cerquiglini-Toulet, 'L'imaginaire du livre à la fin du Moyen Age: Pratiques de lecture, théorie de l'écriture', *Modern Language Notes* 108.4 (1993), 680–95 (693–4).

the intractable surplus of meanings already contained, *in potentia*, within in the poem we have been reading all along. The *Rose* is a poem in which the art of love is truly and self-consciously *enclosed*—locked up but irretrievable, and locked up specifically in language and in 'unnatural' poetic artifice. Although it ends in penetration, the poem itself and the mysterious significance of the Rose/*Rose*, remains hermeneutically impenetrable. The Rose/*Rose* remains an equivocal signifier that can simultaneously denote a flower, a woman, the female genitalia, or a poem, and finally turns out to be a mere receptacle, a featureless 'feminine' surface waiting to be inscribed by the male, writerly or readerly gaze of its many later readers, annotators, continuators, and imitators—Jean de Meun first of all.[202] Given the absence of any real woman from this poem, the body of the text itself finally becomes feminized, turning into a feminine entity that stubbornly resists any hermeneutic penetration, deferring and occluding any genuine experiential understanding of sexuality.[203] In this sense the text is quite literally impenetrable to the male, authorial or hermeneutic agency, oriented towards a moment of climactic closure, fulfilment, and control. After all the pages have been turned, after all the leaves been plucked out, and all the layers removed, the reader is left with nothing except the possibility of copulating in turn with a poetic text, in the hope that it will bear some sort of *profit*—or, at the very least, procure some experience of *delit* that may in turn constitute the grounds and object of such *profit*.

How, then, are we to read the poem's ending and its scattering of seed? For Sylvia Huot, 'Jean de Meun thus inseminates not just the boutonet, like amant (21699), but the whole roman—achieving narrative consummation.'[204] As Huot points out, however, the consummation is purely *narrative*—it is neither sexual

---

[202] My reading here differs from Noah Guynn's, who sees the *Rose* as an aggressively masculine text that 'marks the exaltation of phallic power through dissemination and insemination' (*Allegory and Sexual Ethics*, pp. 170): 'If the plucking of the Rose is coded as an act of *dissemination* (one that proliferates alternate meanings and resists deciphering), it is also a transparently violent and phallic act of insemination' (ibid., pp. 138–9). Masculine aggression is undoubtedly an important element in this ending, but rather than signalling Jean's genuine confidence in his own project of authorial agency and control, it seems to me, this display of aggression is ironic and bathetic/pathetic, signalling a desperate masculine desire to regain interpretive control through sexual/textual violence. For a reading emphasizing the futility and negativity of such displays of masculine phallic power and hermeneutic control, see Lamy, 'The Romance of the Non-Rose'. It is worth noting, however, that such disagreements over whether the *Rose* represents poetic activity as an inherently 'masculine' or 'feminine' process, are more apparent than real: not only does the *Rose* frustrate such identification by presenting itself as a 'hermaphroditic' poetic work, as David Rollo has argued (*Kiss my Relics*, pp. 145–213), but it also tends to erode some of the most fundamental conceptual binaries such as body and soul, male and female, matter and form—on which see discussion above, and n. 40.

[203] On deferral of desire as a characteristically feminine function of language, see Lee Patterson, '"For the Wyves love of Bathe"'; reworked as ibid., 'Feminine Rhetoric and the Politics of Subjectivity: La Vieille and the Wife of Bath', in *Rethinking the Romance of the Rose*, ed. Huot and Brownlee, pp. 316–58.

[204] Sylvia Huot, *From Song to Book: the Poetics of Writing in Old French Lyric and Lyrical Narrative Poetry* (Ithaca: Cornell University Press, 1987), p. 97.

nor hermeneutic.[205] The consummation is strictly metaphorical, and marks the culmination of metaphor itself: in exacerbating the deferral of meaning, it amounts to an aggressive affirmation of the poem's relentless metamorphic energies. As a refusal to resolve or conclude the poem's endless metamorphosis, the ending of the *Rose* contains a signifying potential that invariably exceeds that of any single interpretation, calling for the multiplication of meanings and the further proliferation of poetic language by engendering a whole discourse of interpretation. The seeds scattered at the end of the poem already contain, *in potentia*, the entire reception history of the *Rose*, ready to be activated by the work of later scribes, annotators, commentators, imitators, adapters, translators, and poets, all trying to make sense of the *Rose*, seeking to continue the work of interpretation and trying— and failing—to bring it to completion.[206] By performing a mock-sexual satisfaction and simultaneously frustrating hermeneutic closure, the *Rose* manages, as it were, to engender its own reception history, inseminating an as yet formless, feminine posterity with its potent, emphatically masculine seeds or forms, and thus effectively reproducing itself.

The lover's insemination of the Rose during this climax thus functions as a carefully staged, highly self-conscious, and truly 'seminal' moment of late medieval vernacular poetry as a whole—a scene that asks readers of the *Rose* to reflect on the very nature of such an insemination or dissemination, and on the generative, reproductive, and metamorphic potentialities of textuality, metaphor, and the poetic imagination. As I've tried to show, this seminal moment is the fruit of Jean's ambivalence towards his own art, and the culmination of an open-ended theoretical reflection on the value of poetic writing. It also marks the beginning of late medieval vernacular tradition of authorial ambivalence and sometimes anxiety, characterized by an invariably complex and sceptical exploration of the value of poetry—its rhetorical pleasures, its moral and epistemological limitations or pitfalls, and its ethical and intellectual potentialities. Guillaume de Deguileville's place in this later reception history is crucial: not only does he provide the most sustained and most complex early response to the *Rose*, but does so in ways that durably shape the course of later *Rose*-reception, including the responses of English poets such as Chaucer, Langland, Gower, and the Gawain-poet.

---

[205] For a different view, see Brownlee, 'Pygmalion, Mimesis, and the Multiple Endings of the *Rose*', 196, who maintains that 'Jean de Meun's continuation and expansion of Guillaume does finally succeed in simultaneously representing fulfilled desire and effecting narrative closure'.

[206] This logic too is already ingrained in the first *Rose* written by Guillaume, which deliberately associates its own seminal quality with the ephemeral, necessarily unfinished form of his poetic project, aiming at the elusive vanishing point of the absent 'rose'. See Emmanuèle Baumgartner, 'L'absente de tous les bouquets . . ', in Jean Dufournet, ed., *Etudes sur le Roman de la Rose de Guillaume de Lorris* (Paris: Champion, 1984), pp. 37–52.

PART II

DEGUILEVILLE

Introduction to Part II

Modern readers and critics have struggled, on the whole, to account for the remarkable popularity of Guillaume de Deguileville's *Pèlerinage de Vie Humaine* (*PVH*) with medieval readers, and the poem is still widely misunderstood whenever it is not overlooked or dismissed out of hand. Recent years, however, have seen a growth of interest in the success of *PVH* (1331) as well as the later *Pèlerinages* trilogy, which includes a second, revised version of *Pèlerinage de Vie Humaine* (*PVH2*, 1355), the *Pèlerinage de l'Âme* (*PA*, 1356), and the *Pèlerinage Jhesucrist* (*PJC*, 1358). This growth of interest has produced a number of studies of the poem's circulation, translation, reception, and influence in Europe in the period *c.* 1360–1600[1]—a welcome development, but one that may also have distracted our attention somewhat from the internal workings of this influential, rich, and complex corpus of texts. As Fréderic Duval observes, Deguileville studies are still in their infancy, and considerable amounts of work remain to be carried out to shed light on the intellectual, literary, cultural, and political context in which his poems were produced.[2] The development of the trilogy over time, and the survival of two rather different versions of the first *Pèlerinage—PVH1* (1331) and *PVH2* (1355)— further complicate the picture. However, this complex situation also affords us a

---

[1] For an overview of the state of research, see Kablitz and Peters; Kamath and Nievergelt; Duval and Pomel. See further Kamath, *Authorship and First-Person Allegory*; Nievergelt, *Allegorical Quests*; Maupeu, *Pèlerins de vie humaine*; Marie Bassano, Esther Dehoux and Catherine Vincent, eds, *Le 'Pèlerinage de l'âme' de Guillaume de Digulleville (1355–1358): Regards Croisés Actes du colloque Université Paris-Ouest-Nanterre-La Défense / Université Paris-Descartes (29–30 mars 2012)* (Turnhout: Brepols, 2014).

[2] For such a call to return to the *Pèlerinage de Vie Humaine* in itself, see Frédéric Duval, 'Interpréter le *Pèlerinage de vie humaine* de Guillaume de Digulleville (vers 1330)', in Hélène Bellon-Méquelle *et al.*, eds, *La moisson des lettres: l'invention littéraire autour de 1300* (Turnhout: Brepols, 2011), 233–52. For two recent studies that make a consistent effort in placing the poem in its broader intellectual context, see Robertson, *Nature Speaks*, pp. 177–222; and Rosenfeld, *Ethics and Enjoyment in Late Medieval Poetry*, pp. 111–28.

118 MEDIEVAL ALLEGORY AS EPISTEMOLOGY

rare opportunity for tracing the evolution of an author's poetic vision over time, with its many shifts, internal contradictions, and transformations.[3]

Despite such recent developments, critical opinion on Deguileville's poetry continues to be shaped by the more extreme and reductive views of earlier critics. Dissatisfied with its idiosyncratic allegorical aesthetics, early twentieth-century readers dismissed his work as hopelessly boring, 'anaemic', 'ignoble', 'monstrous', and 'repellent'.[4] Such value judgements continue to determine the critical responses of otherwise sensitive modern readers. The poem thus been described as 'sans audace et d'un grand conformisme',[5] and it has been felt that in comparison with *Piers Plowman* the *Pèlerinages* 'lack the uncertainties of where authority might be found that pervade and vitalize or disorder *Piers Plowman*'.[6] In what follows I will be proposing a rather more complex assessment of the poem. This builds on recent readings that have insisted precisely on the conflicted status of authority in Deguileville's poems; the discrepancies between his poetic ideal and its practical execution; the poet's own doubts and reservations about the value of his poetic vision; his hesitations about the effectiveness of allegorical fiction as a didactic tool for moral instruction; the generally unsettled, shifting nature of Deguileville's poetic project. I will be arguing that far from being conventional and derivative, the poems are intellectually challenging and highly ambitious, albeit often unsuccessful in resolving some of the complex philosophical problems they seek to confront and resolve.

PVH in particular ought to be recognized as a poem outlining an ambitious epistemological programme in the shape of an allegorical quest-narrative—a programme that is both carried further but also substantially modified by the later 'trilogy' (1355–8). As others have suggested, the poem is underpinned by a broadly 'Augustinian' and hence largely conservative epistemology.[7] But this choice, I argue, is far from being the result of cultural and intellectual inertia, and turns out to be highly conflicted and problematic. Deguileville in effect struggles to defend

---

[3] For *PVH1*, see Guillaume de Deguileville, *Le Pèlerinage de Vie Humaine*, ed. Stürzinger. For *PVH2*, see Guillaume de Deguileville, *Le Livre du pèlerin de vie humaine (1355)*, ed. Maupeu and Edwards.

[4] For some examples along these lines, see variously C. S. Lewis, *The Allegory of Love: A Study in Medieval Tradition* (Oxford: Clarendon Press, 1936), pp. 264–71; Arthur Piaget, 'Un poème inédit de Guillaume de Digulleville: *Le Roman de la fleur de lis*', *Romania* 62.247 (1936), 317–58 (317–18); Marion Lofthouse, '*Le Pèlerinage de vie humaine* by Guillaume de Deguileville: With Special Reference to the French MS 2 of the John Rylands Library', *Bulletin of the John Rylands Library* 19.1 (1935), 170–215. The notable exception is Rosemond Tuve's prescient and sensitive discussion in *Allegorical Imagery: Some Medieval Books and Their Posterity* (Princeton: Princeton University Press, 1966), pp. 145–218. For an overview of critical reception from the eighteenth until the later twentieth century, see Pomel, *Les voies*, pp. 527–8, and the introduction to Duval and Pomel, pp. 11–13.

[5] Badel, *Le Roman de la Rose au XIVe siècle*, p. 409.

[6] Andrew Galloway, *The Penn Commentary on 'Piers Plowman': Volume 1* (Philadelphia: University of Pennsylvania Press, 2006), p. 9. For echoes of Deguileville's *Pèlerinages*-trilogy, see the numerous references in the index.

[7] The term 'Augustinian' is inherently problematic, as I have already pointed out (e.g. Introduction, nn. 86, 99), and I use it here as a shorthand term to subsume a wide range of very different intellectual habits and affinities that I examine in greater detail over the next three chapters.

such an Augustinian epistemology against the perceived threats of more recent, more strongly 'Aristotelian' intellectual developments. These include the dominance of scholastic logic in University culture very broadly; the rise of terminist semantics and theories of equivocal signification in language; Aristotelian theories of the soul and its cognitive faculties; and the emerging controversies between intellectualists and voluntarists. Far from being detrimental to the poem's appeal, the author's efforts to rehabilitate a conservative system of thought and understanding makes *PVH* a particularly relevant and exciting text. Indeed, it could be said that it is precisely because of the poem's difficulties, *aporias*, and contradictions in seeking to rehabilitate an Augustinian epistemology that *PVH* is such an intellectually sophisticated, complex, engaging, and historically significant poem. *PVH* in effect registers contemporary debates and controversies in ways that are both remarkably informed and precise, but also demonstrates a considerable degree of experimental inventiveness, particularly in the use of allegorical fiction as a tool for intellectual speculation. It is therefore precisely the inner contradictions, hesitations, and tentative character of the author's thought that make *PVH* such an interesting text from the point of view of intellectual history.

This, at the very least, was the opinion of William Langland, who has been described as 'a poet who is more perceptive than any other contemporary philosopher on what constitutes the grounds of philosophy and thought, questioning those very bases'.[8] As I argue in Part III of this study (Chapters 5–7), Langland's sustained, obsessive interest in Deguileville's poetry is a result of the English poet's fascination with the many philosophical and epistemological difficulties that Deguileville's poem attempts, but ultimately *fails* to resolve. Langland, I argue, is primarily interested in the flaws, ruptures, and difficulties that Deguileville encountered while writing the *Pèlerinages*, and particularly in the divergence between the first and second versions of the *Pèlerinage de Vie Humaine*. Not only does Langland invest his energies in attempting to think through some of these difficulties in turn, but he often uses instances of intellectual crisis and paralysis in Deguileville's poetry as catalysts for his own process of intellectual speculation and poetic composition. I therefore argue that many quintessentially 'Langlandian' idiosyncrasies are in fact best explained as emerging out of the English poet's extremely close, meticulous, and critical engagement with the work of Deguileville—and, through it, with Jean de Meun's *Rose*.

In chapter 2, I will begin by examining the epistemology of *PVH* by focusing on the poem's interest in questions of language, signification, and hermeneutics. I will argue that *PVH* must be read as a response to the *Rose*, but that it cannot be understood merely as a pious rewriting and homiletic counterpart of Jean's

---

[8] Andrew Galloway and Andrew Cole, 'Christian Philosophy in *Piers Plowman*', in Cole and Galloway, pp. 136–59 (142).

erotic allegory. Instead, I suggest, it must be read as an attempt to recuperate processes of allegorical interpretation as viable instruments for spiritual development. Concurrently, this amounts to an assertion of the sapiential and salvific power of Deguileville's own allegorical poetry. Where Jean de Meun had pushed allegory's potential for arbitrary equivocation to its limits, Deguileville attempts to harness and regulate the mechanisms of allegorical signification to foster the spiritual development of the reader. More broadly, I read Deguileville's sustained interest in language and signification as a direct response to the radically anti-authoritarian and relativistic understanding of language and knowledge presented by Jean's *Rose*, in turn influenced by Baconian semantics. In particular, Deguileville attempts to rehabilitate three important ideas about language that Jean's *Rose* had consistently eroded or undermined. Firstly, he attempts to restore some degree of confidence in the possibility of determining secure discursive authority (2.1). Secondly, he seeks to appropriate Aristotelian dialectic as a tool for spiritual growth within a broadly Augustinian understanding of the soul's journey towards its heavenly home (2.2). Thirdly and most importantly, he seeks to codify processes of linguistic signification, and specifically the mechanisms of allegorical interpretation within an overarching spiritual perspective (2.3). As I argue in a fourth section, Deguileville's redefinition of the mechanisms of allegorical signification is shaped by scholastic discussion of specifically sacramental signs, in turn based on Augustinian semiotics (2.4). I conclude the chapter by reviewing the *aporias* and limitations of Deguileville's project in the light of his deeply ambivalent attitude towards his main source, the *Roman de la Rose* (2.5).

As I argue in chapter 2 as a whole, then, *PVH* is far from being a 'naïve' didactic allegory. Instead, it must be seen as a highly sophisticated allegorical narrative that employs first-person dream narrative to theorize the hermeneutic and epistemological principles upon which its own interpretation ought to rest. This is a highly ambitious programme that is only partially successful, and Deguileville repeatedly founders in his attempt to produce a viable, regulated system for allegorical reading and interpretation. Deguileville himself is keenly aware of the difficulties of controlling human interpretation and language use more broadly, and in Chapter 3 I argue that he ultimately seeks to ground his pilgrim's quest for spiritual truth not in language, but in a kind of self-knowledge that arises from greater awareness of the mental, cognitive, and intellective processes at work in the human mind and soul. Despite an extended overview of a number of problems and debates in late medieval philosophy of mind and cognition, however, Deguileville's pilgrim nonetheless realizes the insufficiency of individual will and intellect to pursue individual salvation in effective manner. In Chapter 4, I accordingly examine Deguileville's understanding of the human experience of grace, and its impact on both human cognitive abilities and the problem of individual will, agency, and salvation.

2

Language

Chi s'ensieut li pelerinage qui est uns biaux miroir de sauvement. Et
le compila uns grans clers en divinite moines de labbie de chaalis. Et
est fais par poetrie comme li livre de la rose qui est en grant partie de
philosophie mes cilz pelerinage est de theologie & des sacrements des
vertus & des vices et de cognoistre lame.[1]

1. *Predicatio*: Allegory and the Place of Authority

The *Pèlerinage de Vie* is by far the most popular poem of Deguileville's trilogy. It survives in around ninety MSS, often richly illustrated, and was variously
translated, reworked, adapted, and printed over the two centuries that follow its
appearance. The poem presents an account of a dream vision, and features a pilgrim persona who is simultaneously dreamer, first-person narrator, protagonist,
and expositor of the significance of his dream. This complex narrative configuration of the subject is taken over directly from the *Roman de la Rose*,[2] and
PVH1 (1331) famously opens with a mention of Jean de Meun's poem, explicitly identified as the principal source of inspiration for Deguileville's own dream
vision:

Une vision veul nuncier	I want to recount to you a vision that
Qui en dormant m'avint l'autrier.	came to me the other night as I was
En veillant avoie lëu,	sleeping. While I was awake I had read,
Considere et bien vëu	studied, and looked closely at the
Le biau roumans de la Rose.	beautiful *Romance of the Rose*. I am
Bien croi que ce fu la chose	sure that this was what moved me most
Qui plus m'esmut a ce songier	to have the dream I will tell you about
Que ci apres vous vueil nuncier.	in a moment.[3]
(*PVH1* 7–14)	

---

[1] MS Arras, BM 532 (formerly 845), fol. 74v, containing both the *Pèlerinage de Vie Humaine* and
selected extracts from the *Rose*, rearranged by the scribe/editor of the MS. See also discussion in Huot,
The Romance of the Rose and its Medieval Readers, pp. 231–8.

[2] See especially Kamath, *Authorship and First-Person Allegory*, pp. 19–58.

[3] Unless otherwise indicated, all English translations are taken from *The Pilgrimage of Human Life*,
trans. Eugene Clasby (New York: Garland, 1992).

Medieval Allegory as Epistemology. Marco Nievergelt, Oxford University Press.
© Marco Nievergelt (2023). DOI: 10.1093/oso/9780192849212.003.0003

122   MEDIEVAL ALLEGORY AS EPISTEMOLOGY

Considering the identity of the author and the avowedly moral and homiletic aspirations of his poem, the choice of the *Rose* as a literary model is bound to raise a few eyebrows: what on earth is a Cistercian monk doing reading a smutty erotic allegory like the *Rose*? Existing criticism has accordingly focused on this perceived incompatibility, characterizing *PVH* variously as 'a religious, edifying, unequivocal counterpart' of the earlier poem [une contrepartie réligieuse, édifiante, sans équivoques],[4] or as a transformation of the former into a 'journey to Paradise' [voie de paradis].[5] *PVH1* undeniably seeks to harness the energies of first-person allegorical narrative to spiritual and salvific ends, and existing readings have traced Deguileville's careful handling and re-imagining of specific elements, motifs, and characters from the *Rose* in this sense.[6]

The relationship between the two poems, however, cannot be reduced to that of a simple palimpsest. As well as substituting spiritual for erotic referents, *PVH* equally attempts to transform and redefine the mechanisms and principles of allegorical signification itself, reacting against the referential and hermeneutic slipperiness of Jean de Meun's poem. More specifically, *PVH* makes a consistent effort to locate authority more firmly, attempting to resolve the radical dialogism of the *Rose* into a more strongly monologic spiritual allegory. As Sarah Kay's discussion of *PVH* has suggested, however, such monologism is neither inherently reductive nor uncomplicated. In her study of the 'complexity of one' in late medieval poetry she therefore argues that when texts have

> a pious agenda [. . .] the desire to transmit a unified message leads them to realise that 'oneness' is problematic, and 'one' meaning difficult if not impossible to assign. It is because of this difficulty that 'placing' thought is ultimately so attractive to [. . .] poets [. . .]—it offers them the hope of fixing and determining meaning in the visual field—and so elusive, as the place itself retreats into invisibility. What I have called 'the complexity of one' is a poetic practice that, at once intellectually and aesthetically challenging, is not to be confused with dogmatism and intolerance.[7]

This intense and troubled desire for an elusive 'oneness' provides a remarkably fitting description of *PVH*, particularly in terms of its response to the pluralistic,

---

[4] Badel, *Le Roman de la Rose au XIVe siècle*, pp. 362–76 (365).

[5] Fabienne Pomel, '*Le Roman de la Rose* comme voie de paradis: transposition, parodie et moralisation de Guillaume de Lorris à Jean Molinet', in Bel and Braet, *De la Rose*, pp. 355–75.

[6] See especially Steven Wright, 'Deguileville's *Pèlerinage de vie humaine* as "Contrepartie édifiante" of the *Roman de la Rose*', *Philological Quarterly* 68.4 (1989), 399–422; and Huot, *The Romance of the Rose and its Medieval Readers*, pp. 207–38. Among more recent discussions, see especially Pomel, '*Le Roman de la Rose* comme voie de paradis'; Philippe Maupeu, '*Bivium*: l'écrivain nattier et le *Roman de la Rose*', in Duval and Pomel, pp. 21–41; Maupeu, *Pèlerins de vie humaine*, esp. 48–55; Kamath, *Authorship and First-Person Allegory*, pp. 19–58.

[7] Kay, *Place of Thought*, p. xi, and further pp. 3–6, 177–85 for a discussion of dialogism and monologism, and pp. 70–94 for her reading of *PVH* in this sense.

LANGUAGE   123

subversive, and centrifugal energies of the *Rose*. In what follows, I will therefore describe this relationship repeatedly as an endemic tension between unity and multiplicity, stasis and movement, monologism and dialogism.

One of the most important and conspicuous 'places' in Deguileville's poetry that provides the focus for such an aspiration to 'oneness', to adopt Sarah Kay's terms, is the image of the Holy City, glimpsed during the opening vision of the dreamer/ pilgrim/ narrator figure:

Avis m'ert si com dormoie	As I was sleeping, I dreamed I was a
Que je pelerins estoie	pilgrim eager to go to the city of
Qui d'aler estoie excite	Jerusalem. I saw this city from afar in a
En Jherusalem la cite.	mirror that seemed to me large beyond
En un mirour, ce me sembloit,	measure,
qui sanz mesure grans estoit	
Celle cite aparceue	
Avoie de loing et veue.	
(*PVH1* 35–42)	

The opening vision thus provides a proleptic image of the pilgrim's final destination, but also defines his very identity as a human *viator* in terms of his relation to this heavenly 'place'—our 'homeland' (*patria*), in Augustine's influential formulation.[8] The implication of this vision and of the ensuing urge to set out on pilgrimage is clear: only by reaching the heavenly city can the pilgrim attain a state of union and repose, restored to his original prelapsarian 'place' *in patria*, in the presence of the divine original in whose image he is made as *imago dei*.[9] It is only in such *patria* that the pilgrim's proper subjectivity can be apprehended not as individual selfhood (*ipséité*), but as self-identity and 'sameness' (*mêmeté*), to adopt the terminology of Paul Ricœur.[10] This vision of depersonalized oneness or 'citizenship' becomes the ultimate *telos* of the poem as a whole: just as it becomes the destination of the first-person *viator* and protagonist of the dream, it also becomes the ultimate referent and vanishing point of allegorical interpretation for the poem's readers. The underlying implication is that the act of reading and interpretation is itself endowed with salvific efficacy. As a work of allegorical fiction, then, *PVH* is not so much a didactic work that simply exposes its teaching in the

---

[8] See e.g. *De doctrina christiana* I.4.4. I used *De doctrina christiana*, ed. Joseph Martin, CCSL 32 (Turnhout: Brepols, 1962) and the translation provided in Augustine of Hippo, *On Christian Teaching*, ed. R. P. H. Green (Oxford: Oxford World's Classics, 1997). For a discussion of Augustine's ideas of pilgrimage, see Chapter 2.2.

[9] Again it is Augustine who most famously and influentially developed the idea of the human soul as the image of God. The notion emerges in his early work, and is most fully elaborated in the *De trinitate*, X and XIV. For an overview of Augustine's image theology, see especially Isabelle Bochet, 'Le statut de l'image dans la pensée augustinienne', *Archives de Philosophie* 72.2 (2009), 249–70.

[10] I here adopt the vocabulary of Paul Ricœur, in turn based on a close reading of Augustine—*Soi-même comme un autre*, pp. 140 ff; *Oneself as Another*. Trans. Kathleen Blamey. (Chicago and London: The University of Chicago Press, 1992), pp. 115 ff.

124   MEDIEVAL ALLEGORY AS EPISTEMOLOGY

speeches of a number of personified characters and mouthpieces, but a programmatic allegory that involves its readers actively, as fellow pilgrims, in the gradual retrieval of an ultimate, transcendental reality figured as the heavenly city.

The images and ideas brought into play by this opening vision conjure up an unmistakeably Augustinian anthropology, which equally determines the poem's adoption of the framing motif of the pilgrimage, to which I will turn in Chapter 2.3. The 'placement' of this vision of the Heavenly City within a mirror is in turn significant, and provides important clues about Deguileville's poetic method and his approach to the allegorical mode. On the one hand, the mirror establishes the importance of the perceptual, mental, and cognitive processes that will be set in motion during the pilgrim's journey—topics I will address in Chapter 3. On the other hand, the mirror figures the workings of specifically allegorical imagination and interpretation. The association is well-established, and goes back to Augustine's discussion of the *speculum in aenigmate* from 1 Cor. 13:12 in *De trinitate* XV.9.15 (cf. also *De doctrina* II.7). The association becomes commonplace during the twelfth century, when it is widely used by the Neoplatonic philosophical poets. Alan of Lille's *De planctu naturae*, for instance, ends by framing the preceding vision within just such an allegorical mirror:

> When the mirror of this imaginary vision was withdrawn, the sight of the previous mystical apparition left me awakened from my strange ecstatic dream. (*The Plaint of Nature*, 18.20)[11]

The mirror glimpsed by the dreamer at the start of *PVH* similarly functions as a metonymy for Deguileville's poem, announcing its unmistakeably spiritual and salvific *telos*.[12] The precise significance of this meta-allegorical mirror is particularly evident when compared with the many mirrors that disrupt and disorganize the allegory of the *Rose*, a palace of mirrors that is itself a 'Mirror for Lovers' [*Miroër aus Amoreus, RR* 10,621].[13] Instead of gazing into the treacherous fountain/mirror of Narcissus to see an elusive and equivocal 'Rose', and

---

[11] 'Huius imaginariae visionis subtracto speculo, me ab extasis excitatum insompnio prior misticae apparitionis dereliquit aspectus.' See Alan Of Lille, *Literary Works*, ed. and trans. Winthrop Wetherbee (Cambridge, MA: Dumbarton Oaks, 2013), p. 217. On the use of mirrors to explore the processes of allegorical writing and the literary imagination, see especially several contributions in Fabienne Pomel, ed., *Miroirs et jeux de miroirs dans la littérature médiévale* (Rennes: Presses Universitaires de Rennes, 2003).

[12] For a discussion of the symbolism of mirrors in the poem, see Anne-Marie Legaré and Fabienne Pomel, 'Les Miroirs du *Pèlerinage de Vie humaine*: le texte et l'image', in Pomel, ed., *Miroirs et jeux de miroirs dans la littérature médiévale*, pp. 125–55; Katharina Mertens-Fleury, 'Spiegelungen: Metaphern der Retexualisierung im *Pèlerinage de vie Humaine* und den Prologen der Pilgerfahrt des träumenden Mönchs', in Kablitz and Peters, pp. 587–618 (esp. section II); and Susan K. Hagen, *Allegorical Remembrance: A Study of 'The Pilgrimage of the life of Man' as a Medieval Treatise on Seeing and Remembering* (Athens, GA and London: University of Georgia Press, 1990), pp. 7–29. I return to mirrors below, in relation to both Deguileville (in Chapters 2.3 and 3.5) and Langland (in Chapters 6.3 and 7.1).

[13] For a concise discussion of the play of mirrors in the *Rose*, see Morton and Nievergelt, 'Introduction', pp. 9–13. For further discussion of the mirror/fountain of Narcissus, see especially Claire Nouvet,

setting out on an erratic quest through a poem saturated with mirrored 'illusions produced [. . .] by such visions' [deceptions / qui vienent par tex visions, *RR* 18261–2], the dreamer in *PVH* apprehends and identifies the object of his quest immediately and unambiguously.[14] The semiotic indirections and equivocations of the *Rose* have been supplanted by the far more focused, linear momentum of spiritual pilgrimage, geared towards a final object whose ultimate nature is apprehended at the very beginning of the quest. Deguileville's allegory, then, immediately stakes its claim to function as a transparently spiritual allegory with a clear, unambiguous objective—a 'beautiful mirror of salvation' [biaux miroir de sauvement], as the poem is designated in a manuscript containing both *PVH* and selected extracts from the *Rose*.[15] The opening of Deguileville's poem can thus be read as containing an unambiguous statement of purpose. Just as the pilgrim is about to embark on a pilgrimage to the Heavenly Jerusalem, and just like an image must be understood in relation to its ultimate object, the allegory we are about to read must be deciphered in relation to the kingdom of heaven. The reader's hermeneutic progress through the semiotic wilderness of the poem therefore evolves in parallel with the pilgrim/protagonist's moral, intellectual, and spiritual advance through the allegorical dreamscape. The adoption of an 'open', depersonalized first-person dreamer/narrator/protagonist reinforces this homology between fictional protagonist and the individual reader.[16]

Concurrently, however, the choice of a first-person *acteur* also poses a number of difficulties for differentiating between the multiple discursive instances involved: how, exactly, are we invited to understand the 'I' of the text? Does the grammatical pronoun denote the poem's historical author writing his spiritual autobiography, a partially fictionalized narrator, an entirely fabricated protagonist, or a depersonalized and exemplary 'Everyman'? As A. C. Spearing's recent work has shown, the popularity of late medieval first-person narratives is in large part determined by the range of different possibilities opened up by such referential instability. But while such a radically de-centred and fluctuating 'I' is admirably well-suited to an exploratory, playful, and ultimately subversive poem like the *Rose*, its effects are far more troublesome in a poem with strongly didactic ambitions such as *PVH*. As a consequence, Deguileville is repeatedly forced to disambiguate the status of his poem's 'I', in order to restore the kind of firm

---

'An Allegorical Mirror: The Pool of Narcissus in Guillaume de Lorris' *Romance of the Rose*', *Romanic Review* 91.4 (2000), 353–74; and David Hult, 'The Allegorical Fountain: Narcissus in the *Roman de la Rose*', *Romanic Review* 72.2 (1981), 125–48; and further discussion in Chapter 3.3 and 3.5.

[14] See also Huot, *The Romance of the Rose and its Medieval Readers*, pp. 208–9.

[15] See above, n. 9. See further Kamath, *Authorship*, 31 n. 27; Maupeu, *Pèlerins de vie humaine*, p. 274; and discussion of this manuscript in Huot, *The Romance of the Rose and its Medieval Readers*, pp. 231–8.

[16] See Kamath and Nievergelt, 'Introduction', pp. 9–11; Maupeu, *Pèlerins de vie humaine*, pp. 98–107. More generally on the status of the 'open' status of the 'I' in allegorical dream poetry, see Helen Phillips, 'Frames and Narrators in Chaucerian Poetry', in Helen Cooper and Sally Mapstone, eds, *The Long Fifteenth Century: Essays for Douglas Gray* (Oxford: Oxford University Press, 1997), pp. 71–97 (80), cited and discussed in Spearing, *Medieval Autographies*, p. 19.

126   MEDIEVAL ALLEGORY AS EPISTEMOLOGY

expository authority upon which a monologic reading of the allegory ultimately depends. This effort to differentiate between multiple instances of the 'I' begins with Deguileville's authorial self-presentation at the beginning of *PVH1*. Here he presents himself as the real-life monk from the Cistercian abbey of Chaalis, urging a flock of laypeople to assemble and listen to his predication. His 'sermon' takes the form of an extended account of his dream, doubled by an intermittent exposition of the dream's significance (*PVH1* 15–27). The self-portrait leaves little doubt about the author's didactic aims, and functions as an iconic affirmation of authorial design, intention, and control. To echo again the terms of Sarah Kay's model, Deguileville can be said to assert the monologic aspirations of his allegory by 'placing' his authorial voice in the figure of the preacher, 'fixing and determining meaning in the visual field'.

The image of the Cistercian monk preaching to an assembled flock of laypeople from his pulpit appears to have enjoyed considerable success, and almost invariably occurs as part of the elaborate iconographical programme featured in many manuscripts of *PVH1*.[17] Deguileville's choice of the image is not innocent. On one level the motif is simply meant to remind readers of the poet's superior religious and moral standing, as a Cistercian monk and representative of the institutional and doctrinal authority of the Christian church. But the image also has to be read with reference to the *Rose*, where the image had been used to 'place' the sermon of that most egregiously unreliable figure of authority—the irresistibly subversive Genius, dispenser of the poem's preposterous 'diffinitive santance' (*RR* 19,474; see Chapter 1.4). Genius mounts on an elevated scaffold/pulpit (19,464), unfolding a physical 'chartre' (19,467) to read and expose the meaning of its 'letre' (19,462) for the benefit of the assembled 'barons' (19,671), eager to hear his sermon. This scene too is abundantly illustrated in *Rose* manuscripts, and as Joyce Coleman has shown, the motif did not only influence later authors in localized and circumscribed ways, but became ingrained in the literary imagination of late fourteenth-century England as a whole.[18] Deguileville too appears to have registered the spatial and iconographic coordinates used to 'place' Genius's troubling *santance*, together with the figure's role in 'dis-placing' the very idea of textual, discursive, and intellectual authority. Deguileville's poem indeed redeploys a whole cluster of symbolic attributes and activities associated with Genius: the use of the pulpit; the adoption of a magisterial posture; his use of written documents to authorize his *santance*; his claim to expound the significance of its 'letre'. As will be seen in the following chapters, all of these symbolic activities come to occupy a

---

[17] See Michael W. Camille, 'The Illustrated Manuscripts of Guillaume de Deguileville's *Pèlerinages*, 1330–1426', 2 vols (PhD dissertation, University of Cambridge, 1985).

[18] Joyce Coleman, 'Translating Iconography: Gower, *Pearl*, Chaucer, and the *Rose*', in Susanna Fein and David Raybin, eds, *Chaucer: Visual Approaches* (University Park: Penn State University Press, 2016), pp. 177–94 (188–92); and ibid., 'Where Chaucer Got His Pulpit: Audience and Intervisuality in the Troilus and Criseyde Frontispiece', *Studies in the Age of Chaucer* 32 (2010), 103–28 (114–28).

LANGUAGE 127

pivotal position in both Deguileville's and Langland's poems, where they acquire an increasingly complex and problematic range of meanings and implications.

Deguileville's adoption of the role of preacher in his own poem, then, already signals his desire to restore an overarching and tightly unified *intentio auctoris*, against the supremely evasive and duplicitous authorial self-presentation we find in the jointly authored and authorially disjointed *Rose*. Recuperating the symbolic and spatial attributes of Genius—a magisterial figure of authority entrusted with the mission of expounding the *santance* of all the events previously rehearsed in the poem [fez devant contez, *RR* 19,463]—Deguileville labours to 're-place' authority, locating it specifically within the voice of his own, first-person author/preacher/expositor figure. Clearly the opening vignette of a fictionalized *predicatio* provides a fundamental reference point for *PVH* as a whole:[19] it provides both a narrative framework and an interpretive focus for the subsequent action, allowing the reader to differentiate between the 'I' understood as instance of authorial intention and didactic exposition (preacher), and the 'I' understood as an often hapless and naïve protagonist (the pilgrim). The implication is that all of the pilgrim's subsequent mistakes, misadventures, disputes, and backslidings are rhetorically subsumed and contained within the framework of the poet-preacher's master-discourse, whose authorial voice distils such misadventures into a pedagogical, didactic project through allegorical interpretation. Choosing to locate the vision of his authorial 'I' within the Abbey of Chaalis in this opening section (*PVH1* 33) further enhances its authority: uttered from within the monastic enclosure—pre-figuration of the Heavenly City—the predication is delivered, symbolically speaking, from within the New Jerusalem towards which all pilgrims are travelling. This renewed instance of 'placing' authority once more emphasizes the salvific *telos* that drives the poem.

This technique places the idea of reading and allegorical interpretation at the heart of Deguileville's instructional project. As was seen in Chapter 1, the *Rose* had revealed that allegorical poetry, with its abundant use of equivocal figures and tropes, is a metamorphic literary form that inherently frustrates closure. Since he adopts the same form of first-person allegory inaugurated the *Rose*, Deguileville is forced to counteract this tendency by stabilizing interpretation from the inside. This takes the form of an ongoing expository commentary, using what Philippe Maupeu, following Paul Zumthor, calls 'integrated glossing' (*glose intégrée*).[20] Deguileville thus employs his self-conferred magisterial role in order to extrapolate the allegorical meaning of his own dream-narrative for the benefit of his audience/readership. Such a technique rests on the belief in the possibility of ensuring something like a correct, definitive, and unequivocal interpretation of

---

[19] On *predicatio* as master-discourse in *PVH*, see especially Maupeu, *Pèlerins de vie humaine*, pp. 98, 107–18.
[20] Maupeu, *Pèlerins de vie humaine*, pp. 98–128, cf. Paul Zumthor, *Essai de poétique médiévale* (Paris: Seuil, 1972), p. 157; Maupeu, '*Bivium*', pp. 29–32.

128 MEDIEVAL ALLEGORY AS EPISTEMOLOGY

the dream poem, pointing to an unambiguous *intentio auctoris*. Concurrently, however, this reliance on embedded exposition also implicitly acknowledges the slipperiness of allegorical expression, reminding the reader of its dependence on a supplementary *glose* to stabilize interpretation. It is from this central paradox that Deguileville's insoluble difficulties emerge, forcing him to return again and again to the cognitive and hermeneutic difficulties crystallized by Jean's *Rose*.

Deguileville also uses more subtle strategies that go beyond the exposition of moral precept and benevolent pastoral instruction. In particular, he aims to equip his readers with the kind of intellectual, cognitive, and interpretive abilities necessary to navigate the allegorical wilderness of his own poem, and thus ultimately derive positive salvific benefits from the experience of reading. Two specific strategies stand out. On the one hand, Deguileville attempts to reconstruct a systematic hierarchy of precedence among the multitude of personifications that populate his allegory, reacting against the *Rose*, where allegorical personifications often behave in erratic, surprising, and undisciplined manner, at odds with the faculties or realities they ostensibly personify. This had produced an unreasonable Raison, an unnaturally digressive Nature, Genius as an improbable bishop preaching the gospel of free love, and a pilgrim whose 'devotion' is similarly outrageous. While the personifications that populate *PVH1* are every bit as troublesome and overweening as their counterparts in the *Rose*, Deguileville's poem ultimately seeks to organize their discourses into a clear and functional hierarchy by scrutinizing their truth value and their relative authority within a larger overarching system. The principal tool used to achieve this is debate, as the 'I' witnesses or becomes embroiled in a series of pseudo-scholastic *disputationes*. The implication is that through an adequate use of language and dialectic, understood in the traditional sense as an *ars de bene disputandi* or *ars discernendi verum a falso*, the pilgrim/reader too is able to discern the true significance of the various events, characters, speeches, and situations in the allegory. Instead of being fundamentally flawed, misleading, fallacious, and inconclusive as in the *Rose*, *disputatio* in *PVH1* appears to be geared towards producing a stable and systematic epistemology, resolving itself into an overarching authorial discourse figured as *predicatio*.[21] Deguileville's second strategy for educating the reader in the art of spiritual discernment and self-knowledge consists in determining criteria for the 'correct' interpretation of the allegory itself—an activity that is understood as having a cognitive dimension that is also inherently salvific. Even more than dialectic, then, it is the pilgrim/reader's ability to decipher the signs of the allegorical universe he inhabits that ensures his ability to labour actively for his salvation. The pilgrim's journey, then, figures an induction into a new, soteriological hermeneutics

---

[21] See also Marco Nievergelt, 'From *disputatio* to *predicatio*—and Back Again: Dialectic, Authority and Epistemology between the *Roman de la Rose* and the *Pèlerinage de Vie Humaine*', *New Medieval Literatures* 16 (2015), 135–71.

LANGUAGE 129

that is underpinned by a much wider, distinctively Augustinian semiotics and epistemology. I examine both of these strategies in detail in the following two sections.

2. Learning to Argue

Despite its monologic and salvific aspirations, *PVH1* is not a narrowly didactic, morally prescriptive poem. The emphasis of *PVH* is placed not so much on *doing* the right thing, but on *knowing* and *understanding*, specifically on the importance of discerning truth from falsehood, with the aim of training the pilgrim/reader's cognitive and interpretive abilities within a wider soteriological perspective.[22] 'Discernment' accordingly holds pride of place in the teaching administered by Sapience, who together with Grace Dieu is the principal figure of authority in the poem. As Sapience states, the entire art of dialectic—*ars discernendi verum a falso*—hinges on the ability to define, differentiate, and discern:

'L'entendement [. . .] enfourmoie	'I have formed and instructed the
A arguer et desputer	understanding to argue and dispute,
Et a jugier et discerner	to judge and discern between the
Entre le bon et le mauves.'	good and the bad.'
(*PVH1* 3012–15)[23]	[translation emended]

Since the ability to discern is central in Sapience's pedagogical programme, much of the poem takes the form of edifying dialectical *disputationes* between the various characters and personifications. Either with the help of Sapience and Grace Dieu or on his own, the pilgrim too engages in such debates with a wide range of personifications whose intentions are often unclear: he must scrutinize their arguments, see through their verbal deception, correctly identify their nature, name, and intention, or learn to appreciate the precise significance of their often complex teaching.[24] Relying on the reader's ability to project their own thinking

---

[22] A reading in this sense is proposed by Hagen, *Allegorical Remembrance*. Hagen however sees *PVH* as an essentially unproblematic and internally unified allegory, and focuses largely on Lydgate's translation of *PVH2*. This obscures the specificities of Deguileville's poem in its different versions, and glosses over its internal tensions and contradictions that determine the intellectual complexity of the work. For Lydgate's version, see *The Pilgrimage of the Life of Man*, trans. John Lydgate, ed. F. J. Furnivall and Katharine B. Locock, 3 vols, EETS OS 78, 83 and 92 (London: Kegan Paul, Trench, Trübner & Co., 1899–1904).

[23] The importance of this ability to 'discern' is reiterated throughout the poem. It is first introduced to allegorize the Sword as *Verbum dei* (Heb. 4:12), whose point signifies discernment and discretion (*PVH1* 1083–1118, cited and discussed below). On the related notion of *discretion*, often applied to the pilgrim's *jugement* or *entendement*, see further passages at *PVH1* 1085, 1118, 1242, 1260, 1703, 3078.

[24] For a useful overview of Deguileville's use of personification allegory in this sense, see for instance Rosemond Tuve, *Allegorical Imagery*, pp. 145–218, and Eugene Clasby, 'Introduction', *The Pilgrimage of Human Life*, trans. Eugene Clasby (New York: Garland, 1992), pp. xv–xxvii.

130 MEDIEVAL ALLEGORY AS EPISTEMOLOGY

process onto the depersonalized 'I' of the *viator*, the poem therefore fosters the development of the reader's own dialectical abilities.

It is evident that this interest in the positive, disambiguating potential of scholastic *disputatio* is a direct response to the *Rose*, where dialectic's ability to produce knowledge (*faciens scire*) is subjected to a sustained critique, as I argued in Chapter 1. As if to signal his engagement with the *Rose* more clearly, Deguileville populates his allegorical universe with a number of personified abstractions that are lifted wholesale from Jean de Meun's poem: Nature, Raison, Huiseuse/Oiseuse, Venus, and several others. In contrast with Jean de Meun, however—who gives us mostly unpredictable, erratic, and highly undisciplined personifications— Deguileville labours to realign personifications with their actual names and inner natures. Nature, Grace, Raison, Sapience, and even Aristotle all return to occupy what is seen as their rightful place in a hierarchically structured, tightly organized, and functional allegorical universe. This produces a more harmonious and predictable cast of characters, but is also intended to enable a more stable and systematic interpretation of the allegorical action in the poem. Dialogism and conflict are thus ultimately subsumed within a larger monologic order of being that slowly emerges into full view as the reader moves forward through the poem. Using Sapience and Grace Dieu as mouthpieces for the dominant discourse that organizes the poem, Deguileville begins to articulate, bit by bit, the epistemological and ontological underpinnings of his allegory for the benefit of the reader/*viator*. In the process, *PVH* seeks to reconstruct a functional, systematic epistemology from the relativistic and inconclusive debris of the *Rose*.

In order to illustrate Deguileville's strategy, I want to analyse an extended dispute over Eucharistic matters that involves a range of personifications: Sapience and Grace Dieu on the one hand, and Nature, Raison, and Aristotle on the other (*PVH1* 1431–3306).[25] The passage helps to shed light not only on Deguileville's complex attitude towards dialectic, but also on his broader ideological affiliations. Notably, it brings into focus his reservations about Aristotelian natural science, his views on the relationship between profane philosophy and sacred theology, and his commitment to a distinctly Augustinian, 'sapiential' epistemology. What emerges from Deguileville's handling of this and other pseudo-scholastic *disputationes* that take place over the course of the pilgrim's journey is a deeply conflicted

---

[25] The episode has attracted more critical attention than any other section of the poem. For earlier discussions, see Hagen, *Allegorical Remembrance*, pp. 43–8; Kay, *Place of Thought*, pp. 76–81; Rosenfeld, *Ethics and Enjoyment*, pp. 122–5; Stephanie A. V. G. Kamath, 'Rewriting Ancient *Auctores* in the *Pèlerinage de la vie humaine*', in Kablitz and Peters, pp. 321–42; Robertson, *Nature Speaks*, pp. 191–205; Rebecca Davis, *Piers Plowman and the Books of Nature* (Oxford: Oxford University Press, 2016), pp. 69–76; Nicolette Zeeman, *The Arts of Disruption: Allegory and Piers Plowman* (Oxford: Oxford University Press, 2020), pp. 144–53. On the challenges posed by the doctrine of the Eucharist for late medieval Aristotelian science more broadly, see Marilyn McCord Adams, 'Aristotle and the Sacrament of the Altar: a Crisis in Medieval Aristotelianism', *Canadian Journal of Philosophy* 21 (1991), 195–249.

LANGUAGE 131

and ambivalent attitude towards University culture, and more specifically towards the eminently Aristotelian art of dialectic as well as natural science.

Such ambivalence is at least partially a function of the specific cultural and intellectual environment in which Deguileville moved, lived, and wrote, and it will be useful to provide some general considerations on this context before proceeding with my analysis of this series of 'disputational' exchanges in the poem. As Fréderic Duval pointed out almost ten years ago, any serious study of Deguileville's poetry needs to begin with a much more thorough investigation of its broader historical, cultural, and intellectual context. Given the low literary status of this Cistercian author among modern critics, work on this question is extremely scarce, but it is nonetheless possible to draw up at least a vague outline of Deguileville's intellectual biography.[26] Born in *c.* 1295, he enters the Cistercian Abbey of Chaalis approximately around the age of twenty-one, in 1316, as Edmond Faral discusses in his classic biography of the author, on the basis of internal allusions in *PVH2*.[27] Rather than confining him within a monolithic, strictly contemplative intellectual environment, however, his presence at Chaalis would have enabled him to participate in the abbey's rich and varied cultural, intellectual, and political life. Firstly, the Cistercian order itself had evolved considerably from its early commitment to the ideals of simplicity, monastic rigour, and secluded contemplation of its early days, and had begun playing an important social, economic, political, and intellectual role by the fourteenth century. Chaalis in particular—a mere forty kilometres North-East of Paris—was well placed to play an active role in the intellectual and political life of its day, and did so particularly under Jacques de Thérines, Abbot of Chaalis between 1310 and 1318, covering the period during which Deguileville would have joined the order. Thérines was a remarkable scholar in his own right, who before his appointment had been regent master in theology at the University of Paris, where the Cistercians had their own Collège de Saint-Bernard. In William Chester Jordan's words,

The college was the centre of Cistercian learning in France and Christendom. The monks there and the scholars at other colleges of the University experienced a bubbling cauldron of rigorous learning, distracting activity, bitter rivalries, and intellectual arrogance. The experience had the potential to seduce many into a permanent desire for the academic life. It turned many others off to the posturing. And it provoked ambivalent feelings, comprising both repulsion and attraction, among still others.[28]

---

[26] Duval, 'Interpréter le *Pèlerinage de vie humaine*'.

[27] Édmond Faral, 'Guillaume de Digulleville, moine de Chaalis', in *Histoire littéraire de la France*, Vol. 39 (Paris: Imprimerie Nationale, 1962), p. 6.

[28] William Chester Jordan, *Unceasing Strife, Unending Fear: Jacques de Thérines and the Freedom of the Church in the Age of the Last Capetians* (Princeton: Princeton University Press, 2005), p. 2.

132   MEDIEVAL ALLEGORY AS EPISTEMOLOGY

Thérines, himself author of an impressive set of quodlibetal questions he reworked at Chaalis,[29] accordingly encouraged learning among the younger monks at Chaalis, which like other Cistercian monasteries would have sent at least one out of every twenty monks to study at the Collège Saint-Bernard in Paris.[30] Jordan's evocative description of the atmosphere there provides a neat picture of what may well have been Deguileville's own experience as a student in nearby Paris, in the years immediately following Thérines' tenure as Abbot.[31]

The Abbey of Chaalis itself also provided ample opportunity for cultivating scholarly interests. According to the revised statutes of 1300, every Cistercian monastery with more than sixty monks would have been required to employ a lector capable of dispensing teaching in grammar and logic to the monks.[32] Furthermore, the monks had access to a well-stocked library that included recent Aristotle commentaries alongside work by the usual monastic and patristic authors.[33] During this period of rapid cultural change within the order, we also find a number of Cistercians producing scholastic works of the highest order, such as Humbert de Preuilly, author of a commentary on Aristotle's *Metaphysics* and *De anima* (manuscripts of both were held at Chaalis);[34] John of Mirecourt, condemned in 1347 for espousing Ockhamist views;[35] and Pierre Ceffons, a most interesting figure who cites Jean de Meun's *Rose* on multiple occasions, notably in his *Sentences* commentary, and who also produced—in addition to his more standard scholastic output—an extended dream-vision account to denounce recent changes of confessional practice within the order (1349), and the hugely popular fictional

---

[29] Jordan, *Unceasing Strife*, pp. 9–17, 39–40.

[30] Caroline Obert-Piketty, 'La promotion des études chez les cisterciens à travers le recrutement des étudiants du Collège Saint-Bernard de Paris au moyen âge', *Cîteaux* 39 (1988), 65–78 (67).

[31] See further Guillaume de Digulleville, *Le Dit de la Fleur de Lis*, ed. Duval, pp. 36–40.

[32] Obert-Piketty, 'La promotion des études chez les cisterciens', p. 67, n. 6.

[33] See especially Kamath, 'Rewriting Ancient *Auctores*', who notes the presence of a commentary on Aristotle's *Metaphysics* by Humbert of Preuilly, himself a Cistercian, for which see Humbertus de Prulliaco, *Sententia Super Librum Metaphisice Aristotelis Liber I-V*, ed. Monica Brinzei and Nikolaus Wicki (Turnhout: Brepols, 2013). For the reconstructed contents of Chaalis Library, see Anne Bondéelle-Souchier and Patricia Stirnemann, 'Vers une reconstitution de la bibliothèque ancienne de l'abbaye de Chaalis: inventaires et manuscrits retrouvés', in Monique Goullet, ed., *Parva pro magnis munera—études de littérature tardo-antique et médiévale offertes à François Dolbeau par ses élèves* (Turnhout: Brepols, 2009), pp. 9–73. A commentary by Humbert on Aristotle's *De anima*, now lost, was equally held at Chaalis, as pointed out by Monica Brinzei Calma, 'Le commentaire des Sentences d'Humbert de Preuilly', *Bulletin de Philosophie Médiévale* 53 (2011), 81–148 (82, nn. 5 and 6), based on Carolus de Visch, *Bibliotheca Scriptorum S. Ordinis Cisterciensis* (Cologne, 1656), 165.

[34] On Humbert of Preuilly, see the preceding note.

[35] Mauricio Bechot, 'John of Mirecourt', in Jorge J. E. Gracia and Timothy N. Noone, eds, *A Companion to Philosophy in the Middle Ages* (Oxford: Blackwell, 2002), pp. 377–81; Madalina-Gabriela Pantea, 'Johannes de Mirecuria', in Henrik Lagerlund, ed., *Encyclopedia of Medieval Philosophy: Philosophy between 500 and 1500*, 2nd edition. 2 vols (Dordrecht: Springer, 2020), I: 916–22.

LANGUAGE   133

Epistola luciferi (1352, source of the Wycliffite *Epistola sathanae ad cleros*).[36] Cistercian monasticism in the fourteenth century, then, provided fertile ground for the development of scholastic thought.

Internal evidence also suggests that Deguileville had more than a passing acquaintance with scholastic writings and methods of inquiry. A single but rather telling example will suffice here, as I will discuss this question more fully in Chapter 3. During his description of the seven deadly sins later in the poem, Deguileville describes Trahison (Treason), mounted on Envie (Envy), disguised in a cloak and 'faus visage' (false face/mask, *PVH1* 8340, cf. also 8210):

'Se dehors paree me vois	'Although you can see me in my
Pour ce, voir, ne me connois.	clothes, you do not really know me.
On ne connoist pas aus drapiaus	You cannot know people based on
Les gens ne les vins aus sarciaus.'	their robes, just as you can't tell
(*PVH1* 8453–6)	about wine from mere barrel hoops.'
	[translation mine]

While the mention of the contrast between 'gens' and 'drapiaus' is proverbial—it redeploys the motif of the monk's habit, used to conceal his evil intentions, as in the case of Faux Semblant in the *Rose* (cf. *RR* 11,024–8)—the mention of 'vins' and 'sarciaus' appears more cryptic. There clearly is, however, a 'source' for this abstruse image, which actually is a stock example discussed in scholastic treatises on semantics. The *circulum vini* (a barrel hoop), refers to the sign hung outside a tavern, which ordinarily denoted the presence of wine inside the premises; logicians routinely discussed the situation where all the wine in the tavern had been drunk, and sought to determine whether in these special circumstances the sign still signified according to its original imposition or whether its signification had been modified or corrupted.[37] In Deguileville's hands, the motif becomes a figure for the duplicity and hypocrisy of Trahison, dissimulating her vices under a mask and cloak, and thus behaving like a misleading, false *signum*. While in this particular case the familiarity with this 'source' does little to enhance our understanding of this otherwise unproblematic passage, it confirms that Deguileville had more than a superficial acquaintance with scholastic learning, and more specifically with treatises on logic and semantics, where such discussions of linguistic reference would occur. As will become apparent in what follows, it appears to be precisely in the area of semiotics, semantics, and cognitive and perceptual theory that Deguileville engaged most intensely with recent scholastic developments, often

---

[36] All of these display intriguing affinities with Deguileville, from the use of the dream vision framework, the device of letters authored by Satan and Christ (as in *PA*), and the interest in the *Rose*. On Ceffons, see especially Christopher Schabel, '*Lucifer princeps tenebrarum* . . . The *Epistola Luciferi* and Other Correspondence of the Cistercian Pierre Ceffons (fl. 1348–1353)', *Vivarium* 56 (2018), 126–75. On his citation of the *Rose*, see McWebb, *Debating the Roman de la Rose*, pp. 15, 26.

[37] On the recurrence of this classic example, see Rosier-Catach, *La parole efficace*, pp. 64–5, 72–3, 496 n. 35; and Marmo, *La semiotica del XIII secolo*, pp. 16, 27–8, 77, 88.

134 MEDIEVAL ALLEGORY AS EPISTEMOLOGY

in critical, creative, but also well-informed fashion. More specifically, Deguileville
responds creatively to such recent theories and debates, often adopting and reformulating such ideas in a more strongly moralized register that recalls other hybrid,
pastoral-scholastic works such as Peter of Limoges' *Tractatus moralis de oculo*.[38]
In doing so, Deguileville occupies a highly complex position in relation to institutional discourses of learning, balancing resistance and defensiveness with a keen
and creative interest in advanced theoretical debates on questions of epistemology.

The first episode I want to discuss begins with Raison's baffled, outraged reaction to the unnatural miracle of transubstantiation (*PVH1* 1488–90), inexplicable
according to the principles of Aristotelian natural science. Raison immediately
retires to her tower to sulk (*PVH1* 1502; cf. Raison's tower in *RR* 4196–8), and
determines to raise the matter with Lady Nature in person as soon as possible:
'And I will certainly tell Nature, as soon as I see her' [Et vraiement je le dirai /
A Nature quant la verrai, *PVH1* 1491–2]. When Nature arrives on the scene she
defends her own sphere of influence against the perceived trespasses of Grace: 'I
come to you to argue and defend what is mine' [a vous je vien / Tencier pour def-
fendre le mien, *PVH1* 1519–20]. Nature seeks to relegate Grace to the heavenly
sphere, claiming for herself the sovereign mastery of the sublunary world, and
drawing a clear boundary ('bonne') between their respective jurisdictions:

'Entre moi et vous assise Fu bonne qui nous devise [...]	'A boundary was set up between you and me, dividing us . . .
Celle roe si nous depart A chascune donne sa part De hors est la vostre partie [...]	[T]his [sublunary] sphere separates us, and gives each of us their part . . .
Mais par dedens trestout est mien. Maistresse sui des elemens.' (*PVH1* 1541–59)	[W]ithin this [realm] everything is mine. I am mistress of the elements.'

Instead of merely resolving this dispute in favour of Grace Dieu, Deguileville
tries to show that the argument itself is based on mistaken premises. It quickly
emerges that Nature misunderstands the metaphor she herself adopts to stake her
claim: she understands the heavenly spheres as marking a boundary between two
entirely separate, mutually exclusive areas of competence, whereas in fact they
define a vertical and hierarchical system of concentric circles. Here the authority of Nature is necessarily, always and already subsumed within, and dependent
on, the workings of Grace. Accordingly Grace Dieu reminds her: 'the barrier that

---

[38] Peter of Limoges, *The Moral Treatise on the Eye*, ed. Richard Newhauser (Toronto: PIMS, 2013).
For a critical study of moralized discussions of optics in the period, see also Dallas G. Denery II,
Seeing and Being Seen in the Later Medieval World: Optics, Theology and Religious Life (Cambridge:
Cambridge University Press, 2005).

LANGUAGE   135

is between us prevents you from trespassing, but not me' [le bonnage / Qui est mis entre vous et moy / [...] il vous bonne, non pas moy, *PVH1* 1720–2]—a strikingly concise defence of the divine prerogative to govern *de potentia absoluta*.[39] Rather than making any subtle metaphysical point, however, the exchange is primarily intended to highlight Nature's own shortcomings as a disputant, exposing the premises of her argument as deeply flawed. In particular, Deguileville ridicules Nature's combative and aggressive stance in ways that suggest a broader criticism of contemporary academic practice. The allusions are evident in the recurrent use of the term *tencier* ('to argue, to quarrel, to dispute', at *PVH1* 1515, 1520, 1649, 1702, 1780, 1818, 1832)[40] to describe Nature's antagonistic attitude. Her combative disposition, the pilgrim observes, marks her out immediately as a scholastic disputant rather than a preacher and theologian, casting doubt on her motives and authority even before she begins to speak: 'she seemed more inclined to quarrel and dispute than to preach' [Preste me sembla de *tencier* / Mont plus assez que de preschier, *PVH1* 1515–16, my emphases].[41] The contrast being drawn up between *tencier* and *preschier* is clearly intended to remind us of Deguileville's own *predicatio*, the master-discourse within which all of the poem's dialectical disputes and uncertainties are ultimately meant to be subsumed.

Predictably, Grace Dieu berates Nature for her anger, which inevitably clouds her discernment:

'Quar gens ires a deporter	'One must bear with angry people,
Sont, pour ce que voir discerner	because they cannot see the truth
Ne peuent pas bien clerement	clearly, since their understanding is
Pour leur trouble entendement.'	troubled.'
(*PVH1* 1679–82)	[translation emended]

The clash between Nature's confrontational attitude and the more equanimous wisdom of Grace Dieu also resonates with late thirteenth-century debates over the respective spheres of competence of theology and philosophy. This notably crystallized in the condemnations at the University of Paris during the 1270s, and more broadly in the general hostility against the trespassing *philosophi theologizantes* by members of the Theology Faculty.[42] By deliberately casting Nature as an irascible and aggressive disputant, Deguileville assimilates her to the claims for the emancipation of a science of nature independent of theology voiced—supposedly—by members of the Parisian Arts Faculty at the close of the previous century.[43] Nature

---

[39] See Robertson, *Nature Speaks*, p. 203, and wider discussion, 191–205.

[40] Dee *DMF*, http://www.atilf.fr/dmf/definition/tancer.

[41] Compare also Henri d'Andeli's characterization of 'Logique' as a 'science ... qui toz jors tence', *Bataille des VII ars*, line 6, in les *Dits d'Henri d'Andeli*, ed. Corbellari.

[42] See *La condamnation parisienne de 1277*, ed. Piché and Lafleur, especially pp. 163, 168–76.

[43] Such claims for an independence of philosophical thought may have been more imagined than real, as suggested by recent work. Also the long-term consequences of the conflict are now considered to have been less fractious and traumatic than formerly believed. See e.g. Andreas Speer, 'Sapientia

136   MEDIEVAL ALLEGORY AS EPISTEMOLOGY

proudly identifies herself as a 'Maistresse' (*PVH1* 1559), a parodic and feminized *magister in artibus* who must be reminded that she is Grace's chambermaid—much like philosophy needed to be reminded by Étienne Tempier, Bonaventure, and others 'involved in the condemnations that she was *ancilla theologiae*:[44] 'I am mistress and you chambermaid' [Moi maistresse et vous chambriere, *PVH1* 1706], according to Grace Dieu, who reduces Nature to her 'tool or instrument' ['oustil ou instrument', 1796]. By implicating her in a debate she can never win, Deguileville thus highlights the helplessness of an emancipated 'terrestrial' philosophy, and her need to be subordinated to, and integrated within, the higher aims and methods of a 'celestial' theology.[45]

Deguileville's ironic and condescending treatment of 'Maistresse Nature' is clearly not, however, an outright dismissal of the dialectical method. On the contrary, Nature's passionate, angry investment in the debate becomes an extreme example of *disputatio* spinning out of control. With the appearance of the figure of Aristotle in the poem, Deguileville's anxiety about the arts of debate becomes more focused, allowing him to articulate his own understanding of what he considers to be the legitimate remit and purpose of dialectic.[46] As well as being 'Nature's clerk' (*PVH1* 2918–20)—and thus an advocate for Aristotelian natural science[47]—Aristotle also becomes a defender of the dialectical method, which leads to a wider debate about its fundamental principles, purpose, and limitations. Significantly, Aristotle too adopts the persona of disputant on entering the poem, and begins his speech by accusing Sapience of fallacious reasoning, and points out that he, unlike Sapience, does not use 'argumens' (*PVH1* 2936) like a 'sophiste' (*PVH1* 2942). Sapience pointedly rejects all accusations of 'Sophistical reasoning, fraud and deception, caused by a lack of discretion/discernment' [sophisterie, / De fraude et de deception / Par faute de discretion, *PVH1* 3076–8], and then turns the argument around by claiming ownership of the art of dialectic. Instead of simply dismissing Aristotle's insistence on the importance of sound 'argumens', then, Sapience sets out to redefine the nature of argumentation. In the process she redefines the nature of the art of dialectic as a whole, transforming it to serve the higher aims of theology. Sapience explains how she instituted two schools at the behest of Grace Dieu. In the first she trained Nature to produce natural forms, while in the second she taught her daughter Science the art of reasoning and dialectic:

---

nostra: zum Verhältnis von philosophischer und theologischer Weisheit in den Pariser Debatten am Ende des 13. Jahrhunderts', in Aertsen, Emery and Speer, eds, *Nach der Verurteilung*, pp. 249–75, along with other contributions in the same volume. This does not, however, diminish the intensity with which this threat may have been *perceived* by some of the more conservative theologians at the time.

[44] Piché, *La condamnation*, pp. 183–225.

[45] For the complexity of the representation of Nature and natural philosophy in the poem, see however Robertson, *Nature Speaks*, pp. 177–222.

[46] For important previous discussions of Aristotle in *PVH*, see also the items listed above, n. 32.

[47] On the history of the motif, see especially John Monfasani, 'Aristotle as the Scribe of Nature: The Title-Page of ms Vat. Lat. 2094', *Journal of the Warburg and Courtauld Institutes* 69 (2006), 193–205.

'En l'autre escolle j'enseignoie	'In the other school, I instructed the
L'entendement et l'enfourmoie,	understanding and taught it how to
A arguer et desputer	argue and dispute, to judge and
Et a jugier et discerner	distinguish between good and evil ...
Entre le bon et le mauves	
[...]	
Et la estait ma sage fille	Science, my wise and clever daughter,
Science qui est si soutille,	and she held discussions and
Qui i tenoit les parlemens,	formalised arguments.'
Et s'i fourmoit les argumens.'	
(*PVH1* 3011–22)	

It is in this second school that Aristotle too becomes a fellow student, drawn in by his love for Science. As Sapience explains, however, she also withheld some of her secrets from her 'apprentice' Aristotle [aprentis, *PVH1* 3028, 3067–71]. Suddenly Aristotle himself appears as a flawed practitioner of the 'Aristotelian' dialectic method, suitor to Science, daughter of Sapience. Dialectic is no longer an 'Aristotelian' science under the aegis of Aristotle, but literally a 'sapiential' science founded by Sapience herself. Since Sapience now claims ownership and control over the science of dialectic, she also sets out to redefine its prerogatives and objectives, recuperating it for strongly theological and soteriological ends.

Sapience's appropriation of the art of dialectic is rhetorically effective, but also produces a rather peculiar brand of dialectic that many Aristotelians would have trouble recognizing. Notably, it allows Sapience to state that the real presence in the Eucharist must be 'firmly believed, without speculating about it' [crëu fermement / Sans faire en adevinement, *PVH1* 3117–18], demanding a leap of faith that leaves next to no room for dialectical argumentation of any kind. A similarly dubious logic appears to govern also the earlier exchange between Nature and Grace Dieu. Here Aristotle is invoked by Grace Dieu to support her claims for unfettered divine power, above and beyond the ordinary laws of sublunary nature:

'Aristote qui fu paiens,	'Aristotle who was a pagan, who knew
Qui verite par argumens	the truth through argumentation, I
Bien connut, fas mon advocat	make my advocate against you in this
Encontre vous dans ce debat.	debate. He says, and he proves by
Il dit et preuve par raison	reason, that generation is caused by
Que faite est generation	my sun, of which I have spoken.'
Par mon soleil dont j'ai parle.'	
(*PVH1* 1757–63)	

The Aristotelian attribution is of course correct—presumably alluding to Aristotle's idea of generation through the sun (cf. e.g. Aristotle, *Physics* II.2, 194b13)—but it is rather more difficult to see how exactly this idea supports Grace Dieu's case. In

138 MEDIEVAL ALLEGORY AS EPISTEMOLOGY

particular, it seems rather disingenuous to present Aristotle's theory of generation through the sun as an *argumens* with any real 'argumentative' or dialectical force—let alone a claim with 'demonstrative' value, as is suggested by the use of the verb 'preuve' (*PVH1* 1761). Unsurprisingly, then, Grace does little more than elaborating a loosely Neoplatonic analogy: just as the sun exists in a sphere far beyond the sublunary world, and yet determines the ability of the natural world to generate life, Grace Dieu claims, so the operation of Lady Nature is directly dependent on, and determined by, the transcendent and celestial authority of Grace Dieu herself. While this is certainly an evocative analogy, it is hardly an accurate representation of Aristotle's *argumens*, in the *Physics* or anywhere else. Grace's *determinatio* is therefore highly dubious by the standards of dialectic, however defined, and smacks of playground antics rather than the schoolroom:

'Et pour ce, se l'avoie oste,	'And therefore, if I had removed it
Vostre pouoir vous perdrïez	[i.e. the sun], you would lose your
Et rien faire ne pourrïes.'	power and could do nothing about it.'
(*PVH1* 1764–6)	[translation mine]

Despite the adoption of the language of Aristotelian dialectic to present them, the effect of the various *argumens* brought into play by Sapience and Grace Dieu is largely rhetorical, and the arguments themselves do not stand up to close scrutiny. For all of Sapience's and Grace Dieu's assertiveness, then, Deguileville's attempt to recuperate dialectic for sapiential purposes rests on shaky foundations.

The debate on transubstantiation continues in a similar vein, as Aristotle's request for clarifications is met with similar rhetorical evasions and sleights of hand. Perplexed by the doctrine of the real presence, Aristotle asks Sapience to clarify how exactly the body of Christ might be contained within the sacrament:

'Entendez vous que locaument,	'How exactly are these things enclosed
Vertuaument ou autrement	in the place you have named? Do you
Soient mises celles choses	mean this *localiter*, *virtualiter* or
Es lieus qu'avez dit et encloses [?]'	otherwise?'[48]
(*PVH1* 3221–4)	[translation mine]

Sapience's use of these same terms in her response clearly lends her reply a veneer of scholastic authority, but again the substance of her argument points in a very different direction. Indeed, her reply ultimately amounts to a rejection of these

---

[48] Here and in the quotation that follows my use of Latin terms to translate the French follows Lydgate, in order to stress the learned, academic resonance of such terms. As Kamath observes, Lydgate's translation 'increases the resemblance of the debate to medieval scholastic exchanges'; see Kamath, 'Rewriting Ancient *Auctores*'. Lydgate translates *PVH2*, but the passage is largely identical in *PVH1*. For the corresponding lines, see *PVH2* 3377–408, and *The Pilgrimage of the Life of* Man, 6013–60.

scholastic terms of reference altogether, reaffirming the orthodox position in ways that sound dogmatic and doctrinaire rather than persuasive:

'... dedens ce pain
Est vraiement mis le bien souvrain,
Non pas voir imaginaument,
Non representativement,
Non vertuablement sans plus,
Ainsi i est mis et contenus
Corporelment et reaument,
Presentement et vraiement,'
   (*PVH1* 3243–50)

'In this bread is truly placed the sovereign good, neither *ymaginativae*, nor *representativae*, nor *virtualiter*, but *corporaliter* and *realiter*, *presencialiter* and also *veraciter*.'
[translation mine]

Once more the use of scholastic terminology, rendered even more conspicuous in the Lydgate translation, amounts to a purely rhetorical move. It is merely intended to persuade us, along with Aristotle, that Sapience really masters the techniques of dialectical reasoning and disputation employed in the medieval University.

Deguileville's attempt to recuperate and redefine the art of dialectic to serve his own sapiential ends in *PVH1* therefore produces mixed results at best. The extended dispute over Eucharistic matters is clearly intended to present Sapience as a genuinely proficient practitioner, and indeed founder of the art of dialectic. For an attentive reader, however, the effect is almost bound to be the reverse. If anything, the scene exposes Sapience's inability to engage Aristotle on his own terms, making her attempt to dress up Christian dogma in the rhetorical garb of dialectical reasoning appear rather fraudulent and defensive. Aristotle accordingly leaves the scene—and exits the poem—more exasperated than persuaded, observing that debate under such conditions is impossible:

'j'apercoif bien
Qu'a vous je ne gaignerai rien.
Miex vaut assez moi en aler
Que contre vous plus arguer.'
   (*PVH1* 3295–8)

'I see clearly that I will win nothing against you. It is much better for me to go away than to argue with you any longer.'

On closer scrutiny, then, it becomes clear that the problem posed by Aristotle has been not so much solved as pushed aside. For attentive readers this stratagem only strengthens the sense of Deguileville's pervasive discomfort with the practice of academic *disputatio* as well as Aristotelian natural science.

It is nonetheless remarkable that the poet—a Cistercian with an evident contemplative and sapiential bias—should even *attempt* to recuperate dialectic instead of dismissing or ignoring advanced scholastic methods altogether. Also, the attempt is all the more arresting for being tentative, defensive, and largely rhetorical. So, although the many debates in the poem unmistakeably employ the form and terminology of scholastic *disputationes*, these encounters are primarily designed to

140 MEDIEVAL ALLEGORY AS EPISTEMOLOGY

validate and buttress positions of authority that are already given, and not to conduct a genuinely dialectical and heuristic inquiry into the issues raised. The objections of Nature, Raison, and Aristotle are not so much countered but brushed aside by the forceful, dismissive, and often patronizing interventions of Grace Dieu and Sapience.[49] The often unsophisticated arguments and defensive attitude deployed by his authority figures suggest that Deguileville himself realized that his own strategy was only partially successful. Deguileville appears caught in a paradox: on the one hand he rejects, and even ridicules the possibility of proving doctrinal truths by argument in the manner of the scholastics; on the other he tries to appropriate dialectic methods to do precisely that, with the aim of legitimizing the monologic discourse of his authority figures through proof and argument. This produces what are ultimately inconclusive, abortive, and at times counterproductive *disputationes*: some of the poem's most fundamental certitudes suddenly appear 'debatable', being subjected to extended, increasingly meandering, and ultimately ineffectual demonstrations, objections, and counterarguments. Deguileville's confidence in his own strategy and in the larger aims of his poem thus appears fragile and tentative at best, leading to a gradual turn away from advanced intellectual speculation in his late poetry (see Chapter 4).

3. Learning to Read

As well as providing an induction into the arts of reasoning and disputation, *PVH1* also aims to initiate the reader into a system of allegorical interpretation. In some sense it could be said that the poem is a kind of *primer* for allegorical reading in narrative form, building up its readers' interpretive skills as they follow the account of the pilgrim's quest. In what precedes I have suggested that the central reason behind Deguileville's ambivalent attitude towards Jean de Meun's allegory was the dialectical slipperiness of the *Rose*, specifically its interrogative and relativistic hermeneutics, and its deliberate evasiveness concerning its own 'diffinitive santance'. In response to the *Rose*, Deguileville produces an allegory that attempts to become hermeneutically stable, with the ultimate aim of rehabilitating the sapiential and salvific potential of the allegorical mode more widely. In this respect, the choice of the pilgrimage narrative as a framing motif is doubly meaningful, figuring a rectilinear and teleological forward movement: on the one hand the poem is presented as the experiential account of the *viator*'s journey towards the Heavenly City, momentarily glimpsed by the dreamer in the poem's opening vision (*PVH1* 35–42); on the other, however, this journey in turn figures an interpretive and

---

[49] Parts of my argument have been inspired by Nicolette Zeeman's considerations on Deguileville in a paper on 'Debate and its Contradictions', given at the Medieval English Seminar in Oxford on 22 May 2013, now published as part of *Arts of Disruption*, pp. 144–53. I would like to thank Prof. Zeeman warmly for generously sharing her original typescript and for stimulating subsequent conversation.

LANGUAGE 141

cognitive development whose final referent is again the Heavenly City. The entire poem is therefore postulated on a broad homology between the pilgrim's 'I' and the reader's own subjectivity, engaged in an interpretive quest that parallels that of the dreamer/protagonist.

The notion of a 'hermeneutic pilgrimage' draws its appeal from a wide range of well-established traditional ideas, such as the idea of language itself as a 'reading road', developed by early grammarians and etymologists. The idea is already present in Priscian's definition of the individual letter as a 'leg-iter-a', etymologically speaking a 'reading-road', because 'it provides a path for reading' (*Institutiones grammaticae*, I. 'De litera')—a notion that achieves still wider circulation thanks to Isidore's discussion in the *Etymologiae* (I.3.3).[50] An equally influential but more elaborate development of this notion of reading-as-pilgrimage is found in the thought of Augustine: pilgrimage is employed to visualize the journey of the human soul towards its original heavenly home or *patria*, variously understood as pertaining to the history of the individual (as in the *Confessions*) or to the history of the Church (as in the *City of God*).[51] It is, however, in the massively influential *De doctrina christiana* that we find Augustine's clearest articulation of the notion of a 'pilgrimage of reading', understood as a hermeneutic, cognitive, and ethical process that produces a higher form of self-awareness and self-understanding. In Brian Stock's words, in the *De doctrina* Augustine elaborated the fundamental notion that 'reading [. . .] lies at the root of our ability to acquire salvific knowledge'.[52] The *De doctrina* is itself imagined as a book traversed by the pilgrim-reader, and functions as an induction into scriptural hermeneutics, an experience that in turn enables the reader to engage in a process of self-discovery. The stakes of correct interpretation are therefore essentially ethical: 'change in the person is [. . .] brought about by an elimination of ambiguity in what one reads'.[53] Linguistic, more strictly grammatical and rhetorical education thus serves as a preparation for a discovery of the self, or rather its 'recovery': since the prelapsarian self is defined as being made in the image of God, the journey is conceived as a restorative experience, as a recovery of the divine resemblance of the human

[50] See example and discussion given in Copeland and Sluiter, eds, *Medieval Grammar and Rhetoric*, pp. 19, 173, 235.

[51] Kuntz, 'From *Homo Erro* to *Homo Viator*'; Robert J. O'Connell, *St Augustine's Confessions: The Odyssey of Soul* (Cambridge, MA: Harvard University Press, 1969); M. A. Claussen, '*Peregrinatio* and *Peregrini* in Augustine's *City of God*', *Traditio* 46 (1991), 33–75.

[52] Brian Stock, *Augustine the Reader: Meditation, Self-Knowledge, and the Ethics of Interpretation* (Cambridge, MA: Belknap Press, 1996), p. 197. For a more sustained development of the points made here about *De doctrina*, see ibid, pp. 7–9; 190–206.

[53] Stock, *Augustine the Reader*, p. 204. For Augustine's awareness of the limitations of his own allegorical hermeneutics, and the impossibility of definitively overcoming the ambiguity and obscurity of scripture—an experience that is itself understood as a mark of human finitude—see John D. Dawson, 'Sign Theory, Allegorical Reading, and the Motions of the Soul in *De doctrina christiana*', in Duane W. H. Arnold and Pamela Bright, eds, *De doctrina christiana: A Classic of Western Culture* (Notre Dame: University of Notre Dame Press, 1995), pp. 123–41 (131–5).

142   MEDIEVAL ALLEGORY AS EPISTEMOLOGY

soul obscured by the Fall. This process is enabled by appropriate allegorical interpretation of scripture—a foundational and recurrent idea in Augustine's thought,
variously developed not only in the *De doctrina*, but also by the *De trinitate* and
the *Confessions*.[54]

The *De doctrina* in many ways serves as a touchstone text for *PVH1*, and Augustine's larger aim of expounding a systematic theory of signs, signification, and
interpretation underpins the poem as a whole.[55] Seen from this Augustinian angle,
Deguileville's poem functions as a pilgrimage used to figure another pilgrimage—
or as an allegory of allegorical reading.[56] It provides a double initiation into
scriptural exegesis and allegorical hermeneutics, but does so obliquely, through
the narrative of the author's own dreamed experience of pilgrimage. This notion
of an underlying analogy between the act of reading and the return of the human
viator to the Heavenly City had achieved wide currency by the time Deguileville
sat down to write *PVH1*. It occurs, for instance, in condensed form in Gregory's
Moralia: 'we are not led to the eternal world at once, but by a progression of cases
and of words as though by so many steps' (*Moralia*, II.20.35).[57] Hugh of St. Victor's
Didascalicon, in turn deeply influenced by Augustine's *De doctrina*, develops the
motif with systematic reference to the usefulness of the liberal arts, understood as
enabling an orderly and systematic progression towards the restoration of man's
original divine likeness:

> This, then, is what the arts are concerned with, this is what they intend, namely,
> to restore within us the divine likeness. (*Didascalicon*, 2.1)[58]

---

[54] This is the central contention of Stock's *Augustine the Reader*. On reading/writing and interiority
in Augustine, see further also Colish, *The Mirror of Language*, pp. 1–54; John Fyler, 'St. Augustine, Genesis, and the Origin of Language', in Edward B. King and Jacqueline T. Schaefer, eds, *Saint Augustine
and His Influence in the Middle Ages* (Sewanee: Press of the University of the South, 1988), pp. 69–78;
Eric Jager, *The Tempter's Voice: Language and the Fall in Medieval Literature* (Ithaca: Cornell University Press, 1996), pp. 51–98; ibid., 'The Book of the Heart: Reading and Writing the Medieval Subject',
Speculum 71.1 (1996), 1–26; Eugene Vance, *Marvelous Signals*, pp. 34–50.

[55] For a reading of *PVH* that emphasizes its 'Augustinian epistemology', see also Sarah Kay's chapter
on Deguileville in *The Place of Thought*, pp. 70–94. On Augustine's sign theory in the *De doctrina*, see
B. Darrell Jackson, 'The Theory of Signs in St. Augustine's *De doctrina christiana*', in *Revue des Études
Augustiniennes* 15 (1969), 9–49.

[56] This idea also underpins Deguileville's *Dit* (or *Roman*) *de la fleur de lys*, which has equally been
referred to as 'an allegory of allegorical writing', for which see Pomel, *Les voies*, pp. 506–8, and *Dit de
la fleur de lys*, ed. Duval, pp. 81–8. See also the second part of my discussion of Deguileville's semiotics
in Chapter 4.4.

[57] 'Quia igitur non repente sed causarum uerborum que incrementis, quasi quibusdam ad aeterni-
tatem passibus ducimur, intus apud eum quadam die aliquid factum dicitur, qui ipsa quoque tempora
sine tempore contuetur.' *Moralia in Iob*, ed. M. Adriaen, 3 vols. CCSL 143, 143A, 143B (Turnhout:
Brepols, 1979), I:81. Translation from Gregory the Great, *Morals on the Book of Job by St Gregory the
Great, Translated with Notes and Indeces*, trans. James Bliss, 3 vols (Oxford and London: John Henry
Parker and J. G. F. and J. Rivington, 1844).

[58] 'hoc ergo omnes artes agunt, hoc intendunt, ut divina similitudo in nobis reparetur', in Hugh of
St. Victor. *Hugonis de Sancto Victore Didascalicon De Studio Legendi*, ed. Charles H. Buttimer (Washington DC: Catholic University Press, 1939). Translation from Hugh of St. Victor, *The 'Didascalicon' of*

LANGUAGE   143

For these, one might say, constitute the best instruments, the best rudiments, by which the way is prepared for the mind's complete knowledge of philosophic truth. Therefore they are called by the name *trivium* and *quadrivium*, because by them, as by certain 'ways' (*viae*), a quick mind enters into the secret places of wisdom. (*Didascalicon*, 3.3)[59]

The adventures of the pilgrim in the first half of PVH are designed to outline exactly such a progression, providing a set of preparatory steps exploring the nature of human language and interpretation within an explicitly soteriological perspective.

I shall return to the *De doctrina* later in this section, to tease out some of the deep and important parallels between Deguileville's and Augustine's pedagogical projects. But I want to begin this discussion by turning to the poem itself, and more specifically the paradigmatic encounter between the Pilgrim and the character Rude Entendement ('Untrained Understanding'). Rude Entendement is the first character met by the pilgrim after he finally sets out on his journey, following his preparatory conversations with Grace Dieu, Sapience, Nature, and Raison, discussed in the preceding section (Chapter 2.2). It is therefore particularly appropriate that Rude Entendement should personify the fundamental resistance against any kind of allegorical interpretation. The churl is described as

Un grant villain mal faconne,	A big misshapen churl, husky and
Ensourcillie et reboule,	scowling. He was carrying a club of
Qui un baston de cornoullier	cornel-wood and he seemed to be a
Portoit et bien mal pautonnier	very nasty rogue and a bad pilgrim.
Sembloit estre et mal pelerin,	
Ai encontre en mon chemin.	
(*PVH1* 5095–6000)	

A number of critics have already provided perceptive discussions of this figure and his wider significance in the poem,[60] and in what follows I build on such earlier

---

Hugh of St. Victor: a Medieval Guide to the Arts, trans. Jerome Taylor (New York: Columbia University Press, 1961).

[59] 'sunt enim quasi optima quedam instrumenta et rudimenta quibus uia paratur animo ad plenam philosophice ueritatis notitiam. hinc triuium et quadriuium nomen accepit, eo quod his, quasi quibusdam uiis, uiuax animus ad secreta sophie introeat.' For a fuller discussion of the impact of *De doctrina* on the Victorines, see especially Margaret T. Gibson, 'The *De doctrina christiana* in the School of St. Victor', Grover A. Zinn, 'The Influence of *De doctrina christiana* on the Writings of Hugh of St. Victor'; and Eileen C. Sweeney, 'Hugh of St. Victor: The Augustinian Tradition of Sacred and Secular Reading Revised'; all in Edward D. English, ed., *Reading and Wisdom: The 'De Doctrina Christiana' of Augustine in the Middle Ages* (Notre Dame: University of Notre Dame Press, 1995), pp. 41–7, 48–60, 61–84 respectively. See particularly Gibson, pp. 42–3 on the importance on the pilgrimage metaphor as figure of an educational process.

[60] See Fabienne Pomel, 'L'épisode de Rude Entendement: Mots et choses, bons et mauvais lecteurs, du *Roman de la Rose* au *Pèlerinage de Vie humaine* et d'une version l'autre', in Kablitz and Peters, pp. 265–86; Kamath, *Allegory and Authorship*, pp. 40–5; Maupeu, *Pèlerins de vie humaine*, pp. 132–5;

144 MEDIEVAL ALLEGORY AS EPISTEMOLOGY

readings to tease out the resonances of this episode with contemporary scholastic discussions of semantics and linguistic reference, earlier analyses of scriptural non-contradiction, and with Augustine's larger theory of signs and interpretation.

On a primary level, Rude Entendement is essentially a personification of narrow literalism. It is therefore perfectly fitting that Rude Entendement should block the pilgrim's path, impeding, as it were, the forward movement of his interpretive quest. Significantly, too, it is by means of a *baston* (club), called 'Obstination' (5240) that the churl blocks the pilgrim's path. A crude and primitive item, this 'baston' is the perfect counterexample to the 'bourdon' carried by the pilgrim, which I discuss more fully below. Instead of denoting the articulated symbolic movement of interpretation like the pilgrim staff, the 'baston' is an inert material object that represents the impossibility of figural hermeneutics. This also explains its association with Jewish Old Testament literalism:

Ce baston si est anemis	This club is an enemy to those she
A ceus que veut avoir amis.	[i.e. 'Grace Dieu'] wants to have as
Se il ne fust, a li venissent	friends. If it did not exist, the Jews
Les Juis et se convertissent,	would come to her and convert, all
Touz herites si laisassent	heretics would mend their errors and
Leurs erreurs et s'amendassent.	leave their ways.
(*PVH1* 5599–604)	

The club of Obstinacy represents the refusal of an adequate figural reading of the New Testament, and thus precludes any act of conversion. By association, it also represents the negation of the interpretive and salvific possibilities associated with the pilgrim/reader's forward movement through Deguileville's own text. Augustine too elaborates this analogy between Jewish literalism and the resistance to conversion in the *De doctrina*, following on immediately from his observations on the 'spiritual slavery' of carnal misreading:

Emily Steiner, *Documentary Culture and the Making of Medieval English Literature* (Cambridge: Cambridge University Press, 2006), pp. 36–46; Huot, *The Romance of the Rose and its Medieval Readers*, pp. 218–20; Wright, 'Contrepartie édifiante', 411–13; Tuve, *Allegorical Imagery*, pp. 190–2. I remain unconvinced, however, by the suggestion that the encounter with Rude Entendement ought to be read with reference to the rise of 'nominalism' or 'Ockhamism', as suggested for instance by Pomel, 'L'épisode de Rude Entendement', and Duval, 'Introduction' to Guillaume de Deguileville, *Le Dit de la fleur de lys*, p. 82. Quite apart from nuances of textual interpretation, difficulties with chronology make the possibility of direct influence seem very unlikely, as the Ockhamist controversy only developed in the later 1330s, and primarily concerned Ockham's physics, notably his reduction of Aristotle's categories in number from ten to two (substance and quality), and not his logic or theology; see further Courtenay, *Ockham and Ockhamism*, esp. pp. 100–3, 127–43. While Ockham assigned a central place to improper signification—a move reminiscent of Bacon's suggestions about the equivocal nature of all language (see Chapter 1.3)—this was not the object of the famous 1340 condemnation, which concerned Ockham's excessively rigid application of supposition theory that denied the validity of authoritative statements that were untrue on the literal level (*de virtute sermonis*, or in terms of their *suppositio propria*). For further discussion, see William J. Courtenay, 'Force of Words and Figures of Speech: The Crisis over *virtus sermonis* in the Fourteenth Century', in ibid., *Ockham and Ockhamism: Studies in the Dissemination and Impact of his Thought*. Leiden: Brill, 2008, pp. 209–28.

LANGUAGE 145

But the form this slavery took in the Jewish people was very different [. . .]. [t]hey observed the signs of spiritual things in place of the things themselves. (*De doctrina* III.6; cf. also ibid. III.7–8)[61]

Rude Entendement's club of Obstinacy thus becomes a symbol for the carnal misreading of the scriptural text, figuring the spiritual inertia of those who refuse to set out on the hermeneutic and transformative journey from the 'signs of spiritual things' towards 'the things themselves'. Significantly, Augustine's *De doctrina* also identifies obstinate literalism as the first major obstacle on a reader's path towards accurate interpretation:

'the letter kills and the spirit gives life' [2 Cor. 3:6] For when something meant figuratively is interpreted as if it were meant literally, it is understood in a carnal way (*carnaliter*) [. . .]. It is, then, a miserable kind of spiritual slavery to interpret signs as things, and to be incapable of raising the mind's eye above the physical creation so as to absorb the divine light. (*De doctrina* III.5)[62]

The debate between Rude Entendement and the Pilgrim assisted by Raison explores these ideas in further detail. Rude Entendement's objection to the pilgrim's journey, it turns out, is itself based on a literalistic misreading of scripture. Rude Entendement mistakes Christ's words from the Gospel for a legalistic royal injunction:

'Et pour quoi es et tex et quiex	'How come you dare to break the law
Quë oses la loi trespasser	the king has chosen to establish? The
Qu'a voulu le roi ordener?	king long ago forbade anyone to take
Piec'a le roi deffense fist	a scrip and to carry it with him or to
Que nul escherpe ne prëist,	use a staff.'
Que nul o soi ne la portast	
Et que bourdon ne maniast.'	
(*PVH1* 5122–8)	

As becomes clear from the subsequent discussion (5407–516), the 'law' evoked by Rude Entendement alludes to the Gospel of Luke 9:3, where Christ commands the apostles to 'take nothing for the journey, neither staff, nor haversack, nor bread

---

[61] 'quae tamen seruitus in iudaeo populo longe a ceterarum gentium more distabat, quandoquidem rebus temporalibus ita subiugati erant, ut unus eis in omnibus commendaretur deus. et quamquam signa rerum spiritalium pro ipsis rebus obseruarent nescientes, quo referrentur, id tamen insitum habebant, quod tali seruitute uni omnium, quem non uidebant, placerent deo.' For a discussion of the 'carnal' tendencies within man in terms of the duality of masculine vs. feminine, bodily vs. spiritual, see also *De trinitate* XII.12.17.

[62] 'et ad hoc enim pertinet, quod ait apostolus: littera occidit, spiritus autem uiuificat. cum enim figurate dictum sic accipitur, tamquam proprie dictum sit, carnaliter sapitur. [. . .] ea demum est miserabilis animi seruitus, signa pro rebus accipere; et supra creaturam corpoream, oculum mentis ad hauriendum aeternum lumen leuare non posse.'

146   MEDIEVAL ALLEGORY AS EPISTEMOLOGY

nor money', which Rude Entendement interprets as an injunction forbidding the practice of pilgrimage.

Raison now retorts that even scriptural injunctions—in this case the prohibition of carrying the pilgrim's attributes of scrip and staff (Luke 9:3)—are not necessarily absolute and unconditional, but must be contextualized (cf. also *De doctrina* III.3): depending on the context, Raison explains, the authority of an injunction can be reiterated, maintained, modified, suspended, or displaced (5527–32). And indeed, as Raison observes, in Luke's gospel, 'This prohibition was completely turned around and reversed long ago.' [Celle deffense fu piec'a / Autrement toute tournee / Et au contraire (re)muee, *PVH1* 5420–2], since Christ later invites his disciples to set out on a pilgrimage with the previously proscribed attributes (cf. Luke 22:35–7):

'Escherpe vous ara mestier   'You will need a scrip as well as a staff
Et bourdon pour vous apuier.   to lean on. You must be pilgrims once
Pelerins vous faurra restre   more and set out on the road again.'
Et a la voie vous remetre.'
  (*PVH1* 5493–6)

Rude Entendement predictably rejects Rasion's arguments: she accuses Raison herself of behaving like a like a trickster and sophist, denying the authority of scripture and conjuring up fabulous, unfounded interpretations (*PVH1* 5519–20; 5543–54). Rude Entendement's accusation echoes conventional stereotypes of Jewish objections to New Testament hermeneutics. In Gilbert Crispin's *Disputatio Iudei et Christiani*, for instance, the Jewish disputant attacks Christian exegetical practice in almost identical terms: 'You do violence to Scripture, twisting it.'[63] The issue of apparent contradictions in the scriptural text was indeed a major subject of debate among Christian exegetes: how was it possible to reconcile what appear to be mutually contradictory statements in the scriptural text, in this case two diametrically opposite injunctions in the Gospel of Luke?[64] The analysis and resolution of scriptural contradiction attains its most sophisticated development in the twelfth century with authors like Zachary of Besançon and especially Peter the Chanter, who employed advanced grammatical and logical terminology to elaborate the exegetical principle of non-contradiction. This exegetical tradition and ideas may well have influenced Deguileville: the monastic library at

---

[63] Gilbert Crispin, *Disputatio Iudei et Christiani*, ed. Bernhard Blumenkranz (Utrecht and Antwerp: Spectrum, 1956), p. 51, 1–2. Quoted and discussed in Evans, *The Language and Logic of the Bible*, I:25.

[64] On the issue more broadly, see especially Ineke Van't Spijker, ed., *The Multiple Meaning of Scripture: the Role of Exegesis in Early Christian and Medieval Culture* (Leiden: Brill, 2008), esp. pp. 155–330. On the broader impact of theories of non-contradiction on medieval intellectual culture beyond strictly scriptural exegesis, see especially Catherine Brown, *Contrary Things: Exegesis, Dialectic, and the Poetics of Didacticism* (Stanford: Stanford University Press, 1998), particularly pp. 15–35 on the exegetical background.

LANGUAGE 147

Chaalis contained a copy of Zachary's *Super unum ex quatuor*,[65] and Peter the Chanter ended his days as a fellow Cistercian at Longpont.[66] At least two of the manuscript of the *De tropis loquendi*—his most important work in this respect—are of Cistercian provenance.[67] Both authors emphasized that consideration of the immediate scriptural context was paramount in guiding exegesis, and made abundant use of the 'mantra' of scriptural non-contradiction: *diversa sed non adversa*.[68]

The principle is echoed in Raison's defence of the 'variety' of scriptural interpretation:

'Non fait, dist Raison, quar drois est	'Not so', said Reason, 'for it is right to
Le temps savoir qui passe est,	know about the past, how they acted,
Comment on fist, comment on dist,	how they spoke, why this was so,
Pour quoi ce fu, quel cause i gist,	what was the cause of that, why there
Pour quoi i ot mutations	were changes in what was done and
De fais et de narrations;	in the narratives. The Gospel is not
Et pour ce n'est pas reprouvee	false or refuted for that, but it is more
L'Euvangile ne faussee,	elegant and pleasing to those of good
Ains en est aus bien entendans	understanding. The more varied the
Plus gracieuse et plus plaisans.	flowers in the field, the more elegant
Plus a u pre diverses fleurs,	it is, and the more diverse their
Plus gracieus en est li liex,	shapes the more gladly one looks
Et plus diverse est leur facon,	upon them.'
Plus volentiers les regarde on.'	

(*PVH1* 5526–40; my emphasis)

Even if Raison's explanation does not match the technical sophistication of anything found in Peter the Chanter's *De tropis loquendi*, she clearly engages with this tradition, combining it with the exegetical commonplace about the superabundant, inexhaustible pleasures of scriptural interpretation (e.g. Augustine, *De doctrina*, II.6).[69] Yet the florid language used here cannot avoid simultaneously evoking the *Rose*, which also represents the varied pleasures of textual interpretation and rhetorical ornamentation by using floral metaphors. Where Deguileville's

---

[65] Bondéelle-Souchier and Stirnemann, 'La bibliothèque ancienne de l'abbaye de Chaalis', p. 73.

[66] Evans, *The Language and Logic of the Bible*, I:146–7.

[67] Luisa Valente, *Phantasia contrarietatis: contraddizioni scritturali, discorso teologico e arti del linguaggio nel 'De tropis loquendi' di Pietro Cantore (1197)* (Florence: Olschki, 1997), pp. 29, 215–16.

[68] See variously Valente, *Phantasia contrarietatis*, pp. 42–6; Evans, *The Language and Logic of the Bible*, I:140–63; Gillian R. Evans, 'A Work of "Terminist Theology"? Peter the Chanter's *De Tropis Loquendi* and Some *Fallacie*', *Vivarium* 20.1 (1982), 40–58. On the history of the formula more widely, see Henri de Lubac, 'A propos de la formule: *Diversi sed non adversi*', *Recherches de Science Religieuse* 40 (1952), 27–40.

[69] See further J. Patout Burns, 'Delighting the Spirit: Augustine's Practice of Figurative Interpretation', in Arnold and Bright, *De doctrina christiana: A Classic of Western Culture*, pp. 182–94; and Jager, *The Tempter's Voice*, pp. 84–6.

148   MEDIEVAL ALLEGORY AS EPISTEMOLOGY

Raison describes the Gospel as a 'gracieus liex', a 'pre' covered in 'diverses fleurs', the God of Love in the *Rose*, dwelling in the Garden of 'Deduit', wears an ornate rhetorical mantle (*pallium, panno, vestis*)[70] entirely made of flowers:

[...] ovree de flors	It was made of flowers of various
par diversite de colors	colours. There were flowers of many
Flors i avoit de maintes guises,	different kinds, most skilfully
qui furent par grant sens asises.	arranged. No summer flower was
Nule flor en esté ne nest	absent.
qui n'i fust.	
(*RR* 883–8).	

Raison's adoption of such flowery rhetoric to describe scriptural interpretation both evokes and glosses over the *Rose*: the pleasures of scriptural exegesis have displaced the rhetorical, courtly, carnal, and ultimately narcissistic pleasures of Guillaume's garden. The pleasurable diversity of figurative rhetorical 'flowers' now represents the boundless expressive possibilities of the scriptural text and its ability to signify transcendence through textual and interpretive excess. This move suggests that such diversity might be contained within the larger master discourse of the *predicatio* that frames Deguileville's allegory as a whole, and harnessed for explicitly spiritual purposes. For Raison, it seems, polysemous diversity can ultimately be reconciled with an overarching sapiential hermeneutics that is both monologic and yet infinitely diverse[71]—echoing again Augustine's seminal discussion of different kinds of interpretive pleasure in the *De doctrina*. Here the gratuitous and adulterous pleasures of a 'carnal' reading—a form of adulterous textual fornication (esp. *De doctrina* III.5–9)—is displaced by the superabundant delights of inspired interpretation guided by the spirit. In the latter case, the familiar Augustinian opposition between 'use' and 'enjoyment' is all but annulled, since

---

[70] For an illuminating early rhetorical treatise on metaphor, the *Flores rhetorici* (*c.* 1160, possibly authored by Bernardus Silvestris), presented in terms of its ability to 'cover' direct expression under a veil/mantle of colours and flowers, see Martin Camargo, 'A Twelfth-Century Treatise on "Dictamen" and Metaphor', *Traditio* 47 (1992), 161–213.

[71] For a perceptive discussion of the openness to such excess within the monastic *lectio divina*, and a criticism of the misleading emphasis among modern scholars on a reductively 'preemptive hermeneutics' supposedly shaped by Augustine's *De doctrina* and its often misunderstood invocation of the *regula fidei*, see especially Brown, *Contrary Things*, p. 24–8, and Kay, *Place of Thought*, esp. pp. 177–85. Augustine scholars have similarly shifted away from the earlier emphasis on the supposedly restrictive systematization of interpretation, towards a better appreciation of the tolerance and delight in the multiple interpretive possibilities afforded by scripture (e.g. *De doctrina* I.36.40; III.27)—an attitude that directly influenced many later discussions of figurative language by scholastic figures such as Thomas Aquinas and Henry of Ghent, on which see Joseph Wawrykow, 'Reflections on the Place of the *De Doctrina Christiana* in High Scholastic Discussions of Theology', in English, *Reading and Wisdom*, pp. 99–125, esp. 114. For John Scotus Eriugena too, the interpretation of Scripture is boundless ('sacrae scripturae interpretatio infinitae est'; *Periphyseon* II, *PL* 122:560a), an idea again expressed in terms of the endless spectrum of colours found in the peacock's tail (*Periphyseon* IV, *PL* 122:749c).

here 'the idea of enjoying someone or something is very close to that of using someone or something together with love' (*De doctrina* I.33.20–1).[72]

The encounter with Rude Entendement marks an essential step in establishing a scriptural hermeneutics that provides the basis for Deguileville's own sapiential allegorical poetics. The exchange is thus designed to clarify the processes of reading and interpretation that underpin Deguileville's poem as a whole, and which the reader/pilgrim must begin to master. The paradigmatic nature of the episode becomes evident in the second half of the exchange, which moves on from the discussion of scriptural hermeneutics to examining the nature and identity of lady Raison herself. In focusing attention specifically on questions of naming and signification, the debate provides a template for later encounters, during which the pilgrim must learn to 'read' and identify the various personifications he encounters based on their appearance, attributes, attitude, and speech. This is particularly evident in his encounters with the personified Seven Deadly Sins, where the act of naming is specifically understood as conferring power through knowledge.[73] This ability to recognize the sins for what they are and to conceptualize their nature through language will allow the pilgrim to circumscribe, etymologically 'define', and therefore contain and control the nature of sin through language, an activity that is by definition both ethical and cognitive. Crucially, then, language here serves not only an exegetical and interpretive function in the narrow, textual sense, but also confers the kind of cognitive and ethical agency that enables both self-knowledge and the ability to decipher the outside world.

It is again the encounter with Rude Entendement that establishes the power of language as its central theme of the poem. Significantly it is Raison who comes to the pilgrim's aid in this case, and she is presented specifically in terms of her linguistic skill, as an embodiment of the power of both *ratio* and *logos*:[74]

C'ert dame Raison, la saige	It was lady Reason, the wise, who is
Que on connoist bien au langage,	easily recognised by her words. For
Quar rien ne dit que ordene	she says nothing that is not
Ne soit bien et discipline.	well-ordered and measured.
(*PVH1* 5151–4)	

---

[72] 'quamquam etiam uicinissime dicitur frui cum delectatione uti. Cum enim adest, quod diligitur, etiam delectationem se cum necesse est gerat, per quam si transieris eam que ad illud ubi permanendum est rettuleris, uteris ea et abusiue, non proprie diceris frui.' On these two competing forms of pleasure to be derived from reading, see also Jager, *The Tempter's Voice*, pp. 82–8. On the binary pair of use and enjoyment in relation to interpretation, see further discussion below, and references in preceding notes.

[73] A similar point is also made by Tuve, *Allegorical Interpretation*, pp. 174–5, 178–81; Hagen, *Allegorical Remembrance*, p. 40; Pomel, 'L'épisode de Rude Entendement', Maupeu, *Pèlerins de vie humaine*, pp. 132–5; Clasby, 'Introduction', *The Pilgrimage of Human Life*, pp. xviii–xxiii.

[74] See also Pomel, 'L'épisode de Rude Entendement'.

150 MEDIEVAL ALLEGORY AS EPISTEMOLOGY

The wording here insists on the importance of ordered and disciplined speech, preparing us for a larger discussion of the power of language, specifically the power of naming. Raison begins by asking Rude Entendement for his name (*PVH1* 5169), and the latter likewise reacts to Raison's enquiries by asking her for 'your commission, so I will know your *name* at least' [votre commission, / Si sarai au mains votre *non*, *PVH1* 5177–8; my emphasis]. Raison presents her commission, inviting the fellow to read it, 'so you will know my *name*' [si saras bien mon *non*, *PVH1* 5190; my emphasis], but it emerges that Rude Entendement is in fact illiterate, and therefore unable to establish Raison's legitimate name and identity: 'I am certainly no clerk [. . .] I know nothing about these papers of yours' [ne sui pas clers / Ne rien ne sai en vos feullez', *PVH1* 5193–4]. Raison counters his dismissive rejection of her 'feulles' with the observation that they are highly prized and authorized (*PVH1* 5199–200), and eventually invites the pilgrim himself to act as her 'clers' (*PVH1* 5205). Here again the ability to read is understood in terms of the knowledge conferred by exegetical skill: Raison asks the pilgrim to physically 'unfold' the document and metaphorically 'unpack' its significance, 'explicating' its meaning in the etymological sense [oste[r] ces letres hors de ploi, *PVH1* 5206].[75] This invitation to the pilgrim/reader to explicate the commission invests him with an active role in countering Rude Entendement's 'mendacious words' [mencongables paroles, *PVH1* 5236], and thereby positions him as an active reader of the vision/allegory/text of which he is the main protagonist. More specifically, the document pre-empts the danger represented by Rude Entendement: since he too is already *named* in the document (*PVH1* 5225–32), the pilgrim literally gains knowledge of his opponent's real nature through an act of *reading*. His ability in deciphering language therefore leads directly to his ability to decipher the outside world.

When Rude Entendement finally learns Raison's name, it emerges that not only is he illiterate, but also he does not understand the basic referential function of language, based on conventional attribution of meaning. In particular, Rude Entendement fails to accept the axiomatic principle that names are assigned according to the will (*ad placitum*) and the re-presentational relation of difference between *res* and *signum*. This reveals the churl's incapacity to grasp and resolve any problems of linguistic ambiguity based on equivocation, homophony, and homography. He therefore interprets 'raison' as meaning exclusively 'a measure (or portion, ration, from Lat. *ratio*) of wheat', associated with the proverbial trickery of millers:

---

[75] For discussion of the exegetical resonances of *explicatio* and related terms, see Brown, *Contrary Things*, p. 21; and Nikolaus M. Häring, 'Commentary and Hermeneutics', in Charles Homer Haskins, ed., *Renaissance and Renewal in the Twelfth Century* (Cambridge, MA: Harvard University Press, 1982), pp. 173–200 (174–80).

'Au moulin, dist, ou j'ai este.
La mesurez vous faussement
Et emblez le ble a la gent.'
  (*PVH1* 5278–80)

'I heard it at the mill', he said. 'You
give false measure there and steal
people's grain.'

The meaning is attested in Middle French,[76] but Raison responds by explaining how in the present case the word 'raison' is used improperly, as a means of dissimulating the real nature of the object. She therefore points to the disjunction between word (*dictio*) and thing (*res*):

'Au moulin par aventure
Avez veu une mesure
Qui raison se fait apeler
Pour sa grant desraison celer;
Mais pour ce n'est ce pas raison
Ainz est fraude et deception.
Entre non et existence
Vueil je bien faire difference.
Autre chose est estre Raison
Et autre chose avoir son non.
Du non faire couverture
Puet on pour couvrir s'ordure.'
  (*PVH1* 5285–96)

'At the mill you have perhaps seen a
measure that is called a "reason" in
order to hide its great unfairness, but
it is not therefore Reason but a fraud
and a deception. I would like very
much to distinguish between name
and existence. It is one thing to be
Reason and another thing to have
that name. People can use names as
covering to hide their filth.'

According to Raison's argument, then, only the primary signification of the term 'raison' is legitimate and acceptable, whereas its secondary meaning is considered not only deviant but dishonest. However, Rude Entendement does not understand the nature of linguistic signification as a binary relation, and assumes the identity of names and natures according to an indissoluble correspondence:

'Quant j'o nommer ou chat ou chien,
  [. . .] buef et vache ce n'est pas,
Ains est.I. chien et est.I. chas [.]
A leur nons connois bien chascun,
Quar *leur nons et eus sont tout un*,'
  (*PVH1* 5322–6; my emphasis)

'When I call something a cat or a dog
it is not an ox or a cow, but the one
thing is a cat and the other is a dog. I
know each one very well by their
names, because they and their names
are the same',

This essentialist belief in an indissoluble link between linguistic sign and its *significatum* is neither a nominalist nor a realist doctrine, but is antithetical to signification altogether as it would have been understood by medieval logicians of *any* denomination. It amounts to a denial of the conventional nature of linguistic signs, negating human agency in instituting, modifying, and extrapolating the

---

[76] *DMF*, 'raison', I.A, 1, 2, 3, at http://www.atilf.fr/dmf/definition/raison. See also Pomel, 'L'épisode de Rude Entendement'.

significance of linguistic terms. This is at odds with the most fundamental principles of medieval logic as a science, and *a fortiori* makes it impossible to envisage cases of equivocal speech and figurative or improper *translatio* of meaning—in scripture, poetry, or ordinary language.

Rather than critiquing Rude Entendement, however, Raison now turns Rude Entendement's own argument against him, by feigning to have learnt his lesson:

'Or voi je bien qu'avez	'Now I see you have had some
De l'art apris et qu'en savez.	schooling and have learnt
Soutilment savez arguer	something', said Reason, 'you know
Et biauz exemples amener.'	how to argue cleverly and how to
(*PVH1* 5339–42)	bring forward good examples.'

As Fabienne Pomel has observed, this is part of a rhetorical strategy of denigration and mockery that runs through the passage as a whole.[77] Raison too now pretends to have fully embraced Rude Entendement's essentialism:

'Quar pas apris encor n'avoie	'Since I had not yet learned that you
Que vous et Rude Entendement	and Rude Wit were one and the same.
Fuissiez tout un conjointement;	But now I see that you are doubtless
Mais or voi bien sans soupeceon	the same, without distinction.'
Qu'estes un sans distinction.'	
(*PVH1* 5370–4)	

The adoption of the mock-essentialism is comical and rhetorical, but is also intended to make an altogether more serious point: in feigning to adopt Rude Entendement's own understanding of linguistic reference, Raison effectively accepts his identity with his name, and thus reduces him to a mere *non*—a grammatical 'noun' that has no semantic content or referential function, and thus signifies only itself and no extrinsic substance. As Raison observes, she now understands that Rude Entendement is truly and properly self-identical, excluded from any referential relation, and deprived of the power of signification:

'Par vos paroles proprement	'I know by your words that you are
Sai que estes Rude Entendement	truly Rude Wit. You can no longer
Plus arguer vous ne pouez	argue that you are merely named
Que seulement ainsi nommez	that, for you are that in fact, with no
Soiez, quar par existence	distinction.'
Ce estes sans point de difference.'	
(*PVH1* 5377–8)	

The precise significance of Rude Entendement's self-referential nature again comes into focus with reference to Augustinian scriptural hermeneutics as exposed in

---

[77] Pomel, 'L'épisode de Rude Entendement'.

the *De doctrina*. While the primary objective of the *De doctrina* is to train the Christian reader in scriptural interpretation, Augustine also strives to train readers in their ability to decipher the meaning of the realm of creation, where things (*res*) act as signs (*signa*) for a higher, divinely ordained reality. Augustine defines such things that are also signs as *signa translata*, differentiating them from purely verbal, rhetorical figuration: '[Signs] are metaphorical (*translata sunt*) when the actual things we signify by particular words are used to signify something else' (*De doctrina* II.10; also *De doctrina* III.8–9 for a fuller elaboration).[78] Also in his commentaries on Genesis Augustine differentiates between 'figures of speech' and 'figures of things',[79] establishing a fundamental difference between fully symbolic and merely rhetorical figuration. The idea is elaborated by a number of later theologians—from Bede, with his influential distinction between *allegoria in factis* and *allegoria in verbis*,[80] to Hugh of St Victor (notably *Didascalicon* V.3), and even Thomas Aquinas (e.g. *ST* 1a q.1, 9–10), both of whom engage closely with the *De doctrina*.[81] As Richard of St Victor observed, 'On the sacred page not only things and the understanding signify, but things themselves signify other things.'[82]

Like all *res* of our transient existence, then, for Augustine the *res* signified by scripture must not be 'enjoyed' for their own sake, but 'used' as a means to grasp the eternal realities that are their ultimate referents (cf. *De doctrina* I.3). The fundamental duality of *res/signa* in Augustinian semiotics is therefore doubled, to some extent, in the binary pair of use vs. enjoyment (*uti/frui*), and indeed for Augustine 'use is defined as a form of decoding and interpretation'.[83] The process of self-discovery/recovery through scriptural interpretation is therefore doubled by a

[78] 'translata sunt, cum et ipsae res, quas propriis uerbis significamus, ad aliquid aliud significandum usurpantur.'

[79] Roland J. Teske, 'Criteria for Figurative Interpretation in St. Augustine', in Arnold and Bright, eds, *De doctrina christiana: A Classic of Western Culture*, pp. 109–22, here 114. See also *De Genesi contra Manichaeos*, I.22.34 and II.2.3.

[80] Armand Strubel, '*Allegoria in verbis, allegoria in factis*', *Poétique* 23 (1975), 242–57.

[81] On Hugh of St Victor's increasing interest in this idea throughout his career, see Zinn, 'The Influence of *De doctrina christiana*', in English, ed. *Reading and Wisdom*, pp. 55–6. On Aquinas, see Wawrykow, 'Reflections on the place of the *De Doctrina Christiana* in High Scholastic discussions of Theology', also in English, *Reading and Wisdom*, pp. 99–125 (esp. 106–7).

[82] 'In divina pagina non solum intellectus et res significant, sed ipsae res alias res significant', Richard of St Victor, *Speculum Ecclesiae*, *PL* 177:375, cited and discussed in Ocker, *Biblical Poetics before Humanism and Reformation*, p. 16 n. 33.

[83] For a particularly lucid and perceptive discussion of Augustinian semiotics and hermeneutics in terms of pilgrimage, and the twin binaries of *res/signa* and *uti/frui*, see Elena Lombardi, 'The Semiotic Universe of Mankind: Augustine's Theory of Things', in her *Syntax of Desire: Language and Love in Augustine, the Modistae, Dante* (Toronto: University of Toronto Press, 2007), pp. 27–37 (here 34). Lombardi also develops ideas from Rowan Williams, 'Language, Reality, and Desire in Augustine's *De Doctrina*', *Journal of Literature and Theology* 3 (1989), 138–58. On the *uti/frui* problem more widely, see Oliver O'Donovan, '*Usus* and *Fruitio* in Augustine, *De doctrina christiana* I.1', *Journal of Theological Studies* 33 (1982), 361–97. On its relationship with the pilgrimage metaphor and the risks of 'idolatrous' use of earthly goods, see Sarah Stewart-Kroeker, 'Resisting Idolatry and Instrumentalisation in Loving the Neighbour: The Significance of the Pilgrimage Motif for Augustine's *Usus–Fruitio* Distinction', *Studies in Christian Ethics* 27.2 (2014), 202–21.

154 MEDIEVAL ALLEGORY AS EPISTEMOLOGY

more important kind of hermeneutic pilgrimage, turned outward to decipher the *res* of the created world as *signa* of divine presence:

> In this mortal life we are like travellers away from our Lord [2 Cor. 5:6; cf. also *De trinitate* XII.10.15]: if we wish to return to the homeland where we can be happy we must use this world [cf. 1 Cor. 7:31], not enjoy it, in order to discern 'the invisible attributes of God, which are understood through what has been made' [Rom. 1.20], or, in other words, to derive spiritual value from corporeal and temporal things. (*De doctrina* I.4)[84]

> To enlighten us and enable us, the whole temporal dispensation was set up by divine providence for our salvation. (*De doctrina* I.35.5–6)[85]

Also in the *De trinitate* (XV.4.6), Augustine insists on the importance of determining the significance of the outward reality, and indeed of the entire created universe, itself a tissue of *res* that are also *signa* or *vestigia* of the divine:

> It is not, after all, only the authority of the divine books which asserts that God is; the universal nature of things which surround us, to which we too belong, proclaims that it has a most excellent author/founder/preserver (*conditor*).[86]

The idea comes to occupy a central place in the exegetical tradition, according to which scripture and the created world constitute two mutually illuminating books authored by God's hand.[87] The idea is prominent in the work of John Scotus Eriugena, and is developed by a number of other authors that would have fallen within the horizon of a monastic writer like Deguileville, such as the Victorines for whom the sensible world is like a book authored by the finger of

---

[84] 'quomodo ergo, si essemus peregrini, qui beate uiuere nisi in patria non possemus, ea que peregrinatione utique miseri et miseriam finire cupientes in patriam redire uellemus, opus esset uel terrestribus uel marinis uehiculis, quibus utendum esset, ut ad patriam, qua fruendum erat, peruenire ualeremus; quod si amoenitates itineris et ipsa gestatio uehiculorum nos delectaret, conuersi ad fruendum his, quibus uti debuimus, nollemus cito uiam finire et peruersa suauitate implicati alienaremur a patria, cuius suauitas faceret beatos, sic in huius mortalitatis uita peregrinantes a domino, si redire in patriam uolumus, ubi beati esse possimus, utendum est hoc mundo, non fruendum, ut inuisibilia dei per ea, quae facta sunt, intellecta conspiciantur, hoc est, ut de corporalibus temporalibus que rebus aeterna et spiritalia capiamus.'

[85] 'hoc ergo ut nossemus atque possemus, facta est tota pro nostra salute per diuinam prouidentiam dispensatio temporalis, qua debemus uti.'

[86] 'Neque enim diuinorum librorum tantummodo auctoritas esse deum praedicat, sed omnis quae nos circumstat, ad quam nos etiam pertinemus, uniuersa ipsa rerum natura proclamat habere se praestantissimum conditorem.'

[87] For a recent overview of the tradition of the 'Book of Nature', see Davis, *Piers Plowman and the Books of Nature*, esp. pp. 35–84. See also the classic accounts by Henri De Lubac, *Medieval Exegesis*, trans. Marc Sebanc and M Macierowski, 4 vols (Grand Rapids, MI / Edinburgh: Eerdmans / T&T Clark, 1998–2009), I.76–80; and Ernst Robert Curtius, *Europäische Literatur und Lateinisches Mittelalter* (Bern: Francke, 1948), pp. 321–7.

God—'quasi [. . .] liber scriptus digito Dei' (Hugh of St Victor, *Didascalicon* VII.4)—or the fellow Cistercian Alain de Lille, in his often quoted poem:[88]

Omnis mundi creatura	Every thing in the created universe is
quasi liber et pictura	like a book for us, a picture, a mirror;
nobis est in speculum;[89]	

Bonaventure too speaks of the created universe as a book (*Itinerarium mentis in deo* I.14; II.11–13), formerly self-explanatory but rendered illegible by the fall, yet restored to legibility by the Incarnation the Word made flesh.[90]

The notion of reading and interpretation as a journey or pilgrimage also shaped the discussion of figures and tropes in the various *Artes poetriae* of the thirteenth century. These discussions built on the definitions provided by late antique grammarians, who described tropes not only in terms of a 'turning' or 'twisting' of meaning (*tropus*) but also as cases of *translatio* and *transumptio*—terms that already imply the notion of a semantic 'movement' of words beyond their primary meanings. Geoffrey of Vinsauf provides a particularly striking example for the analysis of metaphorical signification in terms of a semantic 'pilgrimage'. At the beginning of the section on the rhetorical *ornatus*, he thus encourages poets to 'stray' from normal poetic use:

[. . .] Noli semper concedere verbo	Do not always allow the word to rest
In proprio residere loco; residentia talis	in its usual place; such residence
Dedecus est ipsi verbo; loca propria vitet	does not suit it; let it avoid its proper place and **wander elsewhere**, to find
Et **peregrinetur** alibi sedemque placentem	a pleasing seat in another's ground: let it be a new sojourner there and
Fundet in alterius fundo: sit ibi novus hospes, Et placeat novitate sua.	please by its novelty.
(*Poetria Nova*, 763–8, my emphasis)[91]	

As Katherine Willis has recently argued, Vinsauf's appeal to the *peregrinatio* of metaphor builds on a complex history that far exceeds the boundaries of strictly

---

[88] The reconstructed catalogue of the library at Chaalis shows that it would have contained several works by the Victorines, as well as John Scotus Eriugena's translation of the works of pseudo-Dionysius, with a commentary by Hugh of St Victor, where the analogy of the two books is developed, for which see Bondéelle-Souchier and Stirnemann, 'La bibliothèque ancienne de l'abbaye de Chaalis', p. 67. For further discussion of the impact of Dionysian materials on Deguileville, see Graham Robert Edwards, 'Making Sense of Deguileville's Autobiographical Project', in Kamath and Nievergelt, pp. 129–50 (132).

[89] Alan Of Lille, *Literary Works*, ed. Wetherbee, pp. 544–5.

[90] This too is an idea first found in Eriugena, *Expositions super Ierarchiam caelestem S. Dionysii*, PL 122:125–266 (146C). For Bonaventure, see also *in* I *Sent.* Prol. q. I, *Opera Omnia*. 10 vols (Quaracchi: Collegium S. Bonaventurae, 1882–1902), I:7. Bonaventure also develops an elaborate pilgrimage symbolism as part of his mysticism, see also William Harmless, *Mystics* (Oxford: Oxford University Press, 2008), pp. 79–105, here 93.

[91] Ernest Gallo, *The 'Poetria Nova' and its Sources in Early Rhetorical Doctrine* (The Hague / Paris: Mouton, 1971), pp. 54–5.

156 MEDIEVAL ALLEGORY AS EPISTEMOLOGY

grammatical and rhetorical teaching, drawing inspiration from the use of this motif in religious materials, particularly scriptural exegesis and biblical drama.[92] Vinsauf's idea of a spiritual and cognitive transport enabled by metaphorical understanding usefully converges with other thirteenth-century discussions of the imaginative and affective power of metaphor and the poetic imagination more widely, already discussed in the Introduction.[93] In making *peregrinatio* the master-metaphor of the entire poem, then, Deguileville signals his effort to enable the *translatio* of the pilgrim/reader's own 'I' beyond the present *regio dissimilitudinis* and towards its ultimate destination, the Heavenly Jerusalem, by means of an imaginative and cognitive transference.

While the pilgrimage metaphor that governs the entire signifying logic of the poem builds on a whole range of complex traditional resonances and well-established associations, Deguileville's decision to adopt the pilgrimage framework is also determined by more local circumstances, notably in relation to the *Roman de la Rose*, its most important single source of inspiration. The *Rose* too had employed the allegory of *peregrinatio* as a meta-figural motif in its obscene conclusion. The pilgrim/lover's arrival at the 'sanctuary' of the *Rose* figured not only a subversive mock-sexual climax, but also the *mise-en-abîme* of the reader's own frustrated quest for meaning. Both quests had converged upon the 'Rose'—an unsubstantial object that turns out to be merely another metaphor, deferring closure indefinitely and disseminating meaning into empty space (see Chapter 1.5). *PVH1*, by contrast, seeks to rehabilitate the idea that the pilgrimage of allegorical interpretation leads beyond words, towards tangible earthly *res* that are also *signa* for an ultimate, higher reality that is the ultimate destination of the 'pilgrimage of human life'. This also requires a shift of the figurative operation away from mere words (*verba*) towards the actual things (*res*) that can in turn function as signs (*signa*), following Augustine's distinction between ordinary 'figures of speech' and the 'figures of things'. Seeking to differentiate itself from what it sees as the profane, strictly rhetorical, unsubstantial, and ultimately duplicitous verbal figurations of the *Rose*, *PVH1* is accordingly filled to the brim with material objects and attributes. Such objects are in turn extensively allegorized, and provide the very stuff that Deguileville's allegories is made on: they include the pilgrim's carefully itemized Pauline armour from Ephesians (*PVH1* 3813–4778); the pilgrim staff and scrip (*PVH1* 3307–812); the carpenter's square or PAX (*PVH1* 2383–2638); the attributes and contraptions wielded by the various virtues and vices (brooms, clubs, mirrors, saws, mallets, etc.); the emblem of the lily in the later *Dit de la fleur de lys* (*DFL, c.* 1338).

---

[92] Katherine E. C. Willis, 'The Poetry of the *Poetria Nova*: The *Nubes Serena* and *Peregrinatio* of Metaphor', *Traditio* 72 (2017), 275–300.
[93] See above, pp. 10–15.

It is not accidental that two of the most conspicuous attributes of Deguileville's pilgrim should be the scrip and staff—traditional pilgrim attributes that the *Rose* had notoriously turned into figures for the male sexual organs (cf. *RR* 21324, 21618). *PVH1* designates these attributes by the same terms used in the *Rose*—'escherpe' and 'bourdon' (*PVH1* e.g. 3469)—as if to mark their recuperation as terms of 'proper' signification. Deguileville again appears to be following Augustine's lead, who warns about not only the dangers of literalism, but also the risk of interpreting literal statements figuratively (*De doctrina* III.10). Where Jean de Meun had chosen to read the 'scrip' and 'staff' as equivocal figurative *verba* denoting sexual organs, Deguileville restores these terms to their 'proper', literal valence, denoting actual pilgrim attributes. The distinction here retraces to some extent the difference between the purely linguistic *allegoria in verbis* and the truly figurative *allegoria in factis*: it is precisely because the terms 'scrip' and 'staff' once more designate real physical objects that they can, like scriptural *res*, function as *signa* for a higher spiritual reality in turn—in this case, as figures for the theological virtues of Faith and Hope. The two items are accordingly instrumental in turning the poem's dreamer into a *viator* rather than a simple exile from his heavenly home. The exposition of their significance forms a prelude to the dreamer's actual departure (at *PVH1* 5031), but also provides a conceptual underpinning for the larger master-trope of the allegorical pilgrimage. Both attributes thus function as meta-allegorical signifiers, and simultaneously illustrate the mechanisms of a distinctive type of 'sacramental' signification, as I will argue in the following section.

The meta-allegorical function of these attributes is particularly evident in the case of the pilgrim staff (*PVH1* 3433–66, 3673–748). The staff is described as carrying at its top a 'shining mirror' [mirour luisant], reflecting not only the Heavenly City, ultimate destination of his journey, but also the surrounding landscape that the pilgrim will have to traverse. The mirror on the staff is almost invariably represented in illustrated *PVH* manuscripts,[94] and becomes a crucial element in terms of the larger symbolism elaborated by Grace Dieu's description. The spotless mirror is a figure of Christ (*PVH1* 3691–3), through whom humankind can again find its way back to its heavenly home.[95] The image is rich in implications, and again mobilizes a number of influential Augustinian ideas and motifs. On the one hand, the mirror functions as a mnemonic device, reminding the pilgrim of the ultimate *telos* during his journey through the *regio dissimilitudinis* of earthly life.[96] On the other hand, the mirror also serves a deeper, cognitive function, as a token

---

[94] Tuve, *Allegorical Imagery*, pp. 192–3; Hagen, *Allegorical Remembrance*, pp. 27–8; Pomel and Legaré, 'Les miroirs du *PVH*'.

[95] Pomel and Legaré, 'Les miroirs du *PVH*', and Hagen, *Allegorical Remembrance*, pp. 7–29; Fabienne Pomel, 'Mémoire, mnémotechnique, et récit de voyage allégorique: L'exemple du *Pèlerinage de vie humaine* de Guillaume de Deguileville', in Frank Willaert, Herman Braet, Thom Mertens, and Theofiel Venckeleer, eds, *Medieval Memory: Image and Text* (Turnhout: Brepols, 2004), pp. 77–98.

[96] On the Scrip, Staff, and Carpenter's Square as mnemonic devices, see Hagen, *Allegorical Remembrance*, pp. 56–86.

158   MEDIEVAL ALLEGORY AS EPISTEMOLOGY

for the restoration of the human *viator*'s cognitive abilities through Christ's Incarnation. Finally the mirror of Christ also reflects the pilgrim's own face, alluding to the enhanced possibilities for self-knowledge brought about by the Incarnation, in turn geared towards an eventual restoration of the *viator*'s *imago dei* in a future eschatological moment.[97] This complex and articulated symbolism is essential in lending the staff its main quality, namely its ability to 'support' the pilgrim during his extended journey (e.g. *PVH1* 3681–2, 3689, 3701–2, 3730, 3746). Fittingly, the staff also carries a lower pommel symbolizing the Virgin, and this element too is part of a larger symbolism of progression, return, and restoration:

C'est Marie, virge mere	Mary, the virgin mother who
Qui concut, et porta son pere,	conceived her father. She is a shining
C'est l'escharboucle estincelant,	ruby who lights up the night of the
La nuit du monde enluminant	world. She restores to the right path
Par la quelle sont ravoies	all the lost and the wayward. She
Tous eschampes et forvoies,	enlightens all those in darkness and
Par la quelle enlumine sont	lifts up those who have stumbled and
Touz ceuz qui en tenebres sont,	fallen.
Par la quelle sont redrecies	
Les chëus jus et trebuchiez.	
(*PVH1* 3711–20)	

Symbolized by the lower pommel, the Virgin is presented as the human mediator, restoring access to an obscured *imago dei* figured by the mirror of Christ in the upper pommel of the staff. The Virgin thus perfectly illustrates what Fabienne Pomel has described as the broader 'mediating function' of such symbolic objects in the poem.[98]

As well as being loaded with a powerful incarnational symbolism, the staff also figures the operation of allegorical signification. I have already invoked the symbolism of the mirror from 1 Cor. 13:12, famously employed by Augustine to describe the workings of allegory, *per speculum in aenigmate* (*De trinitate* XV.9.15)—a notion that is clearly at work in the poem's opening vision of the Holy City in a mirror, as discussed above (*PVH1* 35–42). This whole nexus of ideas is being reactivated at this moment in the poem, echoing and refracting the initial vision to infuse its significance within the 'bourdon', always at the pilgrim's side during the journey he is finally about to begin. It is precisely thanks to Christ's Incarnation, in turn enabled by the intercessory role of the Virgin, that the *regio dissimilitudinis*, a fallen world of enigmatic signs and allegories is restored to legibility, opening the path for the journey back towards an encounter with God 'face

---

[97] On Augustine's thought on these questions, see variously Kuntz, 'Augustine: From *Homo Erro* to *Homo Viator*'; Gilson, '*Regio dissimilitudinis* de Platon à saint Bernard de Clairvaux'; Ladner, '*Homo Viator*'; and Bochet, 'Le statut de l'image'.

[98] See Pomel, *Les voies*, pp. 336–45.

to face' (1 Cor. 13:12). The idea of an interpretive journey, relying on the *translatio* from *signa* towards their ultimate, transcendent referents, is thus encoded in the very shape of the staff and in the articulation of its constituent parts.

4. Signs and Sacraments

So far I have argued that Deguileville's response to the *Rose* must be understood not only as a substitution of pious signifiers for obscene ones, but as an effort in rehabilitating an ambitious 'system' for allegorical signification and interpretation, underpinning a still larger soteriological project. Deguileville follows Augustine in trying to exorcise the two primary obstacles to the correct interpretation of figurative language, as described in Book III of the *De doctrina christiana*: the misreading of figurative signs as literal ones, and the misinterpretation of literal signs as figurative ones. In his description of Rude Entendement the poet represents the case of a literalistic misreading of figurative signifiers; in his extended description of the pilgrim's staff, by contrast, he counters the *Rose*'s figurative misreading of a real, 'literal' pilgrimage as an allegory of sexual penetration. Deguileville therefore seeks to define a distinctly Augustinian brand of sapiential poetics, inspired by scriptural exegesis as exposed in the *De doctrina*. The main allegorical signifiers in such a poetics are not the poetic *verba* and *dictiones*, but rather the *res* signified by them, which are in turn endowed with signifying ability as *res* that are also *signa translata* of transcendent, divine realities.

It is this latter signifying relation that becomes central in Deguileville's scripturally inspired allegory. To adopt the terminology of contemporary scholastic treatises on semiotics—in turn based on Augustine (esp. *De doctrina* III.9)—this special kind of signifying relation is most accurately described as 'sacramental'. Discussion of the sacraments was in effect a centrepiece of thirteenth-century semiotic treatises and commentaries as a whole, and the scholastics invariably classified the sacraments as belonging to a special sub-category of conventional signs, *signa data*.[99] While the notion is amply elaborated by Hugh of St Victor in his *De sacramentis*,[100] the *locus classicus* for the definition of sacramental signs for the scholastics is undoubtedly Book IV of Peter Lombard's *Sentences* (IV.I.6),[101] which

---

[99] On the semiotics of the sacraments in the thirteenth century, see especially Irène Rosier, 'Signes et sacrements: Thomas d'Aquin et la grammaire spéculative', *Revue des sciences philosophiques et théologiques* 74 (1990), 392–436; ibid., *La Parole comme acte*, pp. 112–22; Marmo, *La semiotica del XIII secolo*, pp. 12–28. For a full account, see Rosier, *La Parole efficace*. For an argument about the broader impact of sacramental theology, including the semiotics of the sacrament, on the vernacular culture of late medieval England, see especially Aers, *Sanctifying Signs*, especially pp. 1–52.

[100] Hugh of St Victor, *De Sacramentis Christianae fidei*, in *PL* 176:173–617; for an English translation, see *On the Sacraments of the Christian Faith (De Sacramentis)*, ed. Roy J. Deferrari (Cambridge, MA: Mediaeval Academy of America, 1951).

[101] Peter Lombard, *Sententiae in IV libris distinctae*, 2 vols (Grottaferrata: Collegium S. Bonaventurae ad Claras Aquas: 1971 and 1981), II:746.

160   MEDIEVAL ALLEGORY AS EPISTEMOLOGY

introduces the ubiquitous formula reiterated by later scholastics: 'the sacrament causes what it represents' [sacramentum id efficit quod figurat]. According to this definition, the sacramental sign differs from other, ordinary signs instituted by convention in performing not only a referential and cognitive function, but in being endowed with an *operative* function. The sacramental sign also occupies a unique place in the Augustinian semiotic system inherited by the scholastics. Augustine had first divided sings into natural and attributed signs—*signa natu-ralia* and *signa data* (*De doctrina* II.2.2). Sacraments too are *signa data*, but are defined as follows:

> The person who attends to or worships a useful sign, one divinely instituted, and does realize its force and significance, does not worship a thing which is appar-ent and transitory but rather the thing to which all such things are to be related. [...] When an individual understands these [sacramental signs, i.e. Baptism and Eucharist], he recognizes with an inner knowledge what they relate to, and con-sequently venerates them not because of any carnal slavery but because of his spiritual freedom. (*De doctrina* III.9)[102]

While sacramental signs too are based on conventional imposition (*signum datum/institutum*), they are instituted by *divine* as opposed to human authority. Their signifying power was therefore felt to be rooted in the natural *similitudo* linking the sign to the object signified (Augustine, *Epistola* 98.9; cf. *De doctrina* II.25), as noted for instance by Hugh of St Victor:

> A sign only signifies through institution. The sacrament also represents through similitude. [...] In the sacrament there is not only signification, but also efficacy.[103]

This tradition determined the evolution of thirteenth-century discussions of sacra-mental semiotics in their entirety, focused primarily on the question of the adequacy or natural affinity of sacramental signs with their objects (variously defined as *convenientia, aptitudo, competentia,* or *proportionalitas*). Sacraments were therefore often described as hybrid signs that signify both naturally and through convention:[104]

> In signs that are also sacraments two properties are required: a natural aptitude (*aptitudo*) to signify sacred objects (*rem sacram*), and the imposition carried out

---

[102] 'qui uero aut operatur aut ueneratur utile signum diuinitus institutum, cuius uim significationem que intellegit, non hoc ueneratur, quod uidetur et transit, sed illud potius, quo talia cuncta referenda sunt. [...] quae unusquisque cum percipit, quo referantur imbutus agnoscit, ut ea non carnali seruitute, sed spiritali potius libertate ueneretur.'

[103] 'Signum solum ex institutione significat; sacramentum etiam ex similitudine repraesentat. [...] In sacramento autem non sola significatio est, sed etiam efficacia.' Hugh of St Victor, *De sacramentis legis naturalis et scriptae*, PL 176:34d. My translation.

[104] For further detail, see Rosier, 'Signes et sacrements', 394–7, whose account I closely follow here.

LANGUAGE 161

by the will (*ordinatio volontaria*) to signify the latter. (William of Middleton, *Quaestiones de sacramentis*, I.iii q.15 5c)[105]

This definition of sacramental signs played a crucial role in inspiring not only Deguileville's description of the central, meta-allegorical signs/objects that abound in his poem—scrip, staff, mirror, PAX—but also provided the basis upon which he elaborated his understanding of the salvific efficacy of his allegorical poem as a whole.[106] At the same time, I also want to suggest that it is precisely this same sacramental function of signs that is most troublesome for Deguileville's overall project. As I have argued in the preceding section, his poem succeeds to some extent in exorcising or at least in addressing instances of misreading as defined by Augustine. But the poem encounters considerably greater difficulty in attempting to regulate and systematize what it considers to be instances of adequate interpretation of sacramental *res* in the created world, attempting to present them as incontrovertible *signa* for 'the invisible attributes of God, which are understood through what has been made' (Rom. 1:20), as Augustine had affirmed in *De doctrina* I.4. In particular, I want to argue that Deguileville's commitment to the polysemy of the allegorical mode ultimately makes it impossible for him to regulate mechanisms of signification in viable fashion. This paradox lies at the root of Deguileville's endless woes in seeking to codify the mechanisms of allegorical interpretation. It is this same paradox that he already found expressed— in uniquely challenging and irresistibly provocative fashion—in Jean de Meun's *Rose*.[107]

In the preceding section, I suggested that Grace Dieu's description of the pilgrim staff functioned as a corrective to the playful, unregulated, and ultimately carnal and obscene figural hermeneutics of the *Rose*. The staff is therefore presented as an exceptional type of sign, whose operative and salvific function depends on its *similitudo* with the *res* signified, and which places it clearly within the Augustinian category of sacramental signs. However, the extended allegorical 'gloss' provided by Grace Dieu to explain the sacramental significance of the staff tends to undermine the very idea of a 'natural', intrinsically efficacious sacramental signification

---

[105] 'In signo quod est sacramentum proprie duo requiruntur: aptitudo naturalis ad significandum rem sacram, et ordinatio volontaria ad illam significandam.' William of Milton/Middleton (Guillelmi de Militona), *Quaestiones de sacramentis*, ed. Gedéon Gál and Celestin Piana. 2 vols (Quaracchi: Collegium S. Bonaventurae, 1961), I:61. My translation.

[106] For similar arguments concerning Deguileville's quest for an 'adéquation parfaite' between sign and referent more generally, in *PVH* and elsewhere in his poetic corpus, especially *DFL*, see Maupeu, *Pèlerins de vie humaine*, pp. 132–5 (135); Frédéric Duval, 'Introduction', *DFL*, pp. 81–8; Fabienne Pomel, 'Généalogie d'un "vrai signe" politique ou l'investiture allégorique dans le *Roman de la fleur de lys* de Guillaume de Digulleville', in Jean-Christophe Cassard, Elizabeth Gaucher, and Jean Kerhervé, eds, *Vérité poétique, vérité politique. Mythes, modèles et idéologies politiques au Moyen Âge* (Brest: Centre de Recherche Bretonne et Celtique, 2007), pp. 327–41; Pomel, *Les voies*, pp. 506–8.

[107] On the important question of Augustine's own complex attitude towards polysemy, see the references given above, n. 76.

162   MEDIEVAL ALLEGORY AS EPISTEMOLOGY

based on inherent *similitudo*. One is tempted to ask: if the 'bourdon' truly signifies Hope through the qualities that inhere in it, why does the Pilgrim require the detailed verbal expository 'gloss' on its significance provided by Grace Dieu? This deep-seated paradox is even more apparent in conjunction with the *viator*'s second defining attribute, the Scrip of Faith. The 'escherpe' is presented even more explicitly as a sacramental sign, directly associated with the Eucharistic sacrament. And yet, Deguileville again ends up undercutting its ostensibly sacramental efficacy by making its signification dependent on a whole range of additional verbal and textual elucidations.

Like the 'bourdon', the 'escherpe' too is presented as a verbal signifier that must first be restored to its proper, literal valence. The word 'escherpe' is no longer a euphemistic *integumentum* that improperly signifies the male scrotum (cf. *RR* 21,324, 21,618), but a term that properly denotes an actual pilgrim satchel. This in turn enables the object to function as a sacramental *signum* of the theological virtue of Faith. Its first significant feature to be unpacked is its green colour:

'Ceste escherpe est de vert couleur,
Quar tout aussi comme la verdeur
Conforte l'ueil et la veue
Aussi te di que foi ague
Fait vëue d'entendement,
Ne ja l'ame parfaitment
Ne verra, se ceste verdeur
Ne li preste force et viguer;
Et pour ce' elle t'ara mestier
Pour toi en ta voie adrecier,
A ce que de loing tu voies
Le païs ou tu t'avoies.'
  (*PVH1* 3485–96)

'This scrip is colored green, for as the color green refreshes the vision of the eyes, so I say to you that Faith sharpens the vision of the understanding. The soul will never see perfectly unless this green gives it strength and vigor, and therefore it will help to guide you on your way, so that you can see from afar off that country where you may live.'

Instead of having a symbolic or allegorical value, Grace argues, the colour green is endowed with intrinsic qualities that 'sharpen' the eye of the intellect, and thus acquires an operative function thanks to its natural characteristics. Since the scrip's ability to sharpen 'the eye of the mind' [vëue d'entendement] provides a natural *similitudo* for the operation of Faith, it becomes an adequate sacramental sign for the latter. The passage thus carries implicit echoes of 2 Cor. 5:6–7—'we walk by faith and not by sight'—a passage also cited by Augustine in *De doctrina*, as part of an extended discussion of how the Christian reader/pilgrim 'purifies the eye through which God may actually be seen [. . .] as we travel in this life, even though we are citizens of heaven [cf. Phil. 3:20]' (*De doctrina* II.7.11).[108]

---

[108] 'ubi iam ipsum oculus purgat, quo uideri deus potest . . . cum in hic uita peregrinamur, quamuis conuersationem habeamus in caelis.'

A similar point is made about the twelve bells that decorate the scrip:

'Ces.xii. clochetes [...]
Souvent te doivent esveiller
Et sonner a ton oreiller.
[...]
D'autre partie Saint Pol dit
Et aus Roumains il l'a escrit
Que d'ouir tel cloquetement
A on la foi parfaitement,
Si ques la cloqueterie
En l'escherpe ne nuist mie,
Ainciez excite la memoire
En quel guise on doit Dieu croire;'
  (*PVH1* 3529–48)

'These twelve little bells ... should often wake you up and ring in your ear ... Further, Saint Paul says, in his letter to the Romans, that through this ringing one has the faith perfectly. Therefore, the set of bells on the scrip is not harmful at all, but stirs the memory as to the way one should believe in God.'

Here the scriptural echoes are explicit—albeit without the accompanying bells: 'Faith comes by hearing' (Rom 10:17). Once more the pilgrim's scrip is presented as an operative sacramental sign, signifying through affinity with its object, Faith. Grace Dieu now seizes the opportunity to make its sacramental efficacy explicit by directly associating the Scrip of Faith with the principal sacramental sign, the Eucharistic body of Christ:

'Non pas que ce ci seulement
Soufise a croire fermement,
Quar pluseurs autres choses sont
Qui fermement a croire font,
Si com du vin et du pain blanc
Qui mue sont en char et sanc,
De Dieu aussi en trinite.'
  (*PVH1* 3549–55)

'Not that it is sufficient to believe firmly only this, for there are many other things to believe steadfastly, such as the wine and the white bread that are changed into flesh and blood, and the three persons of God united in the Trinity.'

The Eucharist too, like the Scrip of Faith, is presented as a sign that naturally aids or rather 'nourishes' the faith of the individual Christian. The passage also establishes a functional association between the Scrip of Faith and the Eucharist, which further intensifies the sacramental status of the scrip as a sign. Since the scrip serves to carry and contain the sacramental 'bread' [pain] during the pilgrim's journey, the two objects become articulated by an underlying sacramental logic that underpins the poem's larger allegorical poetics, establishing a complex interrelation between the ideas of pilgrimage/Faith/communion/sacramental incorporation:

'L'escherpe est *Foi* apelee,
Sans la quelle ja journee
Tu ne feras qui rien vaille,
Quar ton pain et ta vitaille
Doiz en tous temps avoir.'
  (*PVH1* 3473–7)

'The scrip is called Faith, and without it
you will never make a journey that
amounts to anything, for you must
always keep your bread and your food
in it.'

As a sacramental sign, the scrip also functions as a meta-allegorical signifier, embedded in a wider web of relations of *similitudo* that tie it into the larger figural principles underpinning the poem as a whole. Like other sacramental signifiers, the scrip thus functions also as a metonym for the poem as a whole, which stakes its claim to perform not only a referential and cognitive function, but also an operational, salvific one.

In aspiring to produce a poem that functions like a large-scale sacramental sign, Deguileville set himself a formidable task that creates considerable difficulties. More specifically, the lengthy expositions on the significance of the many sacramental signs/objects that clutter the poem are ultimately self-defeating: if such objects are truly endowed with natural, intrinsic signifying qualities, why does the poet feel compelled to provide such detailed and systematic interpretations of their meanings? This paradox ultimately tends to reveal that such objects are in fact very much dependent on some ulterior act of interpretation, generally mediated by one of the poem's authority figures: Sapience, Grace Dieu, or indeed the author himself. Strikingly, too, such interpretations are often dependent on the availability of supplementary texts or documents embedded within the poem, further undermining any claim in favour of their intrinsic ability to signify 'naturally'. A case in point is the detailed description of the twelve bells adorning the Scrip of Faith:

'Les douze apostres mis i ont
Ces.xij. cloches qui i sont
Et en chascune propre escrit
Qui *proprement* enseigne et dit,
En quelle maniere et comment
On doit croire en Dieu fermement.
Ces.xij. clochetes si sont
Douze articles de foi qui sont
Les quiex tu dois fermement croire.'
  (*PVH1* 3523–31; my emphasis)

'The twelve apostles placed on it these
twelve bells and on each one there is an
appropriate inscription that states and
teaches rightly the way one should
believe steadfastly in God. These twelve
little bells are the twelve articles of faith
and you must believe them firmly.'

Instituted by the apostles, the twelve bells 'properly' represent the twelve articles of the Faith, subdividing the overall significance of the scrip into its component elements. But if the significance of the bells is 'proper' to them, why is it made to depend on what is *inscribed* [escrit] upon them? Are the twelve articles of the faith really intrinsic qualities that inhere in the bells and in the scrip, or are they rather

LANGUAGE   165

attributed meanings, placed there, as it were, by the twelve apostles? And if these meanings are proper to the object itself, why does the pilgrim/reader depend on the exposition provided by Grace Dieu?

It is symptomatic for Deguileville's defensiveness on this point that the poem should repeatedly employ variations of the term 'propre/proprement' to designate the signification of sacramental objects and attributes endowed with ostensibly natural power of signification. The sword of the Cherubim guarding the gate of the Heavenly City glimpsed at the beginning of the poem is thus presented as a transparent allegory of the *verbum dei*, clearly echoing Hebrews 4:12.[109] The sword represents (or embodies) 'discretion' (*PVH1* 1085, 1118) because of its single point and its two blades, and it should never be carried by a 'man who does not know how to discern properly' [hon qui ne scet bien discerner, *PVH1* 1098, cf. also 1108; translation mine]. Its double edge also stands for the duality of the human condition (*PVH1* 1125–32, and since the sign is naturally predisposed to carry such meanings, 'it was truly and *properly* figured' [ce estoit il voirement / Figuree et bien *proprement*, *PVH1* 1009–10, my emphasis]. And yet none of the meanings just reviewed is ever accessible without the detailed expositions supplied by Grace Dieu. A similar paradox again obtains in the case of the Carpenter's square, 'Jewel of Peace', or 'PAX', a gift from Christ himself and formed by God the Father: 'It is a jewel formed and shaped by my father' [C'est un jouel qui fu forme / Forgie et fait et charpente / De mon pere, *PVH1* 2507–9]. Figuring Peace, and loaded with complex symbolic meaning, the inscribed object becomes the sign/seal of Christ's testament, authenticated by his own blood—punning on the two meanings of OF 'saign/seign', i.e. 'a sign', and 'blood'—and serves as archetype of all true covenants:

'Ceste figure et ce patron
Est un saing de tabelion
Du quel doivent estre seigniez
Touz bons testamens et merchiez,
Et de saing publiquement
Ai je seignie mon testament.'
  (*PVH1* 2577–82)

'This form and this design is a notary's seal, and all good testaments should be signed and marked with it. With this seal I have publicly signed my testament.'

Christ himself therefore declares that 'I will truly (properly) legate its exemplar (or "archetype") to those of good understanding' [le patron / En bailleroie *proprement* / A ceus de bon entendement, *PVH1* 2514–16, my emphasis and my translation].

All of these objects—sword, scrip, staff, and PAX—are thus presented as objects/signs that supposedly illustrate the 'proper' workings of sacramental signs,

---

[109] 'For the word of God is living and effectual, and more piercing than any two edged sword; and reaching unto the division of the soul and the spirit, of the joints also and the marrow, and is a discerner of the thoughts and intents of the heart'.

166   MEDIEVAL ALLEGORY AS EPISTEMOLOGY

drawing their operative salvific power from their natural affinity with their objects. Despite Grace's insistence, however, all such objects invariably depend on the availability of additional explanations, verbal or textual, that allow supposedly inherent meanings to become apparent. This underscores the extent to which the significance of Deguileville's sacramental allegorical signs in fact depends, firstly, on the physical inscription of allegorical meanings within/upon the objects themselves, and, secondly, on an extraneous, supplementary verbal *glose* dispensed by the poem's authority figures and/or its author. Far from being operative in their own right, then, such signs acquire their signifying force only by being loaded with further signs in the form of textual expositions of various kinds. This raises serious questions about the poem's ability to signify anything *proprement*, drawing attention to the problematic connotations of the term itself.

Like its Latin equivalent—*significatio propria*, opposed to *significatio impropria/translata*—the notion of 'proper' signification is eminently nebulous, despite being widely attested not only among exegetes in the wake of Augustine (e.g. *De doctrina*, II.10), but also among medieval grammarians since Cicero, Donatus, and Priscian. Already in the contexts of twelfth century logic and theology the connotations of the formula *significatio propria* were highly unstable,[110] and by the middle of the following century the term was so fuzzy as to serve for the description of pretty much any form of signification. The category of 'improper speech' accordingly became increasingly capacious from the late thirteenth century onwards, leading to a multiplication of theories emphasizing the radically equivocal nature of human speech and language. This was the case not only with Roger Bacon, already discussed (see Chapter 1.3), but with several other thinkers of rather different philosophical persuasion—such as Burley and Ockham. Far from being exceptional, 'improper meaning' (*suppositio impropria*) was all but ubiquitous in the writings of ancient poets and *auctores*:

> Thus it is important to determine when a term and a proposition are being taken *de virtute sermonis* and when *secundum usum loquentium* or according to the intention of the author. The reason is because there is hardly a word

---

[110] The point is made, in passing, by Evans, *The Language and Logic of the Bible*, I:77. For an overview, see Luisa Valente, 'Langage et théologie pendant la seconde moitié du XIIe siècle', in Ebbesen, *Sprachtheorien in Spätantike und Mittelalter*, pp. 33–54 (37–9); and for an exhaustive account, ibid, *Logique et théologie: Les écoles parisiennes entre 1150 et 1220*. On the related difficulties of establishing the precise significance of 'the literal sense', see especially Ocker, *Biblical Poetics before Reformation and Humanism*, pp. 1–111; and Rita Copeland, 'Rhetoric and the Politics of the Literal Sense in Medieval Literary Theory: Aquinas, Wyclif and the Lollards', in Walter Jost and Michael J. Hyde, eds, *Rhetoric and Hermeneutics in Our Time: A Reader* (New Haven: Yale University Press, 1997), pp. 335–57; Jon Whitman, *Interpretation and Allegory: Antiquity to the Modern Period* (Leiden: Brill, 2000), pp. 17–18, 54–8; Denys Turner, 'Allegory in Christian Late Antiquity', in Copeland and Struck, *The Cambridge Companion to Allegory*, pp. 71–82 (78–82).

which is not somehow employed equivocally in various places in the books of the philosophers, saints, and authors. And therefore those always wishing to take a word univocally and in just one sense frequently err about the intentions of authors and in the inquiry after truth, since almost all words are employed equivocally.[111]

Both in the exegesis of scripture and in commentaries on secular authors, then, the definition of *significatione propria* was thus beset with endemic and ultimately insurmountable difficulties.

More importantly, perhaps, an attentive reader familiar with Jean de Meun's *Rose* could hardly avoid remembering Raison's notorious claim to speak 'proprement des choses [. . .] sanz metre gloses' (*RR* 7049–50; and 6920–8) when defending her use of the term 'coilles' ('balls', or 'testicles'). As Alastair Minnis has shown, Raison's use of the expression implies a self-conscious and fundamentally subversive play with the dizzying array of divergent connotations of this word, muddying the already imprecise meaning(s) and associations(s) of this slippery term even further.[112] As is often noted, Raison's notion of 'parler proprement' is particularly problematic since it is later opposed to interpretation 'a la letre'— usually a close synonym of *significatio propria*—and is made compatible with speaking 'par paraboles', in the manner of 'integumanz aus poetes' (*RR* 7123–42). Raison's inconsistent use of the 'proprement' in the *Rose* thus appears designed to draw attention to the potential *aporia* in contemporary discussions of *significatio propria*, 'literal' meaning, and 'parabolic' signification, across the boundary of the language arts and theology.[113] Far from merely pointing to the deviant and improper use of language by unruly 'fames . . . en France' (*RR* 7101), then, Jean appears to be drawing attention to the fundamentally improper and unregulated signifying relations at work in human language across the board—in the specialized terminology of grammarians and logicians themselves as much as in casual conversations among neighbours (see especially Chapter 1.3).

---

[111] 'Et ideo multum est considerandum quando terminus et propositio accipitur de virtute sermonis et quando secundum usum loquentium vel secundus intentionem auctorum, et hoc quia vix invenitur aliquod quin in diversis locis librorum philosophorum, et Sanctorum et auctorum aequivoce accipitur; et hic penes aliquem modum aequivocationis. Et ideo volentes accipere semper vocabulum univoce et uno modo frequenter errant circa intentiones auctorum et inquisitionem veritatis, cum fere omnia vocabula aequivoce accipiantur.' William of Ockham, *Summa Logicae*, ed. Philotheus Boehner, Gideon Gál, and Stephen Brown (St Bonaventure: Franciscan Institute, 1974), p. 237. For further discussion, see Courtenay, 'Force of Words and Figures of Speech', in his *Ockham and Ockhamism*, pp. 209–28, whose translation I reproduce (218).

[112] Minnis, *Magister Amoris*, pp. 119–63, esp. 131–40, 159–60.

[113] On these difficulties, see especially Ocker, *Biblical Poetics before Reformation and Humanism*, pp. 1–111, and particularly pp. 5–7, 33–4, 40–1 on the challenges of documenting the cross-fertilization of debates in the Theology and Arts Faculties in the thirteenth century.

168 MEDIEVAL ALLEGORY AS EPISTEMOLOGY

5. 'Parler proprement des choses [. . .], sanz metre gloses' (*RR* 7049–50): Exposé sur le *Roman de la Rose*

In employing this conspicuous, widely attested yet hugely troublesome term, Deguileville brings his main dilemma into focus: in seeking to reclaim the very idea of 'proper signification' to counter the obscene figural improprieties of the *Rose*, Deguileville finally ends up exposing the dependence of ostensibly proper, 'natural' sacramental signification on a disambiguating *glose*. This paradox is symptomatic of Deguileville's overarching difficulties in his ambivalent relationship to the *Rose* as a whole: on the one hand, his response is clearly adversarial, determined to close down the intractable hermeneutic and epistemological difficulties opened up by Jean de Meun's poem. Yet in attempting to do so by writing an allegorical poem of his own, Deguileville opens himself up to the very slippages that he seeks to prevent. The fundamentally paradoxical nature of such a move is encapsulated in Deguileville's explicit mentions of Jean's poem in *PVH1* and *PVH2*.

The first passage I want to discuss appears to suggest a deceptively simple attitude towards the *Rose* on Deguileville's part. In a passage that clearly references the plot of the *Rose*, Raison descends from her tower and offers her eroticized 'friendship' to the pilgrim by declaring her repulsion for vice:

'Quar yvresce et gloutonnie	'Drunkenness and gluttony soon make
Me font tost tourner en fuÿe,	me turn and fly away. Unbridled anger
Ire qui est desmesuree	and violent rage make me leave the
Et felonnie la desvee	house they dwell in. Carnal love drives
Me font vuidier la mansion	me out completely and makes me leave
Ou ont leur habitacion,	immediately. You can see this plainly,
Amour charnel tout hors m'enchace	without any gloss, in the *Romance of*
Et me fait tost vuider la place;	*the Rose.*'
Ce verrez vous tout sans glose	[translation emended]
Ou roumans que' est de la Rose.'	
(*PVH1* 873–82)	

The *Rose* here is characterized as a poem that illustrates how sensuality puts reason to flight, and although Raison is by no means a supreme authority in *PVH1*, her characterization at this stage carries weight and appears to fit with Deguileville's own commitment to abstinence and spiritual ascent.

Yet Raison's formulation in *PVH* is striking: 'Ce verrez vous *tout sans glose* / Ou roumans que' est de la Rose' (my emphasis). This suggests that for Deguileville—or perhaps for lady Raison in his poem—the *Rose* indeed *does* present a straightforward, unmistakeable moral argument against sensuality and in favour of the life of the spirit and intellect. Deguileville's Raison thus provides a reading of the *Rose* that to most modern readers familiar with the poem—except perhaps

LANGUAGE 169

for those of staunchly Robertsonian persuasion—will appear rather reductive. Yet Deguileville's understanding of the *Rose* as a moral, spiritual allegory is also characteristic of a certain type of medieval reader-response to this consistently evasive poem.[114] As Sylvia Huot and Pierre-Yves Badel have shown, many of the medieval reader-responses to the poem take the form of an attempt to 'shut down', or at least control or resist the dangerous multiplication of mutually conflicting discourses and interpretations fostered by Jean's poem—and Deguileville's *PVH1* is a conspicuously early and energetic effort in this sense.[115] Sylvia Huot has further suggested that Deguileville may have encountered a B-family *Rose* manuscript, which preserves an early *remaniement* that already reorganizes the allegory so as to turn the poem into a moralizing denunciation of erotic love.[116] Be that as it may, Raison's claim in *PVH1* that the *Rose* presents a clear moral message 'sans glose' is difficult to reconcile with the reality of a poem where nothing is ever said 'sans glose'. As was already seen, in the *Rose* 'plenty of Latin authors are [. . .] glossed—often to within an inch of their lives', and often in deliberately outrageous and subversive fashion (see Chapter 1.1).[117] Under these conditions nothing can ever be said 'sans glose', and Raison's statement in *PVH1* rather short-circuits the irreducible complexity of Jean's poem. By denying the necessity of any ulterior interpretive *glose*, then, Deguileville attempts to sabotage one of the *Rose*'s preferred strategies for interrogating the very possibility of extracting a 'diffinitive santance' (19,474) from any particular text—and above all from itself. In this sense it is rather ironic that Deguileville himself may have known the *Rose* in some form of emended *remaniement* from the B-family of manuscripts, since such a version would have provided him with something that was nothing if not a *glose* on the *Rose*, imposing a heavy-handed moral interpretive grid on the otherwise slippery and evasive allegory.

It is doubly ironic that Deguileville's own *Pèlerinage de Vie Humaine*—itself an unmistakeable *glose* upon the *Rose*—should equally exist in two substantially different versions, *PVH1* and *PVH2*. Critics often observe that Deguileville had developed a much more critical attitude towards the *Rose* by the time he wrote the later, revised version of *PVH* in 1355.[118] I would propose a slightly different interpretation, arguing that the ambivalent attitude that was largely latent and implicit in *PVH1* is now openly revealed. In effect, Deguileville cannot be demonstrated to have held a clear, single, and stable idea about the *Rose* in *PVH2* any more than he did in *PVH1*.[119] The mention of the *Rose* has disappeared from the opening lines of

---

[114] See especially Pomel, 'Le Roman de la Rose comme voie de paradis'.

[115] See Badel, *Le RR au XIVe siècle*; Huot, *The Romance of the Rose and its Medieval Readers*. On Deguileville specifically, see respectively pp. 362–76 in Badel, and pp. 207–38 in Huot.

[116] Huot, *The RR and its Medieval Readers*, pp. 211 and *passim* on pp. 207–38.

[117] Citation from Huot, *Dreams of Lovers, Lies of Poets*, p. 15.

[118] Badel, *Le RR au XIVe siècle*, pp. 375–6; Huot, *The Romance of the Rose and its Medieval Readers*, pp. 225–30. See also the references given above, nn. 5 and 6.

[119] See also Maupeu, 'Bivium', p. 23 and *passim*.

170   MEDIEVAL ALLEGORY AS EPISTEMOLOGY

PVH2, but Raison continues to characterize the *Rose* as a text that unmistakeably opposes reason and sensuality 'sans glose' (*PVH2* 1193–4). Another character in *PVH2*, however, now proposes a diametrically opposing interpretation of the *Rose*, and one that once more plays on the topical rhyme 'rose/glose'. Venus now claims that the *Rose* amounts to a large-scale ideological assault on Chastity:

'Je mesdi de [Chastete] bien souvent	'I often slander Chastity, and ask my
Et fais mesdire par ma gent,	people to slander her, just as can be
Si com il appert sens glose	clearly seen, without gloss, in the
En mon romans dit "La rose",	romance called *The Rose*. There my
Ou Faus Semblant le fais nommer	notary and secretary [i.e. Jean de
Par mon notaire et appeller,	Meun] makes Faux Semblant do this,
Et la cause est car approchier	and this is because she never lets me
Ne me laisse a lui ne touchier.'	come near her or touch her.'
(*PVH2* 8719–26)	

This inner discrepancy inscribed into *PVH2*—whether deliberate or not—is a good measure of the hermeneutically open, unstable nature of the *Rose* itself, and which was later to figure so prominently in the *Quérelle de la Rose*.[120] The inconsistency in *PVH2* suggests that for Deguileville himself the question of interpretive control of this earlier text was far from settled, despite both Raison's and Venus's mutually contradictory claims to the contrary. Venus in effect claims ownership and even perhaps some form of mediated authorship of the *Rose*, presenting it as 'mon romans' (*PVH2* 8722):

'Quar je le fis et il est mien,	'Because I wrote it and it belongs to me,
Et ce puis je prouver tresbien,	and I can prove this without any doubt,
Car du premier jucques au bout,	since from the beginning to the end,
Sans discontinuer, par tout,	without interruption, it speaks about
Il n'y a fors de moi parlé,'	nothing else but me.'
(*PVH2* 8731–5)	

But as soon as this bold claim has been made, it is tempered by Venus' regretful remark that the poem is not, alas, an unadulterated glorification of erotic love. The author—deliberately unnamed so as to deny him authorial status[121]—also included extraneous material that is not concerned with furthering Venus's interests:

---

[120] As David Hult observes, during the *Quérelle* both Christine de Pizan and Jean Gerson 'seem obsessed with the difficulty of pinning down an authorial intention, and on the formal properties of the *Rose* that make it so', Hult, 'Words and Deeds', 356.

[121] Badel, *Le Roman au XIVe siècle*, p. 375; Maupeu, *Pèlerins de vie humaine*, p. 121.

'Ce tant seulement excepté Que mon clerc escrivain embla Et en estranges champs soia; De quoi maintes gens ont cuidié Que en sa terre l'eüst soié, Mes non fist ains partie grant Il en embla en autrui champ.' (*PVH2* 8736–42)	'The only exception being when my clerk and scribe went astray, to harvest and gather from other folks' fields. Many have thought that this was his harvest, when in truth he pilfered much of it in other fields.'
'Laquel chose moult me desplut Car je vousisse que n'eüst Fors seulement de moi escript.' (*PVH2* 8754–6)	'And this I disliked very much, since I would have wanted him to write solely about me.'

Venus complains about the heterogeneous harvest that can be gleaned from the *Rose*, suggesting that her own claim of ownership may be contested due to the presence of crop—and seed—purloined from other fields, sown by other, morally irreproachable *auctores* such as Cicero, Boethius or Alan of Lille.[122] The semantic field of agriculture is particularly relevant in the context of the figurative scattering of seed that concludes the *Rose* (see Chapter 1.5), where Amant/pilgrim tells us that 'un po de greine i espandi' (21,690). Significantly, this image too is brought back and reconfigured at the beginning of *PVH1*—and then significantly removed from *PVH2*. Led by Augustine, numerous 'mestres et docteurs' (*PVH1* 104) scatter the grain of the word for the benefit of the bird-like faithful (*PVH1* 108). This too, then, becomes a motif that Deguileville attempts to recuperate in order to counter the indiscriminate 'dissemination' of meaning performed at the end of the *Rose*, seeking to restore the figure to its 'proper' scriptural connotations.[123] In the very act of doing so, however, Deguileville also necessarily reactivates the latent possibilities for obscene signification that the *Rose* had indelibly grafted onto the expression. The semantic 'fertility' of metaphor revealed by the *Rose*, it seems, has become infused into the very words that Deguileville attempts to recuperate.

This paradoxical relation between *PVH1* and the *Rose* is also encapsulated in one of the recurrent formulas used to describe Deguileville's poem in at least five of its manuscripts: *PVH1* is an 'exposé sur le *Roman de la Rose*'.[124] In presenting itself as an 'exposition' or 'gloss' on this most slippery of poems, Deguileville's *PVH* aspires to produce a stable and definitive interpretation of the earlier poem—which is precisely what appears to elude both Raison and Venus in *PVH2*. As Philippe

---

[122] Huot, *The Romance of the Rose and its Medieval Readers*, pp. 227–8.

[123] See also Huot, *The Romance of the Rose and its Medieval Readers*, p. 210. In performing such a *resémantisation* of obscene signifiers into religious ones Deguileville also anticipates Molinet's *Roman de la Rose Moralisé* (c. 1500), on which see Pomel, 'Le *Roman de la Rose* comme voie de paradis', pp. 366–9.

[124] Maupeu, *Pèlerins de vie humaine*, pp. 275–7.

172 MEDIEVAL ALLEGORY AS EPISTEMOLOGY

Maupeu has argued, the choice of expression here echoes the practice of providing theological *expositiones*, particularly of scriptural texts.[125] Moreover, in presenting itself as a self-conscious 'exposé' of the *Rose*, *PVH1* ultimately aims to provide the long-awaited exposition promised by the author/narrator of the *Rose* itself, a promise that was systematically frustrated by Jean's evasive narrator (see Chapter 1.1). But if *PVH1* presents itself in many ways as an *exposé* or a *glose* on the *Roman de la Rose*, the revised *PVH2* becomes in turn a *glose* on Deguileville's own gloss. Instead of bringing closure to the kind of thinking processes triggered by Jean's frustratingly evasive poem, then, Deguileville is sucked ever deeper into the dialogic and relativistic poetics of the *Rose*, where all 'choses / sont les unes des autres gloses' (*RR* 21,543–4).

The deeply ambivalent and paradoxical attitude of the Cistercian poet towards the *Rose* is also encapsulated in the earliest and most conspicuous allusion to it in Deguileville in his poetic corpus, in the opening lines of *PVH1*.[126] Here the *Rose* is not so much presented as a freely and deliberately chosen literary model to be imitated or criticized, but as a poem that 'moved' the Cistercian poet to experience is own vision, recorded in the poem we are about to read:

En veillant avoie leü	While I was awake I had read, studied,
Consideré et bien veü	and looked closely at the beautiful
Le biau Roumans de la Rose.	*Romance of the Rose*. I am sure that this
Bien croi que fut la chose	was what moved me most to have the
Qui plus m'emust a ce songier	dream.
(*PVH1* 9–13; my emphasis)	

The formulation is remarkably proto-Chaucerian:[127] instead of simply invoking the *Rose* as a formal model for his own poetry, Deguileville actually makes the earlier poem responsible for the *experience* of his dream. He thus situates the *Rose*'s influence at a much deeper, sub-conscious level that seems to defy full authorial and imaginative control on the poet's part. The affective, sub-rational, and thus epistemologically unreliable implications of the verb *esmouvoir* capture both the intensity and the opacity of the intertextual relationship between these two allegories. In the words of Philippe Maupeu, the *Rose* becomes the 'fermenting agent' that produces the dream of *PVH1*,[128] infusing the latter with its own imaginative and speculative processes. Under such circumstances, it appears as difficult to disentangle the two poems from each other as it is to differentiate between mechanisms of 'proper' vs. 'improper' signification.

---

[125] Maupeu, '*Bivium*', pp. 22–3.

[126] My own reading converges most closely with the observations of Maupeu, *Pèlerins de vie humaine*, pp. 118–24.

[127] For the influence of this opening on Chaucer's various instances of the 'text-dazed narrator' in his dream poetry, see especially Kamath, *Allegory and Authorship*, pp. 60–102 (66).

[128] Maupeu, *Pèlerins de vie humaine*, 'le ferment du rêve', p. 54.

LANGUAGE   173

To conclude, then, it seems that despite Deguileville's best efforts to hold the *Rose* at arm's length, Jean's poem continues to speak through *PVH1*, asserting its relentless relativism even as the Cistercian poet attempts to counter it with a different, more tightly regulated form of 'proper' allegorical signification. It will be remembered that signification invariably denotes relation—'signum est in praedicamento relationis' (Bacon, *De signis* §1)—and it is evident that Deguileville's poem attempts to privilege one particular signifying relation above all others: that is, the relation of the poem as a whole to the ultimate divine reality embodied in the Heavenly City—'the thing to which all such things are to be related' (*De doctrina* III.9). All of the poem's countless objects, textual and imaginative, are therefore geared towards a moment of eschatological and epistemic closure. Nonetheless, a different kind of relation also continues to determine the signifying processes at work in Deguileville's poem, reasserting the power of the original act of linguistic dissemination that concludes the *Rose*, and during which Deguileville's own poem—an *exposé sur le roman de la Rose*—was itself conceived.

To some extent this paradoxical, simultaneously adversarial and imitative relation with the *Rose* is characteristic of allegorical intertextuality as described by Judith Anderson. The idea of 'influence' here acquires its full etymological valence, designating a 'flowing into' that far exceeds conscious imitation or resistance, and establishes an open-ended and dynamic relationship between texts.[129] A truly dialogic relation of intertextual 'influence' therefore necessarily introduces a signifying relation that is not univocal but reciprocal, and thereby necessarily unstable and equivocal. In the case of the intertextuality of *PVH1* and the *Rose*, such dialogic possibilities militate against the monologic aspiration that motivates the writing of *PVH1* in the first place. This reciprocity is exacerbated by the Jean de Meun's deliberate and self-conscious commitment to a relentlessly dialectical poetics of 'contreres choses, les unes des autres gloses'. It is as though the *Rose* had always already formulated a pre-emptive *glose* against any subsequent act of interpretation, reception, or appropriation, in turn subjecting such responses to its own proleptic commentary and critique. In this kind of conversation, the *Rose* is bound to have the last word, as if it were anticipating resistance to its radical poetics and engaging its posterity in a two-way dialogue. As David Hult has observed:

> Just as the narrative stages in the future its own writing and the birth of the individual author who will perform that act, it also manages to anticipate in an uncanny fashion, though its manipulative and indecisive debate structure, any response we are likely to make, either by including that response within the text,

---

[129] Judith H. Anderson, *Reading the Allegorical Intertext: Chaucer, Spenser, Shakespeare, Milton* (New York: Fordham University Press, 2008), pp. 1–21, especially 1–5 and 15–17.

174 MEDIEVAL ALLEGORY AS EPISTEMOLOGY

or by deferring responsibility (that is, pronounced authorial intention) through verbal or vocal chicanery.[130]

Even if the *Rose* could be rewritten, it could never be silenced, unmade, or written out of existence. The poem finally remains indomitable, and later attempts to domesticate it become further opportunities for the *Rose* itself to parasite the host-text and to interrogate its poetic and epistemological formulations in turn. Careful and attentive readers could not conscientiously avoid the burden— or temptation—of using the *Rose* as an anterior-yet-ulterior gloss on their own writing- and thinking-processes, becoming engaged in a potentially endless conversation with this seminal and irreducibly talkative poem.

---

[130] Hult, 'Language and Dismemberment', p. 106.

3
Cognition: Theory and Practice

> From words, then, we learn only words. [. . .] when words are spo-
> ken, we either know what they signify or we don't; if we do, then it's
> reminding rather than learning; if we don't, it isn't even reminding,
> though perhaps we recollect that we should enquire.
>
> (*De magistro* XI.36)[1]

In the previous chapter, I argued that in *PVH1* Deguileville essentially attempts to reconstruct a viable system of interpretation of figurative language in the wake of the *Rose*. Following the lead of Augustinian hermeneutics, the poem also signals a larger move away from language, beyond strictly linguistic signs (*signa*) towards things (*res*) denoted by words. Such *res* are in turn endowed with deeper figurative significance, as *signa* of the divine presence in the created world, and their interpretation is accordingly susceptible of causing profound transformations in the individual human subject, understood as a *homo viator* or pilgrim on a quest for individual salvation. Rather than being concerned merely with the exploration of the mechanics of textual interpretation, then, *PVH1* is also a poem dedicated to exploring the cognitive and psychological processes that accompany, underpin, or result from the human effort to interpret encrypted 'signs'—both natural and textual—on a human pilgrimage towards an eschatological heavenly home. It is precisely this combined interest in the mechanics of textual interpretation, human cognition, self-exploration, and individual salvation that determines the distinctly epistemological orientation of Deguileville's poem.

This effort to redefine the remit and mechanics of human interpretation according to an Augustinian model is accompanied by a corresponding examination of the structure of the individual human subject engaged on this journey. In this chapter, I will accordingly focus on Deguileville's anthropology and epistemology, insofar as it can be reconstructed from the poem within its specific intellectual and cultural context. I will be arguing that Deguileville's theory of the structure of the human subject and its cognitive faculties is again deeply

---

[1] 'Verissima quippe ratio est et uerissime dicitur, cum uerba proferentur, aut scire nos quid significent aut nescire; si scimus commemorari potius quam discere, si autem nescimus nec commemorari quidem, sed fortasse ad quaerendum admoneri.' *De magistro*, ed. Green and Daur. Translation in Augustine, *Against Academicians; The Teacher*, ed. King.

Medieval Allegory as Epistemology. Marco Nievergelt, Oxford University Press.
© Marco Nievergelt (2023). DOI: 10.1093/oso/9780192849212.003.0004

176 MEDIEVAL ALLEGORY AS EPISTEMOLOGY

influenced by Augustinian models, and aims to counter the conspicuously sensual and embodied anthropology that underpins the 'carnal' allegory of the *Roman de la Rose*. However, I will also emphasize what appears to be a radical, troubling disconnect between Deguileville's *theory* of the human mind and soul, and the *practical* experience of the poem's first-person protagonist/dreamer/narrator. Thus, on the one hand, Deguileville's authority figures clearly advocate a strongly Augustinian, dualist theory of a disembodied human soul, endowed with accordingly powerful faculties of intellectual cognition. On the other hand, much of the poem's action tends to militate against such a theory, describing a human subject who experiences the world as an ineluctably embodied, fallible human self with limited, radically impaired cognitive abilities, and whose cognitive faculties are inextricably tied up with corporeally mediated sense-perception. The pilgrim's experiences in the poem therefore tend to conform far more closely to a broadly Aristotelian, hylomorphic model of the soul and cognition, which had come to dominate scholastic theories of mind and cognition after the middle of the thirteenth century. Characteristically, then, Deguileville is torn between his ideological allegiance to a largely outdated model of the soul and cognition, and the influence of more recent scientific developments. Far from being the fruit of mere inconsistency or personal idiosyncrasy, however, this lack of clarity in the poem's anthropology and epistemology points to a deeply conflicted, unresolved debate over the true nature of the human soul and individual subjectivity in late medieval intellectual culture. Triggered by the gradual recovery of Aristotle's natural philosophy in the West, this debate dominated European intellectual culture at the time, playing itself out over an extended period from about 1200 until the end of the middle ages. The stakes of such a debate were extremely high, particularly for a Cistercian like Deguileville: the issue at stake was nothing less than the true nature, structure, and faculties of the human rational soul and its capacity to attain salvation on the strength of its own acts. The *Pèlerinage de Vie Humaine* thus provides a particularly revealing insight into one of the most complex, nuanced, yet momentous philosophical debates in the history of pre-modern Western thought, viewed from the perspective of a devout but intellectually adventurous religious writer suspended between tradition and innovation.

First and foremost, Deguileville is concerned with examining the basic structure of the human subject in terms of its cognitive abilities, and its implications for gaining adequate self-knowledge. As noted by the medieval compiler of MS Arras 532 (845), one of the poem's primary objectives is that of 'cognoistre lame',[2] and Deguileville assigns an important place to the discussion of the nature of the soul and its relation to the body, which provides the focus for Chapter 3.1. As I discuss in Chapter 3.2, the *viator*'s examination of the nature of his own soul

---

[2] MS Arras, BM 532 (formerly 845), fol. 74v. See epigraph to Chapter 2 for fuller quotation and references.

becomes the catalyst for the first in a series of reiterated 'inward turns' in the poem, hinting at a gradual reorientation of the poem away from the pursuit of 'knowledge' towards a quest for 'self-knowledge'. This enables Deguileville to present an elaborate, and conspicuously anti-Aristotelian theory of the soul's cognitive powers. Deguileville's suspicion of corporeally mediated knowledge is also conditioned by his reading of the *Rose*, as I argue in Chapter 3.3. In particular, Deguileville uses the extended descriptions of the Seven Deadly Sins in the middle section of *PVH1* to denounce Jean de Meun's equivocal allegorical poetics as a form of carnal misreading according to the definition provided by Augustine. In Chapter 3.4 I will provide a closer examination of the action in the poem, with particular attention to the many descriptions of mental processes and cognitive experiences of the pilgrim/protagonist. Strikingly, these descriptions are largely at odds with the cognitive theory presented earlier in the poem, and tend to conform to the standard Aristotelian account for embodied cognition. This points to a deeper tension at the heart of Deguileville's poem between two radically different, and ultimately incompatible epistemologies and anthropologies, respectively 'Augustinian' and 'Aristotelian'. As I argue in the final section of this chapter, this tension points to a range of long-standing unresolved philosophical problems in late medieval philosophy of mind, but also threatens to undermine Deguileville's own confidence in the epistemological grounding of his own allegorical poetics. The poet's growing anxiety about the epistemic status of the allegorical imagination is particularly evident in his revised *PVH2*, written in 1355, and characterized by a much more hostile attitude towards his original source of inspiration, the *Roman de la Rose*.

1. Augustine's Soul, Avicenna's Flying Man, and Deguileville's Hermeneutics of the Subject

Self-knowledge occupies a central place in Deguileville's poetic project, and emerges as a precondition for any genuine spiritual progress. Since it provides the necessary starting point of every act of perception, cognition, and interpretation, the internal structure and mechanics of the pilgrim's self therefore need to be closely examined.[3] Raison accordingly argues that 'it is much more valuable to know oneself, than to be an emperor, a count, or a king' [Miex vaut assez connoistre soy / Qu'estre empereur, conte ne roy, *PVH1* 5937–8] before launching into a detailed discussion of the nature of the *viator*'s soul and its cognitive faculties (*PVH1* 5686–6502). The passage follows on immediately from the preceding encounter with Rude Entendement, already discussed (Chapter 2.3), and marks a transition from a strictly hermeneutic focus towards broader cognitive and psychological concerns. This is again an unmistakeably Augustinian move: the

---

[3] See also Kay, *Place of Thought*, pp. 70–93, particularly 70–5.

178 MEDIEVAL ALLEGORY AS EPISTEMOLOGY

analogy between self-alienation and linguistic and semiotic obscurity was in effect a fundamental principle in Augustine's thought. For Augustine, human language was itself both product and symptom of a profound ontological fracture determined by the Fall, and was accordingly understood as a collateral result of man's alienation from his self as *imago dei*.[4] More specifically, for Augustine the Fall had the effect of rupturing humanity's direct access to the to the 'inner word', the *verbum in corde* or *verbum mentis*. This *verbum*—unspoken, silent, interior, always equal to itself—constitutes in Augustine's philosophy of mind the one part in the human soul that preserves an originary fullness and self-identity,[5] and thus comes to play a pivotal role in the process of a recovery of the *imago dei* (see especially *De trinitate* XV.9.17–16.26).[6] As several commentators have observed, Augustine's theory of the double semiotic and ontological rupture caused by the Fall, and the loss of access to the inner *verbum*, marks nothing less than 'the birth of western hermeneutics'.[7]

Significantly, Augustine's discussion of the lost access to the inner *verbum* is introduced by a reference to the enigmatic mirror from 1 Cor. 13:12, an image that itself provides an *obscura allegoria* for the radical disparity between our present, indirect and enigmatic apprehension of the divine image, and the promised full vision of the deity face to face (*De trinitate* XV.8–9). The divine image carried within one's soul thus remains beneath the mortal bodies or 'garments of skin' ('tunicas pellicias', *De Genesi contra Manichaeos* II.21.32), a recurrent image in Augustine's writing, elaborated on the basis of Origen (*In Leviticum homiliae*, 6.2):[8] 'So it is that stripped naked of their first robe they earned the skin garments of mortality' (*De trinitate* XII.11.16).[9] Tellingly the clothing provided by

---

[4] See particularly *De doctrina christiana*. II.4.5. See further Jackson, 'The Theory of Signs', 27; Fyler, *Language and the Declining World*, p. 23; Fyler, 'St. Augustine, Genesis, and the Origin of Language'. In his later thought, exemplified by the *De Genesi ad litteram*, Augustine slightly modified this view by claiming that the Fall did not introduce, but merely complicated the process of signification (e.g. *De trinitate* XV.14–16). See Vance, 'Seeing God'; Sirridge, '"Quam videndo intus dicimus"'; Jager, *Tempter's Voice*, pp. 53–4; Jackson, 'The Theory of Signs', 27. See also references in 'Introduction', nn. 21 and 22.

[5] Joseph Rivera, 'Figuring the Porous Self: St. Augustine and the Phenomenology of Temporality', *Modern Theology* 29.1 (2013), 83–103 (91–4); Richard Kearney, 'Time, Evil, and Narrative: Ricoeur on Augustine', in John D. Caputo, and Michael J. Scanlon, eds, *Augustine and Postmodernism: Confessions and Circumfession* (Bloomington and Indianapolis: Indiana University Press, 2005), pp. 144–58 (148–9).

[6] Romele, *L'esperienza del Verbum in corde*, pp. 44, 47–52.

[7] See particularly Jager, *Tempter's Voice*, pp. 51–98, from whom I borrow the expression; Stock, *Augustine the Reader*, pp. 243–78; Fyler, *Language and the Declining World*, pp. 1–59. It has often been suggested that Augustine's theory of signs is based upon a duality that converges, to some degree, with the Saussurian distinction of signifier and signified, or even anticipates post-structuralist linguistics. See variously Louis G. Kelly, 'Saint Augustine and Saussurean Linguistics', *Augustinian Studies* 6 (1975), 45–64, and Luke Ferretter, 'The Trace of the Trinity: Christ and Difference in Saint Augustine's Theory of Language', *Literature and Theology* 12.3 (1998), 256–67.

[8] See Augustine of Hippo, *De Genesi contra Manichaeos*, ed. Weber; ibid., *On Genesis: Two Books on Genesis against the Manichees; On the Literal Interpretation of Genesis: an Unfinished Book*, ed. and trans. Matthew J. O'Connell (Washington, DC: Catholic University of America Press, 1999).

[9] 'inde est quod nudati stola prima pelliceas tunicas mortalitate meruerunt.'

COGNITION: THEORY AND PRACTICE   179

the fig leaves and skin garments worn by the first couple is widely assimilated with the 'letter', the obscure veils of the scriptural text that need to be removed to access inner meaning.[10] Under the present, postlapsarian existential conditions this obscured *imago dei* can never be contemplated or signified directly, but only improperly and indirectly, through the obscure coverings provided by a fundamentally opaque, corporeally mediated human experience on the one hand, and a deeply ambiguous human language on the other.[11]

The broad analogy between the mechanics of linguistic signification and the structure of the human soul imply a distinctly dualist anthropology, positing the existence of the human soul and body as fundamentally separate or separable entities. Deguileville's understanding of the nature of the human soul is unmistakeably aligned with such a dualist Augustinian anthropology, as emerges quite clearly from a paradigmatic episode that describes the separation of the pilgrim's soul from his body. The separation occurs as part of an extended discussion of selfhood and cognition between Raison and the pilgrim, closely intertwined with the hermeneutic discussions that precede it. Significantly, the discussion comes about as the result of the pilgrim's failure to understand the allegorical logic of his own journey, echoing in many ways the literalism of Rude Entendement. Unable to carry his cumbersome Armour of Faith, the pilgrim receives a further lecture from Raison, who alerts him to his lack of self-knowledge: "'Do you know who you are", she asked "whether you are alone or double'" ['Ses tu, dist elle, qui tu es, / Se tu es seul ou double es?', *PVH1* 5733–4]. It quickly turns out that "'You should know that you nourish someone who is your great enemy [...]. He was given to you to serve you, but you have become his servant'" ['Tu doiz savoir que tu nourris / Cil qui est tes grans anemis. [...] Pour toi servir baillie te fu, / Mes tu ses sers es devenu', *PVH1* 5747–56]. In the immediate sense the pilgrim is simply unable to carry the Pauline armour given to him at the beginning of his journey because it

[10] See especially Jager, *Tempter's Voice*, pp. 69–72.

[11] See especially *De quantitate animae; The Measure of the Soul; Latin Text, with English Translation and Notes*, ed. Francis A. Tourscher (Philadelphia: The Peter Reilly company/London: B. Herder, 1933), XXXII.66, and discussion in Christopher Kirwan, 'Augustine's Philosophy of Language', in Norman Kretzmann and Eleonore Stump, eds, *The Cambridge Companion to Augustine* (Cambridge: Cambridge University Press, 2001), pp. 186–204. For the history of the motif before Augustine, and with specific reference to Alexandrinian theories of allegorical interpretation, see David Dawson, 'Plato's Soul and the Body of the Text in Philo and Origen', in Whitman, ed., *Interpretation and Allegory*, pp. 89–107. Howard R. Bloch, *Etymologies and Genealogies: a Literary Anthropology of the French Middle Ages* (Chicago and London: University of Chicago Press, 1986), pp. 47–50. See also, more recently Cervone, *Incarnational Poetics*, pp. 39–43. On the broader issue of the body-soul relation in allegorical literature, see Masha Raskolnikov, *Body against Soul: Gender and 'sowlehele' in Middle English Allegory* (Columbus: Ohio State University Press, 2009). The idea of the body-letter, and soul-signification homology—freed however from its theological and ontological underpinnings—resurfaces also in rhetorical treatises like Geoffrey de Vinsauf's *Poetria nova*, where the *mens*, or 'soul' of the *verbum* is opposed to its external, potentially dissimulating surface—its 'face' or 'cloth/garment' (*facies; panno*). See *Poetria Nova*, ed. Gallo, ll. 742–63. The ideas are also developed in an early, mid-thirteenth commentary on the *Poetria nova*, for which see Marjorie Curry Woods, ed., *An Early Commentary on the 'Poetria Nova' of Geoffrey of Vinsauf* (New York: Garland, 1985), p. 19.

180   MEDIEVAL ALLEGORY AS EPISTEMOLOGY

is too heavy and he is too fat (*PVH1* 3909–32; 4737–814)—an unmistakeable sign of the unnatural subjection of his soul to the whims of his body, according to Raison. However, in the wake of the encounter with Rude Entendement—avatar of Augustine's literalistic carnal reader—the pilgrim's 'carnality' also figures his failure to appreciate the allegorical, non-corporeal nature of the Pauline Armour of Faith, and thus his failure to interpret accurately the allegorical *psychomachia* in which he is engaged.

   This instance of 'misreading' provides Raison with the opportunity to present a broadly Augustinian definition of the body and soul as separate substances. Variations of this kind of Augustinian substance dualism constituted the default position of medieval thinkers on the soul before the absorption of Aristotle's writings on psychology and natural science during the later twelfth and thirteenth centuries in the Latin West, mediated by Arabic commentators.[12] Deguileville's decision to adopt what was in many ways an outdated model of the human soul therefore amounts to an explicit and conspicuous rejection of the more recent, Aristotelian account of the soul and its cognitive faculties. Raison begins by telling the pilgrim that '"then you have two wills and are of two minds"' ['volente / tu as double et double pense', *PVH1* 5917–18] and '"Then you are not alone", she said, "and so your body and you are two"' ['Donques, dist elle, n'es pas seulz, / Ains toi et ton cors estes .ii', *PVH1* 5925–6]. Since the pilgrim fails to understand her factual account, Raison resorts to more evocative figurative language. The soul is hidden and shadowed by the body like the sun behind a cloud (6038–50), or is like the light inside a smoky lantern (6051–74), or like the invisible steersman leading the ship along its right course (6139–58), or is enveloped by the body like the body is enveloped by clothes (6115–38). This latter analogy in particular closely reproduces Augustine's own account of the duality of body and soul (e.g. *Genesi contra Manichaeos* II.21.32), overlaid with a veneer of scholastic terminology:

[Pilgrim:] 'Dame, dis jë, or demant je,	'Lady', I said, 'now I ask you, please,
Je vous en pry, comment est ce	how it is that the soul carries the body,
Que l'ame ainsi porte le cors	when it is inside and the other is
Qui est dedens et il dehors?'	outside?'
[...]	[...]
[Raison:] 'Or entent, dist elle, un petit!	'Now understand something,' she said.
Ton vestement et ton habit,	'Your habit and your clothes contain
Il te contient et es dedens.	you and you are inside them. You would
	be greatly astonished if I told you that

---

[12] I have relied on the following: Haldane, 'Soul and Body'; King, 'Body and Soul'; King, 'Why Isn't the Mind-Body Problem Medieval?'; Pasnau, 'The Mind-Soul Problem'; Pasnau, 'Mind and Hylomorphism'; Stone 'The Soul's Relation to the Body'; Bieniak, *The Soul–Body Problem at Paris, ca. 1200–1250*; Dales, *The Problem of the Rational Soul*; De Boer, *The Science of the Soul*.

Tu feroies grans marremens,
Se disoie qu'il te portast
[...]
En differance je te met
Que l'ame porte et portee est.
Elle porte principaument
Le cors, mes li par accident
La porte en ressortissant
A li sa vertu et rendant.'
  (*PVH1* 6115–38)
	they carried you or controlled you in
	any way.
	  [...]
	[T]his difference I put to you, that the
	soul both carries and is carried. The
	soul carries the body by principle, but
	the body carries the soul by accident,
	taking power from the soul, and
	restoring it to the soul.'

Triggered by the pilgrim's inability to visualize his own dual nature, the exchange thus draws a parallel between the pilgrim's divided subjectivity and his failure to decrypt Raison's allegorical figures: both are ultimately symptoms of the post-lapsarian human condition, characterized by a dislocation that is simultaneously ontological, epistemic, and semiotic. Unable to understand either the constitution of his own self or the figurative power of language as an instrument of self-knowledge, the pilgrim, like Rude Entendement before him, is still a literalistic carnal reader of his pilgrimage experience.

As Raison explains, the pilgrim's failure to grasp her figurative analogies is due precisely to his embodied state:

[...] 'Mont bien croi Que pou m'entens. Scez tu pour quoi? C'est pour le cors qui au devant Fait un obstacle espes et grant.' (*PVH1* 6177–80)	'I am sure you do not understand me very well. Do you know why? Because the body is a great and heavy obstacle in your way.'

The wording is symptomatic: the pilgrim's body—much like Rude Entendement's 'baston'—constitutes an 'obstacle' on his journey, figuring the cognitive and inter-pretive impediments he is required to overcome. Yet Raison's explanation is revealing precisely because it is so unhelpful: it is ultimately because of his own embodied state that the pilgrim is unable to understand (*entendre*) Raison's fig-urative language, and thus cannot visualize his own body as a substance existing separately from his true self, identified solely with his soul. As Raison explains, the pilgrim's fallen corporeal self obscures the previously perfect knowledge of the divinely created human soul. He was originally created '"beautiful and clear-sighted, lighter than a bird on the wing"' ['bel et cler voyant / legier plus quë oysel volant', *PVH1* 5953–4], but the Fall has occluded and deformed the *imago dei* in the human soul:

182 MEDIEVAL ALLEGORY AS EPISTEMOLOGY

'Le cors forsclos dont t'ai parle
Et de touz poins hors separe,
Tu ez de Dieu la portraiture
Et l'ymage et la faiture,
   (*PVH1* 5945–8)
[. . .] ta production pas n'as
D'ome mortel, ains est venue
De Dieu ton pere et descendue.
   [. . .]
Il te fist, quar esperit tu es,
Et te mist ou cors que tu ez.'
   (*PVH1* 5982–4, 5993–4)

'Apart from the body—I have spoken about that, and it is set apart in every way—you are the picture, the image, and the likeness of God.

   [. . .]
you were not made by a mortal man but by God, your Father.

   [. . .]
He made you, for you are a spirit, and placed you in the body that you are.'
   [translation emended]

As a fallen, embodied subject, the pilgrim remains by definition unable to understand Raison's explanation, and fails to visualize his own double nature. He eventually asks to be given an experiential, sensory proof of the existence of his body and soul as two separate substances:

'Se vouliez pour moy tant faire
Que moy de ma nef m'ostissiez
Et du cors despoullissiez,
Que me *moustrissiez* ce contrait,
Cel avugle que tant meffait
   [. . .]
A fin que je peusse *esprouver*
Ce que vous dites.'
   (*PVH1* 6162–70; my emphases)

'If you would be so kind as to take me out of my boat and divest me of my body, *show* me this blind and lame creature that has done me so much harm . . . so that I might *prove/ experience* what you have said.'

Reason eventually satisfies his request, and the soul is disengaged from the body for a brief instant:

Adonc mist main a moi Raison
Et je me mis a son bandon,
Elle sacha et je boutai,
Tant fiz, tant fist et li et moy
Que le contrait fut trebuchie
De dessur moy et deschargie.
Quant destrousse ainsi je fu,
En l'air en haut tout ravi fu.
   (*PVH1* 6199–206)

Then Raison took hold of me and I put myself at her command. She pulled and I pushed, and we made such an effort, she and I, that the crippled one was lifted off me and fell away. When I was unburdened this way, I was carried off high into the air.

The pilgrim's out-of-body experience appears to provide undeniable proof of the separate existence of the soul, as an ontologically superior, separate substance capable of cognitive acts through its own power alone.

The pilgrim's 'cognitive ecstasy'[13] is clearly designed to provide irrefutable evidence for an Augustinian substance dualism, confirming the soul's existence as a separate substance and its identity with the pilgrim's true self. As I want to illustrate in what follows, however, the episode ultimately ends up raising serious doubts about the viability of the doctrine it is intended to validate. If anything, the pilgrim's ecstasy points up the difficulty of describing instances of purely intellectual cognition, supposedly occurring within the incorporeal rational soul and independently of corporeally mediated sense perception. In doing so, I argue, the episode ultimately reveals the untenable status of the anthropological and epistemic model that underpins Deguileville's entire poetic project, when it is measured against subjective experience. Rather than demonstrating the soul's ability to engage in cognitive acts independently of the body—*contra* Aristotle—the episode ends up revealing precisely the inextricable entanglement between soul body, mind and matter, highlighting the tenaciously embodied state of all human cognitive acts.

The precise significance and implications of the pilgrim's cognitive ecstasy largely depend on the epistemic status we decide to attribute to the episode itself. For the pilgrim, the episode functions as an experiential demonstration of the soul's independence and its cognitive abilities. For the poem's readers— invited to project their own subjectivity onto the poem's open 'I'—the episode on the other hand functions as a philosophical thought experiment.[14] The episode in effect appears to be based on an existing thought experiment found in Avicenna's *De anima*, commonly referred to as the thought experiment of the 'flying man' or 'suspended person'. The thought experiment is found in a conspicuous position at the start of the widely circulated twelfth-century Latin translation of Avicenna by Gundissalinus (fifty MSS, of which thirty-five earlier than the fourteenth century).[15] Avicenna's *De anima* as a whole also presents a theory of the soul

---

[13] I borrow the term 'extase cognitive' from Maupeu, *Pèlerins de vie humaine*, p. 165.

[14] There is considerable disagreement over the definitions, mechanisms and epistemological status of thought experiments among contemporary philosophers and intellectual historians, see e.g. the recent collection by Ierodiakonou and Roux, eds, *Thought Experiments in Methodological and Historical Contexts*. Such slipperiness is essential in lending this particular thought experiment its appeal for Deguileville in this specific context. Here I use the term without making definite assumptions about its precise epistemic status, and to designate a visually/mentally simulated situation that is counterfactual, involves a concrete scenario, and is endowed with a clearly discernible cognitive intention—characteristic features of all thought experiments loosely defined, as identified by Sophie Roux, in 'The Emergence of the Notion of Thought Experiments', in Ierodiakonou and Roux, *Thought Experiments in Methodological and Historical Contexts*, pp. 1–36 (4, 19 and *passim*), and Knox, Morton, and Reeve, eds, *Medieval Thought Experiments*. On the problematic, ultimately self-defeating role of thought experiments in Deguileville and in allegory more broadly in the context of *medieval*, as opposed to modern cognitive models, see the conclusion to this chapter, Chapter 3.5, and my 'Can Thought Experiments Backfire? Avicenna's Flying Man, Self-Knowledge, and the Experience of Allegory in Deguileville's *Pèlerinage de Vie Humaine*', in Knox, Morton, and Reeve, *Medieval Thought Experiments*, pp. 41–70.

[15] Hasse, *Avicenna's 'De Anima'*, pp. 7–8.

184 MEDIEVAL ALLEGORY AS EPISTEMOLOGY

that is closely analogous to Deguileville's, and indeed the preface to Gundissalinus's translation provides a useful gloss on Deguileville's general concerns in the body-soul episode:

> It is unworthy of a human being not to know the part of himself by which he knows [. . .]. How could he love himself or God, if he is shown to be ignorant about that which is best in himself? [That is] his soul, in which he carries the likeness of his creator more evidently than the rest.[16]

Such introductory remarks are of course of a highly general order, and would have been available to Deguileville elsewhere in roughly comparable form—for instance the fellow Cistercian Isaac of Stella's *Epistola de anima* (PL 194, 1875–90), or, more likely, in the hugely popular pseudo-Augustinian *De spiritu et anima* (PL 40, 779–832).[17] Avicenna's theory of the soul was not in itself innovative—on the contrary. It was precisely because it seemed to converge so neatly with much earlier, Augustinian theories of the soul that Avicenna's text reached such a wide audience in the Latin West, at a time when scholastic writers were struggling to make sense of Aristotle's far more challenging and 'notoriously murky'[18] theory of the soul in his own *De anima*. Heavily inflected by Neoplatonic ideas, Avicenna's theory of the soul seemed to occupy an intermediary position between Augustine's substance dualism and Aristotle's hylomorphic theory of the self, postulated on the principle that body and soul were, like matter and form, inextricably entangled and mutually activating principles. Avicenna's treatise therefore opened up the possibility for harmonizing Aristotelian Faculty psychology with Augustinian accounts of the soul and cognition, an opportunity that was eagerly seized on by Western scholastics throughout the thirteenth century.[19] Etienne Gilson famously coined

---

[16] 'Indignum siquidem ut illam partem sui qua est sciens, homo nesciat, et id per quod rationalis est, ratione ipse non comprehendat. Quomodo enim iam se vel Deum poterit diligere, cum id quod in se melius est convincitur ignorare [. . .] in qua sui creatoris simulacrum expressius quam ceter gerit.' Avicenna (Ibn Sīnā), *Liber de Anima seu Sextus de Naturalibus: Édition critique de la traduction latine médiévale*, ed. Simone Van Riet. 2 vols (Leiden: Brill, 1968–72), I:3. Translation from Hasse, *Avicenna's 'De Anima'*, p. 5.

[17] Or the *De naturae corporis et animae* by William of St Thierry's, another Cistercian (PL 180: 695–726); or Hugh of St Victor's *De Unione Corporis et Spiritus* (PL 177:285–94). See further Bernard McGinn, *Three Treatises on Man: A Cistercian Anthropology* (Kalamazoo: Cistercian Publications, 1977); Caterina Tarlazzi, 'L'*Epistola de anima* di Isacco di Stella: studio della tradizione ed edizione del testo', in *Medioevo: Rivista di storia della filosofia medievale* 36 (2011), 167–278. Hasse, *Avicenna's 'De Anima'*, pp. 9–12, also points to the wider availability of such ideas since the twelfth century.

[18] Pasnau, *Theories of Cognition in the Later Middle Ages*, p. 12.

[19] On the issue, see particularly the essays in the volume by Lagerlund, *Forming the Mind*. For a concise overview of the questions in the later Middle Ages, see also Haldane, 'Soul and Body', CHMP, I:293–304; and Stone 'The Soul's Relation to the Body, esp. 34–8. For a more focused study of the early thirteenth century, including discussion of Philip the Chancellor, William of Auvergne, and Alexander of Hales as well as Hugh of St Cher, see Bieniak, *The Soul–Body Problem at Paris*, esp. pp. 15–34 for an outline of the general terms of the debate. On the reception of Avicenna, see Hasse, *Avicenna's 'De Anima'*.

COGNITION: THEORY AND PRACTICE   185

the term 'Augustinisme Avicennisant' to describe such theories of the soul,[20] and although Gilson's theory has been much critiqued,[21] the term itself has the advantage of highlighting the largely syncretistic nature of many thirteenth-century discussions of the soul. If anything, recent work has revealed how intense and how dynamic the negotiations between Aristotelian and Augustinian elements in the scholasticism of the period actually were, establishing the extent to which many scholastic thinkers were reluctant to dispense with Augustine altogether even after the supposed 'triumph' of Aristotelian faculty psychology in the mid-thirteenth century.

The specific relevance of Avicenna's *De anima* for Deguileville, however, lies in the Flying Man thought experiment itself—that is, in the imaginative and narrative means used to convey a theory of the soul and cognition that is ultimately reducible to a fairly standard Augustinian substance dualism. There are in effect close parallels between Avicenna's thought experiment and the pilgrim's cognitive ecstasy—as well as important differences. The thought experiment was widely known in the West, not only through Gundissalinus's translation, but also because it was included in further scholastic treatises on the soul, notably by William of Auvergne, Jean de la Rochelle, Peter of Spain, Matthew of Aquasparta, and Vital du Four.[22] It is revealing that many of these scholastic authors use the Flying Man thought experiment in direct conjunction with quotations from Augustinian or pseudo-Augustinian sources.[23] A particularly likely source for Deguileville appears to be Jean de la Rochelle's version of the Flying Man: his treatise on the soul was by far the most influential of the group (fifty manuscripts); he uses the thought experiment as the opening gambit in the very first *quaestio* of his treatise; and his overall sensibility appears to come closest to Deguileville's.[24]

---

[20] Gilson, 'Les sources gréco-arabes de l'augustinisme avicennisant'.

[21] The primary objection concerns Gilson's assumptions regarding the existence of rival 'schools of thought' in the period, Augustinians and Aristotelians—a notion now largely abandoned by intellectual historians. See further Hasse, *Avicenna's 'De Anima'*, pp. v–x; Marrone, *The Light of thy Countenance*, I:2 ff. and *passim*.

[22] See especially Hasse, *Avicenna's 'De Anima'*, pp. 80–92; Juhana Toivanen, 'The Fate of the Flying Man: Medieval Reception of Avicenna's Thought Experiment', *Oxford Studies in Medieval Philosophy* 3 (2015), 64–98; Peter Adamson and Fedor Benevich, 'The Thought Experimental Method: Avicenna's Flying Man Argument', *Journal of the American Philosophical Association* 4.2 (2018), 147–64.

[23] See Toivanen, 'The Fate of the Flying Man', 79 and 82, commenting respectively on Jean de la Rochelle and Matthew of Aquasparta. Jean de la Rochelle, *Summa de anima*, cites not only the Pseudo-Augustinian *De spiritu et anima*, but also Augustine's *De Genesi ad litteram*, *De diversis quaestionibus*, and *De trinitate* in the relevant sections of his treatise (III.14, v.28).

[24] See Jean de la Rochelle, *Summa de anima*, ed. Jacques Guy Bougerol (Paris: Vrin, 1995), I.1, 26–41. Among other noteworthy features shared with Deguileville is Jean's insistence on the divine resemblance of the human soul (II.2, 30–7, V.27–35), and divine illumination (II.3–5), as well as his double, ontological and epistemological emphasis, on which see Toivanen, 'The Fate of the Flying Man', 78–80. As noted by Hasse, *Avicenna's 'De Anima'*, p. 220, Jean de la Rochelle's illuminationist doctrine also demonstrably influenced accounts found in later popular sources such as Vincent of Beauvais' *Speculum naturale*, 27.41, in *Speculum quadruplex, naturale, doctrinale, morale, historiale* (Douai: Balthasar Bellère, 1624), pp. 1946–7, an encyclopaedia that Deguileville would almost certainly have been familiar with. Deguileville's version of the Flying Man, however, also shares a number of features with

186 MEDIEVAL ALLEGORY AS EPISTEMOLOGY

The Flying Man thought experiment occurs twice in the *De anima* (I.1; V.7), and both in its narrative details, philosophical implications, and general purpose it is closely analogous to the pilgrim's cognitive ecstasy:[25]

> We say, therefore, that one of us must imagine himself as created all at once and perfect but with his sight veiled from seeing external things, and that he is created as moving in the air or the void so that the density of the air, which he could perceive, would not touch him, and that he is created with his limbs separate in such a way that they neither meet nor touch each other. He must then see if he affirms the existence of his essence. He would not hesitate to affirm that he exists, but he would not affirm anything external about his members, nor anything hidden about what is inside him, neither his mind nor his brain, nor anything external whatsoever. But he would affirm that he exists without affirming his length, width, or depth.[26]

PVH transposes the idea into the following terms:

Quant destrousse ainsi je fu,	When I was unburdened this way, I was
En l'air en haut tout ravi fu;	carried off high into the air. It seemed
Bien me sembloit que je volasse	to me that I was flying and that I
Et que nulle rien ne pesasse.	weighed nothing. I could go
A mon gre par tout aloie,	everywhere I wanted, both up and
(Et) Sus et jus et loing vëoie.	down, and I could see far away. It
Rien au monde, ce me sembloit,	seemed that nothing in the world was
Mucie ne cele ne m'estoit;	hidden or concealed from me.
(*PVH1* 6205–12)	

Avicenna's own account as translated by Gundissalinus, specifically the emphasis on self-knowledge, very prominent in the translator's prologue, *Liber de anima*, ed. Van Riet, 'prologus', 4–15, p. 3, and the use of an extended analogy of the soul enveloped by the body, compared to a body enveloped by clothing, which Avicenna develops as he repeats the thought experiment of the Flying Man in a later section of the *Liber de anima*, V.7, 51–80, on which see Michael Marmura, 'Avicenna's Flying Man in Context', *The Monist* 69 (1986), 383–95 (389–90), cf. *PVH1* 6115–38. Deguileville's instrumental and more radically dualist attitude to corporality, on the other hand, comes closest to William of Auvergne, *The Soul*, trans. Ronald J. Teske (Milwaukee: Marquette University Press, 2000), 3.11, pp. 139–44.

[25] For discussion of the relevant extracts, see especially Marmura, 'Avicenna's Flying Man in Context'; and Hasse, *Avicenna's 'De Anima'*, pp. 80–92.

[26] 'Dicimus igitur quod aliquis ex nobis putare debet quasi subito creatus esset et perfectus, sed velato visu suo ne exteriora videret, et creatus esset sic quasi moveretur in aere aut in inani, ita ut eum non tangeret spissitudo aeris quam ipse sentire posset, et quasi essent disiuncta membra eius ita ut non concurrerent sibi nec contingerent sese. Deinde videat si affirmat esse suae essentiae: non enim dubitabit affirmare se esse, nec tamen affirmabit exteriora suorum membrorum, nec occulta suorum interiorum nec animum nec cerebrum, nec aliquid aliud extrinsecus, sed affirmabit se esse, cuius non affirmabit longitudinem nec latitudinem nec spissitudinem' (Avicenna, *Liber de anima*, I.1, ed. Van Riet, I.36–7, 49–68). I have used the translation proposed in Toivanen, 'The Fate of the Flying Man', 67, with slight emendation.

COGNITION: THEORY AND PRACTICE 187

Avicenna's conclusions arising from the thought-experiment are equally relevant to Deguileville's cognitive ecstasy:

> And because the essence that he affirms to exist is proper to him in that it is himself and in addition to the body, he who is attentive has the means to be awakened to knowing that the being of the soul is different from the being of the body; indeed, he does not need the body in order to know and perceive the soul. If he were ignorant of it, he would need to be put back on the right track.[27]

The need to put the *viator* 'back on the right track' (*convertire ad viam*) provides a perfectly apt description of the action in Deguileville's allegory: the pilgrim is put back on the right track by a maternal, benevolent if rather patronizing Raison (e.g. 5743–6), reminding her student that '"your body and you are two"' ['toi et ton cors estes .II', *PVH1* 5926] and that '"you are spirit"' ['esperis es', *PVH1* 5993], and finally affirming that it is the soul alone who provides access to knowledge: '"for it is you who can see, and not the body, which is blind both inside and out"' ['Quar tu vois, et non pas le cors / qui avugle est et ens et hors', *PVH1* 6099–100]. The teaching appears to bear fruit, and eventually the pilgrim dutifully rehearses his lesson:

'Je cuidoie que moy et [mon cors]
Fussons un, mes n'est pas ainsi.
Par vous en ay le voir apris
Selonc que j'en ay enquis'
   [...]
'mon cors avez bien distingue
De moy et clerement monstre
Comment il m'est toujours contraire'
   (*PVH1* 6391–4, 6439–41)

'I thought that my body and I were the same, but it is not so. From you I have learned the truth, according to what I asked about it.'
   [...]
'You have distinguished me from my body very well and you have shown clearly how he is always opposed to me in everything good I want to do.'

Deguileville would also have found in Avicenna's *De anima* an ample elaboration of the idea of the body as the soul's clothing, with convenient accidental echoes of Augustine (e.g. *De trinitate* XII.11.16), in a passage that immediately follows the second occurrence of the Flying Man thought-experiment:

> These organs belong to us in reality only as garments, which, due to constant adherence to us have become as parts of our selves. When we imagine our souls, we do not imagine them naked, but imagine them possessing covering garments. The reason for this is constant adherence, with the difference that with real

---

[27] 'Et, quoniam essentia quam affirmat esse est propria illi, eo quod illa est ipsemet, et est praeter corpus eius et membra eius quae non affirmat, ideo expergefactus habet viam evigilandi ad sciendum quod esse animae aliud est quam esse corporis; immo non eget corpore ad hoc ut sciat animam et percipiat eam; si autem fuerit stupidus, opus habet converti ad viam', Avicenna, *Liber de anima* I.1, ed. Van Riet, I.37, 62–8.

188   MEDIEVAL ALLEGORY AS EPISTEMOLOGY

clothes we have become accustomed to taking them off and laying them aside—
something we have not been accustomed to with the bodily organs. Thus our
belief that the organs are part of us is stronger than our belief that garments are
part of us.[28]

Although Avicenna's own theory of the soul is itself problematic—marked by the
double inheritance of Aristotelian ideas on the one hand, and Neoplatonic tradition on the other[29]—the Flying Man thought experiment certainly affirms the
identity of the self with the immaterial rational soul, and identifies its knowledge
as being internally generated rather than conveyed and by information abstracted
from sense perception.[30] Deguileville's version of the thought experiment in *PVH*
similarly aims to establish the identity of the soul with the self—a doctrine that
stands in clear opposition to the Aristotelian model. Aristotle rejected the Platonic
account, which saw the human being as resulting from the conjunction of the two
separate substances of body and soul, and proposed an alternative, hylomorphic
account: instead of being a separate substance, the soul was now understood as the
form that conferred actuality on the material potentiality of the body (*De anima*
II.1, 412a27–8), making its independent existence separately from the body effectively impossible. While Deguileville was not alone in questioning the viability
of the Aristotelian account and its compatibility with Christian doctrine, by 1331
Aristotle's model had been widely accepted. As stipulated at the Council of Vienne
in 1312, the orthodox position held that 'the substance of the rational or intellective
soul is the form of the human body in itself and essentially'.[31] The promulgation

---

[28] Avicenna, *Liber de anima* V.7, ed. Van Riet, II.162–3, 57–64: 'Haec autem membra non sunt vere
nisi sicut vestes; quae, quia diu est quod adhaeserunt nobis, putavimus nos esse illa aut quod sunt sicut
partes nostri; cum enim imaginamur nostras animas, non imaginamur eas nudas, sed imaginamur eas
indutas corporibus, cuius rei causa est diuturnitas adhaerentiae; consuevimus autem exuere vestes at
proiicere, quod omnino non consuevimus in membris: unde opinio quod membra sunt partes nostri,
firmior est in nobis quam opinio quod vestes sint partes nostri.' Of course the idea is not exclusive
to Avicenna, and is found in similar form already in Nemesius of Emesa's fourth-century *De Natura
Hominis*, translated twice into Latin in the eleventh and twelfth centuries. See Nemesius of Emesa,
De natura hominis: Traduction de Burgundio de Pise, ed. G. Verbeke and J. R. Moncho (Leiden: Brill,
1975), pp. 51–2.
[29] Peter Heath, *Allegory and Philosophy in Avicenna (Ibn Sînâ): With a Translation of the Book of
the Prophet Muhammad's Ascent to Heaven* (Philadelphia: University of Pennsylvania Press, 1992),
pp. 53–79.
[30] Heath, *Allegory and Philosophy in Avicenna*, 55–6; Marmura, 'Avicenna's Flying Man in Context';
Deborah Black, 'The Nature of Intellect', in *CHMP* I:324–6, 329–31; Mikko Yrjönsuuri, 'Identity and
Moral Agency', *CHMP*, I:472–83 (474–8).
[31] *Enchiridion Symbolorum, Definitionum et Declarationum de Rebus Fidei et Morum* (Freiburg:
Herder, 1965) nr. 902 (old 481); 'anima rationalis seu intellectiva [. . .] sit forma corporis humani per
se et essentialiter'. It would be tempting to see this as one of the possible reasons behind the conjec-
tural 'condemnation' of Deguileville, evoked in *PVH2*—see Maupeu and Edwards, 'Introduction' to
PVH2, pp. 21–3; Faral, *Guillaume de Deguileville*, pp. 9–10. The passage however survives unchanged
in the second version, with the exception of the substitution of Grace Dieu for Raison as the agent
of the separation. Deguileville's dualistic ship-pilot metaphor (*PVH1* 6139 ff.) similarly transgresses
one of the 1277 condemnations (art. 7 Piché, *La Condamnation*, pp. 82–3 / art. 123 in Roland Hissette, *Enquête sur les 219 articles condamnés à Paris le 7 mars 1277* (Louvain and Paris: Publications

COGNITION: THEORY AND PRACTICE 189

effectively canonizes a position that had been formulated half a century earlier, encapsulated in Aquinas's affirmation that 'the soul is not the whole human being, and my soul is not I.'[32] Aquinas specifically insists on the necessity of the senses to attain perfect knowledge, even in the resurrected body, given the weakness of the human intellect when compared with its angelic counterpart.[33] It has even been suggested that Aquinas, like Albert the Great before him, may have deliberately avoided any reference to Avicenna's popular Flying Man thought-experiment precisely in order to avoid raising the spectre of the soul's capacity for direct and unmediated self-knowledge.[34] It is easy to see how Deguileville is rejecting just such ideas when he stages a body-soul separation that aims to specifically identify the human soul as the source of individual selfhood, and when he clearly asserts— *contra* Aquinas—the angelic nature of the soul's knowledge in its disembodied state:[35]

[. . .] rien	Nothing, not the heavens, the earth, the
A ta noblece comparer	sea, the birds or any other creature,
Ne se puet ciel, terre ne mer,	except the angels, can compare to your
Oisel ne' autre creature	nobility.
Excepte d'angres la nature.	
(*PVH1* 5958–62)	

There is little doubt about the philosophical affinity of Deguileville's model of the soul and cognition, which is strongly Augustinian and even anti-Aristotelian. But it is questionable whether his version of the Flying Man thought experiment ultimately demonstrates the viability of such a doctrine. It is worth considering the epistemic status of Deguileville's thought experiment more closely—especially

---

Universitaires, 1977), pp. 199–201) but equally survives unchanged in *PVH2*. Further on the role of the decree at the council of Vienne, see William Duba, 'The Souls after Vienne: Franciscan Theologians' Views on the Plurality of Forms and the Plurality of Souls, ca. 1315–1330', in Paul J. J. M. Bakker, Sander W. Boer, and Cees Leijenhorst, eds, *Psychology and the other Disciplines: A Case of Cross-Disciplinary Interaction (1250–1750)* (Leiden: Brill, 2012), pp. 171–272.

[32] 'anima autem cum sit pars corporis hominis, non est totus homo, et anima mea non est ego.' Thomas Aquinas, *In I Epist. ad Corinthios*, I.15.2, n. 924, in *Super Epistolas S. Pauli lectura*, ed. Raphael Cai. 2 vols (Turin and Rome: Marietti, 1953) I:411. For a discussion contrasting of Aquinas's and Olivi's conceptualization of the human soul—the latter closely analogous to Deguileville's—see Mikko Yrjönsuuri, 'The Soul as an Entity: Dante, Aquinas, and Olivi', in Lagerlund, *Forming The Mind*, pp. 59–92, and below. Further see Norman Kretzmann, 'Philosophy of Mind', in Norman Kretzmann and Eleonore Stump, eds, *Cambridge Companion to Aquinas* (Cambridge: Cambridge University Press, 1993), pp. 128–59. See also Stone, 'The Soul's Relation to the Body', especially pp. 46–8.

[33] See again *In I Epist. ad Corinthios*, I.15.2, and elsewhere, e.g. *ST* 1a 89.1; for a detailed analysis, see Robert Pasnau, *Thomas Aquinas on Human Nature: A Philosophical Study of 'Summa Theologiae'*, *1a 75–89* (Cambridge: Cambridge University Press, 2002), pp. 380–93.

[34] See especially Deborah J. Brown, 'Aquinas' Missing Flying Man', *Sophia* 40.1 (2001), 17–31; and Therese Scarpelli Cory, *Aquinas on Human Self-knowledge* (Cambridge: Cambridge University Press, 2014), pp. 24–6, 30–2, 183; and ibid., 'The Footprint of Avicenna's Flying Man in Aquinas's Commentary on the *Sentences* I.3.4.5' (https://www.academia.edu/1975062/The_Footprint_of_Avicennas_Flying_Man_in_Aquinass_Commentary_on_the_Sentences_I.3.4.5; retrieved 5 June 2021).

[35] This controversial, originally Victorine doctrine was transmitted by Peter Lombard's *Sentences*, see Bieniak, *The Soul–Body Problem at Paris*, p. 89.

190 MEDIEVAL ALLEGORY AS EPISTEMOLOGY

given the unstable epistemic value of the Flying Man thought experiment more widely as deployed by Latin scholastic authors. Originally, Avicenna had defined the thought experiment as a *tanbih* in the Arabic original, which is best translated as meaning 'a pointer', or 'hint', and one medieval Arabic–Latin translator renders this, in a different context, as a 'nod'.[36] The status of a *tanbih* becomes clearer if we refer to Avicenna's own hierarchy of methods of communicating knowledge.[37] Avicenna identifies three principal methods, all expressing the same truths, but at different levels of fullness and perfection. In ascending order we have the symbolic/allegorical method; the indicative method; and the demonstrative or expository method. The allegorical/symbolic is the most obscure and imperfect mode of communication, and is defined in primarily negative terms as a strategy to conceal or withhold deeper truths from inferior minds that would misapply and misunderstand the actual teachings. The indicative method relies on pointers and allusions, and is accordingly dynamic: its main function is to point, directing the mind towards a higher knowledge that is distantly apprehended, prompting and stimulating the imperfect mind of a promising student to further inquiry. Avicenna's demonstrative method—the highest and most perfect means of accessing and communicating knowledge—consists of syllogistic reasoning as defined by Aristotle: here intelligibles are grasped in the intellect by correctly guessing the middle term of the syllogism. The 'Flying Man' is identified as a *tanbih*, and thus falls in the intermediary category of the indicative method. But such nuances, and the whole epistemic framework they imply, were largely lost on Latin scholastic authors. Most of them describe the thought experiment in terms that tend to assimilate it to a proof or demonstration: it is variously called a *ratio*, a *probatio*, or a *declaratio*.[38] Crucially, however, the indicative, analogical, and counterfactual character of the original thought experiment (*tanbih*) precludes it from serving a strictly demonstrative function that Avicenna defines on the basis of Aristotle's theory of syllogism.

The already nebulous epistemic value of the Flying Man thought experiment is exacerbated in Deguileville's version. The latter is not in fact presented as a theoretical, counterfactual thought experiment at all, but as an actual cognitive ecstasy, an *experience* that is intended to function as an empirical demonstration of the duality of body and soul for the benefit of the Pilgrim. At best, the episode serves

---

[36] See Hasse, *Avicenna's 'De Anima'*, pp. 86–7, 90–2. See also Marmura, 'Avicenna's Flying Man in Context', who argues that Avicenna extrapolates a categorical conclusion from what in reality is merely a hypothetical argument, and thus essentially presents an indemonstrable premise dressed up as a conclusion. Peter of Spain comes closest to Avicenna by emphasizing the imaginative nature of the thought experiment, see Toivanen, 'The Fate of the Flying Man', 76 n. 29.

[37] Gutas, *Avicenna and the Aristotelian Tradition*, pp. 335–58 (cf. pp. 297–318 1st edn). For a complementary approach with a different, more positive emphasis on the role allegory and indeed poetry in fostering the journey and ascent of the human soul, in Avicenna's Arabic Neoplatonic context, see Heath, *Allegory and Philosophy in Avicenna*, pp. 80–106.

[38] Hasse, *Avicenna's 'De Anima'*, pp. 90–2.

as a thought experiment for the reader, who is able to participate vicariously in the Pilgrim's experience. This is a major difference from the scholastic instances of the Flying Man, where the soul is at best *unaware* of its body or ceases to rely on its functions, but is never in fact *separated* from it.[39] But the trick seems to satisfy the Pilgrim's demands to be given a tangible demonstration, 'A fin que je peusse *esprouver* / Ce que vous dites' (ll. 6169–70; see fuller quotation above). The key term here is *esprouver*: it has the Latin *probare* as its root, but in contrast to a scholastic *probatio* the term defines not demonstrative knowledge but experiential, sensory proof. It is the soul itself that directly experiences its own existence as an independent and immaterial substance capable of its own cognitive acts without use of the body.

While the distinctly 'experiential' character of the Flying Man thought experiment as deployed by Deguileville has the advantage of 'thickening' the thought experiment into a more easily graspable, mentally 'plastic' experience, it also tends to undermine the very notion of an incorporeal, purely intellectual cognition. The description of the actual body-soul separation in the poem brings this latent paradox into full view, highlighting the difficulty of providing 'tangible' experiential evidence for the strictly incorporeal, purely intellectual nature of the rational soul. After the separation, the body lies lifeless and numb on the ground, deprived of any perceptual faculty as if to stress its complete lack of cognitive agency:

bien vi mon cors que c'estoit fiens	I saw clearly that my body was
[...]	dung [...]. It lay there stretched out on
A terre estendu se gesoit,	the earth, and *it did not hear nor see*. Its
Ou *il n'ooit ne ne vëoit*;	face showed that it had no power in it.
Sa contenance signe estoit	[translation emended]
Qu'en li nulle vertu n'avoit.	
(*PVH1* 6221–8; my emphasis)	

Yet in order to ascertain that the body is an inert entity, the pilgrim/soul paradoxically does so by *touching* it:

J'alay et ving tout entour li,	I circled all around it to find out if it
A savoir mon së endormy	was asleep. *I felt its pulse*, but
Estoit et *le pous li tastai*,	understand that I did not find, in its
Mes sachiez que je n'i trouvai	nerves, conduits, and veins, any pulse
En nerf, en conduit ne en vaine	or breath, any more than in a log.
Ne qu'en un tronc pous ne alaine;	[translation emended]
(*PVH1* 6229–34; my emphasis)	

---

[39] Another major difference concerns the fact that in most scholastic versions the human soul is imagined *at the moment of creation*, i.e. has not previously obtained any perceptual experience upon which self-awareness might depend.

192 MEDIEVAL ALLEGORY AS EPISTEMOLOGY

The soul's very act of reaching out to *touch* the inert body completely undoes the logic of the thought experiment. It seems that in order to experience its independence from the body, the rational soul relies on sense perception, specifically *touch*—the most bodily of the five senses. This raises serious, possibly insoluble problems, given that sense perception is clearly impossible without reliance on the body's sense organs.[40] Deguileville's notion of a rational soul 'perceiving' its own body—if understood literally and empirically as indeed we are invited to understand it[41]—is inevitably self-defeating: in the very process of seeking to ascertain its separation and independence from the body, the pilgrim's rational soul reveals its continued dependence on the senses, and thus manifests the ineluctably *embodied* condition of the pilgrim's self.[42] The desire to furnish a (literally) 'tangible' proof of the soul's independence from the body finally ends up confirming that self-knowledge depends precisely on the pilgrim's perceptual bodily faculties.[43]

To a certain extent, the poem acknowledges this paradox, and the radical hylomorphism it implies. Despite the sustained efforts to disengage the body from the pilgrim's true self or soul, Raison herself also concedes that body and soul appear to be inextricably enmeshed. Both are constitutive parts of the self-divided subject, by turns a spiritual being made in the image of God, and a tenaciously embodied, material self:

[Dieu] te fist, quar esperit es,	God made you, for you are spirit, and he
Et te mist ou cors *que tu ez*.	placed you in the body *that you are*.
(*PVH1* 5993–4)	[emphasis mine; translation emended]

The formulation is symptomatic, and contradicts the essentially dualistic and instrumental understanding of the body that Raison attempts to instil in the pilgrim throughout this extended passage: rather than being a soul who *has* a body, the pilgrim is a subject who *is*, by turns, soul and/or body.[44]

The conclusion of this episode encapsulates the more fundamental instabilities of the *Pèlerinage*'s anthropology: on the one hand the poet insistently advocates a strongly dualist model of the human self through the mouthpiece of his authority figures; on the other hand, the actual details of the poem's action suggest that this theory may not ultimately provide a reliable explanation for the pilgrim's

---

[40] This principle informs *all* scholastic accounts of sense perception and the sensitive soul. See e.g. King, 'Why isn't the Mind-Body Problem Medieval?'.

[41] Again, the paradox is potentially present in the Latin translation of Avicenna's *Liber de anima*, where the soul perceives (*percipiat*) itself. Deguileville however literalizes Avicenna's allegory, or rather his *tanbih*.

[42] This also contradicts one of the original premises of the Flying Man, namely that the self-aware soul is unaware of its body; see premise nr. 2 in Toivanen's schematic rendering of the argumentative structure of the thought experiment, 'The Fate of the Flying Man', 68.

[43] This touches on yet another related problem discussed by contemporary scholastics, namely proprioception, or the perception of one's own body, on which see e.g. Yrjönsuuri, 'Perceiving One's Own Body'.

[44] A similar point is made by Kay, *Place of Thought*, pp. 85–7.

actual experience of his own cognitive acts in the real world. This tension is not merely an incidental detail, but points to some of the core philosophical difficulties Deguileville had to confront in writing a poem intended to present a complete, totalizing picture of the human condition in the shape of an allegorical quest narrative. In what follows I therefore provide a closer examination of the poet's divided loyalties, emphasizing his theoretical allegiance to a strongly dualist and illuminationst model of active cognition, and his awareness of the practical difficulties in denying or transcending the embodied state that characterizes the human condition on earth.

2. Theory: Divine Illumination and Active Cognition

Deguileville's Flying Man thought experiment serves as a keystone of the poem's anthropology, metaphysics, and epistemology. The cognitive ecstasy marks the midpoint of the narrative, separating the pedagogical emphasis of the first half from the account of the pilgrim's actual experiences on his journey in the second half. Also conceptually speaking the episode plays a pivotal role: it is placed midway between the initial vision of the New Jerusalem—where human souls are shown free from their bodily prison, and 'began to fly, rising high up into the city' [commoncoient a voler, / Pour haut en la cite monter, *PVH1* 121–2]—and the final separation of body and soul at the moment of death, preparing for the resurrection of the body among the fellowship of the blessed, when 'the flesh will decay and it will be born again at the general judgment' [iert la char pourrie, / Et nouvelle regeneree / En la commun assemblee, *PVH1* 13,464–6]. If the poem is understood as a dynamic whole, tracing the trajectory for the *viator*'s journey towards truth, self-knowledge, the recovery of his own divine resemblance, and ultimately salvation, then the success of such a project hinges on this particular moment, where the ontological structure of the human subject is defined.

Since the thought experiment in many ways backfires, however, this episode crystallizes some of the underlying difficulties of *PVH* as a pedagogical, epistemological, and salvific project. As I want to argue in this section, Deguileville's poem makes a concerted effort to reject the dominant, Aristotelian model of cognition, and invokes two alternative theories of cognition that stand in clear and deliberate opposition to Aristotle's philosophy of mind. On the one hand, Deguileville adopts a distinctly illuminationist theory of cognition as developed by Augustine; while such illuminationist theories proved particularly popular during the thirteenth century, they were gradually abandoned by the scholastics at the end of the thirteenth century. Deguileville's advocacy of an illuminationist theory of knowledge thus must be seen as a conspicuous, deliberately reactionary move against the increasing dominance of the Aristotelian model of cognition. On the other hand, Deguileville also proposes a controversial theory of active perception, assigning

194 MEDIEVAL ALLEGORY AS EPISTEMOLOGY

the role of the efficient cause in any process of cognition to the human soul and not to the objects of perception, in direct opposition to Aristotle's passive model of abstractive perception. Both of these theories are unmistakeably anti-Aristotelian, and reveal much about the broader philosophical and ideological affinities of Deguileville's poem in the context of a wide range of scholastic debates on the nature of the soul and cognition.

Deguileville is not alone in rejecting Aristotle's theory because of its ontological implications, but his anti-Aristotelianism appears particularly stark at such a comparatively late date. Western scholastics had struggled throughout the thirteenth century to make sense of Aristotle's 'notoriously murky'[45] theory of the soul as presented in the *De anima*—the Philosopher's 'most frustratingly incoherent and incomplete [. . .] work'.[46] While all scholastics were undeniably 'Aristotelians' of one kind or another, it is difficult to speak of something like a scholastic 'orthodoxy' on the soul until the early fourteenth century, and a whole range of divergent interpretations of Aristotle's own theories were produced. As already mentioned, Avicenna's heavily Neoplatonic take on Aristotle's account did much to ease the process of accommodating Aristotle with Augustine, but also bequeathed to the scholastics a markedly unstable and inconsistent terminology. During the thirteenth century, when Avicenna's influence reached its peak, this produced the various syncretistic models, by turns Platonic and Aristotelian.[47] This produced a number of improbably 'Augustinian' interpretations of Aristotle's thought, such a Robert Grosseteste's commentary on the *Posterior analytics*—surely the least 'Platonic' in spirit of all of Aristotle's works:

If the highest part of the human soul, the so-called intellective part, which is not the actuality of the body and needs no corporeal instrument for its proper operation, were not clouded over (*obnubilata*) and burdened by the weight of the corrupt body, it would have complete knowledge without the aid of sense perception, through an irradiation received from a higher light, just as it will have when the soul has been stripped from the body and perhaps as those who are wholly separated from the love and the phantasms of corporeal things have.[48]

---

[45] Pasnau, *Theories of Cognition in the Later Middle Ages*, p. 12.

[46] Dales, *The Problem of the Rational Soul*, p. 9.

[47] Joseph Owens, 'Faith, Ideas, Illumination and Experience', in *CHLMP*, pp. 440–59; Black, 'The Nature of Intellect', and Noone, 'Divine Illumination' in *CHMP*, respectively I:320–33, I:369–83; Marrone, *The Light of Thy Countenance*.

[48] 'Et similiter si pars suprema anime humane, que vocatur intellectiva et que non est actus alicius corporis neque egens in operatione sui propria instrumento corporeo, non esset mole corporis corrupti obnobilata et aggravata, ipsa per irradiationem acceptam a lumine superiori haberet completam scientiam absque sensus adminiculo, sicut habebit cum anima erit exuta a corpore et sicut forte habent aliqui penitus absoluti ab amore et phantasmatibus rerum corporalium', Grosseteste, *Commentarius in Posteriorum Analyticorum Libros*, I.14, ll. 228–35. Translation from *Robert Grosseteste's Commentary on Aristotle's Posterior Analytics*, trans. Scott MacDonald (Yale University Press, forthcoming), cited in Pasnau, 'Science and Certainty', in *CHMP*, I.357–68 (363).

Grosseteste's interpretation is revealing precisely because of its radically Platonic and illuminationist bias, symptomatic of early attempts to read Aristotle through a strongly Augustinian lens. More specifically, the language of the passage points to the continuing influence of Augustine's doctrine of divine illumination, according to which the human rational soul could receive the light of knowledge directly from a divine source, unmediated by sense perception. Illumination was also thought to be essential for ordinary cognitive processes, as a means to 'validate' information abstracted from acts of sense perception.[49] Several authors even reinterpreted Aristotle's seminal distinction between agent and possible intellect (*De anima* III.5) by identifying the agent intellect with God, source of inner illumination supplying the human soul with immaterial and eternally valid knowledge of essences.[50] Deeply influenced by this tradition, Grosseteste's commentary effectively articulates a strikingly hybrid, and highly improbable, 'Aristotelian Theory of Divine Illumination'.[51]

Deguileville's account of the pilgrim's cognitive ecstasy tends to align his thought with an even more radical kind of illuminationism, as is suggested by Raison's vocabulary. Images of light abound throughout, as in the parables of the smoky lantern or the sun obscured by a cloud (*PVH1* 6038–100), and serve to emphasize the internal enlightenment of the human understanding available to the soul independently from the mediation of corporeal sense perception. Raison tells the pilgrim that 'you are the picture, the image, and the likeness of God' [De Dieu la portraiture / Et l'ymage et la faiture, *PVH1* 5947–8], and that he was originally created 'beautiful and clear-sighted' [bel et cler voyant', *PVH1* 5953]. His cognitive faculties are clouded over by 'the body [that] is a great and heavy obstacle in your way' [le cors qui au devant / Fait un obstacle espes et grant, *PVH1* 6179–80], and insists that the light of his understanding is entirely dependent on the faculties of his intellectual/rational soul:

'Quar tu vois, et non pas le cors
Qui avugle est et ens et hors.'
  (*PVH1* 6099–100)

'For it is you who can see, and not the body, which is blind both inside and out.'

'L'ame qui habitë u cors
Sa clarte espant par dehors
Et fait cuidier aus foles gens

'The soul that live in the body shines outward, and makes foolish people think that everything is illuminated

---

[49] See especially Marrone, *The Light of thy Countenance*, I.1–25. For more general overviews of theories of divine illumination, see e.g. Black, 'The Nature of Intellect'; Noone, 'Divine Illumination'; Owens, 'Faith, Ideas, Illumination and Experience'. On Augustine's own theory, see Schumacher, *Divine Illumination*, and discussion in the introduction above, pp. 32–5.

[50] See especially Hasse, *Avicenna's 'De Anima'*, pp. 203–23.

[51] See especially the detailed account of Christina Van Dyke, 'An Aristotelian Theory of Divine Illumination: Robert Grosseteste's Commentary on the Posterior Analytics', *British Journal for the History of Philosophy* 17.4 (2009), 685–704.

Que tout li enluminemens	by the poor cloud that obscures the
Soit de la povre nuee	soul.
Dont l'ame est obnubilee.	
(*PVH1* 6063–8)	

Raison's use of the term 'obnubile' here is particularly striking, and directly echoes scholastic discussions of faculty psychology. Grosseteste uses the term in the commentary, quoted above, and uses it to designate precisely the clouding effect of the body upon the human rational soul: the soul is 'clouded over and burdened by the weight of the corrupt body' [mole corporis corrupti obnobilata et aggravata]. Deguileville, who uses the term on two further occasions in *PVH1* (6279; 11,304), provides the first attestation for this term in Middle French,[52] which suggests that the term is borrowed directly from Latin scholastic materials such as Grosseteste's commentary. Raison's use of such unmistakeably illuminationist vocabulary is therefore highly conspicuous, especially given the decline of the theory of divine illumination as a whole after the end of the thirteenth century.[53]

It is tempting to dismiss Deguileville's illuminationism as simply belated and reactionary, but this amounts to ignoring it altogether. In many ways the very existence of Deguileville's poem demonstrates that authors outside of strictly scholastic circles continued to invoke theories of divine illumination in their discussions of cognition. This also suggests that the established account of the 'decline' of theories of divine illumination could benefit from being revised with reference to vernacular, instructional, encyclopaedic, and literary texts, producing a more nuanced and differentiated kind of intellectual history that eschews linear and evolutionary narratives.[54]

Deguileville's adoption of an idiosyncratic theory of active cognition is therefore highly conspicuous in intellectual-historical terms, but also participates in a more widely shared and deep-seated dissatisfaction with Aristotle's model of the soul and cognition. Throughout the thirteenth century one of the principal objections to Aristotle's theory of abstractive cognition was that it seemed to represent human cognition as an essentially passive process.[55] Despite attempts to circumvent or

---

[52] See also Béatrice Stumpf, *Lexique des Pèlerinages de Guillaume de Deguileville*, http://stella.atilf. fr/scripts/dmfX.exe?LEM=OBNUBILER;SUIPRE=OBNUBILER;AFFICHAGE=2;XMODE=STE-LLa;FERMER;MENU=menu_dmf;ISIS=isis_dmf2012L.txt;MENU=menu_lexique_PGD;OUVRIR _MENU=2;s=s110a2a00 (accessed 21 Nov 2022). The term 'obnuble' occurs in earlier texts, but invariably with more general connotations, often referring to 'clouds' or 'coverings', for instance Chrétien de Troyes and the *Rose* (*RR* 4755; 4766; 19,042; 20,423–4) as well as Ovidian materials (Godefroy V.555).

[53] Noone, 'Divine illumination', and Marrone, *The Light of thy Countenance*.

[54] See above, 'Introduction', pp. 4–16.

[55] See especially Katherine H. Tachau, 'Seeing as Action and Passion in the Thirteenth and Fourteenth Centuries', in Jeffrey F. Hamburger and Anne-Marie Bouché, eds, *The Mind's Eye: Art and Theological Argument in the Middle Ages* (Princeton, NJ: Princeton University Press, 2006), pp. 336–59. For a broader overview of related debates, see also ibid., 'Approaching Medieval Scholars' Treatment

COGNITION: THEORY AND PRACTICE   197

neutralize the statement, it seemed difficult to deny that Aristotle had maintained that all knowledge was acquired through the senses: as the often reiterated maxim goes, 'nothing is in the intellect that was not previously in senses' [Nihil est in intellectu quod non prius fuerit in sensu', cf. e.g. Aquinas, *Quaestiones disputatae de veritate*, q. 2, a. 3 ad 19]. But as commentators have pointed out, this affirmation appeared to imply that all higher order cognitive acts in the human soul were ultimately caused by corporeally mediated processes of sense perception: how was it possible to accept that an ontologically inferior substance in the physical world could act upon the human soul, a demonstrably superior and incorporeal ontological entity made in the image of God the creator? This was precisely the point made by Robert Kilwardby and Peter John Olivi, both of whom were committed to developing an alternative account of cognition more in line with Augustine's fragmentary remarks on the topic. In order to do so, both of them developed accounts of cognition that attributed active cognitive agency to the human soul, adopting the Augustinian principle that lower substances are by definition prevented from 'acting' upon higher ones.[56]

The difficulties caused by the Aristotelian model coalesced in particular around the concept of sensible and intellectual *species*. First developed by Alhazen and popularized in the West by the writings of Roger Bacon on perspectivist optics, *species* theory maintained that corporeal objects in the physical world emitted sensible *species* or *imagines* that acted upon the sense organs, triggering the process through which the internal senses in the mind would in turn 'abstract' an intellectual species from sense impression.[57] The implications of such an intromissionist theory of perception were problematic precisely because they raised the question of the ontology of different types of *species*—sensible and intellectual—and the related question of individual agency in acts of perception and cognition. Bacon had been far from clear about the precise ontological status and function of *species*, fostering the development of a wide range of divergent accounts of the operation of *species* among later scholastics—accounts that were further hampered by the lack of a precise and consistent terminology.[58] Bacon notably affirmed the essentially

---

of Cognition', in M. C. Pacheco and J. Meirinhos, eds, *Intellect et imagination dans la philosophie médiévale/Intellect and Imagination in Medieval Philosophy/Intelecto e imaginação na Filosofia Medieval: Actes du XIe Congrès International de Philosophie Médiévale de la Société Internationale pour l'Étude de la Philosophie Médiévale (SIEPM). Porto, du 26 au 31 août 2002* (Turnhout: Brepols, 2006), pp. 1–34.

[56] Silva and Toivanen, 'The Active Nature of the Soul in Sense Perception', notably pp. 255–6 on the problem of the soul's ontological superiority over the body.

[57] *De multiplicatione specierum and De speculis comburentibus*, ed. Lidberg; 'Perspectiva', ed. Lindberg; David C. Lindberg, *Theories of Vision from al-Kindi to Kepler* (Chicago and London: University of Chicago Press, 1981), pp. 107–21; Tachau, *Vision and Certitude*, pp. 1–84.

[58] See Spruit, *Species Intelligibilis*, I:6–7, *passim*, and I:150–6 on Bacon specifically. See however Tachau, 'The Notion of Intentional Existence', in Ebbesen, *Medieval Analyses in Language and Cognition*, p. 337 n. 20, for reservations about the accuracy of Spruit's wide-ranging study, and the tendency to reduce the relevance of Bacon, which is crucial in Tachau's own account, *Vision and Certitude*. On the history behind the emergence of the theory of the 'abstraction' of material forms, and on its wider

198   MEDIEVAL ALLEGORY AS EPISTEMOLOGY

material nature of *species in medio* emitted from the object, which was thought to produce a *phantasma* or sensible *species* in the internal senses after reception by the sense organs; but he also maintained that *species* was subsequently 'dematerialized', arguing in favour of the purely abstract and intangible nature of intellectual species once it was processed within the rational/intellective soul[59]—a point on which Henry of Ghent similarly insisted.[60] Indeed Bacon went as far as developing the notion of an imperceptible, incorporeal, but material *species*.[61] The question of the ontological status, mechanics, and degree of agency of various forms of *species* continued to remain the subject of lively debates throughout the thirteenth and fourteenth centuries, as the scholastics attempted to crack the insoluble problem of how material 'things' came to be in the incorporeal human intellect or rational soul.[62]

As other scholars have suggested in recent years, the debate on the nature of Aristotelian *species* also had a considerable impact on the contemporary debates on the cognitive function of the imaginative faculty, and more specifically on discussions of the poetic imagination and allegorical representation.[63] It is worth taking a closer look at the evocative but unsystematic terminology introduced by Bacon's seminal discussion of *species*:

> And this virtue has many names, for it is called 'the similitude of the agent', 'image', 'species', 'idol', 'simulacrum', 'phantasm', 'form', 'intention', 'passion', 'impression', and 'shadow of the philosopher' by authors of works on vision.[64]

Such statements tended to collapse terms with rather diverse associations—such as *species*, generally deemed material at least in the initial stages of perception, and immaterial but real, extramental *intentio* that Avicenna had described as acting upon the estimative faculty alone and not the senses.[65] More broadly, such an account tended to blur any lingering precision and specificity in the terminology invoked, by reducing a range of different terms and concepts to rough analogues.

---

philosophical and anthropological implications, see Martin M. Tweedale, 'Origins of the Medieval Theory that Sensation is an Immaterial Reception of a Form', *Philosophical Topics* 20.2 (1992), 215–31.

[59] Tachau, *Vision and Certitude*, pp. 11, 22–3; Spruit, *Species Intelligibilis*, I:154–5; Hackett, 'Roger Bacon's Concept of Experience'.

[60] Tachau, *Vision and Certitude*, pp. 28–39.

[61] Wood, 'Imagination and Experience', and the remarks in Yrjönsuuri, 'The Soul as Entity', p. 81.

[62] Perler, 'Things in the Mind'.

[63] For previous discussion of the impact of perspectivist optics on medieval allegory (including the tradition of the *Rose*), see especially Akbari, pp. 24–5, 36–7, 93–6 and *passim*, and Nichols, '"The Pupil of your Eye"'. See further Denery, *Seeing and Being Seen in the Later Medieval World*, and, for an explicitly moralized use of optical theory, see Peter of Limoges, *The Moral Treatise on the Eye*.

[64] 'Et hec virtus [...] habet multa nomina: vocatur enim "similitudo agentis", et "ymago" et "species" et "ydolum" et "simulacrum" et "forma" et "intentio" et "passio" et "impressio" et "umbra philosophorum" apud auctores de aspectibus' (Bacon, *De multiplicatione specierum*, I.1). Both text and translation are from *De multiplicatione specierum*, ed. Lindberg, in *Roger Bacon's Philosophy of Nature*, p. 2, ll. 23–6. See also discussion in Tachau, *Vision and Certitude*, pp. 7–8.

[65] Tachau, *Vision and Certitude*, pp. 11–16 and 20–6.

While this was no doubt intended to underline the elusive ontological status of 'intention', it is easy to see how the account finally had the effect of encouraging visualization of *species* as a dangerously material *simulacrum*—a material object acting upon the (passive) perceiver.[66]

As intellectual historians have pointed out, the *species* model is highly problematic since it threatens to fall into one of two opposite yet equally damaging extremes.[67] On the one hand, according to the Aristotelian 'conformality thesis', the *species* held in the sensitive soul and conveyed to the intellectual soul threatens to become dangerously material, entailing a form of philosophical materialism that ascribes a material, corporeal basis to all cognitive processes, including those of the intellectual soul. At the other end, an emphasis on the abstract, strictly mental and representational status of the *species* as a mere 'image'—a position adopted for instance by Aquinas[68]—raises the spectre of representationalism: the risk posed by this second scenario is that the human intellect is ultimately unable to ascertain whether mental images provide accurate representations of their objects, since images are no longer held to have any direct causal and material relationship to their external objects.

This was precisely what troubled authors such as Kilwardby, Olivi, and later Ockham, who variously qualified, reduced, or indeed denied the relevance of *species* to the efficient cause of cognitive acts.[69] Kilwardby explains the operation of *species* as acting merely upon the sense organs, and postulates a subsequent active role of the soul in apprehending the effect of the *species* upon the bodily sense organ by forming its own, further image of that affection. In this manner he sought to separate the material component of sense perception more clearly from the higher order cognitive operations in the mind.[70] Olivi, by contrast, adopted a more radical position, and famously rejects—well before Ockham—the existence of *species* altogether, and in doing so follows a much more explicitly anti-Aristotelian course. Olivi's anti-Aristotelian philosophy of mind ultimately also earned him the dubious privilege of being the primary target of the Decree on the soul promulgated at the council of Vienne in 1312—already discussed.[71] Olivi's

---

[66] Katherine Tachau, 'The Notion of Intentional Existence', p. 347, suggests that this ambivalence produces among perspectivists and later writers the notion of intention as designating 'an intermediary mode of existence, extramental but less "fixed" than body'.

[67] See e.g. Perler, 'Things in the Mind'; Tachau, 'Seeing as Action and Passion'.

[68] Claude Panaccio, 'Aquinas on Intellectual Representation', in Dominik Perler, ed., *Ancient and Medieval Theories of Intentionality* (Leiden: Brill, 2001), pp. 185–201; and ibid. 'Mental Representation', in *CHMP*, I:346–56 (352–4).

[69] To counter such difficulties, Bacon too in fact postulates a complementary, active operation on the part of the perceiving subject to enable actual perception. See Tachau, 'Seeing as Action and Passion'. On the sceptical implications of species theory, see especially Perler, 'Skepticism', *CHMP*, I:384–96 (391–3); Pasnau, *Theories of Cognition*, pp. 236–47.

[70] José Filipe Silva, *Robert Kilwardby on the Human Soul*, pp. 131–76.

[71] The decree stipulated that 'the substance of the rational or intellective soul is the form of the human body in itself and essentially', see Chapter 2 n. 31. For Olivi's views, see *Quaestiones in secundum librum Sententiarum*. Bibliotheca Franciscana Scholastica 4–6, ed. B. Jansen (Quaracchi: Collegium

200 MEDIEVAL ALLEGORY AS EPISTEMOLOGY

primary reason for denying the very existence of *species* was that *species*-theory ultimately implied what is known as 'representationalism': according to Aristotle's theory—Olivi objected—the mind never cognized objects in themselves, but only images that were gradually abstracted from them, which raised serious difficulties regarding the nature of the *species* or *imago* in the mind. Occurring at the end of an indefinitely extended chain of images produced by the multiplication of *species*, human cognitive acts appeared powerless to ascertain the reliability of the image formed in the mind in relation to the object under scrutiny. This, Olivi argued, would have been sufficient reason for the adoption of a fundamental scepticism about human perceptual acts. To circumvent such difficulties Olivi developed an idiosyncratic theory of active perception, according to which the soul was understood as turning its cognitive power directly outwards, towards the objects themselves in the external world. Even though Olivi accepted the existence of intellectual *species*, he denies the material *species in medio* the role of the efficient cause of cognition.[72] In doing so, he develops a theory that displays some loose similarities with the older, broadly extramissionist theory of perception that was widely adopted in the Latin West before the reception of Aristotle's works on natural science. Hugh of Saint Victor, for instance, had similarly argued that the soul itself 'rushes out towards the visible forms of the bodies and, having made contact with them, draws them into itself through imagination' (*Didascalicon*, II.3).[73]

Although it is far less elaborate and systematic than Olivi's theory, the model of perception exposed by Deguileville's Raison's is closely aligned the latter's account. Furthermore—and regardless of any argument about possible 'influence'—it is equally clear that Deguileville's reasons for rejecting the Aristotelian model are exactly the same as Olivi's, and are determined by the claims for the superior ontological status for the soul with relation to the physical world. Just as in Olivi's theory, Raison attributes agency or *virtus* not to the material objects or the *species* they emit, but to the self, previously identified with the soul alone:

'Et aussi comme je te di	'And as I have told you about sight, so I
De la vëue, aussi te di	tell you about hearing and about all
Del'oye et de tous ses sens,	[the body's] senses, for they are only
Quar ce ne sont quë instrumens	instruments by which it receives from
Par les	

S. Bonaventurae, 1922–6), 'Quaestio' 51, 2:104–98. See further Robert Pasnau and Juhana Toivanen, 'Peter John Olivi', section 3, 'Soul and Body', in *The Stanford Encyclopedia of Philosophy* (Summer 2013 Edition), Edward N. Zalta (ed.), http://plato.stanford.edu/archives/sum2013/entries/olivi. See also Robert Pasnau, 'Human Nature', in *Cambridge Companion to Medieval Philosophy*, ed. A. S. McGrade (Cambridge University Press, 2003), pp. 208–30 (212).

[72] Silva and Toivanen, 'The Active Nature of the Soul'; Tachau, *Vision and Certitude*, pp. 39–54; Toivanen, *Perception and the Internal Senses*, pp. 115–222.

[73] 'sed quia per instrumenta sensuum non uniformiter ad sensibilia comprehendenda descendit, eorumque similitudinem per imaginationem ad se trahit.' See also the discussion of perception through intromission as theorized by ancient Greco-Latin tradition, and bequeathed to the pre-thirteenth-century Western tradition, in Smith, 'Perception', pp. 334–5.

quiex de toy [le corps] recoit
Ce quë il a, quar n'ot ne voit
Se n'est par toy tant seulement.'
  (*PVH1* 6103–9)

you what it has. It sees and hears
nothing except through you.'

Raison ascribes a remarkable and unusual degree of agency and intentionality to the human soul, in what is a striking departure from the standard Aristotelian account:[74]

'L'ame qui habitë u cors
Sa clarte espant par dehors
Et fait cuidier aus foles gens
Que tout li enluminemens
Soit de la povre nuee
Dont l'ame est obnubilee.
Mais se la nuee n'estoit,
L'ame si grant lumiere aroit
Qu'elle verroit tout plainement
D'orient jusqu' en occident,
Elle verroit et congnoistroit
Son createur et ameroit.
Les iex du cors pas iex ne sont,
Mais aussi com verrieres sont
Par les queles l'amë au corps
Donne lumiere par dehors
Ne pour ce ne dois pas cuidier
Quë a l'ame de riens mestier
Aient ses iex et ses verrieres,
Quar par devant et par derrieres
Sans fenestrage corporel
Son bien voit esperituel
Et aucune foiz le verroit
Miex, se li cors nus iex n'avoit.'
  (*PVH1* 6063–86)

'The soul that live in the body shines outward, and makes foolish people think that everything is illuminated by the poor cloud that obscures the soul. But if there were no cloud, the soul would have such great light that it would see plainly from east to west, and it would see and know and love its creator. The eyes of the body are not eyes, but windows through which the soul gives light to the body outside. But you must not think, for that reason, that the soul has any need of these eyes, these windows. It sees its spiritual good before and behind it, without bodily windows. And sometimes it would see it better if the body had no eyes.'

Raison here proposes an emphatically active model of cognition, essentially postulating perception not as a passive, receptive act through which information is conveyed to the body from outside, but as an activity of the soul, reaching out to illuminate the material world through its own cognitive acts.

---

[74] On the 'standard', Aristotelian and Avicennan models of perception, see variously the essays in Knuuttila and Kärkkäinen, eds, *Theories of Perception in Medieval and Early Modern Philosophy*, especially essays by Knuuttila and Cristina D'Ancona.

202   MEDIEVAL ALLEGORY AS EPISTEMOLOGY

The philosophical and theological stakes of advocating an active as opposed to a passive model of sense perception are considerable. Indeed, the two models ultimately entail completely incompatible, rival anthropologies. In the case of passive perception, the human sensitive soul is seen as the passive recipient of sensation produced by the external world. In the case of active perception, by contrast, it is the soul itself that acts upon the sensible objects in the external world.

3. The Body of Sin and the Carnal Poetics of the *Rose*

Both Raison's theory of divine illumination and her account of active perception assign a remarkable degree of cognitive agency to the human soul, placing considerable pressure on the Pilgrim to act in accordance with his soul's power. The pilgrim's practical experience of the outside world, however, is riddled with setbacks and misadventures, suggesting that the pilgrim remains vulnerable to the actions and seductions of the physical, corporeal world. This raises serious questions not only about the ability of the soul to control the body, but also about the body's larger 'use', in an Augustinian sense: simply put, if all genuine, reliable knowledge is to be derived from internal illumination of the soul, and if the body constitutes an 'obstacle espes et grant' (*PVH1* 6180) for the direct access to such knowledge, is there any room left for a positive usefulness of the body? In this section I accordingly begin by discussing Raison's teaching about the correct 'use' of corporeal faculties, before examining Deguileville's description of the Seven Deadly Sins in his poem. Throughout this section I want to suggest that Deguileville's technique of 'giving body' to the Sins as personified abstractions is intended to foster both the reader's interpretive skills while enhancing their self-knowledge. More specifically, Deguileville crafts a series of sinful bodies that cry out for allegorical interpretation—an act that enables the pilgrim/reader to transcend the base corporeal nature of the sins themselves, facilitating a recovery of the pilgrim/reader's own true self as a disembodied soul created in the divine image. I will be illustrating how much of Deguileville's description of the Seven Deadly Sins, symptomatically, also reads like a consistent and systematic rejection of the carnal, idolatrous allegorical poetics he associates with the *Roman de la Rose*. In the next section, however, I will address some of the unsuspected difficulties with Deguileville's commitment to such a strongly dualistic poetics, by examining in greater detail the evidence provided by the actual action in the poem. I will argue that far from confirming Raison's optimistic, even exalted account of the cognitive powers of the soul and the soul's ability to triumph over its corporeal opponent, the *viator*'s practical experience of the world as described in the poem ultimately reaffirms his tenaciously embodied condition—despite the poet's considerable efforts to persuade his readers of the contrary, and in direct contradiction with the cognitive theory put forward by the poem's central authority figures.

During the episode of the body-soul separation, Raison begins by clearly warning the Pilgrim to subdue and utterly reject his vile, bodily self:

'c'est un tas de pourreture,	'A pile of corruption, an image made
Un similacre fait d'ordure	of dung, a statue made of mud, a
Une estatue de limon,	scare-crow ... he is powerless and
Un espouentail a coulon.	crippled, deaf, blind, and
[...]	malformed ... a worm that in the
Quar impotent est et contrait,	end will decay and become food for
Sourt, avugle et contrait.	worms.'
[...]	
Un ver qui en la fin sera	
Viande aus vers et pourrira.'	
(PVH1 5813–26)	

Unsurprisingly, the pilgrim falls into the typical dualistic error of seeking to dispose of his bodily self altogether, and asks Raison for leave to kill his 'great enemy' [grans anemis, PVH1 5748]. He thus commits precisely the kind of mistake against which Augustine warns: 'Some say that they would prefer to have no body at all, but they are mistaken. For what they hate is not their body, but its imperfections and its dead weight' (De doctrina I.24.24, cf. Eph. 5:29). Raison now sets about correcting the pilgrim's radical dualism, exhorting him to chastise his body instead, harnessing its positive, instrumental potential. The body is both man's greatest enemy, but also the sole vehicle that can allow the soul to attain salvation, and must be harnessed accordingly:

'Penitance est sa mestresse	'Penance is his mistress and his only
Et sa seule chastierresse,	chastiser, and she takes just vengeance
Celle qui le droit vengement,	on him when it is time and season. If
Quant temps et saison est, en prent.	you bring him to her, she will beat him
Se li bailles, si le batra	so and chastise him so with her
Et si bien le chastiera	switches that he will be a good servant
De ses verges que bon sergent	to you from then on. And you ought to
Te sera des ore en avant.	desire this and seek to accomplish it
Et ce dois tu miex desirrer	rather than kill him, for he is given to
Et miex vouloir et procurer	you to lead it [i.e. your soul] to
Que tu ne doiz faire sa mort,	everlasting life and salvation.'
Quar baillie t'est pour li aport	[translation emended]
De vie et de salut mener.'	
(PVH1 5859–71).	

The reference point for such a metaphysics of penitence is again the De doctrina, where Augustine observes that Christians 'seem to persecute their own body by a kind of repression, and by hardships, [but] their aim (if they are doing it rightly) is

204   MEDIEVAL ALLEGORY AS EPISTEMOLOGY

not to have no body at all but to have one that is subservient and ready for necessary tasks' (*De doctrina* I.24.24).[75] For Augustine such penitential self-discipline is not simply a moral imperative, but enables a productive hermeneutics of the self, bringing into focus the *imago dei* refracted within the individual soul, contained yet obscured by the body. The rebalancing of body and soul therefore again entails a corresponding hermeneutic rebalancing of the letter and the spirit. Instead of being merely an inert and idolatrous 'statue of mud' (*PVH1* 5815), the body too is now urged to participate in the production of salvific meaning.

By insisting on the importance of the instrumental role of the body, however, Raison also establishes the continued interdependence of the two substances of body and soul. This condition can be suspended thanks to the thought experiment of the Flying Man—momentarily freeing the Pilgrim from the limitations of ordinary human cognitive faculties and allowing it to glimpse his own nature as *imago dei*—but it can't be durably transcended.[76] Raison stresses the necessary brevity of the ecstatic 'sequestration' of the soul from the body (*PVH1* 6191–2), reminding the pilgrim that he will have to put on the cloak of his mortal body once more:

'Toutevoies li retrousser	For it is not in my power to keep it off
Te refaurra et rendosser,	you for very long and it is difficult to
Quar mon pouoir pas ne s'estent	even take it off for a single moment.
De li sequestrer longuement	This is the work of death.
De toy et encor y a fort	
D'un seul moment faire en deport.	
A la mort ce ci apartient'	
(*PVH1* 6189–95)	

Such comments resonate with the mystical commonplace about the brevity of ecstatic rapture, as found for instance in Bernard's *De diligendo deo*,[77] or Gregory's *Moralia*.[78] Also Augustine in the *De trinitate* (VIII.2.3) describes the fleeting,

---

[75] 'Quod autem continentia quadam et laboribus quasi persequi uidentur corpora sua, qui hoc recte faciunt, non id agunt, ut non habeant corpus, sed ut habeant subiugatum et paratum ad opera necessaria.'

[76] Evans, *Augustine on Evil*, pp. 39–41, 46–7.

[77] *De diligendo Deo* X.27: 'Et si quidem e mortalibus quispiam ad illud raptim interdum, ut dictum est, et ad momentum admittitur, subito invidet saeculum nequam, perturbat diei malitia, corpus mortis aggravat, sollicitat carnis necessitas, defectus corruptionis non sustinet', in Saint Bernard of Clairvaux, *Opera Omnia*, ed. Jean Mabillon, 2 vols (Paris: Gaume, 1839), I:1351. 'But if sometimes a mere mortal feels the rapture of heavenly joy for an instant, then this earthly life envies his happiness, and the malice of daily routine disrupts it, this mortal body weighs him down, asserts the needs of the flesh, the weakness of corruption cannot sustain it'; translation mine. See further Étienne Gilson, *La théologie mystique de St Bernard* (Paris: Vrin, 1947), pp. 38–47, 142–7.

[78] *Moralia*, XXIII.xi.18–21 discussed in Jean Leclerq, *The Love of Learning and the Desire for God: A Study of Monastic Culture*, trans. Catharine Misrahi, 2nd edn (New York: Fordham University Press, 1974), p. 32.

momentary apprehension of truth as a passing flash of inner, divine light, no sooner experienced than it is already obscured by bodily images:

> Do not ask what truth is; immediately a fog of bodily images and a cloud of fancies will get in your way and disturb the bright fair weather that burst on you the first instant when I said 'truth'. Stay therefore, if you can, in the initial brightness of this sudden blinding flash of light when it is identified as 'truth'. But you cannot; you slide back into these familiar and earthly things. And what weight is it, I ask, that drags you back but the birdlime of greed for the dirty junk you have picked up on your wayward wanderings?[79]

The pilgrim's ecstasy is similarly short-lived, and he is quickly plunged back into the cloud of embodied existence, described in terms closely reminiscent of Augustine's comments:

'Du cors trousse me retrouvai;
Toute la vigueur qu'avoie,
(Et) le bien dont m'esjoissoye
En un moment o adire,
Tout fut mucie, tout absconse
Dessouz la nue obnubilant
Souz qui n'est nul bien cler voyant.'
  (*PVH1* 6274–80)

'I found myself wrapped up in the body right away. In one moment, all the strength I had and all the good I rejoiced in was lost, all hidden, all obscured by the shadowing cloud, under which there is no clear vision.'

The pilgrim's return to the normal state of embodied existence also prepares for the literal eclipse of Dame Raison herself from the narrative at the end of the episode, again expressed in similar terms of covering and obscuring:

'je te dy qu'entre nous .II.
Ara unes fois nuees
Ou des vapeurs eslevees
Ou aucun brullas ou fumee
Par quoi je te seray celee.
Aucune foys espessement
Me verras et obscurement,

'Between us there will sometimes be clouds or vapours arising, or mists of smoke that will hide me from you. Sometimes you will see me darkly and obscurely. At other times you will see me neither more nor less, neither much nor little. And at times

---

[79] 'Noli quaerere quid sit veritas; statim enim se opponent caligines imaginum corporalium et nubila phantasmatum, et perturbabunt serenitatem, quae primo ictu diluxit tibi, cum dicerem: Veritas. Ecce in ipso primo ictu quo velut coruscatione perstringeris, cum dicitur: Veritas, mane si potes; sed non potes. Relaberis in ista solita atque terrena. Quo tandem pondere, quaeso, relaberis nisi sordium contractarum cupiditatis visco et peregrinationis erroribus?' English from *The Trinity*, trans. Hill, p. 244.

206 MEDIEVAL ALLEGORY AS EPISTEMOLOGY

Aucune foys ne tant ne quant
Ne me verras ne pou ne grant,
Et aucune foiz clerement
Me verras et apertement.'
 (*PVH1* 6462–72)

you will see me clearly and openly.'
[translation emended]

The end of the cognitive ecstasy thus also marks the beginning of the pilgrimage proper, with a movement through time and a return to the ongoing practical struggle between flesh and spirit. The actual journey now traces a process of 'becoming' that is essentially articulated in terms of journey and combat, pilgrimage and *psychomachia*—the two archetypal motifs that for Angus Fletcher underpin all forms of allegorical expression and representation.[80] After the Pilgrim's preparatory encounter with Rude Entendement—already discussed (Chapter 2.3)—the quest now continues with the protagonist's arrival at the parting of the ways (*PVH1* 6503–7032). Predictably, he chooses the wrong, left-hand path, and now encounters all Seven Deadly Sins personified before repenting for his ill-advised choice (*PVH1* 7033–11,406), and finally crossing the Sea of the World on the Ship of Religion (*PVH1* 11,407–end). The pilgrim must now demonstrate his ability to 'use' his body in an Augustinian sense, as an instrument of knowledge rather than an idolatrous, carnal self to be enjoyed and endowed with its own contrary will:[81]

'quant par bon chemin vourras
Aler, il t'en destournera
Et par autre aler te fera;
 [...]
Quar quant tu li fais son vouloir,
Tu doiz en verite savoir
Que contre toy tu l'enforcis
Et amenistres ses oustis
Par les quiex il te guerroie
Et destourne de ta voie.'
 (*PVH1* 6404–6; 6425–30)

'Whenever you want to go on a good path, he will turn you aside from it and make you take another.

For when you do what he wants, you must know for certain that you make him stronger against you and give him the weapons to attack you and turn you aside from your way.'

In both Augustine and Deguileville, the ascetic mortification of the flesh is designed to restore the instrumental role of the body on the human pilgrimage of life. Following Augustine, this is achieved primarily though penitential action, initiating a forward movement and transformation that is simultaneously ethical,

---

[80] See particularly Angus Fletcher, *Allegory: Theory of a Symbolic Mode*, pp. 147–80. On Deguileville's influential combination of the two motifs, see Nievergelt, *Allegorical Quests* 23–7.

[81] See e.g. *De trinitate*, IX.8.13 and X.10.13; *De doctrina* I.3.3; I.4; I.22.20–1; I.24.24; I.35.39; I.38.42. See further O'Donovan, '*Usus* and *Fruitio* in Augustine'. For a theological discussion of the dangers of 'idolatrous' enjoyment, particularly in relation to the pilgrimage trope that dominates the *De doctrina*, see Stewart-Kroeker, 'Resisting Idolatry and Instrumentalisation in Loving the Neighbour'.

COGNITION: THEORY AND PRACTICE 207

cognitive, and hermeneutical.[82] This also coincides with the acceptance of one's own embodied status as a self in movement, as an incomplete and evolving 'sign' in need of constant interpretation.[83] Only if it is understood as a *signum* for an intangible *res* (the soul)—like a cloud, smoky glass, or cloak, as a thing to be 'used' and not 'enjoyed' for its own sake—can the human body-soul compound itself function as a sign, and thus become a dynamic agent of forward movement and transformation instead of an inert 'obstacle espes et grant' (cf. *PVH1* 6179–80).

Immediately after the end of her extended lecture, Raison leaves the pilgrim to fend for himself, and he soon arrives at a parting of the ways. There he meets Huiseuse, a young and attractive courtly lady, who invites him to enter the path on the left-hand side [voie senestre, *PVH1* 6517], whereas Labour/Occupant, a seemingly foolish mat-maker invites him to walk along the right-hand path (*PVH1* 6533).[84] Huiseuse/Oiseuse is, of course, a character lifted straight out of Guillaume de Lorris's *Rose*, where she had invited Amant into the delightful garden of *deduit* (*RR* 495–728). Here she similarly invites the pilgrim to enter the 'place of delight, diversion, and pleasure' [lieu de delit, / d'esbatement et de deduit, *PVH1* 6751–2], and the Pilgrim predictably accepts her invitation only to be faced with all Seven Deadly Sins in order.[85] As well as signalling an ethical choice between vice and virtue, the parting of the ways also marks the choice between two rival poetics: the carnal allegorical poetics of the *Rose* on the one, left hand, and the sapiential allegorical poetics of *PVH* itself on the other.[86] The Pilgrim immediately succumbs not only to sensual temptation, but also to the seductions of the self-deceiving carnal poetics that Deguileville associates with the *Rose*. The Pilgrim's misadventures thus provide a further opportunity for the reader to learn about the pitfalls of carnal allegorical 'misreading' as Deguileville understood it. More specifically, the reader is invited to decrypt precisely those allegorical signs that the pilgrim misunderstands or overlooks, thereby rising above the base corporeal reality they 'embody', and programmatically neutralizing the danger they pose for the divinely created human soul. The ability to recognize and identify the sins for what they are is therefore for Deguileville a key skill to be acquired on the path towards the recovery of a functional, salvific allegorical poetics, enabling the reader to decrypt correctly both the poetic text and the world of signs at large. Once more—as in the case of the Flying Man thought experiment—the possibility of adequate salvific knowledge hinges on the ability to transcend any base material reality through an act of interpretation.

---

[82] See especially Lombardi, *Syntax of Desire*, pp. 27–37.

[83] See Colish, *The Mirror of Language*, pp. 51–4.

[84] See especially Maupeu, 'Bivium'; ibid. *Pèlerins de vie humaine*, pp. 118–28, 149–53; Kay, *Place of Thought*, pp. 70–93.

[85] Maupeu, *Pèlerins de vie humaine*, pp. 122–7; Huot, *The Romance of the Rose and its Medieval Readers*, pp. 211–12, and 229–30 on further similar echoes in *PVH2*.

[86] Maupeu, 'Bivium', esp. 27–31; ibid., *Pèlerins de vie humaine*, pp. 118–28. I will return to the character of 'Occupant' in particular in relation to Langland (see Chapter 6.4).

208   MEDIEVAL ALLEGORY AS EPISTEMOLOGY

After Rude Entendement, Huiseuse thus represents a further obstacle to the correct practice of allegorical interpretation and discernment. If Rude Entendement represented the pure and simple negation of the figurative and polysemous possibilities of allegory, Huiseuse represents their frivolous misuse and perversion for the purpose of seduction, deception, mystification, and sensual pleasure. It is significant, therefore, that Huiseuse should be associated with 'roumans' in general, and specifically with romances of a distinctly fabulous and mendacious sort—an implicit yet unmistakable allusion to the *Rose* itself:

[Huiseuse]: 'Festes songë et dimenches	'I look forward to feast-days and
Pour lire unes foiz elenches,	Sundays, to reading the *Sophistical*
Pour menconges enmanteler	*Refutations*, so as to dress up lies to
Et faire les voir ressembler,	make them appear like the truth. I tell
Pour raconter trufes[87] et fables,	trifles and fables, romances and many
Roumans et choses mençongeables.'	mendacious things.'
(*PVH1* 6851–6)	[translation mine]

The passage is somewhat cryptic and rewards closer scrutiny: Huiseuse associates her reading of dubious courtly 'roumans' with her interest in 'elenches', i.e. Aristotle's *Sophistici elenchi*. The logic behind the analogy is not immediately apparent, but Huiseuse appears to assimilate the two forms because of their problematic truth-value.[88] Huiseuse uses Aristotle's work not so much because it allows the disambiguation of the thirteen types of fallacies as described by Aristotle—including verbal fallacies like equivocation and amphiboly—but rather because it enables her to *create* ambiguities and faulty logic and 'cloak lies' [mensonges enmanteler, *PVH1* 6853] under a veil of ostensible truth. Significantly, the attitude of medieval intellectuals towards the *Sophistici elenchi* was itself ambivalent to say the least, as it was often felt that the work could be used to train readers in the practice of misleading interlocutors through fallacious and sophistic arguments.[89] The assimilation of rhetorical excess with fallacious sophistical reasoning is already established in one of Deguileville's key touchstone texts, Augustine's *De doctrina*:

---

[87] The term 'turfles' is used in ways that resonate with its collocation in the *Rose*, notably at 9041 where it is applied to clothing, as part of an excursus on the ethics of clothing as a form of dissimulation, or at 9278, where it is associated with seductive dressing and 'fornicacion' (*RR* 9280). The term is therefore loaded with overtones of adulterous sexuality and deception. More worryingly still, it is used to describe allegorical dreams like the *Somnium Scipionis*, a category that of course includes both the *Rose* itself and *PVH1*: 'ce n'est for trufle et mançonge, / ainsinc con n'ome qui songe, / qui voit, ce cuide, en leur presances / les esperituex sustances, / si con fist Scipion jadis' (*RR* 18,287–91), on which see further Chapter 3.5.

[88] See further my 'From *Disputatio* to *Predicatio*', 160–3.

[89] Scott G. Schreiber, *Aristotle on False Reasoning: Language and the World in the Sophistical Refutations* (New York: SUNY, 2003), pp. 1–7. Sten Ebbesen, *Commentators and Commentaries on Aristotle's Sophistici Elenchi*, 3 vols (Leiden: Brill, 1981), e.g. I:88.

COGNITION: THEORY AND PRACTICE   209

the word 'sophistical' is also applied to a style which is not captious, but goes in for verbal ornament on a scale that does not suit a serious writer. (*De doctrina*, II.31.48)[90]

In Huiseuse's hands, then, Aristotle's *Sophistici elenchi* serves as an instrument for just this kind of overly 'ornate' rhetorical mystification, of a piece with the duplicitous, sophistical/rhetorical poetics of Faux Semblant and the fruitless poetics of courtly 'roumans' more generally. It hardly a coincidence, therefore, that Faux Semblant himself had invoked the *Sophistici elenchi* in the *Rose* when bragging about his own ability to deceive even the most proficient student in the Aristotelian art of definition and disambiguation (*RR* 11,025–33; see Chapter 1.4).

Following Faux Semblant, then, Huiseuse too employs her knowledge of fallacies not so much to elucidate, but to deceive and mislead. The pilgrim's choice of her suggested path therefore marks his fall into a world of increased dissemblance and illusion. This consists not only of faulty reasoning and the enjoyment of mendacious fables, but also leads to more basic perceptual error. This fall into illusion passes through the appeal to the pilgrim's misguided bodily senses, specifically sight and hearing, *voir et ouir*—the two senses most directly implicated in any cognitive act,[91] and particularly relevant to the decoding of figurative language and allegorical imagery. In terms of hearing (*ouir*), Huiseuse promises access to the delight of courtly song in her garden (*PVH1* 6751–6)—closely and unmistakeably echoing the lover's musical delight in the *Rose* upon entering the Garden of Delight (*RR* 629–66). These delights are in turn echoed during the prelude to the poem's bathetic (anti-)climax, where Pygmalion, caught in his erotomaniac frenzy, sings 'little ditties, instead of the Mass' [an leu de messe, chançonetes], with elaborate musical accompaniment (*RR* 20,999–21,016). The motif is elaborated in some detail later in the *Pèlerinage* during the speech of Flatterie, who identifies the pleasures of the ear with the seductive song of the sirens. This once more echoes the *Rose*, with its ambivalent evocation of the sweet song of sirens (*RR* 667–72). In Deguileville's poem, however, there is little room for ambivalence and playful irony, and the harmful consequences of sensual, courtly song are made explicit:[92]

'Je sui la Seraine de mer	'I am the siren of the sea, and with my
Qui par mon doucement chanter	sweet singing I am often make those
Faiz souvent noyer et perir	who want to hear my song drown and
Ceus qui mon chant veulent oir.'	perish.'
(*PVH1* 8135–8)	

---

[90] 'Quamquam etiam sermo non captiosus, sed tamen abundantius quam grauitatem decet, uerborum ornamenta consectans sophisticus dicitur.'

[91] See Maupeu, '*Bivium*' 26; and Stephen G. Nichols, 'Prologue', in *Rethinking the Senses*, p. vii, with a brief, incidental mention of Deguileville. The episode also prepares the ground for the similarly deceptive assault on the pilgrim's senses by the seven deadly sins, as discussed in the following pages.

[92] See also Huot, *The Romance of the Rose and its Medieval Readers*, p. 230.

210 MEDIEVAL ALLEGORY AS EPISTEMOLOGY

As well as being associated with seductive song, Huiseuse also specializes in visual, imaginative deception, figuring a purely rhetorical, devious use of allegorical poetics to mislead and deceive. She opens the doors to the Pilgrim's gradual descent into the ontologically vacuous and hermeneutically duplicitous universe of carnal, bodily poetics, and is accordingly focalized on the Pilgrim's own exterior appearance—his body and his clothing:

'Je sui l'amie de ton cors;
  [...]
Souvent li donne vert chapel
Et regarder li fais sa pel
S'est belle, et s'est bien agencies
Et bien vestus et bien chauciez.'
  (*PVH1* 6857–64)

'I am your Body's friend ... Often I give him a green garland and make him look at himself to see if he is handsome, if he is well-turned out, well-dressed, and wearing fine shoes.'

This emphasis on clothing is more than a simple marker of vanity: on the one hand the motif resonates with earlier descriptions of the pilgrim's body during the body-soul separation, as a form of extraneous covering concealing the real nature of the self/soul (see Chapter 3.1). On the other hand, Huiseuse exemplifies the ability of allegorical rhetoric to dissimulate truth under a mantle of counterfeit pleasant appearances, echoing the archetypal allegorical deceiver Faux Semblant.

Like Guillaume de Lorris' damsel, Deguileville's Huiseuse also carries a mirror used to contemplate her own image (*PVH1* 6849; *RR* 555). The same kind of self-absorbed mirror is also carried by Flatterie (*PVH1* 7366, 8155–90), and alludes to the possibilities of visual self-infatuation, developing ideas latent in Narcissus's mirror in the *Rose* (*RR* 1423 ff.).[93] In the wider context of *PVH*, Huiseuse's mirror thus also displaces the earlier, spotless mirror of Christ on the Staff of Hope, which was able to refract man's original divine resemblance and illuminate the pilgrim's wanderings (*PVH1* 3439–50), and indeed the Pilgrim later loses his staff and mirror along the path of Huiseuse (*PVH1* 10,693). Huiseuse's mirror thus also represents a rival model for conceptualizing the human self: it remains unable to reflect either Christ or the Heavenly Jerusalem (cf. *PVH1* 3445), denying access to man's original *imago dei*, and thus impedes any genuine, dynamic possibility for self-knowledge and self-transformation. It can only ever reflect the pilgrim's lower bodily self, and inevitably leads him deeper into errance, self-alienation, and exile from his spiritual home.[94] Huiseuse's mirror ultimately negates the dynamic signifying possibilities of language and visual imagination altogether, replacing it with an idolatry of the carnal self. This new, 'narcissistic' mirror is emblematic of the perversions of the allegorical mode that Deguileville associates with the carnal poetics of the *Roman de la Rose* in its entirety.

---

[93] Legaré and Pomel, 'Les Miroirs du *PVH*', pp. 135–6. On mirrors in the *Rose*, see also Chapter 3.5.
[94] See also Pomel and Legaré, 'Les Miroirs du *PVH*', esp. pp. 132–5 for the points made here.

The encounter with Huiseuse also functions as a template for the pilgrim's subsequent encounters with the personified sins along the 'voie senestre', all of whom to some extent replicate the paradoxical nature of Faux Semblant in simultaneously concealing yet revealing their true natures through their appearance. The duplicitous nature of the sins gives rise to a complex double logic of representation in the poem. On the one hand, following the broader interpretive logic of Deguileville's personification allegory, the sins manifest their nature through attributes and behaviour that cry out for allegorical interpretation: so Orgueil carries a stick, spurs, a horn and a bellows, all duly allegorized (*PVH1* 7339 ff.); Avarice's six hands are meticulously glossed to reveal her manifold transactions and extortions (*PVH1* 9427–610), and all other sins are similarly dissected and anatomized.[95] On the other hand the sins are also said to dissimulate their real natures under a 'cloak' of false appearances and various disguises, and can be seen as perverting the mechanisms of allegorical representation, grounded in a disjunction between what is 'overt' and 'covert'.[96] Like Faux Semblant in the *Rose*, Deguileville's Detraction describes her 'pleasant aspect [. . .] and counterfeit fair seeming' [bele chiere . . . [que] contreface et *biau semblant*, *PVH1* 8518–20; my emphasis and my translation], and Trahison 'simulates a fair appearance and pleasant aspect' [fait par simulation / Biau semblant et belle chiere, *PVH1* 8396–7]. The latter is told by her father,

[. . .] 'ton pense	'Hide your thoughts with lies, and
Tu couverras de faussete	look different on the outside than
Et par dehors demonsterras	you are on the inside.'
Autre que dedens ne seras.'	
(*PVH1* 8419–22)	

Luxuria, doubling as Venus—who, it will be remembered, claims the *Rose* as 'her romance' in *PVH2* (8722)—embodies the hermeneutic challenge posed by such duplicity, by hiding her multiple attributes and 'tools' underneath her mantle:

[Venus:] 'S'avoies les oustis vëu	'If you had seen the instruments I have
Que souz ma cotelle ai muciez,	under my robe, you would think even
Se mont n'estoies desvoiez,	less of me, unless you were badly
Encore mains me priseroies.'	misled.'[97]
(*PVH1* 10,658–61; cf. *PVH2* 8874–5)	

The use of cloaking metaphors in this section of the narrative is nearly ubiquitous, notably the use of 'mucier' and its variants. The path of Huiseuse thus emerges as a world of profound dissemblance and carnal misreading—avatar of Augustine's

---

[95] E.g. Tuve, *Allegorical Imagery*, pp. 173–83; Hagen, *Allegorical Remembrance*, pp. 120–3; Maupeu, *Pèlerins de vie humaine*, pp. 159–62.

[96] More broadly on this trait in the tradition of narrative allegory, see Pomel, *Les voies*, pp. 368–9.

[97] All translations from *PVH2* are mine unless otherwise noted.

212   MEDIEVAL ALLEGORY AS EPISTEMOLOGY

regio dissimilitudinis—where the human gaze is prevented from piercing beyond the cloak of the body and the letter. It is symptomatic that the terms used here should overlap so neatly with those employed to designate the obscured, 'obnubilated' cognitive powers of the human soul once it becomes embodied. The soul too is 'all hidden, all obscured by the shadowing cloud, under which there is no clear vision' [Tout fut *mucie*, tout absconse / Dessouz la nue obnubilant / Souz qui n'est nul bien cler voyant, *PVH1* 6278–80, my emphasis]. By contrast the soul's ecstatic, disembodied state is described as perceiving truth directly, free from all veils: 'It seemed that nothing in the world was hidden or concealed from me' [Rien ou monde, ce me sembloit, / *Mucie* ne cele ne m'estoit, *PVH1* 6211–12, my emphasis]. Venus in particular embodies the dangers of deliberately obscure, 'covert' poetics of bodily dissimulation, clearly associated with the *Rose*: 'therefore I carry a false painted face to cover my own face' [pour ce porte .i. painture(s) / Faus visage a couverture, *PVH1* 10,638–9]. Trahison, mounted on Envie, similarly keeps her 'face hidden underneath this false face' [face / *Mucie* souz ce faus visage, *PVH1* 8339–40, my emphasis; see also 8210], and presents herself as dressed up in deceptive clothing:

'Se dehors paree me vois,	'If you see my outside array, you do not
Pour ce, voir, pas ne me connois.	see me truly. One cannot know about
On ne connoist pas aus drapiaus	people by their clothing or about wines
Les gens ne les vins aus sarciaus.'	from mere barrel hoops.'
(*PVH1* 8453–6)	[translation emended]

As is suggested by the use of the classic logic textbook example of the 'vins' and 'serciaus' (discussed in Chapter 2.2), the poet's concern throughout this section is consistently semantic and semiotic as opposed to narrowly moralizing: the emphasis is not so much on condemning immoral behaviour, but on reading the signs for sinful behaviour in the world.

In the case of Venus, Trahison, and indeed all the remaining sins, however, any such specialized knowledge of semantics and semiotics is unlikely to be of much use, since ultimately 'all sins appear under the cloak of the name of their contrary virtue' [Touz vices [. . .] couvert se font / du non de (la) vertu contraire, *PVH1* 5301–3, my translation]. The archetype for such impenetrable deception is of course Faux Semblant, who famously points out how 'the habit does not make the monk' [la robe ne fet pas le moine, *RR* 11,028], and how 'you will certainly not be able to tell by my habit which people I am living with' [par mon habit / ne savrez o quex genz j'abit, *RR* 11,041–2]. Deguileville's vices follow suit, and all sins wear the mantle of Ypocrisie, abundantly described by Orgueil using vocabulary that is saturated with recollections of the *Rose* (*PVH1* 7991–8008, cf. *RR* 11,092–3, 8887–900). Her fashionable tastes are not merely an indictment of aristocratic flamboyance (cf. *PVH1* 7483–506, *PVH1* 7507–18)—a strongly proto-Langlandian concern—but also a negative counterexample to the Pilgrim's armour, cumbersome and unappealing yet functional and rich in elaborate allegorical meanings (*PVH1* 3813–4492). The pilgrim of course has long given up wearing the armour, ignoring Grace Dieu's injunctions (*PVH1* 3925–32), and it is fitting that he should end up in company of the sins precisely because he would rather wear comfortable clothes, not 'used' but 'enjoyed' in themselves to satisfy the needs of the body (e.g. *PVH1* 5758–68).

Avarice indulges in still more sophisticated and more devious forms of sartorial deception, emblematized by her colourful curtain:

'Ceste main est estenderresse	'This hand makes curtains and
De courtines et faiserresse	stretches them out, and she makes
Et fait aus drapiers courtines	curtains for drapers so that the colours
Pour ce que les couleurs plus fines	appear very fine to people. And I tell
Des draps resemblent a la gent.	you that very often she displays good
Et si te di que bien souvent	wares, but when they are purchased,
En monstre bonnes denrees,	she has others of the same colour which
Mais quant puis sont achatees,	she delivers to the buyer.'
Elle a autres de tel couleur	
Qu'elle delivre a l'achateur.'	
(*PVH1* 9927–36)	

The curtain is a particularly complex and loaded symbolic attribute in the intertextual negotiations between the *Rose* and *PVH1*. It is conspicuous at the end of the *Rose*, where Amant, about to consummate his sexual desire, removes the curtain that conceals the precious sexualized 'relics' in their sanctuary (*RR* 21,575–82). The motif of the curtain in Deguileville's poetic corpus, by contrast, signals the presence of incarnational and sacramental signs on a number of different occasions, and often demarcates a space for the numinous manifestation of the divine.[98] As noted by Fabienne Pomel, this symbolic use of the curtain effectively restores its original biblical and liturgical significance, which had been subverted by Jean de Meun for the ending of the *Rose*. Avarice's curtain, by contrast, is of a piece with its deviant use at the end of the *Rose*, exemplifying the tendency of the sins to appropriate and pervert sacramental allegorical signifiers more widely—curtains, staffs, and scrips among them. The 'couleurs plus fines' of Avarice's curtain further underline her rhetorical skill in dissimulating rapacious carnality under a mantle of refined courtly fabrics—alluding to the *colores rhetorici*, i.e. stylistic ornamentation as described in most medieval treatises on rhetoric.[99]

---

[98] Fabienne Pomel, 'La courtine chez Guillaume de Digulleville: la scénographie de la révélation et de l'incarnation du signe dans les *Pèlerinages* et le *Roman de la fleur de lys*', in Catherine Croisy-Naquet, ed., *Littérature et révélation. Espace et révélation*, Littérales n∘45 (Paris: Université de Paris Ouest-La Défense, 2010), pp. 219–47.

[99] Leonid Arbusow, *Colores rhetorici: Eine Auswahl rhetorischer Figuren und Gemeinplätze als Hilfsmittel für akademische Übungen an mittelalterlichen Texten* (Geneva: Slatkine, 1974/1948).

214 MEDIEVAL ALLEGORY AS EPISTEMOLOGY

Similar references to the deceptiveness of rhetorical 'colourings' abound in the *Rose*. This is particularly noticeable in connection with the many mirrors found throughout the poem—all serving as metonyms for the allegory as a whole—first and foremost, Guillaume de Lorris' Mirror of Narcissus:[100]

ausi con li mireors montre	Just as the things placed in front of the
les choses qui sont a l'encontre	mirror are reflected in it, and their
et i voit l'en sanz couverture	appearance and colour are seen quite
et lor *color* et lor *figure*,	plainly,
(*RR* 1553–6, my emphasis)	

Typically for the *Rose*, the statement is self-defeating: through the very act of insisting on the mirror's 'transparency', the narrator reminds us that all forms of representation are mediated, and hence potentially 'coloured' and 'figured' by the very process of transmission. Such mendacious rhetorical 'colouring' also features among the defining characteristics of Oiseuse in the *Rose*. As Claire Nouvet has observed, Oiseuse herself is in fact not so much a real person but an elaborate, unsubstantial compound of rhetorical commonplaces: mirror, flowers, colours, clothing, and comb, cf. *RR* 525–72.[101] Jean de Meun provides many further instances of such rhetorical colouring, inviting us to question the truth value of such dubiously rhetorical *couverture*. The speech of the Jaloux, for instance, is saturated with allusions to rhetorical artifice figured in terms of clothing, with abundant references to other classic rhetorical *loci*—clothing, colouring, flowers (*RR* 8867–71; 8878–83; 8891–900). The same applies to the description of Nature's 'novele robe' at the outset of the poem, consisting of a 'cloak' made up entirely of unsubstantial and artificial *flores* and *colores rhetorici*:

lors devient la terre si gobe	Then the earth becomes so proud that
qu'el velt avoir novele robe,	it desires a new dress, and is able to
si set si cointe robe feire	make a dress so lovely that there are a
que de colors i a .C. peire;	hundred pairs of colours in it. This is
l'erbe et les flors blanches et perses	the dress that I describe and devise,
et de maintes colors diverses, c'est la	and in which the earth takes pride.
robe que je devise,	[translation emended]
por quoi la terre mielz se prise	
(*RR* 59–66)	

The description further draws attention to the central paradox that haunts the poem: how is one to 'represent' the natural, and to what extent can a personified abstraction fabricated by the artifice of a poet really hope to provide an accurate representation of 'the natural'? From the very beginning of his poem Guillaume

---

[100] I echo the readings of Nouvet, 'An Allegorical Mirror'; and Hult, 'The Allegorical Fountain'.
[101] Nouvet, 'An Allegorical Mirror', 364–5.

can be seen to deliberately emphasize his own agency in crafting this colourful and flowery mantle: this is not only a robe that he 'details' through his description, but one which he himself 'devises'.[102] The only thing that is truly 'revealed' by such a process is the artifice at the heart of his dream poem, a rhetorical 'covering' for an ultimate truth that remains as elusive and as stubbornly 'enclosed' as the Rose/*Rose* itself. All such unsubstantial instances of flowery rhetorical 'colouring', then, accumulate to constitute the substance of the Rose or *Rose* itself: both the final object of the poem's quest, and the poem itself, may amount to nothing more than an inflated accumulation of rhetorical ornaments.

For a reader like Deguileville, the rhetorical/allegorical shenanigans of the *Rose*—echoed in the descriptions of Huiseuse and the Seven Deadly Sins in *PVH1*—embody not so much the negation of allegorical hermeneutics but its perversion, according to the definition of carnal, idolatrous misreading provided by Augustine.[103] Idolatry or spiritual fornication arises from a fundamental misconception of the semiotic relations between things and signs in the created world: 'What the apostle said about idols and the sacrifices made in their honour [cf. 1 Cor. 10:19–20] must guide our attitude to all these fanciful signs which draw people to the worship of idols or to the worship of the created order or any parts of it as if they were God' (*De doctrina* II.23.36).[104] Conversely, a misunderstanding of the signifying power of created things (*res*) entails a broadly 'idolatrous' understanding of the Book of Nature, denying its semiotic power, as Augustine develops in book III:

> [W]e are instructed to love and worship the one God who created all these things of which they venerate images, whether they do so by treating them as gods or as signs or representations of the gods. If, then, it is a carnal form of slavery to follow a sign divinely instituted for a useful purpose instead of the thing that it was instituted to represent, is it not far worse to accept as things the humanly instituted signs of useless things?
>
> [...]
>
> But the person who attends to or worships a useful sign, one divinely instituted, and does realize its force and significance, does not worship a thing which is only apparent and transitory but rather the thing to which all such things are to be related. (*De doctrina* III.7.11; 9.13)[105]

---

[102] These are two of the available meanings of the term in Middle French, on which see http://www.atilf.fr/dmf/définition/deviser; and Godefroy, II.703c–704c. See further my 'Textuality as Sexuality', pp. 123–4.

[103] See further Stewart-Kroeker, 'Resisting Idolatry and Instrumentalisation'.

[104] 'Quod autem de idolis et de immolationibus, quae honori eorum exhibentur dixit apostolus, hoc de omnibus imaginariis signis sentiendum est, quae uel ad cultum idolorum, uel ad creaturam eiusque partes tamquam deum colendas trahunt.'

[105] 'sed nobis unus diligendus et colendus deus praecipitur, qui facit haec omnia, quorum illi simulacra uenerantur uel tamquam deo uel tamquam signa et imagines deorum. Si ergo signum utiliter

216 MEDIEVAL ALLEGORY AS EPISTEMOLOGY

While Deguileville's reading of the *Rose* as a poem celebrating such forms of idolatry is clearly reductive, it is evident that Jean de Meun is acutely aware of the idolatrous resonances of his own poem. This is particularly evident during the obscene *dénouement* of Jean's *Rose*, describing a palpably idolatrous form of eroticized religious worship, where scrip, staff, curtain, and Rose are finally revealed to denote nothing beyond the carnal reality of sexual organs. Significantly, the scene is saturated with religious language, preparing the reader for the stripping away of the rhetorical garments, colours, and figures that conceal the ultimate (absent?) object of Amant's quest.[106] The mantle of rhetoric is here re-imagined as a curtain, rich in sacramental associations,[107] and Amant becomes a devout pilgrim worshipping the priceless relics at a sanctuary:[108]

m'agenoilloi san demourer,	I knelt without delay, for I was
car mout oi grant fain d'aourer	consumed with desire to worship at
le biau saintuaire honorable	that lovely and venerable shrine . . .
[. . .]	
Trés an sus un po la courtine	I partly raised the curtain that screened
qui les reliques ancourtine;	the relics, and, drawing near to the
de l'ymage lors m'apressai	image that I knew to be close to the
que du saintuaire pres sai;	sanctuary, I kissed it devoutly.
mout la besai devostemant;	
(*RR* 21,561–3; 21,569–70)	

This configuration of motifs is picked up by Deguileville in *PVH2*, as part of his renewed and increasingly anxious attempt to dissociate his own, salvific allegorical poetics from the deviant allegorical figurations of the *Rose*.[109] In a newly added episode, the pilgrim encounters a conspicuously Pygmalion-like carpenter, kneeling just like Amant at the end of the *Rose*, worshipping a freshly completed idol shrouded in sacrificial incense:

Devant li a genoux estoit	In front of it knelt a churl who was
Un grant vilain qui l'encensoit	venerating it with the smoke of incense.
Et lui faisait la fumee	
(*PVH2* 14,049–51)	

---

institutum proipsa re sequi, cui significandae institutum est, carnalis est seruitus, quanto magis inutilium rerum signa instituta pro rebus accipere? [. . .] qui uero aut operatur aut ueneratur utile signum diuinitus institutum, cuius uim significationemque intelligit, non hoc ueneratur, quod uidetur et transit, sed illud potius, quo talia cuncta referenda sunt.'

[106] See especially Minnis, *Magister Amoris*, pp. 82–118.

[107] Pomel, 'La courtine chez Guillaume de Digulleville', 235–6.

[108] See also Minnis, 'From *Coilles* to *Bel Chose*'.

[109] As I argue in Chapter 4.4, Deguileville's second version is characterized by a much greater anxiety about the 'idolatrous' potential of allegorical imagery and visual imagination. See further Maupeu, 'Statut de l'image'; Michael Camille, 'The Iconoclast's Desire: Deguileville's Idolatry in France and England', in Jeremy Dimmick, James Simpson and Nicolette Zeeman, eds, *Images, Idolatry and Iconoclasm in Late Medieval England: Textuality and the Visual Image* (Oxford University Press, 2002), pp. 151–71.

COGNITION: THEORY AND PRACTICE   217

The idol is lifeless and static, 'unable to move its feet' [ses piés ne puet remuer, *PVH2* 14,105], as if to underline its inability to participate in the forward movement of Deguileville's allegorical pilgrimage. But unlike the literalistic and inert Rude Entendement, the idol is also a simulacrum of sacramental efficacy and agency, since he relays the wilfully obscure, duplicitous speech of Satan with the aim of confounding human understanding and interpretation:

[...] a cel ydole la,	Satan goes to that idol there whenever
Ou le Sathan quant il plait va,	he pleases, and speaks some obscure
pour li dire aulcun mot trouble	and ambiguous words to it.
Qui entendement ait double	
(*PVH2* 14,083–6)	

The encounter enables Deguileville to formulate a rival theory of profitable, orthodox devotion to images through the mouthpiece of the Pilgrim. Again echoing Augustine's definition of idolatry (*De doctrina* III.8–9), this theory also doubles as an apology for the sapiential and sacramental efficacy of allegorical interpretation. Both allegorical interpretation and orthodox devotion avoid the pitfalls of idolatry and spiritual fornication precisely because they imply a functional, dynamic, and ultimately spiritual semiotics and hermeneutics, expressed in terms of specifically textual interpretation:

Les ymages pas n'äourons	We do not venerate images, and we do
Et houneur point ne leur faisons,	not worship them, but worship the
Mes aus sains pour qui sont faites,	saints in whose honour they are
[...]	made...
Siques ce nous est grant proffit,	And therefore this is of great benefit to
Mesmement a ceulx qui l'escript	us, and also for those who do not
Ne scevent pas: c'est leur livre,	understand the written word: this is
Tel com il leur faut pour lire.	their book, and this what they need to
(*PVH2* 14,151–3; 14,161–4)	read.

A similar kind of idolatry also features as part of the description of Avarice. In addition to wielding a mystifying 'courtine' with its 'couleurs plus fines' (*PVH1* 9927–36), she also deceives the faithful with false and fabricated relics (*PVH1* 9941–4). Like Chaucer's Pardoner, Avarice too goes the extra mile, and endows her forged saintly 'images' (*PVH1* 9946) with the semblance of life, devising a mechanical system to make them ooze with sweat (*PVH1* 9945–74) to deceive credulous worshippers: 'They call it a miracle, and say that the statue did it' [Il le reputent a miracle / Et dient que c'a fait l'image, *PVH1* 9971–2]. The idol has become an automaton, metonymy for the duplicitous nature of the sins' rhetorical bodies as a whole: monstrously mechanical, physiologically animated, larger than life, yet ultimately hollow and unsubstantial. The episode betrays Deguileville's intensified anxieties about the harmful potential of images, yet it is symptomatic that

218 MEDIEVAL ALLEGORY AS EPISTEMOLOGY

Avarice combines this ability for *visual* deception with more strictly *textual* and *linguistic* forms of dissimulation. Deceptive speech accordingly blurs the boundaries of truth and illusion, rendering 'crooked' (*tort*) that which was once 'straight' (*droit*)—alluding to the equivocal figural 'troping' of poetic language:[110]

'Tel maniere de langueter	'This kind of babbling, changing and
Et de muer et bestourner	twisting right into wrong and wrong
Le tort en droit et droit en tort',	into right.' [lit. 'crooked into straight']
(*PVH1* 10,085–7)	

This ability to 'twist' truths out of joint also characterizes Detraction, who delights in providing warped misinterpretations of texts and intentions:

[...] 'tout le bien que trouver puis	'I know how to interpret falsely all the
Je le sai bien en mal muer	good I can find and turn it into evil.'
Et faussement enterpreter.'	
(*PVH1* 8582–4)	

Like Avarice's curtain, Detraction's duplicity is presented as a perversion of the sacramental possibilities harboured by orthodox and salvific figuration. Detraction does not only change good into bad ('bien en mal muer') but also reverses the process of Eucharistic transubstantiation by changing wine back into water:

'Bien sai en eaue muer vin	'I know how to turn wine into water
Et en venin triacle fin.	and fine medicine into poison. I know
Bien sai honnir les bonnes pommes	how to spoil good apples and defame
Et diffamer vaillans hommes,	honourable people, and then I devour
Et puis ainsi comme char crue	them and eat them like raw flesh.'
Je les deveure et les mengue.'	
(*PVH1* 8585–90)	

The sins thus embody the perversion of Deguileville's own sacramental allegorical poetics, denying any possibility of spiritual development, and turning back upon their own bodies. They manifest an allegorical poetics that is both carnal and cannibalistic—turning Christ's sacramental body into human flesh, devoured raw.

As well as presenting the Seven Deadly Sins as embodiments of the perversion of meaningful allegorical signification, Deguileville suggests that they lack any solid ontological grounding. As negations or perversions of the corresponding virtues, they are in fact antithetical to being—echoing Augustine's definition of Evil as a 'lack' of substance[111]—and are accordingly endowed with deformed,

---

[110] The multiple meanings of *tort*—both 'twisted/crooked' and 'false', from Lat. *torquere*—are lost in any English translation. *FEW* XIII-2, 86b–87a.

[111] Gillian R. Evans, *Augustine on Evil* (Cambridge: Cambridge University Press, 1990), pp. 34–40.

disproportionate, but ultimately vacuous bodies.[112] They signify nothing beyond their inflated materiality, entirely dissociated from any substantial being. This is perfectly exemplified by Orgueil, whose own self-revelation is mere empty speech and 'windy puffery' [venteuses sifleries, *PVH1* 7596], and who becomes inflated beyond all proportion, in an allusion to 1 Cor. 8.1 (*sapientia inflat* 'knowledge puffs up'; see also *De doctrina* II.41.62), and contains merely wind and smoke (*PVH1* 7595–602, 7623–4). This paradoxical metaphysical emptiness is best encapsulated by Flatterie, bloodless and dried out, feeding on the emptiness she herself engenders in others: 'The leanness of others nourishes me' [Autri megrece me nourrit, *PVH1* 8261; *PVH1* 8201–2]. Similarly, Peresce grinds herself into dust and nothingness through her favoured activity—which is pure inertia:

'Et tout ainsi com se defrie	'And just as a millstone grinds itself into
Mole tant que n'a que moudre	powder and dust, when it has nothing
Et se fait farine et poudre,	to grind, so I watch myself grinding
Ausi ie me vois defriant	and consuming myself with sloth.'
Par ennui et degastant.'	
(*PVH1* 7172–6)	

If measured against Deguileville's Augustinian semiotics, the purely material, idolatrous bodies of the sins represent the absolute negation of a hermeneutics of the self. They are purely self-referential, unable to signify anything beyond their own inert physicality, exemplifying the negation of signification of any kind—a *fortiori* the kind of figurative signification where *res* are also *signa*, and particularly sacramental signification, where all signs ultimately point 'to the thing to which all such things are to be related' (*De doctrina* III.13). The sins become hollow figures, aberrant signifiers, purely rhetorical bodies deprived of any genuine, positive semantic or ontological content. This is well illustrated in Orgueil's description of the bellows of Vaine Gloire, used to sound pipes and flutes 'devoid of virtue or sense' [vuit de bien / ou qui de sens n'ont en eus rien, *PVH1* 7745–6]. Here their lack of *sens* denotes not only their irrational, 'senseless' quality but also their meaninglessness, their lack of semiotic and ontological content and their failure to signify anything 'other' than themselves. Like Rude Entendement, then, the sins ore ostensibly reducible to their hollow verbal and rhetorical forms. Deguileville ultimately suggests that despite their corporeal excess and rhetorical 'density' in the allegory, the nature of sin is fundamentally hollow and negative. In this sense the empty, idolatrous yet mechanically animated bodies of the seven deadly sins are, like the pilgrim's own body, not so much the subject of the allegory, but that which the allegory must process, overcome, exorcize and finally evacuate. To adapt

---

[112] I develop the ideas of Philippe Maupeu, 'Corps et langage dans le *PVH*: la mécanique des vices', unpublished paper delivered at the Congress on *Guillaume de Deguileville in Europe*, University of Lausanne, July 2011. I would like to thank the author for kindly sharing the typescript with me.

220 MEDIEVAL ALLEGORY AS EPISTEMOLOGY

Philippe Maupeu's formula, the process of allegorical interpretation cannot allow any corporeal residue, since according to the logic of allegorical representation, everything must finally 'make sense' and generate meaning (*faire sens*), acting as sign and never as a mere 'thing'.[113] In the process the bodies of the sins themselves are, as it were, sublimated out of existence, revealed as the unsubstantial, purely negative realities they are.

4. Practice: Eyes, Ears, and the Spectre of Aristotle

This, at least, is the theoretical principle that underpins the allegorical hermeneutics of Deguileville's first *Pèlerinage*. In practice, however, corporeal realities prove far more resistant to any such process of interpretive, cognitive, and ontological sublimation. This casts serious doubt not only on the Pilgrim's ability to put his instruction into practice, but also raises the possibility that the optimistic, even exalted theory of the soul's agency and independence from the body may not, after all, provide a viable model for describing the experiences of a human *viator* on a quest for salvific knowledge. In this section, I will accordingly propose a closer examination of the narrative action in the poem, paying particular attention to the numerous and meticulous descriptions of the mental processes and cognitive phenomena experienced by the first-person protagonist. I will argue that far from being aligned with the poet's dualistic understanding of the human soul and its active powers, the Pilgrim's experience of the outside world ultimately conforms to a very different, broadly Aristotelian and inherently embodied, hylomorphic model of cognition. Strikingly, the poet is at least partially aware of this inner contradiction, and finds himself forced to formulate a series of competing theories of cognition to account for the Pilgrim's actual experiences. As I will argue in the final section of this chapter, this not only destabilizes Deguileville's confidence in the epistemic and anthropological models that underpin his poem, but also threatens his trust in the ability of his own poem, and allegorical poetry more generally, to serve as a viable corrective to the carnal allegorical poetics of the *Rose*.

As I have previously argued, the description of the Pilgrim's protracted struggle against the Seven Deadly Sins is clearly intended to sharpen the reader's interpretive skills and train the cognitive powers of the soul. The Pilgrim himself, however, clearly lacks the necessary distance from the events recounted, and is literally submerged by the poem's action. His previously silent and lifeless body now regains agency, and prompts the pilgrim to opt for the path of Huiseuse against the better advice of Raison and that of his own soul (*PVH1* 6695–733). As soon as the Pilgrim enters the 'voie senestre' he is viciously attacked by the seven deadly sins, first

---

[113] Maupeu, 'Corps et langage': 'La lecture allégorique ne doit pas laisser de corps résiduel: tout doit faire signe' [allegorical interpretation cannot leave any corporeal residue: everything must signify].

individually and sequentially, and then collectively, until he becomes physically submerged by them—an idea well rendered in an evocatively cluttered illumination from Oxford, Bodleian Library MS Douce 300, fol. 69r.[114] In this long section of the poem, the sins—far from being vacuous and inert signifiers—relentlessly *act upon* the pilgrim, repeatedly attacking his body, which they threaten to variously maim, deform, or paralyse.[115] Their agency is so powerful that they eventually manage to deform and distort the *imago dei* in the pilgrim's soul, as his accusers observe in the *Pèlerinage de l'Âme*:[116]

'Tel est et a tousjours este	'This is what he is and always has been,
Ce las chetif tout defforme,	this poor miserable sinner, deformed,
Defigure et contrefait,	disfigured, and dissimulating, whom
Que le roy du ciel avoit fait	the King of the Heavens had created in
A sa semblance et figure	his image and likeness, without
Sens mehaing et sens laidure.'	blemish or unpleasantness.'

 (*PA* 665–70; see also
 PA 1257–60, 4119)

Allegorically speaking, the sins are of course manifestations the pilgrim's own uncontrolled bodily self,[117] suggesting that this deformity arises from the harmful action of the pilgrim's own corporeal self upon his soul. But the pilgrim's failure to resist the attacks of the sins does not only stem from the weakness of his will, but suggests that Raison's theory of active cognition through the soul fails to adequately describe the practical realities of human cognition in the world. Everything about the Pilgrim's actual experience on his quest exposes the vulnerability of his soul in the face of the corporeal and carnal world into which he has fallen.

The Pilgrim's misadventures are at odds with Raison's model of active perception to such a degree that Deguileville is forced to articulate a further, radically different, and fundamentally passive theory of sense perception and cognition. According to this second model the five senses are imagined as the gateways through which sensation enters the body and affects the soul. As Penitance explains,

---

[114] https://digital.bodleian.ox.ac.uk/objects/b891d227-826c-4db9-adc1-0165aa391511/surfaces/65ff3f9d-d156-452b-9606-9a73d154b800/, accessed 21 November 2022.
[115] On Deguileville's interest in physical, 'artisanal' agency as means for spiritual development, see also Lisa H. Cooper, *Artisans and Narrative Craft in Late Medieval England* (Cambridge: Cambridge University Press, 2011), pp. 106–45.
[116] See also Hagen, *Allegorical Remembrance*, p. 122; and Dolores Grmača, 'Body Trouble: The Impact of Deguileville's Allegory of Human Life on Croatian Renaissance Literature', in Kamath and Nievergelt, pp. 189–208 (esp. 201–2).
[117] See also Kay, *Place of Thought*, pp. 92–3.

222 MEDIEVAL ALLEGORY AS EPISTEMOLOGY

'En la meson dont sui baiesse
et Grace Dieu est la maistresse,
.VI. portes sont dont .V. i a
Par ou l'ordure dedens va.
L'une est la porte d'odourer,
L'autre d'oyr et d'escouter,
L'autre de goust, l'autre de tast
Et l'autre si est de regart.
Par ces .V. portes, ne doutez,
Entre souvent ordure assez.'
   (*PVH1* 2221–30)

'The house where I am servant and
Grace Dieu is mistress, there are six
gates, and filth enters through five of
them. There is one gate of smelling,
another of hearing, another of tasting,
another of touch, and another of
seeing. Through these five gates, you
may be sure, much filth often enters,'
   [translation emended]

The fundamentally negative conception of sensation proposed here is clearly shaped by ascetic and monastic ideals—unsurprisingly for a Cistercian author.[118] This same notion also underpins the logic of the Pauline armour of Faith from Ephesians, amply allegorized later in the poem. The helmet in particular offers protection against the sensual assaults aimed at the pilgrim from the outside world:

'Le heaume, si com dois savoir,
Est Attrempance de vëoir,
D'escouter et dë odourer
Choses qui te peuent grever;'
   (*PVH1* 4083–6)

'The helmet, you should know, is
Temperance, in seeing, hearing, and
smelling things that might harm you;'
   [translation emended]

The eye in particular is vulnerable to temptations being fired at it in the form of arrows:

'Tout aussi attrempance sert
De garder l'ueil que trop ouvert
Ne soit et trop abandonne
A folie et vanite,
Quar se n'ert euillere estroite,
Entrer pourroit ens (tel) saete
Qui droit au cuer pourroit aler
Et sans remede a mort navrer.'
   (*PVH1* 4089–96)

'So Temperance serves to guide the eye
so that it is not too open or too
vulnerable to folly and vanity. If the
visor were too narrow, an arrow could
enter and go straight to the heart and
wound it mortally.'

---

[118] On such architectural symbolism, and the senses as gates or windows to the castle of the human body, see especially Elizabeth Sears, 'Sensory Perception and its Metaphors in the Time of Richard de Fournival', in William F. Bynum and Roy Porter, eds, *Medicine and the Five Senses* (Cambridge: Cambridge University Press, 1993), pp. 17–39, particularly 17–20 and 37–9. See also C. M. Woolgar, *The Senses in Late Medieval England* (New Haven and London: Yale University Press, 2006), pp. 11, 13, 16–17 and the references given there.

COGNITION: THEORY AND PRACTICE   223

This set of metaphors translates a rather different, fundamentally Aristotelian model of sense perception,[119] at odds with the theories of active cognition and divine illumination presented by the poem's authority figures earlier in the poem. Deguileville's highly ambivalent characterization of visual perception in particular is symptomatic for this fundamental tension and irresolution, since the sense of sight appears simultaneously as the most accurate and the most misleading of all the five senses. Ever since Aristotle's *Metaphysics* (I.1)—via Augustine and down to Bacon's *Perspectiva* (I.i.i.3)—sight had been consistently identified as the noblest of the five external senses.[120] In *PVH*, however, sight is a conspicuously misleading guide in the apprehension of spiritual realities, which remain essentially concealed under the veil of appearances and indiscernible to the bodily eye. The prime example of human inability to apprehend divine truths through the corporeal eye is of course the Eucharist, as noted by both Sapience (*PVH1* 3097–8, 3114–16) and Raison (*PVH1* 1477–80; see further Chapter 2.2). *PVH* is saturated with similar reminders of the incommensurable difference between the 'clarity' of internal vision and the comparative 'blindness' of corporeal sight. The opposition has many influential precedents, from Boethius' use of the trope of the 'oculus intelligentiae' (*De consolatione* 5.pr.4.30), Vincent of Beauvais' 'interna visione' (*Speculum Naturale* 27.6 col.1921),[121] or Grosseteste's 'oculus mentis sanus' (*De veritate*).[122] All of these are ultimately instances of Augustine's third and highest type of vision, the 'intellectual vision' or *visio mentis*—the others being 'spiritual' (i.e. mental), and corporeal sight.[123] *Visio mentis* occurred, for Augustine, under modalities that were entirely independent from any physical processes, and amounted to a direct, unmediated apprehension of truth in the human mind through the agency of divine illumination. Corporeal vision is correspondingly devalued, and indeed Augustine repeatedly insisted that sense perception by itself could never convey *sincera veritas* (absolute truth).[124]

---

[119] Illustrations of the body as castle occur in a manuscripts of Aristotle's own *De Sensu et sensatu* as well as Richard de Fournival's work in the thirteenth century. See, respectively, Sears, 'Sensory Perception and its Metaphors'; and Tachau, 'Seeing as Action and Passion', discussing and reproducing Vatican City, Biblioteca Apostolica Vaticana, MS Barberini lat. 165 f. 330r.

[120] On the nobility of sight, see e.g. Denerey, *Seeing and Being Seen*, pp. 5–12; Akbari, *Seeing Through the Veil*, pp. 3–20. On Augustine specifically, see Vance, 'Seeing God'.

[121] Both quoted and discussed in Akbari, *Seeing through the Veil*, pp. 29 and 41–2.

[122] In *Die Philosophischen Werke des Robert Grosseteste, Bischofs von Lincoln*, ed. Ludwig Baur (Münster: Aschendorff, 1912), pp. 130–43 (142).

[123] See Augustine, *De trinitate*, XI.1.1; *De Genesi ad litteram*, ed. Joseph Zycha. CSEL 28.1 (Vienna: Verlag der Österreichischen Akademie der Wissenschaften, 1894), XII.6.15; XII.11.22–6 and *passim*. For the influence of this notion on Victorine anthropology, see also Hugh of St. Victor, *De sacramentis* I.10.2, in *PL* 176:329–30. For further discussion, see Carla Di Martino, *Ratio Particularis*, pp. 65–8; Miles, 'Vision: The Eye of the Body and the Eye of the Mind'; O'Daly, *Augustine's Theory of Mind*, pp. 106–30; Vance, 'Seeing God'.

[124] *De diversis quaestionibus*, q.9; *Contra Academicos* III.37. See further for instance O'Daly, *Augustine's Theory of Mind*, pp. 92–3.

224 MEDIEVAL ALLEGORY AS EPISTEMOLOGY

Despite Raison's ambitious theory of active perception through the soul, in actual practice Deguileville adopts a culturally established suspicion of sense perception as a vehicle for truth. The bodily senses themselves are correspondingly devalued, and often reduced to mere tropes for a form of cognition that does emphatically *not* rely on sense perception, but on internal, divine illumination of human understanding. So when Grace Dieu later alerts the pilgrim-reader to higher, divine truths and realties, her appeal to the specifics of ocular perception is strictly figurative and analogical:

'Ouvrez un pou discretement	'Open the eyes of your understanding
Les yex de vostre entendement!	with a little discretion. If you open up
Quar se bien ouvrez la paupiere,	your eyelids properly . . . you will see
[. . .]	very clearly',
Trouverez tout *apertement*',	[translation emended]
(*PVH1* 1703–7; my emphasis)	

Raison similarly evokes the 'eye' of inner understanding:

'Exemple bailler je t'en vueil,	'I want to give you an example of this,
A fin que se *vëoir a l'ueil*	so that you can see it clearly with your
Puisses clerement et entendre,	own eyes and understand it and
Bien retenir et bien apprendre.'	remember it well.'
(*PVH1* 1317–20; my emphases)	

This insistence on the primacy of inner *entendement*, however, points to a deep paradox that runs through the entire poem. How can Deguileville's poem simultaneously claim to train the pilgrim/reader's mastery of the corporeal senses and yet also urge them to leave sensation behind altogether, in favour of internal contemplation of timeless truths? How is the radical asceticism of this appeal to inner, intellectual vision to be reconciled with the poem's larger aim of providing a pedagogical training ground for a lay readership engaged in a pilgrimage of life through the secular world?[125] This also raises the still more difficult question of the nature, efficacy, and epistemic status of poetic images and imagination in this process of spiritual education: if *PVH* as a whole is intended, like Raison's figural analogies,

---

[125] This also determines the radically ascetic, even monastic bias of Deguileville's didactic project, finally promoting *contemptus mundi* and withdrawal from the active life. This is clearly at odds with the poet's desire to write an exemplary didactic account of the Christian life for a lay, secular audience. Indeed the narrative finally mutates into an allegory of Deguileville's own conversion to the monastic life. On such complex internal tensions, and the shifts from *PVH1* to *PVH2*, see Chapter 4, and the different arguments put forward by Faral, *Guillaume de Deguileville*, pp. 9–10; Hagen, *Allegorical Remembrance*, pp. 114–15; Pomel, *Les voies*, pp. 415–20 and *passim*; Henry, *Manhode*, 'Introduction', pp. xxvii, xxx–xxxi; Maupeu, *Pèlerins de vie humaine*, esp. pp. 197–215; and Nievergelt, *Allegorical Quests*, pp. 41–4.

to 'furnish an example . . . so that you may see clearly with your eye' [Exemple bailler je t'en vueil, / A fin que se vëoir a l'ueil / Puisses clerement et entendre, *PVH1* 1317–19], how exactly does allegorical poetry enhance the human ability to visualize purely intellectual realities in the mind's immaterial 'eye'?

For a while at least it appears that for Deguileville the sense of bodily sight may be assisted and guided by the sense of hearing and its greater claims as a source of accurate and necessary knowledge. The origin of the idea is biblical, with Paul's affirmation that 'Faith comes by hearing' (Rom. 10:17), and the mixing of aural and visual metaphor is again endemic throughout Augustine's writing.[126] So during the discussion of the Eucharist, Grace Dieu clearly establishes how four of the five senses are thoroughly misled, and only hearing can assist man in apprehending the real presence of Christ's body and blood in the bread and wine:

'au taster et au vëoir,
A l'oudourer et au gouster
Et pain et vin te puet sembler,
Quar ces quatre sens decëus
Y sont du tout et fols tenus.
Rien n'i sevent, esbloe sont,
  [. . .]
Mais le sens d'ouir seulement
En enfourme l'entendement;
Celui a tast ici endroit,
Odourement, goust et vëoir,
Cetui connoist plus soutilement
Et apercoit plus clerement.'
  (*PVH1* 2750–62; cf. *PVH2* 2928–40)

'It might seem bread and wine when you touch it, taste it, smell it, or see it, for these four senses are completely deceived and they are foolish. They are stupefied and know nothing . . . But the sense of hearing alone informs the understanding. It knows more subtly and perceives more clearly than touching, smelling, tasting, and seeing.'

Clearly here Grace Dieu develops a broadly 'sapiential' understanding of hearing, defined by its ability to 'savour' the divine presence in the Eucharist in much 'clearer' and more 'subtle' fashion than any of the other senses. While this too is a traditional monastic idea, Grace's point may also resonate with more recent, scholastic discussions of the elusive 'subtlety' of the processes involved in aural perception, often characterized as being of a less material, more abstract and mysterious nature than those of the other senses.[127]

Yet in Grace Dieu's speech, 'hearing' functions primarily as a trope for a form of *entendement* whose actual nature and cognitive mechanics are not, and *cannot*,

---

[126] Miles, 'Vision: The Eye of the Body and the Eye of the Mind', pp. 128–9; Vance, 'Seeing God'.

[127] Deguileville may also have been aware of the generalized scholastic discomfort with accounts of sound, more difficult to explain in terms of the multiplication of the original *species* or 'form' of the perceived object through a material medium as in the case of vision. See Robert Pasnau, 'Sensible Qualities: The Case of Sound', *Journal of the History of Philosophy* 38 (2000), 27–40.

be described, because they are immaterial and thus elude accurate formal analysis. Hearing—just like 'seeing' in the sense of Augustine's *visio mentis*—is used as a trope for otherwise completely immaterial, elusive, and mysterious form of purely intellectual cognition enabled by bending one's ear in a radically improper act of 'troping', twisting and turning of the senses out of joint to 'hear' the voice of the incarnate word (*logos/verbum*). It is of course perfectly appropriate that such an *aporia* of sensory cognition should be triggered precisely by a discussion of the real presence of the incarnate *logos* in the sacrament. Finally it is the profound, absolute alterity of the *logos* in relation to the fallen human body that demands the radically unnatural, 'improper' use of sense perception as an analogical trope. It is the same rupture between postlapsarian humanity and the *logos* that forces language and signification to embrace the equally oblique *alieniloquium* of allegory, in the hope of gesturing towards the absolute alterity of transcendence. Grace accordingly highlights how in her own usage, talk of the Eucharist transgresses the rules of ordinary linguistic signification:

'Pain et vin donc se le nomme,
Je t'avise et si te somme
Que char et sanc soit entendu
   [...]
Aussi ai je en mon usage
De nommer le en tel langage,
Pain l'appelle et pain le nomme
Qui du ciel vient repaistre homme.'
   (*PVH1* 2745–7, 2797–800)

'If I call it bread and wine, then, I advise you and caution you that you must understand and firmly believe that it is flesh and blood ... So it is my custom to call it by that name. I call it bread, the bread that comes down from heaven to feed mankind.'

In the wake of such improper use of language and the senses, the whole semantic field of perception is transposed to serve as an extended trope, stretching and indeed exploding the limits of analogy beyond the affinity of signifier and signified to express a relationship of absolute difference or non-identity between sensation and intellectual vision, body and intellect, letter and spirit.

Despite this seemingly compelling insistence on the absolute alterity of intellectual cognition, however, Deguileville cannot resist the temptation to provide, against all odds, a more precise description of the mechanics of intellectual cognition. Symptomatically, when Grace Dieu speaks of inner, supra-sensual 'hearing' as a process that 'informs the understanding' of the Pilgrim (*PVH1* 2758, quoted above; cf. also 2786), she uses a term with potent Aristotelian associations. The term *enfourmer* evokes precisely the Aristotelian notion of 'form', and along with it the hylomorphic principle of an embodied soul and the corresponding theory of cognition invariably dependent on sense perception. The notion of an 'informed' understanding therefore also implies a model of fundamentally abstractive cognition, postulated on the agency (*virtus*) of the sensible *species* or *forma* upon the

COGNITION: THEORY AND PRACTICE   227

sense organs and thence upon the internal senses. As was already seen in relation to a passage from Roger Bacon's writings (Chapter 3.2), the terms *forma* and *species*, as well as *ymago*, were in effect widely used as synonyms in the period, in order to designate mental images that were abstracted from sense experience. According to the species theory, however, even the incorporeal intellectual *species* preserved some form of material existence as 'spiritual matter', determining its fundamental, ontological difference from strictly intellectual vision as postulated by Augustine, occurring in the purely immaterial rational or intellective soul. In wishing to 'inform' the pilgrim's understanding, then, Grace once more reintroduces the problem of the seemingly irreducible materiality of human cognition.

The frequently discussed 'eyes-in-ears' passage from *PVH2* (3515–24) brings such latent internal contradictions to a head,[128] pointing to the huge difficulties created by Deguileville's desire to reject the Aristotelian model of cognition while also providing an accurate account of the Pilgrim's experience of the outside world. The episode occurs as part of Grace's lecture on the allegorical significance of the Scrip and Staff—signifiers of Faith and Hope respectively (see Chapter 2.4)—and is characteristic of the more verbose, insistently expository character of Deguileville's 1355 rewriting of his original poem. The exchange follows on directly from the earlier discussion of supra-sensual 'hearing' found in the dispute over Eucharistic transubstantiation, which survives essentially unaltered in *PVH2* (6581–630). Grace Dieu briefly recapitulates the earlier debate as a preamble to her new thought experiment:

'Or enten', dist elle, 'un petit.	'Listen to me for a brief moment', she
Il n'a pas moult qu'il te fu dit,	said. 'A short while ago you were told
Quant du petit pain doubtoies	about the little bread, which astonished
Et de li te merveilloies	you and made you doubt ... that none
[. . .]	of the senses apart from hearing would
Que nul sens ne t'en aprenoit,	ever teach you about it;'
Se seulement l'ouïr n'estoit;'	
(*PVH2* 3535–42)	

Grace Dieu now invites the pilgrim to place his eyes in his ears, to help him 'visualize' the nature of the Theological virtues of Faith and Hope:

'L'escherpe et le bourdon que veus	'The scrip and staff that you want are of
Ont tel condicion en eulx	such a nature that you will not be able
Que vëoir tu ne les pourras,	to see them unless you

---

[128] For further discussion of this conspicuous episode, see especially Nicolette Zeeman, 'Medieval Religious Allegory, French and English', in Copeland and Struck, eds, *Cambridge Companion to Allegory*, pp. 148–61; Vincent Gillespie, 'Dame Study's Anatomical Curse: A Scatological Parody?' in Nicholas Jacobs and Gerald Morgan, eds, *'Truthe is the Beste': A Festschrift in Honour of A. V. C. Schmidt* (Oxford: Peter Lang, 2014), pp. 95–107; Stephen J. Russell, 'Allegorical Monstrosity: The Case of Deguileville', *Allegorica* 5 (1980), 95–103; Hagen, *Allegorical Remembrance*, pp. 30–55.

228 MEDIEVAL ALLEGORY AS EPISTEMOLOGY

Se les yeux es oreilles n'as.
Et croy, se ne les vëoies,
Que trop pou les priseroies.
Si que les yeulx je t'osteray
De la ou sont et les mectray
En tes oreilles par dehors,
Si que vëoir les pourras lors.'
  (*PVH2* 3515–24)

place your eyes in your ears. And
believe me, if you didn't see them, you
wouldn't cherish them sufficiently.
Therefore I will take your eyes from
where they are right now, and place
them outside, in your ears, so that you
will be able to see them.'

Here the human body itself becomes an improperly 'troped', deformed signifier to
apprehend the true nature of Faith and Hope: 'turned into a monster, transformed,
and disfigured' [fusse monstre ou transformés / Ou autrement desfigurés, *PVH2*
3533–4]. The episode develops in a series of stages, with Grace Dieu's explanations initially designed, or so it seems, to exalt the cognitive potential of hearing
by opposing it to knowledge conveyed by the four other senses:

'nul sens ne t'en aprenoit,
Se seulement l'ouïr n'estoit :
Celui en scet tant seulement
Et chascuns des autres y ment.'
  (*PVH2* 3541–4)

'None of the senses could teach you
about it, except for hearing; only
hearing brings knowledge, while all
other senses will deceive you.'

In order to differentiate the unique and superior cognitive potential of hearing,
Grace then launches into a technical excursus on the mechanics of ordinary sense
perception, taking sight as her example. Information perceived by the senses is
brought to the internal senses, usually numbering four or five, but reduced to three
in Deguileville's simplified model:[129] information is received by the Common
Sense (*commun sens*), relayed to the imagination or Fantasy (*fantasie*), and finally
transmitted to the Understanding, or 'estimative/cogitative faculty' (*entendement*)
for elaboration:

'Quant dont regart, portier de l'ueil,
Duquel pour toux parler je vueil,
Voit quelque nouvelle chose,
Onques ne dort ne repose
Devant ce que, par le congié

'When Gaze—porter of the eye—who I
shall take as an example for all other
senses, sees anything novel, it will
never rest until it announces this to
Fantasy—with the permission

---

[129] For the classic account, see Wolfson, 'The Internal Senses in Latin, Arabic and Hebrew Philosophic Texts'. See further Simo Knuuttila, 'Aristotle's Theory of Perception and Medieval Aristotelianism', in Knuuttila and Kärkkäinen, *Theories of Perception in Medieval and Early Modern Philosophy*,
pp. 1–22; Smith, 'Perception', *CHMP*, I:334–45. Deguileville's model here fits with the fourfold model of
internal senses—the most widely adopted by later scholastics as opposed to Avicenna's fivefold model,
see e.g. Wolfson, 114–24. Memory is omitted from Grace's account since it is not directly relevant to
the matter in hand.

Du commun sens, l'ara nuncié	of the Common Sense. Fantasy too
A fantasie qui ne dort	never sleeps, so that it may report this
Affin que sens delay rapport	to the Understanding, who will pass
Elle en face a l'entendement	reliable judgment.'
Pour faire en loyal jugement.'	
(PVH2 3633–42)	

While this is indeed a perfectly orthodox account of perception in line with the of the Aristotelian model, it is completely at odds with Raison's theory of the soul's active powers. But Grace now adds that in some cases—notably in the case of the Eucharist, or indeed the Staff of Hope or Scrip of Faith—the Understanding (*entendement*, here corresponding to the estimative or cogitative faculty in the model of the internal senses) is unable to process the information it has received, and thus rejects the sense-data and returns sense impression to where it came from through a curious case of perceptual reflux:[130]

'Se c'est chose qui a lui duit [à Entendement]	'And if it is a thing that falls under its authority, the Understanding will judge
Il en juge et determine	and determine, and explain everything
Et par raison tout affine;	through reason; and if it does not fall
Et se point ne li appertient,	under its authority, it sends it back
Il la renvoie dont li vient	where it has come from, by means of
Par ceulx qui li apporterent,	those who have carried it there,
Nuncierent et amenerent.'	announced and delivered it.'
(PVH2 3644–50)	

The entire passage is rather baffling, and appears oddly ill-suited to the immediate purpose. Grace Dieu's description appears to be designed simply to expose the inability of ordinary sense perception—and corporeal sight in particular—to apprehend the nature of Faith symbolized by the Pilgrim's scrip. Given the preceding emphasis on the subtlety of 'hearing', we now expect to be given an explanation on how the human mind is able to 'hear' the voice of the *logos*, and perform cognitive operations of a higher order that do not, crucially, rely on corporeally mediated sensation at all; we expect, in short, a description of the nature and mechanics of purely intellectual cognition. Surprisingly, however, Grace Dieu largely repeats her previous description of abstractive cognition based on sense perception, simply applying it to hearing instead of seeing: in attempting to grasp the nature of Faith and Hope on the basis of aural information relayed to it by hearing, the Understanding (*entendement*, i.e. estimative or cogitative faculty) is once more baffled, and once more returns the message to the sender:

---

[130] To my knowledge, this idea is unattested elsewhere.

230 MEDIEVAL ALLEGORY AS EPISTEMOLOGY

'Si dois savoir que l'escherpe
Dont bon pelerin s'escherpe,
A la porte de l'oreille
Le portier, si dort, eveille:
A nulle autre porte ne va
Et de nulle autre cure n'a.
L'ouïe, qui en est portier,
Par sens commun la va nuncier
A fantasie com est dit,
Laquelle tantost le redit
Au grant juge l'entendement,
Lequel, quant musé longuement
Y a, et si est afolé
Et com nonsaichant chaitivé,
Il le baillë et envoie
Par le chemin et la voie
Qu'a li est venu a l'ouïr,
Qui a li l'avoit fait venir.'
  (*PVH2* 3651–68)

'So you must know that scrip donned by every good pilgrim, will awaken the porter of the ear, if he were to be asleep; it won't go to any other door, and does not care for any of the other doors. Hearing—which is porter of the ear—will then go and announce this to Fantasy, by means of the Common Sense, as I have just explained, which in turn repeats it to the great judge Understanding. The latter, after pondering this for a long time, and if it is overcome, and proven ignorant and defeated, will hand it back and send it back the same way to Hearing who had brought it.'

Instead of confirming the ostensibly superior cognitive possibilities of the ear, then, the explanation now aligns hearing with all the other four senses, conforming to a perfectly standard Aristotelian account of the internal senses, here reduced to three as was commonly the case in encyclopaedic materials. Rather than providing a viable description of intellectual cognition, then, all that Grace Dieu manages to achieve is to describe how the internal senses *fail* (predictably) to grasp the nature of Faith and Hope on the basis of ordinary sense perception—including hearing just as much as sight. Given her evident failure in elucidating the nature of intellectual cognition altogether, it is hardly surprising that Grace Dieu herself, defensive and cantankerous, should now be keen to put an end to the conversation, irritably dismissing any further requests for explanation, and merely reiterating her invitation to the pilgrim to place his 'eyes in his ears':

'Si faut que jugé lors en soit,
Pour laquel cause faut par droit
Qui en voudra savoir le voir
Et la verite apparcevoir,
Que la soient ses yeux portés
Et de leur propre lieu ostés.
Or en di ce que tu voudras;
Assés avisé esté as.'
  (*PVH2* 3669–76)

'So the question will need to be considered, and this is why by right, whoever will want to know the truth about this, and apprehend this truth, will have to place their eyes in their ears, removing them from their proper place. So you can say whatever you wish about this—I have instructed you well enough on this matter.'

COGNITION: THEORY AND PRACTICE 231

Medieval readers and scribes evidently struggled with the logical flaws and blatant contradictions of this 'explanation'. The nine manuscripts of *PVH2* show considerable variation in their handling of this confusing exchange,[131] and it is telling that Lydgate modified the passage in the attempt to reconstruct some viable overall meaning in his own translation of *PVH2*. But far from solving the problems created by Deguileville's Grace Dieu, Lydgate—or the lost manuscript he was working from—compounds those problems even further. Since *entendement* fails to decrypt the information brought to it by the other internal senses from the ear, the understanding now appeals—inexplicably—to *hearing* as an aid to supplement the information already relayed by the ear:

> They fyrst vn-to the gatë gon
> Off the Ere, & off Eryng;
>   [...]
> And [Entendement], for lak off knowleychyng,
> 'ffeleth ther-in no maner thyng,
> Thanne of Folye, he chek maat,
> Awhapyd and dysconsolat,
> Sent yt ageyn (yt stondeth so)
> By thylkë gate that yt kam fro;
> for he (shortly, in sentement)
> Koude gyve noon other Iugëment
> ffor al hys wyttys were a-gon,
> Saue that Eryng (amon echon),
> Kam a-noon to hys refuge
> ffor to deme & be a Iuge,
> As yt longede off verray ryht.
> 'ffor smellyng, Tastyng, touch and Syht,
> They wer deceyved euerychon;
>   (*PLM* 6516–17, 6539–53)[132]

The confusions around this particular passage may appear rather peripheral and arcane—especially in a poem of some 18,000 lines. The problems point, however, to a much more deep-seated philosophical difficulty that has important resonances far beyond Deguileville's poem, and that runs through late medieval philosophy of mind as a whole. For a start, Deguileville is pursuing two radically incompatible objectives: on the one hand he is attempting to illustrate the inability of ordinary sense perception and the ensuing cognitive operations in the internal

---

[131] Maupeu and Edwards note that several manuscripts provide alternative readings, suggesting that Deguileville's frankly tortuous elucidations at this stage in the poem were frequently misunderstood. See notes to *PVH2* 3519.

[132] John Lydgate, trans. *The Pilgrimage of the Life of Man*.

232　MEDIEVAL ALLEGORY AS EPISTEMOLOGY

senses of the sensitive soul to convey the intangible nature of Faith and Hope; on the other, he is also attempting to describe the cognitive operations performed by the rational or intellectual soul—the 'third' and highest of the three human souls, whose operations are purely intellectual immaterial. In doing so he succumbs to a distinctly naturalistic, 'Aristotelian' temptation to explain intellective processes that supposedly take place in the immaterial rational soul—processes that are *by definition* immaterial, and thus beyond the grasp of human analysis or even description. Deguileville's Grace Dieu here appears to have become a victim of the same kind of naturalistic fallacy that the poet had earlier held up for ridicule in his portrait of Aristotle, who attempts to explain the transubstantiation of the Eucharist as a 'natural' process.[133] In his desperate attempt—and failure—to describe the mechanics of intellectual cognition, Deguileville finally ends up drawing attention to the very question that Grace Dieu is desperately trying to avoid: how is it possible for the human mind to form concepts and ideas in endogenous fashion, without relying on information ultimately abstracted from the corporeal senses and mediated through the internal senses?

Deguileville's difficulties—and the larger philosophical problem concerning the cognitive operations of the immaterial rational soul—crystallize around his use of the crucial, but ultimately slippery term *entendement*, variously used to denote a wide and inconsistent range of faculties of the soul, both sensitive and intellectual. The term is of course best translated simply as 'understanding', but Deguileville often uses the term in such a context that suggests at least two more precise, but very different and largely incompatible meanings. On the one hand, the term is used most often to designate what in the technical vocabulary of intellectual historians would be identified as 'intellectual cognition', i.e. a process occurring in the rational or intellectual soul—whose nature is by definition immaterial. The term is used in this sense by Raison (*PVH1* 1477), as well as by Grace Dieu, designating the 'eyes of the understanding' or *oculus mentis* involved in the apprehension of intellectual realities (*PVH1* 1704, cf. also *PVH1* 3486–92), and again by Grace Dieu (*PVH1* 2758). In *PVH2*, however, the term is also used to describe what is unmistakeably one of the internal senses, located in the sensitive soul that humans share with other animals *PVH2* (3641, 3662; cf. also Lydgate, *PLM* 6491, 6536, both discussed in what precedes). In this second set of examples, *entendement* clearly designates the *vis aestimativa*. This was the fourth and cognitively most advanced of Avicenna's five internal senses, also named the discriminative faculty (*virtus distinctiva* or *cogitativa*) by certain authors, following Averroës, to underline its greater proximity to the more strictly rational function

---

[133] For a fuller discussion of Deguileville's ambivalent attitude towards the character of Aristotle in his poem, and his attitude to the Aristotelian science of dialectic as well as natural science, my 'From *disputatio* to *predicatio*—and back again', and the related discussion in Chapter 2.1.

COGNITION: THEORY AND PRACTICE   233

of the intellectual soul.[134] A similarly confusing use of the term *entendement* to designate both the ordinary cognitive operations of the sensitive soul as well as the higher order cognitive processes in the intellectual soul again occurs in Deguileville's *Pèlerinage de l'Âme* (respectively *PA* 10,787–9 and 10,910–11 vs. *PA* 10,838–9).

Deguileville was not alone in struggling to draw the boundary between the cognitive operations of the sensitive soul and those in the rational soul. He was in very good company indeed—and the importance of drawing that distinction cannot be overstated, since the capacity for intellectual cognition in the rational soul alone was the one single feature that differentiated humans, created in the image of God, from other animals. Just like Deguileville, then, the scholastics too struggled to draw a clear boundary between sensitive and rational soul, and these difficulties again crystallized on the back of discussions of the 'estimative' or 'cogitative' faculty—the highest and most subtle of the internal senses of the sensitive soul. Far from occupying a clear position even in scholastic accounts—which often misunderstood or distorted their Arabic sources[135]—discussions of the precise role of the *vis aestimativa* brought to a head a whole range of conceptual and terminological difficulties that were endemic in thirteenth- and fourteenth-century models of cognition and perception. The problem was already latent in Aristotle's *De anima*, and was further exacerbated by Avicenna, and then bequeathed to later Arabic and Latin commentators.[136] Debates over the ontological status of the rational soul became particularly heated in early and mid-fourteenth-century Paris with the rise of philosophical materialism, which argued that on the basis of strictly 'scientific' philosophical examination all components of the human soul ultimately appeared to be materially based. A materialist understanding of the human soul was not entirely new—it was originally developed by Alexander of Aphrodisias and transmitted by Averroës—but its implications were potentially cataclysmic, since it amounted to a denial of the immaterial nature of the immortal, rational soul. In the fourteenth century the idea was taken up first William of Ockham and later John Buridan, before the view eventually became widespread in the latter half of the fourteenth century.[137] Ockham's comments in the *Questiones Quodlibetales*,

[134] See Hasse, 'The Soul's Faculties', *CHMP*, I:305–19 (314). For Averroes's *virtus distinctiva*, see Averroës Cordubensis, *Commentarium Magnum in Aristotelis 'De Anima Libros'*, ed. F. Stuart Crawford; CCAA VI.1 (Cambridge, MA: Medieval Academy of America, 1953), e.g. III.6.60, p. 415.

[135] See Deborah L. Black, 'Imagination and Estimation: Arabic Paradigms and Western Transformations', *Topoi* 19 (2000), 59–75; Wood, 'Imagination and Experience'; DiMartino, *Ratio Particularis*. On Aquinas, see further Pasnau, *Thomas Aquinas on Human Nature* (Cambridge: Cambridge University Press, 2002), pp. 267–78.

[136] Heath, *Allegory and Philosophy in Avicenna*, 55–9; Hasse, 'The Soul's Faculties', *CHMP*, I: 314–16; Hasse, *Avicenna's 'De Anima'*, pp. 127–53.

[137] See King, 'Body and Soul', pp. 512–15; Pasnau, 'Mind and Hylomorphism', pp. 493–5; Jack Zupko, 'John Buridan on the Immateriality of the Intellect'; and Olaf Pluta, 'How Matter Becomes Mind: Late Medieval Theories of Emergence', both in Lagerlund, *Forming the Mind*, pp. 129–48 and 149–68.

234   MEDIEVAL ALLEGORY AS EPISTEMOLOGY

dated to 1325–6, provide an uncannily resonant gloss on Deguileville's difficulties, in 1331 and again in 1355, in preserving the notion of an entirely immaterial and incorruptible rational soul, entirely separated from the material processes taking place in the sensitive soul:

> one who follows natural reason would allow that we experience thinking in ourselves as acts of understanding that are the acts of a corporeal and corrupt-ible form; and he would consequently maintain that such acts are received in extended form. However, we do not experience an act of understanding of a sort that is an operation proper to an immaterial substance. And, therefore, we do not, by appealing to acts of understanding, establish that an incorruptible substance exists in us as a form.[138]

Ockham and Buridan stopped short of *affirming* that the rational soul was a mate-rial entity, and merely proposed this possibility as the result of a strictly rational and 'scientific' approach to the problem—hence their materialism is of a strictly *philosophical* order. Yet both Ockham and Buridan also insisted—not unlike the palpably frustrated Grace Dieu at *PVH2* 3669–76 (see above)—that belief in the immaterial nature of the rational soul could only be held on grounds of *faith* and revelation, and not reason. In this sense it is certainly symptomatic that in his sec-ond, revised, more defensive and apologetic version of the *Pèlerinage*, Deguileville no longer assigns the task of disembodying the pilgrim's soul to Raison, but to Grace Dieu (*PVH2* 6255–928). This clearly suggests that Deguileville had come to the conclusion that the human experience of the soul as an independent sub-stance no longer lay within the reach of ordinary human thought, but depended directly on the external intervention of Grace to transcend the ordinary limitations of human understanding.

Such difficulties concerning the respective natures, powers, and epistemic oper-ations of the sensitive and intellectual souls are not unique to Deguileville, but endemic to scholastic faculty psychology as a whole. What Deguileville's prob-lem as a whole brings into focus is precisely a latent, diffuse but pervasive unease concerning the relation between the multiple human souls and the body, and the difficulty of understanding how exactly the information conveyed by sense percep-tion is progressively 'dematerialized' during the process of abstraction. Given such

---

[138] 'concederet sequens naturalem rationem quod experimur intellectionem in nobis, quae est actus formae corporae et corruptibilis; et diceret consequenter quod talis forma recipitur in forma extensa. Non autem experimur illam intellectionem quae est operatio propria substantiae immate-rialis; et ideo per intellectionem non concludimus illam substantiam incorruptibilem esse in nobis tamquam formam.' William of Ockham, *Quodlibeta Septem*. Opera Theologica, vol. 9, ed. Joseph C. Wey (Bonaventure, NY: St Bonaventure University, 1980), I.10, p. 65: 88–94; translation from William of Ockham, *Quodlibetal Questions*, trans. Alfred J. Freddoso and Francis E. Kelley. 2 vols (New Haven and London: Yale University Press, 1991), I.10, p. 58.

COGNITION: THEORY AND PRACTICE   235

an imprecise and shifting topography of the soul and its faculties and the associated problems in terminology, Deguileville's difficulties do little more than reflect
the disagreements of different scholastic accounts already available. But for an allegory explicitly claiming to teach its readers to discriminate between true and false,
body and soul, letter and spirit, however, the author's own increasing inability to
differentiate between literal and metaphorical '*vëue*', between divine illumination
and abstractive cognition, and between sensitive and intellective *entendement*, is
potentially disastrous.

Deguileville's latent doubts about the nature of purely intellectual cognition
raise the related problem of the epistemic status of *PVH* itself. How can the
poem—as a work of fiction characterized by its reliance on powerful, vivid, and
eminently visual mental images to be apprehended by the reader's mind—avoid
the taint of corporeal matter and truly illuminate the eyes of the reader's intellectual
understanding? In what precedes I have argued that Deguileville appears to have
internalized—despite his overt commitment to a broadly Augustinian and illuminationist epistemology—a number of fundamental principles of the mainstream
Aristotelian theory of knowledge. As emerges from his handling of the eyes-in-ears
episode, it seems unavoidable that Deguileville must concur with the Aristotelian
maxim that 'the soul never thinks without an image' [nihil intelligit sine phantasmate anima, cf. *De anima* III.7, 431a16–17]—an idea most assertively put forward
by Aquinas,[139] who particularly stresses the role of bodily images in representing
spiritual realities through analogy:

> Other incorporeal substances we know, in the present state of life, only by way
> of remotion or by some comparison to corporeal things. And, therefore, when
> we understand something about these things, we need to turn to phantasms of
> bodies, although there are no phantasms of the things themselves.[140]

This appears to provide an accurate description for how the trope of the eyes in
ears operates upon the reader, in the light of Grace Dieu's additional explanations: although it is intended to describe a purely intellectual form of cognition,

---

[139] See Aquinas, *ST*, 1a q. 75, a. 7, and ibid., *Quaestiones disputatae de veritate*, ed. A. Dondaine,
Editio Leonina, vol. 22. 3 vols (Rome: Editori di San Tommaso, 1970–6), II: q. 10, a. 2, ad 7. See
further *Thomas Aquinas: Commentary on Aristotle's De Anima*, trans. Robert Pasnau (New Haven and
London: Yale University Press, 1999), ch. 12, 104–95, § 770–6 (pp. 383–5) and ch. 10, 243–9, § 745
(p. 370); and Aquinas famously endorses this statement far more energetically than other scholastic
authors, for whom it remained problematic. See further Mikko Yrjönsuuri, 'The Soul as an Entity:
Dante, Aquinas and Olivi', in Lagerlund, *Forming the Mind*, pp. 59–92; Pasnau, *Aquinas on Human
Nature* pp. 267–95, 366; James Doig, 'Aristotle and Aquinas', and Robert Pasnau, 'Philosophy of Mind
and Human Nature', both in Brian Davies, ed, *Oxford Handbook of Aquinas* (Oxford: Oxford University
Press, 2012), resp. pp. 33–41 and 349–65.
[140] 'alias etiam incorporeas substantias, in statu praesentis vitae, cognoscere non possumus nisi
per remotionem, vel aliquam comparationem ad corporalia. Et ideo cum de huiusmodi aliquid intelligimus, necesse habemus converti ad phantasmata corporum, licet ipsorum non sint phantasmata',
Summa Theologiae 1a q. 84, a. 7, ad 3.

236 MEDIEVAL ALLEGORY AS EPISTEMOLOGY

the trope necessarily causes us to form a mental image of that process; yet the very act of conjuring up a visual mental image runs counter to the very principle of intellectual cognition, and thereby threatens to reassert the mind's dependence on visual/mental images. This entails a second Aristotelian proposition that establishes the perceptual, and hence corporeal origin of all mental forms or *species*: 'nothing is in the intellect that was not previously in sense' [Nihil est in intellectu quod non sit prius in sensu, Aquinas, *Quaestiones disputatae de veritate* q. 2, a. 3, obj. 1]. Together these statements would seem to make it impossible for the human soul or intellect to hold any mental forms, no matter how refined or 'soutile' (cf. *PVH1* 2761), that are not grounded in information previously transmitted by the body and abstracted from sense perception. This may in turn validate Aristotle's highly problematic conformality thesis, describing acts of cognition as consisting in the soul's own transformation through its acquisition of the 'likeness' of the thing known (cf. *De anima* II.5, 418a 5–6; III.4, 429b6; III.8, 431b20; Aquinas, *Quaestiones disputatae de veritate*, q. 1, a. 1). Far from remaining at a safe distance from objects and actions in the external world, then, the reader's mind too is the recipient of external action by the bodies, images, and forms that make up the poem, becoming transformed into the very objects it is continuously urged to renounce.

5. The Long Shadow of the *Rose*: Didacticism, Embodiment, and Experiential Hermeneutics

Despite his best efforts to profess the contrary, then, Deguileville's poetic practice underlines the imbrication of mind and matter as a fundamental, intrinsic feature of allegory as a mode of thought, interpretation, and representation. This is not only an uncomfortable contradiction for a poem that elsewhere advocates a radically different, dualist and illuminationist theory of knowledge, but a realization that threatens to undermine the entire anthropology and epistemology upon which Deguileville's poetic universe is built. More specifically, this *aporia* also compromises Deguileville's attempt to dissociate his own, spiritual allegorical poetics from the carnal bodily poetics of the *Rose*.[141] Strikingly, Deguileville appears to have become increasingly aware of this internal tension between his theory of the imagination and his poetic practice. His growing discomfort with the problematic status of allegorical imagery is particularly evident in *PVH2*, an extended and laborious rewriting of his original poem that was completed some twenty-five years later. As I have already noted, this revised version is also characterized by much greater and more explicit hostility towards the *Rose*. Such

---

[141] On Jean de Meun's engagement with scholastic *species*-theories, the abstractive model of cognition, and the theory of the internal senses, see Pomel, 'Visual Experiences and Allegorical Fiction'.

hostility ultimately springs from Deguileville's growing anxiety about the contingent, ineluctably embodied nature of all knowledge as presented by the *Rose*. As Sylvia Huot and others have argued, the *Rose* 'holds out the promise of [. . .] a knowledge accessed not through language, but through the body', a bodily knowledge fundamentally gendered and eroticized.[142] More threateningly still, it has been suggested that in the *Rose* it is precisely 'the body [that] becomes the goal of reading',[143] and that such a body may not in the end be the site of knowledge, since 'the body no longer signifies anything beyond itself' (see Chapter 1.5).[144]

Deguileville thus registers corporeal knowledge as essentially unreliable and indeed idolatrous, of a piece with the carnal misreading associated with the hollow rhetorical coverings donned by Huiseuse, the Seven Deadly Sins, Faux Semblant, and the radically equivocal poetics of the *Rose* as a whole. But given his own struggle to live up to the exalted theory of active and disembodied cognition in the rational soul alone, Deguileville is also haunted by the possibility that such corporeal entanglement may not so much arise from the *perversion* of allegorical imagination, but that it may be its *norm*. It was precisely this notion of the inescapability of the corporeal, experiential entanglement of the human soul that emerges from the conclusion of the *Rose*. Jean the Meun suggests this possibility by staging an elaborately idolatrous climax during the defloration scene, culminating in the lover's obscene worship of a sculpted, artificial material *simulacrum* or 'ymage' placed on two 'pilierz' (*RR* 21,189, 21,199) and ushered in by yet another instance of idol worship with the retelling of the fable of Pygmalion from Ovid's *Metamorphoses* (Chapter 3.3). As I have argued more fully elsewhere, Jean here goes out of his way to highlight the artificial, fabricated nature of this scene along with the entire poem that builds up to this idolatrous climax. The narrator skilfully uses this scene specifically to highlight his own role as the craftsman responsible for conjuring up this scene, the 'deviser' of this idolatrous image ('cele ymage que *je* devise', *RR* 21,199)—echoing Guillaume de Lorris's similarly cunning self-presentation as an all-too-human fabricator behind the rhetorical mantle used to cover naked Nature in the poem (*RR* 65, see Chapter 3.3). Jean's citation of Guillaume de Lorris thus brings the poem full circle, concluding the lover's phantasmatic, delusional, and idolatrous quest for an allegorical 'Rose' that is merely an empty shell, an elusive mental-yet-material *simulacrum* generated by the dreamer/narrator/lover/pilgrim's own uncontrolled 'troubled vision' [vision desordonnée, *RR* 4352].

The generally negative characterization of visual perception in *PVH* as an assault upon the senses from the outside, while highly traditional, is therefore also

---

[142] Huot, *Dreams of Lovers*, p. 5.

[143] Mann, 'Jean de Meun and the Castration of Saturn', p. 326. See further Kay, 'Women's body of Knowledge'. On the wider issue of the gendering of the spirit-body problem, see Raskolnikov, *Body Against Soul*.

[144] Huot, 'Bodily Peril', 52.

238 MEDIEVAL ALLEGORY AS EPISTEMOLOGY

loaded with more topical resonances in the context of the poem's dialogue with the *Rose*. It is hardly a coincidence that the modality of visual assault on the senses in *PVH* should closely reproduce the process of falling in love as described by Guillaume de Lorris' dreamer-narrator, hit in the heart by the God of Love's arrow, which enters the human body through the eye:

tret a moi par tel devise	Loosed his arrow at me in such a way
que par mi l'ueil m'a ou cuer mise	and with such force that the point
sa saiete par grant roidor;	entered my eye and penetrated my
(*RR* 1691–3)	heart.

And indeed, when the pilgrim in *PVH* meets the seven deadly sins, it is Gloutonnie—somewhat confusingly—who adopts this strategy of attack, just as Grace Dieu had previously warned the Pilgrim (*PVH1* 4089–96, cited and discussed in Chapter 3.4):

Un dart avoit dont me feri	She had a dart, and struck me with it
Tout avant que parlasse a li.	before I could speak to her. It went in
Par l'eul entra, au cuer me vint.	through my eye and entered my heart.
(*PVH1* 10,263–5)	

Deguileville also appears to be remembering another passage in the *Rose*, where Raison represents erotic desire as the result of a harmful, entirely passive visual experience:

'Amors, se bien sui apensee,	'Love, if my judgement is correct, is a
c'est maladie de pensee	mental illness affecting two persons of
antre .II. persones annexe,	opposite sex in close proximity who are
franches entr'els, de divers sexe,	both free agents.'
venanz a genz par ardeur *nee*	
de vision desordenee.	
(*RR* 4347–52; my emphases)	

Thus, while Deguileville's monastic background and his penitential agenda undoubtedly help to explain his broad suspicion of sense perception more generally, his pointed ambivalence towards sight appears to be motivated by the *Rose*, and its association of 'vision desordonne' with erotic infatuation and the ensuing fall into carnal misreading.

This concern over the potentially 'idolatrous' status of the human imagination is considerably exacerbated in *PVH2*. As Michael Camille has observed, Deguileville's later trilogy as a whole (*c.* 1355–8) is particularly anxious about the status of *sculpted*, material 'ymages' as opposed to merely *painted* or imagined ones.[145] This points to the evolving nature of Deguileville's engagement with the *Rose*, a poem that can no longer simply be rewritten, but rather a poem that is itself actively engaged in shaping Deguileville's increasing anxieties about the corporeal entanglements of his own poetic art. Already in *PVH1* Deguileville suggests that he may have internalized the *Rose* in ways that go well beyond a detached, strictly rational engagement, assigning it a remarkable degree of independent agency:

Une vision veul nuncier	I want to recount to you a vision that
Qui en dormant m'avint l'autrier.	came to me the other night as I was
En veillant avoie lëu,	sleeping. While I was awake I had read,
Considere et bien vëu	studied, and looked closely at the
Le biau roumans de la Rose.	beautiful *Romance of the Rose*. I am
Bien croi que ce fu la chose	sure that this was what moved me most
Qui plus m'esmut a ce songier	to have the dream I will tell you about
Que ci apres vous vueil nuncier.	in a moment.
(*PVH1* 7–14)	

It is not only the sensual 'biaute' of the *Rose* that troubles any attempt to provide a definitive *exposé* on the earlier poem, but especially Deguileville's description of a specifically *visual* encounter ('vëu') with what has been defined as 'the most visually excessive of all medieval poems'.[146] The *Rose*'s ability to 'move' (*esmouvoir*) its devout reader lends the poem an additional degree of agency that is highly problematic, positioning Deguileville as the passive 'recipient' of the *Rose*—not unlike the Pilgrim, himself continuously assaulted by the overwhelming power (*virtus*) of the *species, ymago, ydolum, simulacrum* or *phantasma* mediated by sense perception and the imagination.[147] Deguileville's own exposure to the imagistic, sensual onslaught of the *Rose* thus threatens to reproduce the dynamics of 'vision desordonnée' and 'maladie de pensee' (*RR* 4352, 4348) experienced by Amant in the *Rose*. Even though all mention of the *Rose* has disappeared from the prologue to *PVH2*, the consequences of prolonged exposure persist, and the dream experience is still characterized in dangerously visual terms: 'Ung songe *vi* aventureus' (*PVH2* 21, my emphasis).

Given such ubiquitous suspicion of bodily sight and visual imagination, Deguileville's own allegory—an ostensibly salvific 'biau miroir de sauvement'[148]—occupies an increasingly unstable and uncertain place. Yet the *Rose* goes further still, and manages to undermine the visionary, salvific, and soteriological aspirations of Deguileville's allegorical mirror even before they are fully articulated. This

---

[145] Camille, 'Deguileville's Idolatry'. On a still more pervasive anxiety about images, visual and rhetorical, see Maupeu, 'Statut de l'image'.

[146] Camille, 'Deguileville's Idolatry', p. 152.

[147] For the recurrence of such terms, see above p. 198–9.

[148] See above, epigraph to Chapter 2.

240 MEDIEVAL ALLEGORY AS EPISTEMOLOGY

occurs during Nature's extended speech on the reflecting and refracting properties of mirrors (*RR* 18,004–484). The passage explicitly references the theories of
Perspectiva introduced by Alhazen (*RR* 18,004–6), as is apparent from the abundant use of the characteristic terminology of 'fantosmes', 'ymages' and 'ydoles' (*RR*
18,151; 18,224; 18,230), and Nature even provides some *verbatim* translations of
sections from Roger Bacon's work on perspectivist optics.[149] Throughout Nature's
discussion of mirrors, Jean also deliberately highlights how visual illusion becomes
interchangeable with linguistic equivocation and interpretive distortion. The very
first detail provided by Nature concerns the ability of mirrors to magnify *text*, in a
passage that closely paraphrases Bacon's *Opus maius*:[150]

'les forces des mirouers	'The principles and properties of
[. . .] tant ont merveilleus pouers	mirrors: they have such marvellous
que toutes choses tres petites,	powers that all tiny things, tiny letters
letres grelles tres loing escrites	far from the eyes and minute grains of
et poudres de sablon menues,	sand, are perceived so large.'
si granz, si grosses sunt veües.'	
(*RR* 18,015–20; my emphasis)	

As well as highlighting the broad analogy of visual representation and textual interpretation, Nature underlines the potential for distortion and deception in both
cases.[151] The idea is developed further in what appears to be another purely digressive interlude, recounting the adultery of Mars and Venus. If only they had been
equipped with a mirror with magnifying properties, Nature suggests, the lovers
would have been able to see the minute strings ('laz soutilz', *RR* 18,038) strung
across the bedroom by the crafty Vulcan, and this would have given them the
opportunity to escape, or at least prepare a crafty alibi. Venus could have claimed,
for instance, that Vulcan's sight was momentarily troubled as he surprised the
lovers in their bedroom:

'tout l'eüst il neïs veüe,	'Even if he had actually seen it, she
deïst ele que la veüe	would have told him that his sight was
li fust occurcie et troublee,	dim and disturbed; she would have
tant eüst la langue doublee	twisted her tongue into many different
en diverses plications	contortions in order to find excuses.'
a trover excusacions,'	
(*RR* 18,091–6)[152]	

---

[149] *Seeing through the Veil*, pp. 78–113; Nichols, '"The Pupil of your Eye": Vision, Language and Poetry in Thirteenth-Century Paris', in *Rethinking the Senses*, pp. 287–307.

[150] *Opus maius* V.3.3.3, in Lindberg, *Bacon and the Origin of Perspectiva*, pp. 332–5, as identified by Akbari, *Seeing through the Veil*, pp. 92–3.

[151] See further Pomel, 'Visual Experiences and Allegorical Fiction'.

[152] See extended discussion of the passage in Pomel, 'L'art du faux-semblant chez Jean de Meun'.

COGNITION: THEORY AND PRACTICE   241

The advice may sound impractical and baffling—typically for Nature's comically academic lack of pragmatism—but again it closely associates altered vision and the deceptive verbal arts of rhetoric: both are fundamentally analogous means of deception—a nexus of ideas redeployed also by Chaucer in the 'Merchant's Tale' (IV.2368–410), a text saturated with complex intertextual echoes of Jean's *Rose*.[153]

The full epistemological implications of Nature's discussion of optics and vision, and their impact on Deguileville, become apparent as Nature seamlessly moves on from mirrors to talk about the unreliable truth value of dreams (*RR* 18,257–484). As is often noted, the passage's mention of Scipio (*RR* 18,337) echoes and retrospectively undermines Guillaume de Lorris' opening evocation of Macrobius, ostensibly introduced to support the prophetic value of dreams (*RR* 1–20). Yet the discussion as a whole looks forwards as well as backwards in time, and provides a prime example of what David Hult describes as the *Rose*'s ability to 'anticipate in an uncanny fashion [...] any response we are likely to make [...] by including that response within the text'.[154] In this case the *Rose* manages to dismantle Deguileville's own spiritual vision before it even occurs. According to Nature, some dreamers are so profoundly convinced of the truthfulness of their mental imaginings that they set out on pilgrimage, scrip and staff in hand:

'maint an sunt si deceü
que de leur liz s'en sunt meü,
et se chaucent neïs et vestent
et de tout leur hernois s'aprestent
[...]
prannent bourdons, prannent escharpes,
[...]
et vont cheminant longues voies,
et ne sevent ou toutevoies.'
    (*RR* 18,275–84)

'many are so deceived by this (i.e. visions), that they have risen from their beds, put their shoes on, got dressed, and put on their whole armour; they pick up their scrip and staff and wander far and wide, without however knowing where they are going.'
[translation mine]

The primary object of this deconstruction is of course the *Rose* itself, and specifically the opening of the dream as recounted by Guillaume de Lorris', unmistakeably paraphrased at *RR* 18,358–72.[155] Yet the passage also has the effect of destabilizing the truth-claims of *all* allegorical dream narratives—past, present

---

[153] See further e.g. Peter Brown, 'An Optical Theme in the Merchant's Tale' *Studies in the Age of Chaucer* 1984.1 (1984), 231–43.

[154] Hult, 'Language and Dismemberment', p. 106. Sarah Kay similarly speaks of the *Rose*'s ability to function as 'a parody of texts that in fact come after it'. Kay, *Place of Thought*, p. 18. See further above, Introduction, p. 46–7, Chapter 2.5, pp. 173–4.

[155] Jean thus creates a further liar's paradox, by situating Nature's own dismissal of the truthfulness of dreams within what is precisely such a delirious dream, experienced by Amant/the narrator/Guillaume de Lorris/Jean de Meun. See further Morton and Nievergelt, pp. 10–13.

242   MEDIEVAL ALLEGORY AS EPISTEMOLOGY

and future.[156] The parallels with Deguileville's future dream vision are particularly uncanny, since Nature specifically identifies contemplative excess as one of the reasons behind such self-deluding visions:

'Ou qui, par grant devocion,
en trop grant contemplacion,
font apparair en leur pansees
les choses qu'il ont porpansees,
et les cuident tout proprement
voair defors apertement
et ce n'est for trufle et mançonge.'
  (*RR* 18,327–33)

'Or those who, through great devotion and excessive contemplation, generate in their thoughts the things they have pondered upon, and think that they can properly, openly see them on the outside, yet it is nothing but trifles and lies.'
[translation mine]

Deguileville, who presents his dream as a distinctively contemplative vision experienced within a monastic setting (*PVH1* 31–44), could hardly avoid recognizing himself in such a portrait upon rereading the *Rose*. He appears to have internalized such reflections on the epistemologically dubious value of spiritual, mental, and visual images as well as rhetorical artifice of all kinds only too well, finding himself forced to question the self-authorizing strategy of his own allegorical poetics at the very moment when he also produced a second, amended, heavily glossed and deeply anxious *Pèlerinage*.

It is worth ending this chapter by reconsidering the didactic and salvific aspirations of Deguileville's poem in the light of the many internal tensions, conflicts, and contractions I have discussed in what precedes. In particular, I would like to offer some considerations on the imaginative 'efficacy' of the poem as a whole by considering the problematic status of the Seven Deadly Sins. The sins encapsulate the impossibility of Deguileville's allegory to perform its didactic work successfully without also exposing its readers to the physical attacks of the sins themselves— and thus pushing them, paradoxically, to give in to the lures of Huiseuse. Within the abstractive, hylomorphic, and experiential perspective that slowly emerges as the dominant model for the pilgrim's adventures, the bodies of the seven deadly sins are no longer inert, but intensely 'real', materially and spiritually tangible psychic potentialities that act upon the Pilgrim, and whose vivid allegorical portraits—invariably illustrated in the manuscripts—similarly act upon the mind of the reader. The sins need to be experienced in order to be known, and their metaphorical bodies need to be allowed to 'do work' on the body of the reader, assimilated to the first-person *viator*. Their operation as images is ultimately analogous to the operation of the sensible *species*, acting upon the recipient through its inherent *virtus*. The bodies of the sins themselves become much more than programmatic 'personified abstractions', and act as concrete, plastic, embodied manifestations of self-abasement, deformation, and self-alienation. This provides

---

[156] Kay, 'Women's Body of Knowledge', p. 231.

COGNITION: THEORY AND PRACTICE   243

a troubling illustration of Aristotle's conformality thesis, according to which knowledge consists in the soul's acquisition of the 'form' or likeness of the thing known. As Philippe Maupeu suggests, 'displaying the vice—if only to condemn it—already amounts to a contamination.'[157] The reader's visual/aural/mental experience of the sins is therefore analogous to the pilgrim's own corporeal exposure to their physical attacks, particularly in the abundantly illustrated manuscripts of *PVH*—a poem that is every bit as 'visually excessive' as the *Rose* before it.[158]

Deguileville's poem finally falls short of, yet also *exceeds* its projected didactic aims. The enhanced agency of the sins confirms—against the author's declared intentions—the primacy of embodied, experiential cognition. Modern theories of metaphor and cognition can help to flesh out what is already implicit in the Aristotelian anthropological model, insisting on the ability of mental visualization and metaphorical thinking to produce opportunities for fully embodied simulation.[159] Allegorical narrative as a whole, and more particularly the corporeally excessive personification of the sins, can be seen as providing just such opportunities for embodied simulation, where metaphors, allegories, or personifications become vehicles for an individual subject's cognitive experience. This highlights also why Deguileville's thought experiments of the Flying Man and the 'eyes-in-ears' backfire so consistently, visualizing the inevitable implication of the body in *all* its cognitive processes. Both thought experiments appear ultimately self-defeating, and far from confirming the theory they are intended to support suggest that any kind of imaginative act must needs function as embodied simulation. This can also contribute important elements to the ongoing debate about the historical evolution, epistemic function, and ontological status of 'thought experiments'—a problematic and unstable category, as twentieth- and twenty-first-century philosophers have invariably pointed out.[160]

---

[157] 'montrer le vice, fût-ce pour le condamner, c'est déjà en être contaminé', Maupeu, 'Le corps des vices'.

[158] On the illustrations in Deguileville MSS, see Michael Camille, 'The Illustrated Manuscripts of Guillaume Deguileville's *Pèlerinages*, 1330–1426' (PhD thesis, Cambridge University, 1985); on the *Rose* as a visually excessive poem, see again Camille, 'Deguileville's Idolatry', p. 152.

[159] See in particular work by Raymond W. Gibbs, Jr, 'Metaphor Interpretation as Embodied Simulation', *Mind & Language* 21.3 (2006), 434–58; ibid., *Embodiment and Cognitive Science*; Raymond W. Gibbs, Jr. and Teenie Matlock, 'Metaphor, Imagination and Simulation: Psycholinguistic Evidence', in Gibbs, *The Cambridge Handbook of Metaphor and Thought*, pp. 161–76.

[160] For contemporary arguments in favour of the 'embodied' workings of thought experiments, see David C. Gooding, 'What is Experimental about Thought Experiments?', *Proceedings of the Biennial Meeting of the Philosophy of Science Association* (1992), 280–90. For an argument against, see John Zeimbekis, 'Thought Experiments and Mental Simulations', in Ierodiakonou and Roux, *Thought Experiments in Methodological and Historical Contexts*, pp. 193–215. More broadly on the clash between broadly 'Platonic' vs. 'empiricist' understandings of thought experiments—associated respectively with the work of James R. Brown and John D. Norton—see Roux, 'The Emergence of the Notion of Thought Experiment', in Ierodiakonou and Roux, *Thought Experiments in Methodological and Historical Contexts*, pp. 2–3 ff. On medieval thought experiments more specifically, see Knox, Morton, and Reeve, eds, *Medieval Thought Experiments*, and further discussion above 'Introduction', pp. 41–2.

244 MEDIEVAL ALLEGORY AS EPISTEMOLOGY

Despite the author's determination to uphold the agency and immateriality of the rational soul as an independent cognitive agent, then, *PVH* ultimately appears to demonstrate the contrary. As I will argue in my next chapter, Deguileville is demonstrably aware of this tension, and indeed goes some way towards acknowledging, even embracing the inevitably embodied nature of all knowledge. This is particularly apparent in his later work—*PVH2*, the '*Pèlerinages*-trilogy', and his Latin poetry—but is already latent in the concluding section of *PVH1*. Towards the end of the poem Deguileville gradually abandons the pursuit of a hermeneutics of depersonalized transcendence and begins to articulate a different, experiential hermeneutics of individual subjectivity. This reorientation simultaneously entails a shift in the poem's referential and didactic focus: the fictional 'I' no longer defines a paradigmatic space that can be inhabited by the poem's many readers, but crystallizes the lived, autobiographical experience of the poem's own author—the Cistercian monk Guillermus de Deguilevilla.

The pilgrim's encounter with Vieilece is emblematic for this shift. After entering the Abbey of Chaalis and spending the rest of his life within the monastic enclosure, the 'I' is eventually visited by Enfermete and Vieillece, who advocate the virtues of experiential knowledge:

'Vieilece ai non la redoutee, | 'My name is Old Age, the feared, the
La piaucelue la ridee, | pale, the one with wrinkles and a white
Celle qui ai le chief chanu | one—and very often a bald one—the
Et bien souvent de cheveus nu, | one people should honour greatly and
Celle a cui conseil demander | look to for counsel, for I have seen the
On doit et grant honneur porter, | past and have experienced much that is
Quar j'ai vu le temps passe | good and evil. put to the test. These are
Et *maint bien et mal esprouve.* | the glosses of common sense, and the
Ce sont de bon sens les gloses | means to know things. People will
Et ce par quoi on set les choses. | never be wise if they haven't seen things
Ja ne sera nul sciente, | and tested them.'
s'il n'a vëu et esprouve.' | [translation mine]
  (*PVH1* 13,201–12; my emphases) |

Strikingly, it is neither Sapience, nor Raison, nor Grace Dieu who are the depositaries of knowledge in the concluding section of the journey, but Enfermete and Vieillece. And the knowledge they provide access to is emphatically definitive and certain:

'Avoir ne pues messagier qui | 'You could have no more truthful
En puist parler plus vraiement. | messenger. My companion [i.e.
Ma compaigne aucune fois ment | Infirmity] lies at times . . . but nothing
[. . .] mes empeschier | can prevent me from speaking the
Rien ne me puet de vrai noncier.' | truth.'
  (*PVH1* 13,194–200) | [translation emended]

Even more strikingly—after 13,000 lines of text that attempt to provide a valid didactic 'glose' on the *Rose*—such knowledge is emphatically *not* mediated by textuality, but by *experience*: 'ce sont de bon sens les gloses / Et ce par quoi on set les choses' (*PVH1* 13,209–10)—an unmistakeable echo of Jean de Meun's own denial of textual authority and commitment to experiential knowledge, where 'contreres choses, / les unes sunt des autres gloses' (*RR* 21,532–44; see Chapter 1.5). Emphasis has once more been moved away from slippery textual 'glose' to experiential 'choses'—from verbal *signa* to *res*. The key to such 'choses', however, is no longer to be found in the eternal and transcendental *res* of Augustine's scriptural hermeneutics, but the *res* of an experiential phenomenology of the subject in time.

Deguileville's progressive move from textually mediated didacticism to experiential knowledge mirrors the evolution the poem itself over time, from a universalizing and paradigmatic *itinerarium* in *PVH1* to a highly personal, particularizing autobiography in *PVH2*.[161] *PVH* and the tradition it inspires finally contribute to crystallizing individual subjectivity rather than providing a positive, normative and viable roadmap to repatriate an exiled and wandering *viator*.[162] In many ways, then, *PVH1* must be considered as a failed attempt to lift the individual subject above the maze of signs, bodies, and forms that make up Augustine's *regio dissimilitudinis*. As I argue in my next chapter, however, the experience of failure itself can be turned into a major turning point on the spiritual trajectory of a pilgrim who is no longer an exemplary *viator*, but a flawed Everyman, an individual and bounded subject whose cognitive abilities are pathetically yet inevitably limited. The mirror of allegory can still serve as an instrument of self-knowledge, but the 'I' refracted by the *PVH* is thereby also distorted and transformed into a rather different subject from the disembodied *imago dei* that Deguileville sets out to recover. As well as exemplifying the failure of allegory, *PVH* calls out to be read as an allegory of failure—a failure that is spiritually productive and ultimately *necessary*, enabling a genuine 'conversion' of the self according to the Augustinian model of the *Confessions*.

---

[161] See especially Maupeu, *Pèlerins de vie humaine*, pp. 173–266.
[162] Maupeu, *Pèlerins de vie humaine*; Nievergelt, *Allegorical Quests*.

4

Experience

'By experience', says Roger Ascham, 'we find out a short way by a long wandering.' Not seldom that long wandering unfits us for further travel, and of what use is our experience to us then?

Thomas Hardy, *Tess of the D'Urbervilles*, Ch. 15

The episode of the weeping Rock of Penitence (11,245–372), frequently depicted in manuscripts,[1] marks a major turning point in the trajectory of Deguileville's pilgrim. I want to argue that it also signals a very serious crisis of the poem's cognitive aspirations, and a major reorientation of its overarching design, away from its earlier focus on cognition, interpretation, and the acquisition of scientific knowledge towards inner, silent contemplation (Chapter 4.1). In parallel, the poem also returns to its concern with language, but now envisages a radically transformed language—interior, silent, and mysterious (Chapter 4.2). This reorientation also announces a change of direction in Deguileville's poetic *oeuvre* as a whole, introducing a new poetics that will find its fullest expression in his late, Latin poetry (Chapter 4.3). In parallel, I also emphasize the growing intensity of Deguileville's longing for a perfect semiotics that eschews the slippages of allegorical interpretation altogether, notably in the *Dit de la fleur de lis*, completed in 1338 (Chapter 4.4). Deguileville's entire poetic corpus, I suggest, is thus characterized by a persistent but increasingly anxious, obsessive, and finally counterproductive desire to control the vagaries of allegorical interpretation, culminating in the desperate attempts to exorcize misreading and misrepresentation of all kinds in the revised *Pèlerinage de Vie Humaine* (PVH2, *c.* 1355) (Chapter 4.5).

Despite this waning confidence in the ability of allegorical poetry to perform its salvific work, however, Deguileville nonetheless continues to produce poetry in the allegorical pilgrimage register, even after *PVH2*. *PVH2* was already a much expanded, more learned, more troubled and defensive rewriting of his original poem, but this was soon to be followed by two further pilgrimage allegories, the *Pèlerinage de l'Âme* (PA, *c.* 1356) and the *Pèlerinage de Jhesucrist* (PJC, *c.* 1358).

---

[1] Illuminations in the manuscripts are listed and discussed by Julia Drobinsky, 'La roche qui pleure et le cuvier aux larmes: les images de la pénitence', in Duval and Pomel, pp. 81–110 (96–110).

Medieval Allegory as Epistemology. Marco Nievergelt, Oxford University Press.
© Marco Nievergelt (2023). DOI: 10.1093/oso/9780192849212.003.0005

Contrary to the prevailing opinion that sees these three poems as constituting a clearly unified and carefully structured poetic project, I want to argue that the so-called 'trilogy'—and Deguileville's poetic *oeuvre* as a whole—must be seen as a far more conflicted and heterogeneous conglomerate. I will therefore offer a substantial reconsideration of the trajectory and evolution of Deguileville's poetic career as a whole, arguing that his entire *oeuvre* is structured by the dialectic between two radically divergent and largely incompatible poetics: on the one hand we find an allegorical and didactic poetics that aims to instruct, reform, and foster the agency of the pilgrim-reader's depersonalized 'I'; on the other hand we find a contemplative, devotional, and introspective poetics focused on a largely passive and expectant individual subject that is increasingly reducible to the poet's own private self (Chapters 4.3, 4.4, and 4.5).

1. Conversion I: The ABC of Grace and Will

The Pilgrim reaches the Rock of Penitence (*PVH1* 11,239 ff.) after his prolonged struggle against the Seven Deadly Sins in the middle section of the poem (*PVH1* 7033–11,406). Arriving at the Rock, the pilgrim finally realizes the need for subjecting himself to the hardships of penance, resulting in a feeling of contrition that triggers the process of conversion.[2] This is not the first time that the poem introduces the theme: Penitance had made an initial appearance as a personification—a lady carrying a mallet, a whip and broom (*PVH1* 2023 ff.)—and later materialized in the form of the Hedge of Penitence, separating the two ways of Huiseuse and Occupant/Labeur (6503–7056). Yet during these early episodes, the importance of penitence appears abstract and theoretical. In the first case Penitance is merely preaching to an assembled congregation, and she herself stresses how her exposition is a 'lecon' and a 'sermon' (*PVH1* 2123; 2347). Despite its precise, vivid descriptions of the penitential process, this remains a theoretical account: the 'I' of the penitent sinner—'I repent what I have done wrong' [Las, que j'ai fourfait, *PVH1* 2066–7; cf. also 2310–14]—was merely a ventriloquized exemplary and programmatic voice, not the voice of the actual pilgrim, who remains a passive listener at this early stage. During the second episode, the pilgrim repeatedly toys with the idea of crossing through the Hedge of Penitence (6721–4, 6993–7022; 7036), but soon gives up and continues on the path of Huiseuse, thus again postponing any penitential action.[3]

---

[2] For an early discussion of the traditional assimilation of contrition and conversion, see Tertullian, *On Penitence*, 2.4, in *Treatises on Penance: On Penitence and On Purity*, trans. William P. Le Saint (Westminster: Newman Press, 1959), pp. 15–16, 20–1.

[3] See also Kay, *Place of Thought*, pp. 81–5.

248 MEDIEVAL ALLEGORY AS EPISTEMOLOGY

The Rock of Penitence thus replays and finally activates possibilities already glimpsed during earlier stages of the narrative.[4] Fittingly the episode is introduced by the pilgrim's lamentation and regret over missed opportunities:

'He Penitance, Penitance!
Pour quoi fis onques redoutance
De passer ta heïë espineuse?'
  (*PVH1* 10,715–17)

'Ah, Penance, Penance! Why was I ever afraid to pass through your thorny hedge?'

The pilgrim's penitential experience is preceded by his loss of the staff of Hope at the hands of the Seven Sins, which marks the lowest point in his trajectory. The pilgrim's crisis culminates with the fear of a permanent loss of Grace Dieu (*PVH1* 10,713–15). This moment marks the deepest spiritual crisis for the pilgrim, an awakening to his individual moral responsibility and to the need for repentance and amendment—but, crucially, the scene also marks a crisis of cognition. Indeed, the very possibility of a penitential awakening is postulated on the experience of a cognitive failure or *aporia*. It is such cognitive impasse that causes the transformation of the pilgrim's self-image, enabling a genuine 'conversion' of the subject, as explained by Grace Dieu:

'Or entent un pou', dist elle,
'Et tourne devers moi t'orelle!
Celle roche que tu vois la
Est le cuer de celi qui a
A escient aussi com tu
Laissie la voie de salu,
Qui com roche s'est endurci
En son erreur et racorni.
Or te di que, quant l'ai laissie
Ainsi grant piece en son pechie,
Acune foiz pitie de lui
Me prent et son eul devers li
Li fais convertir et tourner
Pour soi, quel s'est fait, regarder;
Et lors quant l'ueil a bien vëu
La durte du cuer, esmëu
Tantost est a forment plourer
Et lermoier et degouter.'
  (*PVH1* 11,253–70)

'Now listen a moment', she said, 'and lend me your ear. The rock you see there is the heart of someone who knowingly left the way of salvation, as you have. It is hardened like a rock and callous in its errors. Now I tell you, when I have let it stay in sin for a long time, I have pity on it at some point, and I make its eye turn around and look inward to see itself as it really is. And when the eye has seen clearly how hard the heart is, it is soon moved to weep bitterly, to shed teardrops.

The emphasis of Grace Dieu's explanation is specifically on the role of the eye, and in the wake of the earlier considerations about physical and intellectual vision in

---

[4] See also Drobinsky, 'La roche qui pleure', pp. 82, 86 and *passim*.

EXPERIENCE   249

the poem, the passage brings to a head a number of related crises that have been building up throughout the narrative up to here. The Bath of Penitence is not only a rewriting of the *Rose*'s fountain-mirror of Narcissus, replacing self-infatuation with the self-knowledge to be gained by a penitential experience;[5] the scene also interrogates and finally dismantles the semantic field of vision altogether—both literal and metaphorical. The eye here no longer apprehends any external, let alone transcendental reality, but merely perceives the seeing subject in his own impotence to see beyond itself, determined by its own sinful state (*PVH1* 11,263–6).[6] The emblem aptly captures a deep epistemological crisis in the poem, which is also the crisis of allegory's belief in its own potential to 'show' or convey the truth *apertement*, to illuminate human *entendement* with direct intellectual vision. This crisis reorganizes the prerogatives of Deguileville's poem in radical fashion, yet paradoxically this loss of confidence in allegory as well as in the capabilities of the human *viator* is spiritually beneficial: it marks a narrative and epistemic *retournement*, a 'turning around' that signals a spiritual 'conversion'[7]—in the etymological, Augustinian sense elaborated here by Grace Dieu. The eye is turned back onto the self, converted to apprehend its own inability to look beyond itself—and suddenly the eye is no longer instrument of vision and discernment, but a spring of penitential tears.

The 'gift of tears' is of course a traditional motif with a long and lively history,[8] yet its particularly powerful resonance at this point in the poem is a function of the narrative build-up that precedes it and of the context in which it occurs. As the culmination or indeed anti-climax of the rationalistic and scientific desire that drives so much of the pilgrimage up to this point, the Rock of Penitence turns the poem itself on its head, away from the desire to see and know, with the eye and the mind, towards the realization of the impossibility of true knowledge for man in the world. The passage thus takes the previous troping of the senses to new extremes (see Chapter 3.4) and appropriately Grace here exhorts the Pilgrim to '*turn* your ear towards me' [*tourne* devers moi t'orelle, *PVH1* 11,254, my emphasis), 'tuning' his ear to hear the voice of Grace, while asking him to 'turn and convert' the eye back onto himself (11,264–5). This produces a troping of the senses that reaches beyond sense perception, beyond synaesthesia and ultimately beyond cognition—'turning', bending, and twisting the senses to a breaking point, where

---

[5] Huot, *The Romance of the Rose and its Medieval Readers*, pp. 213–14.

[6] For similar ideas in Augustine, see Colish, *Mirror of Language*, p. 37.

[7] In its biblical sense of ἐπιστρέφω (epistrephō), conversion signifies precisely a 'turning around'. See Richard V. Peace, *Conversion in the New Testament: Paul and the Twelve* (Grand Rapids: Eerdmans, 1999), pp. 346–9.

[8] The literature is considerable, see e.g. Piroska Nagy, *Le don des larmes au Moyen Age: Un instrument spirituel en quête d'institution (Ve–XIIIe siècle)* (Paris: Albin Michel, 2000). On later, vernacular examples, see especially Geneviève Hasenohr, '*Lacrimae pondera vocis habent*: Typologie des larmes dans la littérature de spiritualité française des XIIIe–XVe siècles', *Le moyen français* 37 (1997), 45–63. On the traditions, analogues and possible sources relevant to Deguileville, see also Drobinsky, 'La roche qui pleure'.

previously defined notions of knowledge also break down. Whereas the quest had begun by gesturing towards an ideal of perfect self-knowledge—understood as the unencumbered, perfect reflection of the *imago dei* in the disembodied, separate substance of the human soul—the poem now produces a very different form of self-knowledge, that of a self that is resolutely limited, fallen, blind, weeping, and embodied.

This transition retraces the tension between two radically contrasting soteriological models—a tension that according to Piroska Nagy determines the very emergence and evolution of the motif of the 'gift of tears' throughout the medieval period. The pilgrim here experiences a transition from rationalistic to affective modes of conceiving penitence, and begins to align himself with a venerable mystical and monastic tradition running through Benedict, Gregory the Great, and Bernard: for this tradition it is primarily the agency of grace itself that initiates the penitential process, not the will or understanding of the individual penitent.[9] In the poem too the self is not so much actively known as passively *experienced*,[10] since it is finally unable to actualize or even envisage its original divine resemblance as theorized by Raison earlier: the poem's 'I' realizes that he is not in fact 'self-sufficient'. The grace-induced tears thus mark the subject's bodily experience of his own intellectual limitations in his present, fallen, embodied state. Such an experience of cognitive failure is, however, inherently salvific in predisposing the flawed, helpless subject to receive the continued operation of God's grace. In proper Augustinian fashion, the experience of one's own fallen self brings with it the obverse experience of the immensity of God's mercy and grace.[11]

This reorientation has very serious implications, firstly for the poem itself as a didactic undertaking, and secondly for the poem's underlying anthropology and epistemology, specifically the respective roles of the intellect and the will in determining the course of individual action and moral choice. I shall address both issues in turn in the remainder of this section. First, then, the fundamental didactic aspirations of the poem are compromised, since these are postulated on the idea that the pilgrimage figures a process through which the *viator*'s self is equipped with enhanced agency and understanding. The poem that had started out by promising to equip its pilgrim-readers with the tools of discernment, understanding, and interpretation necessary to complete the journey, finally spirals down to this single, humbling penitential experience. To some extent this experience of the self through failure implies a rejection of the poem's earlier cognitive aspirations, and even entails a degree of anti-intellectualism. Such anti-intellectualism is written into a fictional, intra-diegetic document that triggers the pilgrim's conversion, the

---

[9] See Nagy, *Le don des larmes*, p. 35 and *passim*. For the relevance of this tradition to Deguileville, see also Drobinsky, 'La roche qui pleure', pp. 93–4.

[10] Nagy, 'Individualité et larmes monastiques'.

[11] See also Zeeman, *Discourse of Desire*, pp. 41–4, who assembles a rich cluster of Augustine's statements on the issue.

EXPERIENCE   251

famous ABC-Prayer also translated by Chaucer.[12] The prayer's first-person speaking voice is still programmatic and universal, but provides a script for the prayer to be addressed by the pilgrim to the Virgin, initiating the penitential performance that culminates at the Rock of Penitence. The rejection of Aristotle's *Ethics* here functions as a metonymy for the renunciation of theoretical and scientific knowledge altogether, specifically moral didacticism:[13]

Ethiques s'avoie lëu,	If I had read the *Ethics*, learned and
Tout recorde et tout scëu	understood all of it, but had put
Et apres rien ne n'ouvrasse,	nothing into practice, then I would be
Du tout seroie decëu	sorely deceived.
(*PVH1* 11,169–72)	[my translation]

The reading of didactic materials is thus itself 'deceptive', in danger of becoming a useless, intellectualized surrogate for the virtuous penitential behaviour or disposition it is intended to promote. While this admission again underscores the pilgrim's inability to turn theory into practice, by implication this also devalues Deguileville's own poem, similarly committed to fostering ethical behaviour in the Christian Everyman through an experience of performative reading and a hermeneutics of the self. The rejection of 'Ethiques' may also carry a more precise meaning in the present context, as a direct disavowal of the scientific and cognitive aspirations of *PVH*. 'Ethics' was often understood to designate precisely the kind of faculty psychology that makes up such large portions of Deguileville's allegory, discussed in the previous chapter. Robert Grosseteste, for one—the author of the most influential standard Latin translation of the *Ethics*—states in his commentary on the *Posterior Analytics* that the task of ethics is precisely the study the cognitive mechanics of the soul that do not rely on logical demonstration. This effectively amounts to subsuming philosophy of mind within ethics, and indeed this is how Grosseteste classifies Aristotle's own *De anima*.[14]

The ABC Prayer also underscores the impossibility of obtaining the kind of knowledge that had been promised to the pilgrim by Grace Dieu earlier in the poem: the 'I' is no longer exhorted to open 'the eyes of your understanding [les

---

[12] See Georgia R. Crampton, 'Chaucer's Singular Prayer', *Medium Ævum* 59.2 (1990), 191–213; Helen Phillips, 'Chaucer and Deguileville: The "ABC" in Context', *Medium Ævum* 62.1 (1993), 1–19; John Thompson, 'Chaucer's "An ABC" in and out of Context', *Poetica* (Tokyo)37 (1993), 38–48; William A. Quinn, 'Chaucer's Problematic Priere: "An ABC" as Artifact and Critical Issue', *Studies in the Age of Chaucer* 23.1 (2001), 109–41.

[13] The stanza is part of the poem's concluding Tyronian & and 9 ('con') section, and suggests the reiterative nature of the prayer. It has no equivalent in Chaucer's translation, which eliminates the final stanzas.

[14] Grosseteste, *Commentarius in posteriorem analyticorum libros*, ed. Rossi, I.19, ll. 178–180: 'De aliis vero viribus anime que non ordinate sunt ad opus demonstrationis non est huius loci pertractare, sed quasdam de aliis pertractat physica in libro de Anima, quasdam vero Ethica.' Discussed in Risto Saarinen, 'Weakness of Will: The Plurality of Medieval Explanations', in Henrik Lagerlund and Mikko Yrjönsuuri, *Emotions and Free Choice from Boethius to Descartes* (Dordrecht: Springer, 2002), pp. 85–97 (90–91).

252   MEDIEVAL ALLEGORY AS EPISTEMOLOGY

yex de vostre entendement, *PVH1* 1704], but to appeal to the Virgin, who alone can become 'light for the blind' [lumiere des non voians, *PVH1* 11,049], as if to insist again on man's intellectual blindness without the intercessory agency of the mother of God. Not only are these two injunctions mutually contradictory, but they are supplied by the same character, Grace Dieu—the central figure of authority in the entire allegory. The appeal to the Virgin thus destabilizes Deguileville's very idea of the pilgrimage as a figure for a pedagogical and hermeneutic programme. And indeed the learning programme and theoretical instruction transmitted to the pilgrim in the initial portion of the poem has remained utterly fruitless. His pilgrimage has remained purely tentative and erratic: the pilgrim has not even advanced to the stage of *homo viator*, and remains a *homo erro*[15] who is still 'lost' [desvoie, *PVH1* 10,992], has gone 'astray' [fourvoie, *PVH1* 10,751], and has 'wandered along the crooked path' [erre par la voie torte, *PVH1* 10,910, all translations mine). What has occurred is not at all the anticipated pilgrimage, but a descent to perdition, a miserable failure to realize the moral and cognitive agency of the soul glimpsed during the earlier cognitive ecstasy. This suggests not only that the pilgrim may have failed to put Raison's teachings into practice, but that Raison's whole anthropology may not be viable. This in turn raises doubts about the didactic and salvific efficacy of the poem as a whole, presented as an exhortatory *predicatio*, ostensibly endowed with positive soteriological efficacy for the reader. The Prayer's 'I'—a pronoun that rhetorically subsumes the identities of the fictional pilgrim/protagonist, of the reader, and of the author/narrator, and is scripted by Grace herself—finally loses confidence in the possibility of continuing the pilgrimage. What the 'I' longs for is no longer forward movement, postulated on the belief in the possibility of active, dynamic agency of the subject, but the desire for 'rest and refuge for all sinners' [repos des recreans, *PVH1* 11,050, my translation].

The imagery used in the ABC Prayer underscores this loss of confidence in the possibility of continuing the journey on the terms established earlier in the poem,[16] and signals a desire for stasis as opposed to movement. What the scripted 'I'-voice wishes for is not to return to the breach, but to flee: 'fleeing to your tent I come' [fuiant m'en vieng a ta tente, *PVH1* 10,953], invoking the Virgin as 'refuge of the world' [du monde le refui, *PVH1* 10,893] in the Prayer's very first line. This is not a pilgrimage, but a retreat into a fortress where it is no longer necessary to be clad in

---

[15] Kuntz, 'From *Homo Erro* to *Homo Viator*'.

[16] On the role of the ABC prayer, and of prayer more widely in Deguileville's corpus, see Denis Hüe, 'L'apprentissage de la louange: pour une typologie de la prière dans les *Pèlerinages* de Guillaume de Deguileville', in Duval and Pomel, pp. 159–84. Hüe argues that 'la suite des *Pèlerinages* constitue en soi une sorte de cheminement de maturation de prière' (p. 161), whereas I see the ABC prayer as being essentially disruptive, as an abrupt change of direction in *PVH1* rather than its logical culmination. Hüe's own observation that the irruption of prayer in the pilgrim's universe is 'tardive, mais [. . .] fondatrice' (p. 167) begs the question of the internal unity and consistency of Deguileville's three *Pèlerinages*. See further discussion in Chapter 4.3.

EXPERIENCE   253

a cumbersome Pauline armour to struggle against worldly temptation: here 'I need not arm myself with weapons' [d'armes ne me faut point ferrer, *PVH1* 11,068], and accordingly the prayer reiterates the desire for such protective enclosure, variously figured as a tent (*PVH1* 10,953), temple (*PVH1* 11,109), and castle (*PVH1* 11,122). The implications of this *claustrophilia* are all the more powerful given that the words uttered by the desperate pilgrim are in reality scripted by Grace Dieu herself, as part of a document that teaches the pilgrim 'how you must pray to the Virgin' [comment prier tu la dois, *PVH1* 10,873). Rather than fostering the pilgrim's belief in his own moral and intellectual capabilities as she had done earlier in the poem, Grace now invites the pilgrim to renounce all active struggle in the world.

After uttering the ABC Prayer the pilgrim regains his Staff of Hope (*PVH1* 11,196)—the emblem of the dynamism of the pilgrimage itself (see Chapters 2.3 and 2.4)—but his journey now develops a set of rather different prerogatives. After securing Grace's assistance once more, the pilgrim now advances to take his Bath of Penitence, a 'second baptism' [baptesme secondaire, *PVH1* 11,281], which underscores the episode's role in marking a new beginning, the birth of a new form of self-understanding for the pilgrim. But the effects of this new baptismal and penitential conversion are short-lived, as the pilgrim decides to step out of his bath prematurely (*PVH1* 11,337), rejecting Grace's exhortation to embrace hardships of a penitential lifestyle (*PVH1* 11,343–72). Mocked as a 'bon chevalier' for his lack of moral prowess and penitential zeal (*PVH1* 11,363), the pilgrim is eventually abandoned by Grace, and pensively wanders along the shore of the Mer du Monde (Sea of the World). There he once more realizes that he lacks the strength and discernment to continue his journey alone:

Or voi je bien qu'avant aler
Ne puis, il me faut retourner
Ou demourer il me faut ci
En attendant vostre merci.
Së ens me met, je suis noie;
    [...]
Ne sai, sire Diex, que j'en face,
Se avis n'ai par vostre grace.
    (*PVH1* 11,445–54)

Now I see I cannot go forward. I must either turn back or stay here, waiting for your mercy. If I go into it, I will drown ... Lord God, I do not know what I will do if I do not have counsel, by your grace.

After his encounters with Satan (*PVH1* 11,464–502) and Heresy (*PVH1* 11, 503–75), Grace Dieu reappears once more and provides an exposition of the Mer du Monde, representing the active life. Here she identifies two main groups of swimmers: the blind, caught in outward illusions and swimming aimlessly (*PVH1* 11,665–684; cf. also 11,615–24), and the proficient swimmers, *in* this world but not *of* this world, since their desire inclines them forward to 'spiritual life' [espiritel vie, *PVH1* 11,633]:

254   MEDIEVAL ALLEGORY AS EPISTEMOLOGY

Quar seulement en la mer sont
Pour cause de necessite,
Mes ailleurs ont leur volente.
  (*PVH1* 11,650–52)

For they are only in the sea out of
necessity, but they have their heart set
elsewhere.

After flying over the Sea of the World with the aid of Jeunece (Youth) it becomes
clear that the pilgrim is unable to muster the determination required to join the
swimmers in their effort to stay afloat in the active life. As he falls into the water,
inevitably dropped by Jeunece, he witnesses how they make charitable donations
to the poor and go on penitential pilgrimage (*PVH1* 12,257–64)—but such activities seem beyond him, 'for I did not know how to swim' [pas noer je ne savoie,
PVH1 12,254]:

C'est la maniere du noer
Que je vi faire en celle mer,
Mes pas ainsi je n'i noai,
Quar seulement je me fiai
En mon bourdon qui sus nooit
Et qui au fons point n'afondoit.
  (*PVH1* 12,265–70)

This is the kind of swimming I saw in
the sea, but I did not swim that way, for
I trusted solely in my staff, which
floated on top and did not sink to the
bottom.

Finally, in the midst of the blows inflicted by Tribulation, the pilgrim once more
cries out to God for 'a hiding place and a haven, where I can go and shelter myself'
[un abri et repostal / Ou je me puisse aler bouter, *PVH1* 12,302–3], or a 'refuge for
me, as you did for Noah through your grace at the time of the deluge' [refuge /
aussi qu'au temps du deluge / Par ta grace a Noë fis, *PVH1* 12,297–9].

The answer to the Pilgrim's burning desire for refuge eventually arrives, in the
form of the Nef de Religion (Ship of Religion), where the pilgrim is finally granted
sanctuary (*PVH1* 12,443 ff.). The Ship, allegory of the monastic life, is presented
as an alternative to the journey originally envisaged for the pilgrim. As described
by Grace Dieu the Ship provides a short-cut to the New Jerusalem, developing the
familiar idea of monasticism as the *via regia*, a direct path free from the tortuous
meanderings of an errant self caught up in the active life:[17]

'Et se vouloies abregier
Ton chemin et bien acourcier
D'aler en la belle cite
O d'aler tu es excite,
Encor bien je t'i merroie
Sans point aler a la longue haie.'
  (*PVH1* 12,411–16)

'And if you want to shorten greatly the
path to the fair city where you are eager
to go, I will lead you there without
going by the long hedge.'

---

[17] See Leclerq, *The Love of Learning*, pp. 102–5.

Similarly the Ship functions both as an alternative to penitence and as its culmination:

'Y aroit bien de Penitance.
Penitance a en lieus divers
Mis ses verges et ses mailles
Et encor plus efficaument
En la voie dont parlement
Te tieng, elle a ses oustis mis,'
　(*PVH1* 12,418–23: cf. also
　13,011–14)

'Penance has put her switches and mallets in various places, and she has put her instruments to even greater effect along the way I have been telling you about.'

Crucially for the present discussion, however, this entry into the monastery is not so much the fruit of the previous efforts—let alone their culmination—but the consequence of their *failure*. The conversion to monasticism occurs almost by default because the pilgrim is incapable of staying afloat in the ordinary, active life as a devout layman. He fails to *use* his body in the Augustinian sense, and is finally unable to implement the mastery of his soul over his sensory and cognitive faculties in accordance with Raison's theory.

The pilgrim's rather abrupt decision to enter the monastic life raises troubling questions not only about the weakness of his will, but also about the viability of Raison's theory of the soul's agency and power. The poem indeed points to the combined failure the pilgrim's intellectual and volitional faculties alike during his flight over the Sea of the World, where he identifies the combined threats of the Homeric Syrtes (instead of Scylla) and Charybdis. Charybdis embodies the dangerous lures of secular learning—reiterating the distrust of 'Ethiques' already expressed in the ABC Prayer:

Caribdis est la sapience
Qui est u monde et la science,
Seculiere implication
Et mondaine occupation.
Tiex choses touz jours circulent,
Touz jours tournent et varient,
Touz jours en leur idem reviennent
　(*PVH1* 11,913–19)

Charybdis is worldly wisdom and cunning, secular concerns and worldly occupation. Such things are always going round and round, always turning about and varying, always coming back in the same way.

The circular movement here represents worldly learning as a dissipation of energy, distracting the *viator* from his straight course on his journey to the New Jerusalem. A more striking allegory is provided by Syrtes (Cyrtes, or 'Sidra'), representing the failure of the individual will ('propre volente'):

Cyrtes est propre volente
Qui comme sablon assemble

Syrtes is self-will, and it makes a mountain in the sea like piled up sands,

Fait une montaigne dans la mer,	Syrtes is self-will, and it makes a
Par ou quant on cuide passer,	mountain in the sea like piled up sands,
Il i faut faire station.	and when people think of passing
(*PVH1* 11,897–11,901)	through, it stops them.

This stigmatization of 'propre volente' is crucial since it allows Deguileville to elaborate on the relationship between intellect and will. Indeed the question surrounding failure of the will has been hanging over the poem since a much earlier stage, and is now exacerbated by the pilgrim's inability to join the other swimmers in their penitential practice in the active life, even *after* his conversion at the Rock of Penitence. Up to this point, the will appears to have played a surprisingly small part in Deguileville's anthropology and epistemology, which is all the more surprising given his strongly 'Augustinian' cast of mind.[18] Before this moment any discussion of the will is reduced to Grace Dieu's casual observation to the pilgrim— all but lost among so many others words of wisdom—that 'you have a double will and double mind' [volente / tu as double, et double pensee, *PVH1* 5917–18; reiterated 6281–6]. This echoes Augustine's thought on the influential Pauline formulation of *invitus facere* and the conflict of the two wills, old and new, in the *Confessions* VIII (especially VIII.5.10–12, also VIII.7.19–11.25 and *passim*; and *De spiritu et littera* 31.53; cf. Rom. 7:15–21).[19] But Grace Dieu's formulation is, if anything, rather unhelpful since it tends to equate 'volente' and 'pensee', and thus precludes any nuanced untangling of the respective roles of the will and intellect in determining the pilgrim's course of action.

This omission of any sustained discussion of the will is particularly surprising in the context of the intense contemporary philosophical debates on the role of the human will and divine grace,[20] and the controversies between intellectualists and voluntarists.[21] The omission is more striking still given Deguileville's intellectual affinity with Olivi, a crucial figure for the development of voluntarism: indeed

---

[18] On the influence of Augustine's thinking on the will, and its later history in medieval scholastic theology, see Risto Saarinen, *Weakness of the Will in Medieval Thought: From Augustine to Buridan* (Leiden: Brill, 1994), pp. 20–43. For the problems linked to the term 'Augustinianism' when applied to the emergence of radically anti-Pelagian theories of grace in the period, especially in the writings of Thomas Bradwardine and Gregory of Rimini, see Ocker, 'Augustinianism in Fourteenth-Century Theology'.

[19] Judith Celius Stark, 'The Pauline Influence of Augustine's Notion of the Will', *Vigiliae Christianae* 43 (1989), 345–61; Eleonore Stump, 'Augustine on Free Will', in Norman Kretzman and Eleonore Stump, eds, *Cambridge Companion to Augustine*, pp. 126–47.

[20] See especially the work of Heiko Oberman, e.g. *Archbishop Thomas Bradwardine, a Fourteenth Century Augustinian: A Study of His Theology in Its Historical Context* (Utrecht: Kemink and Zoon, 1957); and *Gregor von Rimini* (Berlin: De Gruyter, 1981).

[21] See especially Theo Kobusch, 'Willensschwäche und Selbstbestimmung des Willens: zur Kritik am abendländischen intellektualismus bei Heinrich von Gent und in der Franziskanischen Philosophie', in Hoffmann *et al.*, pp. 249–63; Tobias Hoffmann, 'Intellectualism and Voluntarism', in *CHMP*, I:414–27; and Peter S. Eardley 'The Foundations of Freedom in Later Medieval Philosophy: Giles of Rome and his Contemporaries', *Journal of the History of Philosophy* 44 (2006), 353–76.

EXPERIENCE   257

Olivi's theory of active cognition through the soul—echoed by Deguileville's Raison (see Chapter 3.2)—is motivated primarily by his insistence on the nature of the will as an active and therefore free power of the soul.[22] Finally the omission is particularly surprising given the poem's commitment, at least initially, to defend a rather exalted view of the abilities of the human intellect. A stronger, more detailed discussion of the role of the will and its weakness in determining moral choices would have allowed Deguileville to exorcize the possibility of cognitive determinism, and thus preserve his exalted notion of the intellect while also effectively accounting for man's depravity—as did nearly all contemporary philosophers of a broadly voluntarist cast, from Bonaventure to Henry of Ghent and Duns Scotus.[23] Indeed for them the demonstration of the freedom of the will was essentially inseparable from the affirmation of the will's ability to act against the advice of reason. Instead, the lack of any sustained discussion of the will in *PVH* automatically raises the possibility that the pilgrim's infelicitous moral choices are directly determined by his troubled intellectual faculties, or indeed by the disproportionate impact of the bodily appetites on the latter. This suggests a clear fallibility of the intellect, and once more destabilizes Raison's exalted account of human cognition: it reveals the soul to be unable to exercise any kind of effective mastery over the body, and *a fortiori* reveals the supposedly immaterial rational intellect to be destabilized directly by the bodily passions, further weakening any belief in the existence of the soul as an independent substance and active agent of cognition.

The discussion of the problem of the will at this stage in the poem, then, comes rather late in the day, and appears as a retrospective intervention in the poem's anthropology. It is only once the pilgrim has entered the monastery that the will becomes fully personified, suggesting that the will can be conceptualized as a full, independent entity in the allegory only once it has already been overcome and subdued. In the monastery, Obedience now ties the individual will with her ropes and laces:

Ses cordeles et ses lïens	Her cords and her ties are her various
Sont ses divers commandemens	rules, and they bind Self-Will so that it
Qui lient Propre Volente	does nothing as it pleases.
Que rien ne face de son gre;	
(*PVH1* 12,745–8; see also 13,001–14)	

---

[22] Indeed Olivi arguably is *the* most important figure behind the emergence of voluntarism, providing the bases for later, better known developments in the thought of authors such as Ockham and Scotus. See Robert Pasnau, 'Olivi on Human Freedom', in Alain Boureau and Sylvain Piron, eds, *Pierre de Jean Olivi (1248–98): Pensée Scholastique, Dissidence Spirituelle et Société* (Paris: Vrin, 1999), pp. 15–25. On the role of the discussion of the will in the broader theory of active powers of the soul, see ibid p. 25; Silva and Toivanen, 'The Active Nature of the Soul', 267–8; and Kobusch, 'Willensschwäche bei Heinrich von Gent', pp. 257–9. On Olivi's analysis of the fallibility of the will, and its compatibility with the seemingly contradictory position that the will is also 'free', i.e. the highest power in the intellectual soul, see Mikko Yrjönsuuri, 'Free Will and Self-Control in Peter Olivi', in Lagerlund and Yrjönsuuri, *Emotions and Free Choice*, pp. 99–123.

[23] See especially Kobusch, 'Willensschwäche bei Heinrich von Gent'.

258   MEDIEVAL ALLEGORY AS EPISTEMOLOGY

It becomes clear that after the Pilgrim's failure to resist the lures of the Seven Deadly Sins in the secular world, the only means for controlling his wayward will or *voluntas propria* is its subjection to the higher, impersonal *voluntas communis* of the monastic ideal and its radically ascetic lifestyle.[24]

While this late discussion of the fallibility of the will technically preserves the exalted cognitive ability of the intellect, it also severely restricts the practical conditions in which man can benefit from such exalted intellectual abilities. Illumination of the intellect now appears beyond the reach of an embodied Christian self, engaged in a pilgrimage through the active life. The experience of illumination is relocated to the protective enclosure of a monastic cloister, where discipline and contemplation can overcome the inherent depravity of the human will. It is difficult to avoid the impression that the conversion to monasticism also functions as a 'short-cut', a last resort against the pilgrim's inability to engage in a penitential reformation of the individual will. Accordingly, the pilgrim's journey towards God now advances not so much thanks to his own, individual efforts, but thanks to the forward movement of the Ship itself, engaged on the *via regia*. The Ship itself is firmly tied, and its course is emphatically straight and infallible:

Liee est et reliee	It is bound, held together, and fastened
De observances et fretee.	by ties. As long as it is bound together
Tant com liee ainsi sera,	in this way, it will not perish or fail.
Perir ne faillir ne pourra.	
(*PVH1* 12,483–6)	

This fettering of the will stresses the necessity of renouncing individual agency in favour of subjection to the ideal of monasticism and the collective rule of the order—a transition from *voluntas propria* to *voluntas communis*. Indeed Benedict's monastic rule identifies in its first lines the novice as 'whoever you may be, who renounces his own [private] will' (*propriis voluntatibus*) (*Regula Benedicti*, Prologus 3).[25] Accordingly the Ship of Religion itself is equipped with fetters to tie and contain the souls of wayward individual pilgrims, ensuring their strict control, 'so that their weakened and broken souls are tied up within it' [A fin qu'en li soit reliee / L'ame dissolute et roupte, *PVH1* 12,488–9]. *Voluntas communis* here defines not only the subjection to an exterior, institutional discourse, but also the attainment of a fully integrated, eschatological perfection of the will itself beyond its inner divisions—what Augustine influentially terms the *voluntas tota* (*Confessions* VIII.10.24), and William of St Thierry defines as divine simplicity: it 'is

---

[24] On the history of the two terms and their relation, see Irénée Rigolot, 'Contribution au vocabulaire cistercien: *voluntas propria* et *voluntas communis*', *Collectanea Cisterciensia* 55.4 (1993), 356–63, and discussion below.

[25] *RB 1980: The Rule of St Benedict, In Latin and English with Notes*, ed. and trans. Timothy Fry, OSB (Collegeville, MN: Liturgical Press, 1981).

EXPERIENCE   259

properly the will fundamentally turned towards God'.[26] Monastic life thus prefig-
ures, however imperfectly and partially, the eschatological condition to be attained
within Christ's unified mystical body—Deguileville's 'common assembly' [com-
mun assemblee, *PVH1* 13,466].[27] Indeed the familiar etymology of 'monasticism'
itself (Isidore, *Etymologiae* I.13.1), from Greek *monos* (one, single), designates this
state of internally unified existence where the will is at one with itself and with its
divine creator.[28]

The renunciation of *voluntas propria* thus consists in the acceptance of an
emphatically *passive* position of the individual with respect to divine agency,
and the patient endurance of God's painful and incomprehensible workings in
the initial stages of self-knowledge. Given its passive character, this new form
of self-knowledge effectively amounts to self-renunciation, a paradoxical state
that Benedict's rule defines as 'a denial of one's self to enable oneself to follow
Christ' [Abnegare semetipsum sibi ut sequatur Christum, *Regula Benedicti* 4.10).
A characteristic and influential articulation of this idea of painful, active self-
renunciation is found in Gregory's remarks on compunction as a key preparatory
stage to divine contemplation and delectation.[29] Such ideas provide a powerful
source and archetype for the imagery that structures *PVH*'s extended process
of spiritual awakening, triggered at the Rock of Penitence and fleshed out during the subsequent conversion to the monastic life. According to Gregory the
sinner is 'enveloped in the deeper darkness', unable to 'see the deficiency of its
own blindness' (*Moralia* VI.23.40), yet to 'unclose the eyes of the transgressor
[. . .] the inactive soul is touched by the rod' (*flagella*, cf. Grace Dieu's 'verge',
PVH1 11,311). The aim of such humbling chastisement is to awaken sinners to
inquire into the nature of their blindness, and prompt them to explore its underlying nature (*Moralia* VI.23.40).[30] Finally 'the conscience, previously polluted, is
renewed by a baptism of tears, to behold the light within' (*Moralia* XXVII.19.39;

---

[26] *Epistola ad fratres de Monte Dei*, ed. M.-M. Davy (Paris/ Vrin, 1940). I, 13, cited in Leclercq, *The Love of Learning*, pp. 205–6.

[27] See especially the discussion of St Bernard's *De Gratia et Libero Arbitrio* in Christian Trorrmann, 'Bernard de Clairvaux sur la faiblaisse de la volonté et la duperie de soi', in Hoffmann, Müller and Perkams, *Das Problem der Willensschwäche*, pp. 147–72.

[28] See further Ladner, 'Homo viator', pp. 236–9; and Leclercq, *The Love of Learning*, pp. 204–7 on divine simplicity.

[29] See Leclercq, *The Love of Learning*, pp. 29–33.

[30] 'peccatorum mens tanto altius tenebrescit quanto nec damnum suae caecitatis intelligit. Vnde fit plerumque diuini muneris largitate, ut culpam poena subsequatur et flagella oculos delinquentis aperiant quos inter uitia securitas caecabat. Torpens quippe animus percussione tangitur ut excite- tur, quatenus qui statum suae rectitudinis securus perdidit, afflictus consideret quo iacet'. Gregory the Great. *Moralia in Iob*, ed. M. Adriaen, 3 vols. *CCSL* 143, 143A, 143B (Turnhout: Brepols, 1979). Trans- lation from Gregory the Great, *Morals on the Book of Job by St Gregory the Great, Translated with Notes and Indeces*, trans. James Bliss, 3 vols (Oxford and London: John Henry Parker and J. G. F. and J. Riv- ington, 1844). Cf. *PVH1* 6067–8: 'la povre nuee / Dont l'ame est obnubilee'; *PVH1* 6098–99: 'Quar tu vois et non pas le cors / Qui avugle est et ens et hors'. Closely analogous passages from the *Moralia* using nearly identical imagery are equally discussed by Zeeman, *Discourses of Desire*, pp. 55–6.

260 MEDIEVAL ALLEGORY AS EPISTEMOLOGY

also XXIV.6.11).[31] Yet crucially Gregory stresses how such light cannot be 'discerned by the eye of the very mind, whose purpose is changed for the better' (*Moralia* XXVII.20.40),[32] stressing the receptive disposition of the individual soul as opposed to is active cognitive abilities. Elsewhere Deguileville attributes such agency specifically to the Virgin, who is already invoked as the 'lumiere des non-voians' in the ABC prayer (*PVH1* 11,049): in his 'Oratio peregrini' the virgin is similarly exhorted to 'moy regarder de l'ueil de grace / que Penitence vuelle faire'.[33] The experience of the divine in the human mind is thus not an active experience of the seeing subject, but a prayer for the human subject to be 'seen' and acknowledged by the Virgin, and become the passive object of divine action through grace. At best the action of the subject is reduced to prayer, actively renouncing its actions and uttering the desire for penance to occur through the agency of Grace.

The pilgrim's acceptance of the radically passive state of the subject in the experience of the divine turns the poem's earlier commitment to emphatically active forms of knowledge on its head, embracing instead a venerable monastic tradition of experience, patience, and subjection.[34] This is reflected in the iconographical resonances of this entire section of the poem, rich in echoes of monastic commonplaces. In parallel with the pilgrim reorientation away from *vita activa* to life in the cloister, then, the imagery and expressive register of the poem also shift gears: the principal discursive frame of reference is no longer broadly scholastic, cognitive, and didactic, but becomes monastic and contemplative, as the emphasis shifts from the active pursuit of knowledge to the passive, tearful experience of the self as object of divine agency. This also heralds the advent of a new, monastic ideal that displaces the philosophical and scholastic aspirations of the poem, in an iconographical variation on Jerome's influential *dictum*: 'the profession of a monk is to weep, not teach' [Monachus autem non doctoris habet, sed plangentis officium, qui vel se vel mundum lugeat, St Jerome, *Contra vigilantium*, PL 23, col. 351c].[35]

This emphasis on the passive condition of the subject is not entirely new in the poem. To some extent it is already announced by the pilgrim's earlier misadventures at the hands of the Seven Deadly Sins (see Chapters 3.4 and 3.5). This too

---

[31] 'Sed quo uberius culpa fletur, eo altius cognitio ueritatis attingitur, quia ad uidendum internum lumen polluta dudum conscientia lacrimis baptizata renouatur.' cf. *PVH1* 11,267–70: 'Et lors quant l'ueil a bien veu / La durte du cuer, esmeu / Tantost est a forment plourer / Et lermoier et degouter'; 11,278–81: 'Lermes que si voi espandues / [...] C'est un baptesme secondaire.' On the patristic sources that elaborate the analogy between Penitence and baptism underlying this passage, see Drobinsky, 'La roche qui pleure', pp. 87–8 n. 8.

[32] 'Sed iste uisitationis occultae quibus modis se nobis insinuet terror ignoratur; neque ipsius mentis acie comprehenditur, cuius as melius intentio commutatur.'

[33] The 'Oratio peregrini' is edited by Edwards, in Kamath and Nievergelt, *The Pilgrimage Allegories*, here ll. 111–12, p. 144.

[34] See especially Miquel, *Le Vocabulaire Latin de L'Expérience Spirituelle*, esp. pp. 15–22, and pp. 97–162 on the Cistercian tradition; on the 'passive' nature of that experience, see pp. 98–9, 109–10, 120–2.

[35] On the ubiquity of this image and its variations, see Leclercq, *The Love of Learning*, pp. 206–7.

EXPERIENCE 261

is an eminently passive and corporeal experience, and to some extent functions as a preparation for the subsequent experience of spiritual conversion occurring at the Rock of Penitence. The pilgrim's earlier passivity in respect of the sins has now been transformed into openness for the operation of what Gregory terms the 'light within', mediated by Grace Dieu and the various personifications the pilgrim meets—or rather *experiences*—in the cloister. Many of these personifications accordingly replay the earlier actions that the sins had inflicted upon the passive and helpless pilgrim, investing them with new, spiritual meanings associated with the action of grace: Obedience, already mentioned, binds the pilgrim with her laces, ropes and ties [las, cordes, liens, *PVH1* 12,736–7; 12,745] just like Peresce had done earlier with her 'las et [. . .] cordiaus' (*PVH1* 7199); the Porter of the monastery, 'Fear of God' [Paour de Dieu] hits him on the head with a large mace called Vengeance of the Lord [grant macue . . . Venjance Dieu, *PVH1* 12,580; 12,589–90], replaying Peresce's earlier attack with a poleaxe which 'stuns and dazes people like a lead club' [ceste coïgne, / Ennui de vie l'appelle on, / qui ausi com mache de plomb / Estonne et assomme la gent, *PVH1* 7179–81]; Decepline carries a file (*PVH1* 12,673), to counterweight Ire's file and other artisanal tools—saw, hammer, and anvil (*PVH1* 8895–8904 and *passim*); Latria carries a horn (*PVH1* 12,954), displacing the earlier horn Vaunting carried by Orgueil [cornet de vantance, *PVH1* 7787 ff.].[36]

The overwhelmingly physical, even mechanical operations of the sins thus retrospectively appear in a more complex light as part of a larger poetics of experience: they prepare for the pilgrim's conversion in the later stages of the journey, and suggest a more positive and complex role for the experience of sin that goes beyond a simple failure of the will to resist temptation. Maupeu similarly observes how, thanks to the dynamic of conversion that polarizes the narrative in *PVH1*, the violence exercised by the sins can be sublimated into painful contrition at the very moment it occurs.[37] Deguileville's thinking is here in line with a long-standing monastic and theological tradition in which tribulation, temptation, and even the actual experience of sin play an important, spiritually productive, and ultimately positive role: they convert the subject from deceptive self-confidence to humble self-commiseration, gateway to sincere self-knowledge. The personification of Tribulation carries two, seemingly contradictory 'commissions' or letters patent, as if to underline her twofold operation and authority—an idea that deeply informs also Langland's *Piers Plowman*, as Nicolette Zeeman's reading has established:[38] the first commission is authored by Christ, 'Adonai, Roi de Justice (*PVH1* 12,099–12,170), and the second by 'Satan, admiral of the Sea' [L'amiraut de la mer,

---

[36] See also Eugene Clasby's introduction to his translation, *The Pilgrimage of Life*, pp. xxv–xxvi.

[37] Maupeu, *Pèlerins*, p. 179: 'cette souffrance est affectée d'un signe double: comme si, en vertu de la dynamique de conversion qui polarise le récit, la violence du péché se changeait, avant même qu'il ne soit commis, en une douleur de contrition'.

[38] Zeeman, *Discourses of Desire*, Ch. 1, pp. 38–63.

262 MEDIEVAL ALLEGORY AS EPISTEMOLOGY

Sathan, *PVH1* 12,172–206]. Tribulation too, like Ire earlier and Decipline later in the poem, carries a set of artisanal tools with which she sets to work on the pilgrim:

avoit	She had a hide around her waist like a
Ceint comme favresse une pel	smith. She was carrying a large hammer
En sa main un grant martel	and a pair of tongs in her hands.
Et unes tenailles portoit.	
(*PVH1* 11,974–7)[39]	

The role of Tribulation remains deeply ambivalent and complex, but is above all enabling and transformative: redemptive possibilities are thus made dependent on the very experience of sin, suffering, and individual failure.

This nuanced treatment of bodily experience suggests that Deguileville may well be exercising much greater control on his poem's narrative trajectory than I have been suggesting in what precedes. According to such a reading, the Pilgrim's many failures are spiritually *necessary*, since they prepare him for the emphatically corporeal experience of conversion at the Rock of Penitence. This would allow the poem to preserve its exemplary character, as a universalizing account of a *viator's* errance and inevitable failure to complete the journey on his strength alone, and designed to educate its readers *a contrario*. This is indeed what the author claims as his poem draws to a close:

bien vourroie et ai voulu	But I have wanted and very much
Que par le songe qu'ai vëu	desire, that by the dream I have seen all
Tous pelerins se radrecassent,	pilgrims might set themselves straight
Et de fourvoier se gardassent.	again and keep from going astray ...
[...]	
L'erreur et le fourvoiement	The error and waywardness of others
D'autrui doit estre avisement	should be a warning for all to choose a
Que chascun pregne tel chemin	path that leads to a good end.
Qu'il puist venir a bonne fin.	
(*PVH1* 13,527–36)	

The problem with such a reading, however, is that it does not take into account the insistent, passionate investment of Deguileville's authority figures—Raison, Sapience, and Grace Dieu, and indeed Deguileville himself—in a number of discourses that are now being abandoned, superseded, and severely qualified, or even shattered by the sudden conversion of the pilgrim to a very different form of knowledge and self-understanding. The epistemic and hermeneutic system that has been so painstakingly articulated in the poem's first half—with Raison's confident exposition of the soul's nearly unlimited cognitive abilities, Grace Dieu's exhortation

---

[39] On artisanal tools and the work of 'moulding' the moral self in Deguileville, see also Cooper, *Artisans and Narrative Craft*, pp. 106–45.

EXPERIENCE   263

to sharpen the 'eye of understanding', and a carefully articulated ideal of spiritual interpretation influenced by Augustine—gives way to a far darker picture of human cognition, irremediably fallen and compromised. Accordingly, the very nature of the pilgrim's journey is deeply transformed, signalling a genuine crisis for its author as well as its fictional protagonist, and leading to a larger shift of the poem's fundamental frame of reference.

2. Language Redeemed, Language Remade

The pilgrim's entry into the monastery thus marks a complex conversion of the subject, paralleling the reorientation of the poem as a whole away from an active quest for knowledge towards a desire for the passive experience of divine illumination at the hands of a higher, divine power, brought about by the workings of grace and not those of the individual will. At a deeper level, such entry into a protected space of monastic 'enclosure' also retraces what Augustine, in his seminal discussion in *Confessions* VII.10.16, defines as an entry into 'my innermost citadel' in order to 'hear within the heart the immutable light higher than my mind'—an idea in turn echoing the Evangelical injunction to 'enter into thy closet, and when thou hast shut the door, pray' (Mat. 6:6).[40] This retreat into the monastic enclosure in *PVH1* also entails a complex shift away from visual tropes for intellectual cognition towards aural tropes, stressing the interior, often silent, experience of the living Word. The move to a certain extent retraces the evolution in Augustine's own late thought, away from a focus on the image as the instrument of cognition and intellection towards a greater emphasis on the operation of the Word.[41] Monastic authors like Saint Bernard similarly insisted on the need to transcend visual and mental images in advanced forms of devotion, to be attained only within the 'locum quietis' or 'habitaculum pacis' (Bernard, *Super Cantica* 52.3.5, in *Opera*, II:93).[42]

This new verbal turn in *PVH* also leads to a profound transformation of the very notion of language itself, away from the outward, spoken or written language that sustains, feeds and gives 'voice' to the pilgrim's earlier desire for knowledge, towards inner, secluded, passive and ultimately silent speech associated with contemplation. Language as experienced here is no longer the language of

---

[40] 'Et inde admonitus redire ad memet ipsum intraui in intima mea duce te et potui, quoniam factos es adiutor meus. Intraui et uidi qualicumque oculo animae meae supra eundem oculum animae meae, supra mentem meam lucem immutabilem.'

[41] Eugene Vance, 'Seeing God', pp. 23–4; Miles, 'Vision: The Eye of the Body and the Eye of the Mind', pp. 128–9; Sirridge, '"*Quam videndo intus dicimus*"'.

[42] See, however, for a qualification of Bernard's supposed 'iconoclasm', Carruthers, *Craft of Thought*, pp. 84–7. Influential formulations of this Augustinian tension between the visual and aural tropes for the silent contemplation of the inner Word also abound in Gregory, e.g. *Moralia* XXVII.19.39, *Moralia* XXVII.21.41, XXVII.23.43.

264   MEDIEVAL ALLEGORY AS EPISTEMOLOGY

exhortation and instruction—a *predicatio* prompting the reader to exercise his own discernment, or *a fortiori* the language of allegorical exposition, dialectical reasoning, disputation, and philosophical inquiry. Instead it is the language of an essentially mysterious, inward, participative and liturgical experience, rooted in a deeply incarnational understanding of the *logos*. Behind the poem's return to language—or rather its effort to finally redeem language from its digressive, wayward and fallen signifying operations pointed up by the *Rose* and discussed above in Chapters 1 and 2—lies a long-standing, Augustinian tradition of the inner word: *verbum in corde, verbum mentis*, or *oratio in mente*.[43]

Augustine's theorization of the *verbum* is not primarily a semiotic theory, but grows out of his commitment to the development of a Trinitarian theology built around the central event of Christian history, the spiritual engendering of the Son as *logos* by the Father.[44] Crucially Augustine insists that the nature of the inner *verbum* is emphatically 'pre-semiotic', at once enabling signification yet unaffected by such ulterior semiotic processes. The inner *verbum* is thus immaterial, unified and singular, of an utterly different nature from the plural and outward *signa*, linguistic or not, with which the *De doctrina* is concerned (see esp. *Confessions* XI.6.8). The influence of Augustine's thinking on the inner word was immense. It went on to occupy a central position in later debates on Trinitarian theology between Franciscans and Dominicans,[45] but also exercised a deep influence throughout the medieval evolution of mystical theology, from Gregory to Bonaventure, leaving a strong mark upon the monastic tradition, and specifically on the Cistercian order.[46] The idea resurfaces in Hugh of St Victor's *Didascalicon*, where Hugh develops the distinction between the meaning of words in the text of Scripture, and the meaning of the *res* themselves, echoing Augustine's *De doctrina*, before plunging into a discussion of the 'inner word':

> the significance of things is far more excellent than that of words, because the latter was established by usage, but Nature dictated the former. The latter is

---

[43] See also above, Introduction, p. XXX. On the history of 'interior speech' see further Claude Panaccio, *Le Discours Intérieur: de Platon à Guillaume d'Ockham* (Paris: Seuil, 1999), and on Augustine specifically, see Stock, *Augustine the Reader*, pp. 247–59.

[44] See especially the *De trinitate* (IX.7.12–8.13, IX.10.15; XV.10.17–16.26). On the *De doctrina* more specifically, see M. D. Jordan, 'Words and Word: Incarnational Signification in Augustine's *De Doctrina Christiana*', *Augustinian Studies* (1980), 177–96.

[45] See Russell L. Friedman, *Intellectual Traditions in the Medieval University: The Use of Philosophical Psychology in Trinitarian Theology Among the Franciscans and the Dominicans*, 1250–1350. 2 vols (Leiden: Brill, 2012), I:28–37.

[46] On Gregory, see Bernard McGinn, *The Growth of Mysticism: Gregory the Great through the 12th Century*. The Presence of God: A History of Christian Mysticism vol. 2 (New York: Crossroad, 1996), pp. 53–4; on the Cistercian Guerric of Igny, ibid. pp. 276–84. On St Bernard, see Gilson, *La Théologie mystique de St. Bernard*, pp. 133–4, 174–6. On Bonaventure, see Ilia Delio, 'Theology, Spirituality and Christ the Center', in Jay M. Hammond, J. A. Wayne Hellmann, and Jared Goff, eds, *A Companion to Bonaventure* (Leiden: Brill, 2014), pp. 361–402, esp. pp. 376–81, 392–4; and Zachary Hays, 'Bonaventure's Trinitarian Theology', also in *Companion*, pp. 189–246, esp. pp. 224–6 and 236–45.

the voice of men, the former of the voice of God speaking to men. [. . .] The unsubstantial word is the sign of man's perceptions; the thing is a resemblance of the divine idea. What, therefore, the sound of the mouth, which all in the same moment begins to subsist and fades away, is to the idea in the mind, that the whole extent of time is to eternity. The idea in the mind is the internal word, which is shown forth by the sound of the voice, that is, by the external word.[47]

Hugh's discussion is particularly striking since it occurs in the midst of a treatise focusing essentially on language and dialectic in the broad sense: while his primary aim is to foster dialectical and hermeneutic skills, he clearly identifies the limits of the language arts, devaluing them in comparison to the incommensurable operation of the 'inner word'. Hugh's argument here also resonates with echoes of Augustine's early *De magistro*, where he first begins to develop the idea of an inner speech:

> Regarding each of the things we understand, however, we don't consult a speaker who makes sounds outside us, but the truth that presides within over the mind itself, though perhaps words prompt us to consult Him. What is more, He who is consulted, He who is said to dwell in the inner man, does teach: Christ—that is, the unchangeable power and everlasting wisdom of God.[48]

The presence and availability of this internal teacher in the mind thus necessarily determines, for Augustine as it does for Hugh, the limits of any sort of dialectical reasoning, pedagogical discourse, or indeed of any external, spoken utterance.

Such ideas about the interior, inexpressible, but immanent truth of the divine *verbum* in the heart or in the mind played an extremely important part in the constitution of the monastic ideals of silence and inner contemplation.[49] It is against such a background that the pilgrim's subjection to the monastic vow of silence needs to be understood—and this again highlights the poem's abrupt change of direction when measured against the pilgrim's earlier exposure to more broadly

---

[47] 'excellentior valde est rerum significatio quam vocum, quia hanc usus instituit, illam natura dictavit. haec hominum vox est, illa vox Dei ad homines. [. . .] vox tenuis est nota sensum, res divinae rationis est simulacrum. Quod ergo sonus oris, qui simul subsistere incipit et desinit, ad rationem mentis est, hoc omne spatium temporis ad aeternitatem. Ratio mentis intrinsecum verbum est, quod sono vocis, id est, verbo extrinseco manifestatur'. Hugh of St Victor, *Didascalicon*, V.3, translation from the English edition by Taylor, pp. 121–2.

[48] 'De universis autem quae intelligimus non loquentem qui personat foris, *sed intus ipsi menti praesidentem consulimus veritatem*, verbis fortasse ut consulamus admoniti. Ille autem qui consulitur, *docet, qui in interiore homine habitare dictus est Christus*, id est incommutabilis Dei Virtus atque sempiterna Sapientia', *De magistro* XI.38; my emphasis. *De magistro*, ed. Green and Daur, translation from Augustine, *Against Academicians; The Teacher*, ed. King.

[49] Paul F. Gehl, '*Competens Silentium*: Varieties of Monastic Silence in the Medieval West', *Viator* 18 (1987), 125–60, specifically 129–34 on Augustine. See also Joseph A. Mazzeo, 'Augustine's Rhetoric of Silence', *Journal of the History of Ideas* 23 (1962), 175–96; and Marcia Colish, 'St. Augustine's Rhetoric of Silence Revisited', *Augustinian Studies* 9 (1978), 15–24. For a broader perspective, see also Diarmaid MacCulloch, *Silence: A Christian History* (London: Penguin, 2013), especially Part II on monasticism.

266 MEDIEVAL ALLEGORY AS EPISTEMOLOGY

scholastic and scientific forms of knowledge and argumentation. The pilgrim's embrace of monastic silence is essentially an extension of his readiness to renounce his individual agency (*voluntas propria*), as is made clear by the use of analogous binding metaphors to describe both:

La lengue encor traire me fist	She even made me stick out my tongue
Et entour .i. lien me mist	and she put a tie around it and told me I
Et me dist que ne parleroie	should not speak unless I spoke through
Point, se par li je ne parloie.	her. 'This tie is called Silence,' she said.
'Ce lien, dist elle, est nomme	
Silence'.	
(*PVH1* 13031–6)	

The tying of the will thus extends to a tying of the tongue, but language is not so much abolished as redefined, internalized, and redeemed: in this new perspective, the only legitimate linguistic activity is recitation and prayer. The company kept by the pilgrim underscores the devotional, meditative, and liturgical character of his new linguistic activity: Estude/Leçon (*PVH1* 12,835–6), Oroison/Priere (*PVH1* 12,912–13), and Latria (*PVH1* 12,949). Estude (Study) embodies meditative reading to which the pilgrim must patiently submit: instead of being obtained through active, searching intellectual enquiry, knowledge is freely given and mysteriously transmitted through the operation of grace:

'Quar par li, se veus, de legier,	'For through her [i.e. Estude], if you
Des autres aras l'acointance,	want, you will easily become
Et l'amour et la connaissance,	acquainted with the others [i.e. ladies].
Et la grace du Saint Esperit	And the love and grace and wisdom of
Qui comme coulon blanc la suit	the Holy Spirit, who follows her like a
Te dira et anuncera	white dove, will speak to you and tell
Quanque on fait u païs de la.'	you about whatever is done in the
(*PVH1* 12,844–50)	country beyond.'

Priere (Prayer) equally enables an utterly different form of communication, again rooted in the acceptance of the subject's passivity in the face of the action of divine grace. This admission of impotence and humility finally restores the broken link between man and God:

Ell'a eles pour tost voler	She has wings to fly, to climb up to
Et pour tantost u ciel monter	heaven quickly, and deliver her message
Pour tantost faire son message	to God for humankind.
A dieu pour humain lignage.	
(*PVH1* 12,915–18)	

By opening this possibility for vertical communication, Priere is essential in restoring the ability of human language to utter some sort of truth: 'she is messenger of the truth' [De li voir messagiere elle est, *PVH1* 12,919]. Language now performs an utterly different task from the ordinary signifying function of human speech, based on the rupture between the inner and the outer word, signifier and signified, *signum* and *suppositum*, and subject to endless slippage, equivocation, and miscommunication. Instead, prayer can rely on direct access to the internally unified *logos*, and operates through invocation instead of signification, as with Latria: 'her horn is the invocation of God *in adjutorium*' [Son cor est l'invocation/ De Dieu in adjutorium, *PVH1* 12,950–1]. The language of invocation experienced in the cloister relies not so much on the ability of language to signify, i.e. designate an object external to itself, but to be identical with its object. It is a language not of absence, but of participation and immanence,[50] where signification is ultimately replaced by being, and where utterance of the exterior, linguistic word is replaced by the contemplative, 'sapiential' experience of the inner, silent Word.

The recovery of an access to truth through internally unified language is also characterized by the abolition of any hermeneutic binaries of inside/outside, *signa/res* that determine the mechanisms of linguistic signification in the created world, specifically allegorical re-presentation. So the symbolism of a naked Voluntaire Povrete (Voluntary Poverty) draws on a whole semantic field of duplicitous integumental wrappings and dissimulating 'veils', simultaneously evoking, denouncing, and exorcizing the overly ornate, rhetorical, and sophistical allegorical poetics of the *Rose*:

'Voluntaire Povrete	'Voluntary Poverty, she has, of her own
Qui a laissie de son bon gre	free will, left all the goods she had in
Touz biens quë u mondë avoit	the world and whatever she might have.
Et quanque avoir en i pouoit,	You would have seen her naked now, if
De touz poins s'en est devestue;	I had not put on her back the
Maintenant la veisses nue,	gambeson that out of laziness you gave
Si je ne li eusse endosse	to memory to carry.'
Le pourpoint que par laschete	
Baillas a Memoire a porter;'	
(PVH1 12,767–75)	

Unencumbered by clothes, Povrete is free to wear only the 'Pourpoint/gambeson' of the armour of faith, functional and not ornamental, and is otherwise naked (*PVH1* 12,663–4). Nakedness here signifies not merely poverty as a rejection of material goods, but the rejection of any verbal and rhetorical covering in favour of

---

[50] On the influence of similar notions of a 'language of theological participation' on *Piers Plowman*, see Curtis Gruenler, '*Piers Plowman' and the Poetics of Enigma: Riddles, Rhetoric, and Theology* (Notre Dame: University of Notre Dame Press, 2017), esp. pp. 31–80.

268 MEDIEVAL ALLEGORY AS EPISTEMOLOGY

divine simplicity, a unified will, and the coincidence of substance and appearance, seeming and being—the perfect antithesis to Faux Semblant. This state of divine poverty and simplicity both enables and anticipates the entry into the company of the blessed or 'commun assemble' (*PVH1* 13,466), rewriting Amant's entry into the Garden of Deduit as the arrival in the Heavenly City, in turn prefigured by the pilgrim's entrance into the monastic cloister:

'elle n'a rien entour li	'She has nothing with her that will keep
Qui la retiegne de passer	her from passing over to the city where
En la cite ou veus aler.'	you want to go.'
(*PVH1* 12,778–80)	

Povrete herself rejoices in the unencumbered simplicity signified by her nakedness:

'Rien je ne porte avecques moi.	'I carry no burden, I will pass through
Au petit guichet retenue	the gate, for I am all naked.'
Ne serai pas, quar je sui nue'	
(*PVH1* 12,720–2)	

The image thus recuperates, and finally gives 'body' to the pilgrim's initial vision of the naked souls entering the New Jerusalem through the narrow gate:

Quar par la ne laissoit passer	He [i.e. the Porter] let no one pass
Nullui fors povres seulement,	except the poor.
[...]	
Mont fu l'entree soutille,	The entry was very narrow, and all the
Quar a l'entrer se desvestoit	people were taking off their clothes and
Chascuns et nuz se despoulloit.	stripping naked at the entrance.
[...]	
Sa vieille robe laisser hors	They would take off their old clothes
Pour neuve avoir dedens l'enclos.	and leave them outside, in order to have
(*PVH1* 172–3, 178–80, 193–4)	new ones within.
	[translation emended]

The underpinnings of this new, redeemed language are fundamentally sacramental, activating the incarnational possibilities of the revealed, living inner Word of Christ as *logos*. Language accordingly develops a substance and a 'thickness' of its own, relying on a coincidence of word and object, *signum* and *res*, whose ultimate term of reference is the Eucharist, sacramental *signum* of divine presence and archetypal model for perfect, sacramental signification (see Chapter 2.4). So Estude/Leçon becomes a purveyor of a 'lesson' (cf. *lectio divina*) where scriptural textuality has become 'enfleshed' as Christ's body, 'sweet and wholesome meat' carried in a 'vessel made of parchment':

'La dame qu'as vëu aler
Par cloistre et viande porter
Sur parchemin est pitanciere
[...]
Elle est appelee Lecon
Et Estude par son droit non
Et sa viande nommee est
Sainte Escriture qui mise est
En vaissel fait de parchemin,
Pour ce que n'espande en chemin;'
    (*PVH1* 12,827–40)

'The Lady you have seen going through the cloister carrying food on the parchment is the provisioner . . .

She is called Lesson and Study by her right name, and her food is called Holy Scripture. It is placed in a vessel made of parchment, so that it is not scattered on the way.'
    [translation emended]

Such Eucharistic symbolism also develops the monastic ideas of sapience as *sapor*,[51] suggesting the 'tasting', ingestion, and *ruminatio*[52] of genuinely nourishing, substantial knowledge. Such nourishment is not only absorbed by the belly ('pance'), but like the inner *verbum* is experienced in the heart:

'ele donne a mangier a l'ame
Et la repaist qu'elle n'afame.
Le cuer remplist, non pas la pance
De sa douce et bonne viande.'
    (*PVH1* 12,831–4)

'She [i.e. Estude] gives food to the soul, nourishing it so that it does not go hungry. She fills the heart, not the belly, with her sweet and wholesome meat.'

This new experience of the Word as a source of nourishment is again sustained by distant yet powerful echoes of Augustine's *Confessions*. There the convert 'heard in the way one hears in the heart', and 'heard as it were your voice from on high: "I am the food of the fully grown; grow and you will feed on me. And you will not

---

[51] Widely attested—e.g. Jean Leclercq, *Etudes sur le vocabulaire monastique du Moyen Âge* (Rome: Pontificium Institutum S. Anselmi, 1961), pp. 39–79—the idea was particularly prominent in Bernard's writings about the experiential, bodily encounter with God, e.g. *Sermones in Cantica Canticorum* 85.8.21: 'Et forte sapientia a sapore denominatur' [And thus perhaps 'Wisdom' (*sapientia*) is derived from 'Taste' (*sapor*)]; he also mentions the 'cordis palatum' ('palate of the heart'), ibid, 85.8.25, in Bernard of Clairvaux. *Sancti Bernardi Opera*, 8 vols (Roma: Editiones Cistercienses, 1957–77), 2: 312. Gundissalinus also elaborates this in his own *De anima* treatise—different but closely related to his translation of Avicenna's *De anima*; see the edition by Abraham Löwenthal, *Pseudo-Aristoteles über die Seele: Eine Psychologische Schrift aus dem 11. Jahrhundert und ihre Beziehungen zu Salomo ibn Gabriol (Avicebron)* (Berlin: Mayer & Müller, 1891), pp. 124–5. For further references, see Michael Casey, *Athirst for God: Spiritual Desire in Bernard of Clairvaux's Sermons on the Song of Songs* (Kalamazoo: Cistercian Publications, 1988), pp. 297–8. For a survey of the tradition from a late thirteenth-century perspective, see Ella Johnson, 'To Taste (*sapere*) Wisdom (*Sapientia*): Eucharistic Devotion in the Writings of Gertrude of Helfta', *Viator* 44.2 (2013), 175–200. For a broader survey, see Ann W. Astell, *Eating Beauty: The Eucharist and the Spiritual Arts of the Middle Ages* (Ithaca: Cornell University Press, 2006).

[52] Leclercq, *The Love of Learning*, pp. 72–3; Mary J. Carruthers, *The Book of Memory: A Study of Memory in Medieval Culture* (Cambridge: Cambridge University Press, 1992), pp. 202–12.

270 MEDIEVAL ALLEGORY AS EPISTEMOLOGY

change me into you like the food your flesh eats, but you will be changed into me"' (*Confessions* VII.10.16).[53]

This sacramental and Eucharistic understanding of the Word has a transformative effect upon the convert, particularly by redirecting his bodily faculties away from their pursuit of lower ends, and putting them to new, spiritual use. In this incarnational perspective not only language, but also bodily, sensual experience can be rehabilitated. Specifically the sensual pleasures of poetic song may now be legitimately enjoyed in their full right, again echoing monastic traditions of 'spiritual sensation'.[54] The influence of Bernard's *Sermons on the Song of Songs* looms large in this section of the allegory, and Deguileville elsewhere reveals his typically Cistercian fascination with the Canticles.[55] The spiritualized eroticism of the Song of Songs now allows Deguileville to recuperate, finally, the *Rose*'s language of erotic pleasure for his own, salvific ends.[56] The echoes of the *Rose* here are numerous, elaborate, and no doubt deliberate. So the 'cloistre', crowded by the 'merry company of ladies' [belle compagnie / De dames, *PVH1* 12,651–4], clearly evokes the rather different company enjoyed by the lover in the enclosed Garden of Deduit in Guillaume's *Rose*—but only in order to overwrite it. It is above all Latria who redefines the nature of 'deduit' (*PVH1* 12,970), opening the doors to a free enjoyment of the pleasures of song:

A chascune heure sans laschier	At every hour, tirelessly, she blows her
Ainsi elle corne au premier,	horn and then she plays the organ and
Et puis aus orgues s'applique,	the melody rings out, and she takes up
Et la melodie en desclique,	the psaltery, mingling the sounds. Then
Et au psalterion se prent	there is the wonderful music of sweet
Avec entremesleement.	singing and psalmody.

---

[53] 'tamquam audirem uocem tuam de excelso: "Cibus sum grandium: resce et manducabis me. Nex tu me in te mutabis sicut cibum carnis tuae, sed tu mutaberis in me."'

[54] On the performative and imitative use of the body in 'moulding' the mind in monastic education, specifically in the Cluniac tradition, see Isabelle Cochelin, 'Besides the Book: Using the Body to Mould the Mind—Cluny in the Tenth and Eleventh Centuries', in George Ferzoco and Carolyn Muessig, eds, *Medieval Monastic Education* (London: Leicester University Press, 2000), pp. 21–35; on the performative pedagogics inherent in the liturgy, see Susan Boynton, 'Training for the Liturgy as a Form of Monastic Education', in ibid, pp. 7–20. On such monastic 'orthopraxis' more broadly, see Carruthers, *The Craft of Thought*. On the tradition of 'spiritual sensation' see Gavrilyuk and Coakley, *The Spiritual Senses: Perceiving God in Western Christianity*; Rudy. *The Mystical Language of Sensation in the Later Middle Ages*; on Bonaventure more specifically, see Hughes, 'By its Fruits: The Spiritual Senses in Bonaventure's "Tree of Life"'.

[55] For his Latin poem on the Song of Songs—the longest of all his Latin lyrics—see Graham Robert Edwards, '*Hortus Conclusus*: Le Jardin des Cantiques chez Guillaume de Deguileville', in Christophe Imbert and Philippe Maupeu, eds, *Le paysage allégorique: entre image mentale et pays transfiguré* (Rennes: Presses Universitaires de Rennes, 2011), pp. 65–79.

[56] It does not come as a surprise that indeed the *Rose* itself already deploys a carefully constructed, systematic parody of the Song of Songs. See for instance Michael Camille, *The Gothic Idol: Ideology and Image-Making in Medieval Art* (Cambridge: Cambridge University Press, 1989), pp. 321–2, and Alice Lamy, 'The Romance of the Non-Rose', in Morton and Nievergelt, pp. 194–209.

Lors i a grant melodie	And so the instruments are named and
De douz chant et de psalmodie.	called by their names. They are the
Ainsi les instrumens nommes	instruments pleasing to the king, my
Sont par leurs nons et apeles,	father the all-powerful. He greatly loves
Ce sont instrumens plaisant	this organ-music, these sounds, and the
Au roi mon pere tout puissant;	minstrelsy, and because it delights him,
Mont aime tel juglerie,	he makes the one who plays it his
Et tel son et tel orguenerie,	principal entertainer and favourite
Et pour ce que ce bien li plaist,	minstrel. Such a thing is most fitting for
De celle qui en joue a fait	a king, to delight him when it is
Sa principal esbaterresse,	appropriate.
Et s'especial jouglerresse.	
Tel chose a roi bien apartient	
Pour son deduit quant il convient.	
(*PVH1* 12,953–72)	

The passage is replete with echoes of the delights of the *verger* in the *Rose*—where the melody, minstrels, and delight [melodie; jugleors; esbatement, *RR* 705, 746, 718 and *passim*] all conspire to create maximum 'deduit' (*RR* 685). In echoing such musical pleasures at the culminating point of the pilgrim's journey *PVH* also rewrites the ending of Jean de Meun's *Rose*, where Pygmalion prepares to consummate his idolatrous passion (*RR* 20,991–21,029). There the imminent sexual apotheosis is announced by a similar musical overload, cluttered with all sorts of 'estrumanz', 'orgues', and 'psalterion' (*RR* 20,995, 21,007, 21,029; cf. *PVH1* 12,961, 12,955, 12,957). Indeed Deguileville sees himself as restoring a legitimate use of song for purposes of religious worship[57]—an association that is already latent in Jean's comments in the *Rose* itself. There erotic poetry is already characterized—ironically, no doubt—as deviant, as an illegitimate misuse of the sacramental potential of song:

an leu de messe, chançonetes	Then, instead of a mass, he would sing
des jolis secrez d'amoretes,	songs of love's sweet secrets in a voice
et fet ses estrumanz soner	that was loud and full of gaiety. He
qu'en n'i oïst pas Dieu toner,	would play loudly enough to drown
(*RR* 20,993–6)	God's thunder.

The obscene release of sexual energy announced by such 'chançonetes' is now replaced by a concentrated devotional performance, contained within the cloister, which fundamentally redefines the nature of sensual pleasure: here 'esbatement'

---

[57] Liturgically inflected discussions of music and song as cosmic harmony also abound both at the end of *PA* and in *PJC*, as discussed by Maureen Boulton, 'Digulleville's *Pèlerinage de Jésus Christ*: A Poem of Courtly Devotion', in Renate Blumenfeld-Kosinski, Nancy B. Warren, and Duncan Robertson, eds, *The Vernacular Spirit: Essays on Medieval Religious Literature* (New York: Palgrave Macmillan, 2002), pp. 125–44 (132–3).

272 MEDIEVAL ALLEGORY AS EPISTEMOLOGY

(*PVH1* 12,969; cf. *RR* 99, 718, 1300 etc.) and 'juglerie' (*PVH1* 12,970; cf. *RR* 746) are invested with an inherently spiritual significance, enabled by the recuperation of eroticism in the Song of Songs that opens the doors to 'fruition', in its full, Augustinian sense, complete with its sexual overtones.[58] It is surely not a coincidence that elsewhere Deguileville also recuperates Jean's term 'chançonetes' to designate his own, ostensibly trifling lyrics: such Latin 'chançonetes', however, tell the story of a very different sort of 'tres fines amouretes': they sing the praises of the mystical love celebrated in the Song of Songs [En cantiques contenues, *PA* 11,103–5].[59]

The monastic enclosure thus appears both as a reinterpretation of the *vergier de deduit* and as an enclosure preserving the energies of the inner Word from being scattered and 'spent' (cf. 'espandue', *RR* 21,690; see also Chapter 1.5) in an uncontrolled outward utterance of the word, dissipated in a secular *regio dissimilitudinis* of erotic poetry, fallen language, and wayward individual will and desire. This desire to 'contain' and preserve the Word as *logos* reinforces the defensive overtones of monastic enclosure, which are again developed by deploying siege-imagery adopted from the *Rose*. The contemplative, inner peace of the cloister is thus ensured by Chastity, who guards and polices the 'castle', in an extended word-play on 'castle'/'chaste' [Chastete la pourras clamer. / Chastelaine est de ce chastel, *PVH1* 12,812–13]. She defends the inmates—already subjected to Silence, Poverty, and Obedience—against any attack from the outside world, figured in richly allusive terms that unmistakeably recall the rhetorical, sensual, and erotic onslaught of the *Rose*:

Archiere n'i a ne carnel,	She will defend all the arrowslits and
Qu'elle ne veulle defendre	battlements so that no arrow can enter.
Que saiete ni dart n'i entre	
(*PVH1* 12,814–16)	

Here the image of the arrows fired at the castle again evokes a whole set of related tropes from the *Rose* (see Chapter 3.5), while Chastete's defence of the 'archiere' pointedly aims to overwrite the *Rose*'s obscene use of the term to denote the female genitalia (*RR* 20,761, 21,205, 21,321 etc., see Chapter 3.3). The poem here recuperates an entire semantic field associated with erotic intimacy, aligning it with mystical and monastic tropes. Chastity herself is ready to share the pilgrim's bed (*PVH1* 12,791–4), echoing Reason's deliberately equivocal, comical offer of eroticized 'friendship' to the Lover in the *Rose*.[60] Chastity becomes the 'dortouriere' and 'chamberiere' (*PVH1* 12,795–6), the officer in charge of defining and policing a symbolic space, a 'chamber' within which images of sexual intimacy from the *Rose* can be appropriated and transformed. The monastic ideas of mystical

---

[58] Pointed out by Jager, *Tempter's Voice*, p. 87.
[59] See also Edwards, '*Hortus conclusus*', pp. 65–6 and *passim*.
[60] See also Huot, *The Romance of the Rose and its Medieval Readers*, p. 214.

EXPERIENCE 273

'sleep' and 'rest' in the *lectulus, cellula* or *cubiculum* of contemplative vision thus begin to drown out echoes of an eroticized garden, bedchamber, and sexualized 'sanctuary' from the *Rose*.[61] Finally all metaphors of enclosure, sleep, and intimacy are rewired to promote ideals of monastic *otium*, against the lures of secular Oiseuse/Huiseuse.[62]

For all its complex play between ascetic and erotic metaphors, tropes and images, this section of the poem emphasizes how monastic conversion is not merely a 'metaphorical', symbolic experience. The conversion to monastic life exorcizes the threat of seductive but hollow rhetorical figures and tropes by transforming mere metaphors into actual realities: *signa* into *res*, figures into concrete objects, abstractions into sensual experience. The monastic enclosure now 'gives body' to the ideal of unity, simplicity, stability, and protection that had been glimpsed since the beginning of the poem, first with the vision of the fortified New Jerusalem, and later theorized by Raison in her allegorical exposition of the monastic tonsure and its symbolism:

Du lieu tondu qui est enclos	Let me say a few more words about
D'un cercle ront trestout entour	your tonsure. It is enclosed all the way
Aussi com fust chastel ou tour.	around in a circle, like a castle or a
Bien semble estre un courtil ferme	tower. It is much like an enclosed
De haut mur et environne;	garden surrounded by a high wall. The
Le lieu dedens tout descouvert	open space within shows that your
Monstre quë a Dieu soit ouvert	heart should be completely open to
Vostre cuer tout entierement	God, without the least obstacle. The
Sans nul moyen d'empaschement.	circle around it forms an enclosure so
Le cercle ront fait la closture	that you will have no concern for the
Que du monde n'aiez cure	world.
(*PVH1* 890–900)	

Such ideas of enclosure are no longer merely theorized and allegorized, as with Raison's exposition of the tonsure, but *experienced* as a physical reality, corresponding to the bodily tying of the *voluntas propria*. The longing for repose and security expressed by the ABC prayer is finally satisfied through the subjection to the physical, volitional, and spatial strictures of a cloistered and regulated life of devotion and oration in the monastery.

---

[61] The symbolism of the bed originates in the *lectulus floridus noster* of the Song of Songs (1:16). Bernard's *Sermon* 46 provides an ecclesiological interpretation of the *lectulus* as symbolizing precisely the enclosure of the monastery, as a resting place for the soul's contemplation of Christ; see McGinn, *Growth*, p. 205. See further Jean Leclercq, *Otia monastica: études sur le vocabulaire de la contemplation au Moyen âge* (Rome: Pontificium institutum S. Anselmi, Herder, 1963), p. 134; ibid., *The Love of Learning*, p. 67; and Carruthers, *Craft of Thought*, pp. 171–220.

[62] For the etymological derivation of 'oiseux/oiseus(e)' from Lat. *otium/otiosus*, see FEW VII.443a.

274   MEDIEVAL ALLEGORY AS EPISTEMOLOGY

The rhetoric of enclosure, protection, and preservation thus dominates Deguileville's description of the devotional activities in the monastery: the language of prayer itself defines a space of repose and protection, providing as it were an enclosure, a *mansio* to be inhabited by the contemplative mind and resting will. Speaking of Priere/Oroison, Grace Dieu explains that

'Bien te sara lieu aprester Et convenable mansion Ou feras habitation.' (*PVH1* 12,930–2)	'She will know very well how to prepare a place for you, a suitable house where you will live.'

The passage of course develops the idea of prayer as a means of access to an eschatological space, enabling the entry into 'the city where you want to go' [la cite ou veus aler, *PVH1* 12,929], but also suggests that language itself is now understood as being endowed with inherently generative, spatial possibilities. The daily routine of prayer and devotion, *lectio* and *meditatio*, contributes to the creation of an eschatological space *within*, *through*, and *as* language. Language is no longer a signifying tool, but a space of invocation, fruition, and delight that defines a 'place of thought' in its own right. The liturgical experience of study, prayer and devotion in the cloister thus anticipates the eschatological enjoyment of the full divine presence, what Augustine terms the enjoyment of 'perpetual rest' and 'pleasant leisure' [quietem perpetuam; iucundo otio; *De Genesi contra Manichaeos* I.25.43]. This experience of eschatological *delectatio* transcends the duality of both *usus* and *fruitio* as and *res* vs. *signa*, enabling the will to find a resting place where it can already enjoy the divine presence, as if on a station on its ascent to God:

> But if the will is still referred to something else, its resting place which we call its end is rather like what we could call the resting place in the foot in walking, when it is set down in a place in which the other foot can be supported as it takes another step. If however something pleases the will in such a way that it rests in it with a certain delight, and yet is not the thing it is tending toward but is also referred to something else, it should be thought of not as the home country of a citizen but as refreshment, or even a night's lodging for a traveller. (*De trinitate* XI.6.10)[63]

While such a resting of the will remains a form of *fruitio in via*, it also participates in the *fruitio in patria*, carving out a space of repose and fruition, a *mansio*

---

[63] 'Sic est autem requies voluntatis quem dicimus finem, si adhuc refertur ad aliud, quemadmodum possumus dicere requiem pedis esse in ambulando, cum ponitur unde alius innitatur cum passibus pergitur. Si autem aliquid ita placet, ut in eo cum aliqua delectatione voluntas acquiescat; nondum est tamen illud quo tenditur, sed et hoc refertur ad aliud, deputetur non tamquam patria civis; sed tamquam refectio, vel etiam mansio viatoris.'

EXPERIENCE 275

for the *viator*'s legitimate enjoyment of divine presence that anticipates, yet also participates, in eschatological rest.[64]

3. *Hortus Conclusus*: Lyric, Stasis, and Fruition

This renewed delight in the sensual possibilities of song is enabled by confining language to a strictly devotional, liturgical use, as an instrument of prayer and invocation rather than active exhortation towards knowledge and understanding. Such a reorientation necessarily raises numerous questions concerning the epistemic status of poetry as a whole. The pilgrim's radical turning away from the worldly, spoken word of debate, instruction, and intellectual speculation towards the inner Word of silent contemplation threatens the legitimacy of any form of linguistic activity that is not devotional and liturgical. More specifically, this raises the question of the legitimacy and salvific efficacy of allegorical poetry of the kind we find in *PVH*. The reorientation of the pilgrim towards a very different idea of the relationship between language and truth, restricted to prayer and devotion, therefore points to a deeper reorientation of the *intentio auctoris*. Deguileville manages to counter the obscene allegory of the *Rose*, replacing it with an utterly different theory of language and signification along the lines of the eroticized lyrical spirituality of the Song of Songs; but he can do so only at the cost of renouncing the formal qualities, theoretical foundations, and narrative and representational strategies that ultimately underpin his own allegorical poem as well as the *Rose*.

The pilgrim's experience at the Rock of Penitence thus marks a watershed not only for the poem's fictional protagonist, but also for the poetic vision of its author. This reorientation towards very different ideas of language entails the emergence of a new poetics, glimpsed in *PVH1*'s ABC prayer and explored much further in Deguileville's later poetry, particularly through the proliferation of embedded lyrics in the later *Pèlerinage* corpus (1355–8) and in his Latin poetry, whose dating remains more difficult to establish. So far I have argued that the didactic teleology of Deguileville's pilgrimage poem is disrupted by an abrupt experience of conversion, a transition from movement to stasis, from struggle to acceptance and passion, and from speech to silence. This reorientation also carries with it a radical shift of poetic form, which appropriately occurs with—as well as *through* and *within*—the ABC prayer, the only embedded lyric in *PVH1*, and thus the earliest

---

[64] On the terms used here, see especially T. J. Van Bavel, '*Fruitio, delectatio* and *voluptas* in Augustine', *Augustinus* 38 (1993), 499–510; O'Donovan, '*Usus* and *fruitio*'. On the parallels between the volitional binaries of *uti/frui* and the hermeneutic binaries of *res/signa* in Augustine, see Chapter 2.3. On the lively scholastic debates on the question of beatific enjoyment, and the disagreements over the terminology bequeathed by Augustine, see Kitanov, *Beatific Enjoyment in Medieval Scholastic Debates*. On the relevance of such debates for the broad ethical concerns as articulated in fourteenth-century literary texts dealing with human love, see Rosenfeld, *Love After Aristotle*, pp. 74–86.

276 MEDIEVAL ALLEGORY AS EPISTEMOLOGY

one in the whole *corpus*. Significantly, it is within the ABC prayer that the desire for flight, repose, and protective enclosure is given voice, for the first time in the poem. This *claustrophilia* is not only the central theme of the prayer, but also its most striking formal characteristic. The unusual, difficult form of the Helinandian stanzas chosen by Deguileville for the ABC,[65] gives body to the very idea of enclosure with its rhyme scheme (*aab aab bba bba*), as if to highlight the self-contained, interior nature of the prayer's utterances, mirroring themselves internally and closing themselves off from any surrounding space.[66]

The formal strictures of the Helinandian stanza, with its rhymes providing a *mimesis* of enclosure, also lends a textual body to a theological idea that is of central importance for the prayer's deeper meaning: the rhyme scheme enacts the reciprocity between the divine and human (*a* and *b* verses), but the reciprocity is asymmetrical (*aab aab*), highlighting the superabundant disproportion of divine grace in the face of the weakness of human will. This idea is made explicit in the ABC Prayer's 'G' stanza by appealing to the Virgin to make up for man's shortfall in respect of the divine original. It is not thanks to man's own dignity, but through the Virgin's intercession that the *viator* can restore his identity as *imago dei*. This restores the pilgrim's ability to confront God the Father ('pere') once more, not quite as his equal ('per'), but at least as his brother ('frere'). Significantly, this incarnational realignment of the disparity between man and God is reflected in the stanza's rhyme scheme, where the difference between the a and b rhymes is similarly annulled, placing the two terms into a symmetrical and reciprocal relation of identity:

Glorieuse virge mere	Glorious Virgin Mother, never bitter to
Qui a nul onques amere	anyone on earth or sea, show me your
Ne fus en terre ne en mer,	mercy now, and do not let my Father
Ta douceur ore m'apere	cast me away from him. If I appear
Et ne sueffres que mon pere	worthless before him, and I cannot by
De devant li me gete puer.	myself escape the punishment for sin,

---

[65] On the history and development of the Helinandian Stanza—first introduced by Helinand de Froidmont's *Vers de la Mort* (c. 1194–7), and thereafter frequently associated with a distinctly exhortatory, monastic, and contemplative first-person voice, and often characterized by particular stylistic complexity and obscure imagery—see especially J.-P. Bobillot, 'La mort, le moi(ne) et Dieu: une approche de la *ratio formae* dans les *Vers de la Mort* d'Hélinand de Froidmont', *Poétique (Collection)* 77 (1989), 93–111; and especially the special issue of the *Cahiers de recherches médiévales et humanistes* 36.2 (2018), 13–205, ed. Silvère Menegaldo. For an in-depth discussion of a late thirteenth-century manuscript containing exclusively works in Helinandian Stanzas, many of which highlight the formal and spatial qualities of the stanza through graphic *mise-en-page*, see Ariane Bottex-Ferragne, 'Lire, écrire et transcrire en strophe d'Hélinand: un art poétique visuel dans le manuscrit BnF, fr. 2199', *Études françaises* 53.2 (2017), 103–30.

[66] Such poetics of enclosure returns, again in conjunction with the use of Helinandian stanzas, in Deguileville's Latin poetry. See further discussion in this section, below, and Edwards, '*Hortus conclusus*', pp. 71–3.

Se devant li tout vuit j'apper
Et par moi ne puis eschaper,
Que ma faute ne compere,
Tu devant li pour moi t'aper
En li moustrant que s'a li per
Ne sui, si est il mon frere.
  (*PVH1* 10,965–76; my emphasis)

appear for me before him and *show him*
that I am not his equal, yet he is still my
brother.

I have already emphasized how the ABC prayer is saturated with spatial imagery, marked by the pilgrim's *claustrophilia*. But the prayer is also endowed with inherently spatial characteristics, not only through its Helinandian rhyme scheme, but in terms of its placement within the pilgrimage narrative it interrupts. As a document, the ABC prayer opens up a space within the poem for an experience of language that is radically different from that of allegorical signification that dominates the narrative: the pilgrim opens and deploys the document [ouvri; desploiai, *PVH1* 10,883–4), as if to stress the discrete materiality of the prayer, and the ability of ritualized recitation to open up new, unsuspected horizons of transcendence mediated by language. The ABC prayer thus enacts precisely the function that Grace Dieu attributes to personified Priere: it carves out a space for the experience of transcendental truth accessed through the devotional practice of invocation, acting as an instantiation of the reciprocity of man and God. The space circumscribed by the stanzas of the prayer becomes itself a dwelling place, a 'convenable mansion / Ou feras habitation' (*PVH1* 12,931–2, see full citation above)—and Edwards aptly describes Deguileville's sensitivity to space and enclosure in the lyrics as that of a 'textual landscape gardener' [paysagiste textuel].[67] The spatialization of poetic form here also recalls Dante's characterization of the poetic stanza as a *mansio capax*—a container for poetic art but also a space to be inhabited: *stantia* itself in Dante's Latin denotes the poetic stanza as a place of 'stasis' (*stare*) and repose.[68] But unlike for Dante, for Deguileville such lyric stanzas do not function as spaces where the poet's lyrical 'I' is affirmed through its ability to capture and circumscribe the phantasmatic experience of desire through poetic utterance:[69] instead, it functions as a space of invocation, where the 'I' is not the poet's or even the pilgrim's own, but an 'empty' pronoun in a document scripted by Grace Dieu.[70]

---

[67] Edwards, '*Hortus conclusus*', p. 75.

[68] See Dante Alighieri, *De Vulgari Eloquentia*, ed. and trans. by Steven Botterill (Cambridge: Cambridge University Press, 1996), pp. 72–3.

[69] See especially the reading of Agamben, in *Stanze: La parola e il fantasma*, 'Prefazione', pp. xi–xvi, and parts I and III, pp. 5–35 and 73–155.

[70] On the status of the first person as constructed in prayers throughout the three *Pèelerinages*, see also Hüe, 'L'apprentissage de la louange', esp. p. 180. Grace's 'authorship' of the ABC—or at least her role as intermediary—prepares for her role as a provider of authoritative lyric utterances, in the form of inserted Latin lyrics in Deguileville's later poetry: two of the three Latin pieces embedded in *PVH2*, the Pa*ter Noster* and *Ave Maria*, are scripted by Grace (4529–5140), as is the bilingual letter publicly read by Justice in *PA* (1593–1784); see also Stéphanie LeBriz and Géraldine Veysseyre, 'Composition et réception médiévale de la lettre bilingue de Grâce de Dieu au Pèlerin (Guillaume de Digulleville,

278   MEDIEVAL ALLEGORY AS EPISTEMOLOGY

The 'I' is affirmed only insofar as it accepts to place itself in a passive, receptive space in relation to the action of the divine Word, mediated by the prayer and its ultimate author, Grace Dieu.

Critics have frequently discussed the problematic status of 'authorship' in relation to Deguileville's first-person allegorical corpus and its many adaptations, including the role of the ABC Prayer and its translations, notably Chaucer's, in this tradition.[71] But the emphatically 'empty', depersonalized status of this narrative 'I' creates considerable problems for a discussion of authorship in the traditional sense. Firstly—and this applies not only to the ABC prayer but to the *Pèlerinages*-'trilogy' as a whole—it seems important to emphasize that while pilgrim's 'I' overlaps with that of the author and narrator, those instances never fully coincide, diverging and aligning as the narrative progresses. Secondly, the ABC prayer modulates this fluctuating 'I'-voice further, in ways that make its 'authorial' status still more uncertain and oblique: the prayer's 'I' crystallizes a subject who ventriloquizes a prayer that is given to it by Grace Dieu—and ultimately *authored* by Grace Dieu—in order to solicit the active intervention of the Virgin as a mediator. Thirdly, this subjection of the 'I' to divine agency raises the question of authorial control that Deguileville does, or *can*, exercise over his poem: to what extend is this desperate, supplicant 'I' still identical, or even compatible with the more assertive authorial 'I' presented during the poem's opening vignette, of a Cistercian monk preaching to an assembled flock of laypeople (see Chapter 2.1)? The adoption of an expectant posture for the first-person narrator/pilgrim/protagonist during the ABC prayer ultimately announces Deguileville's interest in a very different kind of subjectivity in his later poetry, coinciding with a turn towards a very different, mystical, and contemplative mode of poetic expression and an associated epistemology. This shifting definition of subjectivity, finally, also invites us to interrogate any simple notions of authorial agency and a supposedly unified, internally consistent *intentio auctoris*—a difficulty that is further exacerbated in *PVH2*, as I argue further later (Chapter 4.4). After placing Deguileville's growing concern with the loss of authorial control in the context of his ambitious theory of an ideal, perfected language of participation, I discuss the extent of Deguileville's loss of faith in the salvific efficacy allegorical poetry more broadly at the end of *PVH2* (Chapter 4.5). I will argue that this disillusion Deguileville's growing anxiety about the instability of language is triggered by a traumatic personal experience, allegorically encoded in *PVH2*, and ultimately arising from the hostility of Deguileville's contemporaries towards his literary work.

Le Pèlerinage de l'âme, vers 1593–1784)', in Stéphanie Le Briz and Géraldine Veysseyre, eds, *Approches du bilinguisme latin-français au Moyen Âge: linguistique, codicologie, esthétique* (Turnhout: Brepols, 2010), pp. 283–356 (290–91) and *passim*.

[71] See especially Andreas Kablitz and Ursula Peters, 'The *Pèlerinage* Corpus: A Tradition of Textual Transformation across Western Europe', in Kamath and Nievergelt, pp. 25–46; Kamath, *Authorship and First-Person Allegory*; and Kablitz and Peters.

The privileged site for the articulation of poetic subjectivity is of course the lyric—a form that occupies a privileged position in Deguileville's overall poetic corpus. Deguileville's lyrics take on a variety of forms: vernacular, Latin, macaronic, embedded or not. Particularly the lyrics embedded in the *Pèlerinages* have generated a substantial body of criticism.[72] His later, Latin poetry (*c.* 1355–60?) is seldom discussed and remains unedited, but is equally beginning to attract more attention.[73] It is precisely the Latin poetry that can provide precious information towards a more complete and nuanced picture of Deguileville's poetic 'career' and its trajectory, throwing light, retrospectively as it were, on the use of embedded lyrics in the earlier *Pèlerinages* (1331, and 1355–8).[74] Since an exhaustive analysis of Deguileville's lyrics lies far beyond the present discussion, I will merely emphasize their importance for the argument pursued here. More specifically, I want to argue that the conversion to a different, new form of inner language signalled by the ABC Prayer announces Deguileville's gradual abandonment of didactic narrative allegory altogether, and his increasing interest in the very different expressive possibilities of the lyric.

Discussions of relationship between lyric and narrative in late medieval poetry often emphasize the 'linearity' of narrative and the 'circularity' of the lyric, sometimes held in a fragile but fertile balance, as in the case of narrative sequences, looser collections of lyrics, or the insertions of lyrical poems in larger narrative cycles.[75] More broadly speaking, narrative is associated with a forward movement in time, tracing the linear, incremental, and sequential transformation of a character, subject, or a more complex configuration of persons and/or ideas. Lyric, by

---

[72] Fabienne Pomel, 'Les écrits pérégrins ou les voies de l'autorité chez Guillaume de Deguleville: Le modèle épistolaire et juridique', in Kamath and Nievergelt, pp. 91–112; LeBriz and Veysseyre, 'Composition et réception médiévale de la lettre bilingue'; Hüe, 'L'apprentissage de la louange'; Fréderic Duval, 'Du nouveau sur la tradition latine de Guillaume de Digulleville: le manuscrit-recueil Paris, bibl. de l'Arsenal 507', *Scriptorium* 64.2 (2010), 251–67; ibid., 'Deux prières latines de Guillaume de Digulleville: prière à saint Michel et prière à l'ange gardien', in Duval and Pomel, pp. 185–211; Gérard Gros, *Le Poète Marial et l'Art Graphique: Études sur les Jeux de Lettres dans les Poèmes Pieux au Moyen Âge* (Caen: Paradigme, 1993), pp. 18–21 and *passim*.

[73] Edwards, '*Hortus conclusus*', and ibid., 'Making Sense of Deguileville's Autobiographical Project'; Duval, 'Deux prières Latines'; ibid. 'Du Nouveau sur la Tradition Latine'; Gros, *Le Poète Marial*, pp. 25–9; Martha Dana Rust, *Imaginary Worlds in Medieval Books: Exploring the Manuscript Matrix* (New York: Palgrave Macmillan, 2007), pp. 57–67.

[74] Problems of dating need to be acknowledged at the start, however: even though some of the Latin poetry may have gone through a final stage of revision in 1360–61, this sizeable collection of lyrics running to more than 8,000 lines of poetry was doubtless produced over a much longer period. This is also suggested by the inclusion of Latin lyrics in PVH2, completed in 1355, and especially by the presence of Latin verse expositions of the *Pater Noster* and the *Ave Maria* at the end of an early manuscript of PVH1, datable to 1348 or earlier. On the inclusion of the *Ave Maria* and *Pater Noster* in MS Paris, BnF fr. 1818, see Edwards, 'Making Sense', p. 130 and n. 9, and ibid., '*Hortus conclusus*', pp. 78–9.

[75] Maureen Barry McCann Boulton, *The Song in the Story: Lyric Insertion in French Narrative Fiction, 1200–1400* (Philadelphia: University of Pennsylvania Press, 1993), especially pp. 272–93.

280   MEDIEVAL ALLEGORY AS EPISTEMOLOGY

contrast, tends to encapsulate a more clearly self-contained, instantaneous, static condition, lending it a character that is by turns ephemeral and a-temporal.[76]

Lyric insertions often interrupt the linear narrative flow in the *Pèlerinages*-corpus, and often mark moments of crisis, reorientation, complaint, or repose, often rendered metrically and graphically through a transition to a different, more demanding and limiting verse form. This tends to disrupt the logic of the pilgrimage as a sequential, linear, and systematic learning process, but also provides possibilities for alternative and unexpected, vertical development of the human subject. Fabienne Pomel emphasizes this disruptive quality in her study of the typology of embedded lyrics in the *Pèlerinages*:[77]

> des écrits seconds, morceaux détachables et autonomes, caractérisés par des ruptures formelles et un autre art d'écrire que celui de la narration allégorique: rupture rhétorique, rupture de versification avec changements métriques ou rimiques, rupture linguistique avec l'intrusion du latin, rupture de sens de la lecture avec les acrostiches.[78]

The embedded lyrics are often reified in the form of material documents, and can take a variety of forms, but Pomel emphasizes how they invariably fulfil a soteriological function, (re-)introducing a 'vertical' channel of communication between human agents and divine instances.[79] This can take the form of a descending intervention of transcendental agents in human affairs—for instance with Grace Dieu's gift of the verses on the *Pater Noster* and the *Ave Maria* (*PVH2* 4529–5140), or Grace Dieu's bilingual letter to the Pilgrim from *PA* (1593–1784).[80] Alternatively, such vertical communication can take the form of an 'ascending' invocation, a prayer or plea for such an intervention to occur. In both cases such vertical interventions disrupt the horizontal, linear sequence of the pilgrimage, frustrating the desire for a systematic pedagogical and developmental ordering in Deguileville's allegorical narrative. The experience of the divine enshrined in the lyrics is thus essentially one of disruption and surprise, often coinciding with a conspicuous crisis of the individual subject.

---

[76] See especially Teodolinda Barolini's remarks on the dialectic of narrative movement and lyric stasis in Petrarch's *Canzoniere*, in her 'The Making of a Lyric Sequence: Time and Narrative in Petrarch's *Rerum vulgarium fragmenta*', *Modern Language Notes* 104.1 (1989), 1–38. For discussion of the dialectic between lyricism and narrativity in the French tradition, see especially Ardis Butterfield, *Poetry and Music in Medieval France: From Jean Renart to Guillaume de Machaut* (Cambridge: Cambridge University Press, 2002), pp. 217–71; Philip Knox, 'Circularity and Linearity: The Idea of the Lyric and the Idea of the Book in the *Cent Ballades* of Jean le Seneschal', *New Medieval Literatures* 16 (2016), 213–49. See also Huot, *From Song to Book*, e.g. pp. 326–7.

[77] See also Boulton, *The Song in the Story*, pp. 287–9.

[78] Pomel, 'Les écrits pérégrins', in Kamath and Nievergelt, p. 92.

[79] Pomel, 'Les écrits pérégrins', p. 92; on the ABC specifically, see also Phillips, 'Chaucer and Deguileville: the "ABC" in context', 14 and *passim*.

[80] LeBriz and Veysseyre, 'Composition et réception médiévale de la lettre bilingue de Grâce de Dieu au Pèlerin'.

EXPERIENCE   281

The tension between the verticality of the lyric and the horizontal teleology of narrative is effectively inaugurated by the ABC prayer, the only embedded lyric that disrupts the narrative sequence of octosyllabic rhyming couplets in *PVH1*, and thus the earliest embedded lyric in the whole *corpus*.[81] The central question raised by the ABC is precisely whether such mystical, vertical, and sudden experiences of the inner *logos* can still remain meaningfully 'embedded' within the horizontal, sequential narrative movement of the pilgrimage without disrupting its course. The tensions are extreme since the ABC's emphasis on the overwhelming power of grace tends to implode the volitional logic of pilgrimage, hinting at a very different, unexpected, intermittent, and spasmodic experience of the divine where individual agency and volition has little or no place. Indeed the passage resonates with Augustine's stigmatization of the individual will itself as the agent disrupting the contemplative inner vision in *De trinitate* X.5.7:[82] it is precisely through the renunciation of the individual will that such a contemplative state can be attained or maintained. The agency exercised by the pilgrim—or rather by the open, inclusive, 'I'-voice in the prayer scripted by Grace Dieu—is thus limited to the act of invocation.

The emergence of this new poetics is grounded in a new, distinctly mystical grammar, and amounts to a fundamental redefinition of the relationship between language, knowledge, and truth. As an alphabetic acrostic, the ABC prayer initiates the pilgrim into an entirely new order of devotion and invocation, requiring language to be broken down into its basic, primary constituents. The pilgrim is given a new 'alphabet' or *primer*, with all its associations of elementary childhood education, and thus begins an entirely new and different process of instruction. Far from being the culmination of the journey that precedes, this signals the definitive failure of the poem's original pedagogical project: instead of a structured 'pilgrimage', the preceding journey now appears as a series of aimless cognitive and hermeneutic wanderings. The alphabetical sequence of the prayer thus also signals a new kind of forward movement, arranged into a seemingly linear sequence that is in reality a circular *corona*, defining an enclosed space of reiterated devotion and recitation. The emphasis of this new language falls not so much on the denotative, signifying power of language, but rather on its internal and intrinsic order. Rather than being a tool for dialectical analysis and debate, then, language defines a prescriptive and performative space, and the pilgrim is given the 'fourme' and 'guise' of 'how he is expected to pray' [comment prier . . . devroie, *PVH1* 10,867–9]. This emphasis on form underscores both the formal characteristics of the prayer and

---

[81] While being the only embeddd *lyric* in *PVH1*, the ABC is not, however, the only embedded *document*; we have the Testament of Peace (2459–558), Raison's commission (5173 ff.) as well as Tribulation's two commissions, by God and Sathan, respectively (12,099–12,206); none of these however disrupt the narrative form of octosyllabic rhyming couplets.

[82] Echoing also *De trinitate* VIII.2.3 and *Confessiones* VII.10.16 and IX.10.24. See discussion in Stock, *Augustine the Reader*, pp. 268–70.

282   MEDIEVAL ALLEGORY AS EPISTEMOLOGY

the formal, abstract nature of this new order of language, almost mathematical and Pythagorean in its attention to internal structure and proportion.

Deguileville here elaborates a number of influential Isidorian ideas about grammar,[83] tending to endow the order of language with an ontology and moral logic of its own, independent from the necessarily flawed, contingent signifying relations of practical language use, or the equivocal intentions of individual human speakers.[84] Isidore designates this intrinsic ability of language to signify as a *vis verbi*,[85] a term rich in Augustinian echoes (*De dialectica* 6 and 7; *De magistro* X.38). Since etymological activity is concerned with the retrieval of immanent meaning, *interpretatio* here is not so much a strictly hermeneutic act, but the return to the *origo vocabulorum* (*Etymologiae* I.29.1), associated with the original purity of the Edenic Hebrew spoken in the Garden of Eden before the fall. Not only words, but letters themselves are thus indices of things, and define an independent order of meaning inherent in the most basic constituents of language:

> Letters are the indices of things and the signs of words, in which there is such potency that the words of those absent speak to us without voice. (*Etymologiae* I.3.1)[86]

At the outset of the *Etymologies*, Isidore also develops the idea of a *litera* as 'leg-iter-ae' ('reading road'): letters serve as a 'reading-road' for the reader himself, who 're-iterates' the mystical truth contained in those individual letters on every act of reading (*Etymologiae* I.3.3; see also Chapter 2.3). Letters thus play an essential part in Isidore's wider etymological project:

> The myth of the origin of letters is thus parallel to the theory of writing as externalised memory [. . .]. It is a matter of derived things understood through their origins, but also of these derivatives understood as representational and

---

[83] Unsurprisingly Deguileville had access to a copy of the *Etymologies* in his monastic library, see Bondéelle-Souchier and Stirnemann, 'Vers une reconstitution de la bibliothèque ancienne de l'abbaye de Chaalis'. A number of details from Isidore are echoed in *PVH1*, and in the ABC in particular. So Deguileville's elaborate development of the symbolism of the Tau (*PVH1* 503–32) echoes Isidore's discussion of the same letter, one of only five mystical letters in Greek (I.iii.9); Isidore's symbolism of the 'Y' (I.iii.7) resonates with the extended passage of the pilgrim's *bivium* (*PVH1* 6503 ff.); and finally Isidore's choice of 'Kalendae' as the single word requiring the use of the letter 'K' (I.iv.12), is matched by Deguileville's choice of the same word to begin the 'K' stanza in the ABC Prayer (*PVH1* 11,001–12).

[84] For what follows, see variously Mark E. Amsler, *Etymology and Grammatical Discourse in Late Antiquity and the Early Middle Ages* (Amsterdam: John Benjamins Publishing, 1989), pp. 133–72, esp. 148–51; Martin Irvine, *The Making of Textual Culture: 'Grammatica' and Literary Theory 350–1100* (Cambridge: Cambridge University Press, 2006), pp. 209–43, es 211–25; and Bloch, *Etymologies and Genealogies*, pp. 30–61, esp. 54–8.

[85] Valastro Canale, 'Isidoro di Siviglia: la *vis verbi* come riflesso dell'onnipotenza divina', *Cuadernos de Filología Clàsica. Estudios latinos* 10 (1996), 147–76.

[86] 'Litterae autem sunt indices rerum, signa verborum, quibus tanta vis est, ut nobis dicta absentium sine voce loquantur.'

isomorphic with the realities they disclose. Words preserve knowledge authenticated at the source of meaning; writing preserves the memory of things that words capture. (my emphasis)[87]

Isidore's grammatical mysticism trickled down into early medieval monastic culture, producing such curious mystical poetry on the Latin alphabet as the *Versus de nominibus litterarum* or the *Versus de alphabeto*,[88] or theoretical discussions of the mystical/magical properties of letters like (pseudo-?)Hrabanus Maurus' *De inventione litterarum* (or *linguarum*).[89] Hrabanus Maurus equally produced some spectacularly graphic encrypted poetry with his *De laudibus Sanctae Crucis*,[90] which explores possibilities of verbal-visual representation of letters in analogous ways to Deguileville's more daring visual poetry, such as the 'Chessboard of treason', *de prodicione*, recently discovered by Edwards.[91] While it is impossible to demonstrate that such materials directly influenced Deguileville they provide powerful precedents and analogues for Deguileville's poems, and certainly fall within the latter's cultural horizon.

Such a mystical, Isidorian understanding of language and letters allows Deguileville to evacuate the semantic ambiguity that characterizes both ordinary human language and, *a fortiori*, the slippages of allegory—features that were deliberately exacerbated is Jean de Meun's *Rose* (see Chapter 1.3). In the ABC prayer each individual letter thus becomes a springboard for a meditation that is framed by each of the individual Helinandian stanzas. Martha Rust has observed how in the ABC 'the first word exert[s] a kind of gravitational pull on its linguistic content',[92] and I would suggest that this applies *a fortiori* to the letters themselves, inviting a still more abstract and profound meditation on the most basic constituents of language. The alphabet itself becomes a metaphorical enclosure, providing the pilgrim with a 'toolbox' for the experience of the divine that is essentially mnemonic, in the sense that it enables a 're-membering', a 're-iteration' of the

---

[87] Irvine, *The Making of Textual Culture*, p. 215.

[88] *Aenigmata quaestionum artis rhetoricae ('Bernensia'); Aenigmata; De nominibus litterarum (al. de alphabeto). Expositio alphabeti. De dubiis nominibus*, ed. F Glorie. CCSL 133 A (Turnhout: Brepols, 1962); Lucian Müller, 'Versus scoti cuiusdam de alphabeto', *Rheinisches Museum für Philologie*, 20 [new series] (1865), 357–74; Irvine, *The Making of Textual Culture*, pp. 102–3.

[89] Hrabanus Maurus (?), *De inventione linguarum*, PL 112: 1579–84, briefly discussed in René Derolez, *Runica Manuscripta* (Bruges: De Tempel, 1954), pp. 345–9; and Cécile Treffort, 'De inventoribus litterarum: l'histoire de l'écriture vue par les savants carolingiens', *Summa* 1(2013), 38–53. For a revealing study of the lasting impact of such alphabetic mysticism on later medieval culture more broadly, see Benoît Grévin and Julien Véronèse, 'Les "caractères" magiques au Moyen Âge (XIIe–XIVe siècle)', in *Bibliothèque de l'Ecole des Chartes* 62 (2004), 305–79, on the *inventione linguarum/litterarum* especially pp. 372–9.

[90] *De Laudibus Sanctae Crucis*, PL 107:12B. For a critical edition, see *In honorem sanctae crucis*, ed. M. Perrin, 2 vols. CCCM 100–100A (Turnhout: Brepols, 1997). See further Hans-Jürgen Kotzur, *Rabanus Maurus: Auf den Spuren eines karolingischen Gelehrten* (Mainz: Philipp von Zabern, 2006).

[91] Edwards, 'Making Sense', pp. 148–50, including an image reproducing the chessboard.

[92] Rust, *Imaginary Worlds*, p. 61.

284   MEDIEVAL ALLEGORY AS EPISTEMOLOGY

lost original fullness of the *logos* as *imago dei*. The neatly arranged letters of the alphabet also outline the possibility for an entirely new, 'meaning-ful' linguistic pilgrimage, moving in a reiterated circle through a fixed sequence of recitation that recalls the practice of the rosary.[93] For Deguileville it is as though the failure of his original didactic project—as ventriloquized by Grace Dieu, Raison and Sapience—now required for language to be made anew, not as an instrument of instruction, argumentation, dialectical reasoning, or scientific inquiry of any kind, but as an enclosed space for the inner, silent, sapiential experience of truth through prayer and meditation. After the pilgrim's crooked and inconclusive meanderings through the *regio dissimilitudinis* of allegory, language is restored to its original purity and transparency. The letters themselves become not so much instruments but entities, endowed with an ontology, agency, and mystical significance of their own, independently from the pilgrim's ability or inability to use, control, or combine them into variously arbitrary, contingent, and human constructs necessarily prone to slippage and ambiguity.

Such ideas become more prominent in a later, more rarely discussed Latin abecedarian poem by Deguileville, which helps to put the earlier ABC Prayer into much sharper perspective. This second *abecedarium* is given the title of *munus literarum* ('function/office/vocation of the letters') in the manuscript,[94] and is described in the preface as a *corona laudis* ('crown of praise') for the Virgin and Christ. This idea again emphasizes the circular, self-contained qualities of the lyric, ideally suited to providing an enclosure for the immaculate conception of Christ as *logos*. The *corona* thus constitutes a hermetically sealed whole, facilitating what Martha Rust calls a 'virgin hermeneutics', where an unblemished, perfect, self-contained divine presence can be immaculately 'conceived', experienced, and enjoyed (cf. Augustine's *fruitio*).[95] In the preface to the *munus literarum*, under the heading of *missio pro literis congredandi* ('embassy/appeal to the letters to congregate') the letters themselves are personified, as if to emphasize their intrinsic agency and the author's difficulty in assembling them into a meaningful poetic cluster:

> I, wanting to forge a crown of praise for the Virgin and her son, commanded each of the Latin letters dispersed throughout the diverse regions of sacred scripture

---

[93] See especially Rust, *Imaginary Worlds*, pp. 59–60; and Edmund Reiss, 'Dusting off the Cobwebs: A Look at Chaucer's Lyrics', *Chaucer Review* 1 (1966), 55–65 (57); Alfred David, 'An ABC to the Style of the Prioress', in Mary Carruthers, Elizabeth Kirk, and E. Talbot Donaldson, eds, *Acts of Interpretation: The Text in its Contexts, 700–1600: Essays on Medieval and Renaissance Literature in Honor of E. Talbot Donaldson* (Norman, OK: Pilgrim Books, 1982), pp. 147–57 (150); Quinn, 'Chaucer's Problematic Priere', 126.

[94] I follow the transcription of Troyes, Bibliothèque Municipale MS 1612 given in *Analecta Hymnica Medii Aaevi* 48 (Leipzig: O.R. Riesland, 1905), pp. 351–4.

[95] This is reminiscent of Jean de Meun's own use of the familiar trope of the 'intelligible sphere', on which see especially Edit Lukács, *Dieu est une sphère: La métaphore d'Alain de Lille à Vincent de Beauvais et ses traducteurs* (Rennes: Presses Universitaires de Rennes, 2019).

EXPERIENCE   285

to come especially to pay tribute due by law to the Virgin herself along with her Son, the creator of the same letters.[96]

The idea resonates with the conclusion of *PA*, where Deguileville announces his intention of writing Latin verses in honour of Christ and the Virgin in closely analogous terms, calling on the letters of the alphabet to assemble:[97]

Puis manderai par les rues,	Then I shall have it proclaimed in the
Que liquides, voiex, et mues,	streets, that all liquids, vowels, and
Viengnent a moi toutes letres,	silent consonants—indeed all
Pour porter au roy dëues,	letters—shall come to me, in order to
Houneurs et qui sont scëues	pay tribute and make honour to the
A la royne estre debtes	King, and which are known to be at the
(*PA* 11,108–13)	service of the Queen.

In the actual Latin poem, however, the letters prove remarkably resistant and recalcitrant, complaining about the vexatious treatment that had previously been inflicted upon them by the author—notably in the ABC, and in yet another alphabetical poem (*Ave byssus castitatis*):[98]

> they approached and responded all together: even though we were harassed by you elsewhere, as much in the alphabet *Ave byssus castitatis* as in another French poem, *A toy du monde le refui* etc., nevertheless, behold, we begin again, presenting to you the following, according to our order.[99]

The decision to personify the letters as recalcitrant agents is revealing in a number of complex ways: firstly, it suggests that the agency inherent in the letters is itself transcendental, of a piece with the possibilities opened up by the Incarnation of Christ as *logos*, explicitly identified as the original *fabricator* of these letters in the *munus literarum*. One is reminded here of another Isidorian grammatical poem of Deguileville's, the lyric on the Alpha and Omega, where Christ's Incarnation as the *logos* is understood as a vivification of both *cosmos* and alphabet, world and Word.[100] Secondly, however, the personification of the letters as

---

[96] 'ego, volens coronam laudis beatae virginis et eius filio crudere, mandavi universis literis latinis per diversas sacrae scripturae regiones dispersas, ut venierent, maxime cum ipse virginis filio, earundem fabricatori, de iure servitium impendere tributaque solvere tenerentur.' Translation from Rust, *Imaginary Worlds*, pp. 65–6.

[97] On this, see also Gros, *Le Poète marial*, pp. 26–9, who equally discusses Deguileville's other alphabetical poems.

[98] For which see Arthur Langfors, 'Notice du manuscrit français 24436 de la Bibliothèque Nationale', *Romania* 41 (1912), 206–41 (236).

[99] 'respunderunt unanimiter omnes sic: Licet per te alias vexatae furimus tam in Alphabeto *Ave byssus castitatis* etc. quam in alio Gallico scripto: *A toy du monde le refui* etc., tamen iterato assumus, ecce, timi secundum ordinem nostrum quod sequitur praesentantes.' *Analecta Hymnica*, 48:350; translation from Rust, *Imaginary Worlds*, p. 66.

[100] *Analecta Hymnica*, 48:354–60.

286   MEDIEVAL ALLEGORY AS EPISTEMOLOGY

comically undisciplined agents tends to problematize any notion of an uncomplicated *intentio auctoris*, eroding authorial agency and control. Attributing the creation of the letters to Christ emphasizes their numinous qualities and intrinsic agency while simultaneously drawing attention to Deguileville's own authorial failure to federate, control, and organize the letters according to his own intentions. Quite appropriately, the letters finally accept Deguileville's invitation to congregate, but do so strictly on their own terms and according to their own inherent linguistic and ontological order: *secundum ordinem nostrum*. Such an Isidorian insistence on the letter's ability to 're-iterate' an original, ritualized, and unchangeable linguistic order and rectitude, inevitably brings with it the refusal of those same letters to submit to the clumsy, erratic, and finally self-indulgent compositional experiments of a flawed human poet. Deguileville's own poetic practice, or indeed any poetic composition, thus appears already as a disruption of the inherent order of language, and as an inept, even illegitimate 'plundering' of scripture where such letters have their natural, original, and legitimate dwelling place.[101]

As well as marking the salvific irruption of grace into human affairs, then, the ABC prayer in *PVH1* also points to a wider sense of personal and poetic failure. The prayer expresses a longing for language to transcend individual human fallibility through the agency of grace. This restoration of an original alphabetical order also underscores, *a fortiori*, the 'unnatural' character of allegorical poetry, characterized by an oblique, deviant, erratic, and ultimately wilful abuse of the inherent order of language. This compounds the sense of crisis and reorientation emerging from the loss of confidence in the possibility of continuing the interpretive journey towards the poem's final destination, the Heavenly City. With the gift of the ABC prayer, the dominant mode of expression shifts from the pilgrimage of textual interpretation towards a longing for a divine presence and stasis, encapsulated in the static, self-contained, and self-sufficient spatial possibilities of the ABC lyric itself. Instead of exhorting the 'I' to pursue an active, hermeneutic and narrative movement towards the New Jerusalem, this new poetics as it were brings the Heavenly City to the pilgrim/reader. Such a place is no longer 'elsewhere', but inheres in the very poetry that makes it present, as a language that is no longer duplicitous allegory—an *alieniloquium* or a 'speaking otherwise'—but a self-identical *veriloquium*. The New Jerusalem is no longer the vanishing point of an interpretive teleology, but a lyrical space of experience already present and

---

[101] This again recalls the insistence of early grammarians on the order inherent in the basic constituents of language itself, as opposed to its constructions dictated by contingent human usage. The twelfth-century *Glosulae super Priscianum Maiorem* provide a concise but typical formulation: 'Non enim sunt iudicandae uoces secundum actum constructionis, sed secundum propriam naturam inuentionis' [For words should not be judged according to syntax and construction, but according to the nature of imposition]. See Karin M. Fredborg, 'Notes on the *Glosulae* and its Reception by William of Conches and Petrus Helias', in Irène Rosier-Catach, ed., *Arts du langage et theologie aux confins des XI et XII siècles: Textes, maîtres, débats* (Turnhout: Brepols, 2011), pp. 453–83 (464).

always accessible in the form of silent inner contemplation, amounting to a poetic invocation of the action of the divine *logos* on the helpless individual subject.

There are powerful formal and thematic continuities between the ABC and the later Latin lyrics, hitherto almost completely neglected by critics, and I can merely sketch some of the relevant connections here. I have already mentioned the second abecedarian poem, and have touched in passing on the poem on the Song of Songs. In the latter the recurrent themes of enclosure and eschatological anticipation are fully developed. Again the formal strictures of the Helinandian stanzas, with its demanding rhyme scheme (*aab aab bba bba*), function like walls to frame a *hortus conclusus*. The walls, or stanzas, fulfil an analogous function to the Virgin herself, immaculate and impenetrable source of protection from the outside world:

Si murus est dilectio,	If a wall is love, then I am a wall. The
Ego murus; probatio	proof? It is my characteristic to protect
Nam meum est deffendere	those I enclose and receive [...] I am
Quos claudo et recipio	turned into a defence, since I know how
[...]	to repel and lock out the enemies from
ego deffensio	those places I guard.
Facta sum, sciens pellere	
Hostes acque exludere	
De locis quos custodio.[102]	

It is thanks to these multiple enclosures that poetry can provide a protective space for meditation, eschatological anticipation and fruition, closed off from the exterior, secular world: the poet 'sees, shows, and crafts a vision of the Holy Land by means of the verses of the *Canticle*'.[103] Indeed the words of the Song of Songs, highlighted by underlining in three of the five manuscripts, are themselves enclosed, wrapped up within Deguileville's own poetic stanzas—a technique that recurs in his poem on the *Psalter*.[104] It is these same scriptural words that constitute the connecting tissue of this new kind of poetic experience, lending organic and functional unity to the multiple stanzas of Deguileville's verbal art and allowing it to 'conceive' and circumscribe the presence of the divine.

Also the acrostic prayer to Saint Michael,[105] where the name 'GVILLERMVS DE DEGUILEUILLA' is spelt out by the initial letters of each stanza, elaborates the idea of prayer as a poetic space that anticipates the celestial repose and 'citizenship' in the New Jerusalem. Here the monastic enclosure, still imperfect and 'eccentric',

---

[102] The poem is unedited. I cite the extract quoted and discussed in Edwards, '*Hortus conclusus*', p. 70. Translation mine, with reference to Edwards' translation into modern French.

[103] Edwards, '*Hortus conclusus*', p. 73: 'Guillaume "voit" et fait voir—visionne presque—à travers les versets des *Cantiques*, la terre sainte.' For the obsession with enclosure, see ibid., pp. 69–73, and for his graphic 'enclosure' of underlined words from the Song of Songs within his poem, see p. 75.

[104] Edwards, 'Making Sense', p. 132.

[105] Edited by Fréderic Duval, in Duval and Pomel, pp. 185–211.

288   MEDIEVAL ALLEGORY AS EPISTEMOLOGY

becomes the starting point for a spiritual ascent towards a perfect, eschatological 'claustrum':

Girans Claustrum monasticum	Making the monastic cloister spin in an
Per circulum excentricum	ex-centric circle [...] I determine of my
[...]	own accord to raise my face, as in a
Dignum, duxi me judice	theatre, towards the heavenly cloister,
Erigere theatrice	towards the summit, anticipating the
Vultum ad claustrum celitum,	enigmatic vision of that salvific refuge.
In illa solum apice	
Previdens enigmatice	
Refugium salvificum	
(ll. 1–12)	

Themes, terms, and images familiar from the ABC are developed much further, stressing the crucial role of prayer as a renunciation of individual agency that enables the operation of grace:

Vultum ibidem erigens	There, as I direct myself to raise my
Quamquam nimius me dirigens	face, I see that I can be directed, if the
Pensam posse dirigi,	mediator directs me with love, without
Si dirigat me diligens	spurning me as one undeserving of not
Mediator non abigens	being spurned. May my prayers reach
Indignum me non abigi,	him, so that I may be able to raise
Qui sibi velit porrigi	myself, a poor and guilty one, through
Meas preces ut erigi	his assistance, and that I may be able to
Valeam, reus indigens,	receive his grace, this is what I ask as a
Cujus ope recolligi	supplicant.
Ad graciamque redigi	
Queam, supplex hoc exigens.	
(ll. 13–24)	

The idea itself is displayed through the graphic marginalization of the author's name as an acrostic—'scriptus in margine'[106]—as if to stress his own 'eccentric', unmerited and almost accidental inclusion in the central, timeless and superabundant dispensation of grace channelled by the true 'Mediator'.

Deguileville's Latin poetry has much more to tell us, and the brief overview provided here is merely intended as a contribution to a wider argument about the tension between two contrasting poetic forms—narrative and lyrical—and the radically different poetics associated with each of these forms. On the one hand

---

[106] This is the case also for the bilingual acrostic prayer in *PVH2*, from which I quote 'scriptus in margine' (16,150). For discussion of this further acrostic prayer and its relevance for Langland, see also below, Chapter 6.2.

we find a distinctly allegorical poetics, grounded in the principle of an active narrative and interpretive movement, in turn determining an active development of the individual subject in time; on the other we find a markedly contemplative and ascetic poetics that employs the spatial possibilities of the lyric to articulate a more static, passive subject in a state of mystical expectancy where ordinary temporality has been momentarily suspended or transcended. While this second, lyrical poetics dominates the later stages of Deguileville's poetic career, it is nonetheless present from the very beginning, first signalled in the ABC prayer of *PVH1*.

The thematic and formal continuities between the ABC and the Latin poetry invite a reconsideration of established accounts of Deguileville's poetic career. A number of clarifications are necessary, however, given that the traditional understanding of Deguileville's *œuvre* as a whole, its chronology, and the relationship among its different elements may be almost completely inadequate at this stage. Rather than postulating a precise linear evolution or progression from 'early', allegorical and didactic work towards a more contemplative and mystical mode in the 'late' work, it may be more accurate to say that Deguileville's lyrics and *PJC* explore in greater depth a set of possibilities that is there from the start of Deguileville's poetic writing. I am therefore less concerned with establishing a chronological sequence than in appreciating the coexistence of multiple, often contradictory poetic aims and corresponding poetic forms throughout Deguileville's career, producing a rich, complex, and internally conflicted corpus.

It is customary to refer to Deguileville's 'Pilgrimage trilogy': *PVH1* or *PVH2*, *PA*, and *PJC*. The three works appear together in a number of manuscripts,[107] and they were printed as a single unit as the *Romant des trois pelerinaiges* in the early sixteenth century. However, as Graham Edwards has recently suggested, the very choice of the term 'pilgrimage trilogy' implies a unity of poetic vision and purpose that is essentially misleading, in a number of different ways.[108] Firstly, and quite simply, the 'trilogy' was written in the period 1355–58, nearly 25 years after *PVH1* was originally produced as a stand-alone allegorical narrative. *PVH2*, which I discuss in greater detail in the following section, presents itself explicitly as a 'revision' of the earlier, unfinished text, ostensibly stolen before the author had time to finalize his hastily scribbled notes (*PVH2* 19–90). If Deguileville sees *PVH2* as an improved and augmented reworking of his earlier poem, there are clear signs that his revision extended to include the production a second, separate but closely related allegorical poem, *PA*, as suggested by its opening lines:

---

[107] For a census, catalogue, and discussion of the manuscripts, see especially the work of Géraldine Veysseyre, including her forthcoming *Catalogue des Manuscrits*.

[108] Edwards, 'Making Sense', pp. 129–30. See also Duval, 'Interpréter le *Pèlerinage de Vie Humaine*', p. 238 and *passim*.

290   MEDIEVAL ALLEGORY AS EPISTEMOLOGY

En pensant a ces choses ci	And thinking about these matters, I
Soutainnement me rendormi	suddenly fell asleep again, and I had
Et n'avoit guaires que tourne	hardly turned over onto the other side,
M'estoie sus l'autre couste	I had another dream, which I will tell
Un autre songe ressongai	you about in what follows here. And it
Qu cy apres vous compterai,	seems to me that this second dream
Et me semble que deppendant	depends on the first, to continue the
Est de l'autre songe devant	path I had started on by becoming a
Pour continuer le chemin	pilgrim.
Dont fait estoie pelerin;	
(*PA* 21–30)	

Once the vision begins, *PA* refers back to episodes from *PVH2* in a number of places. The relationship between *PVH2* and *PA* thus appears to be one of clear, direct continuity, where a vision of the soul's journey after death follows on from a vision of the pilgrim's embodied journey of life.

The place of *PJC* in this configuration, by contrast, is far less clear. *PJC* is commonly dated to 1358, and is generally considered as the third and final instalment of this trilogy. Despite the pilgrimage framework shared by all three poems, however, their designation as a 'pilgrimage trilogy' is deeply misleading. In a ground-breaking article, Graham Edwards argues that Deguileville *did* envisage a continuation, or a 'tiers livre' to follow *PVH2* and *PA*, but that this would not have been *PJC* but a collection of his Latin lyrics.[109] Deguileville indeed promises that he will compose a cluster of ten Latin poems in a passage at the end of *PA* (11,078–11,161), which is included in more than half of the surviving manuscripts (twenty-seven out of forty-eight). However, only two *PA* manuscripts actually contain this cluster of Latin poems,[110] which are also preserved in three further manuscripts that do not contain any *Pèlerinages* materials.[111] Edwards' invites us to interrogate established assumptions about Deguileville's authorial project. In particular, it invites us to reconsider the place of *PJC*, by far the most neglected poem of the so-called 'trilogy'.

On closer scrutiny, *PJC* indeed appears to be a very different type of poem from the dual Pilgrim-book constituted by *PVH2* and *PA*.[112] Firstly, while it employs both the familiar pilgrimage framework and the first-person narrative, *PJC* does

---

[109] Edwards, 'Making Sense'.

[110] Paris, BnF MS Français 12,466, and Paris, BnF MS Français 1648. Brief description of contents and short extracts are given at the end of *PA*, ed. Stürzinger, pp. 381–6.

[111] These are, respectively, London, Lambeth Palace Library MS 326, containing a Latin translation of *PA* by Jean Gallopes for the Duke of Bedford (*c.* 1427); Troyes, Bibliothèque Municipale MS 1612, a collection of Latin poetry produced at the Abbey of Clairvaux in the sixteenth century; and finally Paris, BnF MS Latin 14485, newly identified and discussed by Edwards, 'Making Sense', containing an additional three poems of indisputably Deguilevillian origin in addition to the ten Latin lyrics. Edwards provides an edition and translation of all three lyrics.

[112] Edwards, 'Making Sense', pp. 136–7.

clearly *not* continue the narrative of the pilgrim's adventures: indeed the pilgrim here is Jesus—not the first-person narrator/poet/dreamer of *PVH* and *PA*. The dreamer is no longer a protagonist or *acteur* in the proper sense, but essentially a witness to key events in the life of Jesus. Secondly, *PJC* is not a didactic allegory, since it neither instructs the reader about his cognitive faculties nor uses personified abstractions to impart any moral, philosophical, scientific, or theological learning in the same manner as *PVH* and *PA*. Instead it invites readers to immerse themselves into a narrative of Christ's life by using the 'I'-voice that witnesses the events, using the device of the 'dream within the dream'. Thirdly, *PJC* is no longer allegorical in the strict sense—Badel even accuses it of 'perverting' the allegorical mode:[113] the third *Pèlerinage* does not solicit the same kind of interpretive efforts as *PVH*, and its characters are primarily historical, human figures from the life of Jesus and celestial agents such as Saints and angels. Personified abstractions (Justice, Verite, Misericorde, and Sapience) merely appear at the beginning of the narrative for a debate (*PJC* 297–1058), and even here we find only speaking personifications and no allegory requiring interpretation. Thus, essentially, the dominant mode of *PJC* is no longer allegorical but historical and exemplary, since it provides an account of the archetypal, paradigmatic Christian journey: the life of Christ. This third dream poem no longer provides an account of Everyman's journey towards God, but of God's journey towards man—a pilgrimage 'a rebours', turning on its head the normative paradigm of human pilgrimage in a sort of 'inverted mirror':[114]

[Christ:] 'onques pelerinage	'There has never been a pilgrimage of
Ne fu tel ne si sauvage.	this kind, nor one as outrageous as this
Du tout il sera a rebours,	one. It will all be turned upside down,
Quar devers moi dëussent tous	because formerly they all had to come
Droit venir et pereliner	and journey towards me, but it is me
Et il me faut a euz aler'.	who has to go to them.'
(*PJC* 845–50)	

Edwards's reading suggests that it is not so much *PJC*, but Deguileville's Latin lyrics that are to be understood as the third instalment of the trilogy, since they would fulfil the promise for ten Latin poems made at the end of a sizeable number of surviving *PA* manuscripts. Other elements can support such a reading. In the present context, however, I am less interested in the question of the 'trilogy' and its original structure than in the wider, continuing movement, evolution, transformation, and reorientation of Deguileville's poetic vision over the thirty years

---

[113] Badel, 'Le poème allégorique, p. 151. See now also the more recent and sympathetic discussion of *PJC* by Maureen Barry McCann Boulton, *Sacred Fictions of Medieval France: Narrative Theology in the Lives of Christ and the Virgin, 1150–1500* (Cambridge: D.S. Brewer, 2015), especially pp. 170–2 and *passim*.
[114] Legaré and Pomel, 'Les Miroirs', p. 125.

292 MEDIEVAL ALLEGORY AS EPISTEMOLOGY

that follow his earliest poem, *PVH1*. Indeed the very *idea* of a trilogy—of whatever sort—may be a red herring, since it presupposes a unity and consistency of poetic vision that seems incompatible with the internally conflicted and evolving nature of Deguileville's poetic *œuvre*. The bulk of my analysis in the first half of the present chapter has illustrated how even *PVH1*—initially produced as an independent and free-standing poem—cannot be seen as an internally unified project: the fundamental assumptions driving the poem forward are eventually turned on their head by the conversion at the Rock of Penitence and with the ABC prayer. Even in *PVH1*, Deguileville's own 'authorial' implication in the wanderings, backslidings, false starts, and changes of direction of his 'fictional' first-person pilgrim is such that it becomes difficult to speak of a stable and internally unified *intentio auctoris* at all. The pilgrim's 'conversion' to a radically different understanding of the relationship between language, agency, and individual salvation occurring at the Rock of Penitence and with the ABC prayer ultimately triggers the pilgrim's 'flight' into the monastery. If the primary aim of *PVH1* is to provide an exemplary and edifying narrative for an audience of fellow pilgrims, providing them with a toolbox and roadmap for their own 'pilgrimage of life', it seems evident that the poem fails to achieve this. All of this raises troubling questions about the *auctor*'s ability to equip his audience of fellow pilgrims with the cognitive and interpretive tools required to complete their own journey towards the Heavenly City as lay *viatores*, leading an active life in the secular world. Despite its efforts to construct an authoritative narrator through the framing fiction of a *predicatio* (see Chapter 2.1), then, *PVH1* presents an 'I' that is fundamentally self-divided, by turns generic and autobiographical, confident and desperate, authoritative teacher and hapless *viator*, expository *auctor*, and flawed carnal reader.

The problem is exacerbated by the existence of *PVH2*, presented as a revision intended to correct and supersede the earlier poem. The very existence of *PVH2* challenges any claims for the stability and consistency of authorial deign made in the earlier version, now heavily emended and overwritten. Tellingly, the framing fiction of the *predicatio* has now disappeared from the poem, and the dominant mode is no longer didactic and expository, but autobiographical and apologetic, relying far more extensively on very different kinds of authorizing strategies such as internal citation, glossing, auto-exegesis, and extended cross-referencing.[115] I have already suggested that the Latin lyrics are grounded in a very different poetics of contemplation and participation. While this may not be immediately apparent, I want to suggest that this applies also to *PJC*—the most critically neglected poem of the trilogy. In an important series of articles Pamela Sheingorn and Robert Clark have provided a series of readings that illustrate just how well *PJC* is aligned with this new kind of poetics, distancing itself from Deguileville's earlier, more strictly

---

[115] See especially the extended and detailed analysis in Maupeu, *Pèlerins de vie humaine*, pp. 174–268.

allegorical poetry.[116] On the basis of illustrated manuscripts of the text, Sheingorn and Clark argue that *PJC* is a distinctly 'performative' devotional poem. They suggest that 'through the evocation and citation of the narrator's body in both text and image', one manuscript (Paris, Bibl. Sainte-Genevieve MS 1130) 'provides the reader with access to the visual, auditory and musical dimension of this work'. In the manuscript, the miniatures 'visualize the monk-dreamer as he *experiences* the various episodes in the life of Christ that constitute his dream' (my emphasis).[117] As I observed above, the 'I' in *PJC* is not that of a full agent—an *acteur* endowed with his own volitional power—but primarily a passive witness and embodied recipient of actions that are not his own. The inaugural miniatures well emphasize this shift, by representing 'Christ walking on a road and carrying the staff and scrip that identify him as a pilgrim',[118] as if to stress that the narrator/dreamer/reader's 'I' has been displaced from its role as a fully fledged *acteur* to take on the role of a witness and secondary participant in the action. The passive 'I' is emptied of its own volitional subjectivity, and becomes the site of a participative and experiential understanding of Jesus's own incarnational pilgrimage. This in turn invites the reader, as a fellow-'I', to become implicated in the fiction in analogous fashion, replaying and re-enacting in his own body that same paradigmatic event in Christian history, by means of a reading experience that becomes a devotional performance.[119]

The expectant position of the subject in relation to the divine agency of Christ in *PJC* thus resonates with the pilgrim's similarly passive position in relation to the actions of the Word in the Latin lyrics, foreshadowed by the ABC prayer and the Pilgrim's devotional and liturgical experience inside the monastery at the end of *PVH1*. The same ideal of a renunciation of *voluntas propria* is, as it were, a precondition for an apt reading of *PJC*, a poem that finally aims to transmit an 'experiential knowledge of the divine',[120] deeply shaped by monastic ideals of self-renunciation and meditation. This pursuit of experiential knowledge implies, like the pilgrim's entrance into the monastery at the end of *PVH1*, a re-evaluation of bodily sensuality, redeemed through the experience of the Incarnation: 'By soliciting the active participation of the body and the senses, Guillaume's text pushes

---

[116] Robert Clark and Pamela Sheingorn, 'Performative Reading: Experiencing through the Poet's Body in Guillaume de Digulleville's *Pèlerinage de Jhesucrist*', in Eglal Doss-Quinby, Roberta I. Krueger, and E. Jane Burns, eds, *Cultural Performances in Medieval France: Essays in Honor of Nancy Freeman Regalado* (Cambridge: D.S. Brewer, 2007), pp. 135–51; ibid. 'Were Guillaume de Digulleville's *Pèlerinages* Plays? The case of Arras ms 845 as Performative Anthology', *European Medieval Drama*, 12 (2008), 109–47; ibid. 'Encountering a Dream-Vision: Visual and Verbal Glosses to Guillaume de Digulleville's *Pèlerinage Jhesucrist*', in Sarah Blick and Laura Gelfand, eds, *Push Me, Pull You: Imaginative and Emotional Interaction in Late Medieval and Renaissance Art*. 2 vols (Leiden/Boston: Brill, 2011), I:1–38.

[117] Clark and Sheingorn, 'Performative Reading', p. 136.

[118] Ibid., p. 137.

[119] See also Pomel, *Les voies*, pp. 400–5.

[120] Clark and Sheingorn, 'Performative Reading', p. 138.

294   MEDIEVAL ALLEGORY AS EPISTEMOLOGY

beyond an intellectual, readerly experience, proposing instead an affective and performative role.'[121] The participation required reaches so far beyond ordinary language and textuality that we are no longer dealing with the temporal, interpretive, and representational deferrals of allegory, but with the full, corporeal and sacramental experience of Christ, made available through the Incarnation. Maureen Boulton strikes much the same note when she observes that with *PJC* 'the poet is able to move from the realm of didactic exposition to that of affective devotion', collapsing the temporalities of sacred history and subjective time.[122]

If anything, then, *PJC* is not the poem that completes the project first begun in *PVH*, but a very different poem that takes its place, 'dis-placing' the earlier poems. The subject as a first-person 'I' endowed with an independent agency and will has now been obliterated, transcended by participating in the unambiguously redemptive and salvific account of Christ's exemplary *passage* on earth. In this sense *PJC* may be the only poem that can legitimately be called a 'pilgrimage', since *PVH* and *PA* finally relate the vicissitudes of human errance and wandering, at best exhausting the human pilgrim and preparing him to submit to the mysterious action of grace. If *PJC* is the 'consummation' of the trilogy, then the previous pilgrimage poems are effectively *consumed by it*, overwritten and abolished. *PJC* also appears as a more legitimate form of literary endeavour for a monastic poet: here the use of a first-person narrator no longer inclines towards 'autobiographical' self-representation, but at best allows the subject to provide a personal, subjective account of a visionary and bodily experience whose significance and magnitude remains timeless and universal. The dream within the dream that frames *PJC* also opens a breach within the predominantly hermeneutic efforts of the previous two *Pèlerinages*, creating an ulterior and 'deeper' space for a very different experience of transcendence through language. *PJC* finally presupposes ideas about language, truth, and experience that are analogous to those found in the Latin lyrics, similarly committed to fostering a participative and embodied devotional experience of Christ as the living Word. In the process, Deguileville has relinquished all residual aspirations to train the reader's hermeneutic, cognitive, argumentative, and analytical skills. Instead of seeking to train the *viator*/reader's 'I' in the task of deciphering and actively navigating the *regio dissimilitudinis* of allegory, the 'I' now becomes the passive object of an experience of grace and the incarnate Word.

If Deguileville's poetry really underwent the reorientation I have been describing, not many of his early readers appear to have registered this. Few readers, even, would have encountered the relevant texts. Although the indications provided by

---

[121] Ibid., pp. 138–9.
[122] Maureen Boulton, 'A Poem of Courtly Devotion', p. 130. Boulton, however, assumes a greater degree of unity and internal consistency within the 'trilogy'.

surviving manuscripts cannot be truly representative, all available evidence suggests that audiences were interested in *PVH* and *PA*—and not in *PJC* and the Latin lyrics.[123] This may be due to the nature of the 'late' poetry itself, focused on inwardness, contemplation, and meditation, and much of it lacking the distinctively imagistic 'allegorical' aesthetic of the first two *Pèlerinages*. The Latin lyrics are technically demanding, and rely on arcane, hermetic imagery that presupposes considerable familiarity with the mystical tradition. Nonetheless, the ABC prayer in *PVH1*, and the many embedded lyrics in *PVH2* and *PA* clearly point to such a tension between two radically different poetics at the heart of Deguileville's work. As I will argue in part III of this study, William Langland appears to have been alone in registering these internal tensions, and engaging with them repeatedly and creatively as he worked is way through the multiple versions of his own poem over time.

4. 'Car les signes puent faillir' (*PVH2* 14,377): The *fleur de lis*, the Revised *Pèlerinage de Vie Humaine*, and the Search for a Perfect Semiotics

Deguileville's gradual loss of confidence in the allegorical mode is counterpointed by an intensified search for an alternative, perfect semiotics, free from the slippages that characterize allegorical representation. This aspiration is already discernible in *PVH1*, with the presence of sacramental signifiers such as the Scrip, Staff, and Carpenter's square (Chapter 2.4), but acquires new intensity in Deguileville's *Dit de la fleur de lis* (*DFL*, 1338). In this section, I therefore propose to trace the evolution of Deguileville's attitude to signs and signification in the time intervening between *PVH1* (1331) and the later 'trilogy' (1355–8), as confidence is gradually replaced by troubled anxiety. This anxiety is particularly noticeable in *PVH2*, where the poet's concern with the dangers of misreading and misrepresentation reaches obsessive proportions that finally engulf Deguileville's entire poetic project in a terminal crisis of representation.

The *Dit de la fleur de lis* is a short poem of some 1300 lines written in 1338 during the period intervening between *PVH1* and *PVH2*.[124] The poem provides an account the creation of the 'Fleur de Lys', the arms of the French King, as

---

[123] See the work of Géraldine Veysseyre, including her forthcoming *Catalogue des Manuscrits.*
[124] For the recent critical edition, see *Le dit de la fleur de lis*, ed. Duval. For discussions of the poem, see Duval's Introduction to the edition; Pomel, 'Généalogie d'un "vrai signe"'; ibid., 'La courtine chez Guillaume de Digulleville'. For older studies and editions, see also Piaget, 'Un poème inédit de Guillaume de Digulleville'; Edmond Faral, '*Le roman de la fleur de lis* de Guillaume de Digulleville', in *Mélanges de philologie romane et de littérature médiévale offerts à Ernest Hoepffner par ses élèves et ses amis* (Paris: Les Belles Lettres: 1949 Genève: Slatkine, 1974), pp. 327–38.

296 MEDIEVAL ALLEGORY AS EPISTEMOLOGY

a perfect sign.[125] The sign is produced thanks to the offices of the usual suspects, already familiar from *PVH1*: Grace Dieu, Sapience, and Raison. As Raison points out to Sapience, the Lys must function as a perfect sign, signifying through an intrinsic affinity with its object in the manner of a sacramental sign (see Chapter 2.4):

Ains sont tousjourz tes signez vraiz,	And thus your signs are always true,
Car selon la proprieté	because they are marked according to
De ce qu'il signe sont signé.	the property they signify. And in this
Et ainsi, mere, signeras	way, mother, you shall signify the noble
Le noble roy dont parlé as.	King of whom you have spoken.
[...]	
Selon ce tu le signeras	You will signify him according to this,
Et vray signe ly talleras.	and you will craft a true sign for him.
(*DFL* 602–10)	

Deguileville is particularly concerned to emphasize that the Lys is an exceptional kind of sign, of an utterly different kind from ordinary signifiers that denote solely thanks to the conventional imposition of meaning. Even though it is a 'cloak' [parement, *DFL* 183, 235, 265, and *passim*] made out cloth left over from the creation of the firmament, then, we are told that, unlike the mantle worn by the Seven Deadly Sins or Faux Semblant (cf. *PVH1* 7993–4, and *RR* 11,092–3, see further Chapter 3.4), such clothing never conceals or dissimulates anything 'other' than itself:

.ii. piechez de .ii. draps	Two pieces of two cloths ... but they
[...]	were not designed to dress up or
Mais pas n'estoient pour vestir	conceal any villainy.
Villeinalle ne pour couvrir.	
(*DFL* 31–4)	

Developing the sartorial metaphor further, Deguileville points out that the final product must be a literally 'seamless' assemblage of parts, with no apparent seams or stitches, manifesting its intrinsic unity and self-identity:

Et pour ce estoient ordeneez	And for this reason the pieces were
Lez piecez miex et assembleez.	ordered and assembled in superior
Laissié n'y fu nule jointure	fashion. There wasn't any sign of joints,
Et tout onny fu sanz cousture.	and all was unified without any stitches.
(*DFL* 1029–32)[126]	

---

[125] On the semiotics of the *DFL*, see especially Duval, *Le Dit de la fleur de lis*, 'Introduction', pp. 81–8.
[126] See also Pomel, 'Généalogie', p. 329.

The Lys thus differs in fundamental ways from ordinary signs, always characterized by their duality and potential duplicity. The two-headed heraldic (imperial) Eagle is invoked as a typical case in point, providing a perfect counterexample to the Lys:

avec ce il ha figure	And because of this it has a shape that
Que la chose par ly signee	shows the thing to be monstrous and
Est monstrueuse et desguisee,	disguised, and which is duplicitous in
Et que double est en tous cez fais,	all its dealings,
(*DFL* 528–31)	

Beyond the more topical, political resonance of the images of the heraldic eagle and the lily,[127] Deguileville's characterization of the Lys as a perfect sign also reveals his broader interest in theorizing forms of representation that eschew the duality and potential 'duplicity' of ordinary signification, based on a disjunction between signs and their objects. In her speech to Sapience, Raison observes how

lez signez faillent souvent,	Signs often fail, which saddens me
Dont il me desplaist grandement!	greatly! But not the signs that you
Mais pas ne sont ceulz que tu faiz,	make, and therefore your signs are
Ains sont tousjourz tes signez vraiz,	always truthful.
(*DFL* 599–602)	

In contrast to such ordinary signs, the Lys is characterized by a perfect agreement between the sign and its object, making it a sacramental sign endowed with an inherent *similitudo*:

aussi comme lez fais as dis	And thus it is reasonable that signs have
Ou comme lez dis au penseez,	to agree with the thing signified, just as
Lez signez aus chosez signeez	deeds have to correspond to the words,
Doivent respondre par raison.	or words have to match thoughts.
(*DFL* 320–3)	

While the Lys is a unique and exceptional sign, it also emblematizes the longing for a perfectly truthful language, lacking any internal rupture between 'signes' and 'choses'. The Lys therefore crystallizes what is essentially a Cratylist ideal of language, according to which words participate in the nature of the things they designate. While Cratylism was never considered as a viable model of signification in terms of practical language use or logical analysis during the Middle Ages, the *ideal* of Cratylism nonetheless continued to exercise a powerful pull on medieval discussion of signification. Channelled by Isidore (*Etymologiae* I.29.2), and Boethius (*Consolation of Philosophy* 3, pr. 12), Cratylist ideas provided an

---

[127] Duval, 'Introduction' in *DFL*, pp. 72–81.

298 MEDIEVAL ALLEGORY AS EPISTEMOLOGY

important counterpoint to the dominant conventionalist model, transmitted particularly by Boethius's commentaries on Aristotle's *De Interpretatione*. Despite the increasingly 'Aristotelian' tendencies of the language sciences during the scholastic period (see Chapters 1.3 and 2.4), then, the notion of a Cratylist language remained available, if only as an account of an unattainable ideal beyond the reach of fallen human language.[128] More specifically Deguileville here directly echoes—like Chaucer after him—Jean de Meun's influential, yet deeply ironic statement about the adequacy of 'diz' to 'fez', quoting the authority of Sallust:[129]

'car quiconques la chose escrit,	'Whoever does the writing, if he is not
se du voir ne nous velt ambler,	to deprive us of the truth, his words
li diz doit le fet resambler;	must echo the deed, for when words
car les voiz aus choses voisines	rub shoulders with things, they should
doivent estre a leur fez cousines'.	be cousins of the deeds.'
(*RR* 15,158–62)	

Deguileville essentially repeats Jean's own statement—but the implications couldn't be more different. Jean typically invites us to interrogate the very possibility of a perfect language in the light of his poetic practice in the poem as a whole: far from writing a poem that conforms to such principles of adequacy and affinity, Jean invariably pushes the disjunction between 'diz' and 'fez' to its limits. True to the spirit of *alieniloquium*, his poem thus culminates with the account of an act of religious devotion that is in reality an allegory for sexual penetration. Deguileville, however, typically attempts to restore faith in the possibility of restoring a lost, prelapsarian alignment between words and things.

Such a longing for a perfectly adequate, unambiguous language of identity and participation therefore points, *a fortiori*, beyond the disjunctions and obscurities that determine the principles of allegorical signification, widely conceptualized as *alieniloquium* or 'other-speaking'. It is therefore slightly misleading to observe that the 'Fleur de Lys' is a fabricated allegorical sign, and that it even constitutes a sort of matrix for Deguileville's poetic art more broadly.[130] Fabienne Pomel's observation is of course correct in the sense that the poem 'combine une série d'équivalences entre deux isotopes', and relies on a 'décomposition du tout en parties':[131] clearly it is the poet himself who fabricates such symbolic structures—but that is not how Deguileville would like us to understand the Lys. The poet instead seeks to occlude the fabricated nature of the sign by attributing its creation to divine instances,

---

[128] See especially Fyler, *Language and the Declining World*, pp. 17–27.

[129] See especially Fyler, *Language and the Declining World*, pp. 95–100, 179–88. See further Marc M. Pelen, 'Chaucer's "Cosyn to the dede": Further Considerations', *Florilegium* 19 (2002), 91–107, and Paul B. Taylor, 'Chaucer's *Cosyn to the Dede*', *Speculum* 57 (1982), 315–27.

[130] As suggested by Pomel, 'Généalogie', pp. 330 and *passim*, who sees the Lys as 'une métaphore possible de la création allégorique' (p. 340).

[131] Pomel, 'Généalogie', p. 330. Pomel's observation that the *DFL* provides an 'allégorie de l'écriture allégorique' (*Les voies*, pp. 506–8) is similarly evocative but—to my mind—misleading.

in the attempt to present it as an incontrovertibly truthful sacramental sign. The semantic field of craftsmanship works analogically, as becomes obvious when the poet observes that the final product is effectively 'seamless', free from any traces of human artifice and unblemished by any seam or stitching [jointure; cousture, *DFL* 1031–2). If anything, then, the creation of the Lys is not so much a paradigm for the writing of allegory by a human poet, but rather an idealized vanishing point to which Deguileville's allegory aspires[132]—much like the Heavenly Jerusalem constitutes the final destination and ultimate semantic referent of the *viator*'s journey. The perfection and self-identity of the Lys thus provides a *terminus* towards which the movement of Deguileville's pilgrimage allegory is asymptotically organized, but also denotes a kind of self-identity that would render allegorical expression superfluous.[133]

Like the 'Virgin hermeneutics' of Deguileville's lyric poetry (see Chapter 4.3), this desire for semiotic perfection therefore amounts to an implicit rejection of the inferential nature of allegorical interpretation, rooted in the fundamental disjunction between words and things. In some sense, then, the very nature of Deguileville's poetic ideal, emblematized by the Lys, determines the inevitable failure of his own poetic art in practical terms. Despite Deguileville's insistence on the divine origin and perfection of the Fleur de Lys, the sign can only ever become accessible to us in mediated and indirect fashion, through the means of an allegorical poem, *DFL*, indelibly marked by semiotic and ontological rupture. Once more Deguileville is at least intermittently aware of this paradox, and comes close to confronting it in the poem's conclusion. Here he describes the production of his new dream poem in unusually factual terms, directly echoing the conclusion of *PVH1*:

De mon songe memoratis	I concluded I should write down my
[. . .]	memorable dream.
Je me pensay qu'escriroye	
[. . .]	
Escript l'ay, c'en est la copie.	And I have written it down, and this
(*DFL* 1325–9)	is a copy of it.

After a poem dedicated to extolling the virtue of the Lys as a perfect signifier, we are reminded that this vision too is framed by a dream, in turn mediated by a textual 'copie' that places the reader at two removes from such idealized perfection. This raises again the spectre of representationalism: to what extent is the image of the Lys actually real, being doubly framed by a textual copy and a mental vision

---

[132] Fabienne Pomel makes a similar point, *Les voies*, p. 508.

[133] In this sense Duval's observation that the *DFL* is 'un mode d'emploi de l'écriture allégorique' is more precise, see 'Interpréter', p. 241. See also Fabienne Pomel's observations on the 'asymptotic' character of allegorical expression more widely, with extended discussion of Deguileville's poetry, in *Les voies*, pp. 489–511.

300 MEDIEVAL ALLEGORY AS EPISTEMOLOGY

experienced during a dream? The poet is forced to concede that he cannot ensure direct access to transcendental truths through his poetic craft. As in *PVH1* and *PVH2*, he is forced to appeal once more to the interpretive skills of his readers, asking them to sift through an unstable compound of 'songe' and 'mençonge' (cf. *PVH1* 13,517–26; *RR* 1–2; 9853–4; 18,463–4), in the hope that they will be able to retrieve some genuine truth with the help of Grace Dieu:

Së aucun bien il segnefie,	If any good is signified here, let Grace
Grace de Dieu en soit loee	de Dieu, who made all this, be blesses
Qui a ce fait et mercïee.	and thanked. And if there is anything
Et s'il y a riens messeant,	awry, or anything unpleasant in some
Rien mal a point desplaisant,	parts, let that be blamed on dreams,
Cela soit reputé a songe,	since only very few are entirely free
Car pou en sont ou n'ait mençonge.	from lies.
(*DFL* 1330–6)[134]	

Just as in the closing lines of *PVH1*, the poet once more reminds us that for all their spiritual and semiotic perfection, such signs are doubly mediated by his own, individual consciousness and a textual 'copie', blurring spiritual 'bien' with unavoidable 'mençonge'.

The discrepancy between the author's poetic ideals and semiotic theory on the one hand, and the practical challenges of capturing such perfection in a material text also emerge very sharply in connection to *PVH2*, to which I now turn. Crucially, *PVH2* is presented as an improved and authorized rewriting of *PVH1*, which is now dismissed as a hasty and imperfect first draft in the prologue of the new version (*PVH2* 21–8). Manuscript numbers, however, tell a very different story: today we have close to eighty MSS of *PVH1*, the ostensibly unfinished draft, compared with a mere nine for *PVH2*, the authorized and definitive version. This suggests that the reception of Deguileville's *œuvre* clearly did not conform to the author's own wishes and intentions. It is therefore deeply ironic, but also symptomatic, that Deguileville should open *PVH2* precisely by drawing attention to the vagaries of textual reception, circulation, and interpretation. His original, unfinished poem— Guillaume tells us in an extended Prologue—was stolen and circulated without the author's consent, before any corrections could be made (*PVH2* 31–8). Deguileville here follows a well-established monastic tradition,[135] but the vividness of the description suggests lived experience. Deguileville here paints an evocative picture of the impossibility of regaining control of his earlier draft for purposes of revision and amendment: 'I could have amended it much more easily before, when I had it all to myself, than I could do now' [Mieux amender le pouvoye / Quant tout seul

---

[134] A similar caveat is also placed earlier in the poem, questioning the status of the dream, at ll. 51–4.
[135] On this tradition, see especially the observations in Kathryn Kerby-Fulton, 'Langland and the Bibliographic Ego', in Stephen Justice and Kathryn Kerby-Fulton, eds, *Written Work: Langland, Labor, and Authorship* (Philadelphia: University of Pennsylvania Press, 1997), pp. 67–143 (100, n. 115).

EXPERIENCE 301

je le tenoye / Que ne feroie maintenant, *PVH2* 51–3]. The poem has developed a life of its own, and its unauthorized circulation is presented as a process of uncontrolled organic growth, its many manuscript witnesses figured as the spread of a plant's tendrils (prouvains), impossible to retrace, prune, or discipline:[136]

Mes tart pour le bien adrecier	But it reached me too late to deal with it
M'est venu et pour corrigier.	and to make any corrections: it had
En tant de lieus s'est provongné	already spread into so many places, I
Que james n'aroye tracié	could never have tracked down all its
Ses prouvains pour eulx bien tailhier	stray tendrils to cut them back and deal
Et pour eulx a point adrecier;	with all of them.
(*PVH2* 41–6)	

The assigned purpose of the revised version is to rectify this situation. Deguileville now mixes his metaphors, and personifies the revised version of his poem as a Pilgrim and 'loyal messenger' [loyal message, *PVH2* 89], sent out on the road to seek out, hunt down, and prune back any undisciplined stray 'prouvains' of the earlier version:

Pour ce que envoyé le vouldray	And therefore I would like it to be sent
Par tous les lieux ou a esté	everywhere where you have already
Sens mon vouloir et sens mon gré.	been, without my will and blessing.
Si que, songe, tu t'en iras	Therefore, o Dream, you shall go to all
Par toux les lieux ou esté as.	the places where you have been already.
A toux tes prouvains t'envoie	I send you to track down all of your
Pour ce quë y scés la voie.	tendrils, since you know the way: go
De par moy les va toux taillier	and cut them back in my name, and call
Et mectre a point et adrecier.	them all back to order.
(*PVH2* 66–74)	

The formulation 'de par moy'—echoing the standard formula establishing the authority of royal missives[137]—is emblematic for the official character of this mission, and the new pilgrim-poem-messenger is therefore sent out with all the marks of authority that pertain to an official messenger and ambassador. Deguileville now shifts his metaphors further, and personifies both poems as two different types of pilgrims: whereas *PVH2* is ordered to follow the straight course assigned to it by the author, the journey of *PVH1* had been erratic and aimless:

---

[136] See also John Moreau, '"Ce mauvais tabellion": Satanic and Marian Textuality in Deguileville's *Pèlerinage de l'Âme*', in Kamath and Nievergelt, pp. 113–28 (122–4).

[137] Pomel, 'Les écrits pérégrins', p. 105.

Quant sens congié tu y alas,	Formerly you went there without my
Par congié aler y devras.	authorisation; but now I command you
Ne t'avoye pas appellé	to go there again. If I have called you
Pieça « Pelerin » et nommé,	'Pilgrim', it was not to allow you to
Affin que a cheval ne a pié	roam, on foot or on horseback, outside
Allasses hors sens mon congié,	of your assigned course, but so that you
Mes pour ce que (je) te menasse	would accompany me to Jerusalem the
Avec moy quant jë alasse	City.
En Jherusalem la cité	
(*PVH2* 75–83)	

PVH1 has clearly strayed outside of its assigned trajectory, going astray from its assigned course and authorial design.

This discrepancy between the two poems raises a whole range of deeper questions regarding authorial control—not only in terms of circulation, but also in terms of divergent reception and interpretation. Critics have invoked a range of possible reasons to explain Deguileville's disavowal of his first poem. Based on circumstantial evidence from within *PVH2*, Faral was the first to suggest that *PVH1* may have been the object of harsh criticism or censorship. The poem may even have played a role in bringing about legal proceedings against its author—a suggestion to which I will return in the conclusive section of this chapter (Chapter 4.5).[138] Be that as it may, *PVH2* as a whole is clearly characterized by a diffuse but ubiquitous defensiveness: the poem pursues a palpably apologetic agenda, and its author is at pains to ensure what he considers to be an appropriate interpretation of his allegory. He does so by multiplying instances of integrated expository glossing, supplying the poem with an impressive apparatus of quotations from learned Latin *auctoritates*, and variously embedding a selection of fictional charters, lyrics, and documents in Latin and French verse in his poem.[139] The earliest and most important of these paratextual and intradiegetic documents is, of course, the prologue itself, providing an account of the context that necessitated the production and promulgation of an additional, revised and corrected version of the original *Pèlerinage*. But far from solving the existing difficulties, the prologue does little more than raising additional difficulties and alerting the reader's suspicions. How exactly can *PVH2* achieve the kind of the textual and interpretive stability, or 'straightness', that was denied to its headstrong and meandering predecessor once it is released into the world? How exactly can the author prevent the copies of this new poem, however firmly authorized 'de par moy' (73) from going off and following a course of their own, roaming 'hors sens mon congie' (80) like the stray

---

[138] Faral, *Guillaume de Deguileville*, pp. 29, 9–10; *PVH2*, ed. Edwards and Maupeu, 'Introduction'; Maupeu, *Pèlerins de vie humaine*, pp. 197–215; Moreau, '"Ce mauvais tabellion"'; ibid., *Eschatological Subjects: Divine and Literary Judgment in Fourteenth-century French Poetry* (Columbus: Ohio State University Press, 2014), pp. 70–80, 84–7; Pomel 'Enjeux'.

[139] Maupeu, *Pèlerins de vie humaine*, pp. 98–127.

EXPERIENCE   303

'tendrils' of *PVH1*? And, most importantly, can the poet really ensure an adequate, orthodox, and salvific interpretation of his allegorical poem?

Symptomatically, the tone of the author's *envoi* at the end of *PVH2* seems hesitant at best. Far from expressing any confidence in the revised version's ability to clear up any previous misunderstandings once and for all, the author anticipates further interpretive slippage and misreading, reiterating the warnings he had placed at the end of *PVH1* (13,517–18; 13,525–6). Deguileville repeats his original appeal to readerly indulgence, since truth is inextricably entangled with lies:

mon aventureux songe,	If any lies are have become entangled in
Ouquel s'aucune mençonge	my eventful dream . . . nobody ought to
Est meslee ou contenue	be surprised, since it is very rare to see
[. . .]	any wheat grow without some hay
Nul merveillier ne [s'en] devroit,	around it, until one has extracted the
Car onques forment on ne voit	wheat.
Croistre qui entour paille n'ait	
Jusqu'à tant que hors on l'en trait.	
(*PVH2* 17,732–9)	

This is yet another alarming echo of the *Rose*, with its endemic and ironic evocations of the blurring of 'songe/mençonge' (cf. *RR* 1–2; 9853–4; 18,463–4), pointing to its self-conscious, deliberately mystifying compounding of truth and lies that characterizes both the allegorical mode and erotically induced dream-visions.[140] If anything, the anxiety is exacerbated. The author no longer insists just on the potentially flawed status of the vision, but now highlights the hermeneutic instability of the *text*. Despite the poet's numerous and obsessive attempts to stabilize the interpretation of the allegory—through intradiegetic glossing, citation, disambiguation, and exposition—the meaning of the poem continues to depend on the reader's interpretive efforts. In its closing lines, Deguileville thus exhorts the reader to winnow the wheat from the chaff, sorting out the truth from the tissue of lies:

je commet aus bons venneurs	And so I commit myself to the good
Qui scevent hors venner erreurs.	winnowers, who are able to winnow
(*PVH2* 17,750–1)	out any mistakes.

The motif of the winnowed 'wheat' and 'chaff' is, of course, highly conventional. Yet as a concluding remark in a poem that not only aspires to train the interpretive abilities of its readers, but also provides a running commentary to ensure the adequacy of that very interpretation, the appeal amounts to an admission of impotence in the face of the inherent slippages of allegory. The image also acquires

---

[140] On the issue, see especially Huot, *Dreams of Lovers*; and Stakel, *False Roses*; and above, Chapter 1.4. On Deguileville's concern with Oiseuse/Huiseuse as a figure blurring the boundaries of truth and lies, see Chapter 3.3. On the history of the topical rhyme *songe/mensonge* before the *Rose*, see Renate Blumenfeld-Kosinski, 'Remarques sur *Songe/Mensonge*', Romania 101 (1980), 885–90.

304   MEDIEVAL ALLEGORY AS EPISTEMOLOGY

an additional level of unintentional irony when read against the background of the *Rose*, where the motif of the 'wheat and chaff' (*grain* and *paille*, *RR* 11,787) is carefully and systematically deconstructed, along with a range of other integumental and hermeneutic binary pairs (see Chapter 1.4). Read against the *Rose*'s poetics of Faux Semblant, Deguileville's appeal to the skill of the winnowing reader thus sounds increasingly like a desperate last resort. A similar latent irony also undermines the repeated use of metaphors of organic growth in *PVH1* and *PVH2*, specifically in the prologue of the revised *PVH2*, where Deguileville discusses the need to prune back the stray tendrils of his first 'draft'. Metaphors of growth and flowering abound throughout the *Rose*—a poem whose central, and most elusive signifier is itself an equivocal 'flower'. The poem ends with the scattering of sexual/semantic 'seed' (*greine*) during the defloration scene, which functions as an affirmation of the *Rose*'s own ability to engender a potentially infinite 'expansion' of semantic meanings (*RR* 21,690, see Chapters 1.5 and 2.5). Such images draw on widely established motifs: poetic ornamentation, for instance, was widely represented in terms of efflorescence, especially in the tradition of the *flores rhetorici*—a motif that Jean self-consciously references throughout his poem, as I have argued above (see Chapter 2.3). Augustine too had spoken of the ambiguities of figurative language in terms of sprawling vegetative growth: in cases of *aequivoca*, where 'things [. . .] which can be contained in one name and not one definition', 'the tangle of ambiguity grows wildly into infinity'.[141]

Deguileville's poem seeks to harness and control this excess of semantic meanings engendered by poetic figures. In the opening lines of the poem, for instance, Deguileville sets out to re-appropriate and 're-evangelize' the semantic field of seeds and sowing, describing how the doctors of the Church scatter the grain of the word: 'semence [. . .] espandoient' (*PVH1* 108).[142] Later in the poem Raison attempts to recuperate the motif of sprawling organic growth in order to defend the superabundant interpretive possibilities offered by Scripture in her argument with Rude Entendement: Raison speaks of the Gospel as a 'gracious place', made more 'pleasant' by the presence of 'diverse flowers' (*PVH1* 5526–40; see discussion in Chapter 2.3). While this motif survives unaltered in *PVH2*, the idea clearly comes under increased pressure, and the overall tone of this passage has lost the confident playfulness of *PVH1*. As Fabienne Pomel has noted in here comparative reading of the Rude Entendement episode in the two version, the poet's attitude in *PVH2* is far less relaxed in the face of misreadings and miscommunication: the rewriting

---

[141] 'Diximus enim aequivoca esse, quae non ut unum nomine ita etiam una definitione possunt teneri'; 'Nunc aequivoca videamus, in quibus ambiguitatum perplexio prope infinita silvescit' (*De dialectica* X.17 ed. Pinborg trans. Jackson; translation emended). The remark occurs within a wider discussion of linguistic obscurity and ambiguity, and Augustine tellingly represents such interpretive difficulties in terms of his recurrent pilgrimage symbolism: 'obscurity is similar to ambiguity, as when someone who is walking on a road comes upon a junction with two, three, or even more forks of the road, but can see none of them on account of the thickness of a fog' (*De dialectica*, VIII.14).

[142] As discussed by Huot, *The Romance of the Rose and its Medieval Readers*, p. 210.

of this scene is characterized by a 'soupçon persistant de duplicité', and the poet sternly warns of 'le péril du plaisir détaché du profit qui pèse [...] insidieusement sur l'esthétique allégorique'.[143] The encounter with Rude Entendement now loses its humorous tone, as Deguileville's commitment to root out any potential ambiguities from his allegory stifles any potential for ironic slippage and linguistic play in his poem.

PVH2's increasing defensiveness about linguistic slippage and equivocation is widely apparent throughout the poem, and may even be said to constitute its principal tonal shift in comparison with *PVH1*. This is particularly evident due to the newly multiplied instances of textual corruption and scriptural misreading that saturate the poem. This is not an entirely new concern, and was already present in *PVH1*: Heresy too—like Rude Entendement before her—had threatened to interrupt the pilgrim's journey by depriving him of his scrip and staff (*PVH1* 11,517–18), objecting to the 'crooked' articles of Faith inscribed on the little bells of the scrip:

'Es clochetes vois escripture	'On those bells I see writing that
Qui selonc ma regardeure	according to my eye is not at all written
N'est a point n'a droit escripte.'	rightly [lit. 'straight'].'
(*PVH1* 11,524–6)	[my translation]

Heresy is not content with misreading the inscription, and seeks to alter or efface the text itself—perverting *escripture* through her skewed, crooked *lecture*:[144]

'Selonc ce que voi de l'ueil,	'According to what I see with my eye, I
Les escriptures corrigiees	want all these writings to be corrected,
Soient du tout ou despeciees.'	or torn into little pieces.'
(*PVH1* 11,532–4)	[translation emended]

The pilgrim counters that it is not so much the text itself that is crooked, but Heresy's own gaze, once more introducing the analogy between distorted perception and deviant textual interpretation:

'L'escripture est escripte a droit,	'The writing is written perfectly
mais pas n'i regardes a droit.	correctly [lit. 'straight'], but you do not
De borgnes ieulz et traversains	look at them correctly. With only one
Ne puet estre regart bien sains.'	squinting eye, it is impossible to have a
(*PVH1* 11,527–30)	good vision.'
	[translation emended]

---

[143] Pomel, 'L'épisode de Rude Entendement', in Kablitz and Peters, p. 279.

[144] I allude to Genius's allegorization of both homosexuality and sexual continence as unnatural acts of 'misreading', where readers 'pervertissent l'escriture / quand ils viennent à la lecture', *RR* 19,631–2. See further Chapter 1.5.

306 MEDIEVAL ALLEGORY AS EPISTEMOLOGY

The encounter with Heresy is maintained but amplified in *PVH2*, where the implicit analogy between visual impairment, misinterpretation, and the *viator*'s loss of textual/interpretive orientation is more fully developed:

'Heresie suis nommee	'I am called Heresy, persisting in my
En mes erreurs affermee,	error. I always observe the path of those
Qui vois tousjours a reculons	who move steadily forward from
Par rebourses oppinions,	behind, through contrary opinions,
La voie de ceulx guerpissant	and distorting scripture through my
Qui vont tousjours droit et avant	false gaze.'
En bestournant l'escripture	
Par ma fausse regardeure,	
(*PVH2* 12,355–62)	

Similar concerns with interpretive, semiotic, and representational error also emerge from the encounters with a host of new characters, unique to *PVH2*, such as Necromancy, Astrology, Geomancy, Idolatry, Sorcery, Conspiracy, and Esbatement mondain (11,967–14,697).[145] Necromancy and her messenger, for instance, are both characterized by their ability to pervert language and to create fanciful, deceptive semiotic systems. So the pilgrim hears

une personne qui crioit	A person who was screaming and
Moult estrangement et parloit.	speaking most bizarrely. It was neither
François ou latin point ne fu	French nor Latin, nor any language
Ne langage a moi cogneü.	known to me.
(*PVH2* 11,979–82)	

Necromancy's messenger displays 'a large and hideous circle', covered in deviant and obscure signs, figures, and characters [un cercle grant et lé / De pluseurs figures signé, *PVH2* 11,995–6; also 12,077–9], designed to summon evil spirits (*PVH2* 12,177–9). Necromancy's deceptive and fanciful magic symbols thus ultimately provide a counterpoint to—and negation of—Deguileville's meditation on the intrinsic, Isidorian signifying properties of the letters in his abecedarian poems (see Chapter 4.2). Necromancy's ability to invoke mysterious forces 'through mysterious and disguised names' [Par noms estranges deguisiés, *PVH2* 12,091] finally amounts to a blasphemous perversion of the salvific function of language, concealing diabolical learning under the semblance of authorized, orthodox documents carrying the seal of royal authority:[146]

---

[145] Pomel, 'Rude Entendement', pp. 283–4.
[146] The idea also plays on Deguileville's recurrent use of Royal authority as trope for the authority of the Gospel in his poetry.

'Bien voi, dis je, qu'es messagier	'I can easily see, I said, that you are the
Du roy, demander ne le quier:	King's messenger, and there is no need
A ses armes t'ai cogneü	for me to ask you: I recognized you
Et a ses robes qu'as vestu.'	based on your arms, and from the robes
(*PVH2* 12,131–4)	you wear.'

Finally the pilgrim concludes that Necromancy's messenger has forged such royal *insigna* [faussaire . . . Du roy, *PVH2* 12,159–60], counterfeiting official marks of authority found in royal seals ('sëaux', *PVH2* 12,180–1). The passage thus addresses questions of semiotic misuse, obscurity, and dissimulation, but also gives voice to a wider anxiety about the falsification of authoritative documents. This concern over the authority and authenticity of texts and documents is particularly troubling given Deguileville's own complaint over 'textual expropriation' in the poem's new prologue, and the more broadly textual/documentary nature of his self-authorizing strategies.[147]

The encounter with Astrology again revolves around a series of semiotic issues concerning the signifying power of the stars as signs (*PVH2* 13,649–836). As if to signal the strongly semiotic turn of the poem in this section, Deguileville again refers to a stock example found in scholastic treatises on semiotics—a tavern's sign displaying barrel hoops ('cercel', *PVH2* 13,687, also 13,675; also 14,379; cf. *PVH1* 8453–6, see further Chapter 2.2). During the dispute with Astrology the pilgrim questions the signifying power of the stars, but also challenges the authority of the document—the written 'commission' (*PVH2* 13,551), 'written, sealed, and read' [Escript seellé et lëu, *PVH2* 13,558]—which entitles Astrology to practise her arts of divination. The commission turns out to be the text of Genesis, and the pilgrim rectifies its interpretation: he denies any divinatory signifying power to the stars beyond their ability to mark the passing of time and reveal the will of God (*PVH2* 13,640–8). Other personifications complete the picture by crystallizing related problems: Geomancy traces cryptic marks in the sand as means of divination, and is similarly misled by false characters (*PVH2* 13,923–14,004). Next the pilgrim meets Idolatry (*PVH2* 14,025–190), who embodies yet another form of (carnal) misreading by speaking 'obscure words, with duplicitous meaning' [mot trouble / Qui entendement ait double, *PVH2* 14,085–6]—an idea amply explored already in the *Rose* (cf. Chapter 3.4).[148] As in the previous encounter with Heresy, concerns over the orthodoxy of devotional practices are viewed essentially as resulting from erroneous textual interpretation and troubled perception and understanding.

This last encounter with Heresy triggers a wider discussion of the representational status of religious art, which the pilgrim redefines as books for the unlearned

---

[147] See especially Pomel, 'Les écrits pérégrins'; and Kamath, *Authorship and First-person Allegory*, pp. 19–58.

[148] See also Morton, *The 'Roman de la Rose' in its Philosophical Context*, pp. 143–70.

308   MEDIEVAL ALLEGORY AS EPISTEMOLOGY

(*PVH2* 14,163–4).[149] This parallel concern with the status of images as well as texts persists throughout this section, and the pilgrim next encounters Sorcery, who wields various writings and images [escrits et divers ymages, *PVH2* 14,237] among other mysterious trinkets. Sorcery conceives of man, *microcosmus*, as a cluster of signs that she proposes to decipher:

'Pour faire de li jugement:	'To pass judgment on him, I resort to
C'est le visage avec la main	the face and the hand, where I can find
Ou en prent jugement certain	clear indications of man and his
De l'omme et ses condicions,'	condition.'
(*PVH2* 14,312–15)	

Yet the pilgrim reiterates his earlier objections to the kind of determinism propounded by Astrology, and finally denies any signifying power to the human body as a divinatory sign:

'Si n'est il nul qui preïst fons	'And therefore nobody should conclude
Pour conclurre nécessité	that it is necessary for us to carry such
D'estre par droit ainsi signé	signs, since signs are bound to fail.'
Car les signes puent faillir,'	
(*PVH2* 14,374–7)	

Like the barrel hoops displayed outside a tavern, Deguileville tells us—using the motif for the third time in this section of *PVH2*—any such signs are inherently misleading (*PVH2* 14,378–82), and the human body can never serve as a divinatory sign. Here too, then, the controversy over superstitious practices of divination is presented as a debate on semiotics and interpretation.

This ubiquitous concern with misreading and mystification fits with the general tone of *PVH2*, characterized by the poet's obsessive concern with ensuring adequate interpretation of his own poem, in the wake of the troubled reception history of *PVH1* evoked in the new prologue (*PVH2* 19–94).[150] All of the newly added personifications that populate this section of the poem accordingly crystallize different kinds of misreading and/or textual manipulation—from Necromancy's falsification of royal writs and her use of mysterious 'figures et de caras' (*PVH2* 12,077), to Astrology's putative 'commission' (*PVH2* 13,551) entitling her to decipher the signification of the stars, in turn based on her misreading of Genesis, and Sorcery's blind trust in all kinds of 'escrits et divers ymages' (*PVH2* 14,237). The multiplication of such instances of potential misreading in *PVH2*, however, often seems counterproductive: they embroil the poem's 'I'—simultaneously

---

[149] Readers were clearly sensitive to such concerns, which are developed further also in Lydgate's translation from 1427, in the context of the controversy over religious images in post-Arundel English religious culture, on which see Shannon Gayk, *Image, Text, and Religious Reform in Fifteenth-Century England* (Cambridge: Cambridge University Press, 2010), pp. 88–95.

[150] See for instance Pomel, *Les voies*, pp. 524–7; Maupeu, *Pèlerins de vie humaine*, pp. 199–207.

protagonist, reader, and author/narrator—in a number of digressive, laborious, and defensive elucidations and explanations. This also raises the question of the authority and authenticity of textual/documentary evidence provided elsewhere in the poem, so often employed by the pilgrim in his effort to assert his authority against his opponents: what exactly can guarantee the truthfulness, authenticity, and salvific efficacy of the pilgrim's own writs and commissions—such as Christ's Testament of Peace inscribed on the carpenter's square (*PVH1* 2618–20; *PVH2* 2689–93), the *laissez-passer* carried by Raison (*PVH1* 5177–8; *PVH2* 7041–6), or indeed the ABC prayer conveyed by Grace Dieu (*PVH1* 10,893–11,192; *PVH2* 13,051–350)—in a poem increasingly saturated by false, ambiguous, or mendacious documents and commissions?[151] Far from compounding the authority of the narrative voice, then, the multiplication of such 'elucidations', qualifications, and disclaimers on the narrator's part often feels forced, defensive, and overstated, pointing to a much deeper, underlying anxiety about the loss of authorial and interpretive control over the allegory. While this anxiety is undoubtedly conditioned by the negative responses to his first poem, it also points to Deguileville's much deeper loss of confidence in his own ability to control and regulate the mechanisms of allegorical interpretation.

5. The Breakdown of Language and the Experiential Subject

By the time of *PVH2*, then, the poet's desire for an unambiguous and seamless language of participation has mutated into a pervasive anxiety over linguistic ambiguity and equivocation. The problem acquires still more threatening proportions with the figure of Agiographe, whom the pilgrim meets inside the monastery. The inclusion of Agiographe marks a major change from *PVH1*: there the gift of the ABC Prayer, the pilgrim's conversion, and his subjection to the monastic vows had allowed him to transcend the hermeneutic, semiotic, and epistemic challenges that characterized his earlier, inconclusive wanderings through a secular *regio dissimilitudinis*. With the figure of Agiographe, however, such problems follow him into the monastery. This highlights Deguileville's waning confidence in the ability of monastic life to provide a safe enclosure for the silent, mystical, and sapiential 'tasting' of transcendent truth through the contemplative experience of the inner Word. While this need not necessarily undermine Deguileville's belief in the incarnational possibilities opened up by the language of prayer and scripture, it exposes the inability of monastic institutions to 'contain' and preserve such a language effectively, and the failure of such institutions to prefigure a state of eschatological

---

[151] On Deguileville's troubled 'documentary poetics' see especially Steiner, *Documentary Culture*, pp. 36–46 and *passim*; Pomel, 'Les écrits pérégrins'.

310   MEDIEVAL ALLEGORY AS EPISTEMOLOGY

self-identity. This finally forces Deguileville to relocate the Word incarnate to the still more exiguous, internalized personal spaces of his late Latin lyrics.

The pilgrim's encounter with Agiographe interrupts his conversation with Leçon/Estude, and once more raises a range of problems associated with textual interpretation, specifically scriptural exegesis. Agiographe personifies the study of religious texts, and she is subsequently identified with Holy Scripture [Sainte Escripture, *PVH2* 15,453]. But the allegorical and moral significance of the character of Agiographe is far from unambiguous, and fittingly the first thing we learn about her is that she is 'mispartie', divided into two sides: one is obscure, the other dressed in light (*PVH2* 15,169–74). Initially this is explained as an image of the bipartition of the Scriptural text, divided into the Old and New Testaments, darkness and light (*PVH2* 15,225–8). But there is also a second, more complex and troubling interpretation of Agiographe's bipartition. Among the merchandise she offers on her stall we find numerous mirrors (*PVH2* 15,163–8; 15,255–60), many of them deforming (*PVH2* 15,304–18). Two in particular are singled out by the Pilgrim: the first is 'Word of Adulation' [parole d'adulacion, *PVH2* 15,331], the second 'Mirror of Conscience' [miroir de conscience, *PVH2* 15,429].[152] It is the latter mirror, of course, that provides the pilgrim with an accurate self-image, echoing earlier discussions of divine likeness and deformity in terms of mirroring and resemblance (e.g. *PVH1* 5813–26 and 5935–6022; *PVH2* 6319–32 and 6457–542; see Chapters 2.1, 2.3, 3.3, and 3.4).[153] It is here that he can find

vraie experience	A true experience of the revelation of
De monstrer sens menterie,	one's face—without dissimulation,
Sens echo de flaterie,	without echoes of flattery. You shall see
Quel face on a et visage,	a true image of who you are, of what
Quel on est, a quel ymage	your face is like, and you will be figured
On est pourtrait et figuré,	and portrayed, and see how deformed
Et en quoi on est deffourmé.	you are.
(*PVH2* 15,430–6)	

The Mirror of Adulation, by contrast, reflects deceptive words and images, again associating visual and linguistic deception: 'Flattering speech, bred by lies' [Parlement de Flaterie / Engendré de Menterie, *PVH2* 15,333–4]. As well as reflecting the flattery and self-righteousness of degenerate aristocratic Lords (*PVH2* 15, 389–96), the mirror also reflects a cosmetically modified, inflated, but ultimately false self-image for individual gazers:

---

[152] For an evocative illustration of the two mirrors from London, British Library, MS Cotton Tiberius A7, see Hagen, *Allegorical Remembrance*, figs 48, 49, and 50.
[153] In what follows I also draw from Legaré and Pomel, 'Les Miroirs', pp. 137–9.

EXPERIENCE 311

[. . .] leur mespresures	All their trespasses they want to be
Veulent que soient mirees	falsely mirrored and observed, and they
Faussement et regardees,	want the mirror to tell them they are
Que le mirouour les die	beautiful, whereas they aren't at all.
Belles, et ne le sont mie.	
(*PVH2* 15,262–6)	

Predictably, the Pilgrim immediately takes advantage of this wondrous yet deceptive mirror, colouring and glossing over his moral and spiritual deformity:

Le premier me print a farder	The first one started to cover up and
Et a mon visage paindre	paint my face, covering it with feigned
Et dessus tel beauté faindre,	beauty.
(*PVH2* 15,282–4)	

The cosmetic and mendacious qualities of the mirror clearly recall the earlier mirror carried by Huiseuse, in turn echoing the Mirror of Narcissus from the *Rose* (see Chapters 3.3 and 3.4). Agiographe confirms this by admitting that her mirror of Adulation is in reality identical with the mirror carried by Orgueil (*PVH2* 9953–92), previously encountered along the path of Huiseuse:

'Jadis tu le veïs pourter,	'You have seen this mirror before—if
Se tu t'en veuls bien recorder,	you care to remember—carried by the
A la vielle que chevauchoit	old riding hag, Pride, who carried the
Orgueil qui le souflet portoit.	bellows. Some call her Placebo, since
Aucuns l'appellent Placebo,	she knows how to repeat what she hears
Pour ce que scet bien faire echo	being said to whoever is her master.'
En redisant ce qu'ot dire	
A cellui qui est son sire.'	
(*PVH2* 15,335–42)	

While there is nothing new or surprising about the operation of this mirror, its placement in the hands of Agiographe—personification of Holy Scripture— is particularly unsettling. During its earlier appearance the mirror had provided a fitting emblem for the pilgrim's fall into carnal misreading (see Chapter 3.4), but its reappearance *inside* the monastic cloister—*after* the pilgrim has sought refuge from the *regio dissimilitudinis* of worldly existence—is far more troubling. In *PVH2*, it seems, the pilgrim's conversion to monasticism and his sapiential experience of the living *logos* no longer allows him to evacuate the threat of duplicity and falsification. On the contrary, the encounter with the living Word within the cloister now provides further opportunities for self-deception and self-alienation. Agiographe/Escripture's adoption of the mirror effectively turns the scriptural

312   MEDIEVAL ALLEGORY AS EPISTEMOLOGY

text itself into a potential site for the projection of a false self-image, artificially enhanced by spiritual *superbia*.[154]

No doubt aware of the problem, Deguileville places a characteristically convoluted and defensive 'elucidation' in the mouth of Agiographe. She apparently wields Orgueil's mirror not to deceive, but rather to warn all Christian pilgrims about its dangers:

'Nullui je n'en veul decepvoir,	'I do not wish to deceive anyone with it,
Mes les decevances de voir	but I rather want to openly reveal its
Je vueil monstrer appertement.'	duplicity to everyone.'
(*PVH2* 15,301–3)	

The phrase perfectly encapsulates the representational conundrum of *PVH2* as a whole, determined by the poet's dogged determination to reveal *apertement* the nature of *decevances* without deceiving his readers. Considering that the poem is itself a 'biau miroir de sauvement', attentive readers cannot fail to identify the latent paradox—or, to borrow Jean de Meun's words, the 'sophism that poisons the conclusion' [soffime / qui la consequance envenime, *RR* 12,113–14]. Despite the poet's additional efforts to disambiguate the significance of his own didactic *speculum*, then, his message remains inevitably caught up in a duplicitous allegorical mirror, by turns 'miroir de conscience' (*PVH2* 15,429) and 'parole d'adulacion' (*PVH2* 15,331). Deguileville's laborious amplifications and 'elucidations' in this section of the poem are thus fundamentally counterproductive, insistently reminding us that the poem itself remains caught within an inescapably compromised, equivocal double vision. The reader is finally unable to escape an equivocal double reality reminiscent of the archetypal 'miroërs perillus'—the *Roman de la Rose* (*RR* 1569)—similarly framed by the duplicitous mirror containing twin crystals, and refracting an irreducibly double reality (*RR* 1536–1612).

The presence of a such a 'self-divided' (*mispartie*) personification as Agiographe/Sainte Escripture *within* the monastery walls fractures the rhetoric of conceptual enclosure and self-identity that dominated *PVH1*: the slippages of language, allegory, and signification have now caught up with the *viator*'s 'I' in the very space that had previously enabled it to seek refuge from duplicity and ambiguity. The problem is not limited to Agiographe, however, and a group of further characters disrupt this rhetoric of enclosure much further in *PVH2*: Envie, Trahison, Detraction, and Scilla/Conspiracion all break into the cloister (*PVH2* 15,980–16,393), and carry out a particularly vicious and violent attack upon the pilgrim, pulling him down from his horse Bon Non (Renown, *PVH2* 15,952). Apart from Scilla/Conspiracion, the characters are not entirely new, and the pilgrim had encountered the other three in *PVH1* along the path of Huiseuse (*PVH1*

---

[154] *PVH2* as a whole is characterized by an intensified concern with Pride, see also Maupeu, *Pèlerins de vie humaine*, pp. 189–90.

EXPERIENCE   313

8191 ff; *PVH2* 9993 ff.). But only in *PVH2* do the three deformed crones return to attack the Pilgrim a second time, *inside* the walls of the monastery, led by the newly added Scilla/Conspiracion. The walls of the monastery have now become literally permeable, and the contemplative enjoyment of the Word through prayer, devotion, and the liturgy is disturbed by a whole range of personifications that *PVH1* had safely relegated to the secular world outside the cloister.

Elaborating on Faral's suggestions, Philippe Maupeu interprets this second attack in terms of topical, autobiographical references to Deguileville's own real-life experiences within the monastery of Chaalis. These autobiographical allusions remain cryptic and obscure, and we can only speculate about the real events figured by the second attack by Envie, Trahison, Detraction, and Scilla/Conspiracion. As Philippe Maupeu has argued, the onslaught of the quartet alludes to an attack that Deguileville himself suffered at the hands of others.[155] This is an important shift, since the allegory here abandons the strictly psychomachic register, where personifications visualize internal, latent possibilities within the 'I' as a figure for the Christian Everyman. Envy and her acolytes here clearly denote the actions of other, historical persons upon the poet, and the 'I' of *PVH2* is no longer shaped by inner, moral and cognitive struggles alone, but becomes the object of attacks from the outside world. This is particularly alarming since the attack takes place *within* the seemingly protective atmosphere of the cloister, and Deguileville stresses this repeatedly by situating the actions clearly within the 'chastel' (*PVH2* 15,909; 15,920; 15,925; 16,175; 16,219; 16,229; 16,335). The attack completely transforms the status of the poem's 'I' and the narrative mode of the poem itself. In Maupeu's phrase, *PVH2* now crystallizes 'un sujet agi par son histoire et non acteur de celle-ci'. This new attack accordingly therefore becomes for Maupeu the new 'epicentre of the poem', triggering the shift away from the depersonalized and universalizing register of allegory towards the particularizing mode of autobiographical self-representation.[156]

More importantly in the present context, the attack of the four *vieilles* in *PVH2* is of a specifically *linguistic* nature: slander, conspiracy, unfounded accusation, and persecution, denoted primarily by the barking and biting of the dogs of Conspiracion and Detraction (e.g. *PVH2* 14,409–14,444).[157] The violence of the attack is unprecedented, and particularly shocking given *PVH2*'s tendency to tone down

[155] In what follow I largely summarize Maupeu's points, see *Pèlerins de vie humaine*, 80–96, 197–214, 257–63.

[156] Quotations from Maupeu, *Pèlerins de vie humaine*, pp. 214 and 257. See also Philippe Maupeu, 'La tentation autobiographique dans le songe allégorique édifiant de Guillaume de Digulleville: *Le pèlerinage de Vie Humaine*', in Nathalie Dauvois and Jean-Philippe Grosperrin, eds, *Songes et Songeurs (XIIIe–XVIIIe siècle)*. Laval: Presses de l'Université de Laval, 2003, pp. 49–67.

[157] On the place of detraction within the traditional structure of the 'sins of the mouth/tongue', and its consistent association with barking dogs—including numerous references to Deguileville's *PA* and the *Rose*—see especially Giacomo Gambale, '"Par langue les livre a martire . . .": La *potestas nocendi* de la parole', in Bériou, Boudet, and Rosier-Catach, eds, *Le pouvoir des mots au Moyen Âge*, pp. 363–77. Further on the recurrent association between biting dogs and detraction, see also Maupeu, *Pèlerins de*

314 MEDIEVAL ALLEGORY AS EPISTEMOLOGY

the violence of the other sins and to attribute greater will power to the pilgrim. Previous commentators have explained this detail with reference to a range of implied suggestions that can be gleaned from the poem. Deguileville appears to have become involved with some form of legal proceedings within the Cistercian order, which resulted in his having to restore his reputation against malicious and unwarranted slander.[158] Several commentators have also suggested that Deguileville's difficulties appear to have arisen in conjunction with his authorship of *PVH1*— a poem that may have been perceived as unorthodox or doctrinally unsound.[159] This appears to explain Deguileville's determination to produce an amended, officially authorized and doctrinally more circumspect version of his poem, as well as his obsessive determination to ensure an adequate, 'correct' interpretation of the allegory on the part of his readers, as emerges from the new prologue to *PVH2*.[160] More recently Moreau has proposed a compelling reading of the pilgrim's lawsuit proceedings in front of the Tribunal of Saint Michael in *PA*—the 'continuation' of the revised *PVH2*—arguing that *PA* as a whole 'offers further support for the idea that the author himself faced some kind of condemnation for his writing'.[161] Deguileville certainly makes a consistent effort to tighten the doctrinal underpinnings of the revised poem, presenting a more nuanced account of the tensions between grace and free will, avoiding the extreme anti-Pelagianism of *PVH1*, where the individual will was completely and utterly dependent on the actions of grace.[162]

In the present context, the precise circumstances of Deguileville's condemnation and rehabilitation are of secondary importance. What matters most for my present argument is that beneath the cryptic autobiographical references that abound in this section of the poem we can discern a much deeper and more pervasive concern with the breakdown of language, representation, and interpretation, and that such a concern appears to be directly linked to the hostile reception of Deguileville's earliest poem, *PVH1*. The linguistic character of Envie, Detraction, and Trahison is already established during their first appearance along the path of Huiseuse in *PVH1*—retained with minor modifications in *PVH2*. Like other

---

vie humaine, pp. 190–1, quoting Mireille Vincent-Cassy, 'L'Envie au Moyen Âge', *Annales ESC* 1 (1980), 253–71.

[158] Maupeu, *Pèlerins de vie humaine*, pp. 87–96, 197–214, 257–63; Moreau, '"Ce mauvais tabellion"'; ibid., *Eschatological Subjects*, pp. 70–80, 84–7; Faral, *Guillaume de Deguileville*, pp. 29, 9–10; *PVH2*, ed. Edwards and Maupeu, 'Introduction'. Deguileville appears to have lost the lawsuit, which alienated him from the order or even led to his excommunication. Maupeu also evokes the possibility of the author's condemnation for necromancy, yet the specific circumstances or accusations seem difficult to reconstruct.

[159] Faral, *Guillaume de Deguileville*, pp. 29, 33.

[160] See Moreau, '"Ce mauvais tabellion"', pp. 113–28 (113–14); ibid., *Eschatological Subjects*, pp. 84–7. See also Kamath, *Authorship and First-Person Allegory*, p. 83.

[161] Moreau, '"Ce mauvais tabellion"', p. 115.

[162] Maupeu, *Pèlerins de vie humaine*, pp. 178, 190, 262–5; also *PA* may be seen as participating in that effort, see Pomel, *Les voies*, pp. 413–15.

sins, the personifications themselves are disfigured, as if to visualize their tendency to abuse, deform, and distort reality—text, speech, and perceptive/cognitive acts: two spears are projected outward from Envy's eyes (*PVH2* 9999–10,000, 10,089–116), while Detraction carries a *brochette* of human ears (*PVH2* 10,020–21; 10,365–86). The two figures are particularly arresting since they provide a grotesque perversion of the normal operation of 'eyes' and 'ears'—key elements in the allegorical/conceptual vocabulary used by Deguileville to discuss cognitive, perceptual, and intellective processes (see Chapter 3.5). Trahison for her part speaks flattering 'words that are soft and unctuous' [paroles / qui seront oignans et moles, *PVH2* 102,009–10], and with her 'counterfeit face' [visage contrefait, *PVH2* 10,173] is a master in the arts of dissimulation. Detraction can 'transform the good into bad, and interpret it falsely' [le bien en mal muer / Et faussement entrepreter, *PVH2* 10,349–50], but also, significantly, performs various feats of perverted, pseudo-Eucharistic trans-substantiation, already discussed (see Chapter 3.4). This last detail is particularly alarming given that in *PVH2* Detraction also infiltrates the monastic enclosure, which in *PVH1* had provided a safe space for the consumption of the eucharistic, sapiential 'sweet and wholesome meat' of Scripture [douce et bonne viande, *PVH1* 12,834, see Chapter 4.2]. The symbolism is preserved in *PVH2* (15,154), but Estude's speech on her own ability to carry the wholesome, nourishing 'flesh' of scripture in a parchment vessel is now interrupted—significantly—by the appearance of a self-divided, duplicitous Agiographie/Escripture (*PVH2* 15,135–94). The irruption of the quartet of old crones into the monastery later in the passage further destabilizes the sacramental, Eucharistic focus on the Word made Flesh, suggesting that Deguileville here denounces problems that transcend his strictly 'autobiographical' concerns. What begins as a relatively anecdotal and localized complaint over personal misfortune and persecution gradually mutates into an extended meditation on the declining moral standards in Deguileville's own Abbey of Chaalis and within monasticism more broadly.

This wider concern with the erosion of monastic discipline is evident also from other details in this section. The attack occurs while the Porter of the 'castle', Paour the Dieu, is asleep (*PVH2* 15,915; 16,335). Since *timor domini est initium sapientiae*—a ubiquitous monastic *dictum* paraphrased by Paour de Dieu himself (*PVH2* 15,085–6)—clearly Deguileville here refers to a perceived 'loosening' of the monastic rule within the order. Paour de Dieu had insisted that if any sin were to penetrate within the cloister this could only occur 'in spite of me, secretly and through subterfuge' [maugré moi / Repostement et en requoi, *PVH2* 15,091–2]—a remark carried over from *PVH1* (12,587–8), but which acquires a newly ominous resonance here. After entering the monastery, Envie and her gang cause the personified monastic virtues to flee [esbaïr / Firent les dames et fuïr, *PVH2* 15,927–8]—and soon the remaining ladies are imprisoned and immobilized:

316   MEDIEVAL ALLEGORY AS EPISTEMOLOGY

Charité estoit liee	Charity was tied up, and closely
Et forment emprisonnee,	imprisoned, and also Mercy, as I can
Et aussi Misericorde,	distinctly remember, so that they did
Si com tresbien m'en recorde,	not come to me at all, and could not do
Que point a moi ne venissent,	any good for me. And all this was
Et que bien ne me feïssent.	caused by Scilla.
Et tout ce fist faire Scilla.	
(*PVH2* 16,049–55)	

Allegorically speaking, this denotes the paralysis of the devotional and liturgical activities within the monastery itself. The attackers' nature as linguistic sins in particular brings to a halt the monastic routine of prayer, devotion, and *lectio divina*, and fractures the sacramental, incarnational order of language that structures cloistered life. The attack accordingly leads to a decline in Eucharistic fruition, as the monastic community follows Abusion in averting its gaze from the sacrament of the altar:

Point ne regarde devant li	She never looks in front of herself, nor
Ne comment est le roi servi	observes how the King is being
Qui a ce tresprincipaument	worshipped, although that ought to be
Deust entendre et ardamment	her primary and ardent duty.
(*PVH2* 16,594–7)	

While Deguileville uses such a picture to situate his own, personal complaint (esp. 16,065–90), the problems he denounces clearly exceed a narrowly autobiographical concern. Indeed, the poet emphatically renounces any possibility of personal vengeance, introduced with the appearance of Ovid as a character in the poem (*PVH2* 16,081–125). Rehearsing extracts from his own curse-poem *Ibis*, the Latin poet offers to cast a similar curse upon the heads of Deguileville's treacherous 'friends': the pilgrim, however, kindly declines the offer, preferring to defer judgement to the court of heaven (*PVH2* 16,120–25)[163]—unmistakable proleptic allusion to the events narrated in *PA*. Instead the pilgrim produces a poem of his own, of a very different kind (*PVH2* 16,142–16,333): a bilingual complaint containing an account of his own suffering, and crystallizing the poet's own name in the shape of an acrostic: 'GVILLERMUS DE DEGUILEUILLA'. Here, again, emphasis is placed not on the centrality of the authorial subject, but on his marginal, 'eccentric' position in relation to the broader changes affecting the communal life in the monastery. Far from being the poem's central focus, the author's name is 'scriptus in margine' (*PVH2* 16,150), visualizing the author's 'marginal' presence in the process that is being described. The acrostic therefore does not so much affirm, let alone monumentalize, a specifically 'authorial' identity, but rather

---

[163] See discussion of this scene in Maupeu, *Pèlerins de vie humaine*, pp. 87–95, and Kamath, 'Rewriting Ancient *Auctores*'.

EXPERIENCE   317

crystallizes an 'I' whose autobiographical status is strictly apologetic and contingent, forced upon the poet by external events and by the actions and attacks of those around him.[164] The juxtaposition of French and Latin further highlights how the subjective, affective mode of complaint is doubled by a more formal, official, and apologetic mode of expression used to denounce the internal state of affairs within the order, and to exculpate the poet himself from unfounded accusations and uncontrolled slander.

Deguileville's concern with the rules of enclosed, monastic life more broadly, and particularly with the role of language in preserving such an order, is also evident in the events that follow (*PVH2* 16,395–17,113), where the pilgrim departs from his own monastery to visit other monasteries or 'castles' (*PVH2* 16,398–401):

Pour ce que vëoir vouloie	For I wanted to see what manner of
En quel maniere on y vivoit	living I could find there, and what sort
Et quelle l'ordenance estoit	of ordinances were being followed.
(*PVH2* 16,451–3)	

The visits prove to be instructive, and provide an enlarged perspective on the decline of monastic order and discipline. The pilgrim thus visits 'many places where I found great bounty and much religion' [mains liex . . . ou grant bonté / Trouvai et grant religion, *PVH2* 16,405–6], but the vast majority of the monasteries offer a desolate picture. At the first monastery he meets Grace Dieu again, who takes him on a brief tour:

Ou cloistre et par tout me mena	She took me to visit the whole cloister,
Et l'ediffice me monstra	and she showed me the building, which
Du lieu, qui estoit ruyneux	was in ruins and perilous to dwell in.
Et a demourer perilleux	
(*PVH2* 16,458–61)	

Since 'this place was spiritually built and established long ago by St Benedict' [jadis ce lieu ci maçonna / Espirituelment et fist / Saint Benoit, *PVH2* 16,473–5], the crumbling architectural structures denote the decline of monastic ideals and the dismantling of the dwelling place of the living Word.[165] The mason abandons his 'ruler' [ruile, *PVH2* 16,487], and the crumbling mortar of the building signifies the disintegration of monastic discipline, prayer, and communal devotional performance (*PVH2* 16,521–34). Such a vista of ruined monastic architecture gives way

---

[164] My view here differs from the arguments proposed by Kamath and Maupeu, who place greater emphasis on questions of authorial naming and literary self-fashioning. See Maupeu, *Pèlerins*, pp. 197–206; ibid., 'La tentation autobiographique'; Kamath, *Authorship and First-Person Allegory*, pp. 30–8, 45–57. Maupeu rightly notes, however, that Deguileville's authorial 'presence' is troubled and hesitant: while 'L'acrostiche [. . .] monumentalise [le nom de l'auctor] dans la chaîne de ses lettrines', his name remains '"scriptum in margine"', spoken by 'la voix de la Grâce [. . .] dont l'acrostiche n'est que l'écho', *Pèlerins de vie humaine*, pp. 204–5.

[165] On the widespread use of architectural symbolism to structure the work of monastic meditation, see especially Carruthers, *Craft of Thought*, pp. 7–24, 221–76.

318 MEDIEVAL ALLEGORY AS EPISTEMOLOGY

to a sequence of images of disrupted rectitude, and a loosening of structure, ordi-
nances, and devotion, eventually leading to a loss of monastic *stabilitas*. Ideas of
monastic stability, enclosure, permanence, and self-identity are replaced by images
of wandering, dissociation, and dislocation, plunging the *viator* back into a *regio
dissimilitudinis* he thought he had escaped:

Cloistre n'y a mais, ne Leçon,	There is neither cloister nor Study,
Discipline, ne Oroison;	Discipline, or Worship. Everyone
Chascun ou il veult va vaguier	wanders where they please.
(*PVH2* 16,546–8)	

Abusion embodies this process of dissolution of the inner unity of monasticism,
'removing herself from ancient unity and fraternity' [En soi ostant dë unité / Ancienne et fraternité, *PVH2* 16,638–9]. Finally the monastic *hortus conclusus* is left
uncultivated, and threatens to revert to a state of uncontrolled wilderness, 'like a
desert left uncultivated' [Com desert laissé sens cure, *PVH2* 16,579].

The spatial rhetoric that organizes monastic life as a structured enclosure is thus
dismantled, as if to signify the dissolution of the concentrated focus on the power
of the Word incarnate through *lectio divina*, prayer, and sacramental communion.
After an extended survey of the self-serving greed that contributes to undermine
the foundations of monasticism (*PVH2* 16,612–964), the pilgrim on his return
to his own monastery finally meets Apostasy. She too has fled the strictures of
monastic enclosure to roam freely (*PVH2* 17,010–12). Her disregard for monastic
obedience eventually compromises her very ability to speak:

en balbuciant me dist	Stuttering she told me that she had a
Que la langue fouchee avoit	forked tongue, and was struggling to
Et a malaise elle parlait.	speak. 'Formerly,' she said, 'I made
'Jadis, dist elle, je promis	great promises and great vows to the
Et grans veus et promesses fis	King, that I would serve him and
Au roy, que le serviroie	would always be one of his own; and I
Et tousjours a li seroie;	paid homage to him for this, both with
Et homage li fis pour ce,	my hands and with my mouth.'
Tant de mains comme de bouche'.	
(*PVH2* 16,991–9)	

Apostasy is therefore unable to participate in the daily routine of prayer, devotion,
and the liturgy, and finally manifests her utter loss of direct access to the salvific
power of the Word:

Ta langue aussi condempnee	Your tongue is therefore utterly
Est du tout et affolee.	condemned and confounded: it could
Dire ne pourroit oroison,	never sing the praises of the King or
Ne faire supplicacion	make a supplication . . . so that all your
Au roy [. . .]	words or deeds will be mere frivolities

Si que tes fais et paroles	to the King, as long as you persist in
Au roy ne sont que frivoles	this state.
Tant com en tel estat seras,	
(*PVH2* 17,062–70)	

The encounter with Apostasy concludes an extended section of *PVH2* where we also find the majority of alterations to the original narrative of *PVH1*. I have argued that the common theme of these changes is an exacerbated, obsessive concern with a whole range of semiotic troubles, specifically the slipperiness and potential misuse of language. Intervening at a moment in the narrative that in *PVH1* marked the pilgrim's deliverance from the cognitive and hermeneutic inconclusiveness that characterized his errance through the *regio dissimilitudinis* of a fallen secular existence, this extended section crystallizes an exacerbated epistemic anxiety and a declining confidence in the ability of language, in any of its forms, to serve unambiguously salvific ends. It is no longer allegory alone that appears problematic and duplicitous, but even forms of linguistic activity that previously enabled a safe and direct experience of the silent inner Word. *PVH2* thus also records a disillusion with religious institutions, encoded as an 'autobiographical' account of a slanderous attack on the poet's own craft, combined with a meditation on the decline of the devotional and linguistic order that structures the communal sapiential 'tasting' of the Word of scripture and the Eucharistic sacrament.

This disillusion with enclosed monastic life emerges with particular clarity from Deguileville's self-naming acrostic complaint. He redeploys the symbolism of the tonsure, which early in *PVH1* had served as a trope to visualize the state of fulfilled, protected existence to be attained in the monastery—'as though it were a castle or tower, it seems to be an enclosed court, surrounded by a high wall' [Aussi com fust chastel ou tour. / Bien semble [estre] un courtil ferme / De haut mur et environne, *PVH1* 892–4 and *PVH2* 1202–4][166]—and prefiguring the state of the blessed citizens of the New Jerusalem. Yet by 1355 this seamless, hermetically sealed protection afforded by the tonsure, cloister, or fortress appears fractured. The pilgrim/poet's 'I' now bitterly notes the futility of such an attempt to seek refuge in the cloister:

J'ai ma paine perdue	I wasted my efforts, and entered in vain
Et castrum supervacue	into this castle, to have my head
Pour avoir teste tondue	tonsured, and above everything else my
Intravi, nam praecipue	hope has been shattered.
M'esperance y est rompue.	
(*PVH2* 16,257–61)	

---

[166] See *PVH1* 889–900 (=*PVH2* 1201–12), and *PVH1* 917–20 (=*PVH2* 1229–32).

320 MEDIEVAL ALLEGORY AS EPISTEMOLOGY

In the following stanza, Deguileville evokes his personal frustration in sacramental terms, as an inability to partake in the 'fruition of the great harvest' (*fruerer magna messe*). Playing on the combined meanings of Latin and French *messe* ('harvest', and 'mass') he now announces his reluctant desire to depart from the cloister to perform his liturgical duties elsewhere:

Ut servirem virgae Iesse	As a servant of the branch of Jesse,
M'i mist Grace Dieu en lesse;	Grace Dieu took me under her wing,
Quod fruerer magna messe	and also promised me that I would
Me fist aussi grant promesse:	benefit from a rich harvest. But now I
Sed video nunc expresse,	see clearly, which pains me greatly, that
Dont grant douleur mon cuer presse,	it is necessary for me to go and sing my
Quod egredi est necesse	mass elsewhere.
Pour chanter ailleurs ma messe.	
(*PVH2* 16,262–9)	

Far from settling down to a participative enjoyment of the Word, the 'I' is prompted to take up his pilgrimage once more, wandering the world and visiting further cloisters. Yet this need to relocate sacramental fruition *ailleurs* also points towards an utterly different kind of 'space', beyond crumbling monastic structures that are no longer able to 'contain' and preserve the redemptive operation of the Word incarnate. Such longing finally points forward towards the 'inward turn' that characterizes Deguileville's later, mystical poetry, moving from the physical and institutional enclosure of the monastery to the mental, spiritual, and formal enclosures of lyrical contemplation and fruition.

Despite the pilgrim's decision to return to Chaalis at the end of the poem, *PVH2* thus lacks the sense of triumphal closure and accomplishment that concludes *PVH1*. The ending of *PVH2* thus both reiterates and reinforces the poet's longing to transcend temporal contingencies of any kind, first glimpsed in *PVH1*'s ABC prayer. But while the monastic cloister initially appears to have provided the *refui* associated with the Virgin in the prayer (*PVH1* 10,894; *PVH2* 13,051, see further Chapter 4.1), in *PVH2* the monastery no longer provides any safe protection against the linguistic perversions and abuses of Detraction and her acolytes. The ending also marks a further stage in Deguileville's progressive disillusion with the endless deferrals of narrative allegory, forever falling short of the experience of total participation to which it aspires, and forever prone to the slippages, abuses, and duplicity of Faux Semblant, whose vicious and underhand attack is ultimately replayed by the four *vieilles*. Like human language and any other man-made sign system, the *alieniloquium* of allegory is bound to fail—'car les signes puent faillir' (*PVH2* 14,377). These two conjoined experiences of failure play a major role in pushing Deguileville to experiment with very different forms and modes of writing with his late Latin lyrics. Only there language appears to some extent freed

EXPERIENCE   321

from its semiotic duplicity, and manages to capture the living presence of the silent inner Word by inviting its action upon a humbled, expectant individual subject.

The analysis I have presented over the last three chapters suggests that the established account of Deguileville's poetic career and its evolution over time may have to be modified in important ways. Most importantly, I hope to have demonstrated that Deguileville's poetic *œuvre* is far more complex, intellectually ambitious, and internally conflicted than many modern critics have hitherto assumed. This matters not only because it allows us to better understand the place of Deguileville's work in the history of late medieval literary and intellectual culture, but because it enables us to re-evaluate its impact on later fellow poets in France and Europe more widely. While most of his medieval readers appear to have used his poems primarily as repertories of proverbial moral wisdom in narrative form—as is suggested by the manuscript tradition and the larger patterns of reception[167]—*some* readers *did* engage with the more philosophical and intellectually challenging aspects of his work. As I want to argue in the third part of this study, this included William Langland. Much work remains to be done to assess Deguileville's impact on English literature more widely, including the work of Chaucer,[168] but Langland appears to occupy a particularly privileged position in the English reception history of the *Pèlerinages*. Uniquely, Langland engaged not only with the philosophical aspects of Deguileville's *Pèlerinages*-corpus, but appears to have been extraordinarily sensitive to the internal tensions, conflicts, and ruptures that occur in the *Pèlerinages*-corpus, and which concurrently shape the French poet's complex, shifting, and ambivalent attitude towards his own poetic craft. More specifically, I will argue that the evolving structure of *Piers Plowman*, with its own internal ruptures, false starts, visions, and *re*-visions, essentially grows out of Langland's sustained engagement with Deguileville's *Pèlerinages*, and, through the latter, with Jean de Meun's *Rose*.

---

[167] On this, see especially the work of Géraldine Veysseyre, e.g. 'Manuscrits à voir, manuscrits à lire, manuscrits lus: Les Marginalia du *Pèlerinage de Vie Humaine* comme indices de sa réception médiévale', in Kamath and Nievergelt, pp. 47–64, and especially the forthcoming annotated catalogue of Deguileville manuscripts.

[168] For some recent work, see Kamath, *Authorship and First-Person Allegory*; Nievergelt, *Allegorical Quests from Deguileville to Spenser*; ibid., 'Invisible Itineraries: The Textual Wanderings of Guillaume Deguileville's *Pèlerinage de Vie Humaine* in Sixteenth-Century England and Europe', in Kablitz and Peters, pp. 721–46; Cooper, *Artisans and Narrative Craft*, pp. 106–45; Gayk, *Image, Text, and Religious Reform in Fifteenth-Century England*, pp. 88–95.

PART III

LANGLAND

Introduction to Part III

Over the previous chapters, I have argued that Deguileville's *Pèlerinage de Vie Humaine*, in its two versions, is a far more complex, intellectually challenging, and internally conflicted work than most critics have assumed. In particular, I have examined the epistemological problems that crystallize in *PVH1*. Many of these problems are taken up again in *PVH2*, but this revised version of the poem finally exacerbates existing difficulties rather than resolving them. I have also suggested that Deguileville is at least intermittently aware of the difficulties created by his attempt to rewrite his own poem twenty-five years later. As Deguileville maintains in the prologue to the revised version, the writing of *PVH2* itself appears to have been motivated by the poet's growing concern over his inability to control the circulation, reception, and interpretation of his work. *PVH2* therefore manifests an exacerbated, obsessive concern with semiotic difficulties, reflected in particular in the proliferation of instances of misreading, dissimulation, and idolatry within the allegory itself. This increased anxiety over erroneous representation and interpretation erodes the poet's confidence in the ability of narrative allegory to serve as a moral, spiritual, and epistemic 'roadmap' for its pilgrim-readers. While this loss of faith in allegorical narrative culminates with Deguileville's 'conversion' to a very different kind of contemplative poetry in his late Latin lyrics, such a reorientation is already adumbrated in *PVH1*, with the disruptive insertion of the ABC prayer and the experience of conversion at the Rock of Penitence. More broadly, this sudden narrative and discursive *retournement* points to a much deeper, underlying tension between divergent modes of poetic thought in Deguileville's poetry, respectively associated with loosely scholastic vs. monastic ideas about knowledge. Deguileville's poetic *oeuvre* as a whole materializes in the space between an active, rationally driven quest for spiritual knowledge on the one hand, and an affective, embodied, and often passive and overwhelming experience of the divine on the other.

It is only in the wake of this sustained reconsideration of Deguileville's poetic *oeuvre* that it is possible to examine the question of Langland's debt to the

324   MEDIEVAL ALLEGORY AS EPISTEMOLOGY

Pèlerinage de Vie Humaine—or rather to the plural *Pèlerinages* that constitute the 'trilogy'. Readers who are intimately familiar with Langland's poem may already have glimpsed a number of powerful resonances and continuities, which I will explore in the remainder of this book. In Chapter 5 I discuss the continuity between the strictly epistemological and cognitive concerns found respectively in Deguileville's *Pèlerinages* and in the various versions of Langland's *Piers Plowman*, with particular attention to the A and B texts. This will take the form of a series of close readings of some of the most salient and relevant passages in the middle sections of the poem (*passus* VIII–XII in the B text), in the context of the work already undertaken in preceding chapters. In Chapter 6 I turn my attention to larger, structural elements in *Piers Plowman*, along with the question of the deeper nature, method, and dynamics of Langland's poetic vision and re-vision, particularly as it emerges from the events in *passus* XIII to XV. I will pay particular attention to questions of revision and rewriting, narrative and cognitive closure, and poetic method. In all of these areas, I argue, Langland's vision is deeply shaped by his engagement with Deguileville's *Pèlerinages*-trilogy. In Chapter 7, finally, I will examine the conclusive section of Langland's poem in the B text, arguing that Langland's thinking on the problem of closure—narrative, poetic, and epistemic— emerges out of his engagement with the many ruptures, crises, pitfalls, false starts and abortive endings in Deguileville's poetry. More specifically, it is Deguileville's troubled and never-ending obsession with the cognitive difficulties highlighted by the *Rose* that lies behind Langland's unique ability to place the personal experience of poetic failure within a broader, eschatological perspective.

The readings I present in what follows point towards a number of broader conclusions concerning the ability of narrative allegory to function as a vehicle for intellectual, philosophical, and theological speculation, particularly in relation to questions of cognition and subjectivity. Those readings, however, also help to shed light on several prominent debates in Langland criticism, which have wider resonances within the poem's broader historical context. This includes, for instance, the poem's attitude towards scholasticism (Chapters 5.1 and 5.2), its penitential logic (Chapters 5.3, 5.4), Langland's understanding of experience and 'kynde knowyng' and related ideas of subjectivity and agency (Chapters 5.2, 5.3, 5.6, 5.7, 6.3, and 7.3), the poem's attitude towards the problems grace, free will, and Predestination (throughout), the role of sacramental thinking in the poem and its relation to Langland's understanding of allegory (Chapters 5.6 and 7.1), but also questions regarding Langland's 'authorial' self–understanding (Chapters 6.2, 6.3, and 7.2) and his development of a distinctive kind of reiterative poetics (Chapter 6.4). In all of these areas *Piers Plowman* shows important signs of the impact of Deguileville's poetry: the *Pèlerinages*, I argue, were not merely a source among many others for Langland, but played a pivotal role in shaping the overall form and evolution of his poetic vision, over the narrative trajectory of the poem's plot as elaborated in the B-version, but also in terms of the poem's evolution over time, as it moves through its successive versions. Deguileville's corpus therefore seems to be the single most important literary intertext for Langland's poem, and I believe that further work on this connection is susceptible of bringing further clarity to our understanding of Langland's poetic method and compositional process. The role of *PA* in particular deserves much closer scrutiny.

While I remain agnostic concerning the possibility of Langland's identity, the suggestions put forward by Robert Adams regarding William de la Rokele would fit remarkably well with the account provided here. Adams paints the portrait of a man on the cusp between the courtly and the religious life, a well-connected eccentric with easy access to many of the texts and ideas discussed throughout this study. In particular, William de la Rokele—'a mature, sophisticated cleric, skilled in both French and Latin, a person of established character'[1]—appears to have benefited from the relatively advanced training provided by a well-equipped Cathedral school (Worcester?); was tonsured and ordained after being married at a younger age; was active also as private secretary or domestic chaplain; and was living a withdrawn existence relying on powerful friends for protection; and was possibly writing from a position of encrypted anonymity. The association with the Beauchamps is particularly tantalizing, as is the presence of a William de la Rokele on a diplomatic mission to Brittany in the company of the young Thomas Beauchamp in 1368.[2] Far from being an eccentric and raggedy urban malcontent dreaming of the distant Malvern Hills, then, William would have been ideally placed to access the kind of courtly, ethical, and allegorical literature epitomized by the *Rose* and the *Pèlerinages*, which circulated extensively among aristocratic English readers during this period, two generations before the 'Lancastrian cult of Deguileville' took on sufficient magnitude to foster a flurry of English translations of his work during the 1410s and 1420s.[3]

Langland and French Allegory

A number of scholars have touched on the question of Deguileville's influence on Langland in the past. I provide a brief overview before proposing a modified approach, arguing for a much deeper, more sustained, and more productive engagement with Deguileville on Langland's part. The connection was first proposed by Jusserand in 1893. Jusserand observes that Langland appears to have

[1] Adams, *Langland and the Rokele Family*, p. 107.
[2] Adams, *Langland and the Rokele Family*, p. 106.
[3] I cite Derek Pearsall, 'Hoccleve's *Regement of Princes*: The Poetics of Royal Self-Representation', *Speculum* 69.2 (1994), 386–410 (408). For a summative account of Deguileville's reception in the Anglo-French sphere, see Kamath and Nievergelt, 'Introduction', pp. 13–18. For a discussion of Manuscript evidence, see Josephine Houghton Meyer, 'The Works of Guillaume Deguileville in Late Medieval England: Transmission, Reception, and Context with Special Reference to Piers *Plowman*'. Unpublished PhD dissertation, University of Birmingham, 2007).

326 MEDIEVAL ALLEGORY AS EPISTEMOLOGY

known Deguileville along with the *Roman de la Rose* and with the works of Rute-beuf, and identifies Deguileville as the only French poet from whom Langland borrows extensively.[4] The possibility of a direct influence was next discussed by Dorothy Owen, who identifies a number of common features that are seen as signs for a possible connection. Owen's emphasis is primarily comparative, but she also provides an itemized concordance of features that are shared by the two poems, suggesting the possibility of direct influence.[5] Later discussions provide stronger arguments in favour of direct influence, notably Rosemary Woolf in 1969, who concentrates on the status of written documents such as charters, prayers and pardons in Langland's allegory, arguing that Deguileville's *Pèlerinage de l'Âme* provides an important model.[6] Next is Guy Bourquin's long study of literary genesis of Langland's three versions, where a considerable amount of energy is dedicated to exploring Langland's use of French sources in the attempt to reconstruct an intricate picture of Langland's compositional process. Even if the author is not primarily concerned with establishing the influence of French allegories on *Piers Plowman*, a useful overview of parallels with Deguileville is provided.[7] Stephen Barney offers a useful assessment of the general correspondences between Langland's poem and earlier French allegories, including *PVH*, without however making any precise claims concerning influence,[8] while similar observations concerning the analogous role of personified Reason in the *Rose*, Deguileville, and *Piers Plowman* are offered by Gillian Rudd in 1994.[9] J. A. Burrow in 1993 equally finds a number of structural and thematic parallels between Langland's poetry and Deguileville's, notably concerning the multiple dream-frame or the concern with the abuses of the judicial system, but also identifies specific parallels in phrasing and suggests that Langland may have known the trilogy as a whole, not *PVH* alone.[10] Emily Steiner, in 2003, also argues that '[c]learly [Deguileville's] trilogy provided a model for William Langland's *Piers Plowman*', and then goes on to highlight a number of points of contact throughout her study.[11] Steiner has again emphasized the importance of this relationship in her more recent work, suggesting also that Langland's engagement with Deguileville ought to be understood

---

[4] J. J. Jusserand, *Piers Plowman: A Contribution to the History of English Mysticism* (London: Fisher Unwin, 1894), pp. 183, 209–14.

[5] *Piers Plowman: A Comparison with some Earlier and Contemporary French Allegories* (London: London University Press, 1912), *passim*, especially pp. 6–9, 19–22, 27–31, 154–66.

[6] Rosemary Woolf, 'The Tearing of the Pardon', in S. S. Hussey, ed., *Piers Plowman: Critical Approaches* (London: Methuen, 1969), pp. 50–75 (58–60).

[7] Guy Bourquin, Piers Plowman: *Etudes sur la genèse littéraire des trois versions* (Paris: Honoré Champion, 1978), pp. 780–98.

[8] Stephen Barney, 'Allegorical Visions', in John Alford, ed., *A Companion to Piers Plowman* (Berkeley and Los Angeles: University of California Press, 1988), pp. 117–34 (126–8).

[9] Gillian Rudd, *Managing Language in 'Piers Plowman'* (Cambridge: D.S. Brewer, 1994), pp. 45–52.

[10] J. A. Burrow, *Langland's Fictions* (Oxford: Oxford University Press, 1993), pp. 113–18, Appendix A: 'Langland and Deguileville'.

[11] Steiner, *Documentary Culture*, pp. 28–46, 111, 222, and *passim*.

within the broader framework of the influence of the *Rose*, profoundly shaping the work of both Langland and Deguileville with its promise of the 'luxury of total vision'.[12]

In her 2007 thesis, Josephine Houghton-Meyer has produced what is the fullest discussion to date, combining an extremely valuable study of the circulation and availability of Deguileville manuscripts in late medieval France and England with a discussion of sense perception and ideas of ageing in the two poems.[13] Although absolute certainty for direct influence is impossible given the absence of external evidence for the material presence of the text in fourteenth-century England, the author comes to the conclusion that 'the similarities between the texts are so numerous that the balance of probabilities weighs heavily in favour of Langland's knowledge of Deguileville's work.'[14] A number of further scholars in recent years have emphasized the importance of this connection, such as Mishtooni Bose, who suggests that Deguileville is not merely a source but an instrument for Langland to 'think with',[15] or Lawrence Clopper, who frames his discussion of the continuities in the allegorical techniques of description and personification employed by both poets within a wider discussion of the problematic, largely artificial opposition between 'nominalist' and 'realist' doctrines often invoked by critics of the poem.[16] In the first volume of the monumental 5-volume *Penn Commentary on Piers Plowman*, Andrew Galloway again notes that the influence of the *Pelerinage de vie humaine* is 'widely assumed', and goes on to discuss its general impact together with specific examples of its possible influence.[17] The fifth volume of the commentary equally identifies a number of examples of Deguileville's influence.[18] Other scholars such as Nicolette Zeeman and Vincent Gillespie have recently provided powerful readings of Langland that rely on Deguileville, with Gillespie arguing for direct influence of *PVH2* more specifically[19]—an important contention to which I will return. There is, therefore, a well-established and growing consensus among *Piers Plowman* scholars concerning Langland's familiarity with Deguileville.

Despite the frequent references to Deguileville in Langland criticism, however, scholars have not attempted to produce a more extensive, precise, and nuanced

---

[12] Emily Steiner, *Reading Piers Plowman* (Cambridge University Press, 2013), p. 13, cf. also pp. 24–5, 103, 152. Steiner again comments on the triangle Rose-Deguileville-Langland in her '*Piers Plowman* and Institutional Poetry'.

[13] Houghton Meyer, 'The Works of Guillaume Deguileville in Late Medieval England'.

[14] Houghton Meyer, 'The Works of Guillaume Deguileville in Late Medieval England', p. 9.

[15] Mishtooni Bose, 'On not being French: Thinking with Deguileville', paper presented at the International Medieval Congress in Kalamazoo in 2006.

[16] Lawrence M. Clopper, 'Langland and Allegory: A Proposition', *YLS* 15 (2001), 35–42.

[17] Galloway, *Penn Commentary on Piers Plowman. Volume One*, pp. 5, 9, 16 for discussion of Deguileville. For isolated echoes, see the numerous references in the index.

[18] Stephen Barney, *Penn Commentary on Piers Plowman. Volume Five: C Passus 20–22; B Passus 18–20* (Philadelphia: University of Pennsylvania Press, 2006), indexed references pp. 33, 81, 94, 104–5.

[19] Zeeman, 'Late Medieval, Religious and Vernacular Allegory', pp. 148–61; Vincent Gillespie, 'Dame Study's Anatomical Curse: A Scatological Parody?', in Nicholas Jacobs and Gerald Morgan, eds, '*Truthe is the Beste*': A Festschrift in Honour of A. V. C. Schmidt (Oxford: Peter Lang, 2014), pp. 95–107.

account of the intertextual dynamics that obtain between the two poems. This is primarily due to the critical neglect of Deguileville's poetry itself, but is also a consequence of the wider lack of interest in Langland's engagement with francophone literature and culture. As Emily Steiner has noted, Langland is still thought of as a 'resolutely insular poet'[20] whose adoption of an insular poetic form—the alliterative long line—occludes his less visible yet profound debt to francophone poetic traditions, especially those of narrative allegory and the lyric. So, while critics often acknowledge the parallels or similarities between Langland's dream poem and the *Roman de la Rose*, for instance, the exact nature and significance of this relationship is often underestimated, trivialized, or misunderstood. As is suggested by recent developments, much interesting work remains to be done on 'Langland and the French Tradition', and the *Rose* is likely to occupy a pivotal place in future resarch on the topic.[21] The *Rose* may well turn out to be an implicit, latent but crucially important intertext for Langland, influential in its own right, but also as a poem that determines the modalities of Langland's encounter with a number of further texts in the tradition of didactic narrative allegory and satire—not only Deguileville, but also works like the exuberantly satirical *Roman de Fauvel* or the more subtle, artfully ironic poetry of Machaut.[22]

Discussions of the relationship between Langland and Deguileville often focus on broad, general similarities between isolated episodes in the two poems. More often than not such similarities are identified only for the purpose of highlighting the differences of the two allegories, and to stress the greater complexity

---

[20] Steiner, '*Piers Plowman* and Institutional Poetry', p. 306. See further my forthcoming chapter, 'William Langland: European Poet?', in Sif Ríkharðsdóttir and Raluca Radulescu, eds, *A Companion to Medieval English Literature in a Trans-European Context, 1100–1500* (London: Routledge, 2022), pp. 300–310.

[21] See especially the cluster of essays in Ryan D. Perry and Lisa Strakhov, eds, 'Langland and the French Tradition', *YLS* 30 (2016), 175–306; and Nicolette Zeeman, 'Tales of Piers and Perceval: *Piers Plowman* and the Grail Romances', *YLS* 22 (2008), 199–236.

[22] As suggested by Andrew Galloway, 'Madame Meed: *Fauvel*, Isabella, and the French Circumstances of *Piers Plowman*', and Sarah Wilma Watson, 'Grace Holds the "Clicket" to the Heavenly "Wiket": *Piers Plowman*, the *Roman de la Rose*, and the Poetics of Penetration', both in *YLS* 30 (2016), pp. 227–52 and 206–26 respectively. On *Fauvel*, see also Bourquin, *Etudes sur la génèse littéraire*, pp. 178–92. See also Roberta D. Cornelius, '*Piers Plowman* and the *Roman de Fauvel*', *PMLA* 47.2 (1932), 363–7. The *Rose*, PVH2 and *Fauvel* all share with *Piers Plowman*, for instance, a sustained concern with visual and linguistic deception, reflected for instance in the ubiquity of metaphors of wrapping, dissimulation, clothing, disguising, and infiltration/penetration. In all four poems, this concern is closely tied to reflections on the ethical challenges confronting the author of didactic allegory, specifically its satirical developments: despite satire's claim to expose abuses to the 'naked eye', the poet's own adoption of the satirist's cloak threatens to function merely as one further disguise, yet another mask of Faux Semblant. See further Marco Nievergelt, 'L'ombre de *Faux Semblant*: fiction, vérité, et tromperie dans la poésie du xivème siècle (France, Angleterre, Italie)', in *L'Homme Comme Animal Politique et Parlant au Moyen Âge*, ed. Gianluca Briguglia et Sonia Gentili. *Philosophical Readings* XII.1 (2020), 161–71. For Study's warning against the adoption of the role of the satirist, see B X.283–91, and for the debate with Lewte on the legitimacy of denunciation, B XI.84–107. See further Priscilla Martin, *The Field and the Tower* (London: Macmillan, 1979), pp. 66–70; Anne Middleton, 'William Langland's "Kynde Name": Authorial Signature and Social Identity in Late Fourteenth-Century England', in Anne Middleton, *Chaucer, Langland and Fourteenth-Century Literary History*, ed. Steven Justice (London: Routledge: 2013), pp. 199–262 (231–4).

and superior artistic value of Langland's poem. A typical, influential example of this procedure may be found in David Aers' 1975 book on *Piers Plowman and Christian Allegory*,[23] which may have contributed to perpetuating the rather uncharitable, aesthetically biased judgments of early twentieth-century scholars such as Arthur Piaget or C. S. Lewis.[24] As well as pointing out general similarities, critics have often focused on more localized *topoi*, individual episodes, personifications, or isolated plot-developments, and until very recently little effort has been made to understand *how*, and *why* exactly Langland is reading, using, re-reading and re-writing Deguileville. As I've already suggested, this is in turn a function of a reductive understanding of the discursive complexities and internal ruptures of Deguileville's poem. Even Andrew Galloway, who identifies numerous fertile echoes of Deguileville's trilogy in the first volume of the *Penn Commentary to Piers Plowman*, finally states that the three *Pèlerinages* 'lack the uncertainties of where authority might be found that pervade and vitalize or disorder *Piers Plowman*'.[25] Yet more recent readings of Deguileville, by contrast, have insisted precisely on the conflicted status of authority in his poems, on the discrepancies between Deguileville's poetic ideal and its practical execution, on the poet's own doubts and reservations about the value of his poetic vision, and on the generally unsettled, shifting nature of Deguileville's poetic project as a whole.[26] Furthermore, Langland's tireless, even obsessive re-reading and rewriting of his own poetic work suggests that his engagement with the work of earlier poets may have been equally probing, intense, and reiterative. Given the complexity of Deguileville's poem as discussed in the preceding chapters, and its ambition to conjure up the 'total vision' that the *Rose* promises but finally withholds, it appears highly reductive to claim that Langland simply plundered the *Pèlerinages* for narrative matter to be redeployed elsewhere, in a radically different poem of far superior artistic value. On the contrary I suggest that Langland was an acute reader of the *Pèlerinages*—far more acute, in fact, than most modern critics—and that he valued Deguileville's allegories precisely because of their internal *aporias*, contradictions, and breakdowns, including the French author's own reservations about the viability of his own didactic project, and the value and legitimacy of vernacular allegorical poetry more generally.

Taking my cue from Steiner, then, I suggest that it is precisely the totalizing scope and ambition of the allegorical tradition of the *Rose* and the *Pèlerinages* that makes Langland's poetic project a concrete, historically and poetically real

---

[23] David Aers, *Piers Plowman and Christian Allegory* (London: Edward Arnold, 1975).
[24] See citations given above, p. 118 n.4.
[25] Galloway, *Penn Commentary on Piers Plowman. Volume 1*, p. 9. For echoes of Deguileville's *Pèlerinages* trilogy, see the numerous references in the index. On the *Rose*, see ibid. pp. 3–4 and index (de Lorris).
[26] See especially groundbreaking discussions by Pomel, *Les voies de l'au-delà*, and Maupeu, *Pèlerins de vie humaine*. For further recent work on Deguileville, see Kablitz and Peters; Kamath and Nievergelt; Duval, 'Interpréter le *Pèlerinage de vie humaine*'.

possibility. More specifically, I claim that Langland's poetry grows out of the *failure* of both earlier poems to live up to their own grand promises of a 'total vision'—a failure that is pre-programmed and deliberate in the *Rose*, but far more unexpected, traumatic, but also spiritually enabling in *PVH*. Langland thus inherits the dialectic between the two poems, and internalizes both the radically sceptical and interrogative energies of the *Rose*, along with Deguileville's constantly frustrated yet irresistible desire for narrative, interpretive, and epistemic closure. The influence of the *Pèlerinages* in particular should be sought not only at the level of specific themes or episodes, but also at the deeper level of narrative logic, poetic method, and the structuring of poetic vision—fortuitous and providential as well as intentional or authorial. Indeed, both Langland and Deguileville appear to have grappled with a number of closely analogous problems regarding the epistemic limits of poetic vision and the pitfalls of both interpretation and authorial agency and control. For both authors this uncertainty concerning the viability of their respective poetic visions in enabling access to 'Truth'—or at least to true self-knowledge—raised still more troublesome and fundamental questions regarding the spiritual, ethical, and didactic legitimacy of allegorical dream-poetry in the vernacular. Both poets therefore engage with such concerns in deeply similar manner, notably by producing sustained and elaborate 're-visions' of their respective dream-allegories. As I will be arguing in Chapter 6, Langland's debt to Deguileville appears to be most intense during moments of major structural and discursive transition, crisis, and reorientation within *Piers Plowman*. Deguileville's *Pèlerinages* thus play a major role in determining the shifting architecture of Langland' vision over time: without the *Pèlerinages* Langland's poem would simply not exist as we know it, with its multiple sequential dreams, and in the multiple versions and revisions that have come down to us as the A, B, and C texts.

5

The Desire for Knowledge and the Experience of Conversion

(*Piers Plowman* B VIII–XIII.215)

Fides non habet meritum vbi humana racio prebet experimentum
(Piers Plowman, B XI.250a)

1. Learning, Crisis, and Conversion

In the preceding chapters I suggested that the role of learning in *PVH*, and particularly scholastic learning, is highly problematic. On the one hand the poem's authority figures, Grace and Sapience, underline the inadequacy of scholastic formulations and methods: the science of dialectic, Aristotelian natural science, and all forms of profane scientific and philosophical learning are deemed irrelevant for advancing the pilgrim on his soteriological pilgrimage. On the other hand, however, those same authority figures also invoke (pseudo-)scholastic terms and discourses to foster the pilgrim's self-knowledge and to support their own claims to authority, and thus finally seek to appropriate scholastic learning for sapiential and salvific ends (see Chapter 2.2). This attempt, however, remains unsuccessful, and the pilgrim's experience at the Rock of Penitence and with the ABC Prayer finally marks a more radical rejection of academic intellectual traditions, and signals a point of non-return for both pilgrim and poet (see Chapter 4.1). The poem's attitude towards scholastic ideas, theories and practices, then, is fluctuating and deeply ambivalent. Langland's own ambivalence towards academic forms of learning, while more controlled and carefully managed, is no less profound, and I want to suggest that this conflicted, at times confrontational attitude towards scholastic philosophy, Aristotelian *scientia*, and faculty psychology emerges in part out of Langland's reading of Deguileville's *Pèlerinage de Vie Humaine* in one or indeed both of its two versions. As I discussed in Chapter 3, *PVH1* is particularly concerned with defining the mechanisms of human cognition, mind, and perception—a preoccupation that is further exacerbated in *PVH2*.

In the present chapter I want to argue that when Langland engages with such problems in the central and most introspective section of *Piers Plowman*

Medieval Allegory as Epistemology. Marco Nievergelt, Oxford University Press.
© Marco Nievergelt (2023). DOI: 10.1093/oso/9780192849212.003.0006

332 MEDIEVAL ALLEGORY AS EPISTEMOLOGY

(B VIII–XIII.215), he does so with close reference to Deguileville's poem, and more specifically with reference to the internal tensions and contradictions that unsettle *PVH2*. As I discussed in Chapter 3, Deguileville's reliance on multiple, often mutually incompatible accounts of mind and cognition in *PVH2* ended up creating a number of epistemological difficulties that threaten to undermine Deguileville's didactic and salvific project as a whole, specifically because of the tension between a broadly illuminationist theory of cognition on the one hand, and an abstractive/Aristotelian theory on the other (see Chapters 3.2 and 3.5). A point of particular difficulty concerned the cognitive status of mental/visual images in representing spiritual, and therefore transcendent and immaterial truths. The most conspicuous effort in this sense is the famous 'eyes in ears' episode—an episode that in many ways brings to a head the epistemic tensions and contradictions that pervade Deguileville's allegory as a whole (Chapter 3.5). With her convoluted efforts to explicate her own 'eyes in ears' metaphor in terms of the cognitive processes involved in human attempts to grasp the nature of the theological virtues of Faith and Hope, then, Deguileville's Grace bequeathed to later readers an account of intellectual cognition that is ultimately self-contradictory and finally self-defeating. As suggested by Lydgate's desperate attempt to make sense of the passage in his 1427 translation, the *Pilgrimage of the Life of Man*, medieval readers were indeed puzzled by Grace's laborious, and finally counterproductive allegorical 'elucidations'.

There are strong indications that Lydgate was not the only English poet puzzled by Grace Dieu's rather absurd explanations in this particular episode. Langland too appears to have engaged with the contradictions of Deguileville's 'eyes-in-ears' thought experiment in ways that may appear anecdotal, but that touch on the deeper principles that lie at the heart of Langland's poetic epistemology more widely. Vincent Gillespie and Jessica Rosenfeld have both recently suggested—concurrently and independently—that Langland's Dame Study may in fact be recasting Deguileville's convoluted 'eyes-in-ears' thought experiment as a scatological parody.[1] Punning on this arresting episode in Deguileville, Study figures such immoderate probing of 'goddes pryvetee' in terms of a far more extreme, obscene form of sensory and corporeal *translatio*: here, eyes are no longer transferred into 'ears', but into 'arse':

> For alle þat wilneþ to wyie þe whyes of God almyȝty,
> I wolde his eiȝe were in his ers and his fynger after
> That euere wilneþ to wite why þat God wolde
> Suffre Sathan his seed to bigile,
> Or Iudas þe Iew Iesu bitraye.

(B X.124–8)

---

[1] Gillespie, 'Dame Study's Anatomical Curse'; Rosenfeld, *Ethics and Enjoyment*, p. 128 n. 77.

THE DESIRE FOR KNOWLEDGE AND THE EXPERIENCE OF CONVERSION   333

Gillespie emphasizes the parodic function of Study's anatomical metaphor, hinging on Langland's substitution of 'ers' for what should be 'eres'—a change that is clearly deliberate as Gillespie demonstrates on the basis of manuscript evidence. Langland's recasting of Grace Dieu's thought experiment, then, uses an extreme, unnatural, and finally sodomitical image of sensory troping to figure an immoderate desire for theological knowledge. This reading also fits with the savage tone of Study's attack on other forms of excessive 'coveitise of learning' in this passage,[2] presented in a series of memorable variations on the theme of '*non plus sapere quam oportet*' (B X.118a). Study specifically deplores the presumption of unqualified lay 'argueres' (B X.118), who 'carpen as þei clerkes were' (B X.104). The whole passage is already introduced by Study's condemnation of idle, pseudo-theological table talk by unqualified and presumptuous laymen—another instance of inordinate desire for theological knowledge represented in terms of uncontrolled bodily appetites and excesses:

> Ac if þei carpen of Crist, þise clerkes and þise lewed,
> atte mete in hir murþes whan mynstrals beþ stille,
> Thanne telleþ þei of þe Trinite how two slowe þe þridde,
> And bryngen forþ a balled reson, taken Bernard to witnesse,
> And puten forþ presumpcioun to preue þe soþe.
> Þus þei dryuele at hir deys þe deitee to knowe,
> And gnawen God wiþ þe gorge whanne hir guttes fullen.
>
> (B X.51–7; cf. A XI.38–44)[3]

In commenting on this passage and on this section more broadly, Zeeman insists on the 'materialism of those who misuse learning', arguing that 'the corporality of this language figures carnality, the misuse of psychological powers.'[4] Such carnality is taken to extremes when in the effort to envisage the ineffable, human eyes are paradoxically re-embodied in the grossest, most material and obscene bodily *locus* of the arse. Langland's parodic *translatio* thus deliberately highlights how Grace's effort to transplant the pilgrim's eyes into his ears spectacularly backfires. Instead of accepting her own image as an analogical trope pointing beyond ordinary, corporeally mediated perception and cognition, Grace ends up providing a *physiological* description of what ought to be—by its very definition—a strictly intellectual, and thus *immaterial* cognitive phenomenon. The absurdity of such a procedure was not lost on Langland, who takes this process still further by re-literalizing and

---

[2] Daniel M. Murtaugh, *Piers Plowman and the Image of God* (Gainesville: The University Presses of Florida, 1978), pp. 64–5.

[3] See also further discussion of this passage in Chapter 5.4.

[4] Zeeman, *Discourses of Desire*, p. 123. The idea of a corporeal, specifically alimentary abuse of religious learning figured as a concretized 'word', resurfaces later in the poem, at the Feast of Patience, in relation to the extravagant eating habits of the 'Maister' (B XIII.61–73). See again Zeeman, *Discourses of Desire*, pp. 259–60, and below, Chapter 5.4.

334   MEDIEVAL ALLEGORY AS EPISTEMOLOGY

re-embodying Grace's abstruse metaphors in the grossest, most obscene fashion. Langland's Study suggests that rather than granting access to *super*natural truths, such troping is merely *un*natural and sodomitical. Such efforts are not only mystifying but spiritually dangerous, since such 'maistres [. . .] maken men in mysbileve þat muse moche on hire wordes' (B X.115–16).[5] Instead of providing any genuine insight into the mysterious nature of intellectual vision (*visio mentis*), Study suggests that Grace Dieu's convoluted allegorical figurations ultimately entail spiritual blindness and deafness. Such 'elucidations' amount to mere 'hauylons [i.e. tricks] to ablende mennes wittes / [. . .] now deef mote he worþe'; B X.131–2). Wit's reaction, for all its apparent negativity, is of a piece with Study's argument, as he shuts down all of his senses and withdraws: "he bicom so confus he kouþe noȝt loke, / And as doumb as deeþ, and drouȝ hym arere' (B X.138–9).

In the immediate context of the action, the primary object of Study's parody are the presumptuous carnal 'argueres', but it is more difficult to determine the real, ultimate object of Study's ferocious attack. Study's criticism in this section as a whole raises problems not only about the status of learning, but also about the status of visual/mental imagination, and indeed about the kind of 'visionary' allegorical poetry that both Deguileville and Langland are writing. Study's tirade in B X is thus at least partially motivated by Wit's irresponsible decision to impart knowledge to Will—a typical case of casting pearls before swine in Study's opinion (B X. 5–12). Gillespie thus reads Study's anatomical curse and the wider episode as 'an implicit rebuke to the ambitious Will, who in this part of the poem is on the verge of valorizing intellect and academic speculation above common sense'.[6] Will's excessive enthusiasm for academic, scholastic learning takes a variety of forms, one of which is his adoption of the posture and rhetoric of a scholastic disputant. Indeed Will, as is often observed, enters the third vision in the role of a disputant, who upon encountering the two Friars immediately launches into a *Contra*, and 'as a clerc [. . .] comsed to disputen' (B VIII.20). To borrow Anne Middleton's words, Langland here unmistakeably 'establish[es] the represented maker of this poem as an aspirant to a specifically clerical and learned legitimacy'.[7] From the beginning of this extended section, then, Will himself is explicitly assimilated to the 'argueres' who 'carpen as thei clerkes were' (B X.118, 104). Such 'argueres' gain no additional insight into God's workings despite their protracted disputations, as Study declares: 'al worþ as [God] wolt, whatso we dispute!' (B X.130).

The episode and Study's speech as a whole clearly participate in a larger exploration of the value of learning—specifically scholastic learning and dialectic, but also the natural sciences more broadly. As was already seen (e.g. Chapter 2.2),

---

[5] Compare also Anima's injunction at B XV.70–9.
[6] Gillespie, 'Dame Study's Anatomical Curse', p. 99.
[7] Anne Middleton, '"Kynde Name"', p. 223.

THE DESIRE FOR KNOWLEDGE AND THE EXPERIENCE OF CONVERSION   335

Deguileville's poem is pervaded by a deep ambivalence about the value of rationalistic, scholastic, and scientific learning. Langland's overall reservations about academic practices of disputation in particular, then, ultimately reproduce but also amplify Deguileville's own misgivings. Just as Grace had done in *PVH*, Study now dismisses the scholastic disputation while also praising the science of dialectic, indeed claiming ownership of the *arte de bene disputandi*: as she directs Will onwards to meet Clergie, Study insists that 'Logyk I lerned hire', and goes on to claim that she herself 'Aristotle and oþere mo to argue I tauȝte' (B X.173, 176)—rehearsing in close detail Grace's equally bold claim in Deguileville's poem (*PVH1* 3011–22).[8] The major difference in Langland, however, is that Deguileville's own poem is now seen as participating in the immoderate desire for certainty, knowledge, and demonstration that also characterizes scholastic *scientia*, as is suggested by Study's parodic *translatio* of eyes from 'ears' to 'arse'.

Langland's dismissive attitude towards *scientia naturalis*, too, is strikingly Deguilevillian.[9] Among the potentially harmful sciences that Study lists in this section, we find numerous echoes of the potentially diabolic arts denounced in the revisions of *PVH2* (see Chapter 4.4):

> 'Ac Astronomye is an hard þyng, and yuel for to knowe;
> Geometrie and Geomesie is gynful of speche;
> Whoso þynketh werche with þo two þryueþ ful late –
> For sorcerie is þe souereyn book þat to þe science longeþ.
> Yet ar ther fibicches in forceres of fele mennes makynge.
> Experimentȝ of Alkenamye þe peple to deceyue;
> If thow þynke to dowel, deel þerewiþ neuere!
> Alle þise sciences I myself sotilede and ordeynede,
> And founded hem formest folke to deceyue.
> Tel Clergie þise tokenes, and to Scripture after,
> To counseille þee kyndely to knowe what is Dowel.'
>
> (B X.209–19)

---

[8] Even the punishment administered to lazy students here is unmistakeably Deguilevillian: idle 'girles' are beaten 'wiþ a baleys but if þei wolde lerne' (B X.177–8), echoing Penitance's iconographically striking 'balai' (e.g. *PVH1* 2187), frequently represented in manuscript illuminations. Characteristically, Langland appears to be working from a set of reminiscences that is thematically sharp but rather loose in term of their allegorical and iconographical meanings. Penitance in *PVH* carries three attributes—broom, mallet and whip—associated with the three stages of penance (Contrition, Confession and Satisfaction). While Penitance's 'balai' is essentially associated with the practice of confession, and therefore carried in her 'mouth', it is described in parallel with the 'verges' ('rods'), associated with Satisfaction: 'S'a mon balai soumis il s'est [...] Et bien confez si com j'ai dit, / Adonc pour bien li chastier / De mes cinglans verges le fiers, / Paine lui dons et batement / Pour son bien et amandement' (*PVH1* 2297–2304). Langland thus appears to have transferred the function of Penitance's 'verges' (beating) to Study's 'baleys'. The 'baleis' of Penance, again imagined as a whipping rod wielded by God, makes one further appearance in another unmistakeably penitential context, at the beginning of Ymaginatif's speech, at B XII.12.

[9] See Zeeman, *Discourses of Desire*, 119–31.

336 MEDIEVAL ALLEGORY AS EPISTEMOLOGY

Beginning with Astrology and Geomancy, the sequence of Langland's presentation reproduces exactly the initial stages of Deguileville's *excursus* in *PVH2*—often introduced, as in MS *h* (Paris, BnF MS français 829, 104r), by a miniature representing two characters that personify Astrology and Geomancy. Deguileville begins with a deceptive 'Astrologie, / L'autre part d'Astronomie' (*PVH2* 13,451–2), whose knowledge similarly requires 'grant labeur' (*PVH2* 13,429; cf. 'an hard þyng, and yuel for to knowe', B XI.209). Astrologie is accompanied by 'Geomancie', 'qui escrisoit / Sus le sablon et pointoioit' (*PVH2* 13,375–6)—just like Langland's 'Geomesye' who is similarly personified and 'gynful of speche' (B X.210). Also Langland's personifications of Sorcery and Necromancy have their equivalents in the same section of *PVH2*, as Sorcerie (*PVH2* 14,229) and Nigromancie (12,309), both of which are given miniatures in MS *h*. What is most striking, however, is that Langland should follow Deguileville so closely in identifying all of these personified sciences as posing challenges of a specifically semiotic and representational order: Study even concludes her brief list by declaring that she founded all these sciences in order 'folke to deceyue' (B X.217). Here too, then, knowledge and learning are cast as arts of deception and occultation, echoing the example of Faux Semblant in the *Rose*, archetypal dissimulator and manipulator of scholastic learning (cf. e.g. *RR* 11,026–34, see Chapter 1.4).

Given Study's own ambivalence about the forms of learning she herself devised, it is relevant that she should present *theologie* as an even 'mystier' and 'derker' science (B X.182–3). There has been extended critical debate about the exact meaning of Study's *theologie*, but the slipperiness of the term may well be deliberate. In this passage, Study insists primarily on the importance of Love/Charity at the heart of Christian doctrine: this is for Study the ultimate source and justification for the science of *theologie* (esp. X B.188), an argument that anticipates the more sustained analysis of the mysterious nature of Charity later in the poem, in its most intensely spiritual *passus* (B XV–XVIII). But theology itself, as Zeeman shows, 'is for Langland a term specifically imbued with anxiety about the misuse of scholarly learning'.[10] It is appropriate, then, that Study should launch into the most vehement condemnation of the abuses of academic theology precisely while illustrating the mysterious, rationally inexplicable nature of the Trinity:

> 'Alle þe clerkes vnder Crist ne koude þis assoille,
> But þus it bilongeþ to bileue to lewed þat willen dowel.
> For hadde neuere freke fyn wit þe feiþ to dispute,
> Ne man hadde no merite, myȝt it ben ypreued;'
>
> (B XI.247–50)

---

[10] For this and the following citation, see Zeeman, *Discourses of Desire*, pp. 129–31, including a discussion of critical disagreements and further references.

THE DESIRE FOR KNOWLEDGE AND THE EXPERIENCE OF CONVERSION 337

As Zeeman observes, *theologie* here denotes '[t]oo much of the wrong kind of labour and effort in response to the unknowables and obscurities fundamental to faith', and this finally 'turns *theologie* into intellectual carnality'. Study then suggests that *theologie* too may become—like the diabolic arts of Necromancy and Astrology—a dangerous game with opaque, dark, and mystifying signs. This applies particularly well to the kind of *theologie* practiced by Grace Dieu later in Deguileville's poem, where obscure, analogical metaphors and abstract tropes for spiritual truths like Faith and Hope are forcibly 'elucidated' with reference to scholastic faculty psychology, threatening to generate not only generalized confusion but also erroneous belief and spiritual error (see Chapter 3.5; cf. B X.116–17). It is not accidental, then, that Langland's poem should offer radically different, more 'incarnational' and experiential ways of apprehending Faith and Hope later in the poem, notably through the presence of the historical characters of Abraham (Faith) and Moses (Hope), followed by the advent of Christ (Charity; see Chapter 7.1). This substitution of historically real persons for Deguileville's tortuous allegorical figurations of Faith and Hope by means of the sacramental signifiers of the Staff and Scrip (see Chapter 2.4) underscores the urge of Langland's dreamer to 'know kyndely': as I will argue in Chapter 7, such knowledge is achieved neither through scholastic theological speculation, nor through allegorical imaginings as in Deguileville's *PVH*, but rather through an immersive, performative, experiential retelling of typological sacred history, culminating with its central, spiritually and historically pivotal event, the Incarnation of Christ.[11]

Langland's parodic *translatio* of 'eyes-in-ears' into 'eyes-in-arse', then, is more than an anecdotal reworking of an isolated episode from *PVH2*, but participates in a much wider concern with mind and cognition in this section of *Piers Plowman*, in close and continuous dialogue with Deguileville's poem. The episode in *PVH2* had served as a springboard for an extended discussion of faculty psychology, and also in Langland's B text the wider context for Study's remark is the extended cognitive exploration of the third vision, culminating in the inner dream and the encounter with Ymaginatif. As well as manifesting Study's clear disapproval of idle theological speculation, then, Langland's extreme, parodic *translatio* of sense perception from eyes to ears to arse suggests something about the difficulty of explaining the mechanics of the human ability to apprehend purely intellectual/spiritual truths. But whereas Langland shares Deguileville's doubts about the ability of the scholastic and natural sciences to grasp and elucidate the mysteries of faith, Langland also reflects on the possibility that poetic figuration, too, may lead to spiritual error and blindness.

While Langland clearly uses Deguileville's 'eyes-in-ears' thought experiment to reflect on the limitations of Aristotelian faculty psychology throughout the third vision in the B and C text, it is clearly reductive to conclude that he simply *applies*

---

[11] See also Middleton '"Kynde Name"' pp. 228–9.

338   MEDIEVAL ALLEGORY AS EPISTEMOLOGY

such models to account for the action during that section of the poem.[12] Instead
Langland stages what is at least a partial failure of traditional Aristotelian faculty
psychology to fully account for Will's subjective, complex, and profoundly disori-
entating experience during the inward journey, making it difficult to pin down
the precise cognitive, affective, and salvific significance of that experience.[13] Most
importantly, Langland underlines the failure of Aristotelian philosophy of mind,
with its disproportionate attention to psycho-physiological processes, to enable
any genuine form of self-knowledge and self-understanding. To some extent Will's
inward journey is itself the result of such failure, plunging him into an embodied, affective, and as-yet baffling experience of his own moral and ontological
condition characterized primarily by his intellectual limitations. In some sense,
then, Langland can be seen to reverse Deguileville's approach to the problem of
cognition: instead of beginning with a programmatic, fundamentally illuminationist account that is ultimately disproved by the pilgrim's practical experience
of the outside world, Langland begins with raw experience. The seemingly erratic,
idiosyncratic nature of Will's inward journey—encountering a sequence of personifications that are impossible to map onto any existing model or theory of the soul
and its cognitive faculties—is deliberately intended to foreground the difficulties
of the 'I' in mapping a mental world it simultaneously examines yet also inhabits.

In refusing to adopt any programmatic formulation of the soul and its powers, however, Langland avoids leading the 'I' into a terminal cognitive impasse
in the manner of Deguileville, whose poem finally gets stuck in the gulf divid-
ing theory and practice—postulating an ideal of the active powers of the soul
and yet providing ample evidence for the contrary. As I will argue in the next
section of this chapter, in the B text revisions Langland recognizes the positive, generative potential of this cognitive impasse, and harnesses it in order to
trace the trajectory of the dreamer's subsequent development in ways that both
reproduce but also exorcise the radical, terminal cognitive *aporia* of Deguileville's
poem (see Chapter 3.6). Rather than seeing active and passive modes of knowledge as fundamentally incompatible, like Deguileville had done, Langland finally
labours to integrate the two as part of an evolving, unstable, and dialectical process.
Instead of attempting to formulate a consistent, fully formed theory of the soul and
cognition, then, Langland provides an experiential narrative of continuous, and

---

[12] See especially James Simpson, *Piers Plowman: An Introduction*. 2nd rev. edn. (Exeter: University of
Exeter Press, 2007), pp. 85–90, who discusses Langland's eclectic use, by turns, of Augustinian/monastic
and Aristotelian/scholastic models of psychology. The point is reiterated by Zeeman, *Discourses of
Desire*, p. 64, but already emerges from earlier work such as Joseph S. Wittig, '*Piers Plowman* B IX–XII:
Elements in the Design of the Inward Journey', *Traditio* 28 (1972), 211–80.
[13] My reading here converges closely with Zeeman, *Discourses of Desire*, especially pp. 64–108. Neither the anguished tone nor the fluctuating and disruptive 'structure' of the inner journey seem to me
to correspond very closely to the rather more serene and carefully ordered patterns of Bonaventuran
meditation and spiritual ascent invoked by Michelle Karnes as terms of reference, in 'Will's Imagination in *Piers Plowman*', *JEGP* 108.1 (2009), 27–58, and in her monograph, *Imagination, Meditation,
and Cognition in the Middle Ages* (Chicago: University of Chicago Press, 2011).

THE DESIRE FOR KNOWLEDGE AND THE EXPERIENCE OF CONVERSION   339

potentially endless accommodation, as the mind apprehends its own workings, fluctuations, slippages, and limitations. To adopt a contemporary vocabulary, it could be said that instead of attempting to formulate a systematic epistemology, Langland's poem articulates an evolving, provisional phenomenology of cognition and self-understanding.

Study's ambivalence about a whole range of different forms of knowledge finally produces a fundamental crisis of learning in this section of the poem. The crisis is not merely abstract and theoretical, since this is essentially a crisis of learning experienced in real time by the poem's dreamer. Will, or 'the will', is at a loss regarding the necessity of learning for attaining salvation, and reacts by advocating an extreme form of anti-intellectualism that echoes the concluding sections of *PVH*, discussed in Chapters 3 and 4 above. Will experiences a breakdown in the A, B, and C texts, but this breakdown takes different forms, with variable consequences for the structure of the dreamer's quest and the ideological structure of Langland's poetic project. In the A text the quest—and the poem—simply grinds to a halt. Here the breakdown appears as an inevitable consequence of the patient and pious fideism that the dreamer advocates in the closing lines (A.XI.309–13), which makes any further intellectual and poetic searching appear futile. Yet the dreamer's own position at the end of the A-text, and *a fortiori* Langland's, is also more complicated and paradoxical:[14] the situation is deeply unresolved, and it has become a critical commonplace to observe that the A text of *Piers Plowman* ends 'abruptly', in an 'impasse', 'in crisis', or on a note of 'near-despair'.[15] While the crisis is not resolved in any simple, immediate, and definitive fashion in the B text, clearly Langland's revisions here are designed to move beyond the paralysis that concludes the A text. Movement out of this paralysis is negotiated slowly, painstakingly and through the messy push-and-pull of conflict and debate, false starts, qualifications, and the careful, tentative, and provisional 'solutions' that crystallize between the beginning of Will's first inner vision (B XI.5) and the end of the fourth vision (B XIV.335). The remainder of this chapter will focus on these portions of the text.

Much has been written about the exact nature of the reorientation that leads from A to B, about its deeper significance, and its ability to he transform the overall

---

[14] So on the one hand Will's anti-intellectualism is complicated by the fact that throughout the third vision, it is Will himself who is most consistently rebuked for his excessively academic intellectual leanings; we thus have an intellectual advocating an anti-intellectual position. On the other hand the A-text's abrupt ending makes it impossible to determine if and to what extent Langland himself, as author, would have shared Will's anti-intellectualism. See especially Malcolm Godden, *The Making of Piers Plowman* (London and. New York: Longman, 1990), pp. 74–5.

[15] See respectively R. W. Chambers, '*Piers Plowman*: A Comparative Study', in *Man's Unconquerable mind: Studies of English writers, from Bede to A. E. Housman and W. P. Ker* (London: Jonathan Cape, 1939), pp. 129–31; John Alford, 'The Design of the Poem', in Alford, ed., *A Companion to Piers Plowman*, pp. 29–66 (46); Simpson, *Introduction*, pp. 103–4; Ralph Hanna, 'The Versions and Revisions of *Piers Plowman*', in Andrew Cole and Andrew Galloway, eds, *The Cambridge Companion to Piers Plowman* (Cambridge: Cambridge University Press, 2014), pp. 33–49 (44).

340 MEDIEVAL ALLEGORY AS EPISTEMOLOGY

outlook of the poem on the back of the developments in B XI to XIV.[16] Joseph Wittig, in an important and influential article, discussed the relevance of monastic as opposed to scholastic faculty psychology for the developments of the 'inner journey' in the B text: the reorientation moves Will away from knowledge conceived as mere *scientia* towards *self*-knowledge understood as a stepping stone to *sapientia*.[17] Such ideas have been developed further by James Simpson in a series of articles, where he argues persuasively that this reorientation brings with it a formal and stylistic shift in rhetorical expression in the poem. The reorientation thus leads from speculative and intellectualized modes of thought and expression to affective ones: increasingly 'the modes of the poetry [are] consistently designed to produce a sapiential, experiential, "kynde" knowing of God'—a development that inevitably works to highlight 'the cognitive limitations of academic learning.'[18] Malcolm Godden provides a similar reading but with a different emphasis: he sees the B text revisions as qualifying, but also to a certain degree reaffirming the anti-intellectualism of the A text, pointing the way towards the emergence of a new ideal in the poem, that of simple, patient poverty and a new trust in the free availability of God's mercy.[19] Such different readings are in many ways complementary rather than mutually exclusive: no single satisfactory account of the reorientation can be given, since a wide range of themes and debates radiate outwards from this single crisis moment, and will be developed further throughout the remainder of the poem: the role of predestination and the freedom of the will; the respective importance of learning and experience, or *clergie* and *kynde knowing*; the importance of mercy and grace vs. faith and works; the ideal of patient poverty; the salvation of the heathen—and, from *passus* XV onwards, the mysterious nature of Charity. Critics concur, however, in identifying the transition from *passus* X to XI and the first inner dream as *the* major reorientation in the poem, the central moment of Will's conversion that marks, in Simpson's words, 'the intellectual and emotional pivot of the whole poem.'[20] Bearing all of these suggestions in mind, I would like to concentrate for a moment on a number of more localized poetic and iconographical details at the very beginning of *passus* XI in the B text—details that both signal and inaugurate Langland's sustained engagement with Deguileville's poem. This

[16] For a good overview of scholarly opinions on this points, see Denise N. Baker, '"The Greatest Riddle of the B Text" of *Piers Plowman*: Why Langland Did Not Scrap the A *Vita*', in Bonnie Wheeler, ed., *Mindful Spirit in Late Medieval Literature: Essays in Honor of Elizabeth D. Kirk* (New York: Palgrave MacMillan, 2006), pp. 149–63.

[17] See Joseph S. Wittig, 'Elements in the Design of the Inward Journey', and ibid 'The Dramatic and Rhetorical Development of Will's Pilgrimage', *Neuphilologische Mitteilungen* 76 (1975), 52–76.

[18] James Simpson, 'From Reason to Affective Knowledge: Modes of Thought and Poetic Form in *Piers Plowman*', *Medium Ævum* 55 (1986), 1–23 (14 and 17). See also ibid., 'The Role of *Scientia* in *Piers Plowman*', in Gregory Kratzmann and James Simpson, eds, *Medieval English Religious and Ethical Literature: Essays in Honour of G. H. Russell* (Cambridge: D. S. Brewer, 1986), pp. 49–65; and ibid., *Introduction* 81–123.

[19] *The Making of Piers Plowman*, pp. 79–116.

[20] Simpson, *Introduction*, p. 108, specifically on B XI.116–17.

THE DESIRE FOR KNOWLEDGE AND THE EXPERIENCE OF CONVERSION 341

moment of transition is thus emblematic for the deeper reorientation that occurs, gradually and laboriously, within the rest of the B-text, preparing the ground for its most profoundly spiritual developments in *passus* XVI to XVIII. I will be arguing that Deguileville's poem appears to have played an important, indeed crucial role in enabling this transition. In particular, the episode of the Pilgrim's arrival at the Rock of Penitence provided the inspiration for Langland's own, more extended and nuanced account of the breakdown and reorientation of Will's spiritual quest in the B text.

The reorientation begins with Scripture's rebuke at the head of *passus* XI:

> Thanne Scripture scorned me and a skile tolde
> And lakked me in Latyn, and lyȝt by me she sette,
> And seide '*Multi multa sciunt et seipsos nesciunt*'.
> Tho wepte I for wo and wraþe of hir speche,
> And in a wynkynge worþ til I was aslepe
>
> (B XI.1–5)

Both the emphasis on self-knowledge and the trope of the tears here are monastic commonplaces, and many relevant texts have been invoked to explain this new departure in the poem.[21] Yet the opening of B XI brings together, in a compact and rhetorically powerful manner, the central motifs of the pilgrim's penitential experience at the Rock of Penitence in *PVH*—itself already loaded with monastic echoes that Deguileville's poem goes on to unpack in its closing sections. Scripture's opening rebuke thus provides a brilliant example of Langland's procedure, exploiting the iconographic and emblematic potential of important narrative moments in Deguileville as a springboard for more extended developments and analysis. The Rock of Penitence provides a particularly useful point of reference for Langland, since it ties together a whole cluster of discourses, themes, motifs, ideas and associations that Langland's B text unpacks over the next five *passus* (XI–XV): monastic self-knowledge; conversion as a penitential process; man's realization of the infirmity of his own will and intellect and a corresponding experience of the overwhelming power of grace. The parallels between the two scenes, then, are not limited to superficial iconographical elements, but touch on the deep narrative movements of the two poems, and on the discursive and intellectual structures that underpin them.

One particularly prominent aspect of these parallels is the analogous use of the trope of the eye—site of intellectual vision but also a spring of penitential tears in both accounts of crisis. I have already discussed the ubiquitous use of metaphors of eyesight to denote different forms of cognition in *PVH*. Knowledge of spiritual

---

[21] Especially Wittig, 'Elements in the Design of the Inward Journey'.

342   MEDIEVAL ALLEGORY AS EPISTEMOLOGY

realities in particular is frequently rendered in terms of 'seeing' (cf. Augustine's *visio mentis*) in a poem that begins by presenting its dreamer's vision of the New Jerusalem refracted in an allegorical mirror (see Chapters 3.2 and 3.5). The weeping eye of the Rock of Penitence reactivates, yet also turns on its head such notions of spiritual/intellectual 'seeing' in the poem (see Chapter 4.1). The pilgrim's weeping eye finally displaces his seeing eye, 'converting' the poem's earlier confidence in man's active cognitive abilities into the pursuit of a new, more mysterious kind of self-knowledge grounded in penitential practice. Langland appears to have registered the rupture produced by this radically different, more introspective and penitential understanding of the metaphorical possibilities associated with the human eye, emblematized by Will's tears and his fall into the inner dream. It is certainly not coincidental, therefore, that Will's 'fall' into a different visionary dimension should redeploy Deguileville's inaugural metonymy of the mirror, transformed into Langland's 'myroure that hight Mydlerd' (B XI.9).[22] This suggests that as well as effecting a transformation in the poem's main protagonist, the episode also requires the poem's reader to modify their definition of the 'visionary' and cognitive possibilities harboured by the poem itself, metonymically figured as a 'mirror' in both *PVH* and *Piers Plowman*. The reader too is invited to re-examine the visionary possibilities afforded by the kind of dream-vision allegory that both Langland and Deguileville are writing, and must redefine their own expectations concerning the kinds of truths that such allegory might refract, and the poetic forms that such a new 'vision' might take. Langland's mirror of 'Mydlerd', then, echoes but also displaces the inaugural allegorical vision of Deguileville's New Jerusalem, and figures a larger cognitive shift in the poem. Instead of refracting the heavenly city or indeed man's original *imago dei*, the mirror/poem now conjures up a very different image of Will's fallen, sinful, and divided self, whose cognitive faculties are—like those of the reader—irremediably impaired.

This reorientation is reflected in the complex and confusing temporality of Will's vision in the inner dream, which provides a telescoped, dramatically compressed overview of the dreamer's life up to the present moment.[23] The retrospective and self-denouncing character of Will's inner dream fits particularly well with the emphasis on self-knowledge in both Deguileville's and Langland's crisis moments, and indeed bears out Grace Dieu's exhortation to 'turn around', to

---

[22] For discussion of mirrors in Langland, see especially Steven F. Kruger, 'Mirrors and the Trajectory of Vision in *Piers Plowman*', *Speculum* 66.1 (1991), 74–95, and further references in ibid., n. 6. For a more recent account of the role of the inner dream as a 'mirror' that reconfigures the poem's ideas of (self-)knowledge and poetic 'vision', usefully converging with the account given here, see also Davis, '*Piers Plowman' and the Book of Nature*, pp. 147–52.

[23] I am following here the reading in Middleton, '"Kynde Name"', and 'Narration and the Invention of Experience: Episodic Form in *Piers Plowman*', in her *Chaucer, Langland and Fourteenth-Century Literary History*, pp. 142–7 (163–4). See also Lawrence M. Clopper, 'The Life of the Dreamer, the Dreams of the Wanderer in *Piers Plowman*', *Studies in Philology* 86.3 (1989), 261–85; J. A. Burrow, 'Langland *nel mezzo del cammin*', in P. L. Heyworth, ed., *Medieval Studies for J.A.W. Bennett* (Oxford, Clarendon Press, 1981), pp. 21–41.

THE DESIRE FOR KNOWLEDGE AND THE EXPERIENCE OF CONVERSION   343

convert the human eye to reconsider one's present moral and psychological state as the result of one's accumulated past action—or indeed *inaction* (Chapter 4.1). Will's inner dream similarly functions as a retrospective look at earlier failures, with the purpose of giving a new, different sense of purpose and direction to his quest. The tears falling from Will's eyes at the beginning of the *passus* thus become inextricably associated with his gaze into the mirror of Mydlerd, and the panoramic view over the 'londe of longynge' that opens up within it (B XI.8). What Will sees in the inner dream is not, then, a 'vision' in any easily understood, previously available sense. As Stephen Kruger has suggested, the inner dream 'offers nothing like transcendent vision'—although Kruger's contention that this is therefore a 'false mirror' rather overshoots the mark and short-circuits the problem.[24] The mirror is more profoundly ambiguous, and here too Langland develops ideas made available by *PVH2*. Deguileville had complicated the status of his inaugural allegorical mirror by supplying a further, double mirror of 'parole d'adulacion' (15,331) and 'miroir de conscience' (15,429) carried by Agiographe. As I have argued above, the presence of this further mirror in *PVH2* ultimately prompts a reconsideration of the ability of the poem as a whole—itself a 'beau miroir de sauvement'—to refract any kind of truth in unambiguous and unproblematic fashion (see Chapter 4.5). Significantly, Agiographe in *PVH2* had been identified with 'Sainte Escripture' herself (*PVH2* 15,453), providing a powerful precedent for Langland's own use of personified Scripture to direct Will's gaze into a similarly ambiguous mirror. Rather than being a 'false mirror' in any simple sense, then, Will's mirror of Mydlerd refracts its own form of truth, forcing both Will and the reader to redefine what such truth might 'look like', and announcing the advent of new forms of vision, expression, and self-understanding in the poem.

The reading I have been pursuing suggests that it is precisely because of its refusal to offer a transcendent and totalizing eschatological vision that the mirror of the inner dream provides a higher and far 'truer', indeed painfully accurate image of the dreamer's own degenerate condition in the land of Fortune, *Concupiscientia-Carnis*, Coueitise of Eiȝes, and Pride of Parfit-Lyuynge (B XI.12–15 ff.)—trapped in a 'lond of longynge' (B XI.8) that is clearly an avatar of Augustine's and Bernard's *regio dissimilitudinis*.[25] In allowing such a retrospective vision, the inner dream reproduces the pilgrim's painful, traumatic realization that his own 'pilgrimage', up to the moment of his arrival at the Rock of Penitence, has in fact been no more than a misguided errance through his own version of the *regio dissimilitudinis* along the path of Huiseuse. This retrospective

---

[24] I'm alluding to the different stages in the analysis proposed by Stephen Kruger, 'Mirrors and the Trajectory of Vision', 79–80. Kruger's initial emphasis on the supposedly contrary, positive and negative features of the two mirrors of the C-text seem to me problematic, and indeed his analysis increasingly emphasizes the ambivalence of both mirrors in the later sections of his article.

[25] See Wittig, 'Elements in the Design of the Inward Journey', 232–4, 247–8 and *passim*; Murtaugh, *Piers Plowman and the Image of God*, p. 76; Middleton, '"Kynde Name"', pp. 224–36.

344   MEDIEVAL ALLEGORY AS EPISTEMOLOGY

vision is instrumental in effecting a process of conversion in the fullest sense, and Langland's account of the inner dream demonstrably references *the* paradigmatic account of Christian conversion provided in Augustine's *Confessions*.[26] Although it takes a negative, paradoxical form, the mirror of Will's inner dream refracts its own form of truth, redirecting and redefining the dreamer/wanderer's quest in ways that resonate profoundly with the pilgrim's conversion at the Rock of Penitence in *PVH*. Both travellers experience a paradoxical form of self-knowledge, realizing their own condition as cognitively impaired, seemingly powerless individual agents.

2. Vision and Penitence: 'to se moche and suffre more'

Will's crisis does not simply provide self-knowledge in any simple, easily understood sense, but rather redefines what such self-knowledge might look like—or indeed *feel* like, experientially, in terms of 'Kynde Knowyng'.[27] As in *PVH*, such knowledge takes the paradoxical form of experiencing the impossibility of fully getting to know oneself through one's own efforts. True self-knowledge is acquired through the frustrating experience of such absolute limits, leading to the recognition of the dependence on a larger, higher force to reveal the true nature of the self to itself.

The unexpected and abrupt nature of this new visionary experience is well rendered by the impression of Will's 'fall' into vision at the beginning of the first inner dream. Commenting on Will's tears here, Stephanie Trigg has observed how in this episode 'the dreamer is taken somewhere else through his weeping state', and how 'tears signal the dreamer's transition into a passive state, as dreams and visions come to him'.[28] It is not accidental that both poems should emphasize the eminently *passive* nature of this realization, apprehended in distinctively corporeal, affective manner, and opening the doors to entirely new, contingent and experiential forms of (self-)knowledge. Indeed, several interlocutors in this section of *Piers Plowman* work to redefine the notion of 'vision' itself by progressively abandoning visual tropes of seeing-as-knowledge altogether, prompting Will to

---

[26] Gruenler, *'Piers Plowman' and the Poetics of Enigma*, pp. 206–19.

[27] For some of the most influential studies on Langland's understanding of this term, see Mary Clemente Davlin, '"Kynde Knowyng" as a Major Theme in *Piers Plowman* B', *Review of English Studies* 22 (1971), 1–19; ibid., '"Kynde Knowyng" as a Middle English Equivalent for "Wisdom" in *Piers Plowman*', *Medium Aevum* 50 (1981), 5–17; Britton J. Harwood, 'Langland's "Kynde Knowyng" and the Quest for Christ', *Modern Philology* 80.3 (1983), 242–55; ibid., *Piers Plowman and the Problem of Belief* (Toronto: Toronto University Press, 1992), pp. 2–31; Simpson, 'From Reason to Affective Knowledge'; Simpson, 'Scientia', 49; Hugh White, *Nature and Salvation in 'Piers Plowman'* (Woodbridge: D. S. Brewer, 1988), esp. pp. 3–59. On the centrality of 'experience' in the poem and its relation to 'kynde knowyng', see also Mishtooni Bose, 'Piers Plowman and God's Thought Experiment', in Knox, Morton and Reeve, *Medieval Thought Experiments*, pp. 71–97, esp. 90–1. See also the observations in Galloway's *Penn Commentary 1*, pp. 119–21, 180–2, 200–1.

[28] Stephanie Trigg: 'Langland's Tears: Poetry, Emotion and Mouvance', *YLS* 26 (2012), 27–48 (37).

THE DESIRE FOR KNOWLEDGE AND THE EXPERIENCE OF CONVERSION   345

obtain more direct, experiential, and ultimately sapiential knowledge of spiritual, theological, and doctrinal truths. This development begins with Dame Study's remarks (B X.127–36), discussed above, where visual tropes denote a dangerously abstract, intellectualized, and therefore limited (mis-)understanding of spiritual realities.[29] Other personifications similarly discourage Will from looking into 'Goddes pryvetee' from such an analytical and rationalistic viewpoint, hammering home their point with repeated Latin citations warning against the intellectual 'covetousness' of divine *scrutatores*: [Trajan]: '*melius est scrutari scelera nostra quam naturas rerum*' (B XI.229a), [Anima]: '*sic qui scrutator est maiestatis, opprimatur a gloria*' (B XV.55a).

Following the lead of the pilgrim's conversion in *PVH*, the experience of conversion in *passus* XI thus tends to emphasize the conspicuously passive position of the individual in the face of the agency of divine grace and mercy. Yet unlike Deguileville, Langland also dwells on the positive and enabling consequences of such divine intervention in terms of the newfound agency of the individual will/Will. This allows him to establish a productive if fragile balance between action and passion, avoiding Deguileville's radically anti-Pelagian position. This desire to produce a more nuanced account of the dialectic of individual action and passion comes into focus as the motif of the penitential weeping is picked up again later in the *passus*, as part of Trajan's long speech.[30] There the tearful 'sourness' of suffering becomes the gateway towards the sapiential 'sweetness' of spiritual reward, as Trajan establishes a broad analogy between the penitential process and the experience of patient poverty.[31] Ultimately the tears themselves, and the passive and penitential disposition they denote, paradoxically become a means of individual penitential and devotional *action*, allowing man 'to haue mynde in God and a gre wille/ to wepe and to wel bidde':

> 'And alle þe wyse þat euere were, by auȝt I kan aspye,
> Preisen pouerte for best lif, if pacience it folwe,
> And boþe bettre and blesseder by many fold þan ricchesse.
> Alþouȝ it be sour to suffre, þer comeþ swete after;
> As on a walnote wiþoute is a bitter barke,
> And after þat bitter bark, be þe shelle aweye,
> Is a kernel of confort kynde to restore.
> So is after pouerte or penaunce paciently ytake,
> Makeþ a man to haue mynde in God and a gre wille

---

[29] Zeeman, *Discourses of Desire*, pp. 157–200.

[30] There is some debate about the identity of the speaker in the poem after the appearance of Trajan at XI.140. I follow Simpson, *Introduction*, p. 112, in attributing the whole speech at XI.140–317 to Trajan.

[31] On the importance of the ideal of patient poverty, see especially Godden, *The Making of Piers Plowman*, pp. 78–116, for whom the ideal lies at the heart of the new, revised B version.

346 MEDIEVAL ALLEGORY AS EPISTEMOLOGY

> To wepe and to wel bidde, wherof wexeþ mercy,
> Of which Crist is a kernell to conforte þe soule.'
>
> (B XI.254–64)

Crucially, man's 'willingness' to suffer, weep, and pray, engenders the operation of mercy, and the passive, 'suffering' penitential disposition of the individual meta-morphoses into the act of prayer ('bidde'), making it into a catalyst of divine agency.[32] Both of these passages in *Piers Plowman* thus set up a productive econ-omy of human passion and divine action, individual prayer and devotion and divine mercy. This tempers and modifies the far more radical and bleak picture of a debilitated individual will found in *PVH*.

Langland's use of the binary bark-and-kernel imagery here is also revealing in other ways. The trope is widely available, but again Langland puts a tradi-tional image to strikingly new and complex use. Rather than exploiting the usual exegetical resonances of this binary image—as happens in both *Rose* and *PVH*[33]— Langland uses the image to describe an experience of an utterly different kind, unmediated by textuality. The bitter bark and the sweet nut visualize not so much an interpretive, exegetical access to spiritual truths mediated by reading, but an experiential access to the redeeming effects of divine 'mercy, / Of which Crist is a kernell' (B XI.265–6), evoking ideas of sapiential ingestion (Lat. *sapor*). The image in itself encapsulates the reorientation of Langland's own poem, deeply influenced by Deguileville's turn towards 'sapiential' models of knowledge after the pilgrim's conversion at the Rock of Penitence (see Chapter 4.2). We are mov-ing away from an analytical, explicative, and 'scientific' understanding of divine mysteries—hinging on the hermeneutic and rationalistic agency of the individ-ual *viator*, and postulated on a semiotic disjunction of shell and nut, wheat and chaff (cf. *RR* 11,787; *PVH2* 17,732–43), *signum* and *res*, body and soul—towards an embodied, affective, and largely passive individual experience of their effects through the sacraments, specifically penance and—implicitly—the Eucharistic sacrament itself (see Chapter 5.6).

Despite deep thematic resonances and structural parallels with *PVH*, then, Langland modulates the French poet's rejection of cognitive and hermeneutic desire in distinctive ways. Deguileville's pilgrim is truly overwhelmed by the

---

[32] The same idea of a reciprocal action is again picked up in Ymaginatif's speech in *passus* XII, in the characteristic shape of an imaginative analogy: 'Ac grace is a grasse therefore the grevaunces to abate. / Ac grace ne groweþ noughte til good wil yeve reyne' (XII.59–60). On Ymaginatif's 'synergistic theory' see also Adams, 'Piers's Pardon', 393–4.

[33] See for instance the opposition of *escorce* and *moëlle* in Faux Semblant's speech at *RR* 11,828–30, and *paille* and *grain* at the end of *PVH2* (17,732–43), where Deguileville discusses the interpreta-tion of his own dream/poem (see Chapters 1.4 and 4.4). At *RR* 11,787 Faux Semblant compares the shell (*quoque*) and kernel (*noiaus*) of a nut (*noiz*) to oppose precious and worthless items. Faux Semblant's speech is organized around ideas of deception and dissimulation, and mobilizes the exeget-ical/integumental resonances of the image. Specifically, Faux Semblant compares the 'false Gospel' of the *Evangile pardurable* with the 'true' Gospels of the four Evangelists.

THE DESIRE FOR KNOWLEDGE AND THE EXPERIENCE OF CONVERSION 347

intensity of his conversion at the hands of Grace Dieu, pushing him to withdraw into the monastery and moving the poem towards a radical rejection of its original desire for the kind of rationalistic understanding associated with scholastic *scientia*. It is within the monastery, after the pilgrimage has been broken off and all former desire for active demonstrative and rationalistic knowledge renounced, that the pilgrim can finally *experience* the salvific effects of the word incarnate, through prayer, devotion, and the liturgy. A similar transition occurs in *Piers Plowman*, but rather than breaking off Will's pilgrimage, Langland gives the journey a new, more complex orientation, attempting a more nuanced if unstable integration of action and passion, vision and experience, seeing and suffering. It is therefore perfectly fitting for Will to affirm that do-well is 'to se muche and suffre moore' on waking from his inner dream (B XI.410), formulating an ideal for the perfect if unequal balance between 'seeing' and 'suffering', active search and passive experience. Significantly, this newfound balance depends on the priority of suffering over seeing, emphasizing the passive endurance of lack and ignorance rather than the active effort to overcome it.[34] Clergie's response confirms Will's belated realization, castigating him once more for his renewed bout of cognitive/visual *curiositas*:

> 'Haddestow suffred', he seyde, 'slepyng þo þow were,
> Thow sholdest haue knowen that Clergie can,
> and conceyued moore þoruȝ Reson.
> [...]
> Ac for þyn entremetynge here artow forsake.'
>
> (B XI.411–14)

Crucially, it is the passivity of suffering itself that works as an apt human approximation of Christ's own passion—'who suffreþ moore þan God?' (B XI.379).[35] It is this passive endurance of his own failures and limitations, paradoxically, that ultimately facilitates the operation of 'Resoun', and prepares Will/the will to understand the nature of Charity more fully in the developments in B XV to XVI (see Chapter 6). This in turn allows him—eventually—to receive a fuller, experiential understanding of the Atonement through a re-enactment of sacred history in *passus* XVI to XVIII, culminating with Christ's Incarnation, and Will's Easter Sunday awakening (see Chapter 7).[36]

---

[34] Zeeman, *Discourses of Desire*, pp. 240–2.

[35] See especially Elizabeth D. Kirk, '"Who suffreth more than God": Narrative Redefinition of Patience in *Patience* and *Piers Plowman*', in Gerald J. Schiffhorst, ed., *The Triumph of Patience* (Orlando: University Press of Florida, 1978), pp. 88–104 (100–2); and more recently Rosenfeld, *Love after Aristotle*, pp. 130–1.

[36] A. V. C. Schmidt, 'The Inner Dreams in *Piers Plowman*', *Medium Ævum* 55.1 (1986), 24–40 (34–7); ibid., 'Langland and the Mystical Tradition', in Marion Glasscoe, ed., *The Medieval Mystical Tradition in England: Papers Read at the Exeter Symposium* (University of Exeter, 1980), pp. 17–38 (21–4).

348 MEDIEVAL ALLEGORY AS EPISTEMOLOGY

In emphasizing the passive nature of Will's tearful conversion, Langland thus adopts a central element of the pilgrim's crisis in *PVH*, but also nuances and transforms its significance. Accordingly, the meaning of Will's tears at the start of *passus* XI is more complex and ambivalent,[37] and cannot be reduced to the rather neat didactic explanation provided by Grace Dieu in *PVH*, where tears are interpreted as unmistakeable marks of contrition. Will sheds tears of 'wo and wraþe' (B XI.4) that are not penitential in any immediate and obvious sense: they seem to denote other, less easily identifiable and less obviously penitential emotions such as anger, frustration, or even despair, and Ralph Hanna goes as far as describing the scene as 'a Parody [. . .] of self-abasement'.[38] Yet for all of Langland's creative, disruptive, and idiosyncratic engagement with the image, the scene marks the poem's return to its deep-seated penitential preoccupations. A sustained concern with penitence, then, runs deep underground throughout the following *passus* (B XI–XV), counterpointing Langland's careful reconsideration of the legitimacy of learning or *clergie*.

Penitence has long been recognized as one of Langland's primary concerns in *Piers Plowman*,[39] and this concern emerges well before the middle sections of the poem. *Passus* V as a whole, for instance, is dedicated to an exploration of penitence, and thus serves as a preparation for later and more problematic developments. Significantly, in *passus* V the treatment of penitential themes is once more introduced by Will's tears, preparing us for the emotionally intense confessions of the seven deadly sins later in the *passus*. While the significance of Will's tears in *passus* V is more obviously penitential, Langland already handles traditional iconographical motifs in ways that invite us to explore additional complexities and paradoxes related to the individual *experience* of penance.[40] Indeed, Will's weeping in *passus* V remains curiously disembodied, as if to suggest that Will's experience of penance at this stage remains abstract and programmatic. The narrator here shifts to a third-person account, which has a distancing and de-familiarizing effect:[41]

> Thanne ran Repentaunce and reherced his teme
> And garte Wille to wepe water wiþ hise eiȝen
>
> (B V.60–1)

---

[37] See again Trigg, 'Langland's Tears', 37.

[38] Ralph Hanna, 'Langland's Ymaginatif: Images and the Limits of Poetry', in Dimmick, Simpson, and Zeeman, eds, *Images, Idolatry and Iconoclasm in Late Medieval England*, pp. 81–94 (84).

[39] The fullest study remains unpublished, Nicholas Gray, 'A Study of *Piers Plowman* in relation to the Medieval Penitential Tradition'. Unpublished PhD dissertation, Cambridge University, 1984.

[40] See especially Larry Scanlon, 'Personification and Penance', *YLS* 21 (2007), 1–29, who attributes an important role to Faux Semblant in triggering reflections on the pitfalls and difficulties of Penance—and authorship—in the poetry of both Chaucer and Langland. Further on Faux Semblant, see Chapters 7.2 and 7.4.

[41] Trigg, 'Langland's Tears', pp. 32–4.

THE DESIRE FOR KNOWLEDGE AND THE EXPERIENCE OF CONVERSION   349

In the light of later developments, then, this earlier scene serves to introduce a cluster of penitential motifs and ideas, which are, however, redeployed and made operational only much later in Will's quest.[42] This strategy too appears distinctly Deguilevillian: as discussed in Chapter 4.1, the pilgrim's quest in *PVH* similarly returns to its penitential concern periodically, with growing urgency an intensity— from the programmatic encounter with Penitance personified at the beginning of the poem, carrying broom, mallet, and rods, to the Hedge of Penitence after the pilgrim's encounter with Huiseuse, and finally to the dramatic and tearful conversion at the Rock of Penitence. This tendency of both poems to crystallize a sequence of increasingly powerful yet finally insufficient and provisional explorations of penitence—or what Alford calls the 'repeated narrative shedding of the outer forms of penance'[43]—corroborates the impression that Langland reworked Deguileville's poem far more carefully, deeply, and deliberately than is commonly allowed.

Will's inner dream in B XI works to focus attention more tightly on the question of contrition. Shortly after his tearful fall into the inner dream, Will himself articulates the centrality of contrition for enabling salvation—even if at this stage his understanding remains imperfect and largely theoretical, as is suggested by his reference to the opinion of the 'maistres':

> 'For a baptiȝed man may, as maistres telleþ,
> Throuȝ contricion come to þe heiȝe heuene –
> *Sola contricio delet peccatum*'
>
> (B XI.80–81a)

The centrality of contrition in enabling Will's own conversion becomes more tangible and dramatic when Will, in two 'unbearably postponed lines',[44] observes that all Christians would be condemned to purgatory were it not for the possibility of contrition:

> '[Reson and Conscience] putten hym after in a prison in purgatorie to brenne,
> For hise arerages rewarden hym þere riȝt to ȝe day of dome,
> But if Contricion wol come and crye bi his lyue
> Mercy for hise mysdedes wiþ mouþe and wiþ herte.'
>
> (B XI.133–6)

---

[42] For a systematic discussion of moments of weeping in the poem, see Trigg, 'Langland's Tears'.

[43] John A. Alford, 'The Figure of Repentance in *Piers Plowman*', in David C. Fowler and Mícéal F. Vaughan, eds, *Suche Werkis to Werche: Essays on Piers Plowman in Honor of David C. Fowler* (East Lansing, Colleagues Press, 1993), pp. 3–28 (28).

[44] Simpson, *Introduction*, pp. 110.

350   MEDIEVAL ALLEGORY AS EPISTEMOLOGY

Such evocations of contrition in B XI are in many ways the tip of an iceberg, pointing to the poem's ongoing, even obsessive concern with contrition as *the* keystone of Langland's penitential system, which like so many contemporary accounts by theologians of widely different persuasions emphasizes that *sola contritio delet peccatum*.[45] While a fuller discussion of the complex, growing importance of contrition in the evolving structure of *Piers Plowman* lies beyond the scope of the present analysis, it is worth emphasizing that contrition comes to occupy an increasingly important place in *Piers Plowman*—not only as Will's quest advances, but also as Langland's poetic project evolves through its different versions, culminating in the C text revisions.[46] Deguileville's Rock of Penitence, then, was not only a major touchstone for Langland's movement out of the impasse at the end of the A text and into the B text. This emblematic moment was also instrumental in focusing Langland's attention more strongly on the mysterious, profoundly paradoxical and transformative role of contrition in enabling the individual to participate in a wider, freely available yet often opaque and inscrutable economy of salvation. In the passage from B XI.133–6, just quoted, contrition is unmistakably personified, intervening in the life of an individual Christian by 'crying' on his account. The formulation is unusual and conspicuous, and works to heighten the impression of an external intervention, an intercession passively experienced by the faithful. Deguileville uses personification in similar if more obvious ways, to visualize a theological point: the whole process of conversion is essentially orchestrated by Grace personified, as if to emphasize man's fundamental dependence on divine intervention to effect such a process of turning around. Langland again departs from Deguileville in avoiding such direct and schematic transposition of doctrinal points, and in mitigating the protagonist's renunciation of personal agency. But the role of grace in Langland's poem from this moment onwards is no less central, if less evidently apparent.[47]

---

[45] See Alan J. Fletcher, 'The Essential (Ephemeral) William Langland: Textual Revision as Ethical Process in *Piers Plowman*', *YLS* 15 (2001), 61–98 (64), referring also to Anne Hudson, *The Premature Reformation: Wycliffite Texts and Lollard history* (Oxford: Clarendon Press, 1988), pp. 404–5.

[46] See variously Alford 'The Figure of Repentance'; and again Fletcher, 'The Essential (Ephemeral) William Langland', esp. 64–8, who identifies the tradition of medieval sermons as a key influence on Langland; and Míceál F. Vaughan, '"Til I gan awake": The Conversion of Dreamer into Narrator in *Piers Plowman* B', *YLS* 5 (1991), 175–92 (188–91). For other treatments of contrition in the poem, see for instance B XII.175–8; B XIV.16 and 83-97 B XIV.282 and 286, B XV.194. In the concluding sections of the poem (for which see Chapter 7), Contrition is finally defeated and exposes the Barn of Unity to the perverted penitential practices of Friar Flatterer. On the centrality of this concern with the erosion of the economy of penitence and its moral and metaphysical logic in the poem, and on the growing importance of this concern with the perversion of contrite repentance across the three versions of the poem, see especially Traugott Lawler 'Harlots' Holiness: The System of Absolution for Miswinning in the C Version of *Piers Plowman*', *YLS* 20 (2006), 141–89. See also Robert Worth Frank, 'The Conclusion of *Piers Plowman*', *JEGP* 49 (1950), 309–16. See however Kathryn Kerby-Fulton, 'Langland and the Bibliographic Ego', in Stephen Justice and Kathryn Kerby-Fulton, eds, *Written Work: Langland, Labor, and Authorship* (Philadelphia: University of Pennsylvania Press, 1997), pp. 67–143 (75), on the newly controversial resonance of the argument for *sola contitio* at B XI.80–1 in the wake of the 1382 Blackfriars council, and Langland's decision to remove references to the question at the time of the C-revisions.

[47] An important, paradigmatic moment of conversion through the operation of grace is to be found in Augustine's *Confessions*, books VII and VIII, as observed by Wittig, 'Elements in the Design of the

THE DESIRE FOR KNOWLEDGE AND THE EXPERIENCE OF CONVERSION   351

Such an emphasis on the overwhelming power of grace brings with it its own set of dangers that Langland is keenly aware of. Indeed much of the action in the poem in B XI to XV is designed to emphasize the centrality of grace, while also exorcizing the dangerously passive fideism that this realization may engender in Will—a mercurial persona always prone to 'wilful' misunderstandings of Christian doctrine in order to justify his own spiritual shortcomings. Throughout the subsequent action, then, Will often displays a complacent, excessively self-assured and even presumptuous tendency to take divine intervention for granted, renouncing any personal agency along with the value of *clergie* altogether. This radical renunciation of individual agency, however, places excessive, nearly absolute pressure on divine agency, thus easily transforming Will's overconfidence into despairing impotence and expectancy, flaring up periodically (e.g. notably at B XI.133–6). The action in B XI–XV is thus intended to highlight the difficulty of steering a middle course between the extremes of a fundamentally anti-intellectual fideism on the one hand, and an inflated valorization of learning and works on the other. The push-and-pull of argument, dispute, and qualification in turn produces a much more nuanced, if unstable, integration of divine grace with *kynde wit* and *clergie*, culminating with Anima's remarks in *passus* XV (see Chapter 6.4).

The figure of Ymaginatif is emblematic of such difficulties and negotiations.[48] Intervening after the dramatic crisis of learning that is played out in *passus* B X and XI, Ymaginatif is often seen as correcting Will's excessive fideism while

---

Inward Journey', 245–63. This emphasis on the crucial role of grace does not, however, necessarily make Langland's attitude aggressively anti-Pelagian or radically Augustinian like Deguileville's in *PVH1*. For a seminal discussion of Langland's receptiveness towards fourteenth-century arguments about the primacy of grace over individual merit, especially those advanced by radical 'Augustinian' theologians, see Denise N. Baker 'From Plowing to Penitence: *Piers Plowman* and Fourteenth-Century Theology', *Speculum* 55.4 (1980), 715–25. See also Woolf, 'The Tearing of the Pardon'. For further discussion emphasizing the complexity and fluidity of Langland's position, see especially Bowers, *The Crisis of Will*. See also e.g. Robert Adams, 'Piers's Pardon and Langland's Semi-Pelagianism', *Traditio* 39 (1983), 367–418; ibid. 'Langland's Theology', in Alford, *Companion*, esp. pp. 95–8; Coleman, *Piers Plowman and the Moderni*, pp. 11–35, 108–46; Murtaugh, *Piers Plowman and the Image of God*, 63–97. For a recent call to redefine Langland's own 'Augustinianism', and to take the nuances of Augustine's own position more seriously, see Aers, *Salvation and Sin*, especially pp. 1–25 on questions of agency and conversion.

[48] The critical literature on Ymaginatif is abundant. In what follows I make no attempt to explore the full complexity of the figure, or indeed to define its status in relation to medieval theories of cognition. As the widely divergent readings of critics demonstrate, it appears increasingly difficult to explain Ymaginatif's role in the poem in terms of scholastic or pre-scholastic accounts of cognition, or indeed to assign an easily circumscribed cognitive function to this figure. For the most important discussions, see Alastair J. Minnis, 'Langland's Ymaginatif and Late-Medieval Theories of Imagination', *Comparative Criticism: A Yearbook* 3 (1981), 71–103; Ernest N. Kaulbach, 'The *Vis Imaginativa* and the Reasoning Powers of Ymaginatif in the B-Text of *Piers Plowman*', *JEGP* 84.1 (1985), 16–29; Hugh White, 'Langland's Ymaginatif, Kynde and the *Benjamin Major*', *Medium Ævum* 55.2 (1986), 241–8; Simpson, *Introduction*, pp. 136–9; Laurence M. Eldredge, 'Some Medical Evidence on Langland's Imaginatif', *YLS* 3 (1989), 131–36; Thomas A. Ryan 'Scripture and the Prudent Ymaginatif', *Viator* 23 (1992), 215–30; Harwood, *Piers Plowman and the Problem of Belief*, pp. 84–90; Patrick J. Gallacher, 'Imaginatif and the Sensus Communis', *YLS* 6 (1992), 51–60; Mary Carruthers, 'Imaginatif, Memoria, and The Need for Critical Theory in *Piers Plowman* Studies', *YLS* 9 (1995), 103–20; Hanna, 'Langland's Ymaginatif'; Karnes, 'Will's Imagination in *Piers Plowman*'.

352   MEDIEVAL ALLEGORY AS EPISTEMOLOGY

also effecting a reconciliation of *clergie* and *kynde wit* (esp. B XII.81–100).[49] Following on from earlier developments, Ymaginatif insists on the mysterious nature of grace, impervious to intellectual analysis: 'grace is a gifte of God and of greet loue spryngeþ; / Knew neuere clerk how it comeþ forth, ne kynde wyt þe weyes' (B XII.68–9). Ymaginatif also discourages excessive intellectual probing, and condemns Will for his foolish attempt to outreason Reason herself: 'And so I seye by þee, þat sekest after þe whyes, / and aresonedest Reson, a rebukynge as it were' (B XII.217–18; see also XI.375–6). Yet Ymaginatif also tempers the anti-intellectualism of the previous *passus*, and provides a sustained defence of the value of *clergie*. It is important to emphasize, however, that *clergie* for Ymaginatif does not consist of advanced theological learning, but defines basic literacy and elementary religious instruction.[50] Ymaginatif insists primarily on the central role of simple pastoral and clerical instruction in the scheme of salvation.

Langland's effort to reintroduce the question of the relative value of learning comes as a reaction against Deguileville's far more radical anti-intellectualism, particularly pronounced in *PVH1*. In this sense it is symptomatic that Ymaginatif should also reintroduce tropes of vision in relation to learning, as if to signal Langland's renewed engagement with fundamental questions relating to the value of knowledge understood as 'vision', and to the role of the human will and intellect in ensuring individual salvation. Knowledge is divided into two complementary aspects in Ymaginatif's speech: *clergie* and *kynde wit*, roughly equivalent to book-learning and practical, experiential understanding. Both modes of knowledge are valued—but only in relation to the self-examination they enable, as mirrors for the subject: 'boþe as mirours ben to amenden oure defautes' (B XII.95), in what is yet another use of the recurrent imagery of mirrors in the poem. Further developing the visual semantic field introduced by this latest allusion to the mirror of vision/understanding, Ymaginatif now compares a total lack of *clergie* to blindness: 'For as a man may noȝt see þat mysseþ his eiȝen, / Na moore kan no clerk but if he cauȝte it first þoruȝ bokes' (B XII.99–100), and, expanding the simile, finally goes on to compare the unlearned to a blind wayfarer: 'And riȝt as syȝte serueþ a man to se þe heiȝe strete, / Riȝt so lereþ lettrure lewed men to reson' (B XII.103–4). All of these images develop the Deguilevillian notion of the pilgrim as wayfarer, and reintroduce the fundamental question of the relevance of learning to the Christian *viator*'s ability to complete his pilgrimage and attain salvation,

---

[49] See for instance White, *Nature and Salvation*, pp. 24–5; Karnes, 'Will's Imagination', pp. 44–6 and *passim*. Karnes' interpretation of *clergie* as a form of revealed knowledge, and her reading of Ymaginatif as a personification of an Aristotelian faculty seem to me rather more debatable.

[50] See especially Hanna, 'Langland's Ymaginatif', who suggests that the main point of reference for the character's striking associative method is to be sought in literature of basic pastoral and grammatical instruction.

during a moment of major crisis and reorientation in the poem. If in Deguileville's *PVH* the searching eye of the intellect is definitively displaced by the weeping eye of the individual penitent, Langland's Ymaginatif allows for a modified, transformed understanding of the role of the intellect and human learning in guiding the wayfarer's quest.

Rather than merely rehabilitating *clergie*, Ymaginatif can thus be said to redefine its limits, its uses, and its prerogatives, along with those of *kynde wit*. This amounts to setting absolute limits to both forms of knowledge in their attempts to explain divine mysteries: 'Clergie ne Kynde Wit ne knew neuere þe cause, / Ac Kynde [i.e. "God"] knoweþ þe cause hymself, no creature ellis' (B XII.224–5). Rather than rendering all knowledge futile, however, the recognition and acceptance of such absolute limits enables both forms of knowledge to recover their proper value, and their legitimate, instrumental place in the scheme of salvation. For Ymaginatif, then, *kynde wit* and *clergie* are not only useful but fundamentally interdependent, since they are deeply 'akin' to each other and 'of a kind' with the divine mysteries they can mediate: 'Forþi I counseille þee for Cristes sake, clergie þat þow louye; / For kynde wit is of his kyn, and neiȝe cosynes boþe / To Oure Lord, leue me—forþi loue hem, I rede' (B XII.92–4). In a soteriological perspective, however, *clergie* plays a far more important role than *kynde wit*. Of the latter, Ymaginatif declares that 'þoruȝ hir science sooþly was neuere no soule ysaued / Ne broȝt by hir bokes to blisse ne to joye' (B XII.133–4). While the knowledge of divine causes eludes both forms of human understanding, *clergie* alone can aid man in attaining the goal of individual salvation.

As part of his recuperation of *clergie*, Ymaginatif also rejects Deguileville's radical anti-Pelagianism, particularly pronounced in *PVH1*. Whereas Deguileville's pilgrim bewails the futility of 'ethical' learning in the ABC prayer (*PVH1* 11169–72, see Chapter 4.1), Ymaginatif emphatically insists that without learning, repentance can occur only with great difficulty: 'he þat knoweþ clergie kan sonner arise / Out of synne and be saaf, þouȝ he synne ofte' (B XII.171–2). A crucial element in Ymaginatif's defence of *clergie*, then, is his insistence that learning is not only broadly valuable, but that it serves a practical salvific, specifically *penitential* purpose. Here Langland clearly departs from Deguileville by emphasizing that *clergie* facilitates contrition—the experience at the heart of penitential process as it is understood by Langland: 'For if þe clerk be konnynge he knoweþ what is synne, / And how contricioun wiþoute confession conforteþ þe soule' (B XII.174–5). This is a major departure from Deguileville, and indeed Ymaginatif here plays not a narrowly cognitive/imaginative role, but develops an emphatically *penitential* function within the larger structure of the poem. This is compounded by the initial thrust of Ymaginatif's speech, ringing variations on the theme of 'Amende þee while þow myȝt' (XII.10)—a feature that often goes unnoticed in the critical literature, overly concerned to explain the character of Ymaginatif with

354 MEDIEVAL ALLEGORY AS EPISTEMOLOGY

reference to Aristotelian faculty psychology.[51] Thus, rather than opposing learning and penitence as Deguileville's Grace Dieu does, Langland's Ymaginatif places them in a functional, productive relationship. *Clergie* is a precious good, but only insofar as it is instrumental in the penitential process, serving an overarching soteriological purpose.

Langland's engagement with *PVH* at this point is again confirmed by Ymaginatif's choice of imagery when discussing the role of learning in fostering the salvific agency of the individual will. The important defence of *clergie* as a gateway to contrition and repentance, just quoted, is in fact preceded by the extended analogy of the two swimmers in the Thames:

> 'That oon haþ konnynge and kan swymmen and dyuen,
> That ooþer is lewed of þat labour, lerned neuere swymme.'
>
> (B XII.162-3)

Ymaginatif here explicitly allegorizes the tides as figuring sin (XII.172, 174), in ways reminiscent of Grace Dieu's exposition of the Sea of the World, allegory of the inherently sinful active life. Also Grace Dieu in *PVH* had identified two categories of swimmers: the proficient ones, embarked on a straight journey ('touz drois i vont', *PVH1* 11,625), and the hapless swimmers with their bandaged eyes, groping about aimlessly in the tides (11,607–84). Deguileville's proficient swimmers were kept afloat and on course by their penitential practices—giving of alms and penitential pilgrimage—whereas the pilgrim himself specifically declares himself unable to swim in such fashion (12,257–70). Tellingly, he merely clings on to his Staff of Hope, unable to continue his journey in the active life, and awaits the rescue of Grace, pointing him to the Ship of Religion, allegory for the monastic life.[52] Significantly, then, neither learning nor practical swimming skills in Deguileville play any role in determining the fate of the swimmers like the pilgrim, who relies entirely on the intervention of Divine Grace and thus renounces any individual moral agency. Ymaginatif's reworking of the imagery to ascribe a central role to *clergie* or *konnynge* in determining the individual swimmers' chances of salvation thus contains an underlying critique of Deguileville's radical anti-Pelagianism, and signals Langland's deliberate rejection of the radical contemplative turn that puts an end to the pilgrim's quest in *PVH*.

In the B and C versions, Langland resists or overcomes the temptation to interrupt Will's journey in the manner of Deguileville's pilgrim, who promptly seeks refuge in the Ship of Religion. The possibility of a retreat to monastic

---

[51] It is evident that during this opening speech Ymaginatif / Langland again employs Deguilevillian tropes, such as the 'baleyses' with which 'God beteth his dere children' (XII.12), echoing Penitence's broom in *PVH*. See above, p. 335 n.8.

[52] This motif too is picked up and developed by Langland, in his extended allegory of Holy Church as Noah's Ark, and the clergy as its 'carpenteres' or 'wrightes', B X.405–19. The crucial difference is of course that for Deguileville the Ship denotes the monastic cloister, whereas for Langland it denotes the Christian Church more broadly.

THE DESIRE FOR KNOWLEDGE AND THE EXPERIENCE OF CONVERSION   355

existence is, however, repeatedly contemplated during this section of the poem, underlining Langland's continued creative dialogue with Deguileville in this section of the poem. Clergie's praise of the stability of cloistered life earlier in the exchange contributes to breeding Will's crisis in the first place, leading to the interruption of the pilgrimage in the A text, and helping to trigger Will's tearful despair in the B and C texts, in turn precipitating the inner dream. Indeed, Clergie's remarks appear to suggest that only monastic *peregrinatio in stabilitate* provides a safe gateway to salvation, providing a foretaste of life in the Heavenly City:[53]

> 'For if heuene be on þis erþe, and ese to any soule,
> It is in cloistre or in scole, by manye skiles I fynde.
> For in cloistre comeþ no man to querele ne to fiȝte,
> But al is buxomnesse þere and bokes, to rede and to lerne.'
>
> (B X.298–301; cf. A XI.207–13)

Other, more incidental mentions of the perfect living of contemplatives recur later, as in *passus* B XV in Anima's speech: 'Ancres and heremytes, and monkes and freres / Peeren to Apostles þoruȝ hire parfit lyuynge' (B XV.416–17).

Several commentators have indeed emphasized that in the wake of the first inner dream, the poem starts modulating its ideal with much stronger reference to monastic and ascetic traditions. Malcolm Godden, for instance, emphasizes how the encounter with Haukyn foregrounds Langland's own, at least partial and conditional rejection of the ideal of the active life, consolidating the poem's movement towards more markedly contemplative ideals of patient poverty.[54] Carl Schmidt has explored Langland's debt to the tradition of mysticism, itself ultimately grounded in monastic practice, while Lawrence Clopper argues that the original structure of the poem as a whole in fact reproduces patterns of contemplative meditation, ultimately based on Augustine's theory of threefold vision in his search to understand the mystery of the Trinity.[55] Most interesting is Galloway's discussion of the relevance of a specifically Cistercian context for an understanding of Langland's complex attitude here. Building on C. H. Talbot's study of the changing role of the Cistercian order in late fourteenth-century England, and emphasizing the problematic coexistence of scholastic learning and more

---

[53] See Elizabeth Orsten, '"Heven on Earth:" Langland's Vision of Life Within the Cloister', *American Benedictine Review* 21 (1970), 526–34. For the earlier history of this well-established sentiment, see R. E. Kaske, 'Langland and the *Paradisus Claustralis*', *MLN* 72 (1957), 481–3.

[54] Godden, *The Making of Piers Plowman*, pp. 111–14 and *passim*; ibid. 'Plowmen and Hermits in Langland's *Piers Plowman*', *RES* n.s. 35.138 (1984), 129–63. Godden also emphasizes, however, that the term 'contemplative' itself was highly problematic for Langland (149), who is clearly engaged in forging a new kind of hybrid, personal ideal rather than choosing between established traditional alternatives. On the clash between active and contemplative lives as embodied by, respectively, Haukyn and Patience in B XIII and XIV, see Nicholas Watson, '*Piers Plowman*, Pastoral Theology, and Spiritual Perfectionism: Hawkyn's Cloak and Patience's *Pater Noster*', *YLS* 21 (2007), 83–118, and discussion below, Chapter 6.2.

[55] Schmidt, 'Langland and the Mystical Tradition'; Lawrence M. Clopper, 'The Contemplative Matrix in Piers Plowman B', *MLQ* 46 (1985), 3–28.

traditional monastic devotion in that particular order (see also Chapter 2.2), Galloway points out the affinity of Will's ambivalent relationship with advanced learning with the Cistercians' own difficulties.[56] Like Galloway, I am not primarily interested in establishing the extent to which Will's or Langland's difficulties actually stem from his direct involvement with the Cistercian order. Rather, in the present context, it seems striking that the characteristic Cistercian ambivalence towards learning described by Galloway finds an almost perfect expression in Deguileville's own fraught attitude towards the relationship between scholastic learning and contemplative withdrawal in *PVH*. Regardless of Langland's involvement with 'real' English Cistercian monks, in *PVH* he would have found an author/narrator/dreamer who repeatedly self-identifies as a Cistercian, and whose entire literary project founders precisely on the seeming incompatibility of advanced academic learning and penitential self-knowledge.

Will's refusal to indulge in contemplative withdrawal from the secular world does not amount to a rejection of the contemplative ideal itself. Indeed, it could be said that monasticism is the only form of institutionalized religious life that Langland does not critique with his usual satirical ferociousness. His decision not to follow in Deguileville's footsteps is motivated by a range of more complex reasons. Firstly, Langland's poetic project is quite simply of a radically different nature: the dreamer's quest is firmly rooted in the active life from the very beginning of the poem, where Will finds himself in 'a fair feeld ful of folk' (B Prol.17). The journey that ensues therefore charts a quest for salvation in a distinctly *secular* world, with continuous reference to social and political institutions and their own role in enabling or hindering salvation for the laity. It is not accidental, then, that shortly after Ymaginatif disappears from the poem, Haukyn or *activa vita* makes his appearance on the scene, as if to remind us that the concern of Langland's poem is not merely the salvation of the individual soul, but also the reformation of the institutions and religious practices upon which individual salvation depends (see Chapter 6.2).[57] In the light of the close and intense dialogue with Deguileville's poem, however, it is evident that Langland's rejection of something like conversion to monasticism has a much more pointed significance. Indeed, Langland appears to have spent considerable energy in processing the possibility of a radical turn towards a contemplative existence in these sections of the poem before rejecting that option.[58]

---

[56] Galloway, '*Piers Plowman* and the Schools'.

[57] See for instance the powerful recent discussion of the unresolved tension and interpenetrations of personal vs. institutional responsibilities of the poem, in James Simpson, 'Religious Forms and Institutions in *Piers Plowman*', in Cole and Galloway, *The Cambridge Companion to Piers Plowman*, pp. 97–114.

[58] Langland's supposed marriage to 'kytte my wif' (B XVIII.426) may have constituted a further obstacle, although Adams raises the possibility of an early death in his account of the biography of the priest William de la Rokele, the most likely author-candidate, in *Langland and the Rokele Family*, pp. 120–3.

THE DESIRE FOR KNOWLEDGE AND THE EXPERIENCE OF CONVERSION   357

Secondly, then, the rejection of monastic contemplation is motivated by Langland's antipathy towards the radical fideism and anti-Pelagianism that underpin the pilgrim's escapist withdrawal to the monastery in *PVH*. In contrast with Deguileville, Langland finally affirms the power, dignity, and moral responsibility of the individual will to exercise at least some degree of agency, and thus contribute to its salvation—an idea to some extent implicit in his very choice of 'Will' as a name for his wayfaring 'I', and thus hardwired into Langland's pilgrimage allegory from the very beginning. Rather than short-circuiting the agency of *voluntas propria* and replacing it with the adoption of a monastic *voluntas communis* and the demands of 'obedience' exhorted by Ymaginatif (B XII.37; see Chapter 4.2 on Deguileville), Langland once more redefines the prerogatives of the individual subject to pursue its journey. From here onwards, Will becomes engaged in the tightrope exercise of leading a 'mixed life', negotiating the benefits and appeals of contemplative life on the one hand, and the pressures and demands of secular existence on the other.[59]

Thirdly, as I will discuss in further detail in Chapter 7, Langland also appears to have heeded Deguileville's warning in the closing section of *PVH2*, concerning the fragility and vulnerability of ecclesiastical institutions themselves. The concluding episodes of *PVH2* indeed suggest—retrospectively in relation to Deguileville, and proleptically in relation to Langland—that rather than being safe and reliable depositaries and purveyors of the divine living Word, monastic institutions too are susceptible to the infiltration of various sins and vices, and as such provide no durable protection against the corruption of poetic, devotional, and sacramental activities. As I will argue in the remainder of this study (especially Chapters 5.5, 6.3, 6.4, 7.2), Deguileville's vivid rendering of his own, personal disillusion with his conversion to monasticism plays a major role in sustaining Langland's own, ambivalent but tenacious determination to defend his own poetic 'makynges' as a legitimate alternative to the contemplative life, foregrounding the salvific efficacy of such idiosyncratic 'work'.

3. The Legitimacy of Poetry: Bidding of Bedes or Meddling with Makynges

Langland's reasons for rejecting Deguileville's reorientation at this point are more profound still, and touch on the very nature of *Piers Plowman* as a poetic project as Langland understood it. As I have argued in the preceding section of this chapter, the experience of the inner dream encodes the spiritual conversion for

---

[59] See especially Ralph Hanna, 'Will's Work', in Justice and Kerby-Fulton, eds, *Written Work*, pp. 23–66; ibid. '"Meddling with Makings" and Will's Work', in Alastair Minnis, ed., *Late-Medieval Texts and their Transmission: Essays in Honour of A. I. Doyle* (Cambridge: D.S. Brewer, 1994), pp. 85–94.

358 MEDIEVAL ALLEGORY AS EPISTEMOLOGY

the dreamer-protagonist. But as Anne Middleton has observed, Will's visionary retrospection and conversion also proclaims 'a new beginning, a re-vision of the nature of his project' for Langland himself—a move that is directly inspired and sustained, I argue, by the rupture and reorientation that unsettles Deguileville's poetic project in *PVH*.[60] In Chapter 4, I argued that the Pilgrim's crisis at the Rock of Penitence in *PVH1* signalled a movement away from the active pursuit of rationalistic knowledge towards a more markedly passive and expectant attitude, facilitating the contemplative experience of spiritual truths by means of prayer, devotion, and the liturgy. This transition was equally accompanied by the gradual initiation into an utterly different kind of language, allowing the pilgrim to experience new order of lyrical, non-narrative expression emblematized by the ABC prayer. Disrupting the previously linear, horizontal narrative logic of the pilgrimage, the ABC prayer also opens up a direct, vertical means of communication between man and God, and refashions the most basic constitutive elements of human language itself, the letters of the alphabet. With the ABC-prayer Deguileville also points forward towards his own disillusion with the didactic aspirations of narrative pilgrimage allegory, initiating his own 'conversion' to an entirely different, devotional, mystical, and sacramental poetic mode attested in his corpus of embedded and freestanding lyrics.

Langland clearly recognized the troubling formal, epistemic, and poetological implications of Deguileville's 'conversion', and uses Will's encounter with Ymaginatif to conduct a more sustained reflection on the ethical legitimacy, epistemic status, and soteriological relevance of his own activity as a poet. Ymaginatif not only criticizes Will's intellectual covetousness or *curiositas*—'þee, þat sekest after þe whyes' (B XII.216)—but also mounts an oblique but scathing attack upon Langland's poem itself:

> 'And þow medlest þee with makynge[s] — and myȝtest go seye þi Sauter,
> And bidde for hem þat ȝyueþ þee breed; for þer ar bokes ynowe
> To telle men what Dowel is, and Dobet, and Dobest boþe'
> (B XII.16–18)

The accusation goes to the heart of the question of the legitimacy of Langland's poetic project as a whole. Ymaginatif suggests that *Piers Plowman* itself as just another, at best superfluous book among many, distracting the author from far more spiritually productive devotional activities such as prayer and the meditative reading of the psalter.[61] As a poem that essentially consists of an extended chronicle of Will's tortuous, digressive, often errant, and arguably inconclusive spiritual and

---

[60] Middleton, "'Kynde Name'", p. 229.

[61] Ralph Hanna has argued—to my mind convincingly—that Ymaginatif here essentially redefines *clergie* as designating basic literacy and elementary doctrinal knowledge, manifested in the form of

THE DESIRE FOR KNOWLEDGE AND THE EXPERIENCE OF CONVERSION   359

intellectual quest, *Piers Plowman* may well be—just like *PVH1*—merely another self-indulgent account of spiritual failure.

Much has been written about Will's attempts to 'excuse' (B XII.20) his own poetic 'makynges' against Ymaginatif's attack.[62] This concern again crystallizes in response to some of the perceived conflicts and pitfalls in Deguileville's *PVH*. Langland's decision to temper and renegotiate the extreme anti-intellectualism that dominates the closing sections of *PVH* thus produces a far more nuanced and ambivalent reflection on the value of poetic fictions themselves. Ymaginatif's indictment of Will's 'makynges' in favour of devotional activities—bidding of beads and reading of the psalter—to some extent reproduces Deguileville's renunciation of his own, inconclusive allegorico-poetical meanderings, and conversion to a radically different order of linguistic signification and its characteristic form of poetic expression, rooted in prayer and monastic devotion. It is important to stress, therefore, that Ymaginatif's injunction to Will to 'go seye þi Sauter' (XII.16) similarly proposes what is—when viewed from Langland's overarching concern with the salvation of Will's soul, and regardless of the many objections levelled by modern critics against what may appear as a strikingly 'unimaginative' substitute for the writing of poetry—an unambiguously *positive* ideal of spiritual action. Following the example of Deguileville's Grace Dieu, Ymaginatif suggests that such 'bidding of bedes' would provide a far more productive use of Will's time and energy.[63] Indeed Ymaginatif hints that in a genuinely salvific perspective such bidding of beads may be the *only* necessary and fully legitimate form of textual activity for Will to pursue: 'for þer ar bokes ynowe' (XII.17). Ymaginatif's condemnation of Will's 'makynges', then, is of a piece with the pilgrim/narrator/poet's conversion away from intellectual *curiositas* in *PVH*, and more particularly Deguileville's own turn away from his speculative, and tortuously explicative allegorical poetry towards more wholesome, traditionally sanctified practices of devotion, oration, and contemplation, and a new poetics grounded in these qualities. But whereas Deguileville's poem actually abandons its own initial speculative and didactic objectives, this radical reorientation is merely a *possibility* in Langland, raised by one of Will's many interlocutors in this extended and unsettling middle section of the poem. The trajectory

---

strikingly 'unimaginative' rote learning and devotion. On this, see Hanna, 'Langland's Ymaginatif', especially pp. 82–4, 92–4. See also Cannon, '*Ars Grammatica*'; Galloway '*Piers Plowman* and the Schools'; and Zeeman, *Discourses of Desire*, pp. 247–8.

[62] See for instance Kruger, 'Mirrors and the Trajectory of Vision', 92–5; Hanna, 'Langland's Ymaginatif', 92–3; A. V. C. Schmidt, *The Clerkly Maker: Langland's Poetic Art* (Woodbridge: Brewer, 1987), esp. 14–19; Godden, *The Making of Piers Plowman*, p. 90 and *passim*; Zeeman, *Discourses of Desire*, p. 248 and *passim*; ibid, '*Piers Plowman* in Theory', in Cole and Galloway, *Cambridge Companion ot Piers Plowman*, 214–29 (226–7); Simpson, *Introduction*, pp. 121–2 ff.; Harwood, *Piers Plowman and the Problem of Belief*, pp. 84–90. More broadly about poetic anxiety, see the work of Anne Middleton, e.g. 'Narration and the Invention of Experience', pp. 164–71.

[63] The idea is already foreshadowed by Trajan's speech in B XI, with emphasis on the specifically penitential significance of 'bidding', inseparable from the weeping of tears of contrition (B XI.261–4, cited and discussed above).

360 MEDIEVAL ALLEGORY AS EPISTEMOLOGY

of the poem itself is deeply modified, and its underlying assumptions are challenged and transformed by Ymaginatif's accusations—but neither the dreamer's quest, nor the poet's 'makynges' are brought to a halt by this. Langland instead modulates this rupture into a more carefully articulated if agonizing transition. Rather than leading to a rejection of the original aspirations of his own pilgrimage poem, Ymaginatif's attack therefore prompts a more carful reconsideration of the limits, dangers, but also the salvific possibilities inherent in Langland's allegorical poetics.

As James Simpson has suggested, Will's defence centres on the claim that while there may be, as Ymaginatif submits, plenty of books about Dowel, Dobet, and Dobest, the failure of official channels and institutions to adequately transmit this teaching justifies the production of at least another book, *Piers Plowman* itself.[64] Implicit in this affirmation is also the related claim that *Piers Plowman* is profoundly different kind of book: rather than being a book designed simply to convey doctrinal teaching in straight-forward, expository fashion, it is a different kind of narrative, an account of the spiritual crises, failures, and pitfalls of the individual will/Will engaged in a journey towards truth, slowly transformed into a quest for salvation. As a 'book', then, *Piers Plowman* itself is the self-conscious account of an experiential, flawed, erratic quest for truth, whose insights remain by definition provisional and imperfect. It is this ongoing *process* of 'working out' or 'figuring out' spiritual truths through writing, and not the final object of the dreamer's quest (Truth), that determines the spiritual efficacy, and hence legitimacy of Will's/Langland's 'makynges'.[65]

Again a comparison with Deguileville is illuminating at this point. Deguileville too had advanced the claim that his *PVH* was in reality the account of an individual failure and errance, rather than the narrative blueprint for an everyman's orderly progress towards the Heavenly Jerusalem (*PVH1* 13,527–36, see Chapter 4.1). This claim, however, provides a clearly inadequate description of the poem's objectives as they emerge from the overall plot and narrative framework. Such negative exemplarism appears incompatible with the investment of Deguileville's principal figures of authority in the very idea of tracing an active path through the *regio dissimilitudinis* of a fallen world back to a heavenly home. The poet's invitation to read the poem as a cautionary tale, then, is essentially an afterthought, a last resort designed to salvage the original didactic aims of the poem. This contradiction already contains the tension between two contrasting interpretations of the 'I's allegorical pilgrimage, which emerge as mutually incompatible possibilities in *PVH2*: the pilgrimage is to be read either as a didactic account of a paradigmatic quest for salvation by a Christian Everyman, or as a confessional, autobiographical, and apologetic account of the misfortunes of GVILLERMVS DE DEGUILEUILLA

---

[64] Simpson, *Introduction*, p. 122; Schmidt, *Clerkly Maker*.
[65] Middleton, 'Narration and the Invention of Experience', pp. 166–71.

THE DESIRE FOR KNOWLEDGE AND THE EXPERIENCE OF CONVERSION   361

(see Chapter 4.3). This tension too, as will be seen in my next chapter, had a pro-found impact on Langland's use of a slippery, simultaneously particularized and yet 'open' first-person everyman/dreamer/narrator/author figure.[66] Indeed, Ymag-inatif's challenge forces the poem's 'I'—refracting the *personae* of Will, the poet, as well as the searching reader—to articulate their own defence of the poem's method and legitimacy.

Despite his frontal attack against Will's and Langland's 'makynges', therefore, Ymaginatif finally enables Langland to redefine the prerogatives of his own poetry in the aftermath of the dreamer's crisis in *passus* B XI. While he denies the legitimacy of Will's poetic trifles, Ymaginatif nonetheless presents himself as an eminently active, restless agent like Will, beginning with the very first line of his speech: '"I am Ymaginatif", quod he; "ydel was I neuere"' (B XII.1). This restless-ness is often interpreted as a symptom of Ymaginatif's identity as a personification of the imaginative faculty, always active even in sleep.[67] Ymaginatif does indeed employ an extended series of vivid imaginative tropes and *exempla* as part of his speech, suggesting that he personifies some form of figurative and analogi-cal thinking. As the opening of his speech makes abundantly clear, however, this imaginative 'restlessness' has a strictly moral, exemplary, and penitential function: 'manye tymes haue [I] meued þee to mynne on þyn ende' (B XII.4). Thus, while rejecting Will's poetic 'makynges', Ymaginatif's operation is in many ways anal-ogous to Langland's own allegorical imaginings and poetic 'makynges', but with explicit reference to the reformation of Will's moral and spiritual state.[68] While his strategy is intended to illustrate the spiritual usefulness of the imaginative fac-ulty,[69] it also lends support to Will's own contention that the poetic imagination can be 'an irreplaceable way of recovering truth'.[70] Just as Langland uses Ymaginatif to redefine the very nature of *clergie* instead of merely rejecting the latter, he also uses that same character to redefine the uses to which the poetic imagination may be put, seeking to recuperate metaphorical and analogical thinking for a spiritual purpose.

As a response to Deguileville's disillusion with the didactic and salvific potential of allegory, Ymaginatif's implicit defence of the human imagination plays a crucial role in the poem. When read against Deguileville's use of poetic allegory, Ymagi-natif's use of poetic figures is particularly striking because of the latter's reliance on conspicuously ordinary, simple, and often bodily and material images, generally drawn from elementary instruction such as that provided in grammar schools.[71]

---

[66] On the question, see e.g. James Simpson, 'The Power of Impropriety: Authorial Naming in *Piers Plowman*' in Kathleen M. Hewett-Smith, *William Langland's Piers Plowman: A Book of Essays* (London: Routledge, 2001), pp. 145–65; Middleton, '"Kynde Name"'.

[67] See especially Minnis, 'Langland's Ymaginatif', 83, 92.

[68] Kruger, 'Mirrors and the Trajectory of Vision', 93–5.

[69] See especially Hanna, 'Langland's Ymaginatif', pp. 84 ff.

[70] Simpson, *Introduction*, p. 122.

[71] Hanna, 'Langland's Ymaginatif'; Cannon, 'Langland's *Ars Grammatica*', 8–9.

362 MEDIEVAL ALLEGORY AS EPISTEMOLOGY

I have already discussed the analogy of the swimmers in the Thames (B XII.160–86); the image of the blind/ignorant wayfarer (B XII.97–112); the idea of God beating his disobedient children with brooms (B XII.12). As I have suggested, many of these images appear to be elaborations of motifs already found in Deguileville. Crucially, however, Ymaginatif uses these images in a section of the poem that corresponds to the crisis that effectively implodes Deguileville's original poetic project. Whereas Deguileville abandons the idea of employing imaginative, allegorical modes of representation to foster the moral agency and responsibility of his pilgrim towards the end of *PVH1*, Langland effectively employs the figure of Ymaginatif to reaffirm that very possibility, under the transformed circumstances brought about by Will's crisis in the third vision and in his first inner dream. Again—as is the case with his redefinition of *clergie*—this amounts recuperating and redefining possibilities that earlier sections of the poem had all but discarded, especially with Study's stern rebuttal of Will's imaginative excess and theological inquisitiveness (see Chapter 5.1).

It is therefore hardly accidental that it should be precisely dame Study who first announces the arrival of Ymaginatif, pointing forward to his role in providing a more nuanced theory of the poetic imagination, and his ability to provide far more substantial spiritual nourishment than the idle theological talk of the 'maistres':

> 'Swiche motyues þey meue, þise maistres in hir glorie,
> And maken men in mysbileue þat muse muche on hire wordes.
> Ymaginatif herafterward shal answere to youre purpos.
> Austyn to swiche argueres he telleþ hem þis teme:
> *Non plus sapere quam oportet.*
>
> (B X.115–18a)

At the same time, Ymaginatif's strikingly simple, elementary imagery also signals a reaction against Deguileville's reliance on an increasingly convoluted, conceptually dense and abstract allegorical imagery in his poem. As I argued in Chapter 3.5, this tendency is exacerbated in *PVH2* in particular, culminating with Grace Dieu 'eyes-in-ears' analogy, accordingly ridiculed by Study in Langland's poem (see Chapter 5.1). By contrast, Ymaginatif's use of such simple, homely imagery, and his adoption of a non-scholastic, figurative, exemplary, and analogical mode of thought at this point,[72] confirm that he embodies a kind of poetic imagination that is intended to provide a viable and productive alternative to academic *scientia*, or 'high' scholastic forms of theological speculation. It is perfectly fitting, then, that Ymaginatif should sing the praises of the conspicuously monastic virtue of 'obedience þat heigh wey is to heuene' (B XII.37). As Hanna and Simpson have noted,

---

[72] See Minnis, 'Langland's Ymaginatif', esp. pp. 79–85.

THE DESIRE FOR KNOWLEDGE AND THE EXPERIENCE OF CONVERSION 363

in the wake of the appearance of Ymaginatif, 'the rest of *Piers Plowman* is written from a position of retrenchment, a withdrawal from efforts of higher speculation'.[73]

The corporeal, imaginatively plastic nature of Ymaginatif's similitudes is particularly remarkable in the present context. In contrast with Deguileville's efforts to maintain a firm dualism of body and soul, Ymaginatif's images are distinctly and confidently material, affective, and embodied. Hanna, for instance, has observed how Ymaginatif employs 'similes which indicate man's imbrication in the world of kind',[74] establishing the concrete, intellectually palpable, plastic nature of human imaginings. To some extent, the tangible materiality of such images is a function of the elementary nature of Ymaginatif's teaching, geared towards the most basic, but also the most fundamental doctrinal truths rather than rarefied theological speculation. Yet the corporeal imagery also has a deeper significance as part of the overarching sacramental, incarnational *telos* of Ymaginatif's speech.[75] I have already emphasized the strongly penitential bias of Ymaginatif's teaching, and his insistence on the importance of *clergie* as a gateway to the sacrament of penance (B XII.10, 171–5, and discussion above). Ymaginatif however articulates a far more elaborate sacramental discourse, and explores a much deeper, doctrinally and poetologically crucial relationship between the sacrament of penance and that of Eucharistic communion.

Ymaginatif argues specifically that it is only through *clergie* that the continued validity and availability of the sacrament of the Eucharist can be guaranteed by the Church, custodian of Christian doctrine on earth: 'For Goddes body myȝte noȝt ben of breed wiþouten clergie' (B XII.85), 'for clergie is kepere vnder Crist of heuene' (B XII.126). It is telling that Ymaginatif's revaluation of learning here should focus specifically on the sacrament of the Eucharist—the most immediate, tangible, corporeal mystery at the heart of Christian sacramental theology as an edible living body/Word, itself a fruit of the Incarnation and the central instrument of the Atonement. The idea is already latent in the poem, introduced by what

---

[73] Hanna, 'Langland's Ymaginatif', p. 91. See also Simpson, 'From Reason to Affective Knowledge', and the relevant sections in his *Introduction*. For a discussion of Patience's pedagogical strategy as a practical application of Ymaginatif's theory, see further Ralph Hanna, 'Hawkin and Patience's Instruction', in ibid., *Patient Reading/Reading Patience: Oxford Essays on Medieval English Literature* (Liverpool: Liverpool University Press, 2017), pp. 319–38.

[74] Hanna, 'Langland's Ymaginatif', p. 87.

[75] I here use 'sacramental' both in its narrow sense as relating to the sacraments of the Church, and in its enlarged, semiotic sense, as discussed in Chapter 2.4, and defined for instance by Aquinas: 'Ergo videtur quod omne signum rei sacrae sit sacramentum. Respondeo dicendum quod signa dantur hominibus, quorum est per nota ad ignota pervenire. Et ideo proprie dicitur sacramentum quod est signum alicuius rei sacrae ad homines pertinenti, ut scilicet proprie dicatur sacramentum, secundum quod nunc de sacramentis loquimur, quod est signum rei sacrae inquantum est sanctificans homines.' Signs are given to men, to whom it is proper to discover the unknown by means of the known. Consequently a sacrament properly so called is that which is the sign of some sacred thing pertaining to man; so that properly speaking a sacrament, as considered by us now, is defined as being the 'sign of a holy thing so far as it makes men holy' (*ST*, 3a, q. 60, a. 2, c). Sacramental signs accordingly entail an epistemology and theology of 'participation'. See further also Gruenler, *Piers Plowman as Enigma*, especially pp. 13–22, 31–80, 271–386.

364   MEDIEVAL ALLEGORY AS EPISTEMOLOGY

Elizabeth Kirk calls Langland's 'most striking metaphysical passage [. . .] on the Incarnation and Atonement',[76] as part of Repentance's evocation of God's Incarnation and sacrifice: 'Feddest þo wiþ þi fresshe blood oure forefadres in derknesse' [. . .] '*Verbum caro factum est et habitavit in nobis*' (B V. 494, 501a). As will be seen below, this idea shapes the poem's use of both literal and symbolic acts of speech and ingestion of food.[77] By presenting the Eucharist specifically as 'God's body' and as 'bread', Ymaginatif further emphasizes the physical, materially 'real', tangible albeit mysterious physical presence of Christ's body in the Sacrament, and its continual presence in the everyday life of each ordinary Christian. Accordingly *clergie*—specifically understood to denote basic literacy and simple religious and sacramental doctrine—becomes an important facilitator of true contrition, itself a necessary gateway to the sacrament of communion, where the individual Christian can finally 'taste' the sapiential and salvific fruit of Christ's Incarnation.

This exploration of the profound links between the sacraments of penance and the Eucharist prepares us for the developments of *passus* XIII, where Eucharistic and penitential elements come together at the Feast of Patience. As Conor McKee has observed, 'the banquet at which a "maister" of the schools is entertained by Conscience and Clergy is a complex treatment of the function of the Eucharistic sacrament'.[78] This Eucharistic symbolism resurfaces later in the poem with the promise of actual sacramental communion—a promise not quite fulfilled and experienced, but rather adumbrated in the poem by Will's Easter Sunday awakening and his desire to receive the Eucharist (B XIX. 1–3), and finally culminates with Conscience's gift of 'bred yblessed and Goddes body þervnder' (B XIX.389, see Chapter 7.1).[79] The rather subdued, intermittent, and unobtrusive exploration of Eucharistic symbolism in the poem does not however detract from its potency—on the contrary. Indeed, the endemic yet essentially implicit presence

---

[76] Elizabeth D. Kirk 'Langland's Narrative Christology', in Robert R. Edwards, ed., *Art and Context in Late Medieval English Narrative: Essays in Honor of Robert Worth Frank* (Cambridge: D.S. Brewer, 1994), pp. 17–35 (34–5).

[77] See especially Jill Mann's influential 'Eating and Drinking in *Piers Plowman*', *Essays and Studies* 32 (1979), pp. 26–43 (39). A. V. C. Schmidt, 'Langland's Structural Imagery of Food and Drink', republished in ibid., *Earthly Honest Things: Collected Essays on Piers Plowman* (Newcastle: Cambridge Scholars Publishing, 2012), pp. 221–36. For a more general discussion, see also Katie L. Walter, *Middle English Mouths: Late Medieval Medical, Religious and Literary Traditions* (Cambridge: Cambridge University Press, 2018), 104–14.

[78] Conor McKee, 'Pedagogic and Dramatic Roles of the Liturgy in *Piers Plowman*', *Cambridge Quarterly*, 45.4 (2016), 343–64 (347).

[79] On the pervasive but unobtrusive concern with the Sacrament of the Eucharist in *Piers*, see especially David Aers, 'The Sacrament of the Altar in *Piers Plowman* and the Late Medieval Church in England', in Dimmick, Simpson, and Zeeman, eds, *Images, Idolatry, and Iconoclasm in Late Medieval England*, pp. 63–80. Contrary to my reading here, however, Aers dismisses Ymaginatif's invocation of the Eucharist to defend the importance of *clergie* as 'opportunistic' and 'theologically superficial' (p. 74). For a reading that emphasizes the seriousness of Ymaginatif's Eucharistic developments here, see Murtaugh, *Piers Plowman and the Image of God*, pp. 94–6, and Zeeman, *Medieval Discourses of Desire*, pp. 253–6. For Aers' further argument on the centrality of the Eucharist and its links with penance in the poem, see Aers, *Sanctifying Signs*, pp. 29–51.

THE DESIRE FOR KNOWLEDGE AND THE EXPERIENCE OF CONVERSION   365

of the Eucharist in the poem ultimately functions as a nearly perfect manifestation of the theological mystery of the 'real presence'. David Aers has best analysed this paradoxical absence-presence of Eucharistic symbolism in Langland's imagination and in the poem. Langland's handling of the Eucharist indeed foregrounds its eschatological significance, its status as a foretaste of the eschatological supper, the reunion of the elect in Christ, prefigured in the unified community of believers of the Church, the mystical body of Christ. *Piers Plowman* in its entirety is thus haunted by the absent presence of the Eucharist: 'Christ's presence and the Sacrament of the Altar are *not yet*, a *not yet* that is at the heart of the poet's sacramental theology' (cf. 1 Cor. 11.26).[80] Langland's Eucharistic imagination, Aers argues, is therefore also enmeshed with his thinking about the role of the Church itself, and particularly the clergy's role in enabling—or indeed disrupting—the continued ritual of mutual incorporation, social as well as spiritual, signified and effected by the sacrament of communion.

Because of this pronounced eschatological emphasis, however, Ymaginatif's discourse on the Eucharist, which prepares us for the Feast of Patience, is also deeply analogous to the mechanisms of allegorical signification, particularly if understood in terms of a provisional, asymptotic process of reference (see Chapters 2.4 and 4.4). Ymaginatif's speech as a whole establishes a powerful link between the imagination, specifically enigmatic imaginative similitudes, analogies, and metaphors, and the real presence in the Eucharist. This chain of associations is picked up again and developed further, *in plenitudo temporis* later in the poem, during the more sustained exploration of the enigmatic signifying mechanisms of St Paul's mirror from 1 Cor. 13.12—only to be deferred once more to an indefinite eschatological future time (see Chapter 7). Indeed, Langland appears to be suggesting that the kind of imaginative operation carried out by Ymaginatif enables a more vivid, more profound, more 'tangible' and ultimately more truthful, 'real', if still provisional and indirect grasp of the central mysteries of Christianity—'in a Mirour / *hic in enigmate, tunc facie ad faciem* (1 Cor. 13.12, cf. XV.162–62a).[81] The difficulty of grasping the central, fundamental tenets of Christianity fully is thus symbolized—or indeed imperfectly 'embodied', as it were—in the absent presence of Christ's own sacrificial body in the poem.

Ultimately, the experience provided by Ymaginatif's compelling speech is full of potent, imaginatively plastic yet also imperfect and provisional images, and gestures towards the kind of 'kynde knowing' that Will originally sets out to acquire on his quest (B I.138–9).[82] Significantly, the exchange with Ymaginatif again opens

---

[80] Aers, 'The Sacrament of the Altar', p. 75.

[81] On the 'incarnational' nature of Langland's thinking about allegorical signification, see especially Cervone, *Poetics of the Incarnation*, esp. pp. 26–31, and *passim*. See also Chapter 7.

[82] My argument here converges closely with the reading of Ymaginatif proposed by Cole and Galloway, 'Christian Philosophy in *Piers Plowman*', pp. 154–6. On 'kynde knowing' see above, n. 27.

366 MEDIEVAL ALLEGORY AS EPISTEMOLOGY

with Will's plea for knowledge. In response to his interlocutor's accusation of idleness, Will affirms that he would stop meddling with his books immediately, if he only had a full understanding of Dowel, Dobet, and Dobest (B XII. 25–8). Will does not employ the term 'kynde knowyng', but variations on the concept are at the heart of Ymaginatif's response, focused on the productive interdependence of practical, empirical and experiential knowledge on the one hand (*kynde knowyng/wit*), and a newly purified and spiritually intensified understanding of the fundamentals of Christian religious doctrine mediated by books and instruction (*clergie*):[83]

> 'Clergie and kynde wit comeþ of siȝte and techyng,
> As þe Book bereþ witnesse to burnes þat kan rede:
> > *Quod scimus loquimur, quod vidimus testamur.*
> Of *quod scimus* comeþ clergie, a konnynge of heuene,
> And of *quod vidimus* comeþ kynde wit, of syȝte of diuerse peple.
> > [...]
> Ac yit is clergie to comende, and kynde wit boþe,
> And namely clergie for Cristes loue, þat of clergie is roote.'
>
> > (B XII.64–71)

Viewed from both a cognitive and a sacramental perspective, Ymaginatif's extended speech thus serves as a preparation for the more sustained, both spiritually and corporeally intensified exploration of the sacrament of the Eucharist during the Feast of Patience. This exploration of Eucharistic knowledge—balancing spiritual understanding with experiential knowledge—is underpinned by the implicit but fundamental awareness that it is through God's Incarnation that a mutual *kynde knowyng* of man and God, creature and creator, can take place (see Chapter 7.1).[84]

4. Eucharistic and Sapiential Knowledge in Deguileville and Langland

The whole of *passus* XIII is conceived, at a very fundamental level, as a symbolic and imaginative exploration of the cognitive and spiritual efficacy of the sacrament of communion, understood as a ritual, performative celebration and

---

[83] 'Kynde knowyng' cannot be reduced to, but rather subsumes the more narrow category of 'kynde witte' (B XII. 45, 55, 70, 93, 125, 128) employed by Ymaginatif here, often understood as direct, empirical knowledge of natural phenomena.

[84] 'And after God auntured hym-self, and toke Adames kynde, / to wyte what he hath suffred' (B XVIII. 222–3). See especially Kirk, 'Langland's Narrative Christology', esp. pp. 27–30; Davlin, '"Kynde Knowyng" as a Major Theme'; Bose, 'God's Thought Experiment', pp. 83, 90–1.

THE DESIRE FOR KNOWLEDGE AND THE EXPERIENCE OF CONVERSION   367

repetition of Christ's paradigmatic Incarnation and sacrifice.[85] This is not to say that the incarnational sacramentalism of *passus* XIII is serene, rapturous, and free from the tensions, failures, clashes, and frustrations that characterize Will's preceding quest—on the contrary. It is precisely through such tensions and renewed disagreements, worked out over the duration of the Feast, that Langland provides yet another instance of his sustained, creative, and critical engagement with Deguileville's *PVH*, specifically its notions of a redeemed language and the new availability of the sacramental word after the pilgrim's entrance into the monastery. In Chapter 4 I argued that the pilgrim's entry into the Cistercian Abbey, figured as a castle on the Ship of Religion, essentially crystallizes a failure of the initial didactic project of the *Pèlerinage de Vie Humaine*. More specifically, I argued that the pilgrim's conversion that immediately precedes his entry into the monastery also signals a turn away from allegory, and a conversion to a different kind of poetry— adumbrated in the 'ABC Prayer', explored further in the many embedded lyrics of the later *Pèlerinages*-trilogy, and finally culminating in Deguileville's late, contemplative Latin lyrics. Importantly, however, this shift to a different order of language is also explored within the closing section of both *PVH1* and *PVH2*, with the pilgrim's entrance into the monastery and his participation in the daily routine of monastic *lectio*, prayer, and the liturgy, within the protective boundaries of the monastic enclosure. This new order of language structuring the pilgrim's life of devotion is represented, I argued, by a series of metaphors that centre on the physical, corporeal, and eminently 'edible' presence of the divine living Word. Rather than being conceived in term of ordinary, dual relations of signification and figuration, this new language allows the pilgrim to experience a relationship of sapiential and sacramental *participation*.

Throughout *passus* XIII, Langland redeploys the tropes, motifs, ideas, and symbolic associations introduced by Deguileville at the end of *PVH*. Clearly the choice of the framing metaphor of the meal or feast is already saturated with echoes of the liturgy, and more specifically with the double allusion to the ingestion of the Eucharist and the consumption of God's word, echoing Matthew 4.4, 'Man shall not live by bread alone, but by every word that proceedeth out of the mouth of God', echoed by Patience at B XIV.45–50. The gathering is not only a textual feast, but also a communal one—another feature shared with Deguileville. *PVH*'s description of the 'chastel' (e.g. *PVH1* 12,635; *PVH2* 15,038) is reconfigured into an account of the festivities inside the lay, aristocratic 'courte' or 'paleis' of Conscience (B XIII.23, 29). Whereas in *PVH1* the pilgrim sees 'Charity, who served and hosted pilgrims, feeding the poor' [Charite, qui servoit / Les pelerins et hebergeoit, [. . .] Pour repaistre la pauvre gent; *PVH1* 12,643–6], Langland rearranges the scene, assigning such charitable tasks of hospitality to Patience, herself in pilgrim's garb: 'Ac Pacience in þe paleis stood in pilgrymes

---

[85] McKee, 'Poetic and Dramatic Roles of the Liturgy', 346–50.

368   MEDIEVAL ALLEGORY AS EPISTEMOLOGY

cloþes / And preyde mete *pur charite* for a pouere heremyte' (B XIII.29–30). The central metaphorical terms of reference for the feast are also analogous. In *PVH*, it is Dame Estude/Leçon who administers textual/sacramental nourishment (*PVH1* 12,827–40; *PVH2* 15,135–58, see Chapter 4.2). Langland expands this idea into a more elaborate and differentiated description of the different textual/devotional/sacramental fare ingested by the guests in Conscience's hall.

Despite these general echoes, the range of the edible texts and the constitution of the banqueting community in *Piers Plowman* are far more heterogeneous and even discordant. *Piers Plowman* does not, like *PVH*, redirect its energies inward, and relocate the consumption of the living word within a closed, homogeneous monastic community, where the individual will has been subsumed within a single overarching *voluntas communis*. Instead, Langland's *passus* B XIII explores the ability of the Eucharist to effect *social* as well as spiritual integration, and—through this—examines the mysterious workings of the Incarnation for the benefit of both the Christian community of laypeople at large as well as the soul of the individual will/Will. Deguileville's metaphorical castle—representing the monastic enclosure—is therefore transformed by Langland into a literal castle, denoting the secular, social, and to some extent public or at least theoretically 'permeable' space of the aristocratic hall. Langland's Feast points not towards a monastic and ascetic experience—with all its implications of spatial and social withdrawal and spiritual elitism—but to a more accessible, permeable, social and vernacular space where the access to the divine living Word is, at least theoretically, freely shared and experienced by the Christian community as a whole. At the heart of this Feast we therefore find at work the most integrative discourse of all, that on the sacrament of the communion in the Eucharist, reconciling the divine with the human through ingestion and reciprocal incorporation, integrating the individual within the community of Christ's mystical body. The Feast of Patience thus rewrites Deguileville's fundamentally ascetic, exclusivist, and at times solipsistic and escapist metaphors of enclosure and spiritual ascent as the account of a different kind of social and sacramental experience, centred on the consumption of a wide range of diverse, more or less adequate symbolic analogues of God's body.

Far from achieving peaceful and harmonious communal integration, however, the Feast of Patience proves highly troublesome in Langland. The fare eaten by the various guests differs—not only according to social status, but also according to their mental, spiritual, and intellectual disposition. Indeed the *passus* may be seen as working through a number of different, at times conflicting ways of 'figuring' the consumption of the Eucharist and its efficacy—imaginatively, cognitively, and spiritually—pitching the mental and devotional habits of the Doctor of Theology against those of Will, Conscience, Clergie, and Patience.[86] The various characters

---

[86] See especially the reading presented by Hanna, 'Conscience's Dinner', in *Patient Reading/Reading Patience*, pp. 303–18. Hanna observes of the banquet that 'this scene effectively explodes those values

THE DESIRE FOR KNOWLEDGE AND THE EXPERIENCE OF CONVERSION   369

involved in this collective debating *symposium* thus function as 'representations of modes of discourse', and their conversation ultimately becomes 'a contest between forms of knowledge'.[87] Indeed the dominant tone of Langland's feast is not so much celebratory as it is satirical: even before the start of the fourth vision Langland sets the scene through Will's waking meditations on ecclesiastical corruption. As he awakens from his latest vision, he sees

> how þat freres folwede folk þat was riche,
>
> [. . .]
>
> And how þis coueitise ouercom clerkes and preestes.
> And how þat lewed men ben lad, but Oure Lord hem helpe,
> Thoru3 vnkonnynge curatours to incurable peynes;
>
> (B XIII.7, 11–13)

This introduces the central theme of the vision as a whole, which is no less than the failure of the institution of the Church to ensure the salvation of the faithful because of the moral and intellectual shortcomings of its officials. Where Deguileville presents us with a celebration of sacramental incorporation through sapiential and textual ingestion, Langland therefore gives us a satire of the ecclesiastical establishment's *failure* to facilitate the adequate sharing of the sacramental flesh/Word of the Eucharist among the faithful. As David Aers observes, 'Langland's haunting satire around the consumption of food often gains force from its allusion to the sacramental which has been set aside', a strategy that serves to highlight the nature of competing and often debased forms of textual/sapiential consumption.[88]

Deguileville's binary opposition between food for the soul ('ame') and food for the gut ('pance', *PVH1* 12,833)—echoed in Holy Church's earlier affirmation that 'it is nou3t al good to þe goost þat þe gut askeþ' (B I.36)—is thus expanded and complicated to produce a wider spectrum of delicacies: Scripture serves up a wholesome and frugal diet of Gospels and Church Fathers: 'serued hem þus soone of sondry metes manye— / Of Austyn, of Ambrose, of alle þe foure Euangelistes' (B XIII.38–9). Will and Patience feast on a 'sour loof' of penitential psalms (31 and 50, with liturgical resonances)[89]—'And [Scripture] brou3te vs of *beati quorum* of *Beatus virres* makynge' (B XIII.48, 52). But neither the Master nor his servant

---

its characters had seemed to instantiate', and 'ends in what for most dinner parties would be social disaster', pp. 304, 305. See further Traugott Lawler, 'Conscience's Dinner', in Mary Teresa Tavormina and Robert F. Yeager, eds, *The Endless Knot: Essays on Old and Middle English in Honor of Marie Borroff* (Cambridge: D.S. Brewer, 1996, pp. 87–103.

[87] For Curtis Gruenler, 'How to Read like a Fool: Riddle Contests and the Banquet of Conscience in *Piers Plowman*', *Speculum* 85. 3 (2010), 592–630 (592; 617)

[88] Aers, 'The Sacrament of the Altar', p. 71.

[89] McKee, 'Poetic and Dramatic Roles of the Liturgy', 348.

370 MEDIEVAL ALLEGORY AS EPISTEMOLOGY

> [. . .] no manere flessh eten.
> Ac þei eten mete of moore cost, mortrews and potages:
> Of þat men myswonne þei made hem wel at ese.
>   [. . .]
> [He] eet manye sondry metes, mortrews and puddynges,
> Wombe cloutes and wilde brawen and egges wiþ grece yfryed.
> (B XIII.40–2; 62–3)

Their taste for the far more outlandish and rarefied pleasures of high gastron-
omy thus points to their interest in equally rarefied, baroque and unsubstantial
theological and intellectual refinements.[90] Rather than denoting sheer animal-
istic gluttony, the Master's diet is that of an overindulgent 'dyuynour' (cf. B
XIII.115) intoxicated—'*de vino*', suggesting a perverted abuse of sacramental
blood/wine[91]—by arcane theological speculation of a distinctly 'Averroistic', i.e.
naturalistic/Aristotelian kind:[92]

> For þis doctour on þe heiȝe dees drank wyn so faste
> (B XIII.61)

> For now he haþ dronken so depe he wole deuyne soone.
> And preuen it by her Pocalips and passion of Seynt Auereys
> (B XIII.90–1)

Inevitably, such an imbalanced diet necessarily leads to the neglect of the far more
wholesome nourishment of Christian fundamentals consumed by the other guests
at the banquet.

It has often been noted that in terms of its symbolic logic, Langland's description of the Master at the Feast provides a direct continuation of Dame Study's
ferocious rebuttal of the presumptuous and ultimately blasphemous amateur theologians in B X.[93] Both scenes develop a set of figurative associations centred
on the multiple and overlapping function of the mouth in a symbolic economy
that includes alimentary, devotional, and sacramental activities. Following a well-
established medieval tradition, the mouth here is envisaged simultaneously as the

---

[90] Zeeman, *Desire*, pp. 258–9.

[91] See David A. Lawton, 'Alliterative Style', in Alford, *A Companion to Piers Plowman*, pp. 223–50
(238).

[92] See further Anne Middleton, 'The Passion of Saynt Averoys (B.13. 91): "Deuynyng" and Divinity in the Banquet Scene', *YLS* 1 (1987), 31–40. The punning wordplay on 'divine' and 'divination' is
prominent and recurrent also in the *Rose*, e.g. *RR* 4373–4, 17,456–7, 19,597–8. The *Rose* also appears
to provide what seems to me a very likely direct source for Langland's own pun on 'wine' and 'divine',
in the mouth of Faux Semblant, who significantly compares himself to a theologian: 'de tres bons
morseaus et de vins / tex con il afixert a devins' (*RR* 11,205–6).

[93] Middleton, 'The Passion of Saynt Averoys'; Simpson, *Introduction*, p. 138; Lawler *Penn Commentary 4*, p. 8.

THE DESIRE FOR KNOWLEDGE AND THE EXPERIENCE OF CONVERSION   371

site for ingestion of food (literal and metaphorical), by turns orderly and excessive, measured and inadequate, as well as the *locus* for a variety of acts of speech, sacred and profane: prayer, confession of mouth, preaching, instruction, and praise—or conversely: blasphemy, uncontrolled or loose talk, deviant song and minstrelsy, deceit, lying, and flattery.[94] This symbolic economy establishes a complex set of correspondences between different actions and functions performed by the mouth: Langland not only identifies these correspondences, but utilizes them for striking poetic, monitory, and philosophical ends. Edwin Craun's analysis of these passages in B X and B XIII has identified the centrality of the contrast between broadly deviant and salvific speech, uncovering a rich tradition of pastoral literature that informs Langland's writing in these sections.[95] At the other end of the symbolic spectrum, a number of studies have explored the important role of eating and drinking symbolism in these two passages, both of which provide 'literal' accounts of communal meals in the distinctively lay and aristocratic setting of the Lord's hall.[96] However, the structural and conceptual centrality of the Eucharistic symbolism within these two episodes has not, in my view, received the attention it deserves. Ultimately, I suggest, it is this unobtrusive but persistent presence of an underlying sacramental symbolism that allows us to understand eating and speaking as complementary symbolic actions concerned with the human experience of the living, incarnated Word. While I cannot propose a full exploration of this question here, juxtaposing these passages with Deguileville's poem allows such important resonances to come into much clearer focus, bringing into view the persistent presence of sacramental concerns within the poem as a whole, as well as highlighting their importance for the evolution of Langland's poetics in the final third of the poem as preserved in the B and C texts.[97]

Passus X already opens by establishing the close association between figurative eating and the problem of the adequate consumption of sacred knowledge: in her opening reproof, Study castigates her husband Wit for attempting to instruct Will, thus effectively casting pearls before swine (cf. Matt 7:6):

---

[94] On the medieval tradition of such Sins of the Mouth/Tongue, see especially Carla Casagrande and Silvana Vecchio, *I peccati della lingua: Disciplina ed etica della parola nella cultura medievale* (Rome: Istituto della Biografia Italiana, 1987); Edwin Craun, *Lies, Slander, and Obscenity in Medieval English Literature: Pastoral Rhetoric and the Deviant Speaker* (Cambridge: Cambridge University Press, 2005); Walter, *Middle English Mouths*. On language more specifically in relation to *Piers Plowman*, and with reference to modern theories of signification, see also Rudd, *Managing Language*.

[95] Craun, *Lies, Slander, and Obscenity*, pp. 157–86. See also Joan Heiges Blythe, 'Sins of the Tongue and Rhetorical Prudence in *Piers Plowman*', in John A. Alford and Richard G. Newhauser, eds, *Literature and Religion in the Later Middle Ages: Philological Studies in Honor of Siegfried Wenzel* (Binghamton: Medieval and Renaissance Texts and Studies, 1995), pp. 119–42.

[96] Mann, 'Eating and Drinking in *Piers Plowman*'; Schmidt, 'Langland's Structural Imagery of Food and Drink'.

[97] For an argument in favour of the centrality of the Eucharist, and an initial analysis of some important aspects, see especially Aers, 'The Sacrament of the Altar', and ibid., *Sanctifying Signs*, pp. 29–51.

372 MEDIEVAL ALLEGORY AS EPISTEMOLOGY

> '*Noli mittere*, man, margery perles
> Amonges hogges þat han hawes at wille.
> Thei doon but dryuele þeron—draf were hem leuere.'
>
> (B X.9–11)

This initial attack chimes with Study's later condemnation of the deviant practices of the aristocratic lords and their clerks—again expressed in terms of 'drivelling':

> 'Thus þei dryuele at her deys þe deitee to knowe,
> And gnawen God wiþ þe gorge whanne her guttes fullen.
> Ac þe carefulle may crie and carpen at þe yate.'
>
> (B X.56–8)[98]

Clearly the main gist of Study's criticism concerns the Lords' utterly inappropriate presumption to discuss delicate theological matters over dinner—out of context, without any appropriate qualification, or without any understanding of, or respect for, the doctrinal points they casually swish around in their mouths and throw across the room:

> 'Ac if þei carpen of Crist, þise clerkes and þise lewed,
> Atte mete in her murþes whan mynstrals beþ stille,
> Thanne telleþ þei of þe Trinite how two slowe þe þridde,
> And bryngen forþ a balled reson, taken Bernard to witnesse,
> And puten forþ presumpsion to preue þe soþe.'
>
> (B X.51–5)

Such careless and pointless lay theologizing is clearly once more associated with the pursuit of pseudo-scholastic theological speculation: 'Freres and faitours han founde vp swiche questiouns / To plese wiþ proude men syn þe pestilence tyme' (B X.71–2).

Most importantly, however, this drivelling theological table talk appears not only as a perversion of salvific speech, but also as a figurative abuse of God's body. Within a culture that theorized the sacramental efficacy of human language through its complex relation to the living divine *logos*,[99] and which embraced a ubiquitous theology of the 'real presence' in the sacrament of the Eucharist,[100]

---

[98] The last line may contain echoes of *PVH2* 16,551–4, describing the ravages of the attack of Envy, Treason, Detraction, and Conspiracy, ejecting Charity from the Cloister: 'Boutee en est hors Charité, / Qui soloit donner a mengier / Aus povres et eux hebergier'.

[99] See especially Rosier-Catach, *La Parole efficace*; Bériou, Boudet, and Rosier-Catach, *Le pouvoir des mots au Moyen Âge*. See also Chapter 2.3.

[100] See especially Miri Rubin, *Corpus Christi: The Eucharist in Late Medieval Culture* (Cambridge: Cambridge University Press, 1991); Sarah Beckwith, *Signifying God: Social Relation and Symbolic Act in the York Corpus Christi Plays* (Chicago and London: University of Chicago Press, 2003); Aers, *Sanctifying Signs*; and the special issue of the *Journal of Medieval and Early Modern Studies* 33.2 (2003).

THE DESIRE FOR KNOWLEDGE AND THE EXPERIENCE OF CONVERSION 373

such 'figurative' linguistic abuses tend to approximate an actual, physical abuse of God's 'real' body. The physicality of Langland's alliteration here conveys a sense of Study's revulsion at such base corporeal abuses:[101] when the lords 'gnawen God wiþ þe gorge' (B X.57, cf. also X.66) or 'carpen as þei clerkes were of Crist and of hise myȝtes, / and leyden fautes vpon þe fader þat formede vs alle' (B X.104–5), they do not merely use language carelessly, but violently dismember the sacramental unity of God's body. Such 'gnawing' talk appears as a bestializing perversion of the human faculties of speech as well as a rejection of civilized food consumption— not to mention the conspicuously uncharitable exclusion of the starving poor at the castle gates (B X.58, 83–4; cf. *PVH2* 16,551–4), which functions as yet another reminder of the imbalance in what ought to be a socially as well as spiritually inte- grative moment. Unsurprisingly, then, such drivelling 'argueres' (cf. B X.118) fail to heed the lesson of charity because they ultimately fail to fully absorb, 'savour', and digest the nourishment provided by God's living body/Word. Langland therefore insistently locates their failed, abortive encounter with both Christ's body/*logos* in the 'gorge'—on the periphery of their own bodies, in a liminal zone that underlines their inability to fully incorporate and absorb it:

> 'God is muche in þe gorge of þise grete maistres,
> Ac amonges meene men his mercy and hise werkes.'
>> (B X.66–7; cf also X.56–8)

> 'Clerkes and oþere kynnes men carpen of God faste,
> And haue hym muche in her mouþ, ac meene men in herte.'
>> (B X.69–70)

Study's attack ultimately points to a double abuse of both the edible and speak- able natures of Christ, understood as the Incarnation of the living Word. Like the Master's later excesses at the Feast of Patience, such cruel and careless eating also appears as an inversion or perversion of the monastic *ruminatio* of prayer and devotion.[102] In the context of the framing episode of the meal, the conspicuously guttural alliteration at B X.57 and 66 points to the perverse, ultimately gluttonous pleasure derived from the prolonged, almost cannibalistic 'gnawing' of God's name in the 'gorge', subverting and mocking the reverent ingestion of God's truly nour- ishing body/Word: 'in gaynesse and in glotonye forglutten hir good hemselue, / And brekeþ noȝt to the beggere as þe Boke techeþ' (B X.83–4). The focus on the 'gorge' or neck is not accidental: the neck is a recurrent site for the experience of Gluttony in pastoral and penitential literature on the Seven Deadly Sins, and

[101] See also Zeeman, *Desire*, pp. 123–4.
[102] See Leclerq, *The Love of Learning*, pp. 72–3. Carruthers, *Book of Memory*, pp. 202–12; ibid. *Craft of Thought*, pp. 104–5. On Langland's debts to this tradition, see Mann, 'Eating and Drinking in *Piers Plowman*', and Curtis R. H. Jirsa, '*Piers Plowman's* Lyric Poetics', *YLS* 26 (2012), 77–110 (98–104).

374   MEDIEVAL ALLEGORY AS EPISTEMOLOGY

Deguileville himself gives us a Gloutonnerie who is both 'avid' and 'curious' (*PVH1* 10,375–6), and who wishes for a longer neck, like a crane, to prolong the pleasure of swallowing (*PVH1* 10,389–92). By analogy, the hollow theological 'gurgling' denounced by Study is both gluttonous and blasphemous—like the deviant speech of the minstrels who entertain the lords—further strengthening the symbolic associations of deviant speech and the immoderate consumption of food: 'Glotonye and grete oþes, þis game þey louyeþ' (B X.50). It is again because of the perverse and immoderate pleasures of empty theological talk that the Master at the Feast of Patience in *passus* XIII is labelled as 'Goddes gloton'. The Master practices—with his mouth—the opposite of what that same mouth has just been preaching:

> 'Ac þis Goddes gloton', quod I, 'wiþ hise grete chekes,
> Haþ no pite on vs pouere: he performeþ yuele
> That he precheþ and preveþ nouȝt', to Pacience I tolde,
>
> (B XIII.78–80)

Also more strictly textual and hermeneutic activities figure amongst the kinds of linguistic abuses denounced in *passus* X and XIII. These consist of techniques for the manipulation and occultation of the meaning of authoritative texts—strategies already familiar from both the *Rose* and Deguileville's trilogy. These include, for instance, the Maister's conveniently selective quotations of the scriptural text— much to the anger of Will:

> 'Ac o worde þei ouerhuppen at ech a tyme þat þei preche
> That Poul in his Pistle to al þe peple tolde:
> *Periculum est in falsis fratribus!*'
>
> (B XIII.69–70a)

Such activities are subsumed within a wider category of textual manipulation and deception characteristic of the Friars—'glosyng': 'Ac I wiste neuere freke þat as a frere yede bifore men on Englissh / Taken it for his teme, and telle it wiþouten glosyng' (B XIII.74–5). Study too had warned against such 'glossators', citing Cato:

> '*Qui simulat verbis, nec corde est fidus amicus,*
> *Tu quoque fac simile; sic ars deluditur arte*:
> Whoso gloseþ as gylours doon, go me to þe same,
> And so shaltow fals folk and feiþlees bigile'
>
> (B X.192–5)

Read against the closing section of Deguileville's *PVH*, these scenes from *passus* X and XIII *Piers Plowman* clearly adopt a complex and organic symbolic vocabulary, linking devotional practice, liturgical experience, the consumption of food,

THE DESIRE FOR KNOWLEDGE AND THE EXPERIENCE OF CONVERSION 375

different forms of religious language, and man's experience of the divine living word. Crucially, however, what in *PVH1* is presented as a consummation, a climax of participation in the divine *logos* through the discovery of a new, redeemed form of language, in Langland turns out to be yet another instance of slippage and at least partial failure. Far from being a moment of wholesome communion with/through the living Word—or, in Patience's terms, participation in a 'proper seruice' (B XIII.51)—the Feast turns out to be an abortive celebration, troubled by the Master's inordinate eating and speaking and Will's own protest, and eventually cut short by the sudden departure of Conscience, Patience, and Will, signalling yet another break with the institutions of learning represented by the Master and Clergie. As Conscience says in her courteous (B XIII.199) but determined parting words: 'Me were leuere, by Oure Lord, and I lyue sholde, / Haue pacience parfitliche þan half þi pak of bokes!' (B XIII.201–2).

5. 'Til I haue preued moore' (B XIII.183)

Significantly, the companions depart in pilgrim's garbs (B X. 183, 216), as if to signal yet another departure, the beginning of yet another modified quest for truth and salvation. This is also Langland's way of signalling his own renewed commitment to the poetic mode of the allegorical pilgrimage, showing us Patience in the act of picking up the essential attribute of pilgrims: a pilgrim scrip filled with newly wholesome, simple fare, once more presented in terms of the dual symbolism of language-as-nourishment: 'Thanne hadde Pacience, as pilgyimes han, in his poke vitailles: / Sobretee and symple speche and sooþfast bileue' (B XIII.217–18; cf. XIV.37–96). Deguileville's pilgrim, by contrast, happily settles down in the company of Leçon/Estude, Povrete, Priere/Oroison, Latria, and the other personifications inhabiting the monastic enclosure, converted to a life of devotion and contemplation in the presence of the living Word.

This, at least, had been the story in *PVH1*. As I argued in Chapter 4, this atmosphere of reverent contemplation and serene monastic devotion is shattered in *PVH2* by the irruption of Conspiracion, Trahison, Envie, and Detraction. More specifically, I argued that the threat posed by this quartet is of an eminently linguistic nature: not only do they personify the misreading, slander, and backbiting that Deguileville himself appears to have been victim of, but they also disrupt the wider devotional and liturgical harmony within the monastery, primarily understood as a celebration of the presence of the living Word in its multiple forms—textual, corporeal, and mystical (see Chapter 4.5). I suggested that the attack in *PVH2* is 'proto-Langlandian', in the sense that it is an episode that displays what Anne Middleton calls an 'explosive disruptive power', characteristic of the repeated instances of crystallization-and-failure that structure Langland's

376   MEDIEVAL ALLEGORY AS EPISTEMOLOGY

poetic and speculative method.[103] As I have already suggested on several occasions, Langland appears to have been familiar with this later, revised version of Deguileville's poem, and appears to have engaged with its often surprising shifts in mood, changes in direction, and traumatic disruptions and failures.

The linguistic disruption embodied by the quartet of *vieilles* in Deguileville is reconfigured by Langland as a series of analogous linguistic abuses performed by the Master and other amateur theologians—including of course Will himself—debasing the salvific value of the divine living Word with their irresponsible and blasphemous pseudo-theological chatter, and necessitating the departure of Will with Conscience and Patience. Significantly, the departure of the fellow pilgrims at this point in the poem is placed under the sign of a renewed commitment to experience. Once more the poem signals a departure from the analytical, argumentative, and broadly rationalistic understanding of the nature of truth and salvation, towards an open-ended quest for some form of experiential 'proof'. It is not accidental that both of these approaches—broadly scholastic theological speculation and dialectical analysis on the one hand, and experiential understanding on the other—should be spoken of in terms of 'proving', as if to highlight the fundamentally equivocal nature of 'proof', denoting two fundamentally different modes of epistemic inquiry. So on the one hand the amateur theologians in *passus* X 'bryngen forþ a balled reson, taken Bernard to witnesse, / And puten forþ presumpcioun to *preue* þe soþe' (B X.54–5, my emphasis), just as the Doctor in *passus* XIII 'wole deuyne soone / And *preuen* it by her Pocalips and passion of Seynt Auereys' (B XIII.90–1, my emphasis). In both cases 'proof' is understood in a strictly argumentative and dialectical sense—a definition that is condemned by Study and Will as a form of manipulative verbal trickery. As Study observes:

> 'Hadde neuere freke fyn wit þe feiþ to dispute,
> Ne man hadde no merite *myȝte it ben ypreued*:
> *Fides non habet meritum ubi humana racio prebet experimentum.*'
> (B X.249–50a)

Significantly the passage goes on to contrast the proofs derived from argumentative and demonstrative reasoning with those derived from experience, and more specifically the experience of one's own cognitive limitations: 'Siþþe is Dobet to suffre for þi soules helþe' (B X.251)—anticipating Will's later insight that Dowell is 'to se muche and suffre moore' (B XI.410). Conscience, by contrast, affirms her determination to 'be pilgrym wiþ Pacience *til I haue proued moore*' (B XIII.183, my emphasis). Crucially here 'proof' is construed in experiential and provisional terms,[104] infinitely perfectible but never, it is implied, susceptible of attaining the

---

[103] Middleton, 'Narrative and the Invention of Experience', pp. 151–2.
[104] See also Lawler, 'Conscience's Dinner', pp. 91–2; Simpson, *Introduction*, p. 133.

THE DESIRE FOR KNOWLEDGE AND THE EXPERIENCE OF CONVERSION   377

definitive certainty of demonstrative proof. Conscience's affirmation thus amounts to a renewed, intensified commitment to the Christian life understood as a pilgrimage where, it seems, there is always 'more' that awaits proving. Tellingly even Clergie, who plays an oppositional role at this stage, recognizes the legitimacy of this project, and endorses it:

> 'That is sooþ', quod Clergie, 'I se what þow menest.
> I shal dwelle as I do, my deuoir to shewe,'
>   [. . .]
> 'Til Pacience haue preued þee and parfit þee maked.'
> (B XIII.212–15, my emphasis)

In doing so, Clergie herself ultimately recognizes her own role not as that of an antagonist, but rather as that of a partner in a genuine reunion and consummation that is, once more, deferred to an indefinite eschatological future. As Conscience states, symmetrically echoing Clergie's own wording

> 'That is sooþ', seide Conscience, 'so me God helpe!
> If Pacience be oure partyng felawe and pryué with vs boþe,
> Ther nys wo in þis world þat we ne sholde amende,'
> (B XIII.205–7)

It is not accidental that this commitment to a re-iterated, and potentially never-ending pilgrimage of *experience*—as opposed to a quest for certain and disembodied knowledge—should be affirmed precisely here, at the very moment where Deguileville's poem grinds to a halt (in *PVH1*) or indeed implodes (in *PVH2*). In *PVH1* the pilgrim's quest is effectively aborted by his conversion at the Rock of Penitence, as the pilgrim lays down the identifying attributes of a pilgrim and definitively redirects his efforts inward to pursue a monastic *peregrinatio in stabilitate*. The linear momentum of pilgrimage is abandoned, transformed into the circular movement of the contemplative routine of an endlessly repeated monastic 'bidding of bedes', removed from the world of the active life. In *PVH2*, however, the viability of this withdrawal into contemplation is cut short, as the monastic routine of oration and devotion is in turn disrupted, and the self-sufficiency and capacity for self-preservation of the living Word comes under serious attack. Langland registers this failure, integrating it within the more complex, articulated, tortuous narrative trajectory of his own poem instead of allowing the latter to implode, as Deguileville had been forced to do. Indeed Langland does not so much dismiss the possibility of a conversion to monasticism, but instead carefully ponders its viability before tracing Will's future trajectory in *passus* B XIV–XX.

Langland can be seen toying with the idea of a conversion to the contemplative life, but after careful examination rejects that possibility. Accordingly, he also registers other troubling difficulties associated with the pilgrim's entrance into the monastery in Deguileville's poem, especially as it is rewritten in *PVH2*. Langland registers this traumatic and disruptive episode not only in terms of its personal, autobiographical resonances, but especially in terms of its broader significance, as a mark of institutional decline, and in terms of its impact on the ready availability of salvation in the form of a secure access to the divine living Word within the monastic enclosure, in turn figuring the larger institution of the Church. Langland appears particularly sensitive to *PVH2*'s larger meditations on the decline of ecclesiastical institutions, specifically the corruption of the monastic ideal. This can be seen from Study's speech in *passus* X. While Study's invective consists of a denunciation of a much broader range of ecclesiastical abuses, she does focus insistently on monastic institutions (B X.265–321), whose decline is presented in terms reminiscent of the complaints of found in *PVH2*. Study emphasizes in particular the dangerous loss of literal and metaphorical 'stability' within a regulated monastic existence (see *PVH2* 16,395–17,113, Chapter 4.5 for comparison):

> 'Gregorie, þe grete clerk and þe goode pope,
> Of religioun þe rule reherseþ in hise *Morales*
> And seiþ it in ensample for þei shulde do þerafter:
> "Whan fisshes faillen þe flood or þe fresshe water,
> Thei deyen for drou3te, whan þei drie ligge;
> Ri3t so religion roileþ and sterueþ
> That out of couent and cloistre coueiten to libbe"'
> (B X.292–8)

> 'Ac now is Religioun a rydere, a romere by stretes,
> A ledere of louedayes and a lond buggere,
> A prikere vpon a palfrey fro manere to manere,
> An heep of houndes at his ers as he a lorde were;'
> (B X.305–8)

It is clear that Study—like Langland—is not attacking the legitimacy of monastic institutions themselves, let alone the monastic ideal. The issue rather concerns the viability of such institutions in terms of their place within the wider social, secular, and historical realities that shape the history of the Church at large. This troubling episode in *PVH2* thus crystallizes a problem that for Langland becomes conceptually and structurally central: the fallibility of human religious practices, officials, and institutions. After the introspective interlude of the third vision, and starting with the Feast of Penitence, Langland focuses his poem increasingly on such problems, culminating with the siege of the Barn of Unity, where he finally unpacks the larger, full implications of the abortive conclusion of Deguileville's *PVH2*, as I illustrate in Chapter 7. Before focusing on such larger historical and eschatological questions, however, Langland continues the narrative of Will's personal pilgrimage. It is here, as I suggest in my next chapter, that Langland works out a more nuanced, fully formed theory of his own allegorical poetics. He does so with close reference to the many shifts, pitfalls, and ruptures that derail Deguileville's original poetic vision, demonstrating a remarkably sharp understanding of the internal conflicts and contradictions that traverse the *oeuvre* of his predecessor.

6

The Experience of Failure and the Architecture of Vision

(*Piers Plowman* B XIII.215–XV)

> Langland (if such were really his name) has no other monument than that which, having framed for himself, he left to posterity to appropriate.
>
> Thomas Dunhelm Whitaker, ed., *The Visions of William Concerning Piers Ploughman* (London: John Murray, 1813), p. vi

In the preceding chapter I have sought to trace Langland's critical and creative dialogue with Deguileville's *Pèlerinage de Vie Humaine*, with particular attention to the shifting definitions of knowledge in their respective poems. Langland's engagement with Deguileville's poem appears to have been particularly intense with respect to its many moments of crisis, failure, slippage, and reorientation, especially as described in *PVH2*. As I will argue in the present chapter, such moments of breakdown and reorientation also enabled Langland to reconsider the workings, aims, and objectives of his own allegorical poem, allowing him to redefine its narrative trajectory and modulate its expressive mode while also interrogating the purpose, efficacy, and legitimacy of his own poetic craft. In particular, I want to examine the deeper, structural and ideational impact of Deguileville's poetry on Langland's evolving poetic vision. I want to argue that the cognitive, epistemic, and interpretive slippages and *aporias* of Deguileville's allegories shaped *Piers Plowman* not only at the level of individual episodes but also in terms of Langland's overarching poetic vision and its evolution over time, helping to shape Langland's distinctive authorial self-understanding and his strategy of authorial self-representation. Langland's creative interest in the difficulties and ruptures crystallized by Deguileville's allegorical corpus, I suggest, allowed him to develop his poem's distinctive episodic and experiential narrative logic.[1]

I began Chapter 5 by discussing how Will's cognitive crisis triggers Langland's sustained and ambivalent reflection on the status, use, and value of his own poetic

---

[1] On this, see especially Middleton, 'Narration and the Invention of Experience'.

Medieval Allegory as Epistemology. Marco Nievergelt, Oxford University Press.
© Marco Nievergelt (2023). DOI: 10.1093/oso/9780192849212.003.0007

'makynges'. This reflection replays and adapts—with important differences—Deguileville's own loss of faith in first-person allegorical fiction, and his gradual conversion to a new kind of poetry rooted in invocation, prayer, and silent inner contemplation. Langland clearly recognizes that Deguileville's initial aspiration of providing tangible, 'visual' knowledge of spiritual truths by means of an allegorical pilgrimage narrative finally places unsustainable demands on his poem, leading it into an inevitable impasse. But instead of abandoning the allegorical mode and the narrative frame of the pilgrimage in favour of the static, contemplative, and sapiential possibilities of the lyric, Ymaginatif's arrival redefines the functions of the poetic/allegorical imagination itself as part of a wider, Incarnation and sacramental logic. In doing so, Langland's poem clearly signals its undiminished, albeit transformed commitment to the imaginative structures of the allegorical 'pilgrimage' narrative, notably with the departure of Conscience in pilgrim's clothes in *passus* XIII. It is significant, therefore, that the protagonist of Langland's poem should be exercising his own prerogative as *Will*—as a personified manifestation of the individual human *voluntas*, endowed with free choice and at least some degree of individual agency. This throws into further relief Langland's critical response to Deguileville's radical anti-Pelagian emphasis on the passivity and impotence of the human will.

I have already argued that in inheriting the narrative configuration of the first-person dream vision from the *Rose* and the *Pèlerinages*, *Piers Plowman* crystallizes a complex, stratified first-person subject—by turns dreamer, protagonist, narrator, everyman, exegete, fictional protagonist, reader, and author.[2] This means that the actions and experiences of the poem's dreamer and protagonist, Will, also figure Langland's evolving self-understanding as an author and poet, albeit in intermittent, oblique, and elusive fashion. Will's departure on pilgrimage in the company of Conscience and Patience thus figures a new beginning also for Langland's poetic craft, and in what follows I want to examine the action of the poem between B XIII.215 until the end of *passus* B XV. Again Langland's response to Deguileville is both critical and creative: he rejects the mode of apologetic autobiography that we see emerging at the end of Deguileville's *PVH2*, but nonetheless responds creatively to Deguileville's strategies of self-representation, particularly the self-naming acrostic in *PVH2* (see Chapters 4.4 and 4.5, and Chapter 6.2 below).

Langland is remarkably sensitive to the numerous pitfalls, internal conflicts, and contradictions that haunt Deguileville's poetic project, but ultimately recognizes

---

[2] Among the most influential studies of this question in *Piers Plowman*, see especially David A. Lawton, 'The Subject of *Piers Plowman*', YLS 1 (1987), 1–30; the essays in Stephen Justice and Kathryn Kerby-Fulton, eds, *Written Work: Langland, Labor, and Authorship*, especially Kerby-Fulton. 'Langland and the Bibliographic Ego'; the essays of Anne Middleton, quoted from the collected gathering in *Chaucer, Langland, and Fourteenth-Century Literary History*, 'Narration and the Invention of Experience', and '"Kynde Name"'; and Simpson, 'The Power of Impropriety'. Throughout my thinking on this question has been much aided by A. C. Spearing's *Textual Subjectivity* and *Medieval Autographies*.

382   MEDIEVAL ALLEGORY AS EPISTEMOLOGY

their positive, poetically and intellectual enabling potential. In my previous chapter I already suggested that Will's crisis at the end of the A-text ought to be read as a self-conscious reiteration of the pilgrim's crisis at the Rock of Penitence in *PVH*, bringing the text to an anti-climactic halt. In the B-text, however, it is precisely this same experience of cognitive breakdown that triggers Will's conversion, precipitating the first inner dream and thus enabling the continuation of the poem beyond the 'impasse' at the end of the A-text (Chapters 5.1 and 5.2). This experience of failure indeed becomes a *necessary* stepping-stone for Langland's B-text to continue where the *PVH* and the A text had imploded: Will's crisis at B XI is both spiritually and poetically productive, and comes to stand as a precondition for the continuation of Will's quest into the fourth vision and beyond, making possible the slow transition to a very different mode of poetic expression (Chapter 5.4). Given the blurring of the identities of the poem's protagonist Will and the poem's author William Langland, however, this transformation of the first-person subject also entails a profound modification of Langland's authorial self-understanding. Recognizing Deguileville's own repeated failures to complete his original poetic project, Langland responds by acknowledging and accepting the inevitability of authorial failure as a foundational principle of his own, distinctively provisional allegorical poetics. More specifically, Langland can be seen to 'stage' and re-play the pitfalls and *aporias* of the earlier poem in the hope of exorcizing and overcoming those very limitations.[3] This allows Langland to develop a far more ambitious, more nuanced, dynamic, and carefully articulated 're-visionary' poetics on the back of Deguileville, postulated on the inevitability of reiterated poetic and visionary failure (Chapter 6.4). Within such a poetics, Will's allegorical quest succeeds only by failing, and by acknowledging its own repeated failures along with the need to fail again—and again, and again. The assumed, necessary fallibility of the 'I'—as dreamer, *viator*, Will/the will, reader, narrator, and author—finally determines the need for an endlessly reiterated, constantly renewed experience of vision and re-vision, in the hope of gesturing towards some ultimate truth that remains resolutely beyond the grasp of the poem itself, in any of its real or hypothetical instantiations.

1. Starting Over

The Feast of Patience ends in at least partial failure, as Conscience departs to 'be pilgrym wiþ Pacience til I haue preued moore' (B XIII.183), looking forward to a personal reconciliation with Clergie, set in an eschatological future that also

---

[3] Many of the most stimulating recent studies of Langland's poetic imagination emphasize the centrality of the experience of *failure* in his experiential poetics. See especially Zeeman, *Discourses of Desire*; Smith, 'Negative Langland'; Ryan McDermott, 'Practices of Satisfaction in *Piers Plowman's* Dynamic Middle', in *SAC* 36 (2014), 169–207.

THE EXPERIENCE OF FAILURE AND THE ARCHITECTURE OF VISION   383

sees the triumph of a unified and purified Christian Church (B XIII.206–11). Conscience's departure also signals Langland's refusal of letting his own poem rest where Deguileville had brought his own journey to a halt, with the pilgrim's arrival in the cloister—'de monde le refui' (*PVH1* 10,893). Where Deguileville's pilgrim retreats into a monastic enclosure that a pre-figures the Heavenly Jerusalem, Will sets out with Conscience and Patience on a pilgrimage that will not stop until he arrives—significantly, as will be seen—in the real, *historical* Jerusalem of Christ's Crucifixion in *passus* B XVIII.[4] This renewed departure manifests the poem's *refusal* to settle down—a move that is significantly repeated at the very end of the poem, with Conscience's final departure in *passus* B XX in search of Piers the Plowman.[5]

What are the implications of this new departure for the poem? And what is its significance in terms of the evolution of Langland's thought, or rather the evolution of Langland's attitude towards his poetic craft, after Will's/Langland's crises as recorded in the abortive A text 'conclusion' and elaborated in B VIII–XIII.215? More specifically: what kind of shift does this departure signal in terms of Langland's understanding of, and attitude towards, his own poetic 'makynges'—a still unresolved question that has been hanging over the poem since the encounter with Ymaginatif? I have previously argued in favour of seeing Will's crisis and 'conversion' in *passus* B XI as the pivotal moment in the poem, signalling what James Simpson and others have described as a transition from analytical, abstract, and scholastic-rationalistic ways of knowing towards affective, embodied, and experiential ones—albeit with important qualifications, notably the gradual realization of the interdependence of *kynde knowyng* and a newly redefined form of *clergie*. But while the conversion occurs at the start of *passus* B XI, its consequences and implications are negotiated and worked out gradually over the following four *passus*, culminating with Anima's instruction in *passus* B XV. As Simpson observes, Will's conversion is reflected also in the shifting poetic texture of Langland's vision at this point, opening up new expressive possibilities for the poet and new modes of cognitive and affective experience for the reader.[6] With the Feast of Patience, 'Will and by implication the reader of the poem, are now being invited to read in a different way, to pass from academic treatment of scriptural texts (associated with the universities), to a more inward, reflective consideration of Scripture, drawn from monastic traditions'.[7] The questions I asked at the start of this paragraph can thus

---

[4] Traugott Lawler, *The Penn Commentary on Piers Plowman, Volume 4: C Passus 15–19; B Passus 13–17* (Philadelphia: University of Pennsylvania Press, 2018), pp. 57–8. This is not however the final destination of the poem either, since the geographical Jerusalem of Christ's first coming is of course in turn supplanted by the New Jerusalem of the second coming, adumbrated in the apocalyptic events of *passus* B XX.

[5] See also the remarks in Lawler, 'Conscience's Dinner'.

[6] See Simpson, 'From Reason to Affective Knowledge', 14. See further Chapters 5.2 and 5.3 above.

[7] Simpson, *Introduction*, p. 128; see also pp. 134–5 and *passim*.

384 MEDIEVAL ALLEGORY AS EPISTEMOLOGY

be reformulated as follows: what kind of shift takes place in Langland's poetics, and in the underlying assumptions concerning the interrelation between language, individual experience, knowledge, learning, spiritual truth, and salvation? This is the question that lies at the heart of this chapter.

Questions regarding the social, ethical, and spiritual function of poetic writing do not appear at first sight to constitute the primary focus of the Feast of Patience. Such themes, however, resurface endemically throughout this section of the poem, and ultimately constitute one of its main thematic reference points. This discussion is often implicit in the extended figurative exploration of the different functions of the mouth: linguistic, alimentary, and sacramental. It is no accident that later in the fourth vision we find multiple references to minstrels and minstrelsy, cross-referencing and glossing the earlier discussion of minstrels in Study's speech from *passus* B X.[8] In Study's earlier speech minstrels exemplified the degenerate practices of the aristocratic household, where mealtimes provide the occasions for presumptuous theological table-talk punctuated by the unholy *turpiloquium* of minstrels (B X.48–55 and *passim*). Indeed the poem's symbolic soundscape clearly invites us to associate the two, viewed as analogous forms of 'drivelling': just as untrained 'hogges [. . .] dryuele [on] al þe precious perree þat in paradyis wexeþ' (B X.10–12) and noble lords 'dryuele at hir deys þe deitee to knowe' (57), so the 'iaperis and iogelours and iangleris of gestes [. . .] / Spitten and spuen and speke foule wordes, / Drynken and dreuelen and do men for to gape' (B X.31, 40–1). Such decline in table manners, speech, and festive decorum points to an underlying lack of respect for the teachings of scripture, figured as a material/textual/edible manifestation of the divine *logos*.[9] The contrast with the respectful and ritualized cultivation of the Word through the reading and rumination of scripture is made explicit: 'Harlotes for hir harlotrie may haue of hir goodes, [. . .] Ac he þat haþ Holy Writ ay in his mouþe [. . .] Litel is he loued' (B X.30–6).

Ultimately the popularity of such 'harlotrie' at court also points to severe dysfunctions in what ought to be the exercise of 'charitable' aristocratic patronage for genuine minstrels along with the starving poor—'Ac þe carefulle may crie and carpen at þe yate' (B X.58). Indeed, Study points out that such new-fangled courtly fashions do *not* in fact deserve to be acknowledged as 'minstrelsy':

> 'Thei konne na moore mynstralcie ne musik men to glade
> Than Munde þe Millere of *Multa fecit Deus*.
> [. . .]

---

[8] On minstrels and minstrelsy in the poem, see discussion in Chapter 6.2, and, notably, E. Talbot Donaldson, *Piers Plowman: The C-text and Its Poet* (Yale: Yale University Press, 1949), pp. 148–55; Simpson, *Introduction*, pp. 135–43; Hanna, 'Will's Work'; Craun, *Lies, Slander, and Obscenity*, pp. 157–86; Lawler, *Penn Commentary 4*, pp. 63–6; Lawrence M. Clopper, *'Songes of Rechelesnesse': Langland and the Franciscans* (Ann Arbor: University of Michigan Press, 1997), especially pp. 181–218.

[9] See also Craun, *Lies, Slander, and Obscenity*, pp. 163, 168–73 and *passim*.

THE EXPERIENCE OF FAILURE AND THE ARCHITECTURE OF VISION 385

> Ac murþe and mynstralcie amonges men is nouþe
> Lecherie and losengerye and losels tales.'
>
> (B X.43–4; 48–9)

Such feats amount to a blasphemous perversion of minstrelsy, as well as a subversion of the divine order of the Word. As is suggested by their monstrous clowning—they 'do men for to gape / Likne men' (B X.41–2)—such jesters embody a perverted caricature of human dignity, defacing the *imago dei* upon which such human dignity depends: 'ayein þe lawe of Oure Lord' (B X.39).

The Feast of Patience provides a forum that enables—or at least *ought* to enable—the elaboration of alternative, more productive and more meaningful uses of the mouth, including a redeemed form of godly minstrelsy. From the beginning the reader is invited to establish correspondences between different eating habits, forms of speech, and forms of poetic performance. Conscience is indeed presented as a sort of minstrel, who 'conforted vs, and carped vs murye tales' (B XIII.58)—an appropriately positive description for the character who also orchestrates the sapiential/Eucharistic consumption of the sacred text: 'Conscience ful curteisly þo comaunded Scripture / Bifore Pacience breed to brynge' (B XIII.46–7). But as a number of compelling readings have pointed out, it is primarily Patience who comes to embody a redeemed and idealized form of spiritual minstrelsy.[10] It is particularly through the use of enigmatic puzzles and riddles inspired by the New Testament that Patience introduces a purified form of minstrelsy, relying on the mysterious, paradoxical, boundless possibilities for playful signification opened up by the Incarnation of the Word made flesh. Patience's riddling antics have been carefully analysed, often in terms of their superabundance of possible meanings.[11] As Curtis Gruenler has observed, the Feast not only stages a conflict of different modes of knowing, but through its lack of resolution propels the poem towards new, mysterious and elusive forms of knowledge that defy precise definition and analysis, and thus rely on oblique signification. The riddling logic that underpins both Clergie's and Patience's memorably mystifying utterances (XIII.120–30; 136–71), ultimately adds 'not only metaphoric richness but a meta-level of reference to the various realms of knowledge that are also signified and put into dialogue by the speakers in the scene.'[12] To begin with Clergie, this shift to a new, semantically and spiritually more capacious from of signification, is encapsulated in the famously

---

[10] See especially Simpson, *Introduction*, pp. 135–8; Gruenler, 'How to Read Like a Fool', 617–25; ibid., '*Piers Plowman' and the Poetics of Enigma*, pp. 153–64.

[11] See e.g. Andrew Galloway, 'The Rhetoric of Riddling in Late-Medieval England: The "Oxford" Riddles, the *Secretum philosophorum*, and the Riddles in *Piers Plowman*', *Speculum* 70 (1995), 68–105.

[12] Gruenler, 'How to Read like a Fool', p. 617. See further Gruenler, *Piers Plowman' and the Poetics of Enigma*, pp. 153–64,

386 MEDIEVAL ALLEGORY AS EPISTEMOLOGY

cryptic appeal to 'two infinites', in response to Will's renewed question regarding the nature of Dowel:

> 'I am vnhardy', quod he, 'to any wy3t to preuen it.
> For oon Piers þe Plouwman haþ impugned vs alle
> And set alle sciences at a sop saue loue one;
> And no text ne takeþ to mayntene his cause
> But *Dilige Deum* and *Domine, quis habitabit,*
> And seiþ that Dowel and Dobet arn two infinites,
> Whiche infinites wiþ a feiþ fynden out Dobest,
> Which shal saue mannes soule:'

(B XIII.123–30)

Crucially, Clergie's answer is prefaced by his admission that he is unable to back up his enigmatic explanation with any ordinary textual or empirical evidence: 'I am vnhardy [. . .] to *preuen* it' (B XIII.123, emphasis mine). This necessarily places the explanations that follow on an epistemic level that does no longer conform to demonstrative proof or textual authority, which otherwise define the remit of the personification of Clergie.

As Anne Middleton has shown in her influential analysis, Clergie here elaborates the notion of Dowel and Dobet as 'infinites' with reference to grammatical terminology.[13] The 'infinity' of Dowel and Dobet is intended to emphasize their predicative nature, their status as verbs and not nouns, as open-ended actions that must be 'infinitely' undertaken, reiterated, and renewed.[14] A collateral implication of this definition is that the nature of the three 'Dos' resists the kind of mental/moral reification that is implicit in Will's question: 'What is Dowel, sire doctour? (B XIII.103)'.[15] Dowel is not so much and object or *res*, but an action, a predicative injunction 'to do well'; similarly, Dobet is the injunction to continue improving one's act of doing well through its reiterated performance. Accordingly when the predicative and operative action of Dowel becomes fossilized into a noun/concept, its cryptic and enigmatic quality is amplified, congealed into an

---

[13] Anne Middleton, 'Two Infinites: Grammatical Metaphor in *Piers Plowman*', *English Literary History* 39.2 (1972), 169–88.

[14] See also Simpson, *Introduction*, p. 130.

[15] Britton Harwood makes a similar point in commenting on Will's disputation with the Friars—'Do-Wel and Do-Yvel mow nought dwelle togidres' (B VIII.23)—which Harwood reads as 'an illustration of the error of identifying 'grammatical and logical forms with ontological realities', *The Problem of Belief*, p. 17, quoting Gordon Leff, *William of Ockham: the Metamorphosis of Scholastic Discourse* (Manchester: Manchester University Press, 1975), p. 166. See also Quilligan, *The Language of Allegory*, pp. 69–71, who argues that the same problem underlies the disagreement over the interpretation of the words of the Pardon between Piers and Will in *passus* VII.

THE EXPERIENCE OF FAILURE AND THE ARCHITECTURE OF VISION   387

opaque object whose real nature and significance remain impenetrable, tied up in a 'bouste'.[16] As Patience affirms

> 'I bere þerinne a bouste, faste ybounde, Dowel
> In a signe of þe Saterday þat sette first þe kalender,
> And al þe wit of þe Wodnesday of the nexte wike after;
> The myddel of þe moone is þe myght of boþe.
> And herwith am I welcome þer I haue it wiþ me.
> Vndo it—late þis doctour se if Dowel be þerinne;'
>
> (B XIII.153–7)

This enigmatic, transumptive and transgressive spiritualization of the science of grammar by Clergie—a personification of institutionalized school learning—is a highly significant move in the context of the Feast of Patience, where academic and sapiential approaches to language are pitched against each other. Indeed Clergie's ability to rely on formalized academic learning while also transcending it through an enlarged, spiritualized *transumptio* of the art of grammar underscores the transitional status of the Feast of Patience itself, as a moment where ordinary school learning is not so much dismissed or surpassed, but rather transfigured.[17] Rather than a rejection of learning, then, this marks the transition from 'trivial' grammar (i.e. belonging to the *trivium*) to a higher kind of mystical grammar. A similar logic also underpins Patience's more extended riddle, hinging on 'half a laumpe lyne in Latyn, *ex vi transicionis*' (XIII.152). As Simpson observes in commenting on this transitional moment in the poem, 'it is Patience's specifically poetic mode here that is itself significant'.[18]

While it is impossible to do justice to the full complexity of this riddle in the present context, it will be useful to retain a number of readings that are particularly relevant for the argument presented here. Curtis Gruenler has recently drawn attention to the realist metaphysics underpinning much medieval riddling, determining its 'capacity [. . .] to manifest the participation of words in reality'. In his reading of the passage, Patience's oracular riddle marks the poem's leap to an utterly different kind of poetic language,[19] 'transiting', as it were, beyond ordinary mechanism of denotative signification. Edward Schweizer, for his part, emphasized the specifically Incarnation overtones of Patience's 'transition', rooted in the echoes of the Jewish feast of the Passover, typological figure for the Passion,

---

[16] In *PVH* Raison's 'commission', which precipitates a similar controversy over literalism (Chapter 2.3), is contained in just such a 'boiste', only to be displayed to the equally clueless, illiterate Rude Entendement (*PVH1* 5183–92). See also Steiner, *Documentary Culture*, pp. 36–46. I follow here the alternative reading of the line from the Kane-Donaldson edition, rejected by Schmidt.
[17] Simpson, *Introduction*, pp. 136–7.
[18] Simpson, *Introduction*, p. 137.
[19] Gruenler, 'How to Read Like a Fool', 613, 620, and *passim*. See also Gruenler, *'Piers Plowman' and the Poetics of Enigma*, pp. 157–9.

388   MEDIEVAL ALLEGORY AS EPISTEMOLOGY

Crucifixion, and Resurrection of Christ, commemorated by the Easter Liturgy.[20] Cynthia Bland, finally, reconsiders the grammatical origin of the term—a feature that Patience's riddle shares, significantly, with Clergie's riddle that precedes it and prepares for it.[21] All of these readings acquire a more pointed relevance in the light of my earlier considerations on the Feast of Patience, and especially within the framework of Langland's continuing dialogue with Deguileville. Patience's riddling allusion to interrelated notions of grammatical, sacramental, and poetic 'transition' manages to condense into a single formulation the most important concerns to emerge from Deguileville's poem after the pilgrim's conversion at the Rock of Penitence. I have already discussed the central role of Sacramental concerns at the Feast of Patience along with the importance of *PVH* in nourishing these developments (Chapter 5.4). But also Langland's emerging interest in alternative, extra-ordinary forms of grammatical signification and associated forms of poetic expression resonates with developments in Deguileville's poem. More specifically, Langland's concern with the mystical and transumptive possibilities of grammar echoes the pilgrim's conversion to an utterly different form of linguistic expression in *PVH*, encapsulated in the new linguistic order of the ABC prayer (Chapter 4.2).

While taking on a very different narrative shape and poetic form, Langland's progressive turn towards an enigmatic and riddling poetic language to some extent reproduces the reorientation of Deguileville's poem, away from ordinary signification towards a numinous language of presence, immanence, and participation. Anne Middleton's observations on the significance of Clergie's definition of Dowel and Dobet as infinites are particularly revealing in this respect: for Middleton, Clergie's cryptic reply signals that the triad of 'Dos' now develops meanings that are not so much 'referential' but purely 'formal', opening the doors to radically different processes of signification. This recalls the important formal as well as tonal rupture provided by the ABC prayer, disrupting the linear flow of narrative as well as disrupting ordinary processes of reference and signification, shifting from horizontal acts of denotation to vertical forms of invocation. But it is particularly Langland's *reasons* for experimenting with new formal and grammatical possibilities that are revealing in relation to Deguileville. Like the conversion of Deguileville's pilgrim, Clergie's appeal to the 'infinite' signifying possibilities of grammatical metaphor must be read, for Middleton, 'as an attempt to purify allegorical language—a medium highly vulnerable to misunderstanding and misuse'.[22] Like Deguileville, then, Langland here seeks to exorcize the ambiguity and fallibility of the allegorical medium itself, envisaging alternative, enigmatic, and

---

[20] Edward C. Schweitzer, '"Half a Laumpe Lyne in Latyne" and Patience's Riddle in *Piers Plowman*', *JEGP* 73.3 (1974), 313–27.
[21] Cynthia Renée Bland, 'Langland's Use of the Term *ex vi transicionis*', YLS 2 (1988), 125–35. See also Vance D. Smith, 'Negative Langland', 44–5.
[22] Middleton, 'Two Infinites', 171–2.

ultimately Incarnation and sacramental mechanisms of linguistic signification. As Middleton points out, an essential component of this shift is the negation of the ordinary referential function of language in favour of a more mysterious and numinous form of linguistic participation. As Vance D. Smith has suggested more recently, then, Clergie's and Patience's riddles—and indeed Langland's entire poem—are in fact postulated on a principle of representational negativity. In Smith's words, this principle produces a poem that 'gestures towards apophasis, a non-predicative language so radically ecstatic [. . .] that it cannot or should not be uttered'.[23] With the Feast of Patience and with the departure that concludes it, Langland's poem exhausts ordinary processes of cognition and signification to reach out towards a new language of enigmatic presence. This language is rooted in the awareness of man's necessarily oblique, mysterious, and ultimately silent inner apprehension of divine realities.

Also Curtis Jirsa has recently discussed the developments of *passus* B XIII in ways that illuminate Langland's critical and reconstructive engagement with Deguileville, particularly in terms of the inspiration provided by embedded lyrics like the ABC prayer. Jirsa argues that a whole range of crucial shifts and developments in the middle sections of Langland's poem ought to be seen as elaborating the expressive, affective, and cognitive possibilities of the medieval lyric in its multiple forms. More specifically, Langland's tendency to 'periodically stage or dramatize the process of creating and consuming lyric forms' is seen as 'bring[ing] into focus one of the poem's most central concerns: the relationship between knowledge and the processes of creating and consuming poetry'.[24] The Feast of Patience in particular is seen as staging a 'metaphoric depiction of a process of lyrical rumination', which provides 'the proper epistemological foundation for textual making'.[25] For Jirsa such developments are inspired by the widespread use of lyric interpolations in fourteenth-century poetry to disrupt the flow of otherwise linear narratives: Jirsa significantly mentions Chaucer and Machaut[26]—but not Deguileville, who in many ways is the most radical and thoughtful practitioner of lyric interpolations, and uses them repeatedly to disrupt the narrative linearity of the kind of pilgrimage-allegory that also underpins *Piers Plowman* itself.[27] Deguileville's seminal ABC prayer, for instance, crystallizes precisely those formal and expressive features of the lyric that Langland himself highlights in visions 3 and 4: it disrupts the horizontal linearity of the pilgrimage narrative; it constitutes a form of 'unpremeditated' textual making; it manifests a distinctly experiential (or *kynde*) poetics, but also reaffirms the validity of authoritative clergical texts

---

[23] Smith, 'Negative Langland', 50.
[24] Jirsa, '*Piers Plowman*'s Lyric Poetics', 80, 78.
[25] Jirsa, '*Piers Plowman*'s Lyric Poetics', 80.
[26] Jirsa, '*Piers Plowman*'s Lyric Poetics', 78.
[27] See especially Pomel, 'Les écrits pérégrins'.

390 MEDIEVAL ALLEGORY AS EPISTEMOLOGY

and doctrines through a description of their effects on the protagonist; it introduces a new form of experiencing language; and finally inaugurates new ways of conceiving the very nature, function, and prerogatives of poetic craft. All of this ultimately signals a complex, and for Langland gradual and qualified, 'conversion' and reorientation towards a new, mystical and contemplative poetry grounded in a radically different, Incarnation epistemology of the Word.

Once more Langland can be seen to adopt but subtly reorganize the motifs, themes, formal features, and ideas introduced by Deguileville. Langland clearly weighs up the possibility of a Deguilevillian retreat from the secular world and from the vernacular, fictional, and didactic work of narrative allegorical 'makyng' into a world of contemplative 'bidding of bedes' (Chapter 5.3), but ultimately resists the temptation to withdraw into the protective enclosure afforded by prayer-like lyric. Accordingly, no formal rupture occurs in the poem, and we do not experience the abrupt shift to formally discrete lyrical poetic forms within the text of *Piers Plowman*. Langland implicitly rejects Deguileville's appeal to the transcendent authority of Grace Dieu, who is presented as the author and scribe of the ABC prayer, a providential and efficacious blueprint 'scripting' the devotional performance the pilgrim is invited to stage. But Langland's refusal to fully shift to lyric forms and his refusal to incorporate a document whose salvific power could in any way approach the efficacy of the ABC, does not ultimately arise from theological reservations about the power of grace/Grace Dieu. I would rather suggest that by omitting anything equivalent to the ABC prayer Langland acknowledges *his own* inability to produce—or indeed receive, spell out, and 're-produce' or transmit, in discrete and detachable textual form—any poetic vision or textual utterance that could hope to function as a viable, unambiguous, transparent, definitive and self-sufficient manifestation of divine truth, presence, or revelation. Langland's poem quite simply refuses to embed within its larger textual body anything as potent, numinous, formally circumscribed and detachable like Deguileville's ABC prayer.[28] On the contrary, Langland's poem seems to militate very deliberately *against* any such a possibility, emphasizing instead the fleeting, elusive, enigmatic, spasmodic, provisional and ultimately 'episodic' nature of Will's textual/cognitive experiences in this section of the poem.[29]

This reluctance to produce or re-produce prescriptive and unassailable forms of textual, institutional, and doctrinal authority is manifested not only in the poem's rejection of 'bidding of bedes' in favour of further 'meddling with makyinges'—a tentative, anxious, dangerous but ultimately defiant gesture—but

---

[28] The clearest evidence for the separable and extractible nature of the ABC prayer, and for its appeal as an independent piece of poetic expression for medieval readers, is of course Chaucer's translation and its independent circulation. See p. 251, n. 12 for further critical literature on Chaucer's ABC.

[29] Middleton, 'Narration and the Invention of Experience'.

THE EXPERIENCE OF FAILURE AND THE ARCHITECTURE OF VISION   391

also, more starkly, in the earlier Tearing of the Pardon.[30] Among a rich array of further resonances, this scene also functions as the inaugural moment announcing the central themes of the poem's extended middle section, focusing on the insufficiency of institutionally and textually mediated doctrine or 'auctoritee' detached from the predicative penitential action and experience of the individual will/Will—or, to adopt the poem's terms, separated from the action of doing well, doing better, and doing best. The Tearing of the Pardon thus prepares for the extended indictment of the desire to obtain a depersonalized, objectified, and textualized 'knowledge' without a correlative experience of embodied knowing-as-doing throughout the third and fourth visions. In John Burrow's formulation, 'Langland's fear, as so often, is that the external form or institution—even though it is acceptable in itself—may come to usurp the place of the inner spiritual reality.'[31] If to this we add Anne Middleton's important insight that 'Piers's vernacular labor was for Langland metonymic of the task of vernacular literary labour,'[32] it becomes clear that the tearing already gestures towards a new, spiritually productive kind of poetic labour. It is therefore significant that Clergie himself, in his reply to Will's renewed questions regarding the nature of Dowel, should reference the earlier episode of the Tearing of the Pardon, at the very moment that marks the poem's transition—*ex vi transicionis*—towards more elusive, enigmatic forms of cognition and linguistic expression:

> 'For oon Piers þe Plowman haþ impugned vs alle
> And set alle sciences at a sop saue loue one,
> And no text ne takeþ to mayntene his cause
> But *Dilige Deum* and *Domine, quis habitabit*,'
>
> (B XIII.124–7)

What is striking is precisely Clergie's insistence on Piers Plowman's rejection of any sort of mediating textual authority—'no text'—apart from the injunction of the Gospel of Mathew 22:37. Later in the poem Piers is again associated with a kind of knowledge that conspicuously eludes the learned clergy, as one who 'parceyueþ moore depper' (B XV.199–201).

---

[30] My reading here converges with that proposed by Quilligan, *The Language of Allegory*, pp. 69–71, for which see above n. 15. The significance of the 'Tearing of the Pardon' is notoriously and tenaciously unclear, as recent work has again emphasized. See especially Traugott Lawler, 'The Pardon Formula in *Piers Plowman*: Its Ubiquity, its Binary Shape, its Silent Middle Term', *YLS* 14 (2000), 117–52; Alastair J. Minnis, 'Piers' Protean Pardon: The Letter and Spirit of Langland's Theology of Indulgences', in Anne Marie D'Arcy and Alan J. Fletcher, eds, *Studies in Late Medieval and Early Renaissance Texts in Honour of John Scattergood* (Dublin: Four Courts Press, 2005), pp. 218–40, reprinted in Minnis, *Translations of Authority*, pp. 68–89; Denise N. Baker, 'Pre-Empting Piers's Tearing of the Pardon: Langland's Revisions of the C Visio', *YLS* 31 (2017), 43–72; Ralph Hanna, 'The "Absent" Pardon-Tearing of Piers Plowman C', *The Review of English Studies* 66.275 (2015), 449–64.

[31] John Burrow, 'The Action of Langland's Second Vision', *Essays in Criticism* 15.3 (1965), 247–68 (260).

[32] Middleton, 'Playing the Plowman: Legends of Fourteenth-Century Authorship', in her *Chaucer, Langland, and Fourteenth-Century Literary History*, pp. 113–42 (132).

392   MEDIEVAL ALLEGORY AS EPISTEMOLOGY

For all his resistance to the dangers of textual and documentary reification, however, Langland does not reject the sapiential, penitential, and sacramental possibilities encapsulated by the 'new' poetic language inaugurated by Deguileville's ABC prayer. Langland ultimately engages with such notions in more subtle, oblique, and critical fashion. Langland concurs with Deguileville that poetic texts do acquire material, and hence sensual and experiential character when produced or consumed by the questing dreamer or *viator* as well as the reader. However, instead of embedding such texts by spelling them out at length as objectified and discrete units of text that can be extracted from the overarching framework of the quest or pilgrimage narrative, Langland's texts remain numinous and ineffable. Langland's texts too become tangible and even portable, yet remain ultimately elusive and inaccessible, as they are never susceptible of definitive reification in material textual form within Langland's poem. My reading therefore differs from the one proposed by Emily Steiner, who like me argues for Langland's sustained engagement with Deguileville's documentary aesthetics, but contends that poems like *Piers Plowman* 'seek their substance in material things, are always verging upon the institutional, and conversely, that the materiality invoked by these poems is institutional in nature'.[33] My own reading, by contrast, identifies Langland's fascination with the material documents that punctuate and structure Deguileville's allegorical quest as a site of major concern and anxiety. While Langland is acutely aware of the power of textual reification, he is above all concerned with its dangers: ultimately his poetry deliberately and determinedly resists any pressures to fixate authority in material, textual, and institutional forms.

Langland's resistance to documentary, institutional, and poetic reification is best seen in the role played by prayer-like texts and documents within the renewed pilgrimage begun by Will in the company of Patience and Conscience at B XIII.216. As the pilgrims depart on their new journey, they are equipped with a single, distinctively Deguilevillian attribute: a pilgrim scrip containing samples of sound doctrine and right belief:

> Thanne had Pacience, as pilgrymes han, in his poke vitailles:
> Sobretee and symple speche and sooþfast bileue,
> To conforte hym and Conscience if þei come in place
> There vnkyndnesse and coueitise is, hungry contrees boþe.
>
> (B XIII.217–20)

The contents of the 'poke' are then served up in the following *passus*, during the encounter with Haukyn. In response to the latter's dismissal of divine providence as spelled out in Ps. 41.4—*volucres celi Deus pascit* (B XIV.34a)— Patience 'out of his poke hente / Vitailles of grete vertues for alle manere beestes'

---

[33] Steiner, '*Piers Plowman* and Institutional Poetry', 299.

THE EXPERIENCE OF FAILURE AND THE ARCHITECTURE OF VISION   393

(B XIV.37–8). It turns out that such wholesome provisions are again made up of textual nourishment:

> 'Quodcumque pecieritis a Patre in nomine meo . . . Et alibi, Non in
> Solo pane viuit homo, set in omni verbo quod procedit de ore Dei'
> But I lokede what liflode it was þat Pacience so preisede,
> and þanne was it a pece of þe Paternoster—Fiat voluntas tua.
> (B XIV 47a–49)

Clearly the notion of such portable and edible texts elaborates a whole series of Deguilevillian motifs and ideas beyond the ABC prayer alone. The motif of Patience's 'poke' itself is clearly modelled on the pilgrim's scrip (*escherpe* or *besace*) in *PVH*, an allegorization of Faith, containing the necessary provisions for the journey (*PVH1* 3473–7; *PVH2* 3773–7; see Chapter 2.4). Like Patience's 'poke', the pilgrim's scrip is a deeply textualized object, spelling out the modalities of correct belief in the shape of the twelve articles of the faith, inscribed on the twelve bells that decorate the satchel (*PVH1* 3324–32). While in *PVH1* the scrip is merely described as carrying the inscription of the twelve articles of Faith, in *PVH2* the poet actually spells out the articles themselves, in a considerably extended treatment of the episode (*PVH2* 3696–3745). More importantly, three further pieces of embedded lyric are associated with this episode in *PVH2*. The first of these consists of an extended Latin lyric elaborating on the text of the *Credo*, and is closely associated with the scrip of Faith (*PVH2* 3927–4442). The second and third of these likewise consist of extended Latin lyrics, elaborating on the words of the *Pater Noster* and *Ave Maria*, both associated with the Staff of Hope (resp. *PVH2* 4529–972; 4973–5140). All three pieces are presented as acrostics of sorts, using the individual words of the Latin Confession of Faith and the two prayers as touchstones for beginning each individual stanza. In exploiting the expressive possibilities of acrostics and in adopting the rhyme scheme of the Helinandian stanza all three pieces clearly echo the aesthetic principles of Deguileville's foundational ABC prayer from *PVH1*. Like the ABC prayer, these three ulterior lyrics are presented as objectified embedded documents, whose authoritative status is further underlined by the adoption of Latin.

Langland's 'pece of the Paternoster' (B XIV.49), fished out from Patience's 'poke', clearly is a further avatar of Deguileville's portable prayers and documents, equally presented as the source of spiritual, and implicitly Eucharistic nourishment. But again the differences are more revealing than the similarities: Langland's decision *not* to spell out, and thus *not* to 'reify' any of these texts as formally discrete and tangible documents and/or inserted lyrics in the manner of Deguileville is conspicuous and significant. Strikingly, the English poem in fact articulates the rationale behind this decision, during Patience's later conversation with Haukyn, which in effect amounts to an extended exposition of the contents of her 'poke'

394   MEDIEVAL ALLEGORY AS EPISTEMOLOGY

(B XIV.50–319). As Patience summarizes the basics of Christian doctrine, she imagines a courtroom drama in which the human soul is arraigned by the Devil, and outlines the strategy of defence and its use of textual evidence—a scenario that is, incidentally, closely reminiscent of the narrative configuration in Deguileville's *Pèlerinage de l'Âme*:[34]

> 'Ac if þe pouke wolde plede herayein, and punysshe vs in conscience,
> He shulde take þe acquaintance as quyk and to þe queed shewen it—
> > *Pateat, etc.: Per Passionem Domini—*
> And putten of so þe pouke, and preuen vs vnder borwe.
> Ac þe parchemyn of þis patente of pouerte be moste,
> And of pure pacience and parfit bileue.
> Of pompe and of pride þe parchemyn decourreþ,
> And principalliche of alle peple, but þei be pore of herte.
> Ellis is al on ydel, al þat euere we wroȝten,
> *Paternoster* and penaunce and pilgrimage to Rome.'
>
> (B XIV.189–97)

On one level the passage clearly draws inspiration from Deguileville's letters, down even to the level of style, with its adoption of the phrasing 'de par le roy', characteristic of formal letters patent or royal edicts.[35] But the underlying logic of the passage ultimately amounts to a *rejection* of Deguileville's reliance on the stability and authority of written documents, understood as codified 'scripts' outlining normative devotional action and prayer.[36] In Langland the passage essentially proposes a rhetorical 'de-materialization' of fundamental Christian doctrine, replacing physical parchment with an abstract, immaterial textual support, an enigmatic parchment made of 'poverty'.[37]

---

[34] See especially Moreau, '"Ce mauvais tabellion"', and ibid, *Eschatological Subjects*, pp. 63–101.

[35] Pomel, 'Écrits pérégrins', p. 98. See above, Chapter 4.4.

[36] See Steiner, *Documentary Culture*, pp. 36–46; ibid., '*Piers Plowman* and Institutional Poetry'; Delphine Connes, 'L'influence coutumière dans la procédure de Guillaume de Deguileville', and Esther Dehoux, 'Des Saints au tribunal: Juges et experts à la cour du Paradis', both in Bassano, Dehoux, and Vincent, eds, *Le 'Pèlerinage de l'âme' de Guillaume de Digulleville (1355–1358)*, pp. 175–84 and 185–98; Pomel, 'Les écrits pérégrins'; Moreau, '"Ce mauvais tabellion"', and ibid, *Eschatological Subjects*, pp. 63–101; Kamath, *Authorship and First-Person Allegory*, pp. 11–12.

[37] On the enigmatic nature of the phrase, see again Gruenler, *Piers Plowman and the Poetics of Enigma*, p. 166, and A. V. C. Schmidt, 'Langland's Structural Imagery of Food and Drink', in ibid, *Earthly Honest Things*, pp. 221–36 (231–5). This elusiveness is contrasted with the conspicuous materiality of the books wielded by Clergie, which ostensibly contain a wealth of information otherwise inaccessible to the pilgrims on their journey, and are used by Clergie to attempt and dissuade them from leaving on their pilgrimage:

> [Clergie:] 'I shal brynge yow a Bible, a book of þe olde lawe
> And lere yow, if yow like, þe leest point to knowe,

'Langland modifies the mechanics of the salvific operation enabled by such texts: the source of their efficacy no longer lies in the outward and material 'letter' of such documents, but in the inner 'spirit' of poverty and selfless charity that ought to sustain their recitation and performance. Clearly the allusion to the 'ydel' and ineffectual nature of a mere *Paternoster* unaccompanied by the appropriate inner disposition is not accidental: it provides us with one more reminder that the contents of Patience's own 'poke' are in themselves powerless and unsubstantial, unless they are employed in accordance with the appropriate moral and spiritual disposition. The perfect example of such mechanistic and ultimately blasphemous misuse of sacramental language is provided by Haukyn, who admits that

> 'Ne neuere penaunce parfornede ne *Paternoster* seide
> That my mynde ne was moore in my good in a doute
> Than in þe grace of God and hise grete helpes'
>
> (B XIII.397–9a)

It is not surprising, then, that Langland should never provide any discrete and extended citations or transcriptions of authoritative Latin texts as detachable embedded lyrics in his poem, here or elsewhere. This would reduce their status to dangerously material 'chaffare', in Langlandian parlance—just like the pardons and indulgences dispensed by the Friars at B XI.53–8.[38] Langland's preferred method of referring to authoritative Latin texts, as critics have often pointed out, is of an utterly different kind, relying on the interjection of brief snippets and fragmentary citations, deliberately incomplete and at times imprecise allusions to multiple texts layered on top of each other.[39] Langland's handling of such authoritative Latin textual 'sources' foregrounds not so much the texts themselves as their absorption within a very different text—his own poem. This turns Langland's poem into 'an extended reading lesson', rooted in a logic of 'dislocation of the refound and reused fragment from its primary site of production', rediscovering the 'productive utility' of such antecedent texts.[40] This points to a very different

> That Pacience þe pilgrym parfitly knew neuere' (B XIII.186–8)
> [...]
> [Conscience:] 'Me were leuere [...]
> Haue pacience parfitliche þan half þi pak of bokes! (B XIII.201–2)

[38] I here echo a point made by Wittig 'The Dramatic and Rhetorical Development of Long Will's Pilgrimage', 67.

[39] See especially Traugott Lawler, 'William Langland', in Roger Ellis, ed., *Oxford History of Literary Translation in English, Vol I: until 1550* (Oxford University Press, 2008), pp. 149–59; ibid., 'Langland Translating', in Andrew Galloway and Frank Grady, eds, *Answerable Style: The Idea of the Literary in Medieval England*, (Columbus: Ohio State University Press, 2013), pp. 54–74; Cannon, 'Langland's *Ars grammatica*'; and John A. Alford, *Piers Plowman: A Guide to the Quotations* (Binghamton: CMERS, 1992).

[40] Anne Middleton, '*Piers Plowman*, the Monsters, and the Critics: Some Embarrassments of Literary History', in Daniel Donoghue, James Simpson, and Nicholas Watson, eds, *The Morton Bloomfield Lectures, 1989–2005* (Kalamazoo: Medieval Institute, 2010), pp. 94–115 (109).

396   MEDIEVAL ALLEGORY AS EPISTEMOLOGY

conception of textual and documentary authority as a whole, and therefore plays an important role in shaping Langland's attitude towards his own poem, towards his poetic craft, and towards the construction of something like an 'authorial persona' (see further Chapter 6.4). Once more, as in the Tearing of the Pardon, Langland moves the emphasis away from the ostensible stability, authority, and permanence of material documents to foreground the importance of absorbing and digesting their teaching, with a view to transforming the user/reader's moral and spiritual disposition.

In *Piers Plowman* such texts are present only implicitly—absorbed, digested, and infused within the main body of the larger poem, at times spliced into the lines of Langland's own poetry and variously ventriloquized but also dislocated by the many skewed mediating voices of his many characters and personifications, including the voice of the dreamer himself. At best, such texts are present in intermittent, fragmentary, and implicit fashion, remaining ultimately 'unreadable' and irrecoverable as discrete and stable textual units. Conversely, however, the very 'implicitness' of such authoritative quotations, and their implication in the account of Will's quest, reminds readers of the importance of *absorbing* them, and experiencing them not merely as reified and static material texts liable to becoming inert, but as manifestations of the living Word to be incorporated, ruminated, and finally acted upon. This fundamental opposition between the 'letter' and the 'spirit', I would suggest, lies at the heart of Langland's move towards a more affective, experiential, and *kynde* poetics. Texts are no longer seen, as in Deguileville, as external, independent, and intrinsically authoritative and efficacious instantiations of truth. Instead, they are shown to function as potential agents of personal understanding and transformation—instances of a kind of language that both transforms and therefore *constitutes* the very 'subject' and 'subjectivity' of Will's, Langland's, and the reader's selves.

To conclude, then, Langland's distinctive attitude to language, knowledge, and authority in B XIII–XIV is simultaneously inspired by Deguileville's longing for a redeemed and numinous language of participation, but also eschews, transcends, and finally rejects the fetishization of documentary textuality implicit in Deguileville's lyrical poetics. On the one hand Langland adopts, and even expands a whole range of Deguilevillian ideas of redeemed and sacramental language, following the lead of Estude, who was seen carrying the 'sweet and wholesome flesh' of Scripture in a 'parchment vessel' to nourish the inmates of the monastery (*PVH1* 12,827–40; cf. *PVH2* 15,135–94).[41] On the other hand, however, Langland ultimately resists and rejects the radical lyrical poetics that results from the pilgrim/author's experience of conversion and inward turn in Deguileville's ABC prayer in *PVH1*, and developed further in many lyrics that punctuate the later poetic corpus. Furthermore, Langland ultimately rejects the

---

[41] See Chapter 4.2.

THE EXPERIENCE OF FAILURE AND THE ARCHITECTURE OF VISION   397

possibility of a radical interruption of his allegorical poetic work, and the conversion to an utterly different, lyrical, and contemplative poetic mode. Instead of abandoning the mode of the allegorical pilgrimage narrative altogether, Langland integrates such new, numinous, and mysterious modalities of lyrical signification *within* the existing narrative structure of his poem, inflecting, modifying, and expanding the expressive possibilities of the allegorical mode itself. More specifically, Langland's distinctive reworking of Deguilevillian ideas of textual reification and absorption becomes an attempt to bridge the gap between *kynde knowinge* (experiential knowledge) and *clergie* (book learning): it is precisely by resisting Deguileville's reification of a putatively transcendent textual authority that texts come to be fully incorporated and truly experienced, and can thus effect a deep transformation of the subject. As I will argue in Chapters 6.3 and 6.4, this is an important precondition for Will's ability to experience the significance of the most important text of all: 'of Good Friday the storye' (cf. B XIII.446). This ultimately enables the poem to move from an allegorical hermeneutics of the self towards a performative retelling and re-enactment of the passion narrative and sacred history as a whole, articulated within the formal framework of a first-person quest narrative that is constantly disrupted and redefined but never abandoned.

2. Haukyn, Guillermus, and Will

I began the previous section of this chapter by insisting on the poetically transformative nature of the events in B XIII and XIV. I have also argued that much of this section of the poem is in fact concerned with defining new, regenerated forms of poetic thought and expression, in the wake of the poem's partial rejection of the more inquisitive, dialectical, and argumentative style of the poem's middle section. It is important to stress that the figure of Will is largely passive throughout this section, from the condemnation of degenerate minstrels at the Feast of Patience until Will's encounter with Anima in the following vision (B XV). Will's adoption of a more passive role clearly signals a major transition in the larger narrative arc of the poem: on the one hand it signals Will's rejection of the analytical modes of knowing characteristic of his earlier persona, the irritable and mercurial disputant of the middle section (B VIII–XIII.215); on the other hand it prepares the ground for subsequent developments where Will becomes a spectator, or rather a 'recipient' and beneficiary of an extended re-enactment of major episodes from salvation history (B XVI–XVIII). Before this is possible, however, Will needs to undergo what appears as a purgative encounter with Haukyn, a figure who in many ways functions as a mirror-image for Will himself, and thus offers the opportunity to confront a number of ethical challenges that continue to threaten the legitimacy of Will's/Langland's poetic 'makynges'.

398   MEDIEVAL ALLEGORY AS EPISTEMOLOGY

The encounter with Haukyn in *passus* XIII and XIV provides numerous direct references to minstrelsy, pointing to the poem's ongoing concern with defining a viable and spiritually productive form of poetic making. There has been considerable debate concerning the significance of Langland's decision to present Haukyn specifically as a 'mynstrall' (B XIII.225), and some commentators have proposed a minimal interpretation of this detail: the term may simply be intended to identify Haukyn as practicing any sort of *ministerium* in the secular world.[42] The subsequent developments of the encounter, however, suggest that Haukyn's minstrelsy is intended to invite the reader to reflect again on the role of poets and minstrels more widely. More specifically, this reintroduces the vexed question of the status, use, and legitimacy of Will's/Langland's own minstrelsy. Haukyn himself insists on the difference between his trade and that of the ordinary 'lordes mynstrals' who 'farten', 'fiþelen at festes' and 'harpen' (B XIII.230, 232), and this suggests that *he*, at least, thinks of himself as representing a higher, non-debased form of poetic activity reminiscent of the genuine 'mynstralcie' and 'musik' whose virtues are extolled by Study at B X.43.[43] Beyond his broad association with a minstrel/poet figure, however, the significance of Haukyn remains stubbornly elusive, especially in the B-text:[44] how exactly are we supposed to interpret his appearance, his behaviour, his words, and his overall role in the poem? Is Haukyn a figure to be condemned and rejected, or rather a typical sinner and fallible human? Are we expected to respond with compassion, or even invited to identify with him? And if he is a sort of double for Will himself, as is often claimed,[45] are we meant to see him as a genuine and viable embodiment of a poetic ideal, or as an example of the pitfalls of poetic activity? The poem provides few unambiguous clues, making it difficult to even determine whether Haukyn is intended to be a positive or a negative figure. Indeed, Haukyn's description cannot be said to amount to the description of a realistic persona at all, because it is saturated in conflicting details and allusions. Significantly, many details in this description are once more drawn from the semantic fields of speech, food consumption, feasting, and Eucharistic symbolism.[46]

I would suggest that the conflicted density and opacity of Haukyn's description is not finally an obstacle to our understanding of his real nature—quite the contrary. As a layman engaged in *Actiua Vita* (B XIII.225), his moral and symbolic

---

[42] See Lawler, *Penn Commentary 4*, pp. 63–6.

[43] Craun, *Lies, Slander, and Obscenity*, pp. 174–5.

[44] *Penn Commentary 4*, pp. 59–62.

[45] James Simpson refers to Haukyn as Will's *alter ego*, 'The Power of Impropriety', p. 161, whereas Adams sees him as Will's *Doppelgänger*, 'Piers's Pardon', p. 381, and for Mary Carruthers, *Search for St. Truth: A Study of Meaning in Piers Plowman* (Evanston: Northwestern University Press, 1973), p. 122, he is 'the most complete and evident mirror image of Will in the poem'. See further e.g. Alford, 'The Design of the Poem', p. 50; Donaldson, *C-Text*, pp. 148–55; Lawler, *Penn Commentary 4*, p. 65.

[46] Simpson, *Introduction*, pp. 139–46; Mann, 'Eating and Drinking'; Watson, 'Haukyn's Cloak', pp. 108–13.

THE EXPERIENCE OF FAILURE AND THE ARCHITECTURE OF VISION   399

opacity is an essential defining feature of his social and spiritual status, which is radically unstable, hybrid, and ambivalent. Haukyn is after all an unclassifiable, hopelessly idiosyncratic figure:

> so singuler by hymself as to sy3te of þe peple
> Was noon swich as hymself, [. . .]
> Yhabited as an heremyte, an ordre by hymselue,
> Religion saun3 rule and resonable obedience;
>
> (B XIII.283–6)

Haukyn ultimately remains a deeply enigmatic figure, referencing and conflating a number of possible *personae* simultaneously: despairing sinner; archetypal penitent; embodiment of the inevitable sinfulness of the active life; working and deserving poor; godly minstrel; even a priestly figure furnishing the community with (Eucharistic?) bread and wafers (e.g. B XIII.227, 236, 241, 242, 261, 263). Ultimately Haukyn seems to crystallize what are possible and hypothetical states of being that are partially and intermittently realized by Will himself—an idea encapsulated also by his identification as a Hermit, dwelling in a liminal and ambivalent social and spiritual space.[47] In this sense, the timing of Haukyn's appearance is essential: appearing on the scene at this precise moment in the poem—after Will's departure from the Feast of Patience, and after his rejection of the forms of communal eating and devotion staged during the banquet—Haukyn, or *Actiua Vita*, reminds us of the difficulties Langland had to confront due to his refusal to embark on a radically ascetic inward turn such as the one that concludes the *Pèlerinage de Vie*. In contrast to Deguileville's monastic pilgrim, Haukyn, like Will, inhabits a space that is intrinsically open, and his social and spiritual identity is therefore precarious and ambivalent, suspended between the desire for penance and redemption on the one hand, and the moral risks of conducting life as a devout but largely unregulated and unattached layperson living in the secular world. Haukyn therefore appears to crystallize a deeply problematic question for Langland: if Will is to reject the ordinary physical labour of ploughing, the life as an inquisitive academic theologian, as well as a monastic existence of prayer and bidding of beads, what, then, might a morally viable and meritorious form of life look like for Will?

On one level, then, Haukyn's role as an embodiment of *Actiua Vita* is clearly meant to stress that Will—unlike Deguileville's pilgrim—forgoes the invitation to short-circuit the cognitive *aporia* of his quest by entering the contemplative life and submitting to its *voluntas communis*, presented in the guise of Ymaginatif's exhortation to submit to a life of 'obedience' and 'bidding of bedes' (cf. B XII.37, 28; see Chapter 5.3). On another, he embodies the difficulties of rejecting

---

[47] On Will/Langland as 'hermit', see Godden, 'Plowmen and Hermits'; Hanna, '"Meddling with Makings" and Will's Work'; ibid., 'Will's Work', in Justice and Kerby-Fulton, *Written Work*, pp. 23–66.

400 MEDIEVAL ALLEGORY AS EPISTEMOLOGY

such a solution while also striving to live up to the highest standards of Christian discipline and morality to ensure his soul's salvation. It is therefore perfectly fitting that Haukyn should be characterized above all by his irreducible 'singularity' (cf. XIII.283–4). It is telling that such singularity should be presented very specifically in terms of his exclusion from any communal and regulated form of religious life: 'Religion saunʒ rule and resonable obedience' (B XIII.286). Interestingly, however, these same motifs of alienation and deregulation characterize the life of Deguileville's pilgrim *after* his forceful expulsion from the monastery in *PVH2*, and during his renewed errance through the secular world (see Chapter 4.5). The pilgrim's condition now is one of isolation, singularity, lack of regulation, loss of identity and orientation: 'I who wander through this world, deprived of any discipline' [Qui en cest monde chemine [. . .] Demourant sans descepline, *PVH2* 16,275–7]. All regularity is lost, and monks are now wandering aimlessly outside the cloister:

Cloistre n'y a mais, ne Leçon,	There is neither cloister nor Study,
Discipline, ne Oroison;	Discipline, or Worship. Everyone wanders
Chascun ou il veult va vaguier	where they please.
(*PVH2* 16,546–8)	

Ultimately this spells the end of the monastic ideal itself, postulated on literal, metaphorical, and devotional *stabilitas* (*PVH2* 16,524–8). The most striking illustration of this state of being is constituted by the figure of Abusion—who functions as a potential double for the pilgrim[48]—memorably equipped with 'the spoon of singularity':[49]

Et que tortueusement va,	And advancing tortuously, and
En abusant de la cuillier	misusing the spoon that she carries, to
Qu'elle porte, pour enseignier	teach everyone her great lechery, and
A tous sa grant lecherie	hideous gluttony. Without reason and
Et villainne gloutonnie,	against all law, through force and
Car li contre droit et raison,	usurpation, and removing herself from
Par force et usurpacion,	ancient unity and fraternity [. . .] And
En soi ostant dë unité	the spoon therefore is called in truth
Ancienne et fraternité,	Singularity.
(*PVH2* 16,631–9)	
[. . .]	
Et pour ce est dite en verité	
La cuillier, Singularité,	
(*PVH2* 16,648–9)	

[48] Maupeu, *Pèlerins de vie humaine*, p. 93.
[49] See especially Stephanie A. V. G, Kamath, 'A Cruel Spoon in Context: Cutlery and Conviviality in Late Medieval Literature', *Études anglaises* 66.3 (2013), 281–96.

THE EXPERIENCE OF FAILURE AND THE ARCHITECTURE OF VISION   401

Abusion walks aimlessly and tortuously, and works against monastic unity[50] and fraternity by wielding a spoon that denotes a form of exclusionist individualism, disrupting the communal eating habits of monastic institutions. This ultimately spells the decay of traditions of charitable hospitality and compassion for the poor, manifested in the literal expulsion of Charity herself from the cloister:

Boutee en est hors Charité, Qui souloit donner a mengier Aus povres et eux herbergier; Misericorde n'y est mais, Par qui souloient estre fais Mains biens aus povres trespassans, Malades et leur pain querans. (*PVH2* 16,551–7)	Charity, who was wont to feed the poor and give them shelter, has now been ejected. Mercy, who used to do much good to the sick and dying, and bring them bread, is no longer present.

Similar ideas and motifs are again redeployed by Langland, but in a significantly different context, in order to denounce the decline of *aristocratic* practices of charity, largesse, and hospitality in the halls of great lords. Again this shift from monastery to great hall arises from Langland's specific interest in the laity and secular society at large—but the use of tropes of enclosure and exclusion to signify the 'contraction' of charity and mercy remains unchanged in Study's denunciation:

> 'Ac þe carefulle may crie and carpen at þe yate,
> Boþe afyngred and afurst, and for chele quake;'
>   [...]
> 'Ne beþ [þe wrecches] plenteuouse to þe pouere as pure charite wolde,
> But in gaynesse and in glotonye forglutten hir good hemselue,
> And brekeþ noȝt to þe beggere as þe Boke techeþ.
>   *Frange esurienti panem tuum, etc.*'
>   [...]
> 'Elenge is þe halle, ech day in þe wyke,
> Ther þe lorde ne þe lady likeþ noȝt to sitte.
> Now haþ ech riche a rule—to eten bi hymselue
> In a pryuee parlour for pouere mennes sake,
> Or in a chambre wiþ a chymenee, and leue þe chief halle.'
>   (B X.58–9; 82–4; 96–100)

---

[50] The line 'se ostant de unité' (*PVH2* 16,638) is possibly echoed in the prophecy of Surquydous and Spille-Love: 'and þei þat ben in Vnite / Shulle come out' (XIX.347–8).

402   MEDIEVAL ALLEGORY AS EPISTEMOLOGY

These images and ideas too are once more reprised in the climactic conclusion of *passus* XIII, as part of what Craun reads as an extended analytical 'sermon' delivered by Will at lines 421–55.[51]

The consequences of Abusion's penchant for singularity, however, are not merely social and moral. Her lack of discipline ultimately also causes widespread neglect of the liturgical duties of religious communities. Abusion openly disrespects the sacrament of the Eucharist by turning her eyes away from it towards the secular world:

Après, quen droit doit regarder	And after, when we are all expected to
Pour faire le roy hounourer,	gaze to show honour to the King, she
Et elle tourne son regart	averts her gaze, and glances at the
Au monde qui est autre part,	world on the other side, openly and
De sa veüe apertement	crassly abusing the power of her sight.
Elle abuse et notairement.	
(*PVH2* 16,624–9)	

Abusion's solipsism finally becomes a figure for a degenerate, self-obsessed priesthood, as the narrator launches into a condemnation of shepherds who deprive their flock of due nourishment, invoking the prophecy of Ezekiel 34:2, and referencing the conspicuously 'Langlandian' trope of false prophets in sheep's clothing from Mat 7:15—once more a throwback to familiar motifs associated with Faux Semblant in the *Rose* (see Chapter 1.4):

Ceste cuisiniere jadis	This cook was just like those cursed by
Fu a ceulx qui furent maudis	the Prophet Ezekiel: 'Beware the
Du prophete Jezechiël	pastors of Israel who want to fest all on
'Vë au pasteurs de Israël	their own!' They have become wolves,
Qui se veulent paistre tous seuls!'	who take for themselves all the fat, and
Et pour tout devourer sont leups,	fail to feed the people, giving them only
Qui devers eulx prennent le gras	the poorest and discarded cuts, until
Et leur peuple ne paissent pas,	they can no more.
Se n'est du maigre et du refus	
Et au moins quë il puent plus.	
(*PVH2* 16,652–62)	

While it would be simplistic to see Abusion as a template or 'source' for Langland's characterization of Haukyn, the latter too is described in terms of an analogous series of tropes that relate notions of vagrancy, self-absorption, deviant speech,

---

[51] Craun, *Deviant Speaker*, pp. 175–85, argues that Will ultimately offers a viable model of linguistic/poetic/charitable economy, pitched against the 'squandering' of charitable resources by wealthy patrons to undeserving deviant minstrels, resulting in the increase of *turpiloquium* and generalized starvation among the deserving poor. As will become apparent below, I read the passage as being far more problematic in terms of its advocacy of the 'legitimacy' of Will's/Langland's poetry, and poetry in general.

THE EXPERIENCE OF FAILURE AND THE ARCHITECTURE OF VISION 403

and the loss of alimentary, sacramental, and festive decorum. And Langland too uses such motifs to explore the difficulties posed by life outside of a tightly regulated religious community and the wider institutional structures of the official church. To anticipate briefly my subsequent analysis, this association of ideas persists into the speech of Anima, large portions of which are dedicated to condemning the deleterious effects of corrupt 'Curatours of Holy Kirke' (B XV.136) on the broader spiritual state of the Christian community (see Chapter 6.3). While Langland focuses more particularly on the avarice and hypocrisy of the priestly class, the tropes he uses to represent the duties of ecclesiastical institutions continue to rely on the same imagery: truly charitable priests are cast as dispensers of meat ('meteзyueres', B XV.147) who 'nourish' their flocks, like Charity, and who keeps nothing to himself: 'And if he soupeþ, eet but a sop of *Spera in Deo*' (XV.180)—unlike the gluttonous doctor of theology at the Feast of Patience (B XIII.40–93). Once more such food is metamorphosed into edible and wholesome scriptural text and thence into charitable action: 'Þouз he bere [poore men and prisones] no breed, he bereþ hem swetter liflode: / Loueþ hem as Oure Lord bit and lokeþ how þei fare' (XV.184–5).

Haukyn too is in the business of procuring what appears to be a kind Eucharistic sustenance, but in his case such a sacramental reading is troubled and complicated.[52] As a waferer, Haukyn is of course primarily a purveyor of literal nourishment—not the transubstantiated and textualized scriptural nourishment whose nutritional virtues are extolled by Patience:

> [Haukyn]: 'For alle trewe trauaillours and tiliers of the erþe
> Fro Mighelmesse to Mighelmesse I fynde hem wiþ wafres'
> (B XIII.239–40)

> 'Al Londoun, I leue, liketh wel my wafres,
> And louren whan þei lakken hem;'
> (B XIII.263–4)

And yet his trade is juxtaposed and contrasted with both the liturgy and with aristocratic feasting in a manner that raises many questions about the nature of those correspondences:

> 'I haue no goode gyftes of þise grete lordes,
> For no bred þat y brynge forþ—saue a benyson on þe Sonday,
> Whan þe prest preieþ the peple hir *Paternoster* to bidde'
> (B XIII.235–7)

---

[52] See also Watson, 'Haukyn's Coat', pp. 108–13.

404　MEDIEVAL ALLEGORY AS EPISTEMOLOGY

Somehow the relationship of analogy and reciprocity between the three terms of
the equation—Haukyn's baking, aristocratic feasting, and the liturgy—appears to
be broken, pointing to a disrupted economy in the social and spiritual circulation
of 'bred'.

While Langland uses this breakdown to castigate all parties within this complex economy—from the priesthood to the aristocracy and to Haukyn himself—in
the present context I am primarily interested in Haukyn's role, and more specifically in the manner in which the shortcomings of his minstrelsy can illuminate
Langland's reflection on the social and spiritual legitimacy of his own poetry. As
a minstrel-poet figure, Haukyn is highly suspect because of his reliance on deceptive, manipulative, and ultimately blasphemous speech, associated with a variety
of excesses of the mouth. His coat is

> bidropped wiþ wraþe and wikkede wille,
> Wiþ enuye and yuel speche entisynge to fyghte,
> Lying and lakkynge and leue tonge to chide;
> Al þat he wiste wikked by any wighte, tellen it,
> And blame men bihynde hir bak and bydden hem meschaunce;
> [. . .]
> And made of frendes foes þoruȝ a fals tonge.
>
> (B XIII.321–8)

> Yet þat glotoun wiþ grete oþes his garnement hadde soiled,
> And foule beflobered it, as wiþ fals speche,
> As, þere no nede ne was, Goddes name an idel—
> Swoor þerby swiþe ofte and al biswatte his cote;
> And moore mete eet and dronk þan kynde myȝte defie
>
> (B XIII.400–4)

Like Abusion and the gluttonous priests castigated by Anima, then, Haukyn too
is a hypocrite, a deceptive wolf in sheepskin, fleecing his fellow Christians—
'Yhabited as an heremyte', 'As a shepsteres shere, ysherewed men and cursed'
(B. XIII.285, 331). Haukyn is accordingly unreceptive to any teachings of the
Gospel and the substance of the *logos*, preferring to busy his mouth with unprof-
itable 'murye tales' (cf. B XIII.352) and listening to dissolute 'wordes of murþe':

> Lyueþ ayein þe bileue and no lawe holdeþ.
> Ech day is a halyday with hym or an heiȝ ferye,
> And if he auȝt wole here, it is an harlotes tonge.
> Whan men carpen of Crist, or of clennesse of soule,
> He wexeþ wroþ and wil noȝt here but wordes of murþe.
>
> (B XIII.414–18)

THE EXPERIENCE OF FAILURE AND THE ARCHITECTURE OF VISION 405

All of these features make Haukyn a disturbingly close double of Will himself, entering the poem clad in

> shroudes as I a sheep were
> In habite as an heremite vnholy of werkes
> Wente wide in þis world wondres to here.
>
> (B Prol.2–4)

Langland highlights this slippage between the personae of Will and Haukyn throughout their encounter in *passus* XIV, and critics have pointed out how the encounter tends to blur the boundaries of voice and agency between the multiple speakers, allowing Haukyn's voice to blend into Will's on multiple occasions.[53] Just as Haukyn's initial presumption to embody a higher form of minstrelsy is dismantled by subsequent developments in XIII and XIV, so are we expected to scrutinize anew Will's/Langland's own latent and implicit vindication of his own poetic 'makynges' as a legitimate and productive form of finding out Truth.

What conclusions can be drawn from Langland's sustained exploration of the symbolic analogies between minstrelsy and other activities—such as feasting, gluttony, vagrancy, singularity, the consumption of salvific text, and the latent Eucharistic symbolism in B XIII–XIV? Both the Feast of Patience and the extended encounter with Haukyn postulate a potentially meaningful but often troubled parallelism between the production of poetic texts and on the one hand, and, on the other, a number of sacramental and devotional practices centred on the mouth, from Eucharistic ingestion to penitential speech acts. Within the overarching soteriological perspective of the poem, the 'nutritional' and hence salvific value of poetic 'makynges' is ultimately measured against the value of sacrament itself, and against the value of all associated verbal and textual instruments for prayer and devotion. What sort of sustenance—Langland seems to be asking—is a poet expected to produce in order to contribute to the greater social and moral good, to the advancement of truth, and to the salvation of souls? Is the kind of poetic effort Langland undertakes in a world where there are 'bokes ynowe' (B XII.17) a sanctioned activity that deserves to be recognized as a form of salvific 'work', or is it a dissolute, spiritually digressive, idiosyncratic, self-indulgent, and finally hypocritical form of self-glorification?[54]

Like Ymaginatif in *passus* XII, who tells Will to abandon any unregulated form of living and poetic activity to 'holde þee vnder obedience, þat heigh wey is to heuene'

---

[53] Craun, *Deviant Speaker*, pp. 175–6; Judith H. Anderson, *The Growth of a Personal Voice: Piers Plowman and The Faerie Queene* (New Haven-London: Yale University Press, 1976), p. 93. See also James Simpson's general observation that 'the narrator's persona [is] fluidly identifiable with actants in the represented world of the poem', 'The Power of Impropriety', p. 159.

[54] See especially Hanna, 'Meddling with Makings'; the various contributions in Justice and Kerby-Fulton, *Written Work*; Bowers, *Crisis of the Will*; John A. Burrow, 'Words, Works and Will: Theme and Structure in *Piers Plowman*' in Hussey, *Piers Plowman: Critical Approaches*, pp. 111–24.

406   MEDIEVAL ALLEGORY AS EPISTEMOLOGY

(B XII.37), the arrival of Haukyn thus highlights the potentially self-indulgent and self-absorbed nature of such poetic meddling. As soon as Haukyn's ostensibly virtuous craft as a minstrel is scrutinized more closely in XIII.225–457, it rapidly emerges that this is in reality a largely self-promoting, sanctimonious and hypocritical form of virtue signalling:

> Wilnynge þat men wende his wit were þe beste,
> Or for his crafty konnynge or of clerkes þe wisest,
> Or strengest on stede, or styuest vnder girdel,
> And louelokest to loken on and lelest of werkes,
> And noon so holy as he ne of lif clennere,
> Or fairest of feitures, of forme and of shafte,
> And most sotil of song oþer sleiyest of hondes,
> And large to lene, loos þerby to cacche,
>   [...]
> Boldest of beggeris; a bostere þat noȝt haþ,
> In towne and in tauernes tales to telle
> And segge þyng þat he neuere seiȝ and for soþe sweren it,
>   [...]
> Al he wolde that men wiste of werkes and of wordes
> Which myȝte plese ȝe peple and preisen hymselue.
>
> (B XIII.292–313)

A similar kind of solipsistic self-glorification is later condemned by Patience, with specific reference to forms of *writing* rather than forms of speech and activities of the mouth. After insisting on the importance of producing evidence of penance and forgiveness, in the shape of a letter patent written on a 'parchemyn [. . .] of pouerte', (B XIV.192), Patience condemns any cynically 'performative' acts of piety and charity, such as ostentatious self-inscription in stained glass windows:

> 'But oure spences and oure spendynge sprynge of a trewe welle;
> Ellis is al oure labour loste—lo, how men writeþ
> In fenestres at þe freres—if fals be þe foundement.'
>
> (B XIV.198–200)

The passage introduces the crucial question of authorial self-naming, and thus prepares us Will's subsequent exchange with Anima, and more specifically his self-identification as one who 'lyued in londe' and calls himself 'Longe Wille' (B XV.152). The significance of this latter, oblique and idiosyncratic act of self-naming has been much debated in Langland scholarship. I suggest that it is again Deguileville's allegorical trilogy that furnishes Langland with many of the motifs,

THE EXPERIENCE OF FAILURE AND THE ARCHITECTURE OF VISION   407

techniques, ideas, and difficulties that go into the making of such a uniquely elusive instance of 'authorial' self-presentation, inflecting Langland's attitude towards other comparable instances of self-naming found in other texts he may have been familiar with. Before exploring Langland's engagement with the 'autobiographical temptations' of Deguileville's revised poem,[55] however, it will be necessary to take a closer look at the latter's authorial self-presentation in *PVH2* (see also Chapter 4.5). *PVH2*'s reflection on singularity, errance, and the decline of religious discipline had been triggered by the poet's reflection on an unmistakeably real, historical event in his personal life. This reflection only occurs in Deguileville's revised *PVH2*, within the narrative sequence that follows the pilgrim's persecution and expulsion from his Abbey of Chaalis. Here the poet had inserted an encrypted allegorical meditation on his real-life experience of persecution—an experience that for Philippe Maupeu constitutes the starting point for Deguileville's rewriting of the first *Pèlerinage* of the trilogy as a whole[56]—which takes the form of an embedded macaronic lyric spelling out a self-naming acrostic 'GVILLERMVS DE DEGUILEUILLA'.

I have already discussed the possible reasons behind such persecution in Chapter 4, and many elements surrounding Deguileville's self-naming acrostic seem to confirm that he incurred the displeasure of his peers, rivals, or superiors specifically because of his poetic activity (see Chapter 4.5). After the attack of Scylla's rabid dogs who pull the pilgrim off his allegorical horse of Bon Non (Good Renown, *PVH2* 15,952), and after being knocked out by Trahison with a mighty cudgel (*PVH2* 16,035) and making himself a wooden stump for his broken leg, the pilgrim receives the visit of Ovid. The choice of Ovid is significant in a wide range of ways, but primarily foregrounds the pattern of destiny shared by these two poets, both exiled because of the displeasure incurred by their poetic 'makyinges'.[57] In his attempt to console and assist the Pilgrim, the classical poet first recites a short poem for the pilgrim/author, adapted from Ovid's own *Ibis*. Ovid's poem effectively consists of a curse—'maledicions grans' (*PVH2* 16,096)—against his unnamed detractor, who is made responsible for his exile from Rome, and is offered to the Pilgrim/protagonist as a means for cursing his own detractors. The pilgrim thanks Ovid for his solidarity, but firmly rejects this particular model of poetic making, deferring judgment to God instead (*PVH2* 16,120–5). Instead of embracing the Ovidian model of a poetic curse, Deguileville finally adopts the register of the complaint. The complaint itself is preceded by an elaborate

---

[55] Maupeu, 'La tentation autobiographique'.

[56] See Maupeu, *Pèlerins de vie humaine*, p. 93, and pp. 87–96, 204–6 for a discussion of the acrostic prayer.

[57] See discussion of this scene in Maupeu, *Pèlerins de vie humaine*, pp. 87–95, and Kamath, 'Rewriting Ancient *Auctores*'.

408   MEDIEVAL ALLEGORY AS EPISTEMOLOGY

self-justification, foregrounding in particular the strictly private, individual, and singular nature of his grief:

Et me sembla que devoie	And it seemed to me that I had to had
Bien dueil faire, [. . .].	to give appropriate shape to my grief
[. . .]	[. . .]. I did this and I wrote it down.
Je le fis et je l'ai escript.	And let nobody reproach me for my
Et ne tiengne nul a despit	work, or if I have placed the letters
Së ou dit duel ai assises	according to my own fancy, according
Les lectres de moi et mises	to the couplets that make up its
Selon les couplés qui y sont	substance from one end to the other.
Et de bout en bout tout au lonc	For this complaint belongs to none
Car a nul tel duel n'appartient	other than myself alone, from whom
Fors à moi seul, dont le dueil vient.	this suffering originates.
(PVH2 16,128–39)	

What is striking about this preamble is that it both asserts the legitimacy of a strictly individual, autobiographical form of self-naming, and yet also depends on literary precedent and poetic convention. Not only the figure of Ovid is relevant in this respect: as Maupeu has convincingly argued, the reference point for the resolutely apologetic and monastic form of individual subjectivity adopted by Deguileville in this passage is provided by Abelard's *Historia Calamitatum*[58]— a text that has been fruitfully compared with Langland's own authorial self-identification in the C text apologia by Katherine Kerby-Fulton.[59] The form of autobiographical self-naming enabled by this kind of literary complaint is therefore of a strictly apologetic order, aimed at restoring an author's renown after a public condemnation, vindicating his moral probity through a literary medium.

A number of critics have commented on the complexity of *PVH2*'s acrostic complaint and its disruptive effect on Deguileville's wider poetic project. The complaint effectively disrupts the linear narrative movement of Deguileville's pilgrimage allegory, breaking also its octosyllabic narrative pace by switching to the stanza form of the lyric. With the shift from exemplary allegory to apologetic autobiography the complaint also marks a fracture of the larger poetic project as a whole: the attempt to produce a paradigmatic narrative of the 'pilgrimage of the human life', intended to serve as a blueprint or roadmap for a Christian Everyman, ultimately cannot stand the test of real-life experience. More specifically, such a project cannot stand the test of the real-life experience of the poem's own author/dreamer/protagonist. Figured by the attack of four personified *vieilles*, the irruption of the personal and contingent explodes the universalizing, didactic, and

[58] Maupeu, *Pèlerins de vie humaine*, pp. 198, 207–9.
[59] Kerby-Fulton, 'Bibliographic Ego', pp. 89–91.

THE EXPERIENCE OF FAILURE AND THE ARCHITECTURE OF VISION   409

salvific aspirations of Deguileville's allegory as a whole, becoming the new 'epi-centre of the poem' and 'the matrix of the process of rewriting'.[60] As Maupeu has suggested, the revisions of *PVH2* thus produce an 'I' who is no longer an active agent in control of either his destiny or his poem—and *a fortiori* the interpreta-tion of his poetic allegory—but a subject who is *acted upon* by a series of external characters, events, agents, and calamities.[61]

What may appear at first sight as a fairly conventional form of authorial self-naming in an acrostic, then, ultimately signals the pilgrim/poet's own inability to bring closure either to his own allegory or to his own subjectivity, 'subjected' to revisions that are imposed on it by external, contingent factors.[62] As Stephanie Kamath observes, then, in *PVH2* Deguileville is forced embrace a far more trou-bling model of authorship than that originally envisaged in *PVH1*: 'Late medieval allegories gesture towards the identity of the author [. . .], but they do not do so in order to enable a stable, external guarantee for the boundary between a fictional world and a reality in which the author resides as an established coherent identity'. As in the case of the *Rose*—the primary model for this kind of authorial 'pres-ence/absence', and for the transgression of the boundaries separating intra- and extradiegetic levels of reference[63]—Deguileville's self-naming strategy 'opens up a space of negotiation between textual and extratextual reality'.[64] Maupeu and Pomel have both explored how this increased awareness of the pressures of extratex-tual reality in *PVH2* produces an intensified concern with temporality, and more specifically with the experiential, non-teleological temporality subjective human existence. For Pomel *PVH2* no longer subsumes the individual human experience of time within the larger salvific teleology of the soul's journey towards God, but time is increasingly experienced in terms of a self-referential existential anguish.[65] For Maupeu too, the pilgrim's body in *PVH2* is increasingly individuated as the site for a kind of experience no longer reducible to a simple soteriological narra-tive relying on the analogical devices of allegory.[66] The frame of reference for the subjective experience of time is no longer strictly eschatological, but has become more markedly existential and individual.[67]

The meta-poetic and experiential reflections that crystallize around Deguileville's 'autobiographical' complaint in *PVH2* play a major role in focusing Langland's own interest in the interconnected questions of authorial agency,

---

[60] Maupeu, *Pèlerins de vie humaine*, p. 93.

[61] Maupeu, *Pèlerins de vie humaine*, p. 214 and *passim*.

[62] See especially Maupeu's analysis, *Pèlerins de vie humaine*, pp. 173–266, developing Paul Ricoeur's ideas about the narrated condition of subjectivity, in *Soi-même comme un autre*.

[63] See Chapter 1.1. See further Luciano Rossi, 'Metalepsis and Allegory', in Morton and Nievergelt, pp. 210–32.

[64] Kamath, *Authorship and First-Person Allegory*, p. 9,

[65] Pomel, *Les voies*, pp. 251, 425–52.

[66] Maupeu, *Pèlerins de vie humaine*, pp. 215–68.

[67] Maupeu, *Pèlerins de vie humaine*, pp. 236–9.

410   MEDIEVAL ALLEGORY AS EPISTEMOLOGY

individuality, and alienation throughout *passus* XIII–XV. As several critics have suggested, Haukyn's singularity represents precisely the condition of social and spiritual alienation that Will has to overcome or exorcize during this section in the poem, as a result of Will's own idiosyncratic 'eccentricity' in relation to established forms of living, both secular and religious, and with reference to both literal agricultural labour, and metaphorical forms of penitential ploughing sanctioned by the intellectual and ecclesiastical institutions of his day.[68] Will's presentation of himself as one 'Longe Wille' who has 'liued in londe' (B XV.152) in many ways constitutes the culmination of this extended reflection on poetic labour, individual selfhood, and 'authorial' presence and agency. A number of critics have already discussed Will's self-naming at this point and throughout the three versions in terms of its affinity with other forms of encrypted self-identification, notably anagrammatic devices and acrostics. Especially Anne Middleton, drawing on earlier work by Chambers and Kane, has explored the ways in which Langland's 'internal signatures' participate in a much wider late medieval culture of authorial self-encryption, but has also emphasized how, crucially, Langland's practice conspicuously *departs* from such conventions in deliberately withholding or occluding the author's own proper name[69]—a strategy of evasion that recent work on the Rokeles brings into still clearer focus.[70] To refocus Middleton's analysis with reference to Deguileville's influence on Langland, then, it can be said that the latter's poetic practice gestures towards, but ultimately *resists* the temptation to perform a 'proper', fully autobiographical self-identification that we find in the work of several contemporaries as well as in *PVH2*.

Again the similarities between the Langland and Deguileville become illuminating only once the differences too are examined more closely. Middleton's statement that in Langland 'moments of signature become moments of poetic reflexivity, disclosures of the literary mode and claims to "truth" that the poet proposes for his work' is certainly applicable to Deguileville too.[71] The same can be said of the claim that such signatures 'are staged with increasing fullness both to evoke excuses and *apologiae* of the subject's insufficiency, and to exact from him a re-examination of his position—in his quest, in his allotted time on earth, and in the trajectory of the work that is the poem', which again aptly describes the condition of both

---

[68] On the various forms of ploughing, see Stephen Barney, 'The Plowshare of the Tongue: the Progress of a Symbol from the Bible to *Piers Plowman*', *Mediaeval Studies* 35 (1973), 261–93. See also Galloway, '*Piers Plowman* and the schools', 94–6.

[69] Anne Middleton, '"Kynde Name"'; R. W. Chambers, 'Robert or William Langland?', *London Medieval Studies* 1 (1948), 430–62. See further George Kane, *Piers Plowman: The Evidence for Authorship* (London: Athlone Press, 1965), and ibid., *The Autobiographical Fallacy in Chaucer and Langland Studies* (London: University of London / H.K. Lewis, 1965).

[70] Adams, *Langland and the Rokele Family*, especially pp. 100–20 on William de la Rokele's 'anonymity' and his patronage network.

[71] '"Kynde Name"', p. 221.

THE EXPERIENCE OF FAILURE AND THE ARCHITECTURE OF VISION   411

Deguileville's and Langland's pilgrim *personae*.[72] But the nature and modalities of the 'truth' crystallized by their respective signatures is profoundly different, as are the ethical and meta-poetic resonances of their respective *apologiae*. While in both poems such signatures coincide with 'moments of subjective crisis', providing 'disruptions of the narrative' occurring 'at the joining of sections' to 'show the "I"' in the act of repeatedly transforming rather than finishing its project',[73] Langland ultimately resists any temptation to abjure or renounce his morally ambiguous and socially deviant poetic making: 'Will does not, like Cynewulf'—or indeed Deguileville—'name himself as penitent hoping for grace and the benefit of his readers' prayers, but declares himself as a writer for whom the business of writing *is finding things out*'.[74] Rather than 'identifying' himself by foregrounding his own authorial singularity through an instance of 'proper' naming[75] Langland presents us with a more elusive subjectivity that continues to be strongly invested in his own textual 'makyng'—inextricably entangled within it, and finally produced *by* it.

3. Willing and Longing; *Makyng* and Suffering

Despite their formal similarities, then, Langland's and Deguileville's respective authorial signatures encode radically different notions of subjectivity. More importantly, their signatures function as powerful markers for their respective authorial self-understanding, pointing to divergent definitions of the value and significance of poetic activity. Deguileville's poetic subjectivity is literally spelled out in the acrostic, becoming visible and textually tangible, as if to affirm the historically real and separable existence of GVILLERMVS DE DEGUILEUILLA—formally marginalized, but in reality at the centre of this new process of poetic revision. As Middleton points out, the efficacy of this kind of acrostic—'seen but not heard'—is entirely dependent on the availability of a physical textual support,[76] which in this case reifies the individual subjectivity of the poet/protagonist as written text. Deguileville's choice of the acrostic, then, is of a piece with his more generalized reverence for material documents, and participates in *PVH2*'s wider tendency to privilege learned, written, and often Latinate authority over the spoken word of disputation or pastoral instruction that had taken centre stage in the earlier *PVH1* (see Chapters 2.1 and 2.2). Most importantly in the present context, this valorization of written documents points to the powerful longing for textual/autobiographical/narrative closure and completion, producing a 'definitive' authoritative *apologia* of one's own life, metaphorically constituted

---

[72] '"Kynde Name"', p. 224.
[73] See variously Middleton, '"Kynde Name"', p. 224; ibid. 'The Invention of Experience', pp. 168–9.
[74] 'The Invention of Experience', pp. 169.
[75] Simpson, 'Power of Impropriety'.
[76] '"Kynde Name"', p. 217.

412 MEDIEVAL ALLEGORY AS EPISTEMOLOGY

as a complete and self-contained physical document affirming the biographical totality, narrative completion, and moral integrity of the individual first-person author-protagonist.[77]

Langland's 'kynde name', by contrast, never even strives to attain a comparable degree of finite and definitive personal 'identity'. His subjectivity remains strictly narrative and provisional, inextricably embedded within the diegesis and infused within the matter of his fictional 'makynges' and ultimately irrecoverable as a discrete objective entity. Instead of identifying himself through the use of a 'proper name' that attempts to signal a stable and unmistakable extra-textual existence, Langland's subjectivity appears to be a function of the continuous labour of textual 'makyng', encrypted within his poem and unable to exist independently. While it is true that Langland's authorial signatures also develop an increasing self-confidence and explicitness throughout the three versions,[78] Langland conspicuously resists the temptation to present his own subjectivity as being somehow extrinsic to the text. In Barbara Newman's words, Langland 'does not have a life that can be imagined to proceed normally on either side of the great vision at its centre'.[79] If anything, Langland reverses the relation between textuality and identity: instead of using reified texts as documents to mark the extrinsic existence of the subject, Langland subsumes personhood within textual labour. The idea memorably crystallizes in the shape of a personified Book—'the most bizarrely Lewis Carroll-like of Langland's personifications'[80]—which also becomes the most strikingly tangible, plastic embodiment of the doctrine of the Incarnation, the Word made Flesh:

> 'By Goddes body!' quod this Book, 'I wol bere witnesse
> That þo þis barn was ybore, þere blased a sterre
> That alle þe wise of þis world in o wit acordeden—
> That swich a barn was ybore in Bethleem þe citee
> That mannes soule sholde saue and synne destroye'.
>
> (B XVIII.231–5)

Accordingly Langland too, in the guise of the errant Will/will, is unable to attain any kind of subjectivity that is extrinsic to his act of visionary and textual 'makyng', engaged in the production of 'the book of his conscience'.[81] The 'real', historical

---

[77] On the notion of *PVH2* as a whole as a missive, see Pomel 'Écrits pérégrins', pp. 104–6, and discussion below.

[78] See e.g. Kerby-Fulton, 'Langland and the Bibliographic Ego', p. 106 and *passim*.

[79] Barbara Newman, 'Redeeming the Time: Langland, Julian, and the Art of Lifelong Revision', *YLS* 23 (2009), 1–32 (12).

[80] Schmidt, 'Langland's Visions and Revisions', 15.

[81] Schmidt, 'Langland's Visions and Revisions', 26.

THE EXPERIENCE OF FAILURE AND THE ARCHITECTURE OF VISION   413

individual William Langland remains fundamentally ephemeral—unattainable and impossible to dissociate from his textual labour.[82]

As well as implying different models of both authorship and self-representation, Deguileville's and Langland's respective poetic signatures point to divergent models of poetic epistemology. To use again Middleton's phrase, it is worth asking: what 'claims for truth' can be captured by first-person poetic fiction according to each of the two poets? Deguileville is concerned with a strictly apologetic *procès*:[83] not only does he attempt to revise and lend definitive closure to the narrative of an individual life (*PVH2*), but he seeks to vindicate its legitimacy by staging a forensic and eschatological process where his own soul is literally put on trial (*PA*). Very appropriately, then, this literal 'weighing up' of individual merit in the balance of St Michael (*PA* 2210–630) produces further forms of self-encryption relying on 'proper naming' in documentary form. This includes, notably, the insertion of a further self-naming acrostic poem that adopts the same verse form as the acrostic complaint from *PVH2*. In *PA*, then, the poet's name again crystallizes in the margins of a letter ostensibly sent by Grace Dieu directly to the Pilgrim, *ad personam* (*PA* 1593–1784).[84] The letter provides a condensed summary of the teachings delivered by Grace Dieu in *PVH*, and is cited in *PA* as evidence incriminating the Pilgrim for his disregard for Grace Dieu's teachings in the earlier poem. The pilgrim, therefore, is individualized specifically because of his *failure* to conform to Grace Dieu's advice. Tellingly it is Verité—Truth personified—who reiterates the accusations against poor Guillaume: 'and therefore it is abundantly clear to me, that he must be put to death' [Et pour ce m'est il bien avis / Quë a mort il doit estre mis, *PA* 1899–1900]. He is saved only through the providential intervention of Misericorde (*PA* 1923–2034), carrying a further document of higher authority, a letter according a special dispensation of grace to the pilgrim: 'a gift of special grace, in addition to the general gift' [don de grace especial / oultre la grand et general', *PA* 2383–4]—and authored by Christ himself (*PA* 2369–2466).

Quite apart from the relevance of this debate to the general tenor of Langland's poem—especially in terms of its use of the Devil's rights tradition and the semantic field of judicial *procès*, and its progression from Old Testament Justice to New Testament Mercy that plays such a central role in James Simpson's important and influential analysis[85]—the episode once more associates authorial self-naming with an overarching penitential and apologetic agenda. Just as in *PVH2*, the self-naming acrostic becomes a marker of failure and misfortune, and crystallizes the

---

[82] I allude here to the arguments presented by Fletcher, 'The "Essential" (Ephemeral) William Langland'.

[83] Moreau, *Eschatological Subjects*, pp. 25–8, 63–101 (28): 'I adopt Lévinas's French term *procès* to refer to the particular conjunction of the poet's endless labor with the "other scene" of a continual, eschatological trial process.'

[84] See discussion in Pomel 'Écrits pérégrins', pp. 98, 99–100, 102–3.

[85] Simpson, *Introduction*.

414   MEDIEVAL ALLEGORY AS EPISTEMOLOGY

pilgrim's subjectivity around his inability to complete his pilgrimage according to the initial didactic programme of the poem. The 'truth' crystallized by the poet's self-naming therefore once more foregrounds the pilgrim/poet's autobiographical singularity, incriminating him for his failure to conform to the exemplary pattern of Everyman's 'pilgrimage' towards the Holy City. Langland's avoidance of any form of referentially 'proper' self-identification, by contrast, is conspicuous and emphatic. This is not to say that Langland is less concerned with the question of the 'truth', legitimacy, and purpose of poetic writing—quite the opposite. But Langland's model is not penitential and apologetic in a simple sense, in that it does not entail any rejection of a past sinful life and/or juvenile poetic activity associated with it—despite the repeated resurgence of the lament *Heu michi, quia sterilem duxi vitam juvenilem* throughout the poem (e.g. B I.141a; V.441a).[86] On the contrary, the penitential dimension of Langland's project is postulated on the *continuation* of the activity of 'finding things out' through writing. Unlike Deguileville—whose entire *PVH2* may be seen as an attempt to simultaneously retract, recuperate, overwrite, and bring definitive closure to his earlier poetic work (see Chapter 4.5)—Langland never produces unambiguous authorial signatures that attempt to signal or perform definitive formal or conceptual closure. Instead, Langland's signatures appear as conspicuously and deliberately fleeting, oblique, momentary, and fragmentary, denoting an imperfect and constantly fluctuating self-understanding. To adopt James Simpson's terms, Langland's poem stubbornly asserts the power of its own 'impropriety': '"Langland" [. . .] has "Will" evade the stabilities and neutralities of proper naming by entering increasingly anonymous discursive territory.'[87] Indeed, Langland's strategy of evasion, Simpson argues, is specifically designed to produce 'a common authorial position,'[88] recording what is both an intensely personal and yet universally significant struggle of the will— radically improper, and beyond the limits determined by its own, idiosyncratic singularity.

Comparison with Deguileville allows us to reconstruct Langland's strategy of self-presentation with much greater precision. Both Middleton and Simpson have observed that Langland's method consists in producing a systematic and carefully structured sequence of instances of self-naming. Middleton in particular has suggested that the appearance of 'Long Will' in XV.152 is already adumbrated during an earlier, equally pivotal moment in the poem, with the advent of the 'lond of longynge' that provides the setting for Will's first inner dream in *passus* XI.8 ff. Importantly, Middleton notes how this earlier, still more elusive authorial signature only acquires its full resonance as part of carefully calibrated evolving 'system' of authorial signatures in the poem.[89] The logic dictating the organization of this

---

[86] See especially discussion in Bowers, *Crisis of Will*, p. 88.
[87] Simpson, 'Power of Impropriety', p. 147.
[88] Simpson, 'Power of Impropriety', p. 148.
[89] Middleton, '"Kynde Name"', 226–34.

THE EXPERIENCE OF FAILURE AND THE ARCHITECTURE OF VISION   415

system of self-encryption comes into sharper focus once it is viewed in terms of its systematic creative redeployment of Deguilevillian motifs and ideas. I have already commented on how Will's 'fall' into the Land of Longing in fact reactivates but also reconfigures the visionary imagery that inaugurates Deguileville's poem—complete with a refracting 'myrour þat hiȝte Middelerþe' (B XI.9), which enables the radical reorientation of the trajectory of 'vision' at this crucial transitional moment in the poem (Chapter 5.2).[90] It is therefore not accidental that it is at this precise moment that Langland should insert his first major oblique self-reference by situating this vision in the 'lond of longynge', providing a perfect illustration of Middleton's point about the coincidence of acts of self-naming with major moments of crisis and transformation in the poem. By the same token, it is also perfectly appropriate that another, analogous mirror should reappear in conjunction with Langland's next internal signature as 'Long Will', marking another major crisis and reorientation of vision during his encounter with Anima in *passus* XV, when Will desires to know the nature of true Charity:

> 'I haue lyued in londe', quod I, 'my name is Longe Wille—
> And fond I neuere ful charite, bifore ne bihynde.'
> [. . .]
> 'Clerkes kenne me þat Crist is in alle places;
> Ac I seiȝ hym neuere sooþly but as myself in a mirour:
> *Hic in enigmate, tunc facie ad faciem.*'
>
> (B XV.152–3; 161–2a)

The self-naming and Will's apprehension of Christ 'as myself in a mirour' are inextricably linked, in an echo of 1 Cor. 13:12: *Videmus nunc per speculum in aenigmate: tunc autem facie ad faciem* ('We see now through a glass in a dark manner: but then face to face'). In Simpson's words, this layered apprehension of oneself as/through the image of Christ provides a strikingly powerful 'riddling preservation and extension of the common force of "Will"'.[91]

Before proceeding with a closer examination of this important move in the poem, it will be helpful to situate the episode within its broader context, and within the larger framework of the poem's thematic and narrative progression. The encounter with Anima opens the poem's fifth vision, and follows on directly from the encounter with Haukyn that concludes the fourth. Will's awakening at the end of *passus* XIV signals that the temptations of deviant and eccentric 'singularity' represented by Haukyn have been left behind, and to some extent resolved or overcome. To be more precise, such possibilities have now crystallized into the choice of a unified disposition of the will/Will geared towards meaningful

---

[90] Middleton, '"Kynde Name"', equally insists on the inaugural qualities of the Lond of Longynge, 'the site of the first episode in the B continuation', p. 226.

[91] Simpson, 'Power of Impropriety', p. 162.

416 MEDIEVAL ALLEGORY AS EPISTEMOLOGY

penitential action[92]—a transition reflected in many B manuscripts (ten), which place the end of 'Dowel' and beginning of 'Dobet' at this juncture.[93] For James Simpson this moment enables a 'psychosynthesis' marking a transition to a mode of thought and expression where the individual, singular 'Will' of the poem's dreamer/narrator/protagonist is finally enlarged and transformed by becoming subsumed within a more capacious 'common will' or *voluntas communis*. 'Will' thus stops denoting a 'singularity produced [. . .] by intellectual arrogance', designating instead 'an authorial "long wille", a *longanimis* common will, the focus of long-suffering charity who speaks for the whole land'.[94]

Simpson's observation is particularly pertinent in the light of comparable narrative and expressive shift in Deguileville's *PVH*, where the Pilgrim's experience at the Rock of Penitence finally results in the attempt to dissolve an infirm individual will into the more inclusive, ostensibly infallible *voluntas communis* of the monastic life adopted by the pilgrim (see Chapters 4.1 and 4.2). Langland once more adopts yet also rewrites this transition, reconfiguring the ethical and meta-poetic significance of this episode during Haukyn's breakdown at the end of XIV:

> 'So hard it is', quod Haukyn, 'to lyue and to do synne.
> Synne seweþ vs euere', quod he, and sory gan wexe,
> And wepte water wiþ hise eyghen and weyled þe tyme
> That euere he dide dede þat deere God displesed;
> Swouned and sobbed and siked ful ofte
>   [. . .]
> [. . .] and cride mercy faste
> And wepte and wailede—and therewiþ I awakede.
>
>   (B XIV.322–6, 331–2)

The scene replays both Will's own tearful fall into vision at the start of B XI,[95] and through it the conversion of Deguileville's Pilgrim at the Rock of Penitence, closing the extended parenthesis of introspection that begins with Will's first inner dream in *passus* XI.

As with Will's earlier shedding of tears at B XI, Haukyn's tears denote a complex set of conflicting emotions, 'on the cusp of despair and contrition'.[96] As an

---

[92] My reading here converges with that proposed by Gruenler, 'How to Read like a Fool', p. 625. See further discussion in Bowers, *The Crisis of Will*, pp. 129–64.

[93] Lawler, *Penn Commentary 4*, p. 141.

[94] Simpson, 'The Power of Impropriety', pp. 156, 161, 163.

[95] See Hanna, 'Haukyn and Patience's Instruction', p. 321.

[96] Gruenler, 'Learning to Read like a Fool', p. 625. Critics have tended to conceive these two possibilities as mutually exclusive. For Nicholas Watson, 'Haukyn's desperate tears [. . .] announce not conversion or even contrition, but self-knowledge and need', in 'Haukyn's Coat', pp. 115–16; for James Simpson what Haukyn experiences is a full 'conversion', 'The Power of Impropriety', pp. 161–2, and Harwood sees 'hints of true contrition' in the scene, *Problem of Belief*, p. 102. As will emerge from what follows, I suggest that these two readings are not only compatible but mutually enabling, and that for

THE EXPERIENCE OF FAILURE AND THE ARCHITECTURE OF VISION 417

embodiment of *Actiua Vita*, Haukyn's crisis to some extent replays the pilgrim's despair in the face of the challenges of the active life in a secular world (*PVH1* 11,445–54, see Chapter 4.1). While neither Will nor Haukyn respond to this crisis by seeking refuge from worldly vicissitudes in a monastic cloister, this is nonetheless a possibility that resurfaces insistently at this moment in the poem. As both Malcolm Godden and James Simpson have pointed out, the possibility of a radical conversion away from the active life is never stronger than in *passus* XIV, where Patience articulates an ideal that comes dangerously close to an ideal of ascetic renunciation.[97] But Will's conversion at the end of the *passus* is of a different kind, yet to be defined and fully conceptualized. Crucially, the poem stresses that this scene of contrite yet despairing impotence is no longer experienced by Will himself, as in *passus* XI, but by his alter ego Haukyn. The experience proves cathartic for Will, leading to his awakening in the last line of *passus* XIV, as if to signal his transition to a further stage in his quest. Haukyn's crisis thus allows Langland to simultaneously experience, but also exorcize and overcome the kind of cognitive and volitional breakdown that brings the journey of the pilgrim Guillermus to a sudden and surprising end, and ultimately drives Deguileville's allegorical poetics into an impasse.

Langland also carefully reconfigures the significance of this transition in terms of its impact on the larger trajectory of Will's quest, and in terms of its wider metapoetic implications. Initially, upon waking from the fourth vision, Will still appears to share in Haukyn's plight. Will—who had first entered the poem clothed, much like Haukyn, 'in habite as an hermite unholy of workes' (B Prol.3; cf. XIII.282–5)—emerges from the dream still more alienated and uncertain about his own place in society, and about his social role and identity: 'folke helden me a fole; and in that folye I raved / tyl Resoun hadde reuthe on me and rokked me aslepe' (B XV.10–11). But this is precisely the moment where Will is reconciled and reunited with Reason—in the shape of Anima, who has been described as enabling a process of 'psychosynthesis' that in many ways concludes Will's extended inward journey (B VIII–XIV, or XI–XIV more particularly), reiterating many of the difficult lessons learned over this extended section.[98] Will can finally pick up the pieces after the many clashes, false starts, arguments, crises, failures, cognitive meanderings, and tentative advances that fill the middle sections of the poem, gathering his psychic energies into a newly balanced agency of the will necessary for a different kind of pilgrimage through the remaining six *passus* (XV–XX). The encounter with Anima thus marks the restoration of Will's access to his own 'reintegrated psyche, the whole soul',[99] marking a shift to a qualitatively different, higher or 'common' level

---

Langland despair becomes instrumental and indeed necessary on the path to true contrition. For a similar argument, see also Hanna, 'Haukyn and Patience's Instruction', p. 321.

[97] Godden, *The Making of Piers Plowman*, pp. 148–9; Simpson, *Introduction*, pp. 145–6.
[98] Simpson, 'Power of Impropriety', p. 156.
[99] Simpson, *Introduction*, p. 153.

418   MEDIEVAL ALLEGORY AS EPISTEMOLOGY

of vision and understanding—a shift that does not, however, presuppose the total renunciation of one's individual will in favour of a larger, utterly depersonalized, institutional, and specifically monastic form of *voluntas communis* as in *PVH*.

As Middleton has shown, a further, more circumscribed context for this instance of self-naming as 'Longe Wille' (B XV.152) is provided by the heightened sensitivity towards the semantic difficulties of 'naming' and related ideas of knowledge, introduced at the very beginning of the encounter with Anima in *passus* XV.[100] Anima is presented as an enigmatic and polysemous personification carrying multiple names to designate its various functions: '*Anima pro diversis accionibus diversa nomina sortitur*' (B XV.39a). Will seeks to crack the riddle of these multiple names, manifesting once more his characteristically immoderate 'will' to gain knowledge and understanding, and prompting Anima to retort with a somewhat enigmatic pun:

> 'now I see þi wille!
> Thow woldest knowe and konne þe cause of alle hire names,
> And of myne'
>   [...]
> [Will:] 'Alle þe sciences vnder sonne and alle þe sotile craftes,
> I wolde I knewe and kouþe kndely in myn herte!'
>
> (B XV.44–9)

Will here is again characterized by his inability to privilege self-knowledge above his obstinate determination to seek secure and definitive *scientia*, 'willing' to gain knowledge of the many names and faculties of Anima instead of recognizing it as an embodiment of his own mental and cognitive faculties and operations. Anima accordingly castigates Will once more for his intellectual curiosity:

> 'Thanne artow inparfit', quod he, 'and oon of Prydes knyȝtes!
> For swich a lust and likyng Lucifer fel from heuene'
>   [...]
> It were ayeins kynde,' quod he, 'and ale kynnes reson
> That any creature sholde konne al, except Criste oone'
>
> (B XV.50–3)

Anima now launches into an extended tirade against intellectual covetousness (B XV.53–148). This reverberates with Study's earlier warning—*Multi multa sciunt et seipsos nesciunt* (B XI.4)—and reprises this theme for one final time in the poem, closing the parenthesis of this extended middle section focused on the human will's

---

[100] Middleton, '"Kynde Name"', p. 227. See also Simpson, 'Power of Impropriety', pp. 156–8.

THE EXPERIENCE OF FAILURE AND THE ARCHITECTURE OF VISION   419

cognitive possibilities, excesses, and limitations (XI–XV).[101] Anima's speech is pervaded by much sententious advice that by now sounds familiar and predictable: '*qui scrutatur est maiestatis opprimitur a gloria*' (B XV.55); '*non plus sapere quam oportet*' (B XV.69). Significantly, however, this fierce sermon focuses specifically on ideas of stasis and inertia vs. movement and action, in ways that help to clarify Langland's rejection of Deguileville's fideistic 'solution' to the problem of the weakness of the will. Tellingly, the problem is once more presented in terms of the symbolism of food and ingestion, appealing to corporeal appetites, or 'licames coueitise' (B XV.67):

> 'The man þat muche hony eet, his mawe it engleymetþ,
> And þe moore þat a man of good matere hereþ,
> But he do þerafter it dooþ hym double scaþe.
> *Beatus est*, seiþ Seint Bernard, *qui scripturas legit,*
> *Et verba vertit in opera* fulliche to his power.'
>
> (B XV.57–61)

The differences from Deguileville's far more radical rejection are subtle but fundamental: both poets bemoan the failure to fully absorb and metaphorically 'digest' the salvific food of moral instruction and scriptural teaching, as in the ABC's memorable rejection of Aristotle's *Ethics* (*PVH1* 11169–72, see Chapter 4.1), paralleling Anima's own point about the priority of penitential action over theoretical knowledge. But while in Deguileville this realization leads to the wholesale rejection of all forms of learning in favour of mystical contemplation, Langland provides a far more qualified rejection of learning by insisting on the central importance of the will's effort in putting learning into practice, 'fulliche to his power'. Crucially Anima's statement insists on the centrality of action (*opera*), but also makes such action dependant on the previous acquisition of knowledge through reading (*legere*). Anima's point therefore highlights the need for learning as a precondition for meaningful penitential action, reprising some of Ymaginatif's most compelling earlier arguments advanced in *passus* B XII (see Chapter 5.3).

Anima's insistence on the importance of works participates in the broadly 'voluntarist' orientation of the poem, often seen as stemming from the influence of loosely 'nominalist' fourteenth-century theology. More specifically, Anima's comments tend to align with post-Ockhamist theology's insistence on the availability of congruous if not condign merit, enabled by God's *acceptatio* of imperfect efforts of the human will, echoed in the familiar formula asserting the sufficiency of

---

[101] See however Richard K. Emmerson, '"Coveitise to Konne", "Goddes Pryvetee", and Will's Ambiguous Dream Experience in *Piers Plowman*', in Fowler, and Vaughan, *Suche Werkis to Werche*, pp. 89–121, who stresses that the danger of intellectual covetousness is never fully overcome in the poem, since the very existence of the dream/poem we are reading is fundamentally determined by the continued appeal of this inordinate desire.

420 MEDIEVAL ALLEGORY AS EPISTEMOLOGY

'*facere quod in se est*'.[102] In the present context, however, it seems more important to emphasize that the point is being made specifically in terms of contrasting attitudes to scripture and associated textual forms. Behind Anima's and Bernard's praise of those who put their learning into practice lies an implicit condemnation of the inertia of the will displayed by readers who merely possess, recite, or revere texts without putting their teachings into practice—or, more succinctly, those who fail to practice what they read and preach.[103] This also provides the rationale for the structure of Anima's otherwise seemingly rambling speech, which begins as a personal rebuke of Will but rapidly metamorphoses into a condemnation of 'Curatours of Holy Kirke' (XV.136).

In its aversion to inert textuality and empty formalism Anima's reproach thus manifests a further facet of the poem's wider, quintessentially Langlandian resistance to fixed and over-determined forms—institutional, mental, textual, and corporeal. As Anima reminds Will, such excessive trust in formal crystallizations of Truth always has idolatrous implications: *Confundantur omnes qui adorant sculptilia* (XV.81a).[104] This injunction to make scriptural knowledge truly operative is thus broadly analogous to other instances of textual, institutional, and conceptual de-materialization, such as the Tearing of the Pardon,[105] the reaffirmation of the predicative and potentially 'infinite' nature of 'doing well', the injunction to write a patent on a 'parchment of poverty', and indeed the infinitely protracted action of Long Will's search for perfect charity 'in londe'. All of this strongly militates against the desire for textual and documentary reification, permanence, and closure that plays such a central importance in Deguileville's poetic corpus. Langland's insistence on predicative and the infinitely reiterative nature of 'doing' thus provides a striking illustration of Angela Leighton's observation about the different modes of cognition enabled by poetic knowing in general, when compared with philosophical demonstration: 'in the end, poetry's knowing remains insufficient, like a verb without an object, or like a suspended participle, something to be found only in the finding, discovered in the discovering, heard and listened for as if in the hearing'.[106] While (Aristotelian) philosophy strives to produce certain, apodictic knowledge of objective realities, 'poetic knowing' can never fully grasp, let alone

---

[102] For arguments in favour of the impact of this particular notion on the poem's theology, see Baker, 'From Ploughing to Pardon'; Adams, 'Piers' Semi-Pelagianism'; Coleman, *Piers Plowman and the Moderni*, pp. 33–5 and *passim*. For a useful overview of the debate and a lucid discussion of Wyclif's position, see Levy, 'Grace and Freedom in the Soteriology of John Wyclif'.

[103] Gruenler, *Poetics of Enigma*, pp. 290–1.

[104] See also Burrow, 'Words, Works, and Will', p. 114.

[105] I here follow Robert Adams's reading, arguing that 'the heart of the priest's objection to the terms of Truth's pardon seems to be that it requires performance', in 'Piers' Pardon', 411, which sees the tearing as a reaction not against its content, but against the inert formalism of this injunction once it acquires the state of a written document.

[106] Angela Leighton, 'Poetry's Knowing: So What Do We Know?', p. 180, in John Gibson, *The Philosophy of Poetry*.

THE EXPERIENCE OF FAILURE AND THE ARCHITECTURE OF VISION 421

define and possess its objects, and prompts a redefinition of knowing as both act and experience rather than an instance of objective proof and demonstration.

It is within this broader context that Langland's authorial signature as 'Longe Wille' acquires its full dramatic, formal, and conceptual significance. In a number of complex ways, I would suggest, Langland's authorial signature deliberately seeks to evade the kinds of closure pursued by Deguileville's authorial signatures: narrative, imaginative, autobiographical/apologetic, cognitive/imaginative, soteriological, and eschatological. As in other crucial moments of crisis and transformation that produce renewed self-understanding in Langland's poem, the progression to a higher level of awareness is unexpectedly precipitated by an experience of *failure*. Here this takes the form of the gaping fracture between an immoderate, self-righteous aspiration towards total knowledge of 'Alle þe sciences vnder sonne and alle þe sotile craftes' (B XV.48) and the painful experience of human intellectual limitations, in this case with specific reference Will's failure to understand the true significance and ultimate nature of Charity:

> 'What is charite', quod I þo.
> [...]
> 'I haue lyued in londe', quod I, 'my name is Longe Wille,
> And fond I neuere ful charité, bifore ne bihynde'.
> [...]
> 'Clerkes kenne me þat Crist is in alle places;
> Ac I sei3 hym neuere sooþly but as myself in a mirour'.
> *Hic in enigmate, tunc facie ad faciem.*
> (B XV.149; 152–3; 161–2)

Langland again affirms the positivity of failure, since it is precisely thanks to Anima's extended tirade against Will's renewed bout of intellectual covetousness that the latter is able to finally recognize himself in an enigmatic mirror as both 'Longe Wille' and a dislocated reflection of the *imago dei*. It is precisely because he realizes his own failure to grasp the magnitude of the significance of Charity—despite his 'long', protracted quest 'in londe'—that Will comes to occupy a position where he is able to experience a higher, inferential understanding of Charity.

Simpson's analysis is particularly relevant here in terms of Langland's reconstructive engagement with Deguileville. Simpson emphasizes the centrality of the experience of 'suffering' in Anima's and Langland's definition of Charity at this moment in the poem—a notion that had already occupied an important place earlier in the poem (see Chapter 5.2):

> 'Amonges Cristene men this myldenesse sholde laste,
> In alle manere angres haue this at herte—
> That þei3 þei suffrede al þis, God suffred for vs moore

> In ensample we sholde do so, and take no vengeaunce
> Of oure foes þat dooþ vs falsnesse—þat is oure Fadres wille.
> For wel may euery man wite, if God hadde wold hymselue,
> Sholde neuere Iudas ne Iew haue Iesu doon on roode,
> Ne han martired Peter ne Poul, ne in prisoun holden.
> Ac he suffrede in ensample þat we sholde suffren also,
> And seide to suche þat suffre wolde þat "*Pacientes vincunt*
> *verbi gratia*", quod he, and verray ensamples manye.'
>
> (B XV.258–68)

For Simpson, Anima finally articulates a 'mysteriously circular, Pauline account of knowing by being known', which 'places the will's own capacity to suffer at the heart of an understanding of Charity'.[107] Langland thus appears to suggest that while the limitations of the singular, individual human will can impede true self-knowledge and the knowledge of Charity, the *experience* of such limitations acquires a truly universal character, lending it a deeply transformative spiritual significance and allowing Will himself to transcend the limits of his own, individual singularity. The moment of this renewed experience of a fractured self coincides with the apprehension of the utmost boundaries of the self—its ultimate horizon or vanishing point provided by the image of Christ glimpsed 'as myself in a mirour'.

Langland's choice of the motif of 'a mirour' to frame this moment of self-discovery is clearly not accidental. In general terms the mirror underlines the double, paradoxical nature of the experience: Will apprehends a doubled, enigmatic reflection of himself, simultaneously mirroring his fallen human condition as well as its divine original as *imago dei*. But Langland's choice is also informed by the more specifically Deguilevillian resonances of the mirror, in turn reminiscent of the many mirrors that structure, re-structure, and de-structure the *Rose* (see Chapters 2.3, 3.5, and 7.1). The encounter with Christ 'as myself in a mirour' signals a major 'restorative rupture'[108] in Will's spiritual quest, and Langland again develops this scene as a response to Deguileville. Far from merely using the *PVH* as a 'source', Langland uses the episode to interrogate and ultimately reconfigure the entire allegorical epistemology that underpins the earlier poem, in order to forge his own, distinctive poetic 're-vision' of Deguileville's allegorical pilgrimage. Unlike Deguileville's mirror—which reflects the perfect and depersonalized geometric outlines of the Heavenly City at the start of *PVH*—Langland's mirror at XV.162 is far more enigmatic, and reflects only the flawed, imperfect human lineaments of Will's own face, while also refracting the image of Christ in an enigmatic play of transparencies and inversions.[109] In that sense Langland's mirror also

---

[107] Simpson, 'Power of Impropriety'.
[108] Middleton, '"Kynde Name"', p. 228.
[109] See also the analysis of Cervone, *Poetics of the Incarnation*, pp. 26–31.

THE EXPERIENCE OF FAILURE AND THE ARCHITECTURE OF VISION   423

recalls a far more problematic mirror that appears in Deguileville's revised poem, the 'miroir de conscience' (*PVH2* 15,429) in which the pilgrim is able to recognize his own state of sinful deformity, and which renders visible the limitations of Deguileville's initial poetic project as they were encapsulated in its initial vision of the Heavenly City. Uniquely, however, Langland also overlays this renewed vision of individual deformity with a second, ghostlike image that opens up the vista onto the final sections of the poem: it is through the very recognition of his own fallen condition that Will is able to dimly apprehend, as in a palimpsest, the lineaments of Christ.

As well as pointing forward to a moment of eschatological closure that will bring all acts of vision to an end—*Hic in enigmate, tunc facie ad faciem*—this new form of doubled self-revelation 'in a mirour' plays an important structural role within Langland's 'system' of signatures, coming to occupy a pivotal position that reflects both backwards and forwards in the narrative progression of the poem. As well as recalling the various mirrors of Deguileville's poem, the mirror from *passus* XV also refracts Will's earlier vision glimpsed in the 'mirour þat hiȝte Middelerþe' (B XI.9), another important step in Langland's systematic reworking of Deguileville. Will's recognition of himself as Christ in the mirror at XV.162 thus both repeats and completes the earlier shock of self-recognition in the mirror of Middle Earth, bracketing all of the action of the middle *passus* (XI–XIV) between two analogous mirrors. More importantly, this image also looks forward to the fuller vision of Christ, *speculum sine macula*, encountered later in Langland's poem in *passus* XVIII (see Chapter 7.1). Long Will's mirror thus signals the transition to yet another level of visionary experience, ushering in both a new form of self-understanding as well as a new understanding of the possibilities of poetic vision. Whereas Deguileville's 'miroir de conscience' (*PVH2* 15,429) refracts only a terminally infected human Everyman, and no longer ensures access to the Heavenly Jerusalem, Langland's mirror reflects *both* Will's present deformity and his original identity with the *imago dei*. If we accept the principle of symbolic analogy that makes such mirrors function as metonymies for the poems in which they occur, Will's mirror implicitly affirms Langland's continued belief in the salvific efficacy of his own poem, enabling the recovery of Will's lost self-identity. Instead of necessitating a desperate, fideistic appeal to the operation of Grace and the Virgin like Deguileville's 'miroir de conscience', Langland's mirror manages to preserve the fundamentally volitional character of the subject and its identity with/as the faculty of the common human 'will', particularized in the form of the poem's endlessly 'willing' protagonist, Will.

In the context of the present analysis it is legitimate to ask whether my suggestion that Deguileville's Rock of Penitence constitutes a major touchstone for both mirroring scenes in *passus* XI and *passus* XV respectively does not diminish or trivialize the significance of the connections I have been tracing. The insights produced by the two moments of mirroring in Langland effectively appear broadly

424 MEDIEVAL ALLEGORY AS EPISTEMOLOGY

analogous in a number of ways: both denote a transition from active ways of knowing to passive ones; both involve some form of authorial signature in conjunction with a moment of major cognitive crisis; both are intensely visual, but also reframe the definition of the 'visionary' aspirations of poetry. I would like to suggest that the similarities do not in fact detract from the expressive power of the two scenes. On the contrary, repetition and incremental development of the same motifs is an integral part both of Langland's poetic method and of his theology: unlike the conversion of Deguileville's pilgrim—which is sudden, immediate, and at least in theory definitive (see Chapter 4.1)—Will's conversions are plural, imperfect, fragmentary, often flawed and essentially provisional and insufficient. This ultimately justifies and indeed *necessitates* the repetition of multiple, broadly analogous instances of crisis and conversion throughout the poem and beyond it, in ways that are profoundly 'Augustinian'.[110] It is therefore highly appropriate that Will should not only continue looking 'bifore' and 'bihynde' (XV.153) at this crucial moment, situating his experience in a temporal and spatial continuum, but that he should step into the fifth vision by noting that 'my wit weex and wanyed' (XV.3), continuing to fluctuate with little chance of settling in a specific place and thus attaining any sort of epistemic closure.

It is also on the formal level, by means of multiple episodic and spasmodic crises that Langland attempts to convey a theologically nuanced message, concerning the productive dialectical relation between the individual acts of the will—forever insufficient and hence necessarily reiterative—and the inexhaustible availability of grace in response to the continued effort of *facere quod in se est*. It is within this dialectic or 'doubled agency'[111] that a salutary economy of true contrition, reiterated conversion, and the gift of special grace (*auxilium dei speciale*) can materialize.[112] Uniquely, Langland's poem affirms the mutually enabling nature of the experiences of failure on the one hand, and that of a continued, constantly renewed and infinitely protracted act of willing on the other—tempering Deguileville's insistence on the will's total dependence on the redemptive operation of Christ/grace with an emphasis on the continued agency of individual

---

[110] See especially the reading of Augustine's understanding of conversion presented in Aers, *Salvation and Sin*, notably p. 24 and *passim*. For Augustine's understanding of conversion as a lifelong process, shaped by his early conversion to Manichaeanism, see especially Jason David BeDuhn, *Augustine's Manichaean Dilemma, I: Conversion and Apostasy, 373–388 C.E.* (Philadelphia: University of Pennsylvania Press, 2010), and *Augustine's Manichaean Dilemma, II: The Making of a 'Catholic' Self, ca. 388–401 C.E.* (Philadelphia: University of Pennsylvania Press, 2013).

[111] Aers, *Sanctifying Signs*, p. 15, borrowing the formula from George Hunsinger, *How to Read Karl Barth: The Shape of His Theology* (Oxford: Oxford University Press, 1991).

[112] I use such loaded Latin *formulae* precisely to suggest that Langland's thought *cannot* be subsumed within either 'school of thought' associated with these recurrent maxims: 'Pelagianism/'Nominalism' with the *facere quod in se est* on the one hand; and the radical Augustinianism of Gregory of Rimini and Thomas Bradwardine with the *auxilium dei speciale*. See further Heiko A. Oberman, '"Facientibus quod in se est Deus non denegat gratiam"'; Christoph P. Burger, 'Das "auxilium speciale Dei" in der Gnadenlehre Gregors von Rimini', in Heiko A. Oberman, ed., *Gregor von Rimini: Werk und Wirkung bis zur* Reformation (Berlin: De Gruyter, 1981), 195–240.

THE EXPERIENCE OF FAILURE AND THE ARCHITECTURE OF VISION 425

voluntas. Long Will's selfhood is thus 'prolonged' through his endlessly reiterated act of longing, which in turn acknowledges and accepts the repeated failure of his acts of the will to grasp any ultimate truth, in turn 'prolonging' the poem's quest for Truth. Long Will's admission that he has 'lyued in londe', and the implied suggestion that this is specifically a 'lond of longynge' (cf. B XI.8), echoes Augustine's own journey through the *regio dissimilitudinis*, where God's voice can only be heard 'de longinquo' ('from afar', *Conf.* VII.10.16), in turn reprising Luke's observations on the departure of the Prodigal Son 'in regionem longinquam' ('into a far country', Luke 15:13).[113]

Will's oblique self-identification, then, functions as a recognition of the irremediably alienated nature of his selfhood in a *regio dissimilitudinis*, determining his inability to differentiate the complementary agency of divine grace and individual will in any viable fashion. As a result, Will's own subjectivity, his 'common will' is necessarily extended in space and distended in time, apprehensible not as a discrete and finite entity but only as narrated form, ever moving towards a vanishing point that recedes into the distance and remains beyond the grasp of a 'proper' naming, beyond the reach of any act of reliable and univocal representation, and ultimately opaque and unknowable in itself.[114] The desire for an ultimate identity with/in/as the *imago dei* therefore functions as a vanishing point, necessarily beyond the grasp of any act of 'proper' linguistic designation. The prospect of self-identity for the poem's 'I' is therefore literally projected beyond the limits of the poem in any of its real or potential forms. The 'lond of longynge' traversed or indeed 'plowed' by 'Long Will' thus gradually turns into a metonymy for both the text and the textual labour that produces it: Long Will is simultaneously subsumed within and produced by the open, infinitely extensible labour that creates the poem/field, determining the poem's fundamentally protean, evolving, organic, metamorphic and unfinishable nature.

4. Vision and Re-Vision: Deguileville's and Langland's Reiterative Poetic

Among the many unique and distinctive traits that define Langland's poetic craft, his commitment to a poetics of revision is often seen as the most idiosyncratic, the most irreducibly 'Langlandian'. In the light of the readings presented so far, however, I would like to suggest that the origins of such a re-visionary poetics are to be sought in Langland's engagement with Deguileville's *PVH* in its two versions and the pilgrimage 'trilogy' as a whole.

---

[113] See also the discussion of this passage in Augustine by Aers, *Sanctifying Signs*, pp. 14, 61.
[114] For a fascinating discussion of Langland's interest in liminality—beginnings as well as endings—see especially D. Vance Smith, *Book of the Incipit: Beginnings in the Fourteenth Century* (Minneapolis and London: University of Minnesota Press, 2001).

426   MEDIEVAL ALLEGORY AS EPISTEMOLOGY

Ralph Hanna has usefully summed up the scholarly consensus on the question of Langland's multiple versions of his poem:

> Langland appears to have written his poem three times, and all three forms had public currency, available to be recorded by copyists. The poet seems to have been at work for an extended period, composing and recomposing. During this period, he promulgated, by means not entirely clear today, the work at various times. But in a situation where anyone who might acquire a copy might make yet another one, Langland had no control over his text, once it had become public. Consequently, second (and third) thoughts required some renewed act of promulgation, and, as a result, substantially different versions of the work were 'public property'—and thus variously available to scribes and readers.[115]

In the same article, Hanna then proceeds to discuss how this production of multiple different versions occurs not so much by accident but by design, as an expression of a unique and idiosyncratic 'revisionist' poetics, where the notion of 're-vision' develops several different but closely interrelated meanings. Firstly, Langland's poem is structured as a sequence of evolving visions from its earliest surviving attestation in the A-text—a technique that is arguably inspired by the tripartite structure of Deguileville's pilgrimage trilogy, constituted by a sequence of three successive dreams, as has been suggested by several scholars from Dorothy Owen to George Kane (see Introduction to Part III above). Secondly, Langland also repeatedly 'revises' his poem, rewriting multiple versions to record his conversations with himself and with his earlier writings. Thirdly, however, Langland also produces—or indeed *experiences*—a sequence of multiple, similar-yet-different visions, where he returns to the same problems from a different and constantly shifting perspective, 're-visioning' earlier insights, and thereby acknowledging and to some extent embracing the reiterative nature of the poetico-visionary process as such:

> *Piers Plowman* is a poem unique in European tradition in being given over to repeated feats of 'visioning' [. . .]. 'Re-visioning' what has already occurred, reopening, commenting upon, and qualifying earlier discussions is the very *métier* of Langland's poetics.[116]

Hanna's characterization of Langland's re-visionary method as an exceptional case in European literary history is compelling, and builds on a long critical tradition that has sought to explain Langland's aims and motivations. Already in 1955, Talbot Donaldson was prompted to wonder whether readers of the poem should

---

[115] Hanna, 'The Different Versions and Revisions of *Piers Plowman*', p. 36.
[116] Hanna, 'The Different Versions and Revisions of *Piers Plowman*', p. 42.

THE EXPERIENCE OF FAILURE AND THE ARCHITECTURE OF VISION   427

in fact view the A, B, and C texts as deliberately promulgated works, or rather snapshots of an ongoing process of revision, 'historical accidents, haphazard milestones in the history of a poem that was begun but never finished, photographs that caught a static image of a living organism at a given but not necessarily significant moment in time'.[117] A. V. C. Schmidt similarly speaks of 'The "dissolution" of *Piers Plowman* from a finished poem into an unfinished process', while nevertheless arguing for the priority of the C-text as representing something like the 'final' result of Langland's poetic process.[118] Barbara Newman notes that 'Langland devoted his whole writing life to the successive versions of *Piers Plowman*, a poem whose startling lack of closure mirrors its author's inability to leave it alone',[119] and Anne Middleton observes of Langland's poem that 'paradoxically, it seems to be a condition of the integrity of his "work", or the defensibility of the project, that it never be fully identifiable or coexistent with any form of its (merely) textual Incarnation'.[120] In a compelling analysis, Alan Fletcher proposes a still more radical reading of Langland's method, insisting on the necessarily provisional nature of *all* versions, real and hypothetical: 'the unfinished [. . .] business of the poem [is] figured poetically in its perpetually deferred ending, but experienced also in practical terms, [. . .], in the restlessness of its process whose traces we have come to call Z, A, B and C'.[121] For Fletcher, this process is endowed with an intrinsic ethical significance, making the constantly shifting form of the poem an integral part of its ethical, epistemological, and theological message: '[Langland's] release into the world of at least three or four version of [his poem] may implicitly acknowledge that provisionality was not only acceptable, but ethically mandatory'.[122]

Langland's work as an obsessive 'serial reviser',[123] however, was not quite so unique and unprecedented as this well-established critical tradition in Langland studies has tended to assume. Indeed, Langland appears to have learnt this particular lesson from Deguileville—who in turn learnt it, the hard way, from the *Rose* (see Chapters 2.5, 3.6, and 4.5). If this irresistible drive to 're-vision' really is 'the métier of Langland's poetics', as Hanna suggests, then it is a very important lesson indeed, and accordingly demands much closer scrutiny. Deguileville's own strategies of poetic re-visioning, re-negotiation, and auto-exegesis therefore provide us with

---

[117] E. Talbot Donaldson, 'MSS R and F in the B-tradition of *Piers Plowman*', *Transactions of the Connecticut Academy* 39 (1955), 177–212 (211), quoted in C. David Benson, *Public Piers Plowman: Modern Scholarship and Late Medieval English Culture* (University Park: Pennsylvania State University Press, 2004), p. 28.

[118] Schmidt, 'Langland's Visions and Revisions', 15.

[119] Newman, 'Redeeming the Time', 16.

[120] Middleton, 'Acts of Vagrancy', p. 289.

[121] Fletcher, 'The Essential (Ephemeral) William Langland', 61. For a powerful reading along comparable lines, but with greater emphasis on the C-text as a work capturing Langland's 'final', or at least latest vision before his death, see again Schmidt, 'Langland's Visions and Revisions'.

[122] Fletcher, 'The Essential (Ephemeral) William Langland', 62.

[123] Schmidt, 'Langland's Visions and Revisions', 13.

428 MEDIEVAL ALLEGORY AS EPISTEMOLOGY

an invaluable tool to better understand the rationale that underpins Langland's incessant reworking of his own poem.

In Chapter 4 I have attempted to define a trajectory for Deguileville's 'literary career', paying particular attention to the dynamics that produced his later corpus and more specifically the so-called 'pilgrimage trilogy', *PVH2* (1355–6), *PA* (1356), and *PJC* (1358). More specifically I have argued that *PVH2* is written from a position of apologetic retrenchment, manifesting not only the poet's defensiveness about the instability of his own text, but revealing his latent anxiety about the slipperiness of allegory itself—ideas that rise to the surface in the new preface (*PVH2* 21–90). The situation of textual and interpretive instability described in the preface provides an apt gloss also on Langland's own situation, similarly aware of the concomitant circulation of multiple divergent and variously imperfect versions of his work. In reading or re-reading the prologue to *PVH2*, Langland would thus have encountered an uncannily resonant account of the kind of loss of textual and interpretive control he would have had to confront in relation to his multiple versions of *Piers Plowman*.[124] Deguileville's story of the theft may have been particularly resonant for Langland if we accept that his own A-text of *Piers Plowman* really was an unauthorized, imperfect or unfinished draft circulated without the author's consent.[125] As I will be arguing in what follows, then, Langland's encounter with Deguileville's reflection on the vagaries of poetic reception and interpretation in both the prologue and the many additional passages in *PVH2* marks a key moment in the development of Langland's poetic vision. Deguileville's act of rewriting finally shapes the evolving architecture of Langland's poetic vision over time, allowing him to formulate a distinctive, highly personal and idiosyncratic poetics of re-vision.

At the heart of the reiterative and revisionist nature of both Langland's and Deguileville's poetics lies the question of the legitimacy of poetic 'meddling'— an activity that appears not only self-indulgent and potentially futile, but also as an obstinately serial offence. While Langland clearly inherits an aesthetics of revision from Deguileville, he radically redefines its ethical and salvific significance. Already in *PVH1* Deguileville articulates something like an ethics and aesthetics of textual revision, during one of the pivotal moments of the allegory. Arriving at a *bivium* or parting of the ways in his journey, the pilgrim encounters two figures who preside over each of the respective paths among which the *viator* has to choose: on one side he sees Huiseuse/Oiseuse, a seductive courtly lady who invites him to enter the 'voie senestre' (*PVH1* 6517); on the other side he sees Labour/Occupant, a seemingly foolish mat-maker who prompts him to

---

[124] On this loss of control over his text, see also Ralph Hanna, 'On the Versions of *Piers Plowman*', in his *Pursuing History: Middle English Manuscripts and Their Texts* (Stanford: Stanford University Press, 1996), pp. 203–43 (240).

[125] For this suggestion, see Hanna, 'On the Versions of *Piers Plowman*', p. 233 and *passim*; Kerby-Fulton, 'Bibliographical Ego', pp. 93–110.

THE EXPERIENCE OF FAILURE AND THE ARCHITECTURE OF VISION   429

continue along the 'chemin destre' (*PVH1* 6533).[126] These two figures do not sim-ply represent a basic moral binarism of vice vs. virtue, but also emblematize two rival forms of textual and poetic labour, and more specifically two competing forms of allegorical interpretation and composition (see Chapter 3.3). The figure of Huiseuse/Oiseuse, lifted wholesale out of the *Rose*, thus comes to represent the idle and sterile rhetorical pleasures of an eroticized, carnal form of allegorical poetics inaugurated by the *Rose*. By contrast, the figure of Occupant clearly functions as an embodiment of monastic *occupatio*, the avoidance of *acedia* that offers the possi-bility of a fundamentally different, ruminative and meditative form of interpretive engagement. As Maupeu's analysis of Occupant demonstrates, his obsessive and seemingly pointless weaving and unmaking of mats figures the specifically monas-tic activities of textual exegesis and commentary, decomposing and recomposing, weaving and unweaving the fabric of the 'text' in order to absorb its sapiential nour-ishment, distilling *senefiance* out of *semblance*.[127] This meditative understanding of poetic composition and interpretation resonates with twelfth-century Platonist ideals of poetry, as in Bernardus Silvestris' *Cosmographia*, which develops an anal-ogy between a cosmic hermeneutics and processes of poetic composition, revision, and interpretation. There Imarmene—who is 'temporal continuity in its aspect as a principle of order'—'weaves together and unravels' [texit et retexit, *Megacosmus* I.13] the universe.[128] Concluding the first part of the *Cosmographia*, the *Megacos-mus*, and leading into the second part, the *Microcosmus*, the act of weaving serves as a paradigm for the creation of poetic fictions, enabling the poet himself to inter-act with the texture of a divinely ordained cosmos. Metonymically speaking, then, Deguileville's own writing of spiritual allegory is presented as being fundamentally analogous to the spiritual labour of the mat-maker, grounded in a salvific poetics of endless composition, exposition, commentary, and recomposition.

The image of repetitive textual making and unmaking acquires a subtly but importantly different significance in Deguileville's reworking of his own poem, *PVH2*. The central activity of Labour, as a mat-maker, remains the same in both versions, as the pilgrim notes: 'I see that you often unmake, what you have already well made and then remake it', [voy que souvent tu deffaiz / Ce qu'as bien fait et le refaiz, *PVH1* 6569–70; cf. *PVH2* 7537–8; my translation). Yet the task of constant weaving and unweaving has lost its meditative monastic appeal, and increasingly appears as a futile, endlessly protracted, solipsistic activity. This is reflected especially in the new role played by Occupant himself in the poem, far less confident and authoritative than in the original version. In *PVH1* the figure of

---

[126] See especially Maupeu, '*Bivium*'; ibid. *Pèlerins de vie humaine*, pp. 118–28, 149–53; Kay, *Place of Thought*, pp. 70–93.
[127] Maupeu, '*Bivium*', 28–30.
[128] Bernardus Silvestris, *Poetic Works*, ed. and trans. Winthrop Wetherbee (Cambridge MA and Lon-don: Harvard University Press, 2015), pp. 74–5. See also Whitman, *Allegory*, p. 255. ibid., *Allegory and Interpretation*, pp. 53–4.

430 MEDIEVAL ALLEGORY AS EPISTEMOLOGY

Labour/Occupant was still presented as a divinely inspired mouthpiece for Grace Dieu's teaching (*PVH1* 6663–6). Yet in *PVH2*, Labour/Occupant relinquishes his role as a reliable guide and figure of authority, and declares himself unable to advise the pilgrim effectively on the choice of the right path:

'Certes', dist, 'pour chemins monstrer
Ne sui pas cy venu ouvrer,
   [. . .]
Si ne t'en çay plus que dire,
Lequel que veulx pues eslire.'
  (*PVH2* 7515–16; 7535–6)

'I haven't set to work here to show people their way [. . .] So I can't tell you any more, chose whatever path you wish'

If, as Maupeu has suggested, the 'Nattier' really is a surrogate authorial persona in disguise, then his refusal to commit himself to any clear instruction has weighty implications. Whereas *PVH1* was produced by a confident author/preacher who was also the expositor of his own poem, the revised version features a 'Nattier' who now doubts the effectiveness and legitimacy of his own textual labour, and fails to provide an adequate interpretation of the allegory he is himself a part of. Whereas the labour of the mat-maker in *PVH1* was intrinsically salvific, it now appears oddly aimless and detached from any overarching sense of purpose and direction. The mat-maker's comments on his own labour also acquire an additional edge in the wake of Deguileville's description of his own labour of textual revision in the prologue: 'there was much to add and to take out, to be corrected and reorganized' [a mectre et a oster, / A corrigier et ordonner, / Y avoit moult, *PVH2* 35–7). Whereas in the early version the activity of composition and recomposition seems to have played an integral and spiritually productive role in Deguileville's poetics, the text now appears to have developed a life of its own, beyond the author's control and no longer reducible to anything like a clearly identifiable authorial design and intention.

The relevance of Deguileville's 'Nattier' to our understanding of Langland's own processes of textual revision has already been suggested by John Bowers in his prescient account of the *Crisis of Will in Piers Plowman* in 1986—although Bowers does not contemplate the possibility of direct influence. Speaking of 'Langland's unspoken attitude towards his writing', Bowers comments on Lydgate's 1427 verse translation of *PVH2*: 'Lydgate, like Deguileville before him, must have understood that Labor's making and unmaking were analogous to the poet's work of writing and revising.'[129] I believe Bowers is also correct in associating Deguileville's Nattier with the figure of Paul the Hermit, an 'archetypally absurd character spending his solitary life in the wastes of Egypt weaving baskets', and whose activity becomes an influential motif in the elaboration of early ideals of monastic and

---

[129] *Crisis of Will*, pp. 215–16. For Paul the Hermit, also see ibid. p. 64.

THE EXPERIENCE OF FAILURE AND THE ARCHITECTURE OF VISION 431

hermitic *occupatio*. Langland's Anima significantly evokes Paul the Hermit as a
foundational figure of monasticism, complete with his activity of weaving baskets:

> 'Poul *primus heremita* hadde parroked hymselue
> That no man miȝte hym se for mosse and for leues.
> Foweles hym fedde fele wyntres wiþ alle
> Til he foundede freres of Austynes ordre.
> Poul, after his prechyng, paniers he made,
> And wan wiþ his hondes þat his wombe neded.'
>
> (B XV.286–91)

While Langland confuses the two St Pauls—a common confusion he shares with
a number of other medieval writers—the image significantly combines a number of ideals that have acquired new centrality in Langland's poem at this stage:
poverty, labour, solitary contemplation, and the hermitic life, all subsumed within
the theme that hangs over this section of Anima's speech: *ne soliciti sitis* (cf. B
VII.131): 'For we ben Goddes foweles and abiden alwey, / Til briddes brynge vs
þat we shulde by lyue' (B XV.313–14).

The ideas that Langland associates with this image, however, suggest a rather
different and more positive attitude towards his own poetic labour than that
found in *PVH2*. For all its interest in the reiterative nature of literary re-visioning,
Deguileville's revision ultimately expresses a profound anxiety about the impossibility of attaining closure: rather than expressing confident serenity in the
intrinsically meditative and devotional value of his own writing, Deguileville's
'Nattier' in *PVH2* crystallizes an obsessive and finally counterproductive desire for
completion and totality, both reifying and fetishizing the documentary status of his
own definitive text, while also coming to realize the impossibility of guaranteeing
interpretive stability and representational closure. Langland's attitude, by contrast,
appears far more confident and equanimous, despite Ymaginatif's accusations and
further, endemic instances of authorial self-doubt. This is manifested not only in
Langland's repeated return to his own one poem, but also in his concerted effort
to recuperate moments of crisis and reorientation inherited from Deguileville,
integrating those within the existing form of the dream vision and pilgrimage allegory and thereby constantly expanding and adapting its visionary remit. As I have
suggested repeatedly, Langland therefore appears to systematically confront and
exorcize the moments of crisis he encounters in Deguileville, employing them not
so much to disrupt and explode the allegorical pilgrimage frame, but in order to
nuance, expand, complicate and articulate its purview into a sequence of multiple,
incremental but open-ended instances of vision and re-vision.

The radically searching, heuristic quality of Langland's poem is also reflected
in the unstable social and professional space occupied by its central
narrator/protagonist. Unlike Deguileville's narrator figure—clearly identified as a

432   MEDIEVAL ALLEGORY AS EPISTEMOLOGY

Cistercian monk in both versions, engaged in an oral *predicatio* during the first version, and in the correction and exegesis of a written text with forensic value in the second version—Langland's narrator/protagonist is consistently elusive and resistant to any kind of permanent identification and socio-economic 'placing': a dubious hermit, vagrant, scrounger, *lollere*, such as those condemned in Anima's tirade (XV.213–14). As Andrew Galloway observes, this instability ultimately allows Will to interrogate the legitimacy of *all* kinds of institutional discourses and attachments, but also creates enormous difficulties in terms of defining and vindicating the writer's own 'vocation'.[130] As I have already suggested, however, Langland's greatest difficulty also provides its own solution: it is precisely by insisting that this kind of salvific poetic work cannot be subsumed within any established profession, discourse, and institution that Langland ends up vindicating the legitimacy of his work as a proper vocation. As Galloway argues, Langland 'is seeking to define a realm of learning and of learned poetry removed both from institutional reification and from the professional or self-serving motives for knowledge presented elsewhere in the poem'.[131] Throughout its multiple versions, then, the poem displays what Anne Middleton calls 'a progressively deeper understanding and more fully conscious acceptance [...] of both the social and literary consequences of developing a philosophic and spiritual quest in the narrative form of a historically specific life-story'.[132]

To be sure, there is nothing self-assured or complacent, let alone triumphant about Langland's poetic labour, whose continuation appears to be postulated on the uncompromising adoption of that great fourteenth-century nominalist mantra: *facere quod in se est*. Despite his 'characteristic distaste for wasting time',[133] and all the while being 'uncomfortably aware [that] the poem is an inadequate substitute for the sort of penance' recommended by Ymaginatif,[134] Langland pursues his work not with a view to its termination or completion but rather with a view to its infinitely re-iterated actualization. As Schmidt observes, for Langland '"redeeming the time" becomes [...] a matter of doing work, that is, "meddling with makyng"'.[135] More recently, Ryan McDermott has argued that Langland's attitude towards his own poetic labour was self-consciously penitential: instead of stressing, like Hanna, the 'inadequacy' of his work as an act of penance, McDermott reads the poem as pursuing a programme of penitential satisfaction, 'according to which writing a poem such as *Piers Plowman* can constitute a work of mercy and therefore count as sacramental satisfaction'.[136] Tellingly, McDermott identifies

---

[130] Galloway, '*Piers Plowman* and the Schools'.
[131] Galloway, '*Piers Plowman* and the Schools', pp. 95–6.
[132] Middleton, '"Kynde Name"', p. 225.
[133] Schmidt, 'Langland's Visions and Revisions', 23.
[134] Hanna, 'Ymaginatif', 92–3.
[135] Schmidt, 'Langland's Visions and Revisions', 23.
[136] McDermott, 'Practices of Satisfaction', 173.

THE EXPERIENCE OF FAILURE AND THE ARCHITECTURE OF VISION   433

such a strategy as an expression of a characteristically Langlandian understanding of Sacramental Theology, in the liminal zone between official institutional doctrine, and more eccentric, if spiritually intense vernacular forms of devotion and belief: 'If Will and William Langland are writing as an act of penitential satisfaction, then they occupy what may seem like a strange place in the medieval economy of salvation, both outside the clerically controlled sacrament of penance, yet also seeking that sacrament's benefits.'[137]

McDermott's characterization of this 'strange place' provides an eloquent and useful picture of Langland's idiosyncratic, yet perfectly calibrated balancing of profoundly orthodox belief in mainstream sacramental theology on the one hand, and an almost obsessive abhorrence of unthinking, empty formalism on the other. Not only does the poem 'hold [. . .] a mechanistic understanding of penance up to critique,'[138] but its re-visionary method and metamorphic structure appears designed to avert the pitfalls of fossilization inherent in the pursuit of settled and fixed forms of all kinds—sacramental, institutional, visionary, cognitive, expressive, interpretive, and textual. As Burrow argued in his discussion of the Tearing of the Pardon, this is also the reason behind the poem's repeated self-destructive moves: 'Langland's fear [. . .] that the external form or institution—even though acceptable in itself—may come to usurp the place of a spiritual reality.'[139] John Bowers strikes a similar note, commenting on 'Langland's hostility toward the types of external show that contribute to a hollow formalism, usurping the place of the inner spiritual reality and cluttering rather than illuminating the life of man.'[140] John Alford too notes that '[h]is fear of the tyranny of form lies not only behind the repeated narrative shedding of the outer forms of penance, pilgrimage, and pardon; it also drives his own restless need to continuously remake his poem.'[141] Paradoxically, then, Langland's continued and continuously re-actualized belief in the spiritual value of his own poetic workings does not obtain *despite* his sense of inadequacy, but precisely *because of it*. In order to maintain its potential for spiritual growth, Langland's work needs to be continuously subjected to the question that for Anne Middleton encapsulates the paradox of Langland's penitential poetics: 'Is a poem like a falsely claimed pardon, offering the illusion of absolution?'[142]

Langland's keen awareness of 'the risks of material and cultural ossification'[143] thus entails an understanding of poetic labour as *inherently* and necessarily provisional, a labour that is actively invested in the periodic unmaking of its concrete textual formations, and whose continued relevance is dependent upon such

---

[137] McDermott, 'Practices of Satisfaction', 173.
[138] McDermott, 'Practices of Satisfaction', 193.
[139] Burrow, 'The Action of Langland's Second Vision', p. 260.
[140] Bowers, *Crisis of Will*, pp. 34–5.
[141] Alford, 'The Figure of Repentance', 27–8.
[142] Middleton, 'Narration and the Invention of Experience', p. 158.
[143] Zeeman, '*Piers Plowman* in Theory', in Cole and Galloway, *Cambridge Companion*, p. 228.

434   MEDIEVAL ALLEGORY AS EPISTEMOLOGY

repeated acts of self-destruction. This also adds an additional layer of significance to Langland's pointed rejection of the kind of realist, materialist, fetishistic documentary poetics he encounters throughout Deguileville's corpus, as discussed above (Chapters 6.1 and 6.2). The tearing of pardons, the rejection of fossilized and ultimately idolatrous false certainties, the dematerialization of parchment into pure poverty, and the predicative and infinitely perfectible understanding of 'do-well' are all manifestations of Langland's characteristic 'fear of the tyranny of form', and much of this fundamental mental disposition in Langland seems to me to be explicable in terms of the latter's engagement with Deguileville. In this sense Langland appears to have embraced the meditative and penitential significance of the labour performed by Paul the Hermit or Deguileville's *Nattier* rather more determinedly and successfully than his French predecessor. It is primarily through his own meaningful experience of the failures of Deguileville's poetic project—failures that he managed to absorb, internalize, re-play, and finally exorcize in *Piers Plowman*—that Langland finally manages to lend his poem a structure that is not merely fluid and dynamic, but geared towards the potentially 'infinite' expansion of spiritual and epistemic possibilities. It is this readiness to contemplate and *experience* his own poetic failure that allows him to forge the re-visionary structural logic that Anne Middleton sees as such a 'pervasive feature of Langland's poetic technique', resulting in 'the elevation of a seemingly fortuitous or peripheral preoccupation into a conscious principle of form'.[144]

Langland's poem is thus unique in the European literary tradition of its time not so much because of its repeated instances of 're-visioning', but rather because of its adoption of a principle of structural slippage and fragmentation, bordering on implosion, as its core structuring principle. As Vance D. Smith puts it, 'The ruptures in the work's form are its essential mode of epistemological disclosure'.[145] Repeated structural breakdown becomes a mimesis of a trans-formative process: the poem is not only continuously metamorphosed through successive and interdependent instances of vision and re-vision, but finally points to the need to transcend form itself. In the context of a widely shared Aristotelian and hylomorphist understanding of form—where both matter and form are mutually actualizing principles, and where their conjunction is co-extensive with existence—*Piers Plowman* points resolutely beyond its own, actual and possible, real and hypothetical material forms, towards a 'place' or 'moment' where the poem ceases to exist by exhausting itself in an apocalyptic *plenitudo temporis*, in the 'fullness of time' (Gal. 4:4–7).[146] It is therefore significant and perfectly fitting that the tenacious counter-current of textual and formal 'un-makyng' that Langland's re-visionary project necessitates, should also become manifested as spatial unmaking, as a gradual

---

[144] Middleton, 'Acts of Vagrancy', p. 247 in *Written Work*.
[145] Smith, *Book of the Incipit*, p. 84.
[146] See J. A Burrow, 'God and the Fullness of Time in *Piers Plowman*'; on the temporal and conceptual elasticity of the expression *plenitudo temporis*, see also Cervone, *Poetics of the Incarnation*, pp. 134–7.

THE EXPERIENCE OF FAILURE AND THE ARCHITECTURE OF VISION 435

dissolution of the material conditions of ordinary earthly existence—a movement that is in the strictest sense eschatological. Since the poem's formal and spatial imaginary is dominated by the master-trope of the 'pilgrimage'—understood as a process of spatial, temporal, intellectual, affective, interpretive, textual, and cognitive movement and transformation—this pilgrimage is *necessarily* geared towards a resolution or closure that is strictly apocalyptic, and thus remains by definition beyond any of the real or hypothetical forms the poem does or could potentially acquire.

This idea is elaborated most fully during Piers the Plowman's own cryptic directions to his fellow pilgrims in *passus* V—a form of allegorical *transumptio* so radical that it unmakes its own forms and analogies, dematerializing the principle of imaginative visualization on which allegory relies for its ability to signify:

> 'Ac if ye wilneþ to wende wel, þis is þe wey þider:
> Ye moten go þourȝ Mekenesse, boþe men and wyues,
> Til ye come into Consciencie, þat Crist wit þe soþe,
> 　[...]
> And so boweþ forþ by a brook, 'Beþ-buxum-of-speche',
> Forto ye fynden a ford, 'Youre-fadres-honoureþ';
> 　*Honora patrem et matrem*, etc.
> Wadeþ in þat water and wassheþ yow wel þere,
> And ye shul lepe þe liȝtloker al youre lif tyme.
> And so shaltow se "Swere-noȝt-but-if-it-be-for-nede-
> And-nameliche-on-ydel-þe-name-of-God-almyȝty".'
> 　　　　　　　　　　　　　　　　　　　(B V.560–2; 566–71)

Unlike Deguileville's New Jerusalem—briefly glimpsed in a mirror, but unmistakably visual, plastic, and imaginatively tangible—Piers's 'courte' is entirely abstract, made of ethereal walls, and containing nothing but the pure light of the sun/Son:

> 'Thanne shaltow come to a court as cler as þe sonne.
> The moot is of Mercy þe manoir aboute,
> And alle þe walles ben of Wit to holden Wil oute.
> The kerneles ben of Cristendom þat kynde to saue,
> Botrased wiþ "Bileef-so-or-þow-beest-noȝt-y-saued";'
> 　　　　　　　　　　　　　　　　　　　(B V.585–9)

The ultimate purpose of this absurdly baroque itinerary is to exhaust any sense of spatial and geographical 'place', producing an inward turn that prepares the pilgrim to receive the gift of grace:

> 'And if Grace graunte þee to go in þis wise
> Thow shalt see in þiselue Truþe sitte in þyn herte

> In a cheyne of charyte, as þow a child were,
> To suffren hym and segge noȝt ayein þi sires wille.'
>
> (B V.605–8)

It is this same drive towards the cathartic, and ultimately *necessary* unmaking of ordinary conditions of existence in time and space that also motivates the poem's final episode—the destruction of the Barn of Unity, its effacement from the face of the earth, and the final, renewed departure of Conscience on yet another unspecified, as yet untold pilgrimage.

7

The Ends of Experience: Incarnation and Apocalypse

(*Piers Plowman* B XVI–XX)

Liber scientie scriptus est in codice;
liber experientie scriptus est in corpore;
liber conscientie scriptus est in corde[1]

Alain de Lille, 'Sermo in die cinerum'

The bulk of Langland's reflections on human ways of knowing, perceiving, and understanding is concentrated into the central portions of the poem, broadly stretching from the beginning of *passus* V to the end of *passus* XV in the B-text. It is also in these deeply introspective sections that Langland's engagement with Deguileville's *PVH* is most intense. As I have suggested over the course of the last two chapters, much of this extended middle section is concerned with 'finding out' newly intensified ways of knowing 'kyndely'.[2] But this preoccupation with *kynde knowing* ultimately traverses the entire poem from its very beginnings, where Will first complains to Holy Church that

> 'Yet have I no kynde knowinge', quod I, 'yet mote ye kenne me bettre
> By what craft in my cors it comseþ and where'.
>
> (B I.138–9)

Will's initial request for greater experiential knowledge, however, is immediately counteracted by Holy Church, as she berates Will for his insufficient book learning:

> 'Thow doted daffe!' quod she, 'dulle are þi wittes.
> To litel Latyn þow lernedest, leode, in þi youþe:
> *Heu michi quia sterilem duxi vitam iuuenilem!*'
>
> (B I.140–1)

---

[1] In Alain de Lille, *Textes inédits*, ed. Marie-Thérèse d'Alverny (Paris: Vrin, 1965), p. 268. For a discussion of the possible influence of Alan's notion on Langland, see Schmidt, 'Appendix to Chapter II: Two Notes on Langland, Alain de Lille and Bernard', in *Earthly Honest Things*, pp. 63–7.

[2] The point is also made by Harwood, *Piers Plowman and the Problem of Salvation*, pp. 4 and 29; Middleton, 'Narration and the Invention of Experience', p. 169. On 'kynde knowing' more broadly, see further Chapter 5, n. 52.

Medieval Allegory as Epistemology. Marco Nievergelt, Oxford University Press.
© Marco Nievergelt (2023). DOI: 10.1093/oso/9780192849212.003.0008

438   MEDIEVAL ALLEGORY AS EPISTEMOLOGY

Holy Church's response appears unhelpful and even infuriating, but it also functions as the inaugural instance of a characteristically 'Langlandian' move, rubbing the reader's face into the interdependence of experience and 'auctoritee'.[3] Similar moves are repeated throughout the poem, reminding us that learning and experiencing, reading and living, are finally two inextricable and mutually enabling opposites—'contreres choses, les unes des autres gloses' (*RR* 21,543–4, see Chapter 1.5).[4]

As scholars like Elizabeth Kirk and Anne Middleton have observed long ago, it seems undeniable that *Piers Plowman* itself, with its multiple visions and re-visions, takes the form of a gradually expanding, open-ended, and potentially infinite dialogue of 'experience and auctoritee':[5] the shortfall of experience prompts engagement with earlier authorities—further books in 'Latyn' or personified representatives of such learned traditions—which produces modified and enhanced experience in the dreamer/protagonist, in turn recorded as poetic text. A similar pattern of alternation obtains during the re-visionary phase: the poet's scrutiny of his own textual attempts to organize the world into meaningful structures produces further experiences through the act of reading, requiring Langland to reconsider established certainties and authorities—including those already crystallized or ventriloquized in his own poem—and in due course necessitating the promulgation of what Hanna calls 'second and third thoughts' recorded in written form.[6] The pattern is not merely reiterative but recursive, and hence circular or cyclical and potentially 'infinite'—exactly like the process through which, according to Piers Plowman, Dowel and Dobet will ultimately 'find out' Dobest with the assistance of Faith:

> '[He] seiþ that Dowel and Dobet arn two infinites,
> Whiche infinites with a feiþ fynden out Dobest,
> Which shal saue mannes soule—þus seiþ Piers þe Plowman'
> (B XIII.128–30)

Critical views on the significance of this interdependence of 'experience and auctoritee' at the heart of *Piers Plowman* differ widely. Does the principle enable a productive dialectic or merely a kind of solipsistic circularity? Is the poem 'recursive' and 'reiterative', or 'developmental' and 'progressive'?[7] For all its seemingly

---

[3] See also Harwood, 'Langland's *Kynde Knowyng* and the Quest for Christ', 242–3.

[4] A similar point is made also by Galloway, *Penn Commentary 1*, pp. 181–2.

[5] Kirk, *The Dream Thought of Piers Plowman*, pp. 33–40; Middleton, 'Narrative and the Invention of Experience', pp. 149–51.

[6] Hanna, 'The Different Versions and Revisions of *Piers Plowman*', p. 36.

[7] I employ the first set of terms as used by Denise N. Baker 'Pre-Empting Piers's Tearing of the Pardon', in her discussion of the Tearing of the Pardon episode, comparing the approaches of Traugott Lawler and Alastair Minnis (cf. Lawler, 'The Pardon Formula in *Piers Plowman*'; and Minnis, "Piers" Protean Pardon: The Letter and Spirit of Langland's Theology of Indulgences'). The second pair of

THE ENDS OF EXPERIENCE: INCARNATION AND APOCALYPSE   439

infinite circularity, the poem does nevertheless progress towards some form of intensified corporeal and experiential apprehension of spiritual truths. This process culminates in *passus* B XVI to XVIII, with the vision of the Tree of Charity and the Trinity, and with a performative retelling of a central episode from the sacred history of the Church, from the arrival of Abraham (Faith) and Moses (Hope) to the Incarnation of Jesus (Charity). Enabled by the momentary conjunction of the temporalities of an individual life and of sacred history, the vision culminates in the participative vision of Christ's Passion and the Harrowing of Hell in *passus* B XVIII—the poem's most beautifully ecstatic vision. At the heart of the poem's quest for *kynde knowyng*, then, lies the miracle of the Incarnation, the event through which the Word is made flesh, and which allows Will to transcend, albeit momentarily, the otherwise ubiquitous binarism of textuality and experience.[8]

In this conclusive chapter, I do not propose to offer a full, detailed account of the poem's final five *passus*. Instead, I simply propose to examine how Langland forges the overarching narrative logic of this final section of the poem out of his close engagement with Deguileville's poetry, with particular attention to the larger structural and conceptual shifts and ruptures that cut across his pilgrimage trilogy as a whole. In particular, I want to suggest that the final poem in the trilogy, the *Pèlerinage Jhesucrist*, provides Langland with a model for his own account of the Incarnation in *passus* B XVIII. More importantly, Langland also demonstrates a nuanced understanding of the highly problematic place of the *Pèlerinage Jhesucrist* in the evolving poetic vision of his predecessor. Langland recognizes that *PJC* essentially amounts to a disavowal of the poet's original didactic project as outlined in *PVH1*, implying a rejection of the salvific potential of allegorical narrative poetry more broadly in favour of a simple, meditative rehearsal of sacred history (Chapter 4). Langland attempts to circumvent a similar breakdown by integrating the account of Christ's life *within* the account of the life of his own pilgrim, Will. Once more Langland redeploys the narrative structures and poetic transition found in Deguileville's trilogy, but considerably modifies their significance, seeking to develop a more complex and articulated, evolving poetic vision out of his predecessor's internally fractured *œuvre* (Chapter 7.1).

The enhanced re-visionary dynamism of Langland's poem, however, also requires him to 'unmake' any sense of closure and resolution that accompanies the culminating vision of the Incarnation in *passus* B XVIII. The poem does so by returning once more to the level of human time, geared towards the promise of Christ's Second Coming, adumbrated but resolutely beyond the grasp of the poem's reiterated acts of narrative and visionary 'finding out'. As I will argue in the

---

terms is used by Middleton, 'Narrative and the Invention of Experience', p. 143. In the light of my own reading as presented here, I'm inclined to suggest that in *Piers Plowman* the recursive is inherently developmental.

[8] This ecstatic culmination is in turn interrupted by Will's awakening due to the sound of the church bells, calling all faithful to attend the Easter Liturgy. See further discussion below.

440   MEDIEVAL ALLEGORY AS EPISTEMOLOGY

second section of this chapter (Chapter 7.2), the partial unmaking of the climactic and historically central moment of the Incarnation takes the form of a return to the temporality of individual and collective human pilgrimage on earth. This movement is initially geared towards the establishment of more solid and durable forms of human religious structures and institutions—the building of the Barn of Unity. In a second phase, however, the poem swiftly moves towards the terminal implosion of such structures, with the arrival of the forces of Antichrist and the erosion of the salvific efficacy of the sacrament of penance. These events once more appear as refigured and re-imagined versions of important and traumatic episodes in Deguileville's trilogy, more specifically *PVH2*—the pilgrim's arrival within the safe precincts of the Ship of Religion, figure for the monastic enclosure and prefiguration of the Heavenly Jerusalem, followed by the dismantling of that idealized religious community. Yet Langland modifies the narrative and historical significance of such events. In *PVH2* the implosion of the religious community is registered as a traumatic, utterly contingent and intractably 'singular' personal event that disrupts the teleological and exemplary momentum of Deguileville's initial plan for producing an allegorical account of the paradigmatic 'pilgrimage of human life'. Langland, by contrast, adopts the formal elements of this irruption of the personal into the universal but modifies their significance, by placing them within a wider, more capacious narrative that remains at least implicitly providential, geared towards an awaited resolution that the poem itself declines to perform. As part of his efforts to accommodate individual and collective human failure within a fully 'apocalyptic' narrative, Langland recuperates the traumatic events that implode Deguileville's poem, assigning them a spiritually enabling, positive valence.[9]

This final stage of historical, institutional, and visionary unmaking is also counterpointed by a parallel process of authorial waning, which necessitates the gradual withdrawal of the poem's 'I' from its act of poetic 'makyng'. Since the poem's author/subject/protagonist is inextricably enmeshed with its own act of poetic 'makyng', and ultimately *produced by it*, the disappearance of such an 'I' marks the end of such a process—its *terminus* if not its ultimate *telos*. In parallel with the unmaking of human institutions and any associated forms of knowledge and devotion, both the agency of the human subject and its authorial programme are finally unmade. This notion is most fully explored during Will's brief but intense encounter with Elde, providing yet another instance of intertextual dialogue with Deguileville, which I discuss in the final section of this chapter (Chapter 7.3). The authority to signify is finally transferred away from written texts altogether, to be inscribed onto the metamorphosing, ageing, passive, powerless and mortal human

---

[9] I use the term 'apocalyptic' in the sense defined by Richard K. Emmerson, 'The Prophetic, the Apocalyptic, and the Study of Medieval Literature', in Raymond-Jean Frontain and Jan Wojcik, eds, *Poetic Prophecy in Western Literature* (Rutherford: Fairleigh Dickinson University Press 1984), pp. 40–54.

THE ENDS OF EXPERIENCE: INCARNATION AND APOCALYPSE   441

body of the poet/Will. This focus on the ailing, suffering, and perishable body of the individual Will crystallizes the limits and ends of experience—but not the end of the pilgrimage narrative, which ultimately projects the poem beyond itself, beyond the necessary formal and material limits of its real and possible bodies, including the decaying body of its visionary 'I'. While the body of the 'I' ceases to be the agent of transformative pilgrimage and embraces its passive position in respect to the suffering inflicted by the passing of time, gradually disappearing from the body of the poem, it is the figure of an increasingly elusive and depersonalized Conscience who finally enables the poem's movement forward, beyond its own formal and material 'endings' towards a further and final 'end', an apocalyptic vanishing point beyond the poem's horizon. It is through such a unique compounding of a terminal decline of the 'suffering' self on the one hand, and a continued commitment to an ongoing, depersonalized 'pilgrimage' on the other, that Langland manages to both conclude his poem and yet project it beyond the finite limits of its textual boundaries.[10]

1. Incarnation and Embodiment: Pilgrimage '*à rebours*'

While clearly Langland is working with a bewildering array of sources and intertexts throughout *passus* B XVI–XVIII, Deguileville's poetic corpus continues to play a major, albeit less easily discernible role in shaping the poem's overall movement and direction. The influence of the *Pèlerinages* on this section of the poem is visible not so much at the level of poetic detail, but rather in terms of the overall shift in register and expression, and at the level of the fundamental logic that underpins the poem's narrative and thematic developments. Accordingly in this section I will concentrate on such deeper tectonic shifts, and shall not attempt to demonstrate how exactly the details of *PJC*'s plot, imagery, and theology may have influenced Langland, as this is a task that would require a separate study in its own right. It is worth pointing out, however, that there are a number of close parallels, although none of these can provide conclusive evidence for Langland's use of *PJC* as a source in the narrow sense. So, for instance, Deguileville provides us with a vision of a tree laden with fruit, falling to the ground in the guise of Adam, and being snatched away to hell (*PJC* 65–84; cf. *PPl* B XVI.69–109); he rehearses a debate between Justice and Misericorde with Verite as arbiter (*PJC* 297–638; cf. *PPl* B XVIII.110–229); he repeatedly and insistently describes the Crucifixion as a chivalric joust and tournament (*PJC* 3314–18; 3349–56; 3369–87; e.g. *PPl* B XVIII.10–20); and he describes the Virgin as a tree laden with fruit, giving in to the irresistible weight of divine grace and willingly humbling itself by bending its branches to nourish the needy, in ways broadly reminiscent of

[10] See also Gruenler, *Piers Plowman and the Poetics of Enigma*, pp. 331–2, 350–66.

442   MEDIEVAL ALLEGORY AS EPISTEMOLOGY

Langland's Plant of Peace (*PJC* 3115–30; cf. *PPl* B I.152–7). A closer and more compelling parallel is provided by the effort of both poems to recount episodes from the chivalric *enfances* or 'apprenticeship' of Jesus—a highly idiosyncratic feature, and one that for Burrow produces one of Langland's 'most unconvincing passages' (cf. *PJC* 3369–78; 3433–9; 3451–6 and *PPl* B XIX.96–107).[11] Further parallels also run through the respective accounts of Gabriel's Annunciation and Mary's response in the two poems, where the Immaculate Conception is described in terms of Christ's dwelling in the 'chamber' of the Virgin's womb, attended by Mary herself as 'handmayden'/'chambriere' (*PJC* 1226–44; B XVI.90–102).

What appears more certain and more relevant, however, is that Langland registered and appropriated the formal and narrative logic that underpins the larger transition of poetic mode and expression that leads from *PVH1* (1331) to *PJC* (1358), via the intermediary stages marked by *PVH2* (1355) and *PA* (1356) (Chapter 4.3). Within the sequence of events that unfold through the fifth and sixth visions (B XVI–XVIII), Langland's poem thus reproduces the large-scale tonal and expressive shifts that move away from the allegorical and didactic mode of *PVH* towards the performative retelling of the Incarnation in *PJC*. This transition from allegory to history, from academic speculation to devotional performance, and from intellectual quest to typological and Christological vision is thus closely analogous to the larger shifts and reorientations that disrupt and reconfigure Deguileville's *Pèlerinage* 'trilogy' and its author's wider poetic corpus. However, what in Deguileville appears as an abrupt, disruptive and uncompromising realignment of poetic, expressive, and epistemic prerogatives, and ultimately requires the poet to abandon the allegorical mode of his original project, becomes in *Piers Plowman* a much more carefully and painstakingly articulated narrative transition, based on the slow, gradual metamorphosis of an original poetic project.

I have already argued in Chapter 4 that *PJC* signals a transition towards very different forms of poetic expression, which in turn presuppose very different models of language, interpretation, and understanding from those that underpin the first-person pilgrimage allegory of *PVH1* and *PVH2* in particular. More specifically, I argued that *PJC* can no longer be seen as an allegorical poem in the full sense, but rather functions as a performative retelling of the historical events from the life of Christ, and thus calls for a fundamentally different kind of interpretive engagement on the part of the reader. Rather than being an instructive allegorical narrative requiring decryption and interpretation, *PJC* invites the reader to re-vision a sequence of historical events from the life of Christ, witnessed and *experienced* vicariously through the dreamer/narrator's 'I' (see Chapter 4.3). While Deguileville provides no explicit authorial statement concerning the nature of

---

[11] Burrow, 'God and the Fullness of Time in *Piers Plowman*', 301.

THE ENDS OF EXPERIENCE: INCARNATION AND APOCALYPSE 443

PJC's relation to any of the earlier pilgrimage poems in his corpus, it is worth stressing that he makes a clear effort to draw attention to the highly unusual, and in some sense subversive nature of his final pilgrimage poem. In his response to Charity's embassy requesting him to descend to earth, Christ himself points out that the journey he is asked to undertake appears to turn on its head the normative Christian conception of 'pilgrimage':

[Christ:] 'Onques maiz ne fu pelerin,	'I have never been a pilgrim as yet; and
Et onques pelerinage	there never was a pilgrimage so strange
Ne fu tel ne si sauvage.	and wonderful. It is all turned upside
Du tout il sera a rebours,	down, since formerly all were required
Quar devers moi dëussent tous	to become pilgrims and come to me,
Droit venir et peleriner	but now it is my turn to go to them.'
Et il me faut a euz aler.'	
(*PJC* 844–50)	

Christ's pilgrimage on earth—like the Incarnation itself (cf. the *disputationes* with Nature in *PVH1* 1633–8 and *PJC* 1995–2146)—appears as an eminently unnatural event, subverting normative dynamics and expectations by enabling God to embark on a journey towards humankind. The first-person dreamer-pilgrim is no longer *acteur*, but rather the passive object and recipient of divine agency manifested in the form of Christ's Incarnation and pilgrimage. St John the Baptist too, later in the text, is similarly incredulous upon encountering God incarnate as a human pilgrim:

[John the Baptist:]	'What is this, Son of God, where are
'Qu'est ce, fil de Dieu, où vas tu?	you going? Have you become a
Es tu pelerin devenu?	pilgrim? You shouldn't be a pilgrim,
Pas ne doiz estre pelerin	since you are the final aim and
Qui es des pelerins la fin	destination where all pilgrims must go
Et le terme où doivent aler	and wander towards, at all times.'
En touz tempz et peleriner.'	
(*PJC* 1491–6)	

What *passus* B XVI–XVIII in Langland's poem share with Deguileville's transition from *PVH* to *PJC* is precisely such an underlying and fundamental shift in poetic, expressive, cognitive, and interpretive possibilities—although that shift is often implicit and concealed from open view in the dense and layered plot of Langland's dream narrative at this point. In Chapter 4, I developed a reading of *PJC* along the lines proposed by Sheingorn and Clark, who argue that 'By soliciting the active participation of the body and the senses, Guillaume's text pushes beyond an

444 MEDIEVAL ALLEGORY AS EPISTEMOLOGY

intellectual, readerly experience, proposing instead an affective and performative role'.[12] This ultimately produces a 'highly idiosyncratic dream vision in which the poet becomes a pilgrim who observes the life of Jesus as a pilgrim to earth, reporting what he sees and hears in a first-person narrative colored by his own emotional responses'.[13] The transition in the final five *passus* in Langland's poem has been described in nearly identical terms. Elizabeth Kirk, for instance, observes that Langland's account of the Incarnation is characterized by its emphasis 'not [on] the events themselves, but on the events as *witnessed*, the events as being *interpreted by observers*' (emphasis in original). Jane Hewett-Smith similarly characterizes the dreamer as 'more a witness of than a participant in these visions, saying and doing less than he has at any other point. [...] [N]arrative interest in Will's quest has been subsumed by an attention to the adventures of Christ, and Piers'.[14] Both poets can therefore be seen to produce a highly personal, defamiliarizing, and idiosyncratic retelling of the Life of Christ.

Also, in both cases this is achieved by shifting the focus away from a psychological and allegorical narrative mode to a historical and typological one.[15] This allows both poets to put an end to their analytical and introspective inquiries into the nature of the human relation to the divine, freeing up their respective poems to explore an embodied, sacramental, and participative experience of the enigmatic central event shaping this relation: the miracle of the Incarnation, 'of Good Friday þe storye' (B XIII.447), which for Patience constitutes the only legitimate subject matter for truly godly 'minstrales' (B XIII.431–56). Crucially, however, in Deguileville this implies a disavowal of the poet's original poetic project, while in Langland this transition takes the form of yet another painstaking reconfiguration of Will's ongoing quest.

In Langland this transition from the primarily dialectical, psychological, and allegorical mode towards an increasingly historical and typological mode of narrative is first signalled during the poem's second inner dream, as the vision of the Tree of Charity slowly metamorphoses into a retelling of the historical circumstances of its growth and development. The scene described is that the Fall of Adam, and the damnation of the various Old Testament prophets, all figured as

---

[12] Clark and Sheingorn, 'Performative Reading', pp. 138–9.

[13] Clark and Sheingorn, 'Rewriting Joseph in the Life of Christ', p. 66.

[14] Kirk, 'Langland's Narrative Christology', p. 22; Kathleen M. Hewett-Smith, '"Nede hath no lawe:" Poverty and the De-Stabilization of Allegory in the Final Visions of *Piers Plowman*', in Kathleen M. Hewett-Smith, ed., *William Langland's Piers Plowman: A Book of Essays* (London: Routledge, 2001), pp. 233–53, 237.

[15] I therefore disagree with Hewett-Smith's contention that *passus* XVIII increasingly relies on 'a more powerfully intellectualized (and intellectualizing) form of the [allegorical] mode', p. 238—a reading that largely results from her readiness to subsume typology within allegory. This does not detract, however, from the validity of Hewett-Smith's important argument concerning the terminal 'destabilization of allegory' that occurs in the final two *passus*, which I discuss below.

THE ENDS OF EXPERIENCE: INCARNATION AND APOCALYPSE   445

metaphorical 'fruit' falling from the tree only to be snatched away by the Devil under the unforgiving standards of Old Testament Justice:[16]

> For euere as þei dropped adoun þe deuel was redy,
> And gadrede hem alle togidres, boþe grete and smale—
> Adam and Abraham and Ysaye þe prophete,
> Sampson and Samuel, and Seint Johan þe Baptist;
> Bar hem forþ boldely—nobody hym lette—
> And made of holy men his hoord in *Limbo Inferni*,
>
> (B XVI.79–84)

The scene ultimately establishes the historical reasons that necessitate the Incarnation and the establishment of the *Lex Cristi* (B XVII.72), a new dispensation of Charity and forgiveness that displaces the Old Law, and thus eventually enables the retrieval of the abducted fruit. The scene of the plenteous fruit falling from the Tree of Charity thus prepares the ground for the much fuller and more elaborate retelling and re-visioning of Old Testament typological history, in the shape of Will's encounter with the prophets Abraham/Faith (B XVI.167–271) and Moses/Hope (B XVII.1–47), in turn serving as a prelude to the encounter with the Samaritan (B XVII.48–352), and finally preparing us for Will's ecstatic visionary experience of the passion of Christ (Charity) in *passus* XVIII.

I shall not be discussing the details of Langland's treatment of the figures of Abraham and Moses at any length, but would simply like to offer a few considerations on Langland's decision to present the theological virtues of Faith and Hope in the guise of the historical figures of these two Old Testament prophets. It will be remembered that in Deguileville's *PVH* Faith and Hope are memorably represented as the pilgrim's Scrip and Staff, sacramental signs that provide the occasion for a detailed and extended exposition of their (meta-)allegorical significance (see Chapter 2.4). I also argued that both of these objects represent the hermeneutic processes that are fostered and theorized by Deguileville's poem as a whole, and it is accordingly appropriate that the stubborn literalist Rude Entendement should object to the pilgrim carrying these attributes (see Chapter 2.3). But the 'I' of the pilgrim-reader persona equally struggles to make sense of these attributes and 'use' them appropriately as part of his efforts to hone his own skills as an allegorical reader/*acteur*. Indeed, it is precisely because of the pilgrim's difficulties in understanding the significance of the central theological virtues of Faith and Hope, allegorized in the form of Scrip and Staff, that in *PVH2* Grace Dieu will resort to her notoriously convoluted trope, exhorting the pilgrim to place his eyes in his ears (*PVH2* 3515–24; see Chapter 3.5). This particular analogy appears to have been

---

[16] I echo in the carefully argued and nuanced account provided by Simpson, *Introduction*, pp. 165–76.

446   MEDIEVAL ALLEGORY AS EPISTEMOLOGY

a source of special irritation for Langland, who responded to Grace Dieu's arcane and convoluted attempts to 'explicate' her own figures with the same kind of impatience he usually reserves for overly zealous and ingenious scholastic *scrutatores* (B XV.55a), glossers (B X.194), 'Maistres' (B XIII.26 ff.) and 'freres and faitoures' (X.71; see Chapter 5.1).

It is significant that Langland should emphatically chose *not* to represent Faith and Hope as elaborately allegorical attributes to be explicated, but rather as historical persons to be encountered, and more specifically Old Testament Prophets who *embody*, rather than merely 'personifying', those virtues while also figuring typologically the advent of Christ/Charity. On the one hand this move is of a piece with Langland's wider response the more convoluted explicative manoeuvres of Deguileville's allegory. On the other hand this choice is motivated by the poem's wider reorientation towards an incarnational and sapiential poetics in the wake of the extended cognitive crisis that runs through *passus* X–XII. To be more precise, not only do Abraham and Moses function as typological figures whose appearance prepares for the coming of Christ that is to follow, but they also establish, through their very *personhood*, the centrality of an incarnational logic within the new signifying mechanisms that come to dominate Langland's poem in *passus* B XVI–XVIII.[17] Instead of continuing to rely on strictly allegorical, hermeneutic, and analytical methods for discovering Truth, with the arrival of Anima—'the integrated soul'—the poem moves into a different realm of embodied cognition and signification, shaped by a more radically enigmatic, participative, sapiential, and sacramental understanding of language, thought, and figuration. Accordingly, at the start of the vision of the Tree of Charity Will expresses his desire to 'savour'—sapientially and sacramentally—the taste of its fruit:

> I preide Piers to pulle adoun an appul, and he wolde,
> And suffre me to assaien what sauour it hadde.
>
> (B XVI.73–4)

At the heart of this new form of knowledge lies a deeply modified understanding of human personhood and subjectivity, ultimately enabled by the experience of Christ's Incarnation and the ensuing restoration of humanity's divine resemblance or *imago dei*. Rather than being fundamentally and terminally alienated, wandering through a region of semantic and ontological 'dissemblance', the individual human self is now absorbed within a larger narrative progression whose shape is determined by the paradigm of sacred history. The incarnational developments of the fifth vision ultimately enable an integration of the micro- and

---

[17] On 'personhood' as a defining characteristic of incarnational figuration, see especially Cervone, *Poetics of the Incarnation*, pp. 6–7, and on *Piers Plowman* specifically pp. 126–38.

macro-historical, of the personal and the cosmic within an apocalyptic perspective. But instead of signalling an abandonment of psychological allegory in favour of historical typology, in Langland's poem the two levels of understanding are effectively integrated within each other. Accordingly, in Simpson's formulation, '[u]nderstanding, or even experience of the passage from the Old to the New Covenant is as much a part of self-hood in Langland's view, as are the functional aspects of the soul (e.g. thinking, desiring). The self, that is, is in its most profound realisation a historical entity.'[18] The poem's first synoptic account of the Incarnation (B XVI.95–166) accordingly marks a crucial transition in the formation or trans-formation of Will's own soul, preparing it to re-vision experientially the foundational events of sacred history with the coming of Abraham, Moses, and Christ (B XVI.167–XVIII.426).

The progressive emergence of an incarnational poetics in this final quarter of *Piers Plowman* has been the object of much excellent recent scholarship, reaffirming the structural and conceptual centrality of Christ's historical and sacramental body in Langland's poetic vision and in Will's quest.[19] I shall not add to these discussions, but would simply like to point out that Langland's poem in this respect is particularly remarkable in comparison with Deguileville's *Pèlerinages*-'trilogy', whose own account of the life of Christ provides Langland with an important source of inspiration. In the 'trilogy' the incarnational logic is primarily explored in *PJC*, while being foreshadowed already in the closing sections of *PVH*, with the ABC prayer and the conversion to a new language of sapiential and liturgical participation in the presence of the divine within the monastery. Rather than appearing as a culmination of the pilgrim's preceding efforts, however, this transition is presented as a conspicuous disruption and even subversion of the normative logic of human pilgrimage that sustains the original allegorical project of *PVH* (see Chapter 4.3). As I have argued in preceding chapters, then, this ultimately amounts to a disavowal of the whole anthropology and epistemology that underpins Deguileville's first allegorical vision, conceived as a hermeneutic and spiritual pilgrimage of the human subject. Langland, by contrast, manages to articulate a progressive integration of ordinary ways of knowing, reading, and understanding with more enigmatic and incarnational ones, rather than simply opposing these two modes of thought and representation. Langland does this by returning once more to the inaugural 'Deguilevillian' master-trope of the mirror, with Will's oblique apprehension of Christ's lineaments 'as myself in a mirour' (B XV.162).

As already suggested (Chapter 6.3), this key moment in the poem points to Langland's continuing investment in an evolving and distinctive specular logic

---

[18] Simpson, *Introduction*, p. 166.
[19] See especially Gruenler, *Poetics of Enigma*, pp. 271–386; Cervone, *Poetics of the Incarnation*; Aers, *Sanctifying Signs*, pp. 29–51; ibid., 'The Sacrament of the Altar'; Kirk, 'Langland's Narrative Christology'.

448 MEDIEVAL ALLEGORY AS EPISTEMOLOGY

that pervades the entirety of the fifth vision.[20] It is worth remembering that both Deguileville and Langland conspicuously associate Christ with such an enigmatic mirror, and that both poems engage in sustained and complex ways with the wider specular and enigmatic logic of 1 Cor. 13:12 in particular. It was already seen that Deguileville presents Christ himself as a literal mirror, carried as a pommel on top of the Pilgrim's Staff of Hope (*PVH1* 3691–3; see Chapter 2.3). As I argued in Chapter 2, this motif serves as an emblem of the poem's underlying allegorical hermeneutics, refracting the Heavenly Jerusalem which in turn functions as a marker of semiotic closure and eschatological fulfilment. Also for Will, who has long lived 'in londe', the mirror serves as guiding instrument, but it does not, crucially, function allegorically in the strict sense. Rather, it provides an instance of a different kind of Christological allegory: instead of refracting the Heavenly City—itself an abstract allegorical construct—it refracts the human lineaments of Christ/Will, reaffirming the paradigmatic role of the Incarnation in a process of self-discovery or self-recovery. Following the lead of Deguileville's poem but modifying its specular logic, this oblique apprehension of Christ allows Will to discern his own true self as a dislocated reflection of the *imago dei*, marking the proper beginning of a process leading to its recovery, culminating in the full vision of the Incarnation during the sixth vision in *passus* XVIII. The notion of the enigmatic Pauline mirror plays a central role both in shaping the trajectory of Will's quest at this particular moment, but also in structuring Langland's poetics as a whole. In her discussion of the C text revisions for this passage—where Will's evocation of a reflection 'in a mirour' in B (XV.162) is replaced by the use of the adjective 'figuratyfly' (C XVI.293)—Cristina Maria Cervone stresses the pointedly Augustinian undertones of this revision, on the basis of Augustine's definition of enigma as an obscure subspecies of allegory (*De trinitate* XV.9.15). Cervone thus stresses the linguistic and hermeneutic undertones of Langland's reading of St Paul via Augustine, alongside the more strictly incarnational interpretation already discussed (see Chapter 6.4): Langland here can be seen thinking through a cluster of associations cutting across the domains of '[l]anguage, embodiment, cognition'.[21] This marks the passage as a major nexus in Langland's evolving reflection on the ability of language to signify transcendence, in the manner of a 'mirror', associating visual imagination and verbal, allegorical figuration in an incarnational context.

Langland's evident interest in signification—and in *allegorical* signification more specifically—is particularly resonant in the present context, since it suggests that he is once more reconsidering the specular and figurative potentialities of allegorical writing in dialogue with Deguileville. Langland redeploys Deguileville's foundational, meta-allegorical motif of the mirror, but also responds

---

[20] See especially Gruenler, *Poetics of Enigma*, pp. 13–29, 271–386.
[21] Cervone, *Poetics of the Incarnation*, pp. 26–31 (31). On Augustine and enigma, see also Gruenler, *Poetics of Enigma*, pp. 194–206, 282–311.

THE ENDS OF EXPERIENCE: INCARNATION AND APOCALYPSE 449

to Deguileville's growing unease with his own poem, presented as 'uns biaux miroir de sauvement' (Chapter 2, epigraph). But while the reduplication of the motif in *PVH2*—as 'miroir de conscience' (*PVH2* 15,429) and 'parole d'adulacion' (*PVH2* 15,331)—crystallizes the Cistercian poet's growing anxieties about the slippages of allegory (see Chapter 4.5), Langland's more strongly Christological use of the Pauline mirror at this juncture expresses much greater confidence in the processes of intellectual speculation and spiritual transformation enabled by this kind of enigmatic allegorical figuration. Langland's very invocation of the 'mirour' thus amounts to a renewed profession of faith in the transformative signifying powers of allegory as a whole: where Deguileville's poem becomes paralysed in a limbo of signification, Langland reaffirms his confidence in the figurative possibilities of the allegorical imagination as a means of access to the divine. As Curtis Gruenler has recently argued, Langland's entire poetic project can in fact be understood as an exploration of an overarching 'Poetics of Enigma', nourished and structured by his recursive engagement with the motif of St Paul's mirror from 1 Cor. 13:12. In providing an extended meditation on the 'enigmatic' nature of the Christian self as *imago dei* throughout the fifth vision, Gruenler argues, Langland ultimately replays Augustine's paradigmatic experience of spiritual awakening, as recounted in Book XV of the *De trinitate* and more fully in the *Confessions*: 'There [Augustine] extends scriptural enigma from the most local (a brief proverb) to whole narratives and, indeed, to the structural relation between the Old and New Testaments, to the human person itself—made in God's image and remade in the Incarnation of the Word—and to all of God's work in History. Langland's dream follows a similar trajectory.'[22]

In Langland, this movement towards more intense, enigmatic, experiential and ultimately incarnational ways of knowing is inextricably tied to the figure Piers Plowman. The significance of Piers in the poem, and his role in precipitating the second inner dream, are complex and much debated, and I do not aim to explain its rich and possibly inexhaustible meanings.[23] In the context of a discussion of the relations between *PJC* and *Piers Plowman*, however, Piers's role as the mediator or prism for the access to enigmatic knowledge made available through Christ's Incarnation appears particularly important.[24] It seems relevant to me that Langland's figure of Piers Plowman radically and deliberately eschews any stable 'identification'—being neither a firmly identifiable historical person, nor a personification of a stable abstract concept. Accordingly the significance of Piers cannot be fully understood in either typological or allegorical terms. As Daniel Murtaugh

---

[22] Gruenler, *Poetics of Enigma*, p. 207.

[23] For a useful overview of critical views, see for instance Hanna, *Penn Commentary 2*, pp. 185–9, 192–3; Lawler *Penn Commentary 4*, pp. 304–5.

[24] See e.g. Aers, *Piers Plowman and Christian Allegory*, p. 95, for whom Piers is 'the visionary mediator through whom we expect to come to Christ', and Gruenler, *Poetics of Enigma*, who sees him as 'the poem's central figure of [. . .] participation in Christ', p. 217, see also ibid. pp. 224–32 and *passim*.

observes, 'Piers functions in the poem not exactly as a personification, but as a realization or discovery of Christ operating in man, individually or in society'.[25] Again comparison with Deguileville is instructive in shedding light on Langland's motives for creating this idiosyncratic figure, whose very *personhood*, I suggest, is specifically designed to assert the centrality of the Incarnation of Christ, as the Word made flesh, in enabling the human *viator* to transcend his ordinary cognitive faculties.

I have previously argued that Deguileville's account of the pilgrim's journey towards the New Jerusalem is essentially the account of the failure of active ways of knowing, ultimately forcing the pilgrim into an utterly passive position where he becomes the recipient of the action of divine Grace, through the gift of the ABC Prayer, which in turn allows him to petition the Virgin to intercede on his behalf. Even Deguileville's earliest poem, *PVH1*, therefore ends with the renunciation of any pursuit of active ways of knowing, precipitating the *viator* into state of passive fideistic retrenchment. This condition of impotent expectancy becomes the dominant perspective from which all of Deguileville's subsequent poetry is written. Langland, who appears conspicuously *un*-interested in traditional notions of Marian devotion,[26] appears to have found Deguileville's highly traditional interest in the figure of the Virgin rather limiting, in the sense that Deguileville's tireless appeals to her intercessory role go hand in hand with the kind of passive fideism that Langland's poem tries so hard to eschew, by seeking to balance active and passive ways of knowing in more nuanced and dynamic fashion (see Chapters 5.3 and 6.3). In this sense the figure of Piers Plowman appears as Langland's response to the perceived limitations of the far more traditional but limiting appeal to the Virgin in the poetry of his French predecessor.

In contrast to the implicit, absent, but central presence of the Virgin in Deguileville's poem, Piers Plowman not only intervenes in the narrative itself through his personal and corporeal presence, but also serves as a paradigm of *human* action as well as divine action. While Piers famously and mysteriously functions as a figure of Christ incarnate—*Petrus, id est, Christus* (B XV.212)—and thus constitutes the 'other' in relation to which we are invited to measure the human will/Will's alienation and singularity, Piers Plowman now also becomes the vanishing point of Will's own subjectivity on his quest for Truth. In Murtaugh's words, 'Piers, embodies "the single Truth" whose "lack" constitutes Will's subjectivity'.[27] Where Deguileville relies on the intangible but powerful agency of the

---

[25] Daniel Murtaugh, '"As myself in a mirour": Langland between Augustine and Lacan', *Exemplaria* 19.3 (2007), 351–85 (378).

[26] See also Watson, 'Grace holds the "Clicket" to the Heavenly "Wiket"', 212–14, on Langland's tendency to picture the Virgin not in terms of her personhood but rather in terms of depersonalized architectural allegory.

[27] Murtaugh, '"As myself in a mirour"', 354.

THE ENDS OF EXPERIENCE: INCARNATION AND APOCALYPSE   451

Virgin as an intercessory mediating figure to be petitioned by a hapless pilgrim, Langland uses Piers as a more dynamic, protean if elusive agent of human contact with the divine, highlighting precisely the unexpected, fluid and enigmatic nature of that reciprocal relationship and of human subjectivity itself. Piers Plowman therefore offers Will the possibility of a momentary identification with Christ through suffering, enabling 'a kind of hypostatic union'.[28] It is therefore significant that soon after inquiring 'what is charite' (XV.149), and after catching an indirect glimpse of Christ 'as myself in a mirour' (XV.162, cf. 1 Cor.13:12), Will should finally be led to a fuller and more vivid vision of Charity in the mirror provided by the second inner dream, through the mediating agency of yet another Christ-like figure, Piers Plowman himself.

At the heart of Piers's mediating role is his capacity for understanding the redemptive significance of 'suffering'—a central concern that recurs repeatedly during Will's extended process of conversion in the wake of his first inner dream, as I've argued in what precedes (see Chapters 5.2 and 6.3). But Langland's understanding of 'suffering' conspicuously eschews the kind of abject passivity embraced by Deguileville's pilgrim, as the figure of Piers allows him to explore the spiritually enabling, paradoxical agency of suffering. As Anima submits, only Piers comprehends the true significance of suffering, and it is only by participating in his knowledge that the true meaning of Charity can become apparent:

> 'Clerkes haue no knowyng', quod he, 'but by werkes and
> by wordes.
> Ac Piers þe Plowman parceyueþ more depper
> That is þe wille, and wherefore þat many wight suffreþ:
> > *Et vidit Deus cogitationes eorum.*
> > > > (B XV.198–200a)

Anima's affirmation simultaneously establishes both Piers Plowman's role in lending positive spiritual significance to such suffering, and his ability to reveal to Will himself the nature of the human 'will'. It is ultimately Piers Plowman who allows Will to gain more advanced self-knowledge, recognizing his own suffering self as functionally analogous with Christ's. It is therefore by becoming the passive object of Piers's knowledge that the will/Will can develop a new form of agency.

The logic of Langland's citation from Luke 11:17 associating Piers with Christ—*Et vidit Deus cogitationes eorum*—seems less than transparent, but James Simpson has invoked an important parallel and possible source to illuminate its significance. Referring to Augustine's discussion of enigma in book XV of the *De trinitate* (8–10), Simpson identifies a cluster of further biblical texts that appear to inform

---

[28] Harwood, *The Problem of Belief*, p. 138. See also Harwood's wider discussion, pp. 135–56.

452 MEDIEVAL ALLEGORY AS EPISTEMOLOGY

Langland's thinking at this juncture (Matt. 9:2–4; Luke 5:21–2), and points out that Augustine associates Jesus's ability to read thoughts with the enigmatic mirror from 1 Cor. 13:12.[29] It is this specular logic that accounts for the paradoxical, baffling yet productive circularity implied by the passage, where Piers Plowman's knowledge of the 'will' enables both an intensified self-knowledge and an intensified knowledge of Christ and Charity by the individual human will/Will—through the agency of Piers/Christ himself. 'Will can know charity [. . .], only by knowing Piers, since Piers knows the will. Will, that is, can know charity only by knowing the figure that knows him, Piers'.[30] The images and biblical quotations brought into play here establish the fundamental reciprocity of these multiple acts and experiences of knowing, pointing forward towards ideas that remain merely latent and implicit in Langland's truncated quotation from 1 Cor. 13. The full Pauline quotation, whose second half is omitted by Langland at XV.162a, in effect supplements the idea of enigmatic knowledge with the promise of an eschatological fulfilment, whose modalities are necessarily circular and paradoxical:

'We see now through a glass in a dark manner: but then face to face. Now I know in part: *but then I shall know even as I am known.*' (my emphasis)

Retrospectively, then, from the vantage point of XV.200a where *vidit Deus cogitationes eorum*, Langland's earlier allusion to 1 Cor. 13:12 is all the more powerful for its refusal to complete the Pauline quotation. By withholding the second half of the passage Langland ultimately provides a formal poetic mimesis of the promised, but as-yet-unfulfilled availability of direct, complete, and perfectly symmetrical reciprocal knowledge experienced 'face to face', deferred to an unspecified and as yet *unspoken* and *unwritten* apocalyptic future.

At the heart of Langland's definition of such paradoxical and reciprocal total knowledge, simultaneously active and passive, lies Piers's ability to truly discern the suffering of the will/Will. This ability to understand suffering is not merely theoretical and disembodied, but is characterized by Piers's ability to perceive 'more depper' (B X.199), implying a physical, and literally 'com-passionate' ability to share in the suffering of the will/Will.[31] It is this ability to participate in the suffering of the will that ultimately lies at the heart of Langland's understanding of Charity. This seemingly incidental mention of 'suffering' prepares the ground for Anima's fuller exposition of the nature of Charity, defined in terms of a full

---

[29] James Simpson, "'*Et vidit deus cogitaciones eorum*:" A Parallel Instance and Possible Source for Langland's Use of a Biblical Formula at B.XV.200a', *Notes and Queries* n.s. 33 (1986), 9–13. See also Gruenler, *Poetics of Enigma*, pp. 282–95, and Lawler, *Penn Commentary 4*, p. 189.

[30] Simpson, *Introduction*, p. 164.

[31] Kirk, '"Who suffreth more than God"', pp. 100–2.

THE ENDS OF EXPERIENCE: INCARNATION AND APOCALYPSE   453

comprehension of the paradigmatic significance of Christ's own suffering during the passion, and the latter's role in bringing about the Atonement:

> 'The mooste liflode þat he [i.e. Charity] lyueth by is loue in Goddes
> passion;
>   [...]
> Amonges Cristene men þis myldenesse sholde laste,
> In alle manere angres haue þis at herte—
> That þoiȝ þei suffrede al þis, God suffred for vs moore
> In ensample we sholde do so, and take no vengeuance
>   [...]
> Ac he suffrede in ensample þat we shulde suffren also,
> And seide to swiche þat suffre wolde þat *Pacientes vincunt.*
> *Verbi gratia*', quod he, and verray ensamples manye.'
>
> (B XV.255, 258–61, 266–8)

Piers's mediating operation in providing access to this new, enlarged and spiritually enabling understanding of human 'suffering' is crucial precisely because it tends to dissolve the boundaries of individual agency and even identity. It does so by introducing the notion that it is precisely by *being known* (by God, who sees our every thought) that humans can attain a higher level of (self-)knowledge. The person of Piers thus serves as a fluctuating and specular point of contact between the human and the divine, a third term or prism through which man can come to experience the redemptive 'action' of the divine, itself paradoxically achieved though Christ's own 'passion'. Man thus comes to share—graciously and gratuitously—in the paradoxical, utterly illogical experience of passion as a means to action, acting by being acted upon, triumphing through suffering. This begins to unpack the full spiritual meaning of the Incarnation, understood as the manifestation of a metaphysical paradox whereby the individual attains a higher degree of agency precisely by allowing itself to *suffer*, to be *acted upon*. It is precisely through such a carefully structured exploration of the paradoxical, and ultimately joyful, reciprocal agency of 'passion' that Langland manages to avert the passive fideism that had ultimately imploded Deguileville's allegorical project. As Jessica Rosenfeld quite rightly observes in a slightly different context, this is quite simply 'an image of a union that Deguileville could not or did not want to dream of'.[32]

This notion of suffering is picked up once more, and given its final and fullest development during the climactic description of the Crucifixion during the sixth vision in *passus* XVIII, where the full force of the paradox of 'passion-as-action' becomes apparent. It is precisely through Christ's Incarnation and passion that the significance of suffering is further transformed and augmented, opening the

---

[32] Rosenfeld, *Love after Aristotle*, p. 133.

454   MEDIEVAL ALLEGORY AS EPISTEMOLOGY

doors to a climactic cognitive-affective experience that transcends the ordinary binaries of joy and woe:

> 'And I shal preie', quod Pees, 'her peyne moot haue ende,
> And wo into wel mowe wende at þe laste.
> For hadde þei wist of no wo, wele had þei noȝt knowen;
> For no wighte woot what wele is, ȝat neuere wo suffrede,
>   [...]
> So God þat bigan al of his goode wille
> Bicam man of a mayde mankynde to saue,
> And suffrede to be sold, to se þe sorwe of deying,
>   [...]
> And siþþe he suffred [Adam] synne, sorwe to feele—
> To wite what wele was, kyndeliche to knowe it.
> And after, God auntrede hymself and took Adames kynde
> To wite what he haþ suffred in þre sondry places,
> Boþe in heuene and in erþe—and now til helle he þenkeþ,
> To wite what al wo is, þat woot of alle joye.'
>   (B XVIII.202–5, 211–13, 219–24)

The affirmation of the spiritual efficacy of suffering thus produces what is paradoxically 'the most joyous *passus* of the B version', where 'suffering as a path towards pleasurable knowledge is emphasised'.[33] The Chiastic structure of the entire passage also reprises the specular and reciprocal logic elaborated on the basis of St Paul's enigmatic mirror from 1 Cor. 13:12 throughout the fifth vision. The passage establishes not only a symmetrical correspondence between the knowledge of joy and suffering, but also between God's understanding of man and man's knowledge of God, mediated by the prism of Piers Plowman. Just as Christ's desire to understand the intensity of both human suffering and joy necessitates his corporeal experience of the human condition, providing Christ himself with an opportunity to effect 'an extension of God's very nature',[34] so Will's understanding of Charity and of his own divine similitude can only pass through a similarly 'kynde' apprehension of Christ's suffering during his vision of the Incarnation and Passion. Peace's insistence that Christ's suffering is motivated by his desire 'To wite what wele was, kyndeliche to knowe it' (B XVIII.220), strongly suggests that such a knowledge also becomes the final vanishing point of Will's own obsessively reiterated desire for *kynde knowying*. The earlier insight into the paradoxical reciprocity of man and God explored in *passus* XV now grows into a still more enigmatic experience that annuls the significance of binary opposites that commonly structure

---

[33] For such a reading of the *passus*, see Rosenfeld, *Love after Aristotle*, pp. 131–4 (131).
[34] Kirk, 'Langland's Narrative Christology', p. 28. See also Mann, 'Eating and Drinking in *Piers Plowman*', pp. 41–2, and Aers, *Christian Allegory*, pp. 107–9.

THE ENDS OF EXPERIENCE: INCARNATION AND APOCALYPSE   455

rational thought, as the experience of suffering itself becomes intrinsically joyous, and man's understanding of divine suffering can finally begin to mirror God's own compassionate understanding of the human condition.

It is not accidental that in his effort to steer clear of the passive fideism that implodes Deguileville's quest for knowledge Langland should once more engage, this time consciously and deliberately, with the intractable and paradoxical epistemology of the *Roman de la Rose*. Langland's analysis of the inextricable interdependence of the experiences of human joy and suffering in *passus* XVIII effectively provides the most important and conspicuous example of direct intertextual echo of the *Rose* in the whole of *Piers Plowman*.[35] More importantly, this citation is merely the tip of an iceberg, pointing to a much deeper and more sustained, albeit often submerged engagement with Jean de Meun's principle of 'contreres choses / qui sont les unes des autres gloses' (see Chapter 1.5).[36] Langland of course tweaks and adapts the significance of Jean's epistemology of 'contrary things' to his own immediate purposes, but like Jean he foregrounds the distinctly experiential and non-rational nature of such knowledge of/through contraries.[37] So, while the principle of opposition of 'contrary things' in the *Rose* is unmistakeably articulated in terms of Aristotelian demonstration and definition, the entire system of Aristotelian *scientia* that they connote is used in purely figurative, and ultimately 'ironic' or 'allegorical' sense:

Ainsinc va des contreres choses,	The nature of opposites is that one
les unes sunt des autres gloses	glosses the other: if you want to define
et qui l'une an veust defenir,	one, you must be mindful of the other,
de l'autre li doit souvenir,	or else you will never achieve a
ou ja, par nule antancion,	definition, however good your
n'i metra diffinicion;	intentions. Unless you know both, you
car qui des .II. n'a connoissance, ja n'i	will never understand the difference
connoistra differance, san quoi ne peut	between them, without which no
venir en place	proper definition can be made.
diffinicion que l'an face.	
(*RR* 21,543–52)	

As a result, the binary terms and definitional processes that are brought into play are effectively deconstructed. Langland redeploys a closely analogous idea in Peace's speech, in a statement that ultimately reaffirms the principle that underlies the *Rose* as a whole.

---

[35] Barney agrees, noting that 'the passage in the *Rose* [. . .] provides so close a parallel as to seem a direct source', in *Penn Commentary 5*, p. 52.

[36] On the pervasive presence of dialectical and oppositional structures of binary contraries throughout *passus* XVIII as a whole, see also Barney, *Penn Commentary 5*, pp. 4–5.

[37] See also White, *Nature and Salvation*, esp. pp. 55–9.

456 MEDIEVAL ALLEGORY AS EPISTEMOLOGY

A similar kind of logical paradox also runs through Raison's earlier promise in the *Rose* to expound the nature of human love and desire by demonstrating the un-demonstrable:

Or te demonstreré sanz fable
chose qui n'est pas demonstrable,
si savras tantost sanz science
et connoistras sanz connoissance
ce qui ne peut estreseü
ne demonstré ne conneü.
  (*RR* 4249–54)

Now I shall soberly demonstrate to you
something that is not demonstrable,
and you will soon know without
knowing and understand without
understanding that which cannot be
known or demonstrated or understood.

Here again the emphasis is placed on the processual and experiential nature of cognition—not on its strictly 'scientific' and demonstrative status, as the use of Aristotelian terminology would suggest. The nature of *eros*, it seems, can never be grasped by the tools of demonstrative Aristotelian science, but only through the experience of an inconclusive, equivocal poetic fiction such as that crystallized by Raison's own exposition, and which implicitly infuses the entirety of the *Rose*. Beneath the surface of the language of Aristotelian syllogistic demonstration, used in purely sophistical fashion, Jean's *Rose* surreptitiously affirms the primacy of both experiential and poetic knowledge in the quest to understand the nature of desire. In Morton's words, 'The *Rose* aims to make its audience experience and thus understand (at least partially) the limits of human knowledge and the workings of desire that rational argument cannot adequately explain.'[38]

At this stage in the poem Langland reconnects with the *Rose*'s interest in paradoxical forms of knowledge precisely because this enables him to move beyond the rather more limiting, expository and explicative forms of knowledge pursued by Deguileville's allegorical poetics. As I argued in Chapter 2, Deguileville's complex and conflicted response to the *Rose* was determined not so much by the erotic subject matter of its allegorical quest narrative, but rather by the poem's radically equivocal hermeneutics and its deliberate deferral of cognitive and interpretive closure. In effect, Jean de Meun's real stroke of genius consisted precisely in associating referential indeterminacy with the erotics of reading and knowing, producing his inimitably 'outrageous miscegenation of sexuality and theology'[39] as part of a wider speculative dialectic of 'contrary things'. In resisting the intrinsically equivocal polysemy of poetic figuration, however, Deguileville ultimately also closes the doors on any opportunity to represent means of knowing and understanding that exceed ordinary, rational, and univocal means of thought, understanding, and representation—and this despite his insistent commitment

---

[38] Morton, *The 'Roman de la Rose' in its Philosophical Context*, p. 35.
[39] Kay, *Place of Thought*, p. 181.

THE ENDS OF EXPERIENCE: INCARNATION AND APOCALYPSE   457

to the ostensibly 'sapiential', higher forms of knowledge represented by personifications such as Grace Dieu and Sapience (on this see Chapter 4.3). Succinctly
put, Deguileville's entire allegorical project militates against the kind of paradoxical and 'illogical' knowledge produced by the experience of interdependent
contraries advocated in the closing sections of the *Rose*. Instead, he sets out to
firmly disambiguate between traditional binaries such as sign and referent, intellect and sensuality, spiritual longing and sexual appetite, soul and body, theology
and obscenity.

Returning to Langland, then, it is revealing that he should return to the *Rose*
precisely at this moment in Will's quest, which moves beyond ordinary ways of
knowing based on binary structures of rational thought, and marks the most
exalted experience of spiritual vision in the entire poem. This may seem a rather
surprising move given that the passage on 'contreres choses' in the *Rose* had
effectively served as a prelude to the poem's most insistently obscene episode:
the allegorical description of the pilgrim's defloration of the Rose. But Langland
appears to have appreciated that the very carnality of the *dénouement* in the *Rose*
is in turn subjected to this same logic of knowledge through/by contraries: it is
not *despite*, but precisely *because* of its outrageously pornographic nature that the
defloration figures a truly incorporeal, spiritual consummation that lies beyond
ordinary representation and understanding. As Alice Lamy has argued in her
analysis of Jean's engagement with negative, apophatic theology, 'The poem's conclusion is too deeply sexualized not to be also profoundly mystical'.[40] Langland
accordingly exploits the logical paradox of 'contreres choses' found in the *Rose*
to characterize the enigmatic nature of the Incarnation, signalling an insight that
transcends and explodes the more ordinary, binary human understanding of both
joy and woe. In doing so Langland also implicitly validates the *Rose*'s claim to
channel a higher form of spiritual vision through its subversion of ordinary mechanisms of cognition, using the *Rose*'s own principle of 'contrary things' to transcend
and explode Deguileville's pious attempt to regulate language, thought, and representation. Just as Jean de Meun in the closing sections of the *Rose*, then, Langland's
Peace in *passus* XVIII advocates the pursuit of a kind of paradoxical and enigmatic
knowledge that violates the Aristotelian law of non-contradiction, and where the
experiences of joy and suffering are inextricably entangled and ultimately coincide.
The nature of such knowledge also has important repercussions on the structure
of the knowing subject. Again following the *Rose*, Langland in fact suggests that
the speculative and cognitive abilities of the human 'I' are amplified as a function
of its willingness to contemplate the infinitely perfectible, and thus radically reiterative nature of its own cognitive journey towards an encounter with the divine,
whose face is fleetingly glimpsed 'as myself in a mirour' (XV.162). Langland can

---

[40] Alice Lamy, 'The Romance of the Non-Rose: Echoes and Subversions of Negative Theology in
Jean de Meun's *Roman de la Rose*', in Morton and Nievergelt, pp. 194–210 (209).

458 MEDIEVAL ALLEGORY AS EPISTEMOLOGY

be seen, like the *Rose*, to 'stag[e] a continual movement between the dissolution of the self and its re-emergence, [representing] the knowledge it offers as a process without end rather than as a series of easily assimilable teachings'.[41]

For Langland this becomes a brilliant way of representing the process whereby Will may apprehend—as opposed to 'defining' or 'demonstrating'—the incommensurable nature of God's gift of Grace and Charity that occurs through Christ's Incarnation. The *Rose* again appears to have provided Langland with powerful inspiration pointing in this direction, by representing the Incarnation as the one single event in history eluding the 'comprehension' of even the sharpest of minds:

C'est la santance de la letre	This is the meaning of the text that
que Platon voust ou livre metre,	Plato desired to include in his book
[...]	[...]. And yet he could not say enough,
Si n'an pot il pas assez dire,	being incapable of understanding
car il ne peüst pas soffire	perfectly that which only a virgin's
a bien parfetemant antandre	womb could comprehend. It is
ce c'onques riens ne pot comprandre,	undoubtedly true that she whose womb
fors li ventres d'une pucele.	was swollen with God understood
Mes, sans faille, il est voirs que cele	more of him than Plato. [...] It was the
a cui le ventres an tandi	triangular circle, the circular triangle
plus que Platon an antandi;	that dwelt within the virgin.
[...]	
C'est li cercles trianguliers,	
c'est li triangle circuliers,	
qui an la vierge s'ostela.	
(*RR* 19,083–115)	

The trap into which Deguileville had fallen was that of attempting to define the boundaries of a sphere that may be intelligible but can never be drawn, seeking to capture the mystery of God's gift to man by explicating, defining, and 'comprehending' its outlines within the body of his own allegorical poem—only to find that this mysterious knowledge necessarily eludes ordinary representation and understanding altogether. In the *Rose*, by contrast, the mystery of love and desire is preserved by the very denial of a transparent representation, and the reliance on necessarily oblique and deforming mirrors that can only ever present distorted and inverted 'figures' (*RR* 18,218) of the truth to the eyes of inquisitive observers ('les ymages revirees / auz eux de ceus qui la se mirent', *RR* 18,224–5). Just like the mystery of Christ's Incarnation is contained and enclosed within the impenetrable body of the virgin, *rosa sine spina*, and just like the 'Rose' is contained within the 'Romanz de la Rose, / ou l'art d'Amors est tote enclose' (*RR* 37–8), so the truth

---

[41] Morton, *The 'Roman de la Rose' in its Philosophical Context*, p. 11.

THE ENDS OF EXPERIENCE: INCARNATION AND APOCALYPSE   459

about the nature of love and desire in all its forms—*agape* as well as *eros*—remains stubbornly and enigmatically 'enclosed', locked up within the poem.

2. The Coming of Antichrist and the Ends of Allegory

The final two *passus* of the poem are marked by the resurgence of societal and institutional concerns, with the establishment of the Barn of Unity in the seventh vision, and the attack of Antichrist on the institutions and sacraments of the Church in the eighth. While this tends to overshadow the poem's concern with Will's quest, the poem continues to trace the progress of the dreamer, which provides an important counterpoint to the expanding apocalyptic focus of the concluding events. As Tavormina notes, 'Apocalypse is no spectator sport', and Will experiences its effects at least indirectly through his vision of the End of Days.[42] In this final section, Langland once more uses Deguileville's poem as a model to explore the relations between a passive, suffering subject and the dismantling of larger institutional structures in order to reassess one final time the value and significance of his own poetic project. In doing so Langland simultaneously replays the pitfalls and contradictions that finally implode Deguileville's allegory, but also manages to utilize his poem to point beyond its own intrinsic limits, into an as yet indefinite and unrealized future. Whereas Deguileville's *PVH2* ends in a crisis of faith in the salvific power of allegorical poetry, undermined by internal *aporia* and external attacks upon the historical 'GVILLERMVS DE DEGUILEUILLA', Langland reaffirms the power of poetic fiction to gesture towards a distant eschatological consummation. He does so, paradoxically, by recognizing and directly confronting the inherent limitations of his own allegorical visionary 'makynges', lending a positive, spiritually enabling significance to the very limitations experienced by the poem's dreaming and desiring 'I'. The poetic subject's experience of its own exhaustion now becomes a counterpoint to a larger and more important pilgrimage narrative, taken forward by the depersonalized and increasingly spiritualized figure of Conscience, beyond the poem and into a providential apocalyptic future.[43] In this section I would therefore like to consider the nature and significance of the 'I's experience of its own failures and limitations during the final two visions.

The purpose and relevance of the two final *passus* has always been the subject of much debate in *Piers Plowman* scholarship. Coming as they do after what appears to be the visionary culmination of *passus* B XVIII, they have been described as

---

[42] M. Teresa Tavormina, *Kindly Similitude: Marriage and Family in 'Piers Plowman'* (Cambridge: D. S. Brewer, 1995), p. 209.

[43] On the increasingly spiritualized role of Conscience towards the end of the B-version, and in the C-version, see especially Sarah Wood, *Conscience and the Composition of 'Piers Plowman'* (Oxford: Oxford University Press, 2012), especially pp. 149–66.

460   MEDIEVAL ALLEGORY AS EPISTEMOLOGY

'anticlimactic' or 'dispiriting', and critics even disagree on whether the poem's ending is to be read as a triumph or a failure.[44] The ecstatic vision of *passus* B XVIII effectively appears to mark the transition from *chronos* to *kairos*, dissolving the subjective temporality of Will's individual pilgrimage of life within the larger temporal movement of sacred history, culminating with the Incarnation.[45] The focus on the arresting, historically and spiritually central event of the Incarnation effectively suspends sequential temporality altogether, creating a narrative texture where historical, individual, and liturgical temporality converge in their shared focus on the sacramental body of Christ, the Word made flesh.[46] To some extent the joyous and trans-historical nature of this ecstatic vision is carried forward into the brief account of Will's waking life that spans the end of *passus* B XVIII and the start of *passus* XIX: significantly, Will awakes at the time of the Easter celebrations—the pivotal moment of the Christian liturgical calendar—as if to signal the emergence of a new, intrinsically salvific, incarnational understanding of human time that provides the framework for Will's individual journey. It is equally significant that in the wake of the Christological developments of the preceding *passus*, Will should now set out no longer on a quest for unspecified knowledge, but with the far more focused aim of rejoining the Easter celebrations in church, in order to receive communion in the form of Christ's sacramental body. This appears to fulfil the promise of the Samaritan in *passus* B XVII, pointing forward to a moment of profound spiritual and corporeal communion and mutual incorporation between Man and God:

> 'May no medicyne vnder molde þe man to heele brynge—
> Neiþer Feiþ ne fyn Hope, so festred be hise woundes,
> Wiþouten þe blood of a barn born of a mayde.
> And be he baþed in þat blood, baptised as it were,
> And þanne plastred wiþ penaunce and passion of þat baby,
> He sholde stonde and steppe—ac stalworþe worþ he neuere,
> Til he haue eten al þe barn and his blood ydronke.'
>
> (B XVII.92–8)

The importance of this vision is also underscored by the fact that it is only now that Langland finally provides, for the first time in this long poem, an explicit

---

[44] See, respectively, Barney, *Penn Commentary 5*, p. 100 and *passim*, and Hanna, 'Conscience's Dinner', p. 311. For a discussion of critical disagreements, see for instance the overview provided in Harwood, *Problem of Belief*, pp. 123–4.

[45] For the use of the contrast between *kairos* and *chronos* to describe the layering of temporalities in Will's vision, see especially Tavormina, *Kindly Similitude*, pp. 207.

[46] See especially the discussion of temporality offered by Cervone, *Poetics of the Incarnation*, pp. 126–38. See further Daniel F. Pigg, 'Apocalypse Then: The Ideology of Literary Form in *Piers Plowman*', *Religion & Literature* (1999), 103–16 (109–13), and Robert Adams, 'The Liturgy Revisited', *Studies in Philology* 73 (1976), 266–84.

THE ENDS OF EXPERIENCE: INCARNATION AND APOCALYPSE   461

and transparent statement about the nature of his hitherto elusive 'work': 'Thus I awaked and wrote what I had dremed' (XIX.1). After a series of oblique, hesitant, evasive, and ambivalent allusions to his status as a poet, such a direct statement of purpose signals that the sixth vision does indeed constitute the culmination of Will's visionary quest.

Following on from the vision of the Incarnation in the preceding section, *passus* B XIX accordingly focuses on the central sacrament of communion, the liturgical and microcosmic re-enactment of Christ's passion. But even before he can receive the sacrament, Will falls asleep once more, as if to suggest that the perfect communion of God and Man figured by the sacrament—and liturgically *contained* and enacted by the Eucharistic host—continues to elude Will.[47] Not even the prospect of a sacramental 'tasting' of Christ's Eucharistic body is able to bring closure to his sapiential hunger and thirst for a definitive, total, and all-consuming *kynde knowyng* of Christ. This compounds the sense that the preceding vision of Christ marks 'a decisive revelation [. . .] beyond which there is no going'.[48] Yet as the very existence of the poem's two final *passus* suggests, however, the vision of the Incarnation is ultimately unable to bring consummation to the poem in a gesture of definitive closure. The Eucharist itself ultimately encapsulates this paradoxical absent presence: in David Aers's words 'it brings worshippers the divine presence, even as it simultaneously acknowledges the absence of the kingdom it represents'; in the temporal, historical perspective adopted in the closing *passus*, it becomes

---

[47] For a discussion of the relationship between Eucharistic theology and allegorical semiotics in the period, and their impact on the poem, see Jennifer Garrison, 'Failed Signification: *Corpus Christi* and *Corpus Mysticum* in *Piers Plowman*', YLS 23 (2009), 97–123. I agree with Garrison that the resonances between the dynamics of allegorical signification and the real presence play an important, even fundamental role in Langland's thought in this section of the poem, and in shaping Langland's allegorical poetics as a whole. As will become apparent in what follows, however, it seems to me that Langland is nonetheless invested in maintaining a firm distinction between allegorical signification and Eucharistic communion despite their convergence. It is precisely this distinction that ultimately lends salvific power to Langland's own, figural/allegorical poetic 'makynges', understood as a form of thought and expression that *approximates* and gestures towards the vanishing point of Eucharistic bodily presence, without ever expecting to *attain* it. A similar tension determines the relationship between sacramental signification and allegorical representation in the poetry of Deguileville, as I argued in Chapter 2.4. For both poets, narrative allegory remains a radically asymptotic and hence provisional, 'fallen' mode of signification. The two poets differ most strongly in their response to this realization: frustration, impotence, and finally resignation in Deguileville; and a mixture of wistful acceptance, equanimity, and dogged determination to pursue the quest in Langland.

[48] This is in some sense inevitable, a necessary consequence of the time-bound condition of the Dreamer, who is bound to remain within an apocalyptic perspective adopted by Langland on this question, as argued especially by David Aers, 'Visionary Eschatology: *Piers Plowman*', *Modern Theology* 16.1 (2000), 3–17 (9). Aers usefully describes Langland's approach to eschatology as strictly 'Christocentric', p. 7. On the inherent limitations of Will's vision in B XVIII, see also e.g. Harwood, *The Problem of Belief*, p. 117. For further studies of Langland's apocalypticism in this vein, see Robert Adams, 'The Nature of Need in *Piers Plowman* XX', *Traditio* 34 (1978), 273–301; E. Talbot. Donaldson, 'Apocalyptic Style in *Piers Plowman* B XIX–XX', *Leeds Studies in English* 14 (1983), 74–81; Emmerson, 'The Prophetic, the Apocalyptic, and the Study of Medieval Literature'; Pigg, 'Apocalypse Then'; Kathryn Kerby-Fulton, *Reformist Apocalypticism and Piers Plowman* (Cambridge: Cambridge University Press, 1990), pp. 153–61.

462   MEDIEVAL ALLEGORY AS EPISTEMOLOGY

evident that 'Christ's presence in this sacrament does not dissolve eschatological frontiers.'[49]

All of this ultimately suggests that Langland crafts these two final *passus* very deliberately to counterpoint, dilute, and to some extent *unmake* the sense of spiritual, visionary, and poetic closure experienced by Will during the sixth dream in conjunction with the vision of the Incarnation. This is borne out also by the structural organization of the seventh vision as a whole, bracketed by two instances of frustrated Eucharistic communion.[50] The seventh vision is both the result of this failure and a sustained reflection upon it, beginning with Will nodding off just before the moment of transubstantiation, 'In myddes of þe Masse, þo men yede to offryng' (B XIX.4), and ending with the failure of 'the comune' to engage in the penitential preparations—*redde quod debes* (B XIX.394)—required to receive the sacrament (B XIX.395–485). It is precisely in the void created between these two instances of purely formal and imperfect communion at the edges of the seventh vision that the absence of Christ is most keenly felt. It is fitting therefore that Grace's prophecy of the coming of Antichrist should be placed at the very centre of this void (B XIX.222–9), anticipating the terminal decline of ecclesiastical institutions as well as penitential and social bonds in *passus* B XX.

This anticlimactic narrative progression in the final sections of the B and C texts is modelled on the pattern of frustrated closure that marks the ending of Deguileville's *PVH2*. Many of the motifs and images brought into play at the start of *passus* B XIX are in effect adapted directly from Deguileville's poem. Like Deguileville's pilgrim (*PVH1* 13,494–8 and *PVH2* 17,727–9) Will is woken from his vision by the sound of ringing bells (B XVIII.427), and like the pilgrim (*PVH1* 13,512–16)[51] this prompts him to declare his intention to record his vision in writing (B XIX. 1)—a series of motifs that Chaucer too appears to have borrowed from Deguileville for the conclusion of his *Book of the Duchess*.[52] But as in earlier sections of the poem, Langland modifies many of the borrowed motifs in accordance with his concern for wider social and spiritual reform, as opposed to the strictly monastic, and increasingly self-referential, autobiographical, and arguably solipsistic focus of Deguileville's closing sections. Unlike the pilgrim of *PVH*, who is woken by the bells of his own Abbey of Chaalis, Will is woken by the bells of his village church, as if to underscore Langland's focus on a far

---

[49] Aers, 'Sacrament of the Altar', pp. 76, 77.

[50] The point is made by Garrison, 'Failed Signification', 98.

[51] In *PVH2* this declaration is less confident, and the action slightly different. After hearing the clock of the monastery, the dreamer attempts but fails to rise, puzzling over the meaning of the dream ('grant pensée [. . .] pour mon aventureux songe', *PVH2* 17,730–1). This provides the occasion for a more defensive authorial disclaimer (*PVH2* 17,733–51).

[52] See variously Kamath, *Authorship and First-Person Allegory*, pp. 72–3; Barney, *Penn Commentary 5*, pp. 104–5.

THE ENDS OF EXPERIENCE: INCARNATION AND APOCALYPSE   463

more inclusive, secular and demotic social space inhabited by 'comune peple' (B XIX.7). Accordingly Langland does not conclude his poem with the description of a heavily allegorized monastic enclosure, figure of the eschatological Heavenly City, but with the account of the building of the 'hous Vnite, Holy Chirche on Englissh' (B XIX.331). This clearly marks a shift of focus away from the vicissitudes of a specific, localized monastic community, towards a much broader concern with the structures that underpin the Christian church as a whole. It also develops *PVH2*'s loosely eschatological focus on the pilgrim's arrival in a figurative Heavenly Jerusalem into a fully fledged apocalyptic narrative modelled on the Book of Revelations.

Despite these fundamental differences, the Barn of Unity is nonetheless allegorized in ways that are reminiscent of Deguileville's monastery, especially as characterized in the revised *PVH2*. In both poems the respective buildings function as allegories of a religious community under threat, and both structures are besieged and eventually stormed by a series of personified linguistic sins, eroding the devotional, sacramental, social, and institutional order that these buildings represent. In both poems, moreover, the accounts of such events function not so much as 'conclusions', but rather as accounts of a process whereby what bears all the promises of a conclusion is effectively unmade and dismantled. In both poems, finally, this account of the demise of communal structures and institutions is offset by a contrapuntal narrative focused on the poet/dreamer's 'I': in parallel with the decline of institutional and communal structures, the visionary powers of the individual poetic self equally unravel. In both poems this takes the form of an irresistible onslaught of Age personified—Elde in Langland, and Vieillesse in Deguileville (see Chapter 7.3). Further parallels emerge at the level of specific poetic detail. So Langland's Barn of Unity is populated by a variety of personified abstractions of moral, theological, and psychological entities, loosely analogous to Deguileville's more markedly monastic virtues. Deguileville has personifications such as Charité (*PVH2* 15,127), Leçon/Étude (15,142 ff.), Agiographe (15,191), Sainte Escripture (15,453), Obedience (15,490), Discipline (15,496), Abstinence (15,527 ff.), Pauvreté Volontaire (15,603), Chastete (15,702), Priere/Oroison (15,780), and Latria (15,847). Langland, by comparison, gives us the personifications of Conscience (B XIX.9 and *passim*), Grace (B XIX.214 ff.), Confession and Contricion (B XIX.334 and *passim*), and Kynde Wit (B XIX.364), along with Langland's characteristically 'naturalistic' and demotic characters— brewers, prostitutes, summoners, 'lewed vicor[ies]', and blaspheming parsons (B XIX.371–8, 400, 413; B XX.221–4).

All of this underscores the shift away from Deguileville's more strictly monastic orientation, focused on life within an idealized monastic community that we are invited to identify with the poet's own monastery of Chaalis, towards Langland's concern with the structures of the Christian Church and English society

464   MEDIEVAL ALLEGORY AS EPISTEMOLOGY

as a whole. Other characters provide more specific parallels, such as the figure of the porter—Päour de Dieu in Deguileville (*PVH2* 15,084) and Peace in Langland (B XX.331). Both allegories place considerable importance on the function of these porters in regulating access to the buildings, emphasizing the disastrous consequences of their inattention (*PVH2* 15,067, 15,915–19, 16,334–9, 16,354–9, 16,426–7; *PPl* B XX.298–304, 323–43, 349–56). While the two edifices are of a fundamentally different kind, and mobilize different semantic fields—a sailing ship in *PVH* (the Ark of the Church, on a journey to salvation), and an agrarian barn in *Piers* (to gather the 'harvest' of the Word)—both are described throughout in distinctly militaristic terms, as fortified allegorical castles under siege (*PVH2* 15,009, 15,045, 15,066, 15,111, 15,909, 16,219, 16,258 and *passim*; *PPl* B XIX.322–31, 355–70, B XX.74–109, 214–27, 298–380). Furthermore, Deguileville too employs metaphors of disrupted ploughing and harvesting, albeit more sporadically, in his characterization of the decline of moral standards within the convent in *PVH2*.[53] Both poets, finally, insistently use the motif of Jesus as the 'King' of the figurative realm or fortress (*PVH2* 15,104, 15,850, 15,919, 16,342; *PPl* B XIX.26–49, 96–107, 136–9, 447).

In both edifices—Cistercian monastery and Barn of Unity—the edible Word of Christ's sacramental body occupies a central position. I have already discussed *PVH*'s interest in the semantic field of sapiential speech and sacramental ingestion as part of the description of monastic life (see Chapter 4.3), as well as Langland's sustained engagement with such ideas in earlier portions of his poem (see Chapters 5.4 and 6.1). This elaborate symbolic articulation of speech, nourishment, and Eucharistic communion culminates in the final two *passus*, where the transubstantiated sacramental Word made flesh plays a fundamental role in preserving the identity, integrity, and corporeal 'unity' of the Christian community. Tellingly Conscience uses the promise of such Eucharistic nourishment as an effective rallying cry, persuading all Christians to labour for the establishment of the Barn of Unity, so that 'there nas Cristene creature [...] / That he ne halp a quantite holynesse to wexe' (B XIX.376–8):

> 'Comeþ', quod Conscience, 'ye Cristene, and dyneþ,
> That han laboured lelly al þis Lenten tyme.
> Here is breed yblessed, and Goddes body þervnder.

---

[53] During his visit to other religious institutions in the wake Conspiracion's attack, the pilgrim encounters the figure of Stérilité, a deformed dwarf who declares that her task consists of blighting the harvest of the monastery (*PVH2* 16,796–803). The most striking element, however, concerns Stérilité's reasons for causing such famine. As she observes, the purpose is that of forcing the community to amend its ways, in ways that are closely reminiscent of Langland's description of the actions of Kynde in XX.80 ff.—as well as Hunger at VI.172 ff. (*PVH2* 16,804). Indeed Stérilité acts not on her own initiative, but as an emissary of Grace Dieu herself (*PVH2* 16,816–19).

THE ENDS OF EXPERIENCE: INCARNATION AND APOCALYPSE   465

> Grace, þoru3 Goddes word, gaf Piers power,
> My3t to maken it, and men to ete it after
> In helpe of hir heele ones in a monþe,
> Or as ofte as þei hadde nede,'

(B XIX.387–93)

Conscience however also insists on the necessity of undergoing the full process of penance, an imperative preparatory sacrament that enables access to the Eucharist. The explanation is given as a response to the common people's objection against the need for penitential restitution—*redde quod debes* (XIX.188, 394; XX.308):[54]

> 'How?' quod al þe comune; 'Þow conseillest vs to yelde
> Al þat we owen any wight ar we go to housel?'
> 'That is my conseil', quod Conscience, 'and Cardinale Vertues;
> Or ech man for3yue ooþer, and þat wole þe *Paternoster*:
>   *et dimitte nobis debita nostra, etc.*
> And so to ben assoiled, and siþþen to ben houseled.'

(B XIX.395–9)

Conscience's insistence on the centrality of penitential restitution is of fundamental importance, since it establishes the nexus of sacramental practice that guarantees the stability of the institution of the Church, mystical body of Christ, figured as an architectural structure that both mirrors and 'contains' the Eucharistic host itself, literal body of Christ.[55] It is precisely by disrupting this key nexus of the sacramental economy organized around the Eucharistic Word made flesh that the forces of Antichrist ultimately manage to breach the walls of Unity. The prophecy of doom uttered by Surquidous and Spille-Loue is accordingly formulated in terms that stress this symbolic rupture of social and sacramental unity: "'And Piers bern worþ ybroke; and þei þat ben in Vnitee / Shulle come out"' (B XIX.347–8). As will become evident during the dénouement in *passus* XX, the fracturing of the community is achieved by eroding the sacrament of penance, compromising its role as a preparatory stage for enabling the redemptive operation of the Eucharist. It is precisely with the arrival of Friar Flatterer or 'Sire *Penetrans-Domos*' (B XX.341)—in response to the many complaints about the hardships of penance (B XX.305–18), and the search for 'any surgien [. . .] in þe sege þat softer koude plastre' (B XX.311)—that the penitential process is undermined, leading to

---

[54] On the specifically sacramental overtones of Restitution, and its relation to penitential Satisfaction, see notably Alford, 'The Figure of Repentance', pp. 11–17, reviewing a range of earlier opinions. See also Barney, *Penn Commentary 5*, pp. 129–31, 164–5.

[55] See Aers, 'The Sacrament of the Altar', pp. 78–80, and ibid, 'Visionary Eschatology', 11–12; Garrison, 'Failed Signification', 117–19.

466 MEDIEVAL ALLEGORY AS EPISTEMOLOGY

the implosion of the entire sacramental system that upholds the institution of the Church:

> Thus he gooþ and gadereþ, and gloseþ þere he shryueþ—
> Til Contricion hadde clene foryeten to crye and to wepe,
> And wake for hise wikked werkes as he was wont to doone.
> For confort of his confessour, contricioun he lafte,
> That is þe souereyneste salue for alle kynne synnes.
>
> (B XX. 369–73)

Langland here insists not only on the crucial functional link that ties together the sacraments of penance and the Eucharist, but also emphasizes their shared focus on activities of the mouth—speech as *confessio oris*; communion as ingestion of the Word made flesh; and the sacrament as a means of 'sapiential' (self)knowledge. Conversely, also the attack upon such 'oral' salvific activities is situated in the mouth, and involves the perversion of the gift of the *logos*: it is precisely through verbal 'glosing' (B XX.369) that Friar Flatterer finally manages to erode the real significance of true contrition, and the assault of his acolytes upon the Barn is similarly described in terms of verbal and semiotic abuses, perpetrated by the 'false prophetes fele, flatereris and gloseris' (B XIX.222) and by means of Lecherye's 'glosynges and gabbynges' (B XX.125).[56]

In exploring such linguistic abuses Langland reconnects with a powerful tradition that flows from the seminal figure of Faux Semblant in the *Rose*, and that had found further avatars in Deguileville's poem in a variety of figures—from Huiseuse to the quartet of Trahison, Detraction, Envie, and Conspiracion (see Chapter 4.5). Like Friar Flatterer and the quartet of 'vieilles' in Deguileville, Faux Semblant besieges and finally infiltrates a fortified building through the misuse and abuse of language. Jean de Meun's Faux Semblant, furthermore, was already closely associated with the idea of a perversion of the sacrament of penance: setting out on a 'pelerinage' (*RR* 12,012) with all the usual trappings—'bourdon' and 'escherpe' (*RR* 12,047, 12,050)—he gains access to the Castle, where he persuades Malebouche to deliver his confession, only to cut his throat with a razor and slaughter the fortress's sleeping garrison (*RR* 11,951–12,350), after what apparently was, we are told, a sincere confession by a true penitent ('veraiz repentanz', *RR* 12,333).[57] Faux Semblant is also identified as a mendicant friar and 'vallez Antecrit' (*RR* 11,683), and Jean famously references the anti-mendicant views of Guillaume

---

[56] Amanda Walling, 'Friar Flatterer: Glossing and the Hermeneutics of Flattery in *Piers Plowman*', *YLS* 21 (2007), 57–76.

[57] See however Scanlon, 'Personification and Penance', for a discussion of the paradoxes inherent in confession itself, as they crystallize both in the *Rose* and in the figure of Faux Semblant in particular, and in Langland's poem.

THE ENDS OF EXPERIENCE: INCARNATION AND APOCALYPSE 467

de Saint Amour's *De Periculis* (cf. *RR* 11,761–814),[58] providing a powerful precedent for Langland's portrait of Sire *Penetrans Domos*—another friar with his own set of impeccably apocalyptic credentials.[59]

Other parallels abound, and point to an engagement that is structured, reasoned, and deliberate rather than incidental. So, for instance, Faux Semblant is described as resembling 'un sainz hermites', but is in reality an 'ypocrites' (*RR* 11,201–2), anticipating the parallel attack of Hypocrisy, who 'at þe yate harde gan fighte, / And woundede wel wikkedly many a wys techere' (B XX.302–3).[60] Deguileville's Detraction engages in a similarly paradoxical self-revelation, 'turn[ing] towards them a pleasant aspect and a fair appearance' [bele chiere [...] [que] contreface et *biau semblant*, *PVH1* 8518–20; my emphasis], while Trahison 'simulates a fair appearance and a pleasant manner' [fait par simulation / Biau semblant et belle chiere, *PVH1* 8396–7], and is told to 'hide your thoughts with lies, and look different on the outside than you are on the inside' [ton pense / Tu couverras de faussete / Et par dehors demonsterras / Autre que dedens ne seras, *PVH1* 8421–2]. Also the wider semantic field of vestimentary/rhetorical disguise that clusters around the figure of Faux Semblant and his companions is adopted and developed by Deguileville (see Chapters 1.3, 3.3, 4.4, and 4.5), and recollections of these moments saturate Langland's description of the siege. Jean's dubious Friar tells us that 'the habit does not make the monk' [la robe ne fet pas le moine, *RR* 11,028]—echoed by Deguileville's Trahison, who reiterates that 'one does not recognize people from their clothes [On ne connoist pas aus drapiaus / Les gens, *PVH1* 8455–6]—while Langland's Antichrist furnishes his fraternal acolytes with similar clothing: he 'made Fals springe and sprede', and 'Freres folwed that fende, for he yaf hem copes' [i.e. 'cloaks, capes, robes'] (B XX.55, 58).[61]

In both the *Rose* and *PVH* these ideas are developed further to establish a homology between sophistical argumentation, manipulative deception, and vestimentary/rhetorical disguise. Faux Semblant is thus presented as a walking sophism (*RR* 12,109–16; see Chapter 1.3). He further insists that not even knowledge of the thirteen types of logical fallacy taught in Aristotle's *Sophistical Refutations* would allow anyone to unmask him (*RR* 11,026–34). Jean's Jaloux had similarly complained of such stratagems in relation to the female arts of

---

[58] See especially Richard K. Emmerson and Ronald B. Herzman, 'The Apocalyptic Age of Hypocrisy: Faus Semblant and Amant in the *Roman de la Rose*', *Speculum* 62.3 (1987), 612–34.

[59] See variously Penn R. Szittya, *The Antifraternal Tradition in Medieval Literature* (Princeton: Princeton University Press, 1986), pp. 3–10, 247–90; Robert Adams, 'Some Versions of Apocalypse: Learned and Popular Eschatology in *Piers Plowman*', in Thomas J. Heffernan, ed., *The Popular Literature of Medieval England* (Knoxville: University of Tennessee Press, 1985), pp. 194–236; Douglas Wurtele, 'The Bane of Flattery in the World of Chaucer and Langland', *Florilegium* 19 (2002), 1–25 (6–10); Kerby-Fulton, *Reformist Apocalypticism*, pp. 153–61; Wendy Scase, *'Piers Plowman' and the New Anticlericalism* (Cambridge: Cambridge University Press, 1989), pp. 118–19.

[60] This set of associations also resonates disturbingly with Langland's earlier portraits of Will himself as a dubious hermit, 'unholy of workes' (B Prol. 3), see Chapter 6.2.

[61] On the symbolism of copes in the poem, see also Barney, *Penn Commentary 5*, pp. 207–8.

468   MEDIEVAL ALLEGORY AS EPISTEMOLOGY

seduction, making explicit the analogy between sophistical fallacies and rhetorical coverings—'silken cloths or brightly coloured and neatly arranged little flowers' [dras de saie ou de floretes / bien colorees et bien nete, *RR* 8869–70]:

[. . .] tel deception	Such deception comes from the eyes'
vient de la fole vision	disordered vision, which sees their
des euz, qui parees les voient,	adornment; hearts are thus so misled
par quoi li queur si s'en desvoient	by the pleasant impression received by
por la plesant impression	the imagination that they are unable to
de leur ymaginacion	distinguish lies from truth or, through
qu'il n'i sevent apercevoir	lack of proper observation, to explicate
ne la mençonge ne le voir,	the sophism.
ne le sophime deviser	
par defaut de bien aviser.	
(*RR* 8891–900)	

Deguileville picks up the theme, albeit in a slightly different key, by casting the seductive Huiseuse, 'friend to your body' [amie de ton cors, *PVH1* 6857], as an amateur disputant engrossed in the sophistical fallacies of Aristotle's 'elenches' (6852)—the *Sophistical Refutations* that Faux Semblant too had invoked—complementing her own vanity and obsession with vacuous vestimentary/rhetorical clothing (*PVH1* 6847–50; see Chapter 3.3).

Langland too adopts this analogy between vestimentary deception, rhetorical covering, and specious scholastic argumentation: Langland's Envy 'heet freres go to scole / And lerne logyk and lawe, and also contemplacion' (B XX.273–4), and 'freres to philosophie he fond hem to scole' (B XX.296). Related ideas are invoked also when Surquidous and Spille-Loue announce that 'Confession and Contricion, and youre carte þe Byleeve / Shal be coloured so queyntely and covered vnder oure sophistrie (B XIX.349–50). Finally, Langland gives us the character of Lecherie, who attacks the fortress "wiþ a laughynge chiere / And wiþ pryuee speche and peyntede wordes", and "Wiþ glosynges and gabbynges [. . .] gyled þe peple" (B XX.114–15, 125). Venus-like (cf. *RR* 20755–86), he "bar a bowe in his hand, and manye brode arewes" (B XX.117) to attack the Barn of Unity.[62] Deguileville too had provided further avatars of these ideas and motifs: Venus(=*luxuria*), who carries "a fals painted face to cover my own face" [porte .i. paintures / Faus visage a couverture', *PVH1* 10,638–9]; Trahison, mounted on Envie, who similarly keeps her 'face and features under a false mask' [face / Mucie souz ce faus visage, *PVH1* 8339–40]; and finally Chastete, 'Chastelaine [. . .] de ce chastel', *PVH1* 12,813),

---

[62] The connection with the *Roman de la Rose* is noted by, among others, Donaldson, 'Apocalyptic Style in *Piers Plowman*', 78; and Barney, *Penn Commentary 5*, p. 213. Both, however, associate the arrows with the allegorized arrows of the God of Love from the earlier section of the poem, written by Guillaume de Lorris (*RR* 1691–3),

THE ENDS OF EXPERIENCE: INCARNATION AND APOCALYPSE   469

charged with defending the fortified monastery against the combined threats of
sensuality and hypocrisy:

Archiere n'i a ne carnel,	She will defend all the arrowslits and
Qu'elle ne veulle defendre	battlements so that no arrow can enter.
Que saiete ni dart n'i entre	
(*PVH1* 12,814–16)	

This wide range of different kinds of linguistic, rhetorical, and sophistical equivocation finally makes up the core strategy of Antichrist's assault on Conscience and
the Barn of Unity, as Grace had warned in *passus* B XIX:

> For Antecrist and hise al þe worlde shul greue,
> And acombre þee, Conscience, but if Crist þee helpe.
> And false prophetes fele, flatereris and gloseris,
> Shullen come and be curatours ouer kynges and erles.
>
> (B XIX.220–3)

In *Piers Plowman*, this rampant epidemic of duplicitous speaking announces a
much deeper, more pervasive, and fully apocalyptic deregulation of the normal
order of speech, knowledge, and belief, along with a profound disruption of the
social and sacramental economy that underpins the Barn. This constitutes a major
development in comparison with Deguileville's *PVH2*. There the attack on the
monastery in the epilogue of the poem had figured a primarily personal catas-
trophe, and although the poet demonstrates serious concern over the decline of
monastic values and institutions, the broader implications of such events remains
clearly circumscribed. Deguileville's account of the attack, however, appears to
have served as a major cue for Langland, who elaborates this same cluster of motifs.
Emphasis is moved away from the register of personal complaint, to foreground
institutional and sacramental dysfunctions within the Church as a whole, within a
fully apocalyptic perspective that had no correlative in Deguileville. Langland thus
appears to have laboured to eschew precisely the kind of 'autobiographical temptation' that characterizes *PVH2*, using Will's encounter with the figure of Haukyn
to exorcize Deguileville's fixation on his own 'singularity' as an impediment to the
completion of his own initial project (see Chapter 6.2). This now allows him to
concentrate on what he sees as the underlying, endemic structural dysfunction
of Christian institutions as a whole, as opposed to the dysfunctions of a specific
monastic community. As David Aers has put it, for Langland '[t]he Church is not,
emphatically not, the kingdom of God'.[63]

The closing two *passus* of the poem, however, are also marked by Langland's
newly intensified engagement with the *Rose*, and particularly with its treatment of

---

[63] Aers, 'Visionary Eschatology', p. 13.

linguistic equivocation, duplicity, representational paradox, and the articulation of a dialectical epistemology of 'contrary things'. It is particularly the markedly apocalyptic orientation of the siege narrative as found in the *Rose*, with Faux Semblant at its centre, that appears to have prompted Langland to develop the account of personal misfortune he found in *PVH2* into a much more ambitious exploration of the workings of Antichrist in subverting the order of Holy Church. At the heart of this apocalyptic reconfiguration lies Langland's concern with the perversion of the economy of penance through flattery and duplicity. This focus on the erosion of penitence, however, is an element in a much wider reflection on the central role of language in determining the salvation of the individual and in shaping the life of the religious community, besieged in the Barn of Unity. Language in all its forms—as speech, writing, poetry, the living *logos*, as the edible Word made flesh, and as a tool wielded by both Christ and Antichrist—appears to be the overarching concern of the closing sections of the poem. Language is simultaneously the immediate target of such attacks upon the sacrament of penance; the ultimate object of these attacks in the form of the Eucharistic Word made flesh, now rendered inaccessible; and it is the means of Antichrist's attack upon the structures of the Church.

3. The Ends of Allegory

It is fitting that Langland should insert within this sustained reflection on the apocalyptic potentialities of language one further, final examination of his own role as a poet engaged in the quest for some ultimate 'Truth' by means of his poetic craft. This examination is again deeply ambivalent, and can be teased out only in relation to Langland's reflections on his own poetic craft elsewhere in *Piers Plowman*. On the one hand, Langland employs the wider reflection on language and deception in this closing section to theorize the epistemology of his own, highly idiosyncratic poetics of paradox—once more in dialogue with Jean de Meun and Deguileville. On the other hand, this rather abstract examination of the nature and modalities of poetic 'makying' also takes a more personal and experiential form. This prompts a reconsideration of the constantly shifting place of the dreaming and writing subject—figured as Will's 'I'—within the visionary world of the poem as it approaches its inconclusive ending.

While Langland rejects Deguileville's insistent focus on personal misfortune at the end of *PVH2* in favour of a broader, fully apocalyptic development, the concern with individual suffering does not disappear from Langland's poem. On the contrary, this question provides a parallel subplot to the main account of the demise of Holy Church. Will's continuing presence as a narrative *acteur*—albeit an increasingly passive and powerless one—is particularly noticeable during the encounters with Nede and Elde in *passus* XX. The encounter with Nede occurs

THE ENDS OF EXPERIENCE: INCARNATION AND APOCALYPSE   471

during one of the extremely rare waking moments of the poem—an important fact that ought to inflect, I believe, any discussion of the significance of this encounter. Existing discussions have often tended to interpret the significance of Nede primarily in relation to Langland's ideals of patient poverty, and specifically in terms of Langland's attitude towards mendicancy. As several recent overviews have shown, interpretations of this kind have tended to become polarized around this central question: is Nede a reliable moral authority advocating a laudable ideal of patient poverty, or rather a cynical opportunist attempting to justify his own parasitical status, and even tempting Will to do likewise?[64] Such readings have offered compelling discussions of how exactly *Piers Plowman* engages with contemporary controversies surrounding the ideals and practices of mendicant orders. Critics, however, have rarely paused to discuss the structural function and allegorical status of Nede within the wider narrative trajectory and visionary geography of the poem. In what follows I would therefore like to approach the question from a different angle, to examine the cognitive, epistemological, and poetological implications of Will's encounter with the slippery 'allegorical' figure of Nede.

Uniquely among personified characters in the poem, Nede does *not* belong to the mental dream-world of moral, psychological, or political abstractions, but to the putatively 'real' world of Will's waking life. I would suggest that the primary, most immediate and elementary function of this figure consists in prompting us to reconsider the articulation between the allegorical dream world as a whole and the waking world of 'existential' individual experience. In this sense I substantially concur with the reading proposed by Kathleen Hewett-Smith, who argues that

> Nede presents the *experience* rather than the authority of need. That is, rather than presenting in his speech to the dreamer any kind of doctrine that must be measured against Christian standards of morality and ethics (and thus judged either suspiciously lacking in integrity, or consistent and worthy of praise), Nede escapes discursive formulation altogether, and provides instead a portrait of the fact of necessity and want.[65]

The character indeed declares that 'Nede ne haþ no lawe' (B XX.10), as if to signal his refusal to confirm to any normative scheme of behaviour, and therefore his resistance to any form of allegorical reduction or conceptual elaboration. Nede operates in a sphere that is emphatically separated from the world of allegorical personifications that populate this section of the poem, and is thus able to prompt

---

[64] The literature on the issue is abundant. For a useful overview, see especially Barney, *Penn Commentary 5*, pp. 186–204, esp. 189 for a survey of earlier critical views; and Hewett-Smith, 'Nede ne hath no lawe', 243–4.

[65] Hewett-Smith, 'Nede ne hath no lawe', p. 245. See also Adams, 'The Nature of Nede in *Piers Plowman* XX': 'Need, though never neutral in effect, is a personification of an ethically neutral condition', p. 279.

472 MEDIEVAL ALLEGORY AS EPISTEMOLOGY

action 'wiþouten conseil of Conscience or Cardynale Vertues' (B XX.21). Need's demands are 'powerfully mundane, deeply individual',[66] and ultimately represent the bare, raw reality of need—pure lack and absence, in itself irreducible to any sort of doctrine, scheme, discourse, philosophy, or referential significance of any kind. As a manifestation of inexhaustible lack, Nede is ultimately antithetical to being and to form, and thus threatens to engulf the very processes of signification, semiosis, cognition, learning, and poetic 'makyng' that constitute the stuff that Langland's allegorical poetry is made on. As the poem approaches its ending—a *terminus* that is not however its *telos*—Nede opens a negative space of non-being, in a gesture that prepares for the poem's ultimate un-making of its own imaginative structures and textual formations.

The abrupt return to the level of Will's waking existence that coincides with the appearance of Nede also reminds us that the ordinary temporality of an individual life has been suspended and reconfigured but not abolished by the poem's shift to a vision of sacred history in *passus* B XVI through XIX. This provides an important framework for the poem's final, imminent apocalyptic vision of Antichrist. Despite its seemingly transhistorical and eschatological nature, that vision too is situated in time: it presupposes the existence of a temporal and material subject, an embodied 'I' who is able to receive and transmit such a vision, and who is subject to the ordinary conditions of corporeal and temporal existence dominated by change and decay. By providing us with a reminder of the subject's own mortality and contingency, Nede ultimately functions as a signal for the imminent need to awake, to stop dreaming, and to start 'doing well'—which for Will includes the act of poetic 'makyng' itself. It is not a coincidence, then, that it is precisely at this point in the poem that Langland should again provide—for the second and last time in the poem—an explicit and transparent statement about his activity as a poet: 'And I awakned þerwiþ, and wroot as me mette' (B XIX.485).

The appearance of Nede ultimately announces the imminent end of Will's vision, and the imminent return to the realm of time-bound waking reality for the poem's readers—and with this, the imminent end of allegory. I have already argued in preceding chapters that during the final quarter of his poem Langland gradually moves away from strictly 'allegorical' modes of representation towards historical and typological ones. The arrival of Nede further destabilizes the imaginative register of allegorical vision, and brings about what Hewett-Smith calls a 'climate of allegorical instability' that dominates *passus* B XX.[67] The closing sections of *Piers Plowman* are therefore not only anticlimactic, but they mark a terminal yet highly 'meaning-ful' crisis of the allegorical mode of expression that Langland has

---

[66] Hewett-Smith, 'Nede ne hath no lawe', p. 247.
[67] Hewett-Smith, 'Nede ne hath no lawe', p. 243.

THE ENDS OF EXPERIENCE: INCARNATION AND APOCALYPSE 473

adopted for his poem.[68] For Hewett-Smith, 'the appearance of Nede explodes the bounds/bonds of allegorical discourse not only by blurring the lines between the visionary and the mimetic, but also [. . .] by thrusting before us the undeniable actualities of indigence'.[69] By reasserting the demands of the flesh and of human time, Nede ineluctably pulls Langland's/Will's vision back down to the level of material, temporal, and corporeal existence, frustrating the poem's insistent, even obsessive desire to transcend and sublimate all kinds of pressing material 'needs' by allegorizing not only agricultural labour, but socio-economic realities as a whole. Ploughing, harrowing, harvesting, and the 'eating' of sacramental bread—all of these activities are allegorized with growing intensity as Will's quest progresses, culminating with the vision of the Barn of Unity, allegory of the Church, in *passus* B XIX; but the increasing spiritualization and dematerialization that underpins the larger movement of the plot is finally counteracted and undercut by the appearance of Nede. Fittingly, Nede begins his speech at start of *passus* B XX by reiterating the unavoidable pressures of 'thre thyinges' that weigh down human existence in the world: 'mete', 'clooth', and drink 'if hym lyst for to lape' (XX.12, 16, 18)— echoing the 'vesture', 'mete', and 'drinke' (I.23, 24, 25) identified by Holy Church as the sole inherently 'nedful' necessities in a divinely ordained cosmos:

> 'And þerfore [Treuthe] hyȝte þe erþe to helpe yow echone
> Of wollene, of lynnen, of liflode at nede
> In mesurable manere to make yow at ese;
> *And comaunded of his curteisie in comune þree þinges:*
> *Are none nedful but þo, and nempne hem I þynke,*
> And rekene hem by resoun—reherce þow hem after'.
>
> (B I.17–22; my emphasis)

Rather than being a set of contingencies to be sublimated by the increasing spiritualization of earthly realities enabled by allegorical vision and interpretation, then, these 'þree þinges' reassert their status as intensely *real*, irreducible necessities at the close of the poem. The arrival of Nede thus clearly gives the lie to the hope in the possibility of transcending or evading the pressures of base, merely physical needs—*ne solliciti sitis* and *patientes vincunt* notwithstanding (e.g. B VII.127; XIV.34a).

Before pushing this analysis a little further and moving on to Elde—another personification that reasserts the inherent pressures of corporeal existence in a time-bound world of change—I want to try to uncover some of the speculative and compositional processes that I believe lie behind Langland's treatment of

---

[68] My own, primarily historical reading, here converges with the one proposed by Sarah Tolmie, using a very different critical and theoretical vocabulary drawn from the work of Wittgenstein's *Tractatus*. See her 'Langland, Wittgenstein, and the End of Language', *YLS* 20 (2006), 115–39.

[69] Hewett-Smith, 'Nede ne hath no lawe', p. 246.

474 MEDIEVAL ALLEGORY AS EPISTEMOLOGY

Nede. Nede's troublesome blurring of the mimetic and the allegorical, the spiritual and the corporeal, appears to reproduce an analogous crisis in Deguileville's
PVH2, precipitated by the late arrival of the quartet of *vieilles* who attack the pil-
grim/author: Trahison, Conspiracion, Envie, and Detraction. Just like Nede, the
four old crones cannot be said to function as personified abstractions within the
established scheme of allegorical signification. Instead, the four ladies appear as
personifications of very concrete, *real* events experienced by the poem's historical
author in his own life. Precisely because they denote the actions of others, real-
life agents, upon the author's 'I'—and not the internal, cognitive, psychological, or
affective movements of the pilgrim's self in the usual manner of *psychomachia*-
allegory—their appearance destabilizes the very principles that underpin the
allegorical mode, and thus unsettle the very foundations of the poem. Their arrival
simultaneously interrupts the progress of the dreamer's allegorical pilgrimage
towards a moment of closure *in patria*, but also shatters the abstractive, universalizing, and spiritualizing aspirations of allegory itself. This event disrupts the
otherwise suspended and unbounded dream state, wrenching the subject away
from his imminent attainment of the eschatological 'citizenship' in the Heavenly
City figured by the monastery of Chaalis (see Chapter 4.5). The dreamer/author
is therefore dragged back—retrospectively, as it happens, fracturing the apparent
closure achieved by *PVH1*—to the reality of an individualized existence in ordinary human time, experiencing his condition as an exile and *viator* with renewed
intensity. As Philippe Maupeu has shown, this shock crystallizes in the physical
and corporeal pain, suffering, and injury caused by the attack, through a series of
acts that effectively inscribe a personal history upon the passive material body of
the dreamer—an 'I' who is no longer an *acteur* of his own pilgrimage allegory, but
rather the object of the actions of others:[70]

[Trahison] en la teste me feri	Treason injured me in the head, and
Et mon sanc a terre espandi	I shed my blood on the ground; she
Et me brisa et jambe et bras,	shattered my arm and leg, and beat me
Et tant bati et tant fis las	and tied me up that I can still feel it,
Qu'encor m'en sent et sentirai	and will continue to feel it as long as
Tout le temps que jamais vivrai	I live.
(*PVH2* 16,034–9)	

Langland once more appears to have taken note of the serious consequences and
implications of this development, and takes care to avoid an analogous slippage of
his poetic project from exemplarist allegory to apologetic autobiography. Will's
encounter with Nede to some extent reproduces the dynamics of the pilgrim's

---

[70] See Maupeu, *Pèlerins de vie humaine*, especially pp. 257–65. *PVH2* 'donne à lire avant tout les
tribulations d'un sujet agi par son histoire et non acteur de celle-ci, en proie à cette succession de
calamitates qui nourrit l'autobiographie apologétique', p. 214.

violent encounter with the four crones in *PVH2*, but Langland firmly and clearly situates this encounter within the realm of Will's *waking* life—'as I went by þe wey, whan I was þus awaked' (XX.I). On one level, this simply has the effect of allowing readers to discriminate more clearly and usefully between different levels of awareness, separating the visionary and speculative insights of Will's dream experience from the realm of time-bound, waking individual existence. At the same time, the sudden but explicit transition from dream to waking life is also designed to prepare the reader for the inevitable, imminent exhaustions of the powers of vision and poetic 'makyng', as both Will's pilgrimage and Langland's work approach their inevitable and inconclusive endings. This abrupt return to the bounded realm of individual temporality therefore also announces an ending that can only ever be provisional and anti-climactic—a *terminus* that is not a *telos*, and that *necessarily* falls short of a direct vision of the Truth 'face to face'.

The poem thus unmistakeably signals its own inability to attain any sort of definitive epistemic closure, but in doing so also prepares the ground for what is yet another experience of controlled, managed, and spiritually meaningful visionary failure. By signalling his awareness of those intrinsic limitations, then, Langland also ensures the continuing validity of his own visionary and re-visionary efforts—not only *despite* their inconclusiveness, but precisely *because* of it. In yet another instance of the logical paradox that dominates these closing sections, it is precisely the failure of Will's vision to attain any narrative and epistemic closure that guarantees its salvific and spiritual efficacy. The very inconclusiveness of the quest thus reaffirms the positivity of failure, establishing its ability to function as an implicit but irresistible call for renewed, multiple, and potentially infinite acts of re-actualization and reiteration, mirrored in the departure of a depersonalized Conscience on yet another, re-*iter*ative pilgrimage at the end of the poem. Such a move also amounts to a final vindication of the salvific relevance of Langland's/Will's allegorical 'makynges', in response to Deguileville's gradual disillusion with the mode in favour of utterly different forms of poetic expression. Langland achieves this by maintaining Deguileville's focus on personal misfortune while deeply transforming its significance and accommodating it within the more capacious internal structure of his poem. Whereas the pilgrim's experience of a personal attack in *PVH2* appears purely contingent and devoid of any allegorical significance and deeper spiritual value, Langland ultimately recuperates the experience of personal suffering within a larger, providentialist and eschatological perspective. This provides yet another, final instance of Langland's insistence on the paradoxical, spiritually enabling significance human suffering—a theme that lies at the very heart of the reorientation undergone by the poem in its final third in both the B and C versions (see Chapters 5.3 and 6.3).

While this abrupt return to the earthly reality of physical 'need' and 'suffering' does not condemn the preceding quest allegory to useless failure, it nevertheless places clear limits on its power, reminding us of its imminent 'end' and yet

476   MEDIEVAL ALLEGORY AS EPISTEMOLOGY

pointing beyond those limits. Hewett-Smith's reading of Nede's wider function in the poem again usefully converges with the reading proposed here: 'the destabilization of allegory provoked by Nede is, finally, a means of redeeming the mode, a means of providing significance within the epistemological void constitutive of allegorical discourse'.[71] Nede's very existence ultimately explodes the binary principles that underlie the signifying relations of allegorical representation, but does so only in order to enable a higher mode of 'signification'—no longer binary and re-presentational, but participatory and experiential. Allegory is simultaneously exploded, but thereby also reaches beyond its own limits, transcending the binary rupture at the heart of *alieniloquium* in order to attain a higher form of non-binary, participatory self-identity.

This is the idea that lies at the heart of Need's speech, as he ventriloquizes the voice of Christ on the cross and urges Will to embrace his affinity with God through their shared experience of 'suffering'—the only philosophical knowledge worthy of that name:

> 'God gouerneþ alle goode vertues;
> And Nede is next hym, for anoon he mekeþ
> And as lowe as a lomb for lakkyng þat hym nedeþ;
> For Nede makeþ nedé fele nedes lowe-herted.
> Philosophres forsoke welþe for þei wolde be nedy.
> And woneden wel elengely and wolde noʒt be riche.
> And God al his grete ioye goostliche he lefte,
> And cam and toke mankynde and bycam nedy.
> So he was nedy, as seiþ þe Book, in manie sondry places,
> That he seide in his sorwe on þe selue roode,
> "Boþe fox and fowel may fle to hole and crepe,
> And þe fissh haþ fyn to flete wiþ to reste,
> There nede haþ ynome me, that I mote nede abide
> *And suffre sorwes ful soure, þat shal to ioye torne*"
> Forþi be noʒt abasshed to byde and to be nedy,
> Siþ he þat wroʒte al þe world was wilfulliche nedy,
> Ne neuere noon so nedy ne pouerer deide.'
>
> (B XX.34–50; my emphasis)

As Hewett-Smith observes, 'the incarnation is figured not only as a merciful redemption of fallen humanity, but also as the necessary fulfilment of divine lack. [...] Behind these daring images is a kind of mutual hunger on the part of both God and man [...]. Such shared need ultimately redeems the rift between human and divine, not by privileging one destination over the other, but by reconfiguring

---

[71] Hewett-Smith, 'Nede ne hath no lawe', p. 233.

THE ENDS OF EXPERIENCE: INCARNATION AND APOCALYPSE   477

that gap as the site for a discourse of mutuality, a recuperative faith'.[72] Again we find the striking reciprocity of suffering that can create a genuine degree of mutual, reciprocal understanding and identification between God and humanity. Within the incarnational perspective of the poem's final developments, and in the context of the epistemology of *contreres choses* established in *passus* B XVIII, the experience of individual need and suffering does not so much 'signify' the ability to transcend suffering, but rather becomes coterminous with the transcendence of suffering itself, allowing suffering to coincide with its polar opposite: joy.

It is significant that Langland here should deliberately avoid using the register of personal, autobiographical complaint in the manner of Deguileville: instead of composing a personal and even autobiographical lament, he chooses to place this reflection into the mouth of the 'allegorical' character of Nede. This allows him to provide a far more detached and philosophical reflection on the significance of the human experience of suffering, understood as a means of 'compassionate' and salvific participation in the paradoxical joy/suffering of the Incarnation. But Langland also complements this rather abstract conversation with a more personal account of the human experience suffering, in the shape of Will's brief encounter with Elde, integrated within the larger account of Antichrist's attack on the Church. This episode therefore marks the return to the dream-world, but also demands to be read thematically as a continuation of the waking encounter with Nede, which is concluded a mere forty-five lines earlier. Elde appears as part of the forces of Kind, summoned by Conscience to persecute the attackers besieging the Barn of Unity:

> Thanne mette þise men, er mynstrals myȝte pipe,
> And er heraudes of armes hadden discryued lordes,
> Elde þe hoore; he was in þe vauntwarde
> And bare þe baner bifore Deeþ—by riȝt he it cleymede.
>
> (B XX.93–6)

Both here and in his subsequent personal attack on Will, Elde is understood as a force for good. His second appearance is even more clearly motivated by moral concerns, since Conscience appeals to Elde in the hope of chastening the citizens of Unity into banishing Despair and amending their ways: 'For care Conscience þo cryde vpon Elde, / And bad hym fonde to fighte and afere Wanhope' (B XX.165–6).

Despite this clear effort to present Elde as a force of moral regeneration, however, the undiscriminating relentlessness of his attack lends the character a terrifying aura that is more difficult to accommodate in terms of clear moral schemata. Instead of being endowed with an intrinsic moral or spiritual significance of its own, Elde, like Nede, functions as a personification of a raw fact of

---

[72] Hewett-Smith, 'Nede ne hath no lawe', pp. 252, 253.

478   MEDIEVAL ALLEGORY AS EPISTEMOLOGY

life and is therefore a fundamentally *a-moral* force. It signifies mere privation or diminution of being, and accordingly resists any firm allegorical interpretation and spiritualization, and even threatens the very project of an allegorical hermeneutics altogether. This considerably complicates the allegorical status of Elde, making it a profoundly ambivalent character whose significance cannot be automatically plotted onto the pattern of binary oppositions between the forces of Holy Church and Antichrist. This impression is enhanced by his savage yet comical attack on Will himself, reminding us that the destiny of Will is closely bound up with the destiny of the Barn of Unity as a whole,[73] while also suggesting that Will, despite his long journey, is *still* in need of serious penitential re-formation:

> And Elde anoon after hym, and ouer myn heed yede,
> And made me balled bifore and bare on the croune;
> So harde he yede ouer myn heed it wol be sene euere.
>   [. . .]
> He buffetted me aboute þe mouþ and bette out my wangteeþ
> And gyued me in goutes—I may noȝt goon at large.
> And of þe wo þat I was inne my wyf hadde ruþe,
> And wisshed ful witterly þat I were in heuene.
> For þe lyme þat she loued me fore, and leef was to feele—
> On nyghtes, namely, whan we naked weere—
> I ne myght in no manere maken it at hir wille,
> So Elde and heo it hadden forbeten.
>
> (B XX.183–5; 191–8)

Deguileville's description of the pilgrim's encounter with the pair Vieillesse (Old Age) and Enfermete (Infirmity) provides the immediate source for this episode, and Langland merges features borrowed from both characters to describe Elde. In both versions of *PVH*, Vieillesse arrives to visit the pilgrim in the company of Enfermete. They are messengers of Mort, and both are equipped with their respective attributes: Vieillesse has feet of lead and carries crutches, while Enfermete is dressed like a wrestler and carries a bed on her head (*PVH1* 13,043–55; *PVH2* 17,113–26). The resonances with Langland's description of Elde are, for once, fairly precise, and seem to me to demonstrate direct influence beyond any reasonable doubt.[74] Where in Langland 'Lif fleiȝ for feere to Phisik after helpe / And bisouȝte hym of socour, and of his salue hadde' (B XX.169–70), and 'Elde auntred hym on Lyf, and at þe laste he hitte / A phisicien with a furred hood, þat he fel in a palsie, / And þere dyed þat doctour er þre dayes after' (XX.175–7),

---

[73] See also Aers, 'Visionary Eschatology', 12.

[74] Barney also suggests a possible influence, *Penn Commentary 5*, p. 219.

THE ENDS OF EXPERIENCE: INCARNATION AND APOCALYPSE   479

Deguileville describes Enfermete her attack upon Sante (Health), guarded by Medicine, complete with her distinctive hood (*huvet*, cf. 'enhuvete'):[75]

'J'ai nom,' dist-elle, 'Enfermete,
Qui par tout ou je truis Sante
Je me preng a li pour luitier,
Pour li vaincre et sousmarchier.
    [...]
Mes pou, si com croi, m'abatist,
S'aucun confort ne li fëist
Medicine l'enhuvetee,
Qui pour moi enchacier fu nee'.
    (*PVH1* 13,097–106;
    cf. *PVH2* 17,168–78)

'My name', she said, 'is Sickness, and wherever I find Health I start to wrestle with her, to trample and conquer her. [...] She would seldom knock me down, I think, if it were not that she is given some help by Medicine, the hooded one, who was born to drive me away'.

Just like Elde's attack is meant to convert those who 'forȝyte sorwe, and ȝyue noȝt of synne' (B XX.155), so Enfermete declares that she acts on the authority of 'he who created nature' [cil qui fist Nature, *PVH1* 13,135; *PVH2* 17,206; cf. 'Kynde' B XX.201 ff.):

'sui celle
Qui ramentoif Penitance
Quant est mise en oubliance,
Qui les devoies ravoie
Et remet en droite voie'.
    (*PVH1* 13,130–4; *PVH2* 17,201–5)

'I am the one who reminds people of Penance, when she has been forgotten, and brings back those who are lost and sets them on the right way again'.

Finally, even the dry, half-sardonic, half-comical tone of Will's response to Elde's attack seems adapted from the pilgrim's reaction to the arrival Enfermete. Will's '"Sire yuele ytauȝt Elde [...] vnhende go wiþ þe! / Siþ whanne was þe way ouer mennes heddes?"' (XX.186–7) neatly matches the pilgrim's laconic '"you are not a messenger to be welcomed warmly"' ['Tu n'es,' dis, 'pas messagiere / A cui doie bonne chiere / Faire', *PVH1* 13,127–9; cf. *PVH2* 17,198–200].

In addition, Vieillesse's unusual characterization provides numerous details that Langland retains, and her description helps to assess the wider significance of this encounter within the two poems. Unusually, Vieillesse is both white-haired and bald [le chief chanu / Et bien souvent de cheveus nu, *PVH2* 17,264–5]—a detail that Langland adopts but transfers to the description of Will (B XX.183–4). More striking is the fact that Deguileville's Vieillesse too—somewhat surprisingly—is bent on pounding the poor dreamer's phallic 'pilgrim staff' into oblivion:

---

[75] See the relevant entry in Béatrice Stumpf's lexicon of the *Pèlerinages*: http://www.atilf.fr/dmf/definition/enhuveter.

480 MEDIEVAL ALLEGORY AS EPISTEMOLOGY

'Je te batrai tant maintenant
Que ja mes n'aras joie grant.
Courbe et impotent te ferai
Des grans coups je te donrrai.'
  (*PVH1* 13,231–4; *PVH2* 17,284–7)

'I will now beat you so hard that you
will never have great joy. I will bend
you and make you impotent with the
great blows I will rain upon you.'
(translation emended)

Compare Will's complaint about sexual impotence, in a characteristically Lang-landian imaginative register and complete with sexual puns of distinctly proto-Shakespearean character at B XX.191–8 (cited above).[76]

Beyond the rather surprising mention of sexual impotence by a Cistercian monk who might have remained rather more sanguine about his declining sexual powers than the apparently married Will,[77] it is especially the *significance* assigned to Vieillesse's debilitating operation that matters. Vieillesse in fact insists on her status as a privileged voice of authority, a messenger granting access to unadulterated truth: '"You cannot find a messenger who will be able to speak more truthfully"' ['Avoir ne pues messagier qui / En puist parler plus vraiement', *PVH1* 13,194–5; cf. *PVH2* 17,255–6). More specifically, she is presented as a medium for a kind of knowledge that transcends textual obscurities and equivocations of all kinds. Her authority, then, is neither textual, nor argumentative, nor even of the order of ratiocination—but of a higher, specifically *experiential* kind:

'Vieillesce ai nom la redoutee
  [. . .]
Celle a cui conseil demander
On doit et grant honneur porter,
Car ja' vëu le temps passe
Et maint bien et mal *esprouve.*
Ce sont de bon sens les gloses
Et ce par quoi on scet les choses,
Ja ne sera nul scienté,
S'il n'a vëu et esprouve.'
  (*PVH1* 13,201, 13,205–12; *PVH2*
  17,262, 17,266–73; my emphases)

'My name is Old Age, the feared [. . .],
the one people should honour greatly
and look to for counsel, for I have seen
the past and I have seen such that is
good or evil put to the test. These are
the glosses of good understanding, and
we understand things through them.
People will never be wise if they have
not seen things and tested them.'
(Translation emended)

The formulation is striking, and unmistakeably refers back to the epistemology of contraries articulated by the narrator of the *Rose*: 'Ainsinc va des contreres choses / les unes des autres gloses' (*RR* 21,543–4). When Vieillesse affirms that only those

---

[76] On Shakespeare's play on sexual 'will', see Joel Fineman, *Shakespeare's Perjured Eye: The Invention of Poetic Subjectivity in Shakespeare's Sonnets* (Berkeley and Los Angeles: University of California Press, 1986), pp. 22–5.

[77] The precise tenor of the term 'impotent' at this point in *PVH1* is open to debate. The restricted meaning of the term to designate specifically 'sexual impotence' is attested (repeatedly) in the writings of Nicolas Oresme in the 1370s, as given in the DMF (http://www.atilf.fr/dmf/definition/impotence) and in the *Ovide Moralisé*, as given in the *Tobler-Lommatzsch* (http://as-bwc-tl.spdns.org/tl/ocr/tl04.html#impotent).

THE ENDS OF EXPERIENCE: INCARNATION AND APOCALYPSE 481

who have tested or experienced both good and evil ('maint bien et mal esprouvé'), are truly wise ('scienté'), she is in effect paraphrasing the advice given by Jean de Meun's narrator, affirming the primacy of experience and commending the ability to suffer ('soffrir', *RR* 21,541) both 'mal' and 'bien', 'ese' and 'mesese' (*RR* 21, 533–4, 21,540–2). In both poems, then, the rhyme 'gloses/choses' is used to highlight the specifically *non*-textual, experiential, corporeal, and seemingly unmediated nature of such knowledge, insisting on its status as a privileged means for the apprehension of a higher degree of truth than that mediated by textual 'glose' of any kind.

As I have already argued in preceding sections of this chapter, this notion of the cognitive potentialities of experiential 'suffering' also becomes a recurrent *Leitmotif* in the entire closing section of *Piers Plowman*, underpinned by Langland's sustained engagement with the epistemology of contraries as articulated in the *Rose*. While Langland does not retain the details and the wording of Vieillesse's explanations, Elde nevertheless enters the poem at a juncture where a similar epistemology of experience has already been established, notably through Nede's quotation of Christ, endorsing experience through his call to 'suffre sorwes ful soure þat shal to ioye torne' (B XX.47). Once more, then, 'suffering' is presented as a paradoxical yet unambiguously truthful experience that enables the knowledge of binary opposites, transcending a merely nominal, indirect, theoretical, and linguistically mediated understanding of concepts such as 'good' and 'evil'.

All three poems present their respective variations on this endorsement of experiential knowledge shortly before their respective conclusions. Inevitably, in all three cases this commitment to emphatically *non*-textual, *non*-verbal knowledge raises serious questions about the authority of the poems themselves: what kind of knowledge, if any, can such allegorical poetry still hope to convey, given its inherent dependence on strategies of interpretive 'glossing' of all kinds? And to what extent is this endorsement of experiential knowledge even credible and viable, since it is ultimately articulated *through language*, within an allegorical poem whose interpretive hermeneutics we are (again) being invited to mistrust? While the ideas, images, and even specific words used by the three poems to articulate this primacy of experiential knowing remain identical, the implications of this experiential turn vary dramatically across the three works. In the *Rose*, the ironic adoption of the language of demonstrative reasoning to promote an utterly different, non-verbal kind of knowledge clearly fits within the poem's wider commitment to relativism and irresolution, specifically its systematic deconstruction of textual authority, linguistic transparency, and its insistence on the limits of demonstrative reasoning. As I argued in Chapter 1, Jean de Meun very deliberately foregrounds the radically slippery status of poetry, figurative language, and even language as a whole, caught in a potentially endless circle of semiosis and equivocation. The promotion of experience at the expense of 'auctoritee'—'choses' over 'gloses'—therefore fits rather neatly within the poem's larger agenda. In Deguileville's *Pèlerinages*, this commitment to an epistemology of embodied experience sits more uneasily with the wider objectives of the poem. At best, Vieillesse's implicit criticism of textuality and hermeneutics marks the communicative, didactic, and cognitive limits of the author's own allegorical poetry. At worst—and particularly in the context of *PVH2*'s enhanced anxiety about misreading—it signals the impossibility of recuperating allegory as a reliable cognitive and salvific tool. Langland once more appears to have pondered the implications of these respective positions very carefully, and modulates his own version of this commitment to experiential knowledge accordingly. Unlike his French predecessors, Langland does not provide any explicit commentary on the 'experiential' significance of Elde's attack. Instead, he simply describes its symptoms and consequences, leaving the reader to ponder their wider significance within the poem. Langland's pointed insistence on Will's impotence—borrowed from Deguileville but intensified and expanded—is particularly arresting. Marie Clemente Davlin long ago pointed out the irony of Langland's insistence on Will's sexual impotence in a passage that leads up to the appearance of natural 'Kynde',[78] the faculty concerned with procreation—but this is merely the tip of a much larger iceberg. Building on the suggestions of several other readers, I want to argue that the loss of sexual vigour and procreative power is intended very specifically to figure the imminent exhaustion of Will's/Langland's powers of poetic creation. After an extended account of his own visions and revisions, the dreamer/narrator/protagonist—figure of the human 'will'—has attained a stage of poetic and cognitive exhaustion, and figures his own imminent withdrawal from the quest and from his inconclusive poetic work. Crucially, however, the declining power of Will/the will does not mark the end of the searching movement that underpins Langland's allegory: as is suggested by the closing lines of *passus* B XX, the forward movement figured by Conscience's own departure on pilgrimage is carried on beyond the end of the poem, even as Will's individual labour grinds to an inevitable halt. Placed in the final *passus* of the poem, this evocative vision of Will's impotence is intended to prompt one further, final reconsideration of the nature, significance, purpose, effects, and legitimacy of Will's poetic 'makynges'.

Langland's final reconsideration of the value of his own poetic labour is formulated with reference to the specifically temporal and experiential perspective introduced by the arrival of Elde.[79] The episode, I suggest, is best understood in terms of its dialogue with the *Rose*, where Jean de Meun had already explored the parallels between clerical literary craft and ideals of male sexual vigour in playful and subversive fashion (see Chapter 1.5).[80] Langland is clearly aware of the *Rose*'s

---

[78] See Davlin, '"Kynde Knowing" as a Major Theme', 17.
[79] On the value of Langland's/Will's poetic labour in terms of its temporality, see John A. Burrow, 'Wasting Time, Wasting Words in *Piers Plowman* B and C', *YLS* 17 (2003), 191–202.
[80] See for instance Minnis, *Magister Amoris*, pp. 164–208, describing 'a humour characteristic of a world without women, wherein the hardships of enforced celibacy are often relieved by elaborate

THE ENDS OF EXPERIENCE: INCARNATION AND APOCALYPSE 483

use of metaphorical language to figure sexual procreation. This includes the ample reliance on the entire semantic field of religious devotion—figuring erotic desire as 'pilgrimage', sexual activity as the adoration of relics, and the play with images of mystical/sexual penetration during the defloration scene[81]—but also the poem's tendency to represent sexual copulation in terms of figurative 'writing', 'forging', and agricultural 'ploughing'. These metaphors are all employed by Genius during his extended and outrageous sermon, delivered to the assembled troops of the God of Love immediately before their final attack on the castle and the ensuing defloration. For a start, Langland is engaged in writing a poem saturated by agricultural metaphors of sowing, ploughing, harrowing, and harvesting—metaphors that are particularly prominent in *passus* B XIX. Langland therefore could not have failed to remember the *Rose*'s memorable and scandalous play on agricultural metaphors to describe sexual procreation. In particular, he must have remembered the 'diffinitive santance' that rounds off Genius's insane sermon (*RR* 19,474 ff.), where he calls upon all barons of the land to plough their fields and sow their seeds: 'Plough, barons, plough for God's sake, and restore your lineage' [Arez, por Dieu, baron, arez, / et voz lignages reparez, *RR* 19,671–2]. Genius employs the metaphor of sexual ploughing throughout his sermon, but for good rhetorical measure also supplements it with two further tropes that figure sexual copulation and natural procreation: writing and forging/hammering. These make up the three metaphors that Genius uses again and again in his relentless tirade, decrying the deviant practices of all those who refuse to perform according to the laws of Nature:

'Bien deüssent avoir grant honte	'They ought to be deeply ashamed,
cil delleal don je vos conte,	those disloyal ones of whom I speak,
quant il ne daignent la main metre	who will not deign to put their hands to
en tables por escrivre letre	the tablets to write a letter nor to make
ne por fere anpreinte qui pere.	any visible mark upon them. Their
Mout sunt d'antancion amere,	intentions are extremely evil, for the
qu'el devandront toutes moussues,	tablets will grow very mossy if left
s'el sint en oiseuse tenues.	unused. When the anvils are allowed to
Quant san cop de martel ferir	go to rack and ruin without a single
lessent les anclumes perir,	hammer-blow being struck, then rust
or s'i peut la rouielle anbatre,	can attack them and no sound of
sanz oïr marteler ne batre.	hammering or beating will be heard. If
Les jaschieres, qui n'i refiche	no one drives the ploughshares into the
le soc, redemourront en friche.	fallow fields,

---

sexual fantasies and sometimes express themselves through an interest in virility which is, in every sense, purely academic' (194). See also Huot, 'Bodily Peril'; Kay, *The Romance of the Rose*, pp. 78–83.

[81] In this point, in addition to Chapter 1 above, see especially Watson, 'Grace Holds the "Clicket"'; and Alice Lamy, 'The Romance of the Non-Rose'.

Vis les puisse l'an anfoïr,	they will remain fallow. These people
quant les oustiz osent foïr	should be buried alive for daring to
que Diex de sa main antailla	neglect the tools that God fashioned
quant a ma dame [Nature] les	with his own hand and gave to my lady.
bailla,	He chose to give them to her so that she
qui por ce les li vost baillier	would be able to make similar ones and
qu'el seüt autex antailler	so give eternal life to mortal creatures.
por doner estres pardurables	
au creatures corumpables.	
(*RR* 19,531–52)	
il despisent la droite raie	They despise the straight furrow of the
du champ bel et planteüreus,	fair and fertile field; those wretches
et vont comme maleüreus	who go tilling the desert ground where
arer en la terre deserte	their seed is wasted, and will not
ou leur semance vet a perte,	plough a straight furrow but overturn
ne ja n'i tandront droite rue,	the plough, justifying their evil ways on
ainz vont bestournant la charrue	the basis of abnormal exceptions when
et conferment leur regles males	they decide to follow Orpheus, who
par exceptions anormales,	could not plough or write or forge on
quant Orpheüs veulent ansivre,	the right forge.
qui ne sot arer ne escrivre	
ne forgier en la droite forge	
[. . .]	[. . .]
ainz pervertissent l'escriture	[thus] they pervert what is written
quant il vienent a la lecture'.	when they come to read it'.
(*RR* 19,612–32)	

All three metaphors employed by Genius—ploughing, hammering, and writing—mobilize binary and gendered sets of tools ('oustiz', *RR* 19,564) that denote active and passive principles, masculine and feminine: plough and arable land ('charrues' and 'jaschieres' *RR* 19,518–19); stylus and wax tablets ('greffes, tables', *RR* 19,516); hammer and anvil ('marteaus, anclumes', *RR* 19,516). As has often been observed, two of the metaphors employed by Genius—writing and hammering—have a much longer history as figures for natural sexual reproduction, and are borrowed directly from Alan of Lille's twelfth-century Neoplatonist cosmological allegory, the *Complaint of Nature*. The exact significance of the suggested homology between the act of writing and sexual procreation in both Alan's and Jean's poems remains a matter of considerable debate, and I will not attempt to resolve this question here.[82] What seems abundantly clear, and what is most

---

[82] On the topic see, among others, Wetherbee, 'The Literal and the Allegorical'; ibid, *Platonism and Poetry*, pp. 187–265; Quilligan, 'Allegory, Allegoresis, and the Deallegorisation of Language';

THE ENDS OF EXPERIENCE: INCARNATION AND APOCALYPSE   485

important for my present purpose, however, is that Alan and Jean contribute to the wider currency of the perceived analogy between textual production and sexual reproduction. While at first sight the correspondence appears to be univocal in both texts—writing is a metaphor for sex, but not vice versa—in reality this very *translatio* of meaning also invites a sexualized understanding of scribal and literary craft. This idea implicitly pervades the entire *Rose*, and invites an extended reflection on the nature, purpose, and legitimacy of artistic, and specifically poetic creation.[83] This same idea is also fundamental for appreciating the full resonances of Langland's insistence on Will's impotence in *passus* B XX of *Piers Plowman*.

It will be useful to retrace the precise articulation of this complex cluster of images and ideas before returning to *Piers Plowman*. At the heart of both Alan's and Jean's interest in the analogy between written production and sexual reproduction is a concern with specifically *poetic* writing: its nature, its significance, its philosophical usefulness, and its social and ethical legitimacy. As lady Nature observes in the *De planctu*, poetry is far from being the most obvious and transparent instrument for expressing philosophical truths. What, Nature asks, is the truth-value or credibility of 'the cloudy fictions of the poets' [*umbratilibus poetarum figmentis*]?

Nonne ea quae in puerilibus cunis poeticae disciplinae discuntur, altioris discretionis lima senior philosophiae tractatus eliminat? An igonras quomodo poetae [. . .] falsitatem quadam probabilitatis ypocrisi palliant, ut per exemplorum imagines hominum animos inhonestae morigerationis incude sigillent?	Does not the more mature study of philosophy rub away with the file of deeper understanding those things which one learns in the childish cradles of poetic study? Do you not know how poets [. . .] clothe falsehood itself with a kind of hypocritical probability, so that through their exemplary images they may stamp the minds of men on the anvil of dishonourable emulation?[84]

In raising the question of the efficacy and legitimacy of poetic language as a vehicle for philosophical truths, both Alan and Jean invoke the categories and definitions provided by late classical grammarians and rhetoricians like Quintilian, Donatus, and Priscian, widely read and commented on throughout the medieval period. In their discussion of linguistic construction and expression, theorists universally concurred in defining poetic language as a form of expression depending on figures and tropes, which transgressed against ordinary rules of grammatical correctness and propriety. This becomes abundantly clear in the description of various subcategories of *tropus*, such as *metaphora, catachresis,*

Ziolkowski, *The Grammar of Sex*; Guynn, *Allegory and Sexual Ethics*, pp. 93–170; Rollo, *Kiss my Relics*, pp. 77–213; Huot, *Dreams of Lovers and Lies of Poets*, pp. 49–50, 55–67; Morton, 'Queer Metaphors'.

[83] See Nievergelt, 'Textuality as Sexuality'.

[84] *De planctu naturae*, 8.17, in Alan of Lille, *Literary Works*, ed. and trans. Wetherbee.

486   MEDIEVAL ALLEGORY AS EPISTEMOLOGY

metalepsis, metonymia, antonomasia, and of course *allegoria*, further subdivided.[85] All such tropes are understood as deliberate 'barbarisms' or 'solecisms' employed for expressive effect, and thus amount to *vitia*—i.e. instances of faulty, irregular, or perverse language use. The idea is also expressed by the very definition of what a trope is and how it operates: from the Greek 'τρόπος' (a 'turn'), a trope is a verbal sign that relies on a turning or 'twisting' of ordinary expressions out of their 'proper', original meaning assigned through the normative imposition of *significata*.[86] Because of its reliance on figures and tropes, poetry was therefore widely understood as a being characterized by a 'twisted', distinctly *unnatural* and deviant use of language, transgressing the ordinary prescriptive rules of grammar.

It Alan of Lille's *De planctu naturae* the unnatural and oblique signifying relations that characterize poetic language serve as metaphors for 'unnatural' sexual copulation. Grammatical *vitia* are thus employed as figures for moral, and specifically sexual, *vitia*. Alan's concern is primarily the denunciation of homosexual relations between men, which are deemed 'unnatural' since they fail to perpetuate the species according to normal paradigms of male-female copulation. But the unnatural sexual acts denounced in the poem also include other forms of non-reproductive sex, all of which are subsumed within the wider category of 'sodomy'.[87] In her account of the processes of natural generation, Nature tells us that

<table>
<tr>
<td>

'Terrestrium animantium materiandae propagini Venerem destinavi, ut varias materias in rebus materiandis excudendo substerneret [. . .]. Et ut instrumentorum fidelitas pravae operationis fermentum excluderet, ei duos legitimos malleos assignavit [. . .]. Incudum etiam nobiles officinas eisdem eosdem malleos adaptando rerum effigiationi fideliter indulgeret, ne ab incudibus malleos aliqua exorbitatione peregrinare permitteret. Ad officium etiam

</td>
<td>

'I delegated to Venus the propagation of earthly life in its material aspect; she was to distribute the various kinds of matter, hammering them out in forming material creatures, [. . .]. And to ensure that the precision of the instruments prevented any taint of flawed workmanship, I assigned her two reliable hammers [. . .]. I also designated splendid anvil forges for the performance of this work, instructing her that in applying the hammers to the

</td>
</tr>
</table>

---

[85] For the categorization in the third book of Donatus' *Ars Maior*, see Holtz, *Donat et la tradition de l'enseignement grammatical: etude et edition critique* (Paris, 1981) pp. 671 ff. See also Copeland and Sluiter, *Medieval Grammar and Rhetoric*, especially pp. 29–38 on figurative language.

[86] See Copeland and Sluiter, *Medieval Grammar and Rhetoric*, p. 29. See also Zeeman, 'The Schools Give a Licence to Poets', pp. 156–60; Morton, 'Queer Metaphors', p. 209.

[87] On the broader issue of the significance of sodomy in the Middle Ages, and especially on the slipperiness and inclusiveness of the concept, see the influential work of Jordan, *The Invention of Sodomy in Christian Theology*, esp. pp. 41–4. On the broad inclusiveness of medieval 'sodomy', see also Frantzen, 'The Disclosure of Sodomy in Cleanness'. On this point in relation to the texts discussed here, see Rollo, *Kiss my Relics*, pp. 82–3; Morton, 'Queer Metaphors', 210–11.

scripturae calamum praepotentem eidem fueram elargita, ut in competentibus cedulis eiusdem calami scripturam poscentibus, quarum meae largitionis beneficio fuerat conpotita, iuxta meae orthographiae normulam rerum genera figuraret, ne a propriae descriptionis semita in falsigraphiae devia eumdem devagare minime sustinit.

Sed cum ipsa, genialis concubitus ordinatis complexionibus, res diversorum sexuum oppositioni dissimiles ad exequendam rerum propaginem connectere teneretur, ut in suis connectionibus artis gramaticae constructiones canonicas observaret, suique artificii nobilitas nullius artis ignorantia suae ferret gloriae detrimentum'.

forming of creatures she should be sure to allow only these to strike those anvils, and not allow hammer to diverge from anvil through any transgressive impulse. For the purpose of inscription I bestowed upon her a most powerful pen, that she might depict the different kinds of creatures, according to the rules of my orthography, on pages, provided through my kind generosity, that were prepared to await the inscriptions of this pen, so that she might never permit its writing to stray from the path of truthful description into the side tracks of false writing.

But since Venus was required by the ordained constitution of generative coition to bring the dissimilar parts of the differing sexes into an opposing connection, to ensure the generation of creatures, I taught her, with a magisterial course of hallowed precepts, that in her connections she should follow the canonical constructions of the great art of grammar, that the nobility of her handiwork might suffer no diminishment of its glory through ignorance of this art'.[88]

Among all living beings on earth, only man chooses *not* to conform to such laws of nature. The following passage well illustrates the almost infinitely adaptable possibilities for describing sexual deviance in terms of the deliberate perversion of the grammatical order through various forms of rhetorical 'troping'.

'Solus homo, meae modulationis citharam aspernatus, sub delirantis Orphei lira delirat: humanum namque genus a sua generositate degenerans, in constructione barbarizans, venereas

'Man alone, scorning the music of my harmonious governance, is deluded by the lyre of a delirious Orpheus. For the human race, fallen away from its noble origin, is barbarous in its construction

---

[88] *De planctu naturae* 10.2–3.

regulas invertendo nimis irregulari utitur metaplasmo. Sic homo, Venere Tiresiatus anomala, directam praedicationem per compositionem inordinate convertit. A Veneris orthographia deviando recedens sophista falsigraphus invenitur. Consequentem etiam Dionaeae artis analogiam devitans, in anastrophem vitiosam degenerat. Dumque in tali constructione me destruit. in sua synaeresi mei themesim machinatur'.	of gender, and practises a most irregular metaplasm that inverts the rules of Venus. Thus a male, Tiresias-like in his strange practice of love, transforms direct predication into composition of an irregular kind. Abandoning the orthography of Venus in his truancy, he shows himself a writer of sophistic falsehood. Evading the natural, analogous path of the Dionean art, he falls into the vice of apostrophe. He works my destruction by such constructions, and his combinations threaten to divide me'.[89]

I want to pause briefly to insist on the role assigned to Orpheus in this passage. Alan's allusion to Orpheus's 'delirious' and 'barbarous constructions' rests on the perceived analogy between his poetic activity—troping and perverting the natural grammatical order—and his homosexuality, similarly pursued in defiance of the 'straight path' of natural order and sexual generation, by transforming 'direct predication into composition of an irregular kind'. What Orpheus homosexuality and poetic activity have in common, then, is that they are both conspicuously *unnatural* acts based on the perversion of the natural order of legitimate and productive sexual/grammatical/semantic relations. But of course the allusion occurs within a poem that itself indulges in the guilty pleasures of poetic troping, if only by determining to use grammatical terminology to 'figure' sexual perversion: as Larry Scanlon and others have noted, 'Alain becomes guilty of the very sin he decries in making the comparison'.[90]

This complex structure of ironies and paradoxes clearly informs the allusion to Orpheus in the *Rose*, where Genius likewise condemns those who 'Orpheüs veulent ansivre, /qui ne sot arer ne escrivre / ne forgier en la droite forge' (*RR* 19,621–3, extended citation above). Despite the seemingly anecdotal nature, this evocation of the figure of Orpheus clearly participates in a much wider, sustained reflection on the nature, purpose, and legitimacy of poetic writing in the closing sections of Jean's poem, as has been argued by various critics.[91] As I have already

---

[89] *De planctu naturae* 8.8.

[90] Larry Scanlon, 'Unspeakable Pleasures: Alain de Lille, Sexual Regulation, and the Priesthood of Genius', *Romanic Review* 86.2 (1995), 213–42 (221). See also Guynn, *Allegory and Sexual Ethics*, pp. 93–135; Rollo, *Kiss my Relics*, pp. 98–123; Morton, 'Queer Metaphor'.

[91] Huot, *Dreams of Lovers*, pp. 55–67; Morton, 'Queer Metaphor'; Minnis, *Magister Amoris*, pp. 165–9.

THE ENDS OF EXPERIENCE: INCARNATION AND APOCALYPSE   489

argued in Chapter 1.5, this reflection on the status of art and poetry finally culminates in Jean's retelling of the fable of Pygmalion, and in the lover's spilling
of 'seed' at the very end of the poem, in turn enabling the meta-figural 'scattering' or 'dissemination' of relations of semantic reference across the poem as a
whole. In such a context the mention of Orpheus clearly foregrounds not only
the problem of the relationship between art and nature—*ars simia naturae*[92]—
but raises the question of the status, purpose, and legitimacy of artistic and poetic
creation: just as homosexuality is concerned with the deviant pursuit of pleasure regardless of any reproductive ends, the analogy implies, so the production
of artificial forms to counterfeit the order of nature amounts to a perverse and
ultimately barren, solipsistic activity. As Morton suggests, Jean de Meun all but
forces us to conclude that poetry, and specifically *allegorical* poetry, is inherently
queer.[93]

Let me now return to Langland, whose familiarity with Alan's *De planctu naturae* as well as Jean's *Rose* is not in doubt.[94] Alan's notion of man's refusal to conform
to the laws of nature in terms of sexual and reproductive behaviour is, in fact,
clearly echoed during an earlier sequence of Will's vision. During the vision of
Kynde in the first inner dream, Will notes how

> Reson I sei3 sooþly sewen alle beestes
> In etynge, drynkynge, and in engendrynge of kynde.
> And after cours of concepcion none took kepe of ooþer
>
> (B XI.334–6)

> Reson rewarded and ruled alle beestes
> Saue man and his make: many tymes and ofte,
> No resoun hem folwede, neiþer riche ne pouere
>
> (B XI.369–71)

As Philip Knox and Isabel Davis have separately observed, this roughly reproduces
the argument of Alan's *De planctu*, with reference to the wording of Jean de Meun's
Dame Nature, who in turn redeploys the ideas and motifs put forward by Alan's
lady Nature:[95]

---

[92] Roger Dragonetti, 'Le singe de nature dans le *Roman de la Rose*', in *Mélanges d'Études Romanes
du Moyen Age et de la Renaissance offerts à Jean Rychner* (Paris: Klincksieck, 1978), pp. 149–60.

[93] Morton, 'Queer Metaphors'.

[94] See for instance White, *Nature and Salvation in Piers Plowman*, pp. 60–88 (esp. 65–6); Isabel
Davis, '*Piers Plowman* and the *Querelle of the Rose*: Marriage, Caritas, and the Peacock's "Pennes".'
New Medieval Literatures 10 (2008), 49–86; Rebecca Davis, *Piers Plowman and the Book of Nature*,
pp. 52–64, 152–64.

[95] Knox, *The 'Romance of the Rose' and the Making of Fourteenth-Century English Literature*, p. 138;
Davis, '*Piers Plowman* and the *Querelle de la Rose*', 59–60.

'Ne ne me plain des autres bestes,
[…]
Li malles vet o sa femele,
ci a couple avenant et bele;
tuit angendrent et vont ansamble
toutes les foiz que bon leur samble;
[…]
Mes seus hom [...] cist me fet pis que
nus louveaus.'
(*RR* 18,969–78; 18,991; 19,024)

'I do not complain of the other animals
[…]. The Male goes with the female to
form a fair and pleasing couple, and
they come together to beget young
whenever it seems good to them. [...]
Only man [...] causes me more distress
than any wolf-cub.'

Langland too therefore introduces the problem of 'unreasonable' human exceptionalism by focusing on the human tendency to deviate from what is perceived as 'natural' sexual behaviour—although he does so, clearly, for reasons that are quite different from Alan of Lille's.[96] Regardless of Langland's specific aim in developing these ideas, however, the passage confirms his acquaintance with the gist of Alan's thought on human sexual deviance. More importantly, it is difficult to imagine that Langland would have ignored the wider tradition of using grammatical terminology figuratively to think about natural or unnatural sexuality. This is suggested, first of all, by Langland's deep interest in the discipline of grammar as a whole: 'grammer' is after all 'ground of al', as Anima reminds us (B XV.371).[97] Moreover, Langland's interest in Grammar is creative and idiosyncratic in ways that are reminiscent of Alan's own 'grammar of sex', in that he uses grammatical terminology allegorically. This can be seen in his description of Dowel and Dobet as grammatical 'infinites', but also in the infamous grammatical allegory of 'two maner relacions, / Rect and indiredt' to describe social interaction and economic exchange in the C III.332–405.[98] Significantly, here too the allegory is conceived as humankind's binary 'relacioun' with reason, as Conscience explains:

> '"Indirect" thyng is as hoso coueytede
> Alle kyn kynde to knowe and to folowe

[96] See also Rebecca Davis, '"Save man allone": Human Exceptionality in *Piers Plowman* and the Exemplarist Tradition', in Christopher Cannon and Maura Nolan, eds, *Medieval Latin and Middle English Literature: Essays in Honour of Jill Mann* (Cambridge: D.S. Brewer, 2011), pp. 41–64; and ibid, *'Piers Plowman' and the Book of Nature*, pp. 52–64, 152–64, 184–6. For a different view, arguing for Langland's critique of the *De planctu* tradition, see Davis, '*Piers Plowman* and the *Querelle de la Rose*', 66–76.

[97] On the centrality of the discipline of Grammar in Langland's thought and poetic method, see especially Cannon, 'Langland's *Ars Grammatica*', and now *From Literacy to Literature*, pp. 126–59.

[98] John Alford, 'The Grammatical Metaphor: A Survey of its Use in the Middle Ages', *Speculum* 57.4 (1982), 728–60; Samuel A. Overstreet '"Grammaticus ludens": Theological Aspects of Langland's Grammatical Allegory', *Traditio* 40 (1984), 251–96; Baker, 'Pre-empting Piers' Tearing of the Pardon', 48–59. See also Chapter 6.1.

THE ENDS OF EXPERIENCE: INCARNATION AND APOCALYPSE   491

> And withoute cause to cache to and come to bothe nombres;
> In whiche ben gode and nat gode, and graunte here noyþer wille.
> And þat is nat resonable ne rect.'
>
> (C III.362–6)

What, then, is the significance of Will's impotence, in the context of this well-established tradition for sexualizing both agricultural and grammatical metaphors? Does Langland represent his own 'ploughing' as a reasonable, productive, fertile activity that has simply run out of steam before reaching its final 'end'? Or is his ploughing a form of self-indulgent, solipsistic, and ultimately barren and foolish performance bound to exhaust itself without any hope of producing real fruit—what grammarians described as a proverbial case of *arare litus* (ploughing sand),[99] and what Jean's Genius describes as 'arer en la terre deserte / ou leur semance vet a perte' (*RR* 19,615–16)? What, finally, is the significance of the injunction to 'lerne to loue' (B XX.208), delivered by Kynde (i.e. 'Nature') only a few lines after Will's impotence has been held up for ridicule and/or commiseration? The injunction to 'lerne to loue' makes it clear that Will has not, in fact, even made a start in the process—at least according to Kynde's admittedly exacting definition of 'loue'. The implied suggestion is that Will's dalliance with his 'wyf', 'On nyghtes, namely, whan we naked weere' (B XX.196), did not in fact qualify as 'loue'. While this evokes the recurrent opposition between sexual love and *caritas* that the poem evokes time and again, it also has much sharper implications in the context: since Kynde ultimately personifies the 'natural' order—regardless of the more specific interpretation we chose to adopt for this particular scene[100]—the implied suggestion is that Will's dalliance with his 'wyf' is itself fundamentally 'unnatural'. Rather than simply condemning Will's *concupiscientia carnis*, then, it seems that Kynde here might be condemning a different, deviant kind of *concupiscientia* figured as a sexual pursuit. Will's impotence no longer simply appears as the inevitable consequence of a 'natural' process culminating with the arrival of Elde, but rather as the (anti-)climax of a protracted indulgence in unnatural, deviant,

---

[99] The phrase goes back to Ovid, *Tristia* V.4.48: 'nec sinet ille tuos litus arare boves', in *Tristia. Ex Ponto*, trans. A. L. Wheeler. Rev. G. P. Goold, Loeb Classical Library 151 (Cambridge, MA: Harvard University Press, 1924); (cf. also Horace, *Satires*, I.1.91). The expression was widely used as a proverbial example of a pointless activity and waste of time ('perdere opus suum'). The irony is that the phrase was also commonly used in treatises of medieval semantics as a common example of amphiboly, exemplifying the 'improper' and equivocal use of language characteristic of poetic diction. See e.g. Lambert of Auxerre/Lagny, *Logica (Summa Lamberti)*, ed. Franco Alessio (Florence: La Nuova Italia, 1971), pp. 153–4. For discussion, see Sten Ebbesen, *Commentators and Commentaries on Aristotle's Sophistici Elenchi: A Study of Post-Aristotelian Ancient and Medieval Writings on Fallacies*. 3 vols (Leiden: Brill, 1983), I:183.

[100] The precise significance of Kynde's advice is of course dependent on the interpretation of this elusive personification, which undergoes considerable fluctuation along the spectrum from 'God' to 'Nature' throughout the poem. On competing interpretations of the 'natural' and the figure of Kynde, see especially Davis, *Piers Plowman and the Books of Nature*, esp. pp. 17–18, 193–218; and White, *Nature and Salvation in Piers Plowman*.

492 MEDIEVAL ALLEGORY AS EPISTEMOLOGY

and ultimately emasculating 'loue'. In the light of the comments that precede, it seems to me that Will's ineffectual sexuality figures the kind of deviant behaviour for which he has been taken to task all along: sterile intellectual *concupiscientia*, and ineffectual poetic meddling.

In this respect it is striking, to say the least, that Langland too—like Alan of Lille and Jean de Meun—should describe sexual copulation and poetic activity in closely analogous fashion, in his case by using language of 'meddling' and 'making'. On the one hand we find the animal world, ordering its procreative impulses to conform to the natural rhythms of the seasons:

> Boþe horse and houndes and alle oþere beestes
> *Medled noȝt wiþ hir makes þat mid fole were.*
>
> (B XI.342–3)

On the other hand—and immediately after the end of the inner dream with the vision of Kynde—we encounter Ymaginatif, reproaching Will for his incurable 'medling' with 'makynge' (B XII.16). As Philip Knox has observed, the resonance invites us to juxtapose the naturally regulated abstinence of animals from 'medling' with their 'makes' with Will's own compulsive, solipsistic, unregulated, and sexualized 'medling' with his own 'makynge'.[101] The implication of Ymaginatif's attack, then, appears to be that such 'makynge' is a doubly inadequate surrogate for natural sexuality: on the one hand such meddling distracts Will from the far more productive devotional activities he ought to perform—'bidding of bedes' (cf. B XII.28)—while on the other they allow him to indulge in the dissolute, sexualized but ultimately barren pleasures of poetic making. At best such meddling is self-indulgent, delusional, masturbatory and hence 'sodomitical',[102] echoing the pleasures of Jean de Meun's Pygmalion. At worst it is an outright caricature of sexual reproduction and a perversion of the act of divine 'making'.

Ymaginatif's attack upon Will does not only distantly chime with Will's much later encounter with Elde in terms of its broader themes and images: the former, I suggest, is in fact deliberately designed to foreshadow the latter. We are accordingly invited to remember this earlier meeting with Ymaginatif once we finally encounter Elde in *passus* B XX. Ymaginatif had warned Will precisely about the inevitable coming of old age and the impeding loss of vigour: 'amende it in þy myddel age, lest myȝt þe faille / In þyn olde elde' (B XII.7–8). More importantly, Ymaginatif also foreshadows Kynde's insistence on the central importance of Christian love as a remedy against the onslaught of age, described it in much the same terms of

---

[101] Knox, *The 'Romance of the Rose' and the Making of Fourteenth-Century English Literature*, pp. 137–41.

[102] On the inclusion of a wide range of non-reproductive sexual acts—including masturbation—in the category of 'sodomy', see the references given above, n. 87.

THE ENDS OF EXPERIENCE: INCARNATION AND APOCALYPSE   493

physical blows later employed to describe Elde's attack on Will's 'forbeten' sexual 'lyme' (B XX.195, 198):

> 'And Dauid in þe Sauter seiþ, of swiche þat loueþ Iesus,
> *Virga tua et baculus tuus, ipsa me consolata sunt, &c*
> "Alþouȝ þow strike me wiþ þi staf, wiþ stikke or wiþ yerde,
> It is but murþe as for me to amende my soule"'
>
> (XII.13–15)

It is debatable whether we are also invited to read Ymaginatif's insistent rhetorical pounding of Will with the threat of 'staf', 'stikke', or 'yerde' as yet another sexualized image—alluding to the displaced, and hence unnatural (homo)erotic pleasures awarded by the master's *virga* in the schoolroom.[103] It is certainly true that in the context of Langland's sustained dialogue with the *Rose*—with its own obscene troping of 'pilgrim staffs' and 'satchels', and with its own eroticization of a misogynistic all-male clerical culture[104]—this possibility no longer seems quite so far-fetched. What is more evident, however, is that with Ymaginatif's insistence on the positive, spiritually enabling significance of physical pain and discipline, we are already offered a first glimpse of the paradoxical epistemology of 'suffering' that will come to dominate the later stages of Will's quest.

One further intra-textual reference informs and complicates the significance of Will's encounter with Elde in terms of the correspondence between visionary poetic 'makyng' and sexual reproduction. This, I suggest, is the episode of Study's 'scatological curse' with which I began my discussion of Langland's response to Deguileville in Chapter 5:

> 'For alle þat wilneþ to wite þe whyes of God almyȝty,
> I wolde his eiȝe were in his ars and his fynger after
> Þat euere wilneþ to wite why þat God wolde
> Suffre Sathan his seed to bigile,
> Or Iudas the Iew Iesu bitraye.'
>
> (B X.124–8)

I have previously argued that in the passage Langland's Study sets out to condemn not only theological curiosity in a general sense, but more specifically the kind of

---

[103] I allude to the ideas presented in Ralph Hanna, 'School and Scorn: Gender in *Piers Plowman*', *New Medieval Literatures* 3 (2000), 213–27, echoed by Zeeman, '*Piers Plowman* in Theory', pp. 226–7. For further discussion of the *Rose*'s influence on Langland's punning habits, especially in the B-text, see also Watson, 'Grace Holds the "Clicket" to the Heavenly "Wiket"'; and Davis, '*Piers Plowman* and the *Querelle de la Rose*', 76–84.

[104] Minnis, *Magister Amoris*, pp. 164–208.

494 MEDIEVAL ALLEGORY AS EPISTEMOLOGY

intellectual and imaginative *concupiscentia* that underpins Deguileville's allegorical poetry. More specifically, I argued that Langland here signals his disapproval of the extreme, convoluted allegorical 'troping' performed by Deguileville's Grace Dieu in *PVH2*, where she invites the pilgrim to place his eyes in his ears in order to visualize the shape of the theological virtues of Faith and Hope (see Chapter 5.1). In the wake of the preceding discussion of tropes as conspicuously 'unnatural' forms of verbal signification broadly analogous with sexual deviance, it seems to me that Study's curse may be more strictly 'sodomitical' as opposed to merely scatological. The butt of the joke, however, is not just Deguileville's Grace Dieu but Will himself, who follows in the footsteps of the incorrigibly inquisitive-yet-obtuse, converted-yet-relapsed pilgrim/author of *PVH2*. Study's attack accordingly foregrounds the perversely 'wilful' nature of a dreamer who 'wilneþ to wite' twice over (X.124, 126), providing yet another encrypted authorial signature. Will's later encounter with Elde, with its evocation of the dreamer's flagging 'lyme' and the implied suggestion of unwholesome sexuality, accordingly reverberates with echoes of Study's earlier outrage about the dreamer's perverse, intellectually sodomitical inclinations.

The possibility that Will's authorial 'makyng' might be seen as a sexualized but sterile, and thus ultimately sodomitical activity, usefully converges with James J. Paxson's reading of Will's encounter with Elde.[105] Paxson too, like Morton—albeit adopting the radically different theoretical foundations of Lacanian psychoanalysis—begins by insisting on 'the link between the un-straightness of the queer and the un-straightness of *tropos*, a turning'.[106] In a dizzying reading of the short but rhetorically overdetermined and 'semiotically strained' encounter between Will and Elde, Paxson sees the latter as a sodomitical 'simulacrum of sexual intercourse'.[107] Since for Paxson troping amounts to a kind of sodomy, and allegory can ultimately be 'equated [. . .] to the queer itself', Langland's entire poetic project is fundamentally sodomitical and solipsistic, 'a metanarrative about the semiotic making of figures and tropes'.[108] Paxson is therefore fundamentally right, I believe, in suggesting that Will's encounter with Elde provides one further, final, highly sexualized and deeply ambivalent authorial signature: it affirms Will's/Langland's paradoxical presence/absence precisely by displaying the exhaustion of his sexual/textual vigour in a scene of poetic emasculation. Elde's 'forbeting' of Will's 'lyme' thus equivocally figures the annihilation of the dreamer's 'will': it announces the failure of a sexualized and gendered authorial project while

---

[105] James J. Paxson, 'Gender Personified, Personification Gendered, and the Body Figuralized in *Piers Plowman*', *YLS* 12 (1998), 65–96; and ibid. 'Inventing the Subject and the Personification of Will in *Piers Plowman*: Rhetorical, Erotic, and Ideological Origins and Limits in Langland's Allegorical Poetics', in Hewett-Smith, *William Langland's Piers Plowman: A Book of Essays*, pp. 195–231.

[106] 'Gender Personified', 91.

[107] 'Inventing the Subject', pp. 199, 200, 222.

[108] 'Inventing the Subject', pp. 222, 223; 'Gender Personified', 91.

THE ENDS OF EXPERIENCE: INCARNATION AND APOCALYPSE   495

also marking the limits of human *voluntas*. The episode thus marks a pivotal point in the poem's paradoxical dialectic between composition and 'unmakyng'—poetic, authorial, and corporeal/experiential. What persists beyond the annihilation of the personal, embodied will/Will, therefore, is the irreducible but strictly *figurative* proliferation of the poem's semantic meanings, detached from any kind of masculine authorial control.

At the heart of this paradoxical affirmation/unmaking of the self lies Langland's persistent, endemic anxiety about the potential barrenness of his literary 'makynges'. This inevitably exacerbates the difficulty of assessing the tone and significance of the poem's ending. Is this merely yet another instance in a potentially endless series of poetic crises, reiterating the *aporia* that already imploded the A text? Or does the poem at least gesture towards some form of closure and satisfaction, where Will can genuinely 'lerne to loue'? It seems to me that once more Langland will have it both ways. His persistent engagement with the paradoxical, non-binary logic of *contreres choses* in this closing section suggests that instead of choosing between these mutually exclusive alternatives, we are invited to recognize their interdependence and ultimate identity. This means that Will's experience of his own impotence becomes meaningful and liberating not so much because it is an inevitable consequence of the natural change brought about by the passing of time and the arrival of Elde—who, like Vieillesse, is a 'messagier [. . .] qui / [. . .] puist parler plus vraiement' (*PVH1* 13,194–5; *PVH2* 17,255–6). Rather, it acquires its full meaning as the culmination of a process through which Will experiences the paradoxical significance of human suffering as a path to love and joy. According to the logic of *contreres choses*, this bathetic sexual anticlimax does not so much *figure*, but *is* the spiritual climax of the poem[109]—suitably understated, and all but overlooked by readers and commentators. Will's impotence thus simultaneously marks a recognition of the intrinsically and irreducibly perverse nature of Will's/the will's wayward 'meddling' and sodomitical tendencies, but thereby also enables Will to purge, exorcize, and to some extent abolish and transcend those same tendencies by withdrawing into a pure, silent, passive lack of agency and being.

This moment of cognitive and ontological reversal that concludes the poem hinges principally on Will's exacerbated, terminal experience of his condition as an embodied, corporeal subject. On one level, this completes the poem's larger, gradual movement away from a sprawling body of supposedly authoritative and revelatory 'texts' and 'glosses' towards the body of the individual subject, understood as the site for more truthful inscription of the human experience of suffering in time. In this final scene, then, Will's body is presented not as a vigorous, reliable, active, masculine, let alone sanctified body, but as an ailing, decaying, fallible, suffering, passive, and feminized one. Within the incarnational perspective introduced by *passus* B XVIII, it is precisely the broken, fallible, and passive human

---

[109] I echo Alice Lamy's comments on the *Rose*, in 'The Romance of the Non-*Rose*'.

body that becomes the site for the paradoxical experience of the divine. Conversely, it is only Langland's own attainment of such a state of exhaustion that can function as a valid proof to himself that he has truly internalized the logic of *facere quod est in se*, reaching the uttermost limits of his own possibilities for 'doing' through/beyond the exhaustion of imaginative, intellectual, poetic, and corporeal forms. Having attained the utmost limits of 'makyng'—understood as a necessarily inadequate, incongruous, infinitely perfectible manifestation of 'doing'—the exhausted Will/will has finally attained a state where participation in the divine appears at least possible. This exhaustion of literal and metaphorical forms—physical, cognitive, poetic, and representational—marks a precondition for the subject's readiness to receive the gift of grace in forms that as yet—and *necessarily* so—lie beyond the poem's own representational power, dimly figured in Conscience's decision to 'bicome a pilgrym' at the end of the poem (B XX.381). Langland's conclusive poetic gesture, then, is one of a spiritually enabling textual 'unmaking', brought about by an analogous unmaking of the corporeal and substantial self within a still wider, apocalyptic perspective. It asserts the primacy of the body as a site of the human experience of time and finitude—and, conversely, as a site for the passive and paradoxical experience of divine omnipotence and transcendence. Such a passive experience, however, can only become accessible through the continuous, repeated, and constantly reiterated exhaustion of the self.

4. False Conclusions

Langland's short but poignant description of the attack of Elde compounds the sense of paradox and anticlimax that dominates the final *passus*, and traces a terminal decline of the author's sexual and textual powers of allegorical 'makyng'. But it does not mark the end of the poem's narrative, which continues with an account of the fall of the Barn of Unity. These events simultaneously mark a final return to the master-narrative of sacred history for humanity as a whole, but also bizarrely stand as a sort of 'coda' to Will's personal and poetic demise. It is in this coda that Langland's reflection on the nature and value of his poetry also takes on a more abstract, philosophical and metaphysical form. Langland achieves this by probing still more deeply the paradoxical logic of *contreres choses*, pointing towards a form of understanding that relies on the coincidence and elimination of binary opposites. He does so by engaging one final time with the paradox crystallized by the haunting figure of Faux Semblant.

I have already mentioned the latter's role as a model for the figure of Langland's Friar Flatterer, who concludes and implodes the poem's final vision. It will be remembered that beyond his obvious associations with apocalypticism and anti-mendicant satire, however, the figure of Faux Semblant in the *Rose* also functions as a surrogate for Jean de Meun's evasive and 'duplicitous' authorial persona

THE ENDS OF EXPERIENCE: INCARNATION AND APOCALYPSE   497

(see Chapter 1.4). As I have argued more fully elsewhere, this aspect of Faux Semblant's description appears to have been registered by later vernacular authors and readers of the *Rose*, who often developed their own models of authorship in response to Jean's shifty character.[110] As a personification of the liar paradox, Faux Semblant is a particularly useful figure to think about the mechanisms of broadly 'allegorical' poetry: based upon a pattern of double signification, and foregrounding the power of figuration inherent in specifically poetic language in order to stake its claim to convey a higher philosophical truth, such poetry is inherently 'duplicitous'. Narrative allegory of the kind popularized by the *Rose* is therefore inherently concerned with its own status as a figurative artefact, whose very ability to produce a surplus of 'philosophical' meaning is wholly dependent upon the *dis*-junction between multiple levels of signification.

Langland's portrait of Friar Flatterer equally participates in this largely abstract and theoretical reflection on the ethics and epistemology of poetic writing. In a powerful study of 'Penance and Personification' in *Piers Plowman*, Larry Scanlon has already identified many of the semiotic and representational paradoxes that underpin both the figure of Faux Semblant and Langland's treatment of penance—without reference however, to Friar Flatterer. In his study, Scanlon argues that Langland's pointed interest in the inherent paradoxes of penance is inextricably associated with his wider interest in the mechanics of poetic representation, specifically those that underpin allegorical personification. Scanlon in effect identifies a common principle of semantic rupture at the heart of both penitential action and poetic expression. In the case of Penance, we encounter a subject who verbally *identifies* with a particular sin—and is therefore rendered identical with it—but who also simultaneously denounces and renounces that identification through the act of confession. Scanlon calls this the 'confessant paradox', which he proceeds to illustrate with the example of Glutton in *passus* B V. This same tension between identification and alterity, being and signification, mimesis and *alieniloquium*, similarly structures the creation of poetic meaning. This is particularly evident in the case of figurative or 'allegorical' signification, based upon a disjunction between the *letre* and *sen* (*RR* 7132-3), *fet* and *diz* (*RR* 11,192), *semblance* and *senefiance*, or what is 'said', and what is 'signified', to adopt once more Donatus's terms. Both poetry and penance, then, signify allegorically for Scanlon, and presuppose 'a structure of intelligibility that finds its significance precisely in the distance between it and the object to which it makes reference'.[111]

Turning to the historical manifestations of this paradox, Scanlon identifies one of its most influential instances in Jean de Meun's figure of Faux Semblant—a

---

[110] Nievergelt, 'L'Ombre de Faus Semblant'.
[111] Scanlon, 'Penance and Personification', 18. For a wider discussion of religious allegory that is 'not so much oblivious to the differences in [...] materials as exhilarated by the challenge of bringing them together', see also Zeeman, 'Medieval Religious Allegory: French and English', in Copeland and Struck, eds, *The Cambridge Companion to Allegory*, pp. 148–61 (154).

498   MEDIEVAL ALLEGORY AS EPISTEMOLOGY

character who is both an embodiment of the liar paradox, an agent of specious confession, and the paradoxical means for obliterating Malebouche's own acts of mis-speaking in a scene of confession-turned-murder (see Chapter 7.2). In doing so, Faux Semblant ultimately crystallizes the ruptures and paradoxes of allegorical expression, and comes to stand as a paradigmatic figure for the maker of poetic allegories:

> To live up to his name, to fulfil properly his allegorical destiny, Faus Semblant must truthfully recount his falseness. It is obvious that the self-reflexive resources of such a figure might seem attractive to producers of poetic fictions. I wish to stress not simply the falseness which Faus Semblant figures but two further points: first, the irreducibility of the figure's service to the truth; and second, the inverse, eccentric nature of its self-reflection. However appropriate this figure might be to poetic fictions generally, it is particularly appropriate to poetic fictions that aspire to transcendent truths. [...] Faus Semblant suggests that the link between poetry and truth is an inverse one. Paradoxically it is when poetry is at its falsest, at its most fictive, in short, at its most poetic, that it best expresses the truth that entirely transcends it. Moreover, the figure makes this suggestion in a manner that is itself inverted, bracketed, set off from the narrative structure it inhabits by its own self-proclaimed falsity. It thus implicates narrative's own intrinsic capacities for self-reflection no less than poetry's relation to truth. That is to say, as a figure whose essence is falsity, in its reflection on its own narrativity it makes narrative self-reflection tantamount to falsification.[112]

These observations seem to me to offer several massively important possibilities in terms of our understanding of the role of Friar Flatterer—another apocalyptic peddler of dubious penance as well as a highly skilled and duplicitous rhetorician. Like Faux Semblant, personification of the liar paradox, Friar Flatterer systematically undermines the very possibility of truthful speech, by subverting signification of all kinds:

> al þe crop of Truþe
> Torned it tyd vp-so-doun, and overtilte the roote,
> And made Fals sprynge and sprede and spede mennes nedes.
> (B XX.53–5; capitals mine)

But if the relation between poetry and truth is really an inverse one, as Scanlon suggests, then Friar Flatterer too calls out to be seen as an 'eccentric' mouthpiece for some higher form of poetic truth. If this is the case, he comes to stand as yet

---

[112] Scanlon, 'Penance and Personification', 18–19.

THE ENDS OF EXPERIENCE: INCARNATION AND APOCALYPSE 499

another implicit authorial alter-ego, invested in the process of 'finding out' Truth that constantly dis- and re-organizes Langland's entire poem.

The question of what this 'truth' might consist of, and how exactly it may be inferred, however, remains more difficult to determine. As a further manifestation of the liar paradox, Friar Flatterer appears as an eminently 'double' figure, whose very determination to deceive conceals a form of higher truth, which can be inferred through its deliberate negation. I would therefore suggest that Langland's use of Friar Flatterer ought to be understood as a further stage in the poem's movement towards increasingly negative and paradoxical forms of knowledge and presence. Indeed, it seems to me that Friar Flatter's own paradoxical status provides one final instance of Langland's engagement with the paradoxical epistemology of *contreres choses* that he adopts from the *Rose*. It seems useful to frame the function of Friar Flatterer also in terms of Langland's commitment to representational negativity, as articulated by Vance Smith. The appearance of sir *penetrans domos* appears to constitute a final, and accordingly extreme and exacerbated manifestation of this principle of paradoxical negativity described by Smith:

> the poem does not merely negate things in the simple sense of the word; it does not cancel out opposites, nor even predicates that we would like to know about but cannot. It is precisely because negation has a kind of presence, because it continues to do something, that the poem's theory of reference is so complex. [. . .] Put in the terms of modern theology, one of the primary motives of this thinking of and around the negative in the poem is a search for a non-predicative language. [. . .] For the large, ongoing project that is *Piers Plowman* perhaps it would be better to speak of a non-predicative literature, which finds its voice in a *surplus* of context. [. . .] [I]f interruption is the supplement that makes the poem by cancelling its own rigid, pastoral proprieties and expositions, negation is also its *modus procedendi*. Indeed negation is, in a sense, the very language of a poem that exists because its search for salvation cannot exist in language. It gestures towards apophasis, a non-predicative language so radically ecstatic (or, to use a favourite word of the poem, 'ravishing') that it cannot or should not be uttered.[113]

According to this logic, Friar Flatterer becomes the means of the poem's supreme self-affirmation, through an episode that recounts the negation and *unmaking* of the very structures—architectural, political, social, and ecclesiastical, but also linguistic, rhetorical, narrative, poetic, epistemic, and imaginative—that the poem has sought to shape and produce, to 'form' and 're-form', envision and re-vision, as part of its socially, psychologically, and spiritually regenerative agenda. Friar Flatterer thus acts simultaneously as an agent who brings formal and narrative closure

[113] Smith, 'Negative Langland'.

to the poem while eschewing any kind of epistemic closure, affirming and celebrating the infinite perfectibility of the knowledge that the poem channels yet fails
to contain and 'comprehend'. In this sense the figure simultaneously signifies both
the definitive unmaking of the allegorical impetus that sustains the poem, and the
ultimate triumph of allegory's ability to function as *alieniloquium*, to be constantly
'other' than itself. By imploding signification altogether, the poem's 'conclusion'
finally affirms its ability to signify its polar opposite, a plenitude utterly beyond the
text: absence here signifies presence, and the culmination of deception amounts
to an affirmation of an unspeakable truth to be sought beyond the poem, in an
inexhaustible '*surplus* of context'.

Bibliography

Note: For abbreviations used here and throughout, please see list at the start of the volume.

Manuscripts

Arras, Bibliothèque Municipale MS 532 (formerly 845)
London, British Library MS Cotton Tiberius A7
London, Lambeth Palace Library MS 326
Oxford, Oriel College MS 15
Oxford, Bodleian Library MS Douce 300
Paris, BnF MS fr. 829
Paris, BnF MS fr. 1648
Paris, BnF MS fr. 1818
Paris, BnF MS fr. 12466
Paris, BnF MS lat. 14845
Paris, BnF MS lat. 16135
Paris, Bibl. Sainte-Genevieve MS 1130
Troyes, Bibliothèque Municipale MS 1612
Vatican City, Biblioteca Apostolica Vaticana MS Barberini lat. 165

Primary

Aenigmata quaestionum artis rhetoricae ('Bernensia'); Aenigmata; De nominibus litterarum (al. de alphabeto). Expositio alphabeti. De dubiis nominibus, ed. F. Glorie. CCSL 133 A. Turnhout: Brepols, 1962.

Alan Of Lille. *Literary Works*, ed. and trans. Winthrop Wetherbee. Cambridge, MA: Dumbarton Oaks, 2013.

Alan Of Lille. 'Sermo in die cinerum', in Marie-Thérèse d'Alverny, ed., *Alain de Lille: Textes inédits*. Paris: Vrin, 1965.

Aquinas, Thomas. *Expositio libri Peryermenias*, ed. René-Antoine Gauthier, Opera Omnia iussu impensaque Leonis XIII edita, 1*. 1. Rome: Commissio Leonina/Paris: Cerf, 1989.

Aquinas, Thomas. *In I Epist. ad Cor.*, in *Super Epistolas S. Pauli lectura*, ed. Raphael Cai. 2 vols. Turin and Rome: Marietti, 1953.

Aquinas, Thomas. *Quaestiones disputatae de veritate*, ed. A. Dondaine, Editio Leonina, vol 22, 3 vols. Rome: Editori di San Tommaso, 1970–6.

Aquinas, Thomas. *Commentary on Aristotle's De Anima*, trans. Robert Pasnau. New Haven and London: Yale University Press, 1999.

Aristotle. *Analytica posteriora*. Translationes Iacobi, Anonymi sive Ioannis Gerardi et Recensio Guillelmi de Moerbeke, ed. Lorenzo Minio-Paluello and Bernard G. Dod, Aristoteles Latinus 4.1–4. Bruges/Paris: Desclée de Brouwer, 1962.

502 BIBLIOGRAPHY

Aristotle. *Metaphysica, lib. I–XIV, Recensio et Translatio Guillelmi de Moerbeka*, ed. Gudrun Villemin-Diem, Aristoteles Latinus, 25. 3. 2. Leiden: Brill, 1995.

Aristotle. *De interpretatione vel Periermenias. Translatio Boethii*, ed. Lorenzo Minio-Paluello; *Translatio Guillelmi de Moerbeka*, ed. G. Verbeke, rev. Lorenzo Minio-Paluello. Bruges and Paris: Desclée De Brouwer, 1965.

Aristotle. *De anima. Translatio 'nova': Iacobi Venetici translationis recensio; Guillelmus de Morbeka revisor translationis Aristotelis secundum Aquinatis librum*. Turnhout: Brepols, 2011.

Aristotle. *The Complete Works of Aristotle: The Revised Oxford Translation*, ed. Jonathan Barnes. 2 vols. Princeton: Princeton University Press, 1984.

Averroës Cordubensis. *Commentarium Magnum in Aristotelis 'De Anima Libros'*, ed. F. Stuart Crawford. CCAA VI.1. Cambridge, MA., Medieval Academy of America, 1953.

Augustine of Hippo. *De quantitate animae; The measure of the soul; Latin text, with English translation and notes*, ed. Francis A. Tourscher. Philadelphia: The Peter Reilly company/ London: B. Herder, 1933.

Augustine of Hippo. *De trinitate libri XV*, ed. W. J. Mountain and F. Glorie, 2 vols, CCSL 50 and 50A. Turnhout: Brepols, 1968.

Augustine of Hippo. *De Genesi ad litteram*, ed. Joseph Zycha. CSEL 28.1. Vienna: Verlag der Österreichischen Akademie der Wissenschaften, 1894.

Augustine of Hippo. *De magistro*, in *Contra academicos; De beata vita; De ordine; De magistro; De libero arbitrio*, ed. W. M. Green and K. D. Daur, CCSL 29. Turnhout: Brepols, 1970.

Augustine of Hippo. *Against Academicians; The Teacher*, ed. and trans. by Peter King. Indianapolis: Hackett, 1995.

Augustine of Hippo. *De Genesi contra Manichaeos*, ed. D. Weber. CSEL 91. Vienna: Verlag der Österreichischen Akademie der Wissenschaften, 1998.

Augustine of Hippo. *On Genesis. On Genesis: A refutation of the manichees; Unfinished literal commentary on Genesis; The literal meaning of Genesis*, ed. and trans Matthew J. O'connell. New York: New City Press, 2002.

Augustine of Hippo. *De doctrina christiana*, ed. Joseph Martin, CCSL 32. Turnhout: Brepols, 1962.

Augustine of Hippo. *De dialectica*, ed. Jan Pinborg and trans. by B. Darrell Jackson. Dordrecht and Boston: Reidel, 1975.

Augustine of Hippo. *The Trinity*, trans. Edmund Hill. New York: New City Press, 1991.

Augustine of Hippo. *On Christian Teaching*, ed. R. P. H. Green. Oxford: Oxford World's Classics, 1997.

Augustine of Hippo. *Confessions*, ed. Carolyn J.-b. Hammond. 2 vols. Loeb Classics Library 26 and 27. Cambridge, MA: Harvard University Press, 2014–16.

Avicenna (Ibn Sīnā). *Liber de Anima seu Sextus de Naturalibus: Édition critique de la traduction latine médiévale*, ed. Simone Van Riet. 2 vols. Leiden: Brill, 1968–72.

Bacon, Roger. *Opus Tertium*, ed. by J. S. Brewer, in *Fr. Rogeri Bacon Opera quaedam hactenus inedita*, vol. 1. London: Longman, Green, Longman and Roberts, 1859.

Bacon, Roger. *The Opus Maius of Roger Bacon*, ed. John Henry Bridges, 3 vols. Oxford, 1897–1900.

Bacon, Roger. *Summulae Dialectices*, ed. Robert Steele. Oxford, 1940.

Bacon, Roger. *De Signis*, ed. K. M. Fredborg, L. Nielsen, and J. Pinborg, 'An Unedited Part of Roger Bacon's *Opus Majus: De Signis*', *Traditio* 34 (1978), 75–136.

Bacon, Roger. *De multiplicatione specierum*. In David C. Lindberg, ed., *Roger Bacon's Philosophy of Nature: A Critical Ed., with English Transl., Introd., and Notes of De multiplicatione specierum and De speculis comburentibus* Oxford: Clarendon Press, 1983.

Bacon, Roger. *De speculis comburentibus*. In David C. Lindberg, ed., *Roger Bacon's Philosophy of Nature: A critical ed., with English transl., introd., and notes of De multiplicatione specierum and De speculis comburentibus* Oxford: Clarendon Press, 1983.

Bacon, Roger. 'Les *summulae dialectices* de Roger Bacon: Parts 1–2: *De termino, De enuntiatione*', and 'Part 3: *De argumentatione*', ed. Alain de Libera, in *AHDLMA* 53 (1986), 139–289; *AHDLMA* 54 (1987), 171–278.

Bacon, Roger. *Compendium of the Study of Theology*, ed. and trans Thomas S. Maloney. Leiden, 1988.

Bacon, Roger. *Perspectiva*. In David C. Lindberg, ed., *Roger Bacon and the origins of 'Perspectiva' in the Middle Ages: A critical edition and English translation of Bacon's 'Perspectiva' with introduction and notes*. Oxford: Clarendon Press, 1996.

Bacon, Roger. *The Art and Science of Logic*, trans. Thomas S. Maloney. Toronto: PIMS, 2009.

Bacon, Roger. *On Signs*, trans. and intr. Thomas S. Maloney. Toronto: PIMS, 2013.

Bacon, Roger. *Des Signes*, translation and commentary by Irène Rosier-Catach, Laurent Cesalli, Frédéric Goubier and Alain de Libera. Paris: Vrin, 2022.

Bartholomaeus Anglicus, *De proprietatibus rerum. On the Properties of Things: John Trevisa's Translation of Bartholomaeus Anglicus 'De Proprietatibus Rerum': a Critical Text*, ed. Michael C. Seymour. 2 vols. Oxford: Clarendon Press, 1975.

Bernard of Clairvaux. *Opera Omnia*, ed. Jean Mabillon, 2 vols. Paris: Gaume, 1839.

Bernardus Silvestris. *Poetic Works*, ed. and trans. Winthrop Wetherbee. Cambridge MA and London: Harvard University Press, 2015.

Boethius of Dacia. *Modi significandi sive quaestiones super Priscianum maiorem*, ed. J. Pinborg and H. Roos. Copenhagen: GAD, 1969.

Bonaventure, *Opera Omnia*. 10 vols. Quaracchi: Collegium S. Bonaventurae, 1882–1902.

Bradwardine, Thomas. *De Causa Dei Contra Pelagium, et de Virtute Causarum, ad suos Mertonenses, libri tres*. London: 1618.

Carolus de Visch, *Bibliotheca Scriptorum S. Ordinis Cisterciensis*. Cologne, 1656.

Christine de Pizan, *et al. Le Débat sur le 'Roman de la Rose'*, ed. Eric Hicks. Paris: Champion, 1977.

Christine de Pizan. *The Debate of the Romance of the Rose*, ed. and trans. David Hult. Chicago: University of Chicago Press, 2010.

Cicero, Marcus Tullius. *De natura deorum*, ed. B.G. Teubner. Turnhout: Brepols, 2010.

Commentators and Commentaries on Aristotle's Sophistici Elenchi, ed., Sten Ebbesen. 3 vols. Leiden: Brill, 1981.

Dante Alighieri, *De Vulgari Eloquentia*, ed. and trans. by Steven Botterill. Cambridge: Cambridge University Press, 1996.

Donatus, *Ars Maior*, in *Donat et la tradition de l'enseignement grammatical: etude et edition critique*, ed. Louis Holtz. Paris: CNRS, 1981.

An Early Commentary on the 'Poetria Nova' of Geoffrey of Vinsauf, ed. Marjorie Curry Woods. New York: Garland, 1985.

Enchiridion Symbolorum, Definitionum et Declarationum de Rebus Fidei et Morum. Freiburg: Herder, 1965.

Flores rhetorici. In Martin Camargo, 'A Twelfth-Century Treatise on "Dictamen" and Metaphor', *Traditio* 47 (1992), 161–213.

504   BIBLIOGRAPHY

Geoffrey of Vinsauf, *Poetria Nova*. In Ernest Gallo, *The 'Poetria Nova' and its Sources in Early Rhetorical Doctrine*. The Hague and Paris: Mouton De Gruyter, 1971.

Gerson, Jean. *Traité contre le 'Roman de la Rose'*, in Christine de Pizan, *et al. Le Débat sur le 'Roman de la Rose'*, ed. Eric Hicks. Paris: Champion, 1977.

Gilbert Crispin. *Disputatio Iudei et Christiani*, ed. Bernhard Blumenkranz. Utrecht and Antwerp: Spectrum, 1956.

Gregory the Great. *Moralia in Iob*, ed. M. Adriaen, 3 vols. *CCSL* 143, 143A, 143B. Turnhout: Brepols, 1979.

Gregory the Great. *Morals on the Book of Job by St Gregory the Great, Translated with Notes and Indeces*, trans. James Bliss, 3 vols. Oxford and London: John Henry Parker and J. G. F. and J. Rivington, 1844.

Grosseteste, Robert. *Die Philosophischen Werke des Robert Grosseteste, Bischofs von Lincoln*, ed. Ludwig Baur. Münster: Aschendorff, 1912.

Grosseteste, Robert. *Commentarius in Posteriorum Analyticorum libros*, ed. by Pietro Rossi. Florence: Olschki, 1981.

Guillaume de Deguileville. *Le Pèlerinage de vie humaine*, ed. J. J. Stürzinger. London: Roxburghe Club, 1893.

Guillaume de Deguileville. *Le Pèlerinage de l'Âme*, ed. J. J. Stürzinger. London: Roxburghe Club, 1895.

Guillaume de Deguileville. *Le Pèlerinage de Jhesucrist*, ed. J. J. Stürzinger. London: Roxburghe Club, 1897.

Guillaume de Deguileville. *The Pilgrimage of Human Life*, trans. Eugene Clasby. New York: Garland, 1992.

Guillaume de Deguileville. *Le Dit de la fleur de lis*, ed. Fréderic Duval. Paris: École des Chartes, 2014.

Guillaume de Deguileville. *Le Livre du pèlerin de vie humaine (1355)*, ed. by Philippe Maupeu and Graham Robert Edwards. Paris: Le Livre de Poche, 2015.

Guillaume de Deguileville [unattributed]. 'munus literarum', in *Analecta Hymnica Medii Aaevi* 48. Leipzig: O.R. Riesland, 1905, pp. 351–4.

Guillaume de Lorris and Jean de Meun. *Le Roman de la Rose*, ed. Félix Lecoy. 3 vols. Paris: Champion, 1965–1970.

Gundissalinus, Dominicus. *Tractatus de Anima*. In *Pseudo-Aristoteles über die Seele: Eine Psychologische Schrift aus dem 11. Jahrhundert und ihre Beziehungen zu Salomo ibn Gabriol (Avicebron)*, ed. Abraham Löwenthal. Berlin: Mayer & Müller, 1891.

Gundissalinus, Dominicus. *De divisione philosophiae*, ed. Alexander Fidora and Dorothee Werner. Freiburg: Herder, 2007.

Henri d'Andeli, *Les dits d'Henri d'Andeli*, ed. Alain Corbellari. Paris: Champion, 2003.

Holcot, Robert. *Quatuor Libros Sententiarum Questiones*. Lyon: 1518.

Hrabanus Maurus (?). *De inventione linguarum, PL* 112:1579–84.

Hrabanus Maurus (?). *In honorem sanctae crucis*, ed. M. Perrin, 2 vols. CCCM 100–100A. Turnhout: Brepols, 1997).

Hugh of St. Victor. *Hugonis de Sancto Victore Didascalicon De Studio Legendi*, ed. Charles H. Buttimer. Washington D. C.: Catholic University Press, 1939.

Hugh of St. Victor. *The 'Didascalicon' of Hugh of St. Victor: a Medieval Guide to the Arts*, trans. Jerome Taylor. New York: Columbia University Press, 1961.

Hugh of St. Victor. *De Sacramentis legis naturalis et scriptae, PL* 176:17–42.

Hugh of St. Victor. *De Sacramentis Christianae fidei. PL* 176, 173–618.

Hugh of St. Victor. *On the Sacraments of the Christian Faith (De Sacramentis)*, ed. and trans Roy J. Deferrari. Cambridge, MA: Mediaeval Academy of America, 1951.

BIBLIOGRAPHY 505

Hugh of St. Victor. *De Unione Corporis et Spiritus. PL* 177, 285–94.

Humbertus de Prulliaco. *Sententia Super Librum Metaphisice Aristotelis Liber I-V*, ed. Monica Brinzei and Nikolaus Wicki. Turnhout: Brepols, 2013.

Isaac of Stella. *Epistola de anima.* In Caterina Tarlazzi, 'L'*Epistola de anima* di Isacco di Stella: studio della tradizione ed edizione del testo', in *Medioevo: Rivista di storia della filosofia medievale* 36 (2011), 167–278.

Isidore of Seville. *Etymologiae sive origines*, ed. W. M. Lindsay. Oxford: Clarendon Press, 1911.

Jehan le Bel, *Li Ars d'Amour, de Vertu, et de Boneurté*, ed. Jules Petit, 2 vols. Brussels: Victor Devaux, 1867–1869.

John of Dacia (Johannes Dacus). *Summa grammatica*, in *Johannis Daci Opera*, ed. Alfred Otto, 2 vols Copenhagen: GAD, 1955.

John of La Rochelle. *Summa de anima*, ed. Jacques Guy Bougerol. Paris: Vrin, 1995.

John Scotus Eriugena (Iohannis Scotti seu Eriugenae). *Periphyseon*, in *Opera quae supersunt Omnia, PL* 122, 439–1022.

John Scotus Eriugena. *Expositiones super Ierarchiam caelestem S. Dionysii*, PL 122, 125–266.

Kilwardby, Robert (Pseudo-). *Commentum super Priscianum Maiorem*, ed. K. M. Fredborg, N. J. Green-Pedersen, and L. Nielsen, J. Pinborg, in 'The Commentary on Priscianus Maior Ascribed to Robert Kilwardby', *CIMAGL* 15 (1975), 1–143.

Lambert of Auxerre (Lagny). *Logica (Summa Lamberti)*, ed. Franco Alessio. Florence: La Nuova Italia, 1971.

Langland, William. '*Piers Plowman': A Parallel-Text Edition of the A, B, C, and Z Versions*, ed. A. V. C. Schmidt, 2nd edn, 2 vols. Kalamazoo: Medieval Institute Publications, 2011.

Laurent de Premierfait, *Des cas des nobles hommes et femmes*, ed. Patricia May Gathercole. Chapel Hill: The University of North Carolina Press, 2017.

Love, Nicholas. *The Mirror of the Blessed Life of Jesus Christ*, ed. Michael Sargeant. Exeter: Exeter University Press, 2004.

Lydgate, John (trans.). *The Pilgrimage of the Life of Man*, ed. F. J. Furnivall and Katharine B. Locock, 3 vols. EETS OS 78, 83 and 92. London: London: Kegan Paul, Trench, Trübner & Co., 1899–1904.

Michel de Marbais. *Summa de modi significandi*, ed. Louis G. Kelly. Stuttgart/Bad Cannstatt: Frommann/Holzboog, 1995.

Molinet, Jean. *Le Roman de la rose moralisé.* Lyon: Guillaume Balsarin, 1503.

Nemesius of Emesa. *De natura hominis: Traduction de Burgundio de Pise*, ed. G. Verbeke and J. R. Moncho. Leiden: Brill, 1975.

Olivi, Peter John. *Quaestiones in secundum librum Sententiarum.* Bibliotheca Franciscana Scholastica 4–6, ed. B. Jansen. Quaracchi: Collegium S. Bonaventurae, 1922–6.

Ovid (Publius Ovidius Naso). *Tristia. Ex Ponto.* Translated by A. L. Wheeler. Revised by G. P. Goold. Loeb Classical Library 151. Cambridge, MA: Harvard University Press, 1924.

Peter Helias (Petrus Helias). *Summa super Priscianum*, ed. Leo Reilly, 2 vols. Toronto: Pontifical Institute of Mediaeval Studies, 1993.

Peter Lombard, *Sententiae in IV libris distinctae*, 2 vols. Grottaferrata: Collegium S. Bonaventurae ad Claras Aquas: 1971 and 1981.

Peter of Limoges. *The Moral Treatise on the Eye*, ed. and trans. Richard Newhauser. Toronto: PIMS, 2013.

Quaestiones super 'Sophisticos elenchos', ed. Sten Ebbesen. Copenhagen: GAD, 1977.

Richard of St Victor, *Speculum Ecclesiae*, PL 177, 375.

Ricœur, Paul. *Temps et Récit 1: L'intrigue et le récit historique.* Paris: Seuil, 1983.

506   BIBLIOGRAPHY

Ricœur, Paul. *Soi-même comme un autre*. Paris: Seuil, 1990.

The Rule of St Benedict, In Latin and English with Notes, ed. and trans. Timothy Fry, OSB. Collegeville: Liturgical Press, 1981.

Siger of Brabant. *Quaestio utrum haec sit vera: Homo est animal, nullo homine existente*, ed. Bernardo Bazàn. Leuven: Publications universitaires de Louvain/Paris: Beatrice Nauwelaerts, 1974.

Stein, Gertrude. *Lectures in America*. Boston: Beacon Press, 1985.

Tertullian. *On Penitence*. In *Treatises on Penance: On Penitence and On Purity*, trans. William P. Le Saint. Westminster: Newman Press, 1959.

Versus de Alphabeto. In Lucian Müller, 'Versus scoti cuiusdam de alphabeto', *Rheinisches Museum für Philologie* 20 [new series] (1865), 357–74.

Vincent of Beauvais' *Speculum naturale*, 27.41, in *Speculum quadruplex, naturale, doctrinale, morale, historiale*. Douai: Balthasar Bellère, 1624.

William of Auvergne, *The Soul*, trans. Ronald J. Teske. Milwaukee: Marquette University Press, 2000.

William of Milton/Middleton (Guillelmi de Militona), *Quaestiones de sacramentis*, ed. Gidéon Gál and Celestin Piana. 2 vols. Quaracchi: Collegium S. Bonaventurae, 1961.

William of Ockham, *Summa Logicae*, ed. Philotheus Boehner, Gideon Gál, and Stephen Brown. St Bonaventure: Franciscan Institute, 1974.

William of Ockham. *Quodlibeta Septem*. Opera Theologica, vol. 9, ed. Joseph C. Wey. Bonaventure, NY: St Bonaventure University, 1980.

William of Ockham. *Quodlibetal Questions*, trans. Alfred J. Freddoso and Francis E. Kelley. 2 vols. New Haven and London: Yale University Press, 1991.

William of St Thierry, *Epistola ad fratres de Monte Dei*, ed. M.-M. Davy (Paris/Vrin, 1940).

William of St Thierry, *De naturae corporis et animae*, PL 180, 695–726.

Secondary

Adams, Robert. 'The Liturgy Revisited', *Studies in Philology* 73 (1976), 266–84.

Adams, Robert. 'The Nature of Need in *Piers Plowman* XX', *Traditio* 34 (1978), 273–301.

Adams, Robert. 'Piers's Pardon and Langland's Semi-Pelagianism', *Traditio* 39 (1983), 367–418.

Adams, Robert. 'Some Versions of Apocalypse: Learned and Popular Eschatology in *Piers Plowman*', in T. Heffernan, ed., *The Popular Literature of Medieval England*. Knoxville: University of Tennessee Press, 1985, pp. 194–236.

Adams, Robert. 'Langland's Theology', in John A. Alford, ed., *A Companion to Piers Plowman*. Berkeley and Los Angeles: University of California Press, 1988, pp. 87–114.

Adams, Robert. *Langland and the Rokele Family: The Gentry Background to Piers Plowman*. Dublin: Four Courts Press, 2013.

Adamson, Peter, and Fedor Benevich, 'The Thought Experimental Method: Avicenna's Flying Man Argument', *Journal of the American Philosophical Association* 4.2 (2018), 147–64.

Aers, David. *Piers Plowman and Christian Allegory*. London: Edward Arnold, 1975.

Aers, David. 'Visionary Eschatology: *Piers Plowman*', *Modern Theology* 16.1 (2000), 3–17.

Aers, David. 'The Sacrament of the Altar in *Piers Plowman* and the Late Medieval Church in England', in Jeremy Dimmick, James Simpson and Nicolette Zeeman, eds, *Images, Idolatry and Iconoclasm in Late Medieval England: Textuality and the Visual Image*. Oxford: Oxford University Press, 2002, pp. 63–80.

Aers, David. *Sanctifying Signs: Making Christian Tradition in Late Medieval England*. Notre Dame, IN: Notre Dame University Press, 2004.

Aers, David. *Salvation and Sin: Augustine, Langland, and Fourteenth-Century Theology*. Notre Dame, IN: University of Notre Dame Press, 2009.

Aertsen, Jan A., and Andreas Speer, eds. *Was ist Philosophie im Mittelalter?*. Berlin and New York: Walter de Gruyter, 1998.

Aertsen, Jan A., Kent Emery, and Andreas Speer, eds. *Nach der Verurteilung von 1277/After the Condemnation of 1277: Philosophie und Theologie an der Universität von Paris im letzten Viertel des 13. Jahrhunderts. Studien und Texte/Philosophy and Theology at the University of Paris in the Last Quarter of the Thirteenth Century. Studies and Texts*. Berlin and New York: Walter de Gruyter, 2001.

Agamben, Giorgio. *Stanze: La parola e il fantasma nella cultura occidentale*. Torino: Einaudi, 1977.

Akasoy, Anna, James E. Montgomery, and Peter E. Pormann, eds. *Islamic Crosspollinations: Interactions in the Medieval Middle East*. Cambridge: The E. J. W. Gibb Memorial Trust, 2007.

Akbari, Suzanne Conklin. *Seeing Through the Veil: Optical Theory and Medieval Allegory*. Toronto: University of Toronto Press, 2004.

Alford, John A. 'The Grammatical Metaphor: A Survey of Its Use in the Middle Ages', *Speculum* 57.4 (1982), 728–60.

Alford, John A., ed. *A Companion to Piers Plowman*. Berkeley and Los Angeles: University of California Press, 1988.

Alford, John A. 'The Design of the Poem', in John Alford, ed., *A Companion to Piers Plowman*. Berkeley and Los Angeles: University of California Press, 1988, pp. 29–66.

Alford, John A. *Piers Plowman: A Guide to the Quotations*. Binghamton: CMERS, 1992.

Alford, John A. 'The Figure of Repentance in *Piers Plowman*', in David C. Fowler and Míceál F. Vaughan, eds, *Suche Werkis to Werche: Essays on Piers Plowman in Honor of David C. Fowler*. East Lansing, Colleagues Press, 1993, pp. 3–28.

Alford, John A. 'Langland's Learning', *YLS* 9 (1995), 1–8.

Alford, John A., and Richard G. Newhauser, eds. *Literature and Religion in the Later Middle Ages: Philological Studies in Honor of Siegfried Wenzel*. Binghamton: Medieval and Renaissance Texts and Studies, 1995.

Amsler, Mark E. *Etymology and Grammatical Discourse in late Antiquity and the early Middle Ages*. Amsterdam: John Benjamins Publishing, 1989.

Anderson, Judith H. *The Growth of a Personal Voice: Piers Plowman and The Faerie Queene*. New Haven-London: Yale University Press, 1976.

Anderson, Judith H. *Reading the Allegorical Intertext: Chaucer, Spenser, Shakespeare, Milton*. New York: Fordham University Press, 2008.

Andrei, Filippo. *Boccaccio the Philosopher: An Epistemology of the Decameron*. Cham: Palgrave Macmillan, 2017.

Arbusow, Leonid. *Colores rhetorici: Eine Auswahl rhetorischer Figuren und Gemeinplätze als Hilfsmittel für akademische Übungen an mittelalterlichen Texten*. Geneva: Slatkine, 1974/1948.

Armisen-Marchetti, Mireille. 'La notion d'imagination chez les Anciens. I: Les philosophes', *Pallas* 26 (1979), 11–51.

Armisen-Marchetti, Mireille. 'La notion d'imagination chez les Anciens. II: La rhétorique', *Pallas* 27 (1980), 3–37.

Armstrong, Adrian, and Sarah Kay. *Knowing Poetry: Verse in Medieval France from the Rose to the Rhétoriqueurs*. Ithaca: Cornell University Press, 2011.

508 BIBLIOGRAPHY

Arnold, Duane W. H., and Pamela Bright, eds. *De doctrina Christiana: A Classic of Western Culture*. Notre Dame: University of Notre Dame Press, 1995.

Ashworth, E. Jennifer. 'Signification and Modes of Signifying in Thirteenth-Century Logic: A Preface to Aquinas on Analogy', *Medieval Philosophy and Theology* 1 (1991), 39–67.

Ashworth, E. Jennifer. 'Terminist Logic', in *CHMP*, I:146–58.

Astell, Ann W. *Eating Beauty: The Eucharist and the Spiritual Arts of the Middle Ages*. Ithaca: Cornell University Press, 2006.

Badel, Pierre-Yves. *Le Roman de la Rose au XIVe siècle: Etude de la Réception de l'Oeuvre*. Geneva: Droz, 1980.

Badel, Pierre-Yves. 'Le poème allégorique', in Daniel Poirion, ed., *Grundriss der Romanischen Literaturen des Mittelalters, vol. VIII.1: La littérature française aux XIVe et XVe siècles*, 11 vols, gen. ed. Hans U. Gumbrecht and Ulrich Mölk. Heidelberg: Carl Winter, 1988, pp. 139–60.

Baker, Denise N. 'From Plowing to Penitence: *Piers Plowman* and Fourteenth-Century Theology', *Speculum* 55.4 (1980), 715–25.

Baker, Denise N. '"The Greatest Riddle of the B Text" of *Piers Plowman*: Why Langland Did Not Scrap the A *Vita*', in Bonnie Wheeler, ed., *Mindful Spirit in Late Medieval Literature: Essays in Honor of Elizabeth D. Kirk*. New York: Palgrave MacMillan, 2006, pp. 149–63.

Baker, Denise N. 'Pre-Empting Piers's Tearing of the Pardon: Langland's Revisions of the C Visio', *YLS* 31 (2017), 43–72.

Bakker, Paul J. J. M., and Johannes M. M. H. Thijssen, eds, *Mind, Cognition and Representation: The Tradition of Commentaries on Aristotle's 'De anima'*. Aldershot: Ashgate, 2008.

Bakker, Paul J. J. M., Sander W. Boer, and Cees Leijenhorst, eds. *Psychology and the other Disciplines: A Case of Cross-Disciplinary Interaction (1250–1750)*. Leiden: Brill, 2012.

Barker, Mark J. 'Experience and Experimentation: The Meaning of *Experimentum* in Aquinas', *The Thomist: A Speculative Quarterly Review* 76.1 (2012), 37–71.

Barney, Stephen A. 'The Plowshare of the Tongue: the Progress of a Symbol from the Bible to *Piers Plowman*', *Mediaeval Studies* 35 (1973), 261–93.

Barney, Stephen A. *Allegories of History, Allegories of Love*. Hamden CT: Archon Books, 1979.

Barney, Stephen A. 'Allegorical Visions', in John Alford, ed., *A Companion to Piers Plowman*. Berkeley and Los Angeles: University of California Press, 1988, pp. 117–34.

Barney, Stephen A. *Penn Commentary on Piers Plowman. Volume Five: C Passus 20–22; B Passus 18–20*. University Park: University of Pennsylvania Press, 2006.

Barolini, Teodolinda. 'The Making of a Lyric Sequence: Time and Narrative in Petrarch's *Rerum vulgarium fragmenta*', *Modern Language Notes* 104.1 (1989), 1–38.

Bassano, Marie, Esther Dehoux and Catherine Vincent, eds. *Le 'Pèlerinage de l'âme' de Guillaume de Digulleville (1355–1358): Regards Croisés Actes du colloque Université Paris-Ouest-Nanterre-La Défense/Université Paris-Descartes (29–30 mars 2012)*. Turnhout: Brepols, 2014.

Baumgartner. 'Emmanuèle. 'L'absente de tous les bouquets . . ', in Jean Dufournet, ed., *Etudes sur le Roman de la Rose de Guillaume de Lorris*. Paris: Champion, 1984, pp. 37–52.

Baumgartner. 'Emmanuèle. 'The Play of Temporalities or, the Reported Dream of Guillaume de Lorris', in Kevin Brownlee and Sylvia Huot, eds, *Rethinking the Romance of the Rose: Text, Image, Reception*. Philadelphia: University of Pennsylvania Press, 1992, pp. 21–38.

Bazàn, Bernardo Carlos, 'La signification des termes communs et la théorie de la supposition chez Maître Siger de Brabant', *Revue Philosophique de Louvain* 77: 35 (1979), 345–72.

Bechot, Mauricio. 'John of Mirecourt', in Jorge J. E. Gracia and Timothy N. Noone, eds, *A Companion to Philosophy in the Middle Ages*. Oxford: Blackwell, 2002, pp. 377–81.

Beckwith, Sarah. *Signifying God: Social Relation and Symbolic Act in the York Corpus Christi Plays*. Chicago and London: University of Chicago Press, 2003.

Bédier, Joseph. *Les Fabliaux*. Paris: Champion, 1893.

BeDuhn, Jason David. *Augustine's Manichaean Dilemma, I: Conversion and Apostasy, 373–388 C.E.* Philadelphia: University of Pennsylvania Press, 2010.

BeDuhn, Jason David. *Augustine's Manichaean Dilemma, II: The Making of a 'Catholic' Self, ca. 388–401 C.E.* Philadelphia: University of Pennsylvania Press, 2013.

Bel, Catherine, and Herman Braet, eds. *De la Rose: texte, image, fortune*. Leuven: Peeters, 2006.

Bell, David N. 'The Tripartite Soul and the Image of God in the Latin Tradition', *Recherches De Théologie Ancienne Et Médiévale* 47 (1980), 16–52.

Bellon-Méquelle, Hélène, *et al.*, eds, *La moisson des lettres: l'invention littéraire autour de 1300*. Turnhout: Brepols, 2011.

Benson, C. David. *Public Piers Plowman: Modern Scholarship and Late Medieval English Culture*. University Park: Pennsylvania State University Press, 2004.

Bermon, Pascale. *L'assentiment et son objet chez Grégoire de Rimini*. Paris: Vrin, 2007.

Biard, Joël, ed. *Raison et démonstration. Les commentaires médiévaux sur les Seconds Analytiques*. Turnhout: Brepols, 2015.

Biard, Joël, and Fosca Mariani Zini, eds. *Ut philosophia poesis: Questions philosophiques dans l'œuvre de Dante, Pétrarque et Boccace*. Paris: Vrin, 2008.

Bieniak, Magdalena. *The Soul–Body Problem at Paris, ca. 1200–1250: Hugh of St Cher and his Contemporaries*. Leuven: Leuven University Press, 2010.

Black, Deborah L. 'The "Imaginative Syllogism" in Arabic Philosophy: A Medieval Contribution to the Philosophical Study of Metaphor', *Mediaeval Studies* 51 (1989), 242–67.

Black, Deborah L. 'Mental Existence in Thomas Aquinas and Avicenna', *Mediaeval Studies* 61 (1999), 45–79.

Black, Deborah L. 'Imagination and Estimation: Arabic Paradigms and Western Transformations', *Topoi* 19 (2000), 59–75.

Black, Deborah L. 'The Nature of Intellect', in *CHMP*, I:320–33.

Blamires, Alcuin. 'Philosophical Sleaze? The "Strok of thought" in the Miller's Tale and Chaucerian Fabliau', *Modern Language Review* 102/3 (2007), 621–40.

Bland, Cynthia Renée. 'Langland's Use of the Term *ex vi transicionis*', *YLS* 2 (1988), 125–35.

Blick, Sarah, and Laura Gelfand, eds. *Push Me, Pull You: Imaginative and Emotional Interaction in Late Medieval and Renaissance Art*. 2 vols. Leiden/Boston: Brill, 2011.

Bloch, Howard R. *Etymologies and Genealogies: a Literary Anthropology of the French Middle Ages*. Chicago and London: University of Chicago Press, 1986.

Bloomfield, Morton W. ed. *Allegory, Myth, and Symbol*. Cambridge, MA: Harvard University Press, 1981.

Blumenfeld-Kosinski, Renate. 'Remarques sur *Songe/Mensonge*', *Romania* 101 (1980), 885–90.

Blumenfeld-Kosinski, Renate. 'Overt and Covert: Amorous and Interpretive Strategies in the *Roman de la Rose*', *Romania* 111 (1990), 432–53.

510 BIBLIOGRAPHY

Blumenfeld-Kosinski, Renate, Nancy B. Warren, and Duncan Robertson, eds. *The Vernacular Spirit: Essays on Medieval Religious Literature.* New York: Palgrave Macmillan, 2002.

Blythe, Joan Heiges. 'Sins of the Tongue and Rhetorical Prudence in *Piers Plowman*', in John A. Alford and Richard G. Newhauser, eds, *Literature and Religion in the Later Middle Ages: Philological Studies in Honor of Siegfried Wenzel.* Binghamton: Medieval and Renaissance Texts and Studies, 1995, pp. 119–42.

Bobillot, J.-P. 'La mort, le moi(ne) et Dieu: une approche de la *ratio formae* dans les *Vers de la Mort* d'Hélinand de Froidmont', *Poétique (Collection)* 77 (1989), 93–111.

Bochet, Isabelle. 'Le statut de l'image dans la pensée augustinienne', *Archives de Philosophie* 72.2 (2009), 249–70.

Bondéelle-Souchier, Anne, and Patricia Stirnemann. 'Vers une reconstitution de la bibliothèque ancienne de l'abbaye de Chaalis: inventaires et manuscrits retrouvés', in Monique Goullet, ed., *Parva pro magnis munera - études de littérature tardo-antique et médiévale offertes à François Dolbeau par ses élèves.* Turnhout: Brepols, 2009, pp. 9–73.

Bos, Egbert P., ed. *Medieval Supposition Theory Revisited.* Special issue of *Vivarium* (51). Leiden: Brill, 2013.

Bose, Mishtooni. '*Piers Plowman* and God's Thought Experiment', in Philip Knox, Jonathan Morton, and Daniel Reeve, eds, *Medieval Thought Experiments: Poetry, Hypothesis, and Experience in the European Middle Ages.* Turnhout: Brepols, 2018, pp. 71–97.

Bottex-Ferragne, Ariane. 'Lire, écrire et transcrire en strophe d'Hélinand: un art poétique visuel dans le manuscrit BnF, fr. 2199', *Études françaises* 53.2 (2017), 103–30.

Bottin, Francesco, ed. *Gregorio da Rimini Filosofo.* Rimini: Raffaelli Editore, 2003.

Boudet, Jean-Patrice, Philippe Haugeard, et al., eds, *Jean de Meun et la culture médiévale: Littérature, art, sciences et droit aux derniers siècles du Moyen Âge.* Rennes: Presses Universitaires de Rennes, 2017.

Boulton, Maureen Barry McCann. *The Song in the Story: Lyric Insertion in French Narrative Fiction, 1200–1400.* Philadelphia: University of Pennsylvania Press, 1993.

Boulton, Maureen Barry McCann. 'Digulleville's *Pèlerinage de Jésus Christ*: A Poem of Courtly Devotion', in Renate Blumenfeld-Kosinski, Nancy B. Warren, and Duncan Robertson, eds, *The Vernacular Spirit: Essays on Medieval Religious Literature.* New York: Palgrave Macmillan, 2002, pp. 125–44.

Boureau, Alain, and Sylvain Piron, eds, *Pierre de Jean Olivi (1248–98): Pensée Scholastique, Dissidence Spirituelle et Société.* Paris: Vrin, 1999.

Bourquin, Guy. *Piers Plowman: 'Etudes sur la genèse littéraire des trois versions.* Paris: Honoré Champion, 1978.

Bowers, John M. *The Crisis of Will in 'Piers Plowman'.* Washington, DC: Catholic University of America Press, 1995.

Bowman, Leonard J. ed. *Itinerarium: The Idea of Journey.* Salzburg: Institut für Anglistik und Amerikanistik, Universität Salzburg, 1983.

Boynton, Susan. 'Training for the Liturgy as a Form of Monastic Education', in George Ferzoco and Carolyn Muessig, eds, *Medieval Monastic Education.* London: Leicester University Press, 2000, pp. 7–20.

Braakhuis, Henricus Antonius Giovanni, Corneille Henri Kneepkens, and Lambertus Marie de Rijk, eds. *English Logic and Semantics, from the End of the Twelfth Century to the Time of Ockham and Burleigh. Acts of the 4th European Symposium on Mediaeval Logic and Semantics, Leiden-Nijmegen, 23–27 April 1979.* Turnhout: Brepols, 1981.

Brantley, Jessica. *Reading in the Wilderness: Private Devotion and Public Performance in Late Medieval England.* Chicago: Chicago University Press, 2007.

Briguglia, Gianluca, and Irène Rosier, eds. *Adam, la nature humaine, avant et après: épistémologie de la chute*. Paris: Presses Universitaires de la Sorbonne, 2016.

Brind'Amour, Lucie, and Eugene Vance, eds. *Archéologie du signe*. Toronto: PIMS, 1983.

Brinzei Calma, Monica, 'Le commentaire des Sentences d'Humbert de Preuilly', *Bulletin de Philosophie Médiévale* 53 (2011), 81–148.

Brljak, Vladimir. 'Introduction: Allegory Past and Present', in ibid., ed., *Allegory Studies? Contemporary Perspectives*. London: Routledge, 2022, pp. 1-41.

Brljak, Vladimir. *Allegory Studies? Contemporary Perspectives*. London: Routledge, 2022.

Brower, Jeffrey E., and Susan Brower-Toland, 'Aquinas on Mental Representation: Concepts and Intentionality', *Philosophical Review* 117.2 (2008), 193–243.

Brown, Catherine. *Contrary Things: Exegesis, Dialectic, and the Poetics of Didacticism*. Stanford: Stanford University Press, 1998.

Brown, Cynthia J. 'Text, Image, and Authorial Self-Consciousness in Late-Medieval Paris', in Sandra Hindman, ed., *Printing the Written Word: The Social History of Books, circa 1450–1520*. Ithaca: Cornell University Press, 1991, pp. 103–42.

Brown, Deborah J. 'Aquinas' Missing Flying Man', *Sophia* 40.1 (2001), 17–31.

Brown, Peter. *Augustine of Hippo*. Berkeley and Los Angeles: University of California Press, 1967.

Brown, Peter. 'An Optical Theme in the Merchant's Tale', *Studies in the Age of Chaucer* 1984.1 (1984), 231–43.

Brownlee, Kevin. 'The Problem of Faux Semblant: Language, History, and Truth in the *Roman de la Rose*', in Marina Scordilis Brownlee, Kevin Brownlee, and Stephen G. Nichols, eds, *The New Medievalism*. Baltimore: Johns Hopkins University Press, 1991, pp. 253–71.

Brownlee, Kevin. 'Pygmalion, Mimesis, and the Multiple Endings of the *Roman de la Rose*', *Yale French Studies* 95 (1991), 193–211.

Brownlee, Kevin. 'The Conflicted Genealogy of Cultural Authority: Italian Responses to French Cultural Dominance in *Il Tesoretto, Il Fiore*, and *La Commedia*', in Kevin Brownlee and Valeria Finucci, eds, *Generation and Degeneration: Tropes of Reproduction in Literature and History, from Antiquity to the Early Modern Period*. Durham and London: Duke UP, 2001, pp. 262–86.

Brownlee, Kevin, and Valeria Finucci, eds. *Generation and Degeneration: Tropes of Reproduction in Literature and History, from Antiquity to the Early Modern Period*. Durham and London: Duke UP, 2001.

Brownlee, Kevin, and Sylvia Huot, eds. *Rethinking the Romance of the Rose: Text, Image, Reception*. Philadelphia: University of Pennsylvania Press, 1992.

Brownlee, Marina Scordilis, Kevin Brownlee, and Stephen G. Nichols, eds, *The New Medievalism*. Baltimore: Johns Hopkins University Press, 1991.

Burger, Christoph P. 'Das "auxilium speciale Dei" in der Gnadenlehre Gregors von Rimini', in Heiko A. Oberman, ed., *Gregor von Rimini: Werk und Wirkung bis zur* Reformation. Berlin: De Gruyter, 1981, 195–240.

Burlin, Robert B. *Chaucerian Fiction*. Princeton: Princeton University Press, 1977.

Burns, J. Patout. 'Delighting the Spirit: Augustine's Practice of Figurative Interpretation', in Duane W. H. Arnold and Pamela Bright, eds, *De doctrina Christiana: A Classic of Western Culture*. Notre Dame: University of Notre Dame Press, 1995, pp. 182–94.

Burrow, J. A. 'The Action of Langland's Second Vision', *Essays in Criticism* 15.3 (1965), 247–68.

Burrow, J. A. 'Words, Works and Will: Theme and Structure in *Piers Plowman*', in S. S. Hussey, ed., *Piers Plowman: Critical Approaches*. London: Methuen, 1969, pp. 111–24.

512 BIBLIOGRAPHY

Burrow, J. A. 'Langland *nel mezzo del cammin*', in P. L. Heyworth, ed., *Medieval Studies for J. A. W. Bennett*. Oxford: Clarendon Press, 1981, pp. 21–41.

Burrow, J. A. 'Wasting Time, Wasting Words in *Piers Plowman* B and C', *YLS* 17 (2003), 191–202.

Burrow, J. A. 'God and the Fullness of Time in Piers Plowman', *Medium Ævum* 79.2 (2010), 300–5.

Butterfield, Ardis. *Poetry and Music in Medieval France: From Jean Renart to Guillaume de Machaut*. Cambridge: Cambridge University Press, 2002.

Butterfield, Herbert. *The Origins of Modern Science, 1300–1800*. London: Bell & Sons, 1949.

Bynum, William F., and Roy Porter, eds. *Medicine and the Five Senses*. Cambridge: Cambridge University Press, 1993.

Camille, Michael. *The Gothic idol: ideology and Image-Making in Medieval Art*. Cambridge: Cambridge University Press, 1989.

Camille, Michael. 'The Iconoclast's Desire: Deguileville's Idolatry in France and England', in Jeremy Dimmick, James Simpson and Nicolette Zeeman, eds, *Images, Idolatry and Iconoclasm in Late Medieval England: Textuality and the Visual Image*. Oxford: Oxford University Press, 2002, pp. 151–71.

Canale, Valastro. 'Isidoro di Siviglia: la *vis verbi* come riflesso dell'onnipotenza divina', *Cuadernos de Filologìa Clàsica. Estudios latinos* 10 (1996), 147–76.

Cannon, Christopher 'Langland's *Ars Grammatica*', *YLS* 22 (2008), 3–25.

Cannon, Christopher. *From Literacy to Literature: England, 1300–1400*. Oxford: Oxford University Press, 2016.

Cannon, Christopher, and Maura Nolan, eds. *Medieval Latin and Middle English Literature: Essays in Honour of Jill Mann*. Cambridge: D. S. Brewer, 2011.

Cantor, Norman. *The Last Knight: The Twilight of the Middle Ages and the Birth of the Modern Era*. New York: Free Press, 2004.

Caputo, John D., and Michael J. Scanlon, eds. *Augustine and Postmodernism: Confessions and Circumfession*. Bloomington and Indianapolis: Indiana University Press, 2005.

Carruthers, Mary J. *Search for St. Truth: A Study of Meaning in Piers Plowman*. Evanston: Northwestern University Press, 1973.

Carruthers, Mary J. *The Book of Memory: A Study of Memory in Medieval Culture*. Cambridge: Cambridge University Press, 1992.

Carruthers, Mary J. Mary Carruthers, 'Imaginatif, Memoria, and the Need for Critical Theory in *Piers Plowman* Studies', *YLS* 9 (1995), 103–20.

Carruthers, Mary J. *The Craft of Thought: Meditation, Rhetoric, and the Making of Images, 400–1200*. Cambridge: Cambridge University Press, 1998.

Carruthers, Mary, Elizabeth Kirk, and E. Talbot Donaldson, eds. *Acts of Interpretation: The Text in its Contexts, 700–1600: Essays on Medieval and Renaissance Literature in Honor of E. Talbot Donaldson*. Norman: Pilgrim Books, 1982.

Casagrande, Carla, and Gianfranco Fioravanti. *La filosofia in Italia nell'età di Dante*. Bologna: Il Mulino, 2016.

Casagrande, Carla, and Silvana Vecchio. *I peccati della lingua: Disciplina ed etica della parola nella cultura medievale*. Rome: Istituto della Biografia Italiana, 1987.

Cerquiglini-Toulet, Jacqueline. *'Un engin si soutil': Guillaume de Machaut et l'écriture au XIV e siècle* Genève: Droz, 1985.

Cerquiglini-Toulet, Jacqueline. 'L'imaginaire du livre à la fin du Moyen Age: Pratiques de lecture, théorie de l'écriture', *Modern Language Notes* 108.4 (1993), 680–95.

Cervone, Maria Cristina. *Poetics of the Incarnation: Middle English Writing and the Leap of Love*. Philadelphia: University of Pennsylvania Press, 2013.

Cesalli, Laurent, and Irène Rosier-Catach. '"*Signum est in praedicamento relationis*": Roger Bacon's Semantics Revisited in the Light of his Relational Theory of the Sign', *Oxford Studies in Medieval Philosophy* 6 (2018), 62–100.

Chambers, R. W. '*Piers Plowman*: A Comparative Study', in *Man's Unconquerable Mind: Studies of English Writers, from Bede to* A. E. Housman and W. P. Ker. London: Jonathan Cape, 1939, pp. 88–171.

Chance, Jane. *Medieval Mythography: From Roman North Africa to the School of Chartres, A.D. 433–1177*. Gainesville: University Press of Florida, 1994.

Charpentier, Françoise, ed. *Le songe à la Renaissance: colloque international de Cannes, 29–31 mai 1987*. Saint-Etienne: Institut d'Études de la Renaissance et de l'Âge classique, Université de Saint-Etienne, 1990.

Clark, Robert, and Pamela Sheingorn, 'Performative Reading: Experiencing through the Poet's Body in Guillaume de Digulleville's *Pèlerinage de Jhesucrist*', in Eglal Doss-Quinby, Roberta l. Krueger, and E. Jane Burns, eds, *Cultural Performances in Medieval France: essays in Honor of Nancy Freeman Regalado*. Cambridge: D.S. Brewer, 2007, pp. 135–51.

Clark, Robert, and Pamela Sheingorn. 'Were Guillaume de Digulleville's *Pèlerinages* Plays? The Case of Arras ms 845 as Performative Anthology', *European Medieval Drama* 12 (2008), 109–47.

Clark, Robert, and Pamela Sheingorn. 'Encountering a Dream-Vision: Visual and Verbal Glosses to Guillaume de Digulleville's *Pèlerinage Jhesucrist*', in Sarah Blick and Laura Gelfand, eds, *Push Me, Pull You: Imaginative and Emotional Interaction in late Medieval and Renaissance art*, 2 vols. Leiden/Boston: Brill, 2011, I:1–38.

Claussen, M. A. '*Peregrinatio* and *Peregrini* in Augustine's *City of God*', *Traditio* 46 (1991), 33–75.

Clopper, Lawrence M. 'The Contemplative Matrix in *Piers Plowman* B', *Modern Language Quarterly* 46 (1985), 3–28.

Clopper, Lawrence M. 'The Life of the Dreamer, the Dreams of the Wanderer in *Piers Plowman*', *Studies in Philology* 86.3 (1989), 261–85.

Clopper, Lawrence M. '*Songes of Rechelesnesse*': Langland and the Franciscans. Ann Arbor: University of Michigan Press, 1997.

Clopper, Lawrence M. 'Langland and Allegory: A Proposition', *YLS* 15 (2001), 35–42.

Cochelin, Isabelle. 'Besides the Book: Using the Body to Mould the Mind—Cluny in the Tenth and Eleventh Centuries', in George Ferzoco and Carolyn Muessig, eds, *Medieval Monastic Education*. London: Leicester University Press, 2000, pp. 21–35.

Cole, Andrew, and Andrew Galloway, 'Christian Philosophy in *Piers Plowman*', in Andrew Cole and Andrew Galloway, eds, *The Cambridge Companion to Piers Plowman*. Cambridge: Cambridge University Press: 2014, pp. 136–59.

Cole, Andrew, and Andrew Galloway, eds. *The Cambridge Companion to Piers Plowman*. Cambridge: Cambridge University Press: 2014.

Coleman, Janet. '*Piers Plowman' and the Moderni*. Rome: Edizioni di Storia e Letteratura, 1981.

Coleman, Joyce. 'Where Chaucer Got His Pulpit: Audience and Intervisuality in the Troilus and Criseyde Frontispiece', *Studies in the Age of Chaucer* 32 (2010), 103–28.

Coleman, Joyce. 'Translating Iconography: Gower, *Pearl*, Chaucer, and the *Rose*', in Susanna Fein and David Raybin, eds, *Chaucer: Visual Approaches*. University Park: Penn State University Press, 2016, pp. 177–94.

Colish, Marcia L. 'St. Augustine's Rhetoric of Silence Revisited', *Augustinian Studies* 9 (1978), 15–24.

514 BIBLIOGRAPHY

Colish, Marcia L. *The Mirror of Language: A Study of the Medieval Theory of Knowledge.* Revised Edition. Lincoln and London: University of Nebraska Press, 1983.

Connes, Delphine. 'L'influence coutumière dans la procédure de Guillaume de Deguileville', in Marie Bassano, Esther Dehoux, and Catherine Vincent, eds, *Le 'Pèlerinage de l'âme' de Guillaume de Digulleville (1355–1358): Regards Croisés Actes du colloque Université Paris-Ouest-Nanterre-La Défense/Université Paris-Descartes (29–30 mars 2012).* Turnhout: Brepols, 2014, pp. 175–84.

Contini, Gianfranco. 'Un nodo della cultura medievale: la serie *Roman de la Rose, Fiore, Divina commedia*', in ibid., *Un Idea di Dante: Saggi Danteschi.* Torino: Einaudi, 1973, pp. 345–83.

Contini, Gianfranco. *Un Idea di Dante: Saggi Danteschi.* Torino: Einaudi, 1973.

Cooper, Helen, and Sally Mapstone, eds. *The Long Fifteenth Century: Essays for Douglas Gray.* Oxford: Oxford University Press, 1997.

Cooper, Lisa H. *Artisans and Narrative Craft in Late Medieval England.* Cambridge: Cambridge University Press, 2011.

Copeland, Rita. *Rhetoric, Hermeneutics, and Translation in the Middle Ages: Academic Traditions and Vernacular Texts.* Cambridge: Cambridge University Press, 1995.

Copeland, Rita, ed. *Criticism and Dissent in the Middle Ages.* Cambridge: Cambridge University Press, 1996.

Copeland, Rita. 'Rhetoric and the Politics of the Literal Sense in Medieval Literary Theory: Aquinas, Wyclif and the Lollards', in Walter Jost and Michael J. Hyde, eds, *Rhetoric and Hermeneutics in Our Time: A Reader.* New Haven: Yale University Press, 1997, pp. 335–57.

Copeland, Rita, and Ineke Sluiter, eds. *Medieval Grammar and Rhetoric: Language Arts and Literary Theory, AD 300–1475.* Oxford: Oxford University Press, 2009.

Copeland, Rita, and Peter T. Struck, eds. *The Cambridge Companion to Allegory.* Cambridge: Cambridge University Press, 2010.

Corbellari, Alain. *Joseph Bédier: Écrivain et Philologue.* Genève: Droz, 1997.

Corbellari, Alain. *La voix des clercs: Littérature et savoir universitaire autour des dits du XIIIe siècle.* Geneva: Droz, 2005.

Cornelius, Roberta D. '*Piers Plowman* and the *Roman de Fauvel*', *PMLA* 47.2 (1932), 363–7.

Courtenay, William J. 'Augustinianism at Oxford in the Fourteenth Century', *Augustiniana* 30.1/2 (1980), 58–70.

Courtenay, William J. *Schools and Scholars in Fourteenth-century England.* Princeton: Princeton University Press, 1987.

Courtenay, William J. 'Force of Words and Figures of Speech: The Crisis over *virtus sermonis* in the Fourteenth Century', in William Courtenay, *Ockham and Ockhamism: Studies in the Dissemination and Impact of his Thought.* Leiden: Brill, 2008, pp. 209–28.

Courtenay, William J. *Ockham and Ockhamism: Studies in the Dissemination and Impact of his Thought.* Leiden: Brill, 2008.

Crabbe, M. James C. *From Soul to Self.* London: Routledge, 1999.

Crampton, Georgia R. 'Chaucer's Singular Prayer', *Medium Ævum* 59.2 (1990), 191–213.

Crane, Tim, and Sarah Patterson, eds. *History of the Mind-Body Problem.* London: Routledge, 2000.

Cranefield, Paul F. 'On the Origin of the Phrase, *Nihil est in intellectu quod non prius fuerit in sensu*', *Journal of the History of Medicine* 25 (1970), 77–80.

Craun, Edwin. *Lies, Slander, and Obscenity in Medieval English Literature: Pastoral Rhetoric and the Deviant Speaker.* Cambridge: Cambridge University Press, 2005.

Crombie, Alistair C. *Robert Grosseteste and the Origins of Experimental Science, 1100–1700*. Oxford: Clarendon Press, 1953.

Cross, Richard. 'Weakness and Grace', in *CHMP*, I:441–53.

Curtius, Ernst Robert. *Europäische Literatur und Lateinisches Mittelalter*. Bern: Francke, 1948.

D'Arcy, Anne Marie, and Alan J. Fletcher, eds. *Studies in Late Medieval and Early Renaissance Texts in Honour of John Scattergood*. Dublin: Four Courts Press, 2005.

Dahan, Gilbert, 'Notes et textes sur la Poétique au Moyen Âge', *AHDLMA* 47 (1980), 171–239.

Dahan, Gilbert. 'Saint Thomas d'Aquin et la métaphore: Rhétorique et herméneutique', *Medioevo* 18 (1992), 85–117.

Dales, Richard. *The Problem of the Rational Soul in the Thirteenth Century*. Leiden: Brill, 1995.

Dauvois, Nathalie, and Jean-Philippe Grosperrin, eds. *Songes et Songeurs (XIIIe–XVIIIe siècle)*. Laval: Preses de l'Université de Laval, 2003.

David, Alfred. 'An ABC to the Style of the Prioress', in Mary Carruthers, Elizabeth Kirk, and E. Talbot Donaldson, *Acts of Interpretation: The Text in its Contexts, 700–1600: Essays on Medieval and Renaissance Literature in Honor of E. Talbot Donaldson*. Norman, OK: Pilgrim Books, 1982, pp. 147–57.

Davies, Brian, ed. *Oxford Handbook of Aquinas*. Oxford: Oxford University Press, 2012.

Davis, Isabel. '*Piers Plowman* and the *Querelle of the Rose*: Marriage, Caritas, and the Peacock's "Pennes"'. *New Medieval Literatures* 10 (2008), 49–86.

Davis, Rebecca. '"Save man allone": Human Exceptionality in *Piers Plowman* and the Exemplarist Tradition', in Christopher Cannon and Maura Nolan, eds, *Medieval Latin and Middle English Literature: Essays in Honour of Jill Mann*. Cambridge: D. S. Brewer, 2011, pp. 41–64.

Davis, Rebecca. *Piers Plowman and the Books of Nature*. Oxford: Oxford University Press, 2016.

Davlin, Mary Clemente. '"Kynde Knowyng" as a Major Theme in *Piers Plowman* B', *RES* 22 (1971), 1–19.

Davlin, Mary Clemente. '"Kynde Knowyng" as a Middle English Equivalent for "Wisdom" in *Piers Plowman*', *Medium Ævum* 50 (1981), 5–17.

Davlin, Mary Clemente. *A Game of Heuene: Word Play and the Meaning of Piers Plowman B*. Woodbridge: D.S. Brewer, 1989.

Dawson, John D. 'Sign Theory, Allegorical Reading, and the Motions of the Soul in *De doctrina christiana*', in Duane W. H. Arnold and Pamela Bright, eds, *De doctrina Christiana: A Classic of Western Culture*. Notre Dame: University of Notre Dame Press, 1995, pp. 123–4.

Dawson, David. 'Plato's Soul and the Body of the Text in Philo and Origen', in Jon Whitman, ed., *Interpretation and Allegory: Antiquity to the Modern Period*. Leiden: Brill, 2000, pp. 89–107.

De Boer, Sander W. *The Science of the Soul: The Commentary Tradition on Aristotle's De anima, c. 1260–c. 1360*. Leuven: Leuven University Press, 2013.

De Libera, Alain. 'Roger Bacon et le problème de l'*appellatio univoca*', in H. A. G. Braakhuis, C. H. Kneepkens, and L. M. de Rijk, eds, *English Logic and Semantics, from the End of the Twelfth Century to the Time of Ockham and Burleigh. Acts of the 4th European Symposium on Mediaeval Logic and Semantics, Leiden-Nijmegen, 23–27 April 1979*. Turnhout: Brepols, 1981, pp. 193–234.

516 BIBLIOGRAPHY

De Libera, Alain. 'Roger Bacon et la reéférence vide: Sur quelques antécédents médiévaux du paradoxe de Meinong', in Jean Jolivet, Zenon Kaluza, Alain de Libera, eds, *'Lectionum varietates', Hommage à Paul Vignaux (1904–1987)*. Paris: Vrin, 1991, pp. 85–120.

De Libera, Alain. *César et le Phénix. Distinctiones et sophismata parisiens du XIIIe siècle*. Pisa: Scuola Normale superiore/Florence: Opus libri, 1991.

De Libera, Alain. *La Querelle des Universaux de Platon à la Fin du Moyen Âge*. Paris: Seuil, 1996.

De Libera, Alain. 'Roger Bacon et la Logique', in Jeremiah Hackett, ed., *Roger Bacon and the Sciences: Commemorative Essays 1996*. Leiden: Brill, 1997, pp. 103–32.

De Libera, Alain. *La Référence vide: Théories de la proposition*. Paris: Presses Universitaires de France, 2002.

De Libera, Alain. *L'unité de l'intellect: Commentaire du 'De unitate intellectus contra Averroistas' de Thomas d'Aquin*. Paris: Vrin, 2004.

De Libera, Alain. *Archéologie du sujet: I. Naissance du sujet*. Paris: Vrin, 2007.

De Libera, Alain. *Archéologie du sujet: II. La Quête de l'identité*. Paris: Vrin, 2008).

De Libera, Alain. *Archéologie du sujet: III. L'Acte de penser: 1. La Double révolution*. Paris: Vrin, 2014.

De Libera, Alain, Abdelali Elamrani-Jamal, and Alain Galaonnier, eds. *Langages et philosophie: Hommage à Jean Jolivet*. Paris: Vrin, 1997.

De Libera, Alain, et Leone Gazziero, 'Le sophisma "Omnis homo de necessitate est animal" du parisinus latinus 16135, f. 99rb–103vb', *AHDLMA* 75/1 (2008), 323–68.

De Looze, Laurence. *Pseudo-Autobiography in the Fourteenth Century: Juan Ruiz, Guillaume De Machaut, Jean Froissart, and Geoffrey Chaucer*. Gainesville: University of Florida Press, 1997.

De Lubac, Henri. 'À propos de la formule: *Diversi sed non adversi*', *Recherches de Science Religieuse* 40 (1952), 27–40.

De Lubac, Henri. *Medieval Exegesis*, trans Marc Sebanc and M Macierowski, 4 Vols. Grand Rapids, MI/Edinburgh: Eerdmans/T&T Clark, 1998–2009.

De Rijk, Lambertus Marie. *Logica Modernorum: A Contribution to the History of Early Terminist Logic*. 2 vols. Assen: Van Grocum, 1962–7.

De Rijk, Lambertus Marie. 'The Origins of the Theory of the Properties of Terms', in *CHLMP*, pp. 159–73.

De Rijk, Lambertus Marie. 'Semantics and Ontology: An Assessment of Medieval Terminism', *Vivarium* 51 (2013), 11–59.

Dehoux, Esther. 'Des Saints au tribunal: Juges et experts à la cour du Paradis', in Marie Bassano, Esther Dehoux, and Catherine Vincent, eds, *Le 'Pèlerinage de l'âme' de Guillaume de Digulleville (1355–1358): Regards Croisés Actes du colloque Université Paris-Ouest-Nanterre-La Défense/Université Paris-Descartes (29–30 mars 2012)*. Turnhout: Brepols, 2014, pp. 185–98.

Delio, Ilia. 'Theology, Spirituality and Christ the Center', in Jay M. Hammond, J. A. Wayne Hellmann, and Jared Goff, eds, *A Companion to Bonaventure*. Leiden: Brill, 2014, pp. 361–402.

Demaules, Mireille. *La corne et l'ivoire: étude sur le récit de rêve dans la littérature romanesque des XIIe et XIIIe siècles*. Paris: Champion, 2010.

Denery, Dallas G. II. *Seeing and Being Seen in the Later Medieval World: Optics, Theology and Religious Life*. Cambridge: Cambridge University Press, 2005.

Denery, Dallas G. II, Kantik Ghosh, and Nicolette Zeeman, eds, *Uncertain Knowledge: Scepticism, Relativism and Doubt in the Middle Ages*. Turnhout: Brepols, 2014, pp. 213–38.

Derolez, René. *Runica Manuscripta*. Bruges: De Tempel, 1954.

Derrida, Jacques. *La Dissémination*. Paris: Seuil, 1972.

Di Martino, Carla. *Ratio particularis: la Doctrine des Sens Internes d'Avicenne à Thomas d'Aquin: Contribution à l'Étude de la Tradition Arabo-Latine de la Psychologie d'Aristote*. Paris: Vrin, 2008.

Dimmick, Jeremy, James Simpson and Nicolette Zeeman, eds. *Images, Idolatry and Iconoclasm in Late Medieval England: Textuality and the Visual Image*. Oxford: Oxford University Press, 2002.

Dixon, Rebecca, and Finn E. Sinclair, eds. *Poetry, Knowledge, and Community in Late Medieval France*. Cambridge: D. S. Brewer, 2008.

Doig, James. 'Aristotle and Aquinas', in Brian Davies, ed., *Oxford Handbook of Aquinas*. Oxford: Oxford University Press, 2012, pp. 33–41.

Donaldson, E. Talbot. *Piers Plowman: The C-text and Its Poet*. New Haven and London: Yale University Press, 1949.

Donaldson, E. Talbot. 'MSS R and F in the B-tradition of *Piers Plowman*', *Transactions of the Connecticut Academy* 39 (1955), 177–212.

Donaldson, E. Talbot. 'Apocalyptic Style in *Piers Plowman* B XIX–XX', *Leeds Studies in English* 14 (1983), 74–81.

Doss-Quinby, Eglal, Roberta l. Krueger, and E. Jane Burns, eds, *Cultural Performances in Medieval France: essays in Honor of Nancy Freeman Regalado*. Cambridge: D.S. Brewer, 2007.

Dragonetti, Roger. 'Le singe de nature dans le Roman de la Rose', in *Mélanges d'Études Romanes du Moyen Age et de la Renaissance offerts à Jean Rychner*. Paris: Klincksieck, 1978, pp. 149–60.

Drobinsky, Julia. 'La roche qui pleure et le cuvier aux larmes: les images de la pénitence', in Duval and Pomel, pp. 81–110.

Duba, William. 'The Souls after Vienne: Franciscan Theologians' Views on the Plurality of Forms and the Plurality of Souls, ca. 1315–1330', in Paul J. J. M. Bakker, Sander W. Boer, and Cees Leijenhorst, eds, *Psychology and the other Disciplines: A Case of Cross-Disciplinary Interaction (1250–1750)*. Leiden: Brill, 2012, pp. 171–272.

Dufournet, Jean, ed., *Etudes sur le Roman de la Rose de Guillaume de Lorris*. Paris: Champion, 1984.

Duval, Frédéric. 'Deux prières latines de Guillaume de Digulleville: Prière à Saint Michel et prière à l'ange gardien', in Duval and Pomel, pp. 185–211.

Duval, Frédéric. 'Du nouveau sur la tradition latine de Guillaume de Digulleville: le manuscrit-recueil Paris, bibl. de l'Arsenal 507', *Scriptorium* 64.2 (2010), 251–67.

Duval, Frédéric. 'Interpréter le *Pèlerinage de vie humaine* de Guillaume de Digulleville (vers 1330)', in Hélène Bellon-Méquelle et al., eds, *La moisson des lettres: l'invention littéraire autour de 1300*. Turnhout: Brepols, 2011, pp. 233–52.

Eardley, Peter S. 'The Foundations of Freedom in Later Medieval Philosophy: Giles of Rome and His Contemporaries', *Journal of the History of Philosophy* 44 (2006), 353–76.

Ebbesen, Sten. *Commentators and Commentaries on Aristotle's Sophistici Elenchi: a Study of post-Aristotelian Ancient and Medieval Writings on Fallacies*. 3 vols. Leiden: Brill, 1983.

Ebbesen, Sten. ed. *Sprachtheorien in Spätantike und Mittelalter*. Tübingen: Günther Narr, 1995.

Ebbesen, Sten. 'The Odyssey of Semantics from the Stoa to Buridan', in *Greek-Latin Philosophical Interaction: Collected Essays of Sten Ebbesen*, 2 vols. Aldershot: Ashgate, 2008, I:21–33.

518 BIBLIOGRAPHY

Ebbesen, Sten. 'Theories of Language in the Hellenistic Age and in the Twelfth and Thirteenth Centuries', in *Greek-Latin Philosophical Interaction: Collected Essays of Sten Ebbesen*, 2 vols. Aldershot: Ashgate, 2008, I:79–96.

Ebbesen, Sten. *Greek-Latin Philosophical Interaction: Collected Essays of Sten Ebbesen*, 2 vols. Aldershot: Ashgate, 2008.

Ebbesen, Sten, and David Bloch, et al., eds. *History of Philosophy in Reverse: Reading Aristotle through the Lenses of Scholars from the Twelfth to the Sixteenth Centuries*. Copenhagen: The Royal Danish Academy of Sciences and Letters, 2014.

Ebbesen, Sten, and Russell L. Friedman, eds, *Medieval Analyses in Language and Cognition*. Copenhagen: Royal Danish Academy of Sciences and Letters, 1999.

Eco, Umberto. *I limiti dell'interpretazione*. Milan: Bompiani, 1990.

Edwards, Graham Robert. '*Hortus conclusus*: Le Jardin des Cantiques chez Guillaume de Deguileville', in Christophe Imbert and Philippe Maupeu, eds, *Le paysage allégorique: entre image mentale et pays transfiguré*. Rennes: Presses Universitaires de Rennes, 2011, pp. 65–79.

Edwards, Graham Robert. 'Making Sense of Deguileville's Autobiographical Project: The Evidence of Paris, BnF MS Latin 14845', in Kamath and Nievergelt, pp. 129–50.

Edwards, Robert R., ed. *Art and Context in Late Medieval English Narrative: Essays in Honor of Robert Worth Frank*. Cambridge: D.S. Brewer, 1994.

Eldredge, Laurence M. 'Some Medical Evidence on Langland's Imaginatif', *YLS* 3 (1989), 131–6.

Ellis, Roger ed. *Oxford History of Literary Translation in English, Vol I: until 1550*. Oxford University Press, 2008.

Emmerson, Richard K. 'The Prophetic, the Apocalyptic, and the Study of Medieval Literature', in Raymond-Jean Frontain and Jan Wojcik, eds, *Poetic Prophecy in Western Literature*. Rutherford: Fairleigh Dickinson University Press 1984, pp. 40–54.

Emmerson, Richard K. '"Coveitise to Konne", "Goddes Pryvetee", and Will's Ambiguous Dream Experience in *Piers Plowman*', in David C. Fowler and Míceál F. Vaughan, eds, *Suche Werkis to Werche: Essays on Piers Plowman in Honor of David C. Fowler*. East Lansing: Colleagues Press, 1993, pp. 89–121.

Emmerson, Richard K., and Ronald B. Herzman. 'The Apocalyptic Age of Hypocrisy: Faus Semblant and Amant in the *Roman de la Rose*', *Speculum* 62.3 (1987), 612–34.

English, Edward D., ed. *Reading and Wisdom: The 'De Doctrina Christiana' of Augustine in the Middle Ages*. Notre Dame: University of Notre Dame Press, 1995.

Evans, Gillian R., 'A Work of "Terminist Theology"? Peter the Chanter's *De Tropis Loquendi* and Some *Fallacie*', *Vivarium* 20.1 (1982), 40–58.

Evans, Gillian R. *The Language and Logic of the Bible: the Earlier Middle Ages*. Vol. 1, and *The Road to Reformation*. Vol. 2. Cambridge: Cambridge University Press, 1984 and 1985.

Evans, Gillian R. *Augustine on Evil*. Cambridge: Cambridge University Press, 1990.

Faral, Edmond. '*Le Roman de la rose* et la pensée française au XIIIe siècle', *Revue des deux mondes* 96 (1926), 430–57.

Faral, Edmond. '*Le roman de la fleur de lis* de Guillaume de Digulleville', in *Mélanges de philologie romane et de littérature médiévale offerts à Ernest Hoepffner par ses élèves et ses amis*. Paris: Les Belles Lettres: 1949/Genève: Slatkine, 1974, pp. 327–38.

Faral, Edmond. 'Guillaume de Digulleville, moine de Chaalis', in *Histoire littéraire de la France*, Vol. 39. Paris: Imprimerie Nationale, 1962.

Fein, Susanna, and David Raybin, eds. *Chaucer: Visual Approaches*. University Park: Penn State University Press, 2016.

Ferretter, Luke. 'The Trace of the Trinity: Christ and Difference in Saint Augustine's Theory of Language', *Literature and Theology* 12.3 (1998), 256–67.

Ferzoco, George, and Carolyn Muessig, eds, *Medieval Monastic Education*. London: Leicester University Press, 2000.

Fidora, Alexander, and Matthias Lutz-Bachmann, eds. *Erfahrung und Beweis. Die Wissenschaften von der Natur im 13. und 14. Jahrhundert/Experience and Demonstration. The Sciences of Nature in the 13th and 14th Centuries*. Berlin: De Gruyter, 2009.

Fineman, Joel. *Shakespeare's Perjured Eye: The Invention of Poetic Subjectivity in Shakespeare's Sonnets*. Berkeley and Los Angeles: University of California Press, 1986.

Fink, Jakob Leth. 'Aristotle and the Medievals on Certainty', in Sten Ebbesen, David Bloch, et al., eds, *History of Philosophy in Reverse: Reading Aristotle through the Lenses of Scholars from the Twelfth to the Sixteenth Centuries*. Copenhagen: The Royal Danish Academy of Sciences and Letters, 2014, pp. 148–65.

Fleming, John V. *Reason and the Lover*. Princeton: Princeton University Press, 1984.

Fletcher, Angus. *Allegory: The Theory of a Symbolic Mode*. Ithaca, NY: Cornell University Press, 1964.

Fletcher, Alan J. 'The Essential (Ephemeral) William Langland: Textual Revision as Ethical Process in *Piers Plowman*', *YLS* 15 (2001), 61–98.

Fowler, David C. and Míceál F. Vaughan, eds. *Suche Werkis to Werche: Essays on Piers Plowman in Honor of David C. Fowler*. East Lansing: Colleagues Press, 1993.

Frank, Robert Worth. 'The Conclusion of *Piers Plowman*', *JEGP* 49 (1950), 309–16.

Franklin-Brown, Mary. *Reading the World: Encyclopaedic Writing in the Scholastic Age*. Chicago and London: University of Chicago Press, 2012.

Frantzen, Allen J. 'The Disclosure of Sodomy in Cleanness', *PMLA* 111 (1996), 451–64.

Fredborg, Karin M. 'Notes on the *Glosulae* and its reception by William of Conches and Petrus Helias', in Irène Rosier-Catach, ed., *Arts du langage et theologie aux confins des XI et XII siècles: Textes, maîtres, débats*. Turnhout: Brepols, 2011, pp. 453–83.

Fredborg, Karin Margareta, 'Roger Bacon on *Impositio vocis ad significandum*', in H. A. G. Braakhuis, C. H. Kneepkens, and L. M. de Rijk, eds, *English Logic and Semantics from the End of the Twelfth Century to the Time of Ockham and Burleigh*. Nijmegen: Ingenium, 1981, pp. 167–91.

Frieden, Philippe. 'Le *Roman de la Rose*: de l'édition aux manuscrits', *Perspectives Médiévales* 34 (2012), n.p.

Friedman, Russell L. *Intellectual Traditions in the Medieval University: The Use of Philosophical Psychology in Trinitarian Theology Among the Franciscans and the Dominicans, 1250–1350*. 2 vols. Leiden: Brill, 2012.

Frontain, Raymond-Jean, and Jan Wojcik, eds, *Poetic Prophecy in Western Literature*. Rutherford: Fairleigh Dickinson University Press 1984.

Fyler, John M. 'St. Augustine, Genesis, and the Origin of Language', in Edward B. King and Jacqueline T. Schaefer, eds, *Saint Augustine and His Influence in the Middle Ages*. Sewanee: Press of the University of the South, 1988, pp. 69–78.

Fyler, John M. *Language and the Declining World in Chaucer, Dante, and Jean de Meun*. Cambridge: Cambridge University Press, 2007.

Galand-Hallyn, Pierrine. 'Le songe et la rhétorique de l'*enargeia*', in Françoise Charpentier, ed., *Le songe à la Renaissance: colloque international de Cannes, 29–31 mai 1987*. Saint-Etienne: Institut d'Études de la Renaissance et de l'Âge classique, Université de Saint-Etienne, 1990, pp. 125–36.

Gallacher, Patrick J. 'Imaginatif and the Sensus Communis', *YLS* 6 (1992), 51–60.

Galloway, Andrew. '*Piers Plowman* and the Schools', *YLS* 6 (1992), 89–107.

520 BIBLIOGRAPHY

Galloway, Andrew. 'The Rhetoric of Riddling in Late-Medieval England: The "Oxford" Riddles, the *Secretum philosophorum*, and the Riddles in *Piers Plowman*', *Speculum* 70 (1995), 68–105.

Galloway, Andrew. *Penn Commentary on 'Piers Plowman': Volume 1*. Philadelphia: University of Pennsylvania Press, 2006.

Galloway, Andrew. 'Madame Meed: *Fauvel*, Isabella, and the French Circumstances of *Piers Plowman*', *YLS* 30 (2016), 227–52.

Galloway, Andrew, and Frank Grady, eds. *Answerable Style: The Idea of the Literary in Medieval England*. Columbus: Ohio State Universit Press 2013.

Gambale, Giacomo. '"Par langue les livre a martire . . .": La *potestas nocendi* de la parole', in Nicole Bériou, Jean-Patrice Boudet, and Irène Rosier-Catach, eds, *Le pouvoir des mots au Moyen Âge*. Turnhout: Brepols, 2014, pp. 363–77.

Garrison, Jennifer. 'Failed Signification: *Corpus Christi* and *Corpus Mysticum* in *Piers Plowman*', *YLS* 23 (2009), 97–123.

Gasquet, Francis A. 'An Unpublished Fragment of a Work by Roger Bacon', *English Historical Review* 12 (1897), 494–517.

Gaunt, Simon. '*Bel Acueil* and the Improper Allegory of the *Romance of the Rose*', *New Medieval Literatures* 2 (1998), 65–93.

Gavrilyuk, Paul L., and Sarah Coakley, eds. *The Spiritual Senses: Perceiving God in Western Christianity*. Cambridge: Cambridge University Press, 2011.

Gayk, Shannon. *Image, Text, and Religious Reform in Fifteenth-Century England*. Cambridge: Cambridge University Press, 2010.

Gehl, Paul F. '*Competens Silentium*: Varieties of Monastic Silence in the Medieval West', *Viator* 18 (1987), 125–60.

Gelber, Hester. *It Could Have Been Otherwise: Contingency and Necessity in Dominican Theology at Oxford, 1300–1350*. Leiden: Brill, 2004.

Gibbs, Raymond W. *Embodiment and Cognitive Science*. Cambridge: Cambridge University Press, 2005.

Gibbs, Raymond W. 'Metaphor Interpretation as Embodied Simulation', *Mind & Language* 21.3 (2006), 434–58.

Gibbs, Raymond W., ed. *The Cambridge Handbook of Metaphor and Thought*. Cambridge: Cambridge University Press, 2008.

Gibbs, Raymond W. and Teenie Matlock. 'Metaphor, Imagination and Simulation: Psycholinguistic Evidence', in Raymond W. Gibbs, ed., *The Cambridge Handbook of Metaphor and Thought*. Cambridge: Cambridge University Press, 2008, pp. 161–76.

Gibson, John, ed., *The Philosophy of Poetry*. Oxford: Oxford University Press: 2015.

Gibson, Margaret T. 'The *De doctrina christiana* in the School of St. Victor', in Edward D. English, ed., *Reading and Wisdom: The 'De Doctrina Christiana' of Augustine in the Middle Ages*. Notre Dame: University of Notre Dame Press, 1995, pp. 41–7.

Gilbert, Neal Ward. 'The Concept of Will in Early Latin Philosophy', *Journal of the History of Philosophy* 1.1 (1963), 17–35.

Gillespie, Vincent. 'From the Twelfth Century to *c.* 1450', in Alastair Minnis and Ian Johnson, eds, *The Cambridge History of Literary Criticism. Volume 2: The Middle Ages*. Cambridge: Cambridge University Press, 2005, pp. 145–235.

Gillespie, Vincent. 'Vernacular Theology', in Paul Strohm, ed., *Medieval English*. Oxford: Oxford University Press, 2007, pp. 401–20.

Gillespie, Vincent. 'Dame Study's Anatomical Curse: A Scatological Parody?', in Nicholas Jacobs and Gerald Morgan, eds, *'Truthe is the Beste': A Festschrift in Honour of A. V. C. Schmidt*. Oxford: Peter Lang, 2014, pp. 95–107.

BIBLIOGRAPHY 521

Gillespie, Vincent. '*Ethice Subponitur*? The Imaginative Syllogism and the Idea of the Poetic', in Philip Knox, Jonathan Morton, and Daniel Reeve, eds, *Medieval Thought Experiments: Poetry, Hypothesis, and Experience in the European Middle Ages*. Turnhout: Brepols, 2018, pp. 297-32.

Gilson, Étienne. 'Les Sources gréco-arabes de l'augustinisme avicennisant', *AHDLMA* 4 (1929-1930), 5-149.

Gilson, Étienne. '*Regio dissimilitudinis* de Platon à saint Bernard de Clairvaux', *Mediaeval Studies* 9 (1947), 108-30.

Gilson, Étienne. further Étienne Gilson, *La théologie mystique de St Bernard*. Paris: Vrin, 1947.

Glasscoe, Marion ed. *The Medieval Mystical Tradition in England: Papers Read at the Exeter Symposium*. Exeter: University of Exeter Press, 1980.

Godden, Malcolm. 'Plowmen and Hermits in Langland's *Piers Plowman*', *RES* n. s. 35.138 (1984), 129-63.

Godden, Malcolm. *The Making of Piers Plowman*. London and. New York: Longman, 1990.

Gonzalez-Doreste, Dulce M. and Maria del Pilar Mendoza Ramos, eds. *Nouvelles de la Rose: Actualités et persepectives du 'Roman de la Rose'*. La Laguna: Servicio de Publicationes, Universidad de La Laguna, 2011.

Gooding, David C. 'What is Experimental about Thought Experiments?' *Proceedings of the Biennial Meeting of the Philosophy of Science Association* (1992), 280-90.

Goris, Wouter. 'The Foundation of the Principle of Non-Contradiction. Some Remarks on the Medieval Transformation of Metaphysics', *Documenti e studi sulla tradizione filosofica medievale* 22 (2011), 527-55.

Goullet, Monique, ed., *Parva pro magnis munera - études de littérature tardo-antique et médiévale offertes à François Dolbeau par ses élèves*. Turnhout: Brepols, 2009.

Gracia, Jorge J. E. 'The Centrality of the Individual in the Philosophy of the Fourteenth Century', *History of Philosophy Quarterly* 8.3 (1991), 235-51.

Gracia, Jorge J. E., and Timothy N. Noone, eds, *A Companion to Philosophy in the Middle Ages*. Oxford: Blackwell, 2002.

Gragnolati, Manuele, Tristan Kay, Elena Lombardi, and Francesca Southerden, eds. *Desire in Dante and the Middle Ages*. Abingdon and New York: Legenda, 2012.

Greenblatt, Norman. *The Swerve: How the World Became Modern*. New York and London: W. W. Norton, 2011.

Greene, Virginie. *Logical Fictions in Medieval Literature and Philosophy*. Cambridge: Cambridge University Press, 2014.

Grellard, Christophe. 'Comment peut-on se fier à l'expérience? Esquisse d'une typologie des réponses médiévales au scepticisme', *Quaestio* 4 (2004), 113-35.

Grellard, Christophe. 'Epistemology', in Henrik Lagerlund, ed., *Encyclopedia of Medieval Philosophy: Philosophy between 500 and 1500*. 2 vols. Dordrecht: Springer, 2011, I:294-300.

Grellard, Christophe. 'Mechanisms of Belief: Jean de Meun's Implicit Epistemology', in Morton and Nievergelt, pp. 27-44.

Grévin, Benoît, and Julien Véronèse, 'Les "caractères" magiques au Moyen Âge (XIIe-XIVe siècle)', in *Bibliothèque de l'Ecole des Chartes* 62 (2004), 305-79.

Grmača, Dolores. 'Body Trouble: The Impact of Deguileville's Allegory of Human Life on Croatian Renaissance Literature', in Kamath and Nievergelt, pp. 189-208.

Gros, Gérard. *Le Poète Marial et l'Art Graphique: Études sur les Jeux de Lettres dans les Poèmes Pieux au Moyen Âge*. Caen: Paradigme, 1993.

522 BIBLIOGRAPHY

Gruenler, Curtis. 'How to Read like a Fool: Riddle Contests and the Banquet of Conscience in *Piers Plowman*', *Speculum* 85. 3 (2010), 592–630.

Gruenler, Curtis '*Piers Plowman' and the Poetics of Enigma: Riddles, Rhetoric, and Theology*. Notre Dame: University of Notre Dame Press, 2017.

Gutas, Dimitri. *Avicenna and the Aristotelian Tradition*, 2nd ed. Leiden: Brill, 2014.

Guynn, Noah. *Allegory and Sexual Ethics in the High Middle Ages*. New York: Palgrave Macmillan, 2007.

Hackett, Jeremiah. '*Scientia experimentalis*: From Robert Grosseteste to Roger Bacon', in James McEvoy, ed., *Robert Grosseteste: New perspectives on his thought and scholarship*. Turnhout: Brepols, 1995, pp. 89–119.

Hackett, Jeremiah. Jeremiah Hackett, 'Roger Bacon: His Life, Career, and Works', in Jeremiah Hackett, ed., *Roger Bacon and the Sciences: Commemorative Essays1996*. Leiden: Brill, 1997, pp. 9–25.

Hackett, Jeremiah. 'Roger Bacon on *Scientia Experimentalis*', in Jeremiah Hackett, ed., *Roger Bacon and the Sciences: Commemorative Essays 1996*. Leiden: Brill, 1997, pp. 277–315.

Hackett, Jeremiah. 'Experience and Demonstration in Roger Bacon: A Critical Review of Some Modern Interpretations', in Alexander Fidora and Matthias Lutz-Bachmann, eds, *Erfahrung und Beweis. Die Wissenschaften von der Natur im 13. und 14. Jahrhundert/Experience and Demonstration. The Sciences of Nature in the 13th and 14th Centuries*. Berlin: De Gruyter, 2009, pp. 41–58.

Hackett, Jeremiah. 'Roger Bacon's Concept of Experience: A New Beginning in Medieval Philosophy?', *The Modern Schoolman* 86.1/2 (2008), 123–46.

Hackett, Jeremiah. 'Roger Bacon', *The Stanford Encyclopedia of Philosophy* (Spring 2015 Edition), ed. Edward N. Zalta, [https://plato.stanford.edu/archives/spr2015/entries/roger-bacon; retrieved 3 June 2021]

Hagen, Susan K. *Allegorical Remembrance: a Study of 'The Pilgrimage of the life of Man' as a Medieval Treatise on Seeing and Remembering*. Athens, GA, and London: University of Georgia Press, 1990.

Haldane, John. 'Soul and Body', in *CHMP*, I:293–304.

Hammond, Jay M., J. A. Wayne Hellmann, and Jared Goff, eds, *A Companion to Bonaventure*. Leiden: Brill, 2014.

Hanna, Ralph. '"Meddling with Makings" and Will's Work', in A. J. Minnis, ed., *Late Medieval Religious Texts and Their Transmission: Essays in Honour of A. I. Doyle*. Woodbridge: D. S. Brewer, 1994, pp. 85–94.

Hanna, Ralph. *Pursuing History: Middle English Manuscripts and Their Texts*. Stanford: Stanford University Press, 1996.

Hanna, Ralph. 'On the versions of *Piers Plowman*', in his *Pursuing History: Middle English Manuscripts and Their Texts*. Stanford: Stanford University Press, 1996, pp. 203–43.

Hanna, Ralph. 'Will's Work', in Steven Justice and Kathryn Kerby-Fulton, eds, *Written Work: Langland, Labor, and Authorship*. Philadelphia: University of Pennsylvania Press, 1997, pp. 23–66.

Hanna, Ralph. 'School and Scorn: Gender in *Piers Plowman*', *New Medieval Literatures* 3 (2000), 213–27.

Hanna, Ralph. 'Langland's Ymaginatif: Images and the Limits of Poetry', in Jeremy Dimmick, James Simpson and Nicolette Zeeman, eds, *Images, Idolatry and Iconoclasm in Late Medieval England: Textuality and the Visual Image*. Oxford: Oxford University Press, 2002, pp. 81–94.

BIBLIOGRAPHY 523

Hanna, Ralph. 'The Versions and Revisions of Piers Plowman', in Andrew Cole and Andrew Galloway, eds, *The Cambridge Companion to Piers Plowman*. Cambridge: Cambridge University Press, 2014, pp. 33–49.

Hanna, Ralph. 'The "Absent" Pardon-Tearing of Piers Plowman C', *RES n. s.* 66.275 (2015), 449–64.

Hanna, Ralph. *Patient Reading/Reading Patience: Oxford Essays on Medieval English Literature*. Liverpool: Liverpool University Press, 2017.

Hanna, Ralph. 'Hawkin and Patience's Instruction', in ibid., *Patient Reading/Reading Patience: Oxford Essays on Medieval English Literature*. Liverpool: Liverpool University Press, 2017, pp. 319–38.

Häring, Nikolaus M. 'Commentary and Hermeneutics', in Charles Homer Haskins, ed., *Renaissance and Renewal in the Twelfth Century*. Cambridge, MA: Harvard University Press, 1982, pp. 173–200.

Harmless, William. *Mystics*. Oxford: Oxford University Press, 2008.

Harwood, Britton J. 'Langland's "Kynde Knowyng" and the Quest for Christ', *Modern Philology* 80.3 (1983), 242–55.

Harwood, Britton J. *Piers Plowman and the Problem of Belief*. Toronto: Toronto University Press, 1992.

Hasenohr, Geneviève. '*Lacrimae pondera vocis habent*: Typologie des larmes dans la littérature de spiritualité française des XIIIe–XVe siècles', *Le moyen français* 37 (1997), 45–63.

Hasse, Dag Nikolaus. *Avicenna's 'De anima' in the Latin West: The Formation of a Peripatetic Philosophy of the Soul, 1160–1300*. London: Warburg Institute, 2000.

Hasse, Dag Nikolaus. 'The Soul's Faculties', in *CHMP*, I:305–19.

Hays, Zachary. 'Bonaventure's Trinitarian Theology', in Jay M. Hammond, J. A. Wayne Hellmann, and Jared Goff, eds, *A Companion to Bonaventure*. Leiden: Brill, 2014, pp. 189–246.

Heath, Peter. *Allegory and Philosophy in Avicenna (Ibn Sînâ): With a Translation of the Book of the Prophet Muhammad's Ascent to Heaven*. Philadelphia: University of Pennsylvania Press, 1992.

Heffernan, Thomas J. ed. *The Popular Literature of Medieval England*. Knoxville: University of Tennessee Press, 1985.

Heller-Roazen, Daniel. *Fortune's Faces: The 'Roman de la Rose' and the Poetics of Contingency*. Baltimore and London: Johns Hopkins University Press, 2003.

Hewett-Smith, Kathleen M. ed. *William Langland's Piers Plowman: A Book of Essays*. London: Routledge, 2001.

Hewett-Smith, Kathleen M. '"Nede hath no lawe:" Poverty and the De-Stabilization of Allegory in the Final Visions of *Piers Plowman*', in Kathleen M. Hewett-Smith, ed., *William Langland's Piers Plowman: A Book of Essays*. London: Routledge, 2001, 233–53.

Heyworth, P. L. ed. *Medieval Studies for J.A.W. Bennett*. Oxford: Clarendon Press, 1981.

Hilder, Gisela. *Der scholastische Wortschatz bei Jean de Meun: die artes liberales*. Tübingen: Niemeyer, 1972.

Hindman, Sandra, ed. *Printing the Written Word: The Social History of Books, circa 1450–1520*. Ithaca: Cornell University Press, 1991.

Hirsh, John C. 'The Experience of God: A New Classification of Certain Late Medieval Affective Texts', *The Chaucer Review* 11. 1 (1976), 11–21.

Hissette, Roland. *Enquête sur les 219 articles condamnés à Paris le 7 mars 1277*. Louvain and Paris: Publications Universitaires, 1977.

Hoffmann, Tobias. 'Intellectualism and Voluntarism', in *CHMP*, I:414–27.

524 BIBLIOGRAPHY

Hoffmann, Tobias, Jörn Müller, and Matthias Perkams, eds. *Das Problem der Willensschwäche in der mittelalterlichen Philosophie/The Problem of Weakness of Will in Medieval Philosophy*. Leuven: Peeters, 2006.

Hölscher, Ludger. *The Reality of the Mind: St Augustine's Philosophical Arguments for the Human Soul as a Spiritual Substance*. London: Routledge, 1986.

Horobin, Simon. 'Manuscripts and Readers of *Piers Plowman*', in Cole and Galloway, pp. 179–97.

Horowitz, Tamara, and Gerald J. Masey, eds. *Thought Experiments in Science and Philosophy*. Savage, MD: Rowman and Littlefield, 1991.

Hudson, Anne. *The Premature Reformation: Wycliffite Texts and Lollard history*. Oxford: Clarendon Press, 1988.

Hüe, Denis. 'L'apprentissage de la louange: pour une typologie de la prière dans les pèlerinages de Guillaume de Deguileville', in Duval and Pomel, pp. 159–84.

Hughes, Kevin L. 'By its Fruits: The Spiritual Senses in Bonaventure's "Tree of Life"', *Medieval Mystical Theology* 28.1 (2019), 36–47.

Hult, David F. 'Closed Quotations: The Speaking Voice in the *Roman de la rose*', *Yale French Studies* 67 (1984), 248–69.

Hult, David F. *Self-Fulfilling Prophecies: Readership and Authority in the First 'Roman de la rose'*. Cambridge: Cambridge University Press, 1986.

Hult, David F. 'Language and Dismemberment: Abelard, Origen and the *Romance of the Rose*', in Kevin Brownlee and Sylvia Huot, eds, *Rethinking the 'Romance of the Rose': Text, Image, Reception*. Philadelphia: University of Pennsylvania Press, 1992, pp. 101–30.

Hult, David F. '1277, 7 March: Jean de Meun's *Roman de la rose*', in Denis Hollier, ed., *A New History of French Literature*. Cambridge MA: Harvard University Press: 1994, pp. 97–103.

Hult, David F. 'Words and Deeds: Jean de Meun's *Romance of the Rose* and the Hermeneutics of Censorship', *New Literary History* 28.2 (1997), 345–66.

Hult, David F. 'Poetry and the Translation of Knowledge in Jean de Meun', in Rebecca Dixon and Finn E. Sinclair, eds, *Poetry, Knowledge and Community in Late Medieval France*. Cambridge: Boydell & Brewer, 2008, pp. 19–41.

Hunsinger, George. *How to Read Karl Barth: The Shape of His Theology*. Oxford: Oxford University Press, 1991.

Huot, Sylvia. *From Song to Book: the Poetics of Writing in Old French Lyric and Lyrical Narrative Poetry*. Ithaca: Cornell University Press, 1987.

Huot, Sylvia. *The Romance of the Rose and its Medieval Readers: Interpretation, Reception, Manuscript Transmission*. Cambridge: Cambridge University Press, 1993.

Huot, Sylvia. 'Bodily Peril: Sexuality and the Subversion of Order in Jean de Meun's Roman de la Rose', Modern Language Review 95 (2000), 41–61.

Huot, Sylvia. *Dreams of Lovers and Lies of Poets: Poetry, Knowledge, and Desire in the Roman de la Rose*. London: Legenda, 2010.

Hussey, S. S, ed. *Piers Plowman: Critical Approaches*. London: Methuen, 1969.

Ierodiakonou, Katerina, and Sophie Roux, eds. *Thought Experiments in Methodological and Historical Contexts*. Leiden: Brill, 2011.

Imbach, Ruedi. *Dante, la philosophie et les laïcs*. Paris/Fribourg: Cerf/Éditions Universitaires, 1996.

Imbach, Ruedi, and Alfonso Maierù, eds, *Gli studi di filosofia medievale fra otto e novecento*. Rome: Edizioni di Storia e Letteratura, 1991.

Imbert, Christophe, and Philippe Maupeu, eds. *Le paysage allégorique: entre image mentale et pays transfiguré*. Rennes: Presses Universitaires de Rennes, 2011.

Irvine, Martin. *The Making of Textual Culture: 'Grammatica' and Literary Theory 350–1100*. Cambridge: Cambridge University Press, 2006.

Jackson, B. Darrell. 'The Theory of Signs in St. Augustine's De doctrina christiana', Revue des Études Augustiniennes 15 (1969), 9–49.

Jager, Eric. *The Tempter's Voice: Language and the Fall in Medieval Literature*. Ithaca: Cornell University Press, 1996, pp. 51–98.

Jager, Eric. 'The Book of the Heart: Reading and Writing the Medieval Subject', *Speculum* 71.1 (1996), 1–26.

Jauss, Hans Robert. 'Entstehung und Strukturwandel der allegorischen Dichtung', in Hans Robert Jauss and Erich Koehler, eds, *Grundriss der romanischen Literaturen des Mittelalters, vol. VI: La Littérature didactique, allégorique et satirique*, 11 vols, gen. ed. Hans U. Gumbrecht and Ulrich Mölk. Heidelberg: Winter, 1968, pp. 146–244.

Jauss, Hans Robert, and Erich Koehler, eds, *Grundriss der romanischen Literaturen des Mittelalters, vol. VI: La Littérature didactique, allégorique et satirique*, 11 vols, gen. ed. Hans U. Gumbrecht and Ulrich Mölk. Heidelberg: Winter, 1968.

Jeanneau, Édouard. 'L'usage de la notion d'integumentum à travers les gloses de Guillaume de Conches', *AHDLMA* 24 (1957), 35–100.

Jirsa, Curtis R. H. '*Piers Plowman's* Lyric Poetics', *YLS* 26 (2012), 77–110.

Johnson, Ella, 'To Taste (*sapere*) Wisdom (*Sapientia*): Eucharistic Devotion in the Writings of Gertrude of Helfta', *Viator* 44.2 (2013),175–200.

Johnson, Ian, and Alastair Minnis, eds. *The Cambridge History of Literary Criticism. Volume 2: The Middle Ages*. Cambridge: Cambridge University Press, 2005.

Johnston, Michael. 'The Clerical Career of William Rokele', *YLS* 33, (2019), 111–25.

Jordan, Mark D. 'Words and Word: Incarnational Signification in Augustine's De Doctrina Christiana', *Augustinian Studies* 11 (1980), 177–96.

Jordan, Mark D. *The Invention of Sodomy in Christian Theology*. Chicago: Chicago University Press, 1997.

Jordan, William Chester. *Unceasing Strife, Unending Fear: Jacques de Thérines and the Freedom of the Church in the Age of the Last Capetians*. Princeton: Princeton University Press, 2005.

Jung, Marc-René. 'Jean de Meun et l'allégorie', *Cahiers de l'Association internationale des études françaises* 28 (1976), 21–36.

Jusserand, J. J. *Piers Plowman: A Contribution to the History of English Mysticism*. London: Fisher Unwin, 1894.

Justice, Steven, and Kathryn Kerby-Fulton, eds. *Written Work: Langland, Labor, and Authorship*. Philadelphia: University of Pennsylvania Press, 1997.

Kablitz, Andreas, and Ursula Peters, 'The Pèlerinage Corpus: A Tradition of Textual Transformation across Western Europe', in Kamath and Nievergelt, pp. 25–46.

Kablitz, Andreas, and Ursula Peters, eds, *Mittelalterliche Literatur als Retextualisierung. Das 'Pèlerinage'-Corpus des Guillaume de Deguileville im europäischen Mittelalter*. Heidelberg: Winter, 2014.

Kamath, Stephanie A. V. G. '*Le Roman de la Rose* and Middle English Poetry', *Literature Compass* 6.6 (2009), 1109–26.

Kamath, Stephanie A. V. G. *Authorship and First-Person Allegory in Late Medieval France and England*. Cambridge: D. S. Brewer, 2012.

Kamath, Stephanie A. V. G. 'A Cruel Spoon in Context: Cutlery and Conviviality in Late Medieval Literature', *Études anglaises* 66.3 (2013), 281–96.

Kamath, Stephanie A. V. G. 'Rewriting Ancient *Auctores* in the *Pèlerinage de la vie humaine*', in Kablitz and Peters, pp. 321–42.

526   BIBLIOGRAPHY

Kamath, Stephanie A. V. G., and Marco Nievergelt, eds. *The Pèlerinage Allegories of Guillaume de Deguileville: Tradition, Authority, and Influence*. Cambridge: D. S. Brewer, 2013.

Kane, George. *Piers Plowman: The Evidence for Authorship*. London: Athlone Press, 1965.

Kane, George. *The Autobiographical Fallacy in Chaucer and Langland Studies*. London: University of London/H.K. Lewis, 1965.

Karger, Elizabeth. 'Mental Sentences According to Burley and to the Early Ockham', *Vivarium* 34.2 (1996), 193–230.

Karnes, Michelle. 'Will's Imagination in *Piers Plowman*', *JEGP* 108.1 (2009), 27–58.

Karnes, Michelle. *Imagination, Meditation, and Cognition in the Middle Ages*. Chicago: University of Chicago Press, 2011.

Kaske, R. E. 'Langland and the *Paradisus Claustralis*', *Modern Language Notes* 72 (1957), 481–3.

Kaulbach, Ernest N. 'The *Vis Imaginativa* and the Reasoning Powers of Ymaginatif in the B-Text of *Piers Plowman*', *JEGP* 84.1 (1985), 16–29.

Kay, Sarah. 'Sexual Knowledge: The Once and Future Texts of the *Romance of the Rose*', in Judith Still and Michael Worton, eds, *Textuality and Sexuality: Reading Theories and Practices*. Manchester: Manchester University Press, 1993, pp. 69–86.

Kay, Sarah. 'Women's Body of Knowledge: Epistemology and Misogyny in the *Romance of the Rose*', in Sarah Kay and Miri Rubin, eds, *Framing Medieval Bodies*. Manchester: Manchester University Press, 1994, pp. 211–35.

Kay, Sarah. *The Romance of the Rose*. London: Grant & Cutler, 1995.

Kay, Sarah. 'The Birth of Venus in the *Roman de la rose*', *Exemplaria* 9 (1997), 7–37.

Kay, Sarah. *Courtly Contradictions: The Emergence of the Literary Object in the Twelfth Century*. Stanford: Stanford University Press, 2001.

Kay, Sarah. *The Place of Thought: The Complexity of One in Late Medieval French Didactic Poetry*. Philadelphia: University of Pennsylvania Press, 2007.

Kay, Sarah, and Miri Rubin, eds. *Framing Medieval Bodies*. Manchester: Manchester University Press, 1994.

Kearney, Richard. 'Time, Evil, and Narrative: Ricœur on Augustine', in John D. Caputo and Michael J. Scanlon, eds, *Augustine and Postmodernism: Confessions and Circumfession* (Bloomington and Indianapolis: Indiana University Press, 2005), pp. 144–58.

Kelly, Louis G. 'Saint Augustine and Saussurean Linguistics', *Augustinian Studies* 6 (1975), 45–64.

Kenny, Anthony. 'Body, Soul, and Intellect in Aquinas', in M. James C. Crabbe, *From Soul to Self*. London: Routledge, 1999, pp. 33–48.

Kent, Bonnie. *Virtues of the Will: The Transformation of Ethics in the Late Thirteenth Century*. Washington, DC: Catholic University of America Press, 1995.

Kerby-Fulton, Kathryn. 'Langland and the Bibliographic Ego', in Steven Justice and Kathryn Kerby-Fulton, eds, *Written Work: Langland, Labor, and Authorship*. Philadelphia: University of Pennsylvania Press, 1997, pp. 67–143.

Kerby-Fulton, Kathryn. *Reformist Apocalypticism and Piers Plowman*. Camridge: Cambridge University Press, 1990.

King, Edward B., and Jacqueline T. Schaefer, eds, *Saint Augustine and His Influence in the Middle Ages*. Sewanee: Press of the University of the South, 1988.

King, Peter. 'Medieval Thought-Experiments: The Metamethodology of Medieval Science', in Tamara Horowitz and Gerald J. Masey, eds, *Thought Experiments in Science and Philosophy*. Savage, MD: Rowman and Littlefield, 1991, pp. 43–64.

King, Peter. 'Two Conceptions of Experience', *Medieval Philosophy and Theology* 11.2 (2003), 203–26.

King, Peter. 'Why Isn't the Mind-Body Problem Medieval?', in Henrik Lagerlund, ed., *Forming the Mind: Essays on the Internal Senses and the Mind/Body Problem from Avicenna to the Medical Enlightenment*. Dordrecht: Springer, 2007, pp. 187–205.

King, Peter. 'Body and Soul', in John Marenbon, ed., *The Oxford Handbook of Medieval Philosophy*. Oxford: Oxford University Press, 2012, pp. 505–24.

Kirk, Elizabeth D. '"Who suffreth more than God": Narrative Redefinition of Patience in *Patience* and *Piers Plowman*', in Gerald J. Schiffhorst, ed., *The Triumph of Patience*. Orlando: University Press of Florida, 1978, pp. 88–104.

Kirk, Elizabeth D. 'Langland's Narrative Christology', in Robert R. Edwards, ed., *Art and Context in Late Medieval English Narrative: Essays in Honor of Robert Worth Frank*. Cambridge: D.S. Brewer, 1994, pp. 17–35.

Klima, Guyla. ed., *Intentionality, Cognition, and Mental Representation in Medieval Philosophy*. New York: Fordham University Press, 2015.

Kirwan, Christopher. 'Augustine's Philosophy of Language', in Norman Kretzmann and Eleonore Stump, eds, *Cambridge Companion Augustine*. Cambridge: Cambridge University Press, 2001, pp. 186–204.

Kitanov, Severin Valentinov. *Beatific Enjoyment in Medieval Scholastic Debates: The Complex Legacy of Augustine and Peter Lombard*. Plymouth: Lexington, 2014.

Kneepkens, Corneille H. 'Roger Bacon on the Double *Intellectus*: A Note on the Development of the Theory of *Congruitas* and *Perfectio*', in Osmond P. Lewry, ed., *The Rise of British Logic*. Toronto: PIMS, 1985, pp. 115–43.

Knox, Philip. 'Circularity and Linearity: The Idea of the Lyric and the Idea of the Book in the *Cent Ballades* of Jean le Seneschal', *New Medieval Literatures* 16 (2016), 213–49.

Knox, Philip. 'Desire for the Good: Jean de Meun, Boethius, and the "homme devisé en deuz"', in Philip Knox, Jonathan Morton, and Daniel Reeve, eds, *Medieval Thought Experiments: Poetry, Hypothesis, and Experience in the European Middle Ages*. Turnhout: Brepols, 2018, pp. 223–50.

Knox, Philip. 'Human Nature and Natural Law in Jean de Meun's Roman de la Rose', in Morton and Nievergelt, pp. 131–48.

Knox, Philip. *The 'Romance of the Rose' and the Making of Fourteenth-Century English Literature*. Oxford: Oxford University Press, 2022.

Knox, Philip, Jonathan Morton, and Daniel Reeve, eds. *Medieval Thought Experiments: Poetry, Hypothesis, and Experience in the European Middle Ages*. Turnhout: Brepols, 2018.

Knuuttila, Simo. 'Supposition and Predication in Medieval Trinitarian Logic', *Vivarium* 51 (2013), 260–74.

Knuuttila, Simo, and Pekka Kärkkäinen, eds. *Theories of Perception in Medieval and Early Modern Philosophy*. New York: Springer, 2008.

Knuuttila, Simo. 'Medieval Theories of Internal Senses', in Simo Knuuttila and Juha Sihvola, eds, *Sourcebook for the History of the Philosophy of Mind*. Dordrecht: Springer, 2014, pp. 131–45.

Knuuttila, Simo, and Juha Sihvola, eds. *Sourcebook for the History of the Philosophy of Mind*. Dordrecht: Springer, 2014.

Kobusch, Theo. 'Willensschwäche und Selbstbestimmung des Willens: zur Kritik am abendländischen intellektualismus bei Heinrich von Gent und in der Franziskanischen Philosophie', in Tobias Hoffmann, Jörn Müller, Matthias Perkams, eds, *Das Problem der*

528 BIBLIOGRAPHY

Willensschwäche in der mittelalterlichen Philosophie/The Problem of Weakness of Will in Medieval Philosophy. Leuven: Peeters, 2006, pp. 249–63.

Kotzur, Hans-Jürgen. *Rabanus Maurus: Auf den Spuren eines karolingischen Gelehrten*. Mainz: Philipp von Zabern, 2006.

Kratzmann, Gregory, and James Simpson, eds, *Medieval English Religious and Ethical Literature: Essays in Honour of G. H. Russell*. Cambridge: D. S. Brewer, 1986.

Kretzmann, Norman. 'Aristotle on Spoken Sounds Significant by Convention', in J. Corcoran, ed., *Ancient Logic and its Modern Interpretations*. Dordrecht: Reidel, 1974, pp. 3–21.

Kretzmann, Norman. 'Philosophy of Mind', in Norman Kretzmann and Eleonore Stump, eds, *Cambridge Companion to Aquinas*. Cambridge: Cambridge University Press, 1993, pp. 128–59.

Kretzmann, Norman, and Eleonore Stump, eds. *Cambridge Companion Augustine*. Cambridge: Cambridge University Press, 2001.

Kruger, Stephen. 'Mirrors and the Trajectory of Vision in *Piers Plowman*', *Speculum* 66.1 (1991), 74–95.

Kruger, Stephen. *Dreaming in the Middle Ages*. Cambridge: Cambridge University Press, 1992.

Kuntz, Paul G. 'Augustine: From *Homo Erro* to *Homo Viator*', in Leonard J. Bowman, ed., *Itinerarium: The Idea of Journey*. Salzburg: Institut für Anglistik und Amerikanistik, Universität Salzburg, 1983, pp. 34–53.

Ladner, Gerhart B. '*Homo Viator*: Mediaeval Ideas on Alienation and Order', *Speculum* 42.2 (1967), 233–59.

Lagerlund, Henrik, ed. *Forming the Mind: Essays on the Internal Senses and the Mind/Body Problem from Avicenna to the Medical Enlightenment*. Dordrecht: Springer, 2007.

Lagerlund, Henrik, ed. *Representation and Objects of Thought in Medieval Philosophy*. London: Routledge, 2007.

Lagerlund, Henrik, ed. *Rethinking the History of Skepticism: the Missing Medieval Background*. Leiden: Brill, 2010.

Lagerlund, Henrik, ed. *Encyclopedia of Medieval Philosophy: Philosophy between 500 and 1500*. 2 vols. Dordrecht: Springer, 2011.

Lagerlund, Henrik, ed. *Encyclopedia of Medieval* Philosophy: Philosophy between 500 and 1500, 2nd edition. 2 vols. Dordrecht: Springer, 2020.

Lagerlund, Henrik, and Mikko Yrjönsuuri, *Emotions and Free Choice from Boethius to Descartes*. Dordrecht: Springer, 2002.

Lakoff, George, and Mark Johnson. *Metaphors we Live By*. Chicago: University of Chicago Press, 1980.

Lakoff, George, and Mark Johnson. *Philosophy in the Flesh*. New York: Basic Books, 1999.

Lamy, Alice. 'The Romance of the Non-Rose: Echoes and Subversions of Negative Theology in Jean de Meun's *Roman de la Rose*', in Morton and Nievergelt, pp. 194–210.

Langfors, Arthur. 'Notice du manuscrit français 24436 de la Bibliothèque Nationale', *Romania* 41 (1912), 206–41.

Largier, Nikolaus. 'Das Glück des Menschen: Diskussionen über *beatitudo* und Vernunft in volkssprachlichen Texten des 14. Jahrhunderts', in Jan A. Aertsen, Kent Emery, and Andreas Speer, eds, *Nach der Verurteilung von 1277/After the Condemnation of 1277: Philosophie und Theologie an der Universität von Paris im letzten Viertel des 13. Jahrhunderts. Studien und Texte/Philosophy and Theology at the University of Paris in the Last Quarter of the Thirteenth Century. Studies and Texts*. Berlin and New York: Walter de Gruyter, 2001, pp. 827–55.

Lawler, Traugott. 'Conscience's Dinner', in Mary Teresa Tavormina and Robert F. Yeager, eds, *The Endless Knot: Essays on Old and Middle English in Honor of Marie Borroff*. Cambridge: D.S. Brewer, 1996, pp. 87–103.

Lawler, Traugott. 'The Pardon Formula in *Piers Plowman*: Its Ubiquity, Its Binary Shape, Its Silent Middle Term', *YLS* 14 (2000), 117–52.

Lawler, Traugott. 'Harlots' Holiness: The System of Absolution for Miswinning in the C Version of *Piers Plowman*', *YLS* 20 (2006), 141–89.

Lawler, Traugott. 'William Langland', in Roger Ellis, ed., *Oxford History of Literary Translation in English, Vol I: until 1550*. Oxford University Press, 2008, pp. 149–59.

Lawler, Traugott. 'Langland Translating', in Andrew Galloway and Frank Grady, eds, *Answerable Style: The Idea of the Literary in Medieval England*. Columbus: Ohio State Universit Press 2013, pp. 54–74.

Lawler, Traugott. *The Penn Commentary on Piers Plowman, Volume 4: C Passus 15–19; B Passus 13–17*. University of Pennsylvania Press, 2018.

Lawton, David A. The Subject of *Piers Plowman*', *YLS* 1 (1987), 1–30.

Lawton, David A. 'Alliterative Style', in John A. Alford, ed., *A Companion to Piers Plowman*. Berkeley and Los Angeles: University of California Press, 1988, pp. 223–50.

LeBriz, Stéphanie, and Géraldine Veysseyre, 'Composition et réception médiévale de la lettre bilingue de Grâce de Dieu au Pèlerin (Guillaume de Digulleville, Le *Pèlerinage de l'âme*, vers 1593–1784)', in Stéphanie Le Briz and Géraldine Veysseyre, eds, *Approches du bilinguisme latin-français au Moyen Âge: linguistique, codicologie, esthétique*. Turnhout: Brepols, 2010, pp. 283–356.

LeBriz, Stéphanie, and Géraldine Veysseyre. *Approches du bilinguisme latin-français au Moyen Âge: linguistique, codicologie, esthétique*. Turnhout: Brepols, 2010.

Leclerq, Jean. *La Spiritualité de Pierre de Celle, 1115–1183*. Paris: Vrin, 1946.

Leclerq, Jean. *Etudes sur le vocabulaire monastique du Moyen Âge*. Rome: Pontificium Institutum S. Anselmi, 1961.

Leclerq, Jean. *Otia monastica: études sur le vocabulaire de la contemplation au Moyen âge*. Rome: Pontificium institutum S. Anselmi, 1963.

Leclerq, Jean. *The Love of Learning and the Desire for God: A Study of Monastic Culture*, trans. Catharine Misrahi, 2nd edition. New York: Fordham University Press, 1974.

Leff, Gordon. *William of Ockham: the Metamorphosis of Scholastic Discourse*. Manchester: Manchester University Press, 1975.

Leff, Gordon. *The Dissolution of the Medieval Outlook*. New York: New York University Press, 1976.

Legaré, Anne-Marie, and Fabienne Pomel, 'Les Miroirs du *Pèlerinage de Vie humaine*: le texte et l'image', in Fabienne Pomel, ed., *Miroirs et jeux de miroirs dans la littérature médiévale*. Rennes: Presses Universitaires de Rennes, 2003, pp. 125–55.

Leibold, Gerhard. 'Ockham und Buridan—Vorgestalten neuzeitlicher Wissenschaft?', in Alexander Fidora and Matthias Lutz-Bachmann, eds, *Erfahrung und Beweis. Die Wissenschaften von der Natur im 13. und 14. Jahrhundert/Experience and Demonstration. The Sciences of Nature in the 13th and 14th Centuries*. Berlin: De Gruyter, 2009, pp. 225–31.

Leighton, Angela. 'Poetry's Knowing: So What Do We Know?', in John Gibson, ed., *The Philosophy of Poetry* Oxford: Oxford University Press: 2015, pp. 162–82.

Leupin, Alexandre. 'Il n'y a pas de rapport sexuel dans le *Roman de la Rose*', talk delivered at the University of California, Berkley, in April 1996.

Levy, Christopher. 'Grace and Freedom in the Soteriology of John Wyclif', *Traditio* 60 (2005), 279–337.

530 BIBLIOGRAPHY

Lewis, Clive Steepleton. *The Allegory of Love: A Study in Medieval Tradition*. Oxford: Clarendon Press, 1936.

Lewry, Osmond P. ed. *The Rise of British Logic*. Toronto: PIMS, 1985.

Lindberg; David C. *Theories of Vision from al-Kindi to Kepler*. Chicago and London: University of Chicago Press, 1981.

Lofthouse, Marion. '*Le Pèlerinage de vie humaine* by Guillaume de Deguileville: With Special Reference to the French MS 2 of the John Rylands Library', *Bulletin of the John Rylands Library* 19.1 (1935), 170–215.

Longeway, John Lee. *Demonstration and Scientific Knowledge in William of Ockham. A Translation of 'Summa Logicae' III-II: De 'Syllogismo Demonstrativo', and Selections from the Prologue to the 'Ordinatio'*. Notre Dame, IN: University of Notre Dame Press, 2007.

Lukács, Edit. *Dieu est une sphère: La métaphore d'Alain de Lille à Vincent de Beauvais et ses traducteurs*. Rennes: Presses Universitaires de Rennes, 2019.

Lynch, Katherine L. *The High Medieval Dream Vision: Poetry, Philosophy, and Literary Form*. Stanford: Stanford University Press, 1998.

MacCulloch, Diarmaid. *Silence: A Christian History*. London: Penguin, 2013.

Maloney, Thomas S. 'Roger Bacon on the *Significatum* of Words', in Lucie Brind'Amour and Eugene Vance, eds, *Archéologie du signe*. Toronto: PIMS, 1983, pp. 187–211.

Maloney, Thomas S. 'The Semiotics of Roger Bacon', *Medieval Studies* 45 (1983), 120–54.

Maloney, Thomas S. 'Roger Bacon on Equivocation', *Vivarium* 22. 2 (1984), 85–112.

Mann, Jill. 'Eating and Drinking in Piers Plowman', Essays and Studies 32 (1979), 26–43.

Mann, Jill. 'Jean de Meun and the Castration of Saturn', in John Marenbon, ed., *Poetry and Philosophy in the Middle Ages: A Festschrift for Peter Dronke*. Leiden: Brill, 2000, pp. 309–26.

Marenbon, John, ed. *Poetry and Philosophy in the Middle Ages: A Festschrift for Peter Dronke*. Leiden: Brill, 2000.

Marenbon, John. 'Latin Averroism', in Anna Akasoy, James E. Montgomery, and Peter E. Pormann, eds, *Islamic Crosspollinations: Interactions in the Medieval Middle East*. Cambridge: The E. J. W. Gibb Memorial Trust, 2007, pp. 135–47.

Marenbon, John, ed. *The Oxford Handbook of Medieval Philosophy*. Oxford: Oxford University Press, 2012, pp. 505–24.

Marenbon, John. 'Jean de Meun, Boethius, and Thirteenth-Century Philosophy', in Morton and Nievergelt, pp. 173–93.

Marmo, Costantino. *Semiotica E Linguaggio Nella Scolastica: Parigi, Bologna, Erfurt, 1270–1330. La Semiotica Dei Modisti*. Rome: Istituto Storico Italiano Per Il Medio Evo, 1994.

Marmo, Costantino. 'Bacon, Aristotle and (all) the Others on Natural Inferential Signs', in Jeremiah Hackett, ed., *Roger Bacon and the Sciences: Commemorative Essays*. Leiden: Brill, 1997, pp. 136–54.

Marmo, Costantino. 'Gregorio da Rimini: Segni, linguaggio e conoscenza: Il pensiero umano tra cani dialettici e angeli introversi', in Francesco Bottin, ed., *Gregorio da Rimini Filosofo*. Rimini: Raffaelli Editore, 2003, pp. 127–54.

Marmo, Costantino. *La Semiotica del XIII secolo: Tra Arti Liberali e Teologia*. Milan: Bompiani, 2010.

Marmo, Costantino. '*De virtute sermonis/verborum*: L'autonomie du texte dans le traitement des expressions figurées ou multiples', in Nicole Bériou, Jean-Patrice Boudet, and Irène Rosier-Catach, eds, *Le pouvoir des mots au Moyen Âge*. Turnhout: Brepols, 2014, pp. 49–69.

Marmura, Michael, 'Avicenna's Flying Man in Context', *The Monist* 69 (1986), 383–95.

BIBLIOGRAPHY   531

Marrone, Stephen P. *The Light of thy Countenance: Science and Knowledge of God in the thirteenth Century*. 2 vols. Leiden: Brill, 2001.

Martin, Priscilla. *The Field and the Tower*. London: Macmillan, 1979.

Matthen, Mohan ed., *The Oxford Handbook of Philosophy of Perception*. Oxford: Oxford University Press, 2015.

Maupeu, Philippe. 'La tentation autobiographique dans le songe allégorique édifiant de Guillaume de Digulleville: *Le pèlerinage de Vie Humaine*', in Nathalie Dauvois and JEan-Philippe Grosperrin, eds, *Songes et Songeurs (XIIIe–XVIIIe siècle)*. Laval: Preses de l'Université de Laval, 2003, pp. 49–67.

Maupeu, Philippe. 'Statut de l'image rhétorique et de l'image peinte dans le *Pèlerinage de Vie Humaine de Guillaume de Deguileville*', *Le Moyen Age* 114.3 (2008), 509–30.

Maupeu, Philippe. 'Bivium: l'écrivain nattier et le Roman de la Rose', in Duval and Pomel, pp. 21–41.

Maupeu, Philippe. *Pèlerins de vie humaine: Autobiographie et allégorie narrative, de Guillaume de Deguileville à Octovien de Saint-Gelais*. Paris: Champion, 2009.

Mazzeo, Joseph A. 'Augustine's Rhetoric of Silence', *Journal of the History of Ideas* 23 (1962), 175–96.

McCord Adams, Marilyn. 'Universals in the Early Fourteenth Century', in *CHLMP*, pp. 411–39.

McCord Adams, Marilyn. 'Aristotle and the Sacrament of the Altar: A Crisis in Medieval Aristotelianism', *Canadian Journal of Philosophy* 21 (1991), 195–249.

McDermott, Ryan. 'Practices of Satisfaction in *Piers Plowman*'s Dynamic Middle', *SAC* 36 (2014), 169–207.

McDonald, Nicola F. ed. *Medieval Obscenities*. Woodbridge: Boydell & Brewer/York Medieval Press, 2006.

McGinn, Bernard. *Three Treatises on Man: A Cistercian Anthropology*. Kalamazoo: Cistercian Publications, 1977.

McGinn, Bernard. *The Growth of Mysticism: Gregory the Great through the 12th Century*. The Presence of God: A History of Christian Mysticism vol. 2. New York: Crossroad, 1996.

McKee, Conor. 'Pedagogic and Dramatic Roles of the Liturgy in *Piers Plowman*', *Cambridge Quarterly*, 45. 4 (2016), 343–64.

McWebb, Christine, ed. *Debating the Roman de la Rose: A Critical Anthology*. New York: Routledge, 2007.

Mertens-Fleury, Katharina, 'Spiegelungen: Metaphern der Retexualisierung im *Pèlerinage de vie Humaine* und den Prologen der *Pilgerfahrt des träumenden Mönchs*', in Kablitz and Peters, pp. 587–618.

Mesqui, Jean. 'La Famille De Meung et ses alliances: Un lignage Orléanais du XIe au XVe siècle', in *Bulletin archéologique et historique de l'Orléanais* 117 (2014), 5–66.

Middleton, Anne. 'Two Infinites: Grammatical Metaphor in *Piers Plowman*', *English Literary History* 39.2 (1972), 169–88.

Middleton, Anne. 'The Passion of Saynt Averoys (B.13. 91): "Deuynyng" and Divinity in the Banquet Scene', *YLS* 1 (1987), 31–40.

Middleton, Anne. '*Piers Plowman*, the Monsters, and the Critics: Some Embarrassments of Literary History', in Daniel Donoghue, James Simpson, and Nicholas Watson, eds, *The Morton Bloomfield Lectures, 1989–2005*. Kalamazoo: Medieval Institute, 2010, pp. 94–115.

Middleton, Anne. *Chaucer, Langland and Fourteenth-Century Literary History*, ed. Steven Justice. Farnham: Ashgate, 2013.

532 BIBLIOGRAPHY

Middleton, Anne. 'Narration and the Invention of Experience: Episodic Form in *Piers Plowman*', in Anne Middleton, *Chaucer, Langland and Fourteenth-Century Literary History*, ed. Steven Justice. Farnham: Ashgate, 2013, pp. 142–71.

Middleton, Anne. 'William Langland's "Kynde Name": Authorial Signature and Social Identity in Late Fourteenth-Century England', in Anne Middleton, *Chaucer, Langland and Fourteenth-Century Literary History*, ed. Steven Justice. Farnham: Ashgate, 2013, pp. 199–262.

Miles, Margaret. 'Vision: The Eye of the Body and the Eye of the Mind in Saint Augustine's *De Trinitate* and *Confessions*', *The Journal of Religion* 63.2 (1983), 125–42.

Miller, Mark. *Philosophical Chaucer: Love, Sex and Agency in the Canterbury Tales*. Cambridge: Cambridge University Press, 2004.

Minnis, Alastair. 'Langland's Ymaginatif and Late-Medieval Theories of Imagination', *Comparative Criticism: A Yearbook* 3 (1981), 71–103.

Minnis, Alastair, ed. *Late-Medieval Texts and their Transmission: Essays in Honour of A. I. Doyle*. Woodbridge: D.S. Brewer, 1994.

Minnis, Alastair. *Magister Amoris: The 'Roman de la Rose' and Vernacular Hermeneutics*. Oxford: Oxford University Press, 2001.

Minnis, Alastair. 'Piers' Protean Pardon: The Letter and Spirit of Langland's Theology of Indulgences', in Anne Marie D'Arcy and Alan J. Fletcher, eds, *Studies in Late Medieval and Early Renaissance Texts in Honour of John Scattergood*. Dublin: Four Courts Press, 2005, pp. 218–40.

Minnis, Alastair. 'Medieval Imagination and Memory', in Alastair Minnis and Ian Johnson, eds, *The Cambridge History of Literary Criticism. Volume 2: The Middle Ages*. Cambridge: Cambridge University Press, 2005, pp. 239–74.

Minnis, Alastair. 'From *Coilles* to *Bel Chose*: Discourses of Obscenity in Jean de Meun and Chaucer', in Nicola F. McDonald, ed., *Medieval Obscenities*. Woodbridge: Boydell & Brewer/York Medieval Press, 2006, pp. 156–78.

Minnis, Alastair. *Translations of Authority in Medieval English Literature: Valuing the Vernacular*. Cambridge: Cambridge University Press, 2009.

Minnis, Alastair. *Medieval Theory of Authorship: Scholastic Literary Attitudes in the later Middle Ages*. Second Edition. Philadelphia: University of Pennsylvania Press, 2010.

Minnis, Alastair. *Fallible Authors: Chaucer's Pardoner and Wife of Bath*. Philadelphia: University of Pennsylvania Press, 2013.

Miquel, Pierre. *Le Vocabulaire Latin de L'Expérience Spirituelle dans la Tradition Monastique et Canoniale de 1050 à 1250*. Paris: Beauchesne, 1989.

Molland, George. 'Bacon, Roger (c.1214–1292?)', Oxford Dictionary of National Biography, Oxford University Press, 2004 [http://www.oxforddnb.com/view/article/1008, retrieved 10 September 2019].

Monfasani, John, 'Aristotle as the Scribe of Nature: The Title-Page of ms Vat. Lat. 2094', *Journal of the Warburg and Courtauld Institutes* 69 (2006), 193–205.

Montefusco, Antonio. 'Contini e il "nodo": l'avventura del *Fiore* (tra *Roman de la Rose* e *Commedia*)', *Ermeneutica Letteraria* 10 (2014), 55–66.

Montefusco, Antonio. 'Sull'autore e il contesto del *Fiore*: Una Nuova Proposta di Datazione', in Natascia Tonelli, ed., *Sulle tracce del Fiore*. Florence: Le Lettere, 2017, pp. 136–58.

Moody, E. A. 'Empiricism and Metaphysics in Medieval Philosophy', *Philosophical Review* 67 (1958), 145–63.

Moody, E. A. 'A Quodlibetal Question of Robert Holcot, O. P., on the Problem of the Objects of Knowledge and Belief', *Speculum* 39 (1964), 53–74.

Moran, Dermot. *Introduction to Phenomenology*. London and New York: Routledge, 2000.

Moreau, John. '"Ce mauvais tabellion": Satanic and Marian Textuality in Deguileville's *Pèlerinage de l'Âme*', in Kamath and Nievergelt, pp. 113–28.

Moreau, John. *Eschatological Subjects: Divine and Literary Judgment in Fourteenth-century French Poetry*. Columbus: Ohio State University Press, 2014.

Morton, Jonathan. 'Queer Metaphors and Queerer Reproduction in Alan de Lille's *De Planctu Naturae* and Jean de Meun's *Roman de la Rose*', in Manuele Gragnolati et al., eds, *Desire in Dante and the Middle Ages*. Abingdon and New York: Legenda, 2012, pp. 208–26.

Morton, Jonathan. *The 'Roman de la Rose' in its Philosophical Context: Art, Nature, and Ethics*. Oxford: Oxford University Press, 2018.

Morton, Jonathan. 'Sophisms and Sophistry in the Roman de la Rose', in Morton and Nievergelt, pp. 90–108.

Mousavian, Seyed N., and Jakob Leth Fink, eds. *The Internal Senses in the Aristotelian Tradition*. Cham: Springer, 2020.

Müller, Franz. *Der 'Rosenroman' und der lateinische Averroismus des 13. Jahrhunders*. Frankfurt: Klostermann, 1947.

Murdoch, John E. 'Pierre Duhem and the History of Late Medieval Science and Philosophy in the Latin West', in Ruedi Imbach and Alfonso Maierù, eds, *Gli studi di filosofia medievale fra otto e novecento*. Rome: Edizioni di Storia e Letteratura, 1991, pp. 253–301.

Murtaugh, Daniel M. *Piers Plowman and the Image of God*. Gainesville: The University Presses of Florida, 1978.

Murtaugh, Daniel M. '"As myself in a mirour": Langland between Augustine and Lacan', *Exemplaria* 19.3 (2007), 351–85.

Nagy, Piroska. *Le don des larmes au Moyen Age: Un instrument spirituel en quête d'institution (Ve–XIIIe siècle)*. Paris: Albin Michel, 2000.

Nagy, Piroska. 'Individualité et larmes monastiques: Une expérience de soi ou de Dieu?', in Gert Melville and Markus Schürer, eds, *Das Eigene und das Ganze. Zum Individuellen im mittelalterlichen Religiosentum*. Münster: Lit Verlag, 2003, pp. 107–30.

Newman, Barbara. 'What Did it Mean to Say "I saw"? The Clash between Theory and Practice in Medieval Visionary Culture', *Speculum* 80.1 (2005), 1–43.

Newman, Barbara. 'Redeeming the Time: Langland, Julian, and the Art of Lifelong Revision', *YLS* 23 (2009), 1–32.

Nichols, Stephen G. 'Rethinking Texts through Contexts: The Case of le *Roman de la Rose*', in Jan-Dirk Müller and Elizabeth Müller-Luckner, eds, *Text und Kontext: Fallstudien und Theoretische Begründungen einer kulturwissenschaftlich angeleiteten Mediävistik*. München: Oldenbourg, 2007, pp. 245–70.

Nichols, Stephen G. 'The Pupil of Your Eye: Vision, Language, and Poetry in Thirteenth-Century Paris', in Stephen G. Nichols, Alison Calhoun, and Andreas Kablitz, eds, *Rethinking the Medieval Senses: Heritage/Fascinations/Frames*. Baltimore: Johns Hopkins University Press, 2008, pp. 286–308.

Nichols, Stephen G., Alison Calhoun, and Andreas Kablitz, eds, *Rethinking the Medieval Senses: Heritage/Fascinations/Frames*. Baltimore: Johns Hopkins University Press, 2008.

Nievergelt, Marco. *Allegorical Quests from Deguileville to Spenser*. Cambridge: D. S. Brewer, 2012.

Nievergelt, Marco. 'Invisible Itineraries: The textual wanderings of Guillaume Deguileville's *Pèlerinage de Vie Humaine* in Sixteenth-Century England and Europe', in Kablitz and Peters, pp. 721–46.

534 BIBLIOGRAPHY

Nievergelt, Marco. 'From *disputatio* to *predicatio*—and Back Again: Dialectic, Authority and Epistemology between the *Roman de la Rose* and the *Pèlerinage de Vie Humaine*', *New Medieval Literatures* 16 (2015), 135–71.

Nievergelt, Marco. 'Allegory', in Robert Rouse and Sian Echard, eds, *The Blackwell Encyclopaedia of British Medieval Literature*, 4 vols. Oxford: Blackwell, 2017, I:50–9.

Nievergelt, Marco. 'Textuality as Sexuality: The Generative Poetics of the *Roman de la Rose*', in Elisabeth Dutton and Martin Rhode, eds, *Medieval Theories of the Creative Act*. Fribourg: Presses Universitaires de Fribourg, 2017, pp 103–30.

Nievergelt, Marco. 'Can Thought Experiments Backfire? Avicenna's Flying Man, Self-Knowledge, and the Experience of Allegory in Deguileville's *Pèlerinage de Vie Humaine*', in Philip Knox, Jonathan Morton and Daniel Reeve, eds, *Thought Experiments and Hypothesis in Medieval Europe, 1100–1400*. Turnhout: Brepols, 2018, pp. 41–69.

Nievergelt, Marco. 'L'ombre de *Faux Semblant*: fiction, vérité, et tromperie dans la poésie du xivème siècle (France, Angleterre, Italie)', in Gianluca Briguglia and Sonia Gentili, eds, *L'Homme Comme Animal Politique et Parlant au Moyen Âge. Philosophical Readings* XII.1 (2020), pp. 161–71.

Nievergelt, Marco. 'Imposition, Equivocation, and Intention: Language and Signification in Jean de Meun's Roman de la Rose and Thirteenth-Century Grammar and Logic', in Morton and Nievergelt, pp. 65–89.

Nievergelt, Marco. 'William Langland: European Poet?', in Sif Ríkharðsdóttir and Raluca Radulescu, eds, *A Companion to Medieval English Literature in a Trans-European Context, 1100–1500*. London: Routledge, 2022, pp. 300–10.

Noone, Timothy. 'Divine Illumination', in *CHMP*, I:369–83.

Nouvet, Claire. 'An Allegorical Mirror: The Pool of Narcissus in Guillaume de Lorris' *Romance of the Rose*', *Romanic Review* 91.4 (2000), 353–74.

O'Connell, Robert J. *St Augustine's Confessions: The Odyssey of Soul*. Cambridge, MA: Harvard University Press, 1969.

O'Daly, Gerard. *Augustine's Philosophy of Mind*. Berkeley and Los Angeles: University of California Press, 1987.

O'Donovan, Oliver. '*Usus* and *Fruitio* in Augustine, De doctrina christiana I.1', *Journal of Theological Studies* 33 (1982), 361–97.

Oberman, Heiko A. *Archbishop Thomas Bradwardine, a Fourteenth Century Augustinian: A Study of His Theology in Its Historical Context*. Utrecht: Kemink & Zoon, 1957.

Oberman, Heiko A. '*Facientibus quod in se est Deus non denegat gratiam*: Robert Holcot, OP and the Beginnings of Luther's Theology', *Harvard Theological Review* 55.4 (1962), 317–42.

Oberman, Heiko A., ed. *Gregor von Rimini: Werk un Wirkung bis zur Reformation*. Berlin: De Gruyter, 1981.

Obert-Piketty, Caroline. 'La promotion des études chez les cisterciens à travers le recrutement des étudiants du Collège Saint-Bernard de Paris au moyen âge', *Cîteaux* 39 (1988), 65–78.

Ocker, Christopher. 'Augustinianism in Fourteenth-Century Theology', *Augustinian Studies* 18 (1987), 81–106.

Ocker, Christopher. *Biblical Poetics before Humanism and Reformation*. Cambridge: Cambridge University Press, 2002.

Orsten, Elizabeth. '"Heven on Earth:" Langland's Vision of Life Within the Cloister', *American Benedictine Review* 21 (1970), 526–34.

Overstreet, Samuel A. '"Grammaticus ludens": Theological Aspects of Langland's Grammatical Allegory', *Traditio* 40 (1984), 251–96.

BIBLIOGRAPHY 535

Owen, Dorothy S. *Piers Plowman: A Comparison with some Earlier and Contemporary French Allegories.* London: London University Press, 1912.

Owens, Joseph. 'Faith, Ideas, Illumination, and Experience', in *CHLMP*, pp. 440–59.

Pacheco, M. C., and J. Meirinhos, eds, *Intellect et imagination dans la philosophie médiévale/Intellect and Imagination in Medieval Philosophy/Intelecto e imaginação na Filosofia Medieval: Actes du XIe Congrès International de Philosophie Médiévale de la Société Internationale pour l'Étude de la Philosophie Médiévale (SIEPM). Porto, du 26 au 31 août 2002.* Turnhout: Brepols, 2006.

Panaccio, Claude. *Le Discours Intérieur: de Platon à Guillaume d'Ockham.* Paris: Seuil, 1999.

Panaccio, Claude. 'Semantics and Mental Language', in Paul Vincent Spade, ed., *The Cambridge Companion to Ockham.* Cambridge: Cambridge University Press, 1999, pp. 53–75.

Panaccio, Claude. 'Aquinas on Intellectual Representation', in Dominik Perler, ed., *Ancient and Medieval Theories of Intentionality.* Leiden: Brill, 2001, pp. 185–201.

Panaccio, Claude. *Ockham on Concepts.* Aldershot: Ashgate, 2004.

Panaccio, Claude. 'Mental Representation', in *CHMP*, I:346–56.

Pantea, Madalina-Gabriela. 'Johannes de Mirecuria', in *Encyclopedia of Medieval Philosophy* (Dordrecht: Springer, 2018), n.p.

Paré, Gérard. *Le 'Roman de la Rose' et la scholastique courtoise.* Paris: Vrin/Ottawa: Institut d'études médiévales, 1941.

Paré, Gérard. *Les idées et les lettres au XIIIe siècle: 'Le Roman de la Rose'.* Montreal: Bibliothèque de Philosophie, 1947.

Paris, Gaston. *Esquisse historique de la littérature française au Moyen Âge.* Paris: A. Colin 1907.

Pasnau, Robert. *Theories of Cognition in the Later Middle Ages.* Cambridge: Cambridge University Press, 1997.

Pasnau, Robert. 'Olivi on Human Freedom', in Alain Boureau and Sylvain Piron, eds, *Pierre de Jean Olivi (1248–98): Pensée Scholastique, Dissidence Spirituelle et Société.* Paris: Vrin, 1999, pp. 15–25.

Pasnau, Robert. 'Sensible Qualities: The Case of Sound', *Journal of the History of Philosophy* 38 (2000), 27–40.

Pasnau, Robert. *Thomas Aquinas on Human Nature: A Philosophical Study of 'Summa Theologiae', 1a 75–89.* Cambridge: Cambridge University Press, 2002.

Pasnau, Robert. 'Human Nature', in A. S. McGrade, ed., *Cambridge Companion to Medieval Philosophy.* Cambridge: Cambridge University Press, 2003, pp. 208–30.

Pasnau, Robert. 'The Mind-Soul Problem', in Paul J. J. M. Bakker and Johannes and M. M. H. Thijssen, eds, *Mind, Cognition and Representation: The Tradition of Commentaries on Aristotle's 'De anima'.* Aldershot: Ashgate, 2008, pp. 3–20.

Pasnau, Robert. 'Id quo cognoscimus', in Knuuttila and Kärkkäinen, *Theories of Perception in Medieval and Early Modern Philosophy*, pp. 131–49.

Pasnau, Robert. 'Science and Certainty', in *CHMP*, I:357–68.

Pasnau, Robert. 'Mind and Hylomorphism', in John Marenbon, ed., *The Oxford Handbook of Medieval Philosophy.* Oxford: Oxford University Press, 2012, pp. 486–504.

Pasnau, Robert. 'Philosophy of Mind and Human Nature', in Brian Davies, ed., *Oxford Handbook of Aquinas.* Oxford: Oxford University Press, 2012, pp. 349–65.

Pasnau, Robert. *After Certainty: A History of our Epistemic Ideals and Illusions.* Oxford: Oxford University Press, 2017.

536 BIBLIOGRAPHY

Pasnau, Robert, and Juhana Toivanen. 'Peter John Olivi', in Edward N. Zalta, ed., *The Stanford Encyclopedia of Philosophy* (Summer 2013 Edition) [http://plato.stanford.edu/archives/sum2013/entries/olivi/; retreived 5 June 2021].

Patterson, Lee. '"For the Wyves love of Bathe": Feminine Rhetoric and Poetic Resolution in the *Roman de la Rose* and the Canterbury Tales', *Speculum* 58.3 (1983), 656–95.

Patterson, Lee. 'Feminine Rhetoric and the Politics of Subjectivity: La Vieille and the Wife of Bath', in Kevin Brownlee and Sylvia Huot, eds, *Rethinking the Romance of the Rose: Text, Image, Reception*. Philadelphia: University of Pennsylvania Press, 1992, pp. 316–58.

Paxson, James J. 'Gender Personified, Personification Gendered, and the Body Figuralized in *Piers Plowman*', *YLS* 12 (1998), 65–96.

Paxson, James J. 'Inventing the Subject and the Personification of Will in *Piers Plowman*: Rhetorical, Erotic, and Ideological Origins and Limits in Langland's Allegorical Poetics', in Kathleen M. Hewett-Smith, ed., *William Langland's Piers Plowman: A Book of Essays*. London: Routledge, 2001, pp. 195–231.

Peace, Richard V. *Conversion in the New Testament: Paul and the Twelve*. Grand Rapids: Eerdmans, 1999.

Pearsall, Derek. 'Hoccleve's *Regement of Princes*: The Poetics of Royal Self-Representation', *Speculum*, 69.2 (1994), 386–410.

Pelen, Marc M. 'Chaucer's "Cosyn to the dede": Further Considerations', *Florilegium* 19 (2002), 91–107.

Perler, Dominik. 'Things in the Mind: Fourteenth-Century Controversies over "Intelligible Species"', *Vivarium* 34 (1996), 231–53.

Perler, Dominik, ed. *Ancient and Medieval Theories of Intentionality*. Leiden: Brill, 2001.

Perler, Dominik. *Zweifel und Gewißheit: Skeptische Debatten im Mittelalter*. Frankfurt am Main: Klosterman, 2006.

Perler, Dominik. 'Skepticism', in *CHMP*, I:384–96.

Perler, Dominik 'Perception in Medieval Philosophy', in Mohan Matthen, ed., *The Oxford Handbook of Philosophy of Perception*. Oxford: Oxford University Press, 2015, pp. 51–65.

Perry, Ryan D., and Lisa Strakhov, eds. 'Langland and the French Tradition', *YLS* 30 (2016), 175–306.

Phillips, Helen. 'Chaucer and Deguileville: The "ABC" in Context', *Medium Ævum* 62.1 (1993), 1–19.

Phillips, Helen. 'Frames and Narrators in Chaucerian Poetry', in Helen Cooper and Sally Mapstone, eds, *The Long Fifteenth Century: Essays for Douglas Gray*. Oxford: Oxford University Press, 1997, pp. 71–97.

Piaget, Arthur. 'Un poème inédit de Guillaume de Digulleville: *Le Roman de la fleur de lis*', *Romania* 62.247 (1936), 317–58.

Piché, David, and Claude Lafleur, eds, *La condamnation parisienne de 1277: nouvelle édition du texte latin, traduction, introduction et commentaire*. Paris: Vrin, 1999.

Pigg, Daniel F. 'Apocalypse Then: The Ideology of Literary Form in *Piers Plowman*', *Religion & Literature* (1999), 103–16.

Pini, Giorgio, 'Species, Concept and Thing: Theories of Signification in the Second Half of the Thirteenth Century', *Medieval Philosophy and Theology* 8.1 (1999), 21–52.

Pluta, Olaf. 'How Matter Becomes Mind: Late-Medieval Theories of Emergence', in Henrik Lagerlund, ed., *Forming The Mind*. Springer: Dordrecht, 2007, pp. 149–67.

Poirion, Daniel, ed. *Grundriss der Romanischen Literaturen des Mittelalters, vol. VIII.1: La littérature française aux XIVe et XVe siècles*. 11 vols, gen. ed. Hans U. Gumbrecht and Ulrich Mölk. Heidelberg: Carl Winter, 1988.

BIBLIOGRAPHY 537

Pomel, Fabienne. *Les voies de l'au-delà et l'essor de l'allégorie au Moyen Âge*. Paris: Champion, 2001.

Pomel, Fabienne. ed., *Miroirs et jeux de miroirs dans la littérature médiévale*. Rennes: Presses Universitaires de Rennes, 2003.

Pomel, Fabienne. 'Mémoire, mnémotechnique, et récit de voyage allégorique: L'exemple du *Pèlerinage de vie humaine* de Guillaume de Deguileville', in Frank Willaert, Herman Braet, Thom Mertens, and Theofiel Venckeleer, eds, *Medieval Memory: Image and Text*. Turnhout: Brepols, 2004, pp. 77–98.

Pomel, Fabienne. 'L'art du faux-semblant chez Jean de Meun ou "la langue doublée en diverses plications"', *Bien dire et bien aprandre* 23 (2005), 295–313.

Pomel, Fabienne. 'Le *Roman de la Rose* comme voie de paradis: Transposition, parodie et moralisation de Guillaume de Lorris à Jean Molinet', in Catherine Bel and Herman Braet, eds, *De la Rose: Texte, image, fortune*. Leiden: Peeters, 2006, pp. 355–76.

Pomel, Fabienne.; Fabienne Pomel, 'Généalogie d'un "vrai signe" politique ou l'investiture allégorique dans le *Roman de la fleur de lys* de Guillaume de Digulleville', in Jean-Christophe Cassard, Elizabeth Gaucher and Jean Kerhervé, eds, *Vérité poétique, vérité politique. Mythes, modèles et idéologies politiques au Moyen Âge*. Brest: Centre de Recherche Bretonne et Celtique, 2007, pp. 327–41.

Pomel, Fabienne. 'La courtine chez Guillaume de Digulleville: la scénographie de la révélation et de l'incarnation du signe dans les *Pèlerinages* et le *Roman de la fleur de lys*', in Catherine Croisy-Naquet, ed., *Littérature et révélation. Espace et révélation*, Littérales no45. Paris: Université de Paris Ouest-La Défense, 2010., pp. 219–47.

Pomel, Fabienne. 'Les écrits pérégrins ou les voies de l'autorité chez Guillaume de Deguleville: Le modèle épistolaire et juridique', in Kamath and Nievergelt, pp. 91–112.

Pomel, Fabienne. 'L'épisode de Rude Entendement: Mots et choses, bons et mauvais lecteurs, du *Roman de la Rose* au *Pèlerinage de Vie humaine* et d'une version l'autre', in Kablitz and Peters, pp. 265–86.

Pomel, Fabienne. 'Visual Experiences and Allegorical Fiction: The Lexis and Paradigm of Fantaisie in Jean de Meun's Rose', in Morton and Nievergelt, pp. 45–64.

Porro, Pasquale, and Costantin Esposito, eds. *Experience/Expérience/Die Erfahrung/L'esperienza*. Special issue of the journal *Quaestio* 4 (2004).

Quilligan, Maureen. 'Words and Sex: The Language of Allegory in the *De planctu Naturae*, the *Roman de la rose*, and Book III of the *Faerie Queene*', *Allegorica* 2 (1977), 195–215.

Quilligan, Maureen. *The Language of Allegory: Defining the Genre*. Ithaca, NY: Cornell University Press, 1979.

Quilligan, Maureen. 'Allegory, Allegoresis, and the De-allegorization of Language: the *Roman de la Rose*, the *De planctu naturae*, and the *Parlement of Foules*', in Morton W. Bloomfield, ed., *Allegory, Myth, and Symbol*. Cambridge, MA: Harvard University Press, 1981, pp. 163–83.

Quinn, William A. 'Chaucer's Problematic Priere: "An ABC" as Artifact and Critical Issue', *Studies in the Age of Chaucer* 23.1 (2001), 109–41.

Raskolnikov, Masha. 'Confessional Literature, Vernacular Psychology, and the History of the Self in Middle English', *Literature Compass* 2.1 (2005), n.p.

Raskolnikov, Masha. *Body against Soul: Gender and 'sowlehele' in Middle English Allegory*. Columbus: Ohio State University Press, 2009.

Read, Stephen. 'Concepts and Meaning in Medieval Philosophy', in Guyla Klima, ed., *Intentionality, Cognition, and Mental Representation in Medieval Philosophy*. New York: Fordham University Press, 2015, pp. 9–28.

538 BIBLIOGRAPHY

Regalado, Nancy Freeman. '"Des contraires choses": la fonction poétique de la citation et des *exempla* dans le *Roman de la rose* de Jean de Meun', *Littérature* 41 (1981), 62–81.

Reiss, Edmund. 'Dusting off the Cobwebs: A Look at Chaucer's Lyrics', *Chaucer Review* 1 (1966), 55–65.

Richards, Earl Jeffrey. '"Les contraires choses": Irony in Jean de Meun's Part of the *Roman de la Rose* and the Problem of Truth and Intelligibility in Thomas Aquinas', in Dulce M. Gonzalez-Doreste and Maria del Pilar Mendoza Ramos, eds, *Nouvelles de la Rose: Actualités et persepectives du 'Roman de la Rose'*. La Laguna: Servicio de Publicationes, Universidad de La Laguna, 2011, pp. 383–98.

Ricœur, Paul. *Temps et Récit 1: L'intrigue et le récit historique*. Paris: Seuil, 1983.

Ricœur, Paul. *Soi-même comme un autre*. Paris: Seuil, 1990.

Ricœur, Paul. *Oneself as Another*. Trans. Kathleen Blamey. Chicago and London: The University of Chicago Press, 1992.

Rigolot, Irénée. 'Contribution au vocabulaire cistercien: *voluntas propria* et *voluntas communis*', *Collectanea Cisterciensia* 55.4 (1993), 356–63.

Rivera, Joseph. 'Figuring the Porous Self: St. Augustine and the Phenomenology of Temporality', *Modern Theology* 29.1 (2013), 83–103.

Robertson, Kellie. *Nature Speaks: Medieval Literature and Aristotelian Philosophy*. Philadelphia: University of Pennsylvania Press, 2017.

Rollo, David. *Kiss My Relics: Hermaphroditic Fictions of the Middle Ages*. Chicago: University of Chicago Press, 2011.

Romele, Alberto. *L'esperienza del 'verbum in corde': Ovvero l'ineffettività dell'ermeneutica*. Milan: Mimesis, 2013.

Rosenfeld, Jessica. *Ethics and Enjoyment in Late Medieval Poetry: Love After Aristotle*. Cambridge: Cambridge University Press, 2011.

Rosenwein, Barbara H. 'Y avait-il un "moi" au haut Moyen Age?', *Revue historique* 633 (2005), 31–52.

Rosier-Catach, Irène. 'Grammaire, Logique, Sémantique, deux positions opposées au XIIIème siècle: Roger Bacon et les modistes', *Histoire Epistémologie Langage* 6.1 (1984), 21–34.

Rosier-Catach, Irène. 'Signes et sacrements: Thomas d'Aquin et la grammaire spéculative', *Revue des sciences philosophiques et théologiques* 74 (1990), 392–436.

Rosier-Catach, Irène. *La Parole Comme Acte: Sur la Grammaire et la Sémantique au XIIIe Siècle*. Paris: Vrin, 1994.

Rosier-Catach, Irène. 'Henri de Gand, le *De dialectica* d'Augustin, et l'imposition des noms divins', *Documenti e studi sulla tradizione filosofica medievale* 6 (1995), 145–253.

Rosier-Catach, Irène. 'Roger Bacon and Grammar', in Jeremiah Hackett, ed., *Roger Bacon and the Sciences: Commemorative Essays 1996*. Leiden: Brill, 1997, pp. 67–102.

Rosier-Catach, Irène. '*Prata rident*', in Alain de Libera, Abdelali Elamrani-Jamal, and Alain Galonnier, eds, *Langages et philosophie: Hommage à Jean Jolivet*. Paris: Vrin, 1997, pp. 155–76.

Rosier-Catach, Irène. 'Modisme, pré-modisme et proto-modisme: vers une définition modulaire', in Sten Ebbesen and Russell L. Friedman, eds, *Medieval Analyses in Language and Cognition*. Copenhagen: Royal Danish Academy of Science and Letters, 1999, pp. 45–81.

Rosier-Catach, Irène. *La Parole Efficace: Signe, Rituel, Sacré*. Paris: Éditions du Seuil, 2004.

Rosier-Catach, Irène. 'Speech Act and Intentional Meaning in the Medieval Philosophy of Language', *Bulletin de philosophie médiévale* 52 (2010), 55–80.

Rosier-Catach, Irène, ed. *Arts du langage et theologie aux confins des XI et XII siècles: Textes, maîtres, débats*. Turnhout: Brepols, 2011.

Rosier-Catach, Irène. 'Babel: Le péché linguistique originel?', in Gianluca Briguglia and Irène Rosier, eds, *Adam, la nature humaine, avant et après: épistémologie de la chute.* Paris: Presses Universitaires de la Sorbonne, 2016, pp. 63–86.

Rossi, Luciano. 'Du nouveau sur Jean de Meun', *Romania* 121 (2003), 430–60.

Rossi, Luciano. 'Encore sur Jean de Meun: Johannes de Magduno, Charles d'Anjou et le Roman de la Rose', *Cahiers de civilisation médiévale* 51 (2008), 361–77.

Rossi, Luciano. 'Jean de Meun e Chrétien de Troyes', *Studi Romanzi* 13 (2017), 9–41.

Rossi, Luciano. 'Jean de Meun et la culture de Panurge', *Revue de linguistique romane* 82 (2018), 289–310.

Rossi, Luciano. 'Metalepsis and Allegory', in Morton and Nievergelt, pp. 210–32.

Rossi, Luciano. '"Frere Seier", i "frati Alberti" e le "pulzellette". Sulla diffusione del *Roman de la Rose* in Italia: da Jean de Meun, a Cino da Pistoia, a Dante', in *Letteratura Italiana Antica* 21 (2020), 21–58.

Roux, Sophie. 'The Emergence of the Notion of Thought Experiments', in Katerina Ierodiakonou and Sophie Roux, eds, *Thought Experiments in Methodological and Historical Contexts*. Leiden: Brill, 2011, pp. 1–36.

Rubin, Miri. *Corpus Christi: The Eucharist in Late Medieval Culture.* Cambridge: Cambridge University Press, 1991.

Rudd, Gillian. *Managing Language in 'Piers Plowman'.* Cambridge: D.S. Brewer, 1994.

Rudy, Gordon. *The Mystical Language of Sensation in the Later Middle Ages.* London: Routledge, 2002.

Russell, Stephen. 'Allegorical Monstrosity: The Case of Deguileville', *Allegorica* 5 (1980), 95–103.

Russell, Stephen. *The English Dream Vision: Anatomy of a Form.* Columbus: Ohio State University Press, 1988.

Rust, Martha Dana. *Imaginary Worlds in Medieval Books: Exploring the Manuscript Matrix.* New York: Palgrave Macmillan, 2007.

Ryan, Thomas A. 'Scripture and the Prudent Ymaginatif', *Viator* 23 (1992), 215–30.

Saarinen, Risto. *Weakness of the Will in Medieval Thought: from Augustine to Buridan.* Leiden: Brill, 1994, pp. 20–43.

Saarinen, Risto. 'Weakness of Will: the Plurality of Medieval Explanations', in Henrik Lagerlund and Mikko Yrjönsuuri, *Emotions and Free Choice from Boethius to Descartes.* Dordrecht: Springer, 2002, pp. 85–97.

Sarnowsky, Jürgen. '*Expertus—experientia—experimentum*: Neue Wege der wissenschaftlichen Erkenntnis im Spätmittelalter', in *Das Mittelalter: Perspektiven mediävistischer Forschung*, 17.2 (2012), 47–59.

Scanlon, Larry. 'Unspeakable Pleasures: Alain de Lille, Sexual Regulation, and the Priesthood of Genius', *Romanic Review* 86.2 (1995), 213–42.

Scanlon, Larry. 'Personification and Penance', *YLS* 21 (2007), 1–29.

Scarpelli Cory, Therese. *Aquinas on Human Self-knowledge.* Cambridge: Cambridge University Press, 2014.

Scarpelli Cory, Therese. 'The Footprint of Avicenna's Flying Man in Aquinas's Commentary on the *Sentences* I.3.4.5' [https://www.academia.edu/1975062/The_Footprint_of_Avicennas_Flying_Man_in_Aquinass_Commentary_on_the_Sentences_I.3.4.5; retrieved 5 June 2021].

Scase, Wendy, *'Piers Plowman' and the New Anticlericalism.* Cambridge: Cambridge University Press, 1989.

Schabel, Christopher. 'Pierre Ceffons', in Henrik Lagerlund and John Marenbon, eds, *Encyclopedia of Medieval Philosophy*. Heidelberg and Dordrecht: Springer, forthcoming.

540 BIBLIOGRAPHY

Schabel, Christopher. 'Lucifer princeps tenebrarum . . . The Epistola Luciferi and Other Correspondence of the Cistercian Pierre Ceffons (fl. 1348–1353)', Vivarium 56 (2018), 126–75.

Schiffhorst, Gerald J., ed. The Triumph of Patience. Orlando: University Press of Florida, 1978.

Schmidt, A. V. C. 'Langland and Scholastic Philosophy', Medium Ævum 38 (1969), 134–56.

Schmidt, A. V. C. 'Langland and the Mystical Tradition', in Marion Glasscoe, ed., The Medieval Mystical Tradition in England: Papers Read at the Exeter Symposium. Exeter: University of Exeter Press, 1980, pp. 17–38.

Schmidt, A. V. C. 'The Inner Dreams in Piers Plowman', Medium Ævum 55.1 (1986), 24–40.

Schmidt, A. V. C. The Clerkly Maker: Langland's Poetic Art. Woodbridge: D.S. Brewer, 1987.

Schmidt, A. V. C. Earthly Honest Things: Collected Essays on Piers Plowman. Newcastle: Cambridge Scholars Publishing, 2012.

Schmidt, A. V. C. 'Langland's Structural Imagery of Food and Drink', in A. V. C. Schmidt, Earthly Honest Things: Collected Essays on Piers Plowman. Newcastle: Cambridge Scholars Publishing, 2012, 221–36.

Schmitt, Jean-Claude. 'La découverte de l'individu: une fiction historiographique?', in ibid., Le corps, les rites, les rêves, le temps: essais d'anthropologie médiévale. Paris: Gallimard, 2001, pp. 241–62.

Schmitt, Jean-Claude. Le corps, les rites, les rêves, le temps: essais d'anthropologie médiévale. Paris: Gallimard, 2001.

Schreiber, Scott G. Aristotle on False Reasoning: Language and the World in the Sophistical Refutations. New York: SUNY, 2003.

Schumacher, Lydia. Divine Illumination: The History and Future of Augustine's Theory of Knowledge. Oxford: Wiley-Blackwell, 2011.

Schweitzer, Edward C. '"Half a Laumpe Lyne in Latyne" and Patience's Riddle in Piers Plowman', JEGP 73.3 (1974), 313–27.

Sears, Elizabeth. 'Sensory Perception and its Metaphors in the Time of Richard de Fournival', in William F. Bynum and Roy Porter, eds, Medicine and the Five Senses. Cambridge: Cambridge University Press, 1993, pp. 17–39.

Silva, José Filipe. Robert Kilwardby on the Human Soul: Plurality of Forms and Censorship in the Thirteenth Century. Leiden: Brill, 2012.

Silva, José Filipe, and Juhana Toivanen. 'The Active Nature of the Soul in Sense Perception: Robert Kilwardby and Peter Olivi', Vivarium 48.3 (2010), 245–78.

Simpson, James. 'From Reason to Affective Knowledge: Modes of Thought and Poetic Form in Piers Plowman', Medium Ævum, 55 (1986), 1–23.

Simpson, James. 'The Role of Scientia in Piers Plowman', in Gregory Kratzmann and James Simpson, eds, Medieval English Religious and Ethical Literature: Essays in Honour of G. H. Russell. Cambridge: D. S. Brewer, 1986, pp. 49–65.

Simpson, James. '"Et vidit deus cogitaciones eorum:" A Parallel Instance and Possible Source for Langland's Use of a Biblical Formula at B.XV.200a', Notes and Queries n. s. 33 (1986), 9–13.

Simpson, James. 'The Power of Impropriety: Authorial Naming in Piers Plowman', in Kathleen M. Hewett-Smith, ed., William Langland's Piers Plowman: A Book of Essays. London: Routledge, 2001, pp. 145–65.

Simpson, James. Piers Plowman: An Introduction. 2nd rev. edn. Exeter: University of Exeter Press, 2007.

Simpson, James. 'Religious Forms and Institutions in Piers Plowman', in Cole and Galloway, The Cambridge Companion to Piers Plowman, pp. 97–114.

Sirridge, Mary. '*Quam videndo intus dicimus*: Seeing and Saying in *De Trinitate* XV', in Sten Ebbesen and Russell L. Friedman, eds, *Medieval Analyses in Language and Cognition.* Copenhagen: Royal Danish Academy of Sciences and Letters, 1999, pp. 317–30.

Slotemaker, John T., and Jeffrey C. Witt. *Robert Holcot.* Oxford: Oxford University Press 2015.

Smith, J-C. ed. *Historical Foundations of Cognitive Science.* Dordrecht: Kluwer, 1990.

Smith, A. Mark 'Perception', in *CHMP*, I:334–45.

Smith, Vance D. *Book of the Incipit: Beginnings in the Fourteenth Century.* Minneapolis and London: University of Minnesota Press, 2001.

Smith, Vance D. 'Negative Langland', *YLS* 23 (2009), 33–59.

Spade, Paul Vincent, ed. *The Cambridge Companion to Ockham.* Cambridge: Cambridge University Press, 1999.

Spade, Paul Vincent. 'The Semantics of Terms', in *CHLMP*, pp. 188–96.

Spade, Paul Vincent. '*Sophismata*', in *CHMP*, I:185–95.

Spearing, Anthony C. *Medieval Dream-Poetry.* Cambridge: Cambridge University Press, 1976.

Spearing, Anthony C. *Textual Subjectivity: the Encoding of Subjectivity in Medieval Narratives and Lyrics.* Oxford: Oxford University Press, 2005.

Spearing, Anthony C. *Medieval Autographies: The" I" of the Text.* Notre Dame: University of Notre Dame Press, 2012.

Speer, Andreas. '*Scientia demonstrativa et universaliter ars faciens scire*: Zur methodischen Grundlegung einer Wissenschaft von der Natur durch Robert Grosseteste', Alexander Fidora and Matthias Lutz-Bachmann, eds, *Erfahrung und Beweis. Die Wissenschaften von der Natur im 13. und 14. Jahrhundert/Experience and Demonstration. The Sciences of Nature in the 13th and 14th Centuries.* Berlin: De Gruyter, 2009, pp. 25–40.

Speer, Andreas. '*Sapientia nostra*: zum Verhältnis von philosophischer und theologischer Weisheit in den Pariser Debatten am Ende des 13. Jahrhunderts', in Jan A. Aertsen, Kent Emery, and Andreas Speer, eds, *Nach der Verurteilung von 1277/After the Condemnation of 1277: Philosophie und Theologie an der Universität von Paris im letzten Viertel des 13. Jahrhunderts. Studien und Texte/Philosophy and Theology at the University of Paris in the Last Quarter of the Thirteenth Century. Studies and Texts.* Berlin and New York: Walter de Gruyter, 2001, pp. 249–75.

Spruit, Leen. *Species Intelligibilis: From Perception to Knowledge*, 2 vols. Leiden:. Brill, 1994 and 1995.

Stakel, Susan. *False Roses: Structures of Duality and Deceit in Jean de Meun's 'Roman de la rose'.* Saratoga, CA: Anma Libri, 1991.

Stark, Judith Celius. 'The Pauline Influence of Augustine's Notion of the Will', *Vigiliae Christianae* 43 (1989), 345–61.

Steiner, Emily. *Documentary Culture and the Making of Medieval English Literature.* Cambridge: Cambridge University Press, 2006.

Steiner, Emily. *Reading Piers Plowman.* Cambridge University Press, 2013.

Steiner, Emily. '*Piers Plowman* and Institutional Poetry', *Etudes Anglaises* 66/2 (2013), 297–310.

Stewart-Kroeker, Sarah. 'Resisting Idolatry and Instrumentalisation in Loving the Neighbour: The Significance of the Pilgrimage Motif for Augustine's *Usus–Fruitio* Distinction', *Studies in Christian Ethics* 27.2 (2014), 202–21.

Still, Judith, and Michael Worton, eds. *Textuality and Sexuality: Reading Theories and Practices.* Manchester: Manchester University Press, 1993.

542 BIBLIOGRAPHY

Stirnemann, Patricia. 'Jean de Meun: Où et pour qui a-t-il travaillé?', in Jean-Patrice Boudet, Philippe Haugeard, et al., eds, *Jean de Meun et la culture médiévale: Littérature, art, sciences et droit aux derniers siècles du Moyen Âge*. Rennes: Presses Universitaires de Rennes, 2017, pp. 107–19.

Stock, Brian. *Augustine the Reader: Meditation, Self-Knowledge, and the Ethics of Interpretation*. Cambridge, MA: Belknap Press, 1996.

Stone, M. W. F. 'The Soul's Relation to the Body: Thomas Aquinas, Siger of Brabant and the Parisian Debate on Monopsychism', in Tim Crane and Sarah Patterson, eds, *History of the Mind-Body Problem*. London: Routledge, 2000, pp. 34–69.

Strohm, Paul, ed., *Middle English*. Oxford Twenty-First Century Approaches to Literature. Oxford: Oxford University Press, 2007.

Strubel, Armand. '*Allegoria in verbis, allegoria in factis*', *Poétique* 23 (1975), 242–57.

Strubel, Armand. *La Rose, Renard et le Graal. La littérature allégorique en France au XIIIe s.* Paris: Champion, 1989.

Strubel, Armand. '*Grant senefiance a*': *Allégorie et littérature au Moyen Âge*. Paris: Honoré Champion, 2002.

Stump, Eleonore. 'Augustine on Free Will', in Norman Kretzmann and Eleonore Stump, eds, *Cambridge Companion Augustine*. Cambridge: Cambridge University Press, 2001, pp. 126–47.

Stumpf, Béatrice. *Lexique des Pèlerinages de Guillaume de Deguileville*. [http://www.atilf.fr/dmf/PelerinagesDigulleville; retrieved 5 June 2021].

Sweeney, Eileen C. 'Hugh of St. Victor: The Augustinian Tradition of Sacred and Secular Reading Revised', in Edward D. English, ed., *Reading and Wisdom: The 'De Doctrina Christiana' of Augustine in the Middle Ages*. Notre Dame: University of Notre Dame Press, 1995, pp. 61–84.

Szittya, Penn R. *The Antifraternal Tradition in Medieval Literature*. Princeton: Princeton University Press, 1986.

Tachau, Katherine H. *Vision and Certitude in the Age of Ockham: Optics, Epistemology, and the Foundations of Semantics, 1250–1345*. Leiden: Brill, 1988.

Tachau, Katherine H. 'The Notion of Intentional Existence', in Sten Ebbesen and Russell L. Friedman, eds, *Medieval Analyses in Language and Cognition*. Copenhagen: Royal Danish Academy of Sciences and Letters, 1999, pp. 331–54.

Tachau, Katherine H. 'Seeing as Action and Passion in the Thirteenth and Fourteenth Centuries', in Jeffrey F. Hamburger and Anne-Marie Bouché, eds, *The Mind's Eye: Art and Theological Argument in the Middle Ages*. Princeton, NJ: Princeton University Press, 2006, pp. 336–59.

Tachau, Katherine H. 'Approaching Medieval Scholars' Treatment of Cognition', in M. C. Pacheco and J. Meirinhos, eds, *Intellect et imagination dans la philosophie médiévale/Intellect and Imagination in Medieval Philosophy/Intelecto e imaginação na Filosofia Medieval: Actes du XIe Congrès International de Philosophie Médiévale de la Société Internationale pour l'Étude de la Philosophie Médiévale (SIEPM). Porto, du 26 au 31 août 2002*. Turnhout: Brepols, 2006, pp. 1–34.

Tavormina, Mary Teresa. *Kindly Similitude: Marriage and Family in 'Piers Plowman'*. Cambridge: D. S. Brewer, 1995.

Tavormina, Mary Teresa, and Robert F. Yeager, eds. *The Endless Knot: Essays on Old and Middle English in Honor of Marie Borroff*. Cambridge: D.S. Brewer, 1996.

Taylor, Paul B. 'Chaucer's *Cosyn to the Dede*', *Speculum* 57 (1982), 315–27.

Teske, Roland J. 'Criteria for Figurative Interpretation in St. Augustine', in Duane W. H. Arnold and Pamela Bright, eds, *De doctrina Christiana: A Classic of Western Culture*. Notre Dame: University of Notre Dame Press, 1995, pp. 109–22.

Thompson, John. 'Chaucer's "An ABC" in and out of Context', *Poetica* (Tokyo) 37 (1993), 38–48.

Toivanen, Juhana. *Perception and the Internal Senses: Peter of John Olivi on the Cognitive Functions of the Sensitive Soul*. Leiden: Brill, 2013.

Toivanen, Juhana. 'The Fate of the Flying Man: Medieval Reception of Avicenna's Thought Experiment', *Oxford Studies in Medieval Philosophy* 3 (2015), 64–98.

Toivanen, Juhana. 'The Personal and the Political: Love and Society in the Roman de la Rose', in Morton and Nievergelt, pp. 111–30.

Tolmie, Sarah. 'Langland, Wittgenstein, and the End of Language', *YLS* 20 (2006), 115–39.

Tonelli, Natascia ed. *Sulle tracce del Fiore*. Florence: Le Lettere, 2017.

Travis, Peter. *Disseminal Chaucer: Rereading the Nun's Priest's Tale*. Notre Dame: Notre Dame University Press, 2010.

Treffort, Cécile. '*De inventoribus litterarum*: l'histoire de l'écriture vue par les savants carolingiens', *Summa* 1(2013), 38–53.

Trigg, Stephanie. 'Langland's Tears: Poetry, Emotion and Mouvance', *YLS* 26 (2012), 27–48.

Trorrmann, Christian. 'Bernard de Clairvaux sur la faiblaisse de la volonté et la duperie de soi', in Tobias Hoffmann, Jörn Müller, Matthias Perkams, eds, *Das Problem der Willensschwäche in der mittelalterlichen Philosophie/The Problem of Weakness of Will in Medieval Philosophy*. Leuven: Peeters, 2006, pp. 147–72.

Turner, Denys. 'Allegory in Christian Late Antiquity', in Rita Copeland and Peter T. Struck, eds, *The Cambridge Companion to Allegory*. Cambridge: Cambridge University Press, 2010, pp. 71–82.

Tuve, Rosamond. *Allegorical Imagery: Some Medieval Books and their Posterity*. Princeton: Princeton University Press, 1966.

Tweedale, Martin M. 'Mental Representations in Later Medieval Scholasticism', in J-C. Smith, ed., *Historical Foundations of Cognitive Science*. Dordrecht: Kluwer, 1990, pp. 35–51.

Tweedale, Martin M. 'Origins of the Medieval Theory that Sensation is an Immaterial Reception of a Form', *Philosophical Topics* 20.2 (1992), 215–31.

Tweedale, Martin M. 'Representation in Scholastic Epistemology', in Henrik Lagerlund, ed., *Representation and Objects of Thought in Medieval Philosophy*. London: Routledge, 2007, pp. 73–90.

Valente, Luisa. 'Langage et théologie pendant la seconde moitié du XIIe siècle', in StenEbbesen, ed., *Sprachtheorien in Spätantike und Mittelalter*. Tübingen: Günther Narr, 1995, pp. 33–54.

Valente, Luisa. *Phantasia contrarietatis: contraddizioni scritturali, discorso teologico e arti del linguaggio nel 'De tropis loquendi' di Pietro Cantore (1197)*. Florence: Olschki, 1997.

Valente, Luisa. *Logique et théologie: Les Écoles Parisiennes entre 1150 et 1220*. Paris: Vrin, 2008.

Valentini, Andrea. *Le remaniement du Roman de la Rose par Gui de Mori. Étude et édition des interpolations d'après le manuscrit*. Leuven: Peeters, 2007.

Van Dyke, Carolynn. *The Fiction of Truth: Structures of Meaning in Narrative and Dramatic Allegory*. Henrik LagerlundIthaca, NY: Cornell University Press, 1985.

Van Dyke, Christina. 'An Aristotelian Theory of Divine Illumination: Robert Grosseteste's Commentary on the Posterior Analytics', *British Journal for the History of Philosophy* 17.4 (2009), 685–704.

544 BIBLIOGRAPHY

Van't Spijker, Ineke, ed. *The Multiple Meaning of Scripture: the Role of Exegesis in Early Christian and Medieval Culture*. Leiden: Brill, 2008.

Vance, Eugene. *Marvelous Signals: Poetics and Sign Theory in the Middle Ages*. Lincoln and London: University of Nebraska Press, 2002.

Vance, Eugene. 'Seeing God: Augustine, Sensation, and the Mind's Eye', in Stephen G. Nichols, Alison Calhoun, and Andreas Kablitz, eds, *Rethinking the Medieval Senses: Heritage/Fascinations/Frames*. Baltimore: Johns Hopkins University Press, 2008, pp. 13–29.

Vaughan, Míceál F. '"Til I gan awake": The Conversion of Dreamer into Narrator in *Piers Plowman* B', *YLS* 5 (1991), 175–92.

Verhuyck, Paul, 'Guillaume de Lorris ou la multiplication des cadres', *Neophilologus* 58.3 (1974), 283–93.

Veysseyre, Géraldine, with Julia Drobinsky and Émilie Fréger. 'Catalogue des manuscrits des Pèlerinages de Guillaume de Deguileville', in Duval and Pomel, pp. 425–53.

Veysseyre, Géraldine. 'Manuscrits à voir, manuscrits à lire, manuscrits lus: Les Marginalia du Pèlerinage de Vie Humaine comme indices de sa réception médiévale', in Kamath and Nievergelt, pp. 47–64.

Vincent-Cassy, Mireille. 'L'Envie au Moyen Âge', *Annales ESC* 1 (1980), 253–71.

Vogt-Spira, Gregor. 'Senses, Imagination, and Literature: Some Epistemological Considerations', in Stephen G. Nichols, Alison Calhoun, and Andreas Kablitz, eds, *Rethinking the Medieval Senses: Heritage/Fascinations/Frames*. Baltimore: Johns Hopkins University Press, 2008, pp. 51–72.

Vulliez, Charles. 'Autour de Jean de Meun, esquisse de bilan des données prosopographiques', in Jean-Patrice Boudet, Philippe Haugeard, et al., eds, *Jean de Meun et la culture médiévale: Littérature, art, sciences et droit aux derniers siècles du Moyen Âge*. Rennes: Presses Universitaires de Rennes, 2017, pp. 23–46.

Walling, Amanda. 'Friar Flatterer: Glossing and the Hermeneutics of Flattery in *Piers Plowman*', *YLS* 21 (2007), 57–76.

Walter, Katie L. *Middle English Mouths: Late Medieval Medical, Religious and Literary Traditions*. Cambridge: Cambridge University Press, 2018.

Warner, Lawrence. *The Lost History of Piers Plowman: The Earliest Transmission of Langland's Work*. Philadelphia: University of Pennsylvania Press, 2011.

Warner, Lawrence. 'Plowman Traditions in Late Medieval and Early Modern Writing', Cole and Galloway, pp. 198–213.

Watson, Nicholas. '*Piers Plowman*, Pastoral Theology, and Spiritual Perfectionism: Hawkyn's Cloak and Patience's *Pater Noster*', *YLS* 21 (2007), 83–118.

Watson, Sarah W. 'Grace Holds the "Clicket" to the Heavenly "Wiket": *Piers Plowman*, the *Roman de la Rose*, and the Poetics of Penetration', *YLS* 30 (2016), 206–26.

Wawrykow, Joseph. 'Reflections on the Place of the *De Doctrina Christiana* in High Scholastic Discussions of Theology', in Edward D. English, ed., *Reading and Wisdom: The 'De Doctrina Christiana' of Augustine in the Middle Ages*. Notre Dame: University of Notre Dame Press, 1995, pp. 99–125.

Wei, Ian. *Intellectual Culture in Medieval Paris: Theologians and the University, c. 1100–1330*. Cambridge: Cambridge University Press, 2012.

Weijers, Olga. 'De la joute dialectique à la dispute scolastique', *Comptes rendus des séances de l'Académie des Inscriptions et Belles-Lettres*, 143.2 (1999), 509–18.

Wetherbee, Winthrop. 'The Literal and the Allegorical: Jean de Meun and the *de Planctu Naturae*', *Mediaeval Studies* 33 (1971), 264–91.

BIBLIOGRAPHY 545

Wetherbee, Winthrop. *Platonism and Poetry in the Twelfth Century: The Literary Influence of the School of Chartres*. Princeton: Princeton University Press, 1972.

Wheeler, Bonnie, ed. *Mindful Spirit in Late Medieval Literature: Essays in Honor of Elizabeth D. Kirk*. New York: Palgrave MacMillan, 2006.

White, Hugh. 'Langland's Ymaginatif, Kynde and the *Benjamin Major*', *Medium Ævum* 55.2 (1986), 241–8.

White, Hugh. *Nature and Salvation in 'Piers Plowman'*. Woodbridge: D.S. Brewer, 1988.

Whitman, Jon. *Allegory: The Dynamics of an Ancient and Medieval Technique*. Oxford: Clarendon Press, 1987.

Whitman, Jon. 'Dislocations: The Crisis of Allegory in the *Romance of the Rose*', in Sanford Budick and Wolfgang Iser, eds, *Languages of the Unsayable: The Play of Negativity in Literature and Literary Theory*. New York: Columbia University Press, 1989, pp. 259–80.

Whitman, Jon, ed. *Interpretation and Allegory: Antiquity to the Modern Period*. Leiden: Brill, 2000.

Willaert, Frank, Herman Braet, Thom Mertens, and Theofiel Venckeleer, eds. *Medieval Memory: Image and Text*. Turnhout: Brepols, 2004.

Williams, Rowan. 'Language, Reality, and Desire in Augustine's *De Doctrina*', *Journal of Literature and Theology* 3 (1989), 138–58.

Willis, Katherine E. C. 'The Poetry of the *Poetria Nova*: The *Nubes Serena* and *Peregrinatio* of Metaphor', *Traditio* 72 (2017), 275–300.

Wippel, John F. 'Essence and Existence', in *CHLMP*, pp. 383–410.

Wippel, John F. 'Essence and Existence', in *CHMP*, II:609–22.

Wittig, Joseph S. '*Piers Plowman* B IX–XII: Elements in the Design of the Inward Journey', *Traditio* 28 (1972), 211–80.

Wittig, Joseph S. 'The Dramatic and Rhetorical Development of Will's Pilgrimage', *Neuphilologische Mitteilungen* 76 (1975), 52–76.

Wolfson, Harry Austryn. 'The Internal Senses in Latin, Arabic, and Hebrew Philosophic Texts', *Harvard Theological Review* 28.2 (1935), 69–133.

Wood, Rega. 'Imagination and Experience: In the Sensory Soul and Beyond: Richard Rufus, Roger Bacon and Their Contemporaries', in Henrik Lagerlund, ed., *Forming the Mind: Essays on the Internal Senses and the Mind/Body Problem from Avicenna to the Medical Enlightenment*. Dordrecht: Springer, 2007, pp. 27–57.

Wood, Sarah. *Conscience and the Composition of 'Piers Plowman'*. Oxford: Oxford University Press, 2012.

Woodruff Smith, David. 'Phenomenology', in Edward N. Zalta (ed.), *The Stanford Encyclopedia of Philosophy*. Summer 2018 Edition [https://plato.stanford.edu/archives/sum2018/entries/phenomenology/; retrieved 31 May 2021].

Woolf, Rosemary. 'The Tearing of the Pardon', in S. S. Hussey, ed., *Piers Plowman: Critical Approaches*. London: Methuen, 1969, pp. 50–75.

Wright, Steven. 'Deguileville's *Pèlerinage de vie humaine* as "Contrepartie édifiante" of the *Roman de la Rose*', *Philological quarterly* 68.4 (1989), 399–422.

Wurtele, Douglas. 'The Bane of Flattery in the World of Chaucer and Langland', *Florilegium* 19 (2002), 1–25.

Yrjönsuuri, Mikko. 'Free Will and Self-Control in Peter Olivi', in Henrik Lagerlund and Mikko Yrjönsuuri, eds, *Emotions and Free Choice from Boethius to Descartes*. Dordrecht: Springer, 2002, pp. 99–123.

Yrjönsuuri, Mikko. 'The Soul as an Entity: Dante, Aquinas, and Olivi', in Henrik Lagerlund, ed., *Forming the Mind*. Dordrecht: Springer: 2007, pp. 59–92.

546 BIBLIOGRAPHY

Yrjönsuuri, Mikko. 'Perceiving One's Own Body', in Simo Knuuttila and Pekka Kärkkäinen, eds, *Theories of Perception in Medieval and Early Modern Philosophy*. New York: Springer, 2008, pp. 101–16.

Yrjönsuuri, Mikko. 'Identity and Moral Agency', in *CHMP*, I:472–83.

Zalta, Edward N., ed. *The Stanford Encyclopedia of Philosophy*. Summer 2018 Edition [https://plato.stanford.edu/archives/sum2018/index.html; retrieved 31 May 2021].

Zeeman, Nicolette. 'The Schools Give a License to Poets', in Rita Copeland, *Criticism and Dissent in the Middle Ages*. Cambridge: Cambridge University Press, 1996, pp. 151–80.

Zeeman, Nicolette. *Piers Plowman and the Medieval Discourse of Desire*. Cambridge: Cambridge University Press, 2006.

Zeeman, Nicolette. 'Imaginative Theory', in Paul Strohm, ed., *Middle English*. Oxford Twenty-First Century Approaches to Literature. Oxford: Oxford University Press, 2007, pp. 222–40.

Zeeman, Nicolette. 'Tales of Piers and Perceval: *Piers Plowman* and the Grail Romances', *YLS 22* (2008), 199–236.

Zeeman, Nicolette. 'Medieval Religious Allegory, French and English', in Rite Copeland and Peter T. Struck, eds, *The Cambridge Companion to Allegory*. Cambridge: Cambridge University Press, 2010, pp. 148–61.

Zeeman, Nicolette. 'Philosophy in Parts: Jean de Meun, Chaucer, and Lydgate', in Dallas G. Denery II, Kantik Ghosh, and Nicolette Zeeman, eds, *Uncertain Knowledge: Scepticism, Relativism and Doubt in the Middle Ages*. Turnhout: Brepols, 2014, pp. 213–38.

Zeeman, Nicolette. '*Piers Plowman* in Theory', in Cole and Galloway, pp. 214–29.

Zeeman, Nicolette. *The Arts of Disruption: Allegory and Piers Plowman*. Oxford: Oxford University Press, 2020.

Zeimbekis, John. 'Thought Experiments and Mental Simulations', in Katerina Ierodiakonou and Sophie Roux, eds, *Thought Experiments in Methodological and Historical Contexts*. Leiden: Brill, 2011, pp. 193–215.

Zink, Michel. *La subjectivité littéraire: autour du siècle de Saint Louis*. Paris: Presses Universitaires de France, 1985.

Zinn, Grover A. 'The Influence of *De doctrina christiana* on the Writings of Hugh of St. Victor', in Edward D. English, ed., *Reading and Wisdom: The 'De Doctrina Christiana' of Augustine in the Middle Ages*. Notre Dame: University of Notre Dame Press, 1995, pp. 48–60.

Ziolkowski, Ian. *Alan of Lille's Grammar of Sex: The Meaning of Grammar to a Twelfth-Century Intellectual*. Cambridge, MA: Medieval Academy of America, 1985.

Zumthor, Paul. *Essai de poétique médiévale*. Paris: Seuil, 1972.

Zupko, Jack. 'John Buridan on the Immateriality of the Intellect', in Henrik Lagerlund, ed., *Forming the Mind*. Dordrecht: Springer: 2007, pp. 129–47.

Unpublished Materials

Bose, Mishtooni. 'On not being French: Thinking with Deguileville', paper presented at the International Medieval Congress in Kalamazoo in 2006.

Camille, Michael W. 'The Illustrated Manuscripts of Guillaume de Deguileville's *Pèlerinages*, 1330–1426', 2 vols. Unpublished PhD dissertation, University of Cambridge, 1985.

Gray, Nicholas. 'A Study of *Piers Plowman* in relation to the Medieval Penitential Tradition'. Unpublished PhD dissertation, University of Cambridge, 1984.

Houghton Meyer, Josephine. 'The Works of Guillaume Deguileville in Late Medieval England: Transmission, Reception, and Context with Special Reference to Piers *Plowman*'. Unpublished PhD dissertation, University of Birmingham, 2007.

Maupeu, Philippe. 'Corps et langage dans le *PVH*: la mécanique des vices', unpublished paper delivered at the Congress on *Guillaume de Deguileville in Europe*, University of Lausanne, July 2011.

General Index (names and themes)

Abelard, Peter, *Historia calamitatum*, 408
Aers, David, 329, 365, 369, 461–2, 469
Agamben, Giorgio, 7
Al-Fārābī, 11, 13, 31
Al-Kindī, 31
Alan of Lille, 62, 171, 490, 492
 De Planctu Naturae, 58, 60–2, 63–4, 113–14, 124, 484–9
 'Omnis mundi creatura', 155
 'Sermo in die cinerum', 437
Albert the Great (Albertus Maguns), 63, 189
 on the intellect, 31
Alexander of Aphrodisias, 233
Alexander of Hales, *Summa fratris Alexandri* (*Summa Halensis*), 106
Alfonso X of Castille, 73
Alford, John, 349, 433
Alhazen (Ibn al-Haytham), 197, 240
allegoria in factis/verbis, 153, 157
Allegory
 as literary genre, 10–11, 13, 46–51, 56–64
 modern theories of, 4, 173
 medieval theories of, 10–11, 153, 485–6
 as rhetorical trope, 10–11, 213–19, 486, 494
Alphabetical poetry, 281–9
Anderson, Judith, 173
Annunciation, 442
Anti-Pelagianism, *see* grace (theory of); Pelagianism and anti-Pelagianism
Antichrist, 79, 459, 462, 465, 466–7, 469, 470, 472, 477, 478
Aquinas, Thomas
 on Grace, 37–9
 In I Epist. ad Corinthios, 189
 on objects of knowledge, 21
 Quaestiones disputatae de veritate, 197, 236
 on the soul and cognition, 30, 189, 199, 235–6
 Summa Theologiae, 31, 36, 38, 153, 235
 on will and intellect, 31, 36
Aristotle, 62
 Analytica posteriora, 8, 17–18, 24, 194, 251
 Arabic commentaries on, 9, 13, 26, 34, 233
 Categoriae, 23
 causality, 16, 20–2, 30, 33, 37, 45, 69, 197, 199–200, 236
 as character (fictional) in *PVH*, 130, 136–40
 conformality thesis, 197–8, 236, 242–3

De anima, 22–3, 25–32, 132, 184, 188, 194, 195, 233, 235, 236, 251
De interpretatione, 10–11, 15, 22–3, 25, 88, 298
demonstrative syllogism, 13, 16, 17–18, 45, 75, 103, 190, 456, 481
'empiricism', 24–5, 103
Ethica, 71, 251, 419
hylomorphism, 25–7, 30, 43, 176, 184, 188, 192, 220, 226, 242, 434
imaginative syllogism, 12–13
Metaphysica, 15, 77, 103–4, 132, 223
natural science, 4, 17, 28, 42, 71, 130, 134, 136, 176, 331, 335
Parva naturalia, 7 n.15
Physica, 137–8
principle of non-contradiction, 15, 457
'rediscovery' of full *organon* in the West (s. XI-XIII), 3, 9, 17–18, 176
scientia (theory of), 8, 12, 15–16, 22–3, 25, 34, 69, 75, 91–2, 102–4, 107, 331, 335, 420–1, 455–6
semantic triangle (*De interpretatione* 16a3–9), 10–11, 88
Sophistici elenchi, 15, 98–9, 208–9, 467
soul (theory of), 25–32, 34–7, 119, 132, 184, 188, 194, 195, 196–7, *see also* Aristotle, *De anima*
artes poetriae, 9, 12–13, 155
Ashworth, Jennifer, 98
Atonement, doctrine of, 38, 347, 363–4, 453
Augustine of Hippo
 as character (fictional) in *PVH*, 171
 cognition (theory of), 9
 divine illumination (theory of), 9, 22, 33–5, 40, 193–202, 223, 224, 228, 235, 236, 258, 263, 332
 on evil, 218
 on the Fall, 141–2, 158–9, 177–9
 on language, 77–8, 83
 on pilgrimage, 45–6, 124, 141–3
 regio dissimilitudinis, 45, 156–8, 212, 245, 272, 284, 294, 311, 318–19, 343, 360, 425
 signs and language (theory of), 21, 105–6, 107, 120, 144–5, 148–9, 152–7, 159–62, 175–7, 215, 219, 274

GENERAL INDEX (NAMES AND THEMES)   549

soul (theory of), 25–7, 32–6, 44–6, 124,
  178–93, 202–5
on spiritual sensation/experience, 43–6
use vs. enjoyment (*uti/frui*), 45, 148–9,
  153–4, 202, 206, 255, 274, 284, 445
verbum in corde/verbum mentis, 9, 178, 226,
  264–5, 267–8, 275, 309–11, 313, 317,
  319–20
vision (tripartite theory of), 9, 223, 226, 334,
  342, 355
  Confessiones, 44, 141, 142, 245, 256, 263,
    269–70, 344
  De Civitate Dei, 141
  De dialectica, 83–4, 282, 304
  De doctrina christiana, 44, 124, 141–9,
    152–4, 157, 159–62, 166, 173, 178, 203–4,
    208–9, 215, 217, 219, 264
  De Genesi contra Manichaeos, 153, 178,
    180, 274
  De magistro, 105–6, 175, 265, 282
  De spiritu et littera, 256
  De trinitate, 25, 35, 44, 124, 142, 154, 158,
    178–9, 187, 204–5, 274, 281, 448, 449,
    451
  Epistola 98, 160
on the will (*voluntas*), 33, 35, 37–8, 250, 256,
  258, 281
'Augustinianism', 26, 34, 38, 118–19, 130, 174–9,
  249, 256, 424
'Augustinisme Avicennisant', 26–7, 184–5
autobiography, 42, 67, 125, 244–5, 278, 292,
  294, 313–19, 378, 407–11, 421, 462, 469,
  474–5, 477
Averroës (Ibn Rushd), 11, 232–3
'Averroism', 74, 370
Avicenna (Ibn Sînâ)
  De anima, theory of mind and knowl-
    edge, 26–7, 30, 34, 183–93, 194, 198,
    232–3
  Neoplatonic elements, 26–7, 184–5, 188, 194

Bacon, Roger, 77–8
  Compendium studii theologiae, 81, 88
  De signis, 55, 80–1, 88–96, 105, 173
  on *experientia/experimentum*, 41–2, 104–5
  and Jean de Meun, 77–97
  Opus Maius, 78–81, 240
  Perspectiva, 79, 223
  semantics, 24, 79–81, 83, 88–97, 105, 107,
    166, 173, 307
  species-theory, 28, 97, 197–8, 226–7, 240, *see
    also* Bacon, Roger, *Perspectiva*
  Summulae Dialectices, 81
Badel, Pierre-Yves, 64, 74, 169, 291
Baptism, 160, 253

Barney, Stephen, 326
Bede, 153
Benedict of Nursia, 250, 317
  Rule of St Benedict (*Regula Benedicti*), 258,
    259
Bernard of Clairvaux, 43, 250, 269–70, 333, 372,
  419–20
  De diligendo deo, 204
  Super cantica canticorum, 263, 270
Bernardus Silvestris, 58, 429
  Cosmographia, 429
Bible
  Biblical exegesis, 141–59, 163, 167, 171–2,
    179, 310–12, 374
  New Testament, 144, 146, 310, 385, 413, 449
  (non-)contradiction in Scripture, 23, 146–9
  Old Testament, 144, 310, 413, 444–6, 449
Biblical citations
  1 Cor. 7:31, 154
  1 Cor. 10:19–20, 215
  1 Cor. 13:12, 124, 158–9, 178, 365, 415, 448,
    449, 451, 452, 454
  2 Cor. 3:6, 145
  2 Cor. 5:6–7, 154, 162
  Eph. 5:29, 203
  Eph. 6:10–17, 156, 179
  Ezk. 34:2, 402
  Gal. 4:4–7, 434
  Genesis, 307, 308
  Heb. 4:12, 165
  Luke 5:21–2, 451–2
  Luke 9:3, 145–6
  Luke 11:17, 451
  Luke 15:13, 425
  Mat. 4:4, 367
  Mat. 6:6, 263
  Mat. 7:6, 371–2
  Mat. 7:15, 402
  Mat. 9:2–4, 452
  Phil. 3:20, 162
  Rom. 1:20, 154, 161
  Rom. 7:15–20, 256
  Rom 10:17, 163, 225
Blamires, Alcuin, 57
Boccaccio, Giovanni, 4, 56
Boethius (Anicius Manlius Severinus), 4, 62, 71,
  75, 171
  *Commentary on Aristotle's De
    Interpretatione*, 15, 298
  Consolation of Philosophy, 57, 223, 297–8

550 GENERAL INDEX (NAMES AND THEMES)

Boethius of Dacia, 84
Bologna, University (Law Faculty), 72–4, 78
Bonaventure, 43, 136, 264
   Itinerarium mentis in deo, 155
   on will and intellect, 31, 36, 257
Book of Nature, 154–5, 215
Bose, Mishtooni, 327
Boulton, Maureen, 294
Bourquin, Guy, 326
Bowers, John, 430–1, 433
Bradwardine, Thomas, on grace, 38–9
Brown, Cynthia, 67
Brown, Peter, 44
Buridan, John, 21
   on the soul, 29 n.82, 233–4
Burley, Walter, 21, 166
Burrow, John A., 326, 391, 433, 442

Camille, Michael, 238–9
Ceffons, Pierre, 132
   Epistola Luciferi, 133
Cerquiglini, Jacqueline, 114
Cervone, Maria Cristina, 448
Chaalis, Abbey of, 126, 127, 131–2, 146–7, 244,
   313, 315, 320, 407, 462, 463–4, 474
   library, 132–3, 146–7
Chambers, R.W., 410
Charles of Anjou, 73
Chartres, 'School of', 58, *see also* Philosophical
   poetry, 'Neoplatonic' (s. XII)
Chaucer, Geoffrey, 116, 172, 217, 241, 278, 321,
   389, 462
   on *experience* and *auctoritee*, 44, 105–7,
   112–13
   influence of Boethius, *Consolation of
   Philosophy*, 57
   influence of the *Roman de la Rose*, 57, 66
Chester-Jordan, William, 131
Christine de Pizan, *see Quérelle de la Rose*
   (1401–3)
Cicero (Marcus Tullius Cicero), 12, 83, 166, 171
Cistercian Order, 131–3, 264, 270, 314, 317,
   355–6, 367
Clarke, Robert, 292–3, 443
Clement IV (Pope), 78
Clopper, Lawrence, 327, 355
Col, Jean and Gonthier, *see Quérelle de la Rose*
   (1401–3)
Coleman, Joyce, 126
Collège de Saint Bernard (Paris), 131–2
complexe significabile, 21
concepts (medieval theory of), 8, 11, 23
conversion, 249–51, 262, 263, 341–2, 383, 417,
   424

Council of Vienne (1312), 188, 199
Craun, Edwin, 371, 402
Crispin, Gilbert, *Disputatio Iudei et
   Christiani*, 146

Dahan, Gilbert, 11
Dante Alighieri, 4
   De vulgari eloquentia, 277
   Divina Commedia, 56
   influence of the *Roman de la Rose*, 56, 66
Davis, Isabel, 498
Davlin, Mary Clemente, 482
De spiritu et anima (pseudo-Augustine),
   26 n.72, 184
demonstrative syllogism, *see* Aristotle,
   demonstrative syllogism
Derrida, Jacques, 110–11
Deschamps, Eustache, 114
devotio moderna, 43
dialectic, dialectical reason-
   ing/argumentation, 120, 128–30,
   136–8, 264–5, 281, 331, 334–5
dictio propria/impropria, 82–3, 85, 87,
   90–6, 151–2, 157, 162, 164–7, 171–3,
   226, 486, *see also* figures and tropes
   (medieval theories of); literal sense;
   translatio/transumptio
didacticism, 4, 47–8, 106, 113, 118, 120, 123–6,
   242–4, 275, 280–1, 358, 360, 482
disputatio, 47, 74–7, 104, 128, 129–40, 264,
   334–5, 411, 443
Donaldson, Talbot E., 426–7
Donatus, 166, 485, 497
   Ars Maior, 10–11
dualism, Augustinian, 14, 25–6, 45, 178–93,
   202–5, 250, 363, *see also* Augustine of
   Hippo, soul (theory of)
dualism, Cartesian, 14
Duval, Frédéric, 117, 131
Dyonisius the Areopagite (Pseudo-), 43

Eco, Umberto, 111
Edwards, Graham R., 277, 283, 289, 290
embodiment, 12–16, 28, 43, 66, 69, 104, 107–16,
   175, 181–93, 202–45, 250, 258, 363, 446,
   448, 472, 495–6
empiricism, 24–5, 41–2, 103, *see also* Aristotle,
   'empiricism'
enargeia, 12–13
encyclopaedism, medieval, 4, 46–7, 56–7, 79,
   196
epistemology (modern discipline), 16, 19
equivocation, 15–16, 23, 58, 76, 77, 79, 81, 93–7,
   98, 103–4, 106–7, 166–7, 481–2

GENERAL INDEX (NAMES AND THEMES) 551

Eucharist, 130, 134–40, 163, 218, 223, 226, 229, 232, 270, 315, 316, 319, 368–75, 385, 393, 398, 402, 405, 464–6, 470
experience vs. *auctoritee*, 3, 40–1, 43, 438, 460–2, 481–2
experientia/experimentum, 41–2
experiential knowledge, 103–4, 107–16, 182–93, 244–5, 293–4, 344, 346, 383, 391, 455–6, 480, 481, *see also* Aristotle, 'empiricism'; Bacon, Roger, on *experientia/experimentum*; empiricism; *experience* vs. *auctoritee*; *experientia/experimentum*; *scientia experimentalis*

facere quod in se est, 39, 420, 424, 432, 442–3, 496
faculty psychology (Aristotelian), 4, 8–9, 11, 17, 22, 27–30, 42, 70, 71, 184–5, 196–8, 228–36, 331, 337–8, 340, 354
  abstractive cognition (Aristotelian), 28, 31–2, 34–5, 42, 193–4, 196, 226–7, 229, 234–5, 332
  internal senses, 198, 228–36, 361
  species-theory, 27–32, 75, 79, 197–9, 226–7, 236, 239, 242
faith, doctrines of, 37, 39, 162–5
Fall (of Adam and Eve), 39, 77–8, 102, 141–2, 155, 158–9, 177–9, 181–2, 263, 342, 444
  impact on language, 77–8, 102, 155, 177–9, 282, 298
fallacies, 98–9, 109, 208, 467–8, *see also* Aristotle, *Sophistici elenchi*; sophism (sophistic argument)
Faral, Edmond, 131, 302, 313
fideism, 5, 339, 351, 357, 419, 423, 450, 453, 455
figures and tropes (medieval theories of), 10–12, 23–4, 45, 83, 87, 92–7, 112, 113–14, 147, 155, 217, 273, 475–6, 484–8
first-person narrator (in medieval poetry), 1–2, 7–8, 67–9, 121–7, 140–2, 176, 183, 244–5, 247, 252, 277–8, 281, 290–3, 313, 316–17, 319–20, 360–1, 381–2, 397, 409, 411–12, 414, 440, 482
five senses (external), 192, 222–32, *see also* faculty psychology (Aristotelian); sense perception
  hearing, 163, 200, 209, 225–31, 334
  sight, 9, 198, 200, 209, 222–36, 237–43, 248–9, 334, 341, 344, *see also* optics (medieval)
  touch, 97, 108, 170, 186, 191–2
  taste, 269, 304, 319, 346, 364, 419, 446, 461
Fletcher, Alan, 427

Fletcher, Angus, 206
Flying Man thought experiment, 183–93, 204, 207, 243, *see also* Avicenna (Ibn Sînâ), *De anima*, theory of mind and knowledge; thought experiments
Franklin-Brown, Mary, 63, 74
Fyler, John, 77–8

Galloway, Andrew, 327, 356, 432
Gawain-poet, 116
Geoffrey of Vinsauf, *Poetria Nova*, 155–6
Gerson, Jean, on the *Roman de la Rose*, 63–4, 104, 110, *see also* Quérelle de la Rose (1401–3)
Gervais du Bus, *Roman de Fauvel*, 328
Gibbs, Raymond W., 14
Gillespie, Vincent, 11–12, 327, 332–4
Gilson, Etienne, 26–7, 184–5
Godden, Malcolm, 340, 355, 417
Godfrey of Fontaines, on will and intellect, 36
Gower, John, 116
grace (theory of), 42, 44, 250, 256, 263
  habitus of grace, 37–9
grammar, medieval, 4, 77–97, 98, 361, 387–8, 484–91, *see also* trivium
  'intentionalist' grammar, 87–97
  modistic grammar/speculative grammar, 85–6, 89–92
  mystical grammar, 281–3, 285–6, 387–8
Gregory of Rimini
  on grace, 38–9
  on objects of knowledge, 21
  on signs, 106
Gregory the Great, 250, 264
  Moralia in Iob, 142, 204, 259–60
  on spiritual sensation/experience, 43, 259–60, 261
Grosseteste, Robert
  Commentary on Aristotle's *Analytica posteriora*, 8, 18, 194–5, 196, 251
  Commentary on Aristotle's *Ethica*, 251
  De veritate, 223
  on *experientia/experimentum*, 41–2
Gruenler, Curtis, 385, 449
Gundissalinus, Dominicus
  De divisione philosophie, 13
  translation of Avicenna, *De anima*, 183–4, 185
Guynn, Noah, 65

Hanna, Ralph, 348, 362–3, 426, 427, 432, 438
Henry of Ghent, 83, 198
  on the will, 257
Hewett-Smith, Jane, 444, 471–3, 476

552 GENERAL INDEX (NAMES AND THEMES)

Hilder, Gisela, 71
Holcot, Robert
  on grace, 38
  on objects of knowledge, 21
  Questions on Peter Lombard's Sentences, 55
Hölscher, Ludger, 44
Horace, 62, 113
Houghton-Meyer, Josephine, 327
Hrabanus Maurus (-Pseudo?)
  De inventione litterarum (/*linguarum*), 283
  De laudibus Sanctae Crucis, 283
Hugh of St Victor
  De Sacramentis Christianae fidei, 159
  Didascalicon, 142, 153, 154–5, 200, 264–5
Hult, David, 47, 64, 173, 241
Humbert of Preuilly, 132
Huot, Sylvia, 65, 66, 107, 114, 169, 237

idolatry, 215–20, 237–9, 206, 420
images (visual), medieval theory of, 217–18,
  237–43, 332
imagination, medieval theories of, 9–10, 13–16,
  32, 76, 198–202, 334, *see also* faculty
  psychology (Aristotelian)
imagination, modern theories of,
  13–15
imaginative syllogism, *see* Aristotle, imaginative
  syllogism
imago dei/Image Theology, 45, 123, 141–2,
  178–82, 184, 192, 195, 202–4, 210, 221,
  233, 245, 250, 276, 283–4, 342, 421, 422,
  423, 435, 446, 448, 449
Immaculate Conception, 442
impositio ad placitum, 81, 84–97, 150, 297–8,
  486
  duplex impositio, 93–6
Incarnation, 3, 37–8, 43, 155, 158, 264, 268–9,
  285–6, 293, 337, 347, 363, 366–7, 439,
  440, 443–9, 453, 460–1
integumentum, 58–60, 94, 101–2, 113, 162,
  167, *see also* Philosophical Poetry,
  'Neoplatonic' (s. XII)
intellect
  agent (active) intellect, 30–1, 34, 195
  Augustine's theory of, 34–7, 42, *see also*
    Augustine of Hippo, soul (theory of)
  intellection, intellectual cognition, 8, 30–1,
    183, 191, 226–7, 230–6, 248–9, 332, 334,
    341
  'intellectualists', *see* 'voluntarists vs.
    intellectualists'
  'monopsychism' (unicity of the intellect), 30
  potential (possible) intellect, 30–1, 195
intellectus primus/secundus (semantics),
  87, 93

Isaac of Stella, *Epistola de anima*, 184
Isidore of Seville, *Etymologiae*, 141, 259, 282–3,
  297–8

James of Venice, 17
Jean de la Rochelle, *Summa de anima*, 185
Jean de Mirecourt, 132
Jean le Bel (Jean d'Arkel), 76
Jerome, *Contra vigilantium*, 260
Jirsa, Curtis, 389–90
John the Baptist, 443, 445
Jung, Marc-René, 64
Jusserand, Jean Jules, 325–6

Kamath, Stephanie A.V.G., 409
Kane, George, 410, 426
Kay, Sarah, 47, 65, 66, 122–3, 126
Kerby-Fulton, Katherine, 408
Kilwardby, Robert, 92, 197, 199
Kilwardby, Robert (Pseudo-), *Commentarium*
  super Priscianum maiorem, 86, 88
King, Peter, 42
Kirk, Elizabeth, 364, 438, 444
Knox, Philip, 489, 492
Kruger, Stephen, 343

Lamy, Alice, 457
Langlois, Ernest, 70
language arts, *see* trivium
Lateran Council, IV (1215), 42
Leff, Gordon, 32
Leighton, Angela, 6, 420
Lewis, Clive Stapleton, 329
liar paradox, 98–100, 102, 106, 497–9
literal sense, 59–62, 97, 101–2, 108, 162, *see also*
  dictio propria/impropria; figures and
  tropes (medieval theories of)
literalism, 144–5, 157, 167, 180, 445
locutio angelica, 106
logic, medieval, 4, 73, 98, 102, 119, 133, 335,
  see also semantics (medieval); terminist
  logic; *trivium*
logos (*verbum*/Word), *see* Augustine of Hippo,
  verbum in corde/verbum mentis
Longpont (Cistercian Abbey), 147
Lydgate, John, *Pilgrimage of the Life of Man*, 231,
  232, 332, 430
lyric, 4, 272, 275–95, 389–90, 408
  acrostic lyrics, 281, 287–8, 316–17, 319, 381,
    393, 407–13
  Helinandian stanza, 276, 277, 283, 287, 393
  macaronic lyrics, 277–80, 316–17, 407

Machaut, Guillaume de, 66, 114, 328, 389
Maloney, Thomas, 96

GENERAL INDEX (NAMES AND THEMES) 553

Malvern Hills, 325
Mann, Jill, 60, 107
Manuscripts
  Paris BnF MS fr. 829, 336
  Arras Bibliothèque Municipale MS 532
    (845), 121, 176
  Oxford Bodleian Library MS Douce 300, 221
  Paris Bibliothèque Sainte Geneviève
    MS 1130, 293
Marmo, Costantino, 95, 110
Marrone, Stephen, 34
Marston, John, on intellect, 31
Martianus Capella, 4
Mathematics (medieval), 42
Maupeu, Philippe, 127, 171–2, 219–20, 243,
  261, 313, 407, 408, 409, 429, 430, 474
McDermott, Ryan, 432–3
memory, 35–6, *see also* Augustine of Hippo, soul
  (theory of)
mental representation (medieval theory of), 8,
  10, 15, 21, 23–4, 32, 236, 241, 332
merit (*meritum de congruo* and *de condigno*), 39,
  419–20
Meung-sur-Loire, 73
Middleton, Anne, 334, 358, 375, 386, 388, 389,
  391, 410, 411, 413, 414, 415, 418, 427,
  432, 433, 434, 438
Miller, Mark, 57
Minnis, Alastair, 57, 65, 83, 167
modi significandi, see grammar, medieval,
  modistic grammar/speculative grammar
modistic grammar (*modistae*), *see* grammar,
  medieval, modistic grammar/speculative
  grammar
Molinet, Jean, 57, 114
  Roman de la Rose moralisé, 57
monasticism/monastic tradition, 4, 43, 250,
  254–5, 259–60, 263–75, 276–7, 283,
  292–4, 300, 311, 315–20, 341, 354–7, 362,
  367, 368, 377–8, 383, 390, 399, 416–18,
  429–31, 463–4, 469
Montreuil, Jean de, *see Quérelle de la Rose*
  (1401–3)
Moreau, John, 314
Morton, Jonathan, 60–1, 64, 456, 489, 494
Murtaugh, Daniel, 449–51
mystical tradition, 43, 250, 264, 271–3, 281, 283,
  320, 355, 358, 419

narrative voice (first-person), *see* first-person
  narrator (in medieval poetry)
natural sciences (medieval), 4, 17, 28, 42, 71,
  130, 134, 331, 334–5
Newman, Barbara, 412, 427

nominalism, 5, 24, 42, 151, 176, 419, 432
Nouvet, Claire, 214

Ockham, William of
  on *experientia/experimentum*, 41–2
  on grace, 38
  on objects of knowledge, 21, 23–4
  Questiones quodlibetales, 233–4
  on the soul, 29 n.82, 233–4
  on *species*, 32, 199–200
  on *suppositio*, 166–7
Olivi, Peter of John
  active perception, theory of, 197–202
  on objects of knowledge, 21
  species, rejection of, 32, 199–200
  on will and intellect, 36, 256–7
opinio, 17–18, *see also* Aristotle, *scientia*
  (theory of)
optics (medieval), 71, 79, 197–8, 239–41
Origen, 43, 178
Orléans, 73
Orpheus, 484–5, 487–9
Ovid, 4, 62, 109, 316, 407–8
  Ibis, 316, 407
  Metamorphoses
  Pygmalion, 109, 237
ovidianism, 4
Owen, Dorothy, 326

paradox, *see* liar paradox
Paré, Gérard, 70–1
Paris, 71–4, 131–2
Paris, University of, 7 n.15, 71–4, 78, 81, 83, 85,
  131–2, 233
  Arts Faculty, 70–1, 74, 78, 83, 85, 135
  Condemnations of Aristotle, 1270 and
    1277, 72, 135–6
Pasnau, Robert, 17–18
Patristic thought, 4, 43, 78
Paul the Hermit, 430–1
Paxson, James J., 494
Pelagianism and anti-Pelagianism, 38, 50, 314,
  345, 353, 354, 357, 381
personification, *see prosopopoeia*
  (personification)
perspectiva, see Bacon, Roger, *Perspectiva*; optics
  (medieval)
Pecham, John, on intellect, 31
penitence/penance, 203–4, 221–2, 246–51, 253,
  256, 261, 348–50, 353–4, 361, 363–4, 414,
  416–17, 419, 432–4, 465–70, 497–8
  contrition, 247, 261, 348–50, 353–4, 364,
  416–17, 424, 466, 470

554 GENERAL INDEX (NAMES AND THEMES)

Peter Lombard, *Sentences*
  on sacraments, 159–60
  on will and intellect, 36
Peter of Limoges, *Tractatus moralis de oculo*, 134
Peter of Spain, 185
Peter the Chanter, *De tropis loquendi*, 147
Petrarch, Francis, 4
phantasma, see faculty psychology (Aristotelian),
    species-theory
phenomenology, 40–1
Philosophical Poetry
  Anglo-French, 4, 6, 12–13, 46–51, 70–7, 98,
    113–16
  antiquity, 4
  Italian, 4, 12
  'Neoplatonic' (s. XII), 4, 58–61, 94, 429
  theory of, 6, 15
Philosophy, medieval (as 'discipline'), 6, 28, 130
physics, *see* Aristotle, natural science; natural
    sciences (medieval)
Piaget, Arthur, 329
Pizan, Christine de, *see Quérelle de la Rose*
  (1401–3)
poetic theory
  medieval, 11–14, 20 n.34
  modern, 13–14
Poetic thought/poetic thinking, 5–7
poetrie, 6, 13
Pomel, Fabienne, 152, 158, 213, 280, 298, 304–5,
  409
potentia dei (*absoluta* and *ordinata*), 38–9, 135
Premierfait, Laurent de
  Des cas des nobles hommes et femmes, 56
  on the *Roman de la Rose*, 56
Priscian, 166, 485
  Institutiones grammaticae, 86, 88, 141
proof, proving, *probare, probatio*, 107, 138, 182,
  190–1, 244, 376, 421, 480
prosimetrum, 4
prosopopoeia (personification), 7, 61, 62, 313,
  446, 449–50, 497–8
psychomachia, 180, 206, 211–20, 313, 474
Ptolemy, 63

Quérelle de la Rose (1401–3), 58, 63–4, 170
Quintilian (Marcus Fabius Quintilianus), 12,
  485

ratio significandi, 84–7, 90–1
regio dissimilitudinis, see Augustine of Hippo,
    regio dissimilitudinis
rhetoric, medieval, 4, 9, 267–8, 467–8,
    see also artes poetriae; figures and

tropes (medieval theories of);
  translatio/transumptio; trivium
colores rhetorici, 213–14
flores rhetorici, 148, 214, 304
ornatus, 155
Richard of St Victor, *Speculum Ecclesiae*, 153
Ricœur, Paul, *Soi-même comme un autre*, 68,
  123
romance, chivalric (literary genre), 4
Rosenfeld, Jessica, 332
Rosier, Irène, 87
Rossi, Luciano, 72–3, 78
Rudd, Gillian, 326
Rufus, Richard, on the intellect, 31
Rust, Martha D., 283, 284
Rutebeuf, 326

sacramental signs, 157, 159–68, 213, 218, 296–7,
  388–9, 396
Sacramental Theology, 23, 433
Sallust (Gaius Sallustius Crispus), 298
Scanlon, Larry, 488, 497
scepticism, 5, 18, 31, 105, 199–200, 268
Schmidt, A.V.C., 355, 427, 432
Schweizer, Edward, 387–8
scientia, see Aristotle, *scientia* (theory of)
scientia experimentalis, 104–5, *see also*
    experiential knowledge
Scotus, John Duns
  on grace, 38
  on *suppositio*, 80
  on the will, 257
Scotus Eriugena, John, 43, 154
self-knowledge, 120, 128, 141, 149, 158, 177–83,
  186–93, 250, 259, 338, 340–4, 414, 418,
  422, 451–3
semantics (medieval), 20–4, 70, 71, 75, 79–97,
  105, 119, 133, 143–4, 151–2, 159–68
sense perception, 8, 22, 25, 27–32, 104, 175, 183,
  191–3, 198–202, 223–36, 249–50, *see also*
  faculty psychology (Aristotelian)
Sheingorn, Pamela, 292–3, 443
Siger of Brabant, on will and intellect, 36
Simpson, James, 340, 360, 362–3, 383, 387, 413,
  414, 415, 416, 417, 421–2, 447, 451
Smith, Vance D., 389, 434, 499
sodomy (medieval discourses of), 114, 332–3,
  486–90, 492, 494–5
sophism (sophistic argument), 98–100, 102–4,
  146, 208, 267, 312, 456, 467–8, 468
sophismata (exercise in medieval logic), 23, 71,
  75
soul (theory of), *see also* Aristotle, soul (theory
  of); Augustine of Hippo, soul (theory of);

GENERAL INDEX (NAMES AND THEMES) 555

Avicenna (Ibn Sînâ); dualism, Augustinian; faculty psychology (Aristotelian); intellect; sense perception
in general, 25–32
immortality, 27
rational/intellective soul, 27, 32, 176, 183, 188, 191–3, 195, 198–9, 232–6, 237, 244, 257
relation to body, 25, 27, 32–3, 43, 45, 66, 113, 175–93, 203–5, 212, 226–36, 257, 346
sensitive/animal soul, 27–9, 31, 198, 228–36
vegetative soul, 27
Spearing, A. C., 125
species-theory of cognition, *see* faculty psychology (Aristotelian), *species*-theory
spiritual sensation/experience, 43
Stein, Gertrude, 'Poetry and Grammar', 56
Steiner, Emily, 326–8, 392
Stock, Brian, 141
subjectivity (medieval understanding of), 40–6, 67, 176, 188–93, 202–3, 210, 221–2, 244, 249–50, 278–9, 288–9, 313, 382, 396, 409, 411–14, 423, 425, 440–1, 446–7, 451, 457–8, 459–60, 463, 470, 474, 495, 496
suppositio (theory of linguistic reference), 20, 23–4, 70, 75, 80, 88–97, 151–2, 166–7, 267

Tavormina, M. Teresa, 459
tears (gift of), weeping, 249–50, 341–2, 344–6, 348, 416
Tempier, Étienne, 136
terminist logic, 22–4
Thames (river), 354, 361–2
Theology, medieval (Faculty and academic discipline), 6, 17, 20–1, 22–3, 28, 73, 130–1, 135, 167
Thérines, Jacques de, 131–2
Thomas Beauchamp, 12th Earl of Warwick, 325
thought experiments, 42–3, 75, 183–93, 243
translatio/transumptio, 87, 92–7, 152–3, 155–6, 159, 166–7, 218, 225–6, 249, 332, 335, 337, 387, 435, 485–8, 494–5, *see also* figures and tropes (medieval theories of)
Travis, Peter, 110
Trigg, Stephanie, 344
Trinitarian Theology, 23, 336, 355
trivium, 4, 20–4, 82–3, 142–3, 167, 298, 387

universals (medieval theory of), 24, 79
Universities, medieval, 4, 8, 17, 19, 20, 70–6, 129–40, *see also* Bologna, University (Law Faculty); Paris, University of

univocatio, 15–16, 77, 95–6, 102
usus loquendi, 87, 91, 166–7

verbum (Word/*logos*), *see* Augustine of Hippo, *verbum in corde/verbum mentis*
Versus de alphabeto, 283
Versus de nominibus litterarum, 283
viator, 45–6, 123–5, 129–30, 140–59, 175, 193, 220, 242, 274–5, 346, 352–3, 362, *see also* Augustine of Hippo, on pilgrimage
Vincent of Beauvais, *Speculum naturale*, 223
vis verbi/virtus verborum, 83, 282
'voluntarists vs. intellectualists', 36–7, 75, 119, 250, 256, 419–20

Wei, Ian, 72, 74
Weijers, Olga, 75
will (*voluntas*, theory of), 32–40, 42, 44, 180, 221, 250, 255–60, 263, 266, 346, 419–20, 424–5, *see also* Augustine of Hippo, soul (theory of)
liberum arbitrium (Free Will), 36, 71, 75, 314
voluntas communis, 258, 318, 357, 368, 399, 416
voluntas propria, 255–6, 257–9, 266, 273, 293, 357, 368, 424–5
William de la Rokele, 50 n.37, 325, 410
William of Auvergne, 185
William of Middleton, *Questiones de sacramentis*, 160–1
William of St Thierry
De naturae corporis et animae, 26 n.72, 184 n.17
Epistola ad fratres de monte dei, 258–9
Willis, Katherine, 155–6
Wittig, Joseph, 340
Wodeham, Adam of, on objects of knowledge, 21
Woolf, Rosemary, 326
Word (as *verbum/logos*) made flesh, *see* Augustine of Hippo, *verbum in corde/verbum mentis*; Eucharist; Incarnation
works (vs. grace), 37, 44, 340, 419–20, *see also* Grace (theory of)
Wyfliff, John, *Epistola sathane ad cleros*, 132–3

Zachary of Besançon, *Super unum ex quatuor*, 146–7
Zeeman, Nicolette, 261, 327, 333, 336–7
Zink, Michel, 67
Zumthor, Paul, 127

Index of passages, motifs, and debates relating to main poetic corpus

(*Le Roman de la Rose*; works of Guillaume de Deguileville; *Piers Plowman*)

Guillaume de Deguileville, *Dit de la Fleur de Lys*, 295–309
lily (symbolic meaning of), 156, 296–9
Guillaume de Deguileville
alphabetical poetry, 281–9, 306, *see also Pèlerinage de Vie Humaine*, ABC prayer
autobiographical elements, 278, 292, 294, 314, 316–17, 319, 357, 360, 381, 407, 408, 414, 440, 462, 469, 474, 477
biography, 131–3
critical reception in modern scholarship, 2, 117–18
documents (fictional and intradiegetic), 126, 150, 164, 250–1, 253, 277, 280–1, 302, 306–9, 326, 390, 392–6, 411–13, 431, 434
intentio auctoris, 127–8, 275–95
lyrics
acrostic lyrics, 281, 287–8, 316–17, 319, 381, 393, 407–13
embedded lyrics (in *Pèlerinages* corpus), 275, 279–81, 295, 302, 358, 367, 392, 393, 395, 396–7, 407–9, *see also Pèlerinage de Vie Humaine*, by lyric title
Helinandian stanza, 276, 277, 283, 287, 393
Latin lyrics, *see separate entry below*
macaronic lyrics, 277–80, 316–17, 407
Marian poetry, 158, 251–3, 260, 276–8, 280, 284–7
Pèlerinages (individual poems), *see separate entries below*
and scholastic learning, 130–40, 180–1
Song of Songs (use of; influence on), 270, 272, 275, 287
'trilogy' of *Pèlerinages* (conception and genesis), 2, 47–8, 117–18, 289–92, 294, 295, 321, 324, 425–6, 428, 447
Jean de Meun
biography and identity (as 'Iohannes de Magduno'), 72–3, 78–9
intentio auctoris, 59–60, 61–2, 64, 96–7, 100–2, 109–14

and Roger Bacon, 77–97
and scholastic learning, 70–7, 78–9, 93–4, 98–9
Guillaume de Deguileville, Latin Lyrics, 272, 275–95, 320–1, 358, 367
Alpha & Omega, 285
Ave byssus castitatis, 285
Ave Maria (*in PVH2*), 280, 393
Credo (in *PVH2*), 393
De prodicione ('chessboard of treason'), 283
Munus litterarum, 284
Oratio peregrini, 260
Paternoster (in *PVH2*), 280, 393
poem on the Psalter, 287
poem on the *Song of Songs*, 272, 287
Prayer to St Michael, 287–8
Guillaume de Lorris and Jean de Meun, *Le Roman de la Rose*: key episodes, motifs, characters, and concepts
Amant (lover), 63, 81–4, 90, 93, 101, 109, 113, 114, 213, 216, 237, 239, 268, 272
defloration, 97–102, 108–16, 171, 213, 216, 237, 304, 457, 483
dreams (interpretation of), 59–60, 68, 97, 101–2, 109–10, 241, 300, 303, *see also Le Roman de la Rose*, interpretation and *senefiance*
Faux Semblant, 97–107, 133, 170, 209–11, 237, 268, 296, 304, 320, 336, 402, 466, 467, 470, 496–8
as alter-ego for Jean de Meun, 100–2
as wolf in sheepskin, 100
Garden of Deduit, 148, 207, 209, 268, 270–2
Genius, 77, 104, 113–14, 126–7, 128, 483, 484, 488, 491
diffinitive santance, 104, 108, 113, 126–7, 140, 483
God of Love, 61, 101, 106, 148, 238, 483
interpretation and *senefiance*, 59–60, 93–4, 98–107, 109–11, 114–16,

INDEX OF PASSAGES, MOTIFS, AND DEBATES   557

see also Le Roman de la Rose, dreams
(interpretation of)
Jaloux, 467
Macrobius, 59–60, 241
Malebouche, 466, 498
Mars, 240
mirrors, 79, 112–13, 124–5, 210, 214, 240–1,
249, 312, 422, 458
naming of the authors, 60, 100–1
Narcissus, 68, 109, 124–5, 210, 214, 249, 312
Nature, 61, 77, 79, 128, 130, 214, 237, 240,
483–4, 489–90
Oiseuse (Huiseuse), 130, 207, 214, 429
Orpheus, 484–5, 488–9
Pygmalion, 109, 112, 209, 216, 237, 270, 489
Raison, 59, 61, 77, 81–5, 90–1, 93–4, 101–2,
128, 130, 167, 168, 456
on figurative language, 59, 93–4
on 'proper speaking' (*parler
proprement*), 81–5, 90–1
Saturn's castration, 81–2
Scipio, 241
Sirens, 209
Venus, 112, 130, 240, 468
Virgin Mary, 458
Vulcan, 240
Guillaume de Lorris and Jean de Meun,
Le Roman de la Rose: themes and critical
issues
and Alan of Lille's *De Planctu Naturae*, 60–2,
113–14, 484–7, 489–90
art and nature, 109–17, 214–15, 237, 484–9
auctoritas (attitude to), *auctoritates* (use
of), 62–6, 95–6, 481
circulation, influence, and reception, 1–2,
56–8, 63–70, 107–16
contreres choses, 102–6, 108, 173, 438, 455–7,
470, 477, 480, 495, 496, 499
dual authorship, 60, 62, 100–1
as *encyclopaedia*, 56–7, 79
narrative voice (first-person), 69, *see also* Jean
de Meun, *intentio auctoris*
obscenity, 64, 81–2, 97–8, 110, 157, 161, 168,
216, 237, 271–3, 275, 456–7, 493
and/as philosophy, 46–7, 56–61, 65–6, 69–79,
93–4, 98, 113–16
Guillaume de Deguileville, *Pèlerinage de l'Âme*
Christ's letter to the Pilgrim, 413
Court (tribunal) of St Michael, 314, 413
Misericorde
on the Pilgrim's soul, 221, 233
relation to Latin lyrics, 290–2
relation to *PVH*, 285, 289–91, 316, 428
self-naming acrostic (letter from Grace Dieu
to the Pilgrim), 413
Verite, 413

Guillaume de Deguileville, *Pèlerinage de
Vie Humaine (PVH1 and PVH2)*:
key episodes, motifs, characters, and
concepts
ABC Prayer, 251–6, 260, 273, 275–9, 281,
283–8, 292–3, 295, 309, 323, 331, 353,
358, 367, 388–90, 392–3, 419, 447, 450
Abstinence, 463
Abusion, 316, 318, 400, 402, 404
Agiographe (Sainte Escripture) (*PVH2
only*), 309–12, 315, 343, 463
Apostasie, 318–19
Aristotle (fictional character), 130, 136–40,
335
Astrologie/Astronomie (*PVH2 only*), 306,
307, 308, 336
auto-exegesis (integrated glossing), 127–8,
164–7, 292–3, 302–3, 432
Ave Maria (*PVH2 only*), 280, 393
Bath of Penitence, 249, 253
besace/escherpe (scrip/satchel of Faith),
144–5, 156–7, 162–4, 227, 229, 230, 295,
305, 332, 337, 392–3, 445, 494
bivium (parting of the ways), 206–10, 220–1,
247, 428
Bon non, 312, 407
bourdon (staff of Hope), 144–5, 156–7, 158,
159, 162, 210, 227, 229, 248, 253, 295,
332, 337, 354, 393, 445, 448, 494
carpenter/idolater (*PVH2 only*), 217
Charite, 316, 367, 401, 463
Chastete, 272, 463, 468
Christ, 157–8, 165, 261
Conspiracion/Scylla/Scilla (*PVH2 only*), 306,
312–13, 316, 375, 466, 474
courtine (curtain), 213
Credo (*PVH2 only*), 393
Decepline, 261, 262, 318, 400, 463
Detraction, 211, 218, 312, 313–15, 320, 375,
466, 467, 474
Enfermete, 244, 478–9
envoi (*PVH2*), 303
Esbatement mondain (*PVH2 only*), 306
Estude (Leçon), 266, 268–9, 310, 315, 318,
368, 375, 396, 400, 463
Eucharist, transubstantiation, 134–40, 163,
218, 223, 226, 229, 232, 270, 315, 316,
319, 368–75, 402
'Eyes-in-Ears' episode (*PVH2 only*), 227–36,
243, 315, 332, 337, 445, 494
Faith, *see Pèlerinage de Vie Humaine*,
besace/escherpe (scrip/satchel of Faith)
Flaterie, 209, 210, 218, 310
Geomancie/Gromancie (*PVH2 only*), 306,
336

558 INDEX OF PASSAGES, MOTIFS, AND DEBATES

Pèlerinage de Vie Humaine (PVH1 and PVH2):
(*Continued*)
Grace Dieu, 129–30, 134–8, 140, 143, 157,
161, 162, 164–6, 213, 222–32, 234–6,
248–9, 251–2, 253, 261–3, 277–8, 280,
281, 284, 296, 300, 317, 320, 331, 332,
342, 347, 348, 350, 354, 359, 362, 390,
413, 423, 430, 446, 450, 457, 494
Heresie, 253, 305–6, 307–8, 333–5, 337
Hope, *see Pèlerinage de Vie Humaine, bourdon*
(staff of Hope)
Huiseuse (Oiseuse), 130, 207–11, 215, 220,
237, 247, 311–12, 314–15, 343, 428–9,
468
Idolatrie (*PVH2* only), 306, 307
Jeunece, 254
Labour/Occupant, 207, 242, 247, 428–30
Latria, 262, 267, 270–1, 375, 463
Medecine, 478–9
Memoire, 267
mirrors, 124–5, 157–8, 161, 210, 310–12, 342,
422–3, 448–9
Misericorde, 291, 316, 401
Nature, 130, 134–8, 140, 143
Nigromancie (*PVH2* only), 306, 307, 308, 336
New Jerusalem, 123–4, 127, 140, 156, 165,
173, 193, 210, 254, 268, 273–4, 286, 292,
298, 302, 319, 342, 360, 414, 422–3, 435,
440, 448, 450, 463, 474
Obedience, 257, 261, 272, 463
Ovid (as fictional character in *PVH2*), 316,
407
Paour de Dieu, 261, 315, 464
Paternoster (*PVH2* only), 280, 393
Pauline Armour (Eph. 6:10–17), 156, 179–80,
212–13, 222, 252–3
PAX (carpenter's square), 156, 161, 165, 295,
309
Penitance, 203–4, 221, 247–51, 349, 479, *see
also Pèlerinage de Vie Humaine*, Bath of
Penitence; *Pèlerinage de Vie Humaine*,
Rock of Penitence
Pilgrim as *viator*, 123–5, 140–59, 175–7, 187,
193, 202, 220, 242, 245, 249–50, 252,
262, 276, 292, 312, 318, 450, 474, *see
also* Augustine of Hippo, on pilgrimage;
viator
Povrete Voluntaire, 267, 272, 320, 375, 463
predicatio (monk preaching), 127, 128, 135,
148, 187, 193, 252, 255, 263–4, 278, 292,
411, 432
Priere (Oroison), 266, 267, 274, 277, 318, 375,
400, 463
Prologue (*PVH2*), 300–2, 304, 428

Raison, 130, 134, 140, 145–52, 168–70, 171,
177, 179–82, 186–93, 195–6, 200–2,
202–7, 210–11, 220–1, 223–4, 229, 234,
250, 252, 255–7, 262, 284, 295–6, 309
Rock of Penitence, 246–51, 256, 259, 261–2,
275, 292, 323, 331, 341, 343–4, 346, 349,
358, 377, 382, 388, 416, 423
Rude Entendement, 143–59, 177, 179, 181,
206, 208, 217, 219, 304–5, 445
Saint Esperit, 266
Sante, 478–9
Sapience, 129–30, 143, 164, 223, 262, 284,
295–6, 331, 457
Sathan, 253, 261–2
Science, 135–6
Scylla/Scilla, *see Pèlerinage de Vie Humaine*,
Conspiracion/Scylla/Scilla (*PVH2* only)
self-naming acrostic complaint (in
PVH2), 316–17, 407–9, 411, 413, 421
Sea of the World, 206, 253–5, 354
Seven Deadly Sins, 133, 149, 177, 202, 207,
211–20, 237, 242, 248, 258, 260–1, 296
Avarice, 211, 213, 217–18, 220
Envie, 133, 312, 313–15, 375, 466, 468, 474
Gloutonnie, 238, 373–4
Ire, 261, 262
Luxure (Venus), 170–1, 211, 212
Orgueil, 211, 212, 219, 262, 311, 312
Peresce, 219, 261, 262
Ship of Religion, 206, 254, 258, 354, 367, 440,
464
Silence, 272
Singularité, 400
Sirens, 209
Sorcerie/Sorcellerie (*PVH2* only), 306, 308,
336
Sword of Discretion (*verbum dei*), 165
Syrtes (Cyrtes, Sidra, i.e. Scylla), 255–6
Trahison, 133, 211, 212, 312, 313–15, 375,
407, 466, 467, 468, 474
Tribulacion, 254, 262
Vaine Gloire, 219
Venus, 170–1, 211, 212
Vieillece, 244, 463, 478, 479–82, 495
Virgin Mary, 158, 251–3, 260, 276–8, 280,
423, 450–1
Ypocrisie (mantle of), 212
Guillaume de Deguileville, *Pèlerinage de Vie
Humaine (PVH1 and PVH2)*: themes
and critical issues
on allegorical interpretation, 123–5, 140–59,
202–20, 264, 275, 302–3, 308–9
circulation, influence, and reception, 1–2,
47–51, 117–18, 314, 323, 325

INDEX OF PASSAGES, MOTIFS, AND DEBATES 559

didacticism, 118, 120, 123–6, 242–4, 250–2, 275, 280–1, 358, 360, 439, 482
iconography, iconographical programme, 126, 242, 336
relation between *PVH1* and *PVH2*, 168–74, 177, 227, 234, 244–5, 289–90, 292–3, 295, 300–2, 305–6, 308, 309–21, 323, 377, 411, 428–9, 432
relation to the *Roman de la Rose*, 121–2, 123–33, 140, 147–8, 156–7, 161, 167–74, 175–7, 202, 207–20, 236–45, 264, 267, 270–3, 275, 283, 303–4, 312, 456
Guillaume de Deguileville, *Pèlerinage Jhésucrist*, 47–8, 117, 289–95, 439–43, 447, 449
Charity, 443
dream within the dream, 294
Justice, 291, 441, 445
Misericorde, 291, 441
relation to *PVH* and *PA*, 289–94, 428, 439, 442–3
Sapience, 291
Verite, 291, 441
Virgin Mary, 441, 442
William Langland, *Piers Plowman*: key episodes, motifs, characters, and concepts
Abraham (Faith), 337, 439, 445–7
Anima, 345, 351, 355, 383, 397, 403, 404, 406, 415, 417–22, 431–2, 446, 451, 452
Antichrist, 459, 462, 465, 466–7, 469, 470, 472, 477, 478
Astronomye, 335–7
Barn of Unity (Holy Church) , 378, 436, 440, 459, 463, 464–70, 473, 477, 478, 496
Book, 412
Christ (Charity), 336, 337, 340, 347, 403, 415, 421, 422, 439, 445–8, 451, 452–3, 454, 458
Clergie, 335, 340, 347, 351–4, 361–4, 366, 368, 375, 377, 382–3, 385, 388–91, 397
Confession, 463, 468
Conscience, 364, 367, 368, 375, 376–7, 381, 383, 385–9, 392, 395, 463–5, 469, 472, 475, 477, 482, 490, 496
Contricion, 463, 466, 468
Dobest, 360, 366, 386, 438
Dobet, 360, 366, 376, 386, 388, 416, 438, 490
Dowel, 335, 360, 366, 376, 386, 387, 388, 391, 416, 438, 490
Easter Sunday liturgy, 347, 364, 387–8, 460
Elde, 440, 463, 470, 473, 475, 477–8, 482, 491, 492–3, 494, 496
Envy, 468, 481
Feast of Patience, 364, 366–75, 378, 382–9, 397, 399, 403, 405

Friar Flatterer, 465–7, 496, 497–9
Geomesie, 335–6
Glutton, 497
grammatical allegory (C-text, III.362–6), 490–1
Harrowing of Hell, 439
Haukyn, 355, 356, 392–3, 395, 397–410, 415, 416–17, 469
Holy Church, 369, 437–8, 473
Hypocrisy, 467
inner dream (first), 340, 342–4, 349, 355, 362, 414–15
inner dream (second), 444, 449, 451
'inward journey' (B VIII-XIII.215), 331–2, 338
Kynde, 353, 477, 482, 491, 492
kynde knowyng, 340, 344, 365–6, 383, 397, 437, 439, 454, 461
kynde wit/Kynde Wit, 351–3, 463
Lecherye, 466, 468
londe of longynge, 343
Master of Divinity (Feast of Patience), 368–70, 373–5, 376
'meddling with makynges', 357–62, 380–1, 383, 390–1, 397, 405, 412, 428, 432, 440, 459, 475, 482, 492, 496
minstrels, minstrelsy, 384, 385, 398, 404, 477
Mirror of Mydlerd, 342–3, 415, 423
mirrors, 342–3, 352, 365, 415, 421, 422–4, 447–8, 451, 457
Moses (Hope), 337, 439, 445–7
Necromancy, 336–7
Nede, 470–7, 481
Paternoster, 393–5, 403
Patience, 367, 368, 369, 375, 376, 381, 385, 389, 386, 392–5, 403, 406, 417
Passion (of Christ), 383, 387–8, 397, 439, 444, 447, 453, 454, 460–1
Peace, 454, 455, 457, 464
Piers the Plowman, 383, 386, 391, 435, 438, 444, 449–51, 452, 453, 454
Plant of Peace, 442
Repentance, 364
Reson, 347, 352, 417
Samaritan, 445, 460
Scripture, 335, 340, 343, 368, 385
Sorcery, 336
Spille-Love, 465, 468
Study, 332–7, 345, 362, 370, 371–2, 374, 376, 378, 384, 398, 401, 418, 493, 494
Surquidous, 465, 468
Tearing of the Pardon, 390–1, 396, 420, 433
Theologie, 336–7
Trajan, 345

560 INDEX OF PASSAGES, MOTIFS, AND DEBATES

Piers Plowman: (*Continued*)
  Tree of Charity, 439, 444, 446
  Trinity, 439
  Virgin Mary, 441–2, 450
  Wanhope, 477
  Will
    in crisis (B XI), 339–44, 380–1, 414–16
    as Haukyn's double, 405–11
    as 'Longe Wille', 410
    as passive spectator, 397, 441, 443–4
    as scholastic disputant, 334, 397
    as *voluntas*, 381–2, 412, 414, 423, 482,
      494–5
  Wit, 334, 371
  Ymaginatif, 337, 351–4, 356–7, 358–66, 381,
    383, 399, 405, 419, 431, 432, 492, 493
William Langland, *Piers Plowman*: themes and
  critical issues
  authorial self-representation, 357–66,
    404–11, 414–16, 425–36
  authorial 'signatures', 405–11, 414–16, 418,
    420, 421, 423, 425
  autobiographical elements in the poetry, 382,
    408

documents and charters, 390–7, 412–13, 420
Eucharist, 346, 363–6, 368–75, 385, 393, 398,
  405, 460–2, 464–6
'glosyng', 374, 466, 470
grace/Grace, 39, 50, 340, 345, 350–2, 390–1,
  435, 458, 462, 496
influence and reception, 1–2
multiple versions (A, B, C-texts), 324–5, 326,
  330, 339–41, 350, 354–5, 382–3, 408, 410,
  412, 426–9, 475, 495
Penance/Penitence, 346, 348–50, 353–4, 361,
  363–4, 405, 414, 419, 432–4, 440, 462,
  465–70, 497–8
pilgrimage, 375, 381, 382–3, 392–3, 410–11,
  433, 435, 441, 447
'suffering', 346, 347, 441, 451–5, 475–7, 481,
  493, 495
William Langland
  debt to Francophone poetry, 325–9
  identity/biography (as William de la
    Rokele?), 325
  learning, attitude to scholasticism, 50, 331, 352,
    356